W9-ADT-828

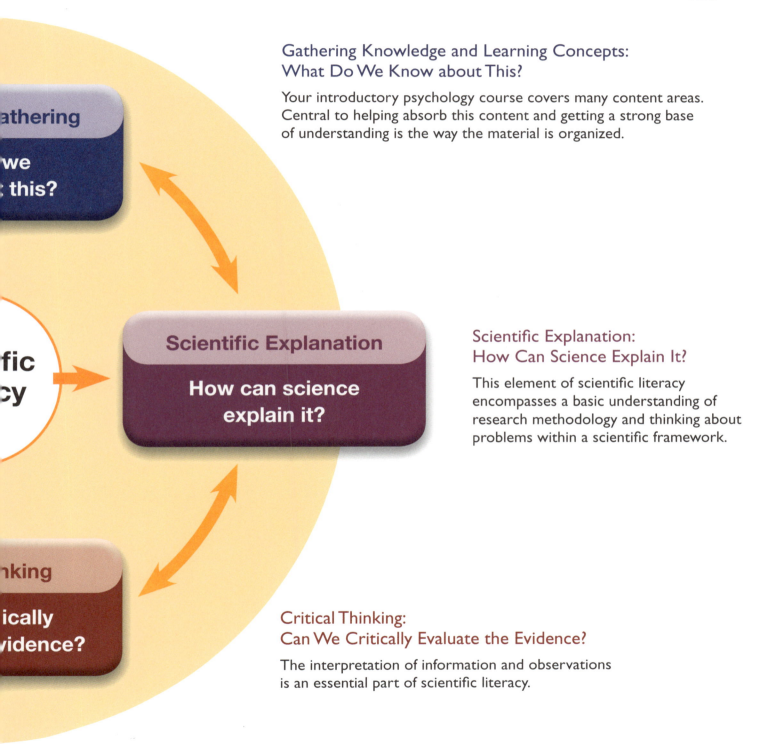

Gathering Knowledge and Learning Concepts: What Do We Know about This?

Your introductory psychology course covers many content areas. Central to helping absorb this content and getting a strong base of understanding is the way the material is organized.

Scientific Explanation: How Can Science Explain It?

This element of scientific literacy encompasses a basic understanding of research methodology and thinking about problems within a scientific framework.

Critical Thinking: Can We Critically Evaluate the Evidence?

The interpretation of information and observations is an essential part of scientific literacy.

PSYCHOLOGICAL SCIENCE

PSYCHOLOGICAL SCIENCE

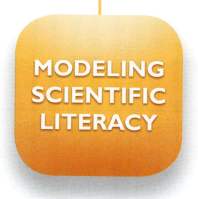

MODELING
SCIENTIFIC
LITERACY

Mark Krause
Southern Oregon University

Daniel Corts
Augustana College

PEARSON

Boston   Columbus   Indianapolis   New York   San Francisco   Upper Saddle River
Amsterdam   Cape Town   Dubai   London   Madrid   Milan   Munich   Paris   Montreal   Toronto
Delhi   Mexico City   Sao Paulo   Sydney   Hong Kong   Seoul   Singapore   Taipei   Tokyo

Editorial Director: Craig Campanella
Editor in Chief: Jessica Mosher
Director of Development: Sharon Geary
Senior Development Editors: Deb Hanlon, Jessica Carlisle
Director of Marketing: Brandy Dawson
Executive Marketing Manager: Jeanette Koskinas
Marketing Manager: Brigeth Rivera
Market Development: Tara Kelly
Marketing Assistant: Craig Deming
Senior Managing Editor: Maureen Richardson
Senior Project Manager/Liaison: Harriet Tellem
Operations Supervisor: Mary Fischer
Operations Specialist: Diane Peirano
Line Art Studio: Precision Graphics

Virtual Brain Line Art Studio: Animated Biomedical
    Productions (ABP)
Art Director, Cover: Leslie Osher
Text and Cover Designer: Charlie Levin, girlcharlie art+design
Cover Art: Trinette Reed/Blend/Glow Images
Media Director: Brian Hyland
Senior Digital Media Editor: Beth Stoner
Media Production Project Manager: Pam Weldin
Assistant Editor: Kerri Hart-Morris
Full-Service Project Management: Douglas Bell/PreMediaGlobal
Composition: PreMediaGlobal
Printer/Binder: Courier/Kendallville
Cover Printer: Lehigh–Phoenix Color

Credits and acknowledgments from other sources and reproduced, with permission, in this textbook appear
on pages C-1–C-8.

Library of Congress Cataloging–in–Publication Data

Krause, Mark A. (Mark Andrew),
    Psychological science : modeling scientific literacy / Mark Krause, Daniel Corts.
        p. cm.
    Includes bibliographical references and index.
    ISBN 978-0-13-173985-7 (alk. paper)
    1. Psychology.   2. Psychology—Study and teaching.   I. Corts, Daniel Paul,   II. Title.
    BF121.K723 2012
    150—dc23

                                                                    2011040997

10 9 8 7 6 5 4 3 2 1

Student Edition (case)
ISBN 10: 0-13-173985-9
ISBN 13: 978-0-13-173985-7

Student Edition (paper)
ISBN 10: 0-205-25586-8
ISBN 13: 978-0-205-25586-3

Annotated Instructor's Edition
ISBN 10: 0-13-173989-1
ISBN 13: 978-0-13-173989-5

Ála Carte Edition
ISBN 10: 0-205-25587-6
ISBN 13: 978-0-205-25587-0

Brief Contents

Contents

INTRODUCING PSYCHOLOGICAL SCIENCE   1

READING AND EVALUATING SCIENTIFIC RESEARCH   36

CONSCIOUSNESS 157

6

LEARNING 194

7

MEMORY 235

9 INTELLIGENCE, APTITUDE, AND COGNITIVE ABILITIES 307

10 LIFE SPAN DEVELOPMENT 345

11

MOTIVATION AND EMOTION   396

12

PERSONALITY   438

13

PSYCHOLOGICAL DISORDERS   475

17

INDUSTRIAL AND ORGANIZATIONAL PSYCHOLOGY 620

About the Authors

Dr. Mark Krause received his Bachelor's and Master's degrees at Central Washington University, and his PhD at the University of Tennessee in 2000. He completed a postdoctoral appointment at the University of Texas at Austin where he studied classical conditioning of sexual behavior in birds. Following this, Krause accepted a research fellowship through the National Institute of Aging to conduct research on cognitive neuroscience at Oregon Health and Sciences University. He has conducted research and published on pointing and communication in chimpanzees, predatory behavior in snakes, the behavioral and brain basis of conditioned sexual behavior, and the influence of testosterone on cognition and brain function. Krause began his teaching career as a doctoral candidate and continued to pursue this passion even during research appointments. His teaching includes courses in general psychology, learning and memory, and behavioral neuroscience. Krause is currently an associate professor of psychology at Southern Oregon University, where his focus is on teaching, writing, and supervising student research. He spends his spare time riding and racing his bike, cooking, reading, and enjoying Oregon's outdoors.

Dr. Daniel Corts received his B.S. in Psychology from Belmont University and his PhD in Experimental Psychology at the University of Tennessee in 1999. He completed a post-doctoral position at Furman University for one year where he focused on the teaching of psychology. Corts is now associate professor of psychology at Augustana College in Rock Island, IL where he has taught for over 10 years. While in graduate school, he focused on language and gesture production. He has since branched out to explore intentional forgetting, and has also published in the area of college student development. Corts also likes to conduct research on just about any topic his students wish to explore. In his spare time, he enjoys spending time with his two children, traveling, camping, and cooking.

Social Media Author & Supplements Coordinator

Dr. Bethany Fleck received her PhD from the University of New Hampshire in 2009 as well as a Master's degree in the Science of College Teaching. She is currently an assistant professor at Metropolitan State College of Denver for the Human Development Major in the psychology department. Her courses include child development, educational psychology, developmental research methods, and cognitive development. She also has teaching experience in statistics and general psychology. Fleck is conducting research in early childhood education, studying memory and social development in the classroom, as well as college teaching pedagogy, including ways to understand and successfully incorporate technology into teaching.

From the Authors

A well-rounded college education requires a healthy dose of science. This means not just a memorized list of scientific terms and famous names, but rather the abilities and disposition that allow students to encounter, understand, and evaluate scientific as well as nonscientific claims. This is true regardless of an individual's personal and career goals. As this text and MyPsychLab program emphasizes, the science of psychology reaches across disciplinary boundaries and addresses numerous complex issues affecting individuals and society. To effectively use what they learn about psychology, students need to carry with them a scientific perspective. *Psychological Science* is written from the perspective of scientific literacy—the ability not only to define scientific terminology, but also to understand how it functions, to critically evaluate it, and to apply it to personal and societal matters.

Psychological science is in a privileged position to help students hone their scientific literacy. It is both a rigorous scientific discipline and a field that studies the most complex of all phenomena: the behavioral, cognitive, and biological basis of behavior. With this focus on behavior, one can rightly argue that psychology resides at the hub or core of numerous other scientific disciplines; it also shares connections with neuroscience, education, and public health, to name a few linkages. From this perspective, the knowledge acquired by studying psychological science should transfer and apply to many other fields. This is great news when you consider that psychology is one of few science courses (if not the only one) that many undergraduates will ever take.

To make scientific literacy the core of our text and MyPsychLab, we developed content and features with the model shown in the graphic as a guide. The competencies that surround the scientific literacy core represent different knowledge or skill sets we want to work toward during the course. The multidirectional nature of the arrows connecting the four supporting themes for scientific literacy demonstrates the interrelatedness of the competencies, which span both core-level skills, such as knowing general information (e.g., terms, concepts), and more advanced skills, such as knowing how to explain phenomena from a scientific perspective, critical thinking, and application of material.

We used this model in developing all aspects of this program, the topics included in the book, the execution of the writing, the learning objectives we established, the quizzes, and other features. We believe a scientific literacy perspective and model will prove useful in addressing two course needs we often hear from instructors—to provide students with a systematic way to categorize the overwhelming amount of information they are confronted with, and to cultivate their curiosity and help them understand the relevance, practicality, and immense appeal of psychological science.

We thank the many instructors and students who have helped us craft this model and apply it to our discipline, and we look forward to your feedback. Please feel free to contact us and share your experiences with *Psychological Science*.

Mark Krause
krausema@sou.edu

Dan Corts
danielcorts@augustana.edu

Content and Features

Students in the general psychology course are inundated with many disparate pieces of information at a time when they are still developing the skills and strategies for organizing and making sense of that information. How does the scientific literacy model and supporting features in *Psychological Science* address this issue?

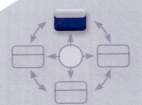

Knowledge Gathering

What do we know about this?

Introductory psychology courses cover a vast amount of content drawn from diverse specialty areas. The organization of the material is central to helping students absorb this content.

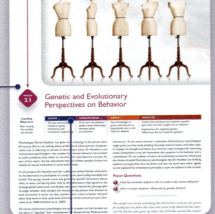

Modules

Chapters are divided into modules to make it easier for students to organize content as well as to self-test and review their learning at regular intervals. For instructors, the modular content makes it easy to customize delivery based on their preferred syllabus.

Learning Objectives

Learning Objectives organized around an updated Bloom's taxonomy that aims to guide students to higher-level understanding. Summaries of the key points related to these objectives are provided at the end of each module. Objectives are listed at four levels of increasing complexity: know, understand, apply, and analyze.

Module Summaries

The major terms, concepts, and applications of the modules are reviewed in the Module Summaries. The summaries also return to and address the original Learning Objectives from the beginning of the module and include application questions (with answers in the back of the book).

Another major set of forebrain structures comprises the **limbic system**, *an integrated network involved in emotion and memory* (see Figure 3.20). One key structure in the limbic system is the almond-shaped **amygdala**, *which facilitates memory formation for emotional events, mediates fear responses, and appears to play a role in recognizing and interpreting emotional stimuli, including facial expressions.* In addition, the amygdala connects with structures in the nervous system that are responsible for adaptive fear responses, such as freezing in position when a possible threat is detected. Just below the amygdala is another limbic region called

Key Terms

Key Terms are defined within the narrative, helping students place them in context, and are then listed again within the Module Summaries. A complete glossary is also included at the end of the text.

Quick Quizzes
End of Chapter Quizzes

Quizzes appear at the conclusion of major sections of the module (typically two to four quizzes per module) as well as the end of the chapter. These quizzes contain multiple-choice questions that enable students to assess their comprehension and better prepare for exams. Like the Learning Objectives, the Quick Quizzes assess understanding at the four levels of Bloom's taxonomy and are marked accordingly.

Active Illustration

For key figures and illustrations, animations are provided within the eText to deliver greater clarity and understanding. For example, readers are much more apt to understand the structures of the brain when they can click on a diagram of it and see a fully rotating illustration. The Pearson eText for *Psychological Science* is designed with alternative delivery models in mind. Highly visual, clearly laid out, and with integrated video and media, it is optimal for online reading and interaction. Students can access their textbook anytime, anywhere, and any way they want, including listening online or downloading it to their iPads.

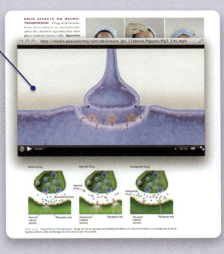

MyPsychLab

MyPsychLab Icons in the margin call out important information students can access online—for example, videos, simulations, and hands-on experiments.

Watch the **Video** on **MyPsychLab**

Listen to the **Chapter Audio** on **MyPsychLab**

Explore the **Concept** on **MyPsychLab**

Simulate the **Experiment** on **MyPsychLab**

Study and **Review** on **MyPsychLab**

PsychTutor

Within the introductory psychology course, some concepts frequently prove to be stumbling blocks for students—such as the difference between an independent variable and a dependent variable, or the difference between negative reinforcement and punishment. To help students move past these bottlenecks, PsychTutor breaks up these key concepts into smaller components, offers further clarification through simulations and provides reinforcement for students through quick self-assessment quizzing. PsychTutor is accessible though the eText, and can be accessed as a web application to students' phones—allowing for easy access to these key threshold concepts.

To view all of the concepts available through PsychTutor download a free QR code reader from the app store and scan this code to access from your phone or tablet (using your MyPsychLab login and password). Add the page to your home screen for easy access.

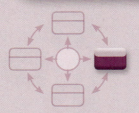

Scientific Explanation

How can science explain it?

This element of scientific literacy encompasses a basic understanding of research methodology and thinking about problems within a scientific framework. *Psychological Science* integrates and reinforces key research methodology concepts throughout the book. This interweaving of methodology encourages students to continue practicing their scientific thinking skills. As noted in the *National Science Education Standards*, learning science is more than accumulating facts; that is, students learn to ask questions, construct explanations, test those explanations, and communicate their ideas to others.

Module Opening Vignettes

Each module opens with a short vignette emphasizing the personal and societal relevance of certain topics to be covered. The vignette concludes with Focus Questions preparing the reader to think about the content found within the module.

Biopsychosocial Perspectives

To emphasize the complexity of scientific explanations, students are reminded throughout each chapter that behavior includes biology, individual thoughts and experiences, and the influence of social and cultural factors.

BIOPSYCHOSOCIAL PERSPECTIVES

Men, Women, and Cognition

Evolutionary psychologists claim that the brain consists of a set of cognitive adaptations for solving problems relating to survival and reproductive fitness. They also hypothesize that male and female brains will differ in some ways because males and females have had to solve a different set of problems in order to survive and reproduce. One sex difference that has been reported involves solving the mental rotation task seen in Figure 3.6.

Instructions

1. Take a close look at standard object #1 below. One of the three objects to the right of it are the same. Which one matches the standard? Repeat this with standard object #2 and the three comparison shapes to the right of it.

2. Many researchers find that, on average, males and females differ in their ability to perform this task. Do you think that:
   - Males perform better than females?
   - Females perform better than males?

Myths in Mind

Many commonly held beliefs people have about behavior before taking a psychology course are half-truths or outright falsehoods. This feature sets the record straight in a concise and informative way. The selected examples are likely to have personal relevance to many readers and deal with important scientific issues.

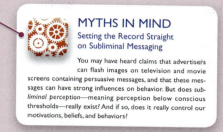

MYTHS IN MIND
Setting the Record Straight on Subliminal Messaging

You may have heard claims that advertisers can flash images on television and movie screens containing persuasive messages, and that these messages can have strong influences on behavior. But does *subliminal perception*—meaning perception below conscious thresholds—really exist? And if so, does it really control our motivations, beliefs, and behaviors?

Experiments Tool

A new Experiments Tool allows students to participate in experiments online to reinforce what they are learning in class and in their book. More than 50 experiments, surveys, and inventories are available through this online tool (available at MyPsychLab).

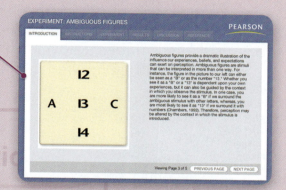

In recent years, an increasing number of instructors have begun to focus on telling students how psychological science fits within the scientific community. Psychology serves, in essence, as a hub science. Through this emphasis on scientific literacy in psychology, students begin to see the practicality and relevance of psychology and become more literate in the fields that our hub science supports.

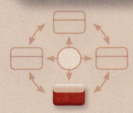

Critical Thinking

Can we critically evaluate the evidence?

Many departments are focusing to an increasing extent on the development of critical thinking, as these skills are highly sought after in society and the workforce. Critical thinking is generally defined as the ability to apply knowledge, use information in new ways, analyze situations and concepts, and evaluate decisions. To develop critical thinking, the module objectives and quizzes are built around an updated Bloom's taxonomy. Objectives are listed at four levels of increasing complexity: know, understand, apply, and analyze. The following features also help students organize, analyze, and synthesize information. Collectively, these features encourage students to connect different levels of understanding with specific objectives and quiz questions.

Scientific Literacy Model

Working the Scientific Literacy Model, introduced in Chapters 1 and 2, and then featured in each module in the remaining chapters, fully integrates the model of scientific literacy. Core concepts are highlighted and students are walked through the steps of knowledge gathering, approaching the problem from a scientific standpoint, using critical thinking, and revealing applications.

Work the Scientific Literacy Model

At the end of every chapter, students have an opportunity to "Work the Scientific Literacy Model" themselves. The Work the Model feature walks students through content from the chapter, providing study tips and reminders for key content areas. Students are asked to critically evaluate what they have learned by accessing a video clip, either through MyPsychLab, the QR code on the page, or YouTube. They are then provided with a question prompting them to apply relevant content to the scenario depicted in the video. These questions can be assigned as either a classroom discussion or a writing assignment. A new automated essay grader available through MyPsychLab allows instructors to easily assign the content as a writing activity, providing writing opportunities that allow students to develop better critical thinking skills by applying the material to real-world situations.

Study Plan

Through MyPsychLab (www.mypsychlab.com), students have access to a *personalized study plan,* based on Bloom's taxonomy, that arranges content from basic level thinking (such as remembering and understanding) to more complex critical thinking (such as applying and analyzing). This layered approach sharpens critical thinking skills, and helps students succeed in the course and beyond.

Study Guide

The Study Guide for *Psychological Science* (ISBN 0131739999), available either as a printed guide or online at MyPsychLab, gives students further opportunities to Work the Scientific Literacy Model. In addition to offering practice tests and study hints, the Study Guide has students walk through the model by using the "Myths in Mind" feature from the text—outlining what we know about the subject and how we know it, asking them to critically evaluate what we know, and helping them see the relevance and application of this topic.

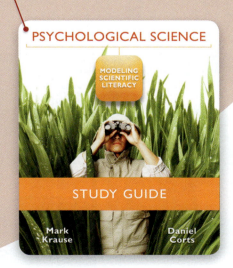

PSYCHOLOGICAL SCIENCE

MODELING SCIENTIFIC LITERACY

STUDY GUIDE

Mark Krause

Daniel Corts

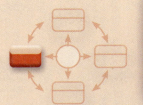

Psychology is a highly relevant, modern science. To be scientifically literate, students should relate psychological concepts to their own lives, making decisions based on knowledge, sound methodology, and skilled interpretation of information.

The "Chapter in Focus" summary found at the end of every chapter reiterates and answers the Focus Questions from the module openers. Links are provided to relevant episodes of the new MyPsychLab Video series—a comprehensive, current, and cutting-edge series featuring 17 original 30-minute videos covering the most recent research, science, and applications and utilizing the most up-to-date film and animation technology.

To view all episodes of the NEW MyPsychLab Video Series, download a free QR code reader from the app store and scan the code to access from your phone or tablet (using your MyPsychLab login and password). Add the page to your home screen for easy access.

PSYCH @

College Parties

Researchers have determined that college students drink significantly more than their peers who do not attend college (Carter et al., 2010). In one study, nearly half of the college student participants binge-drank, one-third drove under the influence, 10% to 12% sustained an injury or were assaulted while intoxicated, and 2% were victims of date rape while drinking (Hingson et al., 2009). Alcohol abuse in our society is widespread, especially during times of celebration (Glindemann et al., 2007; Figure 5.14), so it might seem as if colleges have few options at their disposal to reduce reckless drinking on campus. Psychologists Kent Glindemann, Scott Geller, and their associates, however, have conducted some interesting field studies in fraternity houses at their university. For example, in two separate studies, these researchers measured the typical blood alcohol level at fraternity parties. They then offered monetary awards or entry into a raffle for fraternities that could keep their average blood alcohol level below 0.05 at their next party. The interventions proved to be successful in both studies, with blood alcohol levels being significantly reduced from the baseline (Fournier et al., 2004; Glindemann et al., 2007).

Psych @

The "Psych @" feature reveals an everyday, personally relevant application of psychological science. The content of these features is geared toward issues and concerns that many college students care about.

YouTube Scientific Literacy Site

YouTube has become one of the most popular social media resources for both instructors and students. The challenge, of course, is to find clips that are relevant to key content areas. To help instructors access valuable open-source content and further bring to light the relevance of the discipline of psychology, a YouTube channel, found at

www.youtube.com/scientificliteracy

has been developed to accompany *Psychological Science*. The book provides relevant video links for instructor and student access, in addition to the videos that frame the end of chapter "Work the Scientific Literacy Model" activity.

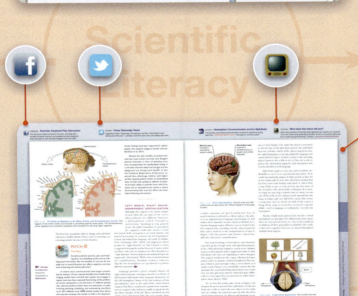

YouTube, Facebook, and Twitter Annotations from the AIE

For instructors interested in bringing more social media content into the classroom, links within the Annotated Instructor's Edition provide guidelines and suggestions for incorporating Facebook and Twitter into the class. Instructors can use the content from the Facebook page created for *Psychological Science*, found at

www.facebook.com/scientific-literacy

on which regular updates highlight relevant news and features, or they can create their own content.

For Instructors

SCIENTIFIC LITERACY is a key course goal for many introductory psychology instructors.

Learning science is an active process. How do we help instructors model scientific literacy in the classroom and online in a way that meets the needs of today's students?

ORGANIZATION

Instructors consistently tell us one of the main challenges they face when teaching the introductory psychology course is organizing engaging, current, and relevant materials to span the breadth of content covered. How do we help organize and access valuable course materials?

DISCUSSION TOPIC :: **Reproductive Strategies**
This is a discussion topic on male-female mating strategies.
ClassPrep Search Term: "reproductive strategies"

Annotated Instructor's Edition

The Annotated Instructor's Edition (AIE) (ISBN 0131739891) contains invaluable tools for teaching an introductory psychology course. Each page integrates relevant teaching resources to help seamlessly incorporate all of the ancillary materials into lectures as well as to continuously foster scientific literacy. The ancillary resources—including lecture launchers, discussion topics, assignments, handouts, video, and animations—are easily accessed through the Annotated Instructor's eText, the Instructor's Manual, and ClassPrep. In addition, for instructors interested in bringing more social media content into the classroom, links within the AIE provide guidelines and suggestions for incorporating social media—YouTube, Facebook and Twitter—into the class.

YouTube Scientific Literacy Site

As mentioned earlier, a YouTube channel, found at www.youtube.com/scientificliteracy, provides a wealth of videos to help engage students and enhance their learning. The ready access provided to these videos, with content spanning the breadth of psychological science, means that instructors no longer have to search for just the right video links to material that meshes with the text's content.

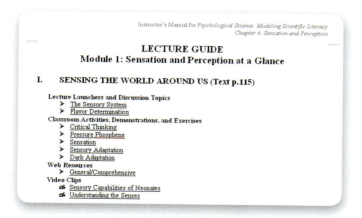

Instructor's Manual

The Instructor's Manual (ISBN 0132368099) includes suggestions for preparing for the course, sample syllabi, and current trends and strategies for successful teaching. Each chapter offers integrated teaching outlines, lists the key terms for each chapter for quick reference, and provides an extensive bank of lecture launchers, handouts, and activities, as well as suggestions for integrating third-party videos and web resources. The electronic format features click-and-view hotlinks that allow instructors to quickly review or print any resource from a particular chapter. This resource saves prep work and helps maximize classroom time.

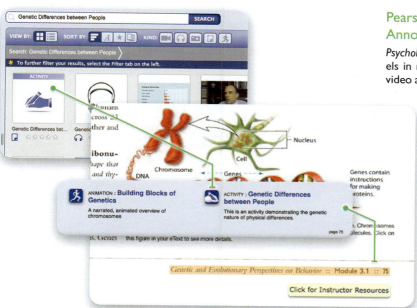

Pearson eText
Annotated Instructor's eText

Psychological Science is designed with alternative delivery models in mind. Highly visual, clearly laid out, and with integrated video and media, it is optimal for online reading and interaction.

Instructors and students can access their textbook anytime, anywhere, and any way they want, including listening online or downloading it to an iPad. In the Annotated Instructor's eText, relevant resources are organized around each topic and available by simply clicking page numbers on the eText—the suggested instructors' resources appear and link to that suggestion, as well as many other resources available through ClassPrep.

Create a Custom Text

For courses with enrollments of at least 25 students, instructors can create their own textbook by combining chapters from best-selling Pearson textbooks or reading selections in a customized sequence. To begin building a custom text, visit

www.pearsoncustomlibrary.com

Instructors can also work with a dedicated Pearson Custom editor to create the ideal text—publishing original content or mixing and matching Pearson content. Contact a Pearson publisher's representative to get started.

PRESENTATION

Instructors consistently tell us making their classroom lectures and online instruction exciting and dynamic is a top priority so they can engage students and bring psychology to life. We have been listening and have responded by creating state-of-the-art presentation resources, putting the most powerful presentation resources at your fingertips.

For maximum flexibility, each half-hour episode features several brief clips that bring psychology to life:

- **The Big Picture** introduces the topic of the episode and provides the hook to draw students fully into the topic.

- **The Basics** uses the power of video to present foundational topics, especially those that students find difficult to understand.

- **Special Topics** dives deeper into high-interest and cutting-edge topics, showing research in action.

- **In the Real World** focuses on applications of psychological research.

- **What's in It for Me?** clips show students the relevance of psychological research to their own lives.

To view the MyPsychLab Video Series download a free QR code reader from the app store and scan this code to access from your phone or tablet (using your MyPsychLab login and password). Add the page to your home screen for easy access.

ClassPrep

Finding, sorting, organizing, and presenting instructor resources is faster and easier than ever before with ClassPrep, which is available in MyPsychLab. This fully searchable database contains hundreds of our best teacher resources, such as lecture launchers and discussion topics, in-class and out-of-class activities and assignments, handouts, and video clips, photos, illustrations, charts, graphs, and animations. Instructors can search or browse by topic, and readily sort their results by type, such as photo, document, or animation. Instructors can create personalized folders to organize and store the content that they like, or can download resources if they prefer. In addition, instructors can upload their own content and present directly from ClassPrep, or make it available online directly to their students. Also available—a ClassPrep app that allows access to all favorite resources via any mobile device.

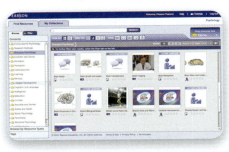

Interactive PowerPoints

Interactive PowerPoint slides (ISBN 0205867375) bring the powerful Krause/Corts design right into the classroom, drawing students into the lecture and providing wonderfully interactive activities, rich visuals, and embedded video clips, which allow instructors an easy and seamless way to show video content without leaving the slide presentation. The slides are built around the Learning Objectives in each Module and offer multiple pathways or links between content areas. Icons sprinkled throughout the slides indicate interactive exercises, simulations, and activities that can be accessed directly from the slides. In addition, simpler lecture slides are provided (ISBN 013173993X), along with key artwork from the texts and "clicker" questions (ISBN 0205860338) for instructors using classroom response systems. All variations of the PowerPoint slides are available on an Instructor's DVD (ISBN 0131739956).

NEW MyPsychLab Video Series

The new MyPsychLab Video series (available through MyPsychLab or on DVD; ISBN 0205035817) is a comprehensive, current, and cutting-edge series featuring 17 original 30-minute videos covering the most recent research, science, and applications and utilizing the most up-to-date film and animation technology. Questions are provided within MyPsychLab so that instructors can assign relevant clips from the series as homework; they may also use the series in the classroom to illustrate the many fascinating topics in the field of psychology as part of their lectures. Guided by the Design, Development, and Review team—a diverse group of introductory psychology instructors—each episode is organized around the major topics covered in the introductory psychology course syllabus. Find out more about the MyPsychLab video at http://www.pearsonhighered.com/showcase/mypsychlab_videos/

Instructors consistently tell us that assessing student progress is a critical component to their course and one of the most time-consuming tasks. Vetted, good-quality, easy-to-use assessment tools are essential. We have been listening and we have responded by creating the absolutely best assessment content available on the market today.

Test Bank

The Test Bank (ISBN 0131739913) contains more than 3,000 questions, many of which were class-tested in multiple classes at both 2-year and 4-year institutions across the country prior to publication. Item analysis is provided for all class-tested items. All questions have been thoroughly reviewed and analyzed line-by-line by a development editor and a copy editor to ensure clarity, accuracy, and delivery of the highest-quality assessment tool. All conceptual and applied multiple-choice questions include rationales for each correct answer and the key distracter. The item analysis helps instructors create balanced tests, while the rationales serve both as an added guarantee of quality and as a time-saver when students challenge the keyed answer for a specific item. The Test Bank includes a two-page Total Assessment Guide, an easy-to-reference grid that organizes all test items by learning objective and question type.

In addition to this high-quality Test Bank, a second bank containing more than 2,000 questions is available for instructors looking for more variation. It has also been class-tested, with item analysis available for each question.

The Test Bank also comes with Pearson MyTest, a powerful assessment generation program that helps instructors easily create and print quizzes and exams. Questions and tests can be authored online, providing instructors with the ultimate in flexibility and the ability to efficiently manage assessments wherever and whenever they want. Instructors can easily access existing questions and then edit, create, and store them using simple drag-and-drop and Word-like controls. The data for each question identifies its difficulty level and the text page number where the relevant content appears. In addition, each question maps to the text's major section and Learning Objective. For more information, go to www.PearsonMyTest.comm

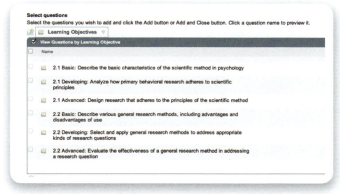

New Design for MyPsychLab

Educators know it. Students know it. It's that inspired moment when something that was difficult to understand suddenly makes perfect sense. MyPsychLab was designed and refined with a single purpose in mind—to help educators create that moment of understanding with their students.

MyPsychLab offers students useful and engaging self-assessment tools, and it provides instructors with flexibility in assessing and tracking student progress. For instructors, MyPsychLab is a powerful tool for assessing student performance and adapting course content to students' changing needs, without requiring instructors to invest additional time or resources to do so.

Instructors and students have been using MyPsychLab for more than 10 years. To date, more than 600,000 students have used MyPsychLab. During that time, three white papers on the efficacy of MyPsychLab have been published. Both the white papers and user feedback show compelling results: MyPsychLab helps students succeed and improve their test scores. One of the key ways MyPsychLab improves student outcomes is by providing continuous assessment as part of the learning process. Over the years, both instructor and student feedback have guided numerous improvements to this system, making MyPsychLab even more flexible and effective.

Pearson is committed to helping instructors and students succeed with MyPsychLab. To that end, we offer a Psychology Faculty Advisor Program designed to provide peer-to-peer support for new users of MyPsychLab. Experienced Faculty Advisors help instructors understand how MyPsychLab can improve student performance. To learn more about the Faculty Advisor Program, please contact your local Pearson representative.

MyPsychLab includes more than 3,000 questions, distinct from the Test Bank, but designed to help instructors easily assign additional quizzes and tests. In addition to the assessment questions, the eText and complete audio files, and the ClassPrep online database of instructor resources, MyPsychLab offers these valuable and unique assessment tools:

MyPsychLab Video Series **NEW**

The MyPsychLab Video Series (available at MyPsychLab or on DVD; ISBN 0205035817) is a comprehensive and cutting-edge series featuring 17 original 30-minute videos covering the most recent research and utilizing the most up-to-date film and animation technology. Multiple choice and short answer essay questions are provided within MyPsychLab so episodes can be assigned as homework.

The greatest strength of MyPsychLab is that it ensures that students are engaging in material outside of class. The videos will grab the attention of the student, and the quizzes will help students know if they are understanding the material. The instant feedback is important. And, because the assignments are graded, students will do the assignments.

Hildur Schilling
Fitchburg State University

MyPsychLab Study Plan

Students have access to a personalized study plan, based on Bloom's taxonomy, that arranges content from less complex thinking (such as remembering and understanding) to more complex critical thinking (such as applying and analyzing). This layered approach promotes better critical thinking skills and helps students succeed in the course and beyond.

The interactive nature of the personalized study plan is an ideal tool for my students, who often feel overwhelmed by the task of reading the textbook. They are unsure of which information is the most important and what they know versus what they don't know.

Chana Etengoff
City College of New York

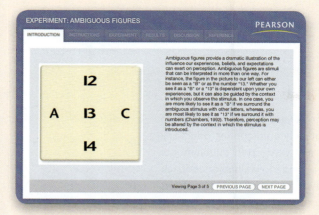

Experiments Tool

Online experiments help students understand scientific principles and practice through active learning. Fifty new experiments, inventories, and surveys are available through MyPsychLab.

*I think it is a great tool—
the best I've seen.*

Darlene Colson
Norfolk State University

For access to all instructor supplements for *Psychological Science: Modeling Scientific Literacy,* go to www.pearsonhighered.com/irc and follow the directions to register (or log in if you already have a Pearson user name and password). Once you have registered and your status as an instructor is verified, you will be emailed a log-in name and password. Use your log-in name and password to access the catalog. Click on the "online catalog" link, click on "psychology" and then "introductory psychology," and finally select the Krause/Corts, *Psychological Science* text. Under the description of each supplement is a link that allows you to download and save the supplement to your desktop.

You can also request hard copies of the supplements through your Pearson sales representative. If you do not know your sales representative, go to www.pearsonhighered.com/replocator and follow the directions to identify him or her.

For technical support for any of your Pearson products, you and your students can contact http://247.pearsoned.com

For more information go to www.mypsychlab.com

APA Assessments

A unique bank of assessment items allows instructors to assess student progress against the American Psychological Association's Learning Goals and Outcomes. These assessments have been keyed to the APA's latest progressive Learning Outcomes (basic, developing, advanced).

The greatest strength of MyPsychLab is being able to see quickly what the students are getting and what they are not. I also think the videos and additional information will help the students to learn more quickly and easily.

Terra Bartee
Cisco College

Development Story

Psychological Science reflects the countless hours and extraordinary efforts of a team of authors, editors, and reviewers that shared a vision for not only a unique introductory psychology textbook, but also the most comprehensive and integrated supplements program on the market. Over 300 manuscript reviewers provided invaluable feedback for making the text and MyPsychLab as accessible and relevant to students as possible. Each chapter was also reviewed by a panel of subject matter experts to ensure accuracy and currency. Over 200 focus group participants helped guide every aspect of the program, from content coverage to the art style and design, to the configuration of the supplements. Over 200 students class tested the full manuscript and Test Bank to ensure the best content possible and over 500 students compared the manuscript to their current textbooks and provided suggestions for improving the prose and design. We thank everyone who participated in ways great and small, and hope that you are as pleased with the finished product as we are!

List of Reviewers

ALABAMA

Susan Anderson
University of South Alabama

Harold E. Arnold
Judson College

Aimee Callender
Auburn University

Lisa Hager
Spring Hill College

Gina Mariano
Troy University

Royce Simpson
Spring Hill College

Amy Skinner
Stillman College

ARIZONA

Suzy Horton
Mesa Community College

Ron Jorgenson
Pima Community College

Patricia Marchok
Paradise Valley Community College, Phoenix

Jennifer Moore
Mesa Community College

Calleen A. Morris
Arizona State University

Jorge Pierce
Mesa Community College

Robert Short
Arizona State University

Belinda Stevens
Pima Community College

Pamela Sulger
Pima Community College

Aaron Tesch
University of Arizona

ARKANSAS

Aneeq Ahmad
Henderson State University

Kathy Brownlee
Henderson State University

Shawn Charlton
University of Central Arkansas

Richard Clubb
University of Arkansas, Monticello

Guyla Davis
Ouachita Baptist University

Robert J. Hines
University of Arkansas, Little Rock

Travis Langley
Henderson State University

Christopher Long
Ouachita Baptist University

Travis P. McNeal
Harding University

Bonnie Nichols
Arkansas Northeastern College

Bernita Patterson
University of Arkansas, Pine Bluff

Sonya Stephens Robinson
Cossatot Community College

Elisabeth D. Sherwin
University of Arkansas, Little Rock

Kenith V. Sobel
University of Central Arkansas

Albert K. Toh
University of Arkansas, Pine Bluff

Jason E. Warnick
Arkansas Tech University

Karen Yanowitz
Arkansas State University

CALIFORNIA

Christina Aldrich
Folsom Lake College

Patricia Bellas
Irvine Valley College

Teesha Barry
San Joaquin Valley College

Matthew Bell
Santa Clara University

Kimberly Brinkman
San Joaquin Valley College

Cari Cannon
Santiago Canyon College

Diane K. Eperthener
California University of Pennsylvania

Christopher Gade
UC Berkeley

Inna Ghajoyan
California State University, Northridge

Melissa Gonzales
San Joaquin Valley College

Kenneth Guttman
Citrus College

Lisa Harrison
California State University, Sacramento

Steven Isonio
Golden West College

Richard Kandus
Mt. San Jacinto College

Fred Leavitt
California State University, East Bay

Margaret Lynch
San Francisco State University

Debra Berry Malmberg
California State University, Northridge

Michelle Pilati
Rio Hondo College

Eileen Roth
Glendale Community College

Angela Sadowski
Chaffey College

Catherine Salmon
University of Redlands

John Slosar
Chapman University

Brenda Smith
Westmont College

Kathleen Taylor
Sierra College

COLORADO

Frederick Coolidge
University of Colorado, Colorado Springs

Roger Drake
Western State College of Colorado

Bethany Fleck
Metropolitan State College of Denver

Peggy Norwood
Community College of Aurora

Brian Parry
Mesa State College

Lisa Routh
Pikes Peak Community College

Randi Smith
Metropolitan State College of Denver

John Walsh
University of Colorado

CONNECTICUT

Daniel Barrett
Western Connecticut State University

Robert Beck
Northwestern Connecticut Community College

Melanie Evans
Eastern Connecticut State University

Ruth Sharf
Yale University, School of Medicine

DC

Morgan Slusher
Community College of Baltimore County

DELAWARE

Gerard Hoefling
Drexel University and University of Warsaw Poland and University of Delaware

John D. Rich, Jr.
Delaware State University

FLORIDA

Susana Barsky
Florida State College, Jacksonville-Downtown Campus

Kathleen Bey
Palm Beach Community College, Central

Gary Bothe
Pensacola Junior College

Michele Camden
Seminole State College of Florida

Greg Fleming
Keiser University, Lakeland

Theresa Foster
Santa Fe College

Peter Gram
Pensacola Junior College

Pamela Hall
Barry University

Deletha Hardin
University of Tampa

Bita Sarah Haynes
Florida State College at Jacksonville

James J. Jakubow
Florida Atlantic University

Dana L. Kuehn
Florida State College at Jacksonville

Alexander Marvin
Seminole State
College of Florida

Christina S. Morris
Seminole State College

Jeanne L. O'Kon
Tallahassee Community
College

Alicia Pfahler
Santa Fe College

Joanna Salapska-Gelleri
Florida Gulf Coast University

Lawrence Siegel
Palm Beach State College

Thomas Westcott
University of West Florida

GEORGIA

Rose Arriaga
Georgia Institute
of Technology

David Brackin
Young Harris College

Deb Briihl
Valdosta State University

Kristen Diliberto-Macaluso
Berry College

Erica Gannon
Clayton State University

Chris Goode
Georgia College and
State University

Adam Goodie
University of Georgia

Michael Hoff
Dalton State College

Heather Kleider
Georgia State University

Diane Kreutzer
Georgia Perimeter College

Pam Marek
Kennesaw State University

David Monetti
Valdosta State University

Christopher K. Randall
Kennesaw State University

Amy Skinner
Gordon College

Clayton Teem
Gainesville College

Chantal Tusher
Georgia State University

HAWAII

Tanya Renner
Kapi'olani Community College

IDAHO

Elizabeth Morgan
Bosie State University

ILLINOIS

Elham Bagheri
Augustana College

Suzanne Bell
DePaul University

John Binning
Illinois State University

Robert Currie
Judson College

Michael Dudley
Southern Illinois
University, Edwardsville

Renee Engeln-Maddox
Northwestern University

Valeri Farmer-Dougan
Illinois State University

Joseph Ferrari
DePaul University

Lisa Fozio-Thielk
Waubonsee Community
College

Allen Huffcutt
Bradley University

Don Kates
College of Dupage

Dawn M. McBride
Illinois State University

Eva Mika
Loyola University, Lakeshore

Derek Montgomery
Bradley University

Joel Nadler
Southern Illinois
University, Edwardsville

Raymond Phinney
Wheaton College

Jane Rose
Augustana College

Joleen Schoulte
Augustana College

Terry Shapiro
Saint Xavier University

James Sichlau
Lincoln Land
Community College

John Skowronski
Northern Illinois University

Jeffrey Wagman
Illinois State University

Mark Watman
South Suburban College

Jill Yamashita
Saint Xavier University

INDIANA

Kristin C. Flora
Franklin College

Mandy Gingerich Hege
Butler University

Karl Nelson
Indiana University Northwest

Sherry Schnake
Saint Mary-of-the-
Woods College

IOWA

Cynthia Bane
Wartburg College

Jennifer Meehan
Brennom Kirkwood
Community College

James Rodgers
Hawkeye Community College

Judith Wightman
Kirkwood Community
College

KANSAS

Stephani Johns-Hines
Cowley County
Community College

Michael Rader
Johnson County
Community College

KENTUCKY

Melissa Burns-Cusato
Centre College

Brian Cusato
Centre College

Janet B. Dean
Asbury University

Sabra Jacobs
Big Sandy Community
and Technical College

Cecile Marczinski
Northern Kentucky
University

Dawn McLin
Big Sandy Community
and Technical College

Richard Miller
Western Kentucky University

Jennifer Sellers
Green Mountain College

Veronica Tinsley
Brescia University

LOUISIANA

Erin Dupuis
Loyola University

Sandra Price
Delgado Community College

Lisa Schulte
Xavier University of Louisiana

MAINE

John Broida
University of Southern Maine

Michael A. Burman
University of New England

Jennifer Coane
Colby College

Trude Cooke Turner
Community College of
Baltimore County, Essex

Kenneth Elliot
University of Maine at Augusta

Rachelle Smith
Husson University

Christine L. B. Selby
Husson University

MARYLAND

Christopher Bishop
Bowie State University

Megan Bradley
Frostburg State University

Katrina Kardiasmenos
Bowie State University

Mike Kerchner
Washington College

Cynthia Koenig
St. Mary's College of Maryland

Marcia McKinley
Mount Saint Mary's University

MASSACHUSETTS

Allison G. Butler
Bryant University

Sarah Rose Cavanagh
Assumption College

Elizabeth Davis
Suffolk University

Christopher Hakala
Western New
England College

Nate Kornell
Williams College

Robin Locke Arkerson
University of Massachusetts,
Dartmouth

Jennifer A. Rivers
Elms College

Eric B. Weiser
Curry College

Summer Williams
Westfield State University

MICHIGAN

Renée L. Babcock
Central Michigan University

Boris Ben Bates
Wayne State University

Christina Brown
Saint Louis University

Marcus Dickson
Wayne State University

Gordon Hammerle
Adrian College

Linda Jackson
Michigan State University

Kari L. McArthur
Hillsdale College

Justin W. Peer
University of
Michigan-Dearborn

MINNESOTA

Mary Bodvarsson
St. Cloud State

Cory Butler
Southwest Minnesota
State University

Kristie Campana
Minnesota State University

Richard Coelho
Lansing Community College

Mark Covey
Concordia College

Ben Denkinger
Augsburg College

Stephanie Gaskin
Concordia College

John Johanson
Winona State University

Marc Mooney
Augsburg College

Emily Stark
Minnesota State
University, Mankato

Dennis Stewart
University of
Minnesota, Morris

Marilyn Swedberg
Fergus Falls Campus
and Minnesota State
Community and Technical
College (M State)

Keilah Worth
St. Catherine University

MISSISSIPPI

Michael Bordieri
University of Mississippi

Scott Drury
Delta State University

Linda Fayard
Mississippi Gulf Coast
Community College

William Goggin
University of Southern
Mississippi

Melissa Lea
Millsaps College

Dawn McLin
Jackson State University

Lindsay R. Trent
University of Mississippi

MISSOURI

Peter J. Green
Maryville University

David Kreiner
University of Central Missouri

David McDonald
University of Missouri,
Columbia

Julie Tietz
Cottey College

Debra Zierenberg
Jefferson College

MONTANA

Flora McCormick
University of Montana,
College of Technology

Fred W. Whitford
Montana State

NEBRASKA

Joseph Benz
University of Nebraska
at Kearney

Wayne Briner
University of Nebraska
at Kearney

Laura Gaudet
Chadron State College

Linda Petroff
Central Community College

Molly Wernli
College of Saint Mary

NEVADA

Evelyn Doody
College of Southern Nevada

Ned Clayton Silver
University of Nevada,
Las Vegas

NEW HAMPSHIRE

Jayne Allen
University of New Hampshire

Jennie Brown
Franklin Pierce University

Mike Mangan
University of New Hampshire

NEW JERSEY

Robert Becklen
Ramapo College of
New Jersey

Gary Kose
Long Island University
of Brooklyn

Gerard La Morte
Rutgers University, Newark

Gary Lewandowski
Monmouth University

Margaret Maghan
Rutgers University, Newark

Nicholas Salter
Ramapo College of
New Jersey

Lynne Schmelter-Davis
Brookdale Community
College

Tim VanderGast
William Paterson University

NEW MEXICO

Ron Salazar
San Juan College

NEW YORK

Brenda Anderson
Stony Brook University

Jeffrey Baker
Monroe Community College

Ellen Banks
Daemon College

Michelle Bannoura
Hudson Valley
Community College

Melody Berkovits
Queens College, CUNY

Cheryl Bluestone
Queens College, CUNY

Kathryn Caldwell
Ithaca College

Martha Leah Chaiken
Hofstra University

Victoria Cooke
Erie Community College

Elizabeth Davis
Suffolk University

Cheryl Dickter
Union College

Dale Doty
Monroe Community College

William Dragon
Cornell University

Marie-Joelle Estrada
University of Rochester

Candice S. Faulring
Genesee Community College

Timothy M. Franz
St. John Fisher College

Phyllis Freeman
New Paltz, SUNY

Elizabeth Gaudino-Goering
Nassau Community College

James Hobbs
SUNY Ulster

Sandra Hunt
College of Staten
Island, CUNY

Yasmine Kalkstein
Mount Saint Mary College

Jean Kubeck
New York City College
of Technology

Jennifer Kyle
Borough of Manhattan
Community College, CUNY

Maria LePadula
New York City Institute
of Technology

Pamela Lusk
Genesee Community College

David S. Malcom
Fordham University

Amy Masnick
Hofstra University

John Mavromatis
St. John Fisher College

Kaneez Naseem
Monroe College

Laurence Nolan
Wagner College

Caroline Olko
Nassau Community College

William Price
North County
Community College

Celia Reaves
Monroe Community College

Claire Rubman
Suffolk County
Community College

Susan Scharoun
Le Moyne College

Paul Schulman
Institute of Technology, SUNY

Keith Shafritz
Hofstra University

Howard Sisco
New York City College
of Technology

Howard Steele
New School for
Social Research

Suzan Tessier
Rochester Institute
of Technology

Ryan Thibodeau
St. John Fisher College

Andreas Wilke
Clarkson University

Karen Wolford
Oswego, SUNY

Jennifer Yanowitz
Utica College

NORTH CAROLINA

Jason C. Allaire
North Carolina
State University

Jennifer Bowler
East Carolina University

Walter Charles
North Carolina
Central University

Sarah Estow
Guilford College

Martha Low
Winston-Salem
State University

Christopher B. Mayhorn
North Carolina
State University

Jutta Street
Campbell University

Nancie Wilson
Southwestern
Community College

OHIO

David Baker
University of Akron

Alicia Doerflinger
Marietta College

Darlene Earley Andrews
Southern Ohio State
Community College

Jessica Hillyer
Kenyon College

Carolyn Kaufman
Columbus State
Community College

Ana M.H. Kehrberg
Muskingum University

Philip Mazzocco
Ohio State University,
Mansfield

Dinah Meyer
Muskingum University

Elizabeth O'Dell
Owens Community College

Barbara Oswald
Miami University

Dennis Shaffer
Ohio State University,
Mansfield

Wayne Shebilske
Wright State University

Albert Smith
Cleveland State University

Colleen Stevenson
Muskingum University

Elizabeth Swenson
John Carroll University

OKLAHOMA

Jared Edwards
Southwestern Oklahoma
State University

John Hensley
Tulsa Community
College, Metro

Alicia MacKay
Tulsa Community College

OREGON

R.H. Ettinger
Eastern Oregon University

Timothy Hackenberg
Reed College

Deana Julka
University of Portland

Chris Koch
George Fox University

Zip Krummel
Columbia Gorge
Community College

Sue Leung
Portland Community College

Jeremy Miller
Willamette University

Melissa Witkow
Willamette University

PENNSYLVANIA

Melissa Terlecki
Cabrini College

Barbara Radigan
Community College of
Allegheny County

Bonnie Green
East Stroudsburg University

Ryan Leonard
Gannon University

Cathy Sigmund
Geneva College

Mark McKellop
Juniata College

David Widman
Juniata College

Robin Musselman
Lehigh Carbon
Community College

Karen Rhines
Northampton
Community College

Rahan Ali
Penn State University

Greg Loviscky
Penn State University

Emily Keener
Slippery Rock University

Natasha Tokowicz
University of Pittsburgh

Catherine Chambliss
Ursinus College

Jennifer Engler
York College of Pennsylvania

RHODE ISLAND

Allison Butler
Bryant University

Lisa Weyandt
University of Rhode Island

SOUTH CAROLINA

Daniel Bellack
Trident Technical College

Maureen Carrigan
University of South
Carolina, Aiken

Michelle Caya
Trident Technical College

Penny S. Edwards
Tri-County Technical College

Chad Galuska
College of Charleston

Chelsea Hansen
Midlands Technical College

Amy M. Kolak
College of Charleston

Echo Leaver
University of South
Carolina, Aiken

Salvador Macias
University of South
Carolina, Sumter

Laura Negel May
University of South
Carolina Aiken

Nancy Simpson
Trident Technical College

Karen Thompson
Columbia College

SOUTH DAKOTA

Brady Phelps
South Dakota State University

TENNESSEE

Karen Baker
Lambuth University

Gayle J. Beck
University of Memphis

Chris S. Dula
East Tennessee
State University

Patricia B. Hinton
Hiwassee College

Jameson K. Hirsch
East Tennessee
State University

Colin Key
University of Tennessee
at Martin

Marvin W. Lee
Tennessee State University

Angelina MacKewn
University of Tennessee
at Martin

Michelle Merwin
University of Tennessee
at Martin

Liz Moseley
Cleveland State
Community College

Tiffany D. Rogers
University of Memphis

Kristin L. Walker
East Tennessee
State University

Lonnie Yandell
Belmont University

TEXAS

Denise Aspell
Northwest Vista College

Kyle Baumbauer
Texas A&M Univeristy

Pamela Brouillard
Texas A&M University,
Corpus Christi

Laura Cavicchi
Northwest Vista College

Jack Chuang
San Jacinto College

Patrick Carroll
University of Texas, Austin

Wanda Clark
South Plains College

Perry Collins
Wayland Baptist
University, Lubbock

Barb Corbisier
Blinn College

Mike Devoley
Lone Star College,
Montgomery

Matt Diggs
Collin College

Wendy Domjan
University of Texas, Austin

Judith Easton
Austin Community College

Patricia Foster
Stephen F. Austin
State University

Perry Fuchs
University of Texas, Arlington

Mark Hartlaub
Texas A&M University,
Corpus Christi

Raquel Henry
Lone Star College, Kingwood

Susan Hornstein
Southern Methodist
University

Stella Lopez
University of Texas,
San Antonio

Bryan Neighbor
Southwestern University

Randall E. Osborne
Texas State University,
San Marco

Kraig Schell
Angelo State University

Carl Scott
University of St. Thomas

Christopher Smith
Tyler Junior College

Victoria Van Wie
Lone Star College, CyFair

Erin Young
Texas A&M University

Acknowledgments

We cannot fathom completing a project like this without the help and support of many individuals. Through every bit of this process has been our families and we thank you for your love, patience, and support. Our departments have also been wonderfully understanding and helpful, offering advice with their various specializations, providing examples and tips, reviewing drafts, and tolerating our occasional absences. It has been an absolute privilege to work with the bright and dedicated people of Pearson Education. We cannot thank Jessica Mosher, Editor in Chief, enough for guiding us through this process, and for staying with us through the hardest as well as the best of times. Sharon Geary, Director of Development, and our Senior Development Editors Deb Hanlon and Jessica Carlisle provided constant encouragement and sage advice. We have also benefitted from the best marketing team in the business, especially Jeanette Koskinas and Brigeth Rivera. Others behind the scenes at Pearson include Kerri Hart-Morris, for supplements management and hiring the supplements writers, and Beth Stoner, for media and MyPsychLab. Our production team was outstanding—we thank Harriet Tellem, Ben Ferrini, Doug Bell, and Marta Johnson. To all of our Pearson team, thank you so much for your guidance, humor, and encouragement along the way.

We also thank Charlie Levin for her outstanding artwork and design. Also, a warm thanks to Bethany Fleck, who has been an invaluable contributor to media and pedagogy. Thanks to David Waxler for his outstanding work on developing our Test Bank.

Finally, the many colleagues and students who reviewed our materials have been immensely helpful. We are very grateful that you shared your expertise in the field of psychology, and in teaching, to help bring this book to life. We value feedback from both instructors and students, and we are sure that we will need it for our Second Edition. Please do not hesitate to offer suggestions or comments by writing to Mark Krause (krausema@sou.edu) and Daniel Corts (danielcorts@augustana.edu).

PSYCHOLOGICAL SCIENCE

1 :: INTRODUCING PSYCHOLOGICAL SCIENCE

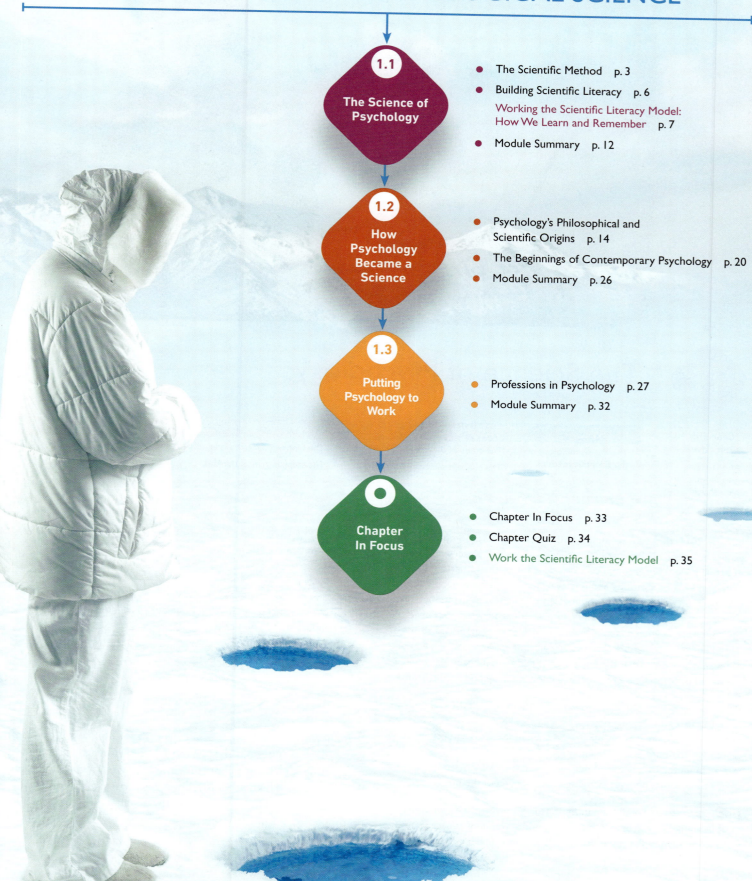

The Science of Psychology

KNOW ...	UNDERSTAND ...	APPLY ...	ANALYZE ...
The key terminology of the scientific method	The steps of the scientific method The concept of scientific literacy	The biopsychosocial model to behavior The steps in critical thinking	The use of the term *scientific theory*

In early 2011, IBM sent its supercomputer, Watson, to compete on the game show *Jeopardy* against highly successful human players, and he (or *it*) actually won! Sure, computers can do a lot of things better than humans—like math or storing and retrieving facts—but most people believe that machines will always lack some essentially human elements: personality, wisdom, maybe a sense of humor, or even (depending on your beliefs) a soul. But imagine yourself finishing up the 15th page of a 15-page term paper when your computer freezes up and all your work is lost. Are you one of those who would treat the computer as if it were human? Many people would call their machine a name, blame it for acting up, and seethe in anger.

Why do we express hostility toward inanimate objects? Psychologists refer to the act of treating objects or animals like people as *anthropomorphism*, and they say it is rather predictable. In fact, it is interesting how readily we attribute elaborate intentions to objects and animals, whether it is a computer that is out to get you, a car that will not cooperate, or even a pet cat that behaves as though she is queen of the house.

Given that we incorrectly see intentions in so many places, what makes people think they are so accurate at understanding the real intentions of other people? If we can be tricked into thinking a computer is outsmarting us, we should be cautious when thinking we understand one another—or even ourselves.

Focus Questions

 How can the human mind, with its quirks and imperfections, conduct studies on itself?

 How can scientific and critical thinking steer us toward a clearer understanding of human behavior and experience?

· · · · · · · · · · · · · · · · · · ·

Which words and images come to mind when you hear that someone is a psychologist? Many of us think of professionals conducting therapy or people in white lab coats watching rats run through mazes. The field of psychology is also viewed through the lens of "pop" psychology—the scores of self-help gurus on TV, on the radio, and in the books lining bookstore shelves. Although these images are not necessarily false, they do not fully capture

Television personalities such as Phil McGraw, experiments involving animals running mazes, and sessions between a therapist and client are common notions about the work of psychologists. But how well do they represent the field?

the scope of the field of psychology. As you will soon discover, some of your expectations about psychology will likely be challenged in your introductory psychology course.

To begin, we should acknowledge that psychology is a vast discipline; in fact, we might do better to consider it to be a collection of disciplines, composed of many overlapping fields of study. Two unifying qualities allow us to group all these fields into the category of psychological science. First, psychology involves the study of behavior that, broadly defined, can include perceptions, thoughts, and emotions. Second, psychologists employ the *scientific method* in their work. On these grounds, we can define **psychology** *as the scientific study of behavior, thought, and experience.* Psychologists share with other sciences a common set of methods and perspectives for understanding the world.

The Scientific Method

What exactly does it mean to be a scientist? A person who haphazardly combines chemicals in test tubes may look like a chemist, but he is not conducting science; a person who dissects a specimen just to see how it looks may appear to be a biologist, but this is not science either. In contrast, a person who carefully follows a system of observing, predicting, and testing *is* conducting science, whether the subject matter is chemicals, physiology, human memory, or social interactions. In other words, whether a field of study is a science, or a specific type of research is *scientific*, is based not on the subject but on the use of the scientific method. The **scientific method** *is a way of learning about the world through collecting observations, proposing explanations for the observations, developing theories to explain them, and using the theories to make predictions.* It involves a dynamic interaction between hypothesis testing and the construction of theories, outlined in Figure 1.1.

HYPOTHESES: MAKING PREDICTIONS Scientific thinking and procedures revolve around the concepts of hypothesis and theory. Both guide the process and progress of the sciences. A **hypothesis** (plural: hypotheses) *is a testable prediction about processes that can be observed and measured.* A testable hypothesis is one that can be confirmed or rejected (you do not *prove* a hypothesis), and a scientific hypothesis *must* be testable. These rules are regularly broken by people claiming to be scientific. For example, astrologers and psychics are in the business of making predictions. An astrologer might tell you, "It's a good time for you to keep quiet or defer important calls or emails." This sounds like a request to not even bother testing the prediction, because it might come true. The horoscope leaves two courses of action: (1) cave in, fully accept the prediction, and heed the advice or (2) take your chances. If you take your chances, it is very likely that by the

Complete the **Survey** *What Do You Know about Psychology?* at **MyPsychLab**

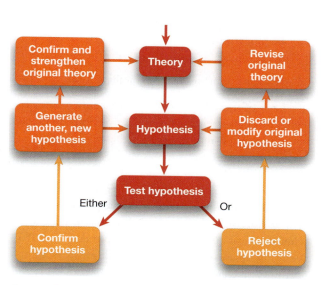

{FIG. 1.1} **The Scientific Method** Scientists use theories to generate hypotheses. Once tested, hypotheses are either confirmed or rejected. Confirmed hypotheses lead to new ones and strengthen theories. Rejected hypotheses are revised and tested again, and can potentially alter an existing theory.

Supporters of psychics and astrologers often point out that scientific fields (such as meteorology) do not always make correct predictions. A key difference between science and pseudoscience is that in science an incorrect hypothesis is rejected and an alternative can be stated and tested.

end of the day you can find at least a grain of truth in the prediction. Horoscopes make *very* general predictions—typically so much so that you could easily find evidence for them if you looked hard enough, and perhaps stretched an interpretation of events a bit. In contrast, a good scientific hypothesis is stated in more precise, and publicly relevant, terms, such as the following:

> "People become less likely to help a stranger if there are others around."
>
> "Cigarette smoking causes cancer."
>
> "Exercise improves memory ability."

Each of these hypotheses can be confirmed or rejected through scientific testing. An obvious difference between science and astrology is that scientists are eager to test hypotheses such as these, whereas astrologists would rather you just take their word for it. We do acknowledge that astrology is a very easy target for criticism, though it is alarming that approximately one in four Americans believes astrology has at least some scientific basis (National Science Foundation, 2010). We bring up astrology only because it provides an opportunity to clarify what a scientific hypothesis is and also to highlight a key difference between science and **pseudoscience**, *which refers to ideas that are presented as science but do not actually utilize basic principles of scientific thinking or procedure.*

THEORIES: EXPLAINING PHENOMENA

Hypotheses are a major component of scientific theories. A **theory** *is an explanation for a broad range of observations that also generates new hypotheses and integrates numerous findings into a coherent whole.* Figure 1.1 shows how hypothesis testing eventually leads back to the theory from which it was based. Theories are built from hypotheses that are repeatedly tested and confirmed; in turn, good theories eventually become accepted explanations of behavior or other natural phenomena. Similar to hypotheses, an essential quality of scientific theories is that they can be proved false with new evidence. In fact, any scientific theory must be *falsifiable*: Just as researchers can discover strong evidence in support of a theory, they can also discover evidence that falsifies a theory. As Figure 1.1 shows, theories can be updated with new evidence. The process helps to ensure that science is self-correcting—bad ideas typically do not last long in the sciences.

The term *theory* is often used very casually, which has led to some persistent and erroneous beliefs that many people have about scientific theories. So to clarify a few common issues:

- **Theories are not the same thing as opinions or beliefs.** Yes, it is certainly true that everyone is entitled to their own beliefs. But the phrase "That's just *your* theory" is neither the correct use of the term "theory," nor an argument that a scientist would make.
- **All theories are *not* equally plausible.** Groups of scientists might adopt different theories for explaining the same phenomenon. For example, several theories have been proposed to explain why people become depressed. This does not mean that anyone can throw their hat into the ring and claim equal status for his or her theory (or belief). There are good theories, and there are not-so-good theories.
- **A measure of a good theory is not the number of people who believe it to be true.** According to a 2009 Gallup Poll, a mere 39% of Americans believe in the theory of evolution by natural selection, despite the fact that it is the most plausible, rigorously tested theory of biological change and diversity.

Testing hypotheses and constructing theories are both part of all sciences. In addition, each science,

"All swans are white" is a falsifiable statement. A swan that is not colored white will falsify it. Falsification is a critical component of scientific hypotheses and theories.

emotions, and personality constitute his or her psychological makeup. Often, behavior can be fully explained only if multiple perspectives are incorporated. This will become particularly apparent as you read about research that tackles complex topics.

Throughout this text, we will apply the biopsychosocial model to many of the topics we will cover. An icon, like the one in the margin, will appear in these sections, prompting you to apply the biopsychosocial model to a specific problem or question about multiple influences on thinking and behavior.

including psychology, has its own unique way of approaching its subject matter. As the study of human behavior and experience, psychology examines the individual as a product of multiple influences, including biological, psychological, and social factors.

THE BIOPSYCHOSOCIAL MODEL Defining psychology as the scientific study of behavior, thought, and experience may sound pretty straightforward, but thinking and behaving are complex subjects with complex explanations. One psychologist might study a single type of cell in the nervous system, whereas another might examine the cultural customs and beliefs that shape daily life for millions of people—all this to explain the same overarching question: Why do we behave the way we do?

Because our thoughts and behaviors have multiple influences, psychologists adopt multiple perspectives to understand them. The **biopsychosocial model** *is a means of explaining behavior as a product of biological, psychological, and sociocultural factors* (Figure 1.2 on p. 6). Biological influences on our behavior involve brain structures, chemicals, hormones, and drug effects. On the other end of the spectrum, your family, peers, and immediate social situation also determine how you think, feel, and behave. Also, a balanced understanding of psychology requires that we always incorporate the influences of ethnicity and gender in our discussion of human behavior. These influences constitute the sociocultural part of the model. In between biology and culture, we can examine how a person's thoughts, experiences,

Quick Quiz 1.1a
The Scientific Method

KNOW…

1 A testable prediction about processes that can be observed and measured is referred to as a(n)_____.

  A theory

  B hypothesis

  C opinion

  D hunch

2 A theory or prediction is falsifiable if:

  A it has been proven false.

  B it is impossible to test.

  C there can be evidence for it or against it.

  D if and only if it comes from pseudoscience.

APPLY…

3 How would you apply the biopsychosocial model to a news report claiming that anxiety is caused by being around other people who are anxious?

  A Recognize that the news report considers all portions of the biopsychosocial model.

  B Recognize that psychologists do not regard biological factors when it comes to anxiety.

  C Recognize that the only effective treatment of anxiety must be drug based.

  D Recognize that the news report only considers one portion of the biopsychosocial model.

ANALYZE…

4 The hypothesis that "exercise improves memory ability" is a scientific one because:

  A it cannot be confirmed.

  B it cannot be rejected.

  C it makes a specific, testable prediction.

  D it can be proven.

Answers can be found on page ANS-1.

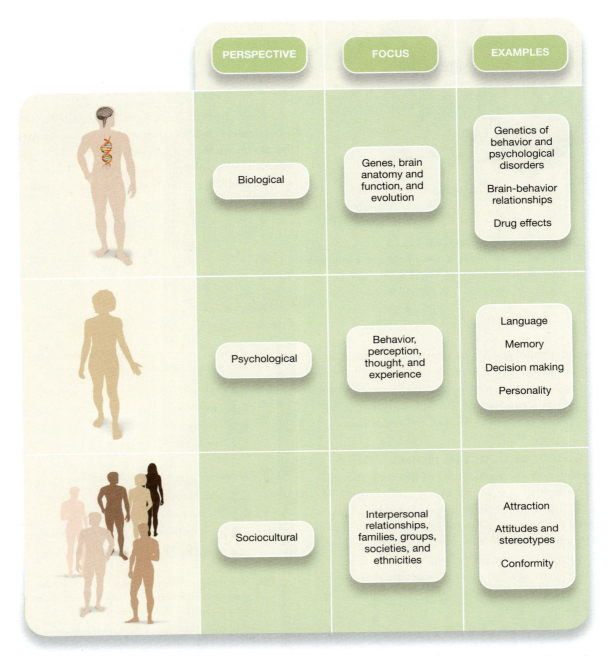

PERSPECTIVE	FOCUS	EXAMPLES
Biological	Genes, brain anatomy and function, and evolution	Genetics of behavior and psychological disorders Brain-behavior relationships Drug effects
Psychological	Behavior, perception, thought, and experience	Language Memory Decision making Personality
Sociocultural	Interpersonal relationships, families, groups, societies, and ethnicities	Attraction Attitudes and stereotypes Conformity

{FIG. 1.2} **The Biopsychosocial Model** Psychologists view behavior from multiple perspectives. A full understanding of human behavior comes from analyzing biological, psychological, social, and cultural factors.

Building Scientific Literacy

A major aim of this book is to encourage the development of the knowledge, skills, and attitudes that are central to the field of psychology. Also, the overarching goal of this textbook is to help students develop **scientific literacy**, *the ability to understand, analyze, and apply scientific information.* Our focal topic is psychology, but the same ways of thinking are applicable to other scientific fields. As you can see in Figure 1.3, scientific literacy has several key components, starting with the ability to learn new information. Certainly this text will provide you with new terminology and concepts, but you will continue to encounter psychological and scientific terminology long after you have completed the course. Being scientifically literate means that you will be able to read and interpret new terminology, or know where to go to find out more.

Knowledge of terminology by itself does not make a person scientifically literate; individuals should also develop an ability to provide explanations that incorporate

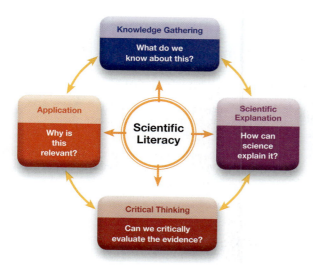

{FIG. 1.3} **A Model for Scientific Literacy** Scientific literacy involves four different skills: gathering knowledge about the world, explaining it using scientific terms and concepts, using critical thinking, and applying and using information.

scientific terms and concepts. Furthermore, being able to apply this ability to real–world situations is crucial. In addition, scientifically literate individuals should be able to use their thinking skills to evaluate information and claims.

WORKING THE SCIENTIFIC LITERACY MODEL
How We Learn and Remember

To develop your scientific literacy skills, in every chapter we will revisit this model and its four components as they apply to a specific psychological topic—a process we call *working the model*. This will help you to move beyond just the vocabulary and toward understanding scientific explanations, thinking critically, and discovering applications of the material. We can demonstrate one component of this process with an example that will be familiar to many: studying vocabulary terms with flashcards.

What do we know about effective studying techniques?

Many college courses, including your psychology course, require that you learn definitions and factual information such as dates, and you may have approached these tasks by studying with flashcards. If so, you have likely stumbled upon a preferred study strategy. Many students do what is called *massing*—they break up a large pile of cards into smaller groups and move through

each pile separately. Another approach is *spacing*—leaving the cards in one big stack and moving through them one at a time. In contrast to massing, spacing means that there is more time between seeing each individual card. The larger the deck, the longer it will be until you return to the beginning. If you used the massing technique (most students prefer it), it is likely because it *seems* easier and it may even give you the sense that it is more effective than spacing. Actually, the two strategies are not equally effective, and spacing is the better of the two.

How can science explain this difference?

To find out which study method really works better, psychologist Nate Kornell (2009) conducted an experiment in which he asked a group of 20 student volunteers to practice studying vocabulary words for a standardized test. Students tried studying using both massing and spacing methods. For the massing study session, they studied 20 vocabulary terms in four sets of five cards each. For the spacing study session, they studied another set of 20 vocabulary terms in one set of 20. As shown in Figure 1.4 (p. 8), the volunteers studied each word four times, regardless of the study method. At the end of the study period, Kornell administered a memory test and discovered that the volunteers could remember significantly more words from the spaced condition than from the massed condition. From these results, he concluded that it is better to study by spacing (despite the fact that the people in his study reported that they preferred massing).

Can we critically evaluate alternative explanations?

As with all research you encounter, there are limitations and other considerations to think about. In this example, the study methods people choose to use are counterintuitive, so it may be difficult to get people to adopt the spacing method. Many students will continue to adopt a massing strategy even though evidence suggests it is not as effective as spacing. Also, this study does not provide evidence that spacing works for all kinds of learning. The terms the students studied were common words that would likely be found on a standardized, general vocabulary test. It would be helpful to see additional studies that apply this research to studying specific topics in sciences and humanities. More importantly, it is not clear how we could apply Kornell's results to other types of studying, such as learning to solve problems or think critically. Therefore, his results may be limited to factual and vocabulary learning.

You have a total of 20 terms to learn.

Massing: Studying a deck of five cards four times in a row. This masses study for an individual card, such as card A in the drawing above.

You have a total of 20 terms to learn.

Spacing: Leaving all 20 cards in one stack and studying the whole deck four times in a row. This spaces the studying for each card, such as card A in the drawing above. However, in both conditions, card A will be studied the same number of times (four).

{FIG. 1.4} **Massed Versus Spaced Practice** In both conditions, volunteers studied each vocabulary word four times. In the massed condition, shown at left, the individual cards were studied closer together whereas in the spaced condition, at right, they were studied further apart. Spaced learning results in better memory for vocabulary terms.

Why is this finding relevant?

Ideally, you will be inspired to apply this material to your own experiences as a student. Each chapter you read in this text includes definitions, and there is a set of flashcards available with the online tools accompanying this text at MyPsychLab, so perhaps you should consider the spacing method when studying key terms for each module. The spacing technique would probably also be useful in other courses, such as history, where you may need to match dates and major historical events, or in a foreign language course, where you are learning new vocabulary and verb conjugations.

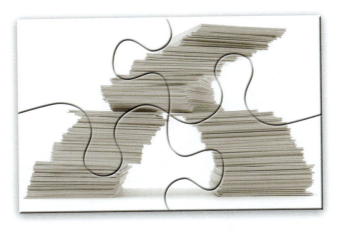

✓●—[Study and **Review** the flashcards for this text at **MyPsychLab**

Now that you have read this feature, we hope you understand how scientific information fits into the four components of the model. But there is still much to learn about working the model: In the next section, we will describe critical thinking skills and how to use them, and Chapter 2 walks you through the specific methods for conducting and evaluating scientific research. You will get a chance to work the scientific literacy model again in Chapter 2, and then in each module in the remaining chapters.

CRITICAL THINKING, CURIOSITY, AND A DOSE OF HEALTHY SKEPTICISM

"Our products are 100% organic."

"These remedies were developed by ancient cultures and have been used for centuries."

"Join now and find your soul mate."

In the 1800s, it was not uncommon for entrepreneurs, in the loosest sense of the term, to rally crowds of people to hear them pitch a brand-new product "guaranteed" to deliver whatever miracle people might be in search of. The term *snake oil salesman* is more fitting than *entrepreneur*, as this was occasionally exactly what they were selling. Modern-day versions of these products are not hard to find on the Internet and television. Misinformation can sometimes seem far more abundant than truth, which is about as good a reason for developing critical thinking skills as we can think of.

Refer back to Figure 1.3 (p. 7). As the model shows, critical thinking is an important element of scientific literacy. Being a psychologist involves more than just developing a set of skills; it also requires having a certain set of attitudes or dispositions. Among these dispositions are the curiosities that drive us to ask thoughtful questions, to look beyond simple answers, and to demonstrate skepticism toward simplistic or outlandish claims. Most importantly, psychology requires us to be reflective—we should know why we believe what we believe, and we should be able to communicate this to others. **Critical thinking** *involves exercising curiosity and skepticism when evaluating the claims of others, and with our own assumptions and beliefs.*

For psychologists, critical thinking means that we apply scientific methods carefully, examine our assumptions and biases, and tolerate ambiguity when the evidence is inconclusive. Curiosity is essential to psychology because many of us think about the causes of behavior only when it affects us negatively or when it

Curiosity helps us ask questions about all behavior—not just problem behavior.

strikes us as unusual. (*Why does my child have problems in school? Why does my dog chew on my shoes?*) People regularly offer reasons why things have gone awry. But as psychologists, we are always curious. We ask questions about all kinds of behaviors—not just the unusual or problematic, but also everyday activities and experiences (*How do we remember where we left our car keys?*). Because we are curious, psychological theories should provide meaningful explanations for *all* behaviors.

It is equally important to approach matters with cautious skepticism. We are constantly being told about amazing products that help us control body weight, improve thinking and memory, enhance sexual performance, and so on. As consumers, there are always going to be claims we really hope to be true. But as critical thinkers, we meet these claims with a good dose of skepticism (*Is there sound evidence that this diet helps people to achieve and maintain a healthy weight?*). Being skeptical can be challenging, especially when it means asking for evidence that we may not want to find. Often the great products that we have always hoped for really are "too good to be true." Wishful thinking is one thing, but when people waste money and become emotionally invested in something that is bound to fail, the results can be quite disheartening. Therefore, we view skepticism, as well as curiosity, as means of raising important questions; both attitudes lead us to search for and evaluate evidence.

Critical thinking involves skills that can be learned and developed, but most of us need to make a conscious effort to apply them (Halpern, 1996). Research points to a core set of habits and skills for developing critical thinking:

1. Be curious. Simple answers are sometimes too simple, and common sense is not always correct (or even close to it—the sun only *appears* to orbit around the Earth).
2. Examine the nature and source of the evidence; not all research is of equal quality.
3. Examine assumptions and biases. This includes your own assumptions as well as the assumptions of those making claims.
4. Avoid overly emotional thinking. Emotions can tell us what we value, but they are not always helpful when it comes to making critical decisions.
5. Tolerate ambiguity. Most complex issues do not have clear-cut answers.
6. Consider alternative viewpoints and alternative interpretations of the evidence.

If you follow these steps, then you will be well on your way to developing critical thinking habits and skills. However, determining what does *not* constitute critical thinking is important as well. Critical thinking is not a philosophy, a belief, or a faith, nor is it meant to make everyone arrive at the same answer. Complex issues often remain ambiguous, and at times a question may have several plausible answers. Although critical thinking cannot guarantee a correct answer—and sometimes it even delivers unpleasant answers—it will help find and justify good answers.

Critical thinking means respecting other viewpoints, but it also means that some ideas can be incorrect. In many cases, one answer emerges as the best one because a large body of evidence converges upon it. Critical thinking does not mean being negatively or arbitrarily critical; it simply means that you intentionally examine knowledge, beliefs, and the means by which conclusions were obtained.

Truly engaging in critical thinking can be challenging. One thing it asks us to do is break some very persistent mental habits employed by nearly everyone, even the best scientists and most rational thinkers. Take, for example, the belief that our own mental activity has some kind of direct effect on physical reality (Pronin et al., 2006). People are prone to ponder their role in the popular but wildly unscientific term *fate*—something we are often advised to avoid tempting. Consider this scenario:

Jon has applied to Stanford to attend graduate school. His highly optimistic mother sent him a Stanford T-shirt to wear before he even learned whether he was accepted. What if:

1. Jon wears the shirt while he awaits the decision from Stanford? Will he be accepted?

   or

2. Jon stuffs the shirt in his drawer and decides to wait until he hears from Stanford? Will he be accepted?

Research participants who read the scenario in which Jon decided to wear the T-shirt were much more likely to guess that Jon would not be accepted (Risen & Gilovitch, 2008). But why? Are people so confused about reality that they honestly believe that wearing a Stanford T-shirt could influence decisions made by the Stanford graduate admissions office? It is not likely. However, people do attach a lot of significance to coincidental events, especially when the outcome is negative. If Jon wore the T-shirt before getting accepted and was subsequently declined, we might see it as at least partially his fault. Fate 1: Jon 0. This is the type of scenario that we (and Jon) would likely remember. If Jon does not wear the shirt and is *either* accepted or declined, we would likely forget about what he did with the T-shirt in the first place. (In the case of the fourth possibility—that Jon wears the shirt and gets accepted—we would now call it his "lucky T-shirt") (Figure 1.5).

Scientists would be the last people to advise that we avoid being curious about how events in the world are related and what causes them to occur. However, in our search for reality, we have to remind ourselves that the human brain is perhaps too willing to make connections. For the mind to study itself—that is, to do psychology or any other science—it needs to carefully steer around the mental barriers to rational thought. This means thinking critically and scientifically.

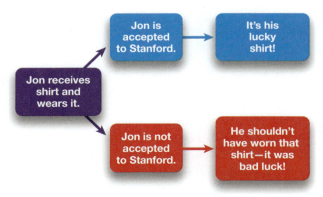

{FIG. 1.5} **Thinking Critically** Was it a mistake to wear the Stanford T-shirt? Many people would answer that it all depends on the outcome. **Click on this figure in your eText to see more details.**

Independent reports of alien abductions often resemble events and characters depicted in science fiction movies.

MYTHS IN MIND
Abducted by Aliens!

Occasionally we hear claims of alien abductions, ghost sightings, and other paranormal activity. Countless television shows and movies, both fictional and documentary based, reinforce the idea that these types of events can and do occur. Alien abductions are probably the most far-fetched stories, yet many people believe they occur or at least regard them as a real possibility. What is even more interesting are the extremely detailed accounts given by purported alien abductees. However, physical evidence of an abduction is always lacking. So what can we make of the validity of alien abduction stories?

Scientific and critical thinking involves the use of the *principle of parsimony*, which means that the simplest of all competing explanations (the most "parsimonious") of a phenomenon should be the one we accept. Is there a simpler explanation for alien abductions? Probably so. Psychologists who study alien abduction cases have discovered some interesting patterns and observations about the people reporting them. First, historical reports of abductions typically spike just after the release of science fiction movies featuring space aliens. Details of the reports often follow specific details seen in these movies. (Clancy, 2005). Second, it probably would not be too surprising to learn that people who report being abducted are prone to fantasizing and having false memories (vivid recollection and belief in something that did not happen; Lynn & Kirsch, 1996). Finally, people who claim to have been abducted are likely to experience sleep paralysis (waking up and becoming aware of being unable to move—a temporary state that is not unusual) and hallucinations while in the paralyzed state (McNally et al., 2004). Following the principle of parsimony typically leads to real, though sometimes less spectacular, answers.

. . . .

Quick Quiz 1.1b :: Building Scientific Literacy

KNOW ...

1 Someone who exercises curiosity and skepticism about assumptions and beliefs is using _____.

   A critical thinking

   B a hypothesis

   C pseudoscience

   D the biopsychosocial model

UNDERSTAND ...

2 Scientific literacy does *not* include _____.

   A gathering knowledge

   B accepting common sense explanations

   C critical thinking

   D applying scientific information to everyday problems

APPLY ...

3 Paul is considering whether to take a cholesterol-reducing medicine that has been recommended by his physician. He goes to the library and learns that the government agency that oversees medications—the FDA—has approved the medication after dozens of studies had been conducted on their usefulness. Which aspect of critical thinking does this *best* represent?

   A Paul has examined the nature and source of the evidence.

   B Paul was simply curious.

   C Paul did not consider alternative viewpoints.

   D Paul was avoiding overly emotional thinking.

Answers can be found on page ANS-1.

Module Summary

Now that you have read this module you should:

Listen to the audio file of this module at **MyPsychLab**

KNOW ...

- **The key terminology of the scientific method:**

biopsychosocial model (p. 5)
critical thinking (p. 8)
hypothesis (p. 3)
pseudoscience (p. 4)

psychology (p. 3)
scientific literacy (p. 6)
scientific method (p. 3)
theory (p. 4)

UNDERSTAND ...

- **The steps of the scientific method.** The basic model in **Figure 1.1 (p. 3)** guides us through the steps of the scientific method. Scientific theories generate hypotheses, which are specific and testable predictions. If a hypothesis is confirmed, new hypotheses may stem from it, and the original theory receives added support. If a hypothesis is rejected, the original hypothesis may be modified and retested, or the original theory may be modified or rejected.

- **The concept of scientific literacy.** *Scientific literacy* refers to the process of how we think about and understand scientific information. The model for scientific literacy was summarized in **Figure 1.3 (p. 7)**. Working the model involves answering a set of questions:

  What do we know about a phenomenon?

  How can science explain it?

  Can we critically evaluate the evidence?

  Why is this relevant?

  You will see this model applied to concepts in each chapter of this text. This includes gathering knowledge, explaining phenomena in scientific terms, engaging in critical thinking, and knowing how to apply and use your knowledge.

APPLY ...

- **The biopsychosocial model to behavior.** This is a model we will use throughout the text. As you consider each topic, think about how biological factors (e.g., the brain and genetics) are influential. Also consider how psychological factors such as thinking, learning, emotion, and memory are relevant. Social and cultural factors complete the model. These three interacting factors influence our behavior.

- **The steps in critical thinking.** To be useful, critical thinking is something not just to memorize, but rather to use and apply. Remember, critical thinking involves (1) being curious, (2) examining evidence, (3) examining assumptions and biases, (4) avoiding emotional thinking, (5) tolerating ambiguity, and (6) considering alternative viewpoints. Try applying these steps below in **Table 1.1** and check your answers on page ANS-1.

ANALYZE ...

- **The use of the term scientific theory.** As you read in this module, the term *theory* is often used very casually in the English language, sometimes synonymously with *opinion*. Thus it is important to analyze the scientific meaning of the term and contrast it with the alternatives. A scientific theory is an explanation for a broad range of observations, integrating numerous findings into a coherent whole. Remember, theories are not the same thing as opinions or beliefs, all theories are not equally plausible, and, strange as it may sound, a measure of a good scientific theory is not determined by the number of people who believe it to be true.

Table 1.1 :: Critical Thinking

Practice applying critical thinking skills to the scenario below:

Magic Mileage is a high-tech fuel additive that actually increases the distance you can drive for every gallon by 20%, while costing only a fraction of the gasoline itself!! Wouldn't you like to cut your fuel expenses by one fifth? Magic Mileage is a blend of complex engine-cleaning agents and patented "octane-booster" that not only packs in extra miles per gallon but also leaves your engine cleaner and running smooth while reducing emissions!

1. How might this appeal lead to overly emotional thinking?
2. Can you identify assumptions or biases the manufacturer might have?
3. Do you have enough evidence to make a judgment about this product?

How Psychology Became a Science

KNOW ...	UNDERSTAND ...	APPLY ...	ANALYZE ...
The key terminology of psychology's history	How various philosophical and scientific fields became major influences on psychology	Your knowledge to distinguish among the different specializations in psychology	How the philosophical ideas of empiricism and determinism are applied to human behavior

Would you pay $45,875 for a tape measure? Or $3 million for a baseball, even if you had the cash to spare? It may sound outrageous, but John F. Kennedy's tape measure went for $45,875 at an auction, and Mark McGwire's record-setting home run baseball sold for $3 million in 1999. Both ancient philosophers and modern psychologists would be curious about *anyone* who would pay this price. Socrates and Aristotle pondered the notion that physical objects have an *essence*—an invisible property that makes them special—but only in the mind of the beholder. As you will see in this module, many of the questions psychologists now test scientifically are not necessarily new—some have been around for centuries. For example, psychologist Paul Bloom (2010) has recently revived and modified the notion of an essence. He uses the term *essentialism* to explain this very human tendency to ascribe significance to certain instances of some objects but not to others. He studies how humans, starting at a very early age, "essentialize" certain objects—consider the child who loses a worn teddy bear and cannot be consoled by a fuzzy new one. Psychologists, like philosophers, are interested in *why* people think and behave in these ways. The main difference between the two is that psychologists apply scientific methods to find answers.

Focus Questions

1. Why did it take so long for scientists to start applying their methods to human thoughts and experience?

2. What has resulted from the application of scientific methods to human behavior?

Psychology has long dealt with some major questions and issues that span philosophical inquiry and scientific study. For example, psychologists have questioned how environmental, genetic, and physiological processes influence behavior. They have wrestled with the issue of whether our behavior is determined by external events, or if we have free will to act. Psychology's search for answers to these and other questions continues, and in this module we put this search into historical context and see how these questions have influenced the field of psychology as it exists today.

Psychology's Philosophical and Scientific Origins

Science is more than a body of facts to memorize or a set of subjects to study. Science is actually a philosophy of knowledge that stems from two fundamental beliefs: empiricism and determinism.

Empiricism *is a philosophical tenet that knowledge comes through experience.* In everyday language, you might hear the phrase "Seeing is believing," but in the scientific sense, empiricism means that knowledge about the world is based on careful observation, not common sense or speculation. Whatever we see or measure should be observable by anyone else who follows the same methods. In addition, scientific theories must be rational explanations of how the observations fit together. Thus, although the empiricist might say, "Seeing is believing," thinking and reasoning about observations are just as important.

Determinism *is the belief that all events are governed by lawful, cause-and-effect relationships.* This is easy enough when we discuss natural laws such as gravity—we probably all agree that if you drop an object, it will fall. But does the lawfulness of nature apply to the way we think and act? Does it mean that we do not have control over our own actions? This interesting philosophical debate is often referred to as *free will versus determinism.* While we certainly feel as if we are in control of our own behaviors—that is, we sense that we have free will—there are some compelling reasons (discussed later in this book) to believe that our behaviors are determined. The level of determinism or free will psychologists attribute to humans is certainly debated, and to be a psychologist, you do not have to believe that every single thought, behavior, or experience is determined by natural laws. But psychologists certainly do recognize that behavior is determined by both internal (e.g., genes, brain chemistry) and external influences.

Psychological science is both empirical and deterministic. Our understanding of behavior comes from observing what we can see and measure, and behavior is caused by a multitude of factors. Psychology arrived at this point over the course of the past couple of centuries and after going through various phases of maturity. For psychology to find its place of origin, there first had to be the right cultural atmosphere.

Once the scientific method started to take hold around 1600, physics, astronomy, physiology, biology, and chemistry all experienced unprecedented growth in knowledge and technology. But why did it take psychology until the late 1800s to become scientific? One of the main reasons is *zeitgeist,* a German word meaning "spirit of the times." **Zeitgeist** *refers to a general set of beliefs of a particular culture at a specific time in history.* It can be used to understand why some ideas take off immediately, whereas other perfectly good ideas may go unnoticed for years.

The power of zeitgeist can be very strong, and there are several ways it prevented psychological science from emerging in the 1600s. Perhaps most important is that people were not ready to accept a science that could be applied to human behavior and thought. To the average person of the 1600s, viewing human behavior as the result of predictable physical laws was troubling. Doing so would seem to imply the philosophy of **materialism**: *the belief that humans, and other living beings, are composed exclusively of physical matter.* Accepting this idea would mean that we are nothing more than complex machines that lack a self-conscious, self-controlling soul. The opposing belief, that there are properties of humans that are not material (a mind or soul separate from the body), is called *dualism.*

Although most early thinking about the mind and behavior remained philosophical in nature, scientific methods were generating great discoveries for the natural sciences of physics, biology, and physiology. This meant that the early influences on psychology came from the natural and physical sciences. (Figure 1.6 provides a timeline that summarizes some of the major events in the history of psychology.)

Most people believe that the behavior of billiard balls will be *determined* by the laws of physics. They roll where the energy directs them, not where they want to go. Could human behavior be determined by natural laws as well?

Late 1700s: Franz Mesmer develops techniques to treat mental illness, including the use of hypnosis.

Around 1850: Gustav Fechner pioneers the study of psychophysics.

1859: Darwin publishes *On the Origin of Species* introducing his theory of natural selection.

1861: Physician Paul Broca discovers a brain area associated with the production of speech, now known as Broca's area, establishing that regions of the brain are specialized to serve different functions.

1879: Wilhelm Wundt establishes the first psychological laboratory in Leipzig, Germany, and two years later he establishes the first journal in psychology.

1883: G. Stanley Hall establishes his laboratory at Johns Hopkins University in Baltimore—the first psychology laboratory in the United States.

1880s: Francis Galton introduces and develops the study of anthropometrics.

1885: Hermann Ebbinghaus begins his scientific study of memory.

1890: William James, founder of the functionalist approach, publishes *Principles of Psychology*.

1892: The American Psychological Association (APA) is established.

AMERICAN PSYCHOLOGICAL ASSOCIATION

1936: Kurt Lewin authors *Principles of Topological Psychology*, which introduces the social psychological formulation that the behavior of individuals is influenced by their social environment.

1929: Psi Chi is founded as the National Honor Society in psychology to recognize and support excellence in academic psychology.

1913: John B. Watson writes "Psychology as the Behaviorist Views It," establishing behaviorism as the primary school of thought in American psychology.

1912: Max Wertheimer establishes the field of gestalt psychology.

1911: Edward Thorndike demonstrates the basic principles of instrumental learning, forming the basis for the study of operant conditioning.

1905: Alfred Binet develops the first intelligence test.

Early 1900s: Ivan Pavlov demonstrates the basic principles of classical conditioning.

1904: Mary Calkins is elected the first female president of the American Psychological Association.

1900: Sigmund Freud writes *The Interpretation of Dreams*, a key book in the development of psychoanalysis.

1896: Lightmer Witmer establishes the first psychological clinic at the University of Pennsylvania.

1894: Margaret Washburn is the first female to receive a PhD in psychology.

1938: B. F. Skinner writes the *Behavior of Organisms*, which furthers the cause of behaviorism.

1951: Carl Rogers writes *Client-Centered Therapy*, which helps establish humanistic psychology.

1952: The first *Diagnostic and Statistical Manual of Mental Disorders*, soon to be in its fifth edition, is published by the American Psychiatric Association.

1967: Ulrich Neisser publishes *Cognitive Psychology*, which introduces a major new subfield of psychology.

1971: B. F. Skinner publishes *Beyond Freedom and Dignity*, stirring controversy over radical behaviorism.

1978: Herbert Simon wins the Nobel Prize in economics for research in cognitive psychology (there is no Nobel Prize dedicated to psychology).

1988: Establishment of the American Psychological Society, now known as Association for Psychological Science (APS).

1980s-early 1990s: Brain-imaging techniques such as magnetic resonance imaging become mainstream methods for studying brain anatomy and function in human subjects.

1990s: President George H. W. Bush proclaims the 1990s to be "The Decade of the Brain," and there is unprecedented growth in neuroscience and biological psychology.

2003: The Human Genome Project is completed.

{FIG. 1.6} **Major Events in the History of Psychology**

INFLUENCES FROM PHYSICS: EXPERIMENTING WITH THE MIND   The initial forays into scientific psychology were conducted by physicists and physiologists. One of the earliest explorations was made by Gustav Fechner (1801–1887), who worked on sensation and perception. As a physicist, Fechner was interested in the natural world of moving objects and energy. He turned his knowledge to psychological questions about how the physical and mental worlds interact. Fechner coined the term **psychophysics**, *which is the study of the relationship between the physical world and the mental representation of that world.*

As an example of psychophysical research, imagine you are holding a one-pound weight in your right hand and a five-pound weight in your left hand. Obviously, your left hand will feel the heavier weight, but that is not what interested Fechner. What if a researcher places a quarter-pound weight in each hand, resting on top of the weight that is already there? Fechner wanted to know which of the quarter-pound weights would be perceived as heavier. Oddly enough, although both weigh the same amount, the quarter-pound weight in your right hand will be more noticeable than the quarter-pound weight added to your left hand, almost as if it were heavier (see Figure 1.7). Through experiments like these, Fechner demonstrated basic principles of how the physical and mental worlds interact. In fact, he developed an equation to precisely calculate the perceived change in weight, and then extended this formula to apply to changes in brightness, loudness, and other perceptual experiences.

INFLUENCES FROM EVOLUTIONARY THEORY: THE ADAPTIVE FUNCTIONS OF BEHAVIOR
Around the same time Fechner was doing his experiments, Charles Darwin (1809–1882) was studying the variety of plants and animals around the world. Darwin noticed that animal groups that were isolated from one another often differed by only minor variations in physical features. These variations seemed to fine-tune the species according to the particular environment in which they lived, making them better equipped for survival and reproduction. Darwin's theory of evolution by *natural selection* was based on his observations that the genetically inherited traits that contribute to survival and reproductive success are more likely to flourish within the breeding population. This theory explains why there is such a diversity of life on Earth.

What does evolution have to do with psychology? As Darwin pointed out in *The Expression of the Emotions in Man and Animals* (1872), behavior is shaped by natural selection, just as physical traits are. Darwin noted that for many species, including humans, survival and reproduction are closely related to an individual's ability to recognize some expressions as threats and others as submission. To Darwin, it appeared that emotional expressions and other behaviors were influenced by natural selection as well. Even before Darwin, humans had selectively bred animals to behave in certain ways (i.e., *artificial* selection of traits, rather than natural selection). Sheep dogs make good herders, whereas their pit bull cousins do not. Retrievers and pointers are good at hunting with humans, but how long would a toy poodle last in this context?

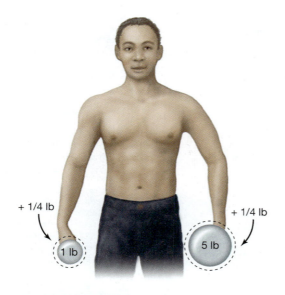

+ 1/4 lb

+ 1/4 lb

1 lb

5 lb

{FIG. 1.7} **The Study of Psychophysics** Gustav Fechner studied relationships between the physical world and our mental representations of that world. For example, Fechner tested how people detect changes in physical stimuli.

Charles Darwin proposed the theory of natural selection to explain how evolution works.

Darwin's recognition that behaviors, like physical traits, are subject to hereditary influences and natural selection was a major contribution to psychology.

INFLUENCES FROM MEDICINE: DIAGNOSES AND TREATMENTS

Medicine contributed a great deal to the biological perspective in psychology, as well as **clinical psychology**, *the field of psychology that concentrates on the diagnosis and treatment of psychological disorders.* One interesting area of medical study was *brain localization*, the idea that certain parts of the brain control specific mental abilities and personality characteristics.

The mid-1800s saw two competing views of localization. The first was *phrenology*, which gained considerable popularity for more than 100 years thanks to physicians Franz Gall (1758–1828) and Johann Spurzheim (1776–1832). Gall, Spurzheim, and their followers believed that the brain consisted of 27 "organs," corresponding to mental traits and dispositions that could be detected by examining the surface of the skull. Phrenology continued to gather supporters for nearly a century before being abandoned by serious scientists. You might have encountered images of the phrenological map of the skull (see Figure 1.8).

The other approach to localization entailed the study of brain injuries and the ways in which they affect

Humans are not unique in their capacity to express emotion with facial expressions.

behavior. This work had a scientific grounding that phrenology lacked. There were many intriguing cases described by physicians of the 1800s, and here are two that provide great examples:

- Physician Paul Broca studied a patient named Tan. Tan received this name because it was the only word he could speak, despite the fact that he could hear and understand perfectly well. Broca identified an area of the left side of Tan's brain that was damaged, and claimed to have found where speech production was localized; that area of the brain is now known as *Broca's area.*

- Motivated by Broca's work, Karl Wernicke identified *Wernicke's area* in 1874. Patients with damage to Wernicke's area could speak in sentences that sounded normal, but with unusual or made-up words. Patients who regained some of their speech later reported that, although they could hear just fine, no speech—not even their own—made sense during the recovery period.

Additional medical influences on psychology came from outside of mainstream practices. Franz Mesmer, an 18th-century Austrian physician practicing in Paris, believed that prolonged exposure to magnets could redirect the flow of metallic fluids in the body, thereby curing disease and insanity. Although his claim was rejected outright by the medical and scientific communities in France, some of his patients seemed to be cured after being lulled into a trance. Modern physicians and scientists attribute these "cures" to belief in the treatment—what we now call *psychosomatic medicine.*

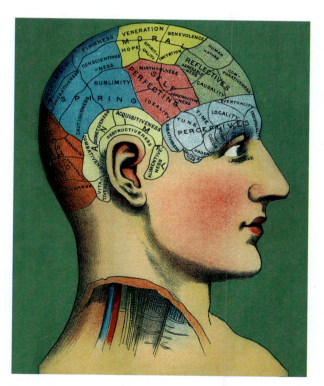

{FIG. 1.8} **A Phrenology Map** Early scholars of the brain believed that mental capacities and personalities could be measured by the contours, bumps, and ridges distributed across the surface of the skull.

Sigmund Freud developed the concept of an unconscious mind and its underlying processes in his theory of psychoanalysis.

The medical establishment eventually grew more intrigued by the trances Mesmer produced in his patients, naming the phenomenon *hypnosis*. This practice also caught the attention of an Austrian physician named Sigmund Freud (1856–1939), who began to use hypnosis to treat his own patients. Freud was particularly interested in how hypnosis seemed to have cured several patients of *hysterical paralysis*—a condition in which an individual loses feeling and control in a specific body part, despite the lack of any known neurological damage or disease. These experiences led Freud to develop his famous theory and technique, called *psychoanalysis*.

Psychoanalysis *is a psychological approach that attempts to explain how behavior and personality are influenced by unconscious processes.* Freud acknowledged that conscious experience includes perceptions, thoughts, a sense of self, and the sense that we are in control of ourselves. However, he also believed in an unconscious mind that contained forgotten episodes from early childhood and urges to fulfill self-serving sexual and aggressive impulses. Freud proposed that because these urges were unconscious, they could exert influence in strange ways, such as restricting the use of a body part (psychosomatic or hysterical paralysis). Freud believed hypnosis played a valuable role in his work. When a person is hypnotized, dreaming, or perhaps medicated into a trancelike state (Freud had a fondness for cocaine during a period of his

career), he thought, the psychoanalyst could have more direct access into the individual's unconscious mind. Once Freud gained access, he could attempt to determine and correct any desires or emotions he believed were causing the unconscious to create the psychosomatic conditions.

Although Freud neglected to conduct scientific experiments, his legacy can be seen in some key elements of scientific psychology. First, many modern psychologists make inferences about unconscious mental activity, just as Freud had advocated. Second, the use of medical ideas to treat disorders of emotions, thought, and behavior—an approach known as the *medical model*—can be traced to Freud's influence. Third, Freud incorporated evolutionary thinking into his work; he emphasized how physiological needs and urges relating to survival and reproduction can influence our behavior. Finally, Freud placed great emphasis on how early life experiences influence our behavior as adults—a perspective that comes up many times in this text.

THE INFLUENCE OF SOCIAL SCIENCES: MEASURING AND COMPARING HUMANS

A third influential force came out of the social sciences of economics, sociology, and anthropology. These disciplines developed statistical methods for measuring human traits, which soon became relevant to the emerging field of psychology. An early pioneer in measuring perception and behavior was Sir Francis Galton. Galton was probably most inspired by his cousin, Charles Darwin, who had just published his theory of evolution by natural selection. Galton believed that heredity (genetics) explained psychological differences among people. The idea of hereditary psychology fit Galton's beliefs about social class. For example, he noticed that great achievement tended to run in families. After all, Galton's cousin was a great naturalist, his uncle Erasmus was a celebrated physician and writer, and Galton himself was no slouch (he began reading as a 2-year-old child, and was into Shakespeare by age 6). To Galton, it seemed natural that people who did better in scholarship, business, and wealth were able to do so because they were *better* people (genetically speaking).

To support his beliefs, Galton developed ways of measuring what he called *eminence*—a combination of ability, morality, and achievement. One observation supporting his claim for a hereditary basis for eminence was that the closer a relative, the more similar the traits. Galton was one of the first investigators to

Francis Galton set up his anthropometric (literally "human measurement") laboratory at the International Health Exhibition in London in 1885.

and brain basis for behavior. Biological psychologists typically work in different specialty areas, such as behavioral genetics, where researchers use various methods to determine how genes affect characteristics such as intelligence and personality. Also, the field of cognitive neuroscience examines relationships between thought and brain function.

scientifically take on the question of **nature and nurture relationships**, *the inquiry into how heredity (nature) and environment (nurture) influence behavior and mental processes.* Galton came down decidedly on the nature side, seemingly ignoring the likelihood that nurturing influences such as upbringing and family traditions, rather than biological endowments, could explain similarities among relatives. Galton also supported his beliefs by ignoring the fact that great people can and do come from very humble beginnings.

Galton's beliefs and biases led him to pursue scientific justification for *eugenics,* which literally translates as "good genes," and promoted the belief that social programs should encourage intelligent, talented individuals to have children, whereas criminals, those with physical or mental disability, and non-White races should be kept out of the English gene pool. The eugenics movement was based largely on what the researchers wanted to believe was true, not quality research methods. It ultimately led to the mistreatment of many individuals, especially first-generation Americans, immigrants, and the descendants of slaves who were not of Galton's own demographic group.

Not all of Galton's contributions to psychology were controversial. He worked on a broad range of topics and is credited with greatly advancing scientific approaches to behavior. The most significant product of Galton's scientific legacy is the use of statistical methods to measure and study behavior and mental processes.

In modern times, biological and genetic approaches to explaining behavior are thriving (and, thankfully, eugenics has vanished). The field of *biological psychology* seeks to explain the underlying genetic, physiological,

Quick Quiz 1.2a
Psychology's Philosophical and Scientific Origins

KNOW…

1 In philosophical terms, a materialist is someone who might believe that:

A money buys happiness.

B species evolve through natural selection.

C personality can be measured by feeling for bumps on the surface of the skull.

D everything that exists, including human beings, are composed exclusively of physical matter.

UNDERSTAND…

2 According to Sigmund Freud, which of the following would be the most likely explanation for why someone is behaving aggressively?

A They are acting according to psychophysics.

B There is something going on at the unconscious level that is causing them to behave this way.

C They are acting out of free will.

D The environment is determining their behavioral response.

APPLY…

3 Jan believes that all knowledge is acquired through experience with the world. Jan is probably _____.

A an empiricist

B a supporter of eugenics

C a clinical psychologist

D a phrenologist

ANALYZE…

4 Francis Galton made a significant contribution to psychology by introducing methods for studying how heredity contributes to human behavior. Which alternative explanation was Galton overlooking when he argued that heredity accounts for these similarities?

A The primary importance of the nature side of the nature versus nurture debate

B The fact that people who share genes live together in families, so they tend to share environmental privileges or disadvantages

C A materialistic account of behavior

D The concept of dualism, which states that the mind is separate from the body

Answers can be found on page ANS-1.

The Beginnings of Contemporary Psychology

As you now know, before psychology became its own discipline, there were scientists working across different fields who were converging on a study of human behavior. It is possible that physicists could have gone on studying psychophysics, physicians could have continued studying brain injuries, and biologists could have kept studying evolutionary influences on behavior. By modern standards, Darwin, Fechner, and others had produced psychological research but it was not referred to as such because the field had not yet formed. Nevertheless, progress toward a distinct discipline of psychology was in the works.

STRUCTURALISM AND FUNCTIONALISM: THE BEGINNINGS OF PSYCHOLOGY Most contemporary psychologists agree that Wilhelm Wundt (1832–1920) established the first laboratory dedicated to studying human behavior and was responsible for establishing psychology as an independent scientific field. Wundt conducted numerous experiments on how people sense and perceive. His primary research method was *introspection*, meaning "to look within." Introspection required a trained volunteer to experience a stimulus and then report each individual sensation he or she could identify through introspection. For example, if the volunteer was given a steel ball to hold in one hand, he would likely report the sensations of cold, hard, smooth, and heavy. To Wundt, these basic sensations were the mental "atoms" that combined to form the molecules of experience. Wundt also developed *reaction time* methods as a way of measuring mental effort. In one such study, volunteers watched an apparatus in which two metal balls swung into each other to make a clicking sound. The volunteers required about one eighth of a second to react to the sound, leading Wundt to conclude that mental activity is not instantaneous, but rather it requires a small amount of effort measured by the amount of time it takes to react. What made Wundt's work distinctly psychological was his focus on measuring mental events and examining how they were affected by his experimental manipulations.

Wundt's ideas made their way to the United States through students who worked with him. One student, Edward Titchener, adopted the same method of introspection used by Wundt to devise an organized map of the structure of human consciousness. **Structuralism** *was an attempt to analyze conscious experience by breaking it down into basic elements, and to understand how these elements work together.* Titchener chose the term *elements* deliberately as an analogy with the periodic table in the physical sciences. He believed that mental experiences were made up of a limited number of sensations, which were analogous to elements in physics and chemistry. According to Titchener, different sensations

German scientist Wilhelm Wundt is widely credited as the "father" of experimental psychology.

William James was a highly influential American psychologist who took a functionalist approach to explaining behavior.

can form and create complex compounds, just like hydrogen and water can combine to form water—H_2O.

The same year Wundt set up his first laboratory, an American scholar named William James (1842–1910) set out to write the first textbook in psychology, *The Principles of Psychology*, which was eventually published in 1890. Trained as a physician, James combined his knowledge of physiology with his interest in the philosophy of mental activity. Among his many interests, he sought to understand how the mind functions. In contrast to structuralism, which looks for permanent, unchanging elements of thought, James was influenced by Darwin's evolutionary principles, so he preferred to examine behavior in context, and explain how our thoughts and actions help us adapt to our environment. **Functionalism** *is the study of the purpose and function of behavior and conscious experience.* The incorporation of Darwin's ideas can be found today in the modern field of *evolutionary psychology,* an approach that interprets and explains modern human behavior in terms of forces acting upon our distant ancestors. According to this approach, our brains and behaviors have been shaped by the physical and social environment that our ancestors encountered.

During the early years of psychology, the pioneers were trying to find a way to use the methods and instruments of the natural sciences to understand behavior. Although some of those techniques, such as Wundt's introspection, are no longer used exclusively, by the turn of the 20th century it was clear that the discipline of psychology was here to stay. With that sense of permanence in place, the second generation of psychologists could focus on refining the subject matter and the methods, and turning psychology into a widely accepted scientific field.

THE RISE OF BEHAVIORISM   Early in the 20th century, biologists became interested in how organisms learn to anticipate their bodily functions. One of the first to do so was Professor Edwin Twitmyer (1873–1943), an American psychologist interested in reflexes. His work involved a contraption with a rubber mallet that would regularly tap the patellar tendon just below the kneecap; this, of course, causes a kicking reflex in most individuals. To make sure his volunteers were not startled by the mallet, the contraption would ring a bell right before the mallet struck the tendon. As is often the case in experiments, the technology failed after a number of these bell-ringing and hammer-tapping combinations: The machine rang the bell, but the hammer did not come down on the volunteer's knee. But the real surprise was this—the volunteer's leg kicked anyway! How did that happen? Because the sound of the bell successfully predicted the hammer, the ringing soon had the effect of the hammer itself, a process now called *classical conditioning.* The study of conditioning would soon become a focus of

Ivan Pavlov (on the right) explained classical conditioning through his studies of salivary reflexes in dogs.

behaviorism, *an approach that dominated the first half of the 20th century of American psychology and had a singular focus on studying only observable behavior, with little to no reference to mental events or instincts as possible influences on behavior.*

At first, Twitmyer's research was coolly received when he announced his findings at the American Psychological Association meeting. Not a single colleague bothered to ask him a question. The credit for discovering classical conditioning typically goes to a Russian physiologist named Ivan Pavlov (1849–1936). Pavlov's Nobel Prize–winning research showed that dogs could learn to salivate to a tone if the tone has a history of sounding just prior to the delivery of food.

Credit for the rise of behaviorism in the United States typically goes to John B. Watson (1878–1958). As research accumulated on the breadth of behaviors that could be conditioned, Watson began to believe that all behavior could ultimately be explained through conditioning. This emphasis on learning also came with stipulations about what could and could not be studied in psychology. Watson was adamant that only observable changes in the environment and behavior were appropriate for scientific study. Methods such as Wundt's introspection, he said, were too subjective to even consider. Perhaps his most famous statement sums it up:

> *Give me a dozen healthy infants, well-formed, and my own specified world to bring them up in and I'll guarantee to take any one at random and train him to become any type of specialist I might select—doctor, lawyer, artist, merchant-chief and, yes, even beggar-man and thief, regardless of his talents, penchants, tendencies, abilities, vocations, and race of his ancestors. (Watson, 1930, p. 82)*

B. F. Skinner revealed how rewards affect behavior by conducting laboratory studies on animals. **Click on this photo in your eText to see more details**.

As you can imagine, Watson believed so much in the power of experience (and so little in the power of genetics) that he was certain he could engineer a personality however he wished, if given enough control over the environment.

After a year of indiscretion involving a female graduate student, Watson was dismissed from his university job, but found his new career—as well as his fortune—in advertising. Most advertisers at the time just assumed they should inform people about the merits of a product. Watson and his colleagues applied a scientific approach to advertising and discovered a consumer's knowledge about the product really was not that important, so long as he or she had positive emotions associated with it. Thus Watson's company developed ads that employed behaviorist principles to form associations between a product's brand image and positive emotions. If Pavlov's dogs could be conditioned to salivate when they heard a tone, what possibilities might there be for conditioning humans in a similar way? Modern advertisers want the logos for their brands of snacks or the trademark signs for their restaurants to bring on a specific craving, and some salivation along the way. We have John B. Watson and his colleagues to thank for this phenomenon.

Taking up the reins from Watson was B. F. Skinner (1904–1990), another behaviorist who had considerable influence over American psychology for several decades. Much like Watson, Skinner believed that psychology was the study of behavior and *not* of the unobservable mind. Mostly working with animal subjects in his laboratory, Skinner sought to discover the principles of how rewards affect behavior. His approach rested on the relatively straightforward observation that organisms repeat behaviors that bring rewards and avoid those that do not. Typically, these studies occurred with animals held in small chambers in which they could manipulate a lever to receive rewards. The experimenter would control when rewards were available, and the animal's task was to learn the reward schedule. You might ask what this work had to do with human behavior. The behaviorists believed that the foundation of psychology could be established through conducting experiments on how rewards and punishment motivate and influence our

behavior. Thus, the same principles ought to apply to any organism—both human and nonhuman.

Watson's and Skinner's concept of behaviorism met with resistance from many psychologists. If our behavior is controlled by external rewards and the satisfaction of motivational drives, then this leaves little room for free will—the notion that we are free to make choices and guide our own behavior without external influence. Many of those who resisted believed that humans could rise above their instinctive, reward-based motivations.

HUMANISTIC PSYCHOLOGY EMERGES The notion that humans have free will and special and unique qualities drew interest in the 1950s by psychologists who were breaking from the predominant perspective of behaviorism. In addition, the field of psychoanalytic psychology developed by Freud did not leave much, if any, room for the possibility of free will.

A new psychological perspective was spawned during this period. **Humanistic psychology** *focuses on the unique aspects of each individual human, each person's freedom to act, his or her rational thought, and the belief that humans are fundamentally different from other animals.* Among the many major figures of humanistic psychology were Carl Rogers (1902–1987) and Abraham Maslow (1908–1970). Both psychologists focused on the positive aspects of humanity and the factors that lead to a productive and fulfilling life. Humanistic psychologists sought to

Carl Rogers helped develop the humanistic psychology movement, which emphasized human strengths and free will.

understand the *meaning* of personal experience. They believed that people could attain mental well-being and satisfaction through gaining a greater understanding of themselves, rather than by being diagnosed with a disorder or having their problems labeled. Both Rogers and Maslow believed that humans strive to develop a sense of self and are motivated to personally grow and fulfill their potential. This view stands in particular contrast to the psychoanalytic tradition, which originated from a medical model and, therefore, focused on illnesses of the body and brain. The humanistic perspective also contrasted with behaviorism in proposing that humans had the freedom to act and a rational mind to guide the process.

THE COGNITIVE REVOLUTION

Behaviorism dominated psychology in the United States throughout the first half of the 20th century. In Europe, however, psychologists retained an emphasis on thinking, and they ignored the Americans' cries to study only what could be directly observed. The European focus on thought flourished through the early 1900s, long before psychologists in the United States began to take seriously the idea that they could study mental processes, even if they could not directly see them. Thus it was the work of European psychologists that formed the basis of the cognitive perspective. Early evidence of an emerging cognitive perspective concerned the study of memory. The German psychologist Hermann Ebbinghaus (1850–1909) produced reams of data on remembering and forgetting. The results of his studies produced numerous "forgetting curves," which showed that most of what a person learns will be forgotten rapidly, but then forgetting slows to a crawl. Not only is the forgetting curve a staple of modern psychology, but some of Ebbinghaus's methods are also still applied to memory research today (you will read more about Ebbinghaus in Module 7.2).

British psychologist Frederick Bartlett (1886–1969) was able to illustrate that memory is an interpretive process that involves cultural knowledge. Think about the last film or television show you saw. Do you remember the exact words in the script? Do you remember what the characters were wearing? Bartlett's work demonstrated that we are more likely to remember the general storyline than any of these other details, and our cultural knowledge shapes what we find important enough to remember (Bartlett, 1932).

Another precursor to cognitive psychology can be seen in the early to mid-1900s movement of **gestalt psychology**, *an approach emphasizing that psychologists need to focus on the whole of perception and experience, rather than its parts*. (*Gestalt* is a German word that refers to the

{FIG. 1.9} **The Whole Is Greater Than the Sum of Its Parts** The Gestalt psychologists emphasized humans' ability to see whole forms. For example, you probably perceive a sphere in the center of this figure, even though it does not exist on the page.

complete form of an object; see Figure 1.9.) This contrasts with the structuralist goal of breaking experience into its individual parts. For example, if Wundt or Titchener were to hand you an apple, you would not think, "Round, red, has a stem …"; you would simply think to yourself, "This is an apple." Gestalt psychologists argued that much of our thinking and experience occur at a higher, more organized level than Wundt emphasized; they believed that Wundt's approach to understanding experience made about as much sense as understanding water only by studying its hydrogen and oxygen atoms.

What do gestalt psychologists mean by "the whole" in terms of perceptual experiences? This concept becomes clearer when you contrast gestalt psychology with Wundt's elements. Imagine you have never seen or heard of apples. If someone gave you an apple and you liked it, you might be inclined to try a pear or a plum because these other fruits have a general resemblance to apples. Even though Wundt would want you to tell him you saw red, round, smooth, and so on when you looked at an apple, gestalt psychologists would point out that you might not be inclined to try everything that had similar elements to it: You would not be at all tempted to take a bite out of your neighbor's shiny new Volkswagen Beetle, no matter how red, round, and smooth it looks.

Around the time humanistic psychology was gaining interest, the interest in mental processes was starting to catch on in the United States. In the 1950s, the scientific study of cognition was becoming accepted practice in American psychology. The invention of the computer gave psychologists a useful analogy for understanding and talking about the mind (the *software* of the brain). Linguists argued that grammar and vocabulary were far too complex to be explained in behaviorist terms;

the alternative was to propose abstract mental processes. There was a great deal of interest in memory and perception as well, but it was not until 1968 that these areas of research were given the name "cognitive psychology" by Ulrich Neisser (born 1928). These events ushered in a new era of psychology in which studies of mental processes and experiences flourished. *Cognitive psychology* is a modern psychological perspective that focuses on processes such as memory, thinking, and language. Thus much of what cognitive psychologists study consists of mental processes that are inferred through rigorous experimentation.

PsychTutor
Click here in your eText for an interactive tutorial on **Schools of Psychology**

SOCIAL AND CULTURAL INFLUENCES The presence of other people affects our behavior in so many different ways. Recognition of this influence can be found in the very early years of psychology. As structuralism and functionalism were taking shape in the late 1800s and early 1900s, psychologists were starting to conduct experiments focusing on how other people influence individual behavior. An American psychologist, Norman Triplett (1861–1931), conducted one of the first formal experiments in this area, observing that cyclists ride faster in the presence of other people than when riding alone. Triplett published the first social psychology research in 1892, and a few social psychology textbooks appeared in 1908.

Despite the early interest in this field, studies of how people influence the behavior of others did not take off until the 1940s. The events in Nazi-controlled Germany that led up to World War II contributed to the development of this new perspective in psychology in at least two ways. First, Adolf Hitler's political machine was explicitly anti-Jewish and anti-intellectual. To escape persecution by the German government, a significant number of German professors and scientists from a range of disciplines fled to the United States. These psychologists brought with them the influence of gestalt psychology and mixed with the mostly behaviorist American psychologists. Second, research on social influences began as a result of collaborations between sociologists (who study populations of humans) and psychologists (who were studying individuals at that time). Together, they attempted to understand how normal individuals could be transformed into brutal prison camp guards, how political propaganda affected people, and how society might address issues of stereotyping and prejudice. In addition, psychologists in this tradition recognized how

important individual, personal factors were in determining behavior. Out of this context sprung the field of *social and personality psychology*, the study of the influence of other people on our behavior along with what makes each individual unique.

Although social psychology was born out of collaboration, Kurt Lewin (1890–1947) is often cited as the founder of modern social psychology. Trained as a gestalt psychologist, Lewin shifted his attention to race relations in the United States. After studying relations between individuals of different groups, he made an observation that is still well known among social psychologists: Behavior is a function of the individual and the environment, or $B = f\{I, E\}$. What Lewin meant was that all behaviors could be predicted and explained through understanding how an individual with a specific set of traits would respond in a context that involved a specific set of conditions. Take two individuals as an example: One tends to be quiet and engages in solitary activities such as reading, whereas the other is talkative and enjoys being where the action is. Now put them in a social situation, such as a wedding reception or a funeral. How will the two behave? Given the disparity between the individuals and between the two settings, we would suspect very different behaviors would emerge. This outcome illustrates the essence of Lewin's formulation of social psychology. On a broader but related scale, *cross-cultural psychology* is the field that draws comparisons about individual and group behavior among cultures; it helps us understand the role of society in shaping behavior, beliefs, and values.

The trends that emerged during this period laid the foundation for modern perspectives and theories in psychology. Psychology was now a clearly established discipline. A set of subject matter had been developed that included thinking and behavior. There were established venues such as professional organizations and journals to disseminate the results of psychological research. What you encounter in the upcoming modules will reflect these early influences. Although modern technology, such as brain scans and computing, would likely baffle psychology's founders, we believe they would find the results of modern research absolutely relevant to their own interests. In the next module, we will explore the settings in which this broad array of psychologists are encountered and what they contribute to society.

Quick Quiz 1.2b :: The Beginnings of Contemporary Psychology

KNOW ...

1 _____ was the study of the basic components of the mind, while _____ was the study of how they work.

- **A** Structuralism; functionalism
- **B** Behaviorism; functionalism
- **C** Functionalism; structuralism
- **D** Humanism; structuralism

UNDERSTAND ...

2 A distinct feature of behaviorism is its:

- **A** search for the deeper meaning of human existence.
- **B** search for patterns that create a whole that is greater than its parts.
- **C** use of introspection.
- **D** exclusive emphasis on observable behavior.

APPLY ...

3 Gwen is in search of the deeper meaning of her life, and would like to learn more about her potential as a human being. Which of the following types of psychologists would likely be most useful to her?

- **A** Humanistic
- **C** Behaviorist
- **B** Gestalt
- **D** Social

4 The gestalt psychologists, with their focus on perception and experience, are closely linked to modern-day _____ psychologists.

- **A** developmental
- **C** cognitive
- **B** social
- **D** evolutionary

Answers can be found on page ANS-1.

Module Summary

Module 1.2

Now that you have read this module you should:

Listen to the audio file of this module at **MyPsychLab**

KNOW ...

● **The key terminology of psychology's history:**

behaviorism (p. 21)
clinical psychology (p. 17)
determinism (p. 14)
empiricism (p. 14)
functionalism (p. 21)
gestalt psychology (p. 23)
humanistic psychology (p. 22)

materialism (p. 14)
nature and nurture relationships (p. 19)
psychoanalysis (p. 18)
psychophysics (p. 16)
structuralism (p. 20)
zeitgeist (p. 14)

UNDERSTAND ...

● **How various philosophical and scientific fields became major influences on psychology.** The philosophical schools of determinism, empiricism, and materialism provided a background for a scientific study of human behavior. The first psychologists were trained as physicists and physiologists. Fechner, for example, developed psychophysics, whereas Titchener looked for the elements of thought. Darwin's theory of natural selection influenced psychologist William James's idea of functionalism—the search for how behaviors may aid the survival and reproduction of the organism.

APPLY ...

● **Your knowledge to distinguish among the different specializations in psychology.** Try the activity in **Table 1.2** and check your answers on page ANS-1.

ANALYZE ...

● **How the philosophical ideas of empiricism and determinism are applied to human behavior.** Psychology is based on empiricism, the belief that all knowledge—including knowledge about human behavior—is acquired through the senses. All sciences, including psychology, require a deterministic viewpoint. Determinism is the philosophical tenet that all events in the world, including human actions, have a physical cause. The deterministic view is also essential to the sciences. Applying determinism to human behavior has been met with resistance by many because it appears to deny a place for free will.

Table 1.2 :: Areas of Specialization within Psychology

Apply your knowledge to distinguish among different specializations in psychology. You should be able to read a description of a psychologist on the left and match her or his work to a specialization on the right. Check your answers on page ANS-1.

1. I am an academic psychologist who studies various methods for improving study habits. I hope to help people increase memory performance and become better students. I am a(n) _____.

2. My work focuses on how the presence of other people influences an individual's acceptance of and willingness to express various stereotypes. I am a(n) _____.

3. I have been studying how childrearing practices in Guatemala, the United States, and Cambodia all share some common elements, as well as how they differ. I am a(n) _____.

4. I am interested in behaviors that are genetically influenced to help animals adapt to their changing environments. I am a(n) _____.

5. I help individuals identify problem areas of their lives and ways to correct them, and guide them to live up to their full potential. I am a(n) _____.

a. social psychologist
b. cross-cultural psychologist
c. cognitive psychologist
d. humanistic psychologist
e. evolutionary psychologist

Putting Psychology to Work: Careers in Psychology and Related Fields

KNOW ...	UNDERSTAND ...	APPLY ...	ANALYZE ...
The key terminology of psychological professions	The various professional settings occupied by psychologists The distinctions among mental health professions in their approaches and educational requirements	Your knowledge to identify the job title of a psychologist based on their work	The claim that psychologists could contribute to virtually any field of work

When you picture a psychologist at work, do you imagine one operating a huge chainsaw and cutting a hole through three feet of ground-level ice? What if the psychologist happened to be in Antarctica studying the behavior of seals, and was creating the hole so that he could capture a glimpse of what these animals were doing beneath the ice? This would describe at least part of the career of Jesse Purdy, a psychology professor who has spent many months in Antarctica recording social behavior of Weddell seals. When not cutting holes through ice and observing seals, Dr. Purdy teaches psychology courses to undergraduate students and conducts research on a bizarre animal called the cuttlefish, a close relative of the octopus. This probably sounds like a far cry from what the stereotypes of psychologists suggest Dr. Purdy is supposed to do. Granted, this example is not exactly mainstream, but it does attest to the wide range of topics and settings where you will find psychologists at work.

We will explore this broad range of activity in this module. Psychologists are engaged in a wide variety of professions dealing with a great range of behaviors. In any field you can think of that involves thinking or behaving, you will probably find a psychologist at work. In fact, it would be a challenge to find an employment sector that does not involve psychologists at some level.

Focus Questions

 How true is the caricature that psychologists constantly analyze people?

 What range of activities do psychologists engage in?

· · · · · · · · · · · · · · · · ·

Professions in Psychology

Psychology is a broad discipline with many applications in the workplace. You will see a wide variety of job titles and descriptions in this module, including some jobs that are not labeled as *psychology* but are closely aligned to it. Despite the diverse roles described here, remember that these are applications of psychology, which means they involve a scientific approach to behavior and thought. Those who earn a doctoral degree (PhD) in psychology work in a variety of settings, with the most common being at colleges and universities (Figure 1.10).

RESEARCH AND TEACHING
Research psychologists typically work at universities, in corporations, in the military, and in governmental agencies (such as the National Institutes of Health and Mental Health). Many psychologists working in these different settings focus on applying basic principles of psychology to real-world settings. **Applied psychology** *uses psychological knowledge to address problems and issues across various settings and professions, including law, education, clinical psychology, and business organization and management.* Some applied psychologists do both basic and applied work; it really depends on where a psychologist is employed.

Your psychology instructor is employed (at least part of the time) in *academic psychology*. Academic psychologists work at colleges and universities, and most combine teaching with conducting research, although some do only one or the other. Psychologists working in academics are not likely to refer to themselves as *academic psychologists*, however. For example, most instructors of psychology courses would describe themselves by their specialization, as in "I am a social psychologist" or "I am a developmental psychologist."

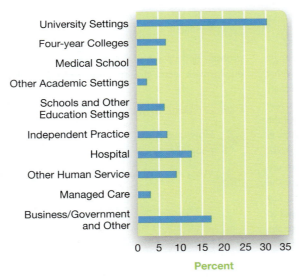

University Settings
Four-year Colleges
Medical School
Other Academic Settings
Schools and Other Education Settings
Independent Practice
Hospital
Other Human Service
Managed Care
Business/Government and Other

0 5 10 15 20 25 30 35
Percent

{FIG. 1.10} **Where Professional Psychologists Work** Primary employment settings for PhD recipients in psychology. **Click on this figure in your eText to see more details.**

PSYCHOLOGICAL HEALTH AND WELL-BEING
For most people, the mental health side comes to mind when they first think of psychology. In fact, the psychologist with notepad in hand listening attentively to a client has become an all-too-common caricature of what psychologists do. This caricature serves to reinforce the belief that psychologists are in the business of analyzing people. Clearly, the mental health field is the largest sector of employment for individuals with advanced degrees in psychology. However, helping professions are not limited to individuals with psychology degrees, as shown in Table 1.3. In fact, we call mental health jobs *the helping professions* because that is what they have in common, rather than specific educational criteria, degrees, or occupational roles.

Why are all these different job descriptions necessary? One reason is to indicate the educational level required; another is to distinguish the treatments considered the most effective by the different professions. For example, **psychiatry** *is a branch of medicine concerned with the treatment of mental and behavioral disorders.* As physicians, psychiatrists are likely to prescribe drugs such as antidepressants. Clinical and counseling psychologists are more likely to emphasize psychological approaches to treat mental health concerns and disorders. Social workers are likely to emphasize the social context of the individuals in treatment, such as the family's dynamics, socioeconomic status, and community.

Psychologists may work with a master's degree in most states, but many go on to pursue doctorates, which provide greater career opportunities. This might include the typical graduate degree for a scientific discipline, the Doctor of Philosophy (PhD), which combines science and practice. However, there is also a specialized Doctor of Psychology (PsyD) degree that focuses almost exclusively on the practice of psychology.

As you can see, mental health providers can be found in many settings and provide numerous services to people in need. The caricature of psychologist as an analyst breaks down even more when we expand our discussion of what psychologists do.

Psychologists can also specialize to practice in specific contexts. **Forensic psychology** *encompasses work in the criminal justice system, including interactions with the legal system and its professionals.* The field is often glorified in movies and TV as criminal profiling and investigation, but it is actually a practical profession involving very little of what is portrayed in these shows. The relatively few criminal profilers work with the FBI and larger law enforcement agencies to develop

Table 1.3 :: Employment in Psychology

Common occupations in the area of mental health, their educational requirements, and the basic roles for each position.

JOB TITLE	EDUCATION	ROLE
Clinical psychologist	PhD or PsyD	Diagnosis and treatment of psychological disorders
Counseling psychologist	Doctorate or master's	Treatment of psychological disorders and less severe psychological difficulties
Neuropsychologist	PhD or PsyD	Diagnosis and evaluation of individuals with neurological damage
School psychologist	EdD, PhD, or master's	Diagnosing behavioral problems and learning disabilities; working in schools to develop personalized programs to help students
Community psychologist	PhD or PsyD	Providing basic mental health services to the community with a focus on education and prevention
Licensed clinical social worker; independent social worker	Master's in social work (MSW)	Counseling individuals and families experiencing mental health and social problems; engaging in community organizations and providing social services
Forensic psychologist	Doctorate or master's	Psychology related to judiciary or criminal issues, such as evaluating an individual's competency to stand trial
Psychiatrist	Medical doctor	Diagnosis and treatment of psychological disorders
Psychiatric nurse	Nursing degree, RN	Working as part of a comprehensive treatment team to manage medical and behavioral treatments on a regular basis
Behavioral health technician; case manager	Bachelor's degree	Overseeing treatment on either an inpatient or outpatient basis, respectively

a set of characteristics that are statistically related to a criminal's methods. You would more likely see forensic psychologists working in prisons, training and evaluating police officers, or assisting with jury selections and evaluating whether defendants are able to stand trial.

School psychology *involves working with students who have special needs, such as those with emotional, social, or academic problems.* Practitioners might address ways to change troubling or disruptive behavior, or a cognitive disability that interferes with learning, such as dyslexia. School psychologists may spend a lot of time observing a child's behavior or administering special psychological tests to identify learning disabilities. These professionals rarely work alone; instead, they are more often part of students' educational teams, which include their parents, teachers, and counselors.

Most of the helping professions we have described have two things in common: (1) graduate degrees (more school after college!) and (2) licensure or certification as approved by individual states. More school and licensing tests may or may not sound appealing, and certainly many individuals prefer to start their careers rather than going for another degree. With a Bachelor's degree, individuals can work in treatment settings on a more

basic level. For example, case managers make regular contact with individuals to ensure they are complying with treatment (e.g., taking medication as prescribed) and make sure their clients are in touch with public and private services that may help them. Behavioral health technicians have similar tasks, except they are for the short term (usually less than 30 days) and on an inpatient basis.

HEALTH AND MEDICAL PROFESSIONS In addition to providing for mental health, an increasing number of psychologists are focusing on physiological health in the field known as **health psychology** (or *behavioral medicine*), *the study of how individual, biological, and environmental factors affect physical health.* Health psychologists identify the behaviors and personality traits that put people

School psychologists often work with children who have behavioral problems in school.

at risk and that, when combined with an unfortunate genetic heritage or infection, lead to disease. For example, overeating, poor food choices, and a sedentary lifestyle have been linked to diabetes and a variety of cardiovascular ailments. Psychological traits such as pessimism and hopelessness are correlated with impaired immune functioning and lower recovery rates from major surgeries, diseases, or accidents. Working long hours at a high-stakes job while sacrificing rich and meaningful relationships can affect one's health as well. Thus psychologists who work in the health fields might be seen as the behavioral counterparts to practitioners of traditional medicine. Whereas physicians treat the physiological effects of a disease, psychologists help to change the related behaviors. Health psychology is the focus of Chapter 16.

PSYCHOLOGY IN THE CORPORATE WORLD

One of the fastest-growing fields within psychology is **industrial and organizational (I/O) psychology**, *a branch of applied psychology in which psychologists work for businesses and other organizations to improve employee productivity and the organizational structure of the company or business.* I/O psychologists may develop tests to hire workers who have the best chance at succeeding, they may assist work teams to improve communication and responsibility, and they may help organizations with the management of change. This approach to psychology is covered in depth in Chapter 17.

Closely related to I/O psychology is *human factors psychology,* the study of how people interact with tools, physical spaces, or products. This is the high-tech branch of applied psychology; a great deal of human factors work applies principles of sensation and perception to complex work environments such as aircraft cockpits or laparoscopic surgical devices. Human factors psychologists may study human–computer interaction to develop user-friendly software and other products. Similarly those who practice *environmental psychology* study factors that improve working and living conditions, but they do so by establishing how the environment affects individuals or groups. Results from this type of research may be used in the design of working and living spaces to foster communication, to reduce distractions, and to prevent or reduce strain, stress, and fatigue.

Many undergraduates who major in psychology go on to marketing and advertising. (In Module 1.2, we mentioned that psychologist John B. Watson made a very successful career for himself in advertising.) What does marketing have to do with psychology? A great deal, it turns out. Marketing involves a lot of research on what consumers prefer, what buyers expect, and what makes shoppers choose one product over another. Marketing professionals conduct surveys and experiments on preferences, such as the taste tests we see reported on television commercials.

I'M NOT PLANNING ON A CAREER IN PSYCHOLOGY...

Not wanting to become a psychologist is fine, too—the world needs only so many psychologists. Based on recent trends, only a small percentage of this year's nearly 100,000 bachelor-level psychology graduates will go on to work in psychological fields—far more (approximately 40%) will go on to work in business settings (Magaletta et al., 2010). But students who major or minor in psychology will be able to apply what they have learned in many different types of work. Because of psychology's emphasis on research methods, psychology majors often turn out to be excellent problem solvers and critical thinkers. Also, psychology majors learn many principles of human behavior, ranging from individual cognition to group dynamics. These skills are needed for marketers, managers, and teachers (see Figure 1.11). So an understanding of behavior works to your advantage regardless of which career you eventually choose.

Even if this is the only course you take in psychology, we hope you enjoy it. We also hope that you come to understand more than just a few principles about human behavior. We anticipate that you will become more aware of the evidence people use when they make claims about behavior. Remember, as members of a capitalist society, our warning is *caveat emptor*—"Buyer, beware!"

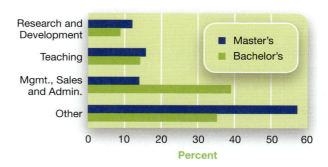

{FIG. 1.11} **Work Settings for People Earning Master's and Bachelor's Degrees in Psychology**

Quick Quiz 1.3a :: Professions in Psychology

KNOW …

1 A professional who would study how stress affects the heart is a(n) _____ psychologist.

   A environmental

   B health

   C clinical

   D I/O

2 A _____ psychologist would likely be asked to evaluate whether different display screens are optimal for work performance.

   A health

   B forensic

   C school

   D human factors

UNDERSTAND …

3 A major difference between most clinical psychologists and psychiatrists is that:

   A clinical psychologists can prescribe medications.

   B psychiatrists prescribe medications.

   C to be a clinical psychologist, you must obtain a Doctorate degree.

   D to be a psychiatrist, you need to obtain only a Master's degree.

APPLY …

4 You meet someone on the bus who is a psychiatrist. From this, you may safely assume that:

   A she completed medical school.

   B she is likely to be analyzing you right now.

   C her work involves profiling criminals.

   D she most likely conducts research and teaches at a university.

ANALYZE …

5 Psychologists could be involved in virtually any field of work because:

   A they study how people behave in multiple situations, including how they carry out the tasks associated with their jobs.

   B there are not enough jobs, so psychologists usually cannot find work in their own field.

   C they are more likely to change careers than most other professions.

   D it is unlikely that they have the social skills needed when working cooperatively with others.

Answers can be found on page ANS-1.

Module Summary

Now that you have read this module
you should:

KNOW ...

- **The key terminology of psychological professions:**

applied psychology (p. 28)   psychiatry (p. 28)
forensic psychology (p. 28)   school psychology
health psychology (p. 29)   (p. 29)
industrial and organizational
   (I/O) psychology (p. 30)

UNDERSTAND ...

- **The various professional settings occupied by
psychologists.** Psychologists work at universities as
researchers and teachers. Of course, many psychologists
work in the mental health care fields. They can be found in
business and industry working in specialized roles geared
toward promoting important factors such as team building,
efficiency, and personnel matters. Professionals in the field
also conduct applied work as specialists in human factors
and environmental psychology. Schools employ psychologists
for their specialized training in learning, thinking, and
development. Some psychologists work in forensics and
primarily work in court and law enforcement settings.

- **The distinctions among mental health professions in
their approaches and educational requirements.** The
many different titles among those working in the mental
health professions can be explained in terms of education
background and specific roles within the work setting.
Typically, an advanced degree (PhD or PsyD) and a state

license is required for clinical psychologists, and, in the
case of psychiatry, an MD is required. Many therapists
and counselors who work directly with clients or patient
populations have master's degrees in clinical, counseling, or
school psychology and social work. Some jobs requiring
a Bachelor's degree involve work with clients in mental
health settings, such as case managers or psychiatric nurses.

APPLY ...

- **Your knowledge to identify the job title of a psychologist
based on their work.** To do this, complete the matching
activity in **Table 1.4** and check your answers on page ANS-1.

ANALYZE ...

- **The claim that psychologists could contribute to
virtually any field of work.** Data show that most
psychologists are employed in mental health settings or in
academics. However, fields such as I/O psychology, human
factors, and environmental psychology have allowed
psychologists to apply their knowledge to just about any
field you can imagine.

Table 1.4 :: Matching Psychologist Titles and Roles

Identify the appropriate job title for each psychologist in the table below. For every job description on the left, there is one correct title on the right
Check your answers on page ANS-1.

1. I am employed at a state penitentiary and work closely with parole officers to make sure parolees have
   a psychological treatment plan to address substance abuse, anger management, impulsiveness, and other
   problems. I am a(n) _____.

2. I conduct research for the military to ensure that computer systems in aircraft are as user-friendly as possible. I am a(n) _____.

3. I went to medical school and then began working at a hospital, where I treat severe psychological disorders with medications and some psychotherapy. I am a(n) _____.

4. I am an independent consultant, and I try to help businesses identify and hire the best possible executives.
   I am a(n) _____.

5. Although I did not go to medical school, I have been working with heart surgery patients to help them
   adjust to life after surgery. This involves psychotherapy to deal with emotions and stress, as well as helping
   the patients adopt healthier behaviors. I am a(n) _____.

a. health psychologist

b. psychiatrist

c. forensic psychologist

d. human factors psychologist

e. I/O psychologist

Module 1.1 :: The Science of Psychology

Focus Questions:

1 How can the human mind, with its quirks and imperfections, conduct studies on itself? After reading this module, you might find the term *quirks and imperfections* to be a matter of interpretation. We could also say that the human tendency to find patterns in the world and connect events together is a hallmark achievement of our species. Unfortunately, this amazing capacity can easily lead people down the path of pseudoscience. Just because someone perceives a pattern or meaning in a set of events does not mean a pattern actually exists. Before taking the first step toward conducting scientific studies on human behavior, we have to recognize the mental traps that await us.

2 How can scientific and critical thinking steer us toward a clearer understanding of human behavior and experience? Scientific and critical thinking bring clarity to any type of inquiry. The scientific method, whether applied to human behavior or atomic particles, involves making predictions in the form of clear, testable hypotheses, and constructing and testing theories that can be supported or falsified. The steps toward critical thinking guide the process of science, as they require us to constantly question the accuracy and source of information, as well as remain aware of how our personal biases can influence our thinking.

> **Watch** *The Basics: A Diverse Approach* in the **MyPsychLab video series**

Module 1.2 :: How Psychology Became a Science

Focus Questions:

1 Why did it take so long for scientists to start applying their methods to human thoughts and experience? The zeitgeist—the cultural and social environment of a given period—that allowed psychology to emerge as a science did not begin until key figures in the natural and physical sciences, including Charles Darwin and Gustav Fechner, began applying scientific thinking to some aspects of human behavior. Key figures including Wilhelm Wundt and Edward Titchener were among the first to conduct studies on mental processes.

2 What has resulted from the application of scientific methods to human behavior? As you read in this module, the scientific method became increasingly applicable to studies of human behavior. As a scientific understanding of human behavior grew, people began asking more questions about different topics. This exploration led to the development of numerous subfields within psychology that focus on specific aspects of behavior, such as biological, social, and cognitive factors.

> **Watch** *Thinking Like a Psychologist: Debunking Myths* in the **MyPsychLab video series**

Module 1.3 :: Putting Psychology to Work: Careers in Psychology and Related Fields

Focus Questions:

1 How true is the caricature that psychologists constantly analyze people? Psychologists probably do not do this any more than people in the general public. Psychologists who do provide mental health services are likely to limit their practice of psychology to areas where they are familiar with the tools and theories of their specific fields. In short, psychologists do not spend all of their waking hours analyzing people! As you read in this module, psychologists can be found in a broad range of settings.

2 What range of activities do psychologists engage in? Psychologists engage in a wide variety of activities. The most typical role is to work as a psychotherapist in a mental health setting, but other psychologists are engaged in research and teaching at universities, improving productivity and satisfaction in work settings, and helping engineers devise better tools and computer systems, among many other jobs.

> **Watch** *The Big Picture: Asking the Tough Questions* in the **MyPsychLab video series**

> **Watch** the complete video series online at **MyPsychLab**

Episode 1: Introduction to Psychology

1. *The Big Picture: Asking the Tough Questions*
2. *The Basics: A Diverse Approach*
3. *Thinking Like a Psychologist: Debunking Myths*
4. *In the Real World Application: Speed Dating*
5. *What's in It for Me? The Myth of Multitasking*

✓●—Study and Review at MyPsychLab

1 Psychology can be considered a collection of many related fields of study. What is one of the features that all of these fields have in common?

- **A** The use of the scientific method
- **B** The study of mental illness
- **C** The belief that the unconscious mind determines human behavior
- **D** The use of introspection

2 _____ are built from _____ that are repeatedly tested and confirmed.

- **A** Theories; hypotheses
- **C** Predictions; observations
- **B** Hypotheses; theories
- **D** Observations; predictions

3 The biopsychosocial model assumes that:

- **A** behavior often can be fully explained only by combining multiple perspectives.
- **B** biological factors are more important than social factors in determining behavior.
- **C** all living organisms form social groups, based on their physical and psychological needs.
- **D** the simplest explanation for behavior is usually the best.

4 Which of the following is true about the concept of *scientific literacy*?

- **A** Only trained scientists are considered scientifically literate.
- **B** Scientific literacy is the ability to answer basic science questions without looking up their answers.
- **C** A person who can understand, analyze, and apply scientific information is demonstrating scientific literacy.
- **D** Knowledge of scientific terminology is the most important part of scientific literacy.

5 _____ is the belief that knowledge comes through observation and experience.

- **A** Determinism
- **C** Skepticism
- **B** Parsimony
- **D** Empiricism

6 Psychology has been a science since:

- **A** around 470 B.C.
- **C** the late 1800s.
- **B** the early 1600s.
- **D** the mid-1900s.

7 How did physiologists and physicists, like Gustav Fechner, contribute to the development of psychology as a science?

- **A** They studied the relationship between the physical world and the mental representation of that world.
- **B** They demonstrated that the brain was responsible for consciousness.
- **C** They identified the locations of specific functions within the brain.
- **D** They extended Darwin's theory of evolution to behavior and cognitive abilities.

8 The belief that the unconscious mind has an influence on a person's behavior is part of which early approach to psychology?

- **A** Structuralism
- **C** Psychoanalysis
- **B** Functionalism
- **D** Behaviorism

9 The question of *nature and nurture relationships* centers on how _____ (nature) and _____ (nurture) influence behavior and mental processes.

- **A** environment; heredity
- **C** emotion; logic
- **B** heredity; environment
- **D** logic; emotion

10 Why was the perspective adopted by Wilhelm Wundt and his followers called structuralism?

- **A** They wanted to identify the major brain structures.
- **B** Their primary goal was to understand the physiology of the mind.
- **C** They focused their efforts on analyzing the elements of the nervous system.
- **D** Their primary focus was on describing the structure of conscious experience.

11 Which school of psychology questioned whether psychologists should study the mind, which was thought to be unobservable?

- **A** Psychoanalysis
- **C** Gestalt psychology
- **B** Behaviorism
- **D** Humanism

12 You attend a lecture by a psychologist who uses terms such as *free will* and *life's meaning*. Which psychological perspective is most consistent with the points the psychologist presented?

- **A** Behaviorism
- **C** Functionalism
- **B** Humanistic psychology
- **D** Psychodynamics

13 _____ psychologists are generally interested in how the behavior of individuals can be influenced by other people.

- **A** Social
- **C** Behavioral
- **B** Gestalt
- **D** Humanistic

14 Dr. Fernwood is a research psychologist. The main focus of her research is the use of psychological knowledge to find ways to reduce bullying in schools. Dr. Fernwood's research could be described as _____ psychology.

- **A** basic
- **C** applied
- **B** forensic
- **D** I/O

15 In which field is someone with a background in psychology likely to work?

- **A** Advertising
- **C** Management
- **B** Teaching
- **D** Any of the above

Work the Scientific Literacy Model : Understanding the Scientific Origins of Psychology

What do we know about psychological science?

Figure 1.6 on page 15 outlined the movement of psychology toward a scientific study of human behavior, including influences from fields such as medicine and physics. Refresh your memory of contemporary psychology, including the rise of behaviorism, humanistic psychology, social psychology, and cognitive psychology, by reviewing the discussion on **pages 20–24.** Psychologists today often use multiple, unique perspectives to study a topic, but they share with other scientists a common set of methods for understanding our world. **Figure 1.1 on page 3** offers a reminder of how psychologists use the scientific method to study human behavior. Of course, approaching any subject scientifically requires that we understand some key concepts. Review the discussion of determinism and empiricism on **page 14.** Psychologists assume that a multitude of factors cause our behavior (determinism), and that our understanding of behavior comes from observing what we can see and measure (empiricism). Here is a tip:

Remember that an **Empirical** approach means knowledge is gained through **Experience**, often by conducting **Experiments**.

How can science explain behavior?

Regardless of their theoretical approach, psychologists rely on the scientific method to gather data. Testing hypotheses and constructing theories are key parts of all scientific endeavors, and the scientific method involves a dynamic interaction between these two tasks. Recall from **page 21** that the proponents of behaviorism, for example, relied almost exclusively on studying observable behavior. Classic studies by Watson and Skinner make up the foundation of our knowledge in those areas today, and you can see the results of Watson's research on behavioral conditioning in the evolution of modern advertising. Moreover, the rise of cognitive psychology eventually allowed the application of the scientific method to phenomena that behaviorists of the time thought were unobservable, such as memory and thought processes.

Why is this relevant?

Watch the accompanying video excerpt on the different psychological perspectives. You can access the video at MyPsychLab or by clicking the play button in the center of your eText. If your instructor assigns this video as a homework activity, you will find additional content to help you in MyPsychLab. You can also view the video by using your smart phone and the QR code below, or you can go to the YouTube link provided.

After you have read this chapter and watched the video, imagine your friend Jake has become very anxious ever since he started taking harder classes in his major. The university's counselor diagnosed him with an anxiety disorder. Compare and contrast how the behavioral, humanistic, and cognitive approaches would view the origins and treatment of Jake's anxiety. Then, describe how each of the three approaches is viewed by psychologists today.

Can we critically evaluate scientific claims?

As outlined on **page 7**, scientific literacy consists of abilities to understand, analyze, and apply scientific information. A key component of scientific literacy—critical thinking—involves exercising curiosity and skepticism when evaluating the claims of others, and when assessing our own assumptions and beliefs. For instance, the alien abductions **Myths in Mind on page 10** reminds us that seeking the simplest of all explanations, also known as applying the principle of parsimony, will generally put you on the path to thinking scientifically and critically. Recall that a key characteristic of a scientific hypothesis is its ability to be tested. We mention astrology as an example, because its predications are typically so general that they cannot be falsified. It is a good idea to be skeptical of any claims that are based on assumptions that cannot be proved or disproved; many times they are couched in pseudoscientific terminology.

**youtube.com/user/
scientificliteracy**

MyPsychLab **Your turn to Work the Scientific Literacy Model:** Watch the accompanying video on YouTube, or on your phone (using the QR code). If your instructor has assigned this as a homework activity, you can find the video clip and additional content at MyPsychLab. Answer the questions that accompany the video clip to test your understanding.

2 :: READING AND EVALUATING SCIENTIFIC RESEARCH

Principles of Scientific Research

Learning Objectives	**KNOW …**	**UNDERSTAND …**	**APPLY …**	**ANALYZE …**
After reading this module you should:	The key terminology related to the principles of scientific research	The five characteristics of quality scientific research How biases might influence the outcome of a study	The concepts of reliability and validity to examples	Whether anecdotes, authority figures, and common sense are reliably truthful sources of information

Does listening to classical music make you smarter? In January 1998, Governor Zell Miller of Georgia placed a $105,000 line in his state budget dedicated to purchasing classical music (Sack, 1998). He even paid the conductor of the Atlanta Symphony to select optimal pieces for this CD. Apparently, Georgia's governor and state legislature believed that providing young children with classical music would make them smarter. There were many reasons to believe this assumption might be true, starting with the observation that most people we know who listen to classical music seem intelligent. At around the same time that Georgia took this step, consumers were being bombarded with advertisements about "the Mozart effect." Suddenly the classical sections at music stores were moved to the front of the store, with signs drawing customers' attention to the intelligence-boosting effects of the CDs. Parents were told that it was never too early to start their children on a Mozart program, even as fetuses residing in the womb. In fact, part of the Georgia budget, as well as the budget in some other states, was dedicated to handing out classical CDs along with hospital birth certificates. Eventually, the hype over the Mozart effect died down, but you may still hear about it from time to time. The whole issue raised some important questions.

Focus Questions

 We hear claims from marketers and politicians every day, but how can we evaluate them?

 Can we evaluate evidence even if we are not scientists?

• • • • • • • • • • • • • • • • • •

Perhaps the single most important aspect of scientific research is that it strives for objectivity. *Objectivity* assumes that certain facts about the world can be observed and tested independently from the individual (e.g., the scientist) who describes them. Everyone—not just the experts—should be able to agree on these facts given the same tools, the same methods, and the same context. Achieving objectivity is not a simple task, however. As soon as people observe an event, their interpretation of it becomes *subjective*, meaning that their knowledge of the event is shaped by prior beliefs, expectations, experiences, and even their mood. A scientific, objective approach to answering questions differs greatly from a subjective one. Most individuals tend to regard a scientific approach as one that is rigorous and demands proof. Although these are not inaccurate characterizations of scientific thinking and research, there is more to explore.

The Five Characteristics of Quality Scientific Research

During the past few centuries, scientists have developed methods to help bring us to an objective understanding of the world. The drive for objectivity influences how scientific research is conducted in at least five ways. Quality scientific research meets the following criteria:

1. It is based on measurements that are *objective, valid,* and *reliable.*
2. It can be *generalized.*
3. It uses techniques that reduce *bias.*
4. It is made *public.*
5. It can be *replicated.*

As you will soon read, these five characteristics of good research overlap in many ways, and they will apply to any of the methods of conducting research that you will read about in Module 2.2.

SCIENTIFIC MEASUREMENT: OBJECTIVITY, RELIABILITY, AND VALIDITY
The foundation of scientific methodology is the use of **objective measurements**, *the measure of an entity or behavior that, within an allowed margin of error, is consistent across instruments and observers.* For example, holding everything constant, a single object should weigh the same using multiple, functioning scales. Weight is something that can be measured objectively. In psychology, behavior is measured objectively. Psychologists' objective measures may include physical recording devices, but more often involve the researchers who do the recording. Thus the objectivity of the measure comes from the person doing the measuring.

The term **variable** *refers to the object, concept, or event being measured.* You are most likely familiar with some instruments to measure variables, such as the speedometer on the dashboard of a car that records observations about the variable we call speed. Similarly, psychologists have developed a variety of instruments to take objective measures of variables related to behavior and thought. Although a device does not yet exist that can objectively read your mind, a wide array of measures are available for psychological observation. These often take the form of behavioral measures. In fact, for much of the 20th century, mainstream psychologists in the United States focused solely on behavioral measures. Naturally, these measures remain the core of psychological research, but in recent decades new technologies—particularly those that have come from the field of neuroscience—have expanded the number of variables that psychologists study. High-tech equipment, such as magnetic resonance imaging (MRI), allows researchers to view the brain (you will read more about this topic in Module 3.3). Other physiological measures might involve gathering samples of blood or saliva, which can then be analyzed for enzymes, hormones, and other biological variables that relate to behavior and mental functioning.

Another common method used by psychologists is **self-reporting**, *a method in which responses are provided directly by the people who are being studied, typically through face-to-face interviews, phone surveys, paper and pencil tests, and web-based questionnaires.* Self-reports are often obtained in the form of a survey that includes scales measuring attitudes, opinions, beliefs, and abilities. Self-report scales may inquire about shyness, mood, or political orientation

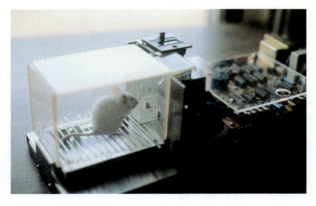

Psychologists make observations using a variety of methods. They might observe and record behavioral responses such as lever pressing for a reward by laboratory animals, or ask people to complete questionnaires that measure thoughts, preferences, emotions, and other variables.

by asking respondents to rate their agreement with a set of statements on, say, a scale of 1 to 7. Other familiar tests, especially for college students, include achievement and intelligence tests that are designed to measure cognitive abilities or performance.

Any method used by a researcher needs to include carefully defined terms. How would you define personality, shyness, or cognitive ability? This is the type of question a researcher would want to answer very carefully, not only for planning and conducting a study, but also when sharing the results of that research. **Operational definitions** *are statements that describe the procedures (or operations) and specific measures that are used to record observations* (Figure 2.1).

The concept of operational definitions would have been helpful to use when the Georgia legislators considered implementing a statewide program based on the Mozart effect. They should have asked, "How do the researchers define the outcome of their study? Do they mean listening to classical music makes you *smarter*, or just that you remember better? Do they claim the effect is permanent, or does it occur only while listening to Mozart?" Here is what the legislators would have found if they had looked up the answers in the scientific reports (Steele et al., 1999):

- Researchers have used several different objective measures of thinking and reasoning in studies of listening to classical music, including objective behavioral measures.
- Based on these measures, the only improvement seems to be in one specific type of thinking called spatial reasoning—that is, the ability to look at objects and mentally manipulate them.

- Researchers have also found that, averaged across a number of studies including 714 individuals, the average increase in spatial reasoning from listening to classical music is only 1½ points on an "IQ"-style intelligence test. (That gain is very small, given the fact that if you took the test twice in a week, it would be perfectly normal for your score to change by as much as 9 points.) In addition, this improvement is short-lived—it disappears after approximately 10 minutes.
- Initially researchers attributed the improvement to classical music (especially piano concertos) because the same result was not found with other types of music or silence. Subsequently, however, researchers found the same type and size of effect after participants listened to a recording of a Stephen King horror novel.

These conclusions make a very strong argument against investing the time, money, and effort in writing policy that relies so heavily on the Mozart effect.

The behavioral measures psychologists make must also be reliable and valid. A measure demonstrates **reliability** *when it provides consistent and stable answers across multiple observations and points in time.* Think of competitive figure skating in which a team of judges simultaneously but independently rates performance. High reliability means that the judges tend to be in agreement; in other words, if one judge gives a high score, then the others should, too. In psychological research, several observers might watch the same individuals to record instances of aggressive behavior. To achieve high reliability, researchers must carefully train the judges how to apply the operational definitions—to accurately identify what counts as aggression versus other types of behavior. What specifically does someone have to do to be considered "aggressive"? How long should the behavior last? What is considered *not* aggressive? In these cases, the instruments doing the measuring are people, but reliability criteria also apply to mechanical instruments used for measurement, such as stopwatches, scales, brain imaging scanners, and questionnaires. All of these instruments need to be consistent in their recordings.

Closely related to reliability is the concept of **validity**—*the degree to which an instrument or procedure actually measures what it claims to measure.* What if a psychologist claimed to measure intelligence based on shoe size? He could give a very clear operational definition of how to measure shoe size, and his measure should be very *reliable*—a simple tape measure should give the same answer (or close to it) each time a specific foot is measured.

Operational Definitions

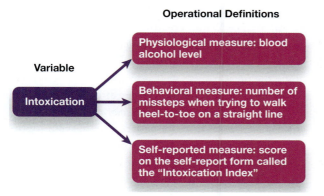

Variable

Intoxication

Physiological measure: blood alcohol level

Behavioral measure: number of missteps when trying to walk heel-to-toe on a straight line

Self-reported measure: score on the self-report form called the "Intoxication Index"

{FIG. 2.1} **Operational Definitions** A variable, such as the level of intoxication, can be operationally defined in multiple ways. This figure shows operational definitions based on physiology, behavior, and self-report measures. **Click on this figure in your eText to see more details.**

But no matter how consistently a tape measure yields a size 6 as a 6, or an 8 as an 8, it is not a *valid* measure of intelligence. Rather than shoe size, valid measures of intelligence might include problem solving and logical thinking—abilities that actually constitute the definition of intelligence.

Reliability and validity are essential components of scientific research. In addition, it is usually very important that knowledge gained from scientific studies have usefulness that extends beyond the laboratory.

GENERALIZABILITY OF RESULTS   Personal testimony can be very persuasive and compelling. Indeed, just a few people claiming great success with a diet supplement or a memory-improvement CD can tempt consumers to believe the product is effective for everyone. Unfortunately, such testimonies are problematic: Although something may appear to be true for an individual (Patrick lost weight while taking a diet supplement), it may not work for everyone else. In fact, we do not even know for sure that it worked for the person making the claim (Patrick's weight loss might have been pure coincidence). When we apply information and findings from one person to another, we are *generalizing*. In psychological research, **generalizability** *refers to the degree to which one set of results can be applied to other situations, individuals, or events.*

One way to increase the possibility that research results will generalize is to study a large group of subjects. By examining and reporting an average effect for that group, psychologists can get a much better sense of how individuals are *likely* to behave. But how large of a group is it possible to study? Ideally, it would be best to study an entire **population**—*the group that researchers want to generalize about.* In reality, the task of finding all population members, persuading them to participate, and measuring their behavior is impossible in most cases. Instead, psychologists typically study a **sample**—*a select group of population members.* Once the sample has been studied, then the results may be generalized to the population as a whole.

To ensure that findings within a sample generalize to a larger population, psychologists prefer to use random sampling whenever possible. In a **random sample**, *every individual of a population has an equal chance of being included.* If you wanted to study the population of students at your school, for example, the best way to obtain a true random sample would

be to have a computer generate a list of names from the entire student body. Your random sample—a subset of this population—would then be identified, with each member of the population having an equal chance of being selected regardless of class standing, gender, major, living situation, and other factors. Obtaining a true random sample can be extremely difficult to do. In practice, psychologists are more likely to settle for **convenience samples**, *which are samples of individuals who are the most readily available*—perhaps even Introductory Psychology students.

Random sampling can help research results generalize across individuals. In addition, research should generalize across time and space. In some situations, the generalizability of research findings can be influenced by where the research takes place. There are two primary research settings: *Laboratory research* includes any study conducted in an environment controlled by the researcher, whereas *naturalistic research* takes place where the behavior would typically occur. As you will see in the next module, many psychologists prefer to conduct their research in the controlled setting of the laboratory so they can see how specific conditions manipulate behavior. However, the artificial nature of the laboratory can sometimes interfere with normal behavior, which in turn would affect the generalizability of the findings. **Ecological validity** *is the degree to which the results of a laboratory study can be applied to or repeated in the natural environment.* For example, if the effects of a cognitive improvement CD were studied by bringing volunteers into the laboratory and measuring their ability to solve problems, the results might not generalize well to a classroom where the students are taking real tests for real grades.

SOURCES OF BIAS IN PSYCHOLOGICAL RESEARCH   While creating objective, reliable, and valid measures is important in quality research, various types of bias can be introduced by the researchers doing the measuring as well as by the people or animals being observed. The **Hawthorne effect** *is a term used to describe situations in which behavior changes as a result of being observed.* Over the past century, psychologists have identified some common sources of bias that can affect research studies, including biases on the part of those who are conducting the experiments (researcher bias), and biases created by participants of studies who are aware that their behavior is under investigation (subject bias).

In the 1920s, researchers in the Chicago area studied the relationship between productivity and working conditions at the Western Electric Company's Hawthorne Works. When the researchers introduced some minor change in working conditions, such as adjustments in the lighting, the workers were more productive for a period of time. When they changed another variable in a different study—such as having fewer but longer breaks—productivity increased again. What was not obvious to the researchers was that any change in factory conditions brought about increased productivity, presumably because the changes were always followed by close attention from the factory supervisors (Adair, 1984; Parsons, 1974). Thus, research results are influenced by both the expectations of those who are observed, as well as those doing the observing.

WORKING THE SCIENTIFIC LITERACY MODEL
Demand Characteristics and Participant Behavior

Results of psychological studies *should* provide uncontaminated views of behavior. In reality, however, people who participate in psychological studies typically enter the research environment with a curiosity about the subject of the study. Researchers need to withhold as much detail as possible to get the best, least biased results possible.

What do we know about how bias affects research participants?

When studying human behavior, a major concern is **demand characteristics**, *inadvertent cues given off by the experimenter or the experimental context that provide information about how participants are expected to behave.* Demand characteristics can range from very subtle to obvious influences on the behavior of research participants (Orne, 1962). They can take the form of responding based on **social desirability** (also known as **socially desirable responding**), *which means that research* *participants respond in ways that increase the chances that they will be viewed favorably.* This type of bias is particularly relevant when the study involves an interview in which the researcher has face-to-face contact with the volunteers. Demand characteristics may also be a problem in laboratory studies, where participants often try to figure out the purpose of the experiment.

Subtle and even obvious cues by the researcher or the experimental context can give away the purpose of the study. For example, imagine you walk into a laboratory and a psychologist asks you to put on a heavy backpack. She then shows you a ramp and asked you to estimate how steep the ramp is. It certainly seems plausible that the experimenter wants to know whether wearing the backpack will affect your judgment of the steepness of the ramp. Even in this simple example there looms the possibility of demand characteristics.

How can science test the effects of demand characteristics on behavior?

Using this same scenario with the backpack, psychologists have tested how, exactly, demand characteristics affect people's judgments (Durgin et al., 2009). In this experiment, undergraduate students were assigned to one of three groups. One group did not wear a backpack during a task, a second group wore a 25-pound backpack with no explanation as to why, and the third group wore a 25-pound backpack and was told that its contents consisted of electrical recording equipment that would measure the muscle activity of their ankles. To increase the believability of this procedure, actual electrodes with wires running to the backpack were attached to the ankles of members of the third group. The participants were taken separately to a room that contained a ramp and were asked to judge how steep they thought it was before and after they stepped onto it. After completing the procedure, the participants sat at a computer and took a survey which included questions in which they guessed the purpose of the study.

The researchers found that the students who wore the backpack without any explanation as to why judged the ramp to be steeper both before and after stepping on it compared with the students who wore the backpack they thought contained recording equipment for the study, as well as the students who did not wear a backpack. In addition, in the follow-up survey students who wore a backpack without explanation believed that the purpose of the experiment was to determine how wearing a backpack affects steepness judgments. Students who did not wear a backpack or, most importantly, who wore one with recording equipment they assumed was critical to the study did not report this belief. Thus demand characteristics affected both perceptual judgment of slope and

participants' beliefs about the purpose of the experiment (Durgin et al., 2009).

How can we critically evaluate the issue of bias in research?

Participants are not the only source of bias when it comes to psychological research. Researchers and observers themselves can introduce bias and unwittingly draw out the responses they desire. Some classic examples of how expectations can influence results come from the research of Rosenthal and colleagues. In one study, researchers told teachers in 18 different classrooms that a group of children had "unusual" potential for learning, when in reality they were just a random selection of students (Rosenthal & Jacobson, 1966). After eight months of schooling, the children singled out as especially promising showed significant gains not just in grades, but in intelligence test scores, which are believed to be relatively stable. Thus, the observers (i.e., teachers) found exactly the results they expected.

Experimenter bias can even be found when people work with animals. When research assistants were told they were handling "bright" rats, it appeared that the animals learned significantly faster than when the assistants were told they were handling "dull" rats. Because it is unlikely that the rats were influenced by demand characteristics—they were not trying to give the researchers what they wanted—the most likely explanation for this difference is that researchers made subtle changes in how they observed and recorded behavior (Rosenthal & Fode, 1963).

Why is this relevant?

Demand characteristics and other sources of bias all have the potential to compromise research studies. Given the time, energy, and monetary cost of conducting research, it is critical that results are as free from contamination as possible. You may be familiar with the **placebo effect**, *a measurable and experienced improvement in health or behavior that cannot be attributable to a medication or treatment.* This term comes from drug studies, in which it is standard procedure for a group, unbeknownst to them, to be given an inactive substance (the placebo) so that this group can be compared to a group given the active drug. What often happens is that people in the placebo group report feeling better. This effect has been reported time and again—not just with drugs, but with other medical and surgical treatments as well. The placebo effect is actually a vigorously researched topic that brings both psychology and medicine together.

PSYCH @

The Hospital: The Placebo Effect

Why do people receiving a placebo claim to feel better? It may be because they expect the drug to make them feel better (it is "all in their head"), because the placebo actually triggers a physiological response that leads to the improvement, or perhaps a combination of the two. The answer is currently up for debate. Large-scale studies have revealed that many people who are given a placebo show physiological evidence of relief from pain and nausea (Hrobjartsson & Gotzsche, 2010). We say "many" people because some individuals do not respond to placebos at all. It appears that the region of the brain that is involved in human pain responses becomes active when research participants or hospital patients simply take a pill, even if it is a placebo (Qiu et al., 2009). Findings such as this tell us that when it comes to pain, the placebo effect is not just a matter of believing that the drug works; instead, the act of taking the drug actively engages a physiological response for reducing pain. As you will read later in this chapter, placebos are an important part of experimental research in psychology and related fields, so it is important to recognize their potential influence on how research participants respond. As we will discuss in Module 2.3, some important ethical issues must be considered when administering placebos to patients.

. . . .

TECHNIQUES THAT REDUCE BIAS   One of the best techniques for reducing subject bias is to provide anonymity and confidentiality to the volunteers. *Anonymity* means that each individual's responses are recorded without any name or other personal information that could link a particular individual to specific results. *Confidentiality* means that the results will be seen only by the researcher. Ensuring anonymity and confidentiality are important steps toward gathering honest responses from research participants. Similarly, participant anxiety about the experiment can be reduced when researchers provide full information about how they will eventually use the data. If volunteers know that the data will not be used to diagnose psychiatric problems, affect their grades, or harm them in some other way, then their concerns about the study will be less likely to affect their performance.

Researchers can reduce biased responding from participants by using what are called *blind* procedures (see Figure 2.3 on p. 44). In a **single-blind study**, *the participants do not know the true purpose of the study, or else do not know which type of treatment they are receiving (for example, a placebo or a drug)*. In this case, the subjects are "blind" to the purpose of the study. Of course, a researcher can introduce bias as well, so an even more effective technique is a **double-blind study**, *in which neither the participant nor the experimenter knows the exact treatment for any individual*. To carry out a double-blind procedure, the researcher must arrange for an assistant to conduct the observations or, at the very least, the researcher must not be told which type of treatment a person is receiving until after the study is completed. Blinding techniques serve to reduce subject and experimenter bias, so ideally researchers should use them whenever possible.

Which kinds of biases might enter into the claims that Mozart's music improves cognitive performance? First, if a researcher stood to make money from a successful test of the product, he or she could introduce bias into the study. Even the most honest and ethical researchers could be unintentionally lenient when evaluating tests from the Mozart group. Also, if volunteers were recruited to help test this hypothesis, they might improve their scores based on the Hawthorne effect—just being watched might make the volunteers try harder. Of course, we cannot be sure that these events would happen in an actual experiment, but is there some way we might explicitly prevent or reduce experimenter and subject bias? As we have seen, a double-blind procedure would accomplish this. Thus, before we give credence to a study's claims about Mozart's music, we would want to confirm that it was conducted with a double blind procedure in place.

SHARING THE RESULTS   Although scientists may secret themselves away as they move toward discovery, once their experiments are completed, everything changes. One of the most important aspects of scientific research (as with any other scholarly endeavor) is

Single-blind   Double-blind

{FIG. 2.3} **Single- and Double-Blind Procedures** In research, being "blind" means that individuals in an experiment do not know which group they were assigned to—a must in an experiment. This constraint can be applied just to the participants (a single-blind study) or, preferably, to both the participants and the researchers (a double-blind study).

making the results public. In Module 1.1, we discussed the scientific method and described the relationship between testing hypotheses and building theories, which are central components of the scientific process. Sharing results is what allows this process to occur among groups of researchers working in different laboratories. In addition, a very important aspect of science is having the opportunity to repeat someone else's study to confirm or reject that researcher's observations and findings. Such processes are made possible by scholarly publications.

Psychology's primary mode of communication comprises academic journals. Academic journals resemble magazines in that they are usually softbound periodicals with a number of articles by different authors (online formats are typically available as well). Unlike magazines, however, journal articles represent primary research or reviews of multiple studies on a single topic. When scientists complete a piece of research, they may write a detailed description of the theory, hypotheses, measures, and results and submit the article for possible publication. You will not find journals or research books in your average mall bookstore because they are too specialized for the general market, but you will find hundreds of them if you check with your school's librarians.

Before research findings can be published, they go through **peer review**—*a process in which papers submitted for publication in scholarly journals are read and critiqued by experts in the specific field of study.* In the field of psychology, peer review involves two main tasks. First, an editor receives the manuscript from the researcher and determines whether it

is appropriate subject matter for the journal (for example, an article on 17th-century Italian sculpture would not be appropriate for publication in the *Journal of Cognitive Neuroscience*). Second, the editor sends copies of the manuscript to a select group of peer reviewers—"peer" in this case refers to another professional working within the same field of study. These reviewers critique the methods and results of the research and make recommendations to the editor regarding the merits of the research. In this process, the editors and reviewers serve as gatekeepers for the discipline, which helps increase the likelihood that the best research is made public.

Science is an ongoing and self-correcting process. The finest, most interesting published research study can quickly become obsolete if it cannot be replicated. **Replication** *is the process of repeating a study and finding a similar outcome each time.* As long as an experiment uses sufficiently objective measurements and techniques, and if the original hypothesis was correct, then similar results should be achieved by later researchers who perform the same types of studies. Results are not always replicated in subsequent investigations, however.

One familiar example is that of the purported Mozart effect. Although the general idea that listening to classical music could make a person smarter had been around for years, one of the first scientific studies of this hypothesis was conducted in 1993 (Rauscher et al., 1995). Other researchers were skeptical of the results and examined the study through partial replications, meaning they employed highly similar methods (e.g., Steele et al., 1997). The original researchers responded by critiquing the replications and recommending a number of changes (Rauscher & Shaw, 1998). Another partial replication was conducted following this advice, but it still did not yield the same results as the original study (Steele et al., 1999). This failure to replicate the original findings does not mean that the authors of the original study were dishonest. It could mean they unintentionally introduced researcher bias, or perhaps the sampling was biased, or perhaps the results were just a fluke. But certainly this example emphasizes the value of replication: Correct hypotheses and sound methods should produce repeatable results.

In the big picture, peer review and replication are self-corrective measures for all disciplines, because they ensure that published results did not occur through carelessness, dishonesty, or coincidence.

Quick Quiz 2.1a
The Five Characteristics of Quality Scientific Research

KNOW …

1 The degree to which an instrument measures what it is intended to measure is known as _____.

A validity   C verifiability

B generalizability   D reliability

2 When psychologists question how well the results of a study apply to other samples or perhaps other situations, they are inquiring about the _____ of the study.

A validity   C verifiability

B generalizability   D reliability

UNDERSTAND …

3 In a single-blind study, the participants do not know the purpose of the study or the condition to which they are assigned. What is the difference in a double-blind study?

A The researcher tells the participants the purpose and their assigned conditions in the study.

B The participants also do not know when the actual study begins or ends.

C The researcher also does not know which condition the participants are in.

D The participants know the condition to which they have been assigned, but the researcher does not.

APPLY …

4 Dr. Rose gives a standardized personality test to a group of psychology majors in January and again in March. Each individual's score remained nearly the same over the two-month period. From this, Dr. Rose can infer that the test is _____.

A reliable   C objective

B generalizable   D verified

Answers can be found on page ANS-1.

Risky Paths to Truth: Anecdotes, Authority, and Common Sense

In the preceding section, you read about what makes for quality research, and it is generally safe to assume that the opposite characteristics detract from the quality of research. Good research uses valid, objective measures; poor research uses subjective measures that are less valid, less reliable, and, therefore, less likely to be replicable. That is good to know, but other issues must also be scrutinized if you hear someone make a scientific-sounding claim. Most claims are accompanied by what might sound like evidence. But evidence can come in many forms. How can we differentiate between weak versus strong evidence?

Poor evidence comes most often in one of three varieties: anecdotes, appeals to authority, and common sense. In an advertisement for a weight loss pill, you might see a statement that an individual lost 200 pounds! This information is just **anecdotal evidence**—*an individual's story or testimony about an observation or event that is used to make a claim as evidence.* In this case, there is no way of knowing whether the diet was responsible for the person's weight loss; the outcome could have been due to any number of things, such as a separate physical problem or changes in food intake and lifestyle that were not part of the diet plan. In fact, you do not even know if the anecdote itself is true: The "before" and "after" photos could easily be doctored.

The second kind of bogus evidence is the **appeal to authority**—*the belief in an "expert's" claim even when no supporting data or scientific evidence is present.* Expertise is not actually evidence; "expert" describes the person making the claim, not the claim itself. It is entirely possible that the expert is mistaken, dishonest, overpaid, or misquoted. True experts are good at developing evidence, so if a claim cites someone's expertise as evidence, then you should see whether the expert offers the corresponding data to support the claim. It is not unusual for people to find that an expert's claim actually has no evidence backing it, but rather is simply an opinion. In other cases, it turns out that the experts have a hidden agenda or a "conflict of interest." It is important to look at what the expert stands to gain by lending his or her name to a product or scientific theory.

Finally, the purported evidence may consist of an **appeal to common sense**—*a claim that appears to be sound, but lacks supporting scientific evidence.* For example, many people throughout history assumed the world was the stationary center of the universe (see Figure 2.4 on p. 46). The idea that the Earth could orbit the sun at blinding speeds was deemed nonsense—the force generated

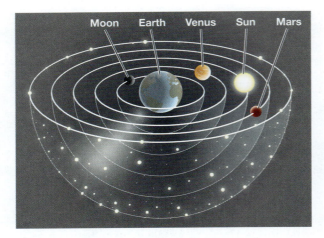

Moon　Earth　Venus　Sun　Mars

{FIG. 2.4} **Beware of "Common Sense" Explanations** For centuries, it was *obvious* that the Earth was at the center of the universe, with the sun and our nearby planets orbiting around our planet—at least the Earth didn't *seem* to be moving. Scientific explanations now tell us differently.

would seemingly cause all the people and objects to be flung into space!

In addition to common sense, beliefs can originate from other potentially unreliable sources. For example, *appeals to tradition* ("We have always done it this way!") as well as their opposite, *appeals to novelty* ("It is the latest thing!"), can lead people to believe the wrong things. Claims based on common sense, tradition, or novelty maybe worthy of consideration, but whether something is true cannot be evaluated by these standards alone.

Quick Quiz 2.1b
Risky Paths to Truth: Anecdotes, Authority, and Common Sense

KNOW …

1　Claiming that something is true because "it should be obvious" is really just _____.

- Ⓐ anecdotal evidence
- Ⓑ an appeal to common sense
- Ⓒ an appeal to authority
- Ⓓ generalizability

UNDERSTAND …

2　Appeals to authority do not qualify as good evidence because:

- Ⓐ they always lack common sense.
- Ⓑ authority figures are likely to distort the truth.
- Ⓒ authority does not mean that there is sound, scientific evidence.
- Ⓓ authority is typically based on anecdotal evidence.

APPLY …

3　Ann is convinced that corporal punishment (e.g., spanking) is a good idea because she knows a child whose behavior improved because of it. Whether or not you agree with her, Ann is using a flawed argument. Which type of evidence is she using?

- Ⓐ Anecdotal
- Ⓑ Objective
- Ⓒ Generalizable
- Ⓓ An appeal to authority

Answers can be found on page ANS-1.

Module Summary

Now that you have read this module you should:

Listen to the audio file of this module at **MyPsychLab**

KNOW ...

- **The key terminology related to the principles of scientific research:**

anecdotal evidence (p. 45)
appeal to authority (p. 45)
appeal to common sense (p. 45)
convenience samples (p. 40)
demand characteristics (p. 41)
double-blind study (p. 43)
ecological validity (p. 40)
generalizability (p. 40)
Hawthorne effect (p. 40)
objective measurements (p. 38)
operational definition (p. 39)
peer review (p. 44)

placebo effect (p. 42)
population (p. 40)
random sample (p. 40)
reliability (p. 39)
replication (p. 44)
sample (p. 40)
self-reporting (p. 38)
single-blind study (p. 43)
social desirability (p. 41)
validity (p. 39)
variable (p. 38)

UNDERSTAND ...

- **The five characteristics of quality scientific research.** These characteristics include (1) that measurements are objective, valid, and reliable; (2) the research can be generalized; (3) it uses techniques that reduce bias; (4) the findings are made public; and (5) the results can be replicated. For example, objective, valid, and reliable measurements make it possible for other scientists to test whether they could come up with the same results if they followed the same procedures. Psychologists mostly study samples of individuals, but usually they are more concerned about describing principles that generalize to a broader population. Single- and double-blind procedures are standard ways of reducing bias. Finally, the process of publishing results is what allows scientists to share information, evaluate hypotheses that have been confirmed or refuted, and, if needed, replicate other researchers' work.

- **How biases might influence the outcome of a study.** Demand characteristics affect how participants respond in research studies—understandably, they often attempt to portray themselves in a positive light, even if that means not answering questions or behaving in a fully truthful manner. Researchers can also influence the outcomes of their own studies, even unintentionally.

APPLY ...

- **The concepts of reliability and validity to examples.** Try this activity to see how well you can apply these concepts. Read the following descriptions, and determine whether each scenario involves an issue with reliability or validity. Check your answers on page ANS-1.

  1. Dr. Tatum is doing very standard physiological recording techniques on human participants. Each morning she checks whether the instruments are calibrated and ready for use. One day she discovered that the instrumentation was way off the mark, and would surely give very inconsistent readings compared to previous days. *Would this affect the reliability or validity of her research? Explain.*

  2. Dr. Nielson uses a behavioral checklist to measure happiness in the children he studies at an elementary school. Every time he and his associates observe the children, they reach near-perfect agreement on what they observed. Another group of psychologists observes the same children in an attempt to identify which children are energetic and which seem tired and lethargic. It turns out that the same children whom Dr. Nielson identifies as happy, using his checklist, are also the children whom the second group of psychologists identify as energetic. *It appears there may be a problem with Dr. Nielson's measure of happiness. Do you think it is a problem of reliability or validity? Explain.*

ANALYZE ...

- **Whether anecdotes, authority figures, and common sense are reliably truthful sources of information.** To evaluate evidence, you should ask several questions. First, is support for the claim based on the words or endorsement of an authority figure? Endorsement by an authority is not necessarily a bad thing, as someone who is an authority at something should be able to back up the claim. But the authority of the individual alone is not satisfactory, especially if data gathered through good scientific methods do not support the claim. Second, is someone supplying anecdotal evidence? As convincing as a personal testimony may be, anecdotal evidence is not sufficient for backing any claim that can be scientifically tested. Common sense also has its place in daily life, but by itself is insufficient as a final explanation for anything. Explanations based on good scientific research should override those based on common sense.

Scientific Research Designs

KNOW ...	UNDERSTAND ...	APPLY ...	ANALYZE ...
The key terminology related to research designs	What it means when variables are positively or negatively correlated	The terms and concepts of experimental methods to research examples	The pros and cons of descriptive, correlational, and experimental research designs
	How experiments help demonstrate cause-and-effect relationships		

Can your attitude affect your health? This is the old question of "mind over matter," and psychologist Rod Martin thinks the answer is definitely yes. He says that if you can laugh in the face of stress, your psychological and physical health will benefit. Martin has found several interesting ways to build evidence for this argument (Martin, 2002, 2007). For example, he developed a self-report instrument that measures sense of humor. People who score high on this measure—those who enjoy a good laugh on a regular basis—appear to be healthier in a number of ways. As interesting as this evidence is, it is not definitive proof that attitude affects health. In this module, you will develop skills in how to ask questions about how research is conducted.

Focus Questions

 What are some of the ways researchers make observations?

 Do some research techniques provide stronger evidence than others?

Psychologists always begin their research with a *research question*, such as "What is the most effective way to study?", "What causes us to feel hungry?", or "How does attitude affect health?" In most cases, they also make a prediction about the outcome they expect—the hypothesis. To test hypotheses, psychologists call on a variety of methods called *research designs*. Research designs guide investigators in (1) organizing the study, (2) making observations, and (3) evaluating the results. Because several types of designs are available, psychologists must choose the one that best addresses the research question and that is most suitable to the subject of their research. Before we examine different research designs, we will focus on the characteristics that all of them have in common.

● *Variables.* Recall from Module 2.1 that a variable is a property of an object, organism, event, or something else that can take on different values. Sense of humor is a variable; some people seem to have more and some have less of it.

- *Operational definitions.* Operational definitions are the details that define the variables for the purposes of a specific study. For sense of humor, this definition might be "the score on the Coping Humor Scale."
- *Data.* When scientists collect observations about the variables of interest, the information they record is called data. For example, data might consist of the collection of scores on the Coping Humor Scale from each individual in the sample.

These characteristics of research designs are important regardless of the design that is used, and the same is true for the five elements of good research you read about in Module 2.1. Next, we will review the different types of designs that allow us to put these principles of research into practice.

Descriptive Research

The beginning of any new line of research must involve descriptive data. Descriptive research is not an attempt to explain a subject—telling why it happened; instead, it is an opportunity to present observations about the characteristics of the subject. Here are a few examples of descriptive research questions:

- How many words can the average two-year-old speak?
- How many hours per week does the typical college student spend on homework?
- What proportion of the population will experience depression or an anxiety disorder at some point in their lives?

As you can see, research questions address the appearance of a behavior, its duration or frequency, its prevalence in a population, and so on. To answer those questions, researchers usually gather data using one or more of the following designs: *case studies, naturalistic observation,* and *surveys and questionnaires.*

CASE STUDIES A **case study** *is an in-depth report about the details of a specific case.* As such, case studies are particularly useful in describing symptoms of psychological disorders and detailed descriptions about specific successes or failures in treatment. One recently published example of a case study did both (Elkins & Moore, 2011). The authors of this study described the experience of a certain type of anxiety disorder and the steps used in therapy to treat the anxiety over a 16-week period. They were able to document how and when changes occurred and the effects of the treatment on other aspects of the individual's life. This level of detail would not be available if the authors had not focused on a single case. A drawback to this method is that a single case may not apply to others, so there is no guarantee that the findings can be generalized to other individuals and situations.

NATURALISTIC OBSERVATION An alternative approach is to observe people (or animals) in their natural settings. When psychologists engage in **naturalistic observation**, *they unobtrusively observe and record behavior as it occurs in the subject's natural environment.* Most students have seen the television programs of scientists in search of chimpanzees in a forest or driving a Range Rover in pursuit of a herd of elephants. This certainly is a form of observation, but there is more to it than just watching animals in the wild. When a scientist conducts naturalistic observation research, she is making systematic observations of specific variables according to operational definitions. Naturalistic observation is also much wider in scope than the nature-programming images would suggest. In fact, one pair of psychologists managed to conduct their research in a bar: They observed the interplay of alcohol consumption and aggressive behavior (Graham & Wells, 2004).

The lesson here is that naturalistic observation can occur anywhere that behavior occurs, and it can apply to any behavior imaginable. But remember—researchers still have to pay attention to specific variables and use operational definitions. Because naturalistic observations may not always provide researchers with the specific types of information they are after, they may need to craft specific questions for participants to answer.

Researchers who use naturalistic observation record behavior in natural, non-laboratory settings and do so as unobtrusively as possible.

SURVEYS AND QUESTIONNAIRES   Finally, in our discussion of objective measurements in Module 2.1, we had our first look at *surveys* and *self-reports*. These methods include face-to-face interviews, phone surveys, paper-and-pencil tests, and web-based questionnaires, and they measure attitudes, opinions, beliefs, and abilities. Despite the range in topics and techniques, their common element is that the individuals speak for themselves. Surveys and questionnaires are still a method of observation, but the observations are provided by the people who are being studied rather than the psychologist.

Quick Quiz 2.2a
Descriptive Research

KNOW …

1 When psychologists observe behavior and record data in the environment where it normally occurs, they are using _____.

  A case studies
  B naturalistic observation
  C the supervisory method
  D artificial observation

2 Any property of an organism, event, or something else that can take on different values is called _____.

  A an operational definition
  B data
  C a variable
  D a case study

APPLY …

3 A psychologist is completing a naturalistic observation study of children's aggressive behavior on a playground. She says that aggression is "any verbal or physical act that appears to be intended to hurt or control another child." She then goes on to list specific examples. It appears that the psychologist is attempting to establish a(n):

  A good relationship with the children.
  B variable.
  C observational definition.
  D operational definition.

Answers can be found on page ANS-1.

Correlational Research

PsychTutor
Click here in your eText for an interactive tutorial on **Correlation Versus Causation**

Psychologists doing descriptive research almost always record information about more than one variable when they are collecting data. In these situations, the researchers may look for an association among variables; they will ask whether the variables tend to occur together in some pattern, or if they tend to occur at opposite times. **Correlational research** *involves measuring the degree of association between two or more variables.* For example, consider these two questions:

- What are the high school graduation rates in each county of your state?
- What are the typical family incomes in each county of your state?

These two questions ask for very different types of information, but their answers may be related. Is it likely that counties with higher graduation rates also tend to have higher income levels? By asking two or more questions—perhaps through a survey—researchers can start to understand the associations among variables. Correlational research may involve any of the descriptive research designs mentioned earlier, but the data are evaluated in such a way that we can see relationships between variables.

Correlations can be visualized when presented in a graph called a *scatterplot*, as shown in Figure 2.5. In scatterplot (a), you can see the data for education and income. The dots show a pattern that slopes upward and to the right, indicating that people with more education tend to have greater income. That correlation is not surprising, but it illustrates one of the two main characteristics that describe correlations:

- Correlations take a *direction* (see Figure 2.5). They may be positive (a), meaning that both variables occur together (such as education and income), or they may be negative (b), meaning that the more of one variable, the less of the other (such as more sleep being associated with lower irritability).
- Correlations have a *magnitude* or *strength*. This magnitude is described in terms of a mathematical measure called the *correlation coefficient*. Correlation coefficients range from -1.0 to $+1.0$, but the closer it is to the absolute value of 1.0, the stronger the relationship. Scatterplot (c) shows a zero-correlation (no association between education and sleep), while the correlation coefficients for scatterplots (a) and (b) are closer to $+1.0$ and -1.0, respectively.

You will encounter many correlations in this text, and it will be important to keep in mind the direction of the relationship—whether the variables are positively or negatively associated. One key point to remember is that the correlation coefficient is a measure of association only—*it is not a measure of causality.* In other words, correlation does not equal causation. In many cases, a correlation gives the *impression* that one variable causes the other, but that relationship cannot be determined from correlational research. For example, we noted in the beginning of the module that a sense of humor is associated with good health—this is a positive correlation. But that does not mean that humor *is responsible for* the good health. Perhaps good health leads to a better sense of humor. Or perhaps neither causes the other, but rather a third variable causes both good health and good sense of humor.

Consider another example. Imagine a researcher found that hot chocolate sales and violent crimes are negatively correlated: As hot chocolate purchases increased, violent crime decreased. Does this mean that hot chocolate prevents violence? Of course not. Correlation coefficients do not by themselves tell us whether one variable caused another. So why would there be a correlation between cocoa sales and violent crime? Could it be that warm, comforting beverages prevent crime? It is not likely. In fact, a more likely explanation suggests there is no causal relationship at all: Crime and hot chocolate purchases, if related at all, would be completely meaningless.

In contrast to hot chocolate and violent crime, it is at least plausible that a meaningful relationship exists between such things as humor and health or sleep and irritability. Even so, we cannot establish that one causes the other because of what is known as the *third variable problem*, which refers to the possibility that a third, unmeasured variable is actually responsible for a well-established correlation between two variables. Consider the negative correlation between sleep and irritability shown in scatterplot (b) of Figure 2.5. Numerous third variables could account for this relationship. Stress, depression, diet, and workload could *cause* both increased irritability and lost sleep. As you can see, correlations must be interpreted with caution. ✳

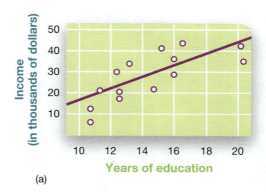
(a)

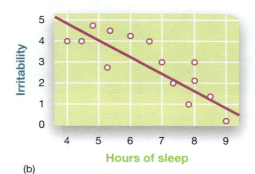
(b)

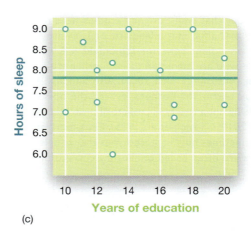
(c)

{FIG. 2.5} **Correlations Are Depicted in Scatterplots** Here we see two variables that are positively correlated (a) and negatively correlated (b). In the example of a zero correlation (c), there is no relationship between the two variables.

✳ Explore the **Concept** *Correlations Do Not Show Causation* at **MyPsychLab**

MYTHS IN MIND
Beware of Illusory Correlations

Chances are you have heard the following claims:

- Crime and emergency room intakes suddenly increase when there is a full moon.
- Opposites attract.
- Competitive basketball players (and even gamblers) get on a "hot streak" where one success leads to the next.

Many common beliefs such as these are deeply ingrained in our culture. They become even more widely accepted when they are repeated with such frequency. It is difficult to argue with a hospital nurse or police officer who *swears* that full-moon nights are the busiest and craziest of all. The conventional, reserved, and studious man who dates a carefree and spirited woman *confirms* that opposites attract. And, after Kobe Bryant has hit a few amazing shots, of course his chances of success just get better and better as the game wears on.

But do they? Each of these three scenarios is an example of what are called *illusory correlations*—relationships that really exist only in the mind, rather than in reality. It

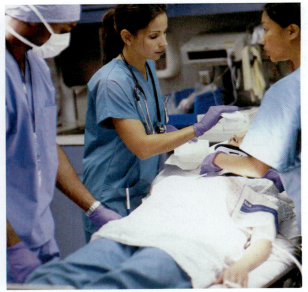

Contrary to *very* popular opinion, a full moon is statistically unrelated to unusual events or increased emergency room visits.

turns out that well-designed studies have found no evidence that a full moon leads to, or is even related to, bizarre or violent behavior (Lilienfeld & Arkowitz, 2009). People who are attracted to each other are typically very similar (Buston & Emlen, 2003). Also, although some games may be better than others, overall the notion of a "hot streak" is not a reality in basketball or in blackjack (Caruso et al., 2010; Gilovich et al., 1985). On a more serious note, the sometimes hurtful stereotypes that people hold about others are often based on illusory correlations (Sherman et al., 2009).

Why do these illusory correlations exist? Instances of them come to mind easily and are more memorable than humdrum examples of "normal" nights in the ER, perfectly matched couples, and all of the times Kobe Bryant misses a shot, even in his best games. However, just because examples are easy to imagine, it does not mean that they represent the patterns in reality.

· · · · · · · · · · · · · · · · · · ·

Quick Quiz 2.2b
Correlational Research

KNOW …

1 Which of the following correlation coefficients shows the strongest relationship between two variables?

Ⓐ +.54   Ⓒ +1.1
Ⓑ −.72   Ⓓ +.10

UNDERSTAND …

2 What does it mean to say that two variables are negatively correlated?

Ⓐ An increase in one variable is associated with a decrease in the other.

Ⓑ An increase in one variable is associated with an increase in the other.

Ⓒ A decrease in one variable is associated with a decrease in the other.

Ⓓ The two variables have no relationship.

ANALYZE …

3 Imagine Dr. Martin finds that sense of humor is positively correlated with psychological well-being. From this, we can conclude that:

Ⓐ humor causes people to be healthier.

Ⓑ health causes people to be funnier.

Ⓒ people who have a good sense of humor tend to be healthier.

Ⓓ people who have a good sense of humor tend to be less healthy.

Answers can be found on page ANS-1.

Experimental Research

Experimental designs improve on descriptive and correlational studies because they are the only designs that can provide strong evidence for cause-and-effect relationships. Like correlational research, experiments have a minimum of two variables, but there are two key differences between correlational research and experiments: the random assignment of the participants and the experimenter's control over the variables being studied. As you will see, these unique features are what make experimental designs so powerful.

THE EXPERIMENTAL METHOD The first unique element of experiments is **random assignment**, *a technique for dividing samples into two or more groups.* For the sake of illustration, consider the example from earlier in this module, about humor helping people cope with stress. To test whether humor causes a reduction in stress, we would need to conduct an experiment. In this scenario, two groups could be formed, with participants randomly assigned to each group. Random assignment allows us to assume the two groups will be roughly equal. If we allowed the participants to choose their own group, we could not be sure that the two groups were similar to start with. When groups are not randomly assigned, all kinds of **confounding variables**— *variables outside of the researcher's control that might affect the results*—could potentially enter the picture. Numerous confounds are possible, and identifying which are most influential will depend on the nature of the study. In studies involving humans, researchers typically cannot control the genes an individual has inherited, the person's mood when he or she participates in an experiment, or the individual's personality.

Now, let us see how random assignment works with experimental manipulation of a variable (Figure 2.6). We need to distinguish between two types of variables.

The first is the **dependent variable**, *which is the observation or measurement that is recorded during the experiment and subsequently compared across all groups.* In our example, the dependent variable is how participants respond to humor, and it is believed to *depend* on whether the participants are exposed to the second variable (hence its name "dependent"). This second type of variable is the **independent variable**, *the variable that the experimenter manipulates to distinguish between the two groups.* In our example, it would be exposure to humor versus no humor. The **experimental group** *is the group in the experiment that is exposed to the independent variable,* which in this specific example would be exposure to humor. The experimental group always receives the treatment. A **control group** *does not receive the treatment and, therefore, serves as a comparison.* In our example, the control group would not be exposed to humor. What if the experimental group showed reduced stress compared to the control group? Assuming that the experiment was well designed and all possible confounds were accounted for, the researchers could conclude that the independent variable—exposure to humor—is responsible for the difference.

THE QUASI-EXPERIMENTAL METHOD Random assignment and manipulation of a variable are required for experiments. They allow researchers to make the case that differences between the groups originate from the independent variable. In some cases, though, random assignment is not possible. **Quasi-experimental research** *is a research technique in which the two or more groups that are compared are selected based on predetermined characteristics, rather than random assignment.* For example, you will read about many studies in this text that compare men to women. Obviously, in this case one cannot flip a coin to randomly assign people to one group or the other. Also, if you gather one sample of men and one sample of women, they could differ in any number of ways that are not necessarily relevant to the questions you are studying. As a result, all sorts of causes could account for any differences that would appear: genetics, gender roles, family history, and so on. Thus quasi-experiments are actually correlational studies—they can point out relationships among preexisting groups and certain variables, but they cannot determine what it is about those groups that lead to the differences.

There are many decisions to make when designing a research study and each method has its pros and cons (Table 2.1 on p. 54). For example, naturalistic research allows psychologists to see behavior as it normally occurs, but it makes experimental control very

Hypothesis: Humor causes a reduction in stress.

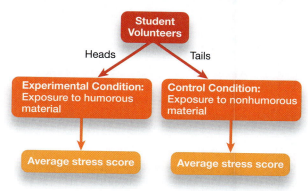

{FIG. 2.6} **Elements of an Experiment** If we wanted to test whether humor causes a reduction in stress, we would first need to randomly assign people in our sample to either the experimental or control condition. The dependent variable, the stress levels, would be measured following exposure to either humorous or neutral material. To test whether the hypothesis is true the average stress scores in both groups would be compared. **Click on this figure in your eText to see more details.**

PsychTutor Click here in your eText for an interactive tutorial on **Experimentation**

Table 2.1 :: Strengths and Limitations of Different Research Designs

METHOD	STRENGTHS	LIMITATIONS
Naturalistic observation	Allows for detailed descriptions of subjects in environments where behavior normally occurs	Poor control over possibly influential variables
Surveys/questionnaires	Quick and often convenient way of gathering large quantities of self-report data	Poor control; participants may not answer honestly, written responses may not be truly representative of actual behavior
Case studies	Yields detailed information, often of rare conditions or observations	Focus on a single subject limits generalizability
Correlational study	Shows strength of relationships between variables	Does not allow researcher to determine cause-and-effect relationships
Experiment	Tests for cause-and-effect relationships; offers good control over influential variables	Risk of being artificial with limited generalization to real-world situations

difficult—some would argue impossible. Conversely, to achieve true random assignment while controlling for any number of confounding variables, the situation may be made so artificial that the results of the study do not apply to natural behavior. Nevertheless, each method has its own advantages, and luckily psychologists do not have to settle on only one. Most interesting topics have been studied using a variety of possible designs, measures, samples, and so on. When a theory's predictions hold up to dozens of tests using a variety of designs, we can be much more confident of its accuracy.

Quick Quiz 2.2c :: Experimental Research

KNOW …

1 The process of setting up two or more groups in an experiment is called _____.

- A correlation
- B observation
- C random assignment
- D selection

UNDERSTAND …

2 A researcher sets up an experiment to test a new antidepressant medication. One group receives the treatment, and the other receives a placebo. The researcher then measures depression using a standardized self-report measure. What is the independent variable in this case?

- A Whether the individuals scored high or low on the depression measure
- B Whether the individuals received the treatment or a placebo
- C Whether the individuals were experiencing depression before the study began
- D Whether the individuals' depression decreased or increased during the study period

APPLY …

3 A researcher compares a group of Republicans and Democrats on a measure of beliefs about poverty. What makes this a quasi-experimental design?

- A The researcher is comparing preexisting groups, rather than randomly assigning people to them.
- B You cannot be both a Republican and a Democrat at the same time.
- C There are two independent variables.
- D There is no operational definition for the dependent variable.

ANALYZE …

4 A researcher is able to conduct an experiment on study habits in his laboratory and finds some exciting results. What is one possible shortcoming of using this method?

- A Results from laboratory experiments do not always generalize to real-world situations.
- B Experiments do not provide evidence about cause-and-effect relationships.
- C It is not possible to conduct experiments on issues such as study habits.
- D Laboratory experiments do not control for confounding variables.

Answers can be found on page ANS-1.

Module Summary

Now that you have read this module you should:

KNOW ...

- *The key terminology related to research designs:*

case study (p. 49)
confounding variable (p. 53)
control group (p. 53)
correlational research (p. 50)
dependent variable (p. 53)
experimental group (p. 53)

independent variable (p. 53)
naturalistic observation (p. 49)
quasi-experimental research (p. 53)
random assignment (p. 53)

UNDERSTAND ...

- *What it means when variables are positively or negatively correlated.* When two or more variables are positively correlated, their relationship is direct—they increase or decrease together. For example, income and education level are positively correlated. Negatively correlated variables are inversely related—as one increases, the other decreases. Substance abuse may be inversely related to cognitive performance—higher levels of substance abuse are associated with lower cognitive ability.

- *How experiments help demonstrate cause-and-effect relationships.* Experiments rely on randomization and the manipulation of an independent variable to show cause and effect. At the beginning of an experiment, two or more groups are randomly assigned—a process that helps ensure that the two groups are roughly equivalent. Then, researchers manipulate an independent variable; perhaps they give one group a drug and the other group a placebo. At the end of the study, if one group turns out to be different, that difference is most likely due to the effects of the independent variable.

APPLY ...

- *The terms and concepts of experimental methods to research examples.* Here are two examples for practice. Check your answers on page ANS-1.

1. Dr. Vincent randomly assigns participants in a study to exercise versus no exercise conditions and, after 30 minutes, measures mood levels. In this case, exercise level is the _____ variable and mood is the _____ variable.

2. Dr. Harrington surveyed students on multiple lifestyle measures. He discovered that as the number of semesters that college students complete increases, their anxiety level increases. If number of semesters and anxiety increase together, this is an example of a(n) _____ correlation. Dr. Harrington also found that the more time students spent socializing, the less likely they were to become depressed. The increase in socializing and decrease in depression is an example of a(n) _____ correlation.

ANALYZE ...

- *The pros and cons of descriptive, correlational, and experimental research designs.* Descriptive methods have many advantages, including observing naturally occurring behavior and providing detailed observations of individuals. In addition, when correlational methods are used in descriptive research, we can see how key variables are related. Experimental methods can be used to test for cause-and-effect relationships. One drawback is that laboratory experiments may be limited in how far their results may generalize to real-world situations.

Module
2.3

Ethics in Psychological Research

	KNOW ...	UNDERSTAND ...	APPLY ...	ANALYZE ...
Learning Objectives After reading this module you should:	The key terminology of research ethics	The importance of reporting and storing data Why animals are often used in scientific research	The ethical principles of scientific research to examples	The role of using deception in psychological research

In 1932, the U.S. Public Health Service began a decades-long study of the long-term effects of syphilis, a disease involving chronic degeneration of the nervous system, dementia, and, if left untreated, death. The human subjects in this study were 399 African American men living in and around the southern Alabama city of Tuskegee. These men were known to be showing the early symptoms of syphilis, but were simply told they had "bad blood." Physicians recruited these men, who were especially vulnerable because of their lack health care resources, to volunteer for what they thought would be treatment for a range of medical problems by offering promises of free medical care, transportation to the clinics, and a square meal. Less than a decade into the study, researchers elsewhere demonstrated that penicillin was a very effective treatment of syphilis. What is most remarkable about this story is that the U.S. Public Health Service elected not to treat any of the volunteers in the Tuskegee study with this cure, even after penicillin became a widely available, well-established method of treating syphilis. The study finally ended in 1974, after many of the men had died from the disease (Cave & Holm, 2003; Thomas & Quinn, 1991).

The *Tuskegee Syphilis Study*, as it has come to be known, is an often-cited example of unethical research on human beings. Although medical experiments since that time have regularly withheld treatment from some individuals in the study—that is the role of the placebo or control condition—the rights of volunteers have changed dramatically. What separates unethical from ethical research? In the past three decades, much more attention has been given to this issue at all levels of society, by international health agencies, federal and local governments, professional organizations (such as the American Psychological Association), and the institutions that host and fund research.

Focus Questions

 Which institutional safeguards are now in place to protect the well-being of research participants?

 Does all research today require that people be informed of risks and consent to participate in a study?

The topics that psychologists study deal with living, sensing organisms, which raises a number of ethical issues that must be addressed before any study begins. These concerns include protecting the physical and mental well-being of participants, obtaining consent from them, and ensuring that their responses remain confidential. The procedures discussed in the next section have been developed as protections for participants; they are critical not only to ensure the individual well-being of the study participants, but also to maintain a positive and trustworthy image of the scientists who conduct research.

Promoting the Welfare of Research Participants

The Tuskegee study certainly is an extreme case—extreme in the harm done to the volunteers, the disregard for their well-being, and its 40-year duration. Today, most research with human subjects involves short-term, low-risk methods, and there are now ethical guidelines and procedures for ensuring the safety and well-being of all individuals involved in research. In the United States, all institutions that engage in research with humans, including colleges and universities, are required to have an **institutional review board (IRB)**, *a committee of researchers and officials at an institution charged with the protection of human research participants.* The IRB is intended to protect individuals in two main ways: (1) The committee weighs potential risks to the volunteers against the possible benefits of the research, and (2) it requires that volunteers agree to participate in the research.

WEIGHING THE RISKS AND BENEFITS OF RESEARCH
The majority of psychological research involves minimal exposure to physical or mental stress. Even so, great care is taken to protect participants. Some research involves exposing individuals to brief periods of stress, such as placing a hand in a tub of freezing water, or to brief periods of exercise. Some studies have even exposed humans to the virus that causes the common cold, or made small cuts to the skin to study factors that affect healing. The benefits that this type of research provides in promoting health and well-being must be weighed against the short-term risks to the people who consent to participate in these studies.

Physical risks are rare in psychological research. More common are measures that involve possible cognitive and emotional stress. Here are a couple of examples:

- *Mortality salience.* In this situation participants are made more aware of death, which can be done in a number of ways. For example, participants may be

asked to read or write about what happens to a human body after death.

- *Writing about upsetting or traumatic experiences.* People who have experienced recent trauma such as the death of a loved one or being laid off from a long-term job might be asked to write about that experience in great detail, sometimes repeatedly.

Another source of risk involves social situations. Humans are social beings with friends, families, and social networks to maintain and reputations to uphold. Some psychological research involves sensitive information that would be damaging if it became known publicly. Think about all the topics in psychology that people might want to keep to themselves: opinions about teachers or supervisors, a history of substance abuse, criminal records, medical records, and so on.

Everyone involved in the research process—the researcher, the IRB, and the potential volunteer—must determine whether the study's inherent risks are worth what can potentially be learned if the research goes forward. Consider again the stressors mentioned previously:

- *Mortality salience.* The stress tends to be short term, and psychologists learn how decisions are influenced by recent events in a person's life, such as the loss of a loved one or experiencing a major natural disaster. These decisions range from making charitable donations to voting for or against going to war.
- *Writing about upsetting experiences.* Although revisiting a stressful experience can be difficult, researchers learn how coping through expression can help emotional adjustment and physical health. In fact, participants who write about stress tend to be healthier—emotionally and physically—than those who write about everyday topics (such as describing their dorms or apartments).

These stressful situations have potential benefits that can be applied to other people. The psychologists who undertake such research tend to be motivated by several factors—including the desire to help others, the drive to satisfy their intellectual curiosity, and even their own livelihood and employment. The IRB serves as a third party that weighs the risks and benefits of research without being personally invested in the outcome. Under today's standards, there is no chance that the Tuskegee syphilis study would have been initiated. The danger to the participants in that study—*victims* might be a better term—far outweighed any scientific benefit in letting the disease go untreated for so long, even if the volunteers had known what they were getting into. Today, it is mandatory that research participants be informed of any risks to which they may be exposed and willfully volunteer to take part in a study. ◉▶

◉▶ Simulate the **Experiment** *Ethics in Psychological Research* at **MyPsychLab**

OBTAINING INFORMED CONSENT In addition to weighing the risks versus the benefits of a study, researchers must ensure that human volunteers truly are *volunteers*. This may seem redundant, but it is actually a tricky issue. Recall that the human subjects at Tuskegee were volunteers only in the sense that they voluntarily sought treatment from the researchers. But did they volunteer to have their disease go untreated? Had the men known the true nature of the study, it is doubtful that any would have continued to participate. Current practice is based on the concept of **informed consent**: *A potential volunteer must be informed (know the purpose, tasks, and risks involved in the study) and give consent (agree to participate based on the information provided) without pressure.*

To be truly informed about the study, volunteers should be told, at minimum, the following details (see also Figure 2.7):

- The topic of the study
- The nature of any stimuli (e.g., images, sounds, smells) to which they will be exposed
- The nature of any tasks (e.g., tests, puzzles) they will complete
- The approximate duration of the study
- Any potential physical, psychological, or social risks involved
- The steps that the researchers have taken to minimize those risks

Ethical practices often involve resolving conflicting interests, and in psychological research the main conflict is between the need for informed consent and the need for "blinded" volunteers. (Recall from Module 2.1 that in the best experimental designs the participants do not know exactly what the study is about, because such information may lead to subject bias.) Consider the mortality salience example. If a researcher told a participant, "We are going to test how a recent stressor you have experienced has affected your behavior," then the experiment probably would not work. In these cases, researchers use **deception**—*misleading or only partially informing participants of the true topic or hypothesis under investigation*. In psychological research, this typically amounts to a "white lie" of sorts. The

---

Informed Consent Statement

You are invited to participate in a research study assessing your attitudes and behaviors related to alcohol. We ask that you read this document before agreeing to participate in this study. Although the legal drinking age is 21, participants do not need to be of age, nor do they need to be regular drinkers. Participants must be at least 18 years of age and be willing to anonymously share opinions about alcohol. The study takes 30 minutes to complete. There are no risks associated with this study.

If you agree to be in this study, you will be asked to complete a survey and rate 40 statements about alcohol and alcohol use in your life. You may refuse to answer any questions and may withdraw from the study without penalty at any time. This research project has been reviewed and approved by the Institutional Review Board.

Thank you for your time.

___ I give consent to participate in this study

Participant Signature: _____ Date: _____

___ I do not wish to participate in this study

{FIG. 2.7} **Informed Consent** Research participants must provide informed consent before taking part in any study. As shown here, the participant must be made aware of the basic topic of the study as well as any possible risks.

---

participants are given enough information to evaluate their own risks. In medical research situations, however, deception can be much more serious. For example, as you learned in Module 2.1, patients who are being tested with an experimental drug may be randomly chosen to receive a placebo. After participating in the research study, participants must undergo a full **debriefing**, *meaning that the researchers should explain the true nature of the study, and especially the nature of and reason for the deception.*

Once participants are informed, they must also be able to give consent. Again, meeting this standard is trickier than it sounds. To revisit the men of Tuskegee, consider what their alternatives were. The men belonged to a socioeconomic group that did not have much access to health care; thus, even if they had been fully informed about the nature of the study, they might not have believed that they had any other options. When treatment options became more available, the researchers discouraged the men from seeking treatment. Such issues affect the nature of consent, so modern psychological research includes the following elements in determining whether full consent is given:

- *Freedom to choose.* Individuals should not be at risk for financial loss, physical harm, or damage to their reputation if they choose not to participate.
- *Equal opportunities.* Volunteers should have choices. For example, if the volunteers are introductory psychology students seeking course credit, they must have nonresearch alternatives available to them for credit should they choose not to participate in a study.
- *The right to withdraw.* Volunteers should have the right to withdraw from the study, at any time, without penalty. The right to give informed consent stays with the participants throughout the entire study.
- *The right to withhold responses.* Volunteers responding to surveys or interviews should not have to answer any question that they feel uncomfortable answering.

Usually, these criteria are sufficient for ensuring full consent. Sometimes, however, psychologists are interested in participants who cannot give their consent that easily. If researchers are studying children or individuals with mental disabilities, some severe psychiatric disorders, or certain neurological conditions, then a third party must give consent on behalf of the participant. This usually amounts to a parent or next-of-kin and, of course, all the rules of informed consent still apply.

THE RIGHT TO ANONYMITY AND CONFIDENTIALITY

A final measure of protection involves anonymity and confidentiality. *Anonymity* means that the data collected during a research study cannot be connected to individual participants. In many cases, volunteers can respond on a survey or through a computer-based experimental task without recording their name. This setup is ideal because it reduces both methodological problems (socially desirable responding) and the social risks to participants. If pure anonymity is not possible—for example, when a researcher must watch the participant perform a task—then confidentiality is a reasonable substitute.

Confidentiality includes at least two parts. First, researchers cannot share specific data or observations that can be connected with an individual. Second, all records must be kept secure (for example, in a password-protected database or locked filing cabinet) so that identities cannot be revealed unintentionally.

THE WELFARE OF ANIMALS IN RESEARCH

Many people who have never taken a psychology course view psychology as the study of *human* behavior, possibly because most psychological research does involve humans. But research with animals is just as important to psychological science for a number of reasons. The simplest and perhaps most obvious is that the study of psychology *does include* the behavior of animals. However, the most significant reason is that scientists can administer treatments to animals that could never be applied to humans. Animal models have proved highly beneficial to modern research on medical treatments and vaccines. In addition, genetic research requires species with much shorter life spans than our own so that several successive generations can be observed. Finally, scientists can manipulate the breeding of laboratory animals to meet the needs of their experimental procedures. Selective breeding allows researchers to study highly similar groups of subjects, which helps control for individual differences based on genetic factors.

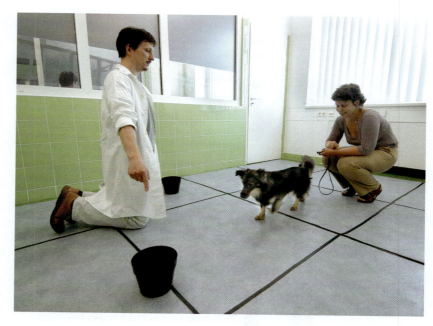

Many psychologists use animals in their research, so ethical codes have been extended to cover nonhuman species. **Click on this photo in your eText to see more details.**

Many ethical standards for animal research were developed at the same time as those for human research. In fact, colleges and universities have established committees responsible for the ethical treatment of animals, which are in some ways similar to IRBs that monitor human research. To be sure, there are differences in standards applied to human research and animal research; for example, we obviously do not ask for informed consent from animals. Nevertheless, similar procedures have been put in place to ensure that risk and discomfort are managed in a humane way, and that the pain or stress an animal may experience can be justified by the potential scientific value of the research. ◉

◉—|Watch the **Video** *Animal Rights Terrorists* at **MyPsychLab**

Three main areas of ethical treatment are emphasized by researchers and animal welfare committees. The first is the basic care of laboratory animals—that is, providing appropriate housing, feeding, and sanitation for the species. The second is minimization of any pain or discomfort experienced by the animals. Third, although it is rare for a study to *require* discomfort, when it is necessary, the researchers must ensure that the pain can be justified by the potential benefits of the research. The same standards apply if animals are to be sacrificed for the research.

Quick Quiz 2.3a
Promoting the Welfare of Research Participants

KNOW …

1 The Institutional Review Board (IRB) is the group that determines:

A whether a hypothesis is valid.

B whether the benefits of a proposed study outweigh its potential risks.

C whether a study should be published in a scientific journal.

D whether animal research is overall an ethical practice.

UNDERSTAND …

2 Which of the following is *not* a requirement for informed consent?

A Participants need to know the nature of the stimuli to which they will be exposed.

B Participants need to understand any potential physical, psychological, or social risks involved in the research.

C Participants need to have a face-to-face meeting with the researcher before volunteering.

D Participants need to know the approximate duration of the study.

ANALYZE …

3 In a memory study, researchers have participants study a list of words, and then tell them it was the wrong list and that they should forget it. This deception is meant to see how effectively participants can forget something they have already studied. If the researchers plan to debrief the participants afterward, would this design meet the standards of an ethical study?

A No, it is not okay to mislead individuals during the course of a study.

B Yes, given that the participants are not at risk and that they will be debriefed, this seems to be an ethical study.

C No, because the researchers should not debrief the participants—it will simply cause them to become angry.

D Yes, because participants fully understood all aspects of the study.

Answers can be found on page ANS-1.

Ethical Collection, Storage, and Reporting of Data

Ethical research does not end when the volunteers go home. Researchers have continuing commitments to the participants, such as the requirement to maintain the anonymity, confidentiality, and security of the data. Once data are reported in a journal or at a conference, they should be kept for a reasonable amount of time—generally, 3 to 5 years is acceptable. The purpose of keeping data for a lengthy period relates to the public nature of good research. Other researchers may request access to the data to reinterpret it, or perhaps examine the data before attempting to replicate the findings. It might seem as though the confidentiality requirement conflicts with the need to make data public, but this is not necessarily true. For example, if the data are anonymous, then none of the participants will be affected if and when the data are shared.

In addition to keeping data safe, scientists must be honest with their data. Some researchers experience great external pressure to obtain certain results. These pressures may relate to receiving tenure at a university, gaining funding from a governmental, industrial, or non-profit agency, or providing evidence that a product (for example, a medical treatment for depression) is effective. Unfortunately, cases of *scientific misconduct* sometimes arise when individuals fabricate or manipulate their data to fit their desired results. These cases seem to be rare and, due to the public aspect of good research, other scientists are likely to find that the study cannot be replicated in such instances. It is also possible to minimize the pressures by requiring researchers to acknowledge any potential conflicts of interest, which might include personal financial gain from an institution or company that funded the work. If you look at most published journal articles, you will see a footnote indicating which agency or organization provided the funds for the study. This annotation is not just a goodwill gesture; it also informs the public when there is the *potential* for a company or government agency to influence research.

Quick Quiz 2.3b
Ethical Collection, Storage, and Reporting of Data

UNDERSTAND ...

1 Researchers should store their data after they present or publish it because:

A other researchers may want to examine the data before conducting a replication study.

B other researchers may want to reinterpret the data using different techniques.

C the process of informed consent requires it.

D both a and b are true.

APPLY ...

2 After completing a naturalistic observation study, a researcher does not quite have enough evidence to support her hypothesis. If she decides to go back to her records and slightly alters a few of the observations to fit her hypothesis, she is engaged in _____.

A scientific forgery

B scientific misconduct

C correcting the data

D ethical behavior

Answers can be found on page ANS-1.

Module Summary

Now that you have read this module you should:

((•—[**Listen** to
the audio file of
this module at
MyPsychLab

KNOW ...

● **The key terminology of research ethics:**

debriefing (p. 58)
deception (p. 58)
informed consent (p. 58)

institutional review board (IRB) (p. 57)

UNDERSTAND ...

● **The importance of reporting and storing data.** Making data public allows scientific peers as well as the general public to have access to the details of research studies. This information includes details about participants, the procedures they experienced, and the outcome of the study. Furthermore, the requirement that data be stored allows fellow researchers to verify reports as well as examine the study for any possible misconduct. Fortunately, such cases are rare.

● **Why animals are often used in scientific research.** First, many research questions that affect medical and public health cannot be answered without animal testing. Second, obvious ethical considerations may not allow such research to be conducted on human subjects. Third, by working with animal models, scientists can control genetic and environmental variables that cannot be controlled with humans.

APPLY ...

● **The ethical principles of scientific research to examples.** For practice, read the following two scenarios and identify why they may fail to meet ethical standards. Check your answers on page ANS-1.

1. Dr. Nguyen wants to expose individuals first to a virus that causes people to experience colds, and then to varying levels of exercise to test whether exercise either facilitates or inhibits recovery. She is concerned that people will not volunteer if they know they may experience a cold, so she wants to give them the informed consent after completing the study.

2. Researchers set up a study on sexuality that involves answering a series of questions in an online survey. At the end of each page of the survey, the software checks whether all of the questions are answered; it will not continue if any questions are left blank. Students cannot advance to the end of the survey and receive credit for participation until they answer all the questions.

ANALYZE ...

● **The role of using deception in psychological research.** It is often the case that fully disclosing the purpose of a study before people participate in it would render the results useless. Thus specific details of the study are not provided during informed consent (although all potential risks are disclosed). When deception of any kind is used, researchers must justify that the benefits of doing so outweigh the costs.

A Statistical Primer

KNOW ...	UNDERSTAND ...	APPLY ...	ANALYZE ...
The key terminology of statistics	How and why psychologists use significance tests	Your knowledge to interpret the most frequently used types of graphs	The choice of central tendency statistics based on the shape of the distribution The conclusions that psychologists can reach based on significance tests

Would you be surprised to learn that even infants and toddlers can think about probability, the foundation of statistics? Professor Allison Gopnik (2010) writes about some interesting experiments showing just how statistically minded young children are. For example, consider the illustration below. If a researcher reached in and randomly selected five balls, would you be more surprised if they were all red or all white? If you are as smart as an infant, you would be more surprised if they were all red. In another experiment, Gopnik's research team placed blue or yellow blocks into a fancy contraption. Yellow blocks appeared to make the machine light up two out of three times, whereas the blue blocks only seemed to work two out of six times. When asked to "make the machine light up," preschoolers selected the yellow blocks, which had a higher probability

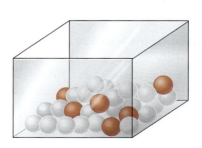

of working. If eight-month-olds and preschoolers can think statistically, adults should also be able to do so!

Focus Questions

 How do psychologists use statistics to describe their observations?

 How are statistics useful in testing the results of experiments?

· · · · · · · · · · · · · · · · · ·

The analysis of psychological data, as well as in other sciences, typically involves initially organizing numbers into ways that can be summarized and visualized to get an overall picture of trends and the outcome of the research. In addition, a critical step is to statistically analyze the data to determine whether the data confirm or refute a hypothesis.

Descriptive Statistics

Once research data have been collected, psychologists use **descriptive statistics**, *a set of techniques used to organize, summarize, and interpret data*. In most research, the statistics used to describe and understand the data are of three types: *frequency*, *central tendency*, and *variability*.

FREQUENCY   Often, the first step in understanding data is to prepare a graph. This depiction of the data allows researchers to see what is often called the *distribution*, the location of where the scores cluster on a number line and to what degree they are spread out. In Figure 2.8, you can see what you probably already know is a *bar graph*. Researchers often present data in a type of bar graph called a *histogram*. Like other bar graphs, the vertical axis shows the **frequency**, *the number of observations that fall within a certain category or range of scores*. These graphs are generally very easy to interpret: The higher the bar, the more scores that fall into the specific range. For example, if you look on the horizontal axis in Figure 2.8, you will see a column of test scores corresponding to people who scored around 500 on the test. Looking over to the vertical axis, you will see there were four individuals in that range. Histograms are a great way to present data but, as you will soon read, we can present the same data with a smooth line called a *curve*.

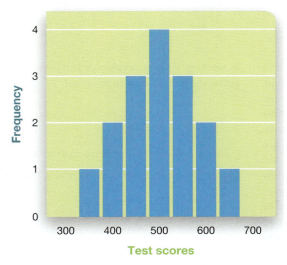

{FIG. 2.8}   **Graphing Psychological Data** The frequency of standardized test scores forming a normal curve.

It is usually easy to describe the distribution of scores from a histogram. By examining changes in frequency across the horizontal axis—basically by describing the heights of the bars—we can learn something about the variable. Where would you say the most scores cluster together? And how would you describe the way they spread out? Although there are specific mathematical ways of answering these questions, we are still safe in making an estimate based on the graph: The scores appear to cluster around 500 and they spread out between 350 and 650. Remember that we are just making estimates, so we can describe this spread as a *symmetrical* curve, meaning that the left half is the mirror image of the right half. A **normal distribution** (sometimes called *the bell curve*) is a *symmetrical distribution with values clustered around a central, mean value*.

Many variables wind up in a normal distribution, such as the scores on most standardized tests or the average high temperature in Sioux Falls, South Dakota, throughout the month of January. Other variables have what is known as a skewed distribution, like the ones shown in Figure 2.9. A **negatively skewed distribution** *occurs when the curve has an extended tail to the left of the cluster*. A **positively skewed distribution** *occurs when the long tail is on the right of the cluster*. Most of the time, skews occur because there is an upper or lower limit to the data. For example, a person cannot take less than 0 minutes to complete a quiz, so a curve depicting times to complete a quiz cannot continue indefinitely to the left, beyond the zero point. In contrast, just one person could take a very long time to complete a quiz, causing the right side of the curve to extend far to the right.

CENTRAL TENDENCY   When we identified the portion of the graph where the scores seem to cluster together, we were estimating **central tendency**—*a measure of the central point of a distribution*. Psychologists choose to calculate central tendency by using one of three measures. The **mean** *is the arithmetic average of a set of numbers*. In Figure 2.10, you can see that the mean is $30,000, which is exactly in the center of the histogram.

A second measure of central tendency is the **median**, *the 50th percentile—the point on the horizontal axis at which 50% of all observations are lower, and 50% of all observations are higher*. The third and final measure of

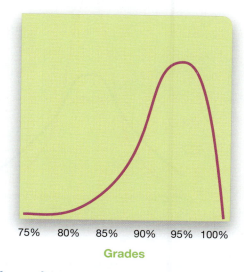

This negatively skewed distribution shows the class grades on a relatively easy quiz.

75% 80% 85% 90% 95% 100%

Grades

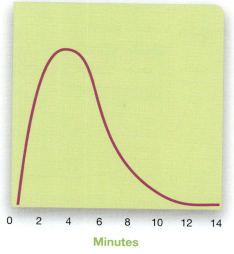

This positively skewed distribution shows that most students finished the quiz in less than 6 minutes— while a small number of students took up to 14 minutes.

0   2   4   6   8   10   12   14

Minutes

{FIG. 2.9}   **Skewed Distributions**   Positively and negatively skewed distributions are clustered on one side and spread out on the other.

central tendency is the **mode**, *which is the category with the highest frequency (that is, the category with the most observations).* In the histogram showing a normal distribution of incomes, the mode is the same as the mean and median—$30,000 has the highest frequency, which, as seen in Figure 2.10, is 3. However, the mean and the median usually give us more information about the central tendency (that is, where the scores cluster), so the mode is typically used when dealing with categories of data. For example, when you vote for a candidate, the mode represents the candidate with the most votes, and (in most cases) that person wins.

Notice that in Figure 2.10 the mean, median, and mode are the same. This is not always the case, but it is true for perfectly symmetrical curves. In contrast, if the histogram spreads out in one direction—in Figure 2.11 (p. 66), it is positively skewed—we are usually better off calculating central tendency by using the median. Notice what happens when you start to add extremely

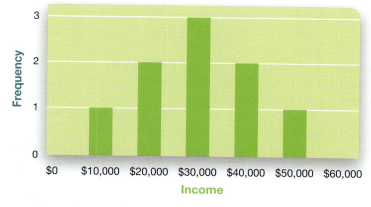

The graph shows that these nine households have the following incomes:

$10,000
$20,000
$20,000
$30,000
$30,000
$30,000
$40,000
$40,000
$50,000

Total = $270,000

Mean income per household:
$270,000 ÷ 9 = $30,000

Median (halfway between the lowest and highest numbers):
$30,000 (10, 20, 20, 30—30—30, 40, 40, 50)

Mode (most frequent number): $30,000

{FIG. 2.10}   **Central Tendency in Symmetrical Distributions**   This symmetrical histogram shows the annual income of nine randomly sampled households. Notice that the mean, median, and mode are all in the same spot—this is characteristic of normal distributions.

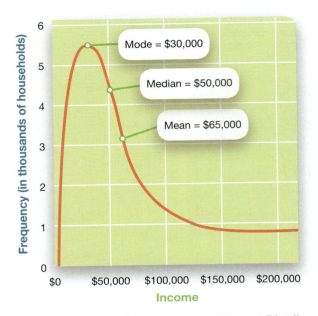

{FIG. 2.11} **Central Tendency in a Skewed Distribution** The mean is not always the ideal measure of central tendency. In this example, the mode and the median are actually more indicative of how much money most people make.

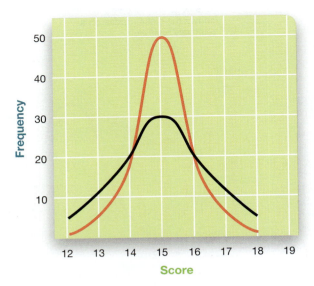

{FIG. 2.12} **Visualizing Variability** Imagine that these curves show how two classes fared on a 20-point quiz. Both classes averaged scores of 15 points. However, the students in one class (depicted in red) scored much more similarly to one another compared to students in another class (depicted in black), whose scores showed greater variability. The class represented by the black line would have a higher standard deviation.

wealthy households to the data set: The tail extends to the right and the mean is pulled in that direction. The longer the tail, the more the mean is pulled away from the center of the curve. By comparison, the median stays relatively stable, so it is a better choice for describing central tendency when dealing with skewed data.

The mean, median, and mode are three favored measures of central tendency. Although you have often heard (and probably used) the terms "average" and "typical," you may not have realized that there were three ways to represent the middle of a distribution. Keep in mind that the function of these statistics is to describe an entire distribution based on a single number. And when you hear someone say, "The typical value is . . . ," remember to stop and investigate whether the measure the researcher chose to report is appropriate for that particular type of distribution.

VARIABILITY Measures of central tendency help us summarize a group of individual cases with a single number by identifying a cluster of scores. In some distributions, however, the scores are more spread out than clustered (see Figure 2.12). **Variability** *is the*

degree to which scores are dispersed in a distribution. When variability is low (as in the red curve in the figure), the measures of central tendency tend to be the same, so they are a good representation of the distribution. But when variability is high (the black curve in the figure), some data are much farther from the center. Therefore, whenever psychologists report data from their research, their measures of central tendency are virtually always accompanied by measures of variability.

The **standard deviation** *is a measure of variability around the mean.* Think of it as an estimate of the *average distance from the mean.* Perhaps the best way to understand the standard deviation is by working through an example. Consider the Graduate Record Examination (GRE), which is a standardized test for admission into many graduate programs. If someone reports that the mean GRE test score is 500 with a standard deviation of 100, you should infer that 500 is in the middle of the pack and most people are within about 100 points on either side of the mean. (More technical calculations would tell us that roughly two-thirds of all individuals would score within 100 points of the mean, which is a range of scores from 400 to 600. You will see this understanding applied later in the intelligence and personality chapters.)

KNOW...

1 The _____ always marks the 50th percentile of the distribution.

   A mean

   B median

   C mode

   D standard deviation

2 The _____ is a measure of variability around the mean of a distribution.

   A mean

   B median

   C mode

   D standard deviation

APPLY...

3 A histogram is created that presents data on the number of mistakes participants in a research study made on a memory test. The vertical axis indicates:

   A the frequency of errors made.

   B the total number of participants.

   C the gender of the participants.

   D the mean number of errors made.

ANALYZE...

4 In a survey of recent graduates, your college reports that the mean salaries of the former students are positively skewed. What are the consequences of choosing the mean rather than the median or the mode in this case?

   A The mean is likely to provide a number that is lower than the largest cluster of scores.

   B The mean is likely to provide a reliable estimate of where the scores cluster.

   C The mean is likely to provide a number that is higher than the largest cluster of scores.

   D The mean provides the 50th percentile of the distribution, making it the best choice to depict this cluster of scores.

Answers can be found on page ANS-1.

Hypothesis Testing: Evaluating the Outcome of the Study

So far, you have learned about central tendency and variability, and perhaps you noticed that you cannot get the full description of what a distribution of scores looks like without one measure of each. You cannot tell where the scores cluster together without central

tendency, and you cannot tell how much scores spread out without a measure of variability. Therefore, if a researcher winds up with normally distributed data—that is, the data appear in the bell-curve shape—she will report both the mean and the standard deviation for each sample studied.

After researchers have described their data, the next step is to test whether the data support their hypothesis. Imagine, for example, that we wanted to test whether text messaging reduces feelings of loneliness in first-year college students. For three days, randomly selected students who regularly send text messages are assigned to one of two groups: those who can text and those who cannot. After three days, the students fill out a survey measuring how lonely they have felt. The diagram in Figure 2.13 shows us the key elements of such an experiment. Individuals are sampled from the population and randomly assigned to either the experimental or control group. The independent variable consists of the two groups, which includes texting or no texting. The dependent variable is the outcome—in this case, loneliness, with larger scores indicating greater loneliness. As you can see, the mean loneliness score of the group who could text message is three points below the mean of the group who did not text message. So, based on this information, are you willing to say that texting causes people to feel less lonely? Or have we left something out?

What we do not know from the diagram is the variability of test scores. We just emphasized that central tendency and variability should *always* be reported together, so we had better follow our own advice. On

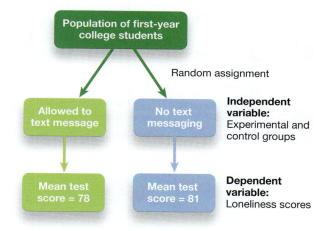

{FIG. 2.13} **Testing a Simple Hypothesis** To conduct an experiment on whether texting reduces loneliness, students would be randomly assigned to either text-messaging or no-text-messaging groups. Their average scores on a loneliness scale would then be compared.

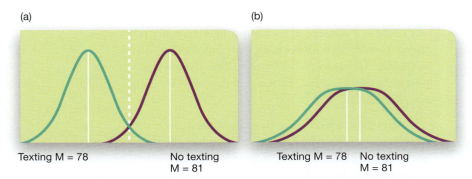

(a) Texting M = 78   No texting M = 81

(b) Texting M = 78   No texting M = 81

{FIG. 2.14} **How Variability Affects Hypothesis Testing** (a) The means (represented by M) differ between the two groups, and there is little overlap in the distribution of scores. When this occurs, the groups are much more likely to be significantly different. (b) Even though the means differ, there is much overlap between the distributions of scores. It is unlikely that these two means would be significantly different.

the one hand, it is quite possible that the scores of the two groups look like the graphs on the left in Figure 2.14. In that situation, the means are three points apart and the standard deviation is very small, so the curves have very little overlap. On the other hand, the scores of each group could have a broad range and therefore look like the graphs on the right. In that case, the group means are three points apart, but the groups overlap so much—the standard deviations are very high—that they seem virtually identical. How, then, would researchers know if the difference in scores is significant? They would rely on the concept of *statistical significance.* If the outcome is like that for the groups on the left,

where there is very little overlap, the difference is likely to have **statistical significance,** *which implies that the means of the groups are farther apart than you would expect them to be by random chance alone.* If this study was replicated several times, members of the group who could text message would almost always report feeling less lonely. But now imagine that the outcome is like the one on the right of the figure, where the scores overlap a great deal. That outcome would be nonsignificant, which means that if we did the study again, the outcomes for the groups might very well be reversed—the group who did not text message might have a lower average loneliness score. Given how much overlap there is between the two distributions, small differences in mean scores will not be significantly different.

When we are describing these examples as significant or not significant, we are just making estimates based on the appearances of the scores. To determine whether their results are significant, researchers analyze data using a **hypothesis test**—*a statistical method of evaluating whether differences among groups are meaningful, or could have been arrived at by chance alone.* The results of a hypothesis test will tell us if the two groups are significantly different (different because of the independent variable) with a certain degree of probability.

Quick Quiz 2.4b :: Hypothesis Testing: Evaluating the Outcome of the Study

UNDERSTAND...

1 A hypothesis test is conducted after an experiment to:

A determine whether the two groups in the study are exactly the same.

B determine how well the two groups are correlated.

C see if the groups are significantly different, as opposed to being different due to chance.

D summarize the distribution using a single score.

ANALYZE...

2 Imagine an experiment where the mean of the experimental group is 50 and the mean of the control group is 40. Given that the two means are obviously different, is it still possible for a researcher to say that the two groups are not significantly different?

A Yes, the two groups could overlap so much that the difference was not significant.

B Yes, if the difference was not predicted by the hypothesis.

C No, because the two groups are so far apart that the difference must be significant.

D No, in statistics a difference of 10 points is just enough to be significant.

Answers can be found on page ANS-1.

Module Summary

Now that you have read this module you should:

((•—|Listen to
the audio file of
this module at
MyPsychLab

KNOW ...

● *The key terminology of statistics:*

central tendency (p. 64)

descriptive statistics (p. 64)

frequency (p. 64)

hypothesis test (p. 68)

mean (p. 64)

median (p. 64)

mode (p. 65)

negatively skewed distribution (p. 64)

normal distribution (p. 64)

positively skewed distribution (p. 64)

standard deviation (p. 66)

statistical significance (p. 68)

variability (p. 66)

UNDERSTAND ...

● *How and why psychologists use significance tests.* Significance tests are statistics that tell us whether differences between groups or distributions are meaningful. For example, the averages of two groups being compared may be very different. However, how much variability there is among individuals within each of the groups will determine whether the averages are significantly different. In some cases, the averages of the two groups may be different, yet not statistically different because the groups overlap so much. This possibility explains why psychologists use significance tests—to test whether groups really are different from one another.

APPLY ...

● *Your knowledge to interpret the most frequently used types of graphs.* Take a look at **Figure 2.15**, a histogram showing the grades from a quiz in a statistics course, at the top of the next column and then answer the following questions and check your answers on page ANS-1.

1. What is the shape of this distribution? Normal, negatively skewed, or positively skewed?

2. What grade range is the mode for this class?

3. How many people earned a grade in the "B" range (between 80 and 89)?

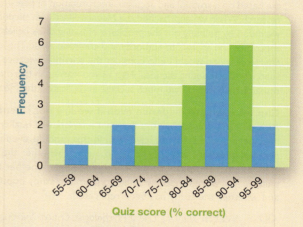

{FIG. 2.15}   Application Activity

ANALYZE ...

● *The choice of central tendency statistics based on the shape of the distribution.* For example, incomes are positively skewed. Suppose one politician claims the mean income level is $40,000, while the other claims that the median income level is $25,000. Which politician is giving the more representative measure? It would seem that the median would be a more representative statistic because it is not overly influenced by extremely high scores.

● *The conclusions that psychologists can reach based on significance tests.* If a significance test reveals that two or more groups are significantly different, it means that chance alone is a very unlikely explanation for why they differ. If the significance test indicates that the groups are not significantly different, then we can conclude that the individuals tested do not differ according to the independent variable for which they were tested.

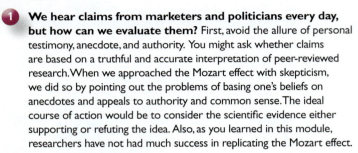

Module 2.1 :: Principles of Scientific Research

Focus Questions:

1 We hear claims from marketers and politicians every day, but how can we evaluate them? First, avoid the allure of personal testimony, anecdote, and authority. You might ask whether claims are based on a truthful and accurate interpretation of peer-reviewed research. When we approached the Mozart effect with skepticism, we did so by pointing out the problems of basing one's beliefs on anecdotes and appeals to authority and common sense. The ideal course of action would be to consider the scientific evidence either supporting or refuting the idea. Also, as you learned in this module, researchers have not had much success in replicating the Mozart effect.

2 Can we evaluate evidence even if we are not scientists? Anyone can ask whether the five characteristics of quality research have been applied. As you have seen in this module, even more detailed questions can also be asked, such as whether the evidence is based on a single- or double-blind procedure, whether the participants were randomly selected from the study population, and whether the study has been replicated.

⊙—[**Watch** *Thinking Like a Psychologist: Critical Thinking* in the **MyPsychLab video series**

Module 2.2 :: Scientific Research Designs

Focus Questions:

1 What are some of the ways researchers make observations? A variety of standard research designs exist, such as correlations, experiments, and quasi-experiments. When psychologists begin their research, they start by choosing one of the research designs that fits their research question. In the module-opening scenario, Dr. Martin used a correlational design that allowed him to say that as one variable (humor) increased, other variables changed in predictable ways.

2 Do some research techniques provide stronger evidence than others? Definitely. Correlational studies, including quasi-experiments, do a great job of describing whether variables are associated. Unfortunately, Dr. Martin is not able to tease out cause-and-effect relationships with his correlational design. However, the experimental design allows researchers to test hypotheses about cause and effect. In this case, the researcher starts with two or more groups of randomly assigned participants, and controls any independent variables that may differentiate the groups during the study.

⊙—[**Watch** *The Basics: The Scientific Method* in the **MyPsychLab video series**

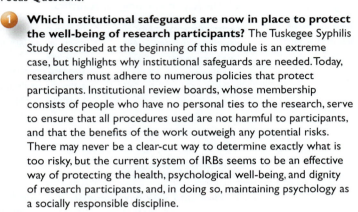

Module 2.3 :: Ethics in Psychological Research

Focus Questions:

1 Which institutional safeguards are now in place to protect the well-being of research participants? The Tuskegee Syphilis Study described at the beginning of this module is an extreme case, but highlights why institutional safeguards are needed. Today, researchers must adhere to numerous policies that protect participants. Institutional review boards, whose membership consists of people who have no personal ties to the research, serve to ensure that all procedures used are not harmful to participants, and that the benefits of the work outweigh any potential risks. There may never be a clear-cut way to determine exactly what is too risky, but the current system of IRBs seems to be an effective way of protecting the health, psychological well-being, and dignity of research participants, and, in doing so, maintaining psychology as a socially responsible discipline.

2 Does all research today require that people be informed of risks and consent to participate in a study? All research participants must be fully informed of any risks associated with their participation in research prior to giving their consent. Furthermore, participants always have the right to discontinue their involvement in a research study.

⊙—[**Watch** *Special Topics: Ethics* in the **MyPsychLab video series**

Module 2.4 :: A Statistical Primer

Focus Questions:

1 How do psychologists use statistics to describe their observations? Familiar statistics such as the mean and the median can be used to describe how scores cluster together. Another important statistical measure reveals how much variation there is among individuals. Measures such as the standard deviation indicate how scores are spread out around a mean.

2 How are statistics useful in testing the results of experiments? It is possible that the difference between an average test score of, say, 450 and 500 may not be meaningful in a statistical sense. This is because scores need to be *significant*, in statistical terms, to be considered truly different.

⊙—[**Watch** *The Big Picture: How to Answer Psychological Questions* in the **MyPsychLab video series**

⊙—[**Watch** the complete video series online at **MyPsychLab**

Episode 2: Research Methods

1 By studying a _____, scientists hope that they can generalize the results of their investigation to the _____.

   A sample; population

   B population; sample

   C convenience sample; random sample

   D random sample; convenience sample

2 Which of the following is an example of demand characteristics affecting an experiment?

   A An experimenter draws the wrong conclusions from a study because she did not use the correct statistical analysis.

   B A participant changes his response to a question because he has the feeling that the experimenter wants him to do so.

   C An experimenter stops using a test because it does not appear to be reliable.

   D A participant in a double-blind experiment believes she is in the control group.

3 Why it is a bad idea to draw conclusions from anecdotal evidence?

   A Such conclusions usually go against common sense.

   B Anecdotes are reliable only if they come from experts, which they rarely do.

   C Anecdotes are a single-blind technique, not a double-blind method.

   D There is no way to know if the anecdote is true or if it will generalize to other people and situations.

4 What does a correlation coefficient of −0.94 indicate about two variables?

   A The variables are weakly associated, with both increasing together.

   B The variables are strongly associated, with both increasing together.

   C The variables are weakly associated, with one increasing as the other decreases.

   D The variables are strongly associated, with one increasing as the other decreases.

5 Most people would agree that anxiety can lead to sleep loss. However, Dr. Jenkins believes that sleep deprivation can also cause increased anxiety. Which research method would allow him to test a cause-effect relationship between the two?

   A Naturalistic observation

   B Experimental

   C Correlational

   D Survey

6 Which of the following statements describes the amount of cognitive and emotional risk to participants allowed in psychological research today?

   A Any amount of risk is acceptable.

   B No amount of risk is acceptable.

   C A little risk is always acceptable, but more than minimal risk is never acceptable.

   D The amount of acceptable risk depends in part on the likely benefits from the study.

7 The use of deception in psychological research is:

   A not a serious issue.

   B never acceptable.

   C generally acceptable when absolutely necessary for the research.

   D acceptable only in nonhuman research.

8 Under which of the following circumstances would the mean be the best measure of central tendency to use?

   A The data have a normal distribution.

   B The data are positively skewed.

   C The data are negatively skewed.

   D The mean is always the best measure of central tendency

9 A teacher notices that on the last science test, some students did very well, while other students performed poorly or had grades in the middle of the pack. If she wanted to measure how "spread out" all of the scores were, which descriptive statistic could she use?

   A Median

   B Mode

   C Standard deviation

   D Mean

10 Keisha performs an experiment with two randomly assigned groups of school children. The first group is allowed 15 minutes of recess play before a math test, while the second group watches a video before the test. When she analyzes the test scores, she finds that there is a statistical difference between the groups, with the recess group scoring higher on average. Which conclusions can be drawn from this result?

   A The difference between the scores for the two groups is probably due to random chance.

   B The difference between the scores for the two groups is likely due to their differing pretest activities, and did not happen by chance.

   C Students who are good at math prefer recess to watching a video.

   D Students who are good at math prefer watching a video to recess.

✓● Study and Review at MyPsychLab

What do we know about scientific research?

On **page 51** we discussed the difference between correlation and causation. Imagine reading a study that states that aggressive people tend to have red bedrooms. Will painting your bedroom red cause you to act aggressively? It simply means that the variables of room color and aggressive acts are statistically related. Only an experiment can show causality, so turn to **Figure 2.6 on page 53** for a review of its elements.

To understand scientific experiments, you should know the difference between a dependent variable, which is the variable that is measured during the experiment and compared across all of the groups, and the independent variable, which is the variable that the researcher manipulates.

To make sure you have correctly labeled the variables in an experiment is, insert the variable names into the following phrase.

How _____ affects _____.
       (i.v.)   (d.v.)

In this case, the room color is the independent variable and aggressiveness is the dependent variable.

How can science help differentiate between different kinds of research designs?

Conducting sound research means not only knowing which questions to ask, but also how to ask them correctly. Early psychological research in the United States was based almost exclusively on observations of behavior and self-reports, but over time new technologies such as magnetic resonance imaging (MRI) expanded the number of variables psychologists can study. In the past few centuries, scientists have developed a variety of research designs suited to answer many new research questions; **Table 2.1 on page 54** offers a snapshot of the strengths and limitations of each. Regardless of the design used, scientific research must be based on objective, reliable measurements; it should generalize to a population from which the sample was drawn; it should avoid bias; and it should be made public so that others can learn from it, evaluate it, and replicate it.

Why is this relevant?

Watch the accompanying video excerpt about the scientific method. You can access the video at MyPsychLab or by clicking the play button in the center of your eText. If your instructor assigns this video as a homework activity, you will find additional content to help you in MyPsychLab. You can also view the video by using your smart phone and the QR code below, or you can go to the YouTube link provided.

After you have read this chapter and watched the video, imagine you have been asked to create an experimental design to test the hypothesis that talking on a cell phone impairs driving skills. Explain why a control condition would be important to include in testing this hypothesis. How should subjects be assigned to conditions? How can the researchers design the experiment so that the only difference between both conditions is the use of a cell phone?

Can we critically evaluate scientific research designs?

Understanding the characteristics of different scientific methods can help you evaluate the claims you encounter in everyday life. Think back to what you know about correlation and causation. The news media in particular often perpetuate the idea that an association, or correlation, between two variables is the same as a cause-and-effect relationship. For example, "Happiness Makes You Live Longer" is more dramatic than the headline "There Is a Positive Correlation between Happiness and Longevity." When evaluating research, notice qualifying words such as "might increase" and "could have an effect," both of which suggest correlation. Similarly, in **Myths in Mind on page 51**, we explored the idea that many common beliefs are actually illusory correlations. When two relatively rare events happen simultaneously, such as a full moon and an uncommonly busy night in the emergency room, then we might overestimate their relationship. That your staunchly conservative friend is dating an equally passionate liberal is more memorable than the fact that most of your coupled friends support the same political candidates.

youtube.com/user/
scientificliteracy

3 :: BIOLOGICAL PSYCHOLOGY

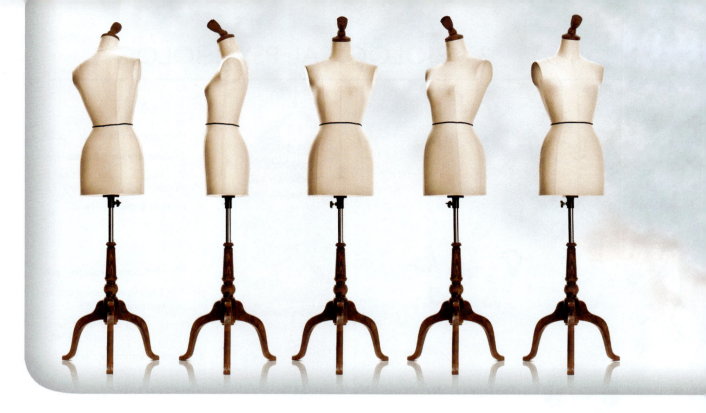

Genetic and Evolutionary Perspectives on Behavior

Learning Objectives

After reading this module you should:

KNOW ...	UNDERSTAND ...	APPLY ...	ANALYZE ...
The key terminology related to genes, inheritance, and evolutionary psychology	How twin and adoption studies reveal relationships between genes and behavior	Your knowledge of genes and behavior to hypothesize why a trait might be adaptive	Claims that scientists have located a specific gene that controls a single trait or behavior Explanations for cognitive gender differences that are rooted in genetics

Psychologist Martie Haselton has given new meaning to the phrase *dress for success*. She is not talking about professional advancement, however; rather, she is referring to success in attracting a mate. Dr. Haselton is an evolutionary psychologist—she studies how human behavior has evolved to solve problems that relate to survival and reproductive success. As part of her work, she has discovered that the clothes people choose are related to sexual motivation in some subtle ways.

In one project, Dr. Haselton and her colleagues invited female volunteers to the laboratory to participate in a study about personality, sexuality, and health. The young women were not given any specific directions about what to wear and during their visit to the laboratory they agreed to be photographed. Later, male and female volunteers viewed the photographs to judge whether they thought the women in the photos had dressed to look attractive. It turns out that women were rated as better dressed when they were in their peak level of fertility of the menstrual cycle (Durante et al., 2008; Haselton et al., 2007).

Of course, evolutionary psychologists are quick to point out that females are not alone in "signaling" their receptiveness for sexual activity. Males provide numerous—if not more obvious—examples. Evolutionary psychologists might point out that body building, flaunting material assets, and other public displays of strength and status are common male strategies for attracting mates. Researchers must ask themselves this question: Is this behavior just a coincidence? Or are millions of years of evolutionary pressures influencing the choice of attire? Evolutionary psychologists like Dr. Haselton are building evidence to argue that how we dress and how we send many other signals can be explained by evolutionary principles, a topic we explore in this module.

Focus Questions

1 How has evolution played a role in modern-day human behavior?

2 How is human behavior influenced by genetic factors?

· · · · · · · · · · · · · · · · · ·

You might have heard something like this before: *Leah gets her passion for reading from her father.* But does that mean Leah inherited this interest? Or did she just grow up with a lot of books around the home?

Are we the products of our genes (nature) or the environment in which we are raised (nurture)? As discussed in Module 1.2, debates about nature and nurture have been going on for many decades; some of the insights that psychology provides into this controversy are discussed in this module. Perhaps one reason people have so often debated nature and nurture relationships is because humans have such a strong tendency to think in either/or categories: yes or no, true or false, black or white. In reality, all of the available evidence suggests that nature and nurture lie along a continuum, with some traits subject to greater influence from genes while others are more environmentally based. Most important, we now know that genes and experience are never independent; instead, they *interact* to make us who we are. Therefore, the modern scientific nature–nurture question does not split them into two exclusive possibilities. Rather, we ask, *How do genes and environment interact to produce behavior?*

Heredity and Behavior

Examples of genetic influences on physical traits easily come to mind because we tend to share our eye color, facial characteristics, stature, and skin coloration with our parents. In fact, research has made it clear that behaviors are influenced by genes just as physical characteristics are. This research typically involves either comparing people of differing levels of relatedness (e.g., identical versus non-identical twins) or studying specific genes at the molecular level. Before we delve into this issue, let's briefly review some basic concepts of genetics.

THE GENETIC CODE   Most of the billions of cells in the human body include a nucleus, which is where we find the entire genetic code. **Genes** *are the basic units of heredity; they are responsible for guiding the process of creating the proteins that make up our physical structures and regulate development and physiological processes throughout the life span.* Genes are organized along **chromosomes,** *structures in the cellular nucleus that are lined with all of the genes an individual inherits.* Humans have approximately 30,000 genes distributed across 23 pairs of chromosomes, half contributed by the mother and half from the father (see Figure 3.1).

Genes are comprised of **DNA (deoxyribonucleic acid)**, *a molecule formed in a double-helix shape that contains four amino acids: adenine, cytosine, guanine, and thymine* (see Figure 3.2). These amino acids are typically abbreviated using the first letter of their names—A, C, G, and T. Each gene is a unique combination of these four amino acids. For example, a sequence of amino acids on a certain gene may be AGCCTAATCG . . . and so on. This sequence represents the *code* used to create proteins. Genes

instruct cells how to behave, which type of molecules to produce, and when to produce them. Traits that show genetic variation, such as eye color, the shape and size of facial features, and even personality, do so because of differences in the amino acid sequencing of A, C, G, and T, as well as through interactions with the environment.

The term **genotype** *refers to the genetic makeup of an organism.* The unique set of genes that compose every chromosome represents the genotype of the individual, whereas the **phenotype** *consists of the observable characteristics, including physical structures and behaviors.* Distinguishing between the genotype and the phenotype is important when it comes to understanding how genes and traits are related. The genotype represents what was inherited, whereas the phenotype represents the physical and behavioral manifestation of the genotype through interactions with the environment.

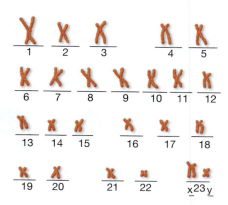

{FIG. 3.1}   **Human Chromosomes** Human DNA is aligned along 23 paired chromosomes. Numbers 1–22 are common to both males and females. Chromosome 23 is sex linked, with males having the XY pattern and females the XX pattern.

Genes come in pairs, one inherited from each parent, aligned along the chromosomes. If two corresponding genes at a given location on a pair of chromosomes are the same, they are referred to as *homozygous*. If the two genes differ, they are *heterozygous*. Whether a trait is expressed depends on which combination of pairs is inherited. For example, the ability to taste a very bitter substance called phenylthiocarbamide (PTC) is based on which combination of genes we inherit from either parent (the genotype; see Figure 3.3 on p. 76). The test for whether you can taste PTC (the phenotype) is typically performed by placing a small tab of paper soaked in the substance on the tongue. Some people are "tasters"; they cringe at the bitter taste of PTC. Others—the

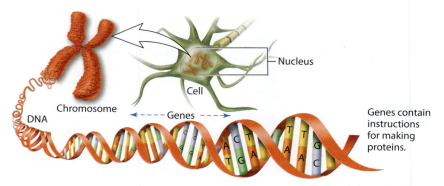

{FIG. 3.2}   **DNA Molecules** The nucleus of a cell contains copies of each chromosome. Chromosomes are composed of the genes arranged in the familiar double helix—a long strand of DNA molecules. **Click on this figure in your eText to see more details.**

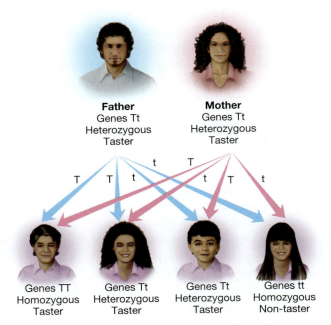

Father
Genes Tt
Heterozygous
Taster

Mother
Genes Tt
Heterozygous
Taster

t T

T T t t t T t

Genes TT
Homozygous
Taster

Genes Tt
Heterozygous
Taster

Genes Tt
Heterozygous
Taster

Genes tt
Homozygous
Non-taster

{FIG. 3.3} **Genetic Inheritance** Whether someone tastes the bitter compound PTC depends on which copies of the gene he or she inherits. Shown here is the statistically probable outcome of two heterozygous (Tt) parents with four children.

Identical twins are genetically the same, whereas fraternal twins are no more closely related than full siblings from different pregnancies. However, fraternal twins do share much of the same prenatal and postnatal environment if they are reared together.

"nontasters"—cannot taste anything other than the tab of paper. Those who are tasters inherit at least one copy of the *dominant* gene for tasting (abbreviated capital "T") from either parent. People can also inherit a *recessive* copy of this gene (t). Those who report tasting PTC are either homozygous dominant (TT) or heterozygous (Tt). Nontasters are homozygous recessive (tt)—they inherited a recessive copy of the gene from both parents. Those who are tasters may find foods such as Brussels sprouts, cauliflower, and cabbage to be unpleasant, or at least too bitter to eat, as these foods contain PTC.

Genetically speaking, the taster versus nontaster example is relatively straightforward and gives us a general sense of how traits are inherited. Human behavior is highly complex, however, and it is rare that normal behavior, or even disorders of the brain, can be explained as simply as in the PTC example. Although the concepts we have just reviewed are helpful, a different approach is needed to provide genetic explanations for human characteristics such as personality, intelligence, and psychological disorders. Specifically, we need an approach that examines the interactions between genes and environment.

BEHAVIORAL GENETICS: TWIN AND ADOPTION STUDIES People have long observed that behavioral characteristics can be inherited. For many centuries, the clearest evidence of this possibility came from animal breeding, where animals such as dogs have been reared to be hunters, herders, protectors, or companions. Because we cannot use the methods of dog breeders to study humans, some alternatives are required. **Behavioral genetics** *is the study of how genes and environment influence behavior.* Behavioral genetic methods applied to humans typically involve comparing people of different levels of relatedness, such as parents and their offspring, siblings, and unrelated individuals, and measuring resemblances for a specific trait of interest.

Twins present an amazing opportunity to conduct natural experiments on how genes influence behavior. One method commonly used in twin studies involves comparing identical and fraternal twins. **Monozygotic twins** *come from a single ovum (egg), which makes them genetically identical.* An ideal comparison group, **dizygotic twins** (fraternal twins) *come from two separate eggs fertilized by two different sperm cells that share the same womb.* Researchers around the world have studied the genetic and environmental bases of behavior by following different sets of twins for many years, often decades. For example, one twin study determined the degree to which anxiety and depression are influenced by genetics in children and adolescents. It was far more likely for both monozygotic twins to show anxiety or depressive symptoms than for both dizygotic twins to do so; thus these results demonstrate the influential role that genes play in depression (Boomsma et al., 2005).

Behavioral geneticists use twin studies to calculate **heritability**—*a statistic, expressed as a number between zero and one, that represents the degree to which genetic differences between individuals contribute to individual differences in a behavior or trait found in a population.* A heritability of 0 means that genes do not contribute to individual differences in a trait, whereas heritability of 1.0 indicates that genes account for all individual differences in a trait. Heritability estimates usually fall somewhere in between these two values; rarely, if ever, is a heritability of 0 or 1.0 found. The estimated heritability found in the study on depression and anxiety described earlier was approximately .76 for 3-year-old identical twin pairs (Boomsma et al., 2005). This tells us that 76% of

There is heritable variation in body height—although environmental factors contribute to variation in height among family members.

BEHAVIORAL GENOMICS: THE MOLECULAR APPROACH As you can see from the research on depression and intelligence, twin studies and adoption studies can provide estimates of heritability, but they do not tell us *how* traits are inherited. To make this determination, researchers go straight to the source of genetic influence—to the genes themselves. **Behavioral genomics** *is the study of DNA and the ways in which specific genes are related to behavior.* The technology supporting behavioral genomics is relatively new, but once it became available, researchers initiated a massive effort to identify the components of the entire human genome—the *Human Genome Project.* This project, which was completed in 2003, resulted in the identification of approximately 30,000 genes. Imagine the undertaking: determining the sequences of the billions of A, C, G, and T amino acids making up the genes, including where each gene begins and ends, and how they are all arranged on the chromosomes. The Human Genome Project itself did not directly provide a cure for a disease or an understanding of any particular behavior. Instead, it has led to an abundance of new techniques and information about where genes are located, and it opened the door for an entirely new era of behavioral genetics (Plomin & Crabbe, 2000). For example, researchers can now examine genes that are present among individuals diagnosed with a disorder that are not present in other persons.

Like any approach to answering scientific questions, behavioral genomic research does have its limitations. For example, although a single gene has been identified as a risk factor for Alzheimer's disease, not everyone who inherits it develops the disease. There is not just one, all-controlling gene for Alzheimer's disease—and the same is true for many other conditions. This brings us to a common misconception about genes and behavior.

individual differences in depression and anxiety at age 3 can be attributed to genetic factors in the population that was studied. Given that experiences inevitably accumulate with time, we sometimes see heritability estimates change as people age. In the Boomsma et al. (2005) study, the heritability of anxiety and depression went from .76 at age 3 to .48 at age 12 for the identical twin pairs. This finding should serve as a reminder that the environment never stops interacting with genes.

Behavioral geneticists also study adopted children to estimate genetic contributions to behavior. The adopted family represents the *nurture* side of the continuum, whereas the biological family represents the *nature* side. On the one hand, if adopted children are more like their biological parents than their adoptive parents on measures of traits such as personality and intelligence, we might conclude that these traits have a strong genetic component. On the other hand, if the children are more like their adoptive, genetically unrelated parents, a strong case can be made that environmental factors outweigh the biological predispositions. Interestingly, young adopted children are more similar to their adoptive parents in intelligence levels than they are to their biological parents. By the time they reach 16 years, however, adopted adolescents score more similarly to their biological parents than their adoptive parents in tests of intelligence (Plomin et al., 1997). Compare this finding to that from the study described in the preceding paragraph: For intelligence, heritability seems to increase with age, whereas the opposite is true for depression and anxiety.

MYTHS IN MIND
Single Genes and Behavior

Just Google the phrase "scientists find gene for" and you will wind up with more hits than you would ever have time to sift through. Although it is true that behavior, both normal and abnormal, can be traced to individual genes, typically *combinations* of genes influence behavior. When it comes to complex characteristics such as personality or disorders like Alzheimer's disease and schizophrenia, there is very little chance that any single gene could be responsible for them (Duan et al., 2010). A person's intelligence and his predisposition to alcoholism, anxiety, shyness, and depression are all examples of traits and conditions with genetic links, but they all involve multiple genes.

Another misconception is that a single gene can affect only one trait. In reality, the discovery that a particular gene predisposes someone to alcoholism does not mean that this gene is *only* relevant to alcohol addiction; it most likely affects other traits as well. For example, genes that are present in people who abuse alcohol are also more likely to be found in individuals who have a history of other problems such as additional forms of drug dependence and antisocial behavior. In other words, there is a "shared genetic liability" (Dick, 2007).

When you encounter a headline beginning "Scientists find gene for . . . ," don't read it as "Scientists found THE gene for. . . ." It would be wise to carefully read on to fully understand what is being reported. It is likely that the news describes the work of scientists who found another one of the many genes involved in a disorder, or, in the case of Alzheimer's disease, a gene that is a risk factor and not the sole cause.

. . . .

Quick Quiz 3.1a
Heredity and Behavior

KNOW...

1 The chemical units that provide instructions on how specific proteins are to be produced are called _____.

- **A** chromosomes
- **B** genes
- **C** genomic
- **D** autosomes

UNDERSTAND...

2 A person who is homozygous for a trait:

- **A** always has two dominant copies of a gene.
- **B** always has two recessive copies of a gene.
- **C** has identical copies of the gene.
- **D** has different copies of the gene.

APPLY...

3 If a researcher wanted to identify an actual gene that put people at risk for developing depression, she would most likely use which of the following methods?

- **A** Behavioral genomics
- **B** A comparison of monozygotic and dizygotic twins
- **C** An adoption study
- **D** Calculation of a heritability

ANALYZE...

4 Imagine you hear a report about a heritability study that claims trait X is "50% genetic." Which of the following is a more accurate way of stating this?

- **A** Fifty percent of individual differences of trait X within a population are due to genetic factors.
- **B** Only half of a population has the trait.
- **C** The trait is homozygous.
- **D** More than 50% of similarities of trait X within a population are due to genetic factors.

Answers can be found on page ANS-1.

Knowing about genes gives us some idea as to why individuals differ. Another issue, explored in the next section, is how these individual differences contribute to behaviors that lead to survival and reproductive success.

Evolutionary Insights into Human Behavior

Genes are the basis for why each individual is unique (except for identical twins) as well as why members of different species are unique. The amazing diversity of behavior found in the animal kingdom has long been of interest to scientists. The best scientific explanation for how this diversity originated remained elusive until Charles Darwin, the 19th-century British naturalist, arrived at a theory for why the anatomical and behavioral traits of animals often seem so fitted to their respective environments. Darwin even applied his ideas to human behavior. Since Darwin's time, psychology has had periods of either embracing or shunning evolutionary explanations of human behavior. The past few decades in particular have seen more embracing than shunning, and we now have a specialized field that uses evolutionary theory to guide explanations of human behavior.

EVOLUTIONARY PSYCHOLOGY Evolutionary psychology, as you will recall from Module 1.2, views modern human behavior as an outcome of the processes of survival and reproduction among our early human ancestors. We now know that genes are important contributors to human behavior. Heritable traits, both physical and behavioral, pass from one generation to the next through sexual reproduction. Some of these traits—called *adaptations*—contribute to survival, health, and sexual behavior. Individuals with these adaptive traits are more likely to pass on their genes to the next generation compared to individuals with traits that do not contribute, or perhaps even hurt, chances for survival and reproduction. Thus, if you had the means to identify and count specific genes within a population, you would see that some of them become more and more widespread over time. This is a major part of the process of **evolution**, *the change in the frequency of genes occurring in an interbreeding population over generations.*

Why do some genes become more frequent and others less so in breeding populations? This was the question Charles Darwin tackled, and natural selection was his answer as to how evolution occurs. **Natural selection** *is the process by which favorable traits become increasingly common in a population of interbreeding individuals, while traits that are unfavorable become less common* (see Figure 3.4). In the grand scheme of things, evolutionary change is gradual—the effects of natural selection on a trait may take numerous generations.

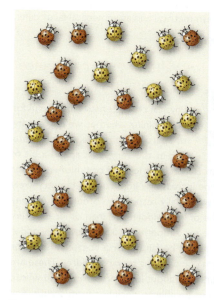

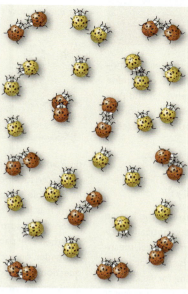

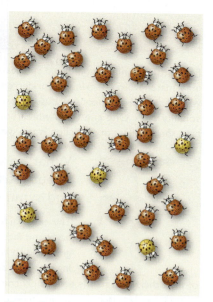

Suppose coloration is a genetically inherited trait in lady bugs.

Suppose a bird that preys on these lady bugs can see the yellow ones better. This brings about a survival and reproductive advantage to red lady bugs that have red-colored offspring.

Genes for red coloration should spread through the population because natural selection favors red lady bugs over yellow lady bugs.

How does this process apply to humans? According to evolutionary psychologists, the human brain contains specialized adaptations for performing certain cognitive and behavioral functions. For example, one adaptation relates to how the brain processes cues that determine whether we are physically attracted to others. At the beginning of this module we described research showing that women dress more attractively when they are ovulating. Likewise, men give off cues to accentuate their masculinity.

Physical attraction is one of many important qualities people value in their mates—whether they are short-term or long-term partnerships. Of course, there are other qualities we look for, particularly when it comes to long-term mates. But what are these qualities, and do members of other cultures value similar characteristics in others? Buss (1989) conducted a survey of more than 10,000 people from 37 different cultures to discover what they most valued in a long-term partner. Across this broad sample, on average, women regarded love and commitment, character, and emotional maturity as the most important qualities in a mate. Women also valued men with strong financial prospects, status, and good health. Men also identified love, commitment, character, and maturity as important to long-term arrangements, but placed a greater emphasis on physical beauty, youth, and other characteristics that relate to reproduction. Buss argues that these cross-cultural "universals" in male and female preferences are psychological adaptations for finding a long-term mate and continuing one's genetic legacy. Female preferences are consistent with the biological fact that there are limits to how many children they can bear in a lifetime. Male preferences are consistent with a motivation to have as many healthy offspring as possible in their lifetime.

Animals of many species use coloration as a way to attract the attention of potential mates, and those who are most colorful are often preferred.

WORKING THE SCIENTIFIC LITERACY MODEL
Attraction and Symmetry

For both human and nonhuman species, the process of finding a mate involves seeking out preferred traits. To determine whether we like someone, we use a host of physical and personality cues. One cue upon which both men and women base their feelings of attraction is the symmetry of the face.

What do we know about attraction and symmetry?

The external features of the human body and face are genetically programmed to be symmetrical, meaning that each side is a mirror image of the other. Even so, the genetic programming for facial symmetry is rarely perfect, and environmental factors such as illness may cause asymmetry of facial features. The eyes may be slightly offset, one ear may be slightly higher than the other, or the chin may be slightly skewed to one side. Psychologists are testing just how sensitive we are to deviations from symmetry, and how our detection of asymmetry affects our preferences for others.

How can science provide evidence that we prefer symmetrical faces?

People can detect even the subtlest bodily asymmetries, and they rate symmetrical faces as more attractive than asymmetrical ones (Gangestad et al., 1994; Rhodes, 2006). For example, view the photos at the bottom of the page.

In studies of facial symmetry and attraction research, participants view sets of photos such as these and rate the ones they most prefer. Clearly, the five photos shown here are of the same individual, and each photo may look identical upon superficial examination. However, if you look more closely, you will likely notice that the sizes of the eyes are asymmetrical in both photos on either side of the center one. Ratings by both males and females indicate that they prefer symmetrical faces of either sex (Rhodes et al., 2009). This preference even occurs when deviations from symmetry are so subtle that participants cannot explain how the symmetrical and asymmetrical faces differ.

Can we critically evaluate the importance of symmetry?

Physical characteristics are useful for determining whether we might want to approach someone, ask for a date, and at the very least spend a bit of time with the person. Beyond this level of commitment, other characteristics become increasingly important. Symmetry likely plays a role in how we initially respond to others. In the long term, it is likely to be of less importance than other qualities. After dating someone for a month or so, we begin to wonder whether our partners will be faithful or a cheater, a saver or a spender, or nurturing or uncaring toward children. These are questions we ask ourselves about long-term mates, and whose answers we would not be able to decipher from scrutinizing body symmetry.

Critics and evolutionary psychologists alike point out that not all behaviors and physical traits are necessarily adaptive, either as they are expressed today or as they were demonstrated by our distant ancestors (Gould & Lewontin, 1979). In other words, not all traits provide an evolutionary advantage. For example, baldness runs in families even though it is unlikely that this characteristic promotes survival and reproductive fitness. Similarly, we cannot assume that all behavioral traits, such as the ability to detect facial asymmetries, have an adaptive function relating to survival and reproductive fitness.

Why is this relevant?

How does research on facial symmetry apply to real-world situations? In evolutionary terms, symmetry is hypothesized to be a physical display of mate quality because it signals that the individual is genetically healthy (Rhodes, 2006). Of course, genetic mutations, exposure to toxins, injury, and other factors may all compromise facial symmetry. Thus symmetry represents an evolutionary ideal trait, which is rarely translated

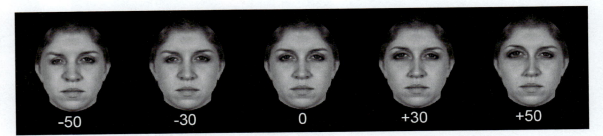

-50   -30   0   +30   +50

Facial Symmetry and Attraction Which face do you prefer of these five? You likely chose the middle face because it has the highest level of symmetry. People can detect this quality without even having to study the faces very closely.

into reality. It is likely, then, that you are actually evaluating health and fitness when you judge how attractive someone is.

With the rise of online dating sites, some people do begin their search for a mate by looking at photographs. However, facial symmetry corresponds to other traits people evaluate as well—this even includes dancing ability. Scientists have discovered that men who have symmetrical facial features are also better dancers, as rated by women who watch their moves (Brown et al., 2005). Dancing ability is probably easier to detect visually than subtle facial asymmetries. Thus the attractiveness of having some good dance moves does not just signal good rhythm, but a more symmetrical face.

CULTURAL AND ENVIRONMENTAL CONTRIBUTIONS TO BEHAVIOR Evolutionary psychologists have opened up new ways of studying and interpreting human behavior, but the field has also generated some controversy. For instance, studies pointing to gender differences in cognitive abilities and sexual motivation have led to debates about what those differences mean and how they arise. Scientists do not dispute that evolution and natural selection have played important roles in shaping the modern human mind, but they do disagree over whether differences among individuals and groups are *hard-wired* in the brain or susceptible to sociocultural influences and personal experiences. For example, researchers can produce lower math test scores among women just by having them read a passage claiming a genetic basis for gender differences prior to taking a math test (a process known as *stereotype threat*). This simple suggestion is enough to redirect brain activity from mathematical problem-solving regions to areas concerned with social interaction (Dar-Nimrod & Heine, 2006; Krendl et al., 2008). Similarly, researchers have been able to prevent or reduce gender differences on math problems by providing female role models and educating test takers about how stereotypes can hurt performance (Johns et al., 2005; Stout et al., 2011). In other words, some gender differences may

occur not because of genes, but simply because people believe that gender differences exist.

Recall that genes and environment are constantly interacting. This dynamic is evident in long-term studies of the relationship between genes, stress, and depression. The brain chemical known as serotonin is related to mood, and imbalances of it are associated with depression (see Module 3.2 and Module 13.3). One identified gene is responsible for the absorption of serotonin in nerve cells. There are two versions of this gene—short and long (referring to length of the DNA strands). Researchers have found that people who inherit two copies of the short version are at greater *risk* for developing depression, whereas those who inherit two long copies are at far less risk (Caspi et al., 2003; Caspi et al., 2010). But what is critical here is not just which genes are inherited, but also how much stress individuals experience. Figure 3.5 shows how this relationship works. As the number of major stressful life events increases, those who inherit two copies of the short version

{FIG. 3.5} **Gene and Environment Interactions** Stress interacts with genes and influences whether someone becomes depressed. People who inherit two copies of the short version of a gene that codes for serotonin activity in nerve cells are at an increased risk for becoming depressed in response to major life stressors. Those who inherit two long copies are buffered from becoming depressed as life stressors accumulate.

Social influences affect performance on examinations.

of this gene are far more likely to develop depression, whereas those who inherit two long copies are buffered from depression. People who inherit one copy of each gene (are heterozygous) show intermediate responses to stressful events. Notice that the type of serotonin gene inherited has no effect on depression after only one or two major stressful events. The gene–environment interaction becomes apparent after an *accumulation* of events. This relationship is just one of many examples of how nature and nurture interact.

BIOPSYCHOSOCIAL PERSPECTIVES

Men, Women, and Cognition

Evolutionary psychologists claim that the brain consists of a set of cognitive adaptations for solving problems relating to survival and reproductive fitness. They also hypothesize that male and female brains will differ in some ways because males and females have had to solve a different set of problems in order to survive and reproduce. One sex difference that has been reported involves solving the mental rotation task seen in Figure 3.6. ⊙➤

⊙➤ Simulate the **Experiment** *Mental Rotation* at **MyPsychLab**

Instructions

1. Take a close look at standard object #1 below. One of the three objects to the right of it are the same. Which one matches the standard? Repeat this with standard object #2 and the three comparison shapes to the right of it.

2. Many researchers find that, on average, males and females differ in their ability to perform this task. Do you think that:
   - Males perform better than females?
   - Females perform better than males?

{FIG. 3.6} **Mental Rotation Task**

Standard	Comparison shapes		
1.	A.	B.	C.
2.	A.	B.	C.

Answers: 1. A; 2. B

Research shows that males are generally able to perform this task more quickly than females, and with greater accuracy. How might the biopsychosocial model account for gender differences in this task? A biological and evolutionary perspective might hypothesize that over the course of human evolution the male brain became specialized for mental rotation tasks (Silverman & Eals, 1992). In fact, researchers have found that males with high testosterone levels were better at solving the task than males with low levels of testosterone (Hooven et al., 2004). Researchers have observed a male advantage in this task across different cultures, suggesting that the finding is not restricted to males at U.S. universities (Silverman et al., 2007). Overall, evidence from many studies suggests that there is a biological and evolutionary explanation for the male advantage in performing this specific task. (In Module 9.3, we give this claim further critical scrutiny.)

· ·

Quick Quiz 3.1b
Evolutionary Insights into Human Behavior

KNOW …

1. For a trait to evolve, it must have a(n) _____ basis.
   - **A** learned
   - **B** adaptive
   - **C** heritable
   - **D** developmental

2. Evolution is best defined as:
   - **A** a gradual increase in complexity.
   - **B** a change in gene frequency over generations.
   - **C** solving the challenge of survival by adapting.
   - **D** a progression toward a complex human brain.

APPLY …

3. In evolutionary terms, why are symmetrical facial features important?
   - **A** They indicate health and, most likely, good genes.
   - **B** They guarantee offspring survival.
   - **C** They make romantic relationships more satisfying.
   - **D** Without them, there is no other way to decide whether you have found a quality mate.

ANALYZE …

4. Evolutionary psychologists have made some claims that gender differences in cognitive abilities are genetically determined. Which of the following is *not* an alternative explanation for such claims?
   - **A** Stereotype threat affects performance.
   - **B** Sociocultural history affects performance.
   - **C** Different educational experiences affect performance.
   - **D** Gender differences do not really exist.

Answers can be found on page ANS-1.

Module 3.1

Now that you have read this module you should:

KNOW ...

- *The key terminology related to genes, inheritance, and evolutionary psychology:*

behavioral genetics (p. 76)
behavioral genomics (p. 77)
chromosomes (p. 75)
dizygotic twins (p. 76)
DNA (deoxyribonucleic acid) (p. 75)
evolution (p. 78)

genes (p. 75)
genotype (p. 75)
heritability (p. 76)
monozygotic twins (p. 76)
natural selection (p. 78)
phenotype (p. 75)

UNDERSTAND ...

- *How twin and adoption studies reveal relationships between genes and behavior.* Both methods measure genetic, environmental, and interactive contributions to behavior. Twin studies typically compare monozygotic twins (genetically identical) and dizygotic twins (full siblings sharing the prenatal environment) to estimate heritability. Adoption studies compare adopted children to their adoptive and biological parents. These designs allow researchers to determine heritability, a number between 0 and 1 that estimates the degree to which individual differences in a trait are due to genetic factors. A heritability of 1.0 would mean that genes contribute to 100% of individual differences. Many human characteristics, including intelligence and personality, have heritability estimates typically ranging between .40 and .70.

APPLY ...

- *Your knowledge of genes and behavior to develop hypotheses about why a trait may be adaptive.* Try putting yourself in an evolutionary psychologist's position and answer the following two questions (check your answers on page ANS-1):

1. Many evolutionary psychologists claim that men are more interested in a mate's physical attractiveness and youth, whereas women are more interested in qualities that contribute to childrearing success, such as intelligence and wealth. If this is the case, then who do you think would express more jealousy over sexual infidelity—men or women?

2. Researchers (Cramer et al., 2008) asked volunteers to rate how upset they would be by sexual infidelity in a mate and then they plotted the results in the graph shown in **Figure 3.7**. Do their results confirm your hypothesis?

ANALYZE ...

- *Claims that scientists have located a specific gene that controls a single trait or behavior.* As you learned in this module, most psychological traits, as well as disorders such as Alzheimer's disease, involve multiple genes, some of which may not even yet be discovered. (See the Myths in Mind feature on page 77.)

- *Explanations for cognitive gender differences that are rooted in genetics.* The Biopsychosocial Perspectives feature on page 82 summarized research showing that males have an advantage when it comes to a specific mental rotation task. Given that this is a relatively consistent gender difference, high testosterone levels are associated with better performance on the task, and the male advantage has been found cross-culturally, it seems plausible that this difference has a genetic basis. In future chapters we will return to issues and discussion of gender-based differences in cognitive abilities.

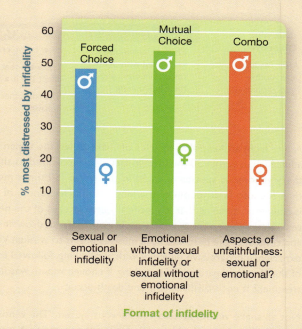

{FIG. 3.7} **Men's and Women's Reactions to Infidelity**
Men find sexual infidelity more distressing than do women, regardless of how a question is framed.

Module 3.2

How the Nervous System Works: Cells and Neurotransmitters

Learning Objectives

After reading this module you should:

KNOW ...	UNDERSTAND ...	APPLY ...	ANALYZE ...
The key terminology associated with nerve cells, hormones, and their functioning	How nerve cells communicate The ways that drugs and other substances affect the brain The roles that hormones play in our behavior	Your knowledge of neurotransmitters to form hypotheses about drug actions	The claim that we are born with all the nerve cells we will ever have

A bite from an Australian species of snake called the taipan can kill an adult human within 30 minutes. In fact, it is recognized as the most lethally venomous species of snake in the world (50 times more potent than the also fatal venom of the king cobra). The venom of the taipan is *neurotoxic*, meaning that it specifically attacks cells of the nervous system. Neurotoxic venom runs a rapid course. First, drowsiness sets in, and control of the head and neck muscles begins to weaken. Victims then experience progressive difficulty with swallowing, followed by tightness of the chest and paralysis of breathing. If enough venom was injected and treatment is not available, coma and death occur.

Not all snake venom attacks the nervous system. The venom found in most rattlesnakes in the United States is not neurotoxic, but rather damages tissue in the vicinity of the bite as well as those tissues it reaches within the bloodstream, particularly the heart. Not exactly comforting news, but compared to other continents, the venom of North American snakes is far less likely to be fatal. Neurotoxic venom is enormously dangerous because it disrupts the functioning of cells that make up the

nervous system, the topic of this module. This leads to some interesting, if not discomforting questions.

Focus Questions

1 Which normal processes of nerve cells are disrupted by a substance like snake venom?

2 What roles do chemicals play in normal nerve cell functioning?

· · · · · · · · · · · · · · · · · · ·

The nervous system acts as a complex communications network, transmitting and receiving information throughout the body. It signals pain, pleasure, and emotion; it controls our reflexive responses as well as our voluntary movements such as reaching and walking; and it even regulates such basic processes as breathing and heart rate. In this module, we explore how nerve cells function individually as well as how they are able to transmit and receive information throughout the network of the nervous system.

Neural Communication

You already know that your body is composed of many different types of cells. Psychologists are most interested in **neurons**, *one of the major types of cells found in the nervous system, which are responsible for sending and receiving messages throughout the body.* Billions of these cells are receiving and transmitting messages during your hours of both waking and sleeping. ✳

Neurons come in many varieties. Some extend from the spinal cord out to the extremities. Others are very short and may end almost as soon as they begin. Regardless of size, most neurons have the same key structures that serve to receive and transmit messages (see Figure 3.8). For starters, the **cell body** (also known as the *soma*) *is the part of a neuron that contains the nucleus that houses the cell's genetic material.* Genes in the cell body synthesize proteins that form the chemicals and structures that allow the neuron to function. **Dendrites**, *the small branches radiating from the cell body, receive messages from other cells and transmit the message toward the cell body.* The **axon** *is the structure that transports information from the neuron to neighboring*

✳ ⊢**Explore** the **Concept** *Neuronal Transmission at* **MyPsychLab**

{FIG. 3.8} **A Neuron and Its Key Components**
Each part of a nerve cell is specialized for a specific task.

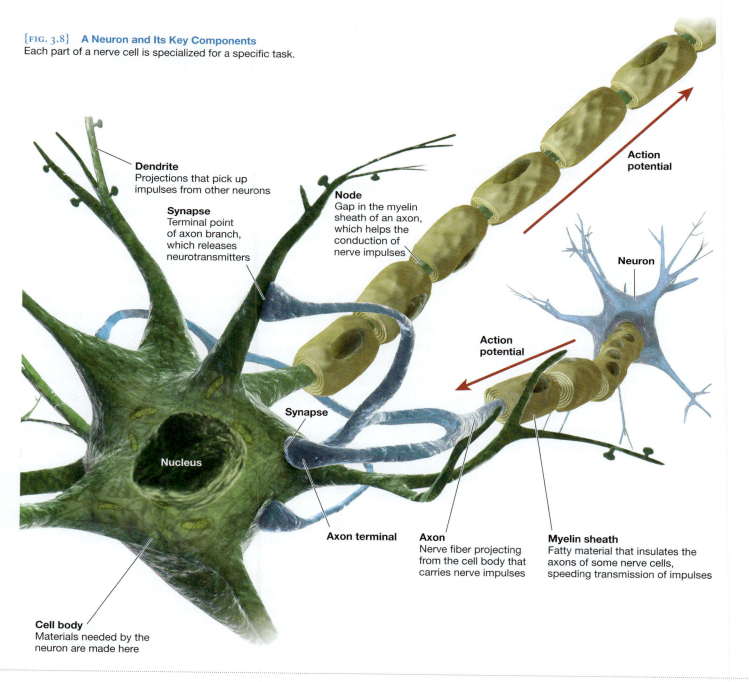

Dendrite
Projections that pick up impulses from other neurons

Synapse
Terminal point of axon branch, which releases neurotransmitters

Node
Gap in the myelin sheath of an axon, which helps the conduction of nerve impulses

Action potential

Neuron

Action potential

Nucleus

Synapse

Axon terminal

Axon
Nerve fiber projecting from the cell body that carries nerve impulses

Myelin sheath
Fatty material that insulates the axons of some nerve cells, speeding transmission of impulses

Cell body
Materials needed by the neuron are made here

A microscopic view of a network of nerve cells.

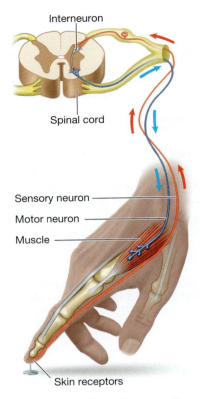

{FIG. 3.9} **Sensory and Motor Neurons** Sensory neurons carry information toward the spinal cord and the brain, whereas motor neurons send messages to muscles of the body. The interneuron links the sensory and motor neurons. This is the pathway of a simple withdrawal response to a painful stimulus.

neurons *in the form of electrochemical reactions.* At the end of the axon are *axon terminals.* Located within the axon terminals are chemicals called **neurotransmitters**, *the chemicals that function as messengers allowing neurons to communicate with each other.* Many different types of neurotransmitters exist, and each has different functions—something we will explore later in more detail. Neurotransmitters are released across **synapses**, *the microscopically small spaces that separate individual nerve cells.*

Each of the structures just described allows neurons to send and receive signals throughout the body and brain. For example, the pain you experience when you stub your toe begins just a fraction of a second after a network of nerve cells sends a message from your toe up to your brain.

Not all neurons are the same—they differ in form and function. *Sensory neurons* fetch information from the bodily senses and bring it toward the brain. Neurons that respond to touch or pain sensations of the skin bring the message toward the spinal cord and to the brain. In contrast, *motor neurons* carry messages away from the brain and spinal cord and toward muscles in order to control their flexion and extension (see Figure 3.9).

GLIAL CELLS One feature shown in Figure 3.8 (p. 85) is a white substance called **myelin**, *a fatty sheath that insulates axons from one another, resulting in increased speed and efficiency of neural communication.* *Multiple sclerosis* is a disease in which the immune system does not recognize myelin and attacks it—a process that can devastate the structural and functional integrity of the nervous system. When myelin breaks down in multiple sclerosis, the resulting symptoms include numbness or tingling sensations caused by the disruption of sensory nerve cell signals that should otherwise reach the brain. Multiple sclerosis is also characterized by problems

with voluntary, coordinated movement, owing to the breakdown of myelin that supports motor nerves.

Myelin is made from a highly abundant type of cell called *glia* (Greek for "glue"). **Glial cells** *are specialized cells of the nervous system that are involved in mounting immune responses in the brain, removing wastes, and synchronizing activity of the billions of neurons that constitute the nervous system.* Glial cells actually outnumber neurons in the brain by a ratio of approximately 10:1. The structural characteristics of glial cells differ from those of the sensory and motor nerves, and they perform different functions. Nevertheless, the activity of neurons is highly dependent on interactions with glial cells.

As you can see, each part of an individual neuron and glial cell performs an important function. Ultimately, however, it is the networking of nerve cells that allows messages to be transmitted within the brain and rest of the body. The actual transmission of these messages is made possible by a combination of electrical and chemical activity.

THE NEURON'S ELECTRICAL SYSTEM: RESTING AND ACTION POTENTIALS The inner and outer environments of a neuron differ in their concentrations of charged atoms called *ions*. In other words, the neuron is polarized. The **resting potential** *of a neuron refers to its*

PsychTutor
Click here in your eText for an interactive tutorial on the **Neuron**

relatively stable state during which the cell is not transmitting messages. At its resting potential, the outside of the neuron has a relatively high concentration of positively charged ions, particularly sodium and potassium, while the interior of the axon has fewer positively charged ions as well as a relatively high concentration of negatively charged chloride ions. This difference in charge between the inside and outside of the cell leaves the inside of the axon with a negative charge of approximately −70 millivolts (−70 mV, see the first panel of Figure 3.10). When stimulated the neuron springs into action, a process referred to as *neural firing*.

What causes a neuron to fire? When a neuron is stimulated, the pores of its membrane surface open up and allow positively charged sodium ions to rush in. If a sufficient number of positively charged ions enter the cell, they will alter the charge to be greater than −70 mV. Each neuron has a specific threshold that must be reached before it will fire. If a threshold of, say, −55 mV is reached, the neuron then initiates an **action potential**, *a wave of electrical activity that originates at the base of the axon and rapidly travels down its length* (see the middle panel of Figure 3.10). The action potential moves down the length of the axon as positively charged ions rush through the membrane pores. As you can see from Figure 3.11, during the action potential the net charge of the cell goes from negatively to positively

 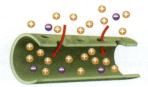 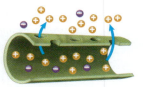

Resting potential.

Positively charged ions rush into the cell during an action potential.

After the nerve has fired the positively charge ions are pumped back out of the cell.

{FIG. 3.10} **Electrical Charges of the Inner and Outer Regions of Nerve Cells** The inner and outer environments of a nerve cell at rest differ in terms of their electrical charge. During the resting potential, there is a net negative charge. When a nerve cell is stimulated, generating an action potential, positively charged ions rush inside the cell membrane. After the cell has fired, the positively charged ions are channeled back outside the nerve cell as it returns to resting state. **Click on this figure in your eText to see more details.**

charged. At each point of the axon, the sodium pores slam shut as soon as the action potential occurs, and the sodium ions are rapidly pumped back out of the cell, returning it to a resting state.

When the action potential reaches the axon terminals at the end of the cell, neurotransmitters are released into the **synaptic cleft**, *the minute space between the terminal button and the dendrite*, and bind to *receptors* on the dendrites of neighboring neurons. Meanwhile, the action potential is followed by a **refractory period**, *a brief period in which a neuron cannot fire*. Within a couple of milliseconds, however, the neuron returns to its resting potential and can fire again if stimulated.

When stimulated, a given neuron always fires at the same intensity and speed. This activity adheres to the **all-or-none principle**: *Individual nerve cells fire at the same strength every time an action potential occurs.* Neurons do not "sort of" fire, or "overfire"—they just fire. That neurons behave this way may seem odd, because we might assume that intense sensations correspond to strong action potentials. In reality, according to the all-or-none principle, action potentials are always the same magnitude and speed. The strength of a sensation is determined by the *rate* at which nerve cells fire as well as by the number of nerve cells that are stimulated. A stimulus is experienced intensely because a greater number of cells are stimulated, and the firing of each cell occurs repeatedly.

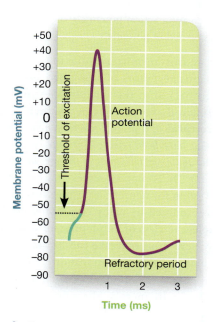

{FIG. 3.11} **Time Course and Phases of a Nerve Cell Going from a Resting Potential to an Action Potential** Nerve cells fire once the threshold of excitation is reached. During the action potential positively charged ions rush inside the cell membrane, creating a net positive change within the cell. Positively charged ions are then forced out of the cell as it returns to its resting potential.

MYTHS IN MIND

We Are Born With All the Brain Cells We Will Ever Have

For decades, neuroscience taught us that nerves do not regenerate; in other words, scientists believed that we are born with all of the brain cells we will ever have. This conclusion made perfect sense because no one had ever seen new neurons form in adults, and severe neurological damage is often permanent.

In the past 15 years or so, however, advances in brain science have challenged this belief. Researchers have observed *neurogenesis*—the formation of new neurons—in a limited number of brain regions, particularly in a region critical for learning and memory (Eriksson et al., 1998; Tashiro et al., 2007). The growth of a new cell, including neurons, starts with stem cells—a unique type of cell that does not have a predestined function. When a stem cell divides, the resulting cells can become part of just about anything—bone, kidney, or brain tissue. The deciding factor seems to be the stem cell's chemical environment (Abematsu et al., 2006).

Our increased understanding of neurogenesis has raised some exciting possibilities—perhaps scientists can discover how to trigger the neural growth in other parts of the nervous system. When this technology is developed, there may finally be hope for recovery from injury and disease in all nerve cells.

· ·

Quick Quiz 3.2a
Neural Communication

KNOW...

1 A positive electrical charge that is carried away from the cell body and down the length of the axon is a(n) _____.

  A refractory period   **C** action potential

  B resting potential   **D** dendrite

2 Which of the following is a function of glial cells?

  A Glial cells slow down the activity of nerve cells.

  B Glial cells manufacture myelin.

  C Glial cells suppress the immune system response.

  D Glial cells contain the nucleus that houses the cell's genetic material.

UNDERSTAND...

3 A neuron will fire when the ions inside the cell body are:

  A in the resting potential.

  B shifted to a threshold greater than the resting potential.

  C shifted to a threshold less than the resting potential.

  D in the refractory period.

4 Sensory and motor nerves differ in that:

  A only sensory neurons have dendrites.

  B only motor neurons have axons.

  C sensory neurons carry messages toward the brain, and motor neurons carry information away from the brain.

  D sensory neurons carry messages away from the brain, and motor neurons carry information toward the brain.

Answers can be found on page ANS-1.

The Chemical Messengers: Neurotransmitters and Hormones

Many different types of neurotransmitters have been identified, each having its own unique molecular shape. Neurons, however, tend to specialize in sending or receiving a limited number of neurotransmitters. A lock-and-key analogy is sometimes used to explain how neurotransmitters and their receptors work: When neurotransmitters are released at the axon terminal, they cross the synapse and fit in a particular receptor of the dendrite like

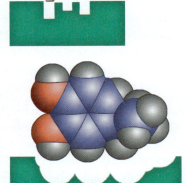

{FIG. 3.12} **The Lock-and-Key Analogy for Matching of Neurotransmitters and Receptors** The molecular structures of different neurotransmitters must have specific shapes in order to bind with the receptors on a neuron.

a key in a lock (see Figure 3.12). If the neurotransmitter binds to the receptor, it will trigger one of two types of reaction in the receiving neuron: The effect can be either *excitatory*, increasing action potentials, or it may be *inhibitory*, decreasing action potentials.

After neurotransmitter molecules have bound to postsynaptic receptors of a neighboring cell, they are released back into the synaptic cleft where they *may* be broken down by enzymes. Others might go through **reuptake**, *a process whereby neurotransmitter molecules that have been released into the synapse are reabsorbed into the axon terminals of the presynaptic neuron* (see Figure 3.13). Reuptake serves as a sort of natural recycling system for neurotransmitters. It is also a process that is modified by many commonly used drugs. For example, the class of antidepressant drugs known as selective serotonin reuptake inhibitors (SSRIs) inhibits reuptake of the neurotransmitter serotonin; in this way, members of SSRI class, such as fluoxetine (Prozac), eventually increase the amount of serotonin available at the synapse.

TYPES OF NEUROTRANSMITTERS The various neurotransmitters listed in Table 3.1 differ in their molecular structure. As a consequence, they also differ in terms of the specific nerve cells they bind to and their effects on behavior.

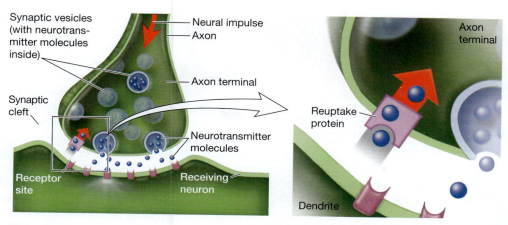

{FIG. 3.13} Major Events at the Synapse As the action potential reaches the axon terminals, neurotransmitters (packed into spherically shaped vesicles) are released across the synaptic cleft. The neurotransmitters bind to the postsynaptic (receiving) neuron. In the process of reuptake, some neurotransmitters are returned to the presynaptic neuron via reuptake proteins. These neurotransmitters are then repackaged into synaptic vessicles.

The *monoamines* are one class of neurotransmitter. Each of the monoamines has its own unique function, although there is some degree of overlap. For example, monoamine neurotransmitters are known to influence mood, and the major antidepressant drugs on the market influence their activity. **Dopamine** *is a monoamine neurotransmitter involved in such varied functions as mood, control of voluntary movement, and processing of rewarding experiences.* **Serotonin** *is a monoamine involved in regulating mood, sleep and appetite.* **Norepinephrine** *is a monoamine synthesized from dopamine molecules that is involved in regulating stress responses, including increasing arousal, attention, and heart rate.*

Acetylcholine *is one of the most widespread neurotransmitters within the body, found at the junctions between nerve cells and skeletal muscles; it is very important for voluntary movement.* As mentioned previously, dopamine is also involved in voluntary movement. Thus the combined activity of both neurotransmitters is required for managing this function. Recall the neurotoxic snake venom discussed at the beginning of this module: Its toxins disrupt activity of acetylcholine transmission at the neuromuscular junctions. Different snakes carry slightly different types of neurotoxic venom. Some types of venom block acetylcholine release at the presynaptic terminals, preventing its release into the synapse. Another type of venom blocks the receptors on the postsynaptic cell, preventing acetylcholine from binding to them (Lewis & Gutmann, 2004). Either way, the effects are devastating. In addition to movement, acetylcholine activity in the brain is associated with arousal and attention.

GABA (gamma-amino butyric acid) *is a primary inhibitory neurotransmitter of the nervous system, meaning that it prevents neurons from generating action potentials.* It accomplishes this feat by reducing the negative charge of neighboring neurons even further than their resting state of −70 mV. When GABA binds to receptors, it causes an influx of negatively charged chloride ions to enter the cell, which is the opposite net effect of what happens when a neuron is stimulated. As an inhibitor, GABA facilitates sleep and reduces arousal of the nervous system. In contrast, **glutamate** *is an excitatory neurotransmitter in the nervous system that is critical to the processes of learning and memory.*

Table 3.1 :: Major Neurotransmitters and Their Functions

NEUROTRANSMITTER	SOME MAJOR FUNCTIONS
Acetylcholine	Movement, attention
Dopamine	Control of movement, reward-seeking behavior, cognition and attention
Norepinephrine	Memory, attention to new or important stimuli, regulation of sleep and mood
Serotonin	Regulation of sleep, appetite, mood
Glutamate	Excites nervous system, memory and autonomic nervous system reactions
GABA (gamma-amino butyric acid)	Inhibits brain activity, lowers arousal, anxiety, and excitation, facilitates sleep

WORKING THE SCIENTIFIC LITERACY MODEL

Pain and Substance P

Each of the neurotransmitters we have discussed thus far serve a variety of functions. An important neurotransmitter we have not yet covered is called substance P.

What do we know about substance P?

Substance P *is a neurotransmitter involved in the experience of pain.* It can be found in sensory nerves in the brain and spinal cord. When tissue on the skin surface is damaged, sensory nerves carry messages to the brain. In turn, the brain releases substance P, giving rise to the perception of pain. One type of stimulus that causes substance P release is *capsaicin*, the pain-inducing compound found on many types of chili peppers. As you are probably aware, pain does not come just from eating them, but also from the peppers making contact with the skin, such as around the eyes.

How can science explain what substance P does?

Much of what is known about substance P comes from a surprising source—the African naked mole rat. This animal seems oblivious to pain: It shows no behavioral response when capsaicin is applied to the skin surface. In contrast, humans, mice, and many other mammalian species show clear signs of pain and irritation. The lack of a pain response in naked mole rats has led to some fascinating discoveries. Researchers who have studied these animals have discovered that they do, in fact, have the same types of sensory neurons that register pain in other mammals. In addition, naked mole rats have the type of receptor on their postsynaptic neurons that substance P can bind to. Yet, they do not show any signs of pain when these nerves are stimulated (Smith et al., 2010). Evidence suggests that the pain pathway within the spinal cord of naked mole rats has been modified via evolution to prevent stimulation of these cells to be "experienced" as pain (Park et al., 2008).

Can we critically evaluate this research?

How could an animal survive without a pain response, which is a very important adaptive means of avoiding bodily harm? People who are born with a rare condition called *congenital insensitivity to pain* lack the ability to perceive pain, and even in early childhood acquire significant damage to the skin, joints, eyes, and other body regions. Because they lack a pain response, these individuals do not take action to prevent physical damage to the body. Researchers believe that naked mole rats, which remain burrowed underground, live in an environment characterized by a high concentration of carbon dioxide. Carbon dioxide exposure actually stimulates the same neurons that send pain signals to the brain (Park et al., 2008). The naked mole rat appears to have evolved a mechanism for avoiding a life of pain, while gaining the benefit of exploiting its underground habitat.

Why is this relevant?

Millions of people in the United States suffer from chronic pain. In addition to compromising the well-being of affected individuals, problems with pain translate into reduced work productivity, increased health care costs, and, for some people, an increased risk of developing dependence or addiction to prescription painkillers. By better understanding the physiological basis of pain, including the information gathered on naked mole rats, researchers may be able to develop more effective drugs and other techniques to help alleviate pain.

The African naked mole rat lacks substance P activity, so it does not appear to experience pain when it comes into contact with a stimulus such as capsaicin.

DRUG EFFECTS ON NEURO-TRANSMISSION Drugs of all varieties, from prescription to recreational, affect the chemical signaling that takes place between nerve cells. **Agonists** *are drugs that enhance or mimic the effects of a neurotransmitter's action.* The well-known drug nicotine is an acetylcholine agonist, meaning that it stimulates the receptor sites for this neurotransmitter. The antianxiety drug alprazolam (Xanax) is a GABA agonist—it causes relaxation by increasing the activity of this inhibitory neurotransmitter. Drugs can behave as agonists either directly or indirectly. A drug that behaves as a direct agonist physically binds to receptors at the postsynaptic cells. A drug that acts as an indirect agonist facilitates neurotransmission by increasing the release and availability of neurotransmitters. For example, a drug that blocks the process of reuptake would be an indirect agonist.

Drugs classified as **antagonists** *inhibit neurotransmitter activity by blocking receptors or preventing synthesis of a neurotransmitter* (see Figure 3.14). You may have heard of the cosmetic medical procedure known as a Botox injection. Botox, which is derived from the nerve-paralyzing bacterium that causes botulism, blocks the action of acetylcholine by binding to its postsynaptic receptor sites (Dastoor et al., 2007). Blocking acetylcholine could lead to paralysis of the heart and lungs; however, when very small amounts are injected into tissue around the eyes, the antagonist simply paralyzes the muscles that lead to wrinkles. When muscles are not used, they cannot stretch the skin—hence the reduction in wrinkling when acetylcholine activity is blocked.

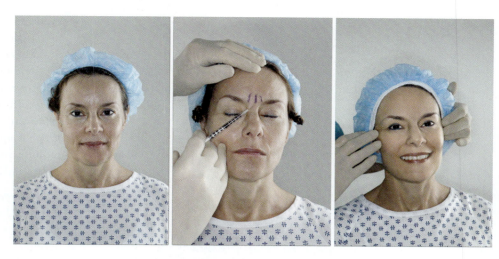

Botox injections paralyze muscles, which can increase youthful appearance in areas such as the face.

HORMONES AND THE ENDOCRINE SYSTEM

Neurotransmitters are not the body's only chemical messenger system. **Hormones** *are chemicals secreted by the glands of the endocrine system.* Generally, neurotransmitters work almost immediately within the microscopic space of the synapse, whereas hormones are secreted into the bloodstream and travel throughout the body. With help from the nervous system, the endocrine system contributes to *homeostasis*—the balance of energy, metabolism, body temperature, and other basic functions that keeps the body working properly (see Figure 3.15 on p. 92).

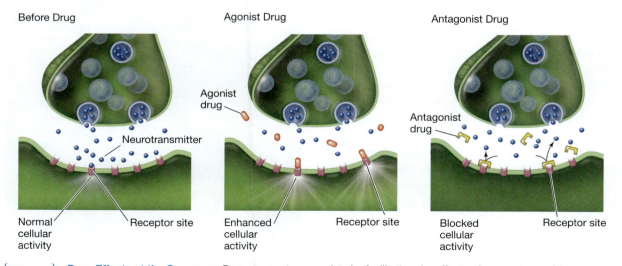

Before Drug — Agonist Drug — Antagonist Drug

Agonist drug · Neurotransmitter · Antagonist drug

Normal cellular activity · Receptor site · Enhanced cellular activity · Receptor site · Blocked cellular activity · Receptor site

{FIG. 3.14} **Drug Effects at the Synapses** Drugs can act as agonists by facilitating the effects of a neurotransmitter, or as antagonists by blocking these effects. **Click on this figure in your eText to see more details.**

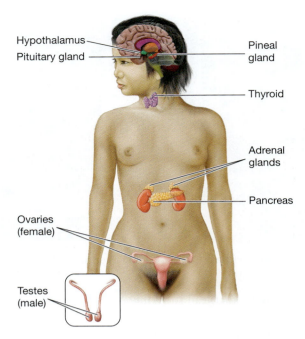

{FIG. 3.15} **The Endocrine System** Glands throughout the body release and exchange hormones. The hypothalamus interacts with the endocrine system to regulate hormonal processes.

The **hypothalamus** *is a brain structure that regulates basic biological needs and motivational systems.* The hypothalamus stimulates the **pituitary gland**—*the master gland of the endocrine system that produces hormones and sends commands about hormone production to the other glands of the endocrine system.* Specialized chemicals called releasing factors are secreted by the hypothalamus and stimulate the pituitary to release specific hormones.

How we respond to stress illustrates nicely how the nervous and endocrine systems are related. In psychological terms, stress is defined as an imbalance between perceived demands and the resources available to meet those demands. Such an imbalance might occur if you suddenly realize your midterm exam is tomorrow at 8:00 A.M. Your resources—time and energy—may not be enough to meet the demand of succeeding on the exam. The hypothalamus, however, sets chemical events in motion that physically prepare the body for stress. It signals the pituitary gland to release a hormone into the bloodstream that in turn stimulates the **adrenal glands**, *a pair of endocrine glands located adjacent to the kidneys that release stress hormones, such as cortisol and epinephrine.* Cortisol and epinephrine help mobilize the body during stress. (In Module 16.2, we will explore stress in greater detail.)

Another important chemical is **endorphin**, *a hormone produced by the pituitary gland and the hypothalamus that functions to reduce pain and induce feelings of pleasure.* Endorphin is released into the bloodstream during events such as strenuous exercise, sexual activity, or injury. It acts on portions of the brain that are attuned to reward, reinforcement, and pleasure, inhibiting the perception of pain and increasing feelings of euphoria (extreme pleasantness and relaxation). Morphine—a drug derived from the poppy plant—binds to endorphin receptors (the term *endorphin* translates to *endogenous [internal] morphine*). Morphine molecules fit into the same receptor sites as endorphins and, therefore, produce the same painkilling and euphoric effects.

Testosterone is a hormone that serves multiple functions, including driving physical and sexual development over the long term, and surging during sexual activity and in response to threats. This hormone is often cited as an explanation for behavior. It can be tempting to conclude that if a behavior has a biological explanation, then the behavior cannot change—and testosterone provides a great example. Because it is related to male sexual development and functioning, this hormone was traditionally targeted as an explanation for why men tend to be more physically aggressive than women. In other words, there was an assumption that testosterone *causes* aggression. (For the record, women have testosterone and it serves many of the same functions in them as it does in men.) In fact, the data do show that the highest levels of violence, aggression, and homicide occur among young males against other young males—that is, within the group whose members tend to have the highest levels of testosterone (Archer, 2004; O'Connor et al., 2004). But the

Extracts from the seeds of some poppy flowers contain opium. Morphine and one of its derivatives, heroin, can be synthesized from these seeds.

truth is much more complicated than simply attributing aggression to testosterone. Testosterone is *correlated* with more aggressive thoughts and feelings, but if aggressive behavior is defined as physical violence, then the relationship between testosterone and aggression is actually rather weak (Archer et al., 2005; Book et al., 2001).

Bear in mind that hormones are secreted in response to experiences. Testosterone levels increase *after* men win sporting or chess matches, and these levels are lower in men who are married or have fathered children (Gray et al., 2002). There is a sociocultural component at play as well. When men from the southeastern United States were bumped and verbally insulted by another male during an experiment, they were more offended, they responded with more aggression, and their testosterone levels rose more than those in men from the northern United States who were subjected to the same treatment (Cohen et al., 1996; discussed in more detail in Module 15.3). Why should geography matter? The culture of the southern United States emphasizes honor and individualism more, whereas the culture of the northern United States is more adapted to dense, urban populations and the accidental bumps and brushes that go along with that kind of lifestyle. Thus, when a Southerner gets bumped in the hallway, he is more likely to interpret it as a threat than is his Northerner counterpart. In this case, it makes sense for his body to prepare for a fight. This research points out the dangers of saying that hormones *cause* behavior; it is probably more accurate to say that hormones *facilitate* behavior.

Quick Quiz 3.2b
The Chemical Messengers: Neurotransmitters and Hormones

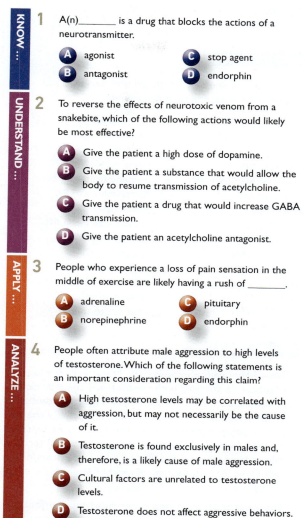

KNOW…

1. A(n)_____ is a drug that blocks the actions of a neurotransmitter.
   - A agonist
   - B antagonist
   - C stop agent
   - D endorphin

UNDERSTAND…

2. To reverse the effects of neurotoxic venom from a snakebite, which of the following actions would likely be most effective?
   - A Give the patient a high dose of dopamine.
   - B Give the patient a substance that would allow the body to resume transmission of acetylcholine.
   - C Give the patient a drug that would increase GABA transmission.
   - D Give the patient an acetylcholine antagonist.

APPLY…

3. People who experience a loss of pain sensation in the middle of exercise are likely having a rush of _____.
   - A adrenaline
   - B norepinephrine
   - C pituitary
   - D endorphin

ANALYZE…

4. People often attribute male aggression to high levels of testosterone. Which of the following statements is an important consideration regarding this claim?
   - A High testosterone levels may be correlated with aggression, but may not necessarily be the cause of it.
   - B Testosterone is found exclusively in males and, therefore, is a likely cause of male aggression.
   - C Cultural factors are unrelated to testosterone levels.
   - D Testosterone does not affect aggressive behaviors.

Answers can be found on page ANS-1.

Module Summary

Now that you have read this module you should:

Listen to the audio file of this module at **MyPsychLab**

KNOW ...

- **The key terminology associated with nerve cells, hormones, and their functioning:**

acetylcholine (p. 89)	hormones (p. 91)
action potential (p. 87)	hypothalamus (p. 92)
adrenal glands (p. 92)	myelin (p. 86)
agonists (p. 91)	neuron (p. 85)
all-or-none principle (p. 87)	neurotransmitters (p. 86)
antagonists (p. 91)	norepinephrine (p. 89)
axon (p. 85)	pituitary gland (p. 92)
cell body (p. 85)	refractory period (p. 87)
dendrite (p. 85)	resting potential (p. 86)
dopamine (p. 89)	reuptake (p. 88)
endorphin (p. 92)	serotonin (p. 89)
GABA (gamma-amino butyric acid) (p. 89)	substance P (p. 90)
glial cells (p. 86)	synapses (p. 86)
glutamate (p. 89)	synaptic cleft (p. 87)

UNDERSTAND ...

- **How nerve cells communicate.** Nerve cells fire because of processes involving both electrical and chemical factors. A stimulated nerve cell goes from resting potential to action potential following an influx of positively charged ions inside the membrane of the cell. As the message reaches the end of the nerve cell, neurotransmitters are released into synapses and bind to neighboring postsynaptic cells. Depending on the type of neurotransmitter, the effect can be either inhibitory or excitatory.

- **The ways that drugs and other substances affect the brain.** Drugs can be agonists or antagonists. A drug is an agonist if it enhances the effects of a neurotransmitter. This outcome occurs if the drug increases the release of a neurotransmitter, blocks reuptake, or mimics the neurotransmitter by binding to the postsynaptic cell. A drug is an antagonist if it blocks the effects of a neurotransmitter. Antagonists block neurotransmitter release, break down neurotransmitters in the synapse, or block neurotransmitters by binding to postsynaptic receptors.

- **The roles that hormones play in our behavior.** Hormones have multiple influences on behavior. The nervous system—in particular, the hypothalamus—interacts with the endocrine system in controlling the release of hormones. A few of humans' many hormonally controlled responses include reactions to stress and pain as well as sexual responses. Some hormones are associated with, though not necessarily a primary cause of, aggressive behavior.

APPLY ...

- **Your knowledge of neurotransmitters to form hypotheses about drug actions.** In this module you read about how SSRIs slow down the reuptake process to increase the amount of serotonin at the synapse. Consider another drug—a monoamine oxidase inhibitor (MAOI).

  1. Based on its name, *monoamine* oxidase inhibitor, which neurotransmitters would be affected by such a drug? (See page 89.)

  2. If monoamine oxidase is an enzyme that breaks down monoamine transmitters, what would happen if a drug inhibits the enzyme? What effect would this action have on levels of the neurotransmitters (i.e., an overall increase or decrease)?

  3. Would the effects of an MAOI resemble those of an SSRI? (SSRIs are discussed on page 88.) Check your answers on page ANS-1.

ANALYZE ...

- **The claim that we are born with all the nerve cells we will ever have.** Earlier in this module, a Myths in Mind feature (page 87) addressed the question of whether we are born with all of the nerve cells we will ever have. Although scientists once believed this to be true, we now know that neurogenesis—the growth of new neurons—takes place in several parts of the brain. One of these regions is the hippocampus, which is involved in learning and memory (see Module 3.3). In many other areas of the brain, neurogenesis has not been observed. Nevertheless, during normal development, neurons make new connections with neighboring cells. This process also occurs following damage to nerve cells, such that surviving nerve cells form new connections left vacant by damaged neurons.

Structure and Organization of the Nervous System

Learning Objectives

After reading this module you should:

KNOW ...	UNDERSTAND ...	APPLY ...	ANALYZE ...
The key terminology associated with the structure and organization of the nervous system	How studies of split-brain patients reveal the workings of the brain	Your knowledge of brain regions to predict which abilities might be affected when a specific area is injured or diseased	Whether psychologists can use technology to map out brain activity

How would you like to have a thought-controlled robot? On your laziest day, you could just think about turning off the alarm clock and a robotic arm would do it for you. It turns out that such a device is closer to reality than science fiction. Neuroscientists such as Nicholas Hatsopoulos have developed techniques to respond to the brain's electrical activity with robotic arms and other devices. This type of technology has some very important applications. Currently, Dr. Hatsopoulos and his colleagues are trying to help people with quadriplegia—paralysis in the arms and legs—regain some of their independence. One of their devices reads the electrical signals of the brain and transfers these data to control the cursor of a computer as a mouse normally would (Hatsopoulos & Donoghue, 2009).

Focus Questions

1 How does the brain control movement?

2 How can we make sense of brain activity as it is actually occurring?

· · · · · · · · · · · · · · · · · ·

In this module, we translate our knowledge of nerve cells into an understanding of how they work as an integrated system. This module is rich with terminology and can be challenging. As you read through it, try to think about how the different parts of the nervous system and brain apply to your own behavior and experiences.

Divisions of the Nervous System

The nervous system is an intricate and highly complex network of nerve cells. This system coordinates both voluntary and involuntary activity in every region of the body. The basic divisions include the peripheral and central nervous systems.

THE PERIPHERAL NERVOUS SYSTEM   The **peripheral nervous system (PNS)** *transmits signals between the brain and the rest of the body and is divided into two subcomponents, the somatic system and the autonomic system* (see Figure 3.16). The **somatic nervous system** *consists of nerves that receive sensory input from the body and control skeletal muscles, which are responsible for voluntary and reflexive movement.* Any voluntary behavior, such as coordinating the movements needed to reach, walk, or move a computer mouse, are governed by the somatic nervous system.

The **autonomic nervous system** *is the portion of the peripheral nervous system responsible for regulating the activity of organs and glands.* It includes two subcomponents: the sympathetic and parasympathetic nervous systems. The **sympathetic nervous system** *is responsible for the fight-or-flight response of an increased heart rate, dilated pupils, and decreased salivary flow—responses that prepare the body for action.* If you hear footsteps behind you as you are walking alone or if you barely avoid an accident while driving, then you will experience *sympathetic* arousal. In this process, blood is directed toward your skeletal muscles, heart rate and perspiration increase, and digestive processes are slowed; each of these responses helps to direct energy where it is most needed. In contrast, the **parasympathetic nervous system** *helps maintain homeostatic balance in the presence of change; following sympathetic arousal, it works to return the body to a baseline, nonemergency state.* Generally speaking, the parasympathetic nervous system does the opposite of what the sympathetic nervous system does (see Figure 3.17).

THE CENTRAL NERVOUS SYSTEM   The **central nervous system (CNS)** *consists of the brain and the spinal cord* (see Figure 3.16). The human brain is perhaps the most complex entity known. Its capacity to store information is apparently limitless. Your personality, preferences, memories, and conscious awareness are all packed into this 3-pound structure made up of approximately 100 billion individual cells. The spinal cord connects the brain with the peripheral nervous system, forming a network that spans the body. This network includes pathways that send commands from the brain out to the glands, muscles, and organs, as well as pathways that relay sensory information back to the brain.

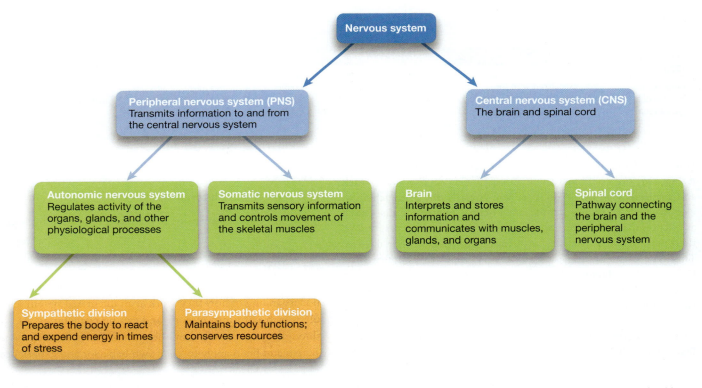

{FIG. 3.16}   **The Organization of the Nervous System**   The nervous system can be divided into several different components, each with a specific set of structures and functions. **Click on this figure in your eText to see more details**.

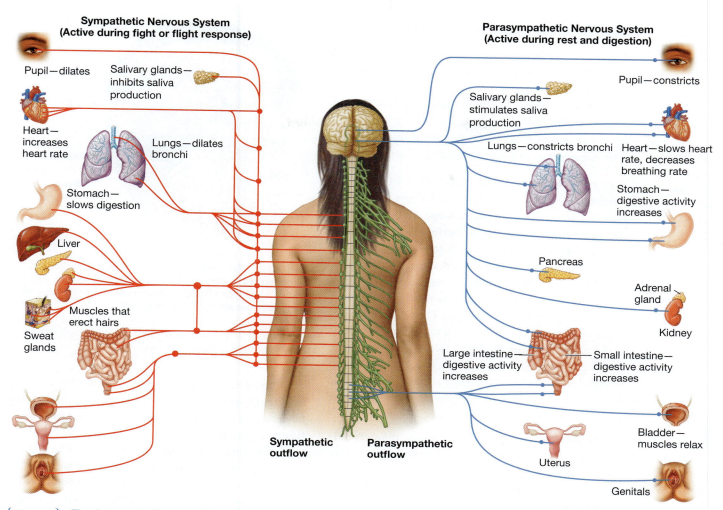

Sympathetic Nervous System
(Active during fight or flight response)

Pupil—dilates

Salivary glands—inhibits saliva production

Heart—increases heart rate

Lungs—dilates bronchi

Stomach—slows digestion

Liver

Muscles that erect hairs

Sweat glands

Sympathetic outflow

Parasympathetic Nervous System
(Active during rest and digestion)

Salivary glands—stimulates saliva production

Pupil—constricts

Lungs—constricts bronchi

Heart—slows heart rate, decreases breathing rate

Stomach—digestive activity increases

Pancreas

Adrenal gland

Kidney

Large intestine—digestive activity increases

Small intestine—digestive activity increases

Bladder—muscles relax

Uterus

Genitals

Parasympathetic outflow

{FIG. 3.17} **The Autonomic Nervous System** The sympathetic and parasympathetic divisions of the autonomic nervous system control and regulate responses by the glands and organs of the body.

Complete the **Survey** *Do You Fly or Fight?* at **MyPsychLab**

Quick Quiz 3.3a :: Divisions of the Nervous System

KNOW …

1 Which division of the peripheral nervous system is responsible for countering much of the activity associated with the sympathetic nervous system?

A Somatic
B Spinal cord
C Central nervous system
D Parasympathetic

2 The central nervous system consists of which of the following?

A The brain and the spinal cord
B The brain and the voluntary muscles
C The brain and the nerves controlling digestion and other automatic functions
D The somatic and autonomic systems

UNDERSTAND …

3 A major difference between the somatic and autonomic branches of the nervous system is that:

A the somatic nervous system controls involuntary responses, and the autonomic nervous system controls voluntary movement.
B the somatic nervous system is located in the brain, and the autonomic nervous system is located peripherally.
C the somatic nervous system controls voluntary movement, and the autonomic nervous system controls involuntary responses.
D the somatic nervous system controls involuntary movement, and the autonomic nervous system controls voluntary responses.

Answers can be found on page ANS-1.

The Brain and Its Structures

The structures of the brain are organized in a hierarchical fashion. The human brain, as well as that of other animals, can be subdivided into three main regions: the hindbrain, the midbrain, and the forebrain (Table 3.2). This system of dividing the brain may tempt you to view it as a mass of separate compartments. Keep in mind that the entire brain is comprised of highly integrated circuitry. ❋

❋⌐Explore the
Concept *Major Brain Structures and Functions* at **MyPsychLab**

THE HINDBRAIN: SUSTAINING THE BODY The hindbrain consists of structures that are critical to controlling basic, life-sustaining processes. At the top of the spinal cord is a region called the **brain stem**, *which consists of the medulla and the pons* (Figure 3.18). Nerve cells in the medulla connect with the body to perform basic functions such as regulating breathing, heart rate, sneezing, salivating, and even vomiting—all those actions your body does with little conscious control on your part. The pons contributes to general levels of wakefulness, and it also appears to have a role in dreaming (see Module 5.1). The *reticular formation* sends signals upward into the cortex, a higher brain center we will describe shortly, to influence attention and alertness. The reticular formation also communicates with cells in the spinal cord involved with motor control.

Another structure of the hindbrain, the **cerebellum** (Latin for "little brain") *is the lobe-like structure at the base of the brain that is involved in the details of movement, maintaining balance, and learning new motor skills.* Although you use other parts of your brain to plan movements, the

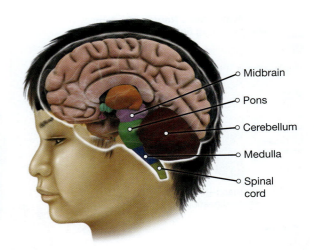

{FIG. 3.18} **The Hindbrain and Midbrain** Structures in the hindbrain are responsible for basic functions that sustain the body. The midbrain includes structures that control basic sensory responses and voluntary movement.

cerebellum is specialized in their coordination and timing (Yamazaki & Tanaka, 2009).

THE MIDBRAIN: SENSATION AND ACTION The **midbrain** *resides just above the hindbrain and primarily functions as a relay station between sensory and motor areas* (Figure 3.18). For example, a midbrain structure called the *tectum* coordinates the sensation of motion with actions. Have you ever walked down a city street and been startled by a pigeon darting in front of you? The pigeon's tectum responded to the impending collision with an object

Table 3.2 :: Major Brain Regions, Structures, and Their Functions

REGIONS AND STRUCTURES	FUNCTIONS
Hindbrain	
Brain stem (medulla and pons)	Breathing, heart rate, sleep and wakefulness
Cerebellum	Balance, coordination and timing of movements
Midbrain	Relay sensory and motor information, voluntary movement
Forebrain	
Basal ganglia	Movement, reward processing
Amygdala	Emotion
Hippocampus	Memory
Hypothalamus	Temperature regulation, motivation (hunger, thirst, sex)
Cerebral Cortex	
Frontal lobe	Thought, planning, language, motor movement
Parietal lobe	Sensory processing, bodily awareness
Occipital lobe	Visual processing
Temporal lobe	Hearing, object recognition, language, emotion

(you) moving toward it, and the pigeon almost instantly swerved away (Wu et al., 2005). Similarly, your own tectum detected a sudden, darting motion and relayed the information to motor areas of your brain. Depending on your experiences with pigeons, you may have flinched or covered your head before you were even conscious of what you were doing. Regions within the midbrain serve a similar function with information that we hear (auditory stimuli). Your reflexive ability to identify the location of sounds around you occurs within the midbrain.

The midbrain also includes neurons that contain very dense concentrations of dopamine receptors and activity. These neurons send messages to higher brain centers involved in the control of movement. Parkinson's disease—a condition marked by major impairments in voluntary movement—is caused by a loss of dopamine-producing cells.

THE FOREBRAIN: EMOTION, MEMORY, AND THOUGHT The **forebrain**, *the most visibly obvious region of the brain, consists of multiple interconnected structures that are critical to such complex processes as emotion, memory, thinking, and reasoning.* We will begin our exploration of the forebrain by looking deep inside of it.

One particular set of structures comprises the **basal ganglia**, *which are involved in facilitating planned movements, skill learning, and are also integrated with the brain's reward system.* (Figure 3.19; Conn et al., 2005). People who are very practiced at a given motor skill, such as playing an instrument or riding a bicycle, have actually modified their basal ganglia through practice to better coordinate engaging in the activity. The basal ganglia are also affected in people who have Tourette's syndrome—a condition marked by erratic and repetitive facial and muscle movements (called tics), heavy eye blinking, and frequent noise making such as grunting, snorting, or sniffing. Contrary to popular belief, shouting of obscenities is actually relatively uncommon in people with Tourette's syndrome. The excess dopamine that appears to be transmitted within the basal ganglia contributes to many of the classic Tourette's symptoms (Baym et al., 2008).

Some parts of the basal ganglia are also involved in emotion, particularly experiences of pleasure and reward. One such area— the *nucleus accumbens*—was inadvertently discovered during an experiment on navigation in rats. Researchers attempted to locate a region of the rat brain that was active in finding paths, but instead they found that this particular area created a pleasurable response. In fact, the rats did nothing but press a bar so long as it brought them the reward of stimulation to the nucleus accumbens. (Olds & Milner, 1954). Subsequent research has confirmed that activity in the nucleus accumbens accompanies all kinds of pleasurable experiences, including sexual excitement and satisfying a food craving (Avena et al., 2008). It is even involved in the rewards and thrills that some people associate with gambling (Breiter et al., 2001). Given that people sometimes claim to be addicted to these experiences, it is probably not surprising that many commonly abused drugs, such as cocaine, target dopamine transmission in the nucleus accumbens (a topic we will cover in Module 5.3).

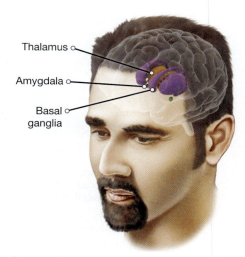

{FIG. 3.19} **The Basal Ganglia** The basal ganglia function in both voluntary movement and processing of rewards. **Click on this figure in your eText to see more details**.

Another major set of forebrain structures comprises the **limbic system**, *an integrated network involved in emotion and memory* (see Figure 3.20). One key structure in the limbic system is the almond-shaped **amygdala**, *which facilitates memory formation for emotional events, mediates fear responses, and appears to play a role in recognizing and interpreting emotional stimuli, including facial expressions.* In addition, the amygdala connects with structures in the nervous system that are responsible for adaptive fear responses, such as freezing in position when a possible threat is detected. Just below the amygdala is another limbic region called

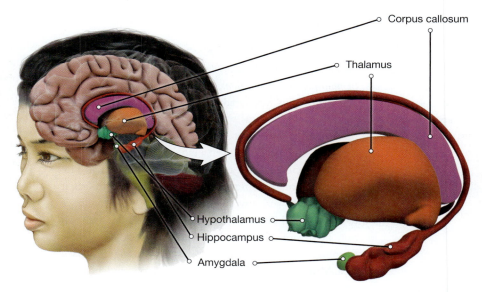

{FIG. 3.20} **The Limbic System** Structures in the limbic system include the hypothalamus, hippocampus, and amygdala, which play roles in regulating motivation, memory, and emotion. **Click on this figure in your eText to see more details**.

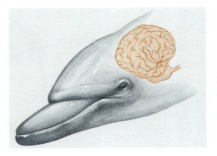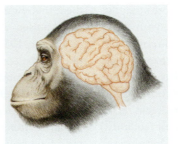

Brain anatomy and complexity vary considerably among different species. One obvious feature found in socially and cognitive-complex animals, such as dolphins and chimpanzees, is the abundance of convolutions across the surface of the brain, compared to the relatively smooth surface of other, less complex species.

the **hippocampus** (Greek for "seahorse"—something it physically resembles), *which is critical for learning and memory, particularly the formation of new memories* (Squire et al., 2007; see Module 7.1).

You have already encountered the hypothalamus (which literally means "below the thalamus") in Module 3.2 when we described its relationship to the endocrine system, and you will encounter it again in Module 11.1 when we describe its influence on the regulation of hunger and thirst. The hypothalamus serves as a sort of thermostat, maintaining the appropriate body temperature, and it regulates drives such as aggression and sex by interacting with the endocrine system. In fact, regions of the hypothalamus trigger orgasm for both females and males (Meston et al., 2004; Peeters & Giuliano, 2007).

The **thalamus** *is involved in relaying sensory information to different regions of the brain.* Most of the incoming sensory information, including what we see and hear, is routed through the thalamus and then proceeds to more specialized regions of the brain for further processing. Many of these regions include the highly complex and advanced cerebral cortex.

PsychTutor
Click here in your eText for an interactive tutorial on the **Brain**

THE CEREBRAL CORTEX The **cerebral cortex** *is the convoluted, wrinkled outer layer of the brain that is involved in multiple higher functions, such as thought, language, and personality.* This highly advanced, complex structure has increased dramatically in size as the primate brain has evolved (Kouprina et al., 2002). The wrinkled surface of the brain seems to have solved a biological problem endured by our species, as well as by many other mammals: The size of the skull is constrained by the birth canal. In fact, if human heads were any bigger at birth, we would all have to be delivered by cesarean sections. Because the skull can only be so large, the brain has countered this constraint by forming a wrinkled surface—thereby increasing its surface area. More surface area means more neurons and, possibly, greater cognitive complexity.

Figure 3.21 shows a slice of the brain revealing contrasting light and dark regions. The dark region is called gray

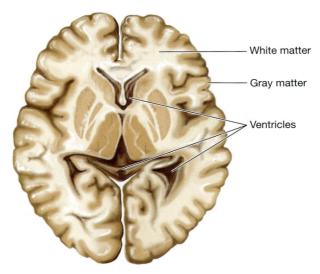

White matter

Gray matter

Ventricles

{FIG. 3.21} **Gray and White Matter of the Brain** The cerebral cortex includes both gray matter and white matter, which consist of myelinated axons. Also seen here are the ventricles of the brain. These cavities within the brain are filled with cerebrospinal fluid that provides nourishment and exchange of chemicals with the brain as well as its protective structure.

matter and is composed of cell bodies and dendrites; the white region is composed of myelinated axons that interconnect the different structures of the brain. Deep within the brain are spaces called *ventricles* (Figure 3.21). Although the ventricles appear hollow, they are filled with cerebrospinal fluid, a solution that helps to eliminate wastes and provides nutrition and hormones to the brain and spinal cord. Cerebrospinal fluid also cushions the brain from impact against the skull. In Figure 3.22, you can see that crossing the midline of the brain is a densely concentrated bundle of nerve cells called the **corpus callosum**, *a collection of neural fibers connecting the two hemispheres.*

The cerebral hemispheres consist of four major areas, known as *lobes*: the frontal, parietal, occipital, and temporal lobes (Figure 3.23). Each of the cerebral lobes has a particular set of functions. Nerve cells from each of the four lobes are interconnected, however, and are also networked with regions of the midbrain and hindbrain already described.

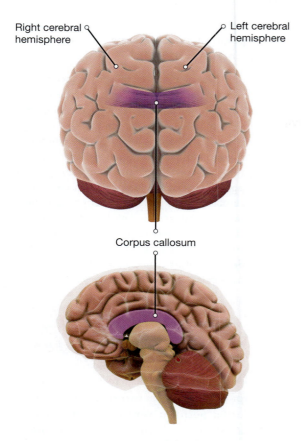

Right cerebral hemisphere — Left cerebral hemisphere

Corpus callosum

{FIG. 3.22} **The Corpus Callosum** The left and right hemispheres of the brain are connected by a thick band of axons called the corpus callosum.

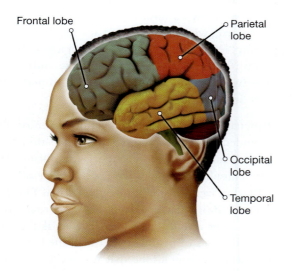

Frontal lobe — Parietal lobe

Occipital lobe

Temporal lobe

{FIG. 3.23} **The Four Lobes of the Cerebral Cortex** The cerebral cortex is divided into the frontal, parietal, occipital, and temporal lobes. **Click on this figure in your eText to see more details.**

The **frontal lobes** *are important in numerous higher cognitive functions, such as planning, regulating impulses and emotion, language production, and voluntary movement* (Goldman-Rakic, 1996). The frontal lobes also allow you to deliberately guide and reflect on your own thought processes.

Toward the rear of the frontal lobes is a thick band of neurons that form the *primary motor cortex*, which is involved in the control of voluntary movement. Figure 3.24 shows how the primary motor cortex corresponds with the region of the body it controls. This and other motor areas of the frontal lobes are active not just when moving the corresponding body part, but also when planning a movement. For this reason, the motor areas of the cortex are a target for researchers who are trying to develop thought-controlled devices. Recall the work of Dr. Hatsopoulos from the beginning of the module: In their experimental procedures, Hatsopoulos and his colleagues have implanted microchips into the motor cortex of healthy monkeys and quadriplegic humans. They can then train the monkeys to make specific movements or ask their human volunteers to do the same. Using the recordings that go along with these movements, the research team has been able to develop thought-controlled robotic arms and computer navigation systems.

The **parietal lobes**, *located behind the frontal lobes, are involved in our experiences of touch as well as bodily awareness.* Adjacent to the primary motor cortex and at the front edge of the parietal lobe is the *somatosensory cortex*—a band of densely packed nerve cells that register touch sensations. Figure 3.24 (p. 102)—a map of the body that corresponds to the somatosensory cortex—is based on the number of sensory receptors present at each respective body region. For instance, the volume of nerve cells in the somatosensory cortex corresponding to the face and hands is proportionally greater than the volume of cells devoted to less sensitive regions like the torso and legs. Regions within the parietal lobes also function in performing mathematical and visuospatial tasks.

The **occipital lobes** *are located at the rear of the brain, where visual information is processed* (vision is covered in more detail in Module 4.2). The **temporal lobes** *are located at the sides of the brain near the ears and are involved in hearing, language, and some higher-level aspects of vision such as object and face recognition.*

What we have described so far are generalities about how the cerebral cortex is organized. However, your own personal experiences have played a role in how the architecture of your cerebral cortex developed. For example, experienced musicians develop a greater density of brain matter in the areas of the motor cortex of the frontal lobe as well as in the auditory cortex (Gaser & Schlaug, 2003).

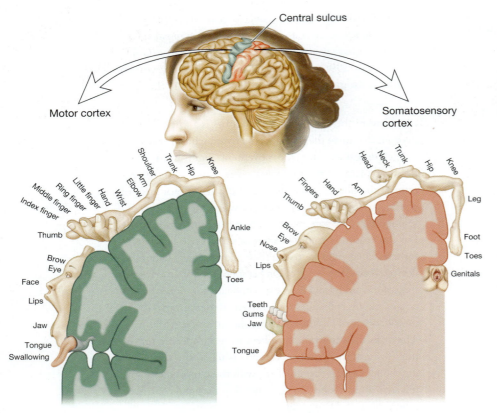

Central sulcus

Motor cortex

Somatosensory cortex

Shoulder · Trunk · Hip · Knee · Little finger · Ring finger · Middle finger · Index finger · Arm · Elbow · Hand · Wrist · Thumb · Brow · Eye · Face · Lips · Jaw · Tongue · Swallowing

Head · Neck · Trunk · Hip · Knee · Fingers · Hand · Thumb · Arm · Brow · Eye · Nose · Lips · Teeth · Gums · Jaw · Tongue · Leg · Foot · Toes · Genitals

Ankle · Toes

{FIG. 3.24} **The Body as Mapped on the Motor Cortex and Somatosensory Cortex** The regions of the motor cortex are involved in controlling specific body parts. The somatosensory cortex registers touch and other sensations that correspond to the body region depicted.

The brain has a remarkable ability to change with individual experience; healthy lifestyle choices, such as exercising, can encourage positive increases in brain function.

PSYCH @

The Gym

Somehow, physical exertion, pain, and breaking down and rebuilding muscle end up making people feel better. But the benefits of exercise do not apply just to mood: Exercise also affects cognitive activities such as learning and memory. But how?

In recent years, neuroscientists have begun unraveling the mystery of how exercise benefits brain health. Brain imaging studies have revealed that people who engage in regular exercise show improved functioning of the prefrontal cortex compared to non-exercisers. In addition, people who exercise perform better than non-exercisers on tasks involving planning, scheduling, and multitasking (see Davis et al., 2011; Hillman et al., 2008). Animal studies have shown that exercise increases the number of cells in the hippocampus, which is critical for memory, and increases the quantity of brain chemicals that are responsible for promoting cell growth and functioning (Cotman & Berchtold, 2002). But animals are not the only beneficiaries of an exercise program:

○▶ **Simulate**
the **Experiment**
Hemispheric
Specialization at
MyPsychLab

Similar findings have been reported for elderly people who regularly engage in aerobic exercise (Erickson et al., 2011).

Despite the clear benefits associated with exercise, many school curricula have dropped physical education in favor of spending more time on preparation for standardized testing. It is not clear that time away from the gym and the playground are having much benefit. In fact, the California Department of Education reported that school-age children with higher aerobic capacity perform better on standardized tests of math and reading. In addition to physical activity's ability to provide some relief from stress and an elevated mood, science is clearly demonstrating that exercise affects the brain basis of learning and memory.

· · · · · · · · · · ·

LEFT BRAIN, RIGHT BRAIN: HEMISPHERIC SPECIALIZATION

Although they appear to be mirror images of each other, the two sides of the cortex often perform very different functions, a phenomenon called *hemispheric specialization*. Speaking in very general terms, the right hemisphere is specialized for cognitive tasks that involve visual and spatial skills, recognition of visual stimuli, and musical processing. In contrast, the left hemisphere is more specialized for language and math (Corballis, 1993; Gazzaniga, 1967, 2000). The degree to which people are "right brained" or "left brained" is often exaggerated in popular media, however. Creative artists and those who rely on intuition are often described as "right brained," whereas logical and analytical types are supposedly "left brained." While these characterizations are simplifications, abundant evidence indicates that the two hemispheres are specialized to perform different functions. ○▶

Language provides a great example: Almost all right-handed people and approximately two-thirds of left-handed individuals show language dominance in the left hemisphere. Some of the first evidence of this specialization came in the mid-1800s, when French surgeon Paul Broca conducted a postmortem examination of a patient who had been unable to speak for the last three decades of his life. Broca identified an area of the man's left frontal lobe that was severely damaged, and reasoned that it played a major role in speech (see Figure 3.25). Countless studies have confirmed that this area, now called *Broca's area*, is responsible for

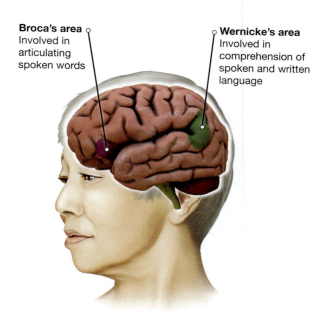

Broca's area Involved in articulating spoken words

Wernicke's area Involved in comprehension of spoken and written language

{FIG. 3.25} **Brain Specialization** Broca's area and Wernicke's area are associated with different aspects of language function.

complex grammar and speech production. Loss of speech function is referred to as *Broca's aphasia*. (An *aphasia* is an impairment of language functioning; we will address these disorders in more detail in Module 8.3.) Another language region, *Wernicke's area*, is located in the left temporal lobe, extending into the adjacent parietal lobe, and is involved in the comprehension of speech (Figure 3.25). Thus patients with *Wernicke's aphasia* have difficulty with speech comprehension.

Our understanding of hemispheric specialization expanded greatly through work with split-brain patients. In the 1960s, physicians hoping to curtail severe epileptic seizures in their patients used a surgical procedure to treat individuals who were not responding to other therapies. The surgeon would sever the corpus callosum, leaving a patient with two separate cerebral hemispheres. This surgery, which is used sparingly today, is not as drastic as it might sound. Patients were remarkably normal after the operation, but several interesting observations were made. One was that split-brain patients responded quite differently to visual input that was presented to either hemisphere alone (Sperry, 1982).

To see how this works, take a look at Figure 3.26. Imagine the person pictured has a split brain. On the one hand, she is able to match the two objects to her right, and can verbalize the match, because the left side of her visual system perceives the objects and language is processed in the left hemisphere of the brain. On the other hand, a visual stimulus presented on the left side of the body is processed on the right side of the brain. As you

can see from Figure 3.26, when the object is presented to the left side of the split-brain patient, the individual does not verbalize which of the objects match, because her right hemisphere is not specialized for language and cannot label the object. If asked to point at the matching object, however, she is able to do so. Thus she is able to process the information using her right hemisphere, but cannot articulate it with language.

Split-brain surgery is very rare, and it would be unthinkable to use it as an experimental procedure—how could you randomly assign a healthy person to have his or her cortex split in two? One alternative method that has been used with healthy individuals is called *Wada testing* (*Wada* is not a technical term, just the name of the researcher who devised the technique). Researchers begin by injecting a sedative into an artery on one side of the body. As the sedative travels upward into the brain, it sedates only one half of the cortex. This creates a temporary state in which one half of the cortex is doing all the work, so researchers can test for a specific ability—such as language or mathematics—in only one hemisphere.

Studies of split-brain patients show that the cerebral hemispheres are specialized for different functions. Again, these are very general terms; it is easy to get caught up in thinking of these generalities as absolutes. The reality is that most cognitive functions are spread throughout multiple brain regions.

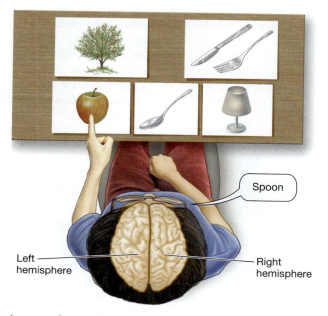

Spoon

Left hemisphere

Right hemisphere

{FIG. 3.26} **A Split-Brain Experiment** This woman has had a split-brain operation. She is able to verbalize which objects match when they are placed to her right side, because language is processed in the left hemisphere. She cannot verbalize the matching objects at left, but can identify them by pointing.

WORKING THE SCIENTIFIC LITERACY MODEL

Neuroplasticity and Recovery from Brain Injury

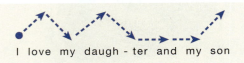

Elementary Level

I love you

Intermediate Level

I love my chil - dren

Advanced Level

I love my daugh - ter and my son

{FIG. 3.27} **Musical Intonation Therapy** During musical intonation therapy, patients are asked to sing phrases of increasing complexity.

Thus far in our discussion of the brain we have emphasized the links between specific brain structures and their functions. It may seem as if structures like Broca's area are as clearly defined as parts of a car's engine, but this is not the case. Although the brain is genetically programmed to be organized in specific ways, it still has a remarkable property called **neuroplasticity**—*the capacity of the brain to change and rewire itself based on individual experience.*

What do we know about neuroplasticity?

An example of neuroplasticity can be found in the brains of adults who received music training as children. The brains of musicians differ from nonmusicians in regions involved in controlling hand movements and in hearing. Experiments have confirmed that the training results in changes in brain anatomy and function (Gaser & Schlaug, 2003; Schlaug et al., 1995).

Neuroplasticity is also very important when it comes to recovery from injury. Traumatic brain damage from strokes and accidents is often permanent because the generation of new neurons seems to be limited to a few specific areas. However, thanks to neuroplasticity, there is a chance that existing areas can be modified to accommodate the injury. For this reason, physicians and therapists attempt to capitalize on neuroplasticity in their treatments. For example, the loss of speech production, Broca's aphasia, often occurs in the aftermath of a stroke. At least partial recovery is often possible by facilitating neuroplasticity. But how is this done?

How can science explain neuroplasticity contributes to stroke recovery?

Researchers have discovered a remarkable technique for facilitating stroke recovery. A surprising observation about stroke patients with Broca's aphasia is that many of them can actually sing using fluent, articulated words, even though they cannot speak those same words. A therapy called Melodic Intonation Therapy (MIT) has been developed to restore speech function through singing (Norton et al., 2009). In a study of this technique, stroke patients with Broca's

aphasia underwent intensive MIT sessions. During these sessions the patients would sing long strings of words using just two pitches, while rhythmically tapping their left hand to the melody. Try this out with the help of Figure 3.27.

The patients underwent 80 or more sessions lasting 1.5 hours each day, 5 days per week. Remarkably, this therapy has worked for multiple patients—after these intensive therapy sessions, they typically regain significant language function (Schlaug et al., 2009). The therapy does not "heal" damaged nerve cells in the left hemisphere at Broca's area. Rather, language function is taken over by the corresponding area of the *right* hemisphere.

You might be wondering why the patients tapped the fingers of their left hand. The researchers suggest that because we typically gesture along with speech, and because speech itself involves motor movements, the tapping may facilitate the recovery process.

Further insight into this work comes from animal studies, which have shown remarkable neuroplasticity following brain damage. This work also demonstrates that chemicals called *trophic factors* facilitate the process of recovery in animals; the same chemicals are most likely responsible for nerve cell recovery in humans (Kleim et al., 2003).

Can we critically evaluate this research?

What about other types of brain damage, such as to the motor areas that control movement that are often damaged in stroke? If one hemisphere is not damaged, might it take over control of movements formerly handled by the damaged area? This is unlikely. Recall from Figure 3.24 that the motor cortex resides in *both* hemispheres, with each hemisphere controlling the opposite side of the body. One side of the motor cortex cannot control both sides of the body.

Does this mean that language function can move because the right hemisphere has a "vacancy"? Definitely not—there is no vacant space in the brain. The claim that we use only 10% of our brain is 100% myth. The right hemisphere does appear to be involved in some aspects of expressive language. For example, the ability to understand metaphors and other figurative language draws upon the right hemisphere (Schmidt et al., 2007). This may be why language can, with great effort, move from left to right hemispheric control.

Why is this relevant?

MIT treatment for stroke patients who have lost language function is not yet commonplace. For decades, other forms of speech therapy have been the primary methods for helping stroke patients recover. Unfortunately, those forms of

speech therapy rarely resulted in significant recovery of function. Given the promising results obtained to date, then, MIT may become increasingly common. It is a remarkable example of neuroplasticity, and may pave the way for therapies needed to restore other functions.

Quick Quiz 3.3b
The Brain and Its Structures

KNOW …

1 The ability to recognize objects is based in which of the cerebral lobes?

  A Frontal   C Temporal
  B Parietal   D Hypothalamus

2 Producing words generally involves the _____ cerebral hemisphere region called _____ area.

  A right; Broca's   C right; Wernicke's
  B left; Broca's   D left; Wernicke's

UNDERSTAND …

3 Why would a person who has undergone a split-brain operation be unable to name an object presented to his left visual field, yet could correctly point to the same object from an array of choices?

  A Because his right hemisphere perceived the object, but does not house the language function needed for naming it

  B Because the image was processed on his left hemisphere, which is required for naming objects

  C Because pointing is something done with the right hand

  D Because the right hemisphere of the brain is where objects are seen

APPLY …

4 Damage to the somatosensory cortex would most likely result in which of the following impairments?

  A Inability to point at an object

  B Impaired vision

  C Impaired mathematical ability

  D Lost or distorted sensations in the region of the body corresponding to the damaged area

ANALYZE …

5 Which of the following statements best summarizes the results of experiments on exercise and brain functioning?

  A Both human and animal studies show cognitive benefits of exercise.

  B Animal studies show benefits from exercise, but the results of human studies are unclear.

  C Exercise benefits mood but not thinking.

  D Exercise only benefits older people.

Answers can be found on page ANS-1.

Windows to the Brain: Measuring and Observing Brain Activity

In the very early days of brain research, scientists had to rely almost exclusively on case studies, such as those used by Broca in his discovery of one of the brain's language centers. Doctors and researchers typically identified symptoms of living patients and then conducted postmortem dissections to see which abnormalities might have been responsible for the problems. Alternatively, they made detailed observations of patients before and after brain surgery, often for tumor removal. There was no way to image the brain of a living, breathing patient or research participant.

Today, perfectly healthy college students can walk into brain imaging research centers found on many college campuses and have their brains scanned during

Before brain imaging technology became available, neurosurgeons had to do quite a bit of guess work. Dr. Harvey Cushing was one of the United States' first neurosurgeons. Dr. Cushing, who operated on patients with brain tumors, had to rely on behavioral symptoms to determine where to target his attempts at removing the tumors.

research studies. Researchers not only take detailed pictures of their brains, but are also able to measure actual brain activity. In this section, we review several methods for examining healthy, normally functioning brains, as well as the brains of individuals who have experienced major injuries or disease.

ELECTROPHYSIOLOGY Module 3.2 discussed the role that electrical activity plays in nerve cell activity. This electrical activity can be recorded using highly sensitive devices. An **electroencephalogram (EEG)** *measures patterns of brain activity with the use of multiple electrodes attached to the scalp.* The neural firing of the billions of cells in the brain can be detected with these electrodes, amplified, and depicted in an electroencephalogram. An EEG can tell us a lot about general brain activity during sleep, during wakefulness, and while patients or research participants are engaged in a particular cognitive activity (see Figure 3.28). The convenience and relatively inexpensive nature of EEGs, compared to other modern methods, make them very appealing to researchers. However, this technique does not allow researchers to probe directly inside the brain.

BRAIN IMAGING To obtain actual images of the brain, researchers turn to techniques such as *positron emission tomography (PET)* scans. In a PET scan, a low level of radioactive glucose is injected into the blood, and its movement to regions of the brain engaged in a particular task is measured (active nerve cells use up the glucose at

a faster rate than do resting cells). This technique allows researchers to monitor brain activity while a person performs a task such as reading or viewing emotionally charged stimuli. The greatest strength of PET scans is that they show metabolic activity of the brain. A drawback is that PET scans take a long time to acquire—which is a problem when you want to see moment-by-moment activity of the brain.

Magnetic resonance imaging (MRI) is a technique that can be used to acquire highly detailed images of brain anatomy via exposure to a strong (and harmless) magnetic field. How does it accomplish this? As you sit reading these words, millions of hydrogen atoms in your brain are spinning around in random directions. If you were to enter an MRI machine, the atoms would align and spin in the same direction due to the application of a magnetic field by the imaging device. Radio waves are then passed through the brain, disrupting the alignment of the atoms. These disruptions produce a signal that can be translated into a detailed, three-dimensional image of the brain.

Like PET, MRI allows us to observe brain activity through a technique called *functional MRI (fMRI).* Blood cells carry oxygen to active nerve cells. Functional MRI measures the difference between blood cells with an oxygen molecule attached versus those without an oxygen molecule attached. In essence, fMRI allows us to see blood flow within the brain, which is closely correlated with brain activity (Logothetis, 2007). Furthermore, fMRI provides a moment-by-moment picture of brain activity (see Figure 3.29).

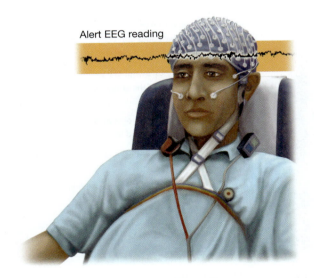

Alert EEG reading

{FIG. 3.28} **Measuring Brain Activity** The electroencephalogram measures electrical activity of the brain by way of electrodes that amplify the signals emitted by active regions.

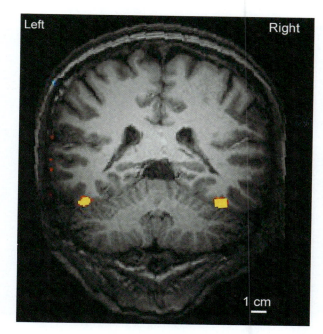

{FIG. 3.29} **Functional Magnetic Resonance Imaging**
Functional MRI technology allows researchers to determine how blood flow, and hence brain activity, changes as study participants or patients perform different tasks. In this image, the colored areas depict increases in blood flow to the left and right temporal lobes, relative to the rest of the brain, during a cognitive task.

Another imaging technique, called *magnetoencephalography (MEG)*, measures the tiny magnetic fields created by the electrical activity of nerve cells in the brain. With this technology, highly sensitive devices that detect magnetic fields surround the skull and detect minute changes in brain activity. MEG records the electrical activity of nerve cells just a few milliseconds after it occurs, which allows researchers to record brain activity at nearly the instant a stimulus is presented. This feature represents an advantage relative to PET and fMRI, which measure glucose consumption and blood flow, respectively, and therefore record responses only after a delay of several seconds.

LESIONING AND BRAIN STIMULATION A number of methods have been developed that, in effect, shut down a portion of the brain to see how it affects behavior. The oldest method based on this idea is brain **lesioning**—*a technique in which researchers intentionally damage an area in the brain* (a *lesion* is abnormal or damaged brain tissue). Researchers interested in how the human brain works obviously cannot perform this procedure in experiments, although many patients have been generous enough to become research participants after stroke, injury, or brain surgery.

Less drastic techniques impair brain activity only temporarily; in fact, some can be applied to humans with no ill effects. The Wada test, used to study hemispheric specialization, is one example. Researchers also study brain function using **transcranial magnetic stimulation (TMS)**, *a procedure in which an electromagnetic pulse is delivered to a targeted region of the brain* (Bestmann, 2008; Terao & Ugawa, 2002). The result is a temporary disruption of brain activity, analogous to the permanent disruption caused by a brain lesion. Interestingly, TMS can also be used to stimulate, rather than temporarily impair, a brain region (Figure 3.30). Not only is this approach a tool for researching the brain, it can also be used to treat serious psychological problems. For example, TMS has been used to stimulate under-active areas associated with depression (Kluger & Triggs, 2007). In addition, researchers have found that the magnetic stimulation provided by TMS may be helpful in promoting stroke recovery by stimulating damaged nerve cells (Schlaug et al., 2008). For example, patients who have damage to the left motor cortex may lose their ability to control regions on the right side of the body. TMS directed at the left motor cortex can help these patients regain some movement.

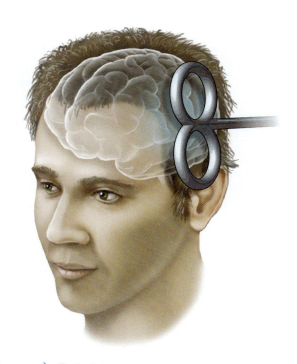

{FIG. 3.30} **Brain Stimulation** Transcranial magnetic stimulation involves targeting a magnetic field to a very specific region of the brain. Depending on the amount of stimulation, researchers can either temporarily stimulate or disable the region.

Quick Quiz 3.3c :: Measuring and Observing Brain Activity

KNOW …

1 The brain imaging technique that involves measuring blood flow in active regions of the brain is called:

A magnetic resonance imaging.

B functional magnetic resonance imaging.

C PET scan.

D transcranial magnetic stimulation.

UNDERSTAND …

2 Which of the following techniques does not provide an actual picture of the brain?

A PET scan

B MRI

C Electroencephalogram (EEG)

D fMRI

APPLY …

3 If a neuroscientist studying vision wanted to temporarily cause someone to lose the ability to see, which technique would be most appropriate?

A Transcranial magnetic stimulation (TMS)

B MRI

C fMRI

D PET scan

ANALYZE …

4 A drawback of PET scans compared to newer techniques, such as magnetoencephalography, is that:

A PET is slower, which means it is more difficult to measure moment-to-moment changes in brain activity.

B PET is faster, which makes it difficult to figure out how brain activity relates to what someone sees or hears.

C PET is too expensive for practical use.

D PET is slower, and it does not provide a picture of the brain.

Answers can be found on page ANS-1.

Module Summary

Now that you have read this module you should:

KNOW ...

- **The key terminology associated with the structure and organization of the nervous system:**

amygdala (p. 99)

autonomic nervous system (p. 96)

basal ganglia (p. 99)

brain stem (p. 98)

central nervous system (CNS) (p. 96)

cerebellum (p. 98)

cerebral cortex (p. 100)

corpus callosum (p. 100)

electroencephalogram (EEG) (p. 106)

forebrain (p. 99)

frontal lobes (p. 101)

hippocampus (p. 100)

lesioning (p. 107)

limbic system (p. 99)

midbrain (p. 98)

neuroplasticity (p. 104)

occipital lobes (p. 101)

parasympathetic nervous system (p. 96)

parietal lobes (p. 101)

peripheral nervous system (PNS) (p. 96)

somatic nervous system (p. 96)

sympathetic nervous system (p. 96)

temporal lobes (p. 101)

thalamus (p. 100)

transcranial magnetic stimulation (TMS) (p. 107)

ANALYZE ...

- **Whether psychologists can use technology to map out brain activity.** Several methods for measuring brain activity were covered in this module. Also, at the beginning of this module, we described a technology that links brain activity with motor movements. For example, researchers are able to detect planned movements by monitoring electrical patterns in the motor cortex. In a sense, they can use technology to identify which types of motions an individual is thinking about. This technology may help people who are paralyzed gain some level of control using brain activity alone. However, we should be cautious about calling this practice "mind-reading." Although we can detect intended movements, there is little or no evidence that psychologists can translate specific types of thoughts from brain activity.

UNDERSTAND ...

- **How studies of split-brain patients reveal the workings of the brain.** Studies of split-brain patients were important in that they revealed that the two hemispheres of the brain are specialized for certain cognitive tasks. For example, studies of split-brain patients showed that the left hemisphere was specialized for language. These studies were carried out before other brain imaging techniques became available.

APPLY ...

- **Your knowledge of brain regions to predict which abilities might be affected when a specific area is injured or diseased.** Review **Table 3.2, (on page 98)** which summarizes each of the major brain regions described in this module. Then try to answer these questions (check your answers on page ANS-2):

1 While at work, a woman suffers a severe blow to the back of her head and then experiences visual problems. Which part of her brain has most likely been affected?

2 If an individual has a stroke and loses the ability to speak in clear sentences, what part of the brain is most likely to have been damaged?

3 If an individual develops a tumor that affects the basal ganglia, which types of behaviors or abilities are likely to be affected?

4 A man suffers a gunshot wound that slightly damages his cerebellum. Which problems might he experience?

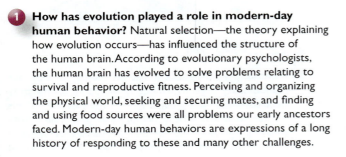

Module 3.1 :: Genetic and Evolutionary Perspectives on Behavior

Focus Questions:

1 How has evolution played a role in modern-day human behavior? Natural selection—the theory explaining how evolution occurs—has influenced the structure of the human brain. According to evolutionary psychologists, the human brain has evolved to solve problems relating to survival and reproductive fitness. Perceiving and organizing the physical world, seeking and securing mates, and finding and using food sources were all problems our early ancestors faced. Modern-day human behaviors are expressions of a long history of responding to these and many other challenges.

2 How is human behavior influenced by genetic factors? Individual differences in behavior and personality are in part due to genetic differences. Also, when comparing how members of various species select mates, defend territories, and perform other survival-enhancing behaviors, we see similarities among human and nonhuman species. For example, humans are not the only species that uses body or facial symmetry when judging attractiveness. Even male honeybees with symmetrically sized left and right wings have better reproductive success than bees with asymmetrical wings (Jaffé & Moritz, 2010). Of course, like all other species, humans have unique and specialized adaptations.

👁—[**Watch** *The Big Picture: Genes, Evolution, and Human Behavior* in the **MyPsychLab video series**

Module 3.2 :: How the Nervous System Works: Cells and Neurotransmitters

Focus Questions:

1 Which normal processes of nerve cells are disrupted by a substance like snake venom? Neurotoxic venom attacks the neurons that secrete and bind to the neurotransmitter acetylcholine. Acetylcholine is important for movement, as it occurs at the junctions between nerve cells and muscles. Neurotoxic venom blocks acetylcholine activity at the synapses between nerve cells, rendering the victim paralyzed.

2 What roles do chemicals play in normal nerve cell functioning? The nervous system relies on numerous chemicals, called neurotransmitters, to perform different functions. Neurons typically produce and receive a limited number of neurotransmitters, though which type depends on the neuron and its location. Also, neurotransmitters play the important roles of both exciting and inhibiting activity.

👁—[**Watch** *The Big Picture: My Brain Made Me Do It* in the **MyPsychLab video series**

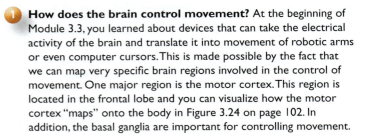

Module 3.3 :: Structure and Organization of the Nervous System

Focus Questions:

1 How does the brain control movement? At the beginning of Module 3.3, you learned about devices that can take the electrical activity of the brain and translate it into movement of robotic arms or even computer cursors. This is made possible by the fact that we can map very specific brain regions involved in the control of movement. One major region is the motor cortex. This region is located in the frontal lobe and you can visualize how the motor cortex "maps" onto the body in Figure 3.24 on page 102. In addition, the basal ganglia are important for controlling movement.

2 How can we make sense of brain activity as it is actually occurring? One step would be to use brain imaging technology reviewed in Module 3.3. Specifically, fMRI, transcranial magnetic stimulation, PET scans, or magnetoencephalography could be used.

👁—[**Watch** *The Basics: How the Brain Works* in the **MyPsychLab video series**

👁—[**Watch** the complete video series online at **MyPsychLab**

Episode 4: Evolution and Genes

1. *The Big Picture: Genes, Evolution, and Human Behavior*
2. *The Basics: Genetic Mechanisms and Behavioral Genetics*
3. *Special Topics: Epigenetics—A Revolutionary Science*
4. *Thinking Like a Psychologist: Evolutionary Psychology— Why We Do the Things We Do*
5. *In the Real World Application: Taking Control of Our Genes*

Episode 3: Biological Psychology

1. *The Big Picture: My Brain Made Me Do It*
2. *The Basics: How the Brain Works? Part 1*
3. *The Basics: How the Brain Works? Part 2*
4. *Special Topics: The Plastic Brain*
5. *Thinking Like a Psychologist: The Prefrontal Cortex: The Good, The Bad, and The Criminal*
6. *In the Real World Application: Too Much, or Too Little, of a Good Thing?*
7. *What's in It for Me? Biology of the High*

1 According to current scientific understanding, which of the following is true about the influence of nature versus nature?

   A Human traits are influenced primarily by nature.

   B Human traits are influenced primarily by nurture.

   C Nature and nurture do not work alone, but instead interact with each other to determine traits.

   D Each human trait is determined either entirely by nature or entirely by nurture.

2 Suppose a researcher studied the occurrence rates of a specific mental illness in monozygotic and dizygotic twins. She finds that if one twin suffers from the mental illness, the other twin is much more likely to also have the mental illness if the pair are monozygotic twins. What conclusion should the researcher draw from this evidence?

   A The incidence of this type of mental illness is strongly influenced by genetics.

   B The incidence of this type of mental illness is completely based on environmental factors.

   C Monozygotic twins are at an increased risk of developing mental illness.

   D Dizygotic twins are at an increased risk of developing mental illness.

3 When behavioral geneticists use adoption studies to estimate the heritability of a behavior, the adoptive family can be thought of as representing _____ , while the biological family can be thought of as representing _____ .

   A adaptive behavior; maladaptive behavior

   B maladaptive behavior; adaptive behavior

   C nature; nurture

   D nurture; nature

4 Which of the following is one of the reasons to be skeptical of news reports claiming that scientists have found the gene for a common mental illness, such as schizophrenia or depression?

   A Mental illnesses are generally caused by environmental factors, not genes.

   B Scientists lack the technology to link specific disorders to only a single gene.

   C Most complicated disorders are influenced by a combination of genes.

   D News reports about science discoveries are almost always biased.

5 In general, the _____ of a neuron receives messages from other cells. The neuron can then pass the message onto another neuron via its _____.

   A axon; dendrites

   B dendrites; axon

   C myelin; cell body

   D cell body; myelin

6 What is a synapse?

   A The site where a "message" is transmitted from one nerve cell to another

   B A chemical substance that is released by a transmitting neuron

   C A fatty coating that increases the rate at which messages travel through neurons

   D The part of the neuron that keeps it alive

7 Which type of drug would a doctor give a patient to *decrease* the activity of the neurotransmitter dopamine in the brain?

   A A dopamine reuptake inhibitor

   B Substance P

   C A dopamine antagonist

   D A dopamine agonist

8 The branch of the autonomic nervous system that prepares the body for quick action in an emergency is the_____ division.

   A central

   B secondary

   C sympathetic

   D parasympathetic

9 Reggie suffered brain damage in a car accident. As a result, he can no longer breathe on his own and needs the help of a respirator. Which structure of his brain was most likely damaged?

   A Pons

   B Medulla

   C Cerebellum

   D Reticular formation

10 Dr. Stearns is studying what happens behaviorally when she temporarily impairs a brain region. Which method is she most likely to be using?

   A Functional MRIs

   B PET scans

   C Transcranial magnetic stimulation

   D Brain lesioning

✔● Study and Review at MyPsychLab

What do we know about structures of the brain?

See **Table 3.2 on page 98** for a list of the major brain regions, structures, and their functions. As you review this material, try to come up with strategies to distinguish these terms. For example, two brain structures commonly confused with each other are the hypothalamus and the hippocampus. Although the hypothalamus and the hippocampus are both part of the limbic system, they have very different functions. The hypothalamus serves as a sort of thermostat, maintaining the appropriate body temperature, and it can affect drives such as aggression and sex. The hippocampus is critical for learning and memory, particularly the formation of new memories. Can you think of a memory device that might help you keep these two brain structures separate? One suggestion: For the hippocampus, think of the last part of the word—"campus." To successfully navigate your college campus, you need to keep in mind where certain buildings are located. This area is exactly the type of task that involves a functioning hippocampus. As you study, try to come up with your own memory devices to help recall the different brain structures and their functions.

How can science help explain brain structure and function?

As discussed on **page 105**, in the very early days of brain research, scientists had to rely almost exclusively on case studies to gather data. There was no way to image the brain of a living, breathing patient or research participant. Today, through brain imaging technology, researchers are able to take detailed pictures of the brain and can examine the actual activity of major structures such as the hypothalamus and the hippocampus while that activity is occurring. Researchers have developed a variety of methods for studying the brain, each of which offers some advantage over the others. See **pages 106–107** for detailed descriptions of methods for measuring and observing brain activity: electroencephalogram (EEG), positron emission tomography (PET) scan, magnetic resonance imaging (MRI), functional MRI (fMRI), magnetoencephalography (MEG), brain lesioning, and transcranial magnetic stimulation (TMS).

Why is this relevant?

Watch the accompanying video excerpt on brain functions. You can access the video at MyPsychLab or by clicking the play button in the center of your eText. If your instructor assigns this video as a homework activity, you will find additional content to help you in MyPsychLab. You can also view the video by using your smart phone and the QR code below, or you can go to the YouTube link provided.

After you have read this chapter and watched the video, imagine that your best friends invite you over for pizza and a friendly game of cards. Describe how the following parts of the brain are involved during your evening of eating pizza, socializing, and playing cards: Broca's area, hippocampus, hypothalamus, and occipital lobe.

Can we critically evaluate claims about brain function?

Modern methods have helped us understand a great deal about brain structures and functions, but many misunderstandings persist. In **Myths in Mind on page 87**, we addressed the question of whether humans are born with all of the nerve cells we will ever have. In the past 15 years or so, advances in brain science have challenged this traditionally held belief. Researchers have observed neurogenesis in a limited number of brain regions, particularly in the hippocampus. Some areas within the hippocampus have the capacity to generate new cells long after birth.

Also, in our discussion of hemispheric specialization on **page 102**, we discussed how the degree to which people are "right brained" or "left brained" is often exaggerated in the popular media. Creative artists are often described as "right brained," whereas logical and analytical types are supposedly "left brained." In reality, most cognitive functions are spread throughout multiple brain regions.

It is easy to get caught up in thinking about these kinds of generalities as absolutes. Whenever you encounter "scientific claims" in the popular media, it is important to properly evaluate the information before embracing it as truth.

MyPsychLab

Your turn to Work the Scientific Literacy Model: You can access the video at MyPsychLab or by clicking the play button in the center of your eText. If your instructor assigns this video as a homework activity, you will find additional content to help you at MyPsychLab. You can also view the video by using your smart phone and the QR code, or you can go to the YouTube link provided.

youtube.com/
scientificliteracy

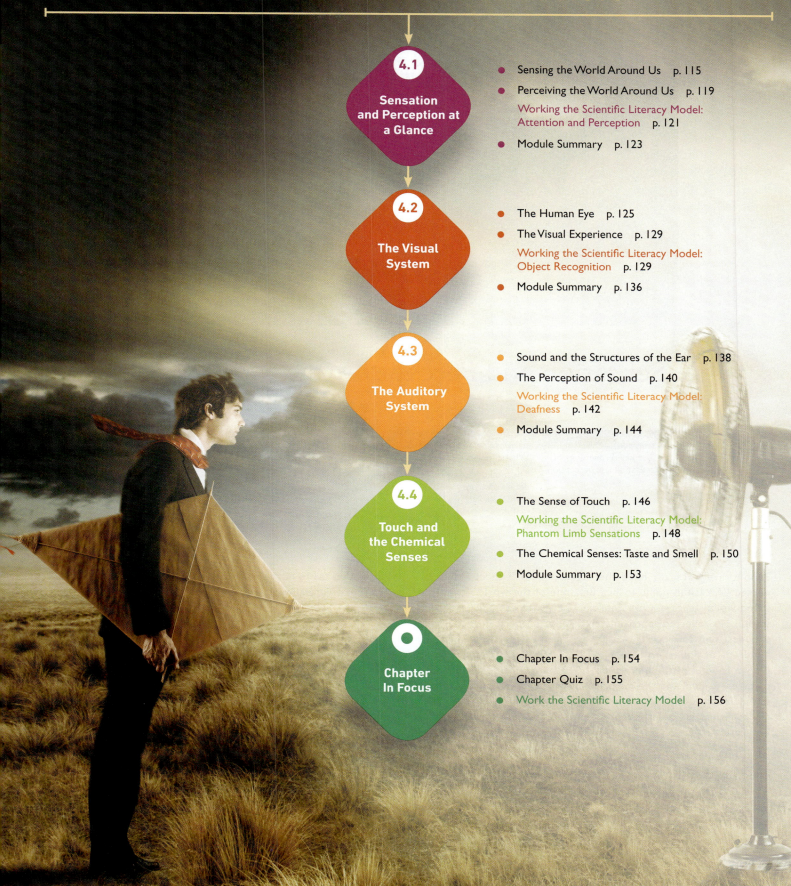

4 :: SENSATION AND PERCEPTION

Sensation and Perception at a Glance

KNOW ...	UNDERSTAND ...	APPLY ...	ANALYZE ...
The key terminology of sensation and perception	What stimulus thresholds are The methods of signal detection theory	Your knowledge of signal detection theory to identify hits, misses, and correct responses in examples	Claims that subliminal advertising can influence your behavior

People rarely actually heed the suggestion to "expect the unexpected." A case in point: Joshua Bell, one of the world's most talented violinists, gave a live concert at a Washington, D.C., subway station. He collected approximately $32 for his performance—quite a modest sum considering that just two days before, people had paid hundreds of dollars to hear him play with the Boston symphony. Only a handful of the more than 1,000 subway passersby stopped to listen to him, and the majority did what people typically do in this situation—they hurried by without stopping to listen or to pitch any coins into his collection. After 45 minutes of playing Bach, Joshua Bell returned his $3.5 million, 18th-century violin to its case and walked away.

This informal, yet remarkable experiment tells us a little bit about Joshua Bell, but it speaks volumes about what the 1,000 other people are like. One lesson is that context plays an extremely important role in what people sense and perceive. No one expects one of the best living violinists to be playing in a subway. Also, many commuters are so busy and

focused they fail to notice amazing events going on around them. It is enough to make you wonder what else we are missing.

Focus Questions

1 What role does attention play in perception?

2 What are the principles that guide perception?

• • • • • • • • • • • • • • • • • •

Sensation and perception are different, yet integrated processes. To illustrate this point, take a look at the Necker cube in Figure 4.1. After staring at it for several seconds, you likely noticed that the perspective changed: The cube seemingly flipped its orientation on the page. Although the cube remains constant on the page and in the way it is reflected in the eye, it can be perceived in different ways.

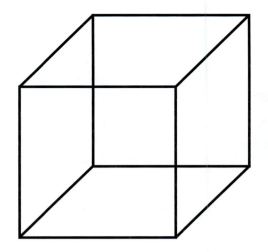

{FIG. 4.1} **The Necker Cube** Stare at this object for several seconds until it changes perspectives.

The switching of perspectives is a perceptual phenomenon that takes place in the brain.

Sensing the World Around Us

The world outside of the human body is full of light, sound vibrations, and natural and artificial chemicals. A walk along the ocean can bring sensations that are rich in color and light, evocative sounds, and distinct smells. The body has an amazing array of specialized processes that allow us to take all of this information in. The first step is **sensation**, *the process of detecting external events by sense organs and turning those events into neural signals*. At the sensory level, the sound of someone's voice is simply noise, and the sight of a person is a combination of color and motion. The raw information of what we sense is relayed to the brain where perception occurs. **Perception** *involves attending to, organizing, and interpreting stimuli that we sense*. Perception includes recognizing the sounds as a human voice and understanding that the colors, shape, and motion together make up the image of a human being.

Sensation gives way to the beginnings of perception when specialized *sensory receptors*—structures that respond to external stimuli—are stimulated. These sensory receptors are spread out over the surface of the skin, inside of the eye, and over the tongue and nasal cavity, and packed within a structure of the ear (summarized in Table 4.1). **Transduction** *is the process in which physical or chemical stimulation is converted into a nerve impulse that is relayed to the brain*. When patterns of light reach receptors at the back of the eye, they are converted into nerve impulses that travel to numerous brain centers where color and motion are perceived, and objects are identified (see Figure 4.2 on p. 116). The transduction of sound takes place in a specialized structure called the cochlea, where what we hear is converted into messages that travel to the hearing centers of the brain (covered in Module 4.3).

Generally speaking, our sensory receptors are most responsive upon initial exposure to a stimulus. For example, when you first walk into a crowded restaurant or when you exit a dark movie theater after a matinee, the sound and light you encounter initially seem intense. Eventually, however, the sensation becomes less intense even if the stimuli remain the same. **Sensory adaptation** *is the reduction of activity in sensory receptors with repeated exposure to a stimulus*. The ongoing sound of your neighbor's loud music or the sound of traffic noise outside is eventually experienced less intensely. Sensory adaptation provides the benefit of allowing us to adjust to our surroundings and shift our focus and attention to other events.

STIMULUS THRESHOLDS How loud does someone have to whisper for you to hear that person? If you touch a railroad track, how sensitive are your fingers to vibrations from a distant train? One early researcher,

Table 4.1 :: **Stimuli Affecting Our Major Senses and Corresponding Receptors**

SENSE	STIMULI	TYPE OF RECEPTOR
Vision (Module 4.2)	Light waves	Light-sensitive structures at the back of the eye
Hearing (Module 4.3)	Sound waves	Hair cells that respond to pressure changes in the ear
Touch (Module 4.4)	Pressure, stretching or piercing of the skin surface	Different types of nerve endings that respond to pressure, temperature changes, and pain
Taste (Module 4.4)	Chemicals on the tongue and in the mouth	Cells lining the taste buds of the tongue
Smell (Module 4.4)	Chemicals contacting mucus-lined membranes of the nose	Nerve endings that respond selectively to different compounds

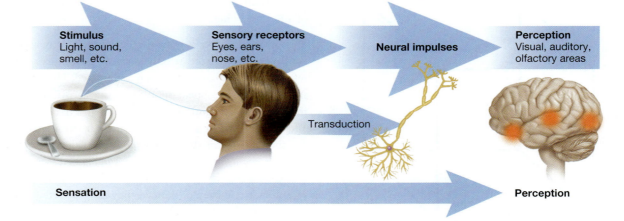

{FIG. 4.2} **From Stimulus to Perception** Sensing and perceiving begin with the detection of a stimulus by one of our senses. Receptors convert the stimulus into a neural impulse, a process called transduction. Our perception of the stimulus takes place in higher, specialized regions of the brain. **Click on this figure in your eText to see more details**.

physicist and philosopher William Gustav Fechner (1801–1887), coined the term **psychophysics**: *the field of study that explores how physical energy such as light and sound and their intensity relate to psychological experience.* Fechner and other early psychophysicists were interested in some basic questions about perceptual experience and sought to understand general principles of perception. A popular approach was to measure the minimum amount of a stimulus needed for detection, and the degree to which a stimulus must change in strength for the change to be perceptible.

Sensory adaptation is one process that accounts for why we respond less to a repeated stimulus—even to something that initially seems impossible to ignore.

See if you can estimate human sensory abilities in the following situations (based on Galanter, 1962):

- If you were standing atop a mountain on a dark, clear night, how far away do you think you could detect the flame from a single candle?
- How much perfume would need to be spilled in a three-room apartment for you to detect the odor?

On a clear night, a candle flame can be detected at 30 miles away. One drop of perfume is all that is needed for detection in a three-room apartment. Each of these values represents an **absolute threshold**—that is, *the minimum amount of energy or quantity of a stimulus required for it to be reliably detected at least 50% of the time it is presented* (Figure 4.3). The minimum amount of pressure, sound, light, or chemical required for detection varies among individuals and across the life span. Also, as you are surely aware, some species-related differences are quite amazing. The family dog may startle, bark, and tear for the door before you can even detect a visitor's approach, and a cat can detect changes in shadows and light that go unnoticed by humans. There is no magic or mystery in either example: These animals simply have lower absolute thresholds for detecting sound and light.

Another measure of perception refers to how well an individual can detect whether a stimulus has changed. A **difference threshold** *is the smallest detectable difference between stimuli.* When you add salt to your food, for example, you are attempting to cross a difference threshold that your taste receptors can register. Whether you actually detect a difference, known as a *just noticeable difference*, depends on the

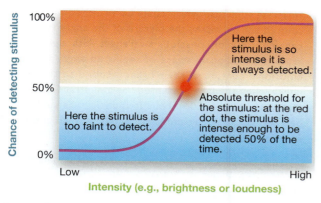

Here the stimulus is so intense it is always detected.

Here the stimulus is too faint to detect.

Absolute threshold for the stimulus: at the red dot, the stimulus is intense enough to be detected 50% of the time.

Chance of detecting stimulus

Intensity (e.g., brightness or loudness)

{FIG. 4.3} **Absolute Thresholds** The absolute threshold is the level at which a stimulus can be detected 50% of the time.

intensity of the original stimulus. The more intense the original stimulus, the more of it that must be added for the difference threshold to be reached. If you add one pinch of salt to a plate of french fries that already had one pinch sprinkled on them, you can probably detect the difference. However, if you add one pinch of salt to fries that already had four pinches applied, you probably will not detect much

Compared to people, dogs have amazingly low thresholds for detecting smells. Dogs have even been trained to detect tumors in people with various types of cancer.

of a difference. Apparently, to your senses, a single pinch of salt does not always equal one pinch.

The study of stimulus thresholds has its limitations. Whether someone perceives a stimulus is determined by self-report—that is, by an individual reporting that she either did or did not detect a stimulus. Someone may claim to see a faint candlelight just because he expects to see it. More importantly, think of a radiologist trying to detect tumors in a set of images, or a lifeguard who is supposed to listen to calls for help. How do we confirm whether these stimuli were truly perceived, or that the individuals were just guessing?

PsychTutor

Click here in your eText for an interactive tutorial on **Perceptual Thresholds**

SIGNAL DETECTION   **Signal detection theory** *states that whether a stimulus is perceived depends on both sensory experience and judgment made by the subject.* Thus the theory requires us to examine two processes: a sensory process and a decision process. In a typical signal detection experiment conducted in the laboratory, the experimenter presents a faint stimulus or no stimulus at all (the *sensory process*), and the subject is asked to report whether it was present (the *decision process*).

How loud does someone need to whisper for you to detect the sound? The answer is unclear: *It depends.* Whether you are able to detect a weak stimulus depends on your expectations, arousal level, and motivation. If you are lost in the woods, you may be better able to notice the sound of someone's voice, the far-off growl of a bear, or the sound of a car on the road than if you are hiking with friends on a well-known trail—even if the surrounding noise level is the same. Is the heightened sensitivity due to enhanced functioning of your ears (the sensory process) or because you are more motivated to detect sounds (the decision process)? Research shows that motivational changes are likely to affect the decision process so that you assume every snapping twig is a bear on the prowl (see Figure 4.4).

In developing signal detection theory, psychologists realized that the sensory judgment process has four possible outcomes. For example, you may be correct that you heard a sound (a *hit*), or correct that you did not hear a sound (known as a *correct rejection*). Of course, you will not always be correct in your judgments—sometimes you will think you heard something that is not there. Psychologists refer to this type of error as a *false alarm*; it could mean that you believed you heard a bear when there were none

	Is there a bear in the woods?	
The individual's response	**Yes**	**No**
"I hear something."	**Hit: Right!** He did hear the bear.	**False Alarm: Wrong!** He must be imagining it.
"I don't hear anything."	**Miss: Wrong!** He didn't hear the bear.	**Correct Rejection: Right!** There is no bear.

{FIG. 4.4} **Signal Detection Theory** Signal detection theory recognizes that a stimulus is either present or absent (by relying on the sensory process) and that the individual either reports detecting the stimulus or does not (the decision process). The cells represent the four possible outcomes of this situation. Here we apply signal detection theory to a man alone in the woods.

"masking stimulus," which could be a colored square. The colored square masks the picture of the angry face, thus keeping it out of conscious awareness. Although people are not consciously aware of seeing an angry face, the emotional centers of their brain respond to the anger, unlike when the face presented has a neutral expression (Critchley et al., 2000). Thus it appears that subliminal perception can occur, and it can produce small effects in the nervous system.

Can subliminal messages lead us to purchase items we would not buy without them—an often-cited example of subliminal messaging? There is no evidence that such messages have much effect at all, and certainly not to the extent that many people fear. At best, flashing a brief message on a screen can have a very temporary effect on thinking. When thirsty research participants watched a drink advertisement that included a subliminal flash of the word "thirst" on the screen, they found the ad to be more persuasive than did nonthirsty people who watched the same ad (Strahan, et al., 2002). Advertisements certainly do affect our behavior, but it is far-fetched to interpret their effects as a form of "mind control."

around. Alternatively, you could experience a *miss*, such as when a bear sneaks up behind you but you fail to detect its presence. Although not perceived, the weak stimulus *could* have a psychological effect even though it would reside below the level of conscious awareness—an issue that brings to mind the saga of subliminal messages.

MYTHS IN MIND
Setting the Record Straight on Subliminal Messaging

You may have heard claims that advertisers can flash images on television and movie screens containing persuasive messages, and that these messages can have strong influences on behavior. But does *subliminal perception*—meaning perception below conscious thresholds—really exist? And if so, does it really control our motivations, beliefs, and behaviors?

The answer to the first question is *yes*, we can perceive subliminal stimuli. This phenomenon has been demonstrated time and again in cognitive psychology experiments (Van den Bussche et al., 2009). To get a subject to register a stimulus unconsciously, a researcher might present a picture such as an angry face for a fraction of a second, immediately followed by what is called a

Do you see a cigarette advertisement in this photo? There is not an obvious one, but you may be reminded of Marlboro cigarettes as you look at this race car. Critics have accused sponsors of this Formula One car of using the barcode design to create an image similar to Marlboro Red cigarettes. Inquiries into attempts at subliminal advertising over this issue ensued.

· · · · · · · · · · · · · · · · · · ·

The study of thresholds and signal detection gives us answers to some very basic questions about how we sense and perceive our environment. Perception, however, can be a very rich experience; to explain it we need a more complex set of principles.

Quick Quiz 4.1a
Sensing the World Around Us

KNOW...

1 _____ is the study of how physical events relate to psychological perceptions of those events.

- **A** Sensation
- **B** Sensory adaptation
- **C** Perception
- **D** Psychophysics

UNDERSTAND...

2 The minimum stimulation required to detect a stimulus is a(n) _____, whereas the minimum required to detect the difference between two stimuli is a(n) _____.

- **A** just noticeable difference; difference threshold
- **B** absolute threshold; difference threshold
- **C** difference threshold; absolute threshold
- **D** just noticeable difference; absolute threshold

3 Signal detection theory improves on simple thresholds by including the influence of:

- **A** psychological factors, such as expectations.
- **B** engineering factors, such as how well a set of speakers is designed.
- **C** whether an individual has hearing or visual impairments.
- **D** the actual intensity of the stimulus.

APPLY...

4 Walking on a crowded downtown sidewalk, Ben thinks he hears his name called, but when he turns around, he cannot find anyone who might be speaking to him. In terms of signal detection theory, mistakenly believing he heard his name is an example of a _____.

- **A** hit
- **B** miss
- **C** bogus hit
- **D** false alarm

ANALYZE...

5 Is it reasonable to conclude that subliminal messages have a *strong* effect on behavior?

- **A** No, research shows that they have no effect whatsoever.
- **B** No, although research shows they might have mild effects.
- **C** Yes, the research shows that subliminal ads are powerful.
- **D** Conclusions about subliminal messages have not been reached by psychologists.

Answers can be found on page ANS-2.

Perceiving the World Around Us

To perceive figures, our perceptual systems make sense of ambiguity and fill in information where it seems to be missing. Figure 4.5 illustrates this principle well. In this figure, we are compelled to see contours where there are none; our brain fills in a nonexistent square.

The contours are referred to as *subjective* contours because they are not physically "there" (except in your brain). Which principles guide this and other perceptual processes?

{FIG. 4.5} **The Kanizsa Square** Can you see a square? Our perceptual systems fill in contours where there are not any to help us perceive familiar shapes.

GESTALT PRINCIPLES OF PERCEPTION In the mid-20th century, a school of psychology emerged out of Germany based on the work of individuals who sought to describe how we perceive form. *Gestalt psychology* is an approach to perception that emphasizes "the whole is greater than the sum of its parts" (see also Module 1.2). In other words, the individual parts of an image may have little meaning on their own, but when combined the whole takes on a significant, perceived form. Gestalt psychologists identified several key principles to describe how we organize features that we perceive.

One basic Gestalt principle is that objects or "figures" in our environment tend to stand out against a background. Gestalt psychologists refer to this basic perceptual rule as the *figure–ground* principle. The text in front of you is a figure set against a background, but you may also consider the letters you see to be figures against the background of the page. This perceptual tendency is particularly apparent when the distinction between figure and ground is ambiguous, as can be seen in the face–vase illusion in Figure 4.6(a). Do you see a vase or two faces in profile? At the level of sensation, there is neither a vase nor two faces—there is just a pattern. What makes it a perceptual illusion is the recognition that there are

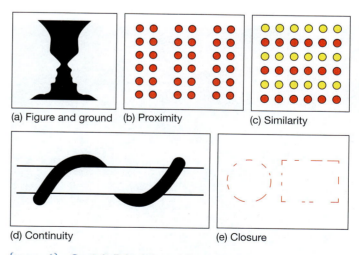

(a) Figure and ground (b) Proximity (c) Similarity

(d) Continuity (e) Closure

{FIG. 4.6} **Gestalt Principles of Form Perception** (a) Figure and ground. (b) Proximity helps us group items together so that we see three columns instead of six rows. (c) Similarity occurs when we perceive the similar dots as forming alternating rows of yellow and red, not as columns of alternating colors. (d) Continuity is the tendency to view items as whole figures even if the image is broken into multiple segments. (e) Closure is the tendency to fill in gaps so as to see a whole object. **Click on this figure in your eText to see more details.**

Animals and insects take advantage of figure–ground ambiguity to camouflage themselves from predators. Can you see the walking stick insect in this photo?

two objects, but there is some ambiguity as to which is figure and which is ground. The figure–ground principle applies to hearing as well. When you are holding a conversation with one individual in a crowded party, you are attending to the figure (the voice of the individual) against the background noise (the ground).

Another set of gestalt principles include *proximity* and *similarity*. We tend to treat two or more objects that are in close proximity to each other as a group. Because of their proximity, a dozen eggs in a carton looks like two rows of six eggs, rather than six rows of two. Similarity can be experienced by viewing the intermixing of sports fans from opposing teams, which typically yields distinct patches of crowd wearing similar clothing. Thus objects are grouped based on similarity of properties such as coloration, shape, and orientation (see Figure 4.6).

Some other key gestalt principles can also be seen in Figure 4.6. *Continuity*, or "good continuation," refers to the perceptual rule that lines and other objects tend to be continuous, rather than abruptly changing direction. The black object snaking its way around the white object is

viewed as a one continuous object rather than two separate ones. A related principle, called *closure*, refers to the tendency to fill in gaps to complete a whole object.

The illusions and figures you have viewed in this section reveal some common principles that guide how we perceive the world. We can take this exploration a step further by discussing the cognitive processes that underlie these principles.

TOP-DOWN AND BOTTOM-UP PROCESSING

Psychologists have identified two different approaches that we take to perceiving the world: top-down and bottom-up.

Sometimes how we perceive a stimulus is based on what we already know. **Top-down processing** *occurs when prior knowledge and expectations guide what is perceived.* For example, the center of Figure 4.7 can be perceived as either the number 13 or the letter B, depending on what you might expect to see—a top-down influence. Similarly, walking into a crowded room to locate a friend is a top-down process because you have a face in mind, and that is how you know what to look for.

At other times, we first perceive the details of a stimulus, and then build up toward a recognizable whole. This is **bottom-up processing**: *constructing a whole stimulus or concept from bits of raw sensory information.* As you might expect, bottom-up processing would occur when you encounter something that is unfamiliar or difficult to recognize. Driving a car in a foreign country for the first time would engage bottom-up processing as you attempt to make sense of what different traffic signals and road signs mean.

These processes can be studied using some interesting stimuli, such as the image in Figure 4.8. When you initially looked at this image, you might have seen either a rat or a man. Unless you are currently surrounded by animals or a lot of people, there was nothing to guide your perception of the image—you were using bottom-up processing. However, when people first look at pictures of animals, they tend to see the rat first; if they first look at pictures of people, the man is first perceived. Thus top-down processes can influence the perception of the image as well. In short, the way we perceive the world is a combination of both top-down and bottom-up processing (Beck & Kastner,

The principle of similarity in action. We perceive groups of sports fans based on the color of their clothing.

A

12   13   14

C

{FIG. 4.7} **Top-Down Processing** Is the center the letter B or the number 13?

{FIG. 4.8} **Expectations Influence Perception** Is this a rat or a man's face? People who look at pictures of animals before seeing this image see a rat, whereas those looking at pictures of faces see the image as a man's face.

2009)—it is difficult to imagine not having some kind of expectation about an experience, and even more difficult to imagine perception without some kind of raw sensation.

Parallel processing refers to the simultaneous use of top-down and bottom-up processing as we perceive and interpret the world (Rumelhart & McClelland, 1986). It is what allows us to attend to multiple features of what we sense. Perceiving the world, whether done from a bottom-up, top-down, or combined direction, requires attending to relevant features.

WORKING THE SCIENTIFIC LITERACY MODEL
Attention and Perception

Attention allows us to focus on a particular stimulus, or even multiple stimuli, depending on the task. In some situations, you use top-down processing and select some particular object or event to attend to, whereas in other situations, you may spread your attention out over multiple stimuli.

What do we know about attention and perception?

Selective attention *involves focusing on one particular event or task*, such as focused studying, driving without distraction, or attentively listening to music or watching a movie. In contrast, **divided attention** *involves paying attention to several stimuli or tasks at once*. Simultaneously playing a video game and holding a conversation, challenging as it may be, involves divided attention. Whether we engage our selective or divided attention systems depends on several factors, including the familiarity

and complexity of the tasks at hand, and our mental energy level. One approach is not necessarily superior to the other. Nevertheless, there are some common misconceptions about multitasking. One is the belief that people can be "good multitaskers" or "bad multitaskers," as though there is a *type* of person when it comes to engaging in divided attention.

How can science explain attention and perception?

Psychologists have adopted some interesting methods for studying how multitasking influences attention and perception. In one study, research participants first reported how often they use different forms of media, including music, television, print media, phone, and computer-based applications (e.g., Internet, word processing) and, importantly, how often they use these media simultaneously. Based on their responses, the participants were labeled as high or low multitaskers. All participants then performed several cognitive tasks that measured their abilities to concentrate, remember, and think. It turns out that participants who were more likely to multitask did *worse* on cognitive tests than those who tended not to multitask. These high multitaskers were easily distracted by irrelevant information and actually performed worse than low multitaskers when it came to switching from one task to another (Ophir et al., 2009). It appears that those who multitask the most are the ones who should do it least.

Additional research has shown that multitasking can result in significantly reduced learning and remembering. In one investigation, university students listened to lists of words they were told they would need to later remember. Half of the students were given a second task to work on simultaneously, while the others gave their full attention to the words. Students who multitasked while attempting to learn the words struggled to remember them compared to students who gave their full attention to listening to the words. Furthermore, students who multitasked during the memory test, but not while originally hearing the words, also remembered fewer words than students who were not distracted (Fernandes & Moscovitch, 2000).

Can we critically evaluate this research?

Does this evidence mean that we should completely isolate ourselves from any possible distraction when working or studying? On the one hand, it certainly suggests that we should at least minimize distracters and the urge to multitask. On the other hand, psychologists have found that the brain is designed to effectively do more than one cognitive task at a time, provided the two tasks can be processed by different brain structures. For example, when participants in one study engaged in one mental task, the left side of the frontal lobe of the brain was active; when a second, very similar task was added, the right frontal lobe became activated, and performance did not suffer (Charron & Koechlin, 2010). Thus the brain is able to multitask up to a point.

Even so, it is important to avoid believing that just because someone *likes* to multitask that the individual is a *good* multitasker. In fact, research shows just the opposite. Also, multitasking while trying to learn new information, such as classroom and textbook material, is not advised.

Why is this relevant?

Perhaps you use several types of media, such as multiple websites and music, while studying. A common belief among students is that they perform better on exams if they listen to music while taking them—the reason being that they listen to music while studying the material, too. The research discussed previously would indicate that multitasking during both learning (studying) and remembering (exam taking) can impair cognitive performance. Unlikely as it may seem, the many professors who forbid the use of headphones while taking exams are looking out for your best interests.

MISSING THE OBVIOUS: INATTENTIONAL BLINDNESS   Missing the obvious can be surprisingly easy—especially if you are focused on just one particular aspect of your environment. **Inattentional blindness** *is a failure to notice clearly visible events or objects because attention is directed elsewhere.* Imagine you are asked to watch a video of students dressed in white T-shirts actively moving around while passing a ball to one another. Your task is to count the number of times the ball is passed. To complicate matters, there are also students in black T-shirts doing the same thing with another ball, but you are instructed to ignore them. This is a top-down task because you are to selectively attend to a single set of events. If this sounds easy—it

is. In an experiment asking participants to do just this, most were able to accurately count the number of passes, give or take a few.

But what if a student wearing a gorilla suit walked through the video, stopped, pounded her chest, and walked off screen? Who could miss that? Surprisingly, about half the participants failed to even notice the gorilla (Simons & Chabris, 1999). You can imagine how shocked the participants were when they watched the film again without selectively attending to one thing and realized they had completely missed the gorilla. Inattentional blindness shows that when we focus on a limited number of features, we might not pay much attention to anything else.

Inattentional blindness accounts for many common phenomena. For example, those who witness auto accidents or criminal behavior may offer faulty or incomplete testimony. This is not necessarily because they failed to remember, but because they did not even notice critical events (Chabris et al., 2011).

Do you think you would fail to notice the student in the gorilla suit at a basketball game (top photo, Simons & Chabris, 1999)? In another study of inattentional blindness, researchers discovered that when participants were focused on running after a confederate at night, only 35% of the subjects noticed a staged fight going on right in their pathway, and during the day only 56% noticed (Chabris et al., 2011).

Quick Quiz 4.1b :: Perceiving the World Around Us

Module Summary

Module 4.1

((•— Listen to the audio file of this module at **MyPsychLab**

Now that you have read this module you should:

KNOW …

- **The key terminology of sensation and perception:**

absolute threshold (p. 116)
bottom-up processing (p. 120)
difference threshold (p. 116)
divided attention (p. 121)
inattentional blindness (p. 122)
perception (p. 115)
psychophysics (p. 116)

selective attention (p. 121)
sensation (p. 115)
sensory adaptation (p. 115)
signal detection theory (p. 117)
top-down processing (p. 120)
transduction (p. 115)

UNDERSTAND …

- **What stimulus thresholds are.** Stimulus thresholds can be either *absolute* (the minimum amount of energy to notice a stimulus) or based on *difference* (the minimum change between stimuli required to notice they are different).

- **The methods of signal detection theory.** Signal detection theory involves testing whether a participant perceives stimuli by measuring hits (stimulus was presented and detected), misses (stimulus was presented and undetected), false alarms (stimulus was not presented and reported as present), and correct rejections (stimulus was not presented and not perceived).

APPLY …

- **Your knowledge of signal detection theory to identify hits, misses, and correct responses in examples.** For practice, consider **Figure 4.4 (p. 118)**, along with this example: Imagine a girl who has seen a scary television program and now, while trying to go to sleep, worries about monsters in the closet. Identify which of the four events (A-D) goes within the correct box; that is, identify it as a hit, a miss, a false alarm, or a correct rejection.

Warning: For half of these events, you may have to assume there really are monsters in the closet. You can check out our answers on page ANS-2.

Hit:	False alarm:
Miss:	Correct rejection:

A. There is no monster in the closet, and the girl is confident that she has not heard anything.

B. There really are monsters in the closet, but the girl has not heard them.

C. There really is a monster in the closet and she hears it.

D. There is no monster in the closet, but the girl insists that she heard something.

ANALYZE …

- **Claims that subliminal advertising can influence your behavior.** As you read in the Myths in Mind feature, we certainly can perceive stimuli below the level of awareness, and this perception can affect our behavior in some ways. As for the often-repeated claim that subliminal advertising can control consumer behavior, it seems safe to conclude that it alone will not cause you to mindlessly part with your money.

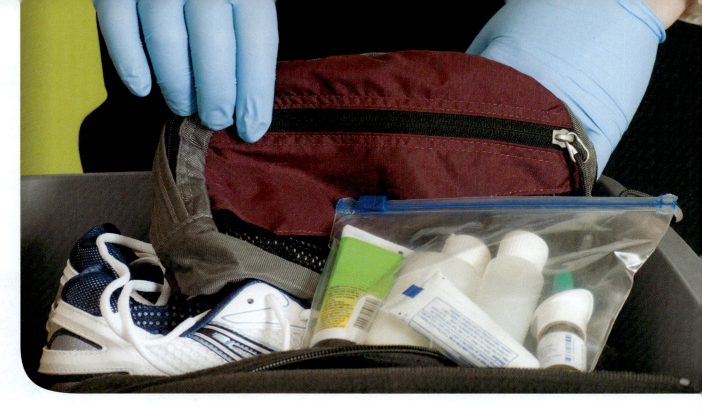

The Visual System

KNOW ...	UNDERSTAND ...	APPLY ...	ANALYZE ...
The key terminology relating to the eye and vision	How visual information travels from the eye through the brain to give us the experience of sight The theories of color vision	Your knowledge to explain how we perceive depth in our visual field	How we perceive objects and faces

In 2008, Gregory Hinkle of West Virginia passed through airport security with a loaded gun, only to return to the security checkpoint and turn it in after realizing the lapse. (He was charged with a misdemeanor.) Amazing as it may sound, these incidents are often accidental—passengers simply forget that they packed a weapon. More importantly, you might wonder how a gun could pass through security screening in the first place. A spokesman for the Transportation Security Authority (TSA) reported that across the United States screeners found an average of two guns each day (CNN, 2008). This tells us how often TSA employees are successful at finding weapons. Another question that is much more difficult to answer is how many undetected weapons make it through security— and why do such lapses happen? TSA employees have the same perceptual systems as the rest of us. Even though they have technology at their disposal and training to enhance detection of certain objects, they are still susceptible to the same types of errors that we all make.

Focus Questions

 How do we recognize and perceive objects?

 Why do errors such as failing to perceive a dangerous object at security checkpoints occur?

· · · · · · · · · · · · · · · · · ·

The world is a visual place to most humans. Traffic signs and road maps, for example, are all visually based. Likewise, museums, restaurant menus, computer screens, and the textbook in front of you were designed to be absorbed through sight. In this module, we explore how vision works—starting out as patterns of light entering the eye, and ending up as a complex, perceptual experience. We

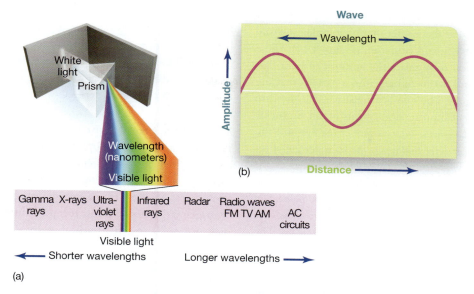

(b)

(a)

{FIG. 4.9} **Light Waves in the Electromagnetic Spectrum** (a) The electromagnetic spectrum: When white light is shined through a prism, the bending of the light reveals the visible light spectrum. The visible spectrum falls within a continuum of other waves of the electromagnetic spectrum. (b) Wavelength is measured by amplitude and distance.

begin with an overview of the basic physical structures of the eye and brain that make vision possible, and then discuss the *experience* of seeing.

The Human Eye

The human eye is one of the most remarkable of the human body's physical structures. It senses an amazing array of information, and then relays it back to the brain for complex, perceptual processing. To ensure that this process occurs correctly, the eye needs specialized structures that allow us to regulate how much light comes in, to start decoding the various colors, and to maintain a focus on the most important objects in a scene.

HOW THE EYE GATHERS LIGHT The term "light" actually refers to radiation that occupies a relatively narrow band of the electromagnetic spectrum, shown in Figure 4.9a. Light travels in waves that vary in terms of two different properties: length and amplitude. The term *wavelength* refers to the distance between peaks of a wave—differences in wavelength correspond to different colors on the electromagnetic spectrum. As you can see from Figure 4.9a, long wavelengths correspond with the reddish colors and short wavelengths with the bluish colors. Also, the *amplitude* (or height; see Figure 4.9b) of the peaks of a wave give different experiences. Low-amplitude waves correspond with dim colors, and high-amplitude waves with bright colors. Some organisms, such as bees, can see in ultraviolet, and some reptiles can sense infrared light. The prism in Figure 4.9a

separates out the basic colors of the spectrum. We do not typically see such pure coloration as depicted in this figure. Rather, what we see is based on a mixture of wavelengths that vary by *hue* (colors of the spectrum), *intensity* (brightness), and *saturation* (colorfulness, or density) (see Figure 4.10).

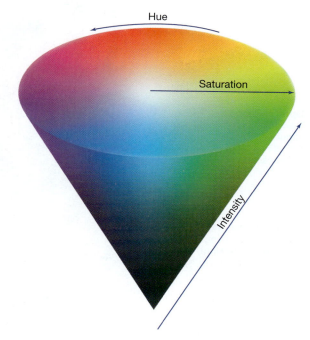

{FIG. 4.10} **Hue, Intensity, and Saturation** Colors vary by hue (color), intensity (brightness), and saturation (colorfulness or "density").

THE STRUCTURE OF THE EYE The eye consists of specialized structures that gather up this complex mixture of light hue, intensity, and saturation (Figure 4.11). These structures function to regulate the amount of light that enters the eye, and organize light into a pattern that the brain can interpret. The eye is a sensitive and delicate structure, so physical protection of this organ is crucial. The **sclera** *is the white, outer surface of the eye* and the **cornea** *is the clear layer that covers the front portion of the eye and also contributes to the eye's ability to focus.* Light enters the eye through the cornea and passes through an opening called the pupil. The **pupil** *regulates the amount of light that enters by changing its size; it dilates to allow more light to enter and constricts to allow less light into the eye.* The

iris *is actually a round muscle that adjusts the size of the pupil; it also gives the eyes their characteristic color.* Behind the pupil is the **lens**, *a clear structure that focuses light onto the back of the eye.* The rear portion of the eye consists of a layer of specialized receptors that convert light into a message that the brain can then interpret.

The Retina: From Light to Nerve Impulse The **retina** *lines the inner surface of the eye and consists of specialized receptors that absorb light and send signals related to the properties of light to the brain.* The specialized receptors of the retina are called *photoreceptors.* Two general types of photoreceptors line the retina—*rods* and *cones*—each of which responds to different

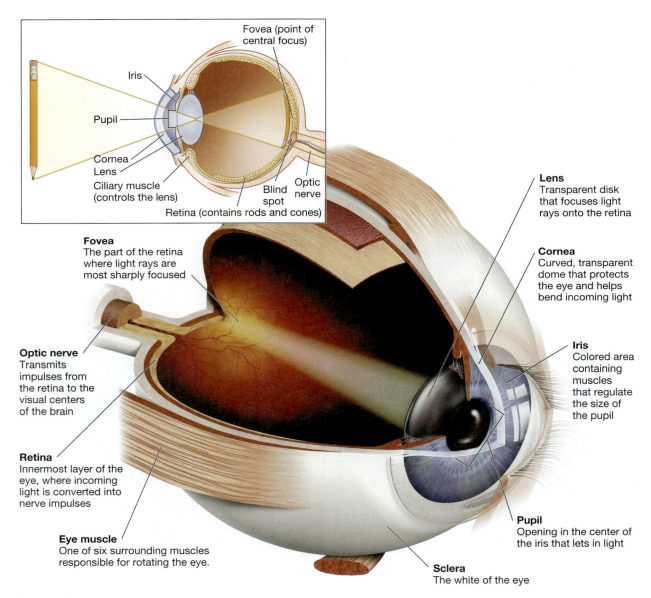

Fovea (point of central focus)

Iris

Pupil

Cornea
Lens

Ciliary muscle
(controls the lens)

Blind spot

Optic nerve

Retina (contains rods and cones)

Fovea
The part of the retina where light rays are most sharply focused

Optic nerve
Transmits impulses from the retina to the visual centers of the brain

Retina
Innermost layer of the eye, where incoming light is converted into nerve impulses

Eye muscle
One of six surrounding muscles responsible for rotating the eye.

Lens
Transparent disk that focuses light rays onto the retina

Cornea
Curved, transparent dome that protects the eye and helps bend incoming light

Iris
Colored area containing muscles that regulate the size of the pupil

Pupil
Opening in the center of the iris that lets in light

Sclera
The white of the eye

{FIG. 4.11} **The Human Eye and Its Structures** Notice how the lens inverts the image that appears on the retina (see inset). The visual centers of the brain correct the inversion.

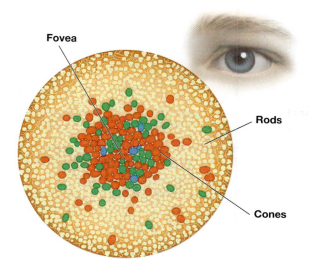

Fovea

Rods

Cones

{FIG. 4.12} **Distribution of Rods and Cones on the Retina** Cones are concentrated at the fovea, the center of the retina, while rods are more abundant in the periphery.

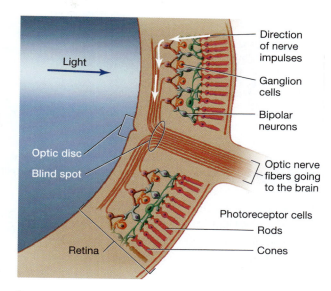

Light

Direction of nerve impulses

Ganglion cells

Bipolar neurons

Optic disc

Blind spot

Optic nerve fibers going to the brain

Photoreceptor cells

Rods

Cones

Retina

{FIG. 4.13} **Arrangement of Photoreceptors in the Retina** Bipolar and ganglion cells collect messages from the light-sensitive photoreceptors and converge on the optic nerve, which then carries the messages to the brain.

characteristics of light. **Cones** *are photoreceptors that are sensitive to the different wavelengths of light that we perceive as color.* The **fovea** *is the central region of the retina that contains the highest concentration of cones;* its functioning explains why objects in our direct line of vision are the clearest and most colorful relative to objects in the periphery. **Rods** *are photoreceptors that occupy peripheral regions of the retina; they are highly sensitive under low light levels.* As we move away from the fovea, the concentration of cones decreases and the concentration of rods increases (see Figure 4.12).

In daylight or under artificial light, the cones in the retina are more active than rods—they help us detect differences in the color of objects and discriminate the fine details of them. In contrast, if the lights suddenly go out or if you enter a dark room, at first you see next to nothing. Over time, however, you gradually begin to see your surroundings more clearly. **Dark adaptation** *is the process by which the rods and cones become increasingly sensitive to light under low levels of illumination.* This process explains why we can gradually see more objects at very low light levels. The complete process of dark adaptation typically takes approximately 20 minutes, although most of the changes occur within the first 10 minutes of darkness. We do not see color at night or in darkness because rods do not detect color—rods are more active under low light levels than cones.

The Optic Nerve Light stimulates chemical reactions in the rods and cones, and these reactions initiate neural signals that pass through an intricate network of cells in the retina, which in turn send impulses to the brain. The

initial steps of the visual pathway are shown in Figure 4.13. Each eye has an **optic nerve**, *a cluster of neurons that gather sensory information, exit at the back of the eye, and connect with the brain.* This nerve presents a challenge to the brain. Because it travels through the back of the eye, it creates an area on the retina with no rods or cones, called the optic disc. The result is a *blind spot*—a space in the retina that lacks photoreceptors. Discover your own blind spot by performing the activity described in Figure 4.14.

The blind spot illustrates just how distinct the processes of sensation and perception are. Why do we fail to notice a completely blank area of our visual field? If we consider only the process of sensation, we cannot answer this question. We have to invoke perception: The visual areas

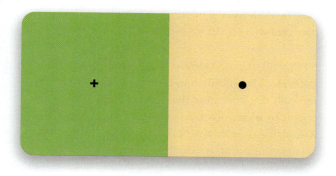

+   •

{FIG. 4.14} **Finding Your Blind Spot** To find your blind spot, close your left eye and, with your right eye, fix your gaze on the + in the green square. Slowly move the page toward you. When the page is approximately 6 inches away, you will notice that the black dot on the right disappears because of your blind spot. Not only does the black dot disappear, but its vacancy is replaced by yellow: The brain "fills it in" for you.

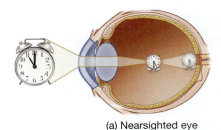

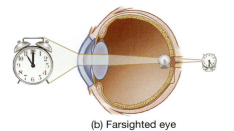

(a) Nearsighted eye

(b) Farsighted eye

{FIG. 4.15} **Near-Sightedness and Far-Sightedness** Near-sightedness and far-sightedness result from misshapen eyes. If the eye is elongated, or too short, images are not centered on the retina. **Click on this figure in your eText to see more details**.

of the brain are able to "fill in" the missing information for us (Ramachandran & Gregory, 1991). Not only does the brain fill in the missing information, but it does so in context. Thus, once the black dot at the right of Figure 4.14 reaches the blind spot, the brain automatically fills in the vacancy with yellow.

Common Vision Disorders The delicate and highly sensitive structures of the eye are prone to various problems that can impair vision. Some of the most common conditions affect the ability to focus—a task performed by the cornea and lens, which are responsible for focusing images on the retina. Some common visual impairments result from changes in eye shape. *Nearsightedness* occurs when the eyeball is slightly elongated, causing the image that the cornea and lens focus on to fall short of the retina (see Figure 4.15). People who are nearsighted can see objects that are relatively close up but have difficulty focusing on distant objects. Alternatively, if the length of the eye is shorter than normal from front to back, the result is *farsightedness*. In this case, the image is focused *behind* the retina (Figure 4.15). Farsighted people can see distant objects clearly but not those that are close by. Both types of impairments can be corrected with contact lenses or glasses.

THE VISUAL PATHWAYS TO THE BRAIN The information contained in the cells that constitute the optic nerve travels to numerous areas of the brain. The first major destination is the *optic chiasm,* the point at which the optic nerves cross at the midline of the brain (see Figure 4.16). For each optic nerve, about half of the nerve fibers travel to the same side of the brain, and half of them travel to the opposite side. Fibers from the optic nerves first connect with the visual area of the thalamus

at a region called the *lateral geniculate nucleus (LGN)*. The LGN then sends messages to the visual cortex, located in the occipital lobe, where the complex processes of visual perception begin (Figure 4.16).

How does the visual cortex make sense of all this incoming information? It starts with a division of labor among specialized cells. One set of cells in the visual cortex are referred to as *feature detection cells*; they respond selectively to simple and specific aspects of a stimulus, such as angles and edges (Hubel & Wiesel, 1962). Researchers have been able to map which feature detection cells respond to specific aspects of an image by investigating the visual cortex in lab animals

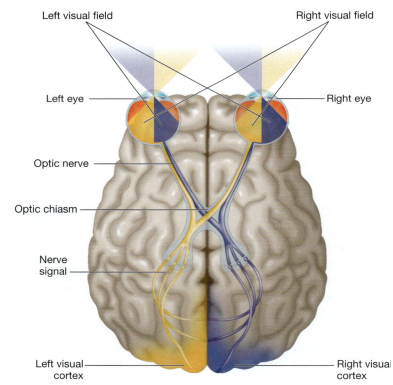

{FIG. 4.16} **Pathways of the Visual System in the Brain** The optic nerves route messages to the visual cortex. At the optic chiasm, some of the cells remain on the same side and some cross to the opposite side of the brain. This organization results in images appearing in the left visual field being processed on the right side of the brain, and images appearing in the right visual field being processed on the left side of the brain. **Click on this figure in your eText to see more details**.

PsychTutor
Click here in your eText for an interactive tutorial on **Feature Detectors**

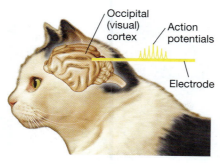

Occipital (visual) cortex

Action potentials

Electrode

The Visual Experience

Our visual experiences are not limited to the lines of various angles and orientations that stimulate feature detection cells. Instead, they are rich, meaningful experiences that arise from higher brain centers of the cerebral cortex. Here we discover how we recognize and experience whole objects such as people, cars, houses, and your pet dog or cat.

{FIG. 4.17} **Measuring the Activity of Feature Detection Cells** Scientists can measure the activity of individual feature detector cells by inserting a microscopic electrode into the visual cortex of an animal. The activity level will peak when the animal is shown the specific feature corresponding to that specific cell.

(Figure 4.17). Feature detection cells of the visual cortex are thought to be where visual input is organized for perception, but further processing is required as well and involves additional neural pathways. From the visual cortex, information about shapes and contours is sent to other cortical areas. For example, the *ventral stream* is a pathway extending from the visual cortex to the temporal lobe and is where object recognition occurs. The *dorsal stream* extends from the visual cortex to the parietal lobe of the cortex and is where depth and motion are perceived.

Quick Quiz 4.2a
The Human Eye

KNOW …

1 Cones are predominantly gathered in a central part of the retina known as the _____.

  A fovea   **C** blind spot

  B photoreceptor   **D** optic chiasm

2 The _____ in the thalamus is where the optic nerves from the left and right eyes converge.

  A fovea   **C** lateral geniculate nucleus

  B optic chiasm   **D** retina

UNDERSTAND …

3 A familiar person walks into the room. Which of the following choices places the structures in the appropriate sequence required to recognize the individual?

  A Optic chiasm, visual cortex, photoreceptors, optic nerve

  B Visual cortex, optic chiasm, photoreceptors, optic nerve

  C Photoreceptors, optic nerve, optic chiasm, visual cortex

  D Photoreceptors, optic chiasm, optic nerve, visual cortex

Answers can be found on page ANS-2.

WORKING THE SCIENTIFIC LITERACY MODEL
Object Recognition

Objects in our world can be seen from many different perspectives—that is, they can be seen from near or far, under varying levels of light, and from different angles. Given the numerous variations in how objects can be sensed, how is it that we still perceive them in the same, unified way?

What do we know about object recognition?

Despite the diverse ways that an object can be sensed, it is still perceived as the same object. This observation highlights what is called **perceptual constancy**, *the ability to perceive objects as having constant shape, size, and color despite changes in perspective*. What makes perceptual constancy possible is our ability to make relative judgments about shape, size, and lightness. For *shape constancy*, we judge the angle of the object relative to our position (see Figure 4.18 on p. 130). *Color constancy* allows us to recognize an object's color under varying levels of illumination. For example, a bright red car is recognized as bright red when in the shade or in full sunlight. *Size constancy* is based on judgments of how close an object is relative to one's position as well as to the positions of other objects. Also, our perception of objects involves distinguishing them individually, and identifying objects that appear frequently or rarely. As it turns out, the process of identifying objects can be much more complicated than just seeing and naming them.

How can science explain how object recognition occurs?

Psychologists who specialize in visual perception have attempted to identify conditions in which we are likely to succeed or fail to detect objects. It

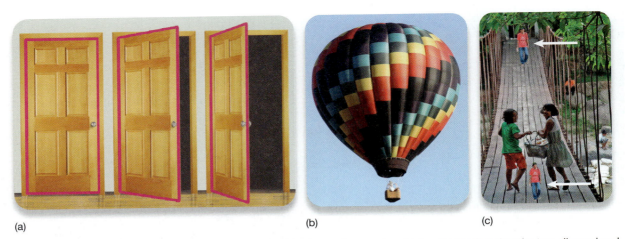

(a)   (b)   (c)

{FIG. 4.18} **Perceptual Constancies** (a) We perceive the door to be a rectangle despite the fact that the two-dimensional outline of the image on the retina is not always rectangular. (b) Color constancy: We perceive colors to be constant despite changing levels of illumination. (c) Size constancy: the person in the red shirt appears normal in size when in the background. A replica of this individual placed in the foreground appears unusually small because of size constancy.

turns out that the frequency with which we encounter objects is closely related to our perception of them.

To see how this works, view the stimulus in Figure 4.19. Scattered around the dark background are offset Ls. One of the objects, however, is actually a T. It is easy to spot and only takes a second or so to locate. Using this type of display, the experimenters flashed a mixture of Ls repeatedly, each time varying their locations. From time to time, the Ts appeared at a random location among the Ls and participants had to determine if any Ts were visible: The Ts appeared either 50% of the time for some participants, or 2% of the time for others. Those participants who were exposed to the Ts 2% of the time failed to detect them far more often than people who could have seen them 50% of the time (Rich et al., 2008).

Ts and offset Ls are great for laboratory experiments, but consider how this finding may apply to real-life

situations, such as at airline security checkpoints. Wolfe and colleagues (2007) obtained photos of screen shots from the U.S. Department of Homeland Security that included luggage with typical travel objects, as well as luggage that included knives and guns. Participants were familiarized with what clothing, sunglasses, keys, and toys, as well as guns and knives, looked like on a security-screening device.

Similar to the experiment with Ls with the occasional T mixed in, the participants often failed to detect guns or knives if they occurred only 2% of the time, compared to 50% of the time (Wolfe et al., 2007). The rare event of a weapon in a suitcase makes these objects less likely to be perceived. Furthermore, little improvement in detecting infrequently placed weapons was noted when participants worked in teams. In summary, when something does not occur very often, you will have more difficulty spotting it.

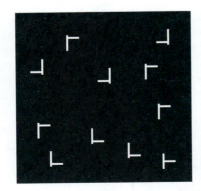

{FIG. 4.19} **Find the T Among this Scattered Array of Offset Ls** It should not take you long to find the T. If you were repeatedly asked to find the T yet it was mixed with the Ls only 2% of the time, however, you would likely miss it quite often.

Can we critically evaluate this evidence?

You might think that knives and guns would be even *more* noticeable when they appear among common objects such as clothing, hairdryers, and magazines. Sometimes the very reason we perceive objects is because they stick out like a sore thumb. This idea may have occurred to you when reading about the research we just described. However, the key issue here is that the more frequent an event is (e.g., a safe suitcase), the less likely an infrequent event (a weapon) will be detected.

Despite the similar findings of these two studies, we might still wonder about the generalizability of this research. In particular, we might question whether volunteers in the studies put forth as much effort as TSA baggage screeners, who have much more at stake.

Why is this relevant?

Clearly, this research has applications beyond our own everyday experiences, although it is certainly still insightful on a personal level. You may be wondering whether people can be trained to overcome the tendency to miss out on infrequent events such as a knife or a gun in a suitcase. It turns out that monitoring and feedback under conditions in which weapons are found frequently improves people's ability to detect these events when they are infrequent (Wolfe et al., 2007). Another important application of this work is in interpretation of medical diagnostic imaging results, such as X-rays and MRIs. If the findings from these studies apply to medical settings, then we might expect that less frequent events such as tumors or other problematic symptoms would be less likely to be detected by a radiologist.

World-renowned chimpanzee researcher Jane Goodall has face blindness (prosopagnosia). Her sister also has it—there appear to be genetic links to the condition. Despite being face-blind, Dr. Goodall and others with this condition use nonfacial characteristics to recognize people, or, in her case, hundreds of individual chimpanzees (Goodall, 1999).

FACIAL RECOGNITION AND PERCEPTION   One of the most important sources of social information comes from the human face—which explains why we have a natural inclination to quickly perceive faces. In fact, there is a region of the brain, located in the lower part of the temporal lobe, that is specialized for facial recognition. Specific genetic problems or damage to this area can result in failure to recognize people's faces (a condition called *prosopagnosia*, or face blindness). People with face blindness are able to recognize voices and other defining features of individuals, but not faces. Some people with face blindness can find ways to compensate for the condition, such as developing heightened abilities to use voice recognition and other nonfacial cues for recognizing individuals (Hoover et al., 2010).

Face blindness also raises interesting questions about when perception and recognition occur. Although they cannot recognize faces consciously, people who are face blind may still exhibit physiological reactions to pictures of family members, but not control-group pictures of unfamiliar faces (Tranel & Damasio, 1985). In addition, people with face blindness can make judgments about famous faces more readily than about unfamiliar faces (Avidan & Behrmann, 2008). These studies suggest that people with face blindness are able to distinguish among faces even if they are unaware that they are doing so. Although this is a rare clinical condition, it does help us understand some basic processes that are involved in perceiving faces. In the absence of this condition, the human brain seemingly insists on seeing faces, even when they are least expected (see Figure 4.20 on p. 132).

Normal perception of faces starts with the very basics. For example, our brain has the reasonable expectation that faces will appear upright. When a face is presented upside down, our ability to recognize the face and facial expressions diminishes. In one experiment, participants correctly recognized different faces 81% of the time when viewed upright, but the level of accuracy fell to 55% when the same faces were inverted (Freire et al., 2000). Also, we are especially attentive to the eyes and mouth when looking at faces. Look at the familiar face in Figure 4.21 (p. 132). These photos are upside down for a reason. As you rotate the page to see the faces upright, you will notice that it becomes increasingly difficult to view one of the pictures as an accurate depiction of the individual. This effect occurs because

{FIG. 4.20} **Seeing Faces** At left is a painting of turnips and other vegetables by the Italian artist Giuseppe Arcimboldo. The image at right is the same image rotated 180 degrees—does it resemble a human face?

Binocular depth cues *are distance cues that are based on the differing perspectives of both eyes.* One type of binocular depth cue, called **convergence**, *occurs when the eye muscles contract so that both eyes focus on a single object.* The sensations that occur as these muscles contract to focus on a single object create the perception of depth. Convergence typically occurs for objects that are relatively close to you. For example, as you track an object that is moving toward you, such as your fingertip toward your nose, your eyes move inward.

One reason why we humans have such a fine-tuned ability to see in three dimensions is that both of our eyes face forward. This arrangement means that we perceive objects from slightly different angles, which in turn enhances depth perception. For example, choose an object in front of you, such as an extended finger, and focus on that object with one eye while keeping the other eye closed. Then open your other eye to look at the object (and close the eye you were just using). You will notice that the position of your finger or object appears to change. This effect demonstrates **retinal disparity** (also called binocular disparity), *the difference in relative position of an object as seen by both eyes, which provides information to the brain about depth.* Your brain relies on cues from each eye individually and from both eyes working in concert—that is, in stereo. Most primates, including humans, have *stereoscopic vision,* which results from overlapping visual fields.

we rely on the unique characteristics of the eyes and mouth most when we recognize a familiar face.

Although objects and faces monopolize our visual experiences, we must also determine where they are in location to ourselves. Without this ability, we would not know how far to reach for an object, nor would we know how to navigate our environment.

DEPTH PERCEPTION   Every image that hits your retina is two-dimensional, so we know that depth perception occurs in your brain. The words on this page, for example, lie on a flat, two-dimensional surface—but look away from your text into a richer environment, and you will experience depth.

Monocular cues *are depth cues that we can perceive with only one eye.* One such cue, called *accommodation,* takes place when the lens of your eye curves to allow you to focus on nearby objects. Close one eye and focus on a nearby object, and then slightly change your focus to an object that is farther away; the lens changes shape again so the next object comes into focus (see Figure 4.22a). *Motion parallax* is another monocular depth cue; it is used when you or your surroundings are in motion. For example, as you sit in a moving vehicle and look out of the passenger

{FIG. 4.21}   **The Face Inversion Effect** After viewing both upside-down faces, you probably noticed a difference between the two pictures. Now turn your book upside-down and notice how the distortion of one of the faces is amplified when viewed from this perspective.

The parakeet on the left, lacking stereoscopic vision, must turn its head to the side to view images directly. In contrast, owls have stereoscopic vision, as indicated by their forward-facing eyes. This gives owls superior depth perception—not to mention outstanding predatory skills.

PSYCH @
The Artist's Studio

Painters are able to create a sense of depth by using a variety of monocular depth cues called *pictorial depth cues*. This can be a very challenging task when working with a two-dimensional surface. So what are some strategies that artists use?

To understand how artists work, view the painting by Gustave Caillebottein shown in Figure 4.23 (p. 134). In this painting, you will notice that the artist used numerous cues to depict depth:

- *Linear perspective*: Parallel lines stretching to the horizon appear to move closer together as they travel farther away. This effect can be seen in the narrowing of the streets and the converging lines of the sidewalks and top of the building in the distance.
- *Interposition*: Nearby objects block our view of far-off objects, such as the umbrellas blocking the view of buildings behind them.
- *Light and shadow*: The shadow cast by an object allows us to detect both the size of the object and the relative locations of objects. In addition, closer objects reflect more light than far-away objects.
- *Texture gradient*: Objects that are coarse and distinct at close range become fine and grainy at greater distances.

window, you will notice objects closer to you, such as the roadside, parked cars, and nearby buildings, appear to move rapidly in the opposite direction of your travel. By comparison, far-off objects such as foothills and mountains in the distance appear to move much more slowly, and in the same direction as your vehicle. The disparity in the directions traveled by near and far-off objects provides a monocular cue about depth.

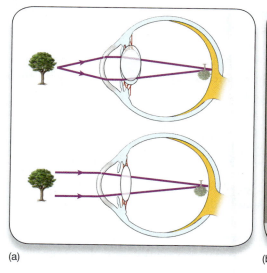

(a) (b) Observer movement

{FIG. 4.22} **Two Monocular Depth Cues** (a) Accommodation. From the top left image light comes from a distant object, and the lens focuses the light on the retina. From the bottom left image the lens changes shape to *accommodate* the light when the same object is moved closer. (b) Motion parallax. Looking out the train window, objects close to you race past quickly and in the opposite direction that you are headed. At the same time, distant objects appear to move slowly and in the same direction that you are traveling.

{FIG. 4.23} **Pictorial Depth Cues** Artists make use of cues such as linear perspective, texture gradient, relative size, and others to create the sense of depth.

In the painting, for example, the texture of the brick street varies from clear to blurred as distance increases.

● *Height in plane*: Objects that are higher in our visual field are perceived as farther away than objects low in our visual field. The base of the main building in the background of the painting is at about the same level as the man's shoulder, but we interpret this effect as distance, not as height.

● *Relative size*: If two objects in an image are known to be of the same actual size, the larger of the two must be closer. This can be seen in the various sizes of the pedestrians.

After identifying these depth cues in the painting in Figure 4.23, it should be clear that non-artists can also

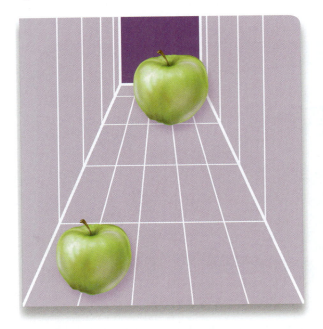

{FIG. 4.24} **The Corridor Illusion** Linear perspective and height in plane create the perception of depth here. The result is that the object at the "back" of the drawing appears to be larger than the one in the foreground; in reality, they are identical in size.

recognize them. Actually, nonhumans can, too. Baboons can detect what is called the corridor illusion (see Figure 4.24), which includes the depth cues of linear perspective and height in plane (Barbet & Fagot, 2007).

. . . .

Monocular and binocular depth cues combine to give us very detailed depth perception. Each individual eye can adjust so that depth can be perceived, and the eyes working together create even a greater sense of depth. In addition to depth, our visual experiences are greatly enriched by our ability to see color.

COLOR PERCEPTION Our experience of color is based on how our visual system *perceives* different wavelengths on the electromagnetic spectrum (refer back to Figure 4.9). Color is not actually a characteristic of objects themselves, but rather an interpretation of these wavelengths by the visual system. As you learned earlier, the cones of the retina are specialized for responding to different wavelengths of light that correspond to different colors. However, the experience of color occurs in the brain. Exactly how this system works has been a long source of scientific debate.

One theory suggests that three different types of cones exist, each of which is sensitive to different wavelengths on the electromagnetic spectrum. These three types of cones were initially identified in the 18th century by physicist Thomas Young and again in the 19th century by scientist Hermann von Helmholtz. The relative responses of the three types of cones allow us to perceive many different colors on the spectrum (see Figure 4.25). For example, yellow is perceived by combining the stimulation of red- and green-sensitive cones, whereas light that stimulates all three cones equally is perceived as white. The **trichromatic theory** (or **Young–Helmholtz theory**) *maintains that color vision is determined by three different cone types that are sensitive to short, medium, and long wavelengths of light*. Modern technology has been used to measure the amount of light that can be absorbed in cones and confirmed that each type responds to different wavelengths.

Not all color experiences can be explained by the trichromatic theory. Stare at the image in Figure 4.26 for about a minute and then look toward a white background. After switching your gaze to a white background, you will see the colors of red, white, and blue, which are the opponent colors of green, black, and yellow. This *negative afterimage* is so named because you see one color after another color is removed. This demonstration suggests that we see color in terms of opposites, rather than combinations of activity by different cones in the retina as described by the trichromatic theory.

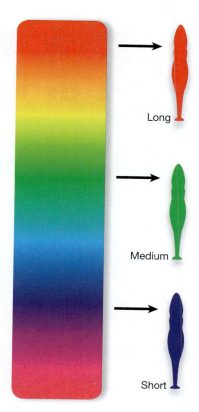

{FIG. 4.25} **The Trichromatic Theory of Color Vision** According to this theory, humans have three types of cones that respond maximally to different regions of the color spectrum. Color is experienced by the combined activity of cones sensitive to short, medium, and long wavelengths.

In the 19th century, Ewald Hering proposed the **opponent-process theory**, *which states that we perceive color in terms of opposite ends of the spectrum: red to green, yellow to blue, and white to black.* The experience of color takes place because of activity within specialized neurons that transmit messages via the optic nerve to the brain. A cell that is stimulated by red is inhibited by green, for example,

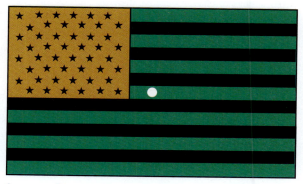

{FIG. 4.26} **The Negative Afterimage: Experiencing Opponent-Process Theory** Stare directly at the white dot within the flag above and avoid looking away. After about a minute, immediately shift your focus to a white background. What do you see?

whereas a cell stimulated by blue inhibits yellow. These cells are responsible for either exciting or inhibiting cells that are responsive to different wavelengths.

The workings of the trichromatic theory concern different types of cone photoreceptors, while the opponent-process theory focuses on the existence of specialized nerve cells for perceiving color. Both the trichromatic and opponent-process theories are correct—and both are required to explain how we see color.

Quick Quiz 4.2b
The Visual Experience

KNOW …

1 Also called face-blindness, which of the following conditions is the inability to recognize faces?

  (A) Prosopaganosia (C) Trichromatism
  (B) Farsightedness (D) Astigmatism

2 Which of the following conditions occur when the eye becomes elongated, causing the image to fall short of the retina?

  (A) Prosopaganosia (C) Farsightedness
  (B) Motion parallax (D) Nearsightedness

UNDERSTAND …

3 Light waves from a blue shirt stimulate different photoreceptors than light waves coming from a red shirt. The fact that we see these shirts as two different colors can be explained by _____.

  (A) trichromatic theory
  (B) hyperopia
  (C) opponent process theory
  (D) motion parallax

APPLY …

4 Michelle looks out of the train window and judges that one cactus is farther away than another because it appears to be moving more slowly. Michelle is relying on _____ to make this judgment.

  (A) binocular cues (C) texture gradient
  (B) motion parallax (D) trichromatic theory

ANALYZE …

5 Some people claim to be unable to perceive faces, yet scientists think that they may be able to do so unconsciously. What is the evidence for this?

  (A) Individuals with face blindness can guess the names that go with faces from pictures without knowing why.
  (B) Individuals with face blindness recognize faces but believe they are imposters.
  (C) Individuals with face blindness have physiological responses to familiar faces that they do not have for strangers.
  (D) When asked to make up names for faces, individuals with face blindness are often correct.

Answers can be found on page ANS-2.

Module Summary

Now that you have read this module you should:

KNOW ...

- **The key terminology relating to the eye and vision:**

binocular depth cues (p. 132)
cones (p. 127)
convergence (p. 132)
cornea (p. 126)
dark adaptation (p. 127)
fovea (p. 127)
iris (p. 126)
lens (p. 126)
monocular cues (p. 132)

opponent-process theory (p. 135)
optic nerve (p. 127)
perceptual constancy (p. 129)
pupil (p. 126)
retina (p. 126)
retinal disparity (p. 132)
rods (p. 127)
sclera (p. 126)
trichromatic theory (p. 134)

UNDERSTAND ...

- **How visual information travels from the eye through the brain to give us the experience of sight.** Light is transformed into a neural signal by photoreceptors in the retina. This information is then relayed via the optic nerve through the thalamus and then to the occipital lobe of the cortex. From this location in the brain, neural circuits travel to other regions for specific levels of processing, such as to the temporal lobe, where object recognition occurs.

- **The theories of color vision.** The two theories reviewed in this module are the trichromatic and opponent-process theories. According to trichromatic theory, the retina contains three different types of light-sensitive cones. Color is experienced as the net combined stimulation of these receptors. The trichromatic theory is not supported by phenomena such as the negative afterimage. Opponent-process theory, which emphasizes how color perception is based on excitation and inhibition of opposing colors (e.g., red–green, blue–yellow, white–black), explains negative afterimages. Taken together, both theories help explain how we perceive color.

APPLY ...

- **Your knowledge to explain how we perceive depth in our visual field.** For practice, take a look at the accompanying photo. Can you identify at least four monocular depth cues that are present in the image below? Check out our answers on p. ANS-2.

ANALYZE ...

- **How we perceive objects and faces.** These tasks are accomplished by specialized perceptual regions of the temporal lobe. Perceptual constancies allow us to recognize objects even though their shape, size, and color may appear to change because their orientation, distance, and lightness in relation to us are not always the same. Facial recognition is a distinct perceptual process, which is supported by evidence from people who are face blind but are otherwise successful at recognizing objects.

The Auditory System

KNOW ...	UNDERSTAND ...	APPLY ...	ANALYZE ...
The key terminology relating to the ear and hearing	Different characteristics of sound and how they correspond to perception How technology is used to restore hearing	Your knowledge of sound localization	The assumption that deafness is something people are motivated to "overcome"

What would the soundtrack to your life sound like? Although each of us has our own musical preferences, some songs have the power to evoke similar emotions in large groups. Stadiums pump out songs that unite and energize fans; DJs at school dances or clubs select songs that fit the themes of friendship, love, and relationships; and even in the workplace certain types of music can harmonize people focusing on a common goal. Daniel Levitin, a psychologist and musician, believes that we are hardwired not just to hear music, but to *feel* a significant emotional connection to it. Each of our lives' soundtracks would probably be different, but Dr. Levitin argues that human identity has music at its core, and that common themes in music include love, friendship, knowledge, religion, relationships, and joy (Levitin, 2008). Music is perceived both at a basic level of sound and at a much deeper emotional level.

Focus Questions

1. How does the auditory system sense and perceive something complex like music?

2. How might the ability to hear be lost?

· · · · · · · · · · · · · · · · · ·

In this module we will explore characteristics of sound, the physical structures that support the sensation of sound, and the pathways involved in its perceptual processing. In addition, we will consider how hearing can become impaired and what can be done in case of such a disability, and discuss some issues associated with deafness.

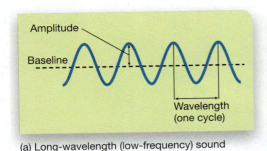

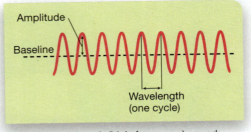

(a) Long-wavelength (low-frequency) sound

(b) Short-wavelength (high-frequency) sound

{FIG. 4.27}   **Characteristics of Sound: Frequency and Amplitude** The frequency of a sound wave (cycles per second) is associated with pitch, while amplitude (the height of the sound wave) is associated with loudness.

Sound and the Structures of the Ear

The function of the ear is to gather sound waves, and the function of *hearing* is to inform you about the nature of the sound source, such as someone calling your name, the phone, an alarm, or a vehicle coming toward you. How do people gain so much information from invisible waves that travel through the air?

SOUND The function of that remarkably sensitive and delicate device, the human ear, is to detect *sound waves*—which are simply changes in mechanical pressure transmitted through solids, liquids, or gases. Sound waves have two important characteristics: frequency and amplitude (see Figure 4.27). *Frequency* refers to wavelength and is measured in hertz (Hz), the number of cycles a sound wave travels per second. **Pitch** *is the perceptual experience of sound wave frequencies.* High-frequency sounds,

such as tires screeching on the road, have short wavelengths and a high pitch. Low-frequency sounds, such as those produced by a bass guitar, have long wavelengths and a low pitch. The *amplitude* of a sound wave determines its loudness: High-amplitude sound waves are louder than low-amplitude waves. To put it simply, our ears are specialized structures for gathering information about the frequency and amplitude of sound waves.

Humans are able to detect sounds in the frequency range from 20 Hz to 20,000 Hz. Figure 4.28 compares the hearing ranges of several different species. Look closely at the scale of the figure—the differences are of a much greater magnitude than could possibly fit on this page using a standard scale. The comparisons show that mice, for example, can hear frequencies close to five times greater than humans.

Loudness—a function of sound wave amplitude—is typically expressed in units called decibels (dB). Table 4.2 compares decibel levels ranging from nearly inaudible to injury inducing.

THE HUMAN EAR The human ear is divided into outer, middle, and inner regions (see Figure 4.29).

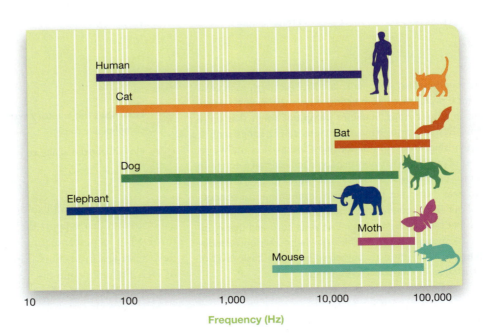

{FIG. 4.28}   **A Comparison of Hearing Ranges in Different Species**

Table 4.2 :: Decibel Levels for Some Familiar Sounds

SOUND	NOISE LEVEL (DB)	EFFECT
Jet engines (near)	140	We begin to feel pain at about 125 dB
Rock concerts (varies)	110–140	
Thunderclap (near)	120	Regular exposure to sound over 100 dB for more than one minute risks permanent hearing loss
Power saw (chainsaw)	110	
Garbage truck/Cement mixer	100	No more than 15 minutes of unprotected exposure is recommended for sounds between 90 and 100 dB
Motorcycle (25 ft)	88	85 dB is the level at which hearing damage (after eight hours) begins
Lawn mower	85–90	
Average city traffic	80	Annoying; interferes with conversation; constant exposure may cause damage
Vacuum cleaner	70	Intrusive; interferes with telephone conversation
Normal conversation	50–65	Comfortable hearing levels are under 60 dB
Whisper	30	Very quiet
Rustling leaves	20	Just audible

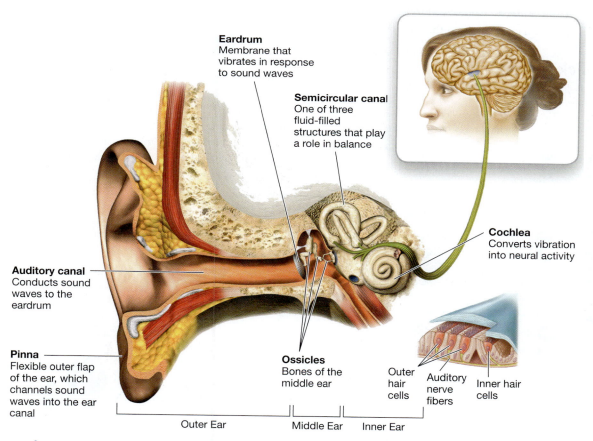

Eardrum Membrane that vibrates in response to sound waves

Semicircular canal One of three fluid-filled structures that play a role in balance

Cochlea Converts vibration into neural activity

Auditory canal Conducts sound waves to the eardrum

Pinna Flexible outer flap of the ear, which channels sound waves into the ear canal

Ossicles Bones of the middle ear

Outer hair cells

Auditory nerve fibers

Inner hair cells

Outer Ear   Middle Ear   Inner Ear

{FIG. 4.29}   **The Human Ear**   Sound waves travel from the outer ear to the eardrum and middle ear, and then through the inner ear. The cochlea of the inner ear is the site at which transduction takes place through movement of the tiny hair cells lining the basilar membrane. The auditory cortex of the brain is a primary brain region where sound is perceived. **Click on this figure in your eText to see more details.**

Explore the **Concept** Virtual Brain: Mechanisms of Perception at **MyPsychLab**

The most noticeable part of your ear is the *pinna*, the outer region that helps channel sound waves to the ear and allows you to determine the source or location of a sound. The *auditory canal* extends from the pinna to the eardrum. Sound waves reaching the eardrum cause it to vibrate. Even very minute sounds, such as a faint whisper, produce vibrations of the eardrum. The middle ear consists of three tiny moveable bones, called *ossicles* (known individually as the hammer, anvil, and stirrup). The eardrum is attached to these bones, so any movement of the eardrum due to sound vibrations results in movement of the ossicles.

The ossicles attach to an inner ear structure called the **cochlea**—*a fluid-filled membrane that is coiled in a snail-like shape and contains the structures that convert sound into neural impulses.* Converting sound vibrations to neural impulses is possible because of hair-like projections that line the basilar membrane of the cochlea. The pressing and pulling action of the ossicles causes the fluid within the cochlea to move, displacing these tiny hair cells. When hair cells move, they stimulate the cells that comprise the auditory nerves. The auditory nerves are composed of bundles of neurons that fire as a result of hair cell movements. These auditory nerves in turn send signals to the auditory cortex, located within the temporal lobe.

Quick Quiz 4.3a
Sound and Structures of the Ear

KNOW …

1 The _____ is the quality of sound waves that is associated with changes in pitch.

  A frequency   C pinna
  B amplitude   D decibel

2 The _____ is a snail-shaped, fluid-filled organ that converts sound waves into a neural signal.

  A ossicle   C cochlea
  B pinna   D outer ear

3 The amplitude of a sound wave determines its loudness; _____-amplitude sound waves are louder than _____-amplitude waves.

  A low; high   C wide; narrow
  B short; tall   D high; low

Answers can be found on page ANS-2.

The Perception of Sound

It is quite remarkable that we are able to determine what makes a sound and where the sound comes from by simply registering and processing sound waves. In this section we examine how the auditory system accomplishes these two tasks, starting with the ability to locate a sound in the environment. ✳

SOUND LOCALIZATION: FINDING THE SOURCE Accurately identifying and orienting oneself toward a sound source has some obvious adaptive benefits. In nature, failure to do so could result in an animal becoming someone's dinner; in human terms, it could result in a comparable disaster. **Sound localization**, *the process of identifying where sound comes from,* is handled by a midbrain structure called the *inferior colliculus.*

There are two ways that we localize sound. First, we take advantage of the slight time difference between a sound hitting both ears to estimate the direction of the source. If your friend shouts your name from your left side, the left ear gets the information just a fraction of a second before the right ear. Second, we localize sound by using differences in the intensity in which sound is heard by both ears—a phenomenon known as a *sound shadow* (Figure 4.30). If the source of the sound is to your left, the left ear will experience the sound more intensely than the right because the right ear will be in the sound shadow. The inferior colliculi (plural) detect differences in the times when sound reaches the left versus the right ear, as well as the intensity of the sound between one side and the other, allowing us to identify where it is coming from.

THEORIES OF PITCH PERCEPTION To explain how we perceive pitch, we will begin in the cochlea and work toward brain centers that are specialized for hearing. How does the cochlea pave the way for pitch perception? One explanation has to do how hair cells are arranged along the basilar membrane. Not all hair cells along the basilar

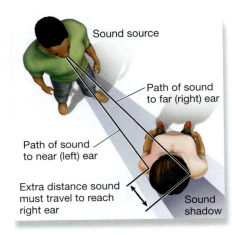

Sound source

Path of sound to far (right) ear

Path of sound to near (left) ear

Extra distance sound must travel to reach right ear

Sound shadow

{FIG. 4.30} **How We Localize Sound** To localize sound, the brain computes the small difference in time at which the sound reaches each of the ears. The brain also registers differences in loudness that reach both ears.

membrane are equally responsive to sounds within the 20 to 20,000 Hz range of human hearing. High-frequency sounds stimulate hair cells closest to the ossicles, whereas lower-frequency sounds stimulate hair cells toward the end of the cochlea (see Figure 4.31). The pattern in which sound affects the cochlea is akin to the pattern seen when snapping a long piece of rope. As you snap the rope, the high-frequency waves occur closer to you, but then become progressively smaller toward the end of the rope. This comparison helps us visualize the **place theory of hearing**, *which states that how we perceive pitch is based on the location (place) along the basilar membrane that sound stimulates.* Early experiments on guinea pigs and human cadavers confirmed the validity of place theory (von Békésy, 1957). As it turns out, place theory works well to explain hearing at higher frequencies, but hair cells for detecting lower frequencies are not so conveniently laid out at the end the cochlea.

Another determinant of how and what we hear is the rate at which the ossicles press into the cochlea, sending a wave of activity down the basilar membrane. According to **frequency theory**, *the perception of pitch is related to the frequency at which the basilar membrane vibrates.* A 70-Hz sound, at 70 cycles per second, stimulates the hair cells 70 times per second. Thus 70 nerve impulses per second travel from the auditory nerves to the brain, which interprets the sound frequency in terms of pitch (Figure 4.31). However, we quickly reach an upper limit on the capacity of the auditory nerves to send signals to the brain: Neurons cannot fire more than 1,000 times per second. Given this limit, how can we hear sounds exceeding 1,000 Hz?

The answer lies in the *volley principle.* A single neuron cannot fire more than 1,000 times per second, but a group of neurons could certainly accomplish this feat. According to the volley principle, groups of neurons fire in alternating (hence the term "volley") fashion. A sound measuring 5,000 Hz can be perceived because groups of neurons fire in rapid succession such that their message is of sufficient magnitude.

Currently, the place, frequency, and volley concepts are all needed to explain our experience of hearing. Place theory is most applicable to high-pitched noises. Frequency theory, in combination with the volley principle, better explains how we hear low-pitched noises. When we hear complex stimuli, such as music, the place, frequency, and volley principles are likely all functioning at the sensory level. Perceiving music, voices, and other important sounds occurs in specialized regions of the brain.

The **primary auditory cortex** *is a major perceptual center of the brain involved in perceiving what we hear.* The auditory cortex is organized in very similar fashion to the cochlea. Cells within different areas across the auditory cortex respond to specific notes. For example, high musical notes are processed at one end of the auditory cortex, and progressively lower notes are heard as you move to the opposite end (Wang et al., 2005). The auditory cortex and surrounding areas are responsible for perceiving and interpreting sound. At the beginning of this module, we discussed the important emotional information conveyed by music. Not surprisingly, music

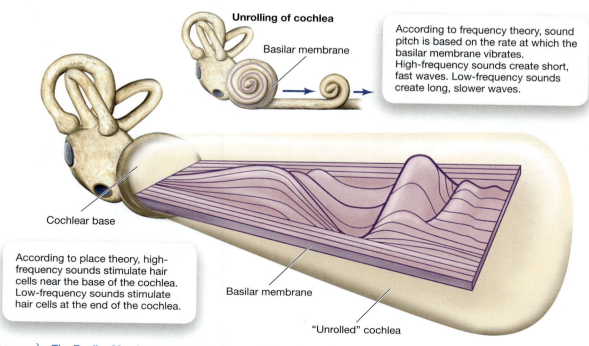

Unrolling of cochlea

Basilar membrane

According to frequency theory, sound pitch is based on the rate at which the basilar membrane vibrates. High-frequency sounds create short, fast waves. Low-frequency sounds create long, slower waves.

Cochlear base

According to place theory, high-frequency sounds stimulate hair cells near the base of the cochlea. Low-frequency sounds stimulate hair cells at the end of the cochlea.

Basilar membrane

"Unrolled" cochlea

{FIG. 4.31} **The Basilar Membrane of the Cochlea and Theories of Hearing**

perception also involves the emotional brain centers, such as those found in the limbic system (see Module 3.3; Bhatara et al., 2011; Koelsch, 2010).

For most people, hearing is something easily taken for granted. But a substantial number of people live without sound. Some people are born without hearing, but hearing loss or complete deafness can also be brought on by factors such as aging, inheritance or genetic mutation, and head trauma (Aggarwal & Saeed, 2005).

What do we know about deafness?

Because the eardrum and ossicles are delicate structures, repeated or even single exposure to loud sounds or injury can cause permanent hearing loss. A **conduction hearing loss** *results when any of the physical structures that conduct sound waves to the cochlea are damaged.* Rupturing or puncturing the eardrum will result in conduction hearing loss, even if the cochlea and the auditory nerves remain intact. Breakage or hardening of the connective tissue between the ossicles can also result in a conduction hearing loss.

Some amazing technological advances have been developed to help people overcome hearing loss, or even profound deafness. One especially notable advance is the *cochlear implant* for people who experience sensorineural loss (see Figure 4.32). **Sensorineural hearing loss** *results from damage to the cochlear hair cells (sensory) and the neurons composing the auditory nerve (neural).* Cochlear implants are small electronic devices that consist of a microphone, speech processor, and electrodes. The speech processor is affixed behind the ear, and a wire is routed through the skull and into the cochlea. Thousands of tiny electrodes placed along the wire stimulate the intact nerve endings, effectively replacing the activity of hair cells.

How can science be used to help people with hearing loss?

The process of adjusting to cochlear implants can be slow and arduous. At first, the sound of people speaking, or *any* sound for that matter, can be disorienting and even unpleasant. As the auditory system and brain adjusts to the input, people with implants can begin perceiving speech sounds.

Researchers have tracked the effects of cochlear implants on language development in children. In one study researchers followed children over a three-year period after receiving cochlear implants, to assess how well they expressed and understood language. Prior to cochlear implantation, the children (who were younger than five at the beginning of the study) were acquiring words at a very low rate, as would be predicted given their hearing impairment. At the end of the three-year study period, the children had greatly improved in both language comprehension and expression (Niparko et al., 2010).

Success with cochlear implants is not restricted to children. Elderly adults can also benefit from these devices (Carlson et al., 2010).

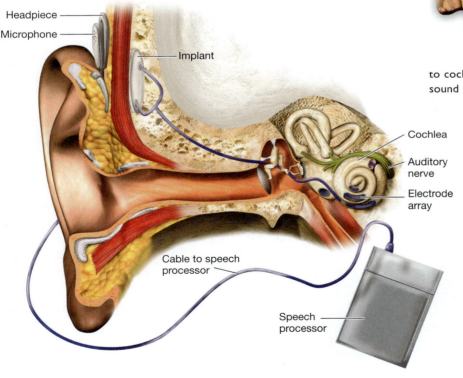

Headpiece —
Microphone —
Implant
Cochlea
Auditory nerve
Electrode array
Cable to speech processor
Speech processor

{FIG. 4.32} **A Cochlear Implant** The speech processor and microphone are located just above the pinna. A wire with tiny electrodes attached is routed through the cochlea.

Can we critically evaluate this information?

Given that cochlear implants have become increasingly common, it may come as a surprise to learn that many deaf people choose not to obtain them. The reasons for rejecting this technology do not necessarily reflect the expense or concern about the process of rehabilitation, however. Rather, the very notion that someone *must* be able to hear is inconsistent with the belief systems of many people who are deaf. Those who are not familiar with people who are deaf may be surprised that the very idea of cochlear implants, and of gaining or regaining hearing, can be quite unwelcome.

Why is this relevant?

The fact that the brain successfully makes this adjustment is remarkable evidence of its plasticity (as discussed in Module 3.3). The first cochlear implants were designed to help users gain or regain the ability to detect speech sounds. Unfortunately, other sounds, such as music or even the sound of a person's voice from a telephone, can be very unpleasant to implant users. This effect occurs because hearing-related areas of the auditory cortex are under-stimulated and, therefore, become rewired to perform other brain functions. Newer devices have been designed that allow some users the opportunity to enjoy music again. In addition, intensive speech therapy and family support are essential for successful use of cochlear implants. Successful surgeries have even been performed on infants.

BIOPSYCHOSOCIAL PERSPECTIVES
Deafness and Culture

Decide whether each of the following statements is true or false:

- Most deaf people would prefer to gain the ability to hear.
- Most deaf people recognize their condition as a disability.
- Signed, gestural languages are fundamentally the same as spoken languages.

The word *deaf* has more than one meaning. The medically based definition refers to hearing loss, ranging from hard-of-hearing to completely deaf. The second meaning is more complex. The Deaf community consists of those individuals who have a hearing impairment and interact with others who also have hearing impairments, hearing people who grew up with deaf family members, and others who have immersed themselves within Deaf communities (Padden & Humphries, 2005). Let's look a little deeper into Deaf culture by discussing the three statements presented above.

- *Most deaf people would prefer to gain the ability to hear.* **False.** In fact, many members of the Deaf community are uncomfortable with the choice of having cochlear implants. Joining the hearing community through these devices, or learning lip reading and attempting to fully integrate within hearing communities, may be frowned upon by deaf people.
- *Most deaf people recognize their condition as a disability.* **False.** A common belief held in Deaf culture is that hearing loss is not a disability, but rather an *ability* to interact in a way that does not require hearing. Language is the primary driving force that brings a culture together, and as such it is major force of cultural identity, especially among the Deaf community.
- *Signed, gestural languages are fundamentally the same as spoken languages.* **True.** Signed languages have the same basic properties of spoken language, including a rich vocabulary, grammatical structure, and rules and norms for usage. In addition, many of the brain regions that support spoken language do the same for signed languages (MacSweeney et al., 2008).

In this chapter, we mostly focus on the normal workings of the sensory and perceptive modalities of vision, hearing, touch, taste, and smell. As research about Deaf culture shows, however, differences in auditory perception invoke complex biopsychosocial issues.

• • • • • • • • • • • • • • • • • •

Quick Quiz 4.3b :: The Perception of Sound

KNOW...

1. _____ hearing loss results from damage to the cochlear hair cells and the neurons making up the auditory nerve.

   A Temporary
   B Conduction
   C Sensorineural
   D Puncturing

UNDERSTAND ...

2. _____ explains pitch perception when hair cells are stimulated at the same rate that a sound wave cycles.

   A Place theory
   B Frequency theory
   C The volley principle
   D Switch theory

3. Neurons cannot fire fast enough to keep up with high-pitched sound waves. Therefore, they alternate firing according to the _____.

   A place theory
   B frequency theory
   C volley principle
   D switch theory

APPLY ...

4. While crossing the street, you know a car is approaching on your left side because:

   A the left ear got the information just a fraction of a second before the right ear.
   B the right ear got the information just a fraction of a second before the left ear.
   C the right ear experienced the sound more intensely than the left ear.
   D both ears experienced the sound at the same intensity.

Answers can be found on page ANS-2.

Module Summary

Module 4.3

((•— **Listen** to the audio file of this module at **MyPsychLab**

Now that you have read this module you should:

KNOW ...

- **The key terminology relating to the ear and hearing:**

cochlea (p. 140)
conduction hearing loss (p. 142)
frequency theory (p. 141)
pitch (p. 138)

place theory of hearing (p. 141)
primary auditory cortex (p. 141)
sensorineural hearing loss (p. 142)
sound localization (p. 140)

UNDERSTAND ...

- **Different characteristics of sound and how they correspond to perception.** Sound can be analyzed based on its frequency (the number of cycles a sound wave travels per second) as well as on its amplitude (the height of a sound wave). Our experience of pitch is based on sound wave frequencies. Amplitude corresponds to loudness: The higher the amplitude, the louder the sound.

- **How technology is used to restore hearing.** Cochlear implants are remarkable devices that can restore much of a person's hearing, but only if the hearing loss is sensorineural in nature. These implants include a microphone that picks up sounds from the environment and a transmitter that relays electrical signals to the auditory nerve in the cochlea.

APPLY ...

- **Your knowledge of sound localization.** Get a friend to participate in a quick localization demonstration. Have her sit with her eyes closed, covering her right ear with her hand. Now walk quietly in a circle around your friend, stopping occasionally to snap your fingers. When you do this, your friend should point to where you are standing, based solely on the sound. If her right ear is covered, at which points will she be most accurate? At which points will she have the most errors? Use the principles of sound localization to make your predictions.

ANALYZE ...

- **The assumption that deafness is something people are motivated to "overcome."** As you learned in the Biopsychosocial Perspectives feature on page 143, many members of the Deaf culture often have little desire to change and reject the assumption that hearing and speaking are something they should want to gain.

Module
4.4

Touch and the Chemical Senses

KNOW ...	UNDERSTAND ...	APPLY ...	ANALYZE ...
The key terminology of touch and chemical senses	How pain messages travel to the brain The relationship between smell, taste, and food flavor experience	Your knowledge about touch to describe the acuity of different areas of skin Your knowledge to determine whether you or someone you know is a "supertaster"	How cultural factors affect taste preferences

Would you ever describe your breakfast cereal as tasting pointy or round? Probably not. Touch, taste, and smell come together to make your favorite foods, yet we can identify the separate components associated with what is felt, tasted, and smelled, through food texture. A rare condition called *synesthesia* results in blended sensory experiences, such that affected individuals might actually hear colors or feel sounds. For the rare individuals who experience this condition, even letters or numbers may have a color associated with them. To illustrate this effect, find the number 2 below:

55555555555555555555555
55555555555555555555555
55555555555555525555555
55555555555555555555555

People who have a type of synesthesia in which words or numbers have unique colors associated with them find the 2 faster than people without synesthesia. One person stated that the 2 was especially easy to find because it appears orange to him—all he had to find was the number that differed in color (Blake et al., 2005). Synesthesia can also involve blending taste and touch, which certainly can influence dining experiences. People may avoid oatmeal because it tastes mushy, but can you imagine avoiding a food because it tastes "pointy," or relishing another food because of its delicate hints of corduroy? Synesthesia occurs in an estimated 1 in 500 people. For the 499 others, touch, taste, and smell are distinct senses.

Focus Questions

 How are our experiences of touch, taste, and smell distinct?

 In addition to food textures, what else involves touch?

Generally speaking, vision and hearing are the senses that we seem to use the most and, therefore, have occupied the majority of research and questioning in psychological science. In this module, we will explore the senses of touch, taste, and smell. Our putting them together in a single module is not meant to diminish their importance, however. Our quality of life, and possibly survival, would be severely compromised without these senses.

The Sense of Touch

The surface of our skin is equipped to respond to numerous types of stimulation. Generally speaking, pressure, temperature, and pain are three types of stimulation—but we can be even more specific. Pressure upon the skin can be barely detectable or cause bruising. It can also involve stretching the skin, as felt when someone gives you a backrub or when you run your hand over the surface of an object to feel its unique texture. Temperature ranges from freezing cold to boiling hot, and many different sensations may cause pain. Our experiences of touch are attributable to the actions of several types of receptors located just beneath the surface of the skin, and also in the muscles, joints, and tendons.

HOW WE PERCEIVE TOUCH Sensitivity to touch varies across different regions of the body. One simple method of testing sensitivity, or *acuity*, is to use the two-point threshold test shown in Figure 4.33. Regions with high acuity, such as the fingertips, can detect the two separate, but closely spaced pressure points of the device, whereas less sensitive regions such as the lower back will perceive the same stimuli as only one pressure point. Body parts such as the fingertips, palms, and lips are highly sensitive to touch, compared to regions such as the calves and lower back.

Exploring objects in our environment by touch is an active process (Lederman & Klatzky, 2004). Merely laying your hand on the surface of an object does little to help identify it. What we need is an active exploration that stimulates receptors in the hand. **Haptics** *is the active, exploratory aspect of touch sensation and perception.* Active touch involves feedback. For example, as you handle an object, such as a piece of fruit, you move your fingers over its surface to identify whether any faults may be present. Your fingertips can help you determine whether the object is the appropriate shape and can detect bruising or abnormalities that may make it unsuitable. For some people, recognizing objects by haptics is hampered by damage to the somatosensory cortex, a condition called *tactile agnosia.* A person with this condition would struggle to identify common objects and even wooden blocks of common geometric shapes.

Haptics allows us not only to identify objects, but also to avoid damaging or dropping them. Fingers and hands coordinate their movements using a complementary body sense called **kinesthesis**, *the sense of bodily motion and position.* Receptors for kinesthesis reside in the muscles, joints, and tendons. These receptors transmit information about movement and the position of your muscles, limbs, and joints to the brain (Figure 4.34). As you handle an object, your kinesthetic sense allows you to hold it with enough resistance to avoid dropping it, and to keep your hands and fingers set in such a way as to avoid letting it roll out of your hands.

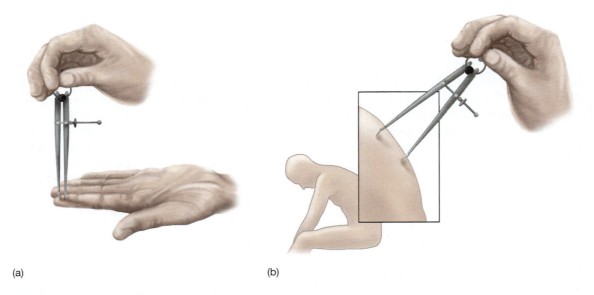

(a) (b)

{FIG. 4.33} **Two-Point Threshold Device for Measuring Touch Acuity** The more sensitive regions of the body can detect two points even when they are spaced very close together. Less sensitive parts of the body have much larger two-point thresholds.

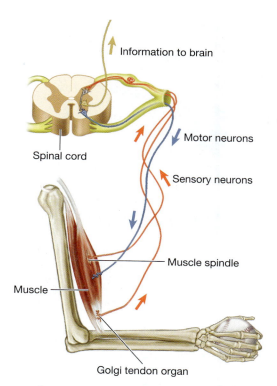

{FIG. 4.34} **The Sense of Kinesthesis** Receptors in muscles and at the joints send sensory messages to the brain, helping us maintain awareness and control of our movements. Muscle spindles and Golgi tendon organs are sensory receptors that provide information about changes in muscle length and tension.

FEELING PAIN Although it might be felt anywhere in the body, pain is perceived by the brain. **Nociception** *is the activity of nerve pathways that respond to uncomfortable stimulation.* Our skin, teeth, cornea, and internal organs contain nerve endings called *nociceptors*, which are receptors that initiate pain messages that travel to the central nervous system (see Figure 4.35). Nociceptors come in varieties that respond to various types of stimuli—for example, to sharp stimulation, such as a pin prick, or to extreme heat or cold (Julius & Basbaum, 2001).

Two types of nerve fibers transmit pain messages. Fast fibers register sharp, immediate pain, such as the pain felt when your skin is scraped or cut. Slow fibers register chronic, dull pain, such as the lingering feelings of bumping your knee into the coffee table. Pain messages first travel to cells in the spinal cord, then move upward to a point where sensory messages branch off to two regions of the brain. One region, the hypothalamus, as you learned in Module 3.3, regulates arousal and emotional responses, which certainly are a part of the experience of pain. The other region, the somatosensory cortex, registers the pain sensations occurring over the entire surface of the body. (Other regions of the cortex are also involved in the experience of pain.)

Pain varies from mild to severe and from acute (brief) to chronic. How do we explain differences in pain experiences? One long-held theory of pain perception is **gate-control theory**, *which explains our experience of pain as an interaction between nerves that transmit pain messages and those that inhibit these messages.* According to this theory, cells in the spinal cord regulate how much pain signaling reaches the brain. Thus the spinal cord serves as a "neural gate" that pain messages must pass through (Melzack & Wall, 1965, 1982). The spinal cord contains small nerve fibers that conduct pain messages and larger nerve fibers that conduct other sensory signals such as those associated with rubbing, pinching, and tickling sensations. Stimulation of the small pain fibers results in the experience of pain, whereas the larger fibers inhibit pain signals. Thus the large fibers close the gate that is opened by the smaller fibers. According to gate-control theory, if you stub your bare toe, rubbing the area around the toe may alleviate some of the pain, because the large fibers carrying the message about touch inhibit the firing of smaller fibers carrying pain signals. Likewise, putting ice on a wound reduces pain by overriding the signals transmitted by the small fibers.

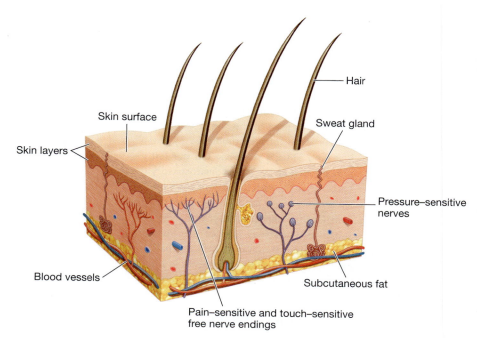

{FIG. 4.35} **Cross-Section of Skin and Free Nerve Endings That Respond to Pain** The nerve endings that respond to pain reside very close to the surface of the skin and, as you are likely aware, are very sensitive to stimulation. **Click on this figure in your eText to see more details.**

WORKING THE SCIENTIFIC LITERACY MODEL
Phantom Limb Sensations

The experience of pain is complex and involves many different biological and subjective factors. Pain is also the source of some deeper mysteries in psychological science and medicine, such as why people experience pain in a region of the body that has been amputated.

What do we know about phantom limb sensations?

Phantom limb sensations are frequently experienced by amputees, who report pain and other sensations coming from the absent limb. It is rather curious that any sensations could be experienced on a nonexistent region of the body. However, both people who are born with a missing limb and those who lose a limb through injury or amputation frequently experience just this phenomenon. Amputees describe such sensations as itching, muscle contractions, and, most unfortunately, pain. The experience of phantom sensations further compromises the well-being of people who are missing a limb. But why do people have this experience and what can be done to help them?

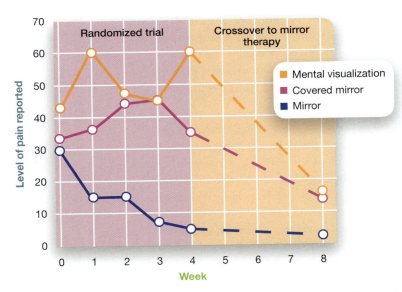

{FIG. 4.36}   **A Mirror Box Used in Therapy for People with Limb Amputation**   In this case, a woman who has lost her left arm can experience some relief from phantom pain by moving her intact hand, such as by unclenching her fist. In turn, she will experience relief from phantom pain corresponding to her left side.

of having both limbs. Amputees often find that watching themselves move and stretch the phantom hand, which is actually the mirror image of the real hand, results in a significant decrease in phantom pain and discomfort (Ramachandran & Altschuler, 2009).

Researchers have conducted experiments to determine how well mirror box therapy works compared both to a control condition and to mentally visualizing the presence of a phantom hand. Over the course of four weeks of regular testing, the people who used the mirror box had significantly reduced pain compared to a control group who used the same mirror apparatus, except the mirror was covered, as well as compared to the group who used mental visualization (Figure 4.37; Chan et al., 2007). Notice in Figure 4.37 that everyone was given mirror

How does science explain phantom limb sensation?

One explanation for phantom pain suggests that rewiring occurs in the brain following loss of the limb. After limb amputation, an area of the somatosensory cortex is no longer stimulated by the lost limb. Thus, if someone has her left arm amputated, the right somatosensory cortex that registers sensations from the left arm no longer has any input from this limb. Healthy nerve cells become hypersensitive when they lose connections. The phantom sensations, including pain, may occur because the nerve cells in the cortex continue to be active, despite the absence of any input.

One ingenious treatment for phantom pain involves the mirror box (Figure 4.36). This apparatus uses the reflection of the amputee's existing limb, such as an arm and hand, to create the visual appearance

{FIG. 4.37}   **Mirror Box Therapy Compared to Mental Visualization and a Control Condition**

therapy after the fourth week of the study, and that the procedure seems to have lasting, positive benefits.

No one is sure why mirror box therapy works, but evidence suggests that the short-term benefits are due to how compelling the illusion is; in the long term, this therapy may actually result in reorganization of the somatosensory cortex (Ramachandran & Altschuler, 2009).

Can we critically evaluate the research on phantom limbs?

A common-sense explanation of phantom pain is that it results from neural activity at the site of the amputation or injury. After all, how could pain in a peripheral body region reside exclusively in the brain? But recall that common sense alone is not sufficient for arriving at accurate answers. Neurologists who specialize in pain treatment have tested the hypothesis that phantom pain comes from free nerve endings at the source of the amputation by applying a local anesthetic to the stump. Even when nerve cells at the stump are numbed, phantom pain continues. This finding confirms that phantom pain and sensations originate in the brain.

Another lesson from research on phantom pain is that the wiring of the brain is not permanent. Rather, over time and with experience, and even following loss of a limb, connections in the brain are dynamic (Ramachandran & Altschuler, 2009).

Why is this relevant?

Mirror box therapy is clearly a useful application of scientific knowledge. It is frequently used in clinical settings to help reduce phantom pain in people who have lost limbs through injury or amputation. Nevertheless, loss of limbs due to amputation is relatively rare compared to other conditions that compromise limb mobility. For example, stroke and other types of brain injury can also result in lost limb functionality and phantom pain sensation. Mirror therapy can be used in these conditions as well. Mirror therapy is not only effective, but also one of the least expensive and easiest to implement medical treatments.

Quick Quiz 4.4a :: The Sense of Touch

KNOW …

1 The sense associated with actively touching objects is known as _____.

  A tactile agnosia   **C** nociception

  B haptics   **D** gestation

2 Phantom limb sensations are:

  A sensations that arise from a limb that has been amputated.

  B sensations that are not perceived.

  C sensations from stimuli that do not reach conscious awareness.

  D sensations from stimuli that you typically identify as intense, such as a burn, but feel dull.

UNDERSTAND …

3 Nociceptors send pain signals to both the _____ and the _____.

  A occipital lobe; hypothalamus

  B cerebellum; somatosensory cortex

  C somatosensory cortex; hypothalamus

  D occipital lobe; cochlea

APPLY …

4 A student gently touches a staple to her fingertip and to the back of her arm near her elbow. How are these sensations likely to differ? Or would they feel similar?

  A The sensation would feel like two points on the fingertip but is likely to feel like only one point on the arm.

  B The sensations would feel identical because the same object touches both locations.

  C The sensation would feel like touch on the fingertips but like pain on the elbow.

  D The sensation would feel like two points on the arm but is likely to feel like only one point on the fingertip.

Answers can be found on page ANS-2.

The Chemical Senses: Taste and Smell

The chemical senses comprise a combination of both taste and smell. Although they are distinct sensory systems, both begin the sensory process with chemicals activating receptors on the tongue and mouth, as well as on the nose.

THE GUSTATORY SYSTEM: TASTE   The **gustatory system** *functions in the sensation and perception of taste.* Food and drink are the most common types of taste stimuli that come to mind. Specifically, the receptors involved in taste sensations are chemical compounds that are water soluble (dissolvable).

Complete the **Survey** *Which Senses Do You Use?* at **MyPsychLab**

Taste is perhaps one of our more indulgent senses. Most of our experiences with the sense of taste involve eating, and rarely do we seek out foods we do not want to put in our mouths. Losing the sense of taste can severely diminish one's quality of life. In the United States, approximately 200,000 people visit their doctors for taste-related disorders each year (National Institutes of Health [NIH], 2009). But our sense of taste does not merely serve the purpose of providing pleasure; rather, it is also useful for identifying potentially poisonous substances in the food we are eating. Imagine if you were not able to detect the awful taste of sour, spoiled milk or rancid meat. Thus taste is adaptive in that it helps ensure that we nourish our bodies and avoid poisoning ourselves.

Taste is registered primarily on the tongue, where roughly 9,000 taste buds reside. On average, approximately 1,000 taste buds are also found throughout the sides and roof of the mouth (Miller & Reedy, 1990). Sensory neurons that transmit signals from the taste buds respond to different types of stimuli, but most tend to respond best to a particular taste. Our experience of taste reflects an overall pattern of activity across many neurons, and generally comes from stimulation of the entire tongue rather than just specific, localized regions. The middle of the tongue has very few

taste receptors, giving it a similar character to the blind spot on the retina (Module 4.2). We do not feel or sense the blind spot of the tongue because the sensory information is filled in, just as we find with vision. Taste receptors replenish themselves every 10 days throughout the life span—the only type of sensory receptor to do so.

Receptors for taste are located in the visible, small bumps (*papillae*) that are distributed over the surface of the tongue. The papillae are lined with taste buds. Figure 4.38 shows papillae, taste buds, and an enlarged view of an individual taste bud and a sensory neuron that sends a message to the brain. The bundles of nerves that register taste at the taste buds send the signal through the thalamus and on to higher-level regions of the brain, including the *gustatory cortex,* which is a deep-seated structure located in the interior of the cortex. Another region, the *secondary gustatory cortex,* processes the pleasurable experiences associated with food.

Approximately 2,500 identifiable chemical compounds are found in the food we eat (Taylor & Hort, 2004). When combined, these compounds give us an enormous diversity of taste sensations. The *primary tastes* include salty, sweet, bitter, and sour. In addition, a fifth taste, called umami, has been identified (Chaudhari et al., 2000). Umami, sometimes referred to as "savoriness," is a Japanese word that refers to tastes associated with seaweed, the seasoning monosodium glutamate (MSG), and protein-rich foods such as milk and aged cheese.

Why do we identify some foods as strong or rich tasting? For one thing, the number of taste buds present on the tongue influences the psychological experience of taste. Although approximately 10,000 taste buds is the average number found in humans, there is wide variation among individuals. Some people may have many times this number. *Supertasters,* who account for approximately 25% of the population, are especially sensitive to bitter

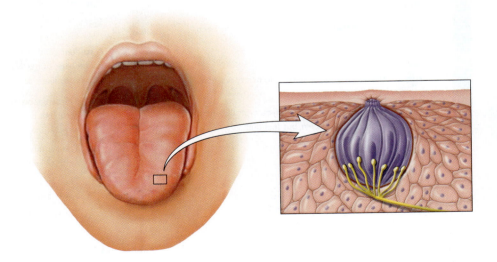

{FIG. 4.38}   **Papillae and Taste Buds** The tongue is lined with papillae (the bumpy surfaces). Within these papillae are your taste buds, the tiny receptors to which chemicals bind.

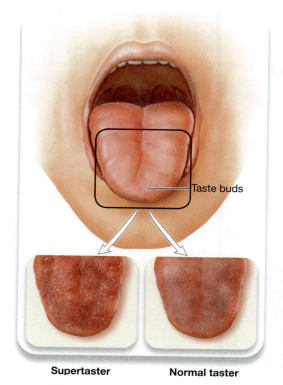

Supertaster   **Normal taster**

{FIG. 4.39} **Density of Papillae, and Hence Taste Buds, in a Supertaster and in a Normal Taster**

tastes such as those of broccoli and black coffee. They typically have lower rates of obesity and cardiovascular disease, possibly because they tend not to prefer fatty and sweet foods. Figure 4.39 shows the number of papillae, and hence taste buds, possessed by a supertaster compared to those without this ability.

Closely related to taste is our sense of smell, which senses the chemical environment via a different mode than does taste.

THE OLFACTORY SYSTEM: SMELL The **olfactory system** *is involved in smell—the detection of airborne particles with specialized receptors located in the nose.* Smell works in concert with taste to give us the experience of flavor. Without smell, a slice of onion might be difficult to discriminate from a slice of apple: The textures of these two foods are quite similar, and our taste buds alone may not be sufficient to discriminate one from the other. The experience of smell makes food enjoyable, but also helps us to identify harmful substances, helps us to recognize individuals, and can warn us of danger.

Our sensation of smell begins with nasal air flow bringing in molecules that bind with receptors at the top of the nasal cavity. Within the nasal cavity is the **olfactory epithelium**, *a thin layer of cells that are lined by sensory receptors called cilia*—tiny hair-like projections that contain specialized proteins that bind with the airborne molecules that enter the nasal cavity (Figure 4.40). The cilia transmit messages to neurons that converge on the *olfactory bulb*, which serves as the brain's central region for processing smell. The olfactory bulb connects with several regions of the brain through the olfactory tract, including the limbic system (emotion) as well as regions of the cortex where the subjective experience of pleasure (or disgust) occurs.

Our perceptual experiences of smell begin with the encoding of sensory information by cells that comprise the olfactory epithelium. The cilia shown in Figure 4.40b

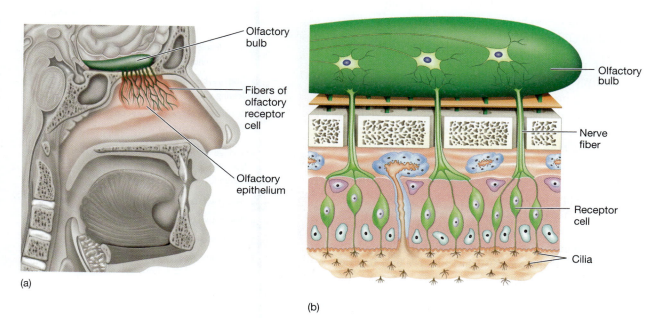

(a)

(b)

{FIG. 4.40} **The Olfactory System** Lining the olfactory epithelium are tiny cilia that collect airborne chemicals, sending sensory messages to the nerve fibers that make up the olfactory bulb. **Click on this figure in your eText to see more details.**

contain specialized proteins that bind to inhaled compounds. (Buck, 1996). This is a complex process, because there are thousands of molecules of differing shapes that correspond to particular odors. Despite the fact that humans have only 1,000 different types of odor receptors, we can detect approximately 10,000 different odors because odor molecules can stimulate several receptors simultaneously. It is the *pattern* of the stimulation, involving more than one receptor, that gives rise to the experience of a particular smell (Buck & Axel, 1991).

DEVELOPING PREFERENCES FOR FLAVORS

The perceptual experience of flavor combines taste and olfactory cues. You have probably noticed that when you have nasal congestion, your experience of flavor is diminished. This loss of taste occurs because approximately 80% of our information about food comes from olfaction (Murphy et al., 1977). Individuals also show much variation in flavor preferences, in part because flavor perception is a subjective experience that is influenced by cultural experiences.

Would you eat a piece of bread smeared with a sticky brown paste that was processed from wasted yeast used to make beer in a brewery? This product, called vegemite, is actually quite popular among people in Switzerland, Australia, and New Zealand. People brought up eating vegemite may love it, while most others find it unbearable. The Masai people of Kenya and Tanzania enjoy eating a coagulated mixture of cow's blood and milk. These foods may sound unappetizing to you. Of course, the foods that many Americans eat—especially highly processed ones—might not sound particularly appealing either if all of their ingredients were revealed.

The process of developing flavor preferences begins early, even before birth. For example, human infants tend to prefer the flavors of the foods consumed by their mothers during gestation (Beauchamp & Mennella, 2009). Soon after starting solid foods, children begin to acquire a taste for the foods prevalent in their culture, even if some of them are inherently unpleasant. A good example is the chili pepper. Rozin (1987) found that chili peppers come to be preferred because of their actual taste, not their anticipated dietary effects. Young children, who typically find chili peppers to be highly aversive, are gradually given increasingly larger amounts of chili in their diets and, as they observe and imitate adults and older children enjoying the taste of chili peppers, come to prefer it as well.

Food preferences, then, show considerable individual and cultural variations. However, it seems clear that these food preferences are learned gradually as a result of being raised within a particular culture. Thus inherently unpleasant foods—from vegemite to chili peppers—can eventually become delicacies.

Quick Quiz 4.4b
The Chemical Senses: Taste and Smell

KNOW…

1 The bumps that line the tongue surface and house our taste buds are called _____.

A epithelia

B gustates

C the gustatory cortex

D papillae

2 Where are the receptor cells for smell located?

A The papillae

B The olfactory epithelium

C The olfactory bulb

D The odor buds

UNDERSTAND…

3 The perceptual experience of flavor originates from:

A taste cues alone.

B olfactory cues alone.

C olfactory and taste cues together.

D haptic and olfactory cues together.

APPLY…

4 After eating grape lollipops, you and a friend notice that your tongues have turned blue. With the change in color, it is easy to notice that there are many more papillae on your friend's tongue. Who is more likely to be a supertaster?

A You are, because you have fewer, and therefore more distinct, papillae.

B Your friend is, because she has many more papillae to taste with.

C You are, because less dye stuck to your tongue, allowing you to taste more.

D It could be either of you because supertasting is unrelated to the number of papillae.

ANALYZE…

5 An exchange student at your school dislikes root beer but often craves seaweed. What is the best explanation for her taste preferences?

A She grew up drinking root beer and is sick of it.

B She grew up consuming seaweed.

C Seaweed is a culturally universal preference.

D These are most likely individual preferences that are unrelated to culture and experience.

Answers can be found on page ANS-2.

Module 4.4

Now that you have read this module you should:

((:•—⌐ **Listen** to the audio file of this module at **MyPsychLab**

KNOW ...

- **The key terminology of touch and chemical senses:**

gate-control theory (p. 147)
gustatory system (p. 150)
haptics (p. 146)
kinesthesis (p. 146)

nociception (p. 147)
olfactory epithelium (p. 151)
olfactory system (p. 151)

UNDERSTAND ...

- **How pain messages travel to the brain.** According to gate-control theory, small nerve fibers carry pain messages from their source to the spinal cord, and then up to, among other regions, the hypothalamus and somatosensory cortex. However, large nerve cells that register other types of touch sensations (such as rubbing) can override signals sent by small pain fibers.
- **The relationship between smell, taste, and food flavor experience.** Both senses combine to give us flavor experiences. Contact with food activates patterns of neural activity among nerve cells connected to the taste buds, and food's odors activate patterns of nerve activity in the olfactory epithelium. The primary and secondary gustatory cortex and the olfactory bulb are involved in the perceptual experience of flavor.

APPLY ...

- **Your knowledge about touch to describe the acuity of different areas of skin.** You can try this yourself by creating a two-point threshold device like the one shown earlier in **Figure 4.33 (page 146)**. We fashioned one out of a straightened paper clip we could hold up to a ruler. Set the two points about ¼ inch apart and gently apply them to different parts of the body—your fingertips, your elbow, your cheek. Which parts of your body are sensitive enough to feel both points, and on which parts does it feel like a single object is touching you? Now try the experiment again with the two points closer together. Can you detect a change in acuity?
- **Your knowledge to determine whether you or someone you know is a "supertaster."** Scientists use a very precise measurement system to identify supertasters, but one less complicated way to do so is to dye your tongue by placing a drop of food coloring on it, or by eating or drinking something dark blue or purple. Next, count the number of papillae you can see in a 4-mm circle. You can accomplish this by viewing the dyed portion of your tongue through the punched hole in a sheet of

loose-leaf notebook paper. If you can count more than 30 papillae, then chances are you are a supertaster. Of course, if you already know that you do not like bitter vegetables like broccoli or asparagus, then perhaps you would expect to find a high number of papillae.

ANALYZE ...

- **How cultural factors affect taste preferences.** Humans share common taste receptors for sweet, sour, salty, bitter, and umami, but much variation exists in food flavor preferences. Experiments and naturalistic observations of people from diverse cultures suggest that early developmental exposure to certain flavors, even those that cause pain (e.g., hot chili peppers), facilitates taste preferences.

Module 4.1 :: Sensation and Perception at a Glance

Focus Questions:

1 **What role does attention play in perception?** Attention is critical to perceiving. Our attentional focus can be either selective (attending to a limited number of features or tasks) or divided (attending to multiple features and tasks). Focusing on a single task makes it more likely we will experience inattentional blindness and miss very obvious events (such as a person in a gorilla suit or a world-famous musician playing at a subway stop). You also learned in this module that some forms of subliminal perception can occur, so some information may be perceived on a subconscious level. The effects of subliminal perception are mild, however, and this phenomenon alone does not result in any significant coercion or manipulation.

2 **What are the principles that guide perception?** The Gestalt psychologists identified many principles, which can be seen in Figure 4.5 and Figure 4.6 (p. 119), including the figure–ground, similarity, proximity, continuity, and closure concepts. Also, how we perceive our world is guided by a combination of bottom-up processing (constructing a whole stimulus or concept from bits of raw sensory information) and top-down processing (when prior knowledge and expectations guide what is perceived). The story about Joshua Bell at the beginning of this module demonstrated how context affects our abilities to sense and perceive. People do not expect to see a world-famous violinist playing in a subway, so they fail to either direct the attentional resources required to notice the event or even perceive what is happening in the first place.

👁 **Watch** *The Big Picture: The Role of Sensation and Perception in Psychology* in the **MyPsychLab video series**

Module 4.2 :: The Visual System

Focus Questions:

1 **How do we recognize and perceive objects?** Objects are recognized within specialized regions of the temporal lobe of the brain. Our experience of objects is aided by perceptual constancies, a phenomenon referring to our ability to recognize an object under different angles, orientations, and light levels.

2 **Why do errors such as failing to perceive a dangerous object at security checkpoints occur?** Typically, we are quite good at spotting unusual features in our visual environment, especially if they stand out. However, when a visual task is repeated over and over—a task required of many security officials—the chance of finding something unusual can actually decrease. Airport security officials who perform luggage screening see far more bags that have no weapons than bags that do. Psychologists have found that the less frequently an object is encountered in an array, the more likely it is missed. This relationship may help explain how

something such as a loaded gun (fortunately, a rare occurrence) has occasionally passed through security checkpoints in U.S. airports.

👁 **Watch** *Special Topics: Facial Recognition* in the **MyPsychLab video series**

Module 4.3 :: The Auditory System

Focus Questions:

1 **How does the auditory system sense and perceive something complex like music?** We have discussed theories of hearing that involve place, frequency, and volley. High- to low-frequency sounds stimulate the basilar membrane at different locations (place theory). Also, high-frequency sounds stimulate hair cells closer to the ossicles, whereas lower-frequency sounds stimulate hair cells located toward the opposite end of the cochlea. Thus the number of times sound waves stimulate the cochlea (frequency) and the recruitment of many nerve cells associated with the hair cells (volley) contribute to the sensory qualities of music.

2 **How might the ability to hear be lost?** Two ways covered in this module are conduction loss and sensorineural loss. Conduction loss involves impairment to the structures that function to transmit sound vibrations to the cochlea—for example, damage to the eardrum or ossicles. Sensorineural hearing loss occurs when there is damage to the cochlea, auditory nerves, and brain centers associated with hearing. In the case of sensorineural hearing loss, cochlear implants have become an option for many affected individuals.

👁 **Watch** *What's in It for Me? Perceptual Magic in Art and Movies* in the **MyPsychLab video series**

Module 4.4 :: Touch and the Chemical Senses

Focus Questions:

1 **How are our experiences of touch, taste, and smell distinct?** Each has a different set of sensory receptors and some unique brain mechanisms responsible for perception. When we eat, however, our senses of touch, taste, and smell are linked with the experience. Although taste and smell have unique sensory receptors and different brain pathways, both contribute to the sensory quality of food we call flavor. Flavor is lost when we have a head cold, but texture is not.

2 **In addition to food textures, what else involves touch?** The somatosensory cortex registers sensations that occur over the entire surface of the body. Haptics involves the direct contact we make with objects and surfaces with our hands, which is distinct in that it allows us to identify objects (imagine trying to discriminate an apple, orange, or softball based on having these objects placed on your lower back). Pain is another distinct sensory experience related to touch.

👁 **Watch** *Thinking Like a Psychologist: Can Smells Alter Mood and Behavior?* in the **MyPsychLab video series**

1 Which of the following requires the greatest amount of cognitive processing?

- A Transduction
- B Sensation
- C Perception
- D Sensory adaptation

2 Research into subliminal perception has found that:

- A human beings are not affected by subliminal stimuli.
- B subliminal advertising is an effective way to influence purchasing habits.
- C human beings can be affected by subliminal stimuli, but the effect is small.
- D subliminal stimuli can be used to induce a form of "mind control."

3 When Keith had to give a presentation to the entire class, his classmate Daniel decided to wear a large fake mustache to make Keith laugh. To Daniel's disappointment, when Keith gave his presentation, he seemed completely unaffected, despite looking at Daniel several times. Afterward, Keith said that he was so focused on the presentation that he didn't even notice the mustache! This scenario is an example of:

- A inattentional blindness.
- B a blind spot.
- C top-down processing.
- D sensory adaptation.

4 At which structure does the transduction of light into a neural signal occur in the visual system?

- A Retina
- B Cornea
- C LGN
- D Lens

5 Which of the following statements is correct regarding the trichromatic and opponent-process theories of color vision?

- A Research suggests that the trichromatic theory is incorrect.
- B Research suggests that the opponent-process theory is incorrect.
- C Both theories are correct; they simply describe color processing at different steps in the visual system.
- D Researchers are still uncertain about which of the two theories is correct.

6 Which of the following depth cues requires two eyes?

- A Motion parallax
- B Retinal disparity
- C Linear perspective
- D Relative size

7 The place theory of hearing states that:

- A the place or location from which a sound is coming is identified based on the difference in intensity between the two ears.
- B the location along the basilar membrane that is stimulated by sound determines how we perceive the sound's pitch.
- C the same frequency sound will have a different sound depending on the location of the sound source relative to the head.
- D the primary auditory cortex is located in the same place in all human brains.

8 Cochlear implants are electronic hearing devices that can "replace" the functioning of which part of the auditory system when it is damaged?

- A The pinna
- B The eardrum
- C The hair cells
- D The ossicles

9 Sally is a ballet dancer. Although she often practices with her eyes closed, she is always aware of exactly where her arms and legs are and how her knees and elbows are bent. This is an example of which bodily sense?

- A Nociception
- B Gustation
- C Haptics
- D Kinesthesis

10 What do taste and smell have in common?

- A Both senses rely on receptors located in structures called papillae.
- B Both senses rely on receptors located on the tongue and in the back of the throat.
- C Both senses are part of the olfactory system.
- D Both senses detect chemicals.

✔ ● Study and Review at MyPsychLab

What do we know about the process of perception?

Review **Figure 4.2 on page 116** for a reminder of the complex processes of sensation and perception. On **page 119**, we discussed the gestalt principles that help us understand how we organize visual information into whole patterns and forms. But what about the cognitive processes that guide this perception? As mentioned on **page 120**, depending on the information available, we process information, or stimuli, in either a top-down or bottom-up direction. Remember that top-down processing happens when our perception of an object is shaped by our existing knowledge or prior information, and bottom-up processing happens when our perception is based only on the information available from the stimulus. Think of it this way: Bottom-up processing occurs when perception starts at the most basic (bottom) level—the stimulus. Top-down processing occurs at a higher (top) level, as you are approaching the stimulus armed with previous knowledge.

Consider a baby's toy giraffe. You are familiar with giraffes and children's toys, so you would process the object from the top down. But giraffes, and even the concept of toys, are new to an infant. Perceiving this stimulus would consist of taking in all of its elements, including its shape, size, and texture. Thus this brand-new object is perceived from the bottom up—from its most basic elements.

How can science help explain how visual perception works?

See **pages 120 and 121** for a discussion of studies that show how top-down and bottom-up processing often work together to help us categorize and identify stimuli. Research has also revealed that our brains have limited resources and, consequently, sometimes make errors in perception. For example, inattentional blindness prevents us from seeing one stimulus if we are focused on another. This was demonstrated in a classic study when subjects viewing a video were asked to attend to one cognitive task (counting the number of times a ball was passed back and forth) and didn't notice a person in a gorilla suit strolling across the screen. This is an example of how processing information in a top-down manner can impede our ability to notice events that, in hindsight, should have been obvious.

On **page 130**, we described research identifying conditions where we fail to see objects—even ones that *should* be highly noticeable—that we are exposed to less often. All of which may lead you to wonder: If perception is flawed, does that mean it can be manipulated? On **page 118**, we reviewed experiments that show we do, indeed, process stimuli at a subconscious level.

Why is this relevant?

Watch the accompanying video excerpt on sensation and perception. You can access the video at MyPsychLab or by clicking the play button in the center of your eText. If your instructor assigns this video as a homework activity, you will find additional content to help you in MyPsychLab. You can also view the video by using your smart phone and the QR code below, or you can go to the YouTube link provided.

Once you have read this chapter and watched the video, consider what you know about the processes of perception. The Gestalt psychologists maintained that when people perceive sensory elements, their tendency is to see things in terms of the entire form or pattern rather than as individual parts. Identify and describe each of the basic principles of perceptual organization from the gestalt perspective, including figure–ground, similarity, proximity, continuity, closure, and symmetry.

Can we critically evaluate claims about perception?

If the frequency with which we encounter objects influences our ability to perceive them, and concentrating on one stimulus can make us blind to another, then is it possible to trick our perceptions through exposure to subliminal stimuli? **Myths in Mind on page 118** notes that while the brain exhibits a small response to subliminal stimuli, the key word is *small*. Your behavior is unlikely to be drastically influenced, either positively or negatively, by subliminal messaging. Also keep in mind how the concept of inattentional blindness can be important when it comes to critically evaluating the value of eyewitness testimony. For example, can a person who witnesses a hit-and-run accident even from a close range, accurately recall the model and color of the car if at the time of the accident her attention was focused on a cell phone conversation?

MyPsychLab **Your turn to Work the Scientific Literacy Model:** You can access the video at MyPsychLab or by clicking the play button in the center of your eText. If your instructor assigns this video as a homework activity, you will find additional content to help you at MyPsychLab. You can also view the video by using your smart phone and the QR code, or you can go to the YouTube link provided.

youtube.com/
scientificliteracy

5 :: CONSCIOUSNESS

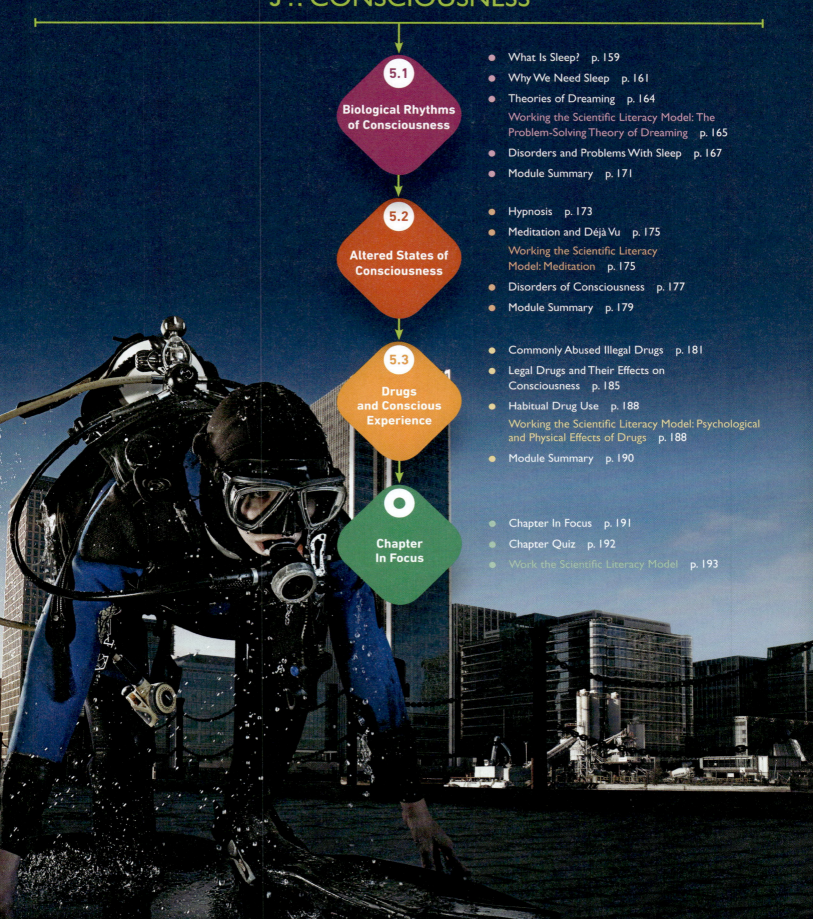

Module
5.1

Biological Rhythms of Consciousness: Wakefulness and Sleep

Learning Objectives

After reading this module you should:

KNOW ...	UNDERSTAND ...	APPLY ...	ANALYZE ...
The key terminology associated with sleep, dreams, and sleep disorders	How the sleep cycle works Theories of why we sleep	Your knowledge to identify and practice good sleep habits	Different theories about why we dream

Smashing through a window in your sleep seems perfectly plausible if it occurs as part of a dream. Mike Birbiglia did just this—but in his case, it was both dream and reality. Birbiglia is a comedian whose show, *Sleepwalk with Me*, is full of stories of personal and embarrassing moments, which include jumping through a second story window of his hotel room while he was asleep. He awoke upon landing; picked his bloodied, half-naked self up; and went to the hotel front desk to notify personnel of what happened. Perhaps his comedy is just his way of dealing with an otherwise troubling sleep problem—a serious condition called REM behavior disorder. People with REM behavior disorder act out their dreams, which clearly has the potential to be very dangerous. In Mike's case, the injury was self-inflicted. Other people with the condition, however, have been known to hit or choke their bed partner. As it turns out, jumping through windows is not entirely uncommon for people with REM behavior disorder (Schenck et al., 2009). In this module, we explore how normal sleep works, and we explain how and why sleep disorders, such as Mike Birbiglia's, occur.

Focus Questions

 What is REM and how is it related to dreaming?

 Why do some people act out their dreams?

· · · · · · · · · · · · · · · · · · ·

Consciousness *is a person's subjective awareness, including thoughts, perceptions, experiences of the world, and self-awareness.* Every day we go through many changes in consciousness—our thoughts and perceptions are constantly adapting to new situations. In some cases, when we are paying close attention to something, we seem to be more in control of conscious experiences. In other situations, such as when we are daydreaming, consciousness seems to wander. These changes in our subjective experiences make consciousness one of the most curious areas of psychological study. We will begin this module by exploring the alternating cycles of consciousness—sleeping and waking.

What Is Sleep?

It makes perfect sense to devote a module to a behavior that humans spend approximately one-third of their lives doing. What happens during sleep can be just as fascinating as what happens during wakefulness. Psychologists and non-psychologists alike have long pondered some basic questions about sleep, such as Why do we need sleep? and Why do we dream? But perhaps we should begin with the most basic question: What is sleep?

CIRCADIAN RHYTHMS Life involves patterns—patterns that cycle within days, weeks, months, or years. Organisms have evolved *biological rhythms* that are neatly adapted to the cycles in the environment. For example, bears are well known for hibernating during the cold winter months. Because this behavior happens on a yearly basis, it is part of a *circannual rhythm* (a term that literally means "a yearly cycle"). **Circadian rhythms** *are internally driven daily cycles of approximately 24 hours affecting physiological and behavioral processes.* They involve the tendency to be asleep or awake at specific times, to feel hungrier during some parts of the day, and even the ability to concentrate better at certain times (Lavie, 2001; Verwey & Amir, 2009).

Think about your own circadian rhythms: When are you most alert? At which times of day do you feel the most tired? Night shift workers and night owls aside, we tend to get most of our sleep when it is dark outside, because our circadian rhythms are regulated by daylight interacting with our nervous and endocrine (hormonal) systems. One key brain structure in this process is the *suprachiasmatic nucleus* (SCN) of the hypothalamus. Cells in the retina of the eye relay messages about light levels in the environment to the SCN. The SCN, in turn, communicates signals about light levels with the pineal gland (see Figure 5.1). The pineal gland releases a hormone called *melatonin*, which peaks in concentration at nighttime and is reduced during wakefulness. Because of this system, light is the primary

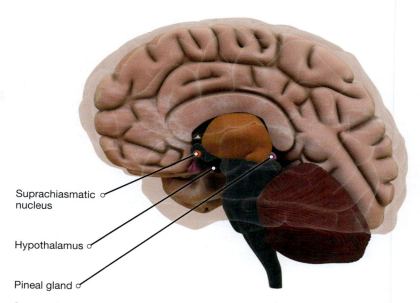

Suprachiasmatic nucleus

Hypothalamus

Pineal gland

{FIG. 5.1}   **Pathways Involved in Circadian Rhythms**   Cells in the retina send messages about light levels to the suprachiasmatic nucleus, which in turn relays the information to the pineal gland, which secretes melatonin.

stimulus regulating the human circadian rhythm. For some people, however, this process is disrupted. For example, people with blindness due to retinal damage cannot send light signals from the retina to the SCN and pineal gland. Thus their circadian rhythms do not synchronize to day–night cycles. However, their cycles can be adjusted using doses of melatonin (Sack et al., 2000).

Our circadian rhythms appear to change with age (Caci et al., 2009). As shown in Figure 5.2, researchers have found that we need much less sleep—especially

PsychTutor
Click here in your eText for an interactive tutorial on **Circadian Rhythms**

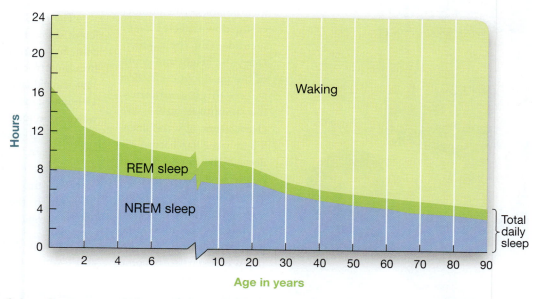

{FIG. 5.2}   **Sleep Requirements Change With Age**   People tend to spend progressively less time sleeping as they age. The amount of a certain type of sleep, REM sleep, declines the most.

a type called REM sleep, which we will discuss in a moment—as we move from infancy and early childhood, and the trend continues even into adulthood. Moreover, people generally experience a change in when they prefer to sleep. In our teens and 20s, many of us become night owls who prefer to stay up late and sleep in. When given the choice, those of us in this age range prefer to work, study, and play late in the day. Later in adulthood, many of us will find ourselves going to bed earlier and getting up earlier, and we may begin to prefer working or exercising before our teenage children even begin to stir. In fact, research shows that these patterns are more than just preferences: People actually do show higher alertness and cognitive functioning during their preferred time of day (Cavallera & Giudici, 2008; Diaz-Morales, 2007).

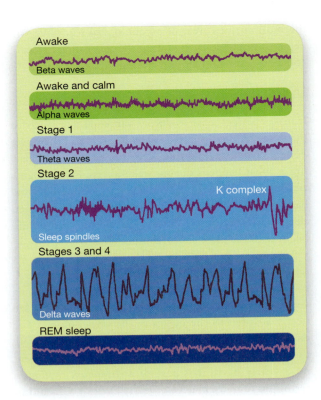

{FIG. 5.3} **EEG Recordings During Wakefulness and Sleep** Brain waves, as measured by the frequency and amplitude of electrical activity, change over the course of the normal circadian rhythm. Beta waves are predominant during wakefulness, but give way to alpha waves during periods of calm and as we drift into sleep. Theta waves are characteristic of stage 1 sleep. As we reach stage 2 sleep, the amplitude (height) of brain waves increases. During deep sleep (stages 3 and 4), the brain waves are at their highest amplitude. During REM sleep, they appear similar to the brain waves occurring when we are awake. **Click on this figure in your eText to see more details.**

PsychTutor
Click here in your eText for an interactive tutorial on **Stages of Sleep**

THE STAGES OF SLEEP We have already seen how sleep fits into the daily rhythm, but if we take a closer look, we will see that sleep itself has rhythms. **Polysomnography** *refers to a set of objective measurements used to examine physiological variables during sleep.* Some of the devices used in this type of study are familiar, such as one to measure respiration and a thermometer to measure body temperature. In addition, electrical sensors attached to the skin measure muscle activity around the eyes and other parts of the body. However, sleep cycles themselves are most often defined by the *electroencephalogram (EEG)*, a device that measures brain waves (also described in Module 3.3).

The output of an EEG is a waveform, like that shown in Figure 5.3. These waves can be described by their *frequency*—the number of up-down cycles every second—and their *amplitude*—the height and depth of the up-down cycle. *Beta waves*—high-frequency, low-amplitude waves—are characteristic of wakefulness. Their irregular nature reflects the bursts of activity in different regions of the cortex, and they are often interpreted as a sign that a person is alert. As the individual begins to shift into sleep, the waves start to become slower, larger, and more predictable; these *alpha waves* signal that a person may be daydreaming, meditating, or starting to fall asleep.

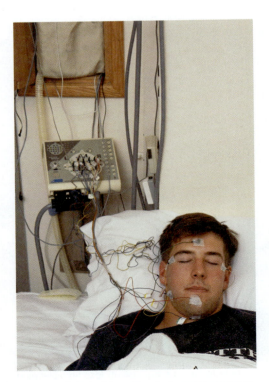

Using physiological recording devices, sleep researchers and doctors can monitor eye movements, brain waves, and other physiological processes.

The EEG signals during sleep move through four different stages. In stage 1, brain waves slow down and become higher in amplitude—these are known as *theta waves*. Breathing, blood pressure, and heart rate all decrease slightly as an individual begins to sleep. After approximately 10 to 15 minutes, the sleeper enters stage 2, during which brain waves continue to slow. As shown in Figure 5.3, stage 2 includes *sleep spindles* and *K complexes,* which are periodic bursts of EEG activity. What these bursts in brain activity mean is not completely understood, but evidence suggests they may play a role in helping maintain a state of sleep and in the process of memory storage (Gais et al., 2002)—a topic we cover more fully later on.

As stage 2 sleep progresses, we respond to fewer and fewer external stimuli, such as lights and sounds. Approximately 20 minutes later, we enter stage 3 sleep, in which brain waves continue to slow down and assume a new form called *delta waves*. The process continues with the deepest stage of sleep, stage 4, during which time the sleeper will be difficult to awaken.

About an hour after falling asleep, we reach the end of our first stage 4 sleep phase. At this point, the sleep cycle goes in reverse and we move back toward stage 1 patterns. Nevertheless, we do not go all the way back to stage 1; instead, we move into a unique stage of **REM sleep**—*a stage of sleep characterized by quickening brain waves, inhibited body movement, and rapid eye movements (REM).* This stage is sometimes known as *paradoxical sleep* because the EEG waves appear to represent a state of wakefulness, despite the fact that we remain asleep. The REM pattern is so distinct that the first four stages are known collectively as *non-REM (NREM) sleep.* At the end of the first REM phase, we cycle back toward deep sleep stages and back into REM sleep again every 90 to 100 minutes.

The sleep cycle through a typical night of sleep is summarized in Figure 5.4. As shown in the figure, the deeper stages of sleep (3 and 4) predominate during the earlier portions of the sleep cycle, but gradually give way to longer REM periods.

REM sleep appears to be critical to a good night's sleep, as we will discuss later. When we are deprived of sleep, we typically experience a phenomenon called *REM rebound*—our brains spend an increased time in REM-phase sleep when given the chance. In fact, the lack of REM sleep may be the most negative aspect of sleep deprivation, rather than the actual amount of lost sleep time. If you usually sleep 8 hours but get only 3 hours of sleep, you can recover from the sleep deficit the next time you sleep with only the normal 8 hours, but your time in REM sleep will increase considerably.

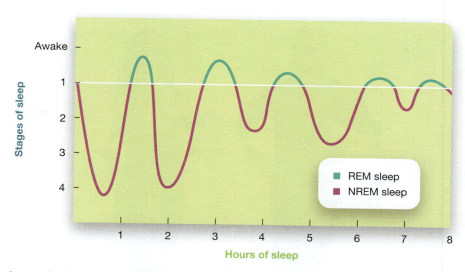

{FIG. 5.4} **Order and Duration of Sleep Stages Through a Typical Night** Our sleep stages progress through a characteristic pattern. The first half of a normal night of sleep is dominated by deep, slow-wave sleep. REM sleep increases in duration relative to deep sleep during the second half of the night. **Click on this figure in your eText to see more details.**

Quick Quiz 5.1a
What Is Sleep?

KNOW …

1 Large, periodic bursts of brain activity that occur during stage 2 sleep are known as _____.

   A beta waves   C delta waves

   B sleep spindles   D alpha waves

UNDERSTAND …

2 Why is REM sleep known as paradoxical sleep?

   A The brain waves appear to be those of an awake person, but the individual seems to be in a very deep sleep.

   B The brain waves resemble those of a sleeping individual, but the person behaves as if he is very nearly awake.

   C The brain wave patterns in REM sleep are totally unlike those produced by brain activity at any other time.

   D The brain waves resemble those of a sleeping individual, and the person seems to be in a very deep sleep.

APPLY …

3 Which of the following is the most likely order of sleep stages during the first 90 minutes of a night of rest?

   A Stages 1-2-3-4-1-2-3-4-REM

   B Stages 1-2-3-4-REM-1-2-3-4

   C Stages 1-2-3-4-3-2-REM

   D Stages REM-4-3-2-1

Answers can be found on page ANS-2.

Why We Need Sleep

Sleep is such a natural part of life that it is difficult to imagine what the world would be like if there were no such thing. It raises another question: Why do humans and other animals need to sleep in the first place?

THEORIES OF SLEEP The most intuitive explanation for why we sleep is probably the **restore and repair hypothesis**, *the idea that the body needs to restore energy levels and repair any wear and tear on the body from the day's activities.* Research on sleep deprivation clearly shows that sleep is a physical and psychological necessity, not just a pleasant way to relax. A lack of sleep eventually leads to cognitive decline, emotional disturbances, and impairs functioning of the immune system. For some species, sleep deprivation can be more detrimental—even fatal—than food deprivation (Rechtschaffen, 1998).

Although there is good evidence supporting the restore and repair hypothesis, it does not account for all the reasons why we sleep. Imagine you have had an unusually active day on Saturday and then spend all day Sunday relaxing. Research shows that you are likely to feel more sleepy

The restore and repair hypothesis suggests that people will need more sleep after a physically demanding day.

on Saturday night, but you will need only slightly more sleep after the high-activity day despite what the restore and repair hypothesis would suggest (Horne & Minard, 1985). The same is true for days filled with mentally challenging activities (De Bruin et al., 2002). Rather than requiring more sleep, it could be that sleep is more efficient after an exhausting day (Montgomery et al., 1987); in other words, more restoring and repairing may go on in the same amount of time.

The **preserve and protect hypothesis** *suggests that two more adaptive functions of sleep are preserving energy and protecting the organism from harm* (Berger & Philips, 1995; Siegel, 2005). To support this hypothesis, researchers note that the animals most vulnerable to predators sleep in safe hideaways and during the time of day when they are most susceptible (Siegel, 1995). For humans and other visually oriented creatures, sleep occurs at night when it is dark and, therefore, when we would be at a disadvantage. Conversely, animals such as lions and bears rarely fall victim to predators, and they may sleep 15 hours per day.

The answer to why we sleep is a complex one. The best explanation seems to that there are multiple reasons that are supported by the research, and the amount that any human or animal sleeps is a combination of its need for restoration and repair along with its need for preservation and protection.

SLEEP DEPRIVATION AND SLEEP DISPLACEMENT

Chances are you have experienced disruptions to your sleep due to jet lag or an occasional late night, or even something as minor as Daylight Savings Time. In fact, researchers have found that over a 20-year period, switching to Daylight Savings in the spring costs workers an average of 40 minutes of sleep and significantly increases work-related injuries (Barnes & Wagner, 2009). The same analysis showed that returning to standard time in the fall produces no significant changes in sleep or injuries.

Sleep deprivation *occurs when an individual cannot or does not sleep.* We have yet to meet a college student who has not experienced this state at some point; approximately two-thirds of college students in one survey reported at least one experience of staying up all night (Thacher, 2008). Whether it is staying up all night to study or to play, the result the next day is predictable—periods during which the sleep deprivation leads to sleepiness, interspersed with other periods during which individuals feel perfectly normal levels of wakefulness. Exactly how sleep deprivation affects daily functioning has been the subject of some very interesting experiments. Volunteers in these studies have stayed awake for days at a time in relatively controlled laboratory settings. The strength of the circadian rhythms was evident; the volunteers generally went through cycles of extreme sleepiness at night, with normal levels of wakefulness in the daytime (especially the afternoon). However, each night saw an increasing level of sleepiness. Tests of cognitive ability, reaction times, and reflexes tend to show similar patterns, with volunteers doing well in the afternoons but getting progressively worse each night (Lavie, 2001).

These laboratory studies may reflect some of your own experiences, but what is perhaps most relevant for you is how sleep deprivation affects your performance at work or school. Research on adolescents shows that for every hour of deprivation, predictable increases in physical illness, family problems, substance abuse, and academic problems occur (Roberts et al., 2009). Among drivers, sleep deprivation is as dangerous as driving while mildly intoxicated (Maruff et al., 2005) and it is one of the most prevalent causes of fatal traffic accidents (Lyznicki et al., 1998; Sagberg, 1999).

Obviously, sleep deprivation is a job hazard for long-haul drivers, but it also presents a problem in other careers that involve shift work. Medical residents and attending physicians often work through the night at hospitals. Research suggests that the resulting sleep deprivation—not the long hours themselves—leads to job stress, burnout, and medical errors (Chen et al., 2008). This finding has motivated some researchers to investigate potential benefits of alternative work schedules; in doing so, they have discovered that reducing sleep-related strain is associated with fewer errors in medical practice (Figure 5.5; Landrigan et al., 2004).

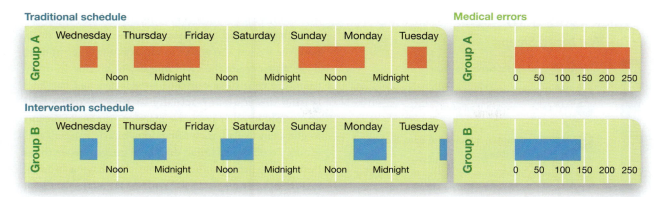

{FIG. 5.5} **The Costly Effects of Sleep Deprivation** The traditional schedule of a medical intern (Group A) requires up to a 31-hour on-call shift, whereas the modified schedule (Group B) divides the 31 hours into two shorter shifts. The latter schedule reduces the effects of prolonged sleep deprivation as measured in terms of medical errors.

Sleep displacement *occurs when an individual is prevented from sleeping at the normal time although she may be able to sleep earlier or later in the day than usual.* Consider a man from Chicago who flies to London for a vacation. The first night in London, he may try to go to bed at his usual 12:00 A.M. time. However, his body's rhythms will be operating six hours earlier—they are still at 6:00 P.M. Chicago time. If he is like most travelers, this individual will experience jet lag for three or four days until he can get his internal rhythms to synchronize with the external day–night cycles. **Jet lag** *is the discomfort a person feels when sleep cycles are out of synchronization with light and darkness* (Arendt, 2009). How much jet lag people experience is related to

how many time zones they cross, and how quickly they do so (e.g., driving versus flying). Also, it is typically easier to adjust when traveling west. When traveling east, a person must try to fall asleep earlier than usual, which is difficult to do. Most people find it easier to stay up longer than usual, which is what westward travel requires.

For someone on a long vacation, jet lag may not be too much of an inconvenience. But imagine an athlete who has to be at her physical best, or a business executive who must remain sharp through an afternoon meeting. For these individuals, it is wise to arrive a week early if possible, or try to adapt to the new time zone before leaving, as shown in Figure 5.6.

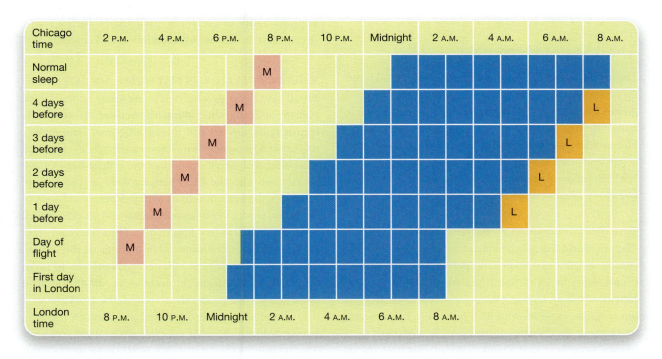

{FIG. 5.6} **Preparing for an Eastward Flight Crossing Six Time Zones** A person who is used to sleeping from midnight until 8:00 A.M. should go to bed an hour earlier each night and stay in bed for eight hours (as indicated by the blue bands). Five hours before bedtime, he should take a melatonin supplement (represented by the pink spaces) and, upon waking, should turn on bright lights (represented by the gold spaces).

Quick Quiz 5.1b
Why We Need Sleep

Complete the **Survey** *Are Dreams Meaningful?* at **MyPsychLab**

Theories of Dreaming

The strange, unpredictable side of dreams has fascinated people for centuries, and it is not uncommon for cultures to search dreams for meaning. Discovering the meaning of dreams by analyzing their content may not be a scientific possibility. However, *why* we dream—what function dreaming serves—better lends itself to scientific testing. We will begin with a brief discussion of one attempt to find meaning in dreams, and then explore some scientific approaches to dreaming.

THE PSYCHOANALYTIC APPROACH

In the Western world, many beliefs about the meaning of dreams come from the psychoanalytic perspective of Sigmund Freud, who in 1899 published his classic work, *The Interpretation of Dreams*. Freud viewed dreams as an unconscious expression of *wish fulfillment*. You can read more about his theories of personality in Module 12.3, but we note here that Freud believed that humans are motivated by primal urges, with sex and aggression being the most dominant. Because giving in to these urges is impractical most of the time (not to mention potentially immoral), we learn ways of keeping these urges suppressed and outside of our conscious awareness. When we sleep, however, we lose the power to suppress our urges; in turn, these drives create the vivid imagery of dreams. In many cases, the **manifest content**—*the images and storylines that we dream about*—actually involve sexuality and aggression. In other cases, the manifest content of dreams might seem like a bunch of random, bizarre imagery and events. Freud would argue that these images are anything but random; instead, he believed they have a hidden, **latent content**—*the actual symbolic meaning of a dream built on suppressed sexual or aggressive urges*. Because the true meaning of the dream is latent, Freud advocated *dream work*, the recording and interpreting of dreams.

Freud's ideas live on in the popular press, and they resonate with mystical beliefs about dreaming. Indeed, there is no shortage of books offering insight into interpreting dreams. There are even dream dictionaries that claim to define certain symbols found in manifest content. These ideas certainly make for good stories, but there is no scientific evidence to support them. In fact, the opposite is true: There is good reason to be skeptical. The content of most dreams is not all that bizarre and, in fact, is usually rather trivial and boring. As a consequence, many dreams are perfectly understandable without symbolic interpretation. Moreover, dream work requires a subjective interpreter to understand dreams, and does not use objective measurements. Therefore, modern dream research focuses much more on the biological activity of dreaming, particularly during REM sleep, when dreams are most common and complex.

THE ACTIVATION–SYNTHESIS HYPOTHESIS

Freud saw deep psychological meaning in the latent content of dreams. In contrast, the **activation–synthesis hypothesis** *suggests that dreams arise from brain activity originating from bursts of excitatory messages from the brainstem*. This electrical activity produces the telltale signs of eye movements and the EEG activity during REM sleep; moreover, the burst of activity activates perceptual areas of the brain, producing imaginary sights and sounds, as well as emotional areas (see Figure 5.7). Thus the brain stem actions initiate the *activation* component of the model. The *synthesis* component arises as the brain tries to make sense of all the images (Hobson et al., 2000). Because these images are randomly activated, the storyline of a dream typically seems disjointed and bizarre. Imagine having a dozen different people each provide you with one randomly selected word, with these words then assembled to look like a single message—you might have to struggle to make sense of the result. This example is analogous to the activation–synthesis theory of dreaming.

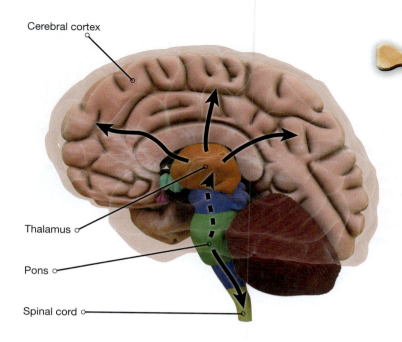

Cerebral cortex

Thalamus

Pons

Spinal cord

{FIG. 5.7} **The Activation–Synthesis Hypothesis of Dreaming** The pons, located in the brain stem, sends excitatory messages through the thalamus to the sensory and emotional areas of the cortex. The images and emotions that arise from this activity are then woven into a story. Inhibitory signals are also relayed from the pons down the spinal cord, which prevents movement during dreaming.

WORKING THE SCIENTIFIC LITERACY MODEL
The Problem-Solving Theory of Dreaming

The rich, symbolic interpretation of dreams in the psychoanalytic tradition has no scientific support. In contrast, the activation–synthesis hypothesis views dream content as random side effects of brain activity with little or no meaning. Given these two extremes, you may be wondering if there is something in between—an approach that allows for some dreams to have meaning that can be scientifically verified.

What do we know about the problem-solving theory of dreaming?

Is it possible to find scientific evidence for meaning in dreams? If you are like most people, your dreams will *sometimes* be highly vivid replays of events from the preceding day. Consistent with these observations, sleep researcher Rosalind Cartwright has proposed the **problem-solving theory**—*the theory that thoughts and concerns are continuous from waking to sleeping, and that dreams may function to facilitate finding solutions to problems encountered while awake.*

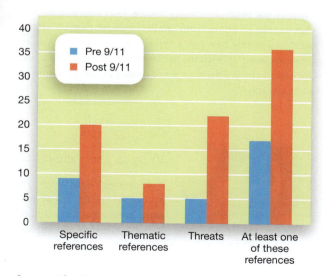

How can science explain whether dreams are problem-solving events?

To test this theory, sleep researchers typically ask volunteers to keep journals of their dream content. One example comes from a group of 14 students who were enrolled in a psychology course in the fall semester of 2001 (Propper et al., 2007). The students had been keeping journals of their dreams at the beginning of the semester. On September 11, 2001, the terrorist attacks on the World Trade Center and Pentagon took place. As they continued journaling after these events, the students reported significant increases in dreams involving objects and events related to the attacks, and had more dreams in which threatening events occurred (see Figure 5.8). Interestingly, the students who watched and listened to the most media coverage of the events were more likely to report attack-related themes and imagery in their dreams. Similar results have been found in other cases of emotional events such as divorce. The amount of waking concern about an ex-spouse correlates with the

{FIG. 5.8} **The Influence of the September 11, 2001 Terrorist Attacks on Dream Content** This graph shows the number of dreams containing specific types of content. *Specific references* include images of box cutters, planes, and the World Trade Center. *Thematic references* include general images of disasters, crashes, or tall buildings. *Threats* involve direct threats and life-threatening situations. The fourth column of the graph summarizes the number of dreams that contained any of these three types of content.

number of times that individual appears in a divorcee's dreams (Cartwright et al., 2006). Together, these studies provide support that waking concerns affect dream content and feeling.

Some additional support for problem-solving theory comes from recent research showing that both sleeping and especially dreaming are important for the formation of new memories (Poe et al., 2010; Stickgold & Walker, 2007). An entire night of sleep is not even necessary for sleep-enhanced memory formation. In one investigation, research participants who studied pictures of people, places, and objects were better able to recognize them when tested after a 90-minute nap in comparison to participants who did not nap (Alger, et al., 2010). Also, it appears that while we sleep, our memories for the emotional events from the day are reinforced during the REM stage (Payne & Kensinger, 2010).

Can we critically evaluate this evidence?

The term "problem-solving theory" seems to imply that the unconscious, sleeping brain is actually devising a solution while we enjoy resting. This is a misleading conclusion to draw from the September 11 and divorce studies just described. Dreaming about events of the waking hours may be beneficial, but there is not much evidence that a solution awaits us when we awaken. When it comes to making a decision you have likely heard the advice to "sleep on it." The clarity that often arises after a night's rest seems to support the problem-solving theory. In reality, the insights that appear to come from "sleeping on it" may be attributable to simply being in a more rested state. Also, many times we wake up with the problem remaining just as it was the night before—perhaps these instances do not come to mind as easily.

Why is this relevant?

If dreaming helps with the processing of information, then the benefits of a good night's rest may go beyond restoring and repairing the body. Also, the fact that a full night of rest—or even just a nap—aids memory formation speaks to the importance of sleeping and dreaming (Payne & Kensinger, 2010; Rasch & Born, 2008). This aspect of problem-solving theory is important to college students everywhere: Pulling an all-nighter prior to an exam may seem like a necessity, but this evidence reminds us that the need to study should be balanced by the need to sleep. The best advice, then, is to study and sleep every night, not just the night before the exam.

Dreams often reflect waking life—but they can also seem bizarre, random, and surreal, just as the activation–synthesis hypothesis predicts. Why we dream, and what dreams mean, remains a scientific mystery. At this point, the activation–synthesis hypothesis and problem-solving theory represent the current state of knowledge about dreaming.

Quick Quiz 5.1c
Theories of Dreaming

KNOW …

1 The problem-solving theory of dreaming proposes that:

   A dreams create more problems than they solve.

   B the problems and concerns we face in our waking life also appear in our dreams.

   C the symbols in our dreams represent unconscious urges related to sex and aggression.

   D we cannot solve complex moral or interpersonal problems until we have dreamed about them.

UNDERSTAND …

2 The *synthesis* part of the activation–synthesis hypothesis suggests that:

   A the brain interprets the meaning of symbolic images.

   B the brain stem activates the cortex to produce random images.

   C the cortex stimulates the brain stem to produce interpretations of dreams.

   D the brain tries to "synthesize," or make sense of, randomly activated images.

ANALYZE …

3 Scientists are skeptical about the psychoanalytic theory of dreaming because the _____ of a dream is entirely subject to interpretation.

   A latent content   C activation

   B sleep stage   D manifest content

Answers can be found on page ANS-2.

Disorders and Problems With Sleep

Throughout this module, we have seen that sleep is an essential biological and psychological process; without sleep, individuals are vulnerable to cognitive, emotional, and physical symptoms. Given this relationship, it is no wonder that so many people seek help getting better sleep.

INSOMNIA   The most widely recognized sleeping problem is **insomnia**, *which is a disorder characterized by an extreme lack of sleep.* Insomnia affects approximately 10% of the U.S. population (Ancoli-Israel & Roth, 1999). Although the average adult may need 7 to 8 hours of sleep to feel rested, substantial individual differences exist. For this reason, insomnia is defined not in terms of the hours of sleep, but rather in terms of the degree to which a person feels rested during the day. This understanding is reflected in the American Psychiatric Association's criteria for insomnia shown in Table 5.1.

Although insomnia is often thought of as a single disorder, it may be more appropriate to refer to *insomnias* in the plural. *Onset insomnia* occurs when a person has difficulty falling asleep (30 minutes or more), *maintenance insomnia* occurs when an individual cannot easily return to sleep after waking in the night, and *terminal insomnia* is a situation in which a person wakes up too early— sometimes hours too early—and cannot return to sleep (Pallesen et al., 2001).

Insomnias stem from internal sleep disturbances, rather than by external stimuli over which one has little control, such as a neighbor's persistent car alarm. *Primary insomnia* refers to cases that arise from an internal source and are not the result of another disorder. Frequently, a person keeps himself awake by worrying about the day's events, an upcoming stressor, or even not getting enough sleep (Harvey, Tang, & Browning, 2005). *Secondary insomnias* are the result of other disorders, such as depression, physical problems such as recovery from back surgery, or use of substances ranging from caffeine and nicotine to illegal drugs such as marijuana, ecstasy, or cocaine (Schierenbeck et al., 2008). In addition, as we will discuss next, a number of other sleep-related disturbances can lead to insomnia.

Insomnia can arise from worrying about sleep. It is among the most common of all sleep disorders.

NIGHTMARES AND NIGHT TERRORS   Certainly, a downside to dreaming is the experience of **nightmares**, *which are particularly vivid and disturbing dreams that occur during REM sleep.* Nightmares can be so emotionally charged that they awaken the individual (Levin & Nielsen, 2007). Almost everyone—as many as 85% to 95% of adults—can remember having bad dreams that have negative emotional content, such as feeling lost, sad, or angry, within a one-year period (Levin, 1994; Schredl, 2003). Not everyone recalls disturbing dreams, however, and data from numerous studies indicate that nightmares are correlated with psychological distress. As problem-solving theory explains, people who are distressed when they are awake are likely to experience distress when they are asleep. This relationship was illustrated in a study of San Francisco and Arizona residents that began before a massive earthquake occurred in 1989. Although both groups began the study reporting similar rates of disturbed dreaming, residents of San Francisco reported a sharp increase in nightmares following the earthquake; residents of Arizona were not directly affected by the disaster and showed no such changes (Wood et al., 1992).

Even worse than nightmares, some people experience **night terrors**—*intense bouts of panic and arousal that awaken the individual, typically in a heightened emotional state.* A person experiencing a night terror may call out or scream, fight back against imaginary attackers, or leap from the bed and start to flee before waking up. Unlike nightmares, night terrors are not dreams. These episodes occur during NREM sleep, and the majority of people who experience them typically do not recall any specific dream content. Night terrors are more common

Table 5.1 :: The American Psychiatric Association's Criteria for Primary Insomnia

1. The person has at least one month of difficulty initiating or maintaining sleep.
2. Sleep loss causes distress or impairment in social, occupational, and other areas.
3. Insomnia does not occur during the course of some other sleep disorder or psychiatric disorder such as depression.
4. The sleep disturbance is not attributable to the effects of substance abuse (e.g., alcohol—which impairs sleep).

Source: Adapted from American Psychiatric Association. (2000). *Diagnostic and statistical manual of mental disorders* (4th ed.).

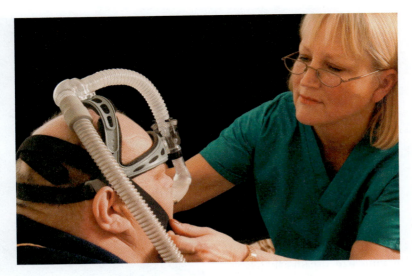

This CPAP device treats apnea by maintaining pressure in the airway.

in young children than in adults, and they increase in frequency during stressful periods, such as when parents are separating or divorcing (Schredl, 2001).

MOVEMENT DISTURBANCES To sleep well, an individual needs to remain still. During REM sleep the brain prevents movement by sending inhibitory signals down the spinal cord. A number of sleep disturbances, however, involve movement and related sensations. For example, **restless legs syndrome** *is a persistent feeling of discomfort in the legs and the urge to continuously shift them into different positions* (Smith & Tolson, 2008). This disorder affects approximately 5% to 10% of the population, and occurs at varying levels of severity. For those individuals who are in constant motion, sleep becomes very difficult. They awake periodically at night to reposition their legs, even though in some cases they do not remember waking the next day.

A more severe and potentially dangerous condition is REM behavior disorder, which was introduced in the beginning of this module. People with this condition do not show the typical restriction of movement during REM sleep; in fact, they appear to be acting out the content of their dreams (Schenck & Mahowald, 2002). Imagine what happens when an individual dreams of being attacked—the dreamed response of defending oneself or even fighting back can be acted out. Not surprisingly, this action can awaken some individuals. Because it occurs during REM sleep, however, some individuals do not awaken until they have hurt themselves or someone else, as occurred with Mike Birbiglia (Schenck et al., 1989).

Somnambulism, or *sleepwalking, is a disorder that involves wandering and performing other activities while asleep.* It is more prevalent during childhood. Sleepwalking is not necessarily indicative of any type of sleep or emotional disturbance, although it may put people in harm's way. People who sleepwalk are not acting out dreams, and they typically do not remember the episode. (For the record, it is not dangerous to wake up a sleepwalker, as is commonly thought. At worst, he will be disoriented.)

SLEEP APNEA **Sleep apnea** *is a disorder characterized by the temporary inability to breathe during sleep* (apnea literally translates to "without breathing"). Although a variety of factors contribute to sleep apnea, this condition appears to be most common among overweight and obese individuals, and it is roughly twice as prevalent among men as among women (Lin et al., 2008; McDaid et al., 2009).

In most cases of apnea, the airway becomes physically obstructed, at a point anywhere from the back of the nose and mouth to the neck (Figure 5.9). Therefore, treatment for mild apnea generally involves dental devices that hold the mouth in a specific position during sleep. Weight-loss efforts should accompany this treatment in most cases, as weight is a contributing factor for many individuals with sleep apnea. In moderate to severe cases, a continuous positive airway pressure (CPAP) device can be used to force air through the nose, keeping the airway open through increased air pressure (McDaid et al., 2009).

Sleep apnea can also be caused by the brain's failure to regulate breathing. This failure can happen for many reasons, including damage to or deterioration of the medulla of the brain stem, which is responsible for controlling the chest muscles during breathing.

You might wonder if disorders that stop breathing during sleep can be fatal. They can be, but rarely so. As

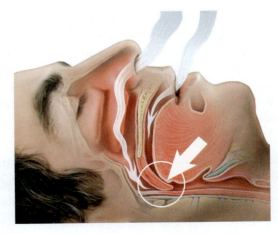

{FIG. 5.9} **Sleep Apnea** One cause of sleep apnea is the obstruction of air flow, which can seriously disrupt the sleep cycle.

breathing slows too much or stops altogether, oxygen levels in the blood rapidly decline, resulting in a gasping reflex and resumed oxygen flow. Actually, gasping may not even result in waking up. People with sleep apnea may not be aware that they are constantly cycling through oxygen loss and gasping as they sleep. It is often the case that affected individuals discover that they have sleep apnea only after visiting their physician.

NARCOLEPSY   While movement disorders, apnea, and night terrors can all lead to insomnia, another condition is characterized by nearly the opposite effect. **Narcolepsy** *is a disorder in which a person experiences extreme daytime sleepiness and even sleep attacks.* These bouts of sleep may last only a few seconds, especially if the person is standing or driving when she falls asleep and is jarred awake by falling, a nodding head, or swerving of the car. Even without such disturbances, the sleep may last only a few minutes or more, so it is not the same as falling asleep for a night's rest.

Narcolepsy differs from more typical sleep in a number of other ways. People with a normal sleep pattern generally reach REM stage after more than an hour of sleep, but a person experiencing narcolepsy is likely to go almost immediately from waking to REM sleep. Also, because REM sleep is associated with dreaming, people with narcolepsy often report vivid dream-like images even if they did not fully fall asleep.

Why does narcolepsy occur? Scientists have investigated a hormone called *orexin* that functions to maintain wakefulness. Individuals with narcolepsy have fewer brain cells that produce orexin, resulting in greater difficulty maintaining wakefulness (Nakamura et al., 2011).

SLEEP MISPERCEPTION   It may come as a surprise, but one sleep problem is simply knowing how long you have slept. **Sleep state misperception (SSM)** *is a condition in which a person underestimates her amount of sleep on a regular basis.* People experiencing SSM are sometimes said to have *paradoxical insomnia*—they believe they cannot sleep enough, but there is no physiological or medical evidence to support that belief (American Academy of Sleep Medicine, 2005; Trinder, 1988). In fact, many people experience SSM without any detriment to their daily functioning. Thus the problem with SSM is primarily the distress a person feels about having insomnia, even though the individual may not actually have insomnia. The opposite condition—**positive sleep state misperception**—*occurs when individuals regularly overestimate their sleep.* This form of misperception produces slightly more problems in that the individual

begins to show signs of sleep deprivation—severe afternoon sleepiness and attention problems—and does not connect these symptoms with poor sleep (Trajanovic et al., 2007).

Think about the difficulty underlying sleep misperception: If you are unconscious when you are asleep, how are you supposed to monitor how long you are sleeping? Yet when researchers compare people's self-rated estimates of how much they sleep with more objective measures—through polysomnography—it turns out that most individuals are relatively accurate. This, however, is not the case in people with SSM. In other words, most sleepers can provide reasonably accurate estimates of their amount of sleep using cues such as the time they went to bed, the time it took to fall asleep, the amount of waking during the night, and the time they first awoke.

OVERCOMING SLEEP PROBLEMS   Everyone has difficulty sleeping at some point, and there are many myths and anecdotes about what will help. For some people, relief can be as simple as a snack or a warm glass of milk; it can certainly be difficult to sleep if you are hungry. Others might have a nightcap—a drink of alcohol—in hopes of inducing sleep, although the effects can be misleading. Alcohol may make you sleepy, but it disrupts the quality of sleep, especially the REM cycle, and may leave you feeling unrested the next day. Fortunately, most people respond very well to psychological interventions. By practicing good sleep hygiene—healthy sleep-related habits—they can typically overcome sleep disturbances in a matter of a few weeks (Morin et al., 2006; Murtagh & Greenwood, 1995). The techniques shown in Table 5.2 (page 170) are effective for many people who prefer self-help methods, but effective help is also available from psychologists, physicians, and even over the Internet (Ritterband et al., 2009; van Straten & Cuijpers, 2009).

Although research supports the use of cognitive and behavioral techniques, people often turn to drugs to help them sleep. A number of sleep aids are available on an over-the-counter basis, and several varieties of prescription drugs have been developed as well. For most of the 20th century, drugs prescribed for insomnia included sedatives such as barbiturates (Phenobarbital) and benzodiazepines (e.g., Valium). Although these drugs managed to put people to sleep, several problems with their use were quickly observed. Notably, people quickly developed tolerance to these agents, meaning they required increasingly higher doses to get the same effect, and many soon came to depend on the drugs so much that they

Table 5.2 :: Nonpharmacological Techniques for Improving Sleep

1. Use your bed for sleeping only, not for working or studying. (Sexual activity is an appropriate exception to the rule.)

2. Do not turn sleep into work. Putting effort into falling asleep generally leads to arousal instead of sleep.

3. Keep your clock out of sight. Watching the clock increases pressure to sleep and worries about getting enough sleep.

4. Get exercise early during the day. Exercise may not increase the amount of sleep, but it may help you sleep better. Exercising late in the day, however, may leave you restless and aroused at bedtime.

5. Avoid substances that disrupt sleep. Such substances include caffeine (in coffee, tea, many soft drinks, and other sources), nicotine, and alcohol. Illicit drugs such as cocaine, marijuana, and ecstasy also disrupt healthy sleep.

6. If you lie in bed worrying at night, schedule evening time to deal with stress. Write down your worries and stressors for approximately 30 minutes prior to bedtime.

7. If you continue to lie in bed without sleeping for 30 minutes, get up and do something else until you are about to fall asleep, and then return to bed.

8. Get up at the same time every morning. Although this practice may lead to sleepiness the first day or two, eventually it helps set the daily rhythm.

9. If you still have problems sleeping after four weeks, consider seeing a sleep specialist to get tested for sleep apnea, restless legs syndrome, or other sleep problem that may require more specific interventions.

Source: Based on recommendations from the American Psychological Association, 2004.

could not sleep without them (Pallesen et al., 2001). Even though benzodiazepines are generally safer than barbiturates, the risk of dependence and worsening sleep problems makes them suitable only for short-term use—generally for a week or two—and only after sleep hygiene efforts have failed.

Modern sleep drugs are generally thought to be much safer in the short term, and many have been approved for long-term use as well. However, few modern drugs have been studied in placebo-controlled experiments, and even fewer have actually been studied for long-term use (e.g., for more than a month; Krystal, 2009).

Quick Quiz 5.1d :: Disorders and Problems with Sleep

KNOW…

1 When people believe they are not getting much sleep, despite physical evidence to the contrary, they are experiencing _____.

A somnambulism

B sleep state misperception

C positive sleep state misperception

D sleep apnea

2 _____ is a condition in which a person's breathing becomes obstructed or stops during sleep.

A Somnambulism

B Sleep state misperception

C Narcolepsy

D Sleep apnea

APPLY…

3 Which of the following is *not* good advice for improving your quality of sleep?

A Use your bed for sleeping only—not homework or watching TV.

B Exercise late in the day to make sure you are tired when it is time to sleep.

C Avoid drinking caffeine, especially late in the day.

D Get up at the same time every morning to make sure you develop a reliable pattern of sleep and wakefulness.

Answers can be found on page ANS-2.

Module Summary

Now that you have read this module you should:

KNOW …

- **The key terminology associated with sleep, dreams, and sleep disorders:**

activation–synthesis hypothesis (p. 164)

circadian rhythms (p. 159)

consciousness (p. 158)

insomnia (p. 167)

jet lag (p. 163)

latent content (p. 164)

manifest content (p. 164)

narcolepsy (p. 169)

nightmares (p. 167)

night terrors (p. 167)

polysomnography (p. 160)

positive sleep state misperception (p. 169)

preserve and protect hypothesis (p. 162)

problem-solving theory (p. 165)

REM sleep (p. 161)

restless legs syndrome (p. 168)

restore and repair hypothesis (p. 161)

sleep apnea (p. 168)

sleep deprivation (p. 162)

sleep displacement (p. 163)

sleep state misperception (SSM) (p. 169)

somnambulism (p. 168)

UNDERSTAND …

- **How the sleep cycle works.** The sleep cycle consists of a series of stages going from stage 1 through stage 4, cycles back down again, and is followed by a REM phase. The first sleep cycle lasts approximately 90 minutes. Deep sleep (stages 3 and 4) is longest during the first half of the sleep cycle, whereas REM phases increase in duration during the second half of the sleep cycle.

- **Theories of why we sleep.** Sleep theories include the restore and repair hypothesis and the preserve and protect hypothesis. According to the restore and repair hypothesis, we sleep so that the body can recover from the stress and strain on the body that occurs during waking. According to the preserve and protect hypothesis, sleep has evolved as a way to reduce activity and provide protection from potential threats, and to reduce the amount of energy intake required. Evidence supports both theories, so it is likely that there is more than one reason for sleep.

APPLY …

- **Your knowledge to identify and practice good sleep habits.** Try completing the Epworth Sleepiness Scale to make sure you are getting enough sleep **(Table 5.3)**. If you score 10 points or higher, you are probably not getting enough sleep. You can always refer to **Table 5.2** (p. 170) for tips on improving your sleep.

ANALYZE …

- **Different theories about why we dream.** Dreams have fascinated psychologists since Freud's time. From his psychoanalytic perspective, Freud believed that the manifest content of dreams could be used to uncover their symbolic, latent content. Contemporary scientists are skeptical about the validity of this approach given the lack of empirical evidence to support it. The activation–synthesis theory eliminates the meaning of dream content, suggesting instead that dreams are just interpretations of haphazard electrical activity in the sleeping brain. The problem-solving theory is a modern alternative proposing that dreams reflect recent events and that they serve as a mechanism for solving problems and facilitating long-term memory storage.

Table 5.3 :: Epworth Sleepiness Scale

Use the following scale to choose the most appropriate number for each situation:
0 = would *never* doze or sleep   1 = *slight* chance of dozing or sleeping
2 = *moderate* chance of dozing or sleeping   3 = *high* chance of dozing or sleeping

SITUATION	CHANCES OF FALLING ASLEEP
Sitting and reading	0 1 2 3
Watching TV	0 1 2 3
Sitting inactive in a public place	0 1 2 3
Being a passenger in a motor vehicle for an hour or more	0 1 2 3
Lying down in the afternoon	0 1 2 3
Sitting and talking to someone	0 1 2 3
Sitting quietly after lunch (no alcohol)	0 1 2 3
Stopped for a few minutes in traffic while driving	0 1 2 3
Your total score	

Source: Johns (1991)

Altered States of Consciousness: Hypnosis, Meditation, and Disorders of Consciousness

Learning Objectives After reading this module you should:	**KNOW ...**	**UNDERSTAND ...**	**APPLY ...**	**ANALYZE ...**
	The key terminology associated with hypnosis, meditation, déjà vu, and disorders of consciousness	The competing theories of hypnosis	Your knowledge of hypnosis to identify what it can and cannot do	Claims that hypnosis can help with memory recovery The effectiveness of meditation for use in therapy

Have you ever walked into a room for the first time and suddenly felt an eerie sense that, although it was not possible, you had been there before? In a sense, you may have visited this place before—albeit not in a past life or through some supernatural means. Psychologists can actually induce this experience, called déjà vu, in research participants. In fact, Dr. Anne Cleary does it quite easily. Dr. Cleary has asked research participants to study pictures of settings such as bowling alleys, landscapes, and rooms from houses. Later, she shows them the same pictures, along with new pictures with a vague resemblance to the originals. These vaguely familiar pictures induce a déjà vu-like experience (Cleary et al., 2009). The same thing happens when she does this experiment using music; songs can also induce déjà vu (Kostic & Cleary, 2009). These experiments help explain the bizarre déjà vu experience, and stimulate additional fascination about our consciousness experiences.

Focus Questions

 Why is déjà vu often accompanied by a strong emotional reaction?

 Is information processed in the background of our awareness?

· · · · · · · · · · · · · · · · · ·

Consciousness varies by degree—much lies between being awake versus being asleep. Humans have a remarkable ability to alter where on this continuum they want to reach. Techniques such as hypnosis and meditation—two topics discussed in this module—are ways of inducing what many regard as an altered state of consciousness. Experiences such as déjà vu highlight the strange, subjective world of conscious experience. Also, injury or illness can temporarily or permanently change a person's level of consciousness. In this module, we examine these topics related to consciousness.

Hypnosis

Chances are that you have seen hypnosis featured in films, television shows, or even live stage performances. The caricature of a pocket watch swung back and forth before an increasingly subdued subject will probably always be around, though it promotes just one of many misunderstandings about hypnosis. **Hypnosis** *is a procedure of inducing a heightened state of suggestibility.* According to this definition, hypnosis is about suggestibility; it is *not* a trance, as is often portrayed in the popular media (Kirsch & Lynn, 1998). The hypnotist simply suggests changes, and the subject is more likely (but not certain) to comply as a result of the hypnosis.

Although one could conceivably make suggestions about almost anything, hypnotic suggestions generally are most effective when they fall into one of three categories:

- *Ideomotor suggestions* are related to specific actions that could be performed, such as adopting a specific position.
- *Challenge suggestions* indicate actions that are not to be performed, so that the subject appears to lose the ability to perform an action.
- *Cognitive-perceptual suggestions* are to remember or forget, or to experience altered perceptions such as reduced pain sensations (Kirsch & Lynn, 1998).

Regardless of the category, hypnotic suggestions will not completely change an individual. In other words, a hypnotist could suggest to someone that the individual's sore hand no longer hurts, thereby helping to diminish the pain. In contrast, the hypnotist could not suggest that an honest person rob a bank and expect the subject to comply.

People who have not encountered scientific information about hypnosis are often skeptical that hypnosis can actually occur or are very reluctant to be hypnotized themselves (Capafons et al., 2008; Molina & Mendoza, 2006). This is probably not surprising given the vast misunderstanding about hypnosis. For all these reasons, it is important to establish a scientific view of the phenomenon.

THEORIES OF HYPNOSIS The word *hypnosis* comes from the Greek *hypno,* meaning "sleep." In reality, scientific research tells us that hypnosis is nothing like sleep. For example, it is even possible to experience

Stage hypnotists often use the human plank demonstration with their subjects. They support an audience volunteer on three chairs. To the audience's amazement, when the chair supporting the mid-body is removed, the hypnotized subject does not fall (even when weight is added, as shown in the photo). However, nonhypnotized subjects also do not fall. (Please do not try this at home—there is a trick behind it!)

hypnosis during periods of high alertness—including during physical exercise (Wark, 2006). So, if hypnosis is not sleep, what is it?

Dissociation theory *explains hypnosis as a unique state in which consciousness is divided into two parts: an observer and a hidden observer.* It may sound magical, but this kind of divided state is actually quite common. Take any skill that you have mastered, such as driving a car or playing an instrument. When you began, it took every bit of your conscious awareness to focus on the correct movements—you were a single, highly focused observer of your actions. After a few years of practice, you could do it automatically while you observed and paid attention to something else. Although we call the familiar behavior automatic, there is still a hidden observer—that is, a part of you that is paying attention to the task. According to dissociation theory, hypnosis splits awareness in a similar way. At one level, the hypnotized individual is focused intently on the suggestions, while at another level of consciousness she is attending to something else (Hilgard, 1994).

Hypnotherapy involves a trained therapist giving hypnotic suggestions to a client.

A more recent approach, **social–cognitive theory**, *explains hypnosis by emphasizing the degree to which beliefs and expectations contribute to increased suggestibility.* This perspective is supported by experiments in which individuals are told either that they will be able to resist ideomotor suggestions or that they will not be able to resist them. In these studies, people tend to conform to what they have been told to expect—a result that cannot be easily explained by dissociation theory (Lynn et al., 1984; Spanos et al., 1985). Similarly, research on hypnosis as a treatment for pain shows that *response expectancy*—whether the individual believes the treatment will work—plays a large role in the actual pain relief experienced (Milling, 2009).

APPLICATIONS OF HYPNOSIS Since hypnosis is a state of heightened suggestibility, why not use it to suggest that an individual in psychotherapy stop thinking depressing thoughts or confront anxiety-provoking situations? Interestingly, hypnosis has been applied to these and other problems. For example, the most frequently used, scientifically supported psychotherapy for depression is known as cognitive-behavioral therapy (CBT; see Module 14.2). Psychotherapy research combining hypnosis with CBT (an approach known as cognitive hypnotherapy) has been shown to be equally effective as, and perhaps even more effective than, CBT alone (Alladin & Alibhai, 2007). Similar research shows that hypnotherapy is an effective addition to medical treatments for anxiety related to post-traumatic stress (Abramowitz et al., 2008). In addition, if you have any anxiety about an oral presentation that lies in your future, cognitive hypnotherapy has been shown to reduce public speaking anxiety (Schoenberger et al., 1997).

Hypnosis is far from a cure-all, however. For example, researchers found that hypnotherapy combined with a nicotine patch is more effective as a smoking cessation intervention than the patch alone. Nonetheless, only one-fifth of the individuals receiving this kind of therapy managed to remain smoke-free for a year (Carmody et al., 2008). Moreover, the individuals receiving hypnotherapy for depression improved only 5% to 8% more on several measures of depressive symptoms than those who received traditional CBT. The best conclusion regarding hypnosis in therapy is that it shows promise, especially when used in conjunction with other evidence-based psychological or medical treatments.

Perhaps the most practical use for hypnosis is in the treatment of pain. If researchers can demonstrate its effectiveness in this application, it may be a preferred method of pain control given painkillers' potential side effects and risk of dependence—not to mention that hypnosis treatments for medical procedures cost only half as much as drugs (Lang et al., 2000). What does the scientific evidence say about the use of hypnosis in treating pain? A review of 18 individual studies found that approximately 75% of all individuals experienced adequate pain relief with this approach beyond that provided by traditional analgesics or no treatment (Montgomery et al., 2000). What happened to the other 25%? Perhaps the failure of the treatment in this group is attributable to the fact that some people are more readily hypnotized than others. In addition, to truly understand pain control, researchers must distinguish among different types of pain. Research has shown that hypnosis generally works as well as drug treatments for *acute pain*, which is the intense, temporary pain associated with a medical or dental procedure (Patterson & Jenson, 2003). Hypnosis is somewhat effective for *chronic pain*, the type of pain that lasts for long periods of time.

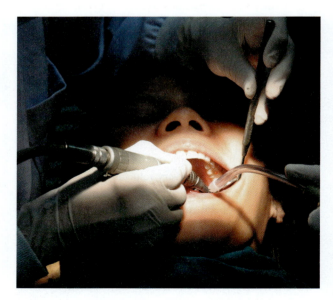

Under hypnosis, people can withstand higher levels of pain for longer periods of time, including the discomfort associated with dental procedures.

MYTHS IN MIND
Recovering Lost Memories Through Hypnosis

Hypnosis has long been used in psychotherapy, and it has many potential benefits in this setting. However, before the limitations of hypnosis were fully understood, professionals working in the fields of psychology and law regularly used this technique for uncovering lost memories. What a powerful tool this would be for a psychologist—if a patient could remember specifics about trauma or abuse it *could* greatly help the individual's recovery. Similarly, law enforcement and legal professionals could benefit by learning the details of a crime recovered through hypnosis—or so many assumed.

As you have read, hypnosis puts the subject into a highly suggestible state. This condition leaves the individual vulnerable to prompts and suggestions by the hypnotist. A cooperative person could certainly comply with suggestions and create a story that, in the end, is entirely false. This has happened time and again. In reality, hypnosis does not improve memory (Kihlstrom, 1997; Loftus & Davis, 2006). Today, responsible psychologists do not use hypnotherapy to uncover or reconstruct lost memories. Also, testimony based on hypnosis sessions alone cannot be submitted as evidence in most U.S. courts.

. . . .

Quick Quiz 5.2a
Hypnosis

KNOW . . .

1. _____ suggestions specify that certain actions cannot be performed while hypnotized.

 A. Ideomotor

B. Challenge

C. Cognitive-perceptual

D. Disassociation

UNDERSTAND . . .

2. Dr. Johnson claims that hypnosis is a distinct state of consciousness in which there is a "hidden" observer. It appears that she is endorsing the _____ theory of hypnosis.

A. social-cognitive   C. dissociation

B. psychoanalytic   D. hypnotherapy

APPLY . . .

3. Hypnosis has been shown to be moderately successful as a therapy for all of the following *except*:

 A. addiction.

B. pain therapy.

 C. causing long-term personality changes.

D. depression and anxiety.

 ANALYZE . . .

4. Which of the following statements best describes the scientific consensus about recovering memories with hypnosis?

A. Memories "recovered" through hypnosis are highly unreliable and should never be used as evidence in court.

B. If the memory is recovered by a trained psychologist, then it may be used as evidence in court.

C. Recovering memories through hypnosis is a simple procedure and, therefore, the findings should be a regular part of court hearings.

D. Memories can be recovered only in individuals who are highly hypnotizable.

Answers can be found on page ANS-2.

Meditation and Déjà Vu

Hypnosis relies on suggestibility, but there are other variations in conscious experience, including those that are intentionally initiated by the individual and those that seem to catch us off guard. Here we will examine meditation and déjà vu.

WORKING THE SCIENTIFIC LITERACY MODEL
Meditation

Meditation is practiced in many forms by members of almost every known culture. You may be familiar with some of these practices, or at least their associated names, such as transcendental meditation and Zen Buddhism. Although these practices may seem beyond the realm of scientific study, researchers have found ways to study and understand them.

What do we know about meditation?

Meditation *is any procedure that involves a shift in consciousness to a state in which an individual is highly focused, aware, and in control of mental processes.* Although meditation includes some century-old practices, scientific interest in it is only a few decades old. Even in the 21st century, researchers have cautioned that we do not know exactly what meditation can accomplish (e.g., Bishop, 2002). Several approaches to meditation have emerged, including *Mindfulness-Based Stress Reduction* (MBSR). MBSR programs have been developed to teach and promote mindfulness as a way of improving well-being and reducing negative experiences. Mindfulness-based interventions are generally well received by patients and can significantly reduce everyday levels of stress, depression, and anxiety, as well as more chronic psychiatric disorders (Chiesa & Serretti, 2010; Olivo et al., 2009).

How can science explain the effects of meditation?

In one study, people who suffered severe social anxiety volunteered to undergo MBSR training (Goldin & Gross, 2010). Prior to the training, the participants' symptoms of social anxiety were assessed, and they were even given brain scans to identify how their emotion centers responded to statements that reminded them of negative self-beliefs regarding social situations (e.g., "I am ashamed of my shyness," "People always judge me"). After this initial assessment, the participants attended eight weekly MBSR training sessions, along with a half-day meditation retreat, that involved focused breathing exercises, bodily awareness, relaxation, and other methods for sustaining a meditative state.

Following the meditation training, the participants improved in their overall well-being, including showing reduced anxiety and depression, and increased self-esteem. Also, the participants received a second brain scan in which their reactions to negative statements about themselves were monitored (Figure 5.10). The emotional centers of the brain that were previously activated by these statements proved to be less responsive at this follow-up test (Goldin & Gross, 2010).

In addition to reducing stress, anxiety, and depression, mindfulness meditation has a strong record of reducing pain, in both short-term experiments (e.g., Zeidan et al., 2010) and in long-term studies with chronic pain patients (Grant & Rainville, 2009; McCracken et al., 2007).

Can we critically evaluate this information?

As these results suggest, a growing body of research supports the use of meditation as a clinical intervention. Before this practice is adopted more widely, however, it is important to address several issues. First, the study did not include a control group which is essential for fully validating a form of therapy. Second, there are many different ways of practicing meditation; the research reviewed here focuses primarily on MBSR. Third, the studies indicate that meditation can make improvements across a wide assortment of variables, but this does not mean that meditation is a *cure*. Instead, meditation should be seen as just one component of a program of treatment that may include medications, psychotherapy, or other interventions, depending on the specific problem.

Why is this relevant?

Stress, anxiety, depression, and pain may seem like a wide range of symptoms to be affected by one type of treatment, but they actually share a similar theme. As you will read in later chapters (in the discussions of stress in Module 16.2 and depression in Module 13.3), each of these conditions can be made worse when individuals focus on the ongoing, seemingly inescapable problem, dwell on it, and emphasize its negative effects. This kind of focus can turn even a minor problem into a catastrophe. Thus the take-home message is that meditation may help you if you have ongoing pain, anxiety, or other negative experiences. Meditation techniques teach individuals to be aware in an accepting, nonjudgmental manner, which seems to be an important cognitive factor in reducing symptoms (Perlman et al., 2010).

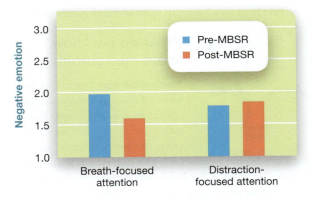

{FIG. 5.10} **Meditation Reduces Negative Emotions** On the left side of the graph, notice that ratings of negative emotions decreased from before MBSR (blue bar) to after (red bar). In contrast, no real difference was apparent when volunteers simply distracted themselves from negative feelings, as shown by the blue and red bars on the right.

DÉJÀ VU At the beginning of this module, we introduced the mysterious conscious experience known as **déjà vu**, *a distinct feeling of having seen or experienced a situation that is impossible or unlikely to have previously occurred.* You may have experienced it yourself—studies indicate that most people have had at least one episode (Brown, 2003). It generally begins with an individual entering a new situation or having a subtle shift of attention, and then it sets in—the feeling that *I've been here before*, doing and seeing the exact same things.

One source of information about déjà vu experiences comes from studies of temporal lobe epilepsy. With this form of epilepsy, seizures tend to occur at the temporal lobes of the cortex. Some individuals with temporal lobe epilepsy experience déjà vu regularly, right at the onset of a seizure (Guedj et al., 2010; O'Connor & Moulin, 2008). Could it be that structures within the temporal lobes are responsible for the intense experience of familiarity? They seem to be likely candidates. The temporal lobes include a structure known as the hippocampus. As you will read in Module 7.1, this structure and the surrounding regions—the parahippocampal area—are important for memory. Brain scans show that individuals prone to temporal lobe epilepsy-induced déjà vu have decreased activity in the parahippocampal regions (Guedj et al., 2010).

Another neurological explanation for déjà vu derives from the fact that the brain contains multiple perceptual pathways. As explained in Module 4.2, the visual system transmits information from the eyes to the left and right hemispheres of the brain. Also, the brain processes information about *what* objects are and *where* they are located in separate pathways. It is possible that déjà vu arises when visual information in one of these pathways is processed a split second earlier than in the other pathway (Brown, 2003). This explanation is very difficult to test, however, and it is certainly contradicted by the finding that people who are blind can also experience déjà vu (O'Connor & Moulin, 2006).

Researchers have also examined déjà vu at the cognitive level, which offers an explanation for this phenomenon based on our experiences with familiarity and recognition (O'Connor & Moulin, 2010). Consider the experience of walking through a grocery store and encountering an acquaintance. Even if you have never seen her in a store before, you can still experience the familiarity of her face as well as something about the context from which you know her. Perhaps déjà vu arises in a situation characterized by both a strong sense of familiarity and an equally strong sense that you could not have encountered it before (Cleary, 2008). Some interesting correlations to support this interpretation exist. For example, people who travel frequently are more prone to the déjà vu experience, as are people who report more dreams (Brown, 2003). These individuals have access to many scenes and situations in memory, which increases the likelihood that they will find something familiar. At the same time, they often have good reason to suspect that they have never experienced something before because they are in an entirely new location.

Quick Quiz 5.2b
Meditation and Déjà Vu

KNOW …

1 Déjà vu is the experience of:

A the feeling of having been in a situation that is impossible or unlikely to have previously occurred.

B forgetting a previous perception.

C failing to perceive the obvious.

D being somewhere familiar but not remembering it.

2 What is one neurological explanation offered for déjà vu?

A Visual information may be processed in two brain regions, albeit slightly faster in one area than in the other.

B There is a déjà vu center in the brain.

C Déjà vu occurs when the brain waves recorded from two regions of the brain are very similar.

D Déjà vu occurs only in people who have problems with temporal lobe functioning.

ANALYZE …

3 What is known about the effects of meditation on pain perception?

A Beliefs about meditation are mostly superstition.

B All forms of meditation have proven effective at reducing pain.

C Some forms of meditation such as MBSR are effective in controlling chronic pain.

D Meditation is not an effective method for controlling pain.

Answers can be found on page ANS-2.

Disorders of Consciousness

It is difficult, if not impossible, to imagine a life without consciousness. However, someone who has dealt with a patient on life support, and certainly the rare individuals who recover from extended periods of lost consciousness, can provide vivid accounts of what it is like.

Take the case of Terri Schiavo, a Florida woman who collapsed in full cardiac arrest and lost consciousness in 1998. She spent more than two months in a coma, was placed on life support, and was diagnosed as being in a persistent vegetative state. Schiavo's physicians and husband were convinced that she had no consciousness, and no hope of ever regaining it. Schiavo's parents disagreed, and a massive court battle ensued to determine whether she should be removed from life support (i.e., a feeding tube), or if she should continue to be kept alive through medical interventions. It was a riveting case that eventually

Terry Schiavo suffered severe brain damage after going into cardiac arrest. She was diagnosed as being in a persistent vegetative state and subsequently taken off of life support in 2005.

At what point should or could an unconscious individual be removed from life support? Medical professionals frame their ethical decision-making process by keeping these disorders of consciousness in mind. For many, the primary challenge is determining whether the patient is conscious or has a chance of regaining consciousness. One approach is to consider the prognosis for individuals in PVS. If they do not recover within 12 months, it is unlikely that they will ever recover. Critics disagree with this contention, arguing that there are some signs of consciousness, even in PVS. For example, some people in PVS have shown rudimentary responses to language. There have been cases of neurological changes in response to one's name (Staffen et al., 2006) as well as the emotional tone of a speaker's voice (Kotchouby et al., 2009). Still other individuals have responded to verbal instructions to imagine themselves completing activities such as playing tennis; their fMRI scans revealed neural activity similar to that of non-PVS controls (Owen & Coleman, 2008; Owen et al., 2006). These patients cannot respond with gesture or speech, so they are classified as having PVS rather than MCS. Clearly, their brain activity is responding in some very interesting ways, but is it a sign of consciousness? The answer remains elusive, because another person's consciousness can only be inferred; it cannot be directly measured.

involved members of the U.S. Congress, the U.S. Supreme Court, and even the president of the United States. Ultimately, the courts sided with Schiavo's husband, and Terri Schiavo was removed from life support in 2005.

To understand cases like that involving Terri Schiavo, we must distinguish among three disorders of consciousness identified by medical personnel: coma, persistent vegetative state, and minimally conscious state. A **coma** *is a state marked by a complete loss of consciousness.* It begins with a serious brain injury or trauma. In response, the patient enters a state that, at least on the surface, looks like sleep—the eyes are closed and the body remains still (except for some reflexes). However, a coma differs from sleep in that some brain stem reflexes are suppressed (e.g., the pupils no longer dilate and contract with changes in brightness).

If a patient in a coma improves slightly, the individual may enter a **persistent vegetative state (PVS)**, *a state of minimal to no consciousness in which the patient's eyes may be open, and the individual will develop sleep–wake cycles without clear signs of consciousness.* For example, PVS patients do not appear to focus on objects in their visual field, nor do they track movement. There is hope for recovery if the patient improves within the first few months of PVS, but the chances for recovery decrease sharply between 6 and 12 months (Wijdicks, 2006).

The least severe of these disorders is the **minimally conscious state (MCS)**, *a disordered state of consciousness marked by the ability to show some behaviors that suggest at least partial consciousness, even if on an inconsistent basis* (Giacino et al., 2002). These behaviors must last long enough or be produced with some consistency to be distinguishable from basic reflexes, which are thought to be possible even without awareness. For example, MCS may be diagnosed if a patient can follow simple instructions, intentionally reach for or grasp objects, provide yes/no answers either verbally or through gestures (regardless of whether they are correct), or produce any intelligible speech.

Quick Quiz 5.2c
Disorders of Consciousness

KNOW...

1 _____ is a disorder of consciousness in which an individual may open the eyes and exhibit sleep–wake cycles but show no specific signs of consciousness.

A A coma

B A persistent vegetative state

C Déjà vu

D A minimally conscious state

2 What is the difference between a persistent vegetative state and a minimally conscious state?

A Nothing—they are both names for the same state.

B Someone in MCS can have conversations, unlike someone in PVS.

C Someone in MCS has sleep–wake cycles, unlike someone in PVS.

D People in MCS show at least some behaviors that indicate consciousness, even if on an irregular basis.

Answers can be found on page ANS-2.

Module Summary

Now that you have read this module you should:

Listen to the audio file of this module at MyPsychLab

KNOW ...

- **The key terminology associated with hypnosis, meditation, déjà vu, and disorders of consciousness:**

coma (p. 178)
déjà vu (p. 176)
dissociation theory (p. 173)
hypnosis (p. 173)
meditation (p. 175)

minimally conscious state (MCS) (p. 178)
persistent vegetative state (PVS) (p. 178)
social-cognitive theory (p. 174)

UNDERSTAND ...

- **The competing theories of hypnosis.** Dissociation theory states that hypnosis involves a division between observer and hidden observer, whereas social-cognitive theory states that hypnosis is a process in which the beliefs and expectations about the process heighten the subject's willingness to follow suggestions.

APPLY ...

- **Your knowledge of hypnosis to identify what it can and cannot do.** Answer the following statements with true or false and check your answers on page ANS-2.

True or False?

Hypnosis could *potentially* work in the following scenarios:

1. Temporarily increasing physical strength
2. Helping someone quit smoking
3. Inducing a hallucination
4. Remembering details of a crime scene
5. Recovering a traumatic memory
6. Helping someone relax
7. Reducing pain sensation

ANALYZE ...

- **Claims that hypnosis can help with memory recovery.** Scientific evidence suggests that hypnosis is not a valid technique for recovering buried memories, but is effective at opening up the subject to suggestion from the hypnotist or therapist. The heightened state of suggestion may result in the construction of memories for events that have not occurred.

- **The effectiveness of meditation for use in therapy.** People who meditate often find that this practice helps reduce symptoms of depression, stress, and anxiety, and provides pain relief. For serious conditions, meditation typically needs to be accompanied by additional therapies or treatments to provide relief.

Drugs and Conscious Experience

KNOW ...	UNDERSTAND ...	APPLY ...	ANALYZE ...
The key terminology related to different categories of drugs and their effects on the nervous system and behavior	Drug tolerance and dependence	Your knowledge to better understand your own beliefs about drug use	The difference between spiritual and recreational drug use The short- and long-term effects of drug use

Could taking a drug-induced trip be a way to cope with traumatic stress or a life-threatening illness? A variety of medications for reducing anxiety or alleviating depression are readily available. However, a few doctors and psychologists have suggested that perhaps a 6-hour trip on psychedelic "magic" mushrooms (called psilocybin) could be helpful to people dealing with difficult psychological and life problems.

In the 1960s, a fringe group of psychologists insisted that psychedelic drugs were the answer to all the world's problems. The outcast nature of this group and the ensuing "war on drugs" prompted mainstream psychologists to shelve any ideas that a psychedelic drug or something similar could be used in a therapeutic setting. This perception appears to be changing, however. Recently, Roland Griffiths from Johns Hopkins University has been conducting studies on the possible therapeutic benefits of psilocybin mushrooms. Cancer patients who were experiencing depression volunteered to take psilocybin as a part of Dr. Griffiths' study. Both at the end of their experience and 14 months later, they reported having personally meaningful, spiritually significant experiences that improved their overall outlook on life (Griffiths et al., 2008). This study

would best be described as preliminary, as additional studies involving controls and follow-up evaluations are needed. It is likely that such investigations will be forthcoming, as Griffiths is one of several researchers who are now exploring the possibility that mushrooms and similar drugs could be used in therapy.

Focus Questions

1. How do we distinguish between recreationally abused drugs and therapeutic usage?

2. Which other motives underlie drug use?

• • • • • • • • • • • • • • • • • •

Every human culture uses drugs. It could even be argued that every *human* uses drugs, depending on your definition of the term. Many of the foods that we eat contain the same types of compounds found in mind-altering drugs. For example, nutmeg contains compounds similar to those found in some psychedelic substances, and chocolate contains small amounts of the same compounds found in amphetamines and marijuana (Wenk, 2010). Of course, caffeine and alcohol—both of which are mainstream parts of our culture—are also drugs. The difference between a drug and a nondrug compound seems to be that drugs are taken because the user has an intended effect in mind. **Psychoactive drugs** *are substances that affect thinking, behavior, perception, and emotion.* From a scientific viewpoint, such drugs are categorized based on their effects on the nervous system. Drugs can speed up the nervous system, slow it down, stimulate its pleasure centers, or distort how it processes the world. Table 5.4 provides an overview of drugs that you should review before and again after reading this module.

Commonly Abused Illegal Drugs

Illicit drugs refer to those drugs whose manufacture, sale, and possession are illegal. As you will see, the boundary between illicit recreational drugs and legal prescription drugs can be razor-thin at times. Many common prescription medications are chemically similar, albeit safer, versions of illicit drugs. It often comes as a surprise to learn that the very substances that people can become

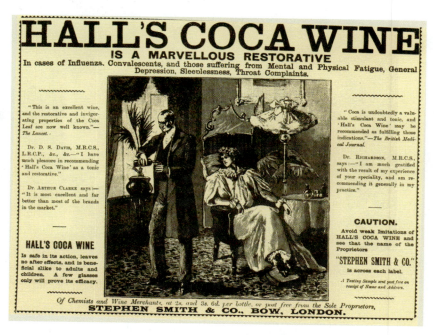

Cocaine was once used as an inexpensive, over-the-counter pain remedy. A concoction of wine and cocaine was popular, and the drug was also added to cough syrups and drops for treating toothaches.

addicted to, or whose possession and use can even land them in prison today, were once ingredients in everyday products.

Table 5.4 :: The Major Categories of Drugs

DRUGS	PSYCHOLOGICAL EFFECTS	CHEMICAL EFFECTS	TOLERANCE	LIKELIHOOD OF DEPENDENCE
Stimulants: cocaine, amphetamine, ecstasy	Euphoria, increased energy, lowered inhibitions	Increase dopamine, serotonin, norepinephrine activity	Develops quickly	High
Marijuana	Euphoria, relaxation, distorted sensory experiences, paranoia	Stimulates cannabinoid receptors	Develops slowly	Low
Hallucinogens: LSD, psilocybin, DMT, ketamine	Major distortion of sensory and perceptual experiences. Fear, panic, paranoia	Increase serotonin activity Blocks glutamate receptors	Develops slowly	Very low
Opiates: heroin	Intense euphoria, pain relief	Stimulate endorphin receptors	Develops quickly	Very high
Sedatives: barbiturates, benzodiazepines	Drowsiness, relaxation, sleep	Increase GABA activity	Develops quickly	High
Alcohol	Euphoria, relaxation, lowered inhibitions	Primarily facilitates GABA activity; also stimulates endorphin and dopamine receptors	Develops gradually	Moderate to high

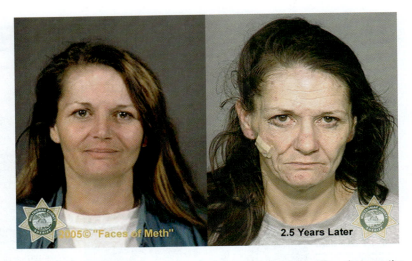

2005© "Faces of Meth" 2.5 Years Later

Theresa Baxter was 42 when the picture on the left was taken. The photo on the right was taken 2½ years later; the effects of methamphetamine are obvious and striking.

STIMULANTS **Stimulants** *are a category of drugs that speed up the nervous system, typically enhancing wakefulness and alertness.* Cocaine, one of the most commonly abused stimulants, is synthesized from cocoa leaves, most often grown in South American countries such as Peru and Colombia. The people who harvest these plants often take the drug in its simplest form—they chew on the leaves and experience a mild increase in energy. However, illicit cocaine appears in other forms as well. It is typically snorted and absorbed into the bloodstream through the nasal passages or, if prepared as crack cocaine, is smoked in a pipe.

Amphetamines, another group of stimulants, come in a variety of forms. Some are prescription drugs, such as methylphenidate (Ritalin) and modafinil (Provigil),

👁 **Watch** the **Video** *Eliminating Meth* at **MyPsychLab**

which are typically prescribed for attention-deficit/ hyperactivity disorder (ADHD) and narcolepsy, respectively. Other abused stimulants, mostly methamphetamine, are not prescribed drugs. Methamphetamine may be even more potent than cocaine when it comes to addictive potential, and is notorious for causing significant neurological as well as external physical problems. For example, chronic methamphetamine abusers often experience deterioration of their facial features, teeth, and gums, owing to a combination of factors. First, methamphetamine addiction can lead to neglect of basic dietary and hygienic care. Second, the drug is often manufactured from a potent cocktail of substances including hydrochloric acid and farm fertilizer—it is probably not surprising that these components can have serious side effects on appearance and health.

Stimulants such as cocaine and methamphetamine affect neural activity in the reward centers of the brain (see Figure 5.11a). Cocaine, for example, blocks reuptake of dopamine by binding to presynaptic terminals (see Figure 5.11b). By blocking reuptake of dopamine, cocaine allows excess amounts of this neurotransmitter to remain in the synapse and continue binding with postsynaptic receptors. Methamphetamine increases presynaptic release of dopamine and norepinephrine, and also slows their reuptake. 👁

The drug **ecstasy (MDMA)** *is typically classified as a stimulant, but also has hallucinogenic effects.* It was developed in the early 1900s as a possible prescription drug. Many decades later, in the 1980s, it was labeled a "club drug" because of its frequent appearance at rave parties. Ecstasy heightens physical sensations and is known to increase

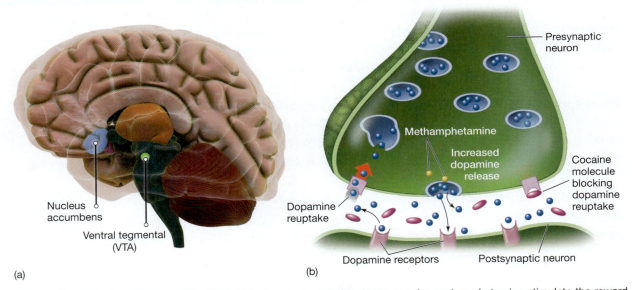

(a) (b)

{FIG. 5.11} **Stimulant Effects on the Brain** (a) Like many addictive drugs, cocaine and amphetamine stimulate the reward centers of the brain, including the nucleus accumbens and ventral tegmental area. (b) Cocaine works by blocking reuptake of dopamine, and methamphetamine works by increasing the release of dopamine at presynaptic neurons. **Click on this figure in your eText to see more details.**

social bonding and compassion among those who are under its influence. Heat stroke and dehydration are major risks associated with ecstasy use, especially when the drug is taken in a rave where there is a high level of physical exertion from dancing in an overheated environment.

HALLUCINOGENS **Hallucinogenic drugs** *are substances that produce perceptual distortions.* Depending on the type of hallucinogen consumed, these distortions may be visual, auditory, and sometimes tactile in nature, such as the experience of crawling sensations against the skin. Hallucinogens also alter how people perceive their own thinking. For example, deep significance may be attached to what are normally mundane objects, events, or thoughts. Commonly used hallucinogens include LSD (lysergic acid diethylamide), which is a laboratory-made (synthetic) drug. Hallucinogenic substances also occur in nature, such as psilocybin (a mushroom) and mescaline (derived from the peyote cactus). Hallucinogens can have very long-lasting effects—more than 12 hours for LSD, for example. These drugs may also elicit powerful emotional experiences that range from extreme euphoria to fear, panic, and paranoia. The two most common hallucinogens, LSD and psilocybin, both act on the transmission of serotonin.

Short-acting hallucinogens have become increasingly popular for recreational use. The effects of two of these hallucinogens, ketamine and DMT (dimethyltryptamine), last for about an hour.

Ketamine (street names include "Special K" and "Vitamin K") was originally developed as a surgical anesthetic to be used in cases where a gaseous anesthetic could not be applied, such as on the battlefield. It has been gaining popularity among college students as well as among people who frequent dance clubs and rave parties. Ketamine induces dream-like states, memory loss, dizziness, confusion, and a distorted sense of body ownership (Morgan et al., 2010). This synthetic drug blocks receptors for glutamate, which is an excitatory neurotransmitter that is important for, among other things, memory.

The short-acting hallucinogen known as DMT occurs naturally in such different places as the bark from trees native to Central and South America and on the skin surface of certain toads. DMT is even found in very small, naturally produced amounts in the human nervous system (Fontanilla et al., 2009). The function of DMT in the brain remains unclear, although some researchers have speculated that it plays a role in sleep and dreaming, and even out-of-body experiences (Barbanoj et al., 2008; Strassman, 2001). DMT is used in the United States primarily for recreational purposes.

BIOPSYCHOSOCIAL PERSPECTIVES

Recreational and Spiritual Uses of Hallucinogens

Salvia divinorum is an herb that grows in Central and South America. When smoked or chewed, salvia induces highly intense but short-lived hallucinations. Use of this drug also leads to *dissociative experiences*—a detachment between self and body (Sumnall et al., 2010).

Test what you know about this drug:

True or False?

1. Sale, possession, and use of salvia are prohibited by the U.S. federal government.

2. Very few younger people in the United States who use drugs have tried salvia.

3. Salvia has profound healing properties.

An exploration of salvia reveals a great deal about how cultural views affect how drugs are perceived. A single drug could be described as recreational, addictive, and a scourge to society in one culture, yet highly valued and spiritually significant to another.

Answers

1. False. Salvia is not regulated by the U.S. federal government. As of 2011, a few states had made it illegal to sell, possess, or use this drug.

The rubber hand illusion occurs when a volunteer places a hand out of view behind a panel, with the rubber hand in plain view. When a researcher brushes the hidden and rubber hands at the same time, the rubber hand appears real to the volunteer. Sober individuals experience this phenomenon, but people under the influence of ketamine have magnified illusory experiences (Morgan et al., 2010).

Salvia divinorum is a type of sage plant that grows naturally in Central and South America. Users of the herb combine juices from the leaves with tea for drinking, or the leaves are chewed or smoked.

2. False. The use of salvia is on the rise among American and Europeans, particularly among younger people (Nyi et al., 2010). Nearly 5.7% of high school seniors have tried it (National Institute of Drug Abuse, 2010). The drug can be legally purchased in most U.S. states.

3. False—there is no scientific evidence that salvia has healing properties. Whether one agrees with this statement, however, depends on who is asked. Among the Mazateca people of Mexico, salvia is used in divine rituals in which an individual communicates with the spiritual world. Shamans of the Mazateca people use salvia for spiritual healing sessions. These people believe the drug has profound medicinal properties.

Head shops in the United States sell salvia in packets for immediate consumption, though this practice may not occur for long if the drug is placed under government regulations.

This type of practice is not uncommon. Some religious groups from South America drink ayahuasca tea, which contains DMT, for spiritual purposes. Cases such as salvia and ayahuasca use provide important lessons. A drug can have standard, narrow effects on brain chemistry, but the subjective experience it provides, and the cultural view of the drug, may vary widely.

· · · · · · · · · · · · · · · · · · · ·

MARIJUANA **Marijuana** *is a drug comprising the leaves and buds of the* Cannabis *plant that produces a combination of hallucinogenic, stimulant, and relaxing (narcotic) effects.* It is among the most commonly abused drugs in the United States. More than one-third of high school students in 2009 reported that they had used marijuana at least once, and one in five identified themselves as current users (Centers for Disease Control and Prevention [CDC], 2010). These high usage rates reflect, in part, the fact that this drug is so readily available.

The bud of the *Cannabis* plant, which is the part that is typically smoked, contains a high concentration of a compound called tetrahydrocannabinol (THC). THC binds to cannabinoid receptors, which are distributed across various regions of the brain. The drug induces feelings of euphoria, relaxation, and heightened and sometimes distorted sensory experiences. One short-term effect of marijuana is memory impairment, likely because of the abundance of cannabinoid receptors in the hippocampus, a key region involved in memory (Ranganathan & D'Souza, 2006).

Researchers had long puzzled over which natural brain chemical is mimicked by THC. It turns out that anandamide, a neurotransmitter found in both brain and peripheral nerves, binds to cannabinoid receptors and is involved in regulating circadian rhythms and sleep, memory, and possibly other functions (Edwards et al., 2010; Vaughn et al., 2010). Marijuana may also reduce the intensity of physical pain, which is one reason why people seek to use it for medicinal purposes (Ware et al., 2010).

OPIATES **Opiates** *(also called narcotics) are drugs such as heroin and morphine that reduce pain and induce extremely intense feelings of euphoria.* These drugs bind to endorphin receptors in the nervous system. Endorphins ("endogenous morphine") are neurotransmitters that reduce pain and produce pleasurable sensations—effects magnified by opiates. Naturally occurring opiates are derived from certain species of poppy plants that are primarily grown in Asia and the Middle East. Opiate drugs are very common in medical and emergency room settings. For example, the drug fentanyl is used in emergency rooms to treat people in extreme pain. A street version of fentanyl, known as "China White," can be more than 20 times the strength of more commonly sold doses of heroin.

Treating opiate addiction can be incredibly challenging. People who are addicted to opiates and other highly addictive drugs enter a negative cycle of having to use these drugs simply to ward off withdrawal effects, rather than to actually achieve the sense of euphoria they may have experienced when they started using. Methadone is an *opioid* (a synthetic opiate) that binds to opiate receptors but does not give the same kind of high that heroin does. A regimen of daily methadone treatment can help people who are addicted to opiates avoid painful withdrawals as they learn to cope without the drug. In recent years, newer alternatives to methadone have been found to be more effective and need to be taken only a few times per week.

Another opioid, oxycodone (OxyContin), has helped many people escape and avoid severe pain with few problems. Unfortunately, this drug has very high abuse potential. It is often misused, especially by those who have obtained it through illegal means (i.e., without a prescription).

Quick Quiz 5.3a
Commonly Abused Illegal Drugs

KNOW…

1. _____ are drugs that increase nervous system activity.

   A Hallucinogens   C Psychoactive drugs

   B Narcotics   D Stimulants

2. Drugs that are best known for their ability to alter normal visual and auditory perceptions are called _____.

   A hallucinogens   C psychoactive drugs

   B narcotics   D stimulants

ANALYZE…

3. Which statement best illustrates the relationship between spiritual and recreational uses of drugs?

   A Drugs that are treated as illegal in the United States are generally considered illegal everywhere.

   B Drugs have different effects on brain chemistry depending on the culture.

   C Drugs can provide different subjective experiences depending on the culture.

   D Drugs that are legal in the United States are usually illegal and considered dangerous in other cultures.

Answers can be found on page ANS-2.

Legal Drugs and Their Effects on Consciousness

So far we have covered drugs that are, for the most part, produced and distributed illegally. Some prescription drugs can also have profound effects on consciousness and, as a consequence, are targets for misuse.

SEDATIVES **Sedative drugs,** *sometimes referred to as "downers," depress activity of the central nervous system. Barbiturates* were an early form of medication used to treat anxiety and promote sleep. High doses of these drugs can shut down the brain stem regions that regulate breathing, so their medical use has largely been discontinued in favor of safer drugs. Barbiturates have a high potential for abuse, typically by people who want to lower inhibitions, relax, and try to improve their sleep. (Incidentally, these agents do not really improve sleep. Barbiturates actually reduce the amount of REM sleep.)

Newer forms of sedative drugs, called *benzodiazepines,* include prescription drugs such as Xanax, Ativan, and Valium. These drugs increase the effects of gamma-aminobutyric acid (GABA), an inhibitory neurotransmitter that helps reduce feelings of anxiety or panic. The major advantage of benzodiazepine drugs over barbiturates is that they do not specifically target the brain regions responsible for breathing and, even at high doses, are unlikely to be fatal. However, people under the influence of any kind of sedative are at greater risk for injury or death due to accidents caused by their diminished attention, reaction time, and motor control.

PRESCRIPTION DRUG ABUSE Prescription drugs are now second only to marijuana as the substances most commonly abused by illicit users (Substance Abuse and Mental Health Services Administration [SAMHSA], 2010; Figure 5.12 on page 186). Surveys have shown that as many as 31% of college students sampled have abused Ritalin, the stimulant commonly prescribed as a treatment for ADHD (Bogle & Smith, 2009). A massive number of prescription drugs are available on the market, including stimulants, opiates, and sedatives. In 2009, 7 million Americans reported having used prescription drugs for nonmedical reasons within the month prior to the survey. This number is actually higher than the number of users of cocaine, heroin, hallucinogens, and inhalants (e.g., paints, glues, gasoline) combined (Volkow, 2010). Users typically opt for prescription drugs as their drugs of choice because they are legal (when used as prescribed), pure (i.e., not contaminated or diluted), and relatively easy to get. Prescription drugs are typically

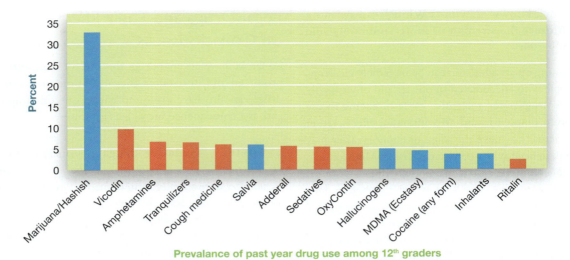

{FIG. 5.12} **Frequency of Drug Use Among High School Seniors** Prescription and over-the-counter drugs (shown as red bars) account for 8 of the 14 most frequently used drugs among high school seniors.

taken at large doses, and administered in such a way to get a quicker, more intense effect—for example, by crushing and snorting stimulants such as Ritalin or injecting liquefied oxycodone (see Figure 5.13).

Curbing prescription drug abuse poses quite a challenge. Approaches to reducing this problem include efforts to develop pain medications that do not act on pleasure and reward centers of the brain. For example, pain can be reduced by administration of compounds that stimulate cannabinoid receptors in peripheral regions of the nervous system thereby avoiding the high associated with stimulation of receptors within the brain. Many communities offer prescription drug disposal opportunities, which helps remove unused drugs from actual or potential circulation. In addition, doctors and other health care professionals are becoming increasingly aware that some individuals seeking prescription drugs are doing so because they are addicted to them.

ALCOHOL Alcohol is by far the most commonly used drug. It can be found in nearly every culture, although some frown on its use more than others. Alcohol use is a part of cherished social and spiritual rituals, but is also associated with violence and accidents. It has the power to change societies, in some cases for the worse. Several decades ago, "problem drinking" was not an issue for the Carib people of Venezuela, for example. During specific yearly festivals, alcohol was brewed and consumed in limited amounts. In more recent years, the influence of Western civilization has led to the emergence of problems with alcohol abuse and alcoholism in this group of people (Seale et al., 2002). Most societies regard alcohol as an acceptable form of drug use, though they may attempt to limit and regulate its use through legal means. Customs and social expectations also affect usage. For example, drinking—especially heavy drinking—is considered more socially acceptable for men than for women.

Alcohol initially targets GABA receptors in the brain, and subsequently affects opiate and dopamine receptors. Stimulation of opiate and dopamine receptors accounts for the euphoria associated with lower doses as well its rewarding effects. Alcohol facilitates the activity of GABA, an inhibitory neurotransmitter. The net effect is to depress the central nervous system, which helps explain the impairments in balance and coordination associated with consumption of alcohol.

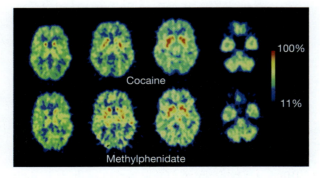

{FIG. 5.13} **Ritalin and Cocaine** Stimulants like methylphenidate (Ritalin) affect the same areas of the brain as cocaine, albeit with different speed and intensity.

But if alcohol increases the release of an inhibitory brain chemical, why do people become *less* inhibited when they drink? One function of the frontal lobe of the cortex is to inhibit behavior and impulses, and alcohol appears to impair the frontal lobe's ability to serve in its regular capacity—in other words, it inhibits an inhibitor.

The lowered inhibitions associated with alcohol may help people muster the courage to perform a toast at a wedding, but many socially unacceptable consequences are also associated with alcohol use. Alcohol abuse has been linked to health problems, sexual and physical assault, automobile accidents, missing work or school, unplanned pregnancies, and contracting sexually transmitted diseases. These effects are primarily associated with heavy consumption. Underage drinkers are at higher risk for binge-drinking, typically defined as consuming five drinks at a setting for males and four drinks for females. Underage drinking is very common in the United States. In a 2009 survey, 42% of people younger than 21 years reported that they drank alcohol, 24% binge-drank, 10% drove after drinking, and 28% rode with a driver who had been drinking (Eaton et al., 2010).

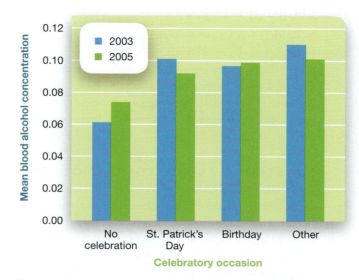

{FIG. 5.14} **Celebrating with Alcohol** Holidays, birthdays, and other celebrations are associated with higher levels of intoxication at fraternity houses as measured by blood alcohol level (Glindemann et al., 2007).

PSYCH @

College Parties

Researchers have determined that college students drink significantly more than their peers who do not attend college (Carter et al., 2010). In one study, nearly half of the college student participants binge-drank, one-third drove under the influence, 10% to 12% sustained an injury or were assaulted while intoxicated, and 2% were victims of date rape while drinking (Hingson et al., 2009). Alcohol abuse in our society is widespread, especially during times of celebration (Glindemann et al., 2007; Figure 5.14), so it might seem as if colleges have few options at their disposal to reduce reckless drinking on campus. Psychologists Kent Glindemann, Scott Geller, and their associates, however, have conducted some interesting field studies in fraternity houses at their university. For example, in two separate studies, these researchers measured the typical blood alcohol level at fraternity parties. They then offered monetary awards or entry into a raffle for fraternities that could keep their average blood alcohol level below 0.05 at their next party. The interventions proved to be successful in both studies, with blood alcohol levels being significantly reduced from the baseline (Fournier et al., 2004; Glindemann et al., 2007).

· · · · · · · · · · · · · · · · · ·

Quick Quiz 5.3b
Legal Drugs and Their Effects on Consciousness

KNOW …

1 Drugs that depress the activity of the central nervous system are known as _____.

Ⓐ stimulants Ⓒ hallucinogens

Ⓑ sedatives Ⓓ GABAs

APPLY …

2 Research shows that one effective way to decrease problem drinking on a college campus is to:

Ⓐ hold informative lectures that illustrate the dangers of drinking.

Ⓑ give up—there is little hope for reducing drinking on campus.

Ⓒ provide monetary incentives for student groups to maintain a low average blood alcohol level.

Ⓓ threaten student groups with fines if they are caught drinking.

ANALYZE …

3 Why are benzodiazepines believed to be safer than barbiturates?

Ⓐ Barbiturates can inhibit the brain's control of breathing.

Ⓑ Benzodiazepines can be prescribed legally, but barbiturates cannot.

Ⓒ No one misuses benzodiazepines.

Ⓓ Both benzodiazepines and barbiturates are viewed as equally dangerous.

Answers can be found on page ANS-2.

Habitual Drug Use

Now that we know how drugs are classified based on their short-term effects, we can turn to the long-term effects of drug use. Society frowns on drug use, and to a great extent this attitude derives from the belief that drugs can have negative long-term consequences. As you will see, some evidence supports these beliefs.

SUBSTANCE ABUSE, TOLERANCE, AND DEPENDENCE

Abuse, tolerance, and dependence are interacting facets of substance use. *Substance abuse* occurs when an individual experiences social, physical, legal, or other problems associated with his drug use. **Tolerance** *occurs when repeated use of a drug results in a need for a higher dose to get the intended effect.* People build up a tolerance to most drugs, including alcohol. Coffee drinkers, for example, are well aware of the phenomenon of tolerance: First-time drinkers may become completely wired and unable to sleep the following night, whereas veteran coffee drinkers can drink a cup of coffee and fall asleep immediately.

Dependence *refers to the need to take a drug to ward off unpleasant physical withdrawal symptoms*; it is often referred to as *addiction*. Caffeine withdrawal can involve head and muscle aches and impaired concentration. Although a hangover after a night of binge-drinking can certainly make a person miserable, withdrawal from long-term alcohol abuse is much more serious. A person who is dependent on alcohol can experience extremely severe, even life-threatening withdrawal symptoms, including nausea, increased heart rate and blood pressure, and hallucinations and delirium.

We can use the biopsychosocial model to help us understand drug dependence. A growing body of evidence supports the idea that there is a genetic component to some addictions, such as alcoholism (Foroud et al., 2010). Current research is aimed at understanding which genes may be responsible and how their actions render people susceptible to alcoholism. Such research suggests that genes are probably not fully responsible, however, because the alcoholism rate is very low among groups that prohibit drinking (e.g., for religious reasons; Chentsova-Dutton & Tsai, 2007; Haber & Jacob, 2007). In addressing this issue from a psychological perspective, researchers have determined that factors such as early experience with alcohol and impulsive personality traits are linked to increased likelihood of substance abuse and addiction (Zernicke et al., 2010).

WORKING THE SCIENTIFIC LITERACY MODEL
Psychological and Physical Effects of Drugs

The short-term effects of drugs obviously involve changes in cognition and behavior. The effects on emotions and perception are a large part of what motivates substance abuse in the first place. However, many of the substances we have covered so far are illegal, or at least their use is highly controlled, because a significant portion of society is worried about the long-term effects of these substances.

What do we know about the psychological and physical effects of drugs?

Depending on the drug, the day or days after its use may involve lingering effects, depression, or further cravings. But what about chronic, long-term use of substances such as marijuana, cocaine, or prescription drugs? How does habitual drug use affect the brain and body? Researchers conducting animal and human studies are tracking the long-term effects of drug use to answer these questions.

How can science explain the long-term effects of drug use?

Research seeking to answer this question typically combines tests of cognitive ability, such as memory and reasoning, with one of many different forms of brain imaging. This dual approach allows researchers to determine what, if any, long-term mental impairments are associated with drug use, and which part of the brain may be damaged. As a result of this work, we now know that long-term exposure to methamphetamine and ecstasy can cause significant damage to nerve cells that transmit dopamine, norepinephrine, and serotonin (Yamamoto et al., 2010). These brain chemicals are important for regulating cognition, emotion, learning, sleep, and many other functions.

To test whether amphetamine abuse alters brain function, researchers compared people with long histories of methamphetamine addiction and abuse with healthy control participants. Compared to the healthy participants, those individuals who had a history of abusing methamphetamine had structural abnormalities of cells in the frontal lobes, which reduced the brain's ability to inhibit irrelevant thoughts

BLUE	**GREEN**	**YELLOW**
PINK	**RED**	**ORANGE**
GREY	**BLACK**	**PURPLE**
TAN	**WHITE**	**BROWN**

{FIG. 5.15} **The Stroop Test** The Stroop test requires you to read aloud the color of the letters of these sample words. The task measures your ability to inhibit a natural tendency to read the word, rather than identify the color. Chronic methamphetamine users have greater difficulty with this task than do non-users. **Click on this figure in your eText to see more details**.

(Tobias et al., 2010). This ability can be measured through the Stroop task (Figure 5.15), which challenges a person's ability to inhibit reading a word in favor of identifying its color. Methamphetamine abusers had greater difficulty with this task than non-users, and they also had reduced activity in the frontal lobes, likely because of the damage described previously (Salo et al., 2010).

Can we critically evaluate this information?

"Methamphetamine Kills Brain Cells" might make for a compelling headline, and it certainly may be true. Even so, there are often multiple possible causes of brain damage in drug abusers. Notably, people who abuse drugs such as methamphetamine and ecstasy rarely just use one drug. Most users also abuse other drugs such as marijuana, alcohol, and possibly other stimulants. Thus it may be these other drugs, or something about their combination, that accounts for any observed cognitive impairments and brain damage (Gouzoulis-Mayfrank & Daumann, 2006). Also, damaged nerve cells and other neurological problems are not necessarily the consequences of drug use. The relationship may go the other way around—people with certain types of neurological problems may be more likely to abuse drugs. Nevertheless, controlled animal studies indicate that the brain damage found in human drug users is likely caused by the toxicity of the drugs (Yamamoto et al., 2010).

In addition, the physical and emotional problems associated with addiction to drugs such as methamphetamine can be reversed, provided the individual is fortunate enough to survive the period of abuse and remains completely abstinent from any further use. When this is the case, recovering methamphetamine addicts show significant, positive increases in neurological and emotional functioning. In fact, they can recover to levels comparable to healthy people with no history of drug abuse (Iudicello et al., 2010).

Why is this relevant?

What does a poor performance on the Stroop task tell us about cognitive functioning? This task measures the ability to focus attention and inhibit one way of thinking (to read) in favor of another (to name colors). The ability to focus attention and think flexibly is an important component of decision making and impulse control. Knowledge about the physical damage wrought by drugs helps psychologists and physicians know what to expect from treatment, and it raises awareness about the significant problems caused by drug use. Of course, it can apply to your own situation as well: If you or someone you know regularly abuses drugs, you should consider the fact that there are serious risks associated with drug use.

Quick Quiz 5.3c
Habitual Drug Use

KNOW...

1 Dependence occurs when:

  A an individual will die if he does not continue to use the drug.

  B an individual desires a drug for its pleasant effects.

  C an individual has to take the drug to prevent or stop unpleasant withdrawal symptoms.

  D an individual requires increasingly larger amounts of a substance to experience its effects.

UNDERSTAND...

2 When does drug tolerance occur?

  A When an individual needs increasingly larger amounts of a drug to achieve the same desired effect

  B When individuals do not pass judgment on drug abusers

  C When an individual experiences withdrawal symptoms

  D When an individual starts taking a new drug for recreational purposes

Answers can be found on page ANS-2.

Module Summary

Now that you have read this module you should:

KNOW ...

- **The key terminology related to different categories of drugs and their effects on the nervous system and behavior:**

dependence (p. 188)
ecstasy (MDMA) (p. 182)
hallucinogenic drugs (p. 183)
marijuana (p. 184)
opiates (p. 184)

psychoactive drugs (p. 181)
sedative drugs (p. 185)
stimulants (p. 182)
tolerance (p. 188)

UNDERSTAND ...

- **Drug tolerance and dependence.** Tolerance is a physiological process in which repeated exposure to a drug leads to a need for increasingly larger dosages to experience the intended effect. Dependence occurs when the user takes a drug to avoid withdrawal symptoms.

APPLY ...

- **Your knowledge to better understand your own beliefs about drug use.** One tool that might help you in this regard is the scale in **Table 5.5**. For each item on the left, circle the number in the column that represents your level of agreement.

ANALYZE ...

- **The difference between spiritual and recreational drug use.** The difference, such as in the case of salvia, is dependent upon cultural factors, the setting in which the drug is used, and the expectations of the user.
- **The short- and long-term effects of drug use.** Review **Table 5.4** (page 181) for a summary of short-term effects of the major drug categories. The long-term effects will depend on the drug. In this module, we focused on the long-term effects of methamphetamine, which can include damage to nerve cells that transmit norepinephrine, serotonin, and dopamine, as well as loss of white matter. Cognitive deficits, such as those involving monitoring thought processes, also occur.

Table 5.5 :: What Are Your Beliefs About Drug Use?

After you have circled an answer for each item, add up all the circled numbers to find your final score.

	STRONGLY DISAGREE	DISAGREE	NEUTRAL	AGREE	STRONGLY AGREE
Marijuana should be legalized.	1	2	3	4	5
Marijuana use among teachers can be just healthy experimentation.	1	2	3	4	5
Personal use of drugs should be legal in the confines of one's own home.	1	2	3	4	5
Daily use of one marijuana cigarette is not necessarily harmful.	1	2	3	4	5
Tobacco smoking should be allowed in high schools.	1	2	3	4	5
It can be normal for a teenager to experiment with drugs.	1	2	3	4	5
Persons convicted for the sale of illicit drugs should not be eligible for parole.	5	4	3	2	1
Lifelong abstinence is a necessary goal in the treatment of alcoholism.	5	4	3	2	1
Once a person becomes drug-free through treatment he can never become a social user.	5	4	3	2	1
Parents should teach their children how to use alcohol.	5	4	3	2	1
Total					

Source: Chappel, Veach, & Krug, 1985.

Note: This scale measures permissive attitudes towards substance use and abuse. Higher scores indicate more permissive attitudes.

Module 5.1 :: Biological Rhythms of Consciousness: Wakefulness and Sleep

Focus Questions:

1 **What is REM and how is it related to dreaming?** REM (rapid eye movement) sleep is the stage of sleep in which dreams are most common. However, dreaming can also occur during deep sleep (stages 3 and 4).

2 **Why do some people act out their dreams?** During REM sleep, the brain sends inhibitory messages down the spinal cord, which renders the muscles that control movement temporarily paralyzed. People with REM behavior disorder, such as Mike Birbiglia who was featured in the vignette at the beginning of Module 5.1, act out their dreams because the brain fails to deliver this inhibitory signal.

👁—Watch *In the Real World Application: REM Sleep and Memory* in the **MyPsychLab video series**

Module 5.2 :: Altered States of Consciousness: Hypnosis, Meditation, and Disorders of Consciousness

Focus Questions:

1 **Why is déjà vu often accompanied by a strong emotional reaction?** There are a few possible reasons for this phenomenon. The surprise that the experience generates is emotional. In addition, the physical scenery, the song, or familiar face that elicits déjà vu may remind the individual of a significant event or person. Also, the emotion centers of the brain are located within the temporal lobes. Déjà vu often precedes seizures in people who have temporal lobe epilepsy.

2 **Is information processed in the background of our awareness?** The déjà vu experience suggests that it is. Déjà vu involves a sense of familiarity that the affected individual struggles to explain. It is likely that the deja vu experience is triggered by a sense of familiarity and recognition for a scene or event that is similar to actual past experiences. However, the individual fails to remember the details of the experience and instead feels an eerie sense of familiarity. Also, patients who are in minimally conscious states often continue to process information, albeit at a very reduced level.

👁—Watch *Thinking Like a Psychologist: Hypnosis—Uses and Limitations* in the **MyPsychLab video series**

Module 5.3 :: Drugs and Conscious Experience

Focus Questions:

1 **How do we distinguish between recreationally abused drugs and therapeutic usage?** Many commonly prescribed drugs are very similar to drugs that are used illegally for recreational purposes. The distinction is primarily based on the dosage of the drug and the intent of the user. Both cocaine and Ritalin have stimulant properties, for example, but dosage and intent of use are two key distinctions between them. In contrast, hallucinogens such as psilocybin have long been regarded as useless for therapeutic purposes, and are not chemically similar to mainstream prescription drugs. Time will tell if they become recognized as therapeutic drugs.

2 **Which other motives underlie drug use?** Drugs such as alcohol and caffeine are used in normal social and personal rituals and habits. Also, in many cultures, drugs are used in spiritual practice.

👁—Watch *What's in It Me? Self-Induced Altered States* in the **MyPsychLab video series**

👁—Watch the complete video series online at **MyPsychLab**

Episode 6: Consciousness
1. *The Big Picture: The State of Our Consciousness*
2. *The Basics: Rhythms of Consciousness*
3. *Special Topics: Sleep Disorders*
4. *Thinking Like a Psychologist: Hypnosis—Uses and Limitations*
5. *In the Real World Application: REM Sleep and Memory*
6. *What's in It for Me?: Self-Induced Altered States*

✓ Study and
Review at
MyPsychLab

1 REM sleep is sometimes referred to as *paradoxical sleep* because:

- **A** the more sleep deprived a person is, the less REM sleep she experiences.
- **B** REM sleep is not really a sleep stage.
- **C** electrical activity in the brain completely shuts down during REM sleep.
- **D** EEG activity in the brain during REM is similar to EEG activity during an awake state.

2 Which of the following statements supports the "preserve and protect" hypothesis of sleep?

- **A** People tend to require more sleep after a hard day of work.
- **B** Sleep deprivation can lead to impaired cognitive abilities.
- **C** Jet lag is usually worse when traveling east than it is when traveling west.
- **D** Many small animals sleep during the day, when they could be easily seen by a predator.

3 Erica tells her friend that last night she dreamed she was asking her boss for a promotion. If Erica's friend believes in the activation–synthesis hypothesis of dreaming, which of the following is she likely to say about the dream?

- **A** "The latent content of the dream is more important than the manifest content."
- **B** "The dream is the result of random activity in the brain and has no deep symbolic meaning."
- **C** "The dream indicates that your brain is trying to figure out how to get you promoted."
- **D** "The dream is your brain's way of forming new memories."

4 Affecting approximately 10% of the U.S. population, _____ is the most widely recognized sleeping problem.

- **A** sleep apnea
- **B** insomnia
- **C** sleep-state misperception
- **D** somnambulism

5 Recently, Zane has been very tired during the day and feels like he hasn't been sleeping well. His wife mentions that he often makes a strange gasping noise several times during the night. Which sleep disorder does Zane most likely have?

- **A** Sleep apnea
- **B** Narcolepsy
- **C** Sleep-state misperception
- **D** Somnambulism

6 Hypnosis is best thought of as:

- **A** a trance.
- **B** a state of increased suggestibility.
- **C** mind control.
- **D** a myth.

7 Which of the following statements is true about the use of hypnosis to recover memories?

- **A** It is generally ineffective, but poses no risks and is harmless.
- **B** Research has shown hypnosis to be an effective way to recover memoires.
- **C** Research indicates that hypnosis does not work, and that it can potentially create false memories.
- **D** While some debate persists regarding the technique's effectiveness, most U.S. courts accept testimony obtained from a person who is placed under hypnosis.

8 Which of the following definitions accurately describes the state of coma?

- **A** A prolonged state of consciousness similar to non-REM sleep
- **B** A state marked by a complete loss of consciousness
- **C** A disordered state of consciousness marked by the ability to show some behaviors that suggest at least partial consciousness, even if on an inconsistent basis
- **D** A state of minimal consciousness, where the patient's eyes may be open, and he or she experiences a sleep–wake cycle

9 Opiates create their euphoric effects by stimulating receptors for:

- **A** GABA.
- **B** endorphins.
- **C** Anandamide.
- **D** Dopamine.

10 Repeated use of drugs over a period of time can result in a need for a higher dose to get the intended effect. This condition is known as:

- **A** addiction.
- **B** dependence.
- **C** withdrawal.
- **D** tolerance.

Work the Scientific Literacy Model :: Understanding the Rhythms of Sleep

What do we know about the stages of sleep?

As part of our circadian rhythm (see **page 159** for a broad overview), sleep follows a relatively predictable pattern. Review **Figure 5.3 on page 160** for a snapshot of the various sleep stages and the brain wavelength activity that characterizes each stage. To get to know your brain waves, review the discussion on **page 160**. As noted there, beta waves are characteristic of wakefulness. Hint: Beta starts with a **b** for "busy"—the activity level of your brain while you are awake. Other wavelengths include alpha (characteristic of a relaxed state), theta (early stages of sleep), and delta (deep sleep). The first four stages of sleep are collectively known as non-REM sleep. REM sleep occurs after the last stage of non-REM sleep and is the stage in which we do most of our dreaming. If you're having trouble remembering the difference between non-REM and REM sleep, note that REM sleep is also called *paradoxical sleep*. During the restorative REM sleep stage, brain activity increases to the point where it resembles wakefulness (beta waves), but your body is paradoxically in a state of sleep and temporary loss of muscle tone. While our need for REM sleep might change from infancy to older adulthood, the stages of sleep we cycle through remain constant.

How can science help explain the importance of sleep?

Devices such as the electroencephalogram (EEG) have allowed modern sleep researchers to isolate sleep stages, differentiate between REM and non-REM sleep, and explore the consequences of sleep deprivation. New information like the suggested link between stage 2 sleep spindles and memory formation is a result of research taking advantage of this kind of technology. Research also shows that even minor sleep disturbances, such as turning the clock forward for Daylight Savings Time or experiencing jetlag, can affect natural sleep rhythms. The negative effects of sleep deprivation are also well documented by research; **page 162** describes a study reporting a correlation between teenagers' lack of sleep and an increase in illness, family problems, and even substance abuse. Researchers have also shown that driving while sleepy can be as dangerous as driving under the influence of alcohol, and that the long, demanding work shifts that deprive doctors and nurses of needed rest can lead to job stress, burnout, and potentially tragic errors in medical care.

Why is this relevant?

Watch the accompanying video excerpt on the rhythms of consciousness. You can access the video at MyPsychLab or by clicking the play button in the center of your eText. If your instructor assigns this video as a homework activity, you will find additional content to help you in MyPsychLab. You can also view the video by using your smart phone and the QR code below, or you can go to the YouTube link provided.

After you have read this chapter and watched the video, imagine that your roommate has been coming back to the dorm at all hours of the night, disrupting your sleep. Describe a typical night's sleep cycle and then describe how your sleep is affected when you are woken up during each of the different stages of sleep. Be sure to differentiate the impact in all the stages.

Can we critically evaluate claims about sleep?

Many people worry that they are not getting enough sleep. Consider what you know about the available research. Do we all need a solid 8 hours of sleep nightly to be functioning members of society? Because we are all unique individuals, our bodies may require more or less sleep. A better rule of thumb than just counting your number of hours slept is to think about how well rested you may feel during the day. When it comes to shift workers and schedules, adjusting the distribution of hours worked (see **Figure 5.5 on page 163**) has a positive effect on cognitive functioning. Also, if you're not feeling well rested, before turning to sleep-aid drugs, consider improving your sleep hygiene by following some of the methods in **Table 5.2 on page 170**.

youtube.com/ scientificliteracy

MyPsychLab

Your turn to Work the Scientific Literacy Model: You can access the video at MyPsychLab or by clicking the play button in the center of your eText. If your instructor assigns this video as a homework activity, you will find additional content to help you at MyPsychLab. You can also view the video by using your smart phone and the QR code, or you can go to the YouTube link provided.

6 :: LEARNING

Module
6.1

Classical Conditioning: Learning by Association

	KNOW ...	UNDERSTAND ...	APPLY ...	ANALYZE ...
Learning Objectives After reading this module you should:	The key terminology involved in classical conditioning	How responses learned through classical conditioning can be acquired and lost The role of biological and evolutionary factors in classical conditioning	The concepts and terms of classical conditioning to new examples	Claims that artificially sweetened beverages are a healthier choice

Are soda consumers drinking themselves fat? Certainly, those individuals who drink a lot of sugary beverages are at greater risk of doing so, but what about the people who appear to be making the more prudent choice of a diet soda? How can we go wrong if the label on the bottle reads "zero calories"? These artificially sweetened beverages are designed and marketed to help people limit their sugar intake. However, as you will see later in this module, trends toward increased diet beverage consumption have not corresponded with weight loss—if anything, the reverse is true. Psychologists have been conducting experiments to figure out why people who drink artificially sweetened beverages may actually gain weight, and the results suggest that the neural and digestive systems of diet soda drinkers may have "learned" an unhealthy lesson. This may come as a surprise to you, given that people typically think of learning as a deliberate process. In fact, classical conditioning—the topic of this module—often takes place without our even knowing it.

Focus Questions

 Which types of behaviors can be learned?

 Do all instances of classical conditioning go undetected by the individual?

· · · · · · · · · · · · · · · · · ·

Learning *is a process by which behavior or knowledge changes as a result of experience.* Learning from experience plays a major role in enabling us to do many things that we clearly were not born to do, from the simplest tasks, such as flipping a light switch, to the more complex, such as playing a musical instrument.

To many people, the term "learning" signifies the activities that students do—reading, listening, and taking tests in order to acquire new information. This process, which is known as *cognitive learning*, is just one type of learning, however. Another way that we learn is by *associative learning*, which is the focus of this module. You probably associate certain holidays with specific sights, sounds, and smells, or foods with specific flavors and textures. We are not the only species with this skill—even the simplest animals such as the earthworm can learn by association. Here we will explore the processes that account for how these associations form. Research on associative learning has a long history in psychology, dating back to Ivan Pavlov (1849–1936), a Russian physiologist and the 1904 Nobel laureate in medicine.

Pavlov's Dogs: Classical Conditioning of Salivation

Watch the Video *Classic Footage of Pavlov* at MyPsychLab

Pavlov studied digestion, using dogs as a model species for his experiments. As a part of his normal research procedure, he collected saliva and other gastric secretions from the dogs when they were presented with meat powder. Pavlov and his assistants noticed that as they prepared dogs for procedures, even before any meat powder was presented, the dogs would start salivating. This curious observation led Pavlov to consider the possibility that digestive responses were more than just simple reflexes in response to food. If dogs salivate in anticipation of food, then perhaps the salivary response can also be learned (Pavlov's lab assistants referred to them as "psychic secretions"). Pavlov began conducting experiments in which he first presented a sound from a metronome, a device that produces ticking sounds at set intervals, and then presented meat powder to the dogs. After pairing the sound with the food several times, Pavlov discovered that the metronome by itself could elicit salivation (see Figure 6.1).

Pavlov's discovery began a long tradition of inquiry into what is now called **classical conditioning**—*learning*

{FIG. 6.1} **Associative Learning** Although much information may pass through the dog's brain, in Pavlov's experiments on classical conditioning an association was made between the tone and the food. (Pavlov used a metronome as well as other devices for presenting sounds. In this module, we use the term "tone" to represent the stimulus that was paired with food in his experiments.)

that occurs when a neutral stimulus elicits a response that was originally caused by another stimulus. In Pavlov's experiments, the neutral stimulus was the sound of the tone, which was paired with meat powder that could by itself elicit salivation (Figure 6.2). After repeated pairings, the dogs learned that the tone predicted meat powder; eventually, just hearing the tone alone could elicit salivation. Classical conditioning, also referred to as *Pavlovian conditioning*, influences many other responses as well and occurs in a variety of settings.

You can think about classical conditioning in mechanical terms—that is, one event causes another. A *stimulus* is an external event or cue that elicits a response. Stimuli (plural), such as food, water, pain, or sexual contact, elicit different types of responses. An **unconditioned stimulus (US)** *is a stimulus that elicits a reflexive response without learning.* In this context, the terms "conditioning" and "learning" are synonymous. Thus the "unconditioned" part of the unconditioned stimulus refers to the fact that it can elicit a response in the absence of any learning. An **unconditioned response (UR)** *is a reflexive, unlearned*

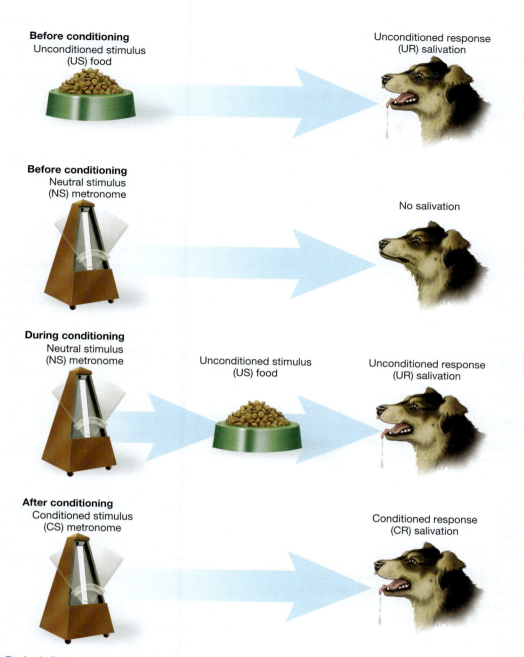

Before conditioning
Unconditioned stimulus
(US) food

Unconditioned response
(UR) salivation

Before conditioning
Neutral stimulus
(NS) metronome

No salivation

During conditioning
Neutral stimulus
(NS) metronome

Unconditioned stimulus
(US) food

Unconditioned response
(UR) salivation

After conditioning
Conditioned stimulus
(CS) metronome

Conditioned response
(CR) salivation

{FIG. 6.2} **Pavlov's Salivary Conditioning Experiment** Food elicits the unconditioned response of salivation. Before conditioning, the tone elicits no response by the dog. During conditioning, the tone repeatedly precedes the food. After conditioning, the tone alone elicits salivation. **Click on this figure in your eText to see more details.**

reaction to an unconditioned stimulus. In Pavlov's experiment, meat powder elicited unconditioned salivation in his dogs (see the top panel of Figure 6.2). The link between the US and the UR is, by definition, unlearned. In addition to food eliciting salivation, other unconditioned stimulus and response relationships include flinching (a UR) in response to a loud sound (US), and blinking (UR) in response to a puff of air to the eye (US).

Recall that a defining characteristic of classical conditioning is that a neutral stimulus comes to elicit a response. It does so because the neutral stimulus is paired with, and therefore predicts, an unconditioned stimulus. In Pavlov's experiment, the tone was *originally* a neutral stimulus because it did not elicit a response, least of all salivation (see Figure 6.2). A **conditioned stimulus (CS)** *is a once neutral stimulus that elicits a conditioned response because it has a history of being paired with an unconditioned stimulus.* A **conditioned response (CR)** *is the learned response that occurs to the conditioned stimulus.* After being repeatedly paired with the US, the once neutral tone in Pavlov's experiment became a conditioned stimulus (CS) because it elicited the conditioned response of salivation. To establish that conditioning has taken place, the tone (CS) must elicit salivation in the *absence* of food (US; see the bottom panel of Figure 6.2).

A common point of confusion is the difference between a conditioned response and an unconditioned response—in Pavlov's experiment, they are both salivation. What distinguishes the two is the stimulus that elicits them. Salivation is a UR if it occurs in response to a US (food). Salivation is a CR if it occurs in response to a CS (the tone). A CS can have this effect only if it becomes *associated* with a US.

PsychTutor
Click here in your eText for an interactive tutorial on **Classical Conditioning**

Quick Quiz 6.1a
Pavlov's Dogs: Classical Conditioning of Salivation

KNOW...

1 The learned response that occurs to the conditioned stimulus is known as the _____.

A unconditioned response

B conditioned stimulus

C conditioned response

D unconditioned response

2 A once neutral stimulus that elicits a conditioned response because it has a history of being paired with an unconditioned stimulus is known as a(n) _____.

A unconditioned response

B conditioned stimulus

C conditioned response

D unconditioned response

APPLY...

3 A dental drill can become an unpleasant stimulus, especially for people who may have experienced pain while one was used on their teeth. In this case, the pain elicited by the drill is a(n) _____.

A conditioned response

B unconditioned stimulus

C conditioned stimulus

D unconditioned response

4 Sylvia used to play with balloons. When she tried to blow up a balloon last week, it popped in her face and gave her quite a scare. Now, blowing up a balloon is so scary that Sylvia will not try it. In this example, the pop is a(n) _____ and the balloon is a(n) _____.

A conditioned stimulus; unconditioned stimulus

B unconditioned stimulus; conditioned stimulus

C unconditioned response; conditioned response

D conditioned response, unconditioned response

Answers can be found on page ANS-2.

Processes of Classical Conditioning

Classically conditioned responses typically involve reflexive actions, but they are still quite flexible. Conditioned responses may be very strong and reliable, which is likely if the CS and the US have a long history of being paired together. Conditioned responding may diminish over time, or it may occur with new stimuli with which the response has never been paired. We now turn to some processes that account for the flexibility of classically conditioned responses.

ACQUISITION, EXTINCTION, AND SPONTANEOUS RECOVERY
Learning involves a change in behavior due to experience, which can include acquiring a new response. **Acquisition** *is the initial phase of learning in which a response is established*; thus, in classical conditioning, acquisition is the phase in which a neutral stimulus is repeatedly paired with the US. In Pavlov's experiment, the conditioned salivary response was *acquired* with numerous tone–food pairings (see Figure 6.3). A critical part of acquisition is the predictability with which the CS and the US occur together. In Pavlov's experiment, conditioning either would not occur or would be very weak if food was delivered only sometimes (i.e., inconsistently) when the tone was sounded. Even once a response is fully acquired, there is no guarantee it will persist forever.

Both in natural situations and in the laboratory, the CS and the US may not always occur together. **Extinction** *is the loss or weakening of a conditioned response when a conditioned stimulus and unconditioned stimulus no longer occur together.* For the dogs in Pavlov's experiment, if a tone is presented repeatedly and no food follows, then salivation should occur less and less, until eventually it may not occur at all (Figure 6.3). This trend probably makes sense from a biological perspective: If the tone is no longer a reliable predictor of food, then salivation becomes unnecessary. However, even after extinction occurs, a once established conditioned response can return.

Spontaneous recovery *is the reoccurrence of a previously extinguished conditioned response, typically after some time has passed since extinction.* Pavlov and his assistants studied the phenomenon of extinction—but also noticed that salivation would reappear when the dogs were later returned to the experimental testing room where acquisition and extinction trials had been conducted. The dogs would also salivate again in response to a tone, albeit less so than at the end of acquisition (Figure 6.3). Why would salivation spontaneously return after the response had supposedly extinguished? Psychologists are not fully sure why, but the fact that responses can be spontaneously recovered suggests that extinction does not result in "forgetting." Rather, the opposite seems to be occurring—namely, extinction involves learning something *new* (Bouton, 1994). In Pavlov's experiment, for example, the dogs learned that in the experimental setting, the tone was no longer a reliable stimulus for predicting food.

Extinction and spontaneous recovery are evidence that classically conditioned responses can change once they are acquired. Further evidence of flexibility of conditioned responding can be seen in some other processes of classical conditioning, including generalization and discrimination learning.

STIMULUS GENERALIZATION AND DISCRIMINATION   Stimulus

generalization is a process in which a response that originally occurs to a specific stimulus also occurs to different, though similar stimuli. In Pavlov's experiment, dogs salivated not just to the original tone (CS), but also to very similar tones (see Figure 6.4). Generalization allows for flexibility in learned behaviors, although it is certainly possible for behavior to be *too* flexible. Salivating in response to *any* sound would be wasteful because not every sound correctly predicts food. Thus Pavlov's dogs also showed **discrimination**, *which occurs when an organism learns*

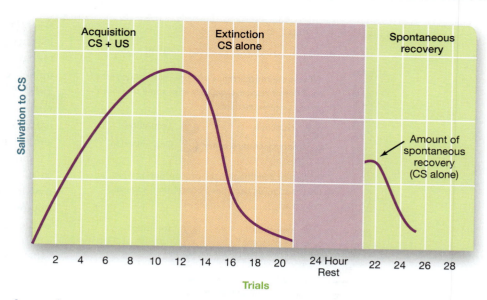

{FIG. 6.3}   **Acquisition, Extinction, and Spontaneous Recovery** *Acquisition* of a conditioned response occurs over repeated pairings of the CS and the US. If the US no longer occurs, conditioned responding diminishes—a process called *extinction*. Often, following a time interval in which the CS does not occur, conditioned responding rebounds when the CS is presented again—a phenomenon called *spontaneous recovery*.

to respond to one original stimulus but not to new stimuli that may be similar to the original stimulus. In salivary conditioning, the CS might be a 1,200-hertz tone, which is the only sound that is paired with food. The experimenter might produce tones of 1,100 or 1,300 hertz as well, but not pair these with food. Stimulus discrimination is said to occur when salivation occurs to the target 1,200-hertz tone, but much less so, if at all, to other tones (Figure 6.4).

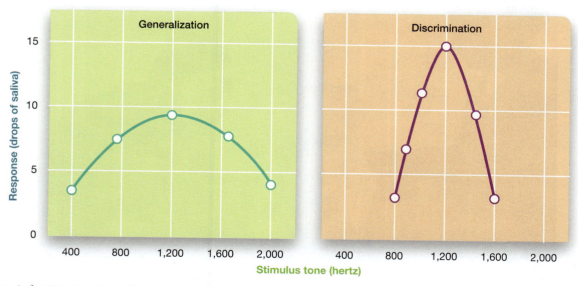

{FIG. 6.4}   **Stimulus Generalization and Discrimination**   A conditioned response may generalize to other similar stimuli. In this case, salivation occurs not just to the 1,200 Hz tone used during conditioning, but to other tones as well. Discrimination learning has occurred when responding is elicited by the original training stimulus, but much less so, if at all, to other stimuli.

Quick Quiz 6.1b
Processes of Classical Conditioning

KNOW...

1 What is the reoccurrence of a previously extinguished conditioned response, typically after some time has passed since extinction?

 A Extinction **C** Acquisition

 B Spontaneous recovery **D** Discrimination

UNDERSTAND...

2 In classical conditioning, the process during which a neutral stimulus becomes a conditioned stimulus is known as _____.

 A extinction **C** acquisition

 B spontaneous recovery **D** discrimination

APPLY...

3 Your dog barks every time a stranger's car pulls into the driveway, but not when you come home. Reacting to your car differently is a sign of _____.

 A discrimination **C** spontaneous recovery

 B generalization **D** acquisition

Answers can be found on page ANS-2.

Applications of Classical Conditioning

Now that you are familiar with the basic processes of classical conditioning, we can begin to explore its many applications. Classical conditioning is a common phenomenon that applies to many different situations, including emotional learning, advertising, aversions to certain foods, and sexual responses.

CONDITIONED EMOTIONAL RESPONSES

Psychologists dating back to John Watson in the 1920s recognized that our emotional responses could be influenced by classical conditioning (Paul & Blumenthal, 1989; Watson & Rayner, 1920). These **conditioned emotional responses** *consist of emotional and physiological responses that develop to a specific object or situation.* Watson and Rayner conducted one of their first studies with an 11-month-old child known as Albert B. (also referred to as "Little Albert"). When they presented Albert with a white rat, he showed no fear at first, and even reached out for the animal. Then, while Albert was in the vicinity of the rat, they startled him by striking a steel bar with a hammer. Watson and Rayner reported that Albert quickly associated the rat with the startling sound; the child soon showed a conditioned emotional response just to the rat. (For the record, ethical standards in modern-day psychological research would not allow this type of experiment to take place.)

The Watson and Rayner procedure may seem artificial because it took place in a laboratory, but here is a more naturalistic example. Consider a boy who sees his neighbor's cat. Not having a cat of his own, the child is very eager to pet the animal—perhaps a little too eager, because the cat reacts defensively and scratches his hand. The cat may become a CS for the boy, which elicits a fear response. Further, if generalization occurs, the boy might be afraid of all cats. Now imagine if this reaction becomes a very intense fear: Conditioned emotional responses like these offer a possible explanation for phobias, which are intense, irrational fears of specific objects or situations (discussed in detail in Module 15.2).

Watson and Rayner generalized Albert's fear of white rats to other furry, white objects. Shown here, Watson tests Albert's reaction to a Santa Claus mask. **Click on this image in your eText to see video footage of Little Albert.**

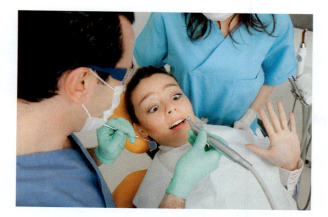

Some commonly feared objects and situations. Psychologists are finding that we are predisposed to fear specific objects that have posed threats over our evolutionary history.

Fear conditioning procedures have frequently been used in the laboratory to address clinical issues beyond phobias. For example, scientists have conducted some fascinating experiments on people diagnosed with psychopathy (the diagnosis of "psychopathy" is very similar to antisocial personality disorder, a topic we expand upon in Module 13.2). People with this disorder are notorious for disregarding the feelings of others. In one study, a sample of people diagnosed with psychopathy looked at brief presentations of human faces (the CS) followed by a painful stimulus (the US). What *should*

have happened is that participants acquired a negative emotional reaction (the CR) to the faces, but this particular sample did not react this way. Instead, these individuals showed very little physiological arousal, their emotional brain centers remained quiet, and overall they did not seem to mind looking at pictures of faces that had been paired with pain (see Figure 6.5;

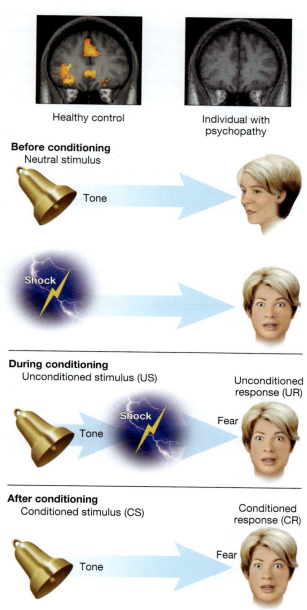

{FIG. 6.5} **Fear Conditioning and the Brain** During fear conditioning, a neutral stimulus (NS) such as a tone or a picture of a human face is briefly presented followed by an unconditioned stimulus (US), such as a mild electric shock. The result is a conditioned fear response to the CS. A procedure like this has been used to compare fear responses in people diagnosed with psychopathy with control participants. The brain images above show that those with psychopathy (right image) show very little responding in their emotional brain circuitry when presented with the CS. In contrast, control participants show strong activation in their emotional brain centers (left image) (Birbaumer et al., 2005).

Birbaumer et al., 2005). People who showed no signs of psychopathy did not enjoy this experience. In fact, following several pairings between CS and US, the control group showed increased physiological arousal and activity of the emotion centers of the brain, and understandably reported disliking the experience of the experiment.

A healthy fear response is important for survival, but not all situations or objects are equally dangerous. Snakes and heights should probably elicit more fear and caution than butterflies or freshly mown grass. In fact, fearing snakes is very common, which makes it tempting to conclude that we have an *instinct* to fear them. In reality, young primates (both human children and young monkeys, for example) tend to be quite curious about, or at least indifferent, to snakes, so this fear is most likely the product of learning rather than instinct.

Psychologists have conducted some ingenious experiments to address how learning is involved in snake fear. For instance, photographs of snakes (the CS) were paired with a mild electric shock (the US). One unconditioned response that a shock elicits is increased palm sweat—known as the skin conductance response. This reaction occurs when our bodies are aroused by a threatening or uncomfortable stimulus. Following several pairings between snake photos and shock in an experimental setting, the snake photos alone (the CS) elicited a strong increase in skin conductance response (the CR). For comparison, participants were also shown nonthreatening pictures of flowers, paired with the shock. Much less intense conditioned responding developed in response to pictures of flowers, even though the pictures had been paired with the shock an equal number of times as the snakes and shock (Figure 6.6; Öhman & Mineka, 2001). Thus it appears we are predisposed to acquire a fear of snakes, but not flowers.

This finding may not be too surprising, but what about other potentially dangerous objects such as guns? In modern times, guns are far more often associated with death or injury than snakes, and certainly flowers. When the researchers paired pictures of guns (the CS) with the shock (US), they found that conditioned arousal to guns among participants was less than that to snake photos, and comparable to that of harmless flowers. In addition, the conditioned arousal to snake photos proved longer lasting and slower to extinguish than the conditioned responding to pictures of guns or flowers (Öhman & Mineka, 2001).

Given that guns and snakes both have the potential to be dangerous, why is it so much easier to learn a fear of snakes than a fear of guns? The term **preparedness** *refers to the biological predisposition to rapidly learn a response to a particular class of stimuli* (Seligman, 1971), such as the finding that we learn to fear snakes more readily than either flowers or guns. Preparedness helps make sense of these research findings from an evolutionary perspective. Over time, humans have evolved a strong predisposition to fear an animal that has a long history of causing severe injury or death (Cook et al., 1986; Öhman & Mineka, 2001). The survival advantage has gone to those who were quick to learn to avoid animals such as snakes. The same is not true for flowers (which do not attack humans) or guns (which are relatively new in our species' history).

CONDITIONED TASTE AVERSIONS

Another example of how biological factors influence classical conditioning comes from food aversions. Chances are there is a food that you cannot stand to even look at because it once made you ill. A **conditioned taste aversion** *is the acquired dislike or disgust of a food or drink because it was paired with illness* (Garcia et al., 1966). In these situations, a taste (the CS) causes the illness (the US). Getting sick is the UR. The CR is the nausea and other signs of disgust in response to the CS (Figure 6.7).

Taste aversions may develop in a variety of ways, such as through illness associated with food poisoning, the flu, medical procedures, or excessive intoxication. Also, as is the case with fear conditioning, only certain types of stimuli are amenable to the development of conditioned taste aversions. When we develop an

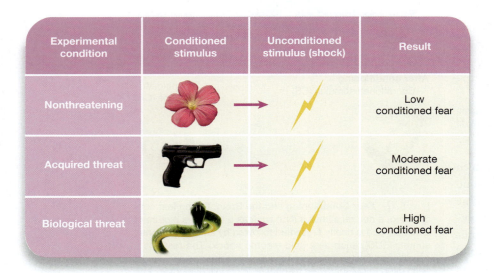

Experimental condition	Conditioned stimulus	Unconditioned stimulus (shock)	Result
Nonthreatening			Low conditioned fear
Acquired threat			Moderate conditioned fear
Biological threat			High conditioned fear

{FIG. 6.6} **Biologically Prepared Fear** Physiological measures of fear are highest in response to photos of snakes after the photos are paired with an electric shock—even higher than the responses to photos of guns. Flowers—something that humans generally do not need to fear in nature—are least effective when it comes to conditioning fear responses.

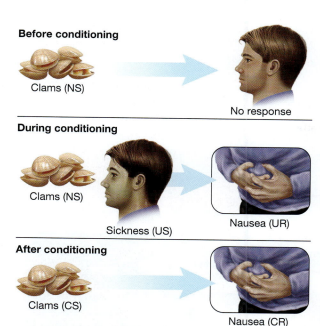

Before conditioning

Clams (NS) → No response

During conditioning

Clams (NS)

Sickness (US) → Nausea (UR)

After conditioning

Clams (CS) → Nausea (CR)

{FIG. 6.7} **Conditioned Taste Aversions** Classical conditioning can account for the development of taste aversions. Falling ill after eating a particular food can result in conditioned feelings of nausea in response to the taste, smell, or texture of the food.

aversion to a particular food, the relationship typically involves the flavor of the food and nausea, rather than the food and *any* stimulus that may have been present during conditioning. For example, if you were listening to a particular song while you got sick from eating tainted spinach, your aversion would develop to the sight, thought, and most definitely taste of spinach, but not to the song that was playing. Thus humans are biologically prepared to associate food, but not sound, with illness (Garcia et al., 1966).

Several unique characteristics are associated with conditioned taste aversions, such as the relatively long delay between tasting the food or beverage (the CS) and sickness (the US). The onset of symptoms from food poisoning may not occur until several hours have passed after the tainted food or beverage was consumed. As a consequence, the interval between tasting the food (CS) and feeling sick (US) may be a matter of hours, whereas most conditioning happens only if the CS and the US occur very closely to each other in time. Another peculiarity is that taste aversions are learned very quickly—a single CS-US pairing is typically sufficient. These special characteristics of taste aversions are extremely important for survival. The flexibility offered by a long window of time separating CS and US, as well as the requirement for only a single exposure, raises the chances of acquiring an important aversion to the offending substance.

Usually, a conditioned taste aversion develops to something we have ingested that has an unfamiliar flavor. If you have eaten the same ham and Swiss cheese sandwich at lunch for years, and you become ill one afternoon after eating it, you will be less prone to develop a conditioned taste aversion. This scenario can be explained by *latent inhibition*, which occurs when frequent experience with a stimulus before it is paired with a US makes it less likely that conditioning will occur after a single episode of illness. Latent inhibition applies to many instances where classical conditioning can occur—not just to conditioned taste aversions. For example, a child who is clawed by the family cat after years of otherwise friendly interactions is less likely to develop a fear of cats than a child who is scratched during her very first encounter with a cat.

WORKING THE SCIENTIFIC LITERACY MODEL
Conditioning and Advertising

Each day hundreds of companies and, depending on the season, political campaigners compete for your attention in the hope of winning your wallet, your vote, or both. For consumers and voters, classical conditioning plays a surprisingly significant role in advertisement.

What do we know about classical conditioning in advertising?

The negative attack ads seen between political opponents rely on similar principles of fear conditioning already described. In contrast, advertisers often use principles of classical conditioning to elicit positive responses in their viewers. Psychologists use the term *evaluative conditioning* to describe the conditioning that occurs through advertisments. Here "evaluative" refers to the conditioned response, which is a positive (like) or negative (dislike) evaluation of a stimulus, typically a brand or product.

How can science help explain the role of classical conditioning in advertising?

To help visualize how classical conditioning can work in advertising, examine Figure 6.8 (p. 204), in which the CS (a product—in this case, a popular brand of perfume) is paired with a US (imagery of two people in a sexually provocative

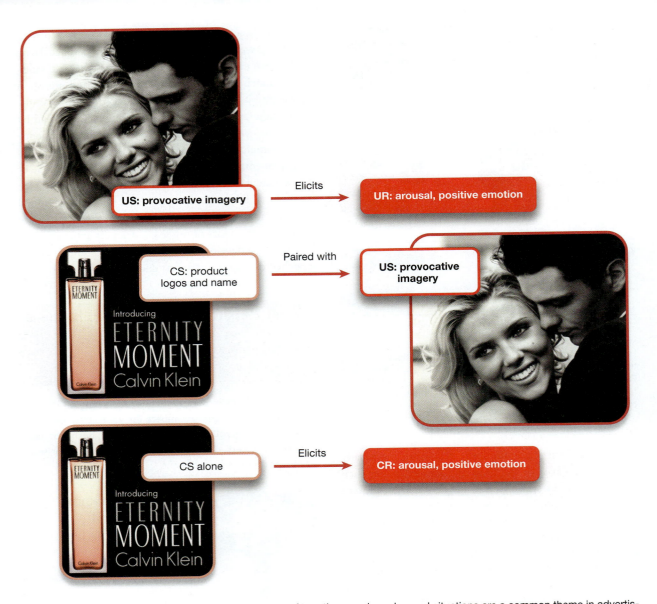

{FIG. 6.8} **Classical Conditioning in Advertisements** Attractive people and sexual situations are a common theme in advertising. By pairing products, brand names, and logos (CSs) with provocative imagery (the US), advertisers hope that viewers become conditioned so that the CSs alone will elicit positive feelings—especially when potential consumers are making choices at stores.

situation). This example alone does not provide scientific confirmation that classical conditioning accounts for why people might be inclined to buy this product. Psychologists, however, have studied this phenomenon in the laboratory to unravel the mysteries of advertisers' appeals. In one study, researchers created a fictitious product they called "Brand L toothpaste." This CS appeared in a slide show several times, along with attractive visual scenery (the US). The participants who experienced the CS and US paired together had positive evaluations of Brand L compared to participants from a control group who viewed the same slides but in an unpaired fashion (Stuart et al., 1987). Recent studies show that both positive and negative evaluations of stimuli can be conditioned in laboratory conditions that mimic what people experience in everyday exposure to advertisements (Stahl et al., 2009).

Can we critically evaluate this information?

Are companies being sneaky and deceitful when they use classical conditioning as a strategy to influence consumer behavior? As discussed in Module 4.1, the effects of subliminal advertising are greatly exaggerated. In reality, images flashed on a screen for a fraction of second can go undetected, yet still elicit subtle emotional and physiological responses. However, this effect is not likely powerful enough to control spending behavior. The imagery in advertisements, by comparison, is presented for longer than a fraction of second, giving viewers time to consciously perceive it. The effect is that you might choose a particular shampoo or body spray because you remember liking the advertisements. Therefore, although classical conditioning in advertisement affects emotional responding, it is not causing us to blindly follow suggestions to purchase products (Stahl et al., 2009).

Why is this relevant?

Advertisements are often perceived as being geared toward instilling and retaining consumer loyalty to products. Another view, of course, is that ads seek to part you and your money. As a thoughtful consumer, you should take a moment to at least ask *why* you are drawn toward a given product. Our emotional responses are not necessarily good guides for decision making. When it comes to deciding whether to make a purchase, you might ask yourself whether the sexy or humorous advertisement for the product is influencing your decision. Alternatively, is your purchase driven by the true value of the product and an actual need for it? Likewise, when you see political advertisements, consider their positive or negative emotional content. Making a reasoned decision about a candidate is preferable to making an emotion-based one.

Quick Quiz 6.1c
Applications of Classical Conditioning

Learning Without Awareness

Common sense might lead us to believe that learning is something we actively *do*, not something that happens to us without our knowledge. In reality, classical conditioning affects very subtle physiological responses, so in some cases we are completely unaware that it is happening. Classical conditioning is involved in physiological reactions that occur during drug taking, sexual arousal and, as we will see, it likely accounts for why diet beverages are seemingly ineffective at promoting weight loss.

DRUG USE AND TOLERANCE   Classical conditioning accounts for some drug-related phenomena, such as cravings and tolerance (see Module 5.3). Cues that accompany drug use can become conditioned stimuli that elicit cravings (Sinha, 2009). For example, a cigarette lighter, the smell of tobacco smoke, or the presence of another smoker can elicit cravings in people who smoke.

Many drugs also have the potential for tolerance, meaning that a decreased reaction occurs with repeated use of the drug. This trend, in turn, leads users to increase their dosage. *Conditioned drug tolerance*, which

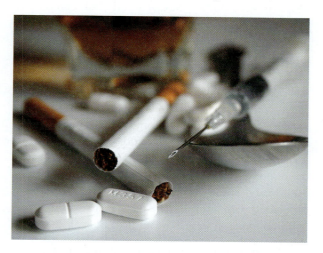

Physiological reactions to drugs are influenced by stimuli that are associated with administration of the drug.

involves physiological responses in preparation for drug administration, appears to underlie this process. It happens when the cues that are associated with drug administration become conditioned stimuli. For example, a heroin user may use the drug in a certain room with a specific set of paraphernalia and rituals for injection. Here, the unconditioned stimulus is the drug. Conditioned drug tolerance develops as the body begins associating environmental cues that accompany drug use with the drug itself. The conditioned responses involve an increase in the physiological processes that metabolize the drug—adaptive responses that prepare the body for something potentially dangerous. Over time, more of the drug is needed to override these preparatory responses so that the desired effect can be obtained.

This phenomenon can have fatal consequences for drug abusers. Psychologist Shepard Siegel (1984) conducted interviews with patients who were hospitalized for overdosing on heroin. Over the course of his interviews a pattern among the patients emerged. Several individuals reported that they were in situations unlike those that typically preceded their heroin injections—for example, in a different environment or even using an injection site that differed from the usual ritual. As a result of these differences, the CSs that were normally paired with delivery of the drug changed, leaving their bodies unprepared for delivery of the drug. Without a conditioned preparatory response, delivery of even a *normal* dose of the drug can be lethal. This finding has been confirmed in animal studies: Siegel and his associates (1982) found that conditioned drug tolerance and overdosing can also occur with rats. When rats received heroin in an environment different from where they experienced the drug previously, mortality was double that in control rats that received the same dose of heroin in their normal surroundings (64% versus 32%).

SEXUAL AROUSAL   Sexual arousal and reproductive physiology can also be influenced by classical conditioning. For example, Domjan and colleagues (2004) have studied conditioned sexual responses in Japanese quail. Males of this species will vigorously copulate with an artificial model (the CS) that has a history of being paired with a female quail (the US). These birds become highly persistent when it comes to copulating with these models—they continue to do so even when actual sexual opportunities have long since vanished. That is, the responses resist the process of extinction described previously. Some have argued that this persistent copulation with an inanimate object mirrors the sexual fetishism found in some humans (Köksal et al., 2004).

A fetish involves sexual attraction and fixation on an object. Some common fetishes involve leather,

Classically conditioned sexual behavior in a male quail. After this object (the CS) is paired with a live female quail (the US), the male quail will direct its sexual responses to the CS alone.

lace, shoes, boots, and undergarments, none of which elicit unconditioned sexual responses (Lalumiere & Quinsey, 1998). A conditioned sexual fetish can form if there is an association between the object (the CS) and sexual encounters (the US). As you can probably imagine, this phenomenon is not often studied in the laboratory. In one rare study, however, male volunteers were conditioned to experience sexual arousal when shown photos of shoes alone after such photos had been paired with sexually explicit photos (Rachman, 1996). Several explanations have been proposed for how sexual fetishes might develop, and classical conditioning certainly appears to play a role (Lowenstein, 2002). Nevertheless, in the case of sexual fetishism (and unlike in the case of the Japanese quail), the conditioning does not seem to function in a way that is conducive to actual reproductive success, given that the fixation on the desired object detracts many affected individuals from normal sexual functioning.

As you can see, the conditioned physiological changes associated with drug tolerance and sexual responses can occur below the level of awareness. It appears that certain types of conditioning involve relatively basic, if not minimal, brain functioning.

CONDITIONING AND TRAUMATIC BRAIN INJURY   Researchers have shown that people who have minimal brain function can still be conditioned. A convincing case comes from work with patients who are comatose or in a persistent vegetative state (see Module 5.3). Patients who have experienced severe brain trauma and are nonresponsive or minimally responsive to outside stimulation can learn to associate a CS and a US (Bekinschtein et al., 2009). Because of their diminished consciousness or nonconscious states, however, these patients cannot report anything about the conditioning experience to the researchers. What demonstrates that they are making an association is a simple conditioned eye blink response that is elicited by the sound of a tone (see Figure 6.9).

THE PARADOX OF "DIET" BEVERAGES

As shown in Figure 6.10, consumption of diet beverages has risen over the last several decades, but so has obesity. Classical conditioning may help explain why diet drinks are seemingly ineffective in helping people lose weight, as described at the beginning of this module (Swithers et al., 2009; Swithers & Davidson, 2005).

Through neural mechanisms linking the brain and digestive system, humans actually become conditioned to the foods and drinks that they consume, including those that contain real sugar. Sweet tastes send a message to the body that a high dose of calories is on the way. For example, the taste of a candy bar is a conditioned stimulus (CS) that tells the body that a large amount of calories (the US) is soon to arrive in the gut. This relationship is an important one for the body to learn, as it helps maintain an energy balance—eventually your body tells you it is time to stop eating sweets and switch to something else, perhaps with fewer calories. Artificially sweetened beverages disrupt this relationship between the sugary sweet CS and high-calorie food US. The artificially sweetened taste of a diet soda is not followed by a high

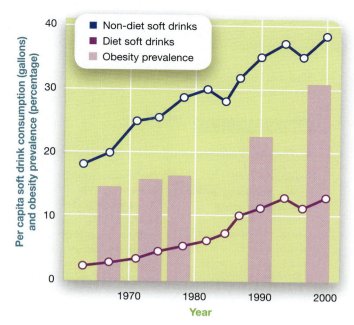

{FIG. 6.10} **Diet Soda Consumption's Association with Increased (Not Decreased) Prevalence of Obesity**

dose of calories that your body "expects." So how does the body respond? It continues to send out hunger messages: Your gut "tells" you to make up for the calories by opening up a bag of cookies or potato chips. This linkage may very well help explain why, overall, artificially sweetened beverages do not promote weight loss.

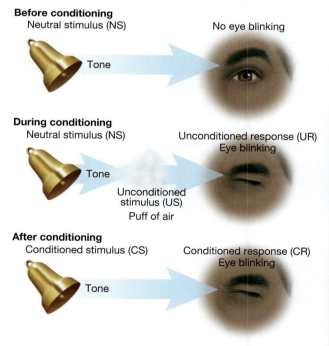

{FIG. 6.9} **Conditioned Eye Blink Responding** Patients who show no signs of consciousness learn to associate a tone (NS) with a puff of air to the eye (US). After several trials this tone alone elicits eye blinking (the CR).

Quick Quiz 6.1d
Learning Without Awareness

KNOW...

1 When a heroin user develops a routine, the needle can become the _____, whereas the body's preparation for the drug in response to the presence of the needle is the _____.

  A CS; CR   **C** US; CR

  B US; UR   **D** CS; US

ANALYZE...

2 Which is the *best* explanation for why diet beverages do not prevent people from gaining weight?

  A Diet beverages actually have more calories than regular beverages.

  B The artificially sweetened beverages seem to stimulate hunger for high-calorie foods.

  C People who drink diet beverages typically eat more food than those who drink only water.

  D Diet drinks elicit conditioned emotional reactions that lead people to overeat.

Answers can be found on page ANS-2.

Module Summary

Listen to the audio file of this module at **MyPsychLab**

Now that you have read this module you should:

KNOW ...

- **The key terminology involved in classical conditioning:**

acquisition (p. 198)
classical conditioning (p. 196)
conditioned emotional response (p. 200)
conditioned response (p. 197)
conditioned stimulus (p. 197)
conditioned taste aversion (p. 202)

discrimination (p. 199)
extinction (p. 198)
generalization (p. 199)
learning (p. 195)
preparedness (p. 202)
spontaneous recovery (p. 198)
unconditioned response (p. 196)
unconditioned stimulus (p. 196)

UNDERSTAND ...

- **How responses learned through classical conditioning can be acquired and lost.** Acquisition of a conditioned response occurs with repeated pairings of the CS and the US. Once a response is acquired, it can be extinguished if the CS and the US no longer occur together. During extinction, the CR diminishes, although it may reappear under some circumstances. For example, if enough time passes following extinction, the CR may spontaneously recover when the organism encounters the CS again.

- **The role of biological and evolutionary factors in classical conditioning.** Not all stimuli have the same potential to become a strong CS. Responses to biologically relevant stimuli, such as snakes, are more easily conditioned than are responses to stimuli such as flowers or guns, for example. Similarly, avoidance of potentially harmful foods is critical to survival, so organisms can develop a conditioned taste aversion quickly (in a single trial) and even when ingestion and illness are separated by a relatively long time interval.

APPLY ...

- **The concepts and terms of classical conditioning to new examples.** Read the three scenarios that follow and identify the conditioned stimulus (CS), the unconditioned stimulus (US), the conditioned response (CR), and the unconditioned response (UR) in each case. [*Hint:* When you apply the terms CS, US, CR, and UR, a good strategy is to identify whether something is a stimulus (something that elicits) or a response (a behavior). Next, identify whether the stimulus automatically elicits a response (the US) or does so only after being paired with a US (a CS). Finally, identify whether the response occurs in response to the US alone (the UR) or the CS alone (the CR).] Check your answers on page ANS-2.

1. Cameron and Tia went to the prom together, and during their last slow dance the DJ played the theme song for the event. During the song, the couple kissed. Now, several years later, whenever Cameron and Tia hear the song, they feel a rush of excitement.

2. Harry has visited his eye doctor several times due to problems with his vision. One test involves blowing a puff of air into his eye. After repeated visits to the eye doctor, Harry starts blinking as soon as the instrument is being applied.

3. Sarah went to a new restaurant and experienced the most delicious meal she has ever tasted. The restaurant starts advertising on the radio, and now every time an ad comes on, Sarah finds herself craving the meal she had enjoyed so much.

ANALYZE ...

- **Claims that artificially sweetened beverages are a healthier choice.** Because of classical conditioning, the digestive system responds to the flavor of the artificially sweetened (CS) beverage as though a high-calorie food source (the US) is on the way. When the low-calorie beverage reaches the digestive system, the gut has already prepared itself for something high in calories (the CR). As a consequence, hunger messages continue to be sent to the brain. Because the "diet" beverage does not deliver on the promise of high calories, the person experiences an increased level of hunger.

Module
6.2

Operant Conditioning: Learning Through Consequences

KNOW ...	UNDERSTAND ...	APPLY ...	ANALYZE ...
The key terminology associated with operant conditioning	The role that consequences play in increasing or decreasing behavior How schedules of reinforcement affect behavior	Your knowledge of operant conditioning to examples	The effectiveness of punishment on changing behavior

Cash and grades are two very strong motivators for college students. Hundreds of students each year spend hours pursuing these valuable rewards through hard work and studying. Recently, a website called Ultrinsic combined these two motivators by enticing students to gamble on their grades. The site, based in New York, allows students at more than 30 colleges and universities in the United States to upload their schedules and authorize access to their academic records through their university. Imagine a student places a wager of $25 that she will earn an A in her general chemistry course. Ultrinsic calculates the odds of this outcome based on course difficulty and the betting student's previous academic record and offers a contribution of perhaps $43. If the student receives any grade less than an A, the $25 is lost. If she earns an A, $68 is paid out to the student.

Gambling among college students is relatively common. In one survey, 42% of college students admitted to gambling within the previous year (see Barnes et al., 2010). Sites like Ultrinsic create additional chances for students to gamble, but in this case the odds are based not on chance, but rather on skill at attaining grades that the student bets on. Ultrinsic certainly has its rightful share of critics who disagree with the idea of students gambling on their grades. Given the myriad problems associated with gambling, its approach is certainly controversial. College students who use the site might argue that the gambling motivates them and brings immediate consequences to their studying, or lack thereof.

Focus Questions

 How do the consequences of our actions—such as winning or losing a bet—affect subsequent behavior?

 Many behaviors, including gambling, are reinforced only part of the time. How do the odds of being reinforced affect how often a behavior occurs?

· · · · · · · · · · · · · · · · · ·

We tend to repeat the actions that bring rewards, and avoid those that lead to punishment. This is about as straightforward a statement about behavior as one can make, but might oversimplify the complex dynamics that occur among our environment, behavior, and consequences. **Operant conditioning** *is a type of learning in which behavior is influenced by consequences.* The term *operant* is used because the individual *operates* on the environment before consequences

Table 6.1 :: Major Differences Between Classical and Operant Conditioning

	CLASSICAL CONDITIONING	OPERANT CONDITIONING
Target response is …	Automatic	Voluntary
Reinforcement is …	Present regardless of whether a response occurs	A consequence of the behavior
Behavior mostly depends on …	Reflexive and physiological responses	Skeletal muscles

can occur. In contrast to classical conditioning, which typically affects reflexive responses, operant conditioning involves voluntary actions such as speaking or listening, starting and stopping an activity, and moving toward or away from something. Whether and when we engage in these types of behaviors depend on our own unique histories with consequences.

Initially the difference between classical and operant conditioning may seem unclear. One useful way of telling the difference is that in classical conditioning a response is *not* required for a reward (or unconditioned stimulus) to be presented; to return to Pavlov's dogs, meat powder is presented regardless of whether salivation occurs. Learning has taken place if a conditioned response develops following pairings between the conditioned stimulus and the unconditioned stimulus. Notice that in this situation that the subject is not required to respond to anything—the dog does not *have* to salivate to receive food. In operant conditioning, a response and a consequence are required for learning to take place. Without a response of some kind, there can be no consequences (see Table 6.1 for a summary of differences between operant and classical conditioning).

Processes of Operant Conditioning

The concept of *contingency* is important to understanding operant conditioning; it simply means that a consequence depends upon an action. Earning good grades is generally contingent upon studying effectively. Excelling at athletics is contingent upon training and practice. The consequences of a particular behavior can be either reinforcing or punishing (see Figure 6.11).

REINFORCEMENT AND PUNISHMENT

Reinforcement *is a process in which an event or reward that follows a response increases the likelihood of that response occurring again.* We can trace the scientific study of reinforcement's effects on behavior to Edward Thorndike, who conducted experiments in which he measured the time it took cats to learn how to escape from puzzle boxes (see Figure 6.12). Thorndike observed that over repeated trials, cats were able to escape more rapidly because they learned which responses worked (such as pressing a pedal on the floor of the box). From his experiments, Thorndike proposed the *law of effect*—the idea that responses followed by satisfaction will occur again, and those that are not followed by satisfaction become less likely. Within a few decades after the publication of Thorndike's work, the famous behaviorist, B. F. Skinner, began conducting his own studies on the systematic relationship between reinforcement and behavior. As was the case with Thorndike, much of Skinner's work took place in the laboratory using nonhuman subjects.

Although operant conditioning is very much a part of our everyday behavior, many of its basic principles stem from laboratory studies conducted on nonhuman species such as pigeons or rats, which were typically placed in an apparatus such as the one pictured in Figure 6.13. *Operant chambers*, sometimes referred to as Skinner boxes, include a lever or key that the subject can manipulate. Pushing the lever may result in the delivery of a reinforcer such as food. In operant conditioning terms, a **reinforcer** *is a stimulus that*

Reinforcement increases behavior.	Punishment decreases behavior.
Behavior: Try the new café on 2nd Avenue.	Behavior: Try listening to the new radio station in town.
Consequence: The meal and service were fantastic!	Consequence: The music is terrible!
Effect: The behavior is reinforced. You'll go there again.	Effect: You won't listen to that station again.

{FIG. 6.11} **Reinforcement and Punishment** The key distinction between reinforcement and punishment is that reinforcers, no matter what they are, increase behavior. Punishment involves a decrease in behavior, regardless of what the specific punisher may be. Thus both reinforcement and punishment are defined based on their effects on behavior. **Click on this figure in your eText to see more details**.

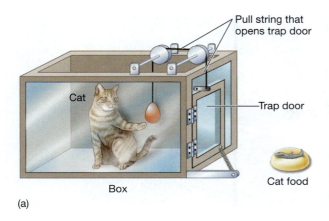

(a)

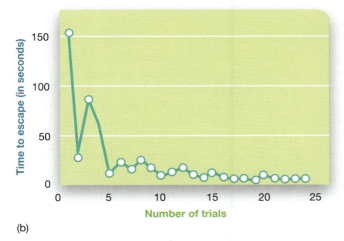

(b)

{FIG. 6.12} **Thorndike's Puzzle Box and the Law of Effect** Thorndike conducted experiments in which cats learned an operant response that was reinforced with escape from the box and access to a food reward (a). Over repeated trials, the cats took progressively less time to escape, as shown in this learning curve (b).

is contingent upon a response, and that increases the probability of that response occurring again. Using operant chambers, researchers record the animal's rate of responding over time (a measure of learning), and typically set a criterion for the number of responses that must be made

before a reinforcer becomes available. As we will discuss later in this module, animals and humans are quite sensitive to how many responses they must make, or how long they must wait, before they will receive a reward.

After studying Figure 6.13, you might wonder whether observations made with this apparatus could possibly apply to real-world situations. In fact, similar machinery can be found in all sorts of nonlaboratory settings. People pull levers on slot machines, press buttons on vending machines, and punch keys on telephones. Researchers use machinery such as operant chambers to help them control and quantify learning, but the general principles of operant conditioning apply to life outside and away from such machines.

Reinforcement involves increased responding, but decreased responding is also a possible outcome of an encounter with a stimulus. **Punishment** *is a process that decreases the future probability of a response.* Thus a **punisher** *is a stimulus that is contingent upon a response, and that results in a decrease in behavior.* Like reinforcers, punishers are defined not based on the stimuli themselves, but rather in terms of their effects on behavior. We will explore some topics related to punishment in this module, but because reinforcement is more central to the topic of operant conditioning, we will elaborate on it more extensively. One key characteristic of reinforcement learning is that it is motivated by the satisfaction of various types of drives.

PRIMARY AND SECONDARY REINFORCERS

Reinforcement can come in many different forms. On the one hand, it may consist of stimuli that are inherently reinforcing, such as food, water, shelter, and sexual contact.

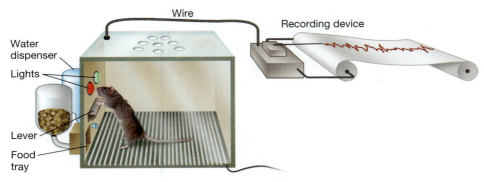

{FIG. 6.13} **An Operant Chamber** The operant chamber is a standard laboratory apparatus for studying operant conditioning. The rat can press the lever to receive a reinforcer such as food or water. The lights can be used to indicate when lever pressing will be rewarded. The recording device measures cumulative responses (lever presses) over time.

Animals pressing levers in operant chambers to receive rewards may seem artificial. However, if you look around you will see that our environment is full of devices that influence our operant responses.

These **primary reinforcers** *consist of reinforcing stimuli that satisfy basic motivational needs.* On the other hand, many stimuli that we find reinforcing, such as money or grades, are reinforcing only after we first *learn* that they have value. **Secondary reinforcers** *consist of reinforcing stimuli that acquire their value through learning.* Think about how you would react if you were handed a $1,000 check to spend as you please, versus how an infant would respond if given the same document. The baby might try to mouth the check before abandoning it for a shiny rattle or something else more reinforcing to her, because she has not learned why it might be reinforcing.

Both primary and secondary reinforcers satisfy our drives, but what underlies the motivation to seek these reinforcers? The answer is complex, but research points to a specific brain circuit including a structure called the *nucleus accumbens* (see Figure 6.14). The nucleus accumbens becomes activated during the processing of all kinds of rewards, including primary ones such as eating and having sex, as well as "artificial" rewards such as using cocaine and smoking a cigarette. Variations in this area might also account for why individuals differ so much in their drive for reinforcers. For example, scientists have discovered that people who are prone to risky behaviors such as gambling and alcohol abuse are more likely to have inherited particular copies of genes that code for dopamine and other reward-based chemicals of the brain (Comings & Blum, 2000). Perhaps the reward centers of gamblers and others who engage in high-risk behaviors are not sufficiently stimulated by natural rewards, making them more likely to engage in behaviors that will give them the rush that they crave.

Secondary reinforcers can be powerful motivators as well, as can be seen in *token economies* (Hackenberg, 2009). Token economies are often used in residential treatment settings to encourage appropriate behaviors while discouraging inappropriate ones. With this approach, caretakers establish a reinforcement system in which tokens serve as secondary reinforcers. A resident can earn tokens through good behavior, which can then be exchanged for something else reinforcing, such as candy or special privileges. Conversely, misbehavior can cost tokens, so these tokens can play a role in punishment as well.

POSITIVE AND NEGATIVE REINFORCEMENT AND PUNISHMENT

Behavior can be reinforced in several different ways. A response can be strengthened because it brings a reward or, alternatively, because it results in the removal of something unpleasant.

Primary reinforcers satisfy basic biological needs, such as hunger or thirst. Secondary reinforcers, such as money, acquire their value and are typically associated with access to primary reinforcers.

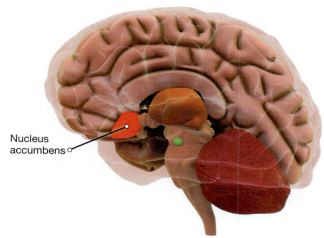

Nucleus
accumbens

{FIG. 6.14} **Reward Processing in the Brain** The nucleus accumbens is one of the brain's primary reward centers.

Positive reinforcement *is the strengthening of behavior after potential reinforcers such as praise, money, or nourishment follow that behavior* (see Table 6.2). With positive reinforcement, a stimulus is added to a situation (the "positive" in positive reinforcement indicates the *addition* of a reward). Positive reinforcement can be a highly effective method of rewarding desired behaviors among humans and other species. In fact, B. F. Skinner devoted most of his career to studying pigeons. In the search for general principles of learning, it mattered less which species was used, and certainly pigeons were easier to keep, feed, and control than human subjects.

Negative reinforcement *involves the strengthening of a behavior because it removes or diminishes a stimulus* (Table 6.2). (In this context, the word "negative" indicates the removal of something.) Much of what we do is for the purposes of avoiding or getting rid of something aversive (unpleasant); these actions serve as examples of negative reinforcement. For instance, taking aspirin is negatively reinforced because doing so removes a painful headache. Similarly, asking someone behind you in a movie theater to stop kicking your seat may remove the annoying

event, thereby reinforcing you and encouraging you to repeat this behavior in future situations.

Negative reinforcement is a concept that students frequently find confusing because it seems unusual that something aversive could be involved in the context of reinforcement. Recall that reinforcement (whether positive or negative) always involves an increase in the strength or frequency of responding. The term "positive" in this context simply means that a stimulus is introduced or increased, whereas the term "negative" means that a stimulus has been reduced or avoided.

Negative reinforcement can be further classified into two subcategories. **Avoidance learning** *is a specific type of negative reinforcement that removes the possibility that a stimulus will occur.* Examples of avoidance learning include taking a detour to avoid traffic congestion on a particular road, and paying bills on time to avoid late fees. In these cases, negative situations are avoided. In contrast, **escape learning** *occurs if a response removes a stimulus that is already present.* Covering your ears upon hearing overwhelmingly loud music is one example. You cannot avoid the music, because it is already present, so you escape the aversive stimulus. The responses of taking a detour and covering your ears both increase in frequency because they have effectively removed the offending stimuli. In the laboratory, operant chambers such as the one pictured in Figure 6.13 often come equipped with a grid metal floor that can be used to deliver a mild electric shock; responses that remove (escape learning) or prevent (avoidance learning) the shock are negatively reinforced.

As with reinforcement, various types of punishment are possible. **Positive punishment** *is a process in which a behavior decreases because it adds or increases a particular stimulus* (Table 6.2). For example, some cat owners use a spray bottle to squirt water when the cat hops on the kitchen counter or scratches the furniture. Remember that the

PsychTutor

Click here in your eText for an interactive tutorial on **Operant Conditioning**

Table 6.2 :: **Distinguishing Types of Reinforcement and Punishment**

	CONSEQUENCE	EFFECT ON BEHAVIOR	EXAMPLE
Positive reinforcement	Stimulus is added or increased.	Increases the response	A child gets an allowance for making her bed, so she is likely to do it again in the future.
Negative reinforcement	Stimulus is removed or decreased.	Increases the response	The rain no longer falls on you after opening your umbrella, so you are likely to do it again in the future.
Positive punishment	Stimulus is added or increased.	Decreases the response	A pet owner scolds his dog for jumping up on a house guest, and now the dog is less likely to do it again.
Negative punishment	Stimulus is removed or decreased.	Decreases the response	A parent takes away TV privileges to stop the children from fighting.

Avoidance and escape learning. Getting caught in road construction is typically an aversive event. Avoidance learning might involve taking precautionary measures, such as starting the trip on an alternative route so you do not encounter the construction at all. Escape responses, such as pulling out of the traffic jam to take a shortcut, occur after the stimulus is already encountered. Either response would be negatively reinforced, as it removes the aversive stimulus of being caught.

term "positive" simply means that a stimulus is added to the situation—in these cases, the stimuli are punishers because they decrease the frequency of a behavior.

Behavior may also decrease as a result of the removal of a stimulus. **Negative punishment** *occurs when a behavior decreases because it removes or diminishes a particular stimulus* (Table 6.2). Withholding someone's privileges as a result of an undesirable behavior is an example of negative punishment. A parent who "grounds" a child does so because this action removes something of value to the child. If effective, the outcome of the grounding will be to decrease the behavior that got the child into trouble.

EXTINCTION, STIMULUS CONTROL, GENERALIZATION, AND DISCRIMINATION

If you read Module 6.1, you know how extinction, generalization, and discrimination apply to classical conditioning. Similar phenomena occur with operant conditioning. In operant conditioning, **extinction** *refers to the weakening of an operant response when reinforcement is no longer available.* If you lose your Internet connection for example, you will probably stop trying to refresh your web browser

because there is no reinforcement for doing so—the behavior will be extinguished.

Once a response has been learned, the organism may soon learn that reinforcement is available under only certain conditions and circumstances. A pigeon in an operant chamber may learn that pecking is reinforced only when the chamber's light is switched on, so there is no need to continue pecking when the light is turned off. This illustrates the concept of a **discriminative stimulus**—*a cue or event that indicates that a response, if made, will be reinforced.* A behavior—in this case, pecking—is under *stimulus control* when a discriminative stimulus reliably elicits a specific response. As with the pigeon in the operant chamber, much of human behavior is under stimulus control. Before we pour a cup of coffee, we might check whether the light on the coffee pot is on—a discriminative stimulus that tells us the beverage will be hot and, presumably, reinforcing.

The processes of generalization and discrimination influence whether organisms respond to discriminative stimuli. Generalization is observed in operant conditioning just as in classical conditioning, albeit with some important differences. In operant conditioning, *generalization* occurs when an operant response takes place to a new stimulus that is similar to the stimulus present during original learning. Children who have a history of being reinforced by their parents for tying their shoes, for example, are likely to demonstrate this same behavior when a teacher or other adult asks them to do so. *Discrimination* occurs when an operant response is made to one stimulus but not to another, even similar stimulus. Perhaps you have learned that reinforcement is associated with only specific behaviors. For example, your behavior of stopping in response to a red traffic light has been reinforced in the past. You would not expect the same reinforcement for stopping at a green traffic light, even though these stimuli are often located closely to each other, and are often the same shape, brightness, and size.

Table 6.3 differentiates among the processes of extinction, generalization, and discrimination in classical and operant conditioning.

Table 6.3 :: Comparing Extinction, Generalization, and Discrimination in Classical and Operant Conditioning

PROCESS	CLASSICAL CONDITIONING	OPERANT CONDITIONING
Extinction	A CS is presented without a US until the CR no longer occurs.	Responding gradually ceases if reinforcement is no longer available.
Generalization	A different CS that resembles the original CS used during acquisition elicits a CR.	Responding occurs to a stimulus that resembles the original discriminative stimulus used during learning.
Discrimination	A CR does not occur in response to a different CS that resembles the original CS.	There is no response to a stimulus that resembles the original discriminative stimulus used during learning.

Quick Quiz 6.2a
Processes of Operant Conditioning

KNOW …

1. _____ removes the immediate effects of an aversive stimulus, whereas _____ removes the possibility of an aversive stimulus from occurring in the first place.

   A Avoidance learning; escape learning

   B Positive reinforcement; positive punishment

   C Negative reinforcement; negative punishment

   D Escape learning; avoidance learning

2. A basic need such as food may be used as a _____ reinforcer, whereas a stimulus whose value must be learned is a _____ reinforcer.

   A primary; continuous   **C** primary; secondary

   B secondary; shaping   **D** continuous; secondary

UNDERSTAND …

3. As a consequence for misbehaving, many teachers use "timeout." How does this consequence affect students' behavior?

   A It adds a stimulus to decrease bad behavior.

   B It takes away a stimulus to decrease bad behavior.

   C It adds a stimulus to increase bad behavior.

   D It takes away a stimulus to increase bad behavior.

APPLY …

4. Lucy hands all of her homework in to her psychology professor on time because she does not want to lose points for late work. This is an example of _____.

   A avoidance learning   **C** escape learning

   B positive reinforcement **D** positive punishment

Answers can be found on page ANS-2.

Applications of Operant Conditioning

Now that we have reviewed the basic processes of operant conditioning, you should have a sense of how much our behavior is influenced by rewards and punishment. In this section, we focus on some specific applications of operant conditioning.

SHAPING   Rats placed in operant chambers do not automatically go straight for the lever and begin pressing it to obtain food rewards. Instead, they must first learn that lever pressing accomplishes something. Getting a rat to press a lever can be done by reinforcing behaviors that *approximate* lever pressing, such as standing up, facing the lever, standing while facing the lever, placing paws upon the lever, and pressing downward. **Shaping** *is a procedure in which a specific operant response is created by reinforcing successive approximations of that response.* Shaping is done in step-by-step fashion until the desired response—in

Applications of shaping. Reinforcement can be used to shape complex chains of behavior in animals and humans.

this case, lever pressing—is learned. Skilled behavioral psychologists can string together long sequences of behavior using shaping techniques. Shaping has some broad applications—a particularly important one is in helping people develop specific skill sets. ✳

✳ **Explore** the **Concept** *The Shaping Process* at **MyPsychLab**

PSYCH @

The Special Needs Classroom

Operant conditioning is the basis for an educational method called *applied behavior analysis* (ABA), which involves using close observation, prompting, and reinforcement to teach behaviors, often to people who experience difficulties and challenges owing to a developmental condition such as autism (Granpeesheh et al., 2009). People with autism are typically nonresponsive to normal social cues from a very early age. This impairment can lead to a deficit in developing many skills, ranging from basic, everyday ones as well as complex skills such as language. For example, explaining how to clear dishes from the dinner table to a child with autism could prove difficult. Psychologists who specialize in ABA often shape the desired behavior using prompts (such as asking the child to stand up, gather silverware, stack plates, and so on) and verbal rewards as each step is completed. These and more elaborate ABA techniques can be used to shape a remarkable variety of behaviors to improve the independence and quality of life for people with autism.

SCHEDULES OF REINFORCEMENT Typically, behavior is rewarded according to some kind of schedule. Skinner and his colleagues (Ferster & Skinner, 1957) recognized the importance of **schedules of reinforcement**—*rules that determine when reinforcement is available*. Reinforcement may be available at highly predictable or very irregular times. Also, reinforcement may be based on how often someone engages in a behavior, or on the passage of time.

Vending machines should deliver a snack every time the correct amount of money is deposited. With such **continuous reinforcement**, *every response made results in reinforcement*, and learning initially occurs rapidly.

Other reinforcers we work to achieve do not come with such regularity; we also encounter situations where reinforcement is available only some of the time. Telephoning a friend may not always get you an actual person on the other end of the call. In this kind of **partial (intermittent) reinforcement**, *only a certain number of responses are rewarded, or a certain amount of time must pass before reinforcement is available*. Four types of partial reinforcement schedules are possible (see Figure 6.15), which have different effects on rates of responding.

Ratio schedules of reinforcement are based on the amount of responding. In a **fixed-ratio schedule**, *reinforcement is delivered after a specific number of responses have been completed*. For example, a rat may be required to press a lever 10 times to receive food. Similarly, an employee working on commission may receive a bonus only after selling a specific number of items.

In a **variable-ratio schedule**, *the number of responses required to receive reinforcement varies according to an average*. Slot machines at casinos operate on variable-ratio reinforcement schedules. The odds are that the slot machine will not give anything back, but sometimes a player will get a modest winning. Of course, hitting the jackpot is very infrequent. The variable nature of the reward structure for playing slot machines helps explain why responding on this schedule can be vigorous and persistent. Slot machines and other games of chance hold out the *possibility* that at some point players will be rewarded, but the unpredictable reward structure tends to promote strong response levels—in other words, a lot of money deposited into the machine.

In contrast to ratio schedules, interval schedules are based on the passage of time, not the number of responses. A **fixed-interval schedule** *reinforces the first response occurring after a set amount of time passes*. If your psychology professor gives you an exam every three weeks, your reinforcement for studying is on a fixed-interval schedule. In Figure 6.15, notice how the fixed-interval schedule shows that responding drops off after each reinforcement is delivered (as indicated by the tick marks). However, responding increases because reinforcement is soon available again. This schedule may reflect how you devote time to studying for your next exam—studying time tends to decrease after an exam, and then builds up again as another test looms.

A slightly different schedule is the **variable-interval schedule**, *in which the first response is reinforced following a variable amount of time*. The time interval varies around an

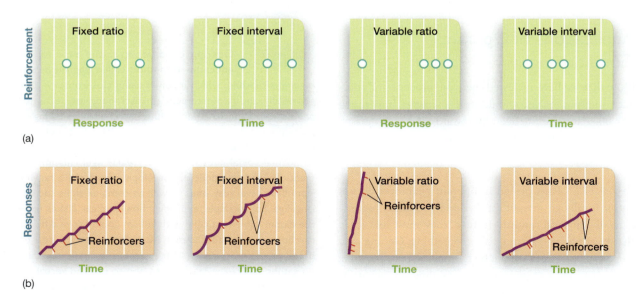

{FIG. 6.15} **Schedules of Reinforcement** (a) Four types of reinforcement schedule are shown here: fixed ratio, variable ratio, fixed interval, and variable interval. Notice how each schedule differs based on when reinforcement is available (interval schedules) and on how many responses are required for reinforcement (ratio schedules). (b) These schedules of reinforcement affect responding in different ways. For example, notice the vigorous responding that is characteristic of the variable ratio schedule, as indicated by the steep upward trajectory of responding. **Click on this figure in your eText to see more details.**

average. For example, if you were watching the nighttime sky during a meteor shower, you would be rewarded for looking upward at irregular times. A meteor may fall on average every 5 minutes, but there will be times of inactivity for a minute, 10 minutes, 8 minutes, and so on.

As you can see from Figure 6.15, ratio schedules tend to generate relatively high rates of responding. This outcome makes sense in light of the fact that in ratio schedules, reinforcement is based on how often you engage in the behavior (something you have some control over) versus how much time has passed (something you do not control). For example, looking up with greater frequency does not *cause* more meteor activity because a variable-interval schedule is in effect. In contrast, a sales person is on a variable-ratio schedule because approaching more customers increases the chances of making a sale.

One general characteristic of schedules of reinforcement is that partially reinforced responses tend to be very persistent. For example, although people are only intermittently reinforced for putting money into a slot machine, a high rate of responding is maintained and may not decrease until after a great many losses in a row (or the individual runs out of money). The effect of partial reinforcement on responding is especially evident during extinction. Being partially reinforced can lead to very persistent responding even if, unbeknownst to the organism, reinforcement is no longer available. The **partial reinforcement effect** *refers to a phenomenon in which organisms that have been conditioned under partial reinforcement resist extinction longer than those conditioned under continuous reinforcement.*

WORKING THE SCIENTIFIC LITERACY MODEL
Reinforcement and Superstition

It is clear that reinforcement can appear in multiple forms and according to various schedules. What all forms have in common is the notion that the behavior that brought about the reinforcement will be strengthened. But what happens if the organism is mistaken about what caused the reinforcement to occur—will it experience reinforcement anyway? This raises the topic of superstition.

What do we know about superstition and reinforcement?

Reinforcement is often systematic and predictable. If it is not, then behavior is eventually extinguished. In some cases, however, it is not

perfectly clear what brings about the reinforcement. Imagine a baseball player who tries to be consistent in how he pitches. After a short losing streak, the pitcher suddenly wins a big game. If he is playing the same way, then what happened to change his luck? Did an alteration in his pre-game ritual lead to the victory? Humans the world over are prone to believing that some ritual or luck charm will somehow improve their chances of success or survival. Psychologists believe these superstitions can be explained by operant conditioning.

How can science explain superstition?

Decades ago, B. F. Skinner (1948) attempted to create superstitious behavior in pigeons. Food was delivered every 15 seconds, regardless of what the pigeons were doing. Over time, the birds started engaging in "superstitious" behaviors. The pigeons repeated the behavior occurring just before reinforcement, even if the behavior was scratching, head-bobbing, or standing on one foot. A pigeon that happened to be turning in a counterclockwise direction when reinforcement was delivered repeated this seemingly senseless behavior.

In a laboratory study involving humans, psychologists constructed a doll that could spit marbles (Wagner & Morris, 1987). Children were told that the doll would sometimes spit marbles at them and that these marbles could be collected and traded for toys. The marbles were ejected at random intervals, leading several of the children to develop superstitious behaviors such as sucking their thumbs or kissing the doll on the nose.

Psychologists have conducted controlled studies to see whether superstitious behaviors have any effect on performance outcomes. In one investigation, college students, 80% of whom believed in the idea of "good luck," were asked to participate in a golf putting contest in which members of one group were told they were playing with "the lucky ball," and others were told they would be using "the ball everyone has used so far." Those who were told they were using the lucky ball performed significantly better than those who used the ball that was not blessed with good luck (Damisch et al., 2010). These effects also occurred in other tasks, such as memory and anagram games, and participants also showed better performance at tasks if allowed to bring a good luck charm.

Can we critically evaluate these findings?

Superstitious beliefs, though irrational on the surface, may enhance individuals' belief that they can perform successfully at a task. Sometimes these beliefs can even enhance performance, as the golf putting experiment revealed. These findings, however, are best applied to situations where the participant has some control over an outcome, such as taking an exam or playing a sport. People who spend a lot of time and money gambling are known to be quite superstitious, but it is important to distinguish between games of chance versus skill in this setting. "Success" at most gambling games is due entirely, or predominantly, to chance. Thus the outcomes are immune to the superstitious beliefs of the players.

Why is this relevant?

Between Skinner's original work with pigeons, and more contemporary experiments with people, it appears that operant conditioning plays a role in the development of some superstitions. Superstitious behavior is frequently displayed by professional athletes, who wear specific (sometimes unwashed) clothing or go through rituals as they prepare to perform. One of the more bizarre rituals was practiced by former Cleveland Indians outfielder Kevin Rhomberg, who believed that if someone touched him he would have bad luck unless he touched that person back. This quirk *may* have been accepted by his teammates, but it also included the opposing players. Thus, if Rhomberg was tagged out while running bases, he could be seen pursuing the player in order to touch him as the teams switched sides (his professional career was short—just 41 games).

Perhaps you have a good-luck charm or a ritual you must complete before a game or even before taking a test. Think about what brings you luck, and then try to identify why you believe in this relationship. Can you identify a specific instance when you were first reinforced for this behavior?

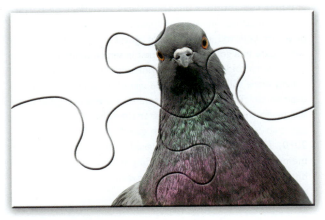

APPLYING PUNISHMENT   People tend to be more sensitive to the unpleasantness of punishment than they are to the pleasures of reward. Psychologists have demonstrated this asymmetry in laboratory studies with college students who play a computerized game where they can choose a response that can bring either a monetary reward or a monetary loss. It turns out that the participants found losing money to be about three times as punishing as being rewarded with money was pleasurable. In other words, losing $100 is three times more punishing than gaining $100 is reinforcing (Rasmussen & Newland, 2008).

The use of punishment raises some ethical concerns—especially when it comes to physical means. A major issue that is debated all over the world is whether corporal punishment (e.g., spanking) is acceptable to use with children. In fact, more than 20 countries, including Sweden, Austria, Finland, Demark, and Israel, have banned the practice. Interestingly, very few people in the United States publicly advocate spanking. This is certainly the case among psychologists. Even so, spanking remains a very common practice. In one recent study, for example, approximately two-thirds of participating families reported spanking their three-year-old child at least once in the past month (Taylor et al., 2010). Parents often use this tactic because it works: Spanking is generally a very effective punisher when it is used for immediately stopping a behavior (Gershoff, 2002). However, one reason why so few psychologists advocate spanking is because it is associated with some major side effects. In multiple studies, spanking has been associated with poorer parent–child relationships, poorer mental health for both adults and children, delinquency in children, and increased chances of children becoming victims or perpetrators of physical abuse in adulthood (Gershoff, 2002; Gershoff & Bitensky, 2007).

Do these findings suggest that corporal punishment should be abandoned altogether? Although few psychologists recommend spanking, further research has shown that the negative side effects are more likely if punishment is particularly severe, such as slapping children in the face. Other research indicates that less harsh forms of corporal punishment, such as light spanking, are effective and unlikely to bring about other negative side effects (Kazdin & Benjet, 2003). In addition, punishment may suppress an unwanted behavior temporarily, but by itself it does not teach which behaviors are appropriate. As a general rule, punishment of any kind is most effective when combined with reinforcement of an alternative, suitable response. Table 6.4 offers some general guidelines for maximizing the effects of punishment and minimizing negative side effects.

Table 6.4 :: Punishment Tends to Be Most Effective When Certain Principles Are Followed

PRINCIPLE	DESCRIPTION AND EXPLANATION
Severity	Should be proportional to offense. A small fine is suitable for parking illegally or littering, but inappropriate for someone who commits assault.
Initial punishment level	The initial level of punishment needs to be sufficiently strong to reduce the likelihood of the offense occurring again.
Contiguity	Punishment is most effective when it occurs immediately after the behavior. Many convicted criminals are not sentenced until many months after they have committed an offense. Children are given detention that may not begin until hours later. Long delays in punishment are known to reduce its effectiveness.
Consistency	Punishment should be administered consistently. A parent who only occasionally punishes a teenager for breaking her curfew will probably have less success in curbing the behavior than a parent who uses punishment consistently.
Show alternatives	Punishment is more successful, and side effects are reduced, if the individual is clear on how reinforcement can be obtained by engaging in appropriate behaviors.

Quick Quiz 6.2b :: Applications of Operant Conditioning

KNOW …

1. Shaping is the process of:

   A. reinforcing a series of responses that approximate the desired behavior.

   B. decreasing the likelihood of a behavior.

   C. reinforcing the basic motivational needs of a subject.

   D. punishing a series of responses that you want to increase.

UNDERSTAND …

2. Pete cannot seem to stop checking the change slots of vending machines. Although he usually does not find any money, occasionally he finds a quarter. Despite the low levels of reinforcement, this behavior is likely to persist due to _____.

   A. escape learning

   B. the partial reinforcement effect

   C. positive punishment

   D. generalization

APPLY …

3. Frederick trained his parrot to open the door to his cage by pecking at a lever three times. Frederick used a _____ schedule of reinforcement to encourage the desired behavior.

   A. variable interval

   B. variable-ratio

   C. fixed interval

   D. fixed-ratio

ANALYZE …

4. A friend regularly spanks his children to decrease their misbehavior. Which statement is most accurate in regard to this type of corporal punishment?

   A. Spanking is an effective method of punishment and should always be used.

   B. Spanking can be an effective method of punishment but carries risks of additional negative outcomes.

   C. Spanking is not an effective method of punishment, so it should never be used.

   D. The effects of spanking have not been well researched, so it should not be used.

Answers can be found on page ANS-2.

Module Summary

Module **6.2**

((•——[**Listen** to

the audio file of

this module at

MyPsychLab

Now that you have read this module you should:

KNOW ...

- **The key terminology associated with operant conditioning:**

avoidance learning (p. 213)

continuous reinforcement (p. 216)

discriminative stimulus (p. 214)

escape learning (p. 213)

extinction (p. 214)

fixed-interval schedule (p. 216)

fixed-ratio schedule (p. 216)

negative punishment (p. 214)

negative reinforcement (p. 213)

operant conditioning (p. 209)

partial (intermittent) reinforcement (p. 216)

partial reinforcement effect (p. 217)

positive punishment (p. 213)

positive reinforcement (p. 213)

primary reinforcer (p. 212)

punisher (p. 211)

punishment (p. 211)

reinforcement (p. 210)

reinforcer (p. 210)

schedules of reinforcement (p. 216)

secondary reinforcer (p. 212)

shaping (p. 215)

variable-interval schedule (p. 216)

variable-ratio schedule (p. 216)

UNDERSTAND ...

- **The role that consequences play in increasing or decreasing behavior.** Positive and negative reinforcement increase the likelihood of a behavior, whereas positive and negative punishment decrease the likelihood of a behavior. Positive reinforcement and punishment involve adding a stimulus to the situation, whereas negative reinforcement and punishment involve removal of a stimulus.

- **How schedules of reinforcement affect behavior.** Schedules of reinforcement can be fixed or variable, and can be based on intervals (time) or ratios (the number of responses). In contrast to continuous reinforcement, intermittent schedules tend to elicit vigorous responding. Our tendency to link our behavior to reinforcement is particularly evident when it comes to superstition—where a ritual is *believed* to bring about reinforcement, regardless of whether it actually does.

APPLY ...

- **Your knowledge of operant conditioning to examples.** The concepts of positive and negative reinforcement and punishment are often the most challenging when it comes to this material. Read the following scenarios and determine whether positive reinforcement, negative reinforcement, positive punishment, or negative punishment explains the change in behavior. Check your answers on page ANS-2.

  1. Steven is caught for cheating on multiple examinations. As a consequence, the school principal suspends him for a three-day period. Steven likes being at school and, when he returns from his suspension, he no longer cheats on exams. Which process explains the change in Steven's behavior? Why?

  2. Ericka earns As in all of her math classes. Throughout her schooling, she finds that the personal and social rewards for excelling at math continue to motivate her. She eventually completes a graduate degree and teaches math. Which process explains her passion for math? Why?

  3. Automobile makers install sound equipment that produces annoying sounds when a door is not shut properly, lights are left on, or a seat belt is not fastened. The purpose is to increase proper door shutting, turning off of lights, and seat belt fastening behavior. Which process explains the behavioral change these sounds are attempting to make?

  4. Hernan bites his fingernails and cuticles to the point of bleeding and discomfort. To reduce this behavior, he applies a terrible-tasting topical lotion to his fingertips; the behavior stops. Which process explains Hernan's behavioral change?

ANALYZE ...

- **The effectiveness of punishment on changing behavior.** Many psychologists recommend that people rely on reinforcement to teach new or appropriate behaviors. The issue here is not that punishment does not work, but rather that there are some notable drawbacks to using punishment as a means to change behavior. For example, punishment may teach individuals to engage in avoidance or aggression, rather than developing an appropriate alternative behavior that can be reinforced.

Cognitive and Observational Learning

Learning Objectives

After reading this module you should:

KNOW ...	UNDERSTAND ...	APPLY ...	ANALYZE ...
The key terminology associated with cognitive and observational learning	The concept of latent learning and its relevance to cognitive aspects of learning	Principles of learning to make your own learning experiences more effective	The claim that viewing violent media increases violent behavior

Are you smarter than a chimpanzee? For years psychologists have asked this question, but in a more nuanced way. More specifically, they have tested the problem-solving and imitative abilities of chimpanzees and humans to help us better understand what sets us apart, and what makes us similar to other animals. Chimps and humans both acquire many behaviors from observing others, but imagine if you pitted a typical human preschooler against a chimpanzee. Who do you think would be the best at learning a new skill just by watching someone else perform it? Researchers Victoria Horner and Andrew Whiten asked this question by showing 3- and 4-year-old children how to retrieve a treat by opening a puzzle box, and then they demonstrated the task to chimpanzees as well. But there was one trick thrown in: As they demonstrated the process, the researchers added in some steps that were unnecessary to opening the box. The children and chimps both figured out how to open it, but the children imitated all the steps—even the unnecessary ones—while the chimps skipped the useless steps and went straight for the treat (Horner & Whiten, 2005).

What can we conclude from these results? Maybe it is true that both humans and chimps are excellent imitators, although it appears the children imitated a little too well, while the chimps imitated in a smarter manner. Clearly, we both share a motivation to imitate—which is a complex cognitive ability.

Focus Questions

1. What role do cognitive factors play in learning?

2. Which processes are required for imitation to occur?

• • • • • • • • • • • • • • • • • •

The first two modules of this chapter focused on relatively basic ways of learning. Classical conditioning occurs through the formation of associations (Module 6.1), and in operant conditioning behavior changes as a result of rewarding or punishing consequences (Module 6.2). In both modules, we emphasized relationships between stimuli and responses, and avoided making reference to an organism that was doing the *thinking* part of the learning process.

When John Watson, B. F. Skinner, and other behavioral psychologists of the time were conducting their research, they assumed that "thought" was unnecessary for a scientific account of how stimuli and responses are related. However, since the 1950s and continuing today, psychologists have recognized that cognitive processes such as thinking and remembering are useful to theories and explanations for how we learn.

Cognitive Perspectives on Learning

Cognitive psychologists have contributed a great deal to psychology's understanding of learning. In some cases, they have presented a very different view from behaviorism by addressing unobservable mental phenomena. In other cases, their work has simply complemented behaviorism by integrating cognitive accounts into even the seemingly simplest of learned behaviors, such as classical conditioning.

Simulate the Experiment *Learning* at MyPsychLab

THE PAST PREDICTS THE FUTURE: COGNITIVE PROCESSES AND CONDITIONING Pavlov's experiments illustrated how classical conditioning involves pairing a conditioned stimulus such as a tone with an unconditioned stimulus of food, resulting in the conditioned response of salivation to the tone alone (Module 6.1). When it comes to the real world, however, learning is rarely so simple. Tones might occur in the absence of food, and food might be available with or without tones. Classical conditioning can take place only if an organism recognizes that there is a consistent relationship between the two stimuli. In other words, an association can form if the conditioned stimulus is a *reliable* predictor of the unconditioned stimulus (Rescorla &

Wagner, 1972). It seems that humans are sensitive to the degree to which stimuli are associated and respond only if there is consistency in their relationship. The same is true for rats. Rats that experience tones and shocks occurring together 100% of the time show more fear in response to a tone than do rats that experience the same number of tones and shocks, but for which the stimuli actually occur together only 50% of the time (see Figure 6.16).

LATENT LEARNING Much of human learning involves absorbing information and then demonstrating what we have learned through a performance task, such as a quiz or exam. Learning, and reinforcement for learning, may not be expressed until there is an opportunity to do so.

Psychologist Edward Tolman proposed that humans, and even rats, express **latent learning**—*learning that is not immediately expressed by a response until the organism is reinforced for doing so.* Tolman and Honzik (1930) demonstrated latent learning in rats running a maze (see Figure 6.17). The first group of rats could obtain food if they navigated the correct route through the maze. They were given 10 trials to figure out an efficient route to the end of the maze, where food was always waiting. A second group was allowed to explore the maze, but did not have food available at the other end until the 11th trial. A third group (a control) never received any food while in the maze. It might seem that only the first group—the one that was reinforced on all trials—would learn how to best shuttle from the start of the maze to the end. After all, it was the only group that was consistently reinforced. This is, in fact, what happened—at least for

{FIG. 6.16} **CS-US Relationships Predict Conditioning** In 12 trials (see top figure), Rat A hears a tone that is followed by a shock every time. Rat B also receives 12 shocks, but hears the tone preceding it in only 50% of the trials. Even though tones are always followed by shocks for both rats, Rat A will show a stronger conditioned response to the tones (bottom figure).

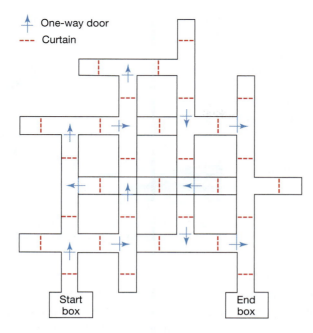

One-way door ↑

Curtain ---

(a)

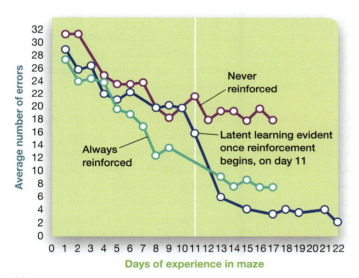

(b)

{FIG. 6.17} **Learning Without Reinforcement** Tolman and Honzik (1930) placed rats in the start box and measured the number of errors they made en route to the end box. Rats that were reinforced during the first 10 days of the experiment made fewer errors. Rats that were reinforced on day 11 immediately made far fewer errors, which indicates that they were learning by a cognitive map of the maze even though reinforcement was not available during the first 10 trials for this group.

If you put yourself in the rat's shoes—or perhaps paws would be more appropriate—you will realize that humans experience latent learning as well. Consider a familiar path you take to work or school. There is probably a spot along that route that you have never visited, simply because there is no reason—perhaps it is a vacant storefront. But imagine you discover one day that a fantastic and inexpensive new restaurant opened up in that spot. You would have no trouble finding it in the future because you have an understanding of the general area. Tolman and Honzik assumed that this process held true for their rats, and they further hypothesized that rats possess a *cognitive map* of their environment, much like our own cognitive map of our surroundings. This classic study is important because it illustrates that humans (and rats) acquire information in the absence of immediate reinforcement and that we can use that information when circumstances allow.

Humans and rats may have latent learning in common, but one characteristic that is unique to human learning is the ability to think about and reflect on strengths and weaknesses in how we learn. Specifically, we can identify what works and what does not work when it comes to learning, and adjust our strategies accordingly.

SUCCESSFUL LONG-TERM LEARNING AND DESIRABLE DIFFICULTIES We humans are highly attuned to our own learning and states of knowledge. When we are sufficiently motivated to learn new information, we tend to share certain goals, including (1) a long-lasting change in behavior and knowledge and (2) the ability to apply new knowledge and skills across a variety of unique situations. All too often, however, we work in ways that provide only short-term effects, and very little improvement over time (Schmidt & Bjork, 1992). There are at least three habits people fall into when trying to learn new behaviors:

● We want clarity about what to learn or do.
● We want very noticeable results.
● We want it all to happen very fast.

the first 10 trials. Tolman and Honzik discovered that rats that were finally rewarded on the 11th trial quickly performed as well as the rats that were rewarded on every trial (see Figure 6.17). It appears that this second group of rats was learning after all, but only demonstrated their knowledge when they received reinforcement worthy of quickly running through the maze.

Thus, if you were learning vocabulary for a foreign language class, chances are you are likely to *cram*. In doing so, you might use a study guide with material for the exam and read through the items repeatedly, testing yourself as you go. As you do so, you might notice that you learned the first few items easily; in turn, you will move on to the next topic as soon as you get the words right. This approach *might* get you through a quiz in your German course in a few hours, but it probably will not help you in actual conversation if you were to fly to Germany next week.

We like these techniques because they are easy and quick, and they seem to be effective. In reality, though, they merely trick us into thinking that we have learned more—or better—than we have. In other words, getting results fast usually causes us to overestimate how well we will remember things in the long run. To really remember and understand something, learning should be a little more difficult—but it should be the right kind of difficult (Schimdt & Bjork, 1992). *Desirable difficulties* are situations that make acquiring new knowledge more challenging and with benefits that are less obvious in the short term. At the same time, desirable difficulties promote long-term learning and the ability to apply the information to new and unique situations. Next, we will discuss two applications of desirable difficulties.

Organization Versus Rearrangement If you have taken other college courses before this one, you have probably filled out instructor evaluation forms at the end of the term. Evaluations almost always ask whether the professor was clear. This seems like an obvious question, because students tend to like course material laid out in a clear and logical manner. But is clarity *always* a good thing? In one study, half of the students in a college course received lecture outlines that fit the lecture perfectly, whereas the

Cramming for four hours does not provide nearly the same benefits as studying for an hour on four separate sessions.

other half of the students received outlines that were scrambled. After the lecture, students were quizzed on their retention for the material. On recognition and cued-recall tests, the students with the organized notes did better. So does that mean students are right in wanting perfect clarity? Not necessarily. On the hard questions—which required inferring the meaning of material or solving problems—the students with the scrambled lecture notes performed better. In other words, the scrambled notes led to more effortful studying and, therefore, more meaningful learning (Mannes & Kintsch, 1987).

Total Time Versus Distributed Practice Students are invariably busy people, and most probably engage in some degree of procrastination. The result is often the need to cram for a final the night before the exam or to write a 15-page paper in one day. Consider this question: Which is better—studying 4 hours the night before an exam or studying in four 1-hour sessions in the days leading up to the exam? Research suggests that the answer is clear. In nearly 200 scientific articles describing more than 300 experiments, distributing 4 hours of study over four separate 1-hour sessions has been proven much better than cramming for the same amount of time (Cepeda et al., 2006). There is not a clear consensus among psychologists as to why this is so, but spreading out study sessions across time seems to provide more opportunities to link concepts together and helps to reinforce memory formation.

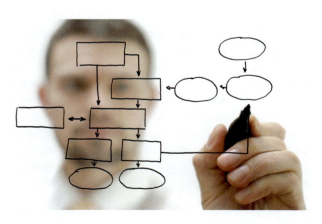

Students benefit from reorganizing information from their notes and readings.

Creating Desirable Difficulties These studies and dozens of others provide compelling evidence that we would be better off creating desirable difficulties for ourselves, rather than trying to make studying as quick and easy as possible.

Before closing this section, it is important to recognize the limits of creating difficulties. There is a

Table 6.5 :: Three Tips for Creating Desirable Difficulties to Promote Learning

Determine the purpose of learning.	On the one hand, if you are learning a three-item grocery list, there is no need to make it difficult. On the other hand, if you are learning a skill for a hobby (e.g., playing guitar) or if you need to remember information for your job (e.g., rules for filing reports), then you will probably want to achieve a thorough understanding.
Consider changing the order.	If you are learning a song on an instrument, do not start at the beginning every time—start halfway through, or one-fourth of the way. If you are learning vocabulary through flashcards, shuffle the order of the words. To learn about more complex ideas—perhaps how nerve cells work—approach the process from a different order each time.
Distribute your learning.	Practicing or studying for four hours can produce varying results, depending on how you spend those four hours. Longer-lasting learning will result if your learning is distributed over a few short study sessions, rather than cramming all at once. Also, you might try the spacing effect: gradually increase the intervals between learning sessions, but start with short ones.

reason researchers included the word "desirable" in the term *desirable difficulty*: If professors were to speak unintelligibly in front of your class, or to give extremely vague assignments with no criteria to work toward or models to follow, you would be right to criticize your instructors—"difficult" does not necessarily equal "desirable."

That leaves us with the most important questions of all: How do we create desirable difficulties for ourselves? And how do we know when a difficulty is desirable? Table 6.5 summarizes what seems to work best. As you can see, learning can be greatly enhanced through awareness and monitoring of your own experiences.

Quick Quiz 6.3a
Cognitive Perspectives on Learning

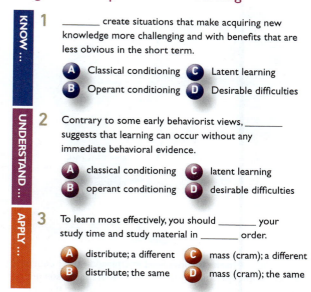

KNOW...

1. _____ create situations that make acquiring new knowledge more challenging and with benefits that are less obvious in the short term.

   A Classical conditioning   C Latent learning

   B Operant conditioning   D Desirable difficulties

UNDERSTAND...

2. Contrary to some early behaviorist views, _____ suggests that learning can occur without any immediate behavioral evidence.

   A classical conditioning   C latent learning

   B operant conditioning   D desirable difficulties

APPLY...

3. To learn most effectively, you should _____ your study time and study material in _____ order.

   A distribute; a different   C mass (cram); a different

   B distribute; the same   D mass (cram); the same

Answers can be found on page ANS-2.

Observational Learning

The first two modules in this chapter focused on aspects of learning that require direct experience. Pavlov's dogs experienced the tone and the food one right after the other, and learning occurred. Rats in an operant chamber experienced the reinforcing consequences of pressing a lever, and learning occurred. However, not all learning requires direct experience, and this is a good thing. Can you imagine if surgeons had to learn by trial and error? Who on earth would volunteer to be the first patient?

Observational learning *involves changes in behavior and knowledge that result from watching others.* Humans have elaborate cultural customs and rituals that spread through observation. The cultural differences we find in dietary preferences, clothing styles, athletic events, holiday rituals, music tastes, and so many other customs exist because of observational learning. Socially transmitting behavior is an efficient approach; indeed, it is the primary way that adaptive behavior spreads so rapidly within a population, even in nonhuman species (Heyes & Galef, 1996). Before setting off in search of food, rats smell the breath of other rats. They will then search preferentially for food that matches the odor of their fellow rats' breath. To humans, this practice may not seem very appealing—but for rats, using breath as a source of information about food may help them survive. By definition, a breathing rat is a living rat, so clearly the food the animal ate did not kill it. Living rats are worth copying. Human children are also very sensitive to social cues about what they should avoid. Curious as they may be, even young children will avoid food if they witness their parents reacting with disgust toward it (Stevenson et al., 2010).

For observational learning to occur, some key processes need to be in place if the behavior is to be successfully transmitted from one person to the next.

Even rats have a special way of socially transmitting information. Without directly observing what other rats have eaten, rats will smell the food on the breath of other rats and then preferentially search for this food.

PROCESSES SUPPORTING OBSERVATIONAL LEARNING Albert Bandura identified four processes involved in observational learning: *attention* to the act or behavior, *memory* for it, the *ability to reproduce it*, and the *motivation* to do so (see Figure 6.18). Without any one of these processes, observational learning would be unlikely—or at least would result in a poor rendition.

First, consider the importance of attention. Seeing someone react with a classically conditioned fear to snakes or spiders can result in acquiring a similar fear—even in the absence of any direct experience with snakes or spiders (LoBue et al., 2010). Also, paying attention to others who are being rewarded or punished, as in operant conditioning, can result in learning by the observer. Observing someone being rewarded for a behavior facilitates imitation of the same behaviors that bring about rewards.

Second, memory is an important facet of observational learning. When we learn a new behavior, there is often a delay before the opportunity to perform it arises. If you tuned into a cooking show, for example, you will need to recreate the steps and processes required to prepare the dish at a later time. Memory for how to reproduce a behavior or skill can be found at a very early age. Infants just nine months of age can reproduce a new behavior, even if there is a 24-hour delay between observing the act and having the opportunity to do so.

Third, observational learning requires that the observer can actually reproduce the behavior. This can be very challenging, depending on the task. Unless an individual has a physical impairment, learning an everyday task—such as operating a can opener—is not difficult. By comparison, hitting a baseball thrown by a professional pitcher requires a very specialized skill set. Research indicates that observational learning is most effective when we first observe, practice immediately, and continue practicing soon after acquiring the response. For example, one study found that the optimal way to develop and maintain motor skills is by repeated observation before and during the initial stages of practicing (Weeks & Anderson, 2000). It appears that watching someone else helps us practice effectively, and allows us to see how errors are made. When we see a model making a mistake, we know to examine our own behavior for similar mistakes (Blandin & Proteau, 2000).

Finally, motivation is clearly an important component of observational learning. On the one hand, being hungry or thirsty will motivate an individual to find out where others are going to find food and drink. On the other hand, a child who has no aspirations to ever play the piano will be less motivated to observe his teacher during lessons.

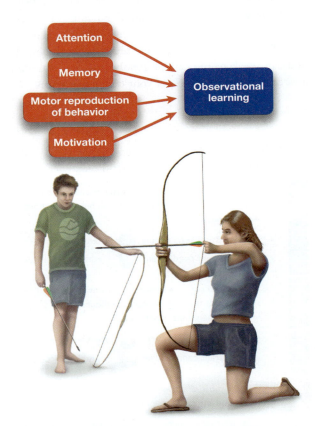

{FIG. 6.18} **Processes Involved in Observational Learning** For observational learning to occur, several processes are required: attention, memory, the ability to reproduce the behavior, and the motivation to do so.

Observational punishment is also possible, but appears to be less effective at changing behavior than reinforcement. Witnessing others experience negative consequences may decrease your chances of copying someone else's behavior. Even so, we are sometimes surprisingly bad at learning from observational punishment. Seeing the consequences of smoking, drug abuse, and other risky behaviors does not seem to prevent many people from engaging in the same activities.

MYTHS IN MIND
Teaching Is Uniquely Human

Teaching is a significant component of human culture and a primary means by which information is learned in classrooms, at home, and many other settings. But are humans the only species with the ability to teach others? Some intriguing examples of teaching-like behavior have been observed in nonhuman species (Thornton & Raihani, 2010). Prepare to be humbled.

Teaching behavior was recently discovered in ants (Franks & Richardson, 2006)—probably the last species we might suspect would demonstrate this complex ability. For example, a "teacher" ant gives a "pupil" ant feedback on how to locate a source of food.

Field researchers studying primates discovered the rapid spread of potato washing behavior in Japanese macaque monkeys (Kawai, 1965). Imo—perhaps one of the more ingenious monkeys of the troop—discovered that potatoes could be washed in salt water, which also may have given them a more appealing taste. Potato washing behavior subsequently spread through the population, especially among the monkeys that observed the behavior in Imo and her followers.

Transmission of new and unique behaviors typically occurs between mothers and their young (Huffman, 1996). Chimpanzee mothers, for example, actively demonstrate to their young the special skills required to crack nuts open (Boesch, 1991). Also, mother killer whales appear to show

Primate researchers have documented the spread of potato washing in Japanese macaque monkeys across multiple generations. Monkeys appear to learn how to do this by observing experienced monkeys from their troop.

Is this killer whale teaching her offspring to hunt for seals? Researchers have found evidence of teaching in killer whales and a variety of other nonhuman species.

their offspring how to beach themselves (Rendell & Whitehead, 2001), a behavior that is needed for the type of killer whale that feeds on seals that congregate along the shoreline.

In each of these examples, it is possible that the observer animals are imitating the individual who is demonstrating a behavior. These observations raise the possibility that teaching may not be a uniquely human endeavor.

• • • • • • • • • • • • • • • • • • •

IMITATION AND OBSERVATIONAL LEARNING

One of the primary mechanisms that allows observational learning to take place is **imitation**—*recreating a motor behavior or expression, often to accomplish a specific goal*. From a very young age, infants imitate the facial expressions of adults (Meltzoff & Moore, 1977). Later, as they mature physically, children readily imitate motor acts produced by a model, such as a parent, teacher, or friend. This ability seems to be something very common among humans.

At the beginning of this module, we raised the topic of human imitation—namely, how children, in contrast to chimpanzees, may imitate *beyond* what is necessary. Psychologists have found that both children from industrialized regions of Australia and children from remote non-industrialized communities in Africa over-imitate the actions of adults who model how to open a contraption using a variety of sticks, switches, and knobs. The adult demonstrating the actions involved in opening the box added irrelevant steps to the

Infants and children actively imitate others, particularly adults.

process—many of which the children were compelled to imitate (Nielsen & Tomaselli, 2010). Perhaps humans are so wired and motivated to learn from others that evolution has given us, but not nonhumans, the tendency to over-imitate.

WORKING THE SCIENTIFIC LITERACY MODEL
Linking Media Exposure to Behavior

Observational learning occurs during our face-to-face interactions with others, but what about all the time people spend observing others through television, movies, the Internet, and even video games?

What do we know about media effects on behavior?

In some cases, learning from the media involves direct imitation; in other cases, what we observe shapes what we view as normal or acceptable behavior. Either way, the actions people observe in the media can raise concerns, especially when children are watching. Given that American children now spend an average of five hours per day interacting with electronic media, it is no wonder that one of the most discussed and researched topics in observational learning is the role of media violence in developing aggressive behaviors and

desensitizing individuals to the effects of violence (Anderson et al., 2003). So how have researchers tackled the issue?

How can science explain the effect of media exposure on children's behavior?

One of the first experimental attempts to test whether exposure to violence begets violent behavior in children was made by Albert Bandura and colleagues (1961, 1963). In a series of studies, groups of children watched an adult or cartoon character attack a "Bobo" doll, while another group of children watched adults who did not attack the doll. Children who watched adults attack the doll did likewise when given the opportunity, in some cases even imitating the specific attack methods used by the adults. The other children did not attack the doll. This provided initial evidence that viewing aggression makes children at least temporarily more prone to committing aggressive acts toward an inanimate object. Decades of research has since confirmed that viewing aggression is associated with increased aggression and desensitization to violence (Bushman & Anderson, 2007).

Exposure to violence can come in many forms, including music. Several genres of popular music tend to have violent lyrical content accompanying aggressive, loud music. Does listening to violent music also increase aggression? Experiments indicate that it can. In one study, undergraduate students listened to either soft music (e.g., classical), heavy metal, or no music while they participated in a laboratory experiment. All of the students completed a self-report on their mood

In Albert Bandura's experiment, children who watched adults behave violently toward the Bobo doll were aggressive toward the same doll when given the chance—often imitating specific acts that they viewed. **Click on this image in your eText to watch video footage of this experiment**.

at the beginning, and then wrote a short essay while listening to the music. Their essay was then taken into another room, where an experimenter provided feedback that was either positive or negative, regardless of the actual content or quality of what they wrote. The purpose of the negative feedback was to provoke aggression in students from each group. After the students received this feedback, their anger and mood levels were measured with a questionnaire. The students who listened to heavy metal music during their participation reported greater feelings of anger in response to negative feedback than those who listened to pleasant music. Also, their overall mood levels declined from the time they started the experiment (Krahé & Bieneck, in press).

Can we critically evaluate this research?

Exposure to violent media and aggressive behavior and thinking are certainly related to each other. However, at least two very important questions remain. First, does exposure to violence *cause* violent behavior or desensitization to violence? Second, does early exposure to violence turn children into violent adolescents or adults? Unfortunately, there are no simple answers to either question, due in large part to investigators' reliance on correlational designs, which are typically used for studying long-term effects. Recall that correlational studies can establish only that variables are related, but cannot determine that one variable (media) causes another one (violent behavior). What is very clear from decades of research is that a positive correlation exists between exposure to violent media and aggressive behavior in individuals, and that this correlation is stronger than those between aggression and peer influence, abusive parenting, or intelligence (Bushman & Anderson, 2007; U.S. Department of Health and Human Services, 2001).

Why is this relevant?

Despite problems establishing a cause-and-effect relationship, we know that, at the very least, media violence is a significant risk factor for future aggressiveness. Many organizations have stepped in to help parents make decisions about which type of media their children will be exposed to. The Motion Picture Association of America has been rating movies, with violence as a criterion, since 1968. Violence on television was being monitored and debated even before the film industry took this step. Since the 1980s, parental advisory stickers have been appearing on music with lyrics that are sexually explicit, reference drug use, or depict violence. Even more recently, due to a drastic upsurge in their popularity and sophistication, video games have been labeled with parental advisory stickers.

Graphic violence in video games has become commonplace.

BIOPSYCHOSOCIAL PERSPECTIVES

Violence, Video Games, and Culture

Can pixilated, fictional characters controlled by your own hands make you more aggressive or even violent? Adolescents, college students, and even a lot of older adults play hours of video games each day, many of which are very violent. Also, because video games are becoming so widespread, concerns have been raised about whether the correlations between media violence and aggression are found across different cultures. What do you think: Do these games increase aggression and violent acts by players? First, test your knowledge and assumptions and then see what research tells us.

True or False?

1. A regular pattern of playing violent video games *causes* violent behavior.

2. Gamers who play violent video games are less likely to behave aggressively if they are able to personalize their own character.

3. Playing violent video games reduces a person's sensitivity to others' suffering and need for help.

4. Gamers from Eastern cultures, who play violent video games as much as Westerners, are less prone to video game-induced aggression.

5. Physiological arousal is not affected by violent video games.

6. Male gamers are more likely to become aggressive by playing video games than female gamers.

Answers

1. *True.* Playing violent video games has both short- and long-term effects on violent thinking and behavior.

2. *False.* Personalizing a character seems to increase aggressive behavior.

3. *True.* People who play violent video games often become less sensitive to the feelings and well-being of others.

4. *False.* Gamers from both Eastern and Western cultures show the same effects.

5. *False.* Players of violent video games show increased physiological arousal during play.

6. *False.* There are no overall gender differences in aggression displayed by gamers.

(These data are from Anderson et al., 2010; Carnagey et al., 2007; and Fischer et al., 2010).

Observing others is clearly an important mechanism for learning new behaviors as well as for learning what to avoid. Dating back to Bandura, psychologists have identified some unique processes involved in observational learning. In addition, learning from others involves cognitive and behavioral principles that are common to classical and operant conditioning.

Quick Quiz 6.3b
Observational Learning

KNOW...

1. Observational learning:
   - **A** is the same thing as teaching.
   - **B** involves a change in behavior as a result of watching others.
   - **C** is limited to humans.
   - **D** is not effective for long term retention.

2. _____ is the replication of a motor behavior or expression, often to accomplish a specific goal.
   - **A** Observational learning
   - **C** Imitation
   - **B** Latent learning
   - **D** Cognitive mapping

APPLY...

3. Nancy is trying to learn a new yoga pose. To obtain the optimal results, research indicates she should:
   - **A** observe, practice immediately, and continue to practice.
   - **B** observe and practice one time.
   - **C** just closely observe the behavior.
   - **D** observe the behavior just one time and then practice on her own.

ANALYZE...

4. Which is the most accurate conclusion from the large body of research that exists on the effects of viewing media violence?
   - **A** Viewing aggression directly causes increased aggression and desensitization to violence.
   - **B** Viewing aggression does not cause increased aggression and desensitization to violence.
   - **C** Viewing aggression is *related* to increased aggression and desensitization to violence.
   - **D** Viewing aggression is not related to increased aggression and desensitization to violence.

Answers can be found on page ANS-2.

Now that you have read this module
you should:

((•●—[Listen to
the audio file of
this module at
MyPsychLab

KNOW ...

- **The key terminology associated with cognitive and observational learning:**

imitation (p. 227)   observational learning
latent learning (p. 222)   (p. 225)

UNDERSTAND ...

- **The concept of latent learning and its relevance to cognitive aspects of learning.** Without being able to observe learning directly, it might seem as if no learning occurs. However, Tolman and Honzik showed that rats can form "cognitive maps" of their environment. They found that even when no immediate reward was available, rats still learned about their environment.

APPLY ...

- **Principles of learning to make your own learning experiences more effective.** Increasing the effectiveness of learning experiences does not mean making your study time easier—in fact, you may need to incorporate some study habits to make learning more difficult so that you have a better understanding and longer-lasting results.

  Use the tips in **Table 6.5** (p. 225) in considering each of the following scenarios (check your answers on page ANS-2):

  1. John forgot that he had an upcoming major examination until 48 hours before the test. Given that it is so close to the examination and he can spend only 12 of the next 48 hours on studying, what is John's best course of action?

  2. Janet is struggling to understand how observational learning involves the four processes of attention, memory, motor reproduction of behavior, and motivation. In class, her professor gave examples that always presented the processes in the exact same order. How might Janet rethink this approach to better understand the concept?

  3. Memorizing schedules of reinforcement seems like something that is relevant only to what goes on in an operant chamber. To Darius, this task seems like busy work. How might he change his mindset to give meaning to this task?

ANALYZE ...

- **The claim that viewing violent media increases violent behavior.** Psychologists agree that observational learning occurs and that media can influence behavior. Many studies show a correlational (noncausal) relationship between violent media exposure and aggressive behavior. Also, experimental studies, going all the way back to Albert Bandura's work of several decades ago, indicate that exposure to violent media can at least temporarily increase aggressive behavior.

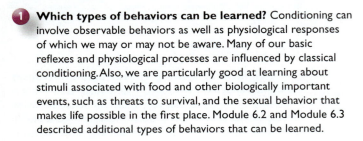

Module 6.1 :: Classical Conditioning: Learning by Association

Focus Questions:

1 **Which types of behaviors can be learned?** Conditioning can involve observable behaviors as well as physiological responses of which we may or may not be aware. Many of our basic reflexes and physiological processes are influenced by classical conditioning. Also, we are particularly good at learning about stimuli associated with food and other biologically important events, such as threats to survival, and the sexual behavior that makes life possible in the first place. Module 6.2 and Module 6.3 described additional types of behaviors that can be learned.

2 **Do all instances of classical conditioning go undetected by the individual?** Clearly, some classical conditioning goes undetected. Conditioning occurs to drugs and cues that accompany drug use. Sexual arousal and physiological responses can be conditioned as well. Drug-related and sexual conditioning often go undetected, but people can become aware that they are responding to cues that are associated with sexual arousal or drug use. The observation that people in vegetative states can be conditioned makes a strong case that awareness is not required for conditioning to occur. Certainly, conditioning that takes place to artificial sweeteners goes undetected—the learning takes place at a very basic physiological level.

👁 **Watch** *The Big Picture: What Does It Mean to Learn?* in the **MyPsychLab video series**

Module 6.2 :: Operant Conditioning: Learning Through Consequences

Focus Questions:

1 **How do the consequences of our actions—such as winning or losing a bet—affect subsequent behavior?** The answer to this question may initially seem obvious: If the consequences are rewarding and we win the bet, we are likely to repeat our behavior. Although that is often the case, consequences are actually somewhat more complex. Consider the concepts of primary and secondary reinforcement. Primary reinforcers satisfy basic biological needs. In contrast, the cash from a bet is a secondary reinforcer, whose value is something we learn. Also, everyone who gambles sometimes wins and sometimes loses, which leads us to the next question. . . .

2 **Many behaviors, including gambling, are reinforced only part of the time. How do the odds of being reinforced affect how often a behavior occurs?** Operant behavior is largely influenced by reinforcement schedules. Some responses are reinforced on a continuous schedule. At other times, reinforcement is not available until a certain number of responses has occurred, or a scheduled amount of time has passed. This kind of intermittent reinforcement can result in vigorous responding. In gambling, rewards are typically obtained only after a gambler has placed many bets that went unrewarded. In the mind of the gambler, the next big reward may be just around the corner—a belief that serves to encourage vigorous, and risky, responding.

👁 **Watch** *Thinking Like a Psychologist: Physical Punishment—You Decide!* in the **MyPsychLab video series**

Module 6.3 :: Cognitive and Observational Learning

Focus Questions:

1 **What role do cognitive factors play in learning?** Even something as seemingly basic as classical conditioning can have a cognitive component. For example, humans and animals both judge the degree to which one stimulus, such as a tone, reliably predicts whether another stimulus, such as food, will be available. In research studies, responding to the tone is strongest when it is consistently followed by food, and animals (including humans) are highly sensitive to changes in this relationship. The concept of desirable difficulties shows that effective learning involves mental organization, rearrangement of information, and awareness of good strategies for learning. Thus one cognitive factor involved in our learning is an awareness of what we know and do not know; we need this ability to use strategies to improve learning.

2 **Which processes are required for imitation to occur?** Imitation, at the very least, requires that the individual pay attention to another individual, that the person remember what was observed, and that the individual has both the motor abilities required for the task and the motivation to learn it. Humans have extraordinary capabilities when it comes to imitation. Indeed, both imitation and "over-imitation" occur at a very young age in humans. This tendency might occur because following cultural conventions is such a strong motivating force for our species—so much so that the motivation to imitate can be stronger than the motivation to solve a problem.

👁 **Watch** *In the Real World Application: Learned Aggression* in the **MyPsychLab video series**

👁 **Watch** the complete video series online at **MyPsychLab**

Episode 7: Learning

1. *The Big Picture: What Does It Mean to Learn?*
2. *The Basics 1: Classical Conditioning: Learning Predictable Signals*
3. *The Basics 2: Operant Conditioning: Learning about Consequences*
4. *Special Topics: Social Anxiety Disorder*
5. *Thinking Like a Psychologist: Physical Punishment—You Decide!*
6. *In the Real World Application: Learned Aggression*
7. *What's in It for Me? Personal Behavior Modification*

6 :: Chapter Quiz

1. In classical conditioning, a(n) _____ becomes a(n) _____, which elicits a response.

   A neutral stimulus; conditioned stimulus

   B neutral stimulus; unconditioned stimulus

   C unconditioned stimulus; conditioned stimulus

   D unconditioned stimulus; neutral stimulus

2. Most mornings, Becky listens to her favorite song as she gets ready for work, including putting in her contacts. One afternoon, Becky hears her favorite song playing, and her eyes start watering—something that usually happens only when she put her contacts in. If this is an example of classical conditioning, what is the unconditioned stimulus?

   A Eye watering

   B Becky's contacts

   C The song

   D Getting ready for work

3. How would John B. Watson have explained why many people have a phobia of flying on airplanes?

   A Flying is unnatural for human beings.

   B The brain has difficulty understanding how something heavy can fly.

   C Extensive news coverage of airplane crashes cause people to associate airplanes with danger.

   D People with a flying phobia are actually afraid of being trapped in small spaces.

4. An important distinction between classical and operant conditioning is that:

   A classical conditioning involves voluntary responding, while operant conditioning involves involuntary responding.

   B classical conditioning involves reinforcement, while operant conditioning involves punishment.

   C cassical conditioning involves cognitive learning, while operant conditioning involves associative learning.

   D responding does not affect the presentation of stimuli in classical conditioning, but in operant conditioning responding has consequences.

5. The word "negative" in the term *negative reinforcement* refers to:

   A the removal of a stimulus.

   B an unwanted conditioned behavior.

   C the use of punishment.

   D the use of inappropriate stimuli.

6. A rat is conditioned to press a lever for food. One day a food pellet jams in the automatic feeder and the rat no longer receives food after pressing the lever. After a few minutes, the rat eventually stops pressing the lever. This is an example of:

   A negative reinforcement.

   B extinction.

   C classical conditioning.

   D avoidance learning.

7. All other things being equal, an animal trained on which of the following schedules of reinforcement should experience extinction most quickly when the reinforcement is removed?

   A Fixed-interval schedule

   B Continuous schedule

   C Variable-ratio schedule

   D Variable-interval schedule

8. Learning that occurs, but is not expressed until later, is called _____.

   A observational learning

   B classical conditioning

   C latent learning

   D discriminative learning

9. In general, studying is more effective when:

   A desirable difficulties are present.

   B the information is organized in outlines that can quickly be reviewed several times.

   C the total amount of studying time is short.

   D all of the studying occurs in one long session.

10. Which of the following statements best describes our current understanding of the relationship between exposure to media violence and future aggression?

    A There is no relationship between media violence and aggression.

    B Media violence clearly causes aggression.

    C There is a positive correlation between media violence and aggression.

    D There is a negative correlation between media violence and aggression.

✓ Study and Review at MyPsychLab

Work the Scientific Literacy Model :: Understanding Reinforcement and Punishment

What do we know about reinforcement and punishment?

Review **Figure 6.11 on page 210** for a summary of operant conditioning, and turn back to **Table 6.2 on page 213** for help distinguishing between reinforcement and punishment. As you review this material, think about how you could mentally organize these concepts. If you are positively reinforced, then some external incentive is given to you. If you are negatively reinforced, then your behavior has resulted in something aversive being removed. For example, the child in line at the grocery store who whines until his dad gives him candy is positively reinforced for whining: He receives something he wants (candy), so the next time the child is at the store, his behavior (whining) is likely to increase. The father is negatively reinforced, because he gives his son the candy and the whining (something he finds aversive) stops. Both father and son were reinforced because each is likely to repeat the behavior that got them what they wanted.

While the father was negatively reinforced in this scenario, no one was *punished*. If you are confused about the difference between negative reinforcement and punishment, consider this: most people find the outcome of negative reinforcement to be desirable but are upset about being punished.

How can science help explain how reinforcement and punishment work?

Page 210 included a discussion of how early research with animal subjects proved that systematic reinforcement can shape behaviors in both animals and humans. Also, on **page 212**, we mentioned how modern researchers have identified a specific region of the brain, the nucleus accumbens, that becomes activated during the processing of rewarding activities such as eating (see **Figure 6.14**). Individual differences in this area of the brain might account for why some people can easily modify their behavior through reinforcement or punishment, whereas others struggle to do so. Research has also revealed that people tend to react more strongly to the unpleasantness of punishment than they do to the pleasures of reward, which raises questions about the effectiveness of punishment versus reinforcement. For example, parents who spank their children often see short-term results when a child stops her undesirable behavior, but studies have found that spanking has several negative side effects. Research also suggests that the negative side effects increase or decrease depending on the severity of the physical punishment.

Why is this relevant?

Watch the accompanying video excerpt on operant conditioning. You can access the video at MyPsychLab or by clicking the play button in the center of your eText. If your instructor assigns this video as a homework activity, you will find additional content to help you in MyPsychLab. You can also view the video by using your smart phone and the QR code below, or you can go to the YouTube link provided.

After you have read this chapter and watched the video, imagine that you are asked by a roommate to help him devise a weight-loss program to increase his chances of making the football team. Create a one-month behavior modification program based on the principles of operant conditioning which will help him get started towards his goal.

Can we critically evaluate claims about reinforcement and punishment?

Do these findings suggest that all punishment is ineffective and that reinforcement is the only way to successfully modify behavior? The discussion of punishment on **pages 213–214** explained that while punishment may temporarily stop an unwanted behavior, it does not teach appropriate behaviors. For example, if the latest fad diet severely restricts the amount and kind of food you can eat, you may lose pounds in the short term, but once the diet is over, you will probably go back to your unhealthy ways and gain back the weight. Generally, punishment of any kind is most effective when it is combined with reinforcing alternative responses. See the guidelines in **Table 6.4 on page 219** for tips on using punishment and minimizing its negative side effects.

MyPsychLab

Your turn to Work the Scientific Literacy Model: You can access the video at MyPsychLab or by clicking the play button in the center of your eText. If your instructor assigns this video as a homework activity, you will find additional content to help you at MyPsychLab. You can also view the video by using your smart phone and the QR code, or you can go to the YouTube link provided.

youtube.com/scientificliteracy

7 :: MEMORY

Module 7.1

Memory Systems

Learning Objectives

After reading this module you should:

KNOW …	UNDERSTAND …	APPLY …	ANALYZE …
The key terminology of memory systems	Which structures of the brain are associated with specific memory tasks and how the brain changes as new memories form	Your knowledge of the brain basis of memory to predict what types of damage or disease would result in certain types of memory loss	The claim that humans have multiple memory systems

Megan's grandmother began showing signs of forgetfulness during day-to-day activities. At first, it was not a big deal, but the problem grew worse and became plainly obvious on the day she forgot who Megan was. As her memory deteriorated, Megan's grandmother seemed to be stuck further and further in the past—she regularly forgot things like other individuals' identities or ages, and whether she had taken her medication. Even so, some things seemed resistant to forgetting, such as her ability to speak or understand English. Curiously, Megan's grandmother did not remember belonging to a quilting group, but when she sat down with the group, she remembered perfectly well how to participate. Yet 10 minutes after leaving the group one afternoon, she forgot she had ever been there. Faced with this difficult situation, Megan had a lot of questions.

Focus Questions

1 How is it possible to remember just long enough to have normal conversations and activities but then to forget them almost immediately?

2 How is it possible to forget some facts that are so important but to remember other things that seem minor?

• • • • • • • • • • • • • • • • • • •

You have probably heard people talk about memory as if it were a single ability:

● I have a terrible memory!
● Isn't there some way I could improve my memory?

But have you ever heard people talk about memory as if it were several abilities?

● One of my memories works well, but the other is not so hot.

As you will learn in this module, *memory* is actually a collection of several systems that store information in different forms

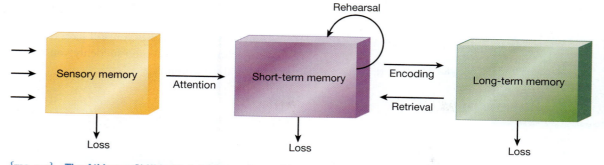

{FIG. 7.1} **The Atkinson-Shiffrin Model** Memory is a multistage process. Information flows through a brief sensory memory store into short-term memory, where rehearsal encodes it to long-term memory for permanent storage. Memories are retrieved from long-term memory and brought into short-term storage for further processing. **Click on this figure in your eText to see more details.**

for differing amounts of time (Atkinson & Shiffrin, 1968). The path that information takes as it is stored in memory can be seen in Figure 7.1.

The Atkinson-Shiffrin Model

In the 1960s, Richard Atkinson and Richard Shiffrin reviewed what psychologists knew about memory at that time and constructed the memory model that bears their name (see Figure 7.1). The first thing to notice about the Atkinson-Shiffrin model is that it includes three memory stores. **Stores** *retain information in memory without using it for any specific purpose;* they essentially serve the same purpose as hard drives serve for a computer. The three stores include sensory memory, short-term memory (STM), and long-term memory (LTM), which we will investigate in more detail later. In addition, **control processes** *shift information from one memory store to another;* they are represented by the arrows in the model. Information enters the sensory memory store through vision, hearing, and other senses, and the control process we call attention selects which information it will pass on to STM. Some information in STM goes through **encoding**, *the process of storing information in the LTM system.* **Retrieval** *brings information from LTM back into STM;* this happens when you become aware of existing memories, such as what you did last week. In this module, we are primarily concerned with the various types of memory stores, so next we will examine each one in detail.

SENSORY MEMORY **Sensory memory** *is a memory store that accurately holds perceptual information for a very brief amount of time*—how brief depends on which sensory system we talk about. Sensory memory holds *iconic memory,* the visual form of sensory memory,

for about one-half to one second. *Echoic memory,* the auditory form of sensory memory, is held for considerably longer, but still only about five seconds (Cowan et al., 1990).

Very precise measurements are needed to identify sensory memory because it disappears faster than an individual can report everything that it can hold. One interesting way to detect iconic memory is by comparing two conditions in a memory experiment: the *whole report* and *partial report* conditions (Sperling, 1960). In the whole report condition, researchers flash a grid of letters on a screen for a split second (Figure 7.2a on p. 238) and participants attempt to recall as many as possible—the *whole* screen. Participants generally can report only three or four of the letters, and those are all in the same line. George Sperling, who developed these techniques, hypothesized that the memory of the letters actually faded faster than participants could report them, and he devised the partial report condition to test this assumption. In this condition, researchers again flash a set of letters on the screen, but the display is followed immediately by a tone that is randomly chosen to be low, medium, or high (Figure 7.2b on p. 238). After hearing the tone, participants are to report the corresponding line—bottom, middle, or top. Under these conditions, participants still report only three or four of the letters, but they can report them from any randomly selected line. Because the tone comes after the screen goes blank, the only way the participants could get the letters right is if they recalled them from memory. Thus Sperling argued that iconic memory could hold all 12 letters as a mental image.

Sensory memory is not just a curious laboratory finding; rather, it functions to hold information long enough for us to determine what to pay attention to (the first control process in the Atkinson-Shiffrin model). If not for iconic sensory memory, our visual experience would

PsychTutor
Click here in your eText for an interactive tutorial on **Stages of Memory: The Atkinson-Shiffrin Model**

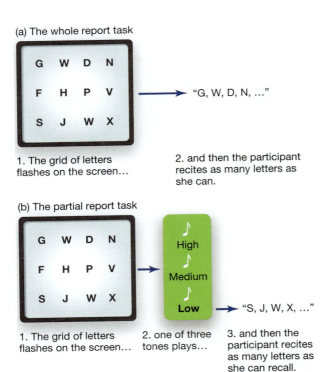

(a) The whole report task

G	W	D	N
F	H	P	V
S	J	W	X

→ "G, W, D, N, ..."

1. The grid of letters flashes on the screen...

2. and then the participant recites as many letters as she can.

(b) The partial report task

G	W	D	N
F	H	P	V
S	J	W	X

→ ♪ High
♪ Medium
♪ Low → "S, J, W, X, ..."

1. The grid of letters flashes on the screen...

2. one of three tones plays...

3. and then the participant recites as many letters as she can recall.

{FIG. 7.2} **A Test of Iconic Sensory Memory** Sperling's participants viewed a grid of letters flashed on a screen for a split second, then attempted to recall as many of the letters as possible. In the whole report condition (a), they averaged approximately four items, usually from a single row. By comparison, as Sperling demonstrated, they could remember more than four items in the partial report condition (b). In these trials, participants could usually name *any* row of four items, depending on the row they were cued to recite.

probably be similar to that of looking around a room with a strobe light flashing—everything would appear to be a series of isolated and still images. Instead, iconic sensory memory holds images long enough to provide smooth, continuous perceptions. Echoic memory is equally

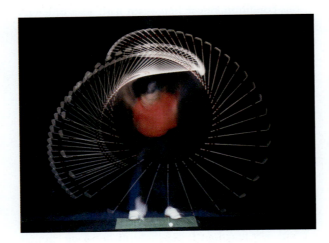

Each time the strobe light flashes, we get a distinct still image. In more typical perceptual experiences, we see continuous movement rather than still images because of our iconic sensory memory.

important. Have you ever experienced the "What? Oh!" phenomenon? Someone asks you a question and you say, "What?" only to realize that you still have the person's voice in echoic memory—and suddenly you say "Oh!" and answer the question.

WORKING THE SCIENTIFIC LITERACY MODEL
Distinguishing Short-Term From Long-Term Memory Stores

Sperling's research identified a very brief memory system, one that you may have never noticed that you had. After we pay attention to specific stimuli in sensory memory, selected information moves into two types of longer-lasting memory systems—the short-term and long-term memory stores.

What do we know about short-term and long-term memory stores?

A major distinction in memory systems is between **short-term memory (STM)**, *a memory store with limited capacity and duration* (less than a minute), and **long-term memory (LTM)**, *a memory store that holds information for extended periods of time, if not permanently.* The distinction between STM and LTM can be revealed with a simple experiment. Imagine everyone in your psychology class studied a list of 15 words and then immediately tried to recall the words in the list. The serial position curve—the U-shaped graph in Figure 7.3—shows what the results would look like according to the **serial position effect**: *In general, most people will recall the first few items from a list and the last few items, but only an item*

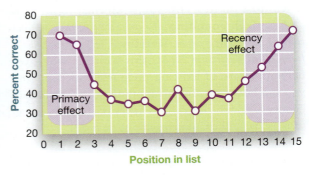

{FIG. 7.3} **The Serial Position Effect** Memory for the order of events is often superior for original items (the primacy effect) and later items (the recency effect). The serial position effect provides evidence of distinct short-term and long-term memory stores. **Click on this figure in your eText to see more details.**

or two from the middle. This finding holds true for many types of information, ranging from simple strings of letters to the ads you might recall after watching the Super Bowl (Laming, 2010; Li, 2010).

The first few items are remembered relatively easily (known as the *primacy effect*) because they have begun the process of entering LTM. They then begin to produce **proactive interference**—that is, *the first information learned (e.g., in a list of words) occupies memory, leaving fewer resources left to remember the newer information.* Yet, we also remember the last few items because they still reside in our STM—a pattern referred to as the *recency effect.* The last few items on the list create **retroactive interference**—that is, *the most recently learned information overshadows some older memories that have not yet made it into long-term memory* (see Figure 7.4).

Sam was asked to remember a list of 10 words: happy, train, carrot, water, bus, sky, cat, candy, hike, telephone.

Happy, Train, Carrot, Water

Bus, Sky, Cat

Candy, Hike, Telephone

After hearing the first four words on the list, *proactive interference* made it difficult to remember additional information.

After hearing the last three words, *retroactive interference* made it difficult to remember the preceding words.

As a result, Sam could not recall the words in the middle of the list.

{FIG. 7.4}   **Proactive and Retroactive Interference Contribute to the Serial Position Effect**

How can science explain the difference between STM and LTM stores?

The evidence from the serial position curve suggests that STM and LTM are distinct systems. To further support this argument, however, scientists should be able to spot the different systems through brain scans. This is exactly what Deborah Talmi and colleagues (2005) set out to look for in one of their studies. They asked 10 volunteers to undergo memory testing during fMRI brain scans. These participants were asked to study a list of 12 words presented one at a time on a computer screen. Next, the computer screen flashed a word and the participants had to determine whether the word was from their study list. Researchers were mostly concerned about the brain activity that occurred when the volunteers correctly recognized words. When volunteers remembered information from early in the serial position curve, the hippocampus was active (this area is associated with the formation of LTM, as you will read about later). By comparison, the brain areas associated with sensory information—hearing or seeing the words—were more active when people recalled items at the end of the serial position curve. Thus the researchers believed they have isolated the effects of two different neural systems, which, working simultaneously; produce the serial position curve.

Can we critically evaluate the distinction between STM and LTM?

Think about how this finding relates to Megan's grandmother in the vignette at the beginning of this module. Does the existence of multiple memory stores seem to be consistent with her experience? Some psychologists would agree: Her grandmother's STM seems to work reasonably well at times because she can remember enough to have conversations. In contrast, she has difficulty with new information like remembering whether she took her medication; this suggests her LTM system is experiencing problems. Thus the functioning in some memory disorders appears to support the distinction between STM and LTM.

Why is this relevant?

This information about multiple memories and the serial position effect also applies to healthy memory functioning, so consider what implications it has for you as a student. If you studied the key terms from this module in alphabetical order, which would you be most likely to forget? We might expect that you would remember the first few words (thanks to the primacy effect) as well as the last few words (thanks to the recency effect). Your knowledge of the terms in the middle of the list would suffer, however. Fortunately, we are not doomed to fall victim to serial position effects: Perhaps you could avoid the problem by constantly shifting the order in which you study the key terms.

KNOW...

1 Which elements of memory do not actually store information, but instead describe how information may be shifted from one type of memory to another?

A Serial position effects **C** Primacy effects

B Recency effects **D** Control processes

2 The distinction between _____ is that it lasts less than a minute, whereas _____ holds information for extended periods of time, if not permanently.

A long-term memory; short-term memory

B short-term memory; sensory memory

C short-term memory; long-term memory

D long-term memory; process memory

APPLY...

3 Chris forgot about his quiz, so he had only 5 minutes to learn 20 vocabulary words. He went through the list once, waited a minute and then went through the list again in the same order. Although he was confident, his grade indicated that he missed approximately half of the words. Which words on the list did he most likely miss, and why?

A According to the primacy effect, he would have missed the first few words on the list.

B According to the recency effect, he would have missed the last few words on the list.

C According to the serial position effect, most of the items he missed were probably in the middle of the list.

D According to the primacy effect, he would have missed all of the words on the list.

ANALYZE...

4 Brain scans show that recently encountered items are processed in one area of the brain, whereas older items are stored in a different area. Which concept does this evidence support?

A Multiple memory stores

B A single memory store

C Complex control processes

D Retrieval

Answers can be found on page ANS-2.

The Working Memory Model: An Active STM System

Imagine you are driving a car when you hear the announcement for a radio contest—*the 98th caller at 1-800-555-HITS will win $98*! As the DJ shouts out the phone number, you do not have a pen or a phone handy, and traffic is swarming, so what do you do? You will probably try to remember the number by using **rehearsal**, *or repeating information* (in this case, the number) *until you do not need to remember it anymore.* Psychological research, however, demonstrates that remembering is much more than just repeating words to yourself. In fact, memory is now viewed as a complex system involving several processes.

Working memory *is a model of short-term remembering that includes a combination of memory components that can temporarily store small amounts of information for a short period of time.* This includes new information such as the specific phone number that will win $98 for you, as well as keeping track of the traffic patterns. Working memory can also draw from older information that is stored in a relatively stable way—the fact that you know what a phone is, how to operate one, and that $98 translates into roughly eight large pizzas.

The working memory model for short-term remembering can be subdivided into three storage components (Figure 7.5), each of which has a specialized role (Baddeley, 2001; Jonides et al., 2005):

- The **phonological loop** *is a storage component of working memory that relies on rehearsal and stores information as sounds, or an auditory code.* It engages some portions of the brain that specialize in speech and hearing, and it can be very active without affecting memory for visual and spatial information.

- The **visuospatial sketchpad** *is a storage component of working memory that maintains visual images and spatial layouts in a visuospatial code.* It keeps you up-to-date on where objects are around you and where you intend to go. To do so, the visuospatial sketchpad engages portions of the brain related to perception of vision and space and does not affect memory for sounds.

- Recent research suggests that working memory also includes an **episodic buffer**—that is, *a storage component of working memory that combines the images and sounds from the other two components into coherent, story-like episodes.* These episodes include the relevant information to make sense of the images and sounds, such as "I was driving to a friend's house when I heard the radio DJ give a number to call."

Finally, working memory includes one component that is not primarily used for storing information. Instead, the **central executive** *is the control center of working memory; it coordinates attention and the exchange of information among the three storage components.* It does so by seeking out

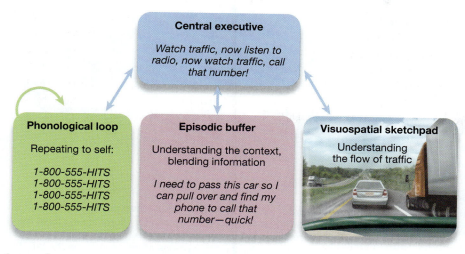

{FIG. 7.5}   **Components of Working Memory Work Together to Manage Complex Tasks**

Within the figure:

Central executive

Watch traffic, now listen to radio, now watch traffic, call that number!

Phonological loop

Repeating to self:

1-800-555-HITS
1-800-555-HITS
1-800-555-HITS
1-800-555-HITS

Episodic buffer

Understanding the context, blending information

I need to pass this car so I can pull over and find my phone to call that number—quick!

Visuospatial sketchpad

Understanding the flow of traffic

what is relevant to the person's goals, interests, and prior knowledge. For example, when you see a series of letters from a familiar alphabet, it is easy to remember the letters by rehearsing them in the phonological loop. In contrast, if you were to look at letters or characters from a foreign language—perhaps you are visiting Seoul and you do not know Korean—you may not be able to convert them to sounds; thus you would assign them to the visuospatial sketchpad instead (Paulesu et al., 1993). Regions within the frontal lobes of the brain are responsible for carrying out these tasks for the central executive.

So how does this system work for you when you cannot pull your car over immediately to place the 98th call? Most of us would rely on our phonological loop, repeating the number to ourselves until we can call. Meanwhile, our visuospatial sketchpad is remembering where other drivers are in relation to our car, even as we look away to check the speedometer, the rearview mirror, or the volume knob. Finally, the episodic buffer binds together all this information into episodes, which might include information such as "I was driving to school," "the DJ announced a contest," and "I wanted to pull over and call the station." In the middle of all this activity is the central executive, which guides attention and ensures that the each component is working on the appropriate task.

Psychologists have long been curious about the dimensions of memory, asking questions about how much information a memory store can hold and for how long. As you will see, measuring memory is not as simple as counting off seconds on a stopwatch. *How much* and *how long* one can remember are affected by the specific information that is being remembered. Therefore, as we address questions of *how much* and *how long*, we will need to understand the methods used to make these measurements. ⊙▶

THE MAGICAL NUMBER 7   The capacity of STM was summed up by one psychologist as *The Magical Number 7 ± 2* (Miller, 1956). In his review, Miller found study after study in which participants were able to remember seven units of information, give or take a couple. One researcher made the analogy between STM and a juggler who can keep seven balls in the air before dropping any of them. Similarly, STM can rehearse only seven units of information at once before forgetting something (Nairne, 1996).

This point leads to an important question: What, exactly, is "a unit of information"? It turns out that, whenever possible, we expand our memory capacity with **chunking**, *organizing smaller units of information into larger, more meaningful units.* Consider these examples:

1. O B A N C H C B S N N C B N C
2. N B C H B O C B S A B C C N N

If we randomly assigned one group of volunteers to remember the first list, and another group to remember the second list, how would you expect the two groups to compare? Look carefully at both lists. List 2 is easier to remember than list 1. Volunteers reading list 2 have the advantage of being able to apply patterns that fit their background knowledge; specifically, they can chunk these letters into five groups based on major television networks:

2b. NBC HBO CBS ABC CNN

In this case, chunking reduces 15 bits of information to a mere 5. Now think back to the example of the radio contest. Can you remember the 11-digit phone number? If so, it is almost certainly because you remembered it in 3 chunks, just as the DJ presented it: *(1-800), (555),* and *(HITS).*

THE PHONOLOGICAL LOOP   The magical number 7 provides a good estimate of STM capacity in general, but to focus more precisely on phonological memories, we should look at how long it takes to pronounce the items. Based on the *word-length effect*, we know that people remember more one-syllable words (*sum, pay, bar,* ...) than four- or five-syllable words (*helicopter,*

⊙▶ **Simulate** the **Experiment**
Digit Span at **MyPsychLab**

university, alligator, ...) in a short-term task (Baddeley et al., 1975). Despite the fact that both *bar* and *alligator* are single chunks, you remember more chunks if they are single syllables. Research indicates that working memory can store as many syllables as can be rehearsed in about two seconds.

The *Brown-Peterson test* (Brown, 1958; Peterson & Peterson, 1959) is a technique for measuring the duration of working memory. This test relies on two main elements—*meaningless stimuli* and *interference*. Here is how the test works: First, participants read a trigram (an unpronounceable series of three letters) that is not associated with anything in LTM. This setup ensures that participants rely on working memory. Immediately afterward, they read a three-digit number, and they must count backward (by threes) from the number to interfere with rehearsal (to make sure they cannot repeat the trigram to themselves). It goes something like this: The participant reads, "CJZ—159" and then counts "159 … 156 … 153 …" until the experimenter says, "Stop." At this point, the participants are to report the trigram (in this case, CJZ). With these particular kinds of stimuli and interference, most of the forgetting takes place within 15 to 18 seconds. Thus the duration of the phonological memory is believed to be approximately 15 seconds.

THE VISUOSPATIAL SKETCHPAD When using the Brown-Peterson task for phonological memory, researchers present test materials that do not sound like familiar words. Likewise, psychologists studying visual and spatial memory often use images that do not resemble familiar objects. Recall that the phonological store can be gauged at several levels—that is, in terms of the number of syllables, the number of words, or the number of chunks. Similarly, items stored in visuospatial memory can be counted based on shapes, colors, and textures. This leads to an important question: Can a smooth, square-shaped, red block count as one chunk? Or do texture, shape, and color of the block act as three separate bits of information? Research has consistently shown that a square-shaped block painted in two colors is just as easy to recognize as the same-shaped block painted in one color (Vogel et al., 2001). Therefore, visuospatial working memory may use a form of chunking. This process of combining visual features into a single unit goes by a different name, however: *feature binding* (see Figure 7.6).

After visual feature binding, visuospatial memory can accurately retain approximately four whole objects, regardless of how many individual features one can find on those objects. Perhaps this is evidence for the

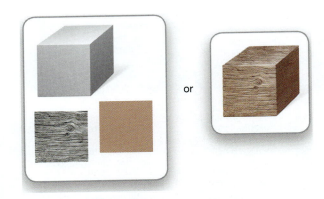

{FIG. 7.6} **Working Memory Binds Visual Features into a Single Chunk** Working memory sometimes stores information such as shape, color, and texture as three separate chunks, like the three pieces of information on the left. For most objects, however, it stores information as a single chunk, like the box on the right.

existence of a second magical number—four (Awh et al., 2007; Vogel et al., 2001).

To put feature binding into perspective, consider the amount of visual information available to you when you are driving a car. If you are at the wheel, watching traffic, you probably would not look at a car in front of you and remember images of red, shiny, and smooth. Instead, you would simply have these features bound together in the image of the car, and you would be able to keep track of three or four such images without much problem as you glance at the speedometer and then back to the traffic around you.

THE EPISODIC BUFFER The episodic buffer is the most recently hypothesized working memory system. Researchers are still examining evidence for and against it, so we can say less about it than the other working memory components (Baddeley, 2001). The episodic buffer seems to hold 7 to 10 pieces of information, which may be combined with other memory stores. This aspect of its operation can be demonstrated by comparing memory for prose (words strung into sentences) to memory for unrelated words. When people are asked to read and remember meaningful prose, they usually remember 7 to 10 more words than when reading a random list of unrelated words. Some portion of working memory is able to connect the prose with LTM (knowledge) to increase memory capacity. Because the phonological loop is not doing the binding, some psychologists have proposed that this phenomenon may demonstrate the episodic buffer at work.

KNOW …

1 Which of the following systems maintains information in memory by repeating words and sounds?

- **A** Episodic buffer
- **B** Central executive
- **C** Phonological loop
- **D** Visuospatial sketchpad

2 Which of the following systems coordinates attention and the exchange of information among memory storage components?

- **A** Episodic buffer
- **B** Central executive
- **C** Phonological loop
- **D** Visuospatial sketchpad

UNDERSTAND …

3 When psychologists ask research participants to remember combinations of letters (such as TJD), why might they have participants engage in distracting tasks such as counting backward by threes?

- **A** Counting backward prevents rehearsal, so researchers can see how long an unrehearsed memory trace will last.
- **B** Researchers try to make the participants forget.
- **C** Counting backward can facilitate episodic binding.
- **D** Researchers are actually interested in backward-counting ability.

APPLY …

4 Nick can remember far more than seven letters if he combines the letters using a strategy called _____.

- **A** the central executive
- **B** chunking
- **C** buffering
- **D** proactive interference

Answers can be found on page ANS-2.

Long-Term Memory Systems: Declarative and Nondeclarative Memories

Figure 7.1 at the beginning of this module (p. 237) suggests that humans have just one type of long-term memory. However, just as working memory has subcomponents, long-term memory can be divided as well. First, we can distinguish between memories that one is aware of versus those that do not require awareness (see Figure 7.7). Some have referred to this distinction as the difference between "knowing *how* and knowing *that*." Specifically, **declarative memories** *are memories that we are consciously aware of and can be verbalized, including facts about the world and one's own personal experiences.* These are the memories you are aware of: knowing that you had breakfast this morning, or knowing that a penguin is a bird, albeit a funny kind of bird.

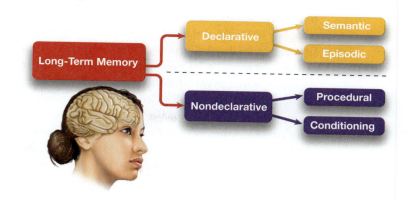

{FIG. 7.7} **Varieties of Long-Term Memory** Long-term memory can be divided into different systems based on the type of information that is stored. **Click on this figure in your eText to see more details.**

Nondeclarative memories *include actions or behaviors that you can remember and perform without awareness.* For example, these memories might consist of **procedural memories**: *patterns of muscle movements (motor memory)* such as how to walk, play piano, or shift gears while driving. Classical conditioning (described in Module 6.1) is another type of nondeclarative memory, as people can be classically conditioned without awareness. Although declarative and nondeclarative memories are distinct types of memory, both are involved in the same day-to-day events. You might know how to ride a bike, which is an example of a nondeclarative procedural memory, but knowing that bikes are two-wheeled vehicles is a declarative memory.

Declarative memory comes in two varieties (Tulving, 1972), and it is easy to distinguish them based on a simple analogy. If your memory is a library, then all of your autobiographical books would be considered episodic memories. **Episodic memories** *are declarative memories for personal experiences that seem to be organized around "episodes" and are recalled from a first-person ("I" or "my") perspective.*

This child may have episodic memories of specific piano lessons, semantic memories about what a piano is and how it works, and procedural memories about how to play a few songs.

Semantic memories *are declarative memories that include facts about the world,* so they would be the nonfiction reference books in your memory library. (Your memory library also includes works of fiction—that is, memories about events that did not actually happen—as discussed in Module 7.3.) Going back to the bicycle example, your semantic memory is your knowledge of what a bike is, whereas episodic memory is the memory of when *you* first (or last) rode a bike, a specific ride that was enjoyable to *you*, or the time *you* rode into a fence. These memories involve bicycles, but episodic memories are specific instances about *you* and *your* bike.

Scientific evidence that semantic and episodic memories are distinct comes from several different sources. First, as people get older, their episodic memory declines more rapidly than their semantic memory (Luo & Craik, 2008). Older people are more likely to forget where they went on vacation five years ago than they are to forget something like the names of state capitals. Psychologists have even reported an extremely rare form of memory loss in which a young, otherwise healthy person lost episodic memory, yet his semantic memory store remained intact (Tulving & Markowitsch, 1998).

Although some very technical debates focus on the difference between *knowing how* and *knowing that*, almost everyone would agree that the declarative memory can be divided into episodic and semantic levels. Such a distinction helps us better understand how memories break down following brain trauma or through conditions such as Alzheimer's disease. It is a helpful distinction to make for students learning about memory loss, which we will address later in this chapter.

Quick Quiz 7.1c
Long-Term Memory Systems: Declarative and Procedural Memories

1 Memories for information that was learned without our being aware of it are known as _____.

   A semantic memories

   B episodic memories

   C nondeclarative memories

   D declarative memories

2 Memories that can be verbalized, whether they are about your own experiences or your knowledge about the world, are called _____.

   A nondeclarative memories

   B procedural memories

   C conditioned memories

   D declarative memories

3 Mary suffered a head injury during an automobile accident and was knocked unconscious. When she woke up in a hospital the next day, she could tell that she was in a hospital room, and she immediately recognized her sister, but she had no idea why she was in the hospital or how she got there. Which memory system seems to be affected in Mary's case?

   A Semantic memories

   B Episodic memories

   C Nondeclarative memories

   D Working memories

Answers can be found on page ANS-2.

The Cognitive Neuroscience of Memory

So far, we have mostly discussed the behavioral and cognitive aspects of memory, but the *biopsychosocial model* reminds us that everything involves a biological component as well. Therefore, psychologists also look at how the nervous system changes with the formation of new memories, and they examine which areas of the brain are actively involved in remembering.

To explore the cognitive neuroscience of memory, we will take a brief look at the neuronal changes that occur as memories are forming and strengthening, and then examine the brain structures involved in long-term storage. Finally, we will use examples of amnesia and other forms of memory loss to understand how our memory models fit with biological data.

MEMORY AT THE NEURAL LEVEL At the neural level, memory formation begins with *long-term potentiation.* This process underlies the permanent changes that occur across numerous brain cells as memories are forming, strengthening, and being stored. **Long-term potentiation (LTP)** *means that there is an enduring increase in connectivity and transmission of neural signals between nerve cells that fire together.* The discovery of LTP occurred when researchers electrically stimulated two neurons in a rabbit's hippocampus—a key memory structure of the brain located in an area called the medial temporal lobes (see Figure 7.8). Stimulation to the hippocampus increased the number of electrical potentials from one neuron to the other. Soon, the neurons began to generate *stronger* signals than before, a change that could last up to a few hours (Bliss & Lømo, 1973).

To see how such microscopic detail relates to memory, consider a very simple case of learning and remembering. Imagine you hear a simple tone right before

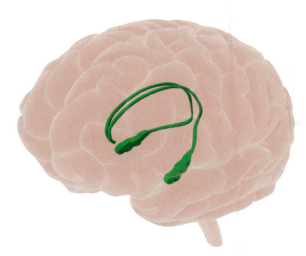

{FIG. 7.8} **The Hippocampus** The hippocampus resides within the temporal lobe and is critical for memory processes.

a puff of air is blown in your eye; you will reflexively blink. After two or three pairings, just the tone will be enough to cause an eye blink—this is an example of classical conditioning, as outlined in Module 6.1. At the neural level, the tone causes a series of neurons to respond, and the puff of air causes another series of neurons to respond. With repeated tone and air puff pairings, the nerves that are involved in hearing the tone, and those that control the blinking response, develop a history of firing together. This simultaneous activation provides the opportunity for LTP to begin, representing the first stages of memory.

Although it is called *long-term* potentiation, it is far from permanent, so LTP might not account for memories that may last days, weeks, or even years. Lasting memories require **consolidation**, *the process of converting short-term memories into long-term memories in the brain*, which may happen at the level of small neuronal groups or across the cortex (Abraham, 2006). When LTP continues long enough or, even better, *often* enough, the neurons will adapt and make the changes more permanent—a process called *cellular consolidation*. Without the consolidation process, LTP eventually fades away, and presumably so does the memory. To demonstrate this effect, researchers administered laboratory rats a drug that allowed LTP, but prevented consolidation from occurring (by blocking biochemical actions). The animals were able to learn a task for a brief period, but they were not able to form long-term memories. By comparison, rats in the placebo group went through the same tasks and formed long-term memories without any apparent problems (Squire, 1986).

MEMORY AT THE CORTICAL LEVEL Long-term declarative memories are distributed throughout the cortex of the brain, rather than being localized in one region—a phenomenon known as *cross-cortical storage* (Paller, 2004). Long-term memory storage of declarative memories requires a critical phase of consolidation that takes place in the hippocampus (Figure 7.9). Although the hippocampus is not where most declarative memories are actually stored, it is still key to the consolidation process. Without a functioning hippocampus, it becomes very difficult to form new long-term memories. For example, laboratory animals with experimental lesions to the hippocampus have little success in learning and remembering spatial information.

The activity of the hippocampus during encoding is part of a second level of consolidation called *systems consolidation* (Abraham, 2006). For this process to occur, the hippocampus maintains LTP until the acquired behavior can form multiple connections throughout the cortex. Once the memory traces are formed in the cortex, the memory is distributed in an entire network of cells. At this point, if an individual experiences damage to the hippocampus, the person would be less likely to lose long-term memories that have been consolidated.

Our long-term memories do not just collect dust after they have formed, however. They can be updated regularly, such as when someone reminds you of an event from years ago, or when you are reminded of information you learned as a child. In this way, memories undergo a process called *reconsolidation*, in which the hippocampus functions to update, strengthen, or modify existing long-term memories (Lee, 2010).

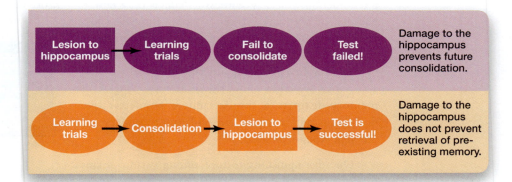

{FIG. 7.9} **Damage to the Hippocampus: Disruption of Consolidation** When the hippocampus is damaged, the injury interferes with consolidation, the formation of long-term memories. Such damage does not prevent recall of preexisting memories, however.

Researchers in London found that the hippocampi of cab drivers, who navigate the complex maze of the city, are larger than the hippocampi of non-cab drivers (Maguire et al., 2000). It is not certain whether people with a larger hippocampus are more likely to take up cab driving, or whether the cab driving increases the size of the hippocampus. Nevertheless, this finding underscores the importance of the hippocampus in memory processes.

Our knowledge of memory consolidation comes from careful laboratory research, but similar effects have been noted to occur outside the laboratory as well. For example, as few as one or two drinks of alcohol reduce the ability of cells in the hippocampus to transmit electrical signals. With binge-drinking (defined as consuming four or five drinks in one sitting), the effects on the hippocampus are quite pronounced and individuals may experience blackouts, also known as *en bloc* memory loss. People who experience blackouts when drinking will have virtually no recollection of what happened while they were intoxicated, yet show no effects on those memories that had already been formed prior to the blackout (Schummers & Browning, 2001; White, 2003).

AMNESIAS AND MEMORY SYSTEMS   Much of our understanding of the brain basis of memory comes from cases of **amnesia**—*a profound loss of at least one form of memory*. Even if you do not personally experience this phenomenon, you may witness its effects on a family member or friend. A variety of types of memory loss exist, however, and each person who experiences amnesia will have slightly different degrees and types of memory loss. To wrap up this module, we will apply what we know about the short-term/long-term memory distinction, the declarative/nondeclarative distinction, and memory consolidation to understand different types of amnesia.

One distinguishing feature among various forms of amnesia is time. When trauma occurs to the brain, it might lead to **retrograde amnesia**, *a condition in which memory for the events preceding trauma or injury is lost*. Retrograde amnesia is usually most severe for recent events; thus, the further back a person tries to recall, the more likely the individual is to retrieve events from the relatively distant past. This phenomenon is all too familiar to people living with Alzheimer's disease. Someone with Alzheimer's disease might have difficulty recognizing her grandchildren as adults because she instead remembers them from long ago. A man who experienced a head injury during a traffic accident may not remember events leading up to that moment, yet have normal memory for events from a week or a month before.

Retrograde is probably the most familiar type of amnesia. The opposite effect of retrograde amnesia is **anterograde amnesia**, *the inability to form new memories for events occurring after a brain injury*. Imagine a person who experienced anterograde amnesia after a stroke 10 years ago. Even with deliberate effort, he may not be able to form new memories based on significant events, such as the fact that he moved to an assisted living facility or that there is now a different president of the United States.

If you examine the timeline in Figure 7.10, you will see the distinction between the two types of amnesia: At the point of the lesion, retrograde amnesia reflects problems with existing memories, whereas anterograde amnesia blocks new memories from forming.

Now that we have defined two types of amnesias, we need to explain how they work in terms of their cognitive and brain basis. When you consider the distinction between STM and LTM, you can see that amnesia affects one of the control processes. If retrograde amnesia is described only as a problem with retrieval, then memory loss would apply to all past events, not just the recent ones. In reality, many less severe retrograde amnesias likely disrupt consolidation that is already in process (Brown, 2002). When memories move from short-term to long-term memory, they are transferred

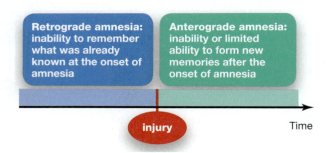

{FIG. 7.10}   **Retrograde and Anterograde Amnesia** The term amnesia can apply to memory problems in both directions. It can wipe out old memories, and it can prevent consolidation of new memories.

into cross-cortical storage through a consolidation process. If this process is disrupted by damage—for example, due to the consumption of too much alcohol in a single sitting, as described earlier—any events currently undergoing this consolidation process will be lost. In contrast, older events have already moved into cross-cortical storage, so they are more resistant to these effects.

Anterograde amnesia also seems to involve a problem with the transfer from short-term to long-term memory; specifically, a disconnect occurs between short- and long-term storage. Individuals with anterograde amnesia can retain their intelligence and memories for events leading up to the brain damage, so some aspects of their retrieval ability seem to work correctly. Cognitive neuroscience tells us that working memory uses regions of the brain involved in sensation, perception, and attention; thus these areas are most likely intact. The problem, once again, is consolidation. Thus we can expect to find some degree of anterograde amnesia, and a failure to consolidate, whenever the hippocampus is damaged (Brown, 2002; Jonides et al., 2005).

Some of the most intriguing stories in psychology are associated with anterograde amnesias, such as the famous case involving a man called H.M. Surgeons removed his right and left hippocampus to relieve him from ongoing problems with seizures. As you know, the hippocampus is essential for consolidating information from short-term to long-term memory stores, so we should assume that someone with this form of amnesia would not be able to remember anything new. H.M., for example, could not learn the names of nurses who were hired to care for him after his surgery, but he could remember those whom he had known before the surgery. Similar memory loss can be found among some people with a long history of severe alcohol abuse.

Another interesting story surrounds a study in which H.M. was repeatedly given the same puzzle to solve. Although he never remembered seeing or playing the game, he was able to improve his performance with practice (Cohen et al., 1985). This outcome points to a distinction between declarative and nondeclarative memory systems. Anterograde amnesia seems to affect declarative memory more so than nondeclarative memory, and it affects episodic memories more than semantic memories. It is clear that H.M. failed to form new episodic memories, but he nevertheless demonstrated learning that would require some procedural and some semantic types of memory.

We can apply this finding to better understand Megan's story from the beginning of this module. It appears that Megan's grandmother retained some procedural memories (such as how to make a quilt) but had difficulty with episodic memories (remembering that she had been in a quilting club).

Quick Quiz 7.1d
The Cognitive Neuroscience of Memory

KNOW…

1 _____ is a process that all memories must undergo to become long-term memories.

  A Consolidation

  B Retrograde remembering

  C Anterograde remembering

  D Chunking

UNDERSTAND…

2 Long-term potentiation can be described as:

  A a decrease in a neuron's electrical signaling.

  B neurons generating stronger signals than before, which then persist.

  C neural networking.

  D an example of working memory.

3 The hippocampus works on _____, which maintains LTP until multiple neural connections can form.

  A systems consolidation C cellular consolidation

  B cross-cortical storage D neural networking

APPLY…

4 Damage to the hippocampus is likely to produce _____.

  A retrograde amnesia C anterograde amnesia

  B consolidation D seizures

Answers can be found on page ANS-2.

Module Summary

Now that you have read this module you should:

Listen to the audio file of this module at **MyPsychLab**

KNOW ...

• *The key terminology of memory systems:*

amnesia (p. 246)
anterograde amnesia (p. 246)
central executive (p. 240)
chunking (p. 241)
consolidation (p. 245)
control process (p. 237)
declarative memory (p. 243)
encoding (p. 237)
episodic buffer (p. 240)
episodic memory (p. 243)
long-term memory (LTM) (p. 238)
long-term potentiation (LTP) (p. 244)
nondeclarative memory (p. 243)

phonological loop (p. 240)
proactive interference (p. 239)
procedural memory (p. 243)
rehearsal (p. 240)
retrieval (p. 237)
retroactive interference (p. 239)
retrograde amnesia (p. 246)
semantic memory (p. 244)
sensory memory (p. 237)
serial position effect (p. 238)
short-term memory (STM) (p. 238)
stores (p. 237)
visuospatial sketchpad (p. 240)
working memory (p. 240)

ANALYZE ...

• *The claim that humans have multiple memory systems.* Consider all the evidence from biological and behavioral research, not to mention the evidence from amnesia. Data related to the serial position effect indicate that information at the beginning and end of a list is remembered differently, and even processed and stored differently in the brain. Also, evidence from amnesia studies suggests that LTM and STM can be affected separately by brain damage or disease. Most psychologists agree that these investigations provide evidence supporting the existence of multiple storage systems and control processes.

UNDERSTAND ...

• *Which structures of the brain are associated with specific memory tasks and how the brain changes as new memories form.* The hippocampus is critical to the formation of new declarative memories. Long-term potentiation at the level of individual nerve cells is the basic mechanism underlying this process. Long-term memory stores are distributed across the cortex. Working memory utilizes the parts of the brain associated with visual and auditory perception, as well as the frontal lobes (for functioning of the central executive).

APPLY ...

• *Your knowledge of the brain basis of memory to predict what types of damage or disease would result in certain types of memory loss.* Try responding to these questions for practice (check your answers on page ANS-2):

1. Dr. Richard trains a rat to navigate a maze, and then administers a drug that blocks the biochemical activity involved in long-term potentiation. What will happen to the rat's memory? Will it become stronger? Weaker? Or is it likely the rat will not remember the maze at all?

2. In another study, Dr. Richard removes a portion of the rat's hippocampus the day after it learns to navigate a maze. What will happen to the rat's memory? Will it become stronger? Weaker? Or will it be unaffected by the procedure?

Encoding and Retrieving Memories

Learning Objectives

After reading this module you should:

KNOW ...	UNDERSTAND ...	APPLY ...	ANALYZE ...
The key terminology related to forgetting, encoding, and retrieval	How the type of cognitive processing employed can affect the chances of remembering what you encounter	What you have learned to improve your ability to memorize information	Whether emotional memories are more accurate than non-emotional ones

The number *pi* is 22/7, or 3.14. For most of us, memorizing the number rounded to two decimal places is sufficient for making it through geometry class, although the number actually goes on infinitely. To memory master Rajan Mahadevan, remembering 3.14 is hardly warming up. Dr. Mahadevan once claimed a world record by reporting 31,811 digits of pi from memory. He developed the skills for this feat at an early age. As a 5-year-old child, he once surprised his parents' guests at a party by repeating the license numbers from all 40 cars of those in attendance—in the order in which they arrived. His ability to rapidly encode and store information into long-term memory is remarkable. However, Dr. Mahadevan does not have a photographic memory. Rather, he has learned strategies for efficiently processing and storing information. Believe it or not, he does forget things from time to time. But perhaps it is not surprising that Dr. Mahadevan grew up to be a cognitive psychologist interested in memory research.

Focus Questions

1. What causes some memories to be strong, while others are weak?

2. How can we improve our memory abilities?

· · · · · · · · · · · · · · · · · ·

To begin this chapter, we covered the different types of memory systems and models that psychologists have developed to explain how memory works. In this module, we explore various factors that influence the encoding and retrieval of memories and explain why we forget. In addition, we offer research-based advice on improving your own memory—tips that every student can put to use.

Encoding and Retrieval

The most familiar aspects of memory are encoding, storage, and retrieval—the processes by which we acquire new memories and then recall them at a later time. In Module 7.1, you read that *encoding* is the process of transforming sensory and perceptual information into memory traces, and *retrieval* is the process of accessing memorized information and returning it to short-term memory. In between these two is the concept of **storage**, *which refers to the time and manner in which information is retained between encoding and retrieval.*

REHEARSAL: THE BASICS OF ENCODING

Common sense suggests that the keys to encoding are (1) rehearsing and repeating information, and (2) intentionally trying to remember that information. This belief is evident among students who try to learn vocabulary terms by reading flashcards with key terms and definitions over and over: They rehearse the information and they intend to learn it. This type of memorization is known as rehearsal to psychologists (although your teachers may have called it *learning by rote*), and it is something probably all of us have tried.

Certainly this approach works some of the time, but is it really the most effective way to remember? Probably not (Craik & Watkins, 1973). In fact, in one experiment, people rehearsed a single word for varying amounts of time before being asked to recall it. Do you think that the individuals remembered the word better after 18 seconds or 4 seconds? After repeating a word 2 times or 20 times? First, review Figure 7.11 to see how this three-step experiment was conducted.

Because participants were trying to remember the digits, they barely paid attention to the word they repeated.

Later, when the researchers surprised the participants by asking them to recall the distracting word they had repeated, what happened? There was virtually no relationship between the duration of rehearsal (between 2 and 18 seconds) and the proportion of individuals who could recall the word (Glenberg, Smith, & Green, 1977). In other words, longer rehearsal did not lead to better recall.

Certainly, rehearsal is associated with better memory at times but, as the study described here shows, rehearsal itself is not very effective, especially for recall. This leaves us with a contradiction: How can rehearsal be both effective and ineffective? It turns out that it is not *how long* we rehearse information, but rather *how* we rehearse it that determines the effectiveness of memory. Individuals in the study just described were engaged in **maintenance rehearsal**—*prolonging exposure to information by repeating it*—which does very little to facilitate encoding that leads to the formation of long-term memories. By comparison, **elaborative rehearsal**—*prolonging exposure to information by thinking about its meaning*—significantly improves the process of encoding. For example, repeating the word *bottle*, and then imagining what a bottle looks like and how it is used, is an elaborative technique. Although maintenance rehearsal helps us remember for a very short time, elaborative rehearsal improves long-term learning and remembering.

This is likely a topic that is important to you as a student. In virtually every class you take, you have key terms to learn and exams to test your progress. You should see how the two types of rehearsal come into play in these processes. Students who simply repeat key terms and their definitions are employing maintenance rehearsal, and are less likely to do well on an exam. The wise strategy is to try to elaborate on the material rather than just repeat it.

PsychTutor
Click here in your eText for an interactive tutorial on the **Information Processing Model of Memory**

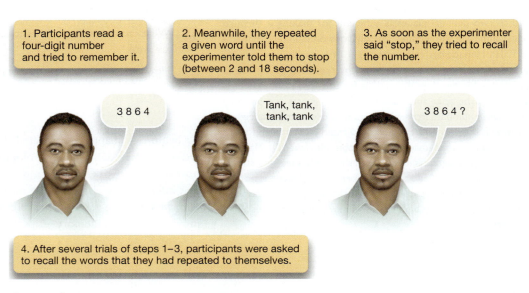

1. Participants read a four-digit number and tried to remember it.

2. Meanwhile, they repeated a given word until the experimenter told them to stop (between 2 and 18 seconds).

3. As soon as the experimenter said "stop," they tried to recall the number.

3 8 6 4

Tank, tank, tank, tank

3 8 6 4 ?

4. After several trials of steps 1–3, participants were asked to recall the words that they had repeated to themselves.

{FIG. 7.11}   **Rote Rehearsal has Limited Effects on Long-Term Memory**

Elaborative and maintenance rehearsal strategies indicate that the more meaningful we make information as we learn it, the more likely we are to remember it. The different ways in which information is encoded and retrieved can be understood by considering what are called *levels of processing* (LOP).

What do we know about levels of processing?

The LOP framework of memory begins with the understanding that encoding is most directly related to *how* information is initially processed. Additionally, but less important, is *how often* the information is encountered or *how long* one is exposed to it (Craik & Lockhart, 1972). Differences in processing can be described as a continuum from shallow processing (which is similar to maintenance rehearsal) to deep processing (which is more similar to elaborative rehearsal). Deep processing is generally the preferred method of encoding information, as it is associated with better retention and retrieval.

How can science explain the levels of processing effect?

Psychologists study LOP effects on encoding with experimental procedures that manipulate how people process information (Craik & Tulving, 1975). For example, research participants may answer questions that require processing at various levels, ranging from very shallow (for example, "Does this word rhyme with *dust*? . . . TRUST") to very deep processing (such as "Is this word a synonym for *locomotive*? . . . TRAIN"). At first, the participants focus solely on answering the questions—they do not expect a memory test. Later, when they are asked to recall the target words such as *trust* or *train*, they remember many more deeply processed words than shallow words. In one study, the differences ranged from recalling as few as 14% of the shallow words to 96% of the deeply processed words. In essence, they were almost 7 times more likely to recall a deep-processed word than one that was processed at only a shallow level.

Does LOP affect short-term and long-term memories in the same way? Rose and his colleagues (2010) adapted the traditional LOP task to focus on working memory processes.

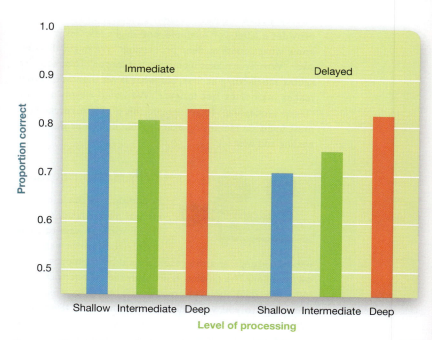

{FIG. 7.12} **Levels of Processing Affect Long-Term Memory, But Not Working Memory** When tested immediately after studying words, levels of processing do not seem to affect memory. In contrast, when there is a gap between studying words and being tested, levels of processing are important. When words are encoded based on their meaning (semantics), they are better retained in long-term memory.

In their study, participants viewed a target word such as *leg* followed by a comparison screen with two words—*arm* and *beg*—written in two different colors. This procedure was repeated for a whole list of target words. The LOP was the important part of this experiment: Researchers instructed volunteers before the study began to process the comparison words in one of three ways. They were instructed to find the word that was the same color as the target word (shallow processing), to find the word that rhymed with the target word (intermediate processing), or to find the word that was meaningfully related to the target word (deep processing). Depending on the instructions they received, the volunteers processed the information at levels ranging from shallow (comparing colors) to deep (comparing meanings). If you understand the definition of LOP, you should be able to anticipate these researchers' hypothesis and results: Rose et al. (2010) predicted that more deeply processed words would be recalled from long-term memory, but not working memory. As you can see in Figure 7.12, the results confirmed their hypothesis.

Can we critically evaluate this evidence?

The LOP framework has been enormously influential on memory research over the past 40 years. However, critics claim that it is simply circular reasoning, meaning that the idea of LOP does not really answer questions about memory, but rather simply provides a label. For example, one might ask, "How do we know what counts as deep processing?" We might then answer, "Whatever makes memories last longer." This response seems satisfactory at first, but what if we then ask, "What makes memories last longer?" We could simply answer, "Deep processing." To get around this problem, researchers must focus on identifying exactly what counts as deep processing and why.

Why is this relevant?

In addition to these experimental manipulations, there are all sorts of ways to think deeply about information in natural settings, and the result should be to improve your own memory. The simplest is probably the *self-reference effect*: When you think about information as it relates to you or how it is useful to you, you will remember it better (Symons & Johnson, 1997). That outcome is not terribly surprising, but it is still helpful to think about when learning material that you might not be interested in at first. Perhaps less intuitive is *survival processing*. Researchers have found that when items are processed as they relate to survival, they are more likely to be recalled (Butler, Kang, & Roediger, 2009). Thus, if you find yourself wanting to remember something, see if you can relate it to your own experiences or identify ways in which the information may aid survival.

ENCODING SPECIFICITY Encoding and retrieval might seem like opposites, given that one brings information in and the other takes it out. In reality, the two processes work together especially well when they share something in common. This is illustrated by the **encoding specificity principle**, which *predicts that retrieval is most effective when it occurs in the same context as encoding*. Context can include internal factors, such as your mood or your level of activity, or external factors, such as the characteristics of the room you are in—even if these factors are completely unrelated to the information you are learning.

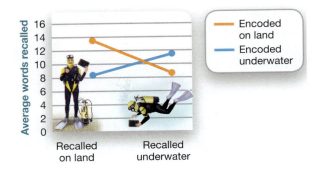

{FIG. 7.13}   **Context-Dependent Learning** Divers who encoded information on land had better recall on land than underwater. Divers who encoded information underwater had the reverse experience, demonstrating better recall underwater than when on land.

There are several ways to observe encoding specificity. The following examples demonstrate that retrieval is superior when the encoding and retrieval situations match up:

- *Context-Dependent Learning.* Retrieval is more effective when it takes place in the physical setting (context) as encoding. In one study, members of a scuba club volunteered to memorize word lists—half while diving underwater, and half while on land. After a short delay, the divers were tested again, but some had switched locations. Those who were tested in the same context as where encoding took place remembered approximately 40% more items than those who switched locations (see Figure 7.13; Godden & Baddeley, 1975).

- *State-Dependent Learning.* Retrieval is more effective when internal conditions—such as heart rate and arousal (physiological state)—match those experienced during encoding. In one study, researchers presented a group of students with a memory task in the presence of snakes or spiders, knowing that the volunteers had phobias about them. Volunteers who were in this anxiety-provoking situation both during the test *and* during the recall task did better than groups who performed either the encoding task or the retrieval task in a relaxed state (Lang et al., 2001).

- *Mood-Dependent Learning.* People remember better if their mood at retrieval matches their mood during encoding. Volunteers in one study generated words while in a pleasant or unpleasant mood, and then attempted to remember them in either the same or a different mood. The results indicated that if the type of mood at encoding and retrieval matched, then memory was superior. However, changes in the intensity of the mood did not seem to have an effect (Balch et al., 1999).

It is usually not difficult to spot these context effects while they are occurring. Almost everyone has had the experience of walking into a room to retrieve something—maybe a specific piece of mail or a roll of tape—only to find that they have no idea what they intended to pick up. We might call this phenomenon *context-dependent forgetting*, if we believe the change in the environment influenced the forgetting. It is certainly frustrating, but can be reversed by the *context reinstatement effect,* which occurs when you return to the original location and the memory suddenly comes back.

Quick Quiz 7.2a
Encoding and Retrieval

KNOW …

1 The time and manner in which information is retained between encoding and retrieval is _____.

- **A** maintenance rehearsal
- **B** storage
- **C** elaborative rehearsal
- **D** recall

2 Prolonging exposure to information by repeating it to oneself is referred to as _____.

- **A** maintenance rehearsal
- **B** storage
- **C** elaborative rehearsal
- **D** recall

UNDERSTAND …

3 According to the levels of processing approach to memory, thinking about synonyms is one method of _____ processing that should _____ memory for that term.

- **A** shallow; decrease
- **B** deep; increase
- **C** maintenance; increase
- **D** dualistic; decrease

APPLY …

4 If you are learning vocabulary for a psychology exam, you are better off using a(n) _____ technique.

- **A** maintenance rehearsal
- **B** elaborative rehearsal
- **C** serial processing
- **D** consolidation

5 When taking a math exam, the concept of _____ would indicate that you would do best if you took the exam in the same physical setting as the setting where you learned the material.

- **A** context-dependent learning
- **B** state-dependent learning
- **C** mood congruence
- **D** elaborative rehearsal

Answers can be found on page ANS-3.

Emotional Memories

The levels of processing research shows that thinking about information helps with remembering it, but can *feelings* about an event do the same? When you think back on distant memories, the ones that likely come to mind first are those that had emotional significance. To clarify matters, however, we should examine the laboratory evidence as well.

The importance of emotion in memory formation has been confirmed in numerous laboratory studies. In one, two groups of volunteers viewed the same slideshow depicting a woman's daily activities, with the final slide showing a bunch of friends gathered outside her door. If that was all the experiment entailed, the two groups would have about an equal chance of remembering the details—but what if one group had been told they were watching the woman on the way to her birthday party, whereas the other group was told that the woman was severely depressed and had thoughts of suicide? The volunteers who had been given the sad scenario actually remembered more details from the slideshow (Laney et al., 2003). Because the two groups were randomly assigned, we assume that the only thing that could have led to the stronger memories was the level of emotion tied to the photos for one of the groups.

Given what we know about levels of processing, it seems that emotions would facilitate deep processing, and research does confirm this effect. Nevertheless, emotional memories may involve more than just a deeper LOP. For example, in another study, participants studied a list of words and were then randomly assigned to view a tape of oral surgery (the emotional condition) or the way to brush your teeth effectively (*not the emotional condition*). After the slideshow, the group members who viewed the surgery tape remembered more of the words (see Figure 7.14 on p. 254) (Nielson et al., 2005). Thus emotions can lead to stronger memory formation, even if the information is not directly related to the emotional event.

This link between emotions and memory also has biological roots in the limbic system (Phelps, 2004). Recall that the limbic system includes the hippocampus (the structure associated with the encoding of long-term memories) and the amygdala (two small structures involved in emotional processing and responding). Brain imaging shows that emotional memories often activate the amygdala, whereas nonemotional memories generated at the same time do not (Sharot et al., 2007). Generally, the emotions associated with experiences tend to solidify memory for

Complete the **Survey** *What Do You Remember?* at **MyPsychLab**

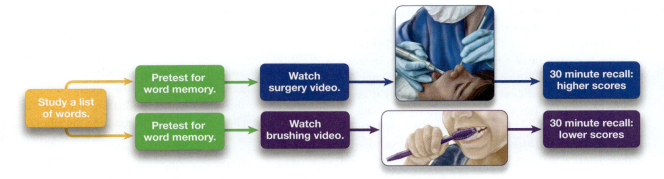

{FIG. 7.14} **Does Emotion Improve Memory?** Both groups remembered approximately the same percentage of words at pre-test, and then watched dentistry videos unrelated to the word lists. The group whose members watched the more emotional video recalled more of the words in the end (Nielson et al., 2005).

them. Of course, this association does not guarantee that all of the details of an experience will be remembered with complete accuracy.

As you thought about the linkage between emotion and memory, you might have begun to recall some of your own emotional memories. Perhaps you even have a **flashbulb memory**—*an extremely vivid and detailed memory about an event and the conditions surrounding how one learned about the event.* These highly charged emotional memories typically involve recollections of location, what was happening at the time of the event, and the emotional reactions of self and others (Brown & Kulik, 1977). Some may be personal memories, such as the memory of an automobile accident. Other events are so widely felt that they seem to form flashbulb memories for an entire society, such as the terrorist attacks of September 11, 2001 (Hirst et al., 2009). One defining feature of

Many people have flashbulb memories of the September 11, 2001, terrorist attacks.

flashbulb memories is that people are highly confident that their recollections are accurate. But is this confidence warranted?

MYTHS IN MIND
The Accuracy of Flashbulb Memories

Although flashbulb memories are very detailed and individuals reciting the details are very confident of their accuracy, it might surprise you to learn that they are not necessarily more accurate than any other memories. For example, researchers examined how college students remember the September 11, 2001, attacks in comparison to an emotional but more mundane event (Talarico & Rubin, 2003). On September 12, 2001, they asked students to describe the events surrounding the moment they heard about the attacks. For a comparison event, they asked students to describe something memorable from the preceding weekend, just two or three days before the attacks. Over several months, the students were asked to recall details of both events, and the researchers compared the accuracy of the two memories. Although their memory for both events was fading at the same rate and they were equal in accuracy, the students acknowledged the decline in memory only for the mundane events. They continued to feel highly confident in their memories surrounding the September 11 attacks, when, in fact, those memories were not any more accurate. The same pattern has been found for other major flashbulb events, such as the 1986 Space Shuttle Challenger explosion and the verdict in the O. J. Simpson murder trial (Neisser & Harsch, 1992; Schmolk et al., 2000).

• • • • • • • • • • • • • • • • • • • •

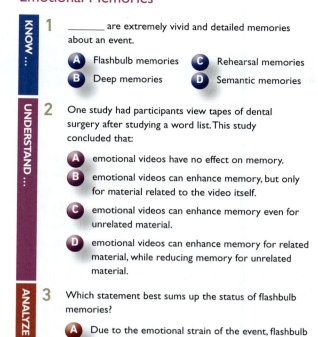

1 _____ are extremely vivid and detailed memories about an event.

  A Flashbulb memories   C Rehearsal memories

  B Deep memories   D Semantic memories

2 One study had participants view tapes of dental surgery after studying a word list. This study concluded that:

  A emotional videos have no effect on memory.

  B emotional videos can enhance memory, but only for material related to the video itself.

  C emotional videos can enhance memory even for unrelated material.

  D emotional videos can enhance memory for related material, while reducing memory for unrelated material.

3 Which statement best sums up the status of flashbulb memories?

  A Due to the emotional strain of the event, flashbulb memories are largely inaccurate.

  B Recall for only physical details is highly accurate.

  C Both emotion and physical details are remembered very accurately.

  D Over time, memory for details decays, similar to what happens with nonflashbulb memories.

Answers can be found on page ANS-3.

Forgetting and Remembering

Few people actually appreciate memory problems as much as the philosopher Friedrich Nietzsche—usually not known for looking on the bright side—who said, "The advantage of a bad memory is that one enjoys *several* times the same good things for the *first* time."

THE FORGETTING CURVE: HOW SOON WE FORGET ...

It might seem odd that the first research on remembering was actually a documentation of how quickly people forget. However, this approach does make sense: Without knowledge of forgetting, it is difficult to ascertain how well we can remember. This early work was conducted by Hermann Ebbinghaus, whom many psychologists consider the founder of memory research. Ebbinghaus used himself as his research subject and he studied hundreds of nonsense syllables for his experiments. His rationale was that because none of the syllables had any meaning, none of them should have

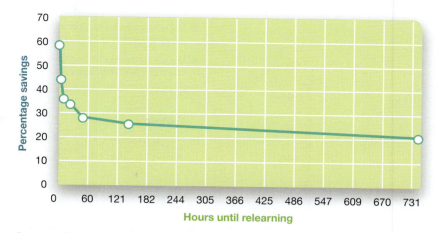

{FIG. 7.15} **Ebbinghaus's Forgetting Curve** This graph reveals Ebbinghaus's results showing the rate at which he forgot a series of nonsense syllables. You can see that there is a steep decline in performance within the first day and that the rate of forgetting levels off over time.

been easier to remember based on past experiences. Ebbinghaus studied lists of these syllables until he could repeat them twice. He then tested himself repeatedly—this is where his persistence really shows—day after day.

How soon do we forget? The data indicated that Ebbinghaus forgot about half of a list in an hour. If Ebbinghaus had continued to forget at that rate, the rest of the list should be lost after two hours. In reality, that was not that case. After a day, he could generally remember one-third of the material, and he could still recall between one-fifth and one-fourth of the words after a week. The graph in Figure 7.15 shows the basic pattern in his test results, which has come to be known as a *forgetting curve*. It clearly shows that most forgetting occurs right away, and that the rate of forgetting eventually slows to the point where one does not seem to forget at all.

These results have stood the test of time. In fact, in the century after Ebbinghaus conducted his research, more than 200 articles were published in psychological journals that fit Ebbinghaus's forgetting curve (Rubin & Wenzel, 1996). How does this finding apply to us as we go about remembering and forgetting things today? Actually, the forgetting curve applies to students quite well. For example, even if you find your psychology course engaging, meaningful, and relevant to your own life, you will likely forget half of the information you learn. Luckily, the forgetting curve will eventually level off and some information will stick with you for the rest of your life. Although we do not have data for psychology students, we do know that the typical forgetting curves apply to high school foreign language students as long as 50 years after graduation (see Figure 7.16 on p. 256; Bahrick, 1984).

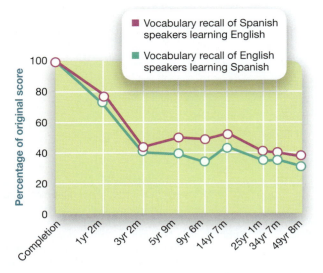

- ■ Vocabulary recall of Spanish speakers learning English
- ■ Vocabulary recall of English speakers learning Spanish

{FIG. 7.16} **Bahrick's Long-Term Forgetting Curve** This forgetting curve indicates the rate at which adults forgot the foreign language they took in high school. Compared to new graduates, those tested two to three years later forgot much of what they learned. After that, however, test scores stabilized (Bahrick, 1984).

This line of research focuses on how *quickly* we forget. Next, we turn to a slightly different question: What can we do to prevent forgetting from happening so quickly?

MNEMONICS: IMPROVING YOUR MEMORY SKILLS

Nietzsche made a good point about forgetting, but for those things we really need to remember, a number of ways to improve our success rates exist; chances are you know some of them already. This section focuses on a few **mnemonics**—*techniques that are intended to improve memory for specific information*—that you can begin using right away.

First, an **acronym** *is a pronounceable word whose letters represent the initials of an important phrase or set of items.* For example, the word "scuba" came into being with the invention of the self-contained underwater breathing apparatus. The **first letter technique** *uses the first letters of a set of items to spell out words that form a sentence.* It is like an acronym, but it tends to be used when the first-letters do not spell a pronounceable word (see Figure 7.17). One well-known example is "Every Good Boy Does Fine" for the five lines on the treble clef in musical notation. It even has

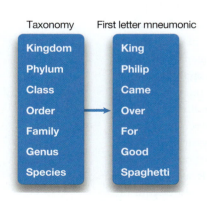

{FIG. 7.17} **The First Letter Technique** Students of biology often use mnemonics, such as this example of the first letter technique, which helps students remember the taxonomic system.

an acronym to go along with it: "FACE" represents the four spaces between E, G, B, D, and F.

These types of mnemonic techniques work by *chunking*—that is, by organizing the information into a pattern that makes more sense than the original information (chunking was discussed in Module 7.1). Acronyms have a meaning of their own, so the learner gets the benefit of both elaborative rehearsal and deeper processing.

A number of mnemonic devices are based on the premise of dual coding. **Dual coding** *occurs when information is stored in more than one form*—such as a verbal description and a visual image, or a description and a sound—and it regularly produces stronger memories than the use of one form alone (Paivio, 1991). Most children growing up in the United States learned the alphabet with the help of a song. In fact, even adults find themselves humming portions of that song when alphabetizing documents in a file cabinet. The simplest explanation for the dual-coding advantage is that twice as much information is stored. These mnemonics also make use of levels of processing by requiring elaboration with the images, and the elaboration seems to be the most important component in ensuring the effectiveness of memory. Although there are a number of ways to use images to improve verbal memory, we will focus on just one here—the method of loci.

The **method of loci** (pronounced "LOW-sigh") is *a mnemonic that connects words to be remembered to locations along a familiar path.* To use the method of loci, one must first imagine a route that has landmarks or easily identifiable spaces—for example, the things you pass on your way from your home to a friend's house. Once the path is identified, the learner takes a moment to visually relate the first word on the list to the first location encountered. For example, if you need to remember to pick up noodles, milk, and soap from the

The method of loci relies on mental imagery of a familiar location or path, like this path that students take to class three times a week.

Restaurant staff often rely on mnemonic devices to remember which diner receives each item.

store and the first thing you pass on the way to your friend's house is an intersection with a stop sign, you might picture the intersection littered with noodles; and so on down the list. When it is time to recall the items, the learner simply imagines the familiar drive, identifying the items to be purchased as they relate to each location along the path.

The application of mnemonic strategies can be found in restaurant waiters who are not allowed to write out orders. These waiters use a variety of the techniques discussed in this chapter. Some use chunking strategies, such as remembering soft drinks for a group of three customers, and cocktails for the other four. Waiters also use the method of loci to link faces with positions at the table. In one study, a waiter was able to recall as many as 20 dinner orders (Ericsson & Polson, 1988). He used the method of loci by linking food type (starch, beef, or fish) with a table location, and he used acronyms to help with encoding salad dressing choices. Thus RaVoSe for a party of three would be ranch, vinegar and oil, and sesame. Waiters, as well as memory researchers, will tell you that the worst thing restaurant patrons can do is switch seats, as it completely disrupts the mnemonic devices used by the waiter (Bekinschtein et al., 2008).

While these mnemonic devices can help with rote memorization, they may not necessarily improve your understanding of material. Researchers have begun to examine other memory boosters that may offer more benefits to you as a student as you prepare for exams. Recall from Module 6.3 that *desirable difficulties* can aid learning. These techniques make studying slower and more effortful, but result in better overall remembering. They include spacing out your studying rather than cramming, and studying material in varying orders.

One popular approach to studying is to use flashcards. Although psychologists have begun to understand how this process benefits students, they also have identified a few pitfalls that can hinder its effects. First is the spacing effect, which was introduced in Module 1.1. When studying with flashcards, it is better to use one big stack rather than several smaller stacks; using the entire deck helps take advantage of the effect of spacing the cards. A second potential problem is the fact that students become overconfident and drop flashcards as soon as they believe they learn the material. In reality, doing so seems to reduce the benefits of overlearning the material (making it more difficult to forget) and spacing out cards in the deck (Kornell, 2009; Kornell & Bjork, 2007). No matter how you study, you should take advantage of the **testing effect**, *the finding that taking practice tests can improve exam performance, even without additional studying.* In fact, researchers have directly compared testing to additional studying and have found that in some cases, testing actually improves memory more (Roediger et al., 2010).

Quick Quiz 7.2c
Forgetting and Remembering

UNDERSTAND …

1. Dual coding seems to help memory by:

   A. allowing for maintenance rehearsal.

   B. ensuring that the information is encoded in multiple ways.

   C. ensuring that the information is encoded on two separate occasions.

   D. duplicating the rehearsal effect.

APPLY …

2. If you are preparing for an exam by using flashcards, you will probably find that you are more confident about some of the items than others. To improve your exam performance, you should:

   A. drop the cards you already know.

   B. keep the cards in the deck even if you feel like you know them.

   C. use elaborative rehearsal.

   D. use the method of loci.

3. If you wanted to remember a grocery list using the method of loci, you should:

   A. imagine the items on the list on your path through the grocery store.

   B. match rhyming words to each item on your list.

   C. repeat the list to yourself over and over again.

   D. tell a story using the items from the list.

Answers can be found on page ANS-3.

Module Summary

Now that you have read this module you should:

Listen to the audio file of this module at **MyPsychLab**

KNOW ...

- **The key terminology related to forgetting, encoding, and retrieval:**

acronym (p. 256)

dual coding (p. 256)

elaborative rehearsal (p. 250)

encoding specificity principle (p. 252)

first letter technique (p. 256)

flashbulb memory (p. 254)

maintenance rehearsal (p. 250)

method of loci (p. 256)

mnemonics (p. 256)

storage (p. 250)

testing effect (p. 257)

UNDERSTAND ...

- **How the type of cognitive processing employed can affect the chances of remembering what you encounter.** Generally speaking, the deeper the processing, the more likely something is to be remembered. Greater depth of processing may be achieved by elaborating on the meaning of the information, through increased emotional content, and through coding in images and sounds simultaneously.

APPLY ...

- **What you have learned to improve your ability to memorize information.** The best way to do so is to give it a try. One mnemonic device that might be helpful is the method of loci. Have someone create a shopping list for you while you prepare yourself by imagining a familiar path (perhaps the route you take to class). When you are ready to learn the list, read a single item on the list and imagine it at some point on the path. Feel free to exaggerate the images in your memory—each item could become the size of a stop sign or might take on the appearance of a particular building or tree that you pass by. Continue this pattern for each individual item until you have learned the list. Then try what Ebbinghaus did: Test your memory over the course of a few days. How do you think you will do?

ANALYZE ...

- **Whether emotional memories are more accurate than non-emotional ones.** Both personal experiences and controlled laboratory studies demonstrate that emotion enhances memory. However, as we learned in the case of flashbulb memories, even memories for details of significant events decline over time, although confidence in memory accuracy typically remains very high.

Module 7.3

Constructing and Reconstructing Memories

Learning Objectives

After reading this module you should:

KNOW ...	UNDERSTAND ...	APPLY ...	ANALYZE ...
The key terminology used in discussing how memories are organized and constructed	How schemas serve as frameworks for encoding and constructing memories How psychologists can produce false memories in the laboratory	What you have learned to judge the reliability of eyewitness testimony	The arguments in the "recovered memory" debate

Imagine you saw a photograph of yourself in a situation you knew you had never been in—perhaps riding in a hot-air balloon when you were five or six years old. Would you believe the picture? More importantly, would you *remember* riding in the balloon, even though it never happened? Psychologist Kimberly Wade and her colleagues have been asking these questions and found some surprising answers. In summary, people who view doctored photographs and videos usually believe what they see and quite often begin to remember the imaginary event. These *false memories* bring up some intriguing questions.

Focus Questions

1. How is it possible to remember events that never happened?

2. Do these false memories represent memory problems, or are they just a normal part of remembering?

• • • • • • • • • • • • • • • • • •

Memory is dynamic. Unlike photographs (that are not altered), memories of details for past events change. Cognitive psychologist and renowned memory researcher Ulric Neisser once recounted what he was doing on December 7, 1941, the day Japan attacked Pearl Harbor. Neisser was sitting in the living room listening to a baseball game on the radio when the program was interrupted with the news (Neisser, 2000). Or was he? He had certainly constructed a very distinct memory for this emotional event, but something must have gone wrong. Baseball season does not last through December. As this example demonstrates, even memory researchers are prone to misremembering. In this module, we will explore how memories are constructed, and describe some of the pitfalls that can occur in the process of reconstruction.

How Memories Are Organized and Constructed

Think about the last time you read a novel or watched a film. What do you recall about the story? If you have a typical memory, you will forget the proper names of locations and characters quickly, but you will be able to remember the basic plot for a very long time (Squire, 1989; Stanhope et al., 1993). The plot may be referred to as the *gist* of the story and it impacts us much more than characters' names, which are often just details. As it turns out, much of the way we store memories depends on our tendency to remember the gist of things.

THE SCHEMA: AN ACTIVE ORGANIZATION PROCESS

In this section, we will focus on the concept of a **schema**, *an organized cluster of memories that constitutes one's knowledge about events, objects, and ideas*. Whenever we encounter familiar events or objects, these schemas become active, and they allow us to know what to expect, what to pay attention to, and what to remember. Because we use these patterns automatically, it may be difficult to understand what they are, even though you have been using them your whole life. Here is an example; just read the following passage through one time.

> The procedure is quite simple. First, you arrange things into different groups. Of course, one pile may be sufficient, depending on how much there is to do. If you have to go somewhere else due to lack of facilities, that is the next step; otherwise, you are pretty well set. It is important not to overdo things. That is, it is better to do too few things at once than too many. At first the whole procedure will seem complicated. Soon, however, it will become just another facet of life. After the procedure is completed, one arranges the materials into different groups again. Then they can be put into their appropriate places. Eventually they will be used once more, and the whole cycle will have to be repeated. (Bransford & Johnson, 1973)

At this point, if you were to write down the details of the paragraph solely from memory, how well do you think you would do? Most people do not have high expectations for themselves, but they would blame it on how vague the paragraph seems. Now, what if we tell you the passage is about doing laundry? If you read the paragraph a second time, you should see that it is easier to understand.

WORKING THE SCIENTIFIC LITERACY MODEL
How Schemas Influence Memory

Although schemas are used to explain memory, they can be used to explain many other phenomena as well, such as the way we perceive, remember, and think about people and situations.

What do we know about schemas?

The laundry demonstration tells us quite a bit about schemas and memory. First, most of us have our own personal schema about the process of doing laundry. Referring back to the definition of schema— a cluster of memories that constitutes your knowledge about an event (gathering clothes, going to the laundromat), object (what clothes are, what detergent is), or idea (why clean clothes are desirable). When you read the paragraph the first time, you probably did not know what the objects and events were. However, when we told you it was about doing laundry, we *activated* your laundry schema—your personal collection of concepts and memories. Once your schema was activated, you were prepared to make sense of the story. Second, we should point out that schemas are involved in all three stages of memory: They guide what we attend to during encoding, organize stored memories, and serve as cues when it comes time to retrieve information.

How can science explain schemas?

Where do schemas come from? They appear to be products of culture and experience (e.g., Ross & Wang, 2010). For example, individuals within a culture tend to have schemas related to gender roles—men and women are each assumed to engage in certain jobs and to behave in certain ways. Even if an individual realizes that these schemas are not 100% accurate (in fact, they can be far from accurate in some cases), he or she is likely to engage in schematic processing when having difficulty remembering something specific.

A study by Heather Kleider and her associates (2008) demonstrates how schemas influence memory quite well. These investigators had research participants view photographs of a handyman engaged in schema-consistent behavior (e.g., working on plumbing) as well as a few schema-inconsistent tasks (e.g., folding a baby's clothing). Mixed in with these photos were images of a stay-at-home mother doing chores, including the same tasks. Immediately after viewing the photographs,

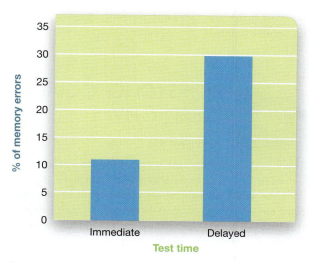

{FIG. 7.18} **Schemas Affect How We Encode and Remember** In this study, memory was accurate when tested immediately, as shown by the small proportion of errors on the "immediate" side of the graph. After two days, however, participants misremembered seeing the schema-inconsistent tasks in line with stereotypes. For example, they misremembered the homemaker stirring cake batter even if they had actually seen the handyman do it (Kleider et al., 2008). **Click on this figure in your eText to see more details**.

participants were quite successful at remembering correctly who had performed what actions. However, after two days, what types of memory mistakes do you think the researchers found? As you can see from Figure 7.18 individuals began making mistakes, and these mistakes are consistent with gender schemas.

Can we critically evaluate the concept of a schema?

The concept of a schema is certainly useful in describing our methods of mental organization, but some psychologists remain skeptical of its validity. After all, you cannot record brain activity and expect to see a particular schema, and individuals generally are not aware that they are using schematic processing. It may even be the case that what we assume are schemas about laundry, gender, or ourselves are different every time we think about these topics. If that is the case, then describing this tendency as a schema might even be misleading. Even so, the concept enjoys some popularity because it is a convenient way to describe a complex set of memory events, and it clearly serves as a guide to some useful therapeutic applications.

Why is this relevant?

Schemas are not limited to memories for other people; in fact, we all have schemas

about ourselves. Clinical psychology researchers have become particularly concerned with the ways in which these *self-schemas* may contribute to psychological problems. Consider a person with clinical depression—a condition that involves negative emotion, lack of energy, self-doubt and self-blame (see Module 13.3 for more details). An individual with depression is likely to have a very negative self-schema, which means that he will pay attention to things that are consistent with the depressive symptoms, and will be more likely to recall events and feelings that are consistent with this schema. Thus the schema contributes to a pattern of thinking and focusing on negative thoughts.

Fortunately, researchers have been able to target these schemas in psychotherapy. The evidence shows that by changing their self-schema, individuals are better able to recover from even very serious bouts of depression (Dozois et al., 2009).

CONSTRUCTING MEMORIES As you have seen, schemas involve a collection of ideas and memories that tell us what to expect in a situation. Research shows that instead of remembering a bunch of accurate details (which would be very time consuming), we remember events using **constructive memory**, *a process by which we first recall a generalized schema and then add in specific details* (Scoboria et al., 2006; Silva et al., 2006).

Here is an interesting story to illustrate how schemas and details interact to construct memories. Imagine visiting an unfamiliar city in the United States. As you are exploring a park downtown, you round a corner and see an elephant on the path. You would probably be quite surprised—what is an elephant doing in the middle of downtown?! But this is exactly what happened to a student of ours.

Schemas tell us what to expect in a situation as well as what is relevant and important. If you have any knowledge of American cities, then your schemas probably provide the gist of what the landscape and buildings look like in a typical downtown. The buildings, roads, and parks are all *schema consistent*. We are just as confident that free-roaming elephants are *not* part of your schema—they are *schema inconsistent*, and quite surprising at that.

Schemas can affect our memory in two ways:

1. *Organization.* When we encounter a new situation, some objects and events will undoubtedly fit our schemas (i.e., our expectations) better than others. When the new information makes sense—that is, when it fits our schema—it can be easier to recall, yet it may be more difficult to recognize or report the exact details.
2. *Distinctiveness.* When we encounter new information, some of it will not fit our schemas. If the new information stands out as weird or unusual, it will be easy to recall. If it does not fit our schema, but is not all that unusual, it will likely be forgotten (Silva et al., 2006).

The effects of organization would be easy to spot if we asked you to recall your encounter with the elephant. Schemas would help you freely recall normal things: There was a walking path, there were grass and shrubbery around, there were tall buildings on the right and a creek on the left. All of these general ideas are correct, and they would be easy to remember because they fit your schema. In contrast, when presented with several details, such as pictures of downtown, you might have difficulty recognizing the exact buildings you passed by on your trip.

Distinctiveness also has obvious effects. Like our student, you would definitely remember the elephant—that was the central point of the story—but there are bound to be other distinctive sights along the way that do not come to mind at all. Perhaps you encountered a discarded shoe on the side of the bike path, or you saw a sign that had been vandalized. Although you probably will not recall those schema-inconsistent objects, if prompted with questions or perhaps a picture, you might very well recognize them.

Here, you can see that schemas and details work together. To use the metaphor of memory construction, the schema provides the framework and structure, and the details are the walls and windows that make each event memorable. Incidentally, as the student continued to round the corner, he saw signs advertising a circus, along with a lot full of large trucks. With the circus schema in place, the encounter immediately made

sense to him—the elephant was simply being let out for some exercise.

BIOPSYCHOSOCIAL PERSPECTIVES
Your Earliest Memories

Think back to the earliest memory you can recall: How old were you? It is likely that you do not have any personal or autobiographical memories from before your third birthday. Psychologists have been trying to explain this phenomenon—sometimes called *infantile amnesia*. Which of the following explanations do you think are supported by scientific evidence?

Yes or no? The nervous system is still developing at birth.
Yes or no? Young children need to develop schemas to help organize and store memories.
Yes or no? Different cultures tend to develop earliest memories at different ages.

Did you say yes to all of these? If so, you are in agreement with what scientific research shows. For example, cross-cultural cognitive research indicates that self-schemas begin to develop around the ages of 18 to 24 months (Howe, 2003). Without these schemas, it is difficult and maybe even impossible to organize and encode memories about the self. This is not a universal phenomenon, however. Other researchers taking a cross-cultural perspective have found that a sense of self emerges earlier among European Americans than among people living in eastern Asia, which correlates with earlier ages of first memories among European Americans (Fivush & Nelson, 2004; Ross & Wang, 2010). Why might this difference arise? The European American emphasis on developing a sense of self encourages thinking about personal experiences, which increases the likelihood that personal events—such as your third birthday party with that scary clown who showed up, or getting chased by a dog—will be remembered. In contrast, Asian cultures tend to emphasize social harmony and collectiveness over individualism, resulting in a schema that is more socially integrated than in Westerners. This may explain the slightly later onset of autobiographical memory in Asian children.

Do these findings mean that we could get infants to remember early life events by teaching them to talk about themselves at an early age? It is not likely. The most plausible reason why we do not have memories that exist before age three years is because the nervous system, including key memory regions, continues to develop through infancy and toddlerhood. Its immaturity limits the degree to which a young person can think, reflect on, and remember their personal experiences (Newcombe et al., 2000).

. . . .

Quick Quiz 7.3a
How Memories Are Organized and Constructed

KNOW…

1 Schemas appear to affect which of the following stages of memory?

A Encoding

B Storage

C Retrieval

D All of these stages

2 The act of remembering through recalling a framework and then adding specific details is known as _____.

A constructive memory

B confabulation

C schematic interpretation

D distinctiveness

UNDERSTAND…

3 Information that does not fit our expectations for a specific context is likely to be forgotten if:

A it is extremely unusual.

B it only fits our expectations for another completely different context.

C it is unexpected, but really not that unusual.

D it is schema consistent.

Answers can be found on page ANS-3.

False Memories: Constructing Memories of What Never Happened

One of the most intriguing aspects of memory and one of the most prolific areas of memory research is **false memory**, *remembering events that did not occur, or incorrectly recalling details of an event*. Although the assertion would be difficult to prove, it is probably the case that everyone has false memories. These incorrect memories do not necessarily indicate a dysfunction of memory, but rather reflect normal memory processes—which are very much imperfect. As we pointed out in our discussion of schemas, the elements of a memory must be reconstructed each time they are revisited. As a result, psychologists agree, memory does not store information as accurately as a video camera would. Instead, remembering is a process of reconstructing stored information.

Every time we reconstruct a memory, there is a possibility that we are getting some of the details incorrect, even those about which we are extremely confident. To better understand how we create false memories, researchers have conducted experiments designed to increase or decrease the occurrence of false memories. Over the past 30 years, a number of methods have emerged that reliably produce false memories, and often very profound memories at that.

THE MISINFORMATION EFFECT A classic method in false memory research involves the **misinformation effect**, *which happens when information occurring after an event becomes part of the memory for that event*. In the original studies pioneered by Elizabeth Loftus (1975), researchers attempted to use the misinformation effect to change the details of people's memories. For example, in one of the first studies on the topic, students viewed a videotaped staged event, such as a car crash. In the experimental conditions, participants were asked about an object that was not in the video. One such question was about the yield sign in the car crash video, even though there was no yield sign, but rather a stop sign. Later, when asked if they had seen a yield sign, participants in the experimental group were likely to say yes. As this experiment demonstrates, one can change the details of a memory just by phrasing a question in a certain way. 👁

THE DRM PARADIGM The Deese-Roediger-McDermott paradigm (*DRM*), named after the psychologists who developed it, is probably the most straightforward procedure used in false memory research. As shown in Figure 7.19 (p. 264), in the **DRM procedure**, *participants study a list of highly related words called semantic associates* (which

👁 **Watch** the **Video** *Memory: Elizabeth Loftus* at **MyPsychLab**

Participants in one study viewed the photo on the left and later were asked about the "yield sign," even though they saw a stop sign. This small bit of misinformation was enough to get many participants to falsely remember seeing a yield sign. Similarly, participants who first viewed the photo on the right could be led to misremember seeing a stop sign with a single misleading question.

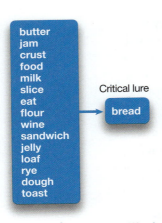

{FIG. 7.19} **A Sample Word List and Its Critical Lure for the DRM Procedure** The words on the left side are all closely related to the word "bread"—but "bread" does not actually appear on the list. People who study this list of words are very likely to mis-remember that "bread" was present.

means they are associated by meaning). The word that would be the most obvious member of the list just happens to be missing. This missing word is called the *critical lure*. What happens when the participants are given a memory test? A significant proportion remember the critical lure, even though it never appeared on the list (Deese, 1959; Roediger & McDermott, 1995). When individuals recall the critical lure, it is called an *intrusion*.

The fact that people make intrusion errors is not particularly surprising. However, the strength of the effect is surprising. In routine studies, the DRM lures as many as 70% of the participants. The most obvious way to reduce this effect would be to simply explain the DRM procedure and warn participants that intrusions may occur. Although this approach has proved effective in reducing intrusions, false memories still occur (Gallo et al., 1997). Obviously, intrusions are very difficult to prevent, but not because memory is prone to mistakes. In fact, memory is generally accurate and extremely efficient, given the millions of bits of information we encounter every day. Instead, the DRM effect reflects the fact that normal memory processes are constructive.

IMAGERY AND FALSE MEMORIES Researchers have found that the more readily and clearly we can imagine events, the more certain we are that the memories are accurate. Based on this evidence, it was not surprising when researchers found that images could be used to lead to false memories in several different ways.

One technique for manipulating memories is known as *guided imagery*. It involves a researcher giving instructions to participants to imagine certain events. Like the misinformation effect, guided imagery can be used to alter memories for actual events, but it can also create entirely false memories. For example, in one study, volunteers were asked to imagine a procedure in which a nurse removed a sample of skin from a finger. Despite the fact that this is not a medical procedure and that it almost certainly never occurred, individuals in the experimental group reported that this event had actually happened to them more often than their peers in the control condition (Mazzoni & Memon, 2003).

IMAGINATION INFLATION **Imagination inflation** *refers to the increased confidence in a false memory of an event following repeated imagination of the event.* To study this effect, researchers created a list of events that may or may not have happened to the individuals in their study (e.g., got in trouble for calling 911, found a $10 bill in a parking lot). The volunteers were first asked to rate their confidence

that the event happened. In sessions held over a period of days, participants were asked to imagine these events, until finally they were asked to rate their confidence again. For each item they were asked to imagine, repeated imagination *inflated* their confidence in the memory of the event (Garry et al., 1996; Garry & Polaschek, 2000).

FALSE PHOTOGRAPHS Perhaps the strongest piece of evidence for image-based false memories comes from doctored photographs, such as the one mentioned at the beginning of this module. The volunteers in the study had to recruit the help of their family. Their parents provided pictures of the participant from early childhood, along with an explanation of the event, the location, and the people and objects in the photo. The researchers took one of the pictures and digitally cut and pasted it into a balloon ride. On three occasions the participants went through the set of pictures, the true originals plus the doctored photo, in a structured interview process (the kind designed to help police get more details from eyewitnesses). By the end of the third session, half the participants had some memory for the balloon ride event, even though it never occurred (Wade et al., 2002).

Photographic images such as the ones used in the hot-air balloon study leave it to the subject to fill in the gaps as to what "happened" on their balloon ride. Other researchers have gone so far as to create false videotaped evidence of an event (Nash et al., 2009). For this method, a volunteer was videotaped watching a graduate student perform an action. Then, researchers videotaped a researcher performing an additional action. Then the videos were spliced together to show the volunteer watching an event that she, in reality, did not actually see. Now imagine you were shown a video of yourself watching an action you had not seen before—would you believe it? In fact, a significant portion of the individuals did form memories of the events they had never witnessed.

Falsely remembering something is not symptomatic of having a weak memory. Psychologists have found that when people recount information that is true, the visual and other sensory areas of the brain become more active. When revealing falsely remembered information, these same individuals have much less activity in the sensory regions—the brain is not drawing on mental imagery because it was not there in the first place (Stark et al., 2010). Of course, being convinced you went on a hot-air balloon ride that never happened is of little consequence. In other circumstances, false remembering can be highly problematic.

THE DANGER OF FALSE REMEMBERING Our ability to organize and construct memories helps us

In one study of false memory, true photos were obtained from volunteers' families (left), and were edited to look like a balloon ride (right). About half of the volunteers in this study came to recall some details of an event that never happened to them.

store large amounts of basic information, yet it also leaves us vulnerable to false memory. A number of personal and social dangers are associated with the confusion between true and false memories. The worst effects of false remembering on individuals have been the well-documented occurrence of false **recovered memories**, *memories of a traumatic event that are suddenly recovered after blocking the memory of that event for a long period of time*, often many years. This idea that we suppress traumatic memories is popularly known as *repression* from Freudian psychoanalysis (you will read more about this topic in Module 12.3). This school of thought suggests that if a repressed memory can be recovered, then a patient can find ways to cope with the trauma. Some therapists espouse this view and use techniques such as hypnosis and guided imagery to try to unearth repressed memories.

Recovered memories, like many other types of long-term memory, are difficult to study because one can rarely determine if they are true or false. The **recovered memory controversy** is a *heated debate among psychologists about the validity of recovered memories* (Davis & Loftus, 2009). On one side of the controversy are some clinical mental health workers (although certainly not the majority) who regularly attempt to recover memories they suspect have been repressed. On the opposing side are the many psychologists who are very skeptical that repression occurs at all and assert that any so-called recovered memory is actually a false memory. This perspective argues that the techniques that might help "recover" a memory bear a striking resemblance to those that are used to create false memories in laboratory research; they often involve instructions to remember, attempts to form images, and

social reinforcement for reporting memories. A neutral party would be correct to point out that, at present, it is virtually impossible to tell what is a true memory versus a false memory without corroborating evidence. Therefore, the debate will likely continue for some time.

What is the danger in a false memory of this nature? The example of Beth Rutherford illustrates the worst that can happen. In the early 1990s, Beth sought the help of her church counselor to deal with personal issues. During their sessions, the counselor managed to convince her that her father, a minister, had raped her. The memory was further elaborated so that she remembered becoming pregnant and that her father had forced her to undergo an abortion using a coat hanger. You can imagine what kind of effects this had on the family. Her father had little choice but to resign from his position, and his reputation was left in shambles. Although it can be difficult to prove some false memories, this incident is particularly disturbing because it *could* have been supported by medical evidence. When a medical investigation was finally conducted, absolutely no evidence was found that Beth had ever been raped or that she had ever been pregnant (Loftus, 1997).

This case is not an isolated one, though fortunately such instances remain rare. Even so, the recovered memory controversy is a serious topic of debate for psychologists. On the one hand, if repression occurs, and if repressed memories affect mental health, then it would be helpful to use memory recovery techniques. On the other hand, most memory recovery techniques are based on the same techniques that cognitive psychologists use to create false memories, especially imagery. Thus the risk for wrongful accusations when this course is pursued is high.

PSYCH @

Court: Is Eyewitness Testimony Reliable?

In the United States, more than 220 individuals convicted of crimes have been exonerated based on DNA evidence; more than 75% of the original convictions were the result of mistaken eyewitness testimony (Innocence Project, 2010; Wells & Quinlivan, 2009). Considering that many cases do not have DNA evidence available (it has been lost or destroyed, or the quality of DNA samples has deteriorated), there are likely to be many more wrongful convictions in this country that we will never know about.

While trying to pinpoint the individual responsible for a crime, investigators often present a lineup of a series of individuals (either in person or in photographs) and ask the eyewitness to identify the suspect. Given the constructive nature of memory, it should come as no surprise to hear that an eyewitness gets it wrong from time to time. The consequences of this kind of wrongful conviction are dire: An innocent person goes to jail while a potentially dangerous person stays free.

How can the science of memory improve this process? Here are the six main suggestions for reforming procedures:

1. *Employ double-blind procedures.* In Module 2.1, we described how double-blind procedures help reduce experimenter bias. Similarly, a double-blind lineup can prevent an investigator from biasing an eyewitness, either intentionally or accidentally.

2. *Use appropriate instructions.* For example, the investigator should include the statement, "The suspect might not be present in the lineup." Eyewitnesses often assume the guilty person is in the lineup, so they are likely to choose a close match. This risk can be greatly reduced by instructing the eyewitness that the correct answer may be "none of the above."

3. *Compose the lineup carefully.* The lineup should include individuals who match the eyewitness's description of the perpetrator, not the investigator's beliefs about the suspect.

4. *Use sequential lineups.* When an entire lineup is shown simultaneously, the witness may assume one of the people is guilty and settle on the best candidate. If the people in the lineup are presented one at a time, witnesses are less likely to pick out an incorrect suspect because they are willing to consider the next person in the sequence.

5. *Require confidence statements.* Eyewitness confidence can change as a result of an investigator's response, or simply by seeing the same suspect in multiple lineups, neither of which make the testimony any more accurate. Therefore, confidence statements should be taken in the witness's own words after an identification is made.

6. *Record the procedures.* Eyewitness researchers have identified at least a dozen specific things that can go wrong during identification procedures. By recording these procedures, expert witnesses can evaluate the reliability of testimony during hearings.

. . . .

Quick Quiz 7.3b

False Memories: Constructing Memories of What Never Happened

KNOW …

1. If you are presented with a list of 15 words, all of which have something in common, you are most likely participating in a study focusing on _____.

   A misinformation effects   C imagination inflation

   B the DRM procedure   D repression

2. Which of the following effects demonstrates that one can change the details of a memory just by how a question is phrased?

   A Misinformation effects   C Imagination inflation

   B The DRM procedure   D Repression

UNDERSTAND …

3. What might happen if a study participant viewed a doctored photograph of an event that did not actually occur?

   A The person could develop a memory for the event and he would *not* recognize that it was a false memory.

   B The person would be unable to form memories of the event.

   C The person could develop a memory for the event, but he would clearly recognize that it was a false memory.

   D We cannot make any predictions about what might or might not happen.

APPLY …

4. Jonathan is choosing a perpetrator from a lineup in a robbery that he witnessed. You can be most confident in his selection if:

   A the authorities smiled after Jonathan's response so that he would feel comfortable during the lineup procedure.

   B the authorities had the lineup presented all at the same time so Jonathan could compare the individuals.

   C the lineup included individuals of different races and ethnicities.

   D Jonathan was given the option to not choose any of the people from the lineup if no one fit his memory.

ANALYZE …

5. Psychologists who study false memories have engaged in a debate over the validity of recovered memories. Why are they skeptical about claims of recovered memories?

   A They have never experienced recovered memories themselves.

   B Many of the techniques used to create false memories in research bear a striking similarity to the techniques used to recover memories in therapy.

   C Brain scans can easily distinguish between true and false memories.

   D Scientists have proved that it is impossible to remember something that you have once forgotten.

Answers can be found on page ANS-3.

Module Summary

Now that you have read this module you should:

((•━ Listen to the audio file of this module at **MyPsychLab**

KNOW ...

- *The key terminology used in discussing how memories are organized and constructed:*

constructive memory (p. 261)
DRM procedure (p. 263)
false memory (p. 263)
imagination inflation (p. 264)
misinformation effect (p. 263)

recovered memory (p. 265)
recovered memory
  controversy (p. 265)
schema (p. 260)

UNDERSTAND ...

- *How schemas serve as frameworks for encoding and constructing memories.* Schemas guide our attention, telling us what to expect in certain circumstances. They organize long-term memories and provide us with cues when it comes time to retrieve those memories.

- *How psychologists can produce false memories in the laboratory.* Psychologists have found that a number of factors contribute to the construction of false memories, including misinformation, imagination inflation, and the semantic similarities used in the DRM procedure.

APPLY ...

- *What you have learned to judge the reliability of eyewitness testimony.* Eyewitness testimony is absolutely crucial to the operation of our legal system, but how reliable is it? **Figure 7.20** summarizes more than 200 cases

of exonerations (convictions that have been overturned due to new evidence after the trial) made possible since 1989, thanks to the help of The Innocence Project. Do eyewitness mistakes seem to play a major role in these reversals? If so, what does this relationship suggest about research on eyewitness testimony? (See our answers on page ANS-3.)

ANALYZE ...

- *The arguments in the "recovered memory" debate.* You should first understand the premise behind the idea of recovered memories: Some people believe that if a memory is too painful, it might be blocked from conscious recollection, only to be recovered later through therapeutic techniques. Others argue that it is difficult to prove that a "recovered" memory is actually recovered. Given how easy it is to create false memories, they argue, any memory believed to be recovered should be viewed with skepticism.

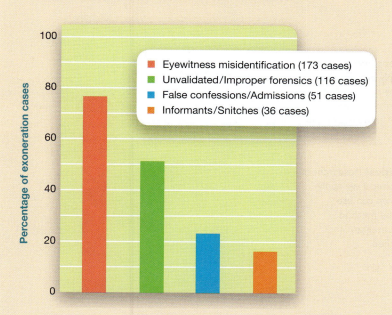

{FIG. 7.20} **The Role of Eyewitness Errors in Wrongful Convictions**

Legend:
- Eyewitness misidentification (173 cases)
- Unvalidated/Improper forensics (116 cases)
- False confessions/Admissions (51 cases)
- Informants/Snitches (36 cases)

y-axis: Percentage of exoneration cases (0–100)

Module 7.1 :: Memory Systems

Focus Questions:

1 **How is it possible to remember just long enough to have normal conversations and activities but then to forget them almost immediately?** Researchers have learned that we have different memory stores, which differ in how long they can store information. In addition, multiple control processes transfer information among these systems. It is possible, as in the case of H.M., to experience memory loss in one of these stores or processes but not another. Therefore, it is not unusual for people with amnesia to have a relatively well-functioning working memory system, even as they experience difficulties learning new information.

2 **How is it possible to forget some facts that are so important but to remember other things that seem minor?** Facts about the world are stored as semantic memories, whereas learned behaviors or skills are stored as procedural memories. The latter types of memories are relatively stable even if an individual has amnesia. Meanwhile, one's experiences are stored throughout the cortex as episodic memories, which are relatively susceptible to memory loss.

Watch *The Basics: Do You Remember When ...?* in the **MyPsychLab video series**

Module 7.2 :: Encoding and Retrieving Memories

Focus Questions:

1 **What causes some memories to be strong, while others are weak?** In general, information that is deeply processed is more likely to be remembered later. Deep processing occurs when a person thinks about the meaning of the information rather than superficial qualities such as the appearance of an object or the sound of a word.

2 **How can we improve our memory abilities?** Researchers have shown that we can remember things better if we apply principles of levels of processing. In addition, we can use a number of mnemonic techniques, such as the method of loci and the first letter technique; these strategies can actually increase the amount of material recalled.

Watch *What's in It for Me?: Making It Stick* in the **MyPsychLab video series**

Module 7.3 :: Constructing and Reconstructing Memories

Focus Questions:

1 **How is it possible to remember events that never happened?** It is remarkably easy to create false memories by taking advantage of the constructive nature of memory. For example, the misinformation effect can combine new information with the original memory to form incorrect memories of how an event unfolded.

2 **Do these false memories represent memory problems, or are they just a normal part of remembering?** False memories do not necessarily arise from memory problems. Instead, they seem to come from normal memory processes that usually serve to make memory more efficient.

Watch *Special Topics: When Memory Fails* in the **MyPsychLab video series**

Watch the complete video series online at **MyPsychLab**

Episode 8: Memory
1. *The Big Picture: The Woman Who Cannot Forget*
2. *The Basics: Do You Remember When ...?*
3. *Special Topics: When Memory Fails*
4. *Thinking Like a Psychologist: Eyewitness Testimony*
5. *In the Real World Application: The Memories We Don't Want*
6. *What's in It for Me?: Making It Stick*

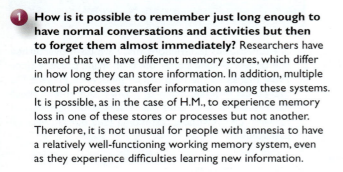

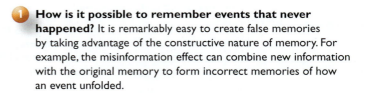

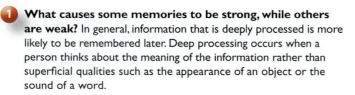

1 Which type of memory can hold information for only a few seconds?

- **A** Semantic memory
- **B** Short-term memory
- **C** Sensory memory
- **D** Long-term memory

2 "About seven" is a famous estimate for:

- **A** the number of memory stores in the human brain.
- **B** the capacity of long-term memory.
- **C** the number of minutes information can stay in short-term memory without rehearsal.
- **D** the capacity of short-term memory span.

3 Latasha remembers visiting Gettysburg on a cloudy day when she was a child. She recalls being bored at the time, but now wishes she had paid more attention. Latasha's memory is an example of a(n)_____ memory.

- **A** episodic
- **B** semantic
- **C** sensory
- **D** nondeclarative

4 Long-term potentiation refers to the ability of neurons to:

- **A** increase their size.
- **B** decrease their size.
- **C** strengthen their signaling with other neurons.
- **D** weaken their signaling with other neurons.

5 Damage to the hippocampus is most likely to lead to the loss of:

- **A** long-term memories that have been consolidated.
- **B** recent short-term memories.
- **C** recent long-term memories that have not yet been consolidated.
- **D** procedural memories.

6 According to the LOP framework, how well we encode long-term information is most directly related to:

- **A** how often we encounter the information.
- **B** how deeply we process the information.
- **C** how long we are exposed to the information.
- **D** how motivated we are to learn the information.

7 Which of the following statements is true about flashbulb memories?

- **A** They are far more accurate than standard memories.
- **B** They are typically no more accurate than standard memories.
- **C** They last for a much shorter period than standard memories.
- **D** They contain fewer details than standard memories.

8 Early research into forgetting by Hermann Ebbinghaus found that forgetting occurs:

- **A** slowly over a long period of time.
- **B** mostly between 12 and 24 hours after the learning event.
- **C** slowly at first, but the rate of forgetting increases over time.
- **D** quickly at first, but the rate of forgetting slows over time.

9 What role are schemas believed to play in memory?

- **A** Schemas store complete memories of events that can be "played back" at will.
- **B** Schemas ensure that memories are highly accurate.
- **C** Schemas organize information so that memories are easier to encode, store, and recall.
- **D** Schemas act as buffers while memories are being consolidated.

10 Terri was mugged one night while she was walking home. Later that same night, a police officer called to tell her that they had arrested a man wearing a red baseball cap who was found in the area. Although Terri's mugger was not wearing a hat when she was mugged, she now recalls the hat when she remembers the mugging. This is an example of the:

- **A** levels of processing effect.
- **B** imagination inflation effect.
- **C** DRM effect.
- **D** misinformation effect.

Work the Scientific Literacy Model :: Understanding How We Remember and Forget

What do we know about the basic processes of memory?

Review **page 250** for the processes involved in memory acquisition and recall. Then review **Figure 7.1 on page 237** for the Atkinson-Shiffrin model of memory storage. Both are important concepts in the chapter, but the details of how they work together can be confusing. Encoding is the process of transforming sensory information into memory, whereas retrieval is the process of accessing and using memory. In addition, there is storage, or how memory is retained after it is encoded. The Atkinson-Shiffrin model organizes these processes as they relate to different types of memory storage—sensory memory, short-term memory (STM), and long-term memory (LTM). Recall that the process of converting short-term memories to lasting memories in the brain is called consolidation; without it, memories cannot become permanent. For example, if an image is encoded to sensory memory, it is stored for a very short time, and then is either forgotten or converted to STM. After it is encoded to STM, the image is stored by way of rehearsal, and then either forgotten or encoded to LTM. Once the image is in long-term memory, the brain will consolidate it and then store the memory for years—maybe even permanently. To see which factors might affect the process of encoding into LTM, you can review the different types of rehearsal on **page 250** and the levels of processing in **Figure 7.12 on page 251**.

How can science help explain how memory works?

Research shows that the hippocampus is crucial to consolidating long-term memories. Support for this idea also comes from outside the laboratory: Binge-drinking has noticeable effects on the hippocampus, which can result in memory loss or blackouts. On **page 247**, we discussed the example of H.M., a man who was unable to form new memories after his hippocampus was surgically removed.

When the structures of the brain are in good working order, the right strategies help us create lasting memories. **Figure 7.11 on page 250** illustrated a study that suggests simple repetition is not as effective as more involved types of rehearsal in creating such memories, and similar research on levels of processing reveals that it is not so much how *long* we try to memorize something, but rather *how* we do so. If thinking about information in a certain way helps us remember something, can feelings about the information do the same? On **page 253**, we mentioned studies that suggest a link between emotions and the quality of memories.

Of course, our memories are not perfect—a point supported by research on the misinformation effect and the DRM paradigm, two procedures used in false memory research.

Why is this relevant?

Watch the accompanying video excerpt on remembering. You can access the video at MyPsychLab or by clicking the play button in the center of your eText. If your instructor assigns this video as a homework activity, you will find additional content to help you in MyPsychLab. You can also view the video by using your smart phone and the QR code below, or you can go to the YouTube link provided.

After you have read the chapter and watched the video, imagine you are reading your textbook and studying for an upcoming exam in psychology. Identify and describe each step in the process required for remembering information from your textbook in order to do well on the exam. Discuss two strategies for improving memory and provide examples of how each could help you on the exam.

Can we critically evaluate claims about memory?

If emotions enhance processing of information, can we completely trust our most vivid and emotional memories? **Myths in Mind on page 254** explored the idea of flashbulb memories. Researchers have found that despite the level of detail involved in memories tied to emotional events, they are ultimately no more accurate than any other type of memories. Similarly, the controversy around recovered memories continues, both because of the difficulty of proving or disproving them and because methods of recovering "lost" memories bear a striking similarity to laboratory experiments that produce false memories.

On a more positive note, **Psych @ Court on page 266** discussed how we can use what we know about the science of memory to improve accuracy in police lineups. A practical application of this chapter's concepts included using what you know about the forgetting curve (**Figure 7.16**) to strategize ways to consolidate memories for easy retrieval when you need them, such as at test time. Using dual-coding in mnemonic strategies, like the method of loci, can aid learning, as can taking your studying beyond basic repetition of information. Finally, on **page 257** we suggested over-learning and creating desirable difficulties to develop a deeper understanding and memory for the material.

MyPsychLab

Your turn to Work the Scientific Literacy Model: You can access the video at MyPsychLab or by clicking the play button in the center of your eText. If your instructor assigns this video as a homework activity, you will find additional content to help you at MyPsychLab. You can also view the video by using your smart phone and the QR code, or you can go to the YouTube link provided.

youtube.com/
scientificliteracy

8 :: THOUGHT AND LANGUAGE

Module
8.1

The Organization of Knowledge

Learning Objectives

After reading this module you should:

KNOW ...	UNDERSTAND ...	APPLY ...	ANALYZE ...
The key terminology associated with concepts and categories	Theories of how people organize their knowledge about the world How experience and culture can shape the way we organize our knowledge	Your knowledge to identify prototypical examples	The claim that the language we speak determines how we think

Your current favorite song is probably the closest approximation of the perfect song for your tastes, but perhaps it could be even better. Maybe there are parts you wish were longer, shorter, or sounded a bit differently. Perhaps your search for the perfect song is not over. Businesses such as Pandora, the Internet radio service, are certainly motivated to lead you to it.

Each of us has a unique concept of what constitutes good music. Recognizing this fact, Pandora has embarked on what it has called the Music Genome Project. In Module 3.1 you read about the Human Genome Project—the decade-long effort to sequence all human genes. The Music Genome Project is a collection of the bits and pieces that make up all of the 800,000-plus songs in its database. Pandora is gathering information about which songs individual listeners play and which ones they block, and then uses a computerized algorithm (a set of rules) to identify a personalized profile for the listener's music tastes (Walker, 2009). In doing so, the company is basically decoding the unique "musical genome" of each listener to determine his or her concept of the perfect song. This is certainly more informative to the individual than the "Top 20 list." The psychological relevance of the Music Genome

Project lies in its recognition that each individual has a unique concept of good music. Concepts and categories are the basis of many of our thought processes. They also reveal unique ways in which individuals and different cultural groups think.

Focus Questions

 How do people form easily recognizable categories from complex information?

 How does culture influence the ways in which we categorize information?

• • • • • • • • • • • • • • • • • • •

Each of us has amassed a tremendous amount of knowledge in the course of our lifetimes. Indeed, it is impossible to put a number on just how many facts each of us knows. Imagine trying to record everything you ever learned about the world—how many books could you fill? Instead of asking how much we know, psychologists are interested in how we keep track of it all. In this module, we will explore what those processes are like and how they work. We will start by learning about the key terminology before presenting theories about how knowledge is stored over the long term.

Concepts and Categories

Concepts and categories are used for memory, decision making, language, and so on; in other words, cognition would not be possible without them. A **concept** *is the mental representation of an object, event, or idea.* As it happens, there are very few independent concepts. You do not have just one concept for *chair*, one for *table*, and one for *sofa*. Instead, each of these concepts can be divided into smaller groups with more precise labels, such as *arm chair* or *coffee table*. Similarly, all of these items can be lumped together under the single label, *furniture*. Psychologists use the term **categories** *to refer to these clusters of interrelated concepts.* We form these groups using a process called *categorization*.

CLASSICAL CATEGORIES: DEFINITIONS AND RULES The earliest approach to the study of categories is referred to as **classical categorization**; *this theory claims that objects or events are categorized according to a certain set of rules or by a specific set of features*—something similar to a dictionary definition (Lakoff & Johnson, 1999; Rouder & Ratcliffe, 2006). Definitions do a fine job of explaining how people categorize items in certain situations. For example, a triangle can be defined as "a figure (usually, a plane rectilinear figure) having three angles and three sides" (*Oxford English Dictionary*, 2011). Using that definition, you should find it easy to categorize the triangles in Figure 8.1.

Classical categorization does not tell the full story of how categorization works. Actually we use a variety of cognitive processes in determining which objects fit which category. One of the major problems we confront in this process is **graded membership**—*the observation that some concepts appear to make better category members than others.* For example, see if the definition in Table 8.1 fits your definition of *bird* and then categorize the items in the table.

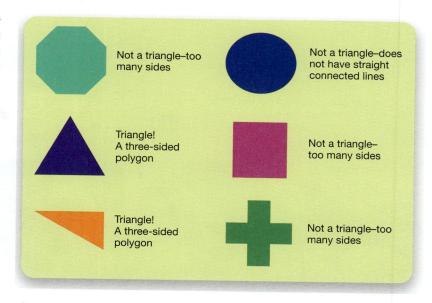

{FIG. 8.1} **Using the Definition of a Triangle to Categorize Shapes**

Ideally, you said yes to the sparrow and penguin, and no to the apple. But did you notice any difference in how you responded to the sparrow and penguin? Psychologists have researched classical categorization using a behavioral measure known as the *sentence-verification technique*, where volunteers wait for a sentence to appear in front of them on a computer screen and respond as fast as they can with a yes or no answer to statements such as *A sparrow is a bird*, or, *A penguin is a bird*. The choice the subject makes, as well as his reaction time to respond, are measured by the researcher. Sentence-verification shows us that some members of a category are recognized faster than others (Olson et al., 2004; Rosch & Mervis, 1975). In other words, subjects almost always answer "yes" faster to sparrow than to penguin. This seems to go against a classical, rule-based categorization system because both sparrows and penguins are equally good fits for the definition, but sparrows are somehow more bird-like than penguins. Thus a modern approach to categorization must explain how "best examples" influence how we categorize items.

PROTOTYPES: CATEGORIZATION BY COMPARISON When you hear the word *bird*, what mental image comes to mind? Does it resemble an ostrich? Or is your

PsychTutor

Click here in your eText for an interactive tutorial on **Conceptual Structure**

Table 8.1 :: Categorizing Objects According to the Definition of *Bird*

Definition: Any of the class Aves of warm-blooded, egg-laying, feathered vertebrates with forelimbs modified to form wings. (American Heritage Dictionary, 2007)

Now categorize a set of items by answering *yes* or *no* regarding the truth of the following sentences.
1. A sparrow is a bird.
2. An apple is a bird.
3. A penguin is a bird.

A prototypical bird might look something like this one on the right.

It combines features of actual birds, such as those below.

{FIG. 8.2} **A Prototypical Bird** Click on this figure in your eText to see more details.

image closer to a robin, sparrow, or blue jay? The likely image that comes to mind at the suggestion to imagine a bird is what psychologists call a prototype (see Figure 8.2). **Prototypes** *are mental representations of an average category member* (Rosch, 1973). If you took an average of the three most familiar birds, you would get a prototypical bird.

Prototypes allow for classification by resemblance. When you encounter a little creature you have never seen before, its basic shape—maybe just its silhouette—can be compared to your prototype of a bird. A match will then be made and you can classify the creature as a bird. Notice how different this process is from classical categorization: No rules or definitions are involved, just a set of similarities in overall shape and function.

The main advantage of prototypes is that they help explain why some category members make better examples than others. Ostriches are birds just as much as blue jays, but they do not resemble the rest of the family very well. In other words, blue jays are closer to the prototypical bird.

Now that you have read about categories based on a set of rules or characteristics (classical categories) and as a

general comparison based on resemblances (prototypes), you might wonder which approach is correct. Research says that we can follow either approach—the choice really depends on how complicated a category or a specific example might be. If there are a few major distinctions between items, we use resemblance; if there are complications, we switch to rules (Feldman, 2003; Rouder & Ratcliff, 2004, 2006). For example, in the case of seeing a bat dart by, your first impression might be "bird" because it resembles a bird. But if you investigated further, you will see that a bat fits the classical description of a mammal, not a bird. In other words, it has hair, gives live birth rather than lays eggs, and so on.

NETWORKS AND HIERARCHIES The connections among ideas can be represented in a network diagram. A **semantic network** *is an interconnected set of nodes (or concepts) and the links that join them to form a category* (see Figure 8.3). *Nodes* are circles that represent concepts, and *links* connect them together to represent the structure of a category as well as the relationships among different categories (Collins & Loftus, 1975).

Something you may notice about Figure 8.3 is that it is arranged in a *hierarchy*—that is, it consists of a structure moving from general to very specific. This organization helps us understand how categories work in daily thought and language by identifying the *basic*

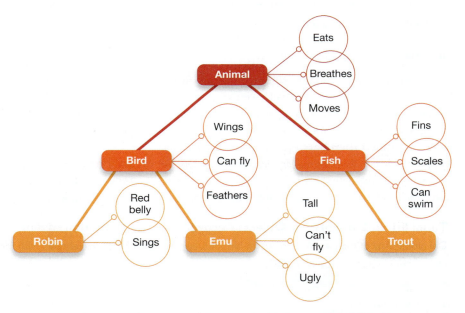

{FIG. 8.3} **A Semantic Network Diagram for the Category "Animal"** The nodes include the basic-level categories, *Birds* and *Fish*. Another node represents the broader category of *Animals,* while the lowest three nodes represent the more specific categories of *Robins*, *Emus*, and *Trout*.

level category, which is located in the middle row of the diagram (where birds and fish are) (Johnson & Mervis, 1997; Rosch et al., 1976). A number of qualities make the basic level category unique:

- Basic level categories are the terms used most often in conversation.
- They are the easiest to pronounce.
- They are the level at which prototypes exist.
- They are the level at which most thinking occurs.

To get a sense for how different category levels influence our thinking, we can compare sentences referring to an object at different levels. Consider what would happen if someone approached you and made any one of the following statements:

- "There's an *animal* in your yard."
- "There's a *bird* in your yard."
- "There's a *robin* in your yard."
- "There's an *emu* in your yard."

The second sentence—"There's a bird in your yard"— is probably the one you are most likely to hear, and it makes reference to a basic level of a category (birds). Many people would respond that the choice of *animal* as a label indicates confusion, claiming that if the speaker knew it was a *bird*, he should have said so; otherwise, it sounds like he is trying to figure out which kind of animal he is looking at. When the speaker identifies a *robin*, it suggests that there is something special about this particular robin. By comparison, when a non-prototypical example is given, it suggests a specific question: *What the heck is an emu doing here?*

Here is an easy test generated by the animal network in Figure 8.3. If you were asked to react to dozens of sentences, and the following two sentences were included among them, which do you think you would mark as "true" the fastest?

- *A robin is a bird.*
- *A robin is an animal.*

As you can see in the network diagram, *robin* and *bird* are closer together; in fact, to connect *robin* to *animal*, you must first go through *bird*. Sure enough, people regard the sentence "A robin is a bird" as a true statement faster than "A robin is an animal."

Now consider another set of examples. Which trait do you think you would verify faster?

- *A robin has wings.*
- *A robin eats.*

Using the connecting lines as we did before, we can predict that it would be the first statement about wings. As research shows, our guess would be correct.

We store thousands upon thousands of concepts and categories in long-term memory, but it is not likely that each of those individual ideas floats around our memory on its own. Instead, concepts and categories are interconnected in vast networks of information.

What do we know about semantic networks?

As you have read, psychologists refer to the millions of associations that connect our concepts and categories as *semantic networks.* You have probably noticed these connections because once you encounter one aspect of a category, related concepts seem to come to mind more easily. Hearing the word "fruit," for example, might lead you to think of an apple, and the apple may lead you to think of a computer, which may lead you to think of a paper that is due tomorrow. These associations illustrate the concept of **priming**—*the activation of individual concepts in long-term memory.*

Priming may cause you to become aware of a related concept, such as when the word "fruit" primes the concept of an apple. At other times, priming just makes you more sensitive to specific concepts without actually becoming aware of them. Even though "fruit" may not lead you to think about a watermelon, for instance, the concept of a watermelon may have been primed nonetheless.

How can science explain priming effects?

Psychologists can test for priming through reaction time measures such as the sentence verification tasks discussed earlier or through a method called the *lexical decision task.* With the lexical decision method, a volunteer sits at a computer and stares at a focal point. Next, a string of letters flashes on the screen. The volunteer responds yes or no as quickly as possible to indicate whether the letters spell a word (see Figure 8.4 on p. 276). Using this method, a volunteer should respond faster that "apple" is a word if it follows the word "fruit" than if it follows the word "bus."

Given that lexical decision tasks are highly controlled experiments, we might wonder if they have any impact outside of the laboratory. One test by Jennifer Coane suggests

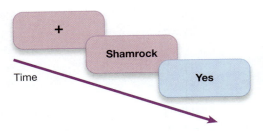

{FIG. 8.4} **A Lexical Decision Task** In a lexical decision task, an individual watches a computer screen as strings of letters are flashed on the screen. The subject must respond as quickly as possible to indicate whether the letters spell a word.

that priming does occur in everyday life (Coane & Balota, 2009). Coane's research team invited volunteers to participate in lexical decision tasks about holidays at different times of the year. The words they chose were based on the holiday season at that time. Sure enough, without any laboratory priming, words such as "nutcracker" and "reindeer" showed priming effects at times when they were *congruent* (or "in season") in December, relative to other times of the year (see Figure 8.5). Similarly, words like "leprechaun" and "shamrock" showed a priming effect during the month of March. Because the researchers did not instigate the priming, it must have been the holiday spirit at work: Decorations and advertisements must serve as constant primes.

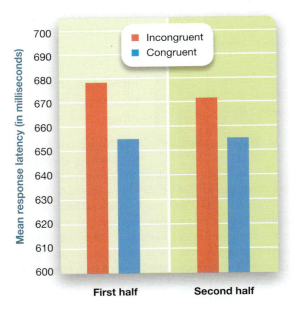

{FIG. 8.5} **Priming Affects the Speed of Responses on a Lexical Decision Task** Average response times were faster when the holiday-themed words were *congruent* (in season), as represented by the blue bars. This finding is consistent for both the first half and second half of the list of words.

Can we critically evaluate this information?

It is important not to generalize the concepts of priming too far, because it might start to seem as if our thoughts are too easily controlled by outside influence. Priming certainly does lead us to think about relatively specific things, and perhaps initiates a chain of associations. It can also elicit emotional reactions. However, those chains of associations appear to be somewhat unique for each of us, and we can typically redirect our attention to something else. For example, an American flag might make you more likely to think of U.S. themes and ideas—but it alone will not cause you to enlist in the military. In short, having a thought activated is not the same as having your thoughts controlled.

Why is this relevant?

Priming effects, while very common, range from subtle to very robust. For example, if you have a birthday that has a month and day that can overlap with a possible time of day (e.g., June 19, or 6:19), you will likely notice it each time you happen to check the clock at 6:19. This will likely catch your attention more so than 6:20 or 7:19. At the more robust end of the spectrum, all kinds of symbols are designed to prime specific thoughts. Yellow ribbons are meant to prime us to think about the military serving overseas, and pink ribbons have become primes to think about breast cancer research. The effects of priming are also evident during political elections. Campaigns for candidates as well as news media outlets use emotional imagery and language to influence voter attitudes and emotions (Miller & Krosnick, 1996).

Quick Quiz 8.1a
Concepts and Categories

KNOW...

1 A _____ is a mental representation of an average member of a category.

A basic level category   **C** similarity principle

B prototype   **D** network

2 _____ refer to mental representations of objects, events, or ideas.

A Categories   **C** Primings

B Concepts   **D** Networks

UNDERSTAND...

3 Classical categorization approaches do not account for _____, a type of categorization that notes some items make better category members than others.

A basic level categorization

B prototyping

C priming

D graded membership

APPLY...

4 In a research study, Ashley participated in a sentence verification technique. How she categorized information in this study was measured by:

A how quickly she responded that a sentence was true or false.

B whether she liked the to-be-categorized stimuli.

C how consistent her responses were with other members of her culture.

D how well she was able to read the questions aloud.

Answers can be found on page ANS-3.

Culture and Categories

The human brain is wired to perceive similarities and differences and, as we learned from prototypes, the end result of this tendency is to categorize items based on these comparisons. However, our natural tendency to do so interacts with our cultural experiences; how we categorize objects depends to a great extent on what we have learned about those objects from others in our culture.

Various researchers have explored the relationships between culture and categorization by studying basic level categories among people from different cultural backgrounds. For example, researchers have asked individuals from traditional villages to identify a variety of plants and animals that are extremely relevant to their diet, medicine, safety, and other aspects of

their lives. Not surprisingly, these individuals referred to plants and animals at a more specific level than U.S. college students would (Bailenson et al., 2002; Berlin, 1974). Thus categorization is based—at least to some extent—on cultural learning. Psychologists have also discovered that cultural factors influence not just how we categorize individual objects, but also how objects in our world relate to one another.

BIOPSYCHOSOCIAL PERSPECTIVES
Culture and Categorical Thinking

Animals, relatives, household appliances, colors, and other entities all fall into categories. However, people from different cultures might differ in how they categorize such objects. In North America, cows are sometimes referred to as "livestock" or "food animals," whereas in India, where cows are regarded as sacred, neither category would apply.

In addition, how objects are *related* to each other differs considerably across cultures. Which of the two photos in Figure 8.6a do you think an American took? Researchers asked both American and Japanese university students to take a picture of someone, from whatever angle or degree of focus they chose. American students were more likely to take close-up pictures, whereas Japanese students typically included surrounding objects (Nisbett & Masuda, 2003). When asked which two objects go together in Figure 8.6b, American college students tend to group cows with chickens—because both are animals. In contrast, Japanese students coupled cows with grass, because grass is what cows eat (Gutchess et al., 2010; Nisbett & Masuda, 2003). These examples demonstrate cross-cultural differences in perceiving how objects are related to their environments. People raised in the United States tend to focus on a single characteristic, whereas Japanese people tend to view objects in relation to their environment.

(a)   (b)

{FIG. 8.6} **Your Culture and Your Point of View** (a) Which of these two pictures do you think a North American would be more likely to take? (b) Which two go together?

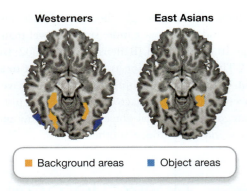

Westerners   **East Asians**

■ Background areas   ■ Object areas

{FIG. 8.7} **Brain Activity Varies by Culture** Brain regions that are involved in object recognition and processing are activated differently in people from Western and Eastern cultures. Brain regions that are involved in processing individual objects are more highly activated when Westerners view focal objects against background scenery, whereas people from East Asian countries appear to attend to background scenery more closely than focal objects.

Researchers have even found differences in brain function when people of different cultural backgrounds view and categorize objects (Park & Huang, 2010). Figure 8.7 reveals differences in brain activity when Westerners and East Asians view photos of objects, such as an animal, against a background of grass and trees. Areas of the brain devoted to processing both objects and background become activated when Westerners view these photos, whereas only areas devoted to background processes become activated in East Asians (Goh et al., 2007). These findings demonstrate that a complete understanding of how humans categorize objects requires application of the biopsychosocial model.

· · · · · · · · · · · · · · · · · · ·

Cultural differences in how people think and categorize items have also led to the idea of **linguistic relativity** (or the **Whorfian hypothesis**)—*the theory that the language we encounter and use determines how we understand the world.* The concept of linguistic relativity was first introduced by Benjamin Whorf. Working as a chemist, Whorf was charged with investigating fires for an insurance company, but in his spare time he became an accomplished linguist. These two interests merged on one occasion when he was investigating the source of a fire at a chemical plant. An employee reported to him that he had tossed a cigarette butt by a gasoline barrel, not suspecting a fire hazard because the barrel was among a group of barrels labeled as *empty*. Of course, what *empty* meant is that the barrel was no longer full in a useful way; in other words, there was not a usable amount of gasoline in it. However, the worker took "empty" in its dictionary sense, assuming that there was absolutely no gasoline in the barrel. Based on the language, the worker failed to notice the fire hazard (Whorf, 1973).

To support the Whorfian hypothesis, evidence would have to show that people from different cultures not only speak differently about the same categories, but think, remember, and behave differently regarding those categories. This idea has been explored in a number of ways and with mixed results. For example, the English language has several color names, such as *black, white, red, blue, green, yellow, purple, orange,* and *pink.* If speakers want to be more specific, they use some combination of other terms, such as *blue-green* or *sky-blue.* By comparison, some cultures have fewer dedicated color words; the Dani people of New Guinea, for example, have one word for blue-green, but no words to distinguish what English speakers consider to be prototypically blue or prototypically green. Do these language differences affect the way individuals categorize and remember colors?

The results of research in this area are mixed. When dividing color samples, similar to what you would find when shopping for paint, English speakers set aside different stacks of cards for samples that seemed more blue and those that seemed more green. In contrast, the Dani included those same samples in one larger blue-green category (Roberson et al., 2000). However, subsequent research has not been able to clarify whether this effect occurred because the language differences led the subjects to actually perceive color differently (true linguistic relativity) or if they were just using language as a means to complete the sorting task. For example, when individuals were asked to use a verbal distracter (producing irrelevant speech), it prevented them from using the color terms for the sorting task. In that case, there are no differences between cultures (Roberson & Davidoff, 2000).

MYTHS IN MIND
How Many Words for Snow?

From time to time, people repeat a bit of "wisdom" about how language relates to thinking. One often-cited example is about the Inuit Eskimos, who are thought to have many words for snow, each with a different meaning. For example, *aput* means snow that is on the ground, and *gana* means falling snow. This observation, which was made in the early 19th century by anthropologist Franz Boas, was often repeated and exaggerated upon with claims that Inuit people had dozens of words for different types of snow. With so many words for snow, it was thought that perhaps the Inuit people perceive snow differently than someone who does not live near it year-round. Scholars used the example to argue that language determines how people categorize the world.

Inuit Eskimos do have multiple words for snow, but so do a lot of other cultures.

Research tells us that we must be careful in over-generalizing the influence of language on categorization. The reality is that Inuits seem to categorize snow the same way a person from the United States does. Someone from Nebraska can tell the difference between falling snow, blowing snow, sticky snow, drifting snow, and so on, just as well as an Inuit who lives with snow year-round (Martin, 1986). Therefore, we see that the linguistic relativity hypothesis is incorrect in this case: The difference in vocabulary for snow does not lead to differences in perception.

• • • • • • • • • • • • • • • • • • •

Quick Quiz 8.1b
Culture and Categories

KNOW...

1 The idea that our language influences how we understand the world is referred to as _____.

  A context specificity
  B sentence verification
  C linguistic relativity
  D priming

ANALYZE...

2 Research on linguistic relativity suggests that:

  A language has a complete control over how people categorize the world.
  B language can have some effects on categorization, but the effects are limited.
  C language has no effect on categorization.
  D researchers have not addressed this question.

Answers can be found on page ANS-3.

Module Summary

Module 8.1

Now that you have read this module you should:

Listen to the audio file of this module at MyPsychLab

KNOW ...

- **The key terminology associated with concepts and categories:**

categories (p. 273)
classical categorization (p. 273)
concept (p. 273)
graded membership (p. 273)
linguistic relativity (Whorfian hypothesis) (p. 278)

priming (p. 275)
prototypes (p. 274)
semantic network (p. 274)

UNDERSTAND ...

- **Theories of how people organize their knowledge about the world.** First, certain objects and events are more likely to be associated in clusters. The priming effect demonstrates this phenomenon; for example, hearing the word "fruit" makes it more likely that you will think of "apple" than, say, "table." More specifically, we organize our knowledge about the world through semantic networks, which arrange categories from general to specific levels. Usually we think in terms of basic level categories, but under some circumstances we can be either more or less specific.

- **How experience and culture can shape the way we organize our knowledge.** One of many possible examples of this influence was discussed. Specifically, ideas of how objects relate to one another differ between people from North America and people from Eastern Asia. People from North America (and Westerners in general) tend to focus on individual, focal objects in a scene, whereas people from Japan tend to focus on how objects are interrelated.

APPLY ...

- **Your knowledge to identify prototypical examples.** Try the following questions for practice (check your answers on page ANS-3):

  1. What is the best example for the category of fish: a hammerhead shark, a trout, or an eel?

  2. What do you consider to be a prototypical sport? Why?

  3. Some categories are created spontaneously, yet still have prototypes. For example, what might be a prototypical object for the category "what to save if your house is on fire"?

ANALYZE ...

- **The claim that the language we speak determines how we think.** Researchers have shown that language can influence the way we think, but it cannot entirely shape how we perceive the world. For example, people can categorize colors even if they do not have specific words for them.

Problem Solving, Judgment, and Decision Making

Learning Objectives	KNOW ...	UNDERSTAND ...	APPLY ...	ANALYZE ...
After reading this module you should:	The key terminology of problem solving and decision making	The characteristics that problems have in common How obstacles to problem solving are often self-imposed	Your knowledge to determine if you tend to be a maximizer or a satisficer	Whether human thought is primarily logical or intuitive

It would seem that one of the greatest benefits of living in a highly technological society is the luxury of choice. We have massive stores filled with all kinds of goods from which to make our selections. For each particular product we might be interested in purchasing, there may be a half-dozen brands, each with seemingly endless permutations of features and designs.

Psychological science has shown that the *luxury* of choice might actually be better described as a *burden*. Barry Schwartz and his colleagues have found that the more choices you have for a product, the less likely you are to be satisfied with your decision. Further, they have found that individuals who regularly strive for perfection in their decisions— *maximizers,* as they are called—are generally less satisfied than people who simply try to find what is good enough to suit their purposes.

Focus Questions

1. How do people make decisions and solve problems?

2. How can having multiple options lead people to be dissatisfied with their decisions?

· · · · · · · · · · · · · · · · ·

Problems and decisions are everywhere. Some decisions are as simple as figuring out which pair of socks to wear, whereas others can be life-defining experiences, such as deciding which career to pursue and who would make a suitable life partner. Psychologists are interested in how all of these decisions are made, but scientific research on problems and decisions focuses largely on the intuitive aspects of thought and the often counterintuitive results they produce.

Defining and Solving Problems

You are certainly familiar with the general concept of a problem, but in psychological terminology, **problem solving** *means accomplishing a goal when the solution or the path to the solution is not clear* (Leighton & Sternberg, 2003; Robertson, 2001). Despite how different individual problems may seem, they all share some key components, and we attempt to solve them in predictable ways.

STATES AND STAGES   Problems are often very recognizable—you know them when you see them—but a description of a problem's three main features allows us to study them in more detail. The *initial state* describes what the condition is at the outset of a problem, and the *goal state* describes what you need or desire as an outcome. Sometimes getting to the goal state is easy, but at other times it can require you to overcome *obstacles*—that is, something that slows or prevents progress toward the goal state. With those three features in place, it is up to you, the problem-solver, to figure out how to overcome the obstacles to reach the goal. The techniques we use to reach the goal state are called *operators*.

You are already aware that there are easy problems and there are hard problems, but it is also important to consider how well a problem is *defined*. A **well-defined problem** *is a problem that has a clear initial state and goal state*, such as the example in Table 8.2. If you know that you are feeling chilly and that a sweater will help, then you can solve your problem rather easily. In contrast, an **ill-defined problem** *is a problem that may be lacking definition in one or more ways, such as an ambiguous initial state or a lack of familiar operators*. In Table 8.2, the ill-defined problem does not have a definite goal state. You could have decided to write about any number of topics, so how did you decide what the goal state was? This problem may become even more abstract if you think about

ill-defined problems such as composing a piece of music or writing a novel. How would you know when the work is done?

PROBLEM-SOLVING STRATEGIES AND TECHNIQUES   Given the number of problems a person could face, there are an infinite number of possible solutions. How do we remember the operators we can use for routine problems? How do we develop operators for nonroutine problems? Although these questions *appear* as if they could have an infinite number of answers, there seem to be only a few basic strategies that we use time and again.

Most theories of cognition describe two general types of thought: One is more objective, logical, and slower, whereas the other is more subjective, intuitive, and quicker (Gilovich & Griffin, 2002; Holyoak & Morrison, 2005). Suppose you are unsure as to whether you would like to accept an invitation for a dinner date. A logical approach might involve listing out the positive and negative attributes of this person before making a decision. An intuitive approach might involve imagining what the date would be like, whether it would be fun or interesting, and using this vision as a guide for the decision.

When we think logically, we rely on **algorithms**, *which are problem-solving strategies based on a series of rules*. As such, they are very logical and follow a set of steps, usually in a preset order. Computers are very good at using algorithms because they can follow a preprogrammed set of steps and perform thousands of operations every second. People, however, are not always so careful. We humans tend to rely on intuition to find operators and solutions that "just seem right." These are called **heuristics**: *problem-solving strategies that stem from prior experiences and provide an educated guess as to what is the most likely solution*. In the example of whether you would like to accept a dinner invitation, the intuitive approach usually makes the most sense.

Certain problems call for different approaches. To further compare algorithms and heuristics, let us

Table 8.2 :: Well-Defined and Ill-Defined Problems

PROBLEM DEFINITION	INITIAL STATE	OPERATOR	GOAL STATE
Well-defined	I'm cold.	Put on a sweater.	I'm comfortable.
Ill-defined	I need to think of a topic for my term paper.	Flip through your favorite chapter in the textbook to find what interests you.	I'm going to write about culture and language.

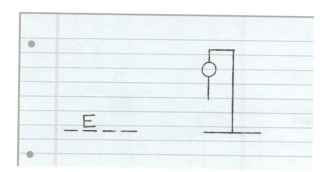

{FIG. 8.8} **Problem Solving in Hangman** In a game of hangman, your job is to guess the letters in the word represented by the four blanks to the left. If you get a letter right, your opponent will put it in the correct blank. If you guess an incorrect letter, your opponent will draw a body part on the stick figure. The goal is to guess the word before the entire body is drawn.

examine a problem with relatively simple strategies and low risk. Think about how you might play the children's word-game known as hangman, shown in Figure 8.8. Here, the goal state is to spell a word. In the initial state, you have none of the letters or other clues to guide you. So your obstacles are to overcome blanks without guessing the wrong letters. How would you go about selecting operators?

On one hand, an algorithm might go like this: Guess the letter *A*, then *B*, then *C*, and so on through the alphabet until you lose or until the word is spelled. However, this would not be a very successful approach. An alternative algorithm would be to find out how frequently each letter occurs in the alphabet and then guess the letters in that order until the game ends with you winning or losing. (According to the *Oxford English Dictionary*, *E* is most frequent, *A* is second most frequent, then *R*, *I*, and so on [OED, 2011.]) On the other hand, a heuristic might be useful. For example, if you discover the last letter is *G*, you might guess that the next-to-last letter is *N*, because you know that many words end with *-ing*.

As you can see, some problems (such as the hangman game) can be approached with either algorithms or heuristics. In other words, most people start out a game like hangman with an algorithm: Guess the most frequent letters until a recognizable pattern emerges, such as *-ing*, or the letters *-oug* (which are often followed by *h*, as in *tough* or *cough*) appear. At that point, you might switch to heuristics and guess which words would be most likely to fit in the spaces.

COGNITIVE OBSTACLES Imagine that you need to climb over the Great Wall of China but you have no rope. This formidable barrier represents an obstacle

to solving the problem. However, when it comes to solving problems, the obstacles standing in your way may not be entirely inherent to the problem. Instead, these obstacles may be based on how you are thinking or approaching a problem. Such cognitive obstacles are more difficult to identify than simply pointing out that one lacks a rope long enough to scale the Great Wall of China. If you believe that climbing a wall requires rope, and you have none, you will forever be on the wrong side. Conversely, if you entertain other possibilities, such as using vines or fallen logs to facilitate the process, you can overcome mental obstacles to problem solving.

Some of the simplest (and maybe most frustrating) forms of cognitive obstacles are self-imposed. The nine-dot problem (Figure 8.9; Maier, 1930) is a good example. The goal is to connect all nine dots using only four straight lines and without lifting your pen or pencil off the paper. Try solving the nine-dot problem before you read further.

Here is something to think about when solving this problem: Most people impose limitations on where the lines can go, even though those limits are not a part of the rules. An explanation of the self-imposed limitation can be found with the solution to the nine-dot problem (see Figure 8.10 on p. 284).

Having a routine solution available for a problem can be great. Sometimes, however, routines may impose cognitive barriers that impede solving a problem if circumstances change such that the routine solution no longer works. A **mental set** *is a cognitive obstacle that occurs when an individual attempts to apply a routine solution to what is actually a new type of problem.* A mental set can also occur when an individual applies a routine solution when a much easier solution is possible.

PsychTutor
Click here in your eText for an interactive tutorial on **Heuristics**

{FIG. 8.9} **The Nine-Dot Problem** Connect all nine dots using only four straight lines and without lifting your pen or pencil (Maier, 1930). The solution to the problem can be seen on page 284 (Figure 8.10).

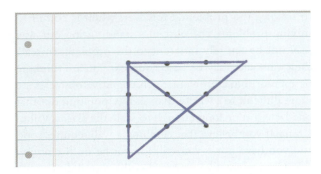

{FIG. 8.10}   **One Solution to the Nine-Dot Problem** In this case, the tendency is to see the outer edge of dots as a boundary, and to assume that one cannot go past that boundary. However, if you are willing to extend some of the lines beyond the dots, it is actually quite a simple puzzle to complete.

{FIG. 8.12}   **The Two-String Problem** Imagine you are standing between two strings and need to tie them together. The only problem is that you cannot reach both strings at the same time (Maier, 1931). In the room with you is a table, a piece of paper, a pair of pliers, and a ball of cotton. What do you do? For a solution, see Figure 8.14 on page 286. **Click on this figure in your eText to see more details.**

Figure 8.11 presents a problem that often elicits a mental set. The answer appears at the bottom of the page, but make your guess before you check it. Did you get it right? If not, then you probably succumbed to mental set. See if you can identify the qualities of the problem that put you into a mental set. If you got the solution right this first time, congratulations! It might be interesting to try this problem on a friend to see if he or she gets caught off guard.

In some situations, a person experiences **functional fixedness**, *which occurs when an individual identifies a potential operator, but can think of only its most obvious function.* For example, Figure 8.12 shows two strings hanging from a ceiling. Imagine you are asked to tie

the strings together. However, once you grab a string, you cannot let go of it until both are tied together. The problem is, unless you have extraordinarily long arms, you cannot reach the second string while you are holding on to the first one (Maier, 1931). So how would you solve the problem? Figure 8.14 on p. 286 offers one possible answer and an explanation of what makes this problem challenging.

Problem solving shows up in every aspect of life, but as you can see, there are basic cognitive processes that appear no matter what the context. We identify initial and goal states, try to determine the best operators, and hope that we do not get caught by unexpected obstacles—especially those we create on our own.

Lala

Lela

Lila

Lola

{FIG. 8.11}   **The Five Daughter Problem** Maria's father has five daughters: Lala, Lela, Lila, and Lola. What is the fifth daughter's name?

Quick Quiz 8.2a
Defining and Solving Problems

KNOW …

1 _____ are problem-solving strategies that provide a reasonable guess for the solution.

A Algorithms   **C** Operators

B Heuristics   **D** Subgoals

2 Steps taken toward reaching the solution of a problem are called _____.

A goal states   **C** operators

B initial states   **D** algorithms

UNDERSTAND …

3 Most problems begin at the _____ and end at the _____.

A algorithm; heuristic   **C** initial state; operator

B initial state; goal state   **D** goal state; initial state

4 When a writer or artist sits down to begin a new piece of work, the creator does not know what it will sound like when it is finished. This is a(n) _____.

A ill-defined problem   **C** algorithm

B well-defined problem   **D** operator state

Answers can be found on page ANS-3.

Judgment and Decision Making

Like problem solving, judgments and decisions can be based on logical algorithms, intuitive heuristics, or a combination of the two types of thought (Gilovich & Griffin, 2002; Holyoak & Morrison, 2005). We tend to use heuristics more often than we realize, even those of us who consider ourselves to be logical thinkers. Here we look more closely at specific types of heuristics and consider how they influence our process of making judgments and decisions.

REPRESENTATIVENESS AND AVAILABILITY One way to illustrate the two types of thought is to examine how individuals make judgments about probabilities and frequencies. For an example, try this problem before reading any further:

> *Linda is 31 years old, single, outspoken, and very bright. She majored in philosophy. As a student, she was deeply concerned with issues of discrimination and social justice, and also participated in antinuclear demonstrations. Which is more likely?*

(A) *Linda is a bank teller.*

(B) *Linda is a bank teller and is active in the feminist movement.*

So which one did you choose? In a study that presented this problem to participants, the researchers report that (B)

was chosen more than 80% of the time. If you chose (B), then you probably do not see anything wrong with the choice, although (A) is actually more likely and would be the correct choice, based on the question asked (Tversky & Kahneman, 1982).

So how is the correct answer (A)? Individuals who approach this problem from the stance of probability theory would apply some simple logical steps. The world has a certain number of (A) bank tellers; this number would be considered the *base rate*, or the rate at which you would find a bank teller in the world's population just by pulling a name out of a hat at random. Among the base group, there will be a certain number of (B) bank tellers who are feminists, as shown in Figure 8.13. In other words, there are many more bank tellers in general than bank tellers who are feminists. As you can see, the heuristic thinking leads people to ignore the base rate of bank tellers in the population. This type of error, known as the *conjunction fallacy*, reflects the mistaken belief that finding a specific member in two overlapping categories (i.e., a member of the *conjunction* of two categories) is more likely than finding any member of one of the larger, general categories.

The conjunction fallacy demonstrates the use of the **representativeness heuristic**: *making judgments of likelihood based on how well an example represents a specific category*. In the bank teller example, we cannot identify any traits that seem like a typical bank teller. At the same time, the traits of social activism really do seem to represent a feminist. Thus the judgment was based on representativeness.

Seeing this type of problem has led many people to question what is wrong with human thought: Why is it so easy to get 80% of the people in a study to give the

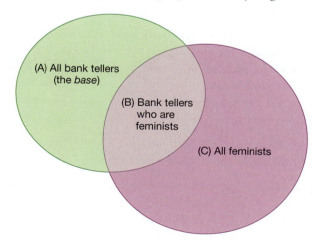

{FIG. 8.13} **The Conjunction Fallacy** There are more bank tellers in the world than there are bank tellers who are feminists, so there is a greater chance that Linda comes from either (A) or (B) than just (B) alone.

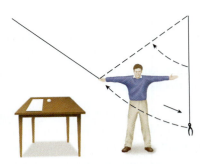

{FIG. 8.14} **A Solution to the Two-String Problem** One solution to the two-string problem from page 284 is to take the pliers off the table and tie them to one string. This provides enough weight to swing one string back and forth while you grab the other. Many people demonstrate functional fixedness when they approach this problem—they do not think of using the pliers as a weight because its normal function is as a grasping tool.

wrong answer? In fact, there is nothing inherently *wrong* with using heuristics; they simply allow individuals to obtain quick answers based on readily available information.

Consider this scenario:

You are in a department store trying to find a product that is apparently sold out. At the end of the aisle, you see a young man in tan pants with a red polo shirt—the typical employee's uniform of this chain of stores. Should you stop and consider the probabilities yielding an answer that was technically most correct?

(A) *A young male of this age would wear tan pants and a red polo shirt.*
(B) *A young male of this age would wear tan pants and a red polo shirt and work at this store.*

Or does it make sense to just assume (B) is correct, and to simply ask the young man for help (Shepperd & Koch, 2005)? In this case, it would make perfect sense to assume (B) is correct and not spend time wondering about the best logical way to approach the situation.

The **availability heuristic** *entails estimating the frequency of an event based on how easily examples of it come to mind.* In other words, we assume that if examples are readily *available,* then they must be very frequent. For example, researchers asked volunteers which was more frequent in the English language:

(A) Words that begin with the letter *K*
(B) Words that have *K* as the third letter

Most subjects chose (A) even though it is not the correct choice. The same thing happened with the consonants *L, N, R,* and *V,* all of which appear as the third letter in a word more often than they appear as the first letter (Tversky & Kahneman, 1973). This outcome reflects the application of the availability heuristic: People base judgments on the information most readily available.

Of course, heuristics often do produce correct answers. Subjects in the same study were asked which was more common in English:

(A) Words that begin with the letter *K*
(B) Words that begin with the letter *T*

In this case, more subjects found that words beginning with T were readily available to memory, and they were correct. The heuristic helped provide a quick intuitive answer.

There are numerous real-world examples of the availability heuristic. Most of us can think of examples of police brutality, kidnapping, and terrorist attacks—these are events that easily come to mind. However, we are also likely to overestimate the risks of each of these events, in part because it is easier to think of examples of these events than to think of all of the times they did *not* occur.

ANCHORING EFFECTS Some heuristics are based on how problems are presented. Issues such as wording, the variety of multiple-choice options, and frames of reference can have a profound impact on judgments. One such effect—known as the **anchoring effect**—*occurs when an individual attempts to solve a problem involving numbers and uses previous knowledge to keep (i.e., anchor) the response within a limited range.* For example, individuals in one study were asked to think aloud when answering questions such as: *When was George Washington elected president?* Participants would reply with thoughts such as "The United States declared independence from England in 1776, and it probably took a few years to elect a president, so Washington was elected in … 1789" (Epley & Gilovich, 2001, p. 392). Thus the signing of the Declaration of Independence in 1776 serves as the *anchor* for Washington's election.

Anchors are more effective when they are generated by the individual making the judgments, but they can also have effects when introduced by the experimenter (Epley & Gilovich, 2006; Kahneman & Miller, 1986). For example, consider what might happen if researchers asked the same question to two different groups, using a different anchor each time:

(A) What percentage of African nations belongs to the United Nations? Is it greater than or less than 10%? What do you think the exact percentage is?
(B) What percentage of African nations belongs to the United Nations? Is it greater than or less than 65%? What do you think the exact percentage is?

Researchers conducted a study using similar methods and found that individuals in group (A), who received the 10% anchor, estimated the number to be approximately 25%. Individuals in the group (B), who received the 65% anchor, estimated the percentage at approximately 45%. In this case, the anchor obviously had a significant effect on the estimates.

PSYCH @

The Stock Exchange

Risk lies at the heart of financial investing—the higher the risk, the bigger the potential for income. When investors buy stocks or mutual funds, they have to wonder, *Will my investment gain or lose money?* Although no investing methods can guarantee profits, some objective rules have been proved effective over time. So why do people so often fail to follow those rules? Psychologist Herbert Simon won a Nobel Prize in economics for demonstrating that humans have *bounded rationality*. In other words, we may be rational up to a point, but then heuristic thinking takes over. Use of heuristics leaves us open to biases and potentially costly mistakes (Garling et al., 2009).

One of the most potent and dangerous biases is *loss aversion*—the tendency to place more value on money lost than on money gained. Psychologists can measure loss aversion by asking participants to rate how happy they would be gaining $10, $100, or $1,000, and then asking other participants to rate how upset they would be by losing $10, $100, or $1,000. It turns out that losing money is a much more negative experience than gaining money is a positive one. In other words, $100 is not always worth $100.

As a consequence of biases such as these, people often ignore sound, objective investing strategies in favor of making an emotional response. For example, people might sell a stock that loses value to avoid losing any more money, even when objective advice would be to keep the stock and let it regain its value. As a result, a new field of study has emerged—behavioral finance. This combination of psychology and finance is aimed at helping investors overcome biases and commit to sound investment strategies.

Stock traders know the basic principles of sound investing, but are also subject to biases such as loss aversion.

. . . .

THE BENEFITS OF HEURISTIC THINKING As you have seen in this section, the heuristics used in making judgments and decisions can lead us astray from time to time. Nevertheless, the point of studying these errors is not to show how naive people can be. Actually, this line of research helps psychologists understand why heuristics are so often beneficial—they help us make decisions as efficiently as possible. While it would be a mistake to think that all human cognition is logical, it would be equally mistaken to take an overly pessimistic view of human thought (Gilovich & Griffin, 2002). Knowing that people are susceptible to errors can help us to be better critical thinkers, allowing us to spend time evaluating our solutions, judgments, and decisions.

BELIEF PERSEVERANCE AND CONFIRMATION BIAS Whenever we solve a problem or make a decision, we have an opportunity to evaluate the outcome to make sure we got it right and to judge how satisfied we are with the decision. That relationship does not always unspool in such a clear-cut manner, however.

Imagine you and several friends sit down for a poker match with an old deck of cards. The dealer removes the cards from the box and counts to make sure they are all present. At first, he comes up with 51 cards—one short. The second try, he gets 52 cards—the correct amount. Now that he has reached the expected number, he goes on to deal the first round. What is wrong with his reasoning in this case?

Belief perseverance *occurs when an individual believes he or she has the solution to the problem or the correct answer for a question* (e.g., How many cards are in this deck?), *and accepts only evidence that will confirm those beliefs.* Our dealer knew the correct number of cards would be 52. He exhibited the belief perseverance by ignoring the count that gave him 51 as some sort of mistake; meanwhile, the count that confirmed his idea that there should be 52 cards was considered to be correct.

Along the same general lines, the **confirmation bias** *occurs when an individual searches for only evidence that will confirm his or her beliefs instead of evidence that might disconfirm them.* This differs from belief perseverance in that the confirmation bias is the search for a particular type of evidence, not a way of evaluating evidence that already exists. In the case of our dealer, he could have laid out all 13 cards from each suite to ensure that he had a full deck—that would have been a logical way to identify if any cards were missing. Instead, he exhibited

Table 8.3 :: Contradictory and Exculpatory Statements for Democratic and Republican Presidential Candidates

SAMPLE STATEMENT SET: GEORGE W. BUSH

Initial: "First of all, Ken Lay is a supporter of mine. I love the man. I got to know Ken Lay years ago, and he has given generously to my campaign. When I'm president, I plan to run the government like a CEO runs a country. Ken Lay and Enron are a model of how I'll do that." —Candidate George Bush, 2000

Contradictory: Mr. Bush now avoids any mention of Ken Lay and is critical of Enron when asked.

Exculpatory: People who know the president report that he feels betrayed by Ken Lay, and was genuinely shocked to find that Enron's leadership had been corrupt.

SAMPLE STATEMENT SET: JOHN KERRY

Initial: During the 1996 campaign, Kerry told a *Boston Globe* reporter that the Social Security system should be overhauled. He said Congress should consider raising the retirement age and means-testing benefits. "I know it's going to be unpopular," he said. "But we have a generational responsibility to fix this problem."

Contradictory: This year [2004], on *Meet the Press*, Kerry pledged that he will never tax or cut benefits to seniors or raise the age for eligibility for Social Security.

Exculpatory: Economic experts now suggest that, in fact, the Social Security system will not run out of money until 2049, not 2020, as they had thought in 1996.

Source: Westen et al., 2006.

the confirmation bias by seeking out only confirmatory evidence.

Confirmation bias and belief perseverance together can dramatically influence a person's beliefs, especially in relation to complex, emotionally charged areas such as religion and politics. In fact, much of the research on these biases shows that people treat evidence in ways that minimize negative or uncomfortable feelings while maximizing positive feelings (Westen et al., 2006). For example, one study examined the brain regions and self-reported feelings involved in interpreting information about presidential candidates during the campaigns. The participants were all deeply committed to either the Republican or Democratic candidate, and

they all encountered information that was threatening toward each candidate, as shown in Table 8.3. As you can see from the results in Figure 8.15, participants had strong emotional reactions to threatening (self-contradictory) information about their own candidate, but not to the alternative candidate, or a relatively neutral person, such as a retired network news anchor. Analyses of the brain scans demonstrated that very different neural processes were at work in each condition. When the threat was directed at the participant's own candidate, brain areas associated with ignoring or suppressing information were more active, whereas few of the regions associated with logical thinking were activated (Westen et al., 2006).

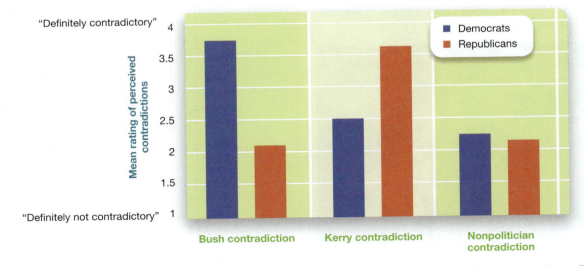

{FIG. 8.15} **Ratings of Perceived Contradictions in Political Statements** Democrats and Republicans reached very different conclusions about candidates' contradictory statements. Democrats readily identified the opponent's contradictions but were less likely to do so for their own candidate; the same was true for Republican responders.

WORKING THE SCIENTIFIC LITERACY MODEL

Maximizing and Satisficing in Complex Decisions

As mentioned in the opening vignette for this module, one privilege of living in a technologically advanced, democratic society is that we get to make so many decisions for ourselves. However, for each decision there can be more choices than we can possibly consider. As a result, two types of consumers have emerged in our society. *Satisficers* are individuals who seek to make decisions that are, simply put, "good enough." In contrast, *maximizers* are individuals who attempt to evaluate every option for every choice until they find the perfect fit. Most people exhibit some of both behaviors, satisficing at times and maximizing at other times. However, if you consider all the people you know, you can probably identify at least one person who is an extreme maximizer—he or she will always be comparing products, jobs, classes, and so on, to find out who has made the best decisions. At the same time, you can probably identify an extreme satisficer—the person who will be satisfied with his or her choices as long as they are "good enough."

What do we know about maximizing and satisficing?

If one person settles for the good-enough option, while another searches until he finds the best possible option, which individual do you think will be happier with the decision in the end? Most people believe the maximizer will be happier, but this is not always the case. In fact, researchers such as Barry Schwartz have no shortage of data about the *paradox of choice*: the observation that more choices can lead to less satisfaction. In one study, the researchers asked participants to recollect both large (more than $100) and small (less than $10) purchases and report the number of options they considered, the time spent shopping and making the decision, and the overall satisfaction with the purchase. Sure enough, those who ranked high on a test of maximization invested more time and effort, but were actually less pleased with the outcome (Schwartz et al., 2002).

In another study, researchers questioned recent college graduates about their job search process. Believe it or not, maximizers averaged 20% higher salaries, but were less happy about their jobs than satisficers (Iyengar et al., 2006). This outcome occurred despite the fact that the opposite would seem to be true—*if* humans were perfectly logical decision makers.

So now we know that just the presence of alternative choices can drive down satisfaction— but how can that be?

How can science explain maximizing and satisficing?

To answer this question, researchers asked participants to read vignettes that included a trade-off between number of choices and effort (Dar-Nimrod et al., 2009). Try this example for yourself:

> *Your cleaning supplies (e.g., laundry detergent, rags, carpet cleaner, dish soap, toilet paper, glass cleaner) are running low. You have the option of going to the nearest grocery store (5 minutes away), which offers 4 alternatives for each of the items you need, or you can drive to the grand cleaning superstore (25 minutes away), which offers 25 different alternatives for each of the items (for approximately the same price). Which store would you go to?*

In the actual study, maximizers were much more likely to spend the extra time and effort to have more choices. Thus, if you decided to go to the store with more options, you are probably a maximizer. What this scenario does not tell us is whether having more or fewer choices was pleasurable for either maximizers or satisficers.

See how well you understand the nature of maximizers and satisficers by predicting the results of the next study: Participants completed a taste test of one piece of chocolate, but they could choose one piece of chocolate from an array of 6 pieces or an array of 30 pieces. When there were 6 pieces, who was happier—maximizers or satisficers? What happened when there were 30 pieces to choose from? As you can see in Figure 8.16, the maximizers are happier when there are fewer choices, but satisficers win out when there is a large variety (Dar-Nimrod et al., 2009). In fact, the maximizers with the large number of choices were least satisfied of all participants!

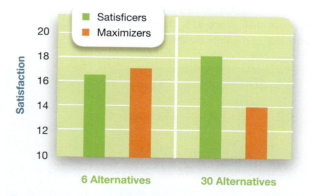

{FIG. 8.16} **Satisfaction of Maximizers and Satisficers** The relative satisfaction of maximizers and satisficers depends on how many choices are available. Maximizers are happier when there are fewer alternatives, whereas satisficers are happier when there are more options.

Can we critically evaluate this information?

One hypothesis that seeks to explain the dissatisfaction of maximizers suggests that they invest more in the decision, so they expect more from the outcome. Imagine that a satisficer and a maximizer purchase the same digital camera for $75. The maximizer may have invested significantly more time and effort into the decision so, in effect, she feels like she paid considerably more for the camera. At the end of the day, however, the two consumers have the same product.

Regardless of the explanation, we should keep in mind that maximizers and satisficers are preexisting categories. People cannot be randomly assigned to be in one category or another, so these findings represent the outcomes of correlational research. We cannot be sure that the act of maximizing leads to dissatisfaction based on these data. Perhaps maximizers are the people who are generally less satisfied, which in turn leads to maximizing behavior.

Why is this relevant?

Although we described maximizing and satisficing in terms of purchasing decisions, you might also notice that these styles of decision making can be applied to other situations, such as multiple-choice exams. Do you select the first response that sounds reasonable (satisficing), or do you carefully review each of the responses and compare them to one another before marking your choice (maximizing)? Once you make your choice, do you stick with it, believing it is good enough (satisficing), or are you willing to change your answer to make the best possible choice (maximizing)? Despite the popular wisdom that you should never change your first response, there may be an advantage to maximizing on exams. Research focusing on more than 1,500 individual examinations showed that when people change their answers, they improve their score 51% of the time and hurt their score only 25% of the time (Kruger et al., 2005).

Quick Quiz 8.2b
Judgment and Decision Making

KNOW...

1 Based on _____, people judge something as more likely if it strongly represents a specific category.

   A anchoring   **C** loss aversion

   B priming   **D** representativeness

2 The_____ occurs when an individual searches for only evidence that will confirm his or her beliefs.

   A availability heuristic   **C** belief perseverance

   B confirmation bias   **D** satisficing

3 When an individual makes judgments based on how easily things come to mind, he or she is employing the _____ heuristic.

   A confirmation   **C** availability

   B representativeness   **D** belief perseverance

UNDERSTAND...

4 Belief perseverance seems to function by:

   A maximizing positive feelings.

   B minimizing negative feelings.

   C maximizing negative feelings while minimizing positive feelings.

   D minimizing negative feelings while maximizing positive feelings.

ANALYZE...

5 Why do psychologists assert that heuristics are beneficial for problem solving?

   A Heuristics increase the amount of time we spend arriving at good solutions to problems.

   B Heuristics decrease our chances of errors dramatically.

   C Heuristics help us make decisions efficiently.

   D Heuristics are considered the most logical thought pattern for problem solving.

6 The fact that humans so often rely on heuristics is evidence that:

   A humans are not always rational thinkers.

   B it is impossible for humans to think logically.

   C it is impossible for humans to use algorithms.

   D humans will always succumb to the confirmation bias.

Answers can be found on page ANS-3.

Module Summary

Now that you have read this module you should:

Listen to the audio file of this module at **MyPsychLab**

KNOW ...

- **The key terminology of problem solving and decision making:**

algorithms (p. 282)

anchoring effect (p. 286)

availability heuristic (p. 286)

belief perseverance (p. 287)

confirmation bias (p. 287)

functional fixedness (p. 284)

heuristics (p. 282)

ill-defined problem (p. 282)

mental set (p. 283)

problem solving (p. 282)

representativeness heuristic (p. 285)

well-defined problem (p. 282)

UNDERSTAND ...

- **The characteristics that problems have in common.** All problems have initial states and goal states. We use operators to achieve goals states. Also, many problems include subgoals. Problems can range from well-defined to ill-defined.

- **How obstacles to problem solving are often self-imposed.** Many obstacles arise from the individual's mental set, which occurs when a person focuses on only one known solution and does not consider alternatives. Similarly, functional fixedness can arise when an individual does not consider alternative uses for familiar objects.

APPLY ...

- **Your knowledge to determine if you tend to be a maximizer or a satisficer.** To do so, rate the following items on a scale from 1 (completely disagree) to 7 (completely agree), with 4 being a neutral response.

  1. Whenever I'm faced with a choice, I try to imagine what all the other possibilities are, even ones that aren't present at the moment.

  2. No matter how satisfied I am with my job, it's only right for me to be on the lookout for better opportunities.

  3. When I am in the car listening to the radio, I often check other stations to see whether something better is playing, even if I am relatively satisfied with what I'm listening to.

  4. When I watch TV, I channel surf, often scanning through the available options even while attempting to watch one program.

  5. I treat relationships like clothing: I expect to try a lot on before finding the perfect fit.

  6. I often find it difficult to shop for a gift for a friend.

  7. When shopping, I have a difficult time finding clothing that I really love.

  8. No matter what I do, I have the highest standards for myself.

  9. I find that writing is very difficult, even if it's just writing to a friend, because it's so difficult to word things just right. I often do several drafts of even simple things.

  10. I never settle for second best.

When you are finished, average your ratings together to find your overall score. Scores greater than 4 indicate maximizers; scores less than 4 indicate satisficers. Approximately one-third of the population scores below 3.25 and approximately one-third scores above 4.75. Where does your score place you?

ANALYZE ...

- **Whether human thought is primarily logical or intuitive.** This module provides ample evidence that humans are not always logical. Heuristics are helpful decision-making and problem-solving tools, but they do not follow logical principles. Even so, the abundance of heuristics does not mean that humans are never logical; instead, they simply point to the limits of our rationality.

Language and Communication

KNOW ...	UNDERSTAND ...	APPLY ...	ANALYZE ...
The key terminology from the study of language	How language is structured How genes and the brain are involved in language use	Your knowledge to distinguish between units of language such as phonemes and morphemes	Whether species other than humans are able to use language

Dog owners are known for attributing a lot of intelligence, emotion, and "humanness" to their canine pals. Sometimes they may appear to go overboard—such as Rico's owners, who claimed their border collie understood 200 words, most of which refer to different toys and objects he likes to play with. His owners claimed that they could show Rico a toy, repeat its name a few times, and toss the toy into a pile of other objects; Rico would then retrieve the object upon verbal command. Rico's ability appeared to go well beyond the usual "sit," "stay," "heel," and perhaps a few other words that dog owners expect their companions to understand.

Claims about Rico's language talents soon drew the attention of scientists, who skeptically questioned whether the dog was just responding to cues by the owners, such as their possible looks or gestures toward the object they asked their pet to retrieve. The scientists set up a carefully controlled experiment in which no one present in the room knew the location of the object that was requested. Rico correctly retrieved 37 out of 40 objects. The experimenters then tested the owners' claim that Rico could learn object names in just one trial. Rico again confirmed his owners' claims, and the researchers concluded that his ability to understand

new words was comparable to that of a three-year-old child (Kaminski et al., 2004).

These researchers answered some interesting questions about language in a nonhuman species, but many still remain.

Focus Questions

 What is the difference between language and other forms of communication?

 Might other species, such as chimpanzees, also be capable of learning human language?

· · · · · · · · · · · · · · · · · ·

Communication happens just about anywhere you can find life. Dogs bark, cats meow, monkeys chatter, and mice can emit sounds undetectable to the human ear when communicating. Honeybees perform an elaborate dance to communicate the direction, distance, and quality of food sources (vonFrisch, 1967). Animals even communicate by marking their territories with their distinct scent. Language is among the ways that humans communicate. It is quite unlike the examples of animal communication mentioned previously. So what differentiates language from these other forms of communication?

What Is Language?

Language, like many other cognitive abilities, flows so automatically that we often overlook how complicated it really is. It is not until we try to learn a new language in adulthood or try to communicate with someone who does not speak our native language that its true complexity becomes clear. **Language** *is a form of communication that involves the use of spoken, written, or gestural symbols that are combined in a rule-based form.* With this definition in mind, we can distinguish which features of language make it a unique form of communication.

What distinguishes human language from animal communication? As we explore different forms of communication, the line between what is and is not language becomes blurred, but a few basic features can help make distinctions (Harley, 2001). One characteristic of language is that we use it to communicate about objects and events that are not in the present time and place. We use language to imagine things that are happening on another planet, or things that are happening inside of atoms. A college student can say, "We're going to order pizza tonight," without her roommate thinking the pizza is already there. But if you tell your dog, "I'll give you a treat later tonight," your dog will hear something like "blar blar TREAT blar blar," without realizing you were displacing the treat to another time. Naturally, that means your dog will expect the treat right away.

Languages can produce entirely new meanings. You alone can produce a sentence that has never been uttered before in the history of humankind. As long as you select English words and use correct grammar, others who know the language should be able to understand it. At worst, this facility allows people to tell tall tales, such as those found in supermarket tabloids: *Bat Boy Found in Cave!* In American culture, "bat boys" are regular kids who keep track of the baseball bats for ball players. In this particular tabloid, the story concerned a completely novel creature that was part bat and part boy. It is bizarre, and we may not believe it, but we can understand it in a number of ways depending on how we decide to put the two words "bat" and "boy"

together. In contrast, dog commands and the signals animals themselves use stand alone. Pairing them together does not produce new meanings. Thus, although dogs may appear to understand many different words, they do not appear to understand their relationships to other words when put into sentences.

Language also differs from other types of communication in that it is passed down from parents to children. Although generation after generation of honeybees will do the same dances, the pattern in which they do this is considered more a biological transmission than a cultural one; in other words, bees will continue to communicate through dances mostly because it is in their genes, not just because they saw their elders do it. And no matter how well your dog responds to commands such as "sit," "stay," or "roll over," the animal isn't able to sit her puppies down and explain the meaning to them.

PHONEMES AND MORPHEMES: THE BASIC INGREDIENTS OF LANGUAGE Languages contain discrete units that exist at differing levels of complexity. When people speak, they assemble these units into larger and more complex units. Some psychologists have used a cooking analogy to explain this phenomenon: We all start with the same basic language ingredients, but they can be mixed together in an unlimited number of ways (Pinker, 1999).

Phonemes *are the most basic of units of speech sounds.* You can identify phonemes rather easily; the phoneme associated with the letter *t* (which is written as /t/, where the two forward slashes indicate a phoneme) is found at the end of the word *pot* or near the beginning of the word *stop.* If you pay close attention to the way you use your tongue, lips, and vocal cords, you will see that phonemes have slight variations depending on the other letters around them. Pay attention to how you pronounce the /t/ phoneme in *stop, stash, stink,* and *stoke.* Your mouth will move in slightly different ways each time, and there will be very slight variations in sound, but they are still the same basic phoneme. Individual phonemes typically do not have any meaning by themselves; if you want someone to stop doing something, asking him to /t/ will not suffice.

Morphemes *are the smallest meaningful units of a language.* Some morphemes are simple words, whereas others may be suffixes or prefixes. For example, the word *pig* is a morpheme—it cannot be broken down into smaller units of meaning. You can combine morphemes, however, if you follow the rules of the language. If you want to

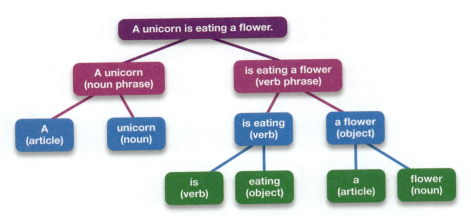

{FIG. 8.17} **Syntax Allows Us to Understand Language by the Organization of the Words** The rules of syntax help us divide a sentence into noun phrases, verb phrases, and other parts of speech.

pluralize *pig*, you can add the morpheme /-s/, which will give you *pigs*. If you want to describe a person as a pig, you can add the morpheme /-ish/ to get *piggish*. In fact, you can add all kinds of morphemes to a word as long as you follow the rules. You could even say *piggable* (able to be pigged) or *piggify* (to turn into a pig). These words do not make much literal sense, but they combine morphemes according to the rules; thus we can make a reasonable guess as to the speaker's intended meaning. Our ability to combine morphemes into words is one distinguishing feature of language that sets it apart from other forms of communication. In essence, language gives us *productivity*—the ability to combine units of sound into an infinite number of meanings.

Finally, there are the words that make up a language. **Semantics** *is the study of how people come to understand meaning from words.* Humans have a knack for this kind of interpretation, and each of us has an extensive mental dictionary to prove it. Not only do normal speakers know tens of thousands of words, but they can often understand new words they have never heard before based on their understanding of morphemes.

As you can see, languages derive their complexity from several elements, including phonemes, morphemes, and semantics. But this is just the shopping list—we still need to figure out how to mix these ingredients together.

SYNTAX: THE LANGUAGE RECIPE Perhaps the most remarkable aspect of language is **syntax**, *the rules for combining words and morphemes into meaningful phrases and sentences*—the recipe for language. Children master the syntax of their native language before they leave

elementary school. They can string together morphemes and words when they speak, and they can easily distinguish between *well-formed* and *ill-formed* sentences. But despite mastering those rules, most speakers cannot tell you what the rules are; syntax just seems to come naturally. It might seem odd that people can do so much with language without a full understanding of its inner workings. Of course, people can also learn how to walk without any understanding of the biochemistry that allows their leg muscles to contract and relax.

The most basic units of syntax are nouns and verbs. They are all that is required to construct a well-formed sentence, such as *Unicorns eat*. Noun–verb sentences are perfectly adequate, if a bit limited, so we build phrases out of nouns and verbs, as the diagram in Figure 8.17 demonstrates.

Syntax also helps explain why the order of words in a sentence has such a strong effect on what the sentence means. For example, how would you make a question out of this statement?

(A) *A unicorn is in the garden.*
(B) IS *a unicorn* _____ *in the garden?*

This example demonstrates that a statement (A) can be turned into a well-formed question (B) just by moving the verb "is" to the beginning of the sentence. Perhaps that is one of the hidden rules of syntax. Try it again:

(A) *A unicorn that is eating a flower is in the garden.*
(B) IS *a unicorn that* _____ *eating a flower is in the garden?*

As you can see, the rule "move *is* to the beginning of the sentence" does not apply in this case. Do you know why? It is because we moved the wrong *is*. The phrase *that is eating a flower* is a part of the noun phrase because it describes the unicorn. We should have moved the *is* from the verb phrase. Try it again:

(A) *A unicorn that is eating a flower is in the garden.*
(B) IS *a unicorn that is eating a flower* _____ *in the garden?*

This is a well-formed sentence. It may be grammatically awkward, but the syntax is understandable (Pinker, 1994).

As you can see from these examples, the order of words in a sentence helps determine what the sentence means, and syntax is the set of rules we use to determine that order.

Table 8.4 :: Pragmatic Rules Guiding Language Use

THE RULE	FLOUTING THE RULE	THE IMPLICATION
Say what you believe is true.	My roommate is a *giraffe*.	He does not *really* live with a giraffe. Maybe his roommate is very tall?
Say only what is relevant.	Is my blind date good-looking? *He's got a great personality.*	She didn't answer my question. He's probably not good looking.
Say only as much as you need to.	I like my lab partner, but he's no *Einstein*.	Of course he's not Einstein. Why is she bothering to tell me this? She probably means that her partner is not very smart.

PRAGMATICS: THE FINISHING TOUCHES If syntax is the recipe for language, pragmatics is the icing on the cake. Unlike syntax, which takes place in your brain, **pragmatics** *is the study of nonlinguistic elements of language use.* It places heavy emphasis on the speaker's behaviors and the social situation (Carston, 2002). Research has shown that pragmatics is guided by the *cooperative principle*, which states that pragmatic rules apply to conversation, so entering into a conversation is essentially agreeing to cooperate.

There is an old joke that deftly explains why the cooperative principle is necessary:

A man walks up to another man, who happens to be standing next to a dog. The first man asks, "Sir, does your dog bite?" The second man replies, "No." But then the dog barks and nips the first man on his fingers. "Ouch! I thought you said your dog does not bite!" the first man complains. To which the second man replies, "I did. But that's not my dog."

In this case, the second man in the conversation was not fully cooperating. The pragmatic aspects of the conversation *should* have been clear to both parties.

Pragmatics reminds us that sometimes *what* is said is not as important as *how* it is said. For example, a student who says, "I ate a 50 pound cheeseburger," is most likely stretching the truth, but you probably would not call him a liar. Pragmatics helps us understand what he implied. The voracious student was actually *flouting*—or blatantly disobeying—a rule of language in a way that is obvious (Grice, 1975; Horn & Ward, 2004). There are all sorts of ways in which flouting the rules can lead to implied, not literal meanings; a sample of those are shown in Table 8.4.

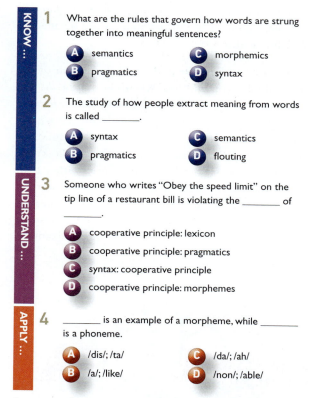

Quick Quiz 8.3a
What Is Language?

KNOW …

1 What are the rules that govern how words are strung together into meaningful sentences?

  A semantics   C morphemics
  B pragmatics   D syntax

2 The study of how people extract meaning from words is called _____.

  A syntax   C semantics
  B pragmatics   D flouting

UNDERSTAND …

3 Someone who writes "Obey the speed limit" on the tip line of a restaurant bill is violating the _____ of _____.

  A cooperative principle: lexicon
  B cooperative principle: pragmatics
  C syntax: cooperative principle
  D cooperative principle: morphemes

APPLY …

4 _____ is an example of a morpheme, while _____ is a phoneme.

  A /dis/; /ta/   C /da/; /ah/
  B /a/; /like/   D /non/; /able/

Answers can be found on page ANS-3.

Language Development, Evolution, and the Brain

Numerous processes are involved in the development and support of human language. These processes require genes, brain regions, and complex interactions of these components that begin during early development. Also, evidence for an evolutionary basis of language comes from work comparing nonhuman species with those of human children. Each of these topics is explored in this section.

LANGUAGE IN THE BRAIN Language involves just about the whole cortex in some aspect or another. Reading requires visual areas, listening involves auditory areas, and the memories that provide ideas and the words to talk about them are distributed throughout the cortex. The most unique and complex aspects of language, however, are based in the left hemisphere (for the vast majority of the human population), in regions known as Wernicke's area and Broca's area, which are named in recognition of the researchers who developed the modern views of their function (Buckingham, 2006; introduced in Module 3.3). The roles of these regions can be illuminated through traditional brain imaging studies, but we can also examine what happens when they malfunction due to injury or disease. **Aphasias** *are language disorders caused by damage to the brain structures that support using and understanding language.* As you will soon see, a number of distinct abilities can be affected by such conditions.

Located toward the middle, back portion of the temporal lobe, you will find **Wernicke's area**, *the area of the brain most associated with finding the meaning of words.* Damage to this area results in *Wernicke's aphasia,* a language disorder in which a person has difficulty understanding the words he or she hears. We know this problem is associated with semantics rather than syntax, because an individual's speech sounds normal at first—the syntax, intonation, accent, and demeanor are normal, but the word choices do not make sense (Akmajian et al., 2001; Caspari, 2005). For example,

one individual with Wernicke's aphasia engaged in this conversation:

> Examiner: Do you like it here in Kansas City?
>
> Person with aphasia: Yes, I am.
>
> Examiner: I'd like to have you tell me something about your problem.
>
> Person with aphasia: Yes, I, ugh, cannot hill all of my way. I cannot talk all of the things I do, and part of the part I can go alright, but I cannot tell from the other people. I usually most of my things. I know what can I talk and know what they are, but I cannot always come back even though I know they should be in, and I know should something eely I should know what I'm doing …

The important thing to look for in this sample of speech is how the wrong words appear in an otherwise fluent stream of utterances. It reads almost like the product of the child's game, Mad Libs, in which a one person fills in missing words from a story while knowing only which parts of speech to produce.

Because of the confusing nature of the speech, a severe case of Wernicke's aphasia could be mistaken for a type of schizophrenia (see Module 13.4 for a description of schizophrenia). Nevertheless, aphasia is a disorder of language, not of other cognitive abilities. Individuals who are fortunate enough to recover some of their language abilities report that, during the worst part of the disorder, they knew when someone was speaking, but they could not understand it—they could not understand even their own speech.

Broca's area *is a frontal lobe structure that controls our ability to articulate speech sounds that compose words.* In Figure 8.18, Broca's area appears adjacent to a strip of the brain known as the motor cortex that helps us control body movements. Given its proximity to the motor cortex, Broca's area has long been associated with the production of speech (Buckingham, 2006). However, its work entails much more than just signaling the muscles to move; it is also involved in adding grammatical flourishes to words that have already been selected and combining them into syntactically appropriate phrases. Broca's area functions in other ways, too. For example, it is active when processing musical notes (Maess et al., 2001).

A person with damage to this area will most likely be diagnosed with *Broca's aphasia* (Akmajian et al.,

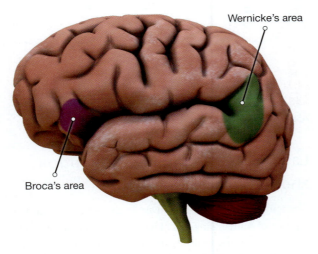

Wernicke's area

Broca's area

{FIG. 8.18} **Two Language Centers of the Brain** Broca's and Wernicke's areas of the cerebral cortex are critical to language function. **Click on this figure in your eText to see more details.**

2001; Dick et al., 2001). Although most of these individuals can still speak, doing so is obviously very difficult for them. As a result, their speech is limited to a series of single words intertwined with filled pauses (uh, er, …); even gesturing with speech can be affected (Skipper et al., 2007). The individual words are often produced without normal grammatical flair: no articles, suffixes, or prefixes. Here is a sample of speech collected during a study of Broca's aphasia:

Examiner: Tell me, what did you do before you retired?

Person with aphasia: Uh, uh, uh, pub, par, partender, no.

Examiner: Carpenter?

Person with aphasia: (Nodding to signal yes) Carpenter, tuh, tuh, twenty year.

Notice that the individual has no trouble understanding the question or coming up with the answer. His difficulty is in getting the word *carpenter* into an appropriate phrase and pronouncing it. Did you also notice the missing morpheme /-s/ from *twenty year*?

Broca's aphasia can include some difficulties in comprehending language as well. In general, the more complex the syntax, the more difficult it will be to understand. Compare these two sentences:

The girl played the piano.

The piano was played by the girl.

These are two well-formed sentences (although the second is somewhat awkward) that have the same meaning but different syntax. An individual with Broca's aphasia is likely to understand the first, more direct method, but much less likely to understand the second sentence, which is more complex. Given the difficulty with producing syntax, we might expect these sentences to be understood as follows:

Girl … play … piano

Piano … ? … play … girl

How does the brain pull all of the language components together to produce coherent speech? Thus far we have focused on two areas on the cerebral cortex: Broca's and Wernicke's areas. Broca's area is needed for word production. Wernicke's area requires inputs from other brain regions, such as the cerebellum, basal ganglia, and hippocampus, to work correctly. The cerebellum, known for its role in balance and coordination, also plays a role in coordinating and organizing speech. The basal ganglia help control voluntary movement, including learning and making speech sounds. The circuitry of the basal ganglia supports our ability to articulate grammatically correct sentences. For example, the basal ganglia helps us articulate "I went to the store," rather than "I wented to the store." Perhaps not surprisingly, people with Parkinson's disease—a condition that adversely affects the basal ganglia—have difficulty using irregular verbs (Ullman et al., 1997). The hippocampus is involved in encoding semantic information, which is critical to language function. As you can see, our amazing faculty of language relies on numerous brain regions.

WORKING THE SCIENTIFIC LITERACY MODEL
Genes and Language

The unique brain specializations underlying human language are likely supported by specific genes. Given that language is a universal trait of the human species, it likely has a genetic substrate that awaits interaction with the environment. How could we possibly find specific genes for this complex ability?

What do we know about genes and language?

Many scientists believe that the evidence is overwhelming that language is a unique feature of the human species, and that language evolved to solve problems related to survival and reproductive fitness. Language adds greater efficiency to thought, allows us to transmit information without requiring us to have direct experience with potentially dangerous situations, and, ultimately, facilitates communicating social needs and desires. Claims that language promotes survival and reproductive success are difficult to test directly with scientific experimentation, but there is a soundness to the logic of the speculation. We can also move beyond speculation and actually examine how genes play a role in human language. As with all complex psychological traits, there are likely many genes associated with language. Nevertheless, amid all of these myriad possibilities, one gene has been identified that is of particular importance.

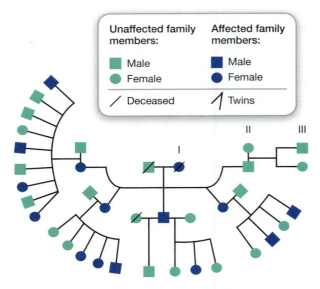

Unaffected family members:
- ■ Male
- ● Female

Affected family members:
- ■ Male
- ● Female

/ Deceased   /\ Twins

{FIG. 8.19} **Inheritance Pattern for the Mutated FOXP2 Gene in the KE Family** Family members who are "affected" have inherited a mutated form of the FOXP2 gene, which results in difficulty with articulating words. As you can see from the center of the figure, the mutated gene is traced to a female family member, and has been passed on to the individuals of the next two generations.

How can science explain a genetic basis of language?

Studies of this gene have primarily focused on the KE family. Many members of this family, whose name is abbreviated to maintain their confidentiality, have inherited a mutated version of a gene on chromosome 7 (see Figure 8.19; Vargha-Khadem et al., 2005). Each gene has a name—and this one is called FOXP2. (All humans carry a copy of the FOXP2 gene, but the KE family passes down a mutated copy.) Those who inherit the mutated copy have great difficulty putting thoughts into words (Tomblin et al., 2009). Thus it appears that the physical and chemical processes that FOXP2 codes for are related to language function.

What evidence indicates that this gene is specifically involved in language? If you were to ask the members of the family who inherited the mutant form of the gene to speak about how to change the batteries in a flashlight, they would be at a loss. A rather jumbled mixture of sounds and words might come out, but nothing that could be easily understood. However, these same individuals have no problem actually performing the task. Their challenges with using language are primarily restricted to the use of words, not with their ability to *think*.

Scientists have used brain imaging methods to further test whether the FOXP2 mutation affects language. One group of researchers compared brain activity of family members who inherited the mutation at FOXP2 with those who did not (Liégeois et al., 2003). During the brain scans, the participants were asked to generate words themselves, and also to repeat words back to the experimenters. As you can see from Figure 8.20, the members of the family who were unaffected by the mutation showed normal brain activity: Broca's area of the left hemisphere became activated, just as expected. In contrast, Broca's area in the affected family members was silent, and the brain activity that did occur was unusual for this type of task.

Can we critically evaluate this evidence?

As you have now read, language has multiple components. Being able to articulate words is just one of many aspects of using and understanding language. The research on FOXP2 is very important, but reveals only how a single gene relates to one aspect of language use. Also, as many scientists have argued, language is a unique product of human evolution and, therefore, has a genetic basis. The studies of FOXP2 actually may not lend much support to this argument of human uniqueness. This gene is found in both mice and birds as well as in humans, and the human version shares a very similar molecular structure to the versions observed in these species. Interestingly, the molecular structure and activity of the FOXP2 gene in songbirds (unlike non-songbirds) is similar to that in humans (Vargha-Khadem et al., 2005). As we will also see later, some other interesting similarities between human and nonhuman language have been identified.

Normal FOXP2
Unaffected group

Mutation at FOXP2
Affected group

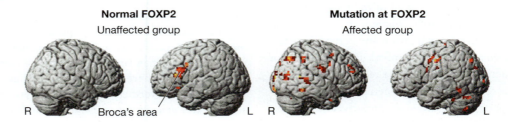

R   Broca's area   L   R   L

{FIG. 8.20} **Brain Scans Taken While Members of the KE Family Completed a Speech Task** The unaffected group shows a normal pattern of activity in Broca's area, while the affected group shows an unusual pattern.

Watch the **Video** *Bilingual Family* at **MyPsychLab**

Why is this relevant?

This work illuminates at least part of the complex relationship between genes and language. Other individual genes that have direct links to language function will likely be discovered someday as well. Also, it is possible that this information could be used to help us further understand the genetic basis of language disorders.

AGE OF ACQUISITION: THE SENSITIVE PERIOD FOR LEARNING A LANGUAGE   Every year, thousands of families move from one country to another, and many of those emigrants will come to the United States. The newcomers may find different customs or a different climate than they are used to, and it is likely that many people will make the adjustment successfully. But a new language presents some unique challenges for immigrant families. The parents may struggle with ESL (English as a Second Language) courses, while the children attend English-speaking schools. Within a few years, the parents may have accumulated some vocabulary but they will likely still have difficulty with pronunciation and grammar. Meanwhile, their children will have picked up

English without much effort, and now have language skills equivalent to those of their classmates; they have roughly the same vocabulary, the same accents, and even the same slang. Most scholastic curricula in the United States postpone teaching a second language to students, in part due to the fear that learning a second language might interfere with mastery of the first. Research actually indicates that learning two languages simultaneously during childhood is advantageous—not only for mastering the languages, but also in providing some cognitive advantages in other areas (Bialystok et al., 2009).

Why do children pick up a language so much more easily than adults? Most psychologists agree that there is a *sensitive period* for language—a time during childhood in which children's brains are primed to develop language skills (see also Module 10.1). Children can absorb language almost effortlessly, but this ability seems to fade away starting around the seventh year. Thus, when families immigrate to a country that uses a different language, the children are able to pick up this language much more quickly than their parents (Hakuta et al., 2003; Hernandez & Li, 2007). Similar results are found when deaf children receive cochlear implants (devices designed to restore hearing; described in Module 4.3). For the first years of life, they cannot hear language, so their development is delayed. Children who receive the implants by age two, however, develop better speech than children who receive them after age four (Nicholas & Geers, 2007).

Other examples come from studies of adults who were born deaf. In one case, Nicaraguan officials asked a researcher who specialized in American Sign Language (ASL) to work with students at the country's newly created school for the deaf. Prior to the establishment of the school, the deaf children lived with virtually no exposure

Signed languages share the same characteristics of spoken languages. They have a rich vocabulary, syntax, and set of pragmatic rules.

to language. They were rarely in contact with other deaf people, and there was no recognized sign language at the time. Once at the school, however, the younger children soon created their own sign language. In addition, the same specialist worked with approximately 300 deaf adults, who seemed unable to learn sign language (Pinker, 1994). Her efforts, along with research in other parts of the world, show that signers who learn later in life will never be as fluent as those who learn it during the sensitive period (Senghas, 2003; Senghas et al., 2004).

PATTERNS OF LANGUAGE ACQUISITION Early psychologists focused only on behavioral approaches to language learning. They believed that language was learned through imitating sounds and being reinforced for pronouncing and using words correctly (Skinner, 1985). Although it is certainly true that imitation and reinforcement are involved in this process, they are only one part of the complex process of learning language (Messer, 2000). Here are a few examples that illustrate how learning through imitation and reinforcement is just one component of language development:

- Children often produce phrases that include incorrect grammar or word forms. Because adults do not use these phrases, it is highly unlikely that such phrases are imitations.
- Children learn irregular verbs and pluralizations on a word-by-word basis. At first, they will use "ran" and "geese" correctly. However, when children begin to use grammar on their own, they over-generalize the rules. A child who learns the /-ed/ morpheme for past tense will start saying *runned* instead of *ran*. When she learns that /-s/ means more than one, she will begin to say *gooses* instead of *geese*. It is also unlikely that children would produce these forms by imitating.
- When children use poor grammar, or when they over-generalize their rules, parents may try to correct them. Although children will acknowledge their parents' attempts at instruction, this method does not seem to work. Instead, children go right back to over-generalizing.

Watch the **Video** *Stimulating Language Development* at **MyPsychLab**

In light of these and many other examples, it seems clear that an exclusive behavioral approach falls short in explaining how language is learned. After all, there are profound differences in the success of children and adults in learning a language: Whereas adults typically struggle, children seem to learn the language effortlessly. If reinforcement and imitation were the primary means by which language was acquired, then adults should be able to learn just as well as children. Also, rapid growth of vocabulary in children has been attributed to a process called **fast mapping**—*the ability to map words onto concepts or objects after only a single exposure.* Rico, the border collie that learned to understand 200 words, also used fast mapping. He was able to learn and remember new words after only one exposure. By comparison, human children seem to have a much broader capacity to do this, as 200 words are just a small fraction of a child's normal vocabulary.

The fact that children seem to learn language differently than adults has led psychologists to use the term *language acquisition* when referring to children instead of *language learning.* The study of language acquisition has revealed remarkable similarities among children from all over the world. Regardless of the language, children seem to develop this capability in stages, as shown in Table 8.5.

CAN ANIMALS USE LANGUAGE? Work with Rico the border collie is just one of many studies of animal language abilities. Psychologists have been studying whether nonhuman species can acquire human language for many decades. Formal studies of language learning in nonhuman species gained momentum in the mid-1950s when psychologists attempted to teach spoken English to a chimpanzee named Viki (Hayes & Hayes, 1951). Viki was **cross-fostered**, *meaning that she was raised as a member of a family that was not of the same species.* Like humans, chimps come into the world dependent on adults for care, so the humans who raised Viki were basically foster parents. Although the psychologists learned a lot about how smart chimpanzees can be, they did not learn that Viki was capable of language—she managed to whisper only about four words after as many years of trying.

Table 8.5 :: Milestones in Language Acquisition

AVERAGE TIME OF ONSET (MONTHS)	MILESTONE	EXAMPLE
1–2	Cooing	Ahhh, ai-ai-ai
4–10	Babbling (consonants start)	Ab-ah-da-ba
8–16	Single-word stage	Up, mama, papa
24	Two-word stage	Go potty
24+	Complete, meaningful phrases strung together	I want to talk to Grandpa.

Washoe was the first chimpanzee taught to use some of the signs of American Sign Language. Washoe died in 2007 at age 42 and throughout her life challenged many to examine their beliefs about human uniqueness.

Psychologists who followed in these researchers' footsteps did not consider the case to be closed. Perhaps Viki's failure to learn spoken English was a limitation not of the brain, but of physical differences in the vocal tract and tongue that distinguish humans and chimpanzees. One project that began in the mid-1960s involved teaching chimpanzees to use American Sign Language (ASL). The first chimpanzee involved in this project was named Washoe. The psychologists immersed Washoe

Kanzi is a bonobo chimpanzee that has learned to use an artificial language consisting of graphical symbols that correspond to words. Kanzi can type out responses by pushing buttons with these symbols, shown in this photo. Researchers are also interested in Kanzi's ability to understand spoken English (which is transmitted to the headphones by an experimenter who is not in the room).

in an environment rich with ASL, using signs instead of speaking and keeping at least one adult present and communicating with her throughout the day. By the time she turned two years old, Washoe had acquired about 35 signs through imitation and direct guidance of how to configure and move her hands. Eventually, she learned approximately 200 signs. She was able to generalize signs from one context to another and to use a sign to represent entire categories of objects, not just specific examples. For example, while Washoe learned the sign for the word "open" on a limited number of doors and cupboards, she subsequently signed "open" to many different doors, cupboards, and even her soda-pop bottles. The findings with Washoe were later replicated with other chimps (Gardner et al., 1989). ●

● Watch the Video Sign Language at MyPsychLab

Instead of using sign language, some researchers have developed a completely artificial language to teach to apes. This language consists of symbols called lexigrams—small keys on a computerized board that represent words and, therefore, can be combined to form complex ideas and phrases. One subject of the research using this language is a bonobo named Kanzi (bonobos are another species of chimpanzee). Kanzi has learned approximately 350 symbols through training, but he learned his first symbols simply by watching as researchers attempted to teach his mother how to use the language. In addition to the lexigrams he produces, Kanzi seems to recognize about 3,000 spoken words. His trainers claim that Kanzi's skills constitute language (Savage-Rumbaugh & Lewin, 1994). They argue that he can understand symbols and at least some syntax; that he acquired symbols simply by being around others who used them; and that he produced symbols without specific training or reinforcement. Those who work with Kanzi conclude that his communication skills are quite similar to those of a young human, in terms of both the elements of language (semantics and syntax) and the acquisition of language (natural and without effortful training).

Findings with apes have inspired psychologists to see if other intelligent, large-brained animals might be able to acquire language. Dolphin trainers have long marveled at how adept their pupils are at responding to gestures. Dolphins can learn that unique gestures can refer to specific objects as well as directions such as right and left. Do the dolphins simply associate a single gesture with a response that, if made, is rewarded with food? As it turns out, the dolphins can respond appropriately when given gestural commands such as one meaning "put the ball on the left into the basket on the right." Thus, they may not merely associate a gesture with an action and a reward, but rather understand the use of gestures as symbols (Herman et al., 1993).

Despite their ability to communicate in complex ways, debate continues to swirl about whether these animals are using language. Returning to chimpanzees, many language researchers point out that their signing and artificial language use is very different from how humans use language. Is the vastness of the difference important? Is using 200 signs different in some critical way from being able to use 4,000 signs, roughly the number found in the ASL dictionary (Stokoe et al., 1976)? If our only criterion for whether a communication system constitutes language is the number of words used, then we can say that nonhuman species acquire some language skills after extensive training. But as you have learned in this module, human language involves more than just using words. In particular, our manipulation of phonemes, morphemes, and syntax allow us to utter an infinite number of words and sentences, thereby conveying an infinite number of thoughts.

Some researchers who have worked closely with language-trained apes observed too many critical differences between humans and chimps to conclude that language extends beyond our species (Seidenberg & Pettito, 1979). For example:

- One major argument is that apes are communicating only with symbols, not with the phrase-based syntax used by humans. Although some evidence of syntax has been reported, the majority of their "utterances" consist of single signs, a couple of signs strung together, or apparently random sequences.
- There is little, reputable experimental evidence showing that apes pass their language skills to other apes.
- Productivity—creating new words (gestures) and using existing gestures to name new objects or events—is rare, if it occurs at all.
- Some of the researchers become very engaged in the lives of these animals and talk about them as friends and family members (Fouts, 1997; Savage-Rumbaugh & Lewin, 1994). This tendency has left critics to wonder the extent to which personal attachments to the animals might interfere with the objectivity of the data.

Finally, we should point out that animal language studies use *human* language as their frame of reference. In an alternate universe where dolphins attempt to teach humans their own system of communication, it is likely they would end up publishing skeptical critiques about the miniscule skills their human subjects acquired. Humans have evolved a remarkably complex capacity to use language for communication, and nonhumans have their own systems serving unique and adaptive functions. ◉

Watch the **Video** *Birds and Language* at **MyPsychLab**

Quick Quiz 8.3b
Development, Evolution, and the Brain

KNOW …

1 What is fast mapping?

A The rapid rate at which chimpanzees learn sign language

B The ability of children to map concepts to words with only a single example

C The very short period of time that language input can be useful for language development

D A major difficulty that people face when affected by Broca's aphasia

UNDERSTAND …

2 The term "sensitive period" is relevant to language acquisition because:

A exposure to language is needed during this time for language abilities to develop normally.

B Broca's area is active only during this period.

C it is what distinguishes humans from the apes.

D it indicates that language is an instinct.

3 Besides being based in a different region of the brain, a major distinction between Broca's aphasia and Wernicke's aphasia is that:

A words from people with Broca's aphasia are strung together fluently, but often make little sense.

B Broca's aphasia is due to a FOXP2 mutation.

C Wernicke's aphasia results in extreme stuttering.

D words from people with Wernicke's aphasia are strung together fluently, but often make little sense.

4 Studies of the KE family and the FOXP2 gene indicate that:

A language is controlled entirely by a single gene found on chromosome 7.

B language is still fluent despite a mutation to this gene.

C this particular gene is related to one specific aspect of language.

D mutations affecting this gene lead to highly expressive language skills.

ANALYZE …

5 What is the most accurate conclusion from research conducted on primate language abilities?

A Primates can learn some aspects of human language, though many differences remain.

B Primates can learn human language in full.

C Primates cannot learn human language in any way.

D There are not enough research data to reach reliable conclusions on this topic.

Answers can be found on page ANS-3.

Module Summary

Listen to the audio file of this module at **MyPsychLab**

Now that you have read this module you should:

KNOW …

- **The key terminology from the study of language:**

aphasias (p. 296)
Broca's area (p. 296)
cross-foster (p. 300)
fast mapping (p. 300)
language (p. 293)
morpheme (p. 293)

phoneme (p. 293)
pragmatics (p. 295)
semantics (p. 294)
syntax (p. 294)
Wernicke's area (p. 296)

UNDERSTAND …

- **How language is structured.** Sentences are broken down into words that are arranged according to grammatical rules (syntax). The relationship between words and their meaning is referred to as semantics. Words can be broken down into morphemes, the smallest meaningful units of speech, and phonemes, the smallest sound units that make up speech.

- **How genes and the brain are involved in language use.** Studies of the KE family show that the FOXP2 gene is involved in our ability to speak. However, mutation to this gene does not necessarily impair people's ability to think. Thus the FOXP2 gene seems to be important for just one of many aspects of human language. Multiple brain areas are involved in language—two particularly important ones are Broca's and Wernicke's areas.

APPLY …

- **Your knowledge to distinguish between units of language such as phonemes and morphemes.** Which of these represent a single phoneme and which represent a morpheme? Do any of them represent both? Check your answers on page ANS-3.

  1. /dis/
  2. /s/
  3. /k/

ANALYZE …

- **Whether species other than humans are able to use language.** Nonhuman species certainly seem capable of acquiring certain aspects of human language. Studies with apes have shown that they can learn and use some sign language or, in the case of Kanzi, an artificial language system involving arbitrary symbols. Critics have pointed out that many differences between human and nonhuman language use remain.

Module 8.1 :: The Organization of Knowledge

Focus Questions:

1 **How do people form easily recognizable categories from complex information?** People are remarkably good at detecting similarities and differences. From this activity, people develop prototypes, which represent the best examples of a category. When distinctions are not so clear, people may resort to using rules to identify whether an example belongs in the category.

2 **How does culture influence the ways in which we categorize information?** Cultural influences on categorization have been compared in people from Western and Eastern backgrounds. Westerners tend to focus on focal objects in scenes, and categorize them according to physical attributes. In contrast, Japanese people tend to categorize objects according to their surroundings and their relationships to each other. Also, research indicates that language—such as the labels we use to indicate different shades of color—can have a slight influence of categorization. However, this influence is sometimes exaggerated, such as in the myth of the number of words Inuit Eskimo have for snow.

👁 **Watch** *Special Topics: Mental Imagery: In the Mind's Eye* in the **MyPsychLab video series**

Module 8.2 :: Problem Solving, Judgment, and Decision Making

Focus Questions:

1 **How do people make decisions and solve problems?** Psychologists have found two broad categories of thought: (1) logical, algorithmic thought, which follows an orderly set of rules, and (2) heuristic thought, which is more intuitive. Research shows that people effectively use heuristic thinking, although sometimes it leads to inaccurate answers. Even so, heuristics are usually beneficial, and they are certainly an efficient way of making judgments and decisions.

2 **How can having multiple options lead people to be dissatisfied with their decisions?** One hypothesis is that when people put extra effort into making a decision, they raise their standards about what to expect. Thus some people will always expect more out of what they have chosen. In addition, personality traits reflect differences among individuals. Maximizing is the tendency to explore all options thoroughly, whereas satisficing is willingness to accept a good enough option. Maximizers are more likely to invest extra time and effort in making decisions, so they are more likely to be dissatisfied with the outcome.

👁 **Watch** *In the Real World Application: A Crash Course in Problem Solving* in the **MyPsychLab video series**

Module 8.3 :: Language and Communication

Focus Questions:

1 **What is the difference between language and other forms of communication?** Many forms of communication exist in the animal kingdom, but language appears to be unique, especially because of its use of syntax. Humans are able to encode and decode meaning based to a large extent on the syntactic structure of sentences.

2 **Might other species, such as chimpanzees, also be capable of learning human language?** Several studies using nonhuman primates have shown that, with extensive training, some animals can demonstrate some incredibly intelligent behavior. For example, the animals can link gestures or symbols to objects and events. In some cases, they have a rudimentary understanding of word order. They certainly seem to have learned some aspects of human language, though many differences remain.

👁 **Watch** *Thinking Like a Psychologist: Multilingualism: When More Is Better* in the **MyPsychLab video series**

👁 **Watch** the complete video series online at **MyPsychLab**

Episode 10: Cognition and Language
1. *The Big Picture: I Am, Therefore I Think*
2. *The Basics: The Mind Is What the Brain Does*
3. *Special Topics: Mental Imagery: In the Mind's Eye*
4. *Thinking Like a Psychologist: Multilingualism: When More Is Better*
5. *In the Real World Application: A Crash Course in Problem Solving*
6. *What's in It for Me?: Making Choices*

8 :: Chapter Quiz

1. According to classical categorization, people use _____ to decide if an object belongs to a specific category.

    A. prototypes

    B. semantic networks

    C. specific rules or features

    D. categorization by comparison

2. The linguist relativity hypothesis suggests that:

    A. the way we think about categories affects the language we use.

    B. there are many different ways to describe the same category.

    C. words are organized mentally based on their relationship to each other.

    D. the language that we use affects how we think about the world.

3. When Kwan's computer stopped working, he called the company's technical support line. The technician followed a predetermined set of steps from a manual to diagnosis and help Kwan fix his computer over the phone. The steps that the technician followed are an example of what type of problem solving strategy?

    A. algorithmic

    B. anchoring

    C. functional fixedness

    D. heuristic

4. People often overestimate the danger of shark attacks because it is fairly easy to think of news stories and reports of shark attacks. This is an example of how the _____ can sometimes lead to poor judgments.

    A. availability heuristic

    B. anchoring effect

    C. functional fixedness effect

    D. representativeness heuristic

5. Han and Bert both bought the same new cell phone. Han spent several weeks reviewing the dozens of different phones and reading reviews online, trying to find the best phone possible for his needs. Bert simply bought the first phone that met his needs. Given the research on maximizers and satisficers, which is most likely to be the outcome?

    A. Han and Bert will end up equally satisfied about their purchases.

    B. Han will be more satisfied with his purchase than Bert.

    C. Bert will be more satisfied with his purchase than Han.

    D. Han will spend less time researching his purchase next time.

6. The smallest units of language that convey meaning are known as:

    A. semantics.

    B. morphemes.

    C. phonemes.

    D. syntaxes.

7. Seth tells his friend that he got two tickets to a big concert next week, to which his friend replies, "Get out of town!" Because of the context, Seth knows his friend is expressing excitement and doesn't really want him to leave town. This is an example of:

    A. pragmatics.

    B. linguistic relativity.

    C. semantics.

    D. syntax.

8. Wernicke's area is most closely associated with:

    A. speech production.

    B. muscle control.

    C. singing.

    D. understanding language.

9. The "sensitive period" for language refers to:

    A. a period of time in our ancestral past when language first evolved.

    B. a period of time during gestation when the language areas of the brain develop.

    C. a time during young adulthood when accents can be reformed.

    D. a time during childhood when children are especially wired to learn language.

10. Studies where researchers have attempted to teach language to non-human animals have generally found that:

    A. chimpanzees and gorillas are the only animal species that can fully learn language.

    B. some animals are capable of learning elements of human language, but they have not convincingly demonstrated human-like language use.

    C. animals are incapable of learning even the most basic elements of human language.

    D. dolphins are the only animal species that can fully learn language.

✓ Study and Review at MyPsychLab

What do we know about problem solving and decision making?

We generally approach problems either logically (with an algorithm) or intuitively (with a heuristic), and usually with some combination of both. As you review problem solving on **page 282**, think of real-life examples that might help you remember these concepts. For example, suppose you are moving to college, and your car is fully packed except for one last box that does not seem to fit. If you took an algorithmic approach to this problem, you might go online to find a physics website. After entering the dimensions of your car's trunk as well as those of each box, you would print out the optimal placement of each box and repack your car according to the step-by-step directions. If you took a heuristic approach, you might remember that your mother always told you to pack the big items first and then squeeze the smaller ones in. Using this general rule of thumb, you would reorganize the trunk.

Now review the idea of cognitive obstacles on **page 283**. Imagine you are thinking ahead to future moves, and shopping for a bigger car. Despite its documented record of poor gas mileage, you decide to buy the model that first comes to mind, being persuaded by all the ads for the car you have recently seen. In this instance, you are displaying the availability heuristic, or making a decision based only on information that is readily available.

How can science help explain the cognitive obstacles to problem solving and decision making?

As mentioned in the discussion on **pages 287–288**, research shows that people often treat evidence in ways that minimize their own discomfort and maximize their positive feelings. Called *confirmation bias,* this situation occurs when we filter information through our existing belief systems and perspectives. We are even more likely to exhibit this bias when the information relates to highly charged issues such as politics or religion. It makes sense, then, that research also reveals that we do something similar when it comes to investing money. In the **Psych @ The Stock Exchange** feature **on page 287**, it was revealed that losing money is a more negative experience than winning money is a positive one, and that the tendency to place more value on money lost than on money gained, also known as loss aversion, has real ramifications in the investment world.

Why is this relevant?

Watch the accompanying video excerpt about making choices. You can access the video at MyPsychLab or by clicking the play button in the center of your eText. If your instructor assigns this video as a homework activity, you will find additional content to help you in MyPsychLab. You can also view the video by using your smart phone and the QR code below, or you can go to the YouTube link provided.

Consider what you know about cognitive shortcuts and obstacles. After you have read this chapter and watched the video, imagine that Maria's method of studying worked effectively throughout high school until she took her first foreign language course. In this course, her grades were much lower than usual. How might a mental set have played a role in Maria's academic problem?

Can we critically evaluate claims about cognitive obstacles?

The fact that people consistently make decisions based on representativeness or availability, and make biased judgments so that they can maintain their sense of comfort in the world, leads many people to wonder what is wrong with human thought processes. Surely they must be flawed! In reality, there is nothing inherently wrong with using heuristics; in fact, they can sometimes be valuable and useful. Heuristics allow people to make quick decisions based on readily available information. While the use of cognitive shortcuts can also open us up to mistakes and bias, being aware that we are fallible encourages us to be more effective critical thinkers and spend more time evaluating our decisions.

MyPsychLab **Your turn to Work the Scientific Literacy Model:** You can access the video at MyPsychLab or by clicking the play button in the center of your eText. If your instructor assigns this video as a homework activity, you will find additional content to help you at MyPsychLab. You can also view the video by using your smart phone and the QR code, or you can go to the YouTube link provided.

youtube.com/
scientificliteracy

9 :: INTELLIGENCE, APTITUDE, AND COGNITIVE ABILITIES

Module 9.1

Measuring Aptitude and Intelligence

Module
9.1

Learning Objectives

After reading this module you should:

KNOW ...	UNDERSTAND ...	APPLY ...	ANALYZE ...
The key terminology associated with intelligence and intelligence testing	The purpose of standardization and norms in intelligence testing	The concepts of test standardization and norms to make judgments about specific test scores	The use of brain size as an estimate of mental ability
	The relationship between reliability and validity in testing		Whether intelligence and aptitude tests make useful predictions about performance

You are probably enrolled in a college-level psychology course, so there is a good chance you were required to take one of the college board exams—namely, the ACT or the SAT. Considering the time and expense that students put into studying, taking the tests, and making sure that the scores are mailed to the right schools on time, one would hope that they are a very good indicator of how well students will perform in their classwork. Not all university administrators place great faith in these exams, however. In fact, the National Association for College Admission Counseling (NACAC) recently issued a report encouraging institutions to consider whether these tests were necessary or even helpful for their institutions. The group concluded that students were diverting time from learning that would develop intellectual skills or prepare them for life and work, in favor of focusing on preparing for the ACT or SAT. It is not clear that the tests actually predict academic success. In fact, the 2008 NACAC report showed that high school grades or scores on the ACT's specific subject tests do a better job predicting success than either of the general exams.

A number of schools (including some of the most prestigious) have stopped requiring the ACT or SAT. Nevertheless, the organizations that provide test coaching, practice test books, and the tests themselves continue to represent a billion-dollar industry. Obviously, some people do believe the tests measure something important, such as intelligence or academic aptitude. In light of these conflicting opinions, psychologists and students are asking important questions about the tests.

Focus Questions

 How are aptitude and intelligence tests constructed, and what are they supposed to measure?

 Is there a perfect way to measure intelligence?

Each of us differs in how we look, act, and feel. Similarly, intelligence appears to differentiate each individual. Intelligent people are described as "brainy," "bright," "wise," or "sharp," while "dim," "slow," and "dense" are less flattering descriptors meant to indicate less intelligence. Typically, these terms are used in reference to how much a person knows, as well as how successful the individual is at solving problems. We can improve upon our everyday notions of intelligence by applying a psychological definition to this concept. **Intelligence** *is the ability to think, understand, reason, and cognitively adapt to and overcome obstacles* (based on Neisser et al, 1996). Thus intelligence reflects not just how much you know, but how you recognize and solve problems. The history of psychology has seen dozens of attempts to define intelligence, and dozens of methods for measuring this very complex entity. We will begin this chapter by examining attempts at measuring intelligence, and then reviewing how these methods have shaped modern views of intelligence.

Achievement and Aptitude

Tests of mental ability come in many different forms to serve various purposes. **Achievement tests** *measure knowledge and thinking skills that an individual has acquired.* On a small scale, the quizzes and tests you take in your college courses are achievement tests. On a much larger scale, statewide and nation-wide achievement tests are given to millions of students every year in an attempt to measure whether individuals, schools, or even demographic groups have mastered the subject matter appropriate to specific grade levels.

In contrast to achievement tests, **aptitude tests** *are designed to measure an individual's potential to perform well on a specific range of tasks.* College entrance exams such as the SAT claim to measure the test taker's potential as a college student, while other aptitude tests are designed to test for specific jobs. The Armed Services Vocational Aptitude Battery (ASVAB) measures aptitude for the entire range of military jobs, from languages and communications to tank and helicopter mechanics. In short, achievement tests measure current abilities and aptitude tests predict future performance.

Most of the intelligence tests we review in this module measure both achievement and aptitude. These tests typically have multiple scales that tap into various facets of mental ability. Some basic rules and procedures are followed in the development and administration of all intelligence tests.

Complete the **Survey** *What Is Intelligence?* at **MyPsychLab**

CONSTRUCTING AND EVALUATING TESTS The task of constructing questionnaires and tests falls under a branch of psychology known as **psychometrics**, *the measurement of psychological traits and abilities—including personality, attitudes, and intelligence.* Items on tests and questionnaires are carefully constructed and evaluated for their relevance to the psychological trait they purport to measure.

Two important concepts in psychometrics, and research methods in general, are reliability and validity. As defined in Module 2.1, *validity* is the degree to which a test actually measures the trait or ability it is intended to measure. When examining validity, a psychologist might ask: *How do we know that the SAT is really measuring the ability to succeed in college?* There are several ways of answering this question, thereby demonstrating the validity of a test. For example, a psychologist might look for *predictive validity*—the degree to which a test predicts future performance. Studies conducted by testing companies and independent university researchers have provided some support for the SAT in this way, showing a positive correlation between SAT scores and first-year grade-point averages (GPAs) (Bridgeman et al., 2000; Coyle & Pillow, 2008). However, at .33 the correlation is quite modest. Thus many other factors play a role in attaining a high GPA. In fact, this correlation between SAT score and college GPA becomes even weaker after students complete their first year of college.

Achievement tests measure knowledge in a certain area. Students may take such tests to evaluate knowledge prior to advancing a grade.

Aptitude tests measure a person's potential to perform a range of specific tasks.

We should also examine whether tests are reliable. Module 2.1 defined *reliability* as the measurement of the degree to which a test produces consistent results. One method of evaluating reliability is through a construct known as *test–retest reliability.* In the same way that you depend on a reliable car to always start, a psychologist should be able to rely on a test to produce consistent scores. Research has shown that students who take the SAT a second time generally increase their score by a small amount, and this increase in scores is not due to changes in intelligence. Therefore, the SAT is not a perfectly reliable test (the retest scores differ from those obtained on the original test). Because these changes are not very large, however, the SAT does demonstrate some degree of reliability (Coyle, 2006).

STANDARDIZATION AND NORMS Another important aspect of test construction is standardization. A **standardized test** *is a test that has a set of questions or problems that are administered and scored in a uniform (in other words,* standardized) *way across large numbers of individuals.* Standardization allows for comparisons across individuals—a critical component of testing.

Intelligence test scores can be compared because of the existence of **norms**: *statistics that allow individuals to be evaluated relative to a typical or standard score.* For most intelligence tests, the *norm* or average score is 100. Another statistic called the *standard deviation* (defined in Module 2.4) measures variability around a mean. In intelligence tests, this can be interpreted as the typical number of points between an individual's score and the mean score. This may sound repetitive, but the standard deviation may be thought of as the average distance away from the average. As shown in Figure 9.1, intelligence tests typically have the standard deviation set to 15 points. Thus, not only do we know what is above or below average, but we also know what is far above average and only slightly below average. Another way to assess this variation is by examining **percentile rank**—*the percentage of scores below a certain point.* For example, a score of 100 has a percentile rank of .50, meaning that 50% of the population scores below this level. A score of 85 has a percentile rank of approximately .16, indicating that 16% of the population scores below it.

Generally, a norm is established by giving the test to hundreds of people and then calculating the mean and the standard deviation. Using a statistical technique, these numbers can be adjusted so that the average and standard deviation are familiar and relatively easy to use, such as 100 and 15, as shown in Figure 9.1. Of course, a test that is "normed" with one set of people may not be representative of another group. In addition, in many cases, a test will be renormed every 10 years or so to ensure that the mean and the standard deviation are still the same.

PSYCH @

The NFL Draft

Every spring, American football fans turn their attention to "the draft," where professional teams in the National Football League (NFL) take turns selecting the best amateur football players to join their teams. Pride, potential championships, and a lot of money are at stake, so teams use all the information they can get to select the players whom they think will contribute the most to the team's success. As a part of the run-up to the draft, the candidates demonstrate their physical aptitude through tests focusing on speed, strength, coordination, and agility by running, lifting, jumping, and clearing obstacles.

But what about the cognitive aspects of the game? American football actually shares some aspects of strategy with games such as chess. Each player must memorize his responsibilities for each possible play. Players must be able to keep in mind the rules for legal tackling and blocks in the midst of the action, not to mention keeping an eye on the boundaries of the field. To assess their intelligence, for the past three decades, candidates participating in the NFL

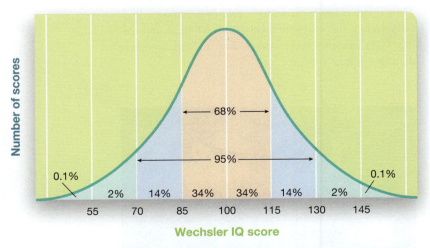

{FIG. 9.1} **The Normal Distribution of Scores for a Standardized Intelligence Test** This distribution of intelligence test scores in the population is standardized to have a mean of 100, so half of the population scores higher than 100, and half score lower than 100. The standard deviation (roughly, the average number of points away from the average) is approximately 15. Note the percentages in the curve. Nearly 68% of the population's scores fall within one standard deviation from the mean (between 85 and 115) and approximately 95% of scores fall within two standard deviations of the mean (between 70 and 130).

The Wonderlic is supposed to predict success in professional football, although it is not always very successful. This failure could be because of low validity.

draft have completed the Wonderlic, a 50-question test that is completed in less than 12 minutes.

The Wonderlic may be a valid scale for predicting success in other careers, but is it a valid predictor for success in professional football? NFL teams do not share test scores, but sports reporters and bloggers are often intrigued and amused by those scores that have leaked out. For example, quarterback Vince Young was expected to be the first pick of the draft in 2006, but many speculated that he would be passed over after his Wonderlic score—16 out of a possible 50—was leaked to the press. Dan Marino, one of the game's all-time great quarterbacks, apparently scored even lower than Vince Young. Without large samples, we cannot tell if these are exceptions to the rule, or if the Wonderlic generally is a poor aptitude test for performance in the NFL.

· · · · · · · · · · · · · · · · · ·

Quick Quiz 9.1a
Achievement and Aptitude

KNOW …

1 The SAT is an example of which kind of test?

A Intelligence test   C Achievement test

B Aptitude test   D Performance test

2 Which statistic, often used for understanding and evaluating standardized tests, measures the average variability around a mean?

A Validity   C Norms

B Standard deviation   D Percentile rank

UNDERSTAND …

3 A test that measures what a researcher intended to measure is _____, while obtaining consistent scores on that test suggests that it is _____.

A reliable; valid   C valid; reliable

B psychometric; reliable   D valid; normed

4 Because of norms in intelligence testing, psychologists are able to:

A evaluate an intelligence test to determine if it is reliable.

B evaluate an intelligence test to determine if it is valid.

C understand why there are learning disabilities.

D evaluate individuals relative to a typical or standard score on an intelligence test.

APPLY …

5 Bill received a score of 115 on his IQ test and as a result is a part of the 84th percentile. In terms of his score compared to the population, this result means that:

A 84% of the population's scores are lower than Bill's score.

B 84% of the population's scores are higher than Bill's score.

C the test must be valid.

D Bill is 84-years-old.

ANALYZE …

6 A high-tech company successfully hired 50 new employees, each of whom scored very high on a standardized achievement test. The employees were assigned to different jobs *based on the needs* of the company. By the end of the year, half were either reassigned or fired. Which is the most likely explanation for this outcome?

A The company should not have assumed intelligent people are needed for high-tech jobs.

B The achievement test was not reliable.

C The company should have given an aptitude test to determine who should work in which sector.

D The company's test was culturally biased.

Answers can be found on page ANS-3.

Approaches to Intelligence Testing

So far we have described the style of testing that is probably most familiar to you—the kind that involves a series of standardized, multiple-choice questions that you can respond to on a bubble sheet or through testing software. Certainly, some intelligence tests are of this variety, but attempts to measure intelligence also include diverse measures ranging from assessment of brain size to recording how fast a person reacts to stimuli. Even so, debate persists over what the tests measure and how they should be interpreted. In this section, we examine several ways that intelligence has been measured.

THE STANFORD-BINET TEST   In 1904, the French government created the Commission on the Education of Retarded Children. As part of this commission, Alfred Binet and Theodore Simon developed a method of assessing children's academic achievement at school (Siegler, 1992). The problem was easy to see: A new law required all children to attend school, and many of the students who showed up were woefully unprepared. Could there be a standardized way of assessing which students would need assistance to catch up, and which students were ahead of the rest? ◉

◉┤Watch the Video *Assessment of Memory with the Stanford-Binet Intelligence Scale* at MyPsychLab

Binet and Simon's work resulted in an achievement test—a measure of how well a child performed at various cognitive tasks relative to other children of his age. Because the focus was on performance at certain age levels, Binet preferred to say that the test measured **mental age**, *the average or typical test score for a specific chronological age*, rather than intelligence. Under this system, a 7-year-old child with a mental age of 7 would be considered average because her mental age matches her chronological age. In contrast, a 10-year-old student who was behind at school might have a mental age of 8, meaning his score was the same as the average 8-year-old child's score. With this information in hand, teachers could determine that the student would need extra help to bring his mental age up to his chronological age.

The practicality of Binet and Simon's test was apparent to others, and soon researchers in California began to adapt it for their own use. Lewis Terman at Stanford University had it translated to English and extended the test beyond school ages to include very high-achieving adults. This modified test, published in 1916, was named the Stanford-Binet Intelligence Scale (Siegler, 1992).

Terman and others almost immediately began describing the **Stanford–Binet test** as *a test intended to measure innate (genetic) intelligence.* Binet, however, had clearly viewed his original test as a measure of achievement, not as a measure of an innate capacity. Nonetheless, soon after, William Stern developed the **intelligence quotient (IQ)**—*a measurement in which the mental age of an individual is divided by the person's chronological age and then multiplied by 100.* For example, a 10-year-old child with a mental age of 7 would have an IQ of $7/10 \times 100 = 70$. The IQ score replaced the idea of a mental age—something that reflects progress in school—with a number purporting to measure a person's ability.

It might seem as if stating a mental age is no different from calculating an IQ ratio, but it certainly can be. Consider these two statements to see if one sounds more optimistic than the other:

- He has a mental age of 7, so he is 3 years behind.
- He has an IQ of 70, so he is 30 points below average.

To many, mental age leaves the door open to catching up because the student is described as behind—after two more years of school his mental age and chronological age could both be 12. The IQ, however, sounds almost like the diagnosis of a permanent condition. If that is the case, then no amount of help or education will affect the student—his IQ will seemingly be the same throughout his life.

THE WECHSLER ADULT INTELLIGENCE SCALE
The **Wechsler Adult Intelligence Scale (WAIS)** *is the most commonly used intelligence test used on adolescents and adults.* Its predecessor, the Wechsler-Bellvue test, was first developed by David Wechsler in 1939, and the WAIS is currently in its fourth edition. (In an ironic twist, Wechsler himself was classified as having mild intellectual disabilities—"feeble minded" was the term used at the time—as a nine-year-old child when his family immigrated to the United States from Romania.)

The WAIS provides a single IQ score for each test taker—the *Full Scale IQ*—but also breaks intelligence into a General Ability Index (GAI) and a Cognitive Proficiency Index (CPI), as shown in Figure 9.2.

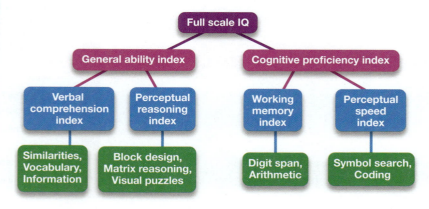

{FIG. 9.2}   **Subscales of the Wechsler Adult Intelligence Scale**

The GAI is computed from scores on the Verbal Comprehension and Perceptual Reasoning indices. These measures tap into an individual's intellectual abilities without placing so much emphasis on how fast he can solve problems and make decisions. The CPI, in contrast, is based on the Working Memory and Processing Speed subtests. It is included in the Full Scale IQ category because greater working memory capacity and processing speed allow more cognitive resources to be devoted to reasoning and solving problems. Figure 9.3 shows some sample test items from the WAIS.

RAVEN'S PROGRESSIVE MATRICES

Many of the original standardized tests required knowledge of the test developer's culture and language. As a result, individuals from different cultures and social classes were at an immediate disadvantage when taking these tests. However, many psychologists reasoned that intelligence is a universal human quality, independent of culture and language. A person should not be penalized on an intelligence test if he or she did not have an English vocabulary, or could not understand what a question meant. If a test could find some way to circumvent culture and language, then psychologists would have a fairer, more valid, "culture-free" test.

In the 1930s, John Raven developed **Raven's Progressive Matrices** (often shortened to just Raven's Matrices), *an intelligence test that emphasizes problems that are intended not to be bound to a particular language or culture.* The main set of tasks found in Raven's Matrices measure the extent to which test takers can see patterns in the shapes and colors within a matrix and then determine which shape or color would complete the pattern (see Figure 9.4). Note how this type of problem does not require knowledge of a specific language, culture, or human-made object or custom.

If you give the problem in Figure 9.4 (p. 314) a try, you will probably notice that it requires some thought—but how does it gauge intelligence? According to Raven, two abilities are key to intelligent behavior: identifying and extracting important information (*deductive reasoning*) and then applying it to new situations (*reproductive reasoning*).

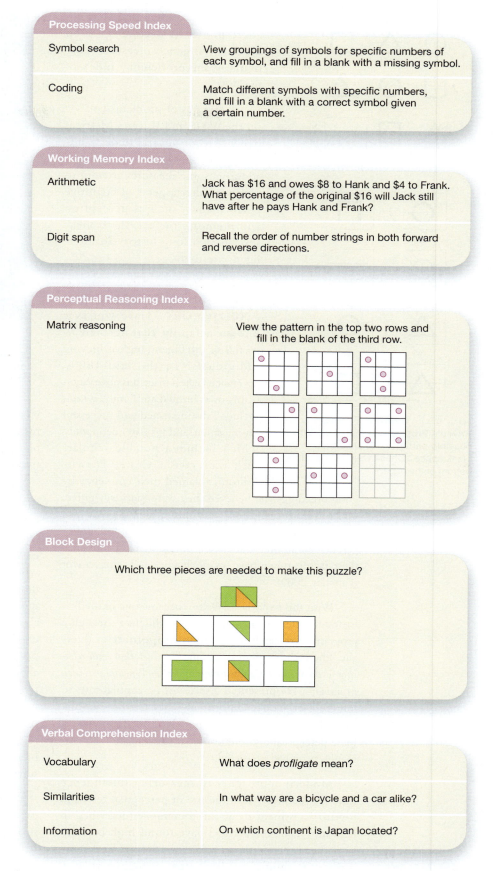

Processing Speed Index	
Symbol search	View groupings of symbols for specific numbers of each symbol, and fill in a blank with a missing symbol.
Coding	Match different symbols with specific numbers, and fill in a blank with a correct symbol given a certain number.

Working Memory Index	
Arithmetic	Jack has $16 and owes $8 to Hank and $4 to Frank. What percentage of the original $16 will Jack still have after he pays Hank and Frank?
Digit span	Recall the order of number strings in both forward and reverse directions.

Perceptual Reasoning Index	
Matrix reasoning	View the pattern in the top two rows and fill in the blank of the third row.

Block Design

Which three pieces are needed to make this puzzle?

Verbal Comprehension Index	
Vocabulary	What does *profligate* mean?
Similarities	In what way are a bicycle and a car alike?
Information	On which continent is Japan located?

{FIG. 9.3} **Types of Problems Used to Measure Intelligence** These hypothetical problems are consistent with the types seen on the Wechsler Adult Intelligence Scale.

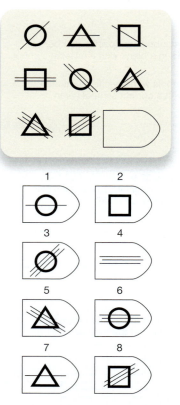

{FIG. 9.4} **Sample Problem from Raven's Progressive Matrices** Which possible pattern (1–8) should go in the blank space? Check your answer at the bottom of the page.

Performance on Raven's Matrices corresponds to performance on other intelligence measures, particularly the proficiency index of the WAIS.

The types of problems you see on the WAIS and Raven's Matrices likely fit your general understanding of how intelligence is tested. In addition, some measures attempt to tap into other aspects of cognitive performance, such as perception and memory. In fact, these measures have a long history in intelligence testing.

MEASURING PERCEPTION AND MEMORY Have you ever known a family that seemed to be full of intelligent, high-achieving individuals? In the mid-1800s, Sir Francis Galton made this observation of his own immediate family, which included distinguished and successful businessmen, and his extended family, which included notable scholars such as his cousin, Charles Darwin. Galton explained their eminence by good breeding—he believed they were *genetically* gifted. Of course, the children were raised with a great deal of privilege, good nutrition, fine schools, and plenty of parental attention—but Galton discounted any influence these factors might have on intelligence and achievement (Fancher, 2009).

With this hypothesis, Galton became one of the first to try to scientifically measure intelligence through a program of research he called **anthropometrics** (literally, "the measurement of people"), *a historical term referring to the method of measuring physical and mental variation in humans.* He presented a series of perceptual tests to hundreds of people. Unfortunately for Galton (but fortunately for those who did not share his family tree), these perceptual tests did not seem to correlate with eminence as he had predicted.

Modern approaches to measuring intelligence have moved away from the use of perceptual tests and toward assessment of working memory (described in Module 7.1). Researchers have found high correlations between working memory capacity and standardized reasoning tests (Kyllonen, 1996). In particular,

Sir Francis Galton believed that intelligence was something people inherit. Thus, he believed that an individual's relatives were a better predictor of intelligence than practice and effort.

working memory tests measure how well one can hold instructions and information in memory while completing problem-solving tasks (Conway et al., 2003) (see Figure 9.5).

Perhaps after examining the operation span measure in Figure 9.5 it is clearer to you why working memory is related to intelligence. Just as Galton equated perceptual abilities with intelligence, some modern psychologists believe that intelligence and working memory are one and the same. However, despite a great deal of overlap in working memory scores and other measures of intelligence, debate persists about exactly how strong this relationship is and why it exists (Ackerman et al., 2005). Perhaps working memory capacity is an expression of intelligence because it allows complex reasoning strategies to be used in short-term storage. Alternatively, working memory processes help us ignore irrelevant and distracting information, which also allows for intelligent behavior to emerge (Unsworth & Engle, 2005). At the very least, working memory tasks seem to tap into abilities that allow us to solve problems and express our mental abilities.

Tests of perception and memory take a biologically oriented approach to measuring intelligence. Thus researchers who study intelligence have also attempted to look directly at the human brain for possible insight into individual differences in intelligence.

1. Study this word

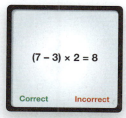

2. Judge whether the math problem is correct or incorrect

Kite

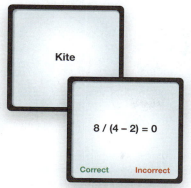

3. Repeat steps 1 and 2 with different words and problems multiple times

House   Pencil

Nose   Kite

4. Identify which words were and were not previously studied

{FIG. 9.5} **A Memory Task for Intelligence Testing** In the operation span task, a series of target words are shown one at a time, interspersed with equations that must be judged for accuracy. Once all of the words have been shown—typically between two and five of them—subjects are asked to pick the words out of a list of containing both target and distracter words.

WORKING THE SCIENTIFIC LITERACY MODEL
Brain Size and Intelligence

As the processor of complex thought and behavior, we can search within the brain to identify which characteristics may account for intelligence. Identifying which specific feature or features of the brain account for individual differences in intelligence, however, has proved challenging.

What do we know about brain size and intelligence?

Brain-based approaches to measuring intelligence rest on a common-sense assumption: Thinking occurs in the brain, so a larger brain should be related to greater intelligence. But does scientific evidence support this common-sense notion? In the days before modern brain imaging was possible, researchers typically obtained skulls from deceased subjects, filled them with fine-grained matter such metal pellets, and then transferred the pellets to a flask to measure the volume. These efforts taught us very little about intelligence and brain or skull size, but a lot about problems with measurement and racial prejudice. In some cases, the studies were highly flawed and inevitably led to conclusions that Caucasian males (and therefore the Caucasian male scientists who conducted these experiments) had the largest brains and, therefore, were the smartest of the human race (Gould, 1981). Modern approaches to studying

the brain and intelligence are far more sophisticated, thanks to newer techniques and a more enlightened knowledge of the brain's form and functions.

How can science explain the relationship between brain size and intelligence?

In relatively rare cases, researchers have two main sources of data available to them: a brain and an intelligence test score. In one study, Sandra Witelson and her colleagues (2006) collected 100 brains obtained following autopsies. Scores on the Wechsler Adult Intelligence Scale were available for each person (or each brain, depending on how you want to look at it). Detailed anatomical examinations and size measurements were made on the entire brain and subregions that support cognitive skills. Overall, approximately 36% of the variation in verbal intelligence scores was accounted for by the size of the cortex.

The size of the brain and its various regions is just one way of looking at intelligence. One of the most obvious features of the human brain is its convoluted surface. These convolutions (called gyri; pronounced "ji-rye") comprise the outer part of the cerebral cortex (see Figure 9.6 on p. 316). The number and size of these cerebral gyri is greater in species that have complex cognitive and social lives, such as elephants, dolphins, and primates (Marino, 2002; Rogers et al., 2010). But what about humans: Are individual differences in intelligence test scores related to convolutions of the cortex? Using brain imaging technology, researchers have scanned the brains of healthy adults

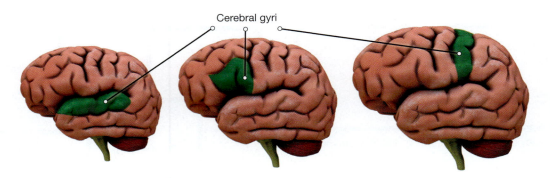

Cerebral gyri

{FIG. 9.6}   **Does Intelligence Increase With Brain Size?** While the size of the brain may have a modest relationship to intelligence, the convolutions or "gyri" along the surface of the cortex are another important factor: Increased convolutions are associated with higher intelligence test scores.

who had completed the WAIS. The degree of convolution across the surface of the cortex was then correlated to the subjects' IQ score. It turns out that the higher the score on the WAIS, the more convolutions seen across several regions of the cortex; the degree of convolutions accounted for approximately 25% of the variability in WAIS scores (Luders et al., 2008).

Can we critically evaluate this issue?

Clearly, the relationship between brain size and intelligence is much more complicated than once thought. One particular exception to the "bigger is better" rule of brain size comes from Albert Einstein. The average human brain is between 1,300 and 1,400 grams. Einstein's brain measured 1,230 grams. Despite this relatively small size, a region of his parietal lobe—one that is associated with mathematical processing—appeared to be approximately 15% larger than normal (Witelson et al., 1999). This single exception does not invalidate all of the work on brain size and intelligence, but it reminds us that other factors may account for individual differences in intelligence. Also, both brain size and IQ, like other physical characteristics, are influenced by factors such as nutrition and physical health (Choi et al., 2008).

Why is this relevant?

The relationship between brain size and IQ can be used to better understand clinical conditions. For example, individuals who experience anorexia nervosa (a psychological disorder marked by self-starvation) or prolonged periods of alcohol abuse appear to lose brain mass along with certain cognitive skills, such as the ability to put together block designs in a standardized test (McCormick et al., 2008; Schottenbauer et al., 2007). Even in relatively healthy adults, brain volume gradually declines as a result of aging; this effect is also correlated with declines in some, but not all, measures of intelligence (Rabbitt et al., 2008).

The size of Albert Einstein's brain was average. However, researchers discovered some peculiar features within his parietal lobe—an area known to be involved in processing mathematical and spatial information.

Quick Quiz 9.1b :: Approaches to Intelligence Testing

KNOW ...

1 Galton developed anthropometrics as a means to measure intelligence based on _____.

  A creativity
  B speed and perception
  C physical size and body type
  D brain convolution

2 Although the WAIS provides a full IQ score as a measure of general intelligence, it also includes subscales for:

  A progression and matrices.
  B working memory and working perception IQs.
  C general ability and cognitive proficiency.
  D reading and writing skills.

UNDERSTAND ...

3 The Raven Matrices were developed to improve upon which issue with intelligence tests?

  A Cross-cultural barriers
  B Inconsistency of scores with retesting
  C The time needed to complete a test
  D Comparisons of old versus young people

APPLY ...

4 If someone's mental age is double her chronological age, what would her IQ be?

  A 100
  B 50
  C 200
  D Cannot be determined with this information

ANALYZE ...

5 Which of the following statements best summarizes the relationship between brain size and intelligence?

  A Brain size is a great predictor of intelligence—the larger the brain, the greater the intelligence.
  B There is no relationship between brain size and intelligence whatsoever.
  C Brain size and intelligence are related only in Caucasian people.
  D There are modest correlations between brain size, convolutions of the cortex, and intelligence.

Answers can be found on page ANS-3.

Module Summary

Now that you have read this module you should:

Listen to the audio file of this module at **MyPsychLab**

KNOW ...

- *The key terminology associated with intelligence and intelligence testing:*

achievement tests (p. 309)
anthropometrics (p. 314)
aptitude tests (p. 309)
intelligence (p. 309)
intelligence quotient (IQ) (p. 312)
mental age (p. 312)
norms (p. 310)
percentile rank (p. 310)

psychometrics (p. 309)
Raven's Progressive Matrices (p. 313)
standardized test (p. 310)
Stanford-Binet test (p. 312)
Wechsler Adult Intelligence Scale (WAIS) (p. 312)

UNDERSTAND ...

- *The purpose of standardization and norms in intelligence testing.* Standardization of testing content as well as the conditions in which tests are administered is critical, as comparisons among scores between individuals cannot be made unless tests are standardized. Establishing norms provides numbers with which individual scores can be compared.

- *The relationship between reliability and validity in testing.* A test that gives similar scores for an individual from one time to the next is reliable. A valid test is one that measures what it is supposed to measure. For a test to be valid, it must be reliable. However, a test can be reliable but not valid.

APPLY ...

- *The concepts of test standardization and norms to make judgments about specific test scores.* Consider this scenario:

On a standardized test with a mean of 500 and a standard deviation of 100, which of the following are typical scores, high scores, or low scores? Student A earned a 550, student B earned a 425, student C earned a 375, and student D earned a 700. Check your answers on page ANS-3.

ANALYZE ...

- *The use of brain size as an estimate of mental ability.* The correlation between brain size and intelligence is very modest. Brain size is a very general measurement; it may be that specific regions of the cerebral cortex, as shown by convolutions of the cortical surface, account for some of the variations across intelligence test scores.

- *Whether intelligence and aptitude tests make useful predictions about performance.* When intelligence and aptitude tests are developed, their creators conduct studies to assess the validity of the instrument. In some cases, they look for predictive validity, which is the ability of a test to predict performance in a specific area. For example, the SAT predicts college GPA to some degree and intelligence tests such as the Wonderlic can predict job success. Conversely, we do not know how well the Wonderlic can predict success in the NFL.

Understanding Intelligence

KNOW ...	UNDERSTAND ...	APPLY ...	ANALYZE ...
The key terminology related to understanding intelligence	Why intelligence is divided into fluid and crystallized types	Your knowledge to identify examples from the triarchic theory of intelligence	Whether teachers should spend time tailoring lessons to each individual student's learning style
	The puzzling "Flynn effect"—a generational rise in IQ scores		

Why is it that we can be so good at one cognitive task, yet struggle with another? Practice, aptitude, and even genetics are part of the answer. The wide chasm between excelling and struggling at a mental task is especially evident in many children with autism. Individuals with autism and related disorders are typically impaired in their abilities to develop social or emotional connections with others, even their parents. They *generally* fare poorly on standardized intelligence tests, scoring in lower percentiles. Asking a child with autism to complete a test that requires several hours of interaction with the test administrator, according to psychologist Michelle Dawson, "is like giving a blind person an intelligence test that requires him to process visual information" (Begley, 2007). Yet Dawson and her colleagues (2007) reported that when students with autism completed a standardized intelligence test (the Raven's Matrices described in Module 9.1), their average IQ score was in the 56th percentile, which is slightly *above* average. Dawson (who has autism) attributes this outcome to the fact that the Raven's test does not require social interaction. Instead, test takers are given an explanation, and then proceed to solve problems on their own. It appears that many children with autism perform poorly on tests that require substantial verbal interaction, but they may perform as well as (if not better than) the rest of the population when it comes to more culture-free tasks that tap into problem-solving ability.

Focus Questions

1 Is intelligence one ability or many?

2 How have psychologists attempted to explain intelligence as a collection of different abilities?

· · · · · · · · · · · · · · · · · ·

Recall that the definition of intelligence incorporates the ability to think, understand, reason, and cognitively adapt to and overcome obstacles. This definition includes a lot of important terms—understanding, adapting, reasoning, and thinking skills are things we typically attribute to intelligent behavior. So what exactly constitutes intelligent behavior? Does it consist of a single capacity, or a bunch of interworking components? As you will learn in this module, a full picture of intelligence involves various perspectives on how many different abilities fall under the term "intelligence."

Intelligence as a Single, General Ability

PsychTutor

Click here in your eText for an interactive tutorial on **Spearman's Theory**

Before you read this section, try the thought experiment in Table 9.1. Randomly select either the left or right column of the table.

The scenario on the left side of Table 9.1 is intended to get you to think in terms of intelligence as a trait that people can apply to all sorts of problems, including math, language, mechanics, and so on. According to this perspective, people who rate high in general intelligence should do well at all sorts of tasks, whereas those who rate low in general intelligence would likely struggle across each of the same tasks.

Scientific arguments and evidence for general intelligence date back to early 20th-century work by Charles Spearman. Spearman (1923) began by developing techniques to calculate correlations among multiple measures of mental abilities. One of these techniques, known as **factor analysis**, *is a statistical technique that reveals similarities among a wide variety of items.* For example, different measures such as vocabulary, reading comprehension, and verbal reasoning might overlap enough to form a "language ability" factor. Similarly, you might find high correlations among the scores on various achievement tests and grades from school grade

reports. If an individual does well in algebra, she is likely to do well in geometry and calculus. Perhaps that is not surprising, given that these subjects are all mathematical in nature. According to the perspective that assumes intelligence is a single factor, someone who is skilled in math subjects will also be skilled in reading and writing.

SPEARMAN'S GENERAL INTELLIGENCE The correlations among different mental abilities led Spearman to hypothesize the existence of a **general intelligence** (abbreviated as "*g*")—*a concept that intelligence is a basic cognitive trait comprising the ability to learn, reason, and solve problems regardless of their nature.* Spearman's concept of *g* is apparent today with college admissions tests and a wide range of intelligence tests administered by psychologists (Johnson et al., 2008).

If human intelligence really is a general ability, then that would certainly explain Spearman's correlational findings: A person with a high *g* score could use his general intelligence to solve problems in any domain he chose, even in fields as different as reading comprehension and algebra. In fact, *g* is related to a number of outcomes that people seek, as shown in Figure 9.7.

The notion of general intelligence may not be consistent with your own experiences. Perhaps you know people whom you would regard as "book smart," but who are not particularly skilled at solving problems as they arise. Conversely, other friends may be the ones you call when your car breaks down, or when you are lost in an unfamiliar place. Perhaps intelligence is similarly divided.

Table 9.1 :: Two Approaches to Intelligence

For this experiment choose either the left or right side. Read and answer both questions posed. Then stop, think about something else for a few minutes, and try the questions on the opposite side.

1(a). If you have attended traditional schools, you have almost certainly compared report cards and standardized test grades (such as the ACT or SAT) with friends and classmates. Have you ever noticed that within any given grade level there are some students who are known to receive high marks no matter which class in involved, whereas other students cannot seem to get better than a D, no matter which subject is involved? Can you list the names of some present or former classmates who fit one of these descriptions?	2(a). Have you ever known a student who does extremely well in mathematics and physical sciences, someone headed toward a career as an engineer, perhaps, but who cannot seem to make any sense of a short story or poem? Or what about the opposite: a student who is constantly reading novels, and who can write beautiful prose without a rough draft, but cannot seem to get 2 + 2 to equal 4? Can you list the names of some present or former classmates who fit one of these descriptions?
1(b). Naturally, factors such as interest and motivation will affect a student's grades but, in general, doesn't it seem that some people are just more intelligent than others?	2(b). Naturally, factors such as interest and motivation will affect a student's grades but, in general, doesn't it seem that everyone is intelligent in some ways but not in others?

Total percentage of the population in this range:

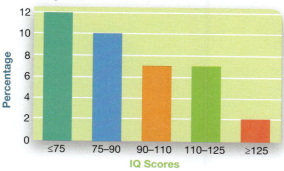

Individuals in this range who divorced within five years:

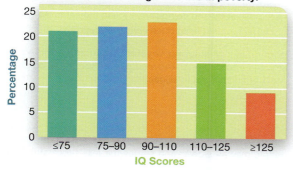

Individuals in this range who live in poverty:

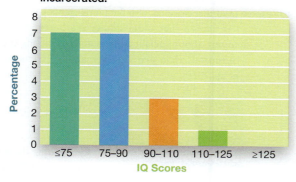

Individuals in this range who have been incarcerated:

{FIG. 9.7}   **General Intelligence Is Related to Various Outcomes**   General intelligence (*g*) predicts not just intellectual ability, but also psychological well-being, income, and successful long-term relationships.

A scientific account of intelligence should be able to explain why intelligent behavior can be expressed in several different ways.

What do we know about different types of intelligence?

Intelligence appears to be divisible into at least two categories. Some types of problem solving and thinking fall into the category of **fluid intelligence (Gf)**, *a type of intelligence that is used to adapt to new situations and solve new problems without relying on previous knowledge.* Tests of Gf involve problems that do not require prior experience with the task or any specialized knowledge, and may include tasks such as pattern recognition and solving geometric puzzles, such as Raven's Matrices (described in Module 9.1). **Crystallized intelligence (Gc)**, like an actual crystal, *is a form of intelligence that relies on extensive experience and knowledge and, therefore, tends to be relatively stable and robust* (Figure 9.8; Cattell, 1971). Intelligence tests measure Gc with vocabulary, similarity/difference, and reading comprehension problems, because all of these tasks require prior knowledge. The idea underlying Gf and Gc probably makes sense, but does scientific evidence support the division of intelligence into these two categories?

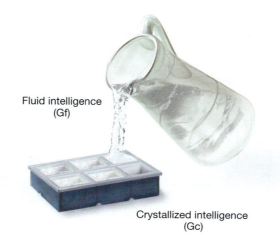

Fluid intelligence (Gf)

Crystallized intelligence (Gc)

{FIG. 9.8}   **Fluid and Crystallized Intelligence**   Fluid intelligence is dynamic and changing, and may eventually become crystallized into a more permanent form.

How can science help distinguish between fluid and crystallized intelligence?

The hypothesis that we have both Gf and Gc intelligence has been tested by examining how each type changes over the life span (Cattell, 1971; Horn & Cattell, 1967). In one study, people aged 20 to 89 years were given a wide array of tasks, including the Tower of London puzzle, Block Design, and tests of reaction time (see Figure 9.3 and Figure 9.9). The researchers found that performance in tasks that require Gf intelligence peaks in early to middle adulthood and declines later in life (Bugg et al., 2006).

Gc, by comparison, involves accumulated knowledge. Thus, as long as an individual keeps learning new information, Gc is less likely to decrease. An example of Gc intelligence is vocabulary and verbal ability (Figure 9.10). Healthy, older adults generally do not show much decline, if any at all, in these skills (Miller et al., 2009). In fact, some evidence indicates that Gc may increase with age (Kaufman, 2001). Observations of decreased fluid and conserved Gc memory abilities in older adults are supported by neurological studies. The functioning of brain regions associated with Gf intelligence tasks declines sooner than the functioning of those regions supporting Gc intelligence tasks (Geake & Hansen, 2010).

Which South American countries are these?

PACIFIC OCEAN

ATLANTIC OCEAN

Do *irony* and *coincidence* mean the same thing?
What does *abstruse* mean?

{FIG. 9.10} **Measuring Crystallized Intelligence** Vocabulary and informational knowledge are thought to be components of crystallized intelligence.

Can we critically evaluate evidence for distinguishing Gc and Gf?

There is certainly a lot of strong evidence that fluid and crystallized intelligence are distinct from each other. The tasks that measure each type of intelligence are very different from each other, and age affects how well people do on them. Nevertheless, we should be careful not to over-generalize these findings. Older

people may be slower and somewhat less successful at tasks measuring reaction time and problem-solving skills, but they also excel in certain domains. Consider social conflicts and dilemmas, which can be highly complex, nuanced, and difficult to resolve (and therefore require fluid intelligence). Research has shown that older adults are better at reasoning about social conflicts and predicting their outcomes than are younger adults (Grossman et al., 2010).

Why is this relevant?

Recognizing the distinctness of Gf and Gc can help to reduce stereotypes and expectations about intelligence in older age. Also, the theory that more than one type of intelligence exists may help explain individual differences in performance on intelligence tests found at any age. The notion of *general intelligence* may not fully capture

Tower of London Test
Shallice (1982)

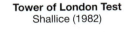

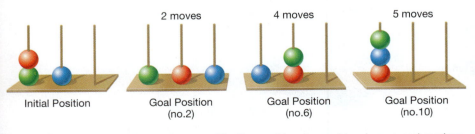

Initial Position   Goal Position (no.2)   Goal Position (no.6)   Goal Position (no.10)

{FIG. 9.9} **Measuring Fluid Intelligence** The Tower of London problem has several versions, each of which requires the test taker to plan and keep track of rules. For example, the task might involve moving the colored beads from the initial position so that they match any of the various end goal positions.

the complex and individualized ways that people express their cognitive skills. Strong evidence supports the contention that intelligence comes in both fluid and crystallized forms—but could there be even more?

Quick Quiz 9.2a
Intelligence as a Single, General Ability

KNOW …

1. The ability to adapt to new situations and solve new problems reflects _____ intelligence(s), whereas the ability to draw on one's experiences and knowledge reflects _____ intelligence(s).

   A fluid; crystallized
   B crystallized; fluid
   C general; multiple
   D multiple; general

2. What is factor analysis?

   A A method of ranking individuals by their intelligence
   B A statistical procedure that is used to identify which sets of psychological measures are highly correlated with each other
   C The technique of choice for testing fluid intelligence
   D The technique of choice for testing crystallized intelligence

UNDERSTAND …

3. Which of the following *is not* a reason why intelligence is divisible into both fluid and crystallized forms?

   A The two types are not equally affected in old age.
   B Valid and unique tests for each type have been developed.
   C Intelligence tests are difficult to score if problems are not divided into categories.
   D The two types of intelligence can more fully capture the complex and individualized ways that people express their cognitive skills.

Answers can be found on page ANS-3.

Intelligence as Multiple, Specific Abilities

Let's return to the thought experiment in Table 9.1 on page 320, this time looking at only the right side. Did you agree that some people seem to be extremely intelligent with regard to some topics but average or below average with regard to other topics? This side of the thought experiment emphasizes multiple, specific abilities. Each of these abilities, like individual components in an engine or a computer, has one specific function that may be unrelated to another ability's function. However, each mental ability contributes to overall thought in the same way that a keyboard, mouse, and memory all contribute to the overall function of a computer.

Even Spearman's own techniques were used to argue against general intelligence. For example, L. L. Thurstone examined scores of general intelligence tests and found seven different clusters of what he termed *primary mental abilities*, including familiar topics such as reading comprehension, spatial reasoning, numerical ability, and memory span. Modern proponents of multiple intelligence types cite other evidence (Gardner, 1983):

- An individual may experience a head injury or stroke and lose one ability (such as language production) without any loss in other aspects of intelligence. For example, an individual might lose the ability to understand sentences that use the passive voice (e.g., "The ball was chased by the dog"), yet still understand sentences that use the active voice (e.g., "The dog chased the ball").

- **Savants** *are individuals with low mental capacity in most domains but extraordinary abilities in other specific areas such as music, mathematics, or art.* If intelligence was a single ability, then we would not expect such brilliance in one area and impaired functioning in others.

- When psychologists look beyond traditional ways of viewing intelligence (i.e., language, math, and problem-solving ability), they find people vary a great deal in terms of physical, social, and artistic skills that are not well explained by *g*.

Recall that the introduction to this module revealed that many people with autism do very well on some measures of intelligence—namely, those that do not involve extensive social interactions with a test giver. Based on all of these examples and evidence, several contemporary psychologists have formulated multifaceted models of intelligence. For example, Robert Sternberg offers an alternative known as the *triarchic theory of intelligence*, a model of intelligence consisting

Stephen Wiltshire is a savant who has autism. Although he has mental impairments in many areas, his artistic skills are amazing. Wiltshire is capable of viewing extremely complex landscapes and drawing them from memory with great accuracy and clarity. (Note: People with autism who are also savants are the exception—contrary to popular belief most people with autism are not savants.)

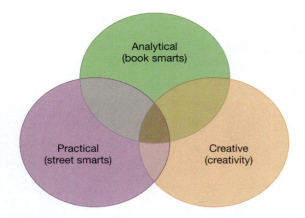

{FIG. 9.11} **The Triarchic Theory of Intelligence** According to psychologist Robert Sternberg, intelligence comprises three overlapping, yet distinct components. **Click on this figure in your eText to see more details.**

PsychTutor

Click here in your eText for an interactive tutorial on **Gardner's Theory**

of three domains: analytical intelligence, practical intelligence, and creative intelligence (see Figure 9.11).

Analytical intelligence is the verbal, mathematical problem-solving type of intelligence that probably comes to mind when we speak of intelligence. It is close to the concept of academic achievement and the notion of intelligence as measured by *g*.

Practical intelligence is the ability to address real-world problems that are encountered in daily life, especially those that occur in an individual's specific work context and family life.

Creative intelligence is the ability to create new ideas to solve problems. Obviously, artists must have some level of creative intelligence, but the same is true for any kind

of designer. It also takes creative intelligence to be a scientist because creative thinking is often required to conceive of good scientific hypotheses and develop ways of testing them (Sternberg et al., 2001).

Howard Gardner (1999) proposed the concept of **multiple intelligences**, *a model claiming that eight different forms of intelligence exist, each independent from the others.* This model has been influential in elementary education. Gardner argued that the eight forms of intelligence listed in Table 9.2 are all unique ways of expressing intellectual abilities. His theory makes intuitive sense: People can be great with language but clumsy and uncoordinated; we know people who have amazing strength, agility, and stamina, but who cannot hum a simple tune or add double-digit numbers without a calculator. But are these really forms of intelligence? For example, does being able to control body movement and balance constitute intelligence, or is this better described as a talent or skill?

These questions are relevant to a number of educational practices that have used the notion of multiple intelligences to promote the idea of **learning styles**, *the hypothesis that individuals are fundamentally different in how*

Table 9.2 :: Gardner's Proposed Forms of Intelligence

Verbal/linguistic intelligence	The ability to read, write, and speak effectively
Logical/mathematical intelligence	The ability to think with numbers and use abstract thought; the ability to use logic or mathematical operations to solve problems
Visuospatial intelligence	The ability to create mental pictures, manipulate them in the imagination, and use them to solve problems
Bodily/kinesthetic intelligence	The ability to control body movements, to balance, and to sense how one's body is situated
Musical/rhythmical intelligence	The ability to produce and comprehend tonal and rhythmic patterns
Interpersonal intelligence	The ability to detect another person's emotional states, motives, and thoughts
Self/intrapersonal intelligence	Self-awareness; the ability to accurately judge one's own abilities, and identify one's own emotions and motives
Naturalist intelligence	The ability to recognize and identify processes in the natural world—plants, animals, and so on
Existential intelligence	The tendency and ability to ask questions about purpose in life and the meaning of human existence

they best acquire information. The most common sets of learning styles include divisions such as visual, auditory, reading/writing, and kinesthetic/tactile (moving and touching)—you probably see the connection with the theory of multiple intelligences. Many educators claim that students tend to learn best using their own personal style. These claims require further critical and scientific scrutiny to test their validity.

MYTHS IN MIND
Learning Styles

The proposal that humans have individual learning styles can be tested scientifically with a simple hypothesis: Individuals should learn and retain more information learned through their preferred learning style than through the other styles. For example, if a person is a visual learner, he should score better on tests for information he learns visually than on tests for information learned through listening. A kinesthetic learner should retain more information she learned through physical interaction than information she learned through listening.

The idea that each individual has his or her own learning style might make intuitive sense, but finding evidence to support it has proved difficult. In fact, dozens of studies have failed to show any benefit for studying according to an individual's learning style; this is true even in large-scale reviews analyzing results of dozens of studies (Pasher et al., 2008). This result probably occurs because regardless of how you encounter something—reading, watching, listening, or moving—you still need to store the *meaning* of the information to retain it over the long term (Willingham, 2004). As a result, it would not make sense for teachers to tailor their instructional styles to fit individual students. Instead, teachers should tailor their teaching to fit the material.

Are there actually "learning styles"? Educators have long argued that individual students learn better if instruction practices are adapted to suit their style of learning, but evidence supporting the existence of different learning styles is virtually nonexistent.

• • • • • • • • • • • • • • • • • •

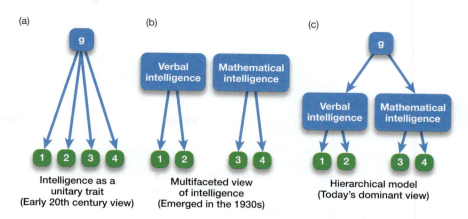

Notes:
• "*g*" stands for general, a single factor underlying all intelligent behavior.
• Numbered boxes represent multiple tests of different intellectual abilities.

{FIG. 9.12} **Differing Perspectives on Intelligence** Spearman proposed a single, general intelligence that could affect scores on *all* varieties of tasks, as shown in (a). Later, Thurstone and others argued for separate, unrelated primary mental abilities as shown in (b). The dominant view today incorporates the evidence in favor of both, as shown in (c). It appears that individuals can have large differences in verbal and mathematical skills (separate abilities), although in the general population, they produce high correlations that support the concept of g (Willingham, 2004).

EVALUATING THEORIES OF SINGLE AND MULTIPLE INTELLIGENCES So is intelligence one ability or many? Decades of scientific inquiry suggest the answer is "It depends." Researchers have found that scores among various types of cognitive tests are positively correlated, supporting the one-ability hypothesis (Johnson et al., 2008; Johnson et al., 2004). However, correlations occur in the population, not in any one individual. Therefore, some individuals may have unusual differences in ability, such as very low mathematical intelligence, but very high language intelligence. In addition, scores on different types of mathematical tests have higher correlations with one another than they do with verbal tests, and vice versa. Thus mathematical and verbal abilities are distinct, but they probably share at least some common source.

Psychologists took these factors into account and developed the hierarchical model shown in Figure 9.12. Diagrams A and B summarize historical views you are now familiar with. Diagram C seems to sum up the modern, general consensus that intelligence can be traced to a single common construct called "*g*," and within it we can separate out verbal and mathematical intelligence. Verbal and mathematical intelligence encompass specific and unique tasks.

It may be easier to understand the advantage of this type of model by using an analogy. Chimps and gorillas are clearly two different types of animals, but both are primates, which also means they are mammals. Thus they are distinct at some levels, but similar at others. That is exactly what research has shown about intelligence. The abilities to comprehend written text and to produce written text may, in fact, be different intelligences, but they are both forms of verbal intelligence, so both contribute to general intelligence.

Quick Quiz 9.2b
Intelligence as Multiple, Specific Abilities

KNOW...

1 Which of the following is *not* part of the triarchic theory of intelligence?

- **A** Practical
- **B** Analytical
- **C** Kinesthetic
- **D** Creative

2 _____ proposed that there are eight different forms of intelligence, each independent from the others.

- **A** Robert Sternberg
- **B** Howard Gardner
- **C** L. L. Thurstone
- **D** Raymond Cattell

ANALYZE...

3 A teacher is struggling to get his students to understand the concept of how electricity works. Based on learning and educational research, what might he need to do to help his students understand?

- **A** Modify his teaching style for this topic.
- **B** Go out into the real world and point to examples.
- **C** Offer separate tutorials for visual and auditory learners.
- **D** Get the class to choreograph an interpretive dance of how electricity works.

4 Which of the following statements is an argument for multiple intelligences?

- **A** Statistical analyses show that all varieties of intelligence tests are highly correlated with one another.
- **B** Most individuals who score high on verbal tests also score high on quantitative and performance tests.
- **C** Some individuals score high on verbal tests but very low on quantitative tests, and vice versa.
- **D** Some people would rather listen to a lecture than view a film because they are "auditory" learners.

Answers can be found on page ANS-3.

The Flynn Effect: Is *Everyone* Getting Smarter?

For reasons that are not yet clearly understood, performance on standardized intelligence tests has been improving at a steady pace for decades. One line of evidence came from the Dutch and French militaries, both of which administered the Raven's Progressive Matrices test (discussed in Module 9.1) to all newly enlisted young adults. From the 1950s to the 1980s, the scores increased approximately 21 points from a mean of 100 to a mean of 121 for the Dutch. Thus the Dutch military personnel's average scores increased roughly 7 points per decade. Similar testing in France revealed even greater increases of about 10 points per decade (Flynn, 1987).

Other evidence of a gradual rise in IQ test performance comes from changing norms on standardized tests. One frequently used test was normed to have an average of 100 in 1953. When a new version of the test was developed 25 years later, psychologists set it up to have a norm of 100 as well. In theory, an adult who scored the average of 100 on the 1947 version of the test should have the same score on the 1978 version—it is the same individual taking basically the same test, after all. However, when researchers actually tried having the same adults take both versions of the test, the participants' average was about 8 points higher on the old test (Flynn, 1984). After reviewing many similar studies that were reported between 1932 and 2007, James Flynn (2007) has estimated that the averages increase about 1 point every three years. This phenomenon has a fitting name: The **Flynn effect** *refers to the steady population level increases in intelligence test scores over time* (Figure 9.13).

Consider the implications of the Flynn effect. Individuals of your generation score, on average, higher than your parents would on the same test. This year's high school class will average 15 points higher than their grandparents' graduating class. How can we explain this increase? An adolescent who learns about the Flynn effect may exclaim, "I knew I was smarter than my parents!" Of course, the parents' response would probably be something along these lines: "Kids are not smarter! They're just being trained to take tests better." These are exactly the kinds of explanations that psychologists are testing. But which side is right?

First, consider this question: Are today's kids smarter than earlier generations? A number of psychologists offered this hypothesis based on factors such as improved nutrition, health care, and early childhood educational programs, but there are reasons to be skeptical of this explanation (Neisser, 1998). Consider what it means for past generations. Recall that the Dutch military personnel's test scores increased 7 points per decade; thus, as shown in Figure 9.13, today's group of 18-year-olds would average 35 points higher than 50 years ago, which means the average Dutch soldier today would score 135 on the 1950 test! This is an improbable result—but the reverse is not any better. If today's Dutch soldiers are of normal intelligence, their grandparents would have scored, on average, 65 points—enough to qualify as severely mentally disabled. That does not seem any more likely.

Now consider the other question: Are younger generations just better at taking tests? People often increase their test scores by taking it a second time. The practice and increased familiarity definitely affect the score on the second attempt, and they may even have long-term effects. Considering that children in the United States and other wealthy countries are taking standardized tests with increasing frequency, it is possible that the practice effects add up over time. Even so, this hypothesis cannot explain the entire Flynn effect. The Flynn effect holds even for infants who take intelligence tests specially adapted for this age group. Certainly infants could not have experience with intelligence testing before birth (Lynn, 2009).

One issue that may help make sense of the Flynn effect concerns technological advances. The technological environment has definitely increased, along with test scores, over the past 60 years. Perhaps the increased exposure to television, computers, and video games enhances individuals' ability to handle visualization tasks and increases their comfort level with tests. The most substantial gains that Flynn has documented involve performance-based scores that measure speed of processing, visualization, and the like.

Whatever led to these increases in IQ scores over time, the most recent data suggest that the Flynn effect might be coming to an end—or may even be reversing—in wealthy countries that have a long history of testing. Not only have intelligence test scores leveled off, but in some cases they have even declined (Sundet, 2004; Teasdale & Owen, 2005). In contrast, developing countries may just be at the beginning of their own run of experiencing the Flynn effect (Daley et al., 2003).

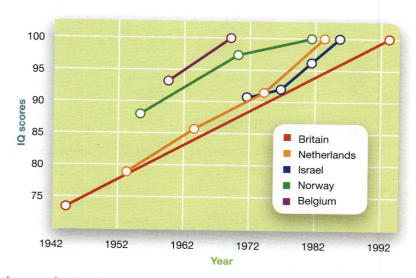

{FIG. 9.13} **The Flynn Effect** For decades, there has been a general trend toward increasing IQ scores. This trend, called the Flynn effect, has been occurring since standardized IQ tests have been administered.

Quick Quiz 9.2c
The Flynn Effect: Is *Everyone* Getting Smarter?

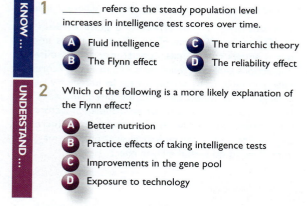

KNOW…

1 _____ refers to the steady population level increases in intelligence test scores over time.

A Fluid intelligence   C The triarchic theory

B The Flynn effect   D The reliability effect

UNDERSTAND…

2 Which of the following is a more likely explanation of the Flynn effect?

A Better nutrition

B Practice effects of taking intelligence tests

C Improvements in the gene pool

D Exposure to technology

Answers can be found on page ANS-3.

Module Summary

Now that you have read this module
you should:

Listen to
the audio file of
this module at
MyPsychLab

KNOW ...

- **The key terminology related to understanding intelligence:**

crystallized intelligence (Gc) (p. 321)

factor analysis (p. 320)

fluid intelligence (Gf) (p. 321)

Flynn effect (p. 326)

general intelligence (g) (p. 320)

learning styles (p. 324)

multiple intelligences (p. 324)

savants (p. 323)

UNDERSTAND ...

- **Why intelligence is divided into fluid and crystallized types.** Mental abilities encompass both the amount of knowledge accumulated and the ability to solve new problems. This understanding is consistent not only with our common views of intelligence, but also with the results of decades of intelligence testing. Also, the observation that fluid intelligence can decline over the life span, even as crystallized intelligence remains constant, lends further support to the contention that they are different abilities.

- **The puzzling "Flynn effect"—a generational rise in IQ scores.** Why the Flynn effect occurs is unclear, but it shows remarkable consistency across different populations and intelligence tests. The rise in IQ scores has been too rapid to be accounted for by hereditary factors. Changes in education, nutrition, increased familiarity with testing procedures, and other environmental factors may be related, but do not alone account for it. Increased experience with a technological environment may have something to do with the Flynn effect.

APPLY ...

- **Your knowledge to identify examples from the triarchic theory of intelligence.** Recall from pages 323–324 that this theory proposes the existence of analytical, practical, and creative forms of intelligence. Classify whether the individual in the following scenario is low, medium, or high in regard to each of the three aspects of intelligence.

    Katrina is an excellent chemist. She has always performed well in school, so it is no surprise that she earned her PhD from a prestigious institution. Despite her many contributions and discoveries related to chemistry, however, she seems to fall short in some domains. For example, Katrina does not know how to cook her own meals and if anything breaks at her house, she has to rely on someone else to fix it.

    Check your answers on page ANS-3.

ANALYZE ...

- **Whether teachers should spend time tailoring lessons to each individual student's learning style.** Certainly, no one would want to discourage teachers from being attentive to the unique characteristics that each student brings to the classroom. However, large-scale reviews of research suggest that there is little basis for individualized teaching based on learning styles (e.g., auditory, visual, kinesthetic).

Heredity, Environment, and Intelligence

Learning Objectives

After reading this module you should:

KNOW ...	UNDERSTAND ...	APPLY ...	ANALYZE ...
The key terminology related to heredity, environment, and intelligence	Different approaches to studying the genetic basis of intelligence	Your knowledge of entity and incremental theories to understand your own beliefs about intelligence	Claims that infant intelligence is increased by viewing educational television programming The meaning of group level differences in intelligence scores

Being the oldest sibling has its advantages. For example, the oldest sibling usually scores highest on IQ tests relative to younger siblings. Researchers have found that the IQ of first-born children is, on average, 3 points higher than that of second-born siblings and 4 points higher than that of third-borns (Kristensen & Bjerkedal, 2007). These are modest, but significant, differences. Why do they occur? Do older siblings somehow monopolize the good genes? Perhaps mothers are more attentive to prenatal care for their first-borns, or parents invest more resources in the first-born. Maybe all of the hand-me-down clothing is just one of many examples of how younger siblings have to settle for second best (or worse). There is not a single explanation for this phenomenon, but the better genes monopoly is definitely not the case—parents do not decide who gets which genes. Prenatal care has also been ruled out as a factor. A more plausible explanation is that older siblings, like it or not, end up tutoring and mentoring younger siblings. Playing the role of tutor may benefit the intellectual development of the older sibling more than the younger sibling (Sulloway, 2007). If something as subtle as this can have a significant impact on IQ, there are likely many other factors that influence intelligence.

Focus Questions

 Which factors have been found to be important contributors to intelligence?

 Is nature or nurture more important when it comes to intelligence?

• • • • • • • • • • • • • • • • • •

It is easy to make intuitive judgments about sources of intelligence. Perhaps you see someone graduating at the top of her high school class and say, "Not surprising—her older brother was valedictorian." Maybe it is not that surprising, but what does this pattern imply about where the high intelligence came from? Perhaps the valedictorians inherited a good set of genes, grew up in an environment that fostered intellectual development, or lived in a school district that provided high-quality teachers and a challenging curriculum. Pondering the sources of intelligence often leads to explanations based on the genes people inherit or the environment they grew up in. As we will see in this module, there are multiple contributors to intelligence—each of which plays a small but significant role.

Intelligence and Heredity

Scientists have been looking for evidence of genetic influences on intelligence ever since the first attempts to measure it. In the 1930s, the anthropologist Samuel Morton measured skull sizes in an attempt to show racial and ethnic differences in cognitive ability, and assumed that skull size—and therefore intelligence—were almost entirely genetically determined. In the 1860s, Sir Francis Galton became motivated to study intelligence to, in effect, prove that certain families were intellectually superior because of the genes they inherited (Module 9.1).

Researchers have continued to approach similar topics, sometimes focusing on ethnicity or gender, but also focusing on differences and similarities within families. In Module 3.1 we described the field of *behavioral genetics*, which examines how genes, environment, and their interaction influence behavior and cognition. Also, some recent advances have revolutionized the way scientists study the nature of intelligence. Thanks to the Human Genome Project (also discussed in Module 3.1) and modern brain imaging techniques, scientists can now view the genetics of intelligence in ways Galton

and Morton could not have imagined. As the researcher Robert Plomin put it, psychologists can study *genetics, genes, and the genome* (Plomin & Spinath, 2004). Plomin and Spinath (2004) describe behavioral genetics as a three-layered approach, with each layer asking different, yet related questions:

- Genetics: To what degree is intelligence an inherited trait?
- Genes: If intelligence does have a genetic component, which genes are involved?
- Genome: If we can identify which genes contribute to intelligence, then how exactly do they contribute to brain development and function?

TWIN AND ADOPTION STUDIES   Decades of research on families, adopted children, and twins has shown that genetic similarity contributes to intelligence test scores. Several important findings from this line of work are summarized in Figure 9.14 (Plomin & Spinath, 2004). The most obvious trend in the figure shows that as the degree of genetic relatedness increases, similarity in IQ scores also increases. Intelligence scores between parents and their children and between siblings are statistically related, with correlations between .40 and .50. Also, identical twins are more alike in intelligence than are fraternal twins. Nevertheless, we cannot jump

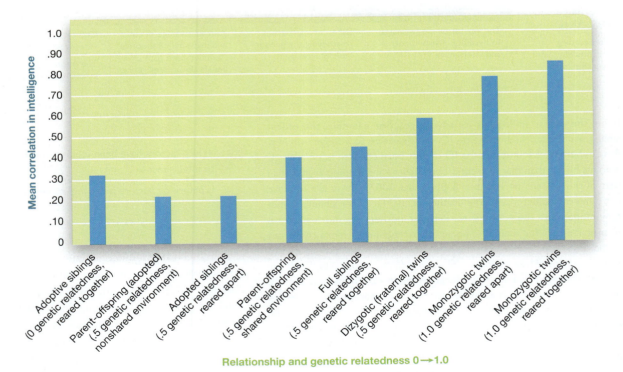

Relationship and genetic relatedness 0 → 1.0

{FIG. 9.14}   **Intelligence and Genetic Relatedness** Several types of comparisons reveal genetic contributions to intelligence (Plomin & Spinath, 2004). Generally, the closer the biological relationship between people, the more similar their intelligence scores. **Click on this figure in your eText to see more details.**

to the conclusion that genes are more important than environmental factors when it comes to intelligence. If you look more closely at Figure 9.14, you will notice that the environment is important, too. Offspring are more similar to the parents with whom they grow up. This can be seen by comparing parents and offspring who share an environment with those who do not, as is the case with adopted children and their parents.

The last two bars on the right of Figure 9.14 present perhaps the strongest evidence for a genetic basis for intelligence. Identical twins share 100% of their genes, and their intelligence scores have a correlation of approximately .85 when they are raised together. This is a higher figure than for fraternal twins—which is quite compelling evidence for a strong genetic component to intelligence. Of course, the twin pairs are growing up in a very similar environment, which could also account for the strong correlation. Yet even when identical twins are adopted and raised apart, their intelligence scores are still correlated at approximately .80—a very strong relationship. In fact, this is about the same number that researchers find when the very same individuals take the same intelligence test twice—now *that* is identical.

BEHAVIORAL GENOMICS Twin and adoption studies show that some of the individual differences observed in intelligence scores can be attributed to genetic factors. But recall that twin and adoption studies give statistical estimates, rather than specifics about which genes account for the differences. To search for specific genes related to intelligence, researchers use **behavioral genomics**—*the study of how specific genes, in their interactions with the environment, influence behavior.* The focus of the behavioral genomic approach to intelligence is to identify genes that are related to increases or decreases in certain types of learning and problem solving (Deary et al., 2010).

Overall, studies scanning the whole human genome show that intelligence levels can be predicted, to some degree, by the collection of genes that individuals inherit (Craig & Plomin, 2006; Plomin & Spinath, 2004). In other words, collections of genes seem to pool together to influence general cognitive ability; each contributes a small amount but, taken as a whole, they can have a very large effect. To date, behavioral genomic studies on humans have identified some good candidate genes that are associated with intelligence, but no definitive conclusions about their roles can yet be drawn (Deary et al., 2009).

Researchers have developed mouse models of intelligence because, unlike humans, there are ethical ways of randomly assigning mice to various genetic and environmental conditions and conducting experiments. **Gene knockout (KO) studies** *involve removing a specific gene thought to be involved in a trait (such as intelligence) and testing the effects of removing the gene by comparing behavior of animals without the gene with those that have it.* In one of the first knockout studies of intelligence, researchers discovered that removing one particular gene disrupted the ability of mice to learn spatial layouts (Silva et al., 1992). Since this investigation was completed, numerous studies using gene knockout methods have shown that specific genes are related to performance on tasks that have been adapted to study learning and cognitive abilities in animals (Robinson et al., 2011).

Scientists can also take the opposite approach to knocking genes out—they can insert genetic material into mouse chromosomes to study the changes associated with the new gene. The animal that receives this so-called gene transplant is referred to as a *transgenic* animal. This approach may sound like science fiction. In fact, researchers have been able to engineer transgenic mice that are better than average learners (Cao et al., 2007; Tang et al., 1999). Transgenic mice that have been given a gene regulating the chemical changes supporting memory formation outperform non-transgenic mice on numerous cognitive tasks (Nakajima & Tang, 2005).

Genes clearly have some effect on intelligence. From the genetics approach, we see correlations of intelligence increase along with genetic similarity. From the gene approach, researchers are narrowing their search for specific genes that support cognitive functioning. How these genes interact with the environment is another key question in the study of intelligence.

The Princeton University lab mouse, Doogie (named for the fictional whiz kid, Doogie Howser, from a 1980s television program), is able to learn faster than other mice thanks to a bit of genetic engineering. Researchers inserted a gene known as NR2B that helps create new synapses and, apparently, leads to quicker learning.

Quick Quiz 9.3a
Intelligence and Heredity

KNOW …

1 When scientists insert genetic material into an animal's genome, the result is called a _____.

- **A** genomic animal
- **C** knockout animal
- **B** transgenic animal
- **D** fraternal twin

UNDERSTAND …

2 How do gene knockout studies help to identify the contribution of specific genes to intelligence?

- **A** After removing or suppressing a portion of genetic material, scientists can look for changes in intelligence.
- **B** After inserting genetic material, scientists can see how intelligence has changed.
- **C** Scientists can rank animals in terms of intelligence, and then see how the most intelligent animals differ genetically from the least intelligent.
- **D** They allow scientists to compare identical and fraternal twins.

ANALYZE …

3 Identical twins reared together and apart tend to score very similarly on standardized measures of intelligence. Which of the following statements does this finding support?

- **A** Intelligence levels are based on environmental factors for both twins reared together and twins reared apart.
- **B** Environmental factors are stronger influences on twins raised together compared to twins reared apart.
- **C** The "intelligence gene" is identical in both twins reared together and reared apart.
- **D** Genes are an important source of individual variations in intelligence test scores.

Answers can be found on page ANS-3.

Environmental Influences on Intelligence

Although genes appear to be important contributors to individual differences in intelligence, there is ample room for environmental factors to play a role. Evidence supporting the influence of environmental factors comes from multiple sources that include both animal and human studies. Controlled experiments with animals show that growing up in physically and socially stimulating environments results in faster learning and enhanced brain development and functioning compared to growing up in a dull environment (Hebb, 1947; Tashiro et al., 2007).

Although it would be impossible to conduct the same kinds of controlled laboratory experiments with human children, psychologists have found higher levels

Growing up in an enriched environment enhances brain development and functioning.

of stress hormones among poor children, which were negatively correlated with measures of cognitive ability (Evans & Schamberg, 2009). Also, children raised in impoverished orphanages show a remarkable recovery in intelligence after getting into foster care homes compared to those who remain behind (Nelson et al., 2007). In this section, we review some of the major environmental factors that, through their interaction with genes, influence intelligence.

HEALTH AND NUTRITION Diet and lifestyle factors influence intelligence. Generally speaking, children who are healthy attend school more frequently and are able to spend more time on schoolwork; thus there have been numerous studies correlating health, schooling, and intelligence. These correlations should not be too surprising when comparing people living in the extremes—children living in poverty and those in affluent households, for example. But according to a Spanish study, even among high-socioeconomic grade-school children, there is a statistically significant relationship between nutrition and intelligence. This relationship holds even after influences of gender and income are removed from the analysis (Arija et al., 2006). As for children who may not consume balanced diets, there is even evidence that nutritional supplements can help overcome this factor (Benton, 2001). It is tempting to assume that nutrition *leads to* better brain functioning, but this link is not fully understood at this time. An alternative would be simply that children who eat well are more prepared to learn during the school day (Kleinman et al., 2002).

INCOME There are very good reasons to believe that income is a relevant environmental contributor to intelligence (Turkheimer et al., 2003). On average, children of affluent parents have higher IQs than children living

Socioeconomic status is related to intelligence. People from low-socioeconomic backgrounds typically have far fewer opportunities to access educational and other important resources that contribute to intellectual growth.

below the poverty level. High-socioeconomic-status students are more likely to enjoy the advantage of better schools and teachers. Low-income households face higher stress levels on a day-to-day basis, and this stress can distract children from school; in addition, the stress responses can negatively impact brain development. Because stimulating environments promote brain development and subsequent learning, perhaps the effect of income arises from the additional enrichment opportunities it affords.

SEASON OF BIRTH AND BIRTH ORDER Children born during the first part of the calendar year have higher verbal and mathematical aptitude, according to a number of sources. Researchers originally hypothesized that temperature, flu season, and other natural factors were responsible for this effect, but longitudinal studies ultimately discounted these explanations. It appears that children who are the oldest in their class get the most out of school, perhaps because they are, on average, slightly more mature and prepared to learn (Lawlor et al., 2006). Also, as you learned from the discussion at the opening of this module, even birth order has a slight impact on IQ scores (Kristensen & Bjerkedal, 2007). It is unlikely that this effect is due to genetic factors. The pattern holds true even if an elder sibling dies during infancy. If there are three siblings, the middle sibling will still score higher than the younger sibling (see Figure 9.15).

EDUCATION Health, nutrition, and season of birth are all related to intelligence, and, if you read published reports on these factors closely, it becomes apparent that they may exert their influence on IQ through education. During school, children not only accumulate factual knowledge and learn basic language and math skills, but also become more

intelligent as a result. A review of the research on education and schooling shows that children's IQ scores are significantly lower if they are not attending school (Ceci & Williams, 1997; Nisbett, 2009). This relationship has been observed in numerous places, such as over long summer breaks from school, in occupied European cities in World War II, and in remote villages where teachers have not been available. One should be careful when assigning causes to these correlations, however: There may be other explanations related to poorer test scores that have to do with nonschool-related stress and quality of life.

These are just a few of the major environmental factors shown to influence intelligence. Parents are often particularly concerned about these factors, given

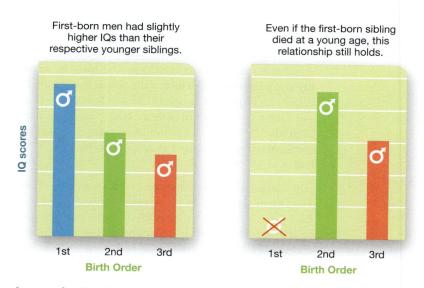

First-born men had slightly higher IQs than their respective younger siblings.

Even if the first-born sibling died at a young age, this relationship still holds.

IQ scores

1st 2nd 3rd
Birth Order

1st 2nd 3rd
Birth Order

{FIG. 9.15} **Birth Order and Intelligence** A study examining records of over 200,000 men enlisted in the Norwegian military revealed that older siblings tend to score slightly higher on intelligence than younger siblings.

Watching television at a very young age may slow the processes of cognitive and intellectual development.

television, the lower their verbal comprehension and performance scores achieved when tested at age 6 or 7 years (Christakis, 2009; Zimmerman & Christakis, 2005). Shows based mostly on pantomime or simplified sing-along songs (rather than narrative) have also been negatively correlated with vocabulary development between 6 months and 2½ years of age (Linebarger & Walker, 2005).

These studies point out the drawbacks of the "electronic babysitter." Even so, television is not all bad. Its effects may be neutral or even positive after age 3 or so, when children can understand more complex programs. Also, regardless of age, it is probably a good idea for a parent to maintain an ongoing conversation with the child about the shows they watch (Barr et al., 2008).

that they have some degree of control over them. For many parents, efforts to increase their child's intelligence begin as soon as they realize a baby is on the way, and intensify the moment the baby arrives. This concern has led to some claims by makers of products designed for infants that intelligence can be accelerated and enhanced by certain types of television programming and DVDs.

MYTHS IN MIND
Can the Media Make Babies Smarter?

A 2010 Nielsen Research Report revealed that 99% of American households have a television, and the average household has more TV sets (2.93) than people (2.5)! Almost two-thirds of children aged 2 years and younger watch television every day, and they average about 80 minutes of TV watching per day (Rideout & Hamel, 2006). Such statistics can make people feel self-conscious, particularly parents of children who spend hours per day in front of the set. But what if the time in front of the TV is spent on educational programs? *Sesame Street*, *Blue's Clues*, and *Square One* (which is, sadly, no longer on the air) can all produce immediate, cognitive benefits for preschoolers and elementary school-aged children (Crawley et al., 1999; Hall et al., 1990).

Companies also market products for viewing by infants. The Disney Corporation has tremendous success with its Baby Einstein DVD series. Intuitively, it seems that exposure to educational media should make people—even infants—smarter. The American Academy of Pediatrics, however, recommends that children younger than age 2 years do not watch television at all.

There seems to be a good reason for this recommendation. The more time infants spend viewing educational

Quick Quiz 9.3b
Environmental Influences on Intelligence

UNDERSTAND …

1. What have controlled experiments with animals found in regard to the effects of the environment on intelligence?

   A Stimulating environments result in faster learning.

   B Deprived environments result in faster learning.

   C Stimulating environments result in slower learning.

   D Deprived environments have no effect on learning.

2. In which way have psychologists studied the major environmental factors that, through their interaction with genes, influence intelligence?

   A By measuring stress hormones among poor and affluent children

   B By depriving some children of education and comparing them to others who attended school

   C By monitoring children's nutrition and then correlating it with intelligence scores

   D Both a and c

ANALYZE …

3. Research on television viewing by children under the age of 2 shows that:

   A TV is especially detrimental to children aged three years or older.

   B there is never any benefit from television, not even from educational programs.

   C infants who watch educational shows are, on average, better learners when they reach school age.

   D even educational programming shows no benefit, and can even slow some aspects of cognitive development.

Answers can be found on page ANS-3.

Group Similarities and Differences in Test Scores

Although psychological tests are designed to be taken by individuals, many people have speculated about the meaning of test results on a much broader scale—between males and females, among various ethnicities, in criminals versus law-abiding citizens, and among other segments of society. Many psychologists who study group differences believe it is important to do so because public policies and laws are often based on assumptions about group equalities or inequalities. Therefore, it is important that society be well informed on the pertinent issues (Hunt & Carlson, 2007).

DO MALES AND FEMALES HAVE UNIQUE COGNITIVE SKILLS? Although a few studies do report that males have a slightly higher average general intelligence, this result is often not replicated in subsequent studies. Furthermore, when differences do turn up, they are truly minor, as shown in Figure 9.16 (Colom et al., 2000; Halpern & LaMay, 2000; Hyde, 2005). A more reliable result is that there appears to be greater variability among males (Deary et al., 2007; Dykiert et al., 2009). Thus, among the top 1% of scores on general intelligence tests, there will be more males, but the same is true of the lowest 1% of all test scores as well (Ceci et al., 2009). In turn, we can conclude that there is little to no difference in overall intelligence test scores for the overwhelming majority of the population. However, if you stumble across a mathematical genius, that person is somewhat more likely to be male than female.

Some researchers have argued that sex differences exist in specific cognitive abilities. For example, average scores on verbal fluency tasks often tip in the favor of

Males and females are not equally distributed across all professions. Do these discrepancies arise because of inherent differences in cognitive abilities, or something else?

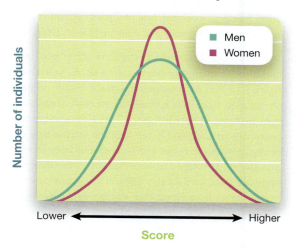

{FIG. 9.16} **Intelligence Distributions for Males and Females** There is very little difference in average IQ scores for males and females; in fact, there is much more overlap than difference. The major sex-related difference is the fact that males usually produce wider variability in test scores than females. Males are more likely to be found in the upper and lower extremes.

females. Conversely, average scores on tests of visual–spatial manipulation ability tend to favor males (see Figure 9.17 on p. 336; Halpern & LaMay, 2000; Lewin et al., 2001; Weiss et al., 2003). This finding is frequently offered as an explanation for why males are more represented in fields of engineering and mathematics. Such a difference *might* give males a sex-based advantage for visual–spatial demands of the physical sciences and math, but we should examine details and explanations of sex differences before wholeheartedly accepting the conclusion that males and females are fundamentally different in some cognitive abilities.

For starters, psychologists should be careful not to over-generalize the concept of visual–spatial ability. Females have, on average, higher test scores on verbal fluency, so it should not be too surprising to find that they apply verbal strategies to solving visual–spatial problems (Pezaris & Casey, 1991). As a result, females

Can you find the match?
One of the three figures below matches the one on top. Males often perform tasks like this mental rotation problem faster than females.

(a)

Conversely, women tend to outperform men on verbal fluency tasks like this one.

In 60 seconds, name as many words that start with the letter "G" that you can think of.

OR

In 60 seconds, name as many different kinds of animals you can think of.

(b)

{FIG. 9.17} **Mental Rotation and Verbal Fluency Tasks** Some research indicates that, on average, males outperform females on mental rotation tasks (a), while females outperform men on verbal fluency (b). **Click on this figure in your eText to see more details.**

greater variability among males provides the "best of the best"—exactly those individuals who fill the top academic positions.

BIOPSYCHO-SOCIAL PERSPECTIVES

Biology, Gender, and Cognition

First, pretest some of your knowledge and assumptions about our topic:

True or False?

1. Hormones such as testosterone and estrogen control growth and physical development *only*.

2. Testosterone and estrogen can be found all over the body, except in the brain.

3. Individual differences in cognitive skills are related to hormonal levels.

Psychologists and nonpsychologists alike have long pondered what to make of gender differences in various aspects of cognition and intelligence. In this module, we mostly focus on issues dealing with the context in which tests are administered and other environmental factors that contribute to some of the observed gender differences. However, we can also apply the biopsychosocial perspective to integrate biological factors.

To answer the questions asked previously:

1. *False.* Although we typically associate sex hormones such as testosterone and estrogen with growth, both are involved in psychological processes.

2. *False.* Testosterone, estrogen, and their receptors are actually found all over the brain, in particular in regions associated with memory and thinking (Raber, 2008).

3. *True.* Individual differences in cognitive ability have been found to be related to hormone levels. As you saw in Figure 9.17 men, on average, outperform women on mental rotation tasks, and women, on average, outperform men on tests of verbal fluency. These differences may potentially be explained in terms of the relative amounts of testosterone in males and females. But keep in mind that just as each individual, regardless of gender, differs on cognitive tasks, so they also differ in testosterone levels. Psychologists have found that women who have higher testosterone levels, compared to other women, do better on mental rotation tasks. Likewise, men with lower testosterone levels do better on verbal fluency tests than men with high testosterone levels (Burton et al., 2005). Thus it may be more accurate to say that hormone levels, rather than being identified as "male" or "female," are related to cognitive skills of various types.

· · · · · · · · · · · · · · · · · ·

actually outperform males when the visual-spatial tasks also rely on verbal skills, such as remembering where specific categories of items are located. Developmental studies help us understand how some sex differences in cognition arise. Boys and girls are born with roughly equal spatial abilities (Spelke, 2005), so any differences that emerge in childhood and beyond could be due to socialization, other experiences, or genetically controlled maturational process. Leaning toward the environmental side, psychologists find ample evidence that stereotypes lead to differential treatment of boys and girls at a very young age, which then can persist throughout life. These differences in treatment bring different opportunities for developing specific skills, as well as a sense of identity (Crawford et al., 1995). 👁

👁 **Watch** the **Video** *Gender Differences: Robert Sternberg* at **MyPsychLab**

What makes the study of sex differences and similarities important? If sex differences are due to socialization and stereotypes, then educational institutions and public policymakers may develop strategies to challenge these stereotypes, thereby bringing more women into the sciences. This movement would help meet a democratic goal of having diverse viewpoints in universities, medicine, and government; after all, many issues directly affect women in ways that do not affect men, and vice versa.

Programs and changes in societal attitudes are helping to increase the presence of women in scientific fields. A 2001 survey showed that roughly half of undergraduate degrees and not quite a third of all PhDs in scientific fields were earned by female students (Ceci et al., 2009). Psychologists favoring the environmental explanation of sex differences argue that education and socialization can erase differences in cognitive ability. Others, however, point to the fact that at the most elite universities only 3% to 15% of science and engineering faculty are women (Ceci et al., 2009). Therefore, they argue, the

RACIAL AND SOCIOECONOMIC SIMILARITIES AND DIFFERENCES

Probably an even more hotly debated topic than gender differences in intelligence are racial and ethnic differences in intelligence. Since the inception of intelligence testing, researchers in this area have generally ranked measures by large geographical groups. In the United States, for example, Asians and Asian Americans score the highest among all groups on intelligence measures, followed by people of European, Latin American, and African heritage (Herrnstein & Murray, 1994; Lynn, 2006). Intelligence test scores also differ among the various social classes in the United States, with a strong correlation between measures of wealth or social status and IQ.

As is the case with comparing males and females, a statistical difference between two groups reflects only averages, not the individuals within those groups. The average differences between European Americans and Asian Americans is negligible—about the same 2- to 5-point range that some researchers find between the sexes, and with greatly overlapping distributions. By comparison, the difference between African Americans and Asian Americans is quite large—approximately 15 points (one standard deviation). If the small differences between males and females have implications for education and public policy, then certainly the large differences among races deserve attention.

From one perspective, Herrnstein and Murray (1994) presented a social argument based on *meritocracy*—a society in which people with the most merit gain the most privilege and status. They concluded that the differences among races were substantial and resistant to change. Therefore, they argued, why should the public spend time and resources trying to compensate for the differences with minority scholarships, Head Start programs, and other interventions? Such a system would be geared toward allowing people with the most merit to rise to the top of society, even if they are almost all Asian Americans and European Americans.

As it turns out, there are some very good reasons to disagree with this argument. For one, differences in social class, rather than genetic heritage, may actually be responsible for the disparity in intelligence scores. As we have learned, the environment influences cognitive abilities in numerous ways. A cycle of poverty, low income, and low opportunity leads to lower scores on intelligence tests. Studies of children who have been adopted, however, suggest that there is a strong environmental influence: It is unlikely that predominately high-IQ individuals are putting more children up for adoption. It is more plausible that adoptive parents (who are carefully screened, trained, and supervised) are themselves more affluent, more intelligent, and more enriching than the average parent. This relationship seems likely because the rise in test scores and school performance occurs in both same-race and mixed-race adoptions (van IJzendoorn & Juffer, 2005).

SUMMARY OF GROUP-DIFFERENCES RESEARCH

Debates about gender and racial differences in intelligence have been ongoing for as long as people have been trying to scientifically study intelligence. In fact, identifying sex and ethnic differences were the primary inspiration driving the work of the first researchers in these areas—Francis Galton, Samuel Morton, and others—and, as you can see, the debate is still going strong (Hunt & Carlson, 2007; Jensen, 2002). How is it that more than a century of work has not been able to resolve these questions? A part of the problem is that these are political as much as psychological issues; they involve moral conflicts about the inherent equality or inequality of people. Whenever individuals have this level of emotion, it can be difficult to resolve differences in opinion.

In addition, the research is almost entirely correlational—it is just not possible to conduct randomized experiments (e.g., randomly assigning someone to a certain socioeconomic class, for example). As you read in Module 2.2, correlations do not provide evidence for cause-and-effect relationships. Therefore, we should not assume that the genetic patterns that contribute to a particular race also account for differences in intelligence. In fact, correlations often support a reasoning error known as the *confirmation bias* (described in Module 8.2): If you believe something is true, then you are likely to interpret a correlation in a way that supports your conviction.

Consider this example: One researcher believes men are genetically more intelligent than women on average, while another researcher believes tests are biased to favor men. If these researchers discover that

How different are racial groups when it comes to scores on standardized intelligence tests?

men score higher on a new intelligence test, both are likely to say, "I told you so!" The data actually support both individuals' positions, even though they have opposite beliefs. The first researcher says that men score higher because they are more intelligent, whereas the second researcher says men and women are equally intelligent but the tests are biased.

In case you think this is a trick example, consider this finding: Brain imaging studies show that women have greater cerebral blood flow (Halpern & LaMay, 2000). This fact could be used by proponents of either side of the argument as well: Perhaps women have greater blood flow because they are less intelligent and, therefore, their brains have to work harder. Conversely, perhaps women are more intelligent than men, and the rich blood supply is simply more evidence in their favor.

Quick Quiz 9.3c
Group Similarities and Differences in Test Scores

KNOW …

1. Which of the following might explain why ethnic groups differ in intelligence scores?

   A Genetic factors

   B Educational history

   C Cultural value placed on education

   D All of the above are possible

2. When psychologists have compared men and women on different cognitive tasks, men tend to perform slightly better on _____ tasks, while women tend to perform better on _____ tasks.

   A verbal fluency; mental rotation

   B mental rotation; verbal fluency

   C fluid; crystallized

   D mental rotation; visual-spatial

ANALYZE …

3. Which of the following is evidence that intelligence can change with experience?

   A People who inherit the right genes can become more intelligent.

   B Children who have been adopted into a life that includes an enriched environment show increases in IQ scores.

   C Giving individuals testosterone injections improves intelligence test scores.

   D The IQ scores of identical twins reared apart are very similar.

Answers can be found on page ANS-3.

Beyond the Test: Personal Beliefs Affect IQ Scores

Assuming you have read through the first part of this module, then you have already begun developing a well-informed, scientific understanding of cognitive abilities. One interesting observation about intelligence is that scientific understanding and beliefs held by the general public can be quite different. To explore this discrepancy, we should examine some commonly held beliefs about intelligence.

Ideas about intelligence have some stability across cultures, but there are differences as well. For example, individuals from the United States often distinguish between "book smarts," the ability to solve complex problems, and "common sense," the ability to make smart decisions in daily life. People the world over make distinctions between different types of intelligence (Grigorenko et al., 2001; Lim et al., 2002; Swami et al., 2008). Regardless of where you call home you can probably identify with this distinction. However, at least one big difference emerged from these studies. Western cultures (the United States and Europe) focus primarily on intellectual intelligence, whereas African and Asian cultures are more likely to include concepts such as respectfulness and empathy. Thus Americans are far more comfortable labeling a person as both brilliant and abrasive—that person would be considered an eccentric genius. In contrast, that same individual might be viewed by members of other cultures as smart, but in a limited way. In summary, Americans are more likely to distinguish book smarts from street smarts.

Another approach to examining nonscientific beliefs about intelligence is to ask individuals to rate their own intelligence and perhaps family members as well; in some cases, these can even be compared to actual intelligence test scores. Trends in this line of research show only a very modest amount of accuracy across the population—there is a low to modest positive correlation between estimated and actual test scores of .10 to .30 in most studies (e.g., Furnham & Chamorro-Premuzic, 2004). Even so, our beliefs about intelligence can have a very strong effect on our personal performance, as well as the expectations we have of others.

WORKING THE SCIENTIFIC LITERACY MODEL
Beliefs About Intelligence

Test scores are not necessarily pure measures of a person's knowledge or intelligence. Social context and personal experiences and beliefs about mental abilities may be contributing factors to such scores.

What do we know about how beliefs affect test scores?

Educators and parents have long been perplexed by students who consistently achieve below what their ability would predict. This is an especially important issue for students, as children's self-perceptions of their mental abilities have a very strong influence on their academic performance (Greven et al., 2009). For some students, it is simply a matter of apathy, but for others, it can be a very frustrating experience.

Thus it was truly a serious matter when psychologist Carol Dweck (2002) responded to a colleague's inquiry about "Why smart people can be so stupid." Her research has found some interesting conclusions in that there seem to be two influential beliefs about the nature of intelligence. First is **entity theory**: *the belief that intelligence is a fixed characteristic and relatively difficult (or impossible) to change.* Second is **incremental theory**: *the belief that intelligence can be shaped by experiences, practice, and effort.* According to Dweck and colleagues, beliefs based on entity theory and incremental theory have different effects on academic performance.

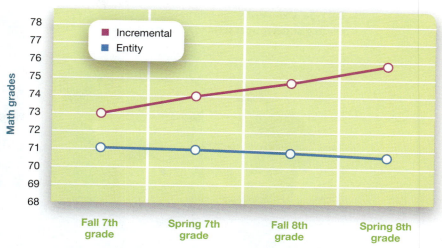

{FIG. 9.18} **Personal Beliefs Influence Grades** Students who hold incremental views of intelligence (i.e., the belief that intelligence can change with effort) show improved grades in math compared to children who believe that intelligence is an unchanging entity (Blackwell et al., 2007).

the school year, whereas the control group's grades actually declined (Figure 9.18). Thus, if you are skeptical about your own abilities, it might pay to look into Dweck's research more closely.

How can science help explain how beliefs affect performance?

According to Dweck's research, the differences between the two theories are not nearly as important as the differences in behavior that result. In experiments by Dweck and her colleagues, students were identified as holding either entity theories or incremental theories. The students had the chance to answer 476 general knowledge questions dealing with topics such as history, literature, math, and geography. They received immediate feedback on whether their answers were correct or incorrect. Those who held entity theories were more likely to give up in the face of highly challenging problems, and they were likely to withdraw from situations that resulted in failure. These individuals believe that successful people were born that way, so why keep punishing yourself if you simply do not have the ability to succeed? By comparison, people with incremental views of intelligence were more resilient (Mangels et al., 2006). If they are motivated to succeed at a task, then they will work through failures and challenges—if intelligence and ability can change, then it makes sense to keep pursuing goals.

Resilience is a desirable trait, so Dweck and her colleagues tested a group of junior high students to see whether incremental views could be taught (Blackwell et al., 2007). In a randomized, controlled experiment, they taught one group of 7th graders incremental theory—that they could control and change their ability. This group's grades increased over

Can we critically evaluate this research?

The work by Dweck and others you will read about later in this module shows how beliefs affect cognitive performance. Their findings encourage a liberal approach to learning—anytime a belief about intelligence can be changed for the better, then that change should probably be made. However, as you have learned in this chapter, psychologists have identified different types of intelligence, including fluid, crystallized, analytical, practical, and others (see Module 9.2). Each of us differs in our relative strengths and limitations for each. Someone who is amazingly analytical may struggle with tasks requiring practical intelligence—even if that person is told that she can change.

Why is this relevant?

As you have learned in this module, intelligence is greatly modified by numerous environmental factors. Awareness of these factors and adoption of an incremental view of intelligence increases students' potential to boost their academic performance. This relationship certainly has important implications for both occupational and classroom work. Actually, Carol Dweck and colleague Lisa Sorich Blackwell have developed a program called Brainology that is designed to help elementary school, middle school, and high school students achieve higher levels of confidence and motivation by teaching them that the brain can be strengthened through experience. Furthermore, this type of knowledge can help people overcome the negative effects that stereotypes seem to have on cognitive performance.

STEREOTYPES UNDERMINE TEST PERFORMANCE

Psychologists have found that Asian Americans score higher on standardized intelligence tests than African Americans—an outcome that meshes with commonly held cultural stereotypes. And psychologists have found that stereotypes can certainly affect how one performs on tests of aptitude and achievement. This linkage is the basis of **stereotype threat**: *When people are aware of stereotypes about their social group, they may fear being reduced to that stereotype* (Steele, 1997). Such a fear can have both short-term and long-term effects. For example, in a math classroom, a female student might experience a subtle reminder of gender stereotypes (perhaps just having a male teacher, or overhearing comments from peers), and the effect would be a distraction and a test score that underestimates her true ability. Over the long term, such experiences may become incorporated into one's self-concept, a process called *disidentification* (Steele, 1997). Disidentification can be seen in African American students who, early in school, have similar test scores to White students, but over time become separated from their White counterparts by an achievement gap. For many Black students, lower scores and grades may have resulted from stereotype threat and other social influences rather than reflecting a lack of skill.

Psychologists have also strengthened the evidence base supporting the theory of stereotype threat by showing how stereotypes take their toll. Dozens of studies have identified at least three influences, many of which create large effects (Nguyen & Ryan, 2008; Schmader et al., 2008). First, stereotype threat leads to physiological anxiety, resulting in more than just physical discomfort during tests. In brain imaging experiments, women who experienced stereotype cues before solving math problems showed less activity in the frontal lobes than members of a control group, and more activity in emotional circuitry. As predicted, these women also solved fewer problems (Krendl et al., 2008). Second, stereotype threat causes individuals to focus more on how they

Just being reminded of a stereotype can reduce performance on mental tasks.

are performing than on the test itself. Third, individuals also try to ignore negative thoughts about their performance. Both of these activities place a high demand on working memory, leaving fewer cognitive resources available to solve the problems (Beilock et al., 2007; Rydell et al., 2009).

Quick Quiz 9.3d
Beyond the Test: Personal Beliefs Affect IQ Scores

KNOW…

1. People who believe that intelligence is relatively fixed are said to advocate a(n) _____ theory of intelligence.

   A incremental
   B entity
   C sexist
   D hereditary

2. _____ is the situation in which when people are aware of stereotypes about their social group, they may fear being reduced to that stereotype.

   A Incremental intelligence
   B Hereditary intelligence
   C Stereotype threat
   D Intelligence discrimination

APPLY…

3. As a major exam approaches, a teacher who is hoping to reduce stereotype threat and promote an incremental theory of intelligence would most likely:

   A remind test takers that males tend to do poorly on the problems.
   B remind students that they inherited their IQ from their parents.
   C cite research of a recent study showing that a particular gene is linked to IQ.
   D let students know that hard work is the best way to prepare for the exam.

Answers can be found on page ANS-3.

Module Summary

Now that you have read this module
you should:

Listen to
the audio file of
this module at
MyPsychLab

KNOW ...

- **The key terminology related to heredity, environment, and intelligence:**

behavioral genomics (p. 331)
entity theory (p. 339)
gene knockout (KO) studies
  (p. 331)

incremental theory (p. 339)
stereotype threat (p. 340)

UNDERSTAND ...

- **Different approaches to studying the genetic basis of intelligence.** Behavioral genetics typically involves conducting twin or adoption studies. Behavioral genomics involves looking at gene–behavior relationships at the molecular level. This approach often involves using animal models, including knockout and transgenic models.

APPLY ...

- **Your knowledge of entity and incremental theories to understand your own beliefs about intelligence.** One way to assess your own beliefs is to complete the incremental and entity theories of intelligence measure developed by Carol Dweck and her colleagues (Dweck et al., 1995). Rate the following five statements on a scale from 1 (strongly agree) to 6 (strongly disagree).

Although the items may sound repetitive, please consider each one carefully before responding to it.

1. I have a certain amount of intelligence and I really can't do much to change it.

2. There are not enough intelligent people in the world.

3. My intelligence is something about me that I can't change very much.

4. I believe I am an intelligent person.

5. I can learn new things but I can't really change my basic intelligence.

Now, add up your responses to statements 1, 3, and 5. If you scored 9 or less, you tend to endorse the entity theory (p. 339) approach to *intelligence*; if you scored 12 or more, you tend to endorse the *incremental* approach. In Dweck's research, approximately 15% of respondents fell in between the two camps, so if you scored between 9 and 12, you endorse some aspects of each type of theory.

ANALYZE ...

- **Claims that infant intelligence is increased by viewing educational television programming.** As you read in the Myths in Mind feature, television viewing appears to have no benefits for cognitive development, and in some cases inhibits it. This relationship is especially strong in children younger than three years old.

- **The meaning of group level differences in intelligence scores.** In some cases, average intelligence scores differ between groups, such as between males and females. It is possible that this variation is due to genetic or brain-based differences. However, there are abundant, plausible explanations based on situational and experiential factors. In the case of male and female comparisons, perhaps there are more males at both ends of the spectrum (with very low and very high IQs), which may account for why a higher proportion of males are represented in fields that rely on mathematical and engineering skill.

Module 9.1 :: Measuring Aptitude and Intelligence

Focus Questions:

1 How are aptitude and intelligence tests constructed, and what are they supposed to measure? Tests such as the ACT, SAT, and other tests you read about in this module are constructed by designing questions and problems that are relevant to the construct they purport to measure. The Stanford-Binet test and the WAIS were designed to measure intelligence. Also, a part of the process of constructing and evaluating these tests is to determine the norm or average of a population taking the test, as well as the variability in scores.

2 Is there a perfect way to measure intelligence? After reading this module, you would probably answer "no" to this question. Certainly, some measures of intelligence are better than others. The Stanford-Binet test and WAIS have a long history and are regularly evaluated to determine the norm and variability among those who take the test. Raven's Progressive Matrices is ideal in some situations, such as when concerns arise about cultural bias or language barriers interfering with the test taker's performance. Other approaches have focused on correlating brain measurements with intelligence test scores, as well as behavioral responses such as working memory and reaction time. Finally, reliability, validity, and standardization are basic requirements for all intelligence tests.

👁 Watch *Special Topics: Intelligence Testing, Then and Now* in the **MyPsychLab video series**

Module 9.2 :: Understanding Intelligence

Focus Questions:

1 Is intelligence one ability or many? To some extent, intelligence is what intelligence tests measure (Boring, 1923). Thus, if a test measures *g* (general intelligence), then it assumes intelligence is just one ability. However, the reality is that many different abilities compose intelligent behavior. Thus psychologists divide intelligence into different categories, such as fluid versus crystallized intelligence, the three categories in the triarchic theory, or the eight categories used in the multiple intelligences model. Michelle Dawson has shown in her research on people with autism that intelligence is more than just a single ability.

2 How have psychologists attempted to explain intelligence as a collection of different abilities? Crystallized and fluid intelligence represent two different types of intelligence, but psychologists have also attempted to expand even further on the idea that intelligence comprises multiple abilities. Sternberg's triarchic theory consists of analytic, practical, and creative intelligences, each of which refers to the ability to solve different types of problems; individuals tend to differ in their

expression of each type of intelligence. Also, Gardner's theory posits the existence of eight different types of intelligence. Although useful in expanding the scope of the discussion of what constitutes intelligent behavior, not all psychologists agree with each of the various theories of multiple intelligences.

👁 Watch *The Basics: Theories of Intelligence* in the **MyPsychLab video series**

Module 9.3 :: Heredity, Environment, and Intelligence

Focus Questions:

1 Which factors have been found to be important contributors to intelligence? You have now read about many of these factors. Intelligence appears to be a cumulative product of numerous variables. At the beginning of Module 9.3, we discussed the possibility that birth order has a small effect on IQ scores (see also the work by Wichman et al., [2007]). In addition, genes are a major contributor, as well as their interactions with environmental factors such as nutrition, education, health, and socioeconomic status.

2 Is nature or nurture more important when it comes to intelligence? This is a question that people often ask. After reading this module, you might see that the way that the question is framed in the first place creates a major problem. The answer is that neither aspect is "more important" than the other. Intelligence comes from dynamic interactions between genes and the environmental factors that influence their expression.

👁 Watch *What's in It for Me? How Resilient Are You?* in the **MyPsychLab video series**

👁 Watch the complete video series online at **MyPsychLab**

Episode 11: Intelligence

1. *The Big Picture: What Is Intelligence?*
2. *The Basics: Theories of Intelligence*
3. *Special Topics: Intelligence Testing, Then and Now*
4. *Thinking Like a Psychologist: Intelligence Tests and Success*
5. *In the Real World Application: Intelligence Tests and Stereotypes*
6. *What's in It for Me? How Resilient Are You?*

Answers on page ANS-3

1 Which of the following is the best psychological definition of intelligence?

- **A** How much a person knows
- **B** The ability to think, understand, reason, and cognitively adapt to and overcome obstacles
- **C** The score on an intelligence test
- **D** The ability to quickly learn new material

2 Jonah receives the results of his intelligence test, which describes his score as having a percentile rank of .70 (or 70%). What does this information indicate about Jonah's intelligence score?

- **A** He has an IQ of 70.
- **B** He has an IQ of 30.
- **C** His score is greater than the score of 70% of the population.
- **D** His score is less than the score of 70% of the population.

3 Using the original formula for the intelligence quotient, an 8-year-old child with a mental age of 10 would have an IQ that:

- **A** is exactly 100.
- **B** is greater than 100.
- **C** is less than 100.
- **D** cannot be determined without more information.

4 Which of the following statements is true about the relationship between brain size and some aspects of intelligence?

- **A** Brain size is moderately related to intelligence.
- **B** There is no relationship between brain size and intelligence.
- **C** Brain size is an almost perfect predictor of intelligence.
- **D** The number and size of cerebral gyri, but not overall brain size, are related to intelligence.

5 Whereas _____ intelligence tends to decrease in later life, _____ intelligence generally does not decline, and may even continue to increase.

- **A** general; crystallized
- **B** general; fluid
- **C** crystallized; fluid
- **D** fluid; crystallized

6 Hussein is a small business owner. He was a C– student in school and does not generally think of himself as very "smart." Nonetheless, Hussein does an excellent job of running his business and dealing intelligently with real-world problems when they arise. According to the triarchic theory of intelligence, which type of intelligence is Hussein demonstrating?

- **A** Creative
- **B** Analytical
- **C** Crystallized
- **D** Practical

7 What does the Flynn effect refer to?

- **A** The increase in average IQ test scores over decades
- **B** The decrease in average IQ test scores over decades
- **C** The higher IQ test average scores for Asian Americans compared to European Americans
- **D** The lower IQ test average scores for African Americans compared to European Americans

8 Which of the following statements supports the theory that intelligence is determined in part by genes?

- **A** The correlation between IQ scores is stronger for fraternal twins than it is for identical twins.
- **B** Diet and lifestyle factors influence intelligence.
- **C** Offspring are more similar to their parents when they grow up with them as opposed to when children are raised apart from their parents.
- **D** Identical twins separated by adoption still have highly correlated IQ scores.

9 Differences between men and women on mental rotation and verbal fluency tests may reflect differences in _____ levels in the brain.

- **A** testosterone
- **B** estrogen
- **C** serotonin
- **D** dopamine

10 Carlos, who is Hispanic, is asked to take an IQ test by a job placement company. As he sits down to take the test, Carlos begins to think about how minorities in the United States, including Hispanics, are often viewed as less intelligent than others. These thoughts cause Carlos to experience discomfort and anxiety during the test, which then have a negative impact on his test result. Carlos's dilemma is an example of what psychologists call _____.

- **A** the Flynn effect
- **B** covert discrimination
- **C** stereotype threat
- **D** confirmation bias

What do we know about testing and evaluating intelligence?

To understand and evaluate intelligence tests—and indeed, any kind of research—you should know the difference between reliability and validity. Review the definitions on **pages 309–310**. If Helen took the same intelligence test twice and she received two very different results, then you would question the *reliability* of the test. If she found an online test that purports to measure IQ depending on how long she could hold her breath, then you would likely question its validity. Without reliability, a test will lack *validity*. Also, just because a test is reliable, that does not mean it is valid. Helen may be able to hold her breath for approximately 20 seconds each time she tries, but the amount of time she can hold her breath will never be a valid test of intelligence. While none of the IQ tests involve holding your breath for any length of time, many intelligence and aptitude tests do appear to measure a single, generalized intelligence.

There is still debate over the exact nature of intelligence; review **Table 9.1 on page 320** for a reminder of the two main approaches. Consider Sternberg's triarchic theory of intelligence (**Figure 9.11 on page 324**) and Gardner's concept of multiple intelligences (**Table 9.2 on page 324**), and think about how each contrasts with Spearman's theory of a general, basic intelligence (g).

Why is this relevant?

Watch the accompanying video excerpt on the theories of intelligence. You can access the video at MyPsychLab or by clicking the play button in the center of your eText. If your instructor assigns this video as a homework activity, you will find additional content to help you in MyPsychLab. You can also view the video by using your smart phone and the QR code below, or you can go to the YouTube link provided.

After you have read this chapter and watched the video, provide real-world examples for the following types of intelligences as theorized by Gardner: verbal/linguistic, body-kinesthetic, and intrapersonal. Present some of the arguments critics have offered against Gardner's research.

How can science help explain theories of intelligence?

As you can see in **Figure 9.7 on page 321**, research has shown a correlation between IQ, which is primarily an indicator of a single intelligence (g), and several other positive outcomes, such as higher income, better physical and psychological health, and successful relationships. Researchers have mixed opinions on the validity of aptitude tests such as the SAT, as there is only a slightly positive correlation between high test scores and later academic performance. By comparison, strong research evidence supports the idea that intelligence can be divided into the dual categories of fluid intelligence (the ability to adapt to new problems) and crystallized intelligence (the ability to solve problems based on past experience). Research involving the existence of savants—people with low mental capabilities in some areas and extraordinary abilities in others—also supports the idea that intelligence has multiple components. Gardner's speculation on the multiple dimensions of intelligence in particular has had a heavy influence on the emphasis on learning styles in educational practice.

Can we critically evaluate claims about intelligence?

Does scientific research confirm that multiple kinds of intelligence exist, driving everything from your artistic ability to how you learn vocabulary terms? Are aptitude tests such as the SAT and the GRE a waste of your time? **Myths in Mind on page 325** highlights how researchers have failed to find evidence that people learn more efficiently when teaching is tailored to their particular learning style. Furthermore, critics of Gardner's theory of multiple intelligences question whether the ability to paint a beautiful picture is intelligence or whether it should just be considered a skill. Before you throw out your SAT scores, also consider that while the research is unclear on whether aptitude tests predict later academic success, the slight correlation between high scores and academic performance, and the relatively minor issues in reliability, have ensured that many colleges and universities still require them for admission.

MyPsychLab **Your turn to Work the Scientific Literacy Model:** You can access the video at MyPsychLab or by clicking the play button in the center of your eText. If your instructor assigns this video as a homework activity, you will find additional content to help you at MyPsychLab. You can also view the video by using your smart phone and the QR code, or you can go to the YouTube link provided.

youtube.com/
scientificliteracy

10 :: LIFE SPAN DEVELOPMENT

Methods, Concepts, and Prenatal Development

Learning Objectives

After reading this module you should:

KNOW ...	UNDERSTAND ...	APPLY ...	ANALYZE ...
The key terminology relating to concepts in developmental psychology and prenatal development	How development proceeds in both stage-like and continuous fashion over the life span	Your understanding to identify research designs	The effects of preterm birth

The pros and cons of cross-sectional and longitudinal designs |

If you listen long enough, you can probably discriminate spoken French from German, even if you do not know either language. But what about crying? Psychologists have discovered that babies actually cry with an accent. Researchers analyzed the crying of 60 babies born to either French or German parents and discovered that their sounds had characteristics of their native tongue. French babies cry with a rising melody contour, meaning that they gradually rise toward a peak of intensity at the end of their cries. In contrast, German babies cry with a falling contour, meaning that they start at high intensity and then trail off. This difference is apparent at only a few days of age and reflects the same sound patterns characteristic of their respective languages (Mampe et al., 2009). Apparently, language development is well under way before birth, and infants are preparing to interact with their worlds before they even enter into them.

Focus Questions

 1 How developed is the brain of a human fetus?

 2 What are newborns able to sense?

· · · · · · · · · · · · · · · · · ·

Developmental psychology *is the study of change and stability of human physical, cognitive, social, and behavioral characteristics across the life span.* Take just about anything you have encountered so far in this text, and you will probably find psychologists approaching it from a developmental perspective. Neuroscientists examine changes in the nervous system that occur even before birth, and track them all the way through old age. Psychologists study how social behavior originates in the context of parent–offspring bonds and flourishes and expands to include extended family, close friends, enemies, romantic relationships, and broader social and cultural groups. This subfield of psychology is absolutely essential because we do not enter into the world as adults, and our psychological qualities and abilities change drastically over time. Also, much of what occurs through early development influences behavior throughout the life span.

In this module, we begin by reviewing the methods for studying development and then explore the beginnings of life, starting with prenatal development.

Measuring Developmental Trends: Methods and Patterns

Studying development requires some special methods for tracking and measuring change. Also, modeling how development occurs involves some key terms and concepts that we explore in this section.

METHODS OF MEASURING DEVELOPMENT

Developmental psychologists generally rely on a few different designs for measuring how psychological traits and abilities change over time. One approach, called a **cross-sectional design**, *is used to measure and compare samples of people at different ages at a given point in time.* Imagine you are designing a study examining the effects of premature birth on learning and thinking abilities from infancy through adulthood. How would you recruit volunteers? One way would be to compare people of different age groups—say, groups of 1-, 5-, 10-, and 20-year-olds who were born prematurely. In contrast, a **longitudinal design** *follows the development of the same set of individuals through time.* With this type of study, you might identify a set of 50 infants and measure their cognitive development annually over the course of 20 years (see Figure 10.1).

A longitudinal study of one group can be costly and time-consuming. This research design is also hampered by the issue of *attrition*, which occurs when participants stop returning mail or phone calls, become ineligible, or otherwise quit participating. Even so, some of the longest-duration studies of this nature have lasted for decades and have been passed from one generation of researchers to the next as the original psychologists retire and young scientists take over the project. For example, researchers at the University of Minnesota are in their third decade of conducting longitudinal studies of twins. In contrast, the cross-sectional design has the advantage of convenience—it is more time- and cost-efficient to compare people of different ages at once, rather than to follow the same individual for, say, 20 years.

One major issue to consider in cross-sectional designs is the potential for **cohort effects**, which *are consequences of being born in a particular year or narrow range of years.* ("Cohort" and "generation" refer to similar things in this context.) Differences across age cohorts can be due to numerous factors, including societal, nutritional, medical, and many other influences on both physical and behavioral development. If you studied the effects of premature birth on cognitive development using a cross-sectional design, for example, you would likely note cohort effects. Some possible effects might include differences in medical care for infants who are born prematurely—infants generally get better care now than their counterparts did 20 years ago, and this improvement is reflected in much higher survival rates (Saigal & Doyle, 2008). It is possible that the 1-year-old cohort might develop differently than the 20-year-old cohort because of differences in infant health care. Longitudinal designs, unlike cross-sectional studies, avoid the problems associated with cohort effects.

Developmental studies yield important data. Information about developmental trends can help researchers and clinicians identify what is "normal" for a given age, such as the normal age range for the onset of language or the typical age at which memory decline might be expected. This information can help professionals determine whether an individual may have a problem that needs to be addressed or, alternatively, whether an individual is exceptional in some ability for a person of his or her age.

In addition to selecting the appropriate design for studying developmental changes, developmental psychologists face the challenge of describing *how* changes take place.

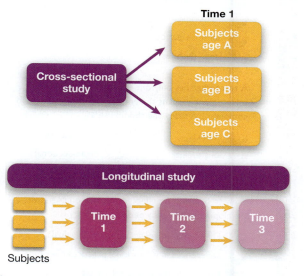

{FIG. 10.1} **Cross-Sectional and Longitudinal Methods** In cross-sectional studies, different groups of people—typically of different ages—are compared at a single point in time. In longitudinal studies, the same group of subjects is tracked over multiple points in time. **Click on this figure in your eText to see more details.**

PATTERNS OF DEVELOPMENT: STAGES AND CONTINUITY

Parents are all too aware of how fast their children seem to grow up; if they blink, they may miss something important in their child's development. A parent away on a business trip might miss her child's first steps or words. A child away at summer camp might come home after undergoing a remarkable growth spurt. These rapid changes are explained by a model that views development as a progression of abrupt transitions in physical or mental skills, followed by slower, more gradual change. Psychologists describe this pattern of change as a series of *stages*. The transition from stage to stage is very much like a growth spurt, except marked by rapid shifts in thinking and behaving rather than size. In addition, stages are more than increases in size, speed, or amount; they also represent a fundamental shift in the *type* of abilities. This understanding can be seen in developmental milestones of motor development (crawling, standing, and walking; see Module 10.2).

Of course, an adult returning from a business trip likely will not observe a similarly drastic change in the behavior of her spouse. Adults tend to change at a slower, steadier pace—what developmental psychologists would call *continuous* change. It is not unusual for adults to complain about putting on a few extra pounds or taking longer to recover from a workout. Cognitively, adults continue learning new words, facts, and skills, but these are gradual or *continuous* changes. Typically, there is nothing fundamentally different about their bodies or minds from week to week. This is not to say that life stages are absent in adulthood. Indeed, older adults still deal with new phases of life such as marriage, parenthood, and retirement (a topic covered in Module 10.4).

What accounts for the rapid physical and behavioral transitions that occur during early development? Complex interactions between genetics and the childrearing environment are constantly determining developmental processes. Also, for change to take place so rapidly during early development, it helps if the individual is particularly sensitive and attentive to the stimulation that facilitates behavioral and cognitive growth. The concept of a sensitive period helps explain how this transformation happens.

THE IMPORTANCE OF SENSITIVE PERIODS

Timing is everything during key stages of development. During infancy and childhood, exposure to specific types of environmental stimulation is critical to healthy development. For example, to become fluent in their native language, infants need to be exposed to speech during their first few years of life. As you have already read, infants even seem to pick up an accent before they are born. A **sensitive period** is *a window of time during which exposure to a specific type of environmental*

stimulation is needed for normal development of a specific ability. Long-term deficits can emerge if the needed stimulation, such as language input, is missing during a sensitive period.

Sensitive periods of development are a widespread phenomenon. They have been found in humans and other species for abilities such as depth perception, balance, and recognition of parents as well as future potential mates. A sensitive period for adopting and identifying with a culture may be uniquely human. Among immigrants of all ages, it is the younger individuals (0 to 20 years) who are quicker to identify more strongly with their new culture (Cheung et al., 2011).

Quick Quiz 10.1a
Measuring Developmental Trends: Methods and Patterns

UNDERSTAND...

1 A developmental psychologist's research suggests that coordination improves gradually over time rather than in short bursts of rapid change. These results reflect a _____ view of developmental change.

- **A** discontinuous
- **B** psychosocial
- **C** continuous
- **D** cohort

2 The effects of language deprivation during infancy and childhood can be irreversible. This fact is best explained by which concept?

- **A** Cohort effects
- **B** Sensorimotor functioning
- **C** Sensitive period
- **D** Stage theories

APPLY...

3 A researcher has only one year to complete a study on a topic that spans the entire range of childhood. To complete the study she should use a _____ design.

- **A** cohort
- **B** longitudinal
- **C** correlational
- **D** cross-sectional

ANALYZE...

4 Which of the following is a factor that would be *least* likely to be a cohort effect for a study on cognitive development in healthy people?

- **A** Differences in genes between individuals
- **B** Differences in educational practices over time
- **C** Changes in the legal drinking age
- **D** Changes in prescription drug use

Answers can be found on page ANS-3.

Prenatal to Newborns: From One Cell to Billions

We begin our exploration of developmental psychology from a very early point in time. As you read earlier in this module, we can start to explore psychological development before birth even happens. In this section we will see how the prenatal environment affects psychological development.

FERTILIZATION AND GESTATION An individual's development does not begin at birth; genetics and environment begin to shape an individual throughout pregnancy (also called *gestation*). The **germinal stage** *is the first phase of prenatal development and spans from conception to two weeks*. It all begins at *fertilization* with the formation of a **zygote**—*a cell formed by the fusion of a sperm and an ovum (egg cell)*. The zygote begins dividing, first into two cells, then into four, then eight, and so on. As the zygote develops, we can measure its developmental progress by its *gestational age*—the estimated time since fertilization. At a gestational age of six days, the zygote, now called a *blastocyst*, contains between 50 and 150 nonspecialized cells. At this point, the blastocyst uses energy and resources provided by the ovum. ◉

The blastocyst moves along the fallopian tubes and becomes implanted in the lining of the uterus (Figure 10.2). Soon after implantation, the blastocyst divides into a group of cells that continues developing into an embryo, and another group that forms the placenta, the structure that allows oxygen and nutrients to pass to the fetus and waste to leave the fetus. The **embryonic stage** *spans weeks two through eight, during which time the* embryo begins developing major physical structures such as the heart and nervous system, as well as the beginnings of arms, legs, hands, and feet.

The **fetal stage** *spans week eight through birth, during which time the skeletal, organ, and nervous systems become more developed and specialized.* Muscles develop and, along with them, the fetus begins to move. Sleeping and waking cycles start and the senses become fine-tuned—even to the point where the fetus is responsive to external cues (these events are summarized in Table 10.1 on page 350).

FETAL BRAIN DEVELOPMENT Human brain development is an extremely lengthy process—spanning all the way to early adulthood. The beginnings of the human brain can be seen during the embryonic stage, between the second and third weeks of gestation. Cells that are genetically programmed to create the nervous system migrate to their appropriate sites and begin to differentiate into nerve cells. The first sign of the major divisions of the brain—the forebrain, the midbrain, and the hindbrain—are apparent beginning at only 4 weeks' gestation (see Figure 10.3 on page 351). By 11 weeks' gestation, the differentiations between the cerebral hemispheres, the cerebellum, and the brain stem are apparent. During the final months of pregnancy, a fatty tissue called myelin builds up around developing nerve cells, a process called *myelination*. Myelin insulates nerve cells, enabling them to conduct messages more rapidly and efficiently (see Module 3.2; Giedd, 2008). At birth, the newborn has an estimated 100 billion neurons and a brain that is approximately 25% the size and weight of an adult brain.

◉ ⌐Watch
the **Video** *Period of the Zygote* at
MyPsychLab

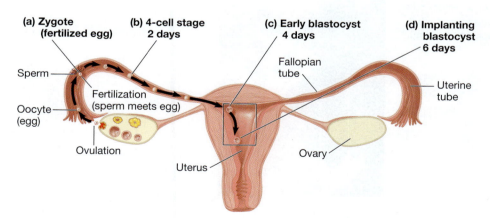

(a) Zygote
(fertilized egg)

(b) 4-cell stage
2 days

(c) Early blastocyst
4 days

(d) Implanting blastocyst
6 days

Sperm

Fertilization
(sperm meets egg)

Oocyte
(egg)

Ovulation

Fallopian
tube

Uterine
tube

Ovary

Uterus

{FIG. 10.2} **The Process of Implantation During Early Pregnancy** Eggs are fertilized in the fallopian tubes. Within six days, the resulting zygote becomes a blastocyst and is implanted along the lining of the uterus.

Table 10.1 :: Phases of Prenatal Development

A summary of the stages of human prenatal development and some of the major events at each.

GERMINAL: 0 TO 2 WEEKS

Major Events

Migration of the blastocyst from the fallopian tubes and its implantation in the uterus. Cellular divisions take place that eventually lead to multiple organ, nervous system, and skin tissues.

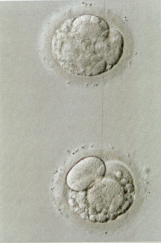

EMBRYONIC: 2 TO 8 WEEKS

Major Events

Stage in which basic cell layers become differentiated. Major structures such as the head, heart, limbs, hands, and feet emerge. The embryo attaches to the placenta, the structure that allows for the exchange of oxygen and nutrients and the removal of wastes.

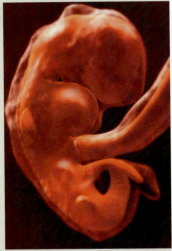

FETAL STAGE: 8 WEEKS TO BIRTH

Major Events

Brain development progresses as distinct regions take form. The circulatory, respiratory, digestive, and other bodily systems develop. Sex organs appear at around the third month of gestation.

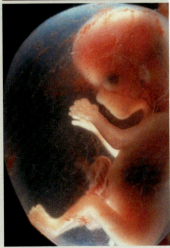

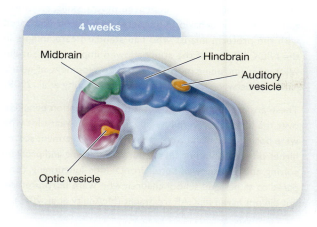

4 weeks

Midbrain

Hindbrain

Auditory vesicle

Optic vesicle

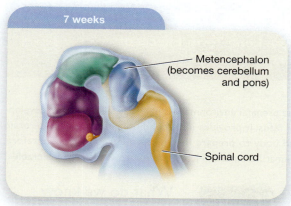

7 weeks

Metencephalon (becomes cerebellum and pons)

Spinal cord

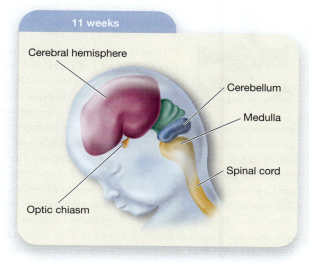

11 weeks

Cerebral hemisphere

Cerebellum

Medulla

Spinal cord

Optic chiasm

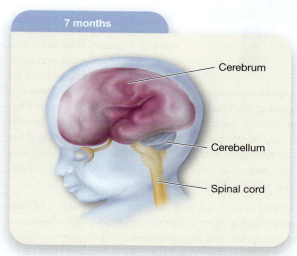

7 months

Cerebrum

Cerebellum

Spinal cord

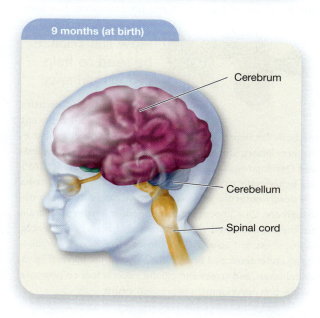

9 months (at birth)

Cerebrum

Cerebellum

Spinal cord

{FIG. 10.3} **Fetal Brain Development** The origins of the major regions of the brain are already detectable at four weeks' gestation. Their differentiation progresses rapidly, with the major forebrain, midbrain, and hindbrain regions becoming increasingly specialized. **Click on this figure in your eText to see more details**.

WORKING THE SCIENTIFIC LITERACY MODEL

The Long-Term Effects of Premature Birth

The prenatal environment is perfectly suited for the developing fetus. It provides ideal conditions for the delicate brain and body to prepare for life outside the womb. Therefore, premature birth can leave a newborn extremely vulnerable.

What do we know about premature birth?

Typically, humans are born at a gestational age of around 37 weeks (9 months). **Preterm infants** *are born at 36 weeks or earlier.* Depending on their gestational age, they can be extremely underweight compared to full-term infants, and vital regions of the brain and body may be underdeveloped. Even with modern medical care, a preterm infant born at 25 weeks has only slightly better than a 50% chance of surviving (Dani et al., 2009; Jones et al., 2005). Fetal development happens very quickly, so survival rates reach 95% at around 30 weeks of gestation, which is still well short of full-term delivery.

Surviving preterm birth is only the first in a series of challenges faced by these vulnerable infants. An underdeveloped nervous system may have both short- and long-term negative effects on psychological and cognitive functioning. Thus a well-established procedure for nurturing preterm infants is needed.

How can science be used to help preterm infants?

Researchers and doctors have compared different methods for improving survival and normal development in preterm infants. One program, called the Newborn Individualized Developmental Care and Assessment Program (NIDCAP), is a behaviorally based intervention in which preterm infants are closely observed and given intensive care during early development. One important component is keeping the brain healthy and protected against potentially harmful experiences. Lights, stress, and other factors can interfere by over-stimulating an underdeveloped brain. NIDCAP calls for minimal lights, sound levels, and stress and painful experiences to promote healthy brain development in preterm infants.

Controlled studies suggest that this program works. Researchers randomly assigned 117 infants born at 29 weeks or less gestational age to receive either NIDCAP or standard care in a prenatal intensive care unit. The infants were periodically tested for neurological and behavioral maturity. Within

9 months of birth, the infants who received the NIDCAP care showed significantly improved motor skills, attention, and other infant behavioral measures. In addition, compared with the preterm infants who had standard care, infants in the NIDCAP arm of the study showed improved brain development (including more advanced development of neural pathways between major brain regions; McAnulty et al., 2009).

These are promising results, but is this intervention beneficial over the long term? In follow-up studies, eight-year-olds who were born preterm and were given NIDCAP treatment scored higher on some (but not all) measures of thinking and problem solving, and also showed better frontal lobe functioning, compared to same-aged school children who were born preterm but did not have NIDCAP treatment (McAnulty et al., 2010).

Can we critically evaluate this research?

Premature birth in no way guarantees that an individual will experience developmental problems. People born preterm do experience slightly higher rates of cognitive impairment as teenagers, but more than half have no cognitive problems associated with premature birth at all (Gray et al., 2007). In fact, the majority of children who survive a preterm birth before 29 weeks' gestational age report typical sensory, emotional, and physical development in adolescence. The research on NIDCAP suggests that some effects may linger through age 8—especially if specialized treatment is not provided to the premature newborn. One important consideration is that the research we have discussed here involved infants and children who generally have reliable access to health care and a supportive environment.

Why is this relevant?

Worldwide, an estimated 9% of infants are born preterm (Villar et al., 2003). For these children, medical advances have increased the likelihood of survival, and behaviorally based interventions, such as NIDCAP, can reduce the chances of long-term negative effects of preterm birth. One application of behaviorally based interventions concerns developing countries where health care services may be minimal, if they even exist. Researchers have found that the risks for physical and cognitive deficits in preterm infants can be reduced with some surprisingly simple interventions. For example, massaging preterm infants for 15 minutes per day can result in a 50% greater daily weight gain compared with preterm infants who are not massaged (Field et al, 2006). Massage therapy also reduces stress-related behavior in preterm infants (Hernandez-Reif et al., 2007). A method called *kangaroo care* focuses on constant, ongoing physical contact between infants and their mothers, as well as breastfeeding. Kangaroo care methods in developing countries, as well as in the

United States, have also been shown to improve the physical and psychological health of preterm infants (Conde-Agudelo et al., 2011).

NUTRITION, TERATOGENS, AND FETAL DEVELOPMENT Nutrition is critical for normal fetal development. Pregnant women typically require an almost 20% increase in energy intake during pregnancy, including foods high in protein and calcium. Malnutrition, illness, and some drugs can result in mild to very severe physical and psychological effects on the developing fetus. A **teratogen** *is a substance, such as a drug, that is capable of producing physical defects.* These defects typically appear at birth or shortly after. Because of this risk, expectant mothers who take certain medications, such as those used to treat epilepsy, are typically advised to stop taking the medication at some point during pregnancy (Cragan et al., 2006). Discontinuing a medication, of course, has to be balanced with the need to ensure that the expectant mother is in good health.

Alcohol and tobacco can be teratogens if they are consumed at the wrong times and in large enough amounts during pregnancy. First described in the 1970s (Jones & Smith, 1973), **fetal alcohol syndrome** *involves abnormalities in mental functioning, growth, and facial development in the offspring of women who use alcohol during pregnancy.* This condition occurs in approximately 1 per 1,000 births worldwide, but is probably underreported (Morleo et al., 2011). Alcohol, like many other substances, readily passes through the placental membranes, leaving the developing fetus vulnerable to its effects. The more alcohol the mother consumes, the more likely these birth defects will appear; nevertheless, detrimental effects on the fetus have been shown with the consumption of as little as one drink per day (O'Leary et al., 2010; Streissguth & Connor, 2001).

Smoking can also expose the developing fetus to teratogens. Smoking decreases blood oxygen and raises uterine concentrations of poisonous nicotine and carbon monoxide, increasing the risk of miscarriage or death during infancy. Babies born to mothers who smoke are twice as likely to have low birth weight and have a 30% chance of premature birth—both factors that increase the newborn's risk of illness or death. Babies exposed to smoke are also as much as three times more likely to die from the mysterious and tragic phenomenon of sudden infant death syndrome—an unexpected and not directly explainable death of a child younger than age one (Centers for Disease Control and Prevention [CDC], 2009; Rogers, 2009). The same risks even apply to expecting mothers who do not smoke but have regular exposure to second-hand smoke (Best, 2009). Children born to mothers who smoked during pregnancy are also at greater risk for having problems with some aspects of emotional development and impulse control (Brion et al., 2010).

Fetal alcohol syndrome is diagnosed based on facial abnormalities, growth problems, and behavioral and cognitive deficits.

Drugs, alcohol, and other prenatal teratogens are of major concern to parents and doctors alike. The health of newborn infants can also be compromised by exposure to other harmful pathogens such as bacteria and viruses. Within their first year after birth, infants are given vaccinations to protect them against conditions such as measles, mumps, and rubella (MMR). A small but vocal group had claimed that the MMR vaccine causes autism, a psychological disorder characterized by impaired social functioning and, typically, mental disabilities; this supposition has been debunked in recent years, however.

MYTHS IN MIND
Vaccinations and Autism

In the late 1990s, a team of researchers claimed that the combined vaccination for measles, mumps, and rubella (MMR) was linked to the development of autism (Wakefield et al., 1998). The MMR vaccination is given to millions of children at around their first birthday; a second dose is administered at approximately the time they start school. Of course, scientific evidence that such a widespread treatment could lead directly to autism alarmed many parents, many of whom refused to have the vaccine given to their young children.

The hypothesis that the MMR vaccine causes autism unraveled when other groups of scientists could not replicate the original findings that called this relationship into question. The knockout blow to the MMR–autism hypothesis came when it was discovered that Andrew Wakefield, the doctor who published the original study in 1998, was found to have financial interests in linking the disease with the vaccine. His research was funded by lawyers who sued makers of vaccines for damages. In 2010, the original 1998 paper was retracted by *The Lancet*, the medical journal that published it. Also, a thorough investigation revealed numerous counts of misconduct by Wakefield, and the UK revoked his medical licence.

Fortunately, such cases of fraud are rare in science. There is no scientific evidence that the MMR vaccine causes autism.

· · · · · · · · · · · · · · · · · ·

SENSORY AND MOTOR ABILITIES OF NEWBORNS
Compared to the offspring of other species, healthy newborn humans are relatively helpless. Horses, snakes, deer, and many other organisms come into the world with a few basic skills, such as walking (or slithering) that ready them for life's challenges. They can move about the world, and at least have a chance of evading predators, from their earliest days. Human infants, in contrast, are born almost completely helpless and require extended care as they develop their senses, strength, and coordination. In this section, we shift our focus to newborns to find out how movement and sensation develop in the first year of life.

Anyone who interacts with infants is probably curious about what their world is like. What can they see, hear, or smell, and what may still be a work in progress? At the beginning of this module, we revealed that the tone of infants' crying has an accent resembling the signature melodies of their native language. Thus sensory experiences, and learning, occur before birth. By month four of prenatal development, the brain starts receiving signals from the eyes and ears. By seven to eight months of gestation, not only can infants hear, but they also seem to be actively listening. How do psychologists know this? In one study, mothers read children's stories, including *The Cat in the Hat,* twice daily during the final six weeks of pregnancy. At birth, their babies were given a pacifier that could be used to control a tape recording of their mother reading the story, as well as stories that were not read before birth. Babies sucked the pacifier much more to hear their mothers read *The Cat in the Hat,* but sucked the pacifier much less if it meant hearing stories she had not read before birth (DeCasper & Spence, 1986).

Psychologists have determined that infants can see objects up to only 12 to 15 inches away at birth (approximately the same distance between the mother's face and a breastfeeding infant) and that they reach the normal 20/20 visual capacity between 6 and 12 months of age. Color vision also appears to take some time to develop, but by at least 2 months infants begin discriminating different colors. By 8 months, infants can usually perceive basic shapes and objects as well as adults do (Csibra et al., 2000; Fantz, 1961).

Like adults, newborns cringe when smelling something rotten or pungent, such as ammonia, and they show a strong preference for the smell of sweets. Odors are strong memory cues for infants as well. For example, infants can learn that a toy will work in the presence of one odor but not others, and they can retain this memory over several days (Schroers et al., 2007). Newborn infants can also discriminate the odor of their own mother's breastmilk from the breastmilk of a stranger. Infants even turn their heads toward the scent of breastmilk, which helps to initiate nursing (Porter & Winberg, 1999). In summary, sensory abilities are in various stages of development when infants are born. Remarkably, their development is well underway well before birth even occurs.

By five months' gestation, the fetus begins to have control of voluntary motor movements. In the last months of gestation and the first months of life, the muscles and nervous system become developed enough to demonstrate basic **reflexes**—*involuntary muscular reactions to specific types of stimulation.* These reflexes provide newborns

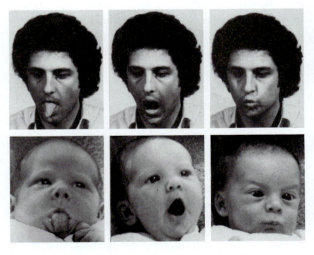

At just a few days of age infants will imitate the facial expressions of others (Meltzoff & Moore, 1977).

Table 10.2 :: Infant Reflexes

THE ROOTING REFLEX

The *rooting reflex* is elicited by stimulation to the corners of the mouth, which causes infants to orient themselves toward the stimulation and make sucking motions. The rooting reflex helps the infant begin feeding immediately after birth.

THE MORO REFLEX

The *Moro reflex*, also known as the "startle" reflex, occurs when infants lose support of their head. Infants grimace and reach their arms outward and then inward in a hugging motion. This may be a protective reflex that allows the infant to hold on to the mother when support is suddenly lost.

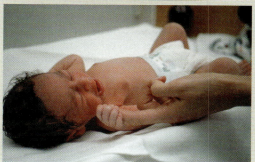

THE GRASPING REFLEX

The *grasping reflex* is elicited by stimulating the infant's palm. The infant's grasp is remarkably strong and facilitates safely holding on to one's caregiver.

and infants with a basic set of responses for feeding and interacting with their caregivers (see Table 10.2). Just a few days after birth, newborns show complex responses to social cues—such as imitating facial expressions of their caregivers (Meltzoff & Moore, 1977).

Quick Quiz 10.1b
Prenatal to Newborns: From One Cell to Billions

KNOW …

1 A developing human is called a(n) _____ during the time between weeks 2 and 8.

   Ⓐ embryo   Ⓒ fetus
   Ⓑ zygote   Ⓓ germinal

2 In which stage do the skeletal, organ, and nervous systems become more developed and specialized?

   Ⓐ Embryonic stage   Ⓒ Germinal stage
   Ⓑ Fetal stage   Ⓓ Gestational stage

UNDERSTAND …

3 Which of the following would not qualify as a teratogen?

   Ⓐ Cigarette smoke
   Ⓑ Alcohol
   Ⓒ Prescription drug
   Ⓓ All of the above are possible teratogens

ANALYZE …

4 Which of the following statements best summarizes the effects of preterm birth?

   Ⓐ Preterm births are typically fatal.
   Ⓑ The worrisome effects of preterm birth are exaggerated. There is little to worry about.
   Ⓒ Some physical and cognitive problems may be present during early development, but eventually are reduced or eliminated with proper treatment.
   Ⓓ Cohort effects make it impossible to answer this question.

Answers can be found on page ANS-3.

Module Summary

Module
10.1

Now that you have read this module
you should:

((•— Listen to
the audio file of
this module at
MyPsychLab

KNOW ...

- **The key terminology relating to concepts
  in developmental psychology and prenatal
  development:**

cohort effect (p. 347)
cross-sectional design (p. 347)
developmental psychology (p. 346)
embryonic stage (p. 349)
fetal alcohol syndrome (p. 353)
fetal stage (p. 349)
germinal stage (p. 349)

longitudinal design (p. 347)
preterm infant (p. 352)
reflexes (p. 354)
sensitive period (p. 348)
teratogen (p. 353)
zygote (p. 349)

UNDERSTAND ...

- **How development proceeds in both stage-like and
  continuous fashion over the life span.** Physical and
  behavioral development in the early years tends to fit a
  stage model of development. Change can also be gradual
  and continuous. Adulthood typically does not involve
  changes as drastic as those observed during infancy and
  childhood, although adults must still face major challenges
  and life phases.

APPLY ...

- **Your understanding to identify research designs.** Read
  the following scenarios and decide whether the research
  design was cross-sectional or longitudinal. Check your
  answers on page ANS-3.

  1. Forty infants were selected at birth to participate
     in a study focusing on the development of facial
     expressions. Researchers used a standard set of stimuli
     for eliciting smiling and frowning to test each infant's
     response at 1 week, 1 month, 6 months, and 12 months
     of age. They compared how the expressions occurred
     for each infant at each point in time.

  2. To test whether happiness and life satisfaction of parents
     increase as their children grow older, researchers
     recruited 100 volunteers. They compared happiness
     and life satisfaction in 25 parents with newborn infants,
     25 parents with children starting kindergarten, 25
     parents with children in grade school, and 25 parents
     with children graduating from high school.

ANALYZE ...

- **The effects of preterm birth.** Health risks increase
  considerably with very premature births (e.g., those
  occurring at just 25 weeks' gestation rather than the
  normal 37 weeks). Use of proper caregiving procedures,
  especially personalized care that emphasizes mother–
  infant contact, breastfeeding, and minimal sensory
  stimulation for the underdeveloped brain, increases the
  chances that preterm infants will remain healthy. Long-
  term studies indicate that with proper care children who
  were born preterm will not be disadvantaged relative to
  peers born at normal term.

- **The pros and cons of cross-sectional and longitudinal
  designs.** Cross-sectional data can be gathered at a single
  point in time, making a study adhering to this design
  less time consuming to complete than a study with a
  longitudinal design. Cross-sectional designs are also
  less likely to be affected by attrition (subjects dropping
  out). However, cross-sectional designs are vulnerable to
  cohort effects—that is, age differences may be due to
  historical factors rather than developmental differences.
  Longitudinal designs are less significantly affected by
  cohort effects because the same individuals are followed
  through the duration of the study.

Infancy and Childhood

KNOW ...	UNDERSTAND ...	APPLY ...	ANALYZE ...
The terminology associated with infancy and childhood	The cognitive changes that occur during infancy and childhood and the ways in which sociocultural influences can shape development The concept of attachment and the different styles of attachment	The stages of cognitive development to examples	Evidence that some cognitive abilities are present at birth

Many parents have turned to Disney's "Baby Einstein" line of books, toys, and DVDs in hopes of entertaining and enriching their children. These materials certainly are entertaining—children watch them. But a major issue concerns whether they provide the advertised long-term benefits of increasing cognitive skills. These products are designed to help babies explore music, art, language, science, poetry and nature through engaging images, characters, and music. The American Academy of Pediatrics, however, recommends that children younger than two years do not watch television at all. This recommendation is consistent with research showing that memory and language skills are slower to develop in infants who regularly watch television (Christakis, 2009). Furthermore, controlled studies show that the DVDs in question have no effect on vocabulary development (Richert et al., 2010; Robb et al, 2009). It turns out that the amount of time parents spend reading to their infants is related to greater vocabulary comprehension and production. As you can imagine, these results might give parents pause before they commit to using the DVDs.

Focus Questions

1. Which types of activities do infants and young children need for their psychological development?

2. Given that social interactions are so important, which specific abilities are nurtured by them?

. . . .

Although human infants are relatively helpless for an extended period of time, the complexity of the human brain and behavior begins to unfold immediately after birth. The physical, cognitive, and social transitions that occur between infancy and childhood are remarkably ordered, yet are also influenced by individual genetic and sociocultural factors. In this module, we integrate some important stage perspectives to explain psychological development through childhood.

Physical Changes in Infancy and Childhood

Infant abilities to move proceeds in stages—from crawling, to standing, to walking—over the course of the first 12 to18 months of life (see Figure 10.4). The age at which children can perform each of these movements differs from one individual to the next. Why do some children develop more rapidly or more slowly than others? In contrast to reflexes, the development of motor skills seems to rely more on practice and deliberate effort. Cross-cultural studies show that children raised in different environments mature at slightly different rates. In some cases, these variations may be attributable to the expectations that parents hold about when young people should be capable of certain tasks (Kelly et al., 2006; van Beek et al., 2006). For example, one study asked mothers of different nationalities when they expected their newborns to perform different actions. As compared to British or Indian mothers, Jamaican mothers gave earlier dates on average for sitting up and walking. Their expectations were confirmed, because the infants born to Jamaican mothers walked at a significantly earlier age, likely because these infants were encouraged to practice

Different childrearing practices and expectations result in cultural variations in the rate at which motor skills develop.

these skills at an earlier age (Hopkins & Westra, 1989; Zelazo et al., 1993).

The major structures of the brain are all present at birth, but their development is ongoing through early adulthood. During childhood, the cerebral cortex thickens, first in the sensory and motor areas, and then in regions involved in perception and eventually higher-order thinking and planning (Gogtay et al. 2004; Marsh et al., 2009). These changes in brain development

(a) (b) (c) (d) (e) (f)

{FIG. 10.4} **Motor Skills Develop in Stages** This series shows infants in different stages of development: (a) raising the head, (b) rolling over, (c) propping up, (d) sitting up, (e) crawling, and (f) walking.

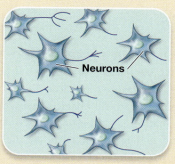

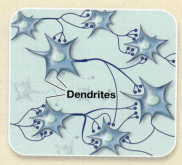

1. At birth, the infant's brain has a complete set of neurons but not very many synaptic connections.

2. During the first year, the axons grow longer, the dendrites increase in number, and a surplus of new connections is formed.

3. Over the next few years, active connections are strengthened, while unused connections disintegrate.

{FIG. 10.5}   **The Processes of Synaptic Pruning**

directly correspond with the development of cognitive abilities through late childhood.

Changes at the level of individual cells include myelination, which begins prenatally (see Module 10.1), accelerates through infancy and childhood, and then continues gradually for several decades. In addition, two events are occurring at the level of synapses—that is, in the junctions between connecting nerve cells (Module 3.2). The formation of billions of new synapses, a process called *synaptogenesis*, occurs at blinding speed through infancy and childhood, and continues through the life span. Along with synaptogenesis, the process of **synaptic pruning**, *the loss of weak nerve cell connections*, accelerates during brain development through infancy and childhood (Figure 10.5). Both synaptogenesis and synaptic pruning serve to increase brain functionality by strengthening needed connections between nerve cells and weeding out unnecessary ones.

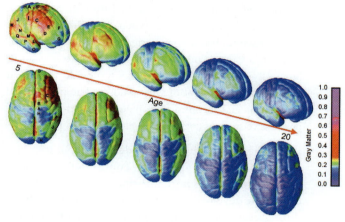

Brain development through early adulthood. Gray matter of the cerebral cortex continues to thicken from childhood all the way through young adulthood (Gogtay et al., 2004).

Quick Quiz 10.2a :: Physical Changes in Infancy and Childhood

KNOW …

1 The cerebral cortex continues thickening and developing after birth. Which of the following best describes the pattern of this process?

A Regions devoted to sensory and motor skills develop sooner than those involved in higher-order thinking.

B Regions devoted to higher-order thinking develop first.

C The physical structure of the brain at the end of childhood is indistinguishable from an adult's brain.

D The cortex is fully developed at birth.

UNDERSTAND …

2 The development of infant motor skills is best described as:

A a genetic process with no environmental influence.

B completely due to the effects of encouragement.

C a mixture of biological maturation and learning.

D progressing in continuous, rather than stage, fashion.

Answers can be found on page ANS-3.

Cognitive Changes: Piaget's Cognitive Development Theory

Jean Piaget (1896–1980) is often credited with initiating the modern science of **cognitive development**—*the study of changes in memory, thought, and reasoning processes that occur throughout the life span.* In his own work, Piaget focused on cognitive development spanning infancy through early adolescence. In this section, we review his theory and offer insight into modern work that builds upon it.

PsychTutor

Click here in your eText for an interactive tutorial on **Stage Theory: Piaget**

Piaget was interested in explaining how different ways of thinking and reasoning develop. According to Piaget, knowledge accumulates and is modified by two processes—assimilation and accommodation. In the case of *assimilation*, children add new information, but interpret it based on what they already know. A young child who is familiar with only the family's pet Chihuahua might develop a concept that all dogs are furry creatures that stand less than a foot tall. Because this is not true, her concept of dogs will eventually be modified through a different process. *Accommodation* occurs when children modify their belief structures based on experience. When this child encounters a Great Dane, she might first refer to it as horse, but will eventually correctly accommodate the Great Dane into her concept of what a dog is. The processes of assimilation and accommodation continue throughout the progressive steps of cognitive development.

Piaget's observations revealed that cognitive development was not one long, continuous process of learning more and more information, but rather that cognition develops in four distinct *stages* from birth through early adolescence: the sensorimotor stage, the preoperational stage, the concrete operational stage, and the formal operational stage. *Developmental milestones* are an important feature of Piaget's theory. As infants and children progress from one stage to the next, they obtain mastery of some important concept or skill (see Table 10.3).

THE SENSORIMOTOR STAGE: OBJECTS AND THE PHYSICAL WORLD When we are adults, if things like our cars, homes, and loved ones are not physically present, we can still imagine their continued existence. Imagination is a type of abstraction—what is in your mind is a representation of the objects and people in your physical environment. Unlike adults, four-month-old infants do not appear to have the ability to form abstract, mental representations. Therefore, infants' thinking and exploration of the world are based on immediate *sensory* (e.g., seeing, touching) and *motor* (e.g., grasping, mouthing) experiences. Piaget put these together and named this earliest period of cognitive development the **sensorimotor stage** (*spanning birth to two years*), *referring to the period in which infants' thinking and understanding about the world is based on sensory experiences and physical actions they perform on objects.*

If Piaget is right and infants think in terms of sensorimotor experience, then what happens when an object is out of sight and out of reach? Very young infants may not understand that the object continues to exist. Notice that this is not a problem for a two-year-old child. He can be very aware that his favorite dinosaur toy awaits him in another room while he has to sit at the dinner table; in fact, he might not be able to get the toy out of his mind. **Object permanence** *is the ability to understand that objects exist even when they cannot be seen or touched,* and Piaget proposed that it is a major milestone of cognitive development. To test for object permanence, Piaget would allow a child to

Table 10.3 :: Piaget's Stages of Cognitive Development

STAGE	DESCRIPTION
Sensorimotor (0–2 years)	Cognitive experience is based on direct, sensory experience with the world as well as motor movements that allow infants to interact with the world. Object permanence is the significant developmental milestone of this stage.
Preoperational (2–7 years)	Thinking moves beyond the immediate appearance of objects. Child understands physical conservation and that symbols, language, and drawings can be used to represent ideas.
Concrete operational (7–11 years)	The ability to perform mental transformations for objects that are physically present emerges. Thinking becomes logical and organized.
Formal operational (11 years–adulthood)	The capacity for abstract and hypothetical thinking develops. Scientific reasoning and thinking becomes possible.

Object permanence is tested by examining reactions that infants have to objects when they cannot be seen. Children who have object permanence will attempt to reach around the barrier or will continue looking in the direction of the desired object.

reach for a toy, and then place a screen or a barrier between the infant and the toy. If the infant stopped reaching for the object—as if looking for something else to do—this behavior indicated a lack of object permanence.

THE PREOPERATIONAL STAGE: QUANTITY AND NUMBERS According to Piaget, once children have mastered sensorimotor tasks, they have progressed to the next stage of development. The **preoperational stage**, *which spans ages two through seven years, is characterized by understanding of symbols, pretend play, and mastery of the concept of conservation.* During this stage, children can look at and think about physical objects, although they have not quite attained abstract thinking abilities. They may count objects and use numbers in their language, yet they remain limited in their use of mental operations (hence the name *preoperational*). One way to illustrate this quality is through the cognitive ability of **conservation**, *the knowledge that the quantity or amount of an object is not related to the physical arrangement and appearance of that object.*

A child's understanding of conservation may be assessed in a number of ways. For example, imagine that a child is presented with two identical rows of seven pennies each, as shown in the bottom of Figure 10.6. Next, the experimenter spreads out one of the rows so that it is longer, but has the same number of coins. If you ask a child, "Which row has more?" a three-year-old child would likely point to the row that was spread out. Here the child in the preoperational stage focuses on the simpler method of answering based on immediate perception, instead of the answer that would require more sophisticated mental operations.

Although Piaget emphasized how developmental changes occur in stages, he and other developmental psychologists recognized that mastery of cognitive tasks such as conservation does not occur overnight. Various other factors, such as motivation, influence whether children appear to understand the task. When three-year-old children are presented with a similar conservation test as the one described previously except with (1) M&Ms instead of pennies and (2) fewer M&Ms present in the row that is spread out, children will pick the row containing more candy—especially if they get to eat the candy from the row they choose (Mehler & Bever, 1967). Furthermore, children late in the preoperational stage will begin to use their hands to point out that there are equal numbers of pennies in two rows, even though they continue to provide the wrong answer verbally (Church & Goldin-Meadow, 1986). Their gesturing suggests that they are getting close to mastering the task.

Before children start to use and understand numbers, they acquire a basic sense for rules about quantity. That is, they seem to have a "number sense" that allows them to discriminate between different quantities (Libertus & Brannon, 2009). Very soon after they are born, infants appear to understand what it means to have less or more of something.

Although abstract thinking abilities are a work in progress for young children, they do begin to understand some basic principles. The children in

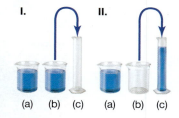

I.   **II.**

(a)   (b)   (c)   (a)   (b)   (c)

Row A
Row B

Which has more, row A or row B, or do they both have the same?

Row A
Row B

Now which has more, row A or row B, or do they both have the same?

{FIG. 10.6} **Testing Conservation** A child views two equal amounts of fluid, one of which is then poured into a taller container. Children who do not yet understand conservation believe that there is more fluid in the tall, narrow container compared to the shorter one. A similar version of this task can be tested using equal arrays of separate objects.

(a)

(b)

(c)

{FIG. 10.7} **Scale Errors and Testing for Scale Model Comprehension** The children in photos (a) and (b) are making scale errors. One child is attempting to slide down a toy slide and another is attempting to enter a toy car. Three-year-olds understand that a scale model represents an actual room (c). The adult pictured is using a scale model to indicate the location of a hidden object in an actual room of this type. At around 3-years children understand that the scale model symbolizes an actual room and will go directly to the hidden object after viewing the scale model.

Figure 10.7 are committing *scale* errors in the sense that they appear to interact with a doll-sized slide and a toy car as if they were the real thing, rather than miniatures (DeLoache et al., 2004).

By 2 to 2½ years, scale errors decline as children begin to understand properties of objects and how they are related. At around 3 years of age children begin to understand symbolic relationships. For example, 3-year-olds understand that a scale model of a room can symbolize an actual room (Figure 10.7). Children who view an experimenter placing a miniature toy within the scale model will quickly locate the actual toy when allowed to enter the room symbolized by the scale model (DeLoache, 1995). Abilities such as this are precursors to more advanced abilities of mental abstraction.

THE CONCRETE OPERATIONAL STAGE: USING LOGICAL THOUGHT Conservation is one of the main skills marking the transition from the preoperational stage to what Piaget called the **concrete operational stage** *(roughly spanning ages 7 to 11 years), when children develop skills in using and manipulating numbers as well as logical thinking.* Children in the concrete operational stage are able to classify objects according to properties such as size, value, shape, or some other physical characteristic. Thinking becomes increasingly logical and organized. For example, a child in the concrete operational stage recognizes that if X is more than Y, and Y is more than Z, then X is more than Z (a property called transitivity). This ability to think logically about physical objects transitions into more abstract realms in Piaget's fourth and final stage of cognitive development.

THE FORMAL OPERATIONAL STAGE: ABSTRACT AND HYPOTHETICAL THOUGHT The **formal operational stage** *(spanning from approximately 11 years of age and into adulthood) involves the development of advanced cognitive processes such as abstract reasoning and hypothetical thinking.* Scientific thinking, such as gathering evidence and systematically testing possibilities is characteristic of this stage. Thinking can exist entirely in hypothetical realms. Additional details on cognitive development at this age can be found in the next two modules where we will discuss adolescent and adult cognitive abilities.

Piaget was immensely successful at opening our eyes to the cognitive development of infants and children. Nevertheless, new methods for testing cognitive development suggest that he may have underestimated some aspects of infant cognitive abilities. For example, infants appear to understand some basic principles of the physical and social worlds very shortly after birth.

What do we know about cognitive abilities in infants?

The **core knowledge hypothesis** *is a view on development proposing that infants have inborn abilities for understanding some key aspects of their environment* (Spelke & Kinzler, 2007). It is a bold claim to say that babies know something about the world before they have even experienced it, so we should closely examine the evidence for this hypothesis.

First, how can *we* know what infants know or what they perceive? One frequently used method for answering this question relies on the habituation–dishabituation response. **Habituation** *refers to a decrease in responding with repeated exposure to an event,* something infants are well known for doing. For example, if an infant views the same stimulus or event over and over, she will stop looking at it. In this case, the habituated response is time spent looking at the event. Conversely, infants are quite responsive to novelty or changes in their environment. Thus, if the stimulus suddenly changes, the infant will display **dishabituation,** *an increase in responsiveness with the presentation of a new stimulus.* In other words, the infant will return her gaze to the location that was once boring.

How can science help explain infant cognitive abilities?

Habituation and dishabituation have been used to measure whether infants understand many different concepts, including abstract numbers—an ability that most people imagine appears much later in development. Elizabeth Spelke and colleagues have conducted numerous experiments on this topic. In

one study, 16 infants just two days of age were shown arrays on a video screen of either 4 or 12 identical small shapes (e.g., yellow triangles, purple circles). The researchers also sounded a tone 4 or 12 times (tu-tu-tu-tu or ra-ra-ra-ra-ra-ra-ra-ra-ra-ra-ra-ra) at the same time they showed the shapes (see Figure 10.8). Sometimes the number of shapes the infants saw matched the number of tones they heard (4 yellow triangles and 4 ra-ra-ra-ra tones); at other times the number of shapes and tones were mismatched (12 ra's and 4 purple circles). Whether the stimuli were circles or triangles and the tones were "ra" or "tu" did not matter: The infants were attentive when what they saw and heard matched. In other words, they looked longer at the shapes when the tone that accompanied them matched in number, compared to when they did not match. The researchers believe that this finding is evidence that even very young infants have a rudimentary appreciation for abstract numbers (Izard et al., 2009).

A popular method for testing infant cognitive abilities is to measure the amount of time infants look at events. Researchers measure habituation and dishabituation to infer what infants understand.

…"da-da-da-da-da-da-da-da-da-da-da-da"…"bu-bu-bu-bu-bu-bu-bu-bu-bu-bu-bu-bu"…
or
…"daaaaa-daaaaa-daaaaa-daaaaa"…"buuuuu-buuuuu-buuuuu-buuuuu"…

Test (4 trials)

{FIG. 10.8} **Testing Infants' Understanding of Quantity** In this study, infants listened to tones that were repeated either 4 or 12 times while they looked at objects that had either 4 or 12 components. Infants spend more time looking at visual arrays when the number of items they see matches the number of tones they hear.

Can we critically evaluate alternative explanations?

Many of the studies of early cognitive development discussed in this module used the "looking time" procedure, although not all psychologists agree that it is an ideal way of determining what infants understand or perceive (Aslin, 2007; Rivera et al., 1999). We cannot know exactly what infants are thinking, and perhaps they look longer at events and stimuli simply because these are more interesting, rather than because they understand anything in particular about them. Also, just like with studies of adults, we cannot necessarily generalize findings from infants, even though they have accumulated only a mere 48 hours of knowledge. In the study of abstract numbers (shapes and tones) just described, only 16 infants managed to complete the study. Forty-five others were too fussy or sleepy to successfully finish the task.

Why is this relevant?

One thing that psychologists can agree on is that habituation seems a lot like boredom. With that being the case, how might we use this information in childrearing? It is a good idea to provide plenty of stimulation for infants. Playing with a variety of toys, hearing various stories and songs, and interacting with different people will not confuse an infant, but instead will encourage the infant's curiosity and stimulate intellectual development.

COMPLEMENTARY APPROACHES TO PIAGET

Piaget's theories have had a lasting impact on modern developmental psychology. Even so, some details of his theories have generated controversy in the decades since they were proposed. In particular, Piaget generally underestimated the abilities of infants and their rates of development, and his strong emphasis on cognitive tasks

Caregivers who are attentive to the learning and abilities of a developing child provide scaffolding for cognitive development.

overlooked sociocultural and biological elements of cognitive growth.

The dynamics that occur between children and their parents, teachers, and peers form the sociocultural context in which cognitive development occurs. Children who try to master a skill alone may find themselves up against obstacles that are difficult to overcome, whereas children who are not allowed to work through problems at all lack opportunities to exercise and improve their abilities. Therefore, it seems that optimal development may occur somewhere in between these two scenarios, an area that psychologist Lev Vygotsky (1978) named the **zone of proximal development**: *Development is ideal when a child attempts skills and activities that are just beyond what he or she can do alone, but the child has guidance from adults who are attentive to his or her progress* (Singer & Goldin-Meadow, 2005). This interactive approach to teaching and learning is a great facilitator of cognitive development in children. **Scaffolding** *is the approach to teaching in which the teacher matches guidance to the learner or student's needs.*

Cross-cultural research on parent–infant interactions shows that scaffolding is exercised in different ways (Rogoff et al., 1993). For example, in one study 12- to 24-month-old children were offered a toy that required pulling a string to make it move. Parents from Turkey, Guatemala, and the United States were observed interacting with their infants as they attempted to figure out how the toy worked. All parents used scaffolding when they spoke and gestured to their children to encourage them to pull the string, but the researchers found cross-cultural variations in the types of scaffolding used. Parents from Turkey and the United States rarely touched or used the direction of their eye gaze to encourage the behavior. In general, members of the mother–child pairs from Guatemala were more communicative with each other, both verbally and through gestures.

KNOW …

1 Recognizing that the quantity of an object does not change despite changes in physical arrangement or appearance is referred to as: _____.

- **A** object permanence
- **C** conservation
- **B** scale comprehension
- **D** number sense

2 Parents who attend to their children's psychological abilities and guide them through the learning process are using: _____.

- **A** scaffolding
- **B** tutoring
- **C** core knowledge
- **D** the zone of proximal development

3 What is the correct order of Piaget's stages of cognitive development?

- **A** Preoperational, sensorimotor, concrete operational, formal operational
- **B** Sensorimotor, preoperational, formal operational, concrete operational
- **C** Sensorimotor, preoperational, concrete operational, formal operational
- **D** Preoperational, concrete operational, sensorimotor, formal operational

APPLY …

4 A child in the sensorimotor stage may quit looking or reaching for a toy if you move it out of sight. This behavior reflects the fact that the child has not developed _____.

- **A** core knowledge
- **C** conservation
- **B** object permanence
- **D** preoperations

ANALYZE …

5 Research on newborns indicates that they have a sense of number and quantity. What does this finding suggest about Piaget's theory of cognitive development?

- **A** It confirms what Piaget claimed about infants in the sensorimotor phase.
- **B** Some infants are born with superior intelligence.
- **C** Piaget may have underestimated some cognitive abilities of infants and children.
- **D** Culture determines what infants are capable of doing.

Answers can be found on page ANS-3.

Social Development: Attachment, Personality, and Reading Others

We know that humans are social creatures; teens and adults are keenly aware of their social status and need for companionship, and they work to form and maintain relationships. But what about newborns—are they interested in social relationships? Do they care who is around them, who likes them, and what others think about them? The optimal developmental course is for infants to form loving and trusting relationships with their primary caregivers, but how does this happen? Do infants simply bond with whoever provides milk and clean diapers? Or is there something more emotional at work?

TYPES OF ATTACHMENT Intense social bonding between humans starts with the dynamic between infant and caregiver. An **attachment** *is an enduring emotional bond formed between individuals.* More than that, attachment is a *motivation* to seek out others for close physical and psychological comfort, especially during stressful situations. In evolutionary terms, safety and survival underlie the motivation to form attachments (Bowlby, 1951).

Attachment is as important to survival as food and water, and this observation led some early psychologists to speculate that infants form attachments to whoever satisfies their hunger and thirst. After all, the caregivers who provide nourishment are usually the persons who share the strongest bonds with the infant. However, it turns out that nourishment is just a small part of the process of forming attachments.

Love, comfort, and protection can be very strong motivating forces. Isolation from others—namely, those who play nurturing and caring roles—can be as disastrous as nutritional starvation. In the 1950s, psychologist Harry Harlow became passionately interested in the topic of bonding and attachment. Through numerous experimental studies on monkeys, Harlow sought to determine just how strong the need for attachment was in monkeys in comparison to other motivators such as food. He showed that monkeys deprived of maternal care clinged compulsively to a piece of terrycloth wrapped around a cylinder of wire mesh that loosely resembled the body shape of an adult monkey. Infant monkeys spent less time with an identical wire object that lacked the terrycloth, even though the infant's food was attached to it. These early experiments suggested that physical contact, rather than food, formed the basis for mother–infant bonding (Harlow, 1958).

A baby monkey clings to a cloth covered object—Harlow called this object the *cloth mother*—even though the wire "mother" provided food.

Further research showed that a lack of bonding does not just affect infant and early childhood behaviors. Primates that are denied social contact during infancy display abnormal social and sexual behaviors in adulthood as well (Harlow et al., 1965). However, these behavioral problems are not necessarily permanent. In subsequent studies, when monkeys that were socially deprived as infants were given regular social contact, their behavior returned to relatively normal levels (Suomi & Harlow, 1972).

Obviously, for ethical reasons Harlow's studies with monkeys cannot be replicated with human participants. Instead, psychologists have developed methods of studying infant attachment that are only mildly stressful and mimic natural situations. One method capitalizes on how infants react to strangers. At around eight months of age, infants can become distressed when they encounter someone unfamiliar, a phenomenon called stranger anxiety. Infants experiencing stranger anxiety may cry and actively seek out their caregivers. Laboratory experiments have used the *strange situation* protocol to characterize the type of attachment infants have toward their mothers or caregivers (Ainsworth, 1978). In this procedure, the primary caregiver brings an infant into a room that has some toys on the floor and a stranger nearby. The mother leaves the room for a few moments and returns; meanwhile, the experimenter monitors the infant. Attachment styles are categorized by the reactions the infants exhibit when the mother leaves and returns (Figure 10.9). Using this procedure, researchers have identified the following categories of attachment (Ainsworth, 1978):

1. *Secure attachment.* The caregiver is a base that the child uses as he or she explores. In the strange situation, the child plays comfortably while the mother is in the room. The child may or may not cry when the mother leaves, and seeks contact with her upon returning.

2. *Insecure attachment.* Three subtypes are distinguished:
   - *Disorganized.* The child does not have a consistent pattern of behavior either when the mother leaves or when she returns. The child might freeze for a moment, seemingly unsure of what to do next.
   - *Resistant.* The child is upset when the mother leaves, but is angry when she returns.
   - *Avoidant.* The child is not upset when the mother leaves, and does not seek contact when she returns.

The anxiety that children experience when their primary caregiver is absent declines after they reach approximately 13 months of age. This transformation does not imply that attachment becomes less important. Infancy is a phase in which the *first* attachments form, but attachment continues to occur across the life span and in other contexts, such as in romantic relationships. Patterns of attachment in romantic relationships reflect back on styles of attachment formed during infancy (Hofer, 2006). A longitudinal study spanning more than 20 years showed that people who were securely attached as infants were better able to recover from interpersonal conflict with their romantic partners (Salvatore et al., 2011). Our attachment styles hold evolutionary advantages in that they lead us to establish secure and long lasting relationships, which, in humans, is an important component of childrearing (Bowlby, 1951; Fraley et al., 2005).

After identifying the main attachment styles, psychologists began to ask how infants develop their characteristic attachment style. The social environment that parents create influences the type of attachment style formed. When emotional and communicative responses between parent and infant are closely coordinated, secure attachment styles result (Hane et al., 2003). By comparison, insecure attachments are more likely if parents respond inconsistently and slowly to their infants.

SOCIAL COGNITION Attachment studies highlight just how strong the motivation for social interaction is in the human species. During infancy and into childhood, the basic need for contact comfort expands as developing children become more aware of the complexity of their social environment. For example, when looking in a mirror, you recognize that it is you who looks back, not some stranger who has invited himself or herself into your bathroom. At approximately 24 months of age, toddlers and young children show evidence of **self-awareness**, *the*

Mother   Stranger

{FIG. 10.9} **The Strange Situation** Studies of attachment by Mary Ainsworth involved a mother leaving her infant with a stranger. Ainsworth believed that the infants' attachment styles could be categorized according to their behavioral and emotional responses to the mother leaving and returning.

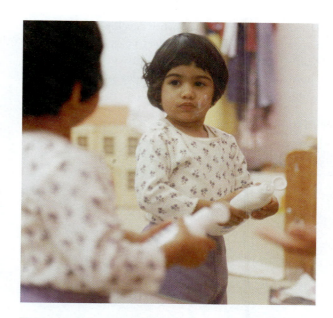

By two years of age, toddlers can recognize themselves in mirrors.

shoes from time to time, but young children may find it next to impossible. Consider the following scenario:

> An experimenter offers three-year-old Andrea a box of chocolates. Upon opening the box, Andrea discovers not candy, but rather pencils. Joseph enters the room and she watches as Joseph is offered the same box. The researcher asks Andrea, "What does Joseph expect to find in the box?"

This is called the *false-belief task*. On the one hand, if Andrea answers "pencils," then she does not understand that Joseph is being misled; more importantly, she believes that Joseph knows the same thing she does. On the other hand, Andrea might tell the experimenter that Joseph expects to see chocolates. If so, she must understand that he is being misled and, therefore, is taking the mental perspective of another. This task is a common method used to study the development of theory of mind (Lillard, 1998; Wimmer & Perner, 1983). Children typically pass this test at ages four to five years, although younger children may pass if they are told that Joseph is about to be tricked. The shift away from egocentric thought does not occur overnight. Older children may still have difficulty taking the perspective of others. The presence of theory of mind in young children suggests that they move away from egocentric thought at an earlier age than once believed, however.

The specific ways that infants and children relate to others is intertwined with their own unique and developing personality characteristics.

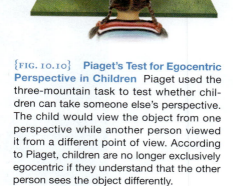

{FIG. 10.10} **Piaget's Test for Egocentric Perspective in Children** Piaget used the three-mountain task to test whether children can take someone else's perspective. The child would view the object from one perspective while another person viewed it from a different point of view. According to Piaget, children are no longer exclusively egocentric if they understand that the other person sees the object differently.

ability to recognize one's individuality. The presence of self-awareness is typically tested by observing infants' reactions to their reflection in a mirror or on video (Bahrick & Watson, 1985; Bard et al., 2006). Self-awareness becomes increasingly sophisticated over the course of development, progressing from early recognition of oneself in a mirror or on video, to having the ability to reflect on one's own feelings, decisions, and appearance. By the time children reach their fifth birthday, they become self-reflective, show concern for others, and are intensely interested in the causes of other people's behavior.

What about awareness of *others*? Young children are sometimes described as **egocentric**, *meaning that they perceive and interpret the world in terms of the self* (Piaget & Inhelder, 1956). This does not imply that children are selfish or inconsiderate. For example, a two-year-old may attempt to hide by simply covering her own eyes. From her perspective, she *is* hidden. Piaget tested for egocentrism by sitting a child in front of an object, and then presenting pictures of that object from four angles. While sitting opposite the child, Piaget would ask him or her to identify which image represented the object from Piaget's perspective, but many children would select the image corresponding to their own perspective (Figure 10.10). Piaget concluded that children were egocentric through the preoperational phase (ending around age seven).

Modern research indicates that children take the perspective of others long before the preoperational phase is complete. Perspective taking in young children has been demonstrated in studies of **theory of mind**—*the ability to recognize the thoughts, beliefs, and expectations of others, and to understand that these can be different from one's own.* Adults may have difficulty putting themselves in another person's

TEMPERAMENT: A GLIMPSE INTO PERSONALITY

Infants differ in **temperament**, *their general emotional reactivity, which is regarded as the root from which several aspects of adult personality grow.* Temperament comes in at least a couple of varieties. High-reactive infants tend to show vigorous activity of their limbs, back arching, and crying when confronted with unfamiliar stimuli. Low-reactive infants show less motor activity and less distress when exposed to unfamiliar stimuli. As high-reactive infants mature, they become timid and react negatively to unfamiliar people, whereas low-reactive infants are more likely to show willingness to approach unfamiliar people and situations (Kagan et al., 1998). Thus emotional reactivity to the strange situation, or any other situation that elicits emotions, also depends on inherited predispositions of infants.

From temperament spawns personality—our unique and enduring personal and social qualities. Erik Erikson (1963) believed that personality develops in eight separate stages, each of which involves a particular *psychosocial crisis*—that is, a struggle between two opposing beliefs about oneself. Each of these stages and the conflicts within are summarized in Table 10.4.

Table 10.4 :: Erikson's Stages of Psychosocial Development

1

Infancy: trust versus mistrust: Developing a sense of trust and security toward caregivers.

3

Preschool/early childhood: initiative versus guilt: Active exploration of the environment and taking personal initiative.

2

Toddlerhood: autonomy versus shame and doubt: Seeking independence and gaining self-sufficiency.

4

Childhood: industry versus inferiority: Striving to master tasks and challenges of childhood, particularly those faced in school. Child begins pursuing unique interests.

Table 10.4 :: Erikson's Stages of Psychosocial Development *(Continued)*

Adolescence: identity versus role confusion: Achieving a sense of self and future direction.

Young adulthood: intimacy versus isolation: Developing the ability to initiate and maintain intimate relationships.

Adulthood: generativity versus stagnation: The focus is on satisfying personal and family needs, as well as contributing to society.

Aging: ego integrity versus despair: Coping with the prospect of death while looking back on life with a sense of contentment and integrity for accomplishments.

PsychTutor

Click here in your eText for an interactive tutorial on **Stage Theory: Erikson**

Erikson's first four stages are applicable to infancy and childhood. During the first year after birth, the psychosocial crisis that infants face is *trust versus mistrust*—the concern over whether basic needs such as food, comfort, and physical contact will be met. Stage two, *autonomy versus shame and doubt*, spans the child's second and third years and involves conflict over whether the individual can take care of himself or herself without constant parental supervision and guidance. Stage three, *initiative versus guilt*, lasts from years three through six and is characterized by the child's attempts to take initiative and become independent. It is not unusual for children to act out their frustrations as their attempts to become independent are redirected by parents and caregivers. During this third stage, children also acquire the ability to feel guilty, which can be experienced when their initiative does not lead to a desired outcome. The fourth stage of Erikson's theory, *industry versus inferiority*, comprises adolescence (age six through puberty). The psychosocial crisis of this phase centers on accomplishing goals, succeeding in school, developing self-confidence, and discovering personal interests and talents.

Two strengths of Erikson's theory are that he identified critical issues we face from infancy onward, and that personality is influenced by the outcome of conflicts we face. A weakness is that the age ranges may not be entirely accurate: We can have conflicts of any type throughout the life span.

Quick Quiz 10.2c
Social Development: Bonding, Attachment, and Reading Others

KNOW…

1 An enduring emotional bond characterized by a strong motivation for physical and psychological comfort is referred to as: _____.

- **A** empathy
- **B** attachment
- **C** object permanence
- **D** theory of mind

2 Temperament refers to:

- **A** whether a child is likely to get angry
- **B** body temperature at birth.
- **C** a child's ability to recognize himself or herself in a mirror.
- **D** general emotional reactivity.

UNDERSTAND…

3 Two-year-old Sarah talks to her brother, who is wearing headphones and looking away, and becomes frustrated that he is (or seems to be) ignoring her. Sarah's misunderstanding is likely to do the fact that she has yet to develop: _____.

- **A** theory of mind
- **B** self-awareness
- **C** egocentrism
- **D** stranger anxiety

APPLY…

4 Two-year-old Jeffrey continues playing when his mother returns home and does not respond to her greetings. His attachment style might be described as: _____.

- **A** avoidant
- **B** resistant
- **C** disorganized
- **D** secure

Answers can be found on page ANS-3.

Module Summary

Now that you have read this module you should:

Listen to the audio file of this module at **MyPsychLab**

KNOW ...

- **The key terminology associated with infancy and childhood:**

attachment (p. 365)
cognitive development (p. 360)
concrete operational stage (p. 362)
conservation (p. 361)
core knowledge hypothesis (p. 363)
dishabituation (p. 363)
egocentric (p. 367)
formal operational stage (p. 362)
habituation (p. 363)

object permanence (p. 360)
preoperational stage (p. 361)
scaffolding (p. 364)
self-awareness (p. 366)
sensorimotor stage (p. 360)
synaptic pruning (p. 359)
temperament (p. 367)
theory of mind (p. 367)
zone of proximal development (p. 364)

UNDERSTAND ...

- **The cognitive changes that occur during infancy and childhood and the ways in which sociocultural influences can shape cognitive development.** According to Piaget's theory of cognitive development, infants mature through childhood via orderly transitions across the sensorimotor, preoperational, concrete operational, and formal operational stages. According to Vygotsky, cognitive development unfolds in a social context between caregivers/teachers and children. Specifically, children's skills are nurtured by adults who are sensitive to the cognitive capacities that individual children have attained.

- **The concept of attachment and the different styles of attachment.** In developmental psychology, attachment refers to the enduring social bond between child and caregiver. Work on nonhuman primates by Harry Harlow demonstrated the strength of attachment motivation. Research involving the "strange situation" reveals the various styles of attachment that may form between children and their caregivers. Children are either securely or insecurely attached, and insecure attachments can be further divided into disorganized, resistant, and avoidant styles.

APPLY ...

- **The stages of cognitive development to examples.** Each of the following scenarios describes behavior and thinking of different children. Read these cases and identify where each child is in terms of cognitive development. Check your answers on page ANS-3.

1. Bridgette's understanding of her world is largely based on her direct interactions with objects, which includes mouthing, grasping, and handling them. Which stage of Piaget's cognitive development is she most likely in? What is a major cognitive milestone that occurs during this stage?

2. Jared is able to add and subtract as long as he is able to use actual objects in computing the problems. According to Piaget, Jared is probably in which stage of cognitive development?

3. Michael and his brother receive $1 for allowance. One week, his father mysteriously gave 100 pennies to his brother, but "only" 10 dimes to Michael. Michael's frustration with this situation is likely due to his being in which stage of cognitive development? Which specific ability does Michael seem to lack?

4. A teacher wants to ask her students to describe what the United States would be like if the country were still run by England. According to Piaget, which stage of cognitive development would the students need to have reached to offer thoughtful answers to this scenario?

ANALYZE ...

- **Evidence that some cognitive abilities are present at birth.** According to the core-knowledge hypothesis, humans come into the world with a rudimentary understanding of various cognitive domains, such as arithmetic and the ways in which physical objects are related. Experiments with newborns and very young infants suggest that, to some extent, our adult understanding of the world builds upon capacities that can be detected from our first days after birth. These studies suggest that Piaget's framework underestimates the cognitive abilities of infants and children at each stage of development.

Adolescence

KNOW ...	UNDERSTAND ...	APPLY ...	ANALYZE ...
The key terminology concerning adolescent development	The different ways in which identity develops The role of status in adolescent relationships	Your understanding of the categories of moral development and identity statuses	The relationship between brain development and adolescent judgment and risk taking

Are Internet use and depression related among adolescents? They may be, but psychologists are finding that this is not an easy question to answer. Research on hundreds of Internet users aged 13 to 18 years suggests that they are related (Lam & Peng, 2010). Considering that adolescents spend more time than any other age group using the Internet, this might be an alarming trend. Since the 1990s, many (but not all) researchers have arrived at the same conclusion—that Internet use negatively affects mental well-being. These problems raise important societal concerns about the well-being of adolescents.

Even so, before we rush to judgment, we must consider several factors that might influence this relationship. Not all adolescents who are frequent Internet users have psychological problems. In fact, it may be that Internet use and depression are linked for only a subset of adolescents, such as those who are socially marginalized even before the Internet factor comes into play. Also, "Internet use" is a very broad term; the ways in which people use the Internet, as well as the types of devices for accessing it, are constantly changing. Moreover, the Internet can be used for many different purposes, including random browsing, research, gaming, social networking, and instant messaging. Perhaps there are also psychological and social benefits to using the Internet.

Focus Questions

 Does Internet use impair or enhance social relationships during adolescence?

 Which other psychological characteristics are major points of change during adolescence?

· · · · · · · · · · · · · · · · · · ·

Adolescents are an interesting group; they are cognitively and socially more sophisticated than children, yet they behave in sometimes very impulsive ways. Their behavior often goes to extremes in terms of energy, curiosity, imagination, and emotion. Individuals during this stage of development also demonstrate rapid and obvious changes in terms of physical growth. In this section, we begin by exploring these physical changes and then move on to discuss the personal and social changes that adolescents face.

Physical Changes in Adolescence

Puberty *marks the physical transition from childhood to adolescence, culminating in reproductive maturity.* Puberty begins at approximately age 11 in girls and age 13 in boys. The changes that occur during puberty are primarily caused by hormonal activity. Physical growth is stimulated by the pituitary gland. The nervous and reproductive systems interact to cause further physical changes of reproductive anatomy. The *hypothalamus* begins stimulating the release of hormones such as testosterone and estrogen, both of which contribute to the development of sex characteristics in boys and girls. The resulting changes affect *primary sex traits,* including the genitals and gonads (testes or ovaries), as well as *secondary sex traits.* In females, the development of secondary sex traits includes growth in breast size and the increased distribution of fat at the hips and buttocks. In males, secondary traits include growth of facial and body hair, a deepening of the voice, increased muscle mass, and fat deposits at the waist (Figure 10.11).

For girls, puberty is also marked by **menarche**—*the onset of menstruation*—which typically occurs around age 12. The timing of menarche is influenced by physiological and environmental factors. Nutrition, genetics, physical activity levels, and illness are just a few of these contributing factors (Ellis & Garber, 2000). Even the absence of a father or the presence of a stepfather during development is known to be associated with early onset of menarche (Bogaert, 2008). Boys are considered to reach sexual maturity at **spermarche**, *their first ejaculation of sperm.* This experience typically takes place at approximately 14 years of age as a nocturnal emission (wet dream).

Hormone surges during adolescence are associated with negative moods and problems with adjustment (Warren & Brooks-Gunn, 1989). Also, the physical changes associated with puberty affect how adolescents perceive themselves and others. Girls who reach puberty early tend to have more emotional difficulty with the experience than do boys. For boys, acquiring masculine traits at an early age may be regarded positively by both the individual and his peers. Early developers do have a greater risk of drug and alcohol abuse and unwanted pregnancies. Along with all of these physical changes and the challenges they bring, adolescents also experience major cognitive and social changes.

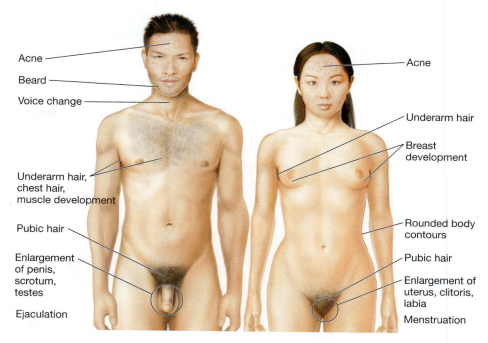

Acne
Beard
Voice change
Underarm hair, chest hair, muscle development
Pubic hair
Enlargement of penis, scrotum, testes
Ejaculation

Acne
Underarm hair
Breast development
Rounded body contours
Pubic hair
Enlargement of uterus, clitoris, labia
Menstruation

{FIG. 10.11} **Physical Changes That Accompany Puberty in Male and Female Adolescents** Hormonal changes accelerate the development of physical traits in males and females. Changes involve maturation of the reproductive system (primary sex traits) as well as secondary sex traits such as enlargement of breasts in women and deepening of the voice in males. **Click on this figure in your eText to see more details.**

Quick Quiz 10.3a
Physical Changes in Adolescence

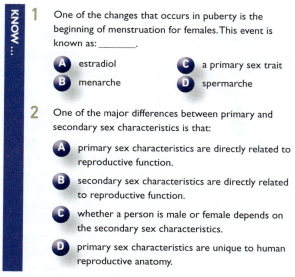

KNOW ...

1 One of the changes that occurs in puberty is the beginning of menstruation for females. This event is known as: _____.

   A estradiol   **C** a primary sex trait

   B menarche   **D** spermarche

2 One of the major differences between primary and secondary sex characteristics is that:

   A primary sex characteristics are directly related to reproductive function.

   B secondary sex characteristics are directly related to reproductive function.

   C whether a person is male or female depends on the secondary sex characteristics.

   D primary sex characteristics are unique to human reproductive anatomy.

Answers can be found on page ANS-3.

Cognitive Development: Thinking and Moral Reasoning

Between the onset of adolescence and young adulthood, cognitive abilities approach their peak. Beginning at approximately 12 years of age, young adolescents show significant improvements in their abilities to use logic and reasoning (what Piaget referred to as *formal operational* thinking; see Module 10.2). Youths of this age begin thinking abstractly about things that are not present and about events or scenarios that are entirely impossible or hypothetical (Klaczynski, 1993). This ability is a major advance beyond the concrete thinking that characterizes late childhood. During this time, adolescents also develop the ability and capacity to think scientifically and view problems from multiple perspectives.

How can science explain brain development and decision making in adolescents?

In addition to looking at changes in brain anatomy over time, we should ask how actual brain activity is affected in adolescents who make risky decisions.

One study sought to address this issue by scanning the brains of adolescents while they played a *Wheel of Fortune* game. Named after the television game show, this task asked participants to view a screen that presented them with two choices. One option—the riskier choice—was to place a $6 bet that a spinning wheel would stop at a target that it had only a 25% chance of hitting. A less risky choice was to bet $1 that the wheel would stop at a target that it had a 50% chance of hitting. The game was set up to simulate a real-life decision between a high-risk choice that has the potential to bring a larger monetary reward and a low-risk choice that offers only a small reward. As the participants played the game, their brains were scanned using functional magnetic resonance imaging. The researchers discovered that adolescents who selected the riskier choice had less brain activity in their prefrontal cortex compared to adolescents who avoided the risky choice (Figure 10.12; Shad et al., 2011). This is just one of many studies pointing to the conclusion that risky decision making by adolescents has a basis in their still-developing frontal cortex.

Can we critically evaluate alternative explanations?

Neurological differences between adolescents and adults in terms of their prefrontal cortex anatomy

Adolescents have the ability to think critically, but this does not mean that they always do. People of any age may take risks or make poor decisions, but adolescents are particularly prone to them, and adolescents' reasoning and decision making do not always lead to the best outcomes (Steinberg, 2007). Unplanned pregnancies, drug and alcohol abuse, accidents, and violence are more common during adolescence than during any other stage of life. Adolescents have greater difficulty inhibiting their impulses than do adults, and they can also be less inclined to plan and envision future consequences of their behavior.

What do we know about adolescence and decision making?

Although adolescents are beginning to show the cognitive and social sophistication of adults, hormonal and neurological changes are still under way, which helps to explain some of the struggles that youths of this age experience. In recent years, psychologists and neuroscientists have implicated ongoing changes in the *prefrontal cortex* as the basis of some of the behavioral issues that are especially likely to occur during adolescence. The prefrontal cortex is involved in impulse control, regulates mood, and facilitates planning, organizing, and reasoning. To the naked eye, an adolescent brain looks like an adult brain. However, as discussed in Modules 10.1 and 10.2, the processes of myelination (growth of brain white matter) and synaptic pruning (loss of useless connections between brain cells) continue through adolescence (Giorgio et al., 2010). Thus the adolescent brain is still developing in critical areas, particularly those involved in decision making and impulse control.

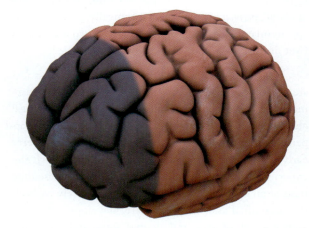

{FIG. 10.12} **Extended Brain Development** The prefrontal cortex (highlighted in blue) continues to develop through adolescence and even into young adulthood. **Click on this figure in your eText to see more details.**

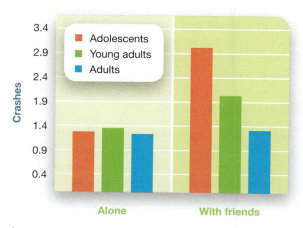

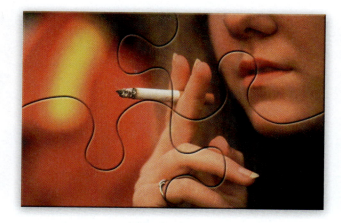

{FIG. 10.13} **What Drives Teenagers to Take Risks?** One key factor in risk taking is simply *other teenagers*. When teens play a driving video game with other teens, they crash more than when playing the same game when alone, and more than adults playing the game (from Steinberg, 2007).

offer a plausible scientific explanation for why adolescents are prone to risk taking and poor decision making. However, a less than fully developed prefrontal cortex does not completely rob adolescents of the capacity for making good decisions and avoiding risk, nor does it relieve them of assuming responsibility for their actions. Adolescents can also be risk averse and make excellent, well-considered decisions, just as they can accept blame and take credit where it is due. In addition, risk taking and decision making are related to temperament and personality characteristics, which vary from one individual to the next, no matter what their age. The study using the *Wheel of Fortune* task showed that some adolescents—namely, those who showed higher activity in their prefrontal cortex—chose to avoid risky bets.

Moreover, situational factors influence whether adolescents take risks. Psychologists have found that in some situations, adolescents are no more likely to engage in risky behavior than adults. When adolescents are with other adolescents, however, this propensity changes (see Figure 10.13). This finding and others like it indicate that strategies for reducing adolescent risk taking and impulsivity should appreciate the important role that situational and social factors play in adolescents' decision making.

Why is this relevant?

Research on the developing adolescent brain helps explain problems with risk and impulse control. But where does it leave us? Scholars, parents, and insurance companies, to name a few concerned parties, regard adolescent risk-taking behavior to be a major public health problem (Steinberg, 2008). Risky behavior and poor decision making lead to both self- and other-inflicted harm and injury. Workers in mental and public health professions have spent countless hours and devoted vast expenditures of public funds to implementing

programs—some successful, some not—that seek to steer adolescents toward making better decisions, such as avoiding unprotected sex, smoking, alcohol, and drug use (Reyna & Farley, 2006).

KOHLBERG'S MORAL DEVELOPMENT: LEARNING RIGHT FROM WRONG Early beliefs about right and wrong form during childhood, particularly as very young children learn which behaviors are punished or rewarded. It is during adolescence that beliefs about right and wrong become increasingly complex and sophisticated. Right and wrong remain important endpoints, but adolescents come to understand that there can be a lot of space between these two alternatives. Psychologists are interested in how moral reasoning develops and how people apply moral beliefs to the various situations they encounter. Traditionally, studies of moral development pose dilemmas to people of different ages and examine the details of their responses. For example, imagine the following scenario, unlikely as it may be:

> *A trolley is hurtling down the tracks toward a group of five unsuspecting people. You are standing next to a lever that, if pulled, would direct the trolley onto another track, thereby saving the five individuals. However, on the second track stands a single, unsuspecting person, who would be struck by the diverted trolley.*

What would you choose to do? Would you pull the lever, allowing five to live but causing one to die? Would you do nothing? Moral dilemmas provide interesting tests of development because they place an individual's values in conflict with each other. Obviously, five lives are more than one—yet most of us recognize that it is not up to us to make such decisions. Unfortunately, this hypothetical dilemma does not include a bullhorn that you could use to warn the unsuspecting people. The only alternative is to pull the switch or do nothing. Saying you would or would not pull the lever is only the starting point to understanding your moral development. Two people could come up with the same answer for very different reasons. It is *how* and *why* you made your choice that is of greater interest to psychologists studying moral development.

Lawrence Kohlberg (1984) examined how people reason about moral dilemmas and identified three stages of moral reasoning. Table 10.5 reviews these stages and illustrates how three individuals might reason through their decisions.

The reasoning behind the answers given is the most important source of information about the development of moral reasoning. A child and an older adult may both claim that they would not flip the switch, but the reasoning behind their decisions would probably be very different. Also, postconventional moral reasoning involves the ability to think abstractly, which (as noted earlier in this module) becomes evident during adolescence.

Kohlberg regarded the three stages of moral reasoning as universal to all humans, but he developed his theory mostly through the study of how *males* reason about moral dilemmas. Clearly, a theory about human behavior cannot be universal if it is based on research involving members of only one gender. Based on later work done by other psychologists interested in moral reasoning, it appears that girls reason *differently* about moral dilemmas than boys (Gilligan, 1982). Females appear to base moral decisions more on caring relationships and less on justice and abstract principles that Kohlberg emphasized (Jaffee & Hyde, 2000).

Knowing that something is right or wrong is very different from *feeling* that it is right or wrong. Early studies of moral development have been criticized because moral reasoning was viewed as a cognitive and problem solving process. To some extent it is, but in our everyday lives our moral decisions are largely based on emotional reactions. According to the *social intuitionist model* of morality, our moral judgments are not guided solely by reason, but also by our emotional, intuitive reactions to a moral dilemma. For example, imagine the following scenario (adapted from Haidt, 2001).

Julie and Steven are brother and sister. They are traveling together in France on summer vacation from college. One night they are staying alone in a cabin near the beach. They decide that it would be interesting and fun if they shared a romantic kiss. At the very least it would be a new experience for each of them. They both enjoy the experience but they decide not to do it again. They keep that night as a special secret, which makes them feel even closer to each other.

How do you react to this scenario? Was what took place between the two siblings acceptable? In deciding on your answer, it is likely that you did not think through the pros and cons of the situation, weighing each carefully and questioning the reasoning behind your arguments, until you reached a decision. The first time people hear a scenario like this, their emotional intuition typically guides them to their initial decision as to whether the act was moral. What generally follows a snap decision (another way of saying "intuitive judgment") is thoughtful and reflective reasoning, which often amounts to an after-the-fact attempt to put into words how one feels about a sexual act between siblings. You might think, "I don't know—it just isn't right because they are brother and sister!" The intuitionist approach to moral decision making complements the more cognitive-based approach that emphasizes logic and reasoning. Moral thinking can be just as much an emotional process as it is a rational one.

Table 10.5 :: Kohlberg's Stages of Moral Reasoning

STAGE OF MORAL DEVELOPMENT	DESCRIPTION	APPLICATION TO TROLLEY DILEMMA
Preconventional morality	*Characterized by self-interest in seeking reward or avoiding punishment.* Preconventional morality is considered a very basic and egocentric form of moral reasoning.	"I would not flip the trolley track switch because I would get in trouble."
Conventional morality	*Regards social conventions and rules as guides for appropriate moral behavior.* Directives from parents, teachers, and the law are used as guidelines for moral behavior.	"I would not flip the switch. It is illegal to kill, and if I willfully intervened I would have probably violated the law."
Postconventional morality	*Considers rules and laws as relative.* Right and wrong are determined by more abstract principles of justice and rights.	"I would flip the switch. The value of five lives exceeds that of one, and saving them is for the greater good of society."

Emotion is a major component of moral thinking and decision making.

BIOPSYCHOSOCIAL PERSPECTIVES

Emotion and Disgust

Moral reasoning draws on our cognitive capacities to think about both real and hypothetical dilemmas. At the same time, moral dilemmas also elicit emotional reactions that influence our decisions about whether something is right or wrong. Disgust—a very primal emotion—often guides our moral reasoning and decision making. For example, people who refuse to eat meat or animal products may do so because they find the practice and the processes involved to be disgusting to them. To cite another example, many Americans love to keep dogs as pets, but members of other cultures think dogs are disgusting vermin, and still other cultures eat them. Whether individuals regard an act as "right" or "wrong" depends on an interaction between their thinking, emotional reactions, and sociocultural background.

Psychologists Jonathan Haidt and his colleagues conceive of disgust as a "moral emotion." They have developed a "Disgust Scale" that takes only a few minutes to complete. This scale will provide you with your own individualized result on how easily disgusted you are, as well as how you compare with others who have completed the scale. The questionnaire can be found at http://www.yourmorals.org/ (first register and then link to "explore your morals" and "disgust scale"). Your responses are anonymous.

After completing the questionnaire and viewing your results, think about the following questions:

1. Your disgust reaction probably kicked in when you read and answered many of the items on the questionnaire. Do you think that some kinds of disgust are more relevant to morality than others (e.g., disgust for contaminations versus disgust for certain types of food)?

2. From a developmental perspective, do you think that moral disgust arises earlier than the ability to reason about moral situations?

· · · · · · · · · · · · · · · · · ·

Quick Quiz 10.3b
Cognitive Development: Thinking and Moral Reasoning

KNOW...

1 A weakening of unused connections between nerve cells is referred to as _____.

  A myelination   **C** synaptic pruning

  B synaptogenesis   **D** neurogenesis

UNDERSTAND...

2 Rachel believes that it is wrong to steal only because doing so could land her in jail. Which level of Kohlberg's moral development scheme is Rachel applying in this scenario?

  A postconventional   **C** preoperational

  B preconventional   **D** conventional

APPLY...

3 Which of the following may help explain why adolescent decision making is sometimes problematic?

  A Adolescents are still in the concrete operational stage of development.

  B Adolescents are limited to inductive and deductive reasoning.

  C Adolescents' decisions are overly based on emotions.

  D Adolescents' prefrontal cortex, which controls decision-making processes, is still developing.

Answers can be found on page ANS-3.

Social Development: Identity and Relationships

Two major changes occurring during adolescence include recognizing what makes each individual unique and the formation of close social relationships that also expand to include romantic and sexual partners. Here we cover both of these critical experiences of adolescence.

WHO AM I? IDENTITY FORMATION DURING ADOLESCENCE   A major issue faced by adolescents is the formation of an **identity**, *a self-image and a perception of one's unique and individual characteristics*. Module 10.2 introduced Erik Erikson's theory of psychosocial development, which includes conflicts that occur through adolescence. Referring back to Table 10.4, you can see that the primary psychosocial conflict occurring during adolescence through early adulthood (ages 14 to 24) is *identity versus role confusion*. During this time, adolescents and young adults are figuring out their personal identities, their desired careers, and their religious and political orientations. Erikson believed that failure to accomplish these tasks results in confusion over which roles the young adult can and should play.

As identity develops, adolescents tend to describe themselves in terms of personal qualities ("I am a good listener"), social qualities ("my family and I are Hindu"), and future goals ("I am going to be an artist") (Harter & Monsour, 1992). They are able to engage in a greater variety of activities and become independent from their parents. Today's adolescents also spend a great deal of time on the Internet, which provides even more opportunities to explore possible identities. The sense of self that develops during adolescence can be a conglomeration of many different ideas; indeed, perhaps we should replace the term "self" with "selves."

Adolescents may actually experience numerous *identity crises* before they reach young adulthood. An identity crisis involves curiosity, questioning, and exploration of different identities. One month a teenage boy might be interested in playing varsity football and lifting weights, and the next month he might ponder abandoning sports to pursue music. All the while, he may be wondering where he would best fit in, be most successful, or make more friends.

Adolescence is also a time for deciding whether to make personal commitments to a set of values and goals. Parents may play an influential role in this aspect of identity formation—but adolescents tend to strive for greater autonomy in making their own decisions about who they are. A girl may decide she no longer wants to attend church with her parents; alternatively, she may embrace this practice and volunteer for additional service opportunities. **Identity statuses** *are the processes and outcomes of identity development that include elements of both crisis and personal commitment.* As an individual questions and tries out different identities and commitments, he or she might be experiencing any one of four possible identity statuses (Marcia, 1980):

- *Identity achievement:* Consideration of different identities, followed by commitment to a particular one.
- *Identity diffusion:* A reluctance or refusal to commit to an identity and respond to identity crises.
- *Identity foreclosure:* A situation in which adolescents do not experience identity crises and commit to the roles and values that are handed down by their parents.
- *Identity moratorium:* Prolonged experimentation with different identities. This can involve delaying commitment to a single identity and frequent identity crises.

Do any of these identity statuses sound familiar to you? In studying them, you may have noticed that one particular status sums up your own experiences. You may even find that more than one of these profiles describes your experiences with identity at different periods of time. Ultimately, the search for identity, no matter how circuitous the route, is a necessary task for adolescents.

PEER GROUPS AND STATUS Friendships are a priority to most adolescents, and teenagers typically spend more time with peers while gaining independence from

For decades, television shows and movies have offered glimpses into life within adolescent cliques and crowds. The portrayals may be exaggerated, but they are often successful because viewers can closely identify with the characters' experiences.

their parents. As they become more interested in social status and romantic relationships, peer relationships can become complicated and layered with different emotional experiences (Brown & Klute, 2006). During adolescence, friendships become very close and involve mutual trust and intimacy, yet also have the potential for pain and sadness. Friendships take place within a broader social context of small groups or *cliques,* and the membership and intensity of friendships within a clique are constantly changing (Cairns & Cairns, 1994). Adolescent *crowds*—often referred to with labels such as "jocks," "geeks," "Goths," "normals," "loners," and "druggies"—are larger than cliques and are characterized by common social and behavioral conventions.

Popularity can be a major issue and concern for adolescents. Popular individuals are those who have high social status within their group. Compared to the effects of low social status, the effects of popularity have been less studied. Psychologists who study popularity categorize individuals into two groups (Cillessen & Rose, 2005):

- *Sociometric popularity:* Individuals who are well known and respected, and who display low levels of aggression. These adolescents may participate in high-status activities such as athletics or cheerleading, but their participation does not translate into aggression toward lower-status individuals.
- *Perceived popularity:* Adolescents who are perceived as popular and may be more well known than sociometrically popular people, but are not necessarily well liked and are more prone to engage in verbally and physically aggressive ways.

As you are probably aware, the individuals falling into these categories use different methods of maintaining their high status. Adolescents who are sociometrically popular are more likely to engage in cooperative and prosocial behaviors to resolve conflict, whereas perceived popular individuals may default to aggression or coercion. During adolescence, aggression typically becomes less physical and more "relational"—meaning that hostility is expressed not through force, but rather through strategies such as exclusion or spreading rumors (Rose et al., 2004).

Social status becomes a central issue for many adolescents. Peer rejection at school and the experience of being of low social status troubles many adolescents. Some turn to virtual social networks for online friendships, while others continue to operate with relatively few social connections. Both psychologists and the media have given low-status adolescents a great deal of attention because of the widespread belief that these individuals are at the highest risk for engaging in antisocial behaviors, particularly those of a violent nature.

Incidents of violence by adolescents who are low in social rank, including school shootings, reinforce this ongoing concern. Homicide rates increase dramatically during adolescence and reach their peak by 24 years of age (CDC, 2010).

At the beginning of this module, we mentioned a study showing that adolescents who use the Internet are more likely to become depressed (Lam & Peng, 2010). Studies like this have had a major impact on news media outlets, making headlines all over the world. However, a close look at the actual study reveals that only those adolescents who developed "pathological" tendencies toward Internet use (e.g., they used the Internet for most of their waking hours) became depressed. Also, this study included only Chinese adolescents and may not generalize across all populations, just as studies of U.S. adolescents may not generalize to other populations and cultures.

The majority of adolescents are not pathological Internet users. However, as a group, adolescents in the United States spend many hours each week online. Initial studies conducted in the 1990s indicated that adolescents were becoming less socially connected as a result of their Internet use (Kraut et al., 1998). More recent studies of Internet use indicate that this medium has exactly the opposite effect: It is making adolescents feel *more* socially connected (Valkenburg & Peter, 2009). Why might this be? A probable reason for this change is that a decade ago adolescents who used the Internet were engrossed in public chat rooms and multiuser games that mostly involved interacting with strangers. In contrast, adolescents today use the Internet and digital media for social networking and instant messaging with *real* friends (Valkenburg & Peter, 2009). Thus their social connectedness may actually be increasing.

One concern with digital media is that interacting with these devices might have a negative impact on the social development of adolescents.

The question remains as to whether the quality of online interactions is inferior to interactions occurring on an in-person basis. Psychologists have found that communicating online promotes even greater self-disclosure, which in turn leads to improved quality of relationships and sense of well-being (Kraut et al., 2002; Valkenburg & Peter, 2009).

As you can see, the issue of whether Internet use is detrimental to adolescent mental health is multifaceted. Certainly, Internet technology has some unfortunate effects, such as "cyberbullying" and other forms of abuse. Online interactions in the context of bullying can be just as hostile and problematic as in-person encounters. The problem of cyberbullying is growing, and because it can be done anonymously and outside of face-to-face encounters, this practice can bring out aggression in people who might not otherwise behave in this fashion. Those who do engage in cyberbullying tend to have problems with emotions, attention, and other behavioral problems (Sourander et al., 2010).

Although problems associated with bullying, popularity, and status are common experiences for many

Cyberbullying can have devastating consequences. Fifteen-year-old Phoebe Prince, thought to be a well-adjusted adolescent, was the victim of relentless cyberbullying. In response to the ongoing harassment, she eventually took her own life. Although other factors may have contributed, the cyberbullying is thought to have played a central role in her decision to commit suicide.

adolescents, the development of peer relationships marks a significant change in the social development of young people. Another major social change occurring during adolescence is the development of intimate partnerships.

ROMANTIC RELATIONSHIPS Romantic relationships take center stage during adolescence. Many teenagers begin dating and exploring romantic interactions; some even get involved in committed relationships. Adolescents who date may experience elevated social status, but also face challenges because their social and emotional maturity is still developing. Coping with particularly strong feelings of attraction, rejection, and loss at a relatively young age is particularly difficult, and many adolescents feel as though their negative experiences are entirely unique.

Dating varies a great deal from generation to generation. The value of dating may be less emphasized by adolescents in the United States today, compared with the last several decades. One reason may be that adolescents see adults marrying later in life and spending more time exploring and developing other aspects of their lives, such as their careers. Adolescents from different cultures also have varying beliefs and values about romance and marriage. For example, Turkish and Moroccan adolescents who identify strongly with their ethnic groups consider marriage to be the ideal arrangement for couples, whereas Dutch adolescents prefer marriage less and believe that couples should cohabitate before they marry (De Valk & Liefbroer, 2007).

Our culture may feel uncomfortable with adolescents exploring and engaging in sexual behavior—but this discomfort does not seem to actually curb the practice. It appears that since the 1990s adolescents have been changing their views about what constitutes virginity and appropriate sexual contact. More than 80% of adolescents report participating in oral sex, mutual masturbation, and other acts that do not involve intercourse before the age of 16 (Bauserman & Davis, 1996). In addition, more teens are engaging in oral sex than in intercourse, believing oral sex to be less risky for one's health and social reputation (Halpern-Felsher et al., 2005).

Same-sex sexual behavior occurs in early adolescence and even childhood. However, as with adults, engaging in sex with a member of the same sex does not mean that adolescents identify themselves as gay, lesbian, or bisexual. As many as 60% of adolescents who identify themselves as being heterosexual have had at least one sexual encounter with a member of the same sex (Remafedi et al., 1992). The negative stigma associated with homosexuality probably leads to underreporting of same-sex behavior, especially among adolescents. Nearly half of all heterosexual adult males who reported same-sex activity during adolescence regarded the sex as a phase of experimentation. In contrast, most women who engaged in same-sex encounters during adolescence also did so during adulthood (Laumann et al., 1994).

Regardless of whether an individual identifies himself or herself as homosexual at adulthood, sexual and emotional interest in members of the same sex generally appears during early adolescence (Savin-Williams & Cohen, 2004). Sexual orientation typically becomes fully recognized during high school or somewhat later (e.g., during college). How adolescents who are homosexual navigate through the process of recognizing their sexual orientation depends on many factors, including how they are perceived by their family and peers, as well as by themselves. Research suggests that psychological well-being is no more affected by homosexual orientation than by heterosexuality (Rieger & Savin-Williams, 2011).

Generally speaking, the period of adolescence experienced by people growing up in the United States can seem prolonged. Are 18-year-olds adults or adolescents? Or are they neither? It turns out that identification of a new life stage may be in order—"emerging adulthood." Not that long ago, when traditional college students moved to campus each year, parents would help them transport their belongings from the car to the dorm room, say goodbye, and go their separate ways. More recently, however, college staff members have noticed a big change—the parents cannot seem to leave, and their close ties with their children do not just end at the dormitory doorstep. One student's parents even attended the first day of class with their daughter, and then marched her up to the registrar's office to drop the class when they were not satisfied. Psychologist Jeffrey Arnett says this occurrence could be evidence of emerging adulthood, a new stage in social development. According to Arnett (2004, 2010), the process of forming an identity occurs during emerging adulthood and can span well into the 20s.

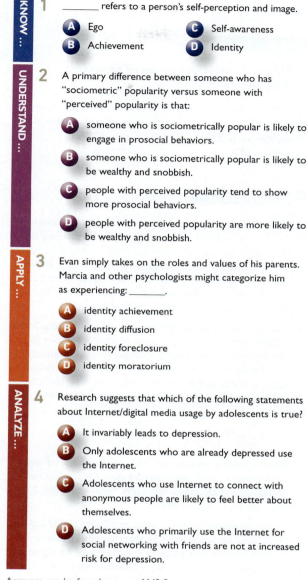

Quick Quiz 10.3c
Social Development: Identity and Relationships

KNOW …

1 _____ refers to a person's self-perception and image.

- **A** Ego
- **B** Achievement
- **C** Self-awareness
- **D** Identity

UNDERSTAND …

2 A primary difference between someone who has "sociometric" popularity versus someone with "perceived" popularity is that:

- **A** someone who is sociometrically popular is likely to engage in prosocial behaviors.
- **B** someone who is sociometrically popular is likely to be wealthy and snobbish.
- **C** people with perceived popularity tend to show more prosocial behaviors.
- **D** people with perceived popularity are more likely to be wealthy and snobbish.

APPLY …

3 Evan simply takes on the roles and values of his parents. Marcia and other psychologists might categorize him as experiencing: _____.

- **A** identity achievement
- **B** identity diffusion
- **C** identity foreclosure
- **D** identity moratorium

ANALYZE …

4 Research suggests that which of the following statements about Internet/digital media usage by adolescents is true?

- **A** It invariably leads to depression.
- **B** Only adolescents who are already depressed use the Internet.
- **C** Adolescents who use Internet to connect with anonymous people are likely to feel better about themselves.
- **D** Adolescents who primarily use the Internet for social networking with friends are not at increased risk for depression.

Answers can be found on page ANS-3.

Module Summary

Now that you have read this module you should:

Listen to the audio file of this module at **MyPsychLab**

KNOW ...

● **The key terminology concerning adolescent development:**

conventional morality (p. 376)
identity (p. 377)
identity statuses (p. 378)
menarche (p. 373)

postconventional morality (p. 376)
preconventional morality (p. 376)
puberty (p. 373)
spermarche (p. 373)

UNDERSTAND ...

● **The different ways in which identity develops.** According to Erikson's model, identity formation is the central issue of adolescence. Successful resolution results in a stable and personally satisfying sense of self. Different outcomes of identity development were described by Marcia, including identity achievement, identity diffusion, identity foreclosure, and identity moratorium.

● **The role of status in adolescent relationships.** Status achievement is also a major issue of adolescence. Its effects can be seen in those who struggle to gain popularity in its different forms (sociometric and perceived). Failure to achieve status and form friendships may lead to isolation and the problematic behaviors discussed in this module.

APPLY ...

● **Your understanding of the categories of moral development and identity statuses.** Read the following scenarios and identify which term applies to each. Check your answers on page ANS-3.

1. Jeff discovers that the security camera at his job that is fixed on some valuable merchandise is disabled. He tells himself it is okay to steal because he could not possibly be charged with breaking the law without videotaped proof. Applying Kohlberg's theory, which type of moral reasoning is Jeff using?

2. Margaret is aware that a person in her class, without provocation, has been sending hostile, damaging text messages to various people at her school. Although she does not receive these messages, and she does not personally know any of the victims, Margaret reports the offending individual to school officials. Applying Kohlberg's theory, which type of moral reasoning is Margaret displaying?

3. Julie avoids committing to choosing a major and finishing college, does not have a stable group of friends to whom she can relate, and avoids any kind of extracurricular pursuits. Which of Marcia's four identity statuses best applies to Julie?

4. Breanna identifies closely with her peer group, plays softball, and has studiously prepared to enter college to study fine arts. Which of Marcia's four identity statuses best applies to Breanna?

ANALYZE ...

● **The relationship between brain development and adolescent judgment and risk taking.** Problems with judgment may involve a region of the brain called the prefrontal cortex, which is involved in planning, reasoning, and emotion and impulse control. This region of the brain continues to change, via myelination and synaptic pruning, during adolescence. The underdeveloped state of this structure may account for the problems with decision making and impulse control observed during adolescence. Nevertheless, this factor by itself does not explain such problems, as adolescents who may avoid risk and make prudent decisions also have cortical areas that are not yet fully mature.

Adulthood and Aging

KNOW ...	UNDERSTAND ...	APPLY ...	ANALYZE ...
The terminology related to adulthood and aging	Age-related disorders such as Alzheimer's disease	Parenting concepts to your own childhood experiences, or even to parenting if you have children	The stereotype that middle and old age are associated with unhappiness
	How memory and cognition change with age, including the difference between fluid and crystallized intelligence		

Everyone (adults in particular) has heard the phrase "use it or lose it." The repetition of such a phrase like this does not always confirm its truth—but when it comes to the brain, there may be solid scientific evidence for this aphorism. As people reach old age, particularly from their 60s onward, the brain changes as cellular connections are lost and gray and white matter volume is slowly reduced. Accompanying these changes are gradual declines in some types of cognitive functioning. However, these changes in the brain do not mean that older people must simply resign themselves to do less with what they have. In fact, the opposite is recommended—the adage "use it or lose it" has some wisdom. Psychologists and neuroscientists who study cognitive and brain changes in older age are discovering that exercising the brain can have major long-term benefits, not just in terms of quality of life and preservation of cognitive ability, but also in terms of resisting the onset of age-related disorders such as Alzheimer's disease. Research indicates that frequent use of puzzles and brain teasers leads to better maintenance of cognitive and brain functioning (Ackerman, Kanfer, &

Calderwood, 2010). Conversely, disuse of the brain in older age allows decline to occur at a faster pace.

Focus Questions

 Which specific types of activities are most beneficial to the aging brain?

 Which mental abilities are more likely to decline with age?

· · · · · · · · · · · · · · · · · ·

As mentioned in Module 10.3, puberty signals the change from childhood to adolescence. In contrast, there is no well-defined biological event that marks the transition from adolescence to young adulthood. In the United States, turning 18 is a somewhat arbitrary threshold to adulthood, but many 18-year-olds do not take on full adult responsibilities. Adulthood is largely determined by sociocultural norms and expectations about establishing a long-term relationship, perhaps having children, buying a house, retiring, and so on. Because there is no true biological or psychological marker that signals adulthood, psychologists who study the entire life span divide adulthood based on age brackets: Young adulthood spans 18 to 40 years, middle adulthood from 40 to 65 years, and older adulthood from 65 years onward.

Physical Changes in Adulthood

The most obvious signs of age-related physical changes in adulthood typically appear at middle adulthood. These include an increased likelihood of weight gain, thinning and graying of the hair, and some decline in sensory abilities such as hearing and sight. For healthy adults, these changes are typically easy to manage. One major physical change affecting women at approximately age 50 is *menopause*, the termination of the menstrual cycle and reproductive ability. The physical changes associated with menopause, particularly the significant reduction in the hormone estrogen, can result in some symptoms such as hot flashes, a reduced sex drive, and mood swings. The severity of these symptoms varies widely among individuals. Men do not experience a physical change as drastic as menopause during middle adulthood, but testosterone production, and sexual motivation typically slow in middle age.

The brain, just like other physical systems, shows normal structural changes and some decline in functioning with age. These changes include reduced volume of white and gray matter of the cerebral cortex, as well as the memory-processing hippocampus (Allen et al., 2005). Aging also puts people at greater risk for developing serious *neurodegenerative* conditions, which are characterized by significant loss of nerve cells and nervous system functioning. **Dementia** *refers to a set of symptoms including mild to severe disruption of mental functioning, memory loss, disorientation, poor judgment, and decision making.* Approximately 14% of people older than 71 years of age have dementia. Nearly 10% of these cases involved a type of dementia called **Alzheimer's disease**—*a degenerative and terminal condition resulting in severe damage of the entire brain* (see Figure 10.14). Alzheimer's disease rarely appears before age 60, and it usually lasts 7 to 10 years from onset to death (although some individuals may live for 20 years with it). Early

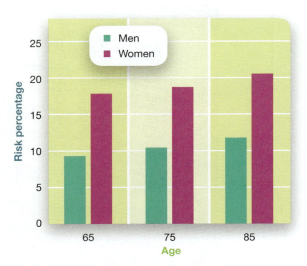

{FIG. 10.14} **Alzheimer's Disease Risk** The chances of developing Alzheimer's disease increase with age.

symptoms include forgetfulness for recent events, poor judgment, and some mood and personality changes. As the disease progresses, people struggle to recognize family members, have frequent memory loss, and experience confusion. In the most advanced stages of Alzheimer's disease, affected individuals may fail to recognize themselves and develop difficulty with basic bodily processes such as swallowing and bowel and bladder control.

What accounts for such extensive deterioration of cognitive abilities and memory? Alzheimer's disease is probably due to a buildup of proteins that clump together in the spaces between neurons, interrupting their normal activity. In addition, another type of protein builds up and forms tangles within nerve cells, which severely disrupts their structural integrity and functioning (Figure 10.15). Many different research groups are currently searching for specific genes that are associated with Alzheimer's disease. The genetic risk (i.e., the heritability of the disease) is very high for people who develop an early-onset form (age 30–60) of Alzheimer's disease. In particular, people who inherit three high-risk genes have a 50% chance of developing early-onset Alzheimer's (Bertram et al., 2010). In those individuals with later-onset (age 60+) disease, the genetic link is not as consistent. However, one study of 56,000 participants discovered five different genes that together may be responsible for the cellular processes that lead to the death of brain cells (Naj et al., 2011).

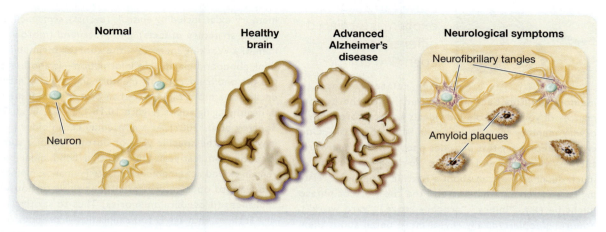

Normal

Neuron

Healthy brain

Advanced Alzheimer's disease

Neurological symptoms

Neurofibrillary tangles

Amyloid plaques

{FIG. 10.15} **How Alzheimer's Disease Affects the Brain** Advanced Alzheimer's disease is marked by significant loss of both gray and white matter throughout the brain. The brain of a person with Alzheimer's disease typically has a large buildup of plaques of a protein called beta-amyloid, which kills nerve cells. Also, tau proteins maintain the structure of nerve cells in the normal brain; these proteins are often found to be defective in the Alzheimer's brain, resulting in neurofibrillary tangles.

Quick Quiz 10.4a
Physical Changes in Adulthood

KNOW …

1 Which of the following is not a symptom of Alzheimer's disease?

- **A** Memory problems
- **B** Disorientation
- **C** Obsessive behaviors
- **D** Personality changes

UNDERSTAND …

2 Deterioration of cognitive abilities and memory in Alzheimer's patients may be attributable to:

- **A** nonprescription drug usage earlier in life.
- **B** a buildup of proteins that clump together in the spaces between neurons, interrupting their normal activity.
- **C** normal aging processes that are unavoidable.
- **D** one gene that definitively determines whether the disease will appear.

Answers can be found on page ANS-3.

Cognitive Development: Wisdom and Change

Through middle to late adulthood, many people begin to show changes in physical and cognitive abilities. These changes may become particularly apparent in old age.

WORKING THE SCIENTIFIC LITERACY MODEL
Aging and Cognitive Change

How does the normal aging process affect cognitive abilities such as intelligence, learning, and memory? People commonly believe that a loss of cognitive abilities is an inevitable part of aging, even for those who do not develop dementia or Alzheimer's disease. This belief, however, may do a disservice by unduly simplifying the relationship between aging and cognitive change.

What do we know about different cognitive abilities?

Some cognitive tasks require the ability to react quickly and have mental flexibility. Such tasks utilize *fluid intelligence*, which involves processes such as problem solving and reasoning. Your elderly relative may have no difficulty in solving a complicated crossword puzzle, a task that taps into *crystallized intelligence*, a type of intelligence based on accumulated experiences and skills (see Module 9.2). Vocabulary and general knowledge, such as knowing U.S. presidents and state capitals, constitute crystallized intelligence. Fluid intelligence reaches a peak during young adulthood and proceeds to decline, whereas crystallized intelligence shows a much slower decline. Memory abilities also change over the course of the life span.

How can science explain age-related differences in cognitive abilities?

Age-related change in memory abilities becomes apparent when the performances of young and old individuals are compared in everyday memory tests as well as in laboratory tasks. One type of laboratory test provides people with a cue word, such as "vacation," and asks the participants to recall as much detail as they can about a specific experience relating to vacation, or whatever else the cue word or phrase might be (e.g., "injury," "grocery store," "yard work"). Younger people typically reveal more detail about their memories than older people (Addis et al., 2008). While a young person might describe a vacation taken a year prior in great detail, older people have difficulty providing this kind of specific information.

Memory for personal events is not just limited to the past. We also envision future personal events. In the study described previously, younger and older people were also asked to envision future events that they might experience that were related to a cue word or phrase. Older people had more difficulty than younger people in elaborating on future events (Addis et al., 2008).

Can we critically evaluate our assumptions about age-related cognitive changes?

Being forgetful is a common expectation people have about older people. But recall from Module 7.1 that many types of memory exist, including *episodic* (events), *semantic* (meaning and structure of facts), and *procedural* (motor skills) memory. Working memory—the shorter-term ability to think about and manipulate information—is another type. On the one hand, episodic memory and working memory decline at a more rapid rate than other types of memory in healthy, aging adults (Figure 10.16; Daselaar et al., 2007; Souchay et al., 2007). As a consequence, an older person may forget the specific year or destination of a summer vacation from last year. On the other hand, older people remain skilled at remembering facts (semantic memories) and ways to operate devices such as tools or household appliances (procedural memories). Thus to say that memory declines with age is too simplistic—it depends on the type of memory system and, most certainly, on the individual. Older adults age differently from one another.

Why is this relevant?

Research on aging has shown that, while declines may be expected in some mental abilities, people have a remarkable amount of control over how they age. Psychologists have found that older people who choose to engage in cognitive tasks are mentally sharper and more satisfied with their mental abilities than are people who feel that they cannot overcome the effects of an aging brain. One important bit of advice seems to be that older adults can benefit greatly from actively engaging in activities that they personally enjoy (rather than ones they are expected to enjoy; Stine-Morrow, 2007). For example, seniors who like to socialize should seek others; if they do not care for crossword puzzles or brain teasers, there is no need

giraffe, lion, zebra, dog, bird, monkey, bear...

giraffe...dog...bird...

{FIG. 10.16} **Memory and Aging** Several types of memory systems exist, not all of which are equally affected by age. An older person's ability to remember events, such as words that appeared on a list (episodic memory), is more likely to decline than his or her memory for facts and concepts (semantic memory).

to do them. These findings have direct applications to how we interact with senior citizens at home and in retirement facilities.

Some changes in perceptual and cognitive abilities may result in impairments that negatively affect the lives of older adults. Even older adults who are otherwise healthy may find that important everyday tasks, such as driving, can become overwhelming and, in some cases, dangerous. Some of these changes may not be reversible. Nevertheless, new technologies and an appreciation for how the aging brain works may help prolong perceptual and cognitive sharpness in older adults.

PSYCH @

The Driver's Seat

Thanks to technology, the current generation of elderly adults faces issues that previous generations never did. Take driving, for example. Many older adults depend on their cars to shop, maintain a social life, and keep appointments. Research, however, has shown that the cognitive and physical changes in old age may take a toll on driving skill. This decline presents a dilemma for many seniors and their families: How can individuals maintain the independence afforded by driving without endangering themselves and other drivers?

To address this problem, psychologist Karlene Ball developed an intervention called Useful Field of View (UFOV) Speed of Processing training. UFOV uses computer-based training exercises to increase the portion of the visual field that adults can quickly process and respond to. Laboratory studies show that UFOV actually increases the speed of cognitive processing for older adults. Records from several states that have studied the UFOV show that drivers who completed the training were half as likely to have had an accident during the study period.

· · · · · · · · · · · · · · · · · ·

Quick Quiz 10.4b
Cognitive Development: Wisdom and Change

KNOW ...

1 Intelligence based on accumulated skills and abilities is referred to as _____.

   (A) longitudinal   (C) deductive

   (B) fluid   (D) crystallized

UNDERSTAND ...

2 John, who is in his 70s, notices that it takes him longer to figure out a brand-new game than it used to. This delay occurs because the skills required to learn the game would most likely rely on: _____.

   (A) crystallized intelligence

   (B) fluid intelligence

   (C) inductive reasoning

   (D) autonomy

3 The cognitive changes that occur in late adulthood and may impair driving:

   (A) are irreversible.

   (B) are minimal.

   (C) can be improved with specific training.

   (D) affect only people with dementia.

Answers can be found on page ANS-3.

Social Development: Intimacy and Commitment

As adolescents transition into adulthood, the nature of their social relationships begins to change as, for many, finding a potential lifelong partner and having a family become focal interests. According to Erikson, the major challenge spanning years 25 through 40 is *intimacy versus isolation* (refer back to Table 10.4 on page 368). At some point, young adults begin to separate from their parents, and become challenged with cultivating caring, compassionate, and intimate relationships. Failure to do so can result in isolation, or entering into a relationship that lacks intimacy and sharing.

The next stage, *generativity versus stagnation* (ages 45 to 65 years), is characterized by the pursuit to produce something of value for future generations. These efforts can include a combination of accomplishments at work as well as with family.

Erikson's final major stage of psychosocial development, spanning 65 years onward, is *ego integrity versus despair*. During this time the older adult contemplates whether he or she lived a full life and fulfilled major accomplishments, or looks back and dwells upon disappointments and failures.

Erikson's theory helps frame some of the major challenges faced in adulthood. In this section, we will explore contemporary findings about some of the major challenges of adulthood, including marriage, parenting, careers, and the changes and experiences of older adulthood.

MARRIAGE   Adults may pair up in the form of marriage, civil unions, or cohabitation (living together as unmarried partners). Overall, marriage appears to benefit physical and mental health. Married couples monitor their medical care more effectively, report greater sexual satisfaction and frequency, and are more financially secure than are unmarried people (Waite & Gallagher, 2000). The most tempting, and perhaps easiest, conclusion is that marriage causes greater physical and mental health, but it is also plausible that people who are healthier are more likely to marry.

What people experience in their marriages largely depends on which attributes they most value in their partners. Marrying someone based on physical attractiveness alone will give rise to a very different marital experience than marrying for emotional support, security, or family arrangements. The characteristics that adults value most in potential partners change with time (Buss et al., 2001). In the 1930s, men and women ranked the character of their partner above mutual feelings of love, emotional stability, and maturity. For men, the importance assigned to having a partner who is a good cook or housekeeper has dropped steadily since the 1930s. In the last 15 years, males and females in heterosexual relationships have ranked feelings of mutual attraction and love as the most important quality in a long-term relationship. Thus, while some aspects of long-term relationship values remain relatively stable, others are sensitive to societal changes.

Unfortunately, divorce is a common outcome of marriage, with approximately half of first marriages and 60% of second marriages ending in divorce. The overall divorce rate in the United States is very high, but (as shown in Figure 10.17) the divorce rate has been in steady decline since 1980. Many different factors can lead to divorce. Psychologist John Gottman and colleagues have conducted numerous longitudinal studies of married couples over the past few decades (Gottman & Levenson, 1992, 2002). In many of these studies, couples are asked to discuss and argue problematic concerns with each other while under close observation by researchers. Key predictors of whether a couple will stay together are the emotional expressions given off during arguments. For example, couples who show contempt for each other during arguments are the most likely to have long-term marital problems. In addition to contempt, Gottman has identified criticism, defensiveness, and stonewalling (becoming unresponsive to the other person) as the most disastrous ways of communicating with one's partner. Conversely, Gottman has found several key predictors of successful marriage, including willingness and ability of *both* partners to give up some level of control, focusing on solving problems that are solvable, and nurturing fondness and admiration toward the other.

PARENTING   Parenting is another major experience that defines the young and middle adult years of many people. This all-consuming activity involves caring for the physical, cognitive, social and emotional needs of children. You have probably noticed that there are many different ways of addressing these needs. In high school, you may have compared notes with friends about how your parents and their parents interacted with you, set expectations for schoolwork and behavior, and enforced rules. If you are not yet a parent, you may be surprised to find out that parents also compare notes—they want to know the best ways to carry out their responsibilities. So what does the research say about parenting practices?

Psychologists have identified multiple parenting styles—that is, different patterns in discipline, guidance, and involvement (see Figure 10.18; Baumrind, 1971; Maccoby & Martin, 1983). **Authoritative parenting** *is characterized by the expression of warmth and responsiveness to the needs of children, but also by*

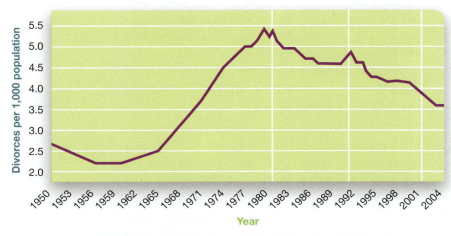

{FIG. 10.17}   **Divorce Trends in the United States Since 1950**   Starting in the late 1950s, U.S. divorce rates rose sharply over a 20-year period. Divorce rates are currently in steady decline.

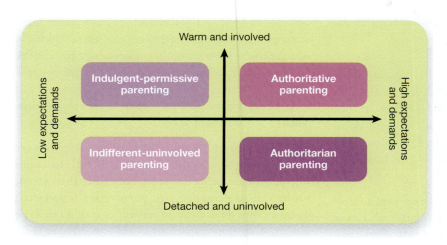

{FIG. 10.18} **Parenting Styles** Psychologists believe that parenting styles can be classified into four categories that vary along the dimensions of warmth versus detachment, and low versus high expectations. **Click on this figure in your eText to see more details**.

exercising control over certain actions and decisions made by children. In contrast, **authoritarian parenting** *emphasizes excessive control over children and less expression of warmth.* Parents who practice **indulgent-permissive parenting** *are warm but indifferent and do not attempt to control their children, even in positive and helpful ways.* Parents who practice **indifferent-uninvolved parenting** *show neither warmth nor control toward their children.* Identifying these categories of parenting might give the impression that we could accurately label parents as one type or another. In reality, parents may switch between different parenting styles depending on the circumstances. For example, authoritative parents might become authoritarian if they feel their sense of power over a child is compromised, or might become more permissive as an adolescent ages and shows that he or she can make good decisions on his or her own.

Psychologists—and parents, of course—are interested in how a specific style of parenting might influence a child's behavior and well-being. Researchers have found that children of authoritative parents tend to be more socially aware, assertive, friendly, and independent than are children consistently exposed to the other three styles (Baumrind, 1991). These findings are not based on experimental research, however, so we cannot be sure the degree to which the parenting is shaping the behavior. Parenting styles that are harsh and lacking in support as well as warm and nurturing parenting styles do tend to be transmitted from one generation to the next (Belsky, 2007).

Parenting can bring overwhelming joy, but it can also reduce personal and marital happiness. On the one hand, children tend to stabilize marriages, as they become the objects of mutual, cooperative focus for the parents. On the other hand, parents report a decline in marital satisfaction within the first two years of having children (Belsky & Rovine, 1990). Marital satisfaction is usually highest before the birth of the first child and declines until children have left home, after which satisfaction tends to rise again (Glenn, 1990). Marital difficulties can increase between parents who may be struggling with adolescent children who are seeking their autonomy (Steinberg, 1987).

You may have heard of the *empty nest* phenomenon. Parents who see their children off to college or other pursuits away from home experience a dramatic change in their own roles—from that of mother and father back to wife and husband. In fact, this phenomenon may lead to the prolonged parenting described at the beginning of the module. Some parents in this situation realize that they no longer have the same things in common; divorce may be the result of this newfound understanding. However, the general trend is quite the opposite—marital satisfaction for both husbands and wives increases dramatically after children leave home. In fact, married older adults are just as likely

Although parents may experience sadness or even divorce when their children move out, the general trend is toward an increase in martial satisfaction.

to report being "very satisfied" with marriage as are newlyweds (Rollins, 1989).

CAREER In addition to parenting, having a satisfying career is a component of generativity in adulthood. Erikson believed that generativity involves having meaningful and productive work, as well as making contributions to future generations. Failure to fulfill these goals leads to being self-absorbed (see Table 10.4 on page 368).

Career choice is a major decision that affects the lifestyle of the majority of adults. Although career changes are very common, most choices that adults make about their career reflect their own self-concept (Super et al., 1996)—that is, what people believe about what they can do well and what they are happy doing influence the jobs they choose. Several variables influence career happiness. For example, salary or wage earnings contribute to career satisfaction, but other factors such as job interest and relationships with managers and supervisors are important as well (Sousa-Poza & Sousa-Poza, 2000).

Most adults who are financially able to do so retire during late adulthood. Primary concerns at this life stage may switch to grandparenting roles, closely monitoring and maintaining health, travel, and leisure activity. Of course, not all adults are able to enjoy the luxuries associated with retirement. For example, African Americans and Mexican Americans retire at an earlier age than do Whites, largely due to factors such as job-related injury and low job satisfaction (Stanford et al., 1991).

EMOTIONAL CHANGES Late adulthood can be a phase of life characterized by considerable change and adjustment. Many older people experience the death of a spouse, the loss of close friends, some loss of personal freedoms such as driving or living without assistance, and one or more physical conditions that require regular medical monitoring and treatment. Older adults also realize and contemplate the reality of dying. It is no wonder why younger people often sympathize with the elderly and often make assumptions that life experiences during the twilight

years are to be feared. Depression in older adults often accompanies other physical illnesses, just as it does in young people. Even so, healthy older adults are actually no more likely to become depressed than are younger people. The reality is that as long as basic emotional and social needs are met, old age can be a very joyous time (Charles & Carstensen, 2009).

Older people are more likely than their younger counterparts to see the glass as half full; in other words, they are generally more optimistic than young adults and adolescents. This perspective is reflected in how they deal with adversity as well as in how they deal with negative emotional experiences from the past. Personality factors also contribute to aging well—low levels of anxiety and hostility and high levels of optimism are associated with better physical health (Smith & Spiro, 2002). However, optimism in older age may not be universal to people of all cultures. Although older people in America tend to be more optimistic than younger adults, older adults in China tend to be *less* optimistic than younger adults (You et al., 2009).

To get a good sense of what it is like to grow older, it is important to consider emotional experience. Researchers who have examined emotions throughout the life span tend to find that negative emotions decline with age while positive emotions increase in frequency (Figure 10.19). **Emotional well-being** is *the subjective experience of both positive and negative emotions, and is measured by life satisfaction, happiness, and the balance between*

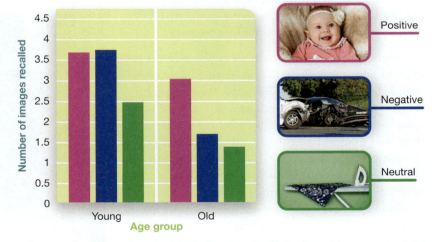

{FIG. 10.19} **Emotion, Memory, and Aging** Younger people have superior memory for whether they have seen positive, negative, or neutral pictures compared with older people. However, notice that younger people remember positive and negative pictures equally, whereas older people are more likely to remember positive pictures (Charles et al., 2003).

negative and positive emotional experiences (Charles & Carstensen, 2009). Emotional well-being tends to increase as people get older. Why might this be? Perhaps this trend runs counter to what we expect as time winds down. One explanation is that with wisdom and experience come the ability to avoid situations that may elicit negative emotions. Older people simply become better at putting themselves in situations that will elicit positive emotions. Also, the goals that older people set differ from those set by younger people. Younger people are planning for a long-term and uncertain future. In contrast, older people are more likely to set goals that emphasize positive emotional and meaningful experiences (Carstensen et al., 1999).

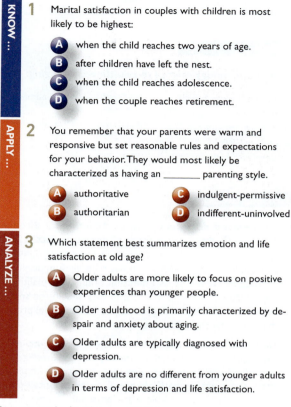

Quick Quiz 10.4c
Social Development: Intimacy and Commitment

KNOW…

1 Marital satisfaction in couples with children is most likely to be highest:

A when the child reaches two years of age.

B after children have left the nest.

C when the child reaches adolescence.

D when the couple reaches retirement.

APPLY…

2 You remember that your parents were warm and responsive but set reasonable rules and expectations for your behavior. They would most likely be characterized as having an _____ parenting style.

A authoritative

B authoritarian

C indulgent-permissive

D indifferent-uninvolved

ANALYZE…

3 Which statement best summarizes emotion and life satisfaction at old age?

A Older adults are more likely to focus on positive experiences than younger people.

B Older adulthood is primarily characterized by despair and anxiety about aging.

C Older adults are typically diagnosed with depression.

D Older adults are no different from younger adults in terms of depression and life satisfaction.

Answers can be found on page ANS-3.

Module Summary

Module
10.4

Listen to
the audio file of
this module at
MyPsychLab

Now that you have read this module
you should:

KNOW ...

- *The terminology related to adulthood and aging:*

Alzheimer's disease (p. 384)

authoritarian parenting (p. 389)

authoritative parenting (p. 388)

dementia (p. 384)

emotional well-being (p. 390)

indifferent-uninvolved parenting
(p. 389)

indulgent-permissive parenting
(p. 389)

UNDERSTAND ...

- *Age-related disorders such as Alzheimer's disease.*
Alzheimer's disease is a form of dementia that is characterized by significant decline in memory, cognition,
and eventually personality and basic bodily functioning. It
is probably caused by two different brain abnormalities—
the buildup of proteins that clump together in the spaces
between neurons, plus degeneration of a structural protein
that forms tangles within nerve cells.

- *How memory and cognition change with age, including
the difference between fluid and crystallized intelligence.*
Episodic memory and working memory abilities typically
show some decline with old age. Crystallized intelligence
consists of relatively stable knowledge and abilities and is
generally maintained in old age, whereas fluid intelligence
involves problem-solving abilities that may decline with time.

APPLY ...

- *Parenting concepts to your own childhood experiences, or even to parenting if you have children*. Read
each scenario and identify which style of parenting best
applies. Check your answers on page ANS-3.

  1. Seventeen-year-old David rarely gets into any serious
trouble. Even so, his parents mandate that David return
straight home from school, punish him if he does not
follow strict house rules, and provide little emotional
or interpersonal affection. Which style of parenting do
David's parents employ?

  2. Stephanie's mother frequently asks how she is doing
in school and with friends, and spends as much time as
she can with her daughter. However, her mother does
not set a time for Stephanie to come home at night,
and she is unconcerned if Stephanie fails some classes
and quits attending school club meetings. Stephanie's
mother seems to display which type of parenting?

  3. Sung's parents enforce some fairly strict rules around
the house, and they establish consequences for doing
poorly in school and for misbehavior. They keep
to these rules consistently and ensure that Sung
understands them. His parents also express love and
warmth toward their son. Which style of parenting
best describes Sung's parents?

ANALYZE ...

- *The stereotype that middle or old age is associated
with unhappiness.* Research shows that older adults
do face issues that might lead to unhappiness—changes
in health, family structure, and activities generally
accompany aging. At the same time, the research shows
that such challenges do not necessarily condemn a person
to unhappiness. In fact, many older adults have a very
positive outlook on life. Optimism and life satisfaction
tend to *increase*, and older adults have the wisdom to put
themselves in situations that will be favorable to their
well-being.

Module 10.1 :: Methods, Concepts, and Prenatal Development

Focus Questions:

1 **How developed is the brain of a human fetus?** At just 11 weeks' gestation, the major divisions of the brain—including the cerebral hemispheres, cerebellum, and brain stem—are differentiated. Also, the nerve cells of the fetal brain are developing myelin sheaths that insulate the cells and increase the efficiency and speed of neural transmission. Although the basic structures are all present at birth, the newborn brain is only one-fourth the size of an adult brain. In addition to growing in size, the number of connections between nerve cells will expand exponentially as the child develops.

2 **What are newborns able to sense?** In addition to a language accent that is detectable in their crying, newborns can recognize the sound of their own mother's voice as well as the smell of her breastmilk. Newborns are equipped with basic reflexes and have a basic sense of disgust, which will help them reject potentially harmful substances. At only a few days of age, newborns can even imitate the facial expressions of others.

👁—**Watch** *Thinking Like a Psychologist: Babies by Design* in the **MyPsychLab video series**

Module 10.2 :: Infancy and Childhood

Focus Questions:

1 **Which types of activities do infants and young children need for their psychological development?** At the beginning of this module, we learned that one activity that children younger than two years of age do *not* need is television viewing (even "Baby Einstein" DVDs). The answer to this question depends on the stage of development. If we incorporate Piaget's stages into this discussion, we see that cognitive development centers on the young child's interactions with physical objects. Later in childhood, such as in the preoperational and concrete operational stages, children advance in their understanding of how objects and physical processes work. Cognitive processes become more advanced as logic and abstract thinking replace basic sensory and motor experience.

2 **Given that social interactions are so important, which specific abilities are nurtured by them?** One of the first major developments of social behavior is the attachment that infants form with their primary caregivers. As social cognition becomes more advanced, young children become less egocentric and better able to take the mental perspective of others, as indicated by the development of theory of mind.

👁—**Watch** *In the Real World Application: Socialization* in the **MyPsychLab video series**

Module 10.3 :: Adolescence

Focus Questions:

1 **Does Internet use impair or enhance social relationships during adolescence?** Not all studies point to the same conclusion. Excessive use of the Internet can lead to depression and social isolation. However, converging evidence indicates that applications such as instant messaging and Facebook are not a replacement for face-to-face interactions, and that forming friendships that involve the use of social networking sites of friends, rather than mostly strangers, actually increases adolescent well-being.

2 **Which other psychological characteristics are major points of change during adolescence?** Social relationships during adolescence expand to include romantic partners. Another major transition during adolescence is the focus on identity formation, which has a variety of possible outcomes. Moral development also begins to take on more adult-like qualities, as adolescents begin thinking abstractly about principles of justice and caring. The adolescent brain also undergoes some fine-tuning, even into early adulthood, particularly in the areas of the cortex involved in impulse control and decision making.

👁—**Watch** *What's in It for Me? Identity* in the **MyPsychLab video series**

Module 10.4 :: Adulthood and Aging

Focus Questions:

1 **Which specific types of activities are most beneficial to the aging brain?** The answer to this question is "It depends." Currently, digital media companies such as Nintendo offer games that are targeted specifically at older adults, claiming that their products will help keep an individual's brain sharp. Some evidence supports their claims. However, the brain, just like our muscles, can be exercised in many different ways. Psychologists advise that the key to exploiting the "use it or lose it" wisdom is to engage in those stimulating activities that the individual prefers. Thus, if a person prefers to engage in exercise or socializing, these activities have greater potential to benefit brain health than forcing oneself to solve puzzles.

2 **Which mental abilities are more likely to decline with age?** Performance on cognitive tasks that rely on reaction time and problem solving (e.g., those requiring crystallized intelligence) tend to decline with age. Keep in mind that this is generally the case—there are exceptions. Also, older adults who are healthy tend to maintain strong cognitive abilities, especially for tasks that tap into crystallized intelligence.

👁—**Watch** *The Big Picture: Different Perspectives on the World* in the **MyPsychLab video series**

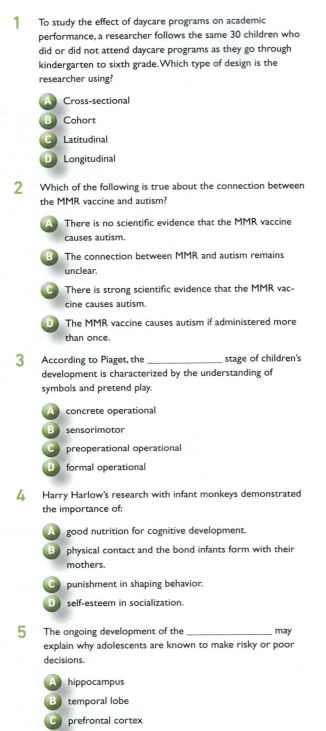

1 To study the effect of daycare programs on academic performance, a researcher follows the same 30 children who did or did not attend daycare programs as they go through kindergarten to sixth grade. Which type of design is the researcher using?

A Cross-sectional

B Cohort

C Latitudinal

D Longitudinal

2 Which of the following is true about the connection between the MMR vaccine and autism?

A There is no scientific evidence that the MMR vaccine causes autism.

B The connection between MMR and autism remains unclear.

C There is strong scientific evidence that the MMR vaccine causes autism.

D The MMR vaccine causes autism if administered more than once.

3 According to Piaget, the _____ stage of children's development is characterized by the understanding of symbols and pretend play.

A concrete operational

B sensorimotor

C preoperational operational

D formal operational

4 Harry Harlow's research with infant monkeys demonstrated the importance of:

A good nutrition for cognitive development.

B physical contact and the bond infants form with their mothers.

C punishment in shaping behavior.

D self-esteem in socialization.

5 The ongoing development of the _____ may explain why adolescents are known to make risky or poor decisions.

A hippocampus

B temporal lobe

C prefrontal cortex

D parietal lobe

6 Unlike many of her friends, Rita never "rebelled" against her parents when she became an adolescent. In fact, as an adult, Rita advocates essentially the same values and roles that her parents instilled in her. Which type of identity status does Rita demonstrate?

A Identity foreclosure   C Identity diffusion

B Identity moratorium   D Identity achievement

7 According to your text, which of the following statements is true regarding same-sex encounters?

A Most individuals who identify as heterosexual have never had a sexual encounter with a member of the same sex.

B If it does occur, sexual interest in members of the same sex is recognized during early adolescence.

C Most women who engage in same-sex encounters during adolescence have strictly heterosexual relationships during adulthood.

D The stigma of same-sex encounters prevents most adolescents from ever engaging in this behavior.

8 A healthy adult with no signs of dementia in his or her 80s is likely to have the most difficulty doing which of the following tasks?

A Remembering how many feet are in a mile

B Recalling the definition of the word "antepenultimate"

C Knowing the names of his or her grandchildren

D Solving a logic problem

9 Which parenting style would you recommend that parents use if they want to maximize the chance that their children will be well balanced?

A Authoritarian

B Authoritative

C Indulgent-permissive parenting

D Indifferent-uninvolved parenting

10 Healthy older adults are:

A more likely to develop depression than younger people.

B less likely to develop depression than younger people.

C no more likely than younger people are to develop depression.

D more likely to develop depression than younger people in the United States, although the opposite is true in China.

Work the Scientific Literacy Model :: Understanding Cognitive Development

What do we know about Piaget's theory of cognitive development?

Table 10.3 on page 360 reviews Piaget's stage approach to cognitive development in children. The discussion on **pages 360–361** offers some strategies for pairing the stage name with the milestones achieved in each phase. Piaget's theory is based on the idea of developmental milestones; that children transition from one stage to the next upon developing a new cognitive skill. Also, two processes supporting cognitive development are the twin concepts of assimilation and accommodation.

If you are having trouble telling the difference between the two, it might help to think about learning motor skills in the sensorimotor stage. Once an infant learns to grasp an object in one hand, he will soon learn to grasp all sorts of things—your finger, a pacifier, or a toy. If you give him a new toy, the child can quickly assimilate the new object and learn to grasp it with one hand—unless, of course, that toy happens to be a great big ball that does not fit in one hand. In that case, the infant must accommodate the new object by modifying what he knows about grasping objects. In this case, the task involves devising a technique that uses both hands.

How can science help explain cognitive development?

Research, such as the study on errors of scale illustrated in **Figure 10.7 on page 362** and the conservation study described in **Figure 10.6 on page 361**, has provided extensive support for Piaget's ideas. More recently, researchers like Elizabeth Spelke have shown that even infants may actually have some appreciation for abstract numbers. Other studies suggest that children may be able to take on the perspective of others as early as 4 or 5 years of age. The dynamics between caregivers and children's cognitive development have been explored via the idea of scaffolding, and the text on **page 364** highlights cross-cultural research on caregiver/child interaction suggesting that cultural issues might also have a noticeable effect on cognitive development.

Why is this relevant?

Watch the accompanying video excerpt on how thinking develops. You can access the video at MyPsychLab or by clicking the play button in the center of your eText. If your instructor assigns this video as a homework activity, you will find additional content to help you in MyPsychLab. You can also view the video by using your smart phone and the QR code below, or you can go to the YouTube link provided.

Once you have read this chapter and watched the video, using specific examples, differentiate between the thinking patterns of a 3-year-old preschooler and a 9-year-old student, according to Piaget's theory of cognitive development.

Can we critically evaluate theories of cognitive development?

Piaget's early work on cognitive development from infancy through adolescence has exerted an enormous influence on developmental psychology, but modern research has raised some questions about when and how children move through each stage. The possibility that children are born with some innate cognitive abilities and the recent studies on egocentrism have added to an already rich discussion. Similarly, evidence of the link between social influences and cognitive development suggests that the interplay between cognitive development and sociocultural factors may be stronger than Piaget originally thought.

youtube.com/ scientificliteracy

MyPsychLab

Your turn to Work the Scientific Literacy Model: You can access the video at MyPsychLab or by clicking the play button in the center of your eText. If your instructor assigns this video as a homework activity, you will find additional content to help you at MyPsychLab. You can also view the video by using your smart phone and the QR code, or you can go to the YouTube link provided.

11 :: MOTIVATION AND EMOTION

Hunger and Eating

KNOW ...	UNDERSTAND ...	APPLY ...	ANALYZE ...
The key terminology of motivation and hunger	The biological, cognitive, and social processes that shape eating patterns The major eating and weight-control problems people face	Your knowledge of hunger regulation to better understand and evaluate your own eating patterns	The roles of texture and taste in satiation

It may be true that "you are what you eat," but recent research has suggested a new twist on this old saying—it may be that "you are *how* you eat." Do you prefer to eat on the run, following the American tradition of fast food? Or do you prefer the French approach of spreading out dinner over hours? It may be that your preference for either mode of eating affects not only what you ingest, but also how you think and behave in other ways. Psychologists have recently discovered that when individuals are exposed to images and thoughts of fast food, they do not just eat fast—they do everything fast (Zhong & DeVoe, 2010). One study had volunteers look at fast-food logos and describe their favorite items from those restaurants. Afterwards, the participants read faster, showed preferences for time-saving products, and even chose to receive small payments immediately rather than waiting a week for larger sums. Think about your own experiences—are you more likely to see a person multitasking, perhaps holding a paperback in one hand and food in the other, at a fast-food place or a fine dining establishment? It appears that the fast-food environment is not just about getting a quick meal, but speeds up other aspects of our thinking and behaving as well.

Focus Questions

 What are some ways that our physical and social environments affect eating?

 What makes us feel hungry or full?

· · · · · · · · · · · · · · · · · ·

The study of **motivation** *concerns the physiological and psychological processes underlying the initiation of behaviors that direct organisms toward specific goals.* These initiating factors, or *motives,* include the thoughts, feelings, sensations, and bodily process that lead to goal–directed behavior. Motivation is essential to an individual's survival because at its most basic level it contributes to **homeostasis**, *the body's physiological processes that allow it to maintain consistent internal states in response to the outer environment.* These states include physiological

{FIG. 11.1} **Maintaining Balance** Homeostasis is the process of maintaining relatively stable internal states. For example, this diagram illustrates how homeostasis regulates thirst and the body's fluid levels.

needs such as appropriate body temperature as well as indicators of hunger and thirst. Take thirst, for example. When bodily water levels fall below normal, cells release chemical compounds that maintain the structure and fluid levels of cells. Receptors in the body respond to the increased concentrations of these compounds, as well as to the lower water volume, and send messages to the brain. These messages trigger thirst signals in the brain, which in turn motivates us to seek water or other fluids, thereby maintaining homeostasis (Figure 11.1).

In addition to satisfying our basic physiological needs, motivation is social in nature. Humans, like many other species of animals, are highly motivated to form social bonds. Motivation addresses some uniquely human goals as well, such as achieving success at school or work. Across the domains of physiological, social, and achievement motivation, psychologists view motives as consisting of two main parts. First, our motivated behavior involves **drives**—*the physiological triggers that tell us we may be deprived of something and cause us to seek out what is needed, such as food.* We also respond to **incentives** (or *goals*) *the stimuli we seek to reduce the drives such as social approval and companionship, food,*

PsychTutor

Click here in your eText for an interactive tutorial on **Drive and Incentive Theories of Emotion**

Drive	Behavior
Water deprivation leads to thirst.	Drink fluids to reduce drive.

Behavior	Incentive
Drink fluids to experience incentive.	Sweetened sports drink

{FIG. 11.2} **Drives and Incentives** Our motivation to reduce a drive, or in response to an incentive, can lead to the same behavior.

water, and other needs (Figure 11.2). These concepts also apply to material covered in the other modules in this chapter. Here we will focus on the motivation to eat.

Physiological Aspects of Hunger

As children, most of us learned to equate *hunger*—the motivation to eat—with a growling stomach. It is tempting to conclude that stomach contractions *cause* hunger; indeed, this belief has been around for a long time (Cannon & Washburn, 1921). In reality, a growling stomach is only one of many physical processes associated with hunger. At the opposite end of the spectrum, a full stomach is only one cue for **satiation**—*the point in a meal when we are no longer motivated to eat.* Thus homeostasis of food intake is balanced between hunger motives and satiation.

The on and off switches involved in hunger can be found in a few regions of the *hypothalamus* (see Module 3.2). Researchers have found that electrically stimulating the *lateral hypothalamus* causes rats to begin to eat; thus this structure may serve as an "on" switch (Delgado & Anand, 1952). In contrast, the *ventromedial region* of the hypothalamus appears to serve as the "off" switch; damage to this area leads to obesity in lab animals. A related area, the *paraventricular nucleus* of the hypothalamus, also signals that it is time to stop eating by inhibiting the lateral hypothalamus (Figure 11.3).

The hypothalamus, like any other brain region, does not work alone. It is generally more accurate to think of the hypothalamus as a busy hub of activity that sends and receives signals throughout the body. When it comes to eating and hunger, this area receives information about tastes, textures, and smells through nerves coming from the mouth and nose, and it exchanges this information with the frontal cortex.

The hypothalamus also takes on the job of monitoring blood chemistry for indicators of the levels of sugars and hormones involved in energy. For example, the hypothalamus detects changes in the level of **glucose**, *a sugar that serves as a primary energy source for the brain and the rest of the body.* Highly specialized neurons called *glucostats* can detect glucose levels in the fluid outside of the cell. When glucose levels drop, glucostats signal the hypothalamus that energy supplies are low, and hunger increases (Langhans, 1996a, 1996b). After food

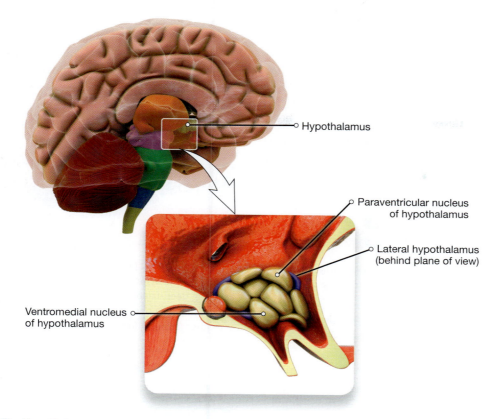

{FIG. 11.3} **The Hypothalamus and Hunger** The hypothalamus acts as an on/off switch for hunger. The lateral region of the hypothalamus signals when it is time to eat, while the ventromedial and paraventricular regions signal when it is time to stop eating.

The rat on the left has swollen to enormous proportions after researchers created lesions to its ventromedial hypothalamus. Compare it to the more typical rat on the right.

reaches the stomach and intestines, sugars are absorbed into the bloodstream and transported throughout the body. *Insulin*, a hormone secreted by the pancreas, helps cells store this circulating glucose for future use. As insulin levels rise in response to consumption of a meal, hunger decreases—but so do glucose levels, which eventually leads to hunger again a few hours later. Glucose, glucostats, and insulin are merely pieces of the hunger puzzle, however. In fact, a psychologist can better predict how much a person will eat by simply asking, "How hungry are you?" than by measuring blood glucose levels (Pittas et al., 2005).

Other hunger-related hormones include *ghrelin*, a hormone secreted in the stomach that stimulates stomach contractions and appetite (Cummings, 2006). Ghrelin is also released by the hypothalamus, where—in contrast to what it does in the stomach—it functions to decrease appetite. Another key chemical in regulating hunger is *cholecystokinin* (CCK) (Badman & Flier, 2005). As the intestines expand, neurons release CCK, which communicates to the hypothalamus that it is time to stop eating. These hormones and other biological processes interact with equally complex psychological factors to determine when and how much we eat.

Quick Quiz 11.1a
Physiological Aspects of Hunger

KNOW...

1 The _____ region of the hypothalamus is associated with the onset of eating, while the _____ region is associated with the offset.

  A lateral; ventromedial   **C** anterior; posterior

  B ventromedial; lateral   **D** anterior; ventromedial

2 _____ is a sugar that serves as a vital energy source for the human body; its levels are monitored by the nervous system.

  A Ghrelin   **C** Glucose

  B CCK   **D** Insulin

UNDERSTAND...

3 Why do psychologists believe the lateral hypothalamus generates hunger signals that contribute to people's motivation to eat?

  A This brain structure responds to glucose levels.

  B When the lateral hypothalamus is stimulated, laboratory animals eat more.

  C Skinny people have smaller nuclei in this area.

  D The lateral hypothalamus releases CCK which reduces hunger.

Answers can be found on page ANS-4.

Psychological Aspects of Hunger

People will go to great lengths to get their favorite treats and will avoid other items that taste bad unless they are extremely hungry. In some situations, food can be a more powerful reinforcer than highly addictive drugs (Christensen et al., 2008). Some people even report cravings for a "sugar fix"—a term that seems to imply that addiction to candy bars is comparable to an addiction to a drug like heroin. The phrase "sugar fix" may seem an exaggeration, but is it possible that sugar actually does act like a drug? Sugar and some addictive drugs share a few interesting similarities. Ordinary sucrose—plain white granulated sugar—can stimulate release of the neurotransmitter dopamine in the *nucleus accumbens*, a brain region associated with the reinforcing effects of substances such as amphetamines and cocaine (Rada et al., 2005). Taste is another powerful force behind our motivation to eat. Thus eating is more than just maintaining homeostasis. In addition to the body's efforts to monitor energy needs, eating is motivated by psychological factors that include physical qualities of food such as its flavor and texture, as well as the availability of food, the social setting, and cravings.

TASTES, TEXTURES, AND EATING If the only factors underlying our motivation to eat were calories and essential nutrients, a few simple foods consumed every day for our entire lives would suffice. However, for those fortunate enough to have plentiful food available, taste and variety motivate decisions about what to eat. One unfortunate consequence of this relationship is that, generally speaking, the most popular foods are the ones that contain the most dietary fat and sugar. Let's look more specifically at fat.

WORKING THE SCIENTIFIC LITERACY MODEL
Why Dietary Fat Can Be So Tempting

Some of the most popular foods in the United States are loaded with fats, including red meat, cheese, ice cream, and anything deep-fried. Psychologists and neuroscientists are discovering why people can be so driven to consume these and other fattening foods.

What do we know about consuming fatty foods?

As we learned in Module 4.4, taste is based on the pattern of stimulation of receptors on the tongue and mouth. These receptors have evolved to help us decide whether to eat or reject a food. Dietary fat presents an interesting paradox: Humans have evolved to have a strong preference for fat, raising the possibility that it is (or was) a dietary necessity. Nevertheless, long-term consumption of foods that are high in fat and cholesterol is associated with cardiovascular disease and other health problems. So why are people motivated to consume dietary fat?

How can science explain the common craving for fattening foods?

Scientists are not 100% sure why, but it is likely we crave fats because we have specialized receptors on the tongue that are sensitive to the fat content of food. Research on animal subjects shows that these receptors send messages to the brain and stimulate the release of endorphins and dopamine—both of which are responsible for the subjective sense of pleasure and reward (Mizushige et al., 2007).

The animal work has involved the use of recording techniques that cannot be employed with humans. To conduct similar experiments with humans, scientists have used brain imaging technology (Rolls, 2010). In one study, participants had their brains scanned while they tasted various substances. At different times the participants tasted either a fatty solution (vegetable oil), sucrose (a sweet taste), or a tasteless control substance. Brain activity was recorded while these different taste stimuli were delivered in liquefied form into the mouths of the participants through a small plastic tube. The participants were also asked to rate the pleasantness of each stimulus. Overall, the participants rated the fatty substance favorably, and the brain scans showed activation in regions of the brain associated with pleasure sensations when they tasted fat (de Araujo & Rolls, 2004).

Can we critically evaluate this research?

A magnetic resonance imaging (MRI) machine hardly approximates the cozy atmosphere of the home dining room or a quaint restaurant. Despite general preferences for fatty foods, few of us sip on vegetable oil. However, if the research results described previously generalize to other experiences, then we can better understand how cravings for fatty foods come about—that is, they directly stimulate pleasure-sensing areas of the brain. But why might we have fat receptors in our mouths, and why would they be linked to brain reward centers in the first place? One possibility is that a preference for high-fat foods has evolved precisely because fats are usually a very rich source of energy. This system would certainly work to enhance our chance of survival when food resources are scarce—which was probably a relatively common experience before the invention of agriculture and grocery stores.

Why is this relevant?

Scientific studies have long confirmed the health risks brought on by high-fat diets. What is less understood is how and why we crave these foods, as opposed to lettuce or carrot sticks. Understanding how fat is sensed in our taste system and its links to the reward centers of the brain may help with treatments for avoiding or reducing excessive consumption of unhealthy foods.

Cells in the orbitofrontal cortex respond to perceptual qualities of food texture, such as the difference between a runny spaghetti sauce and a thick one.

While chemical receptors in the mouth and nose are detecting the tastes and smells of food, touch receptors in the mouth are detecting the textures of the food and relaying this information to the *orbitofrontal cortex,* which in turn contributes information to the overall sensation of eating (Figure 11.4; de Araujo & Rolls, 2004). These cells help us distinguish a runny spaghetti sauce from a thick one, or crunchy peanut butter from the creamy variety. Other cells distinguish between fatty and lean meats, or even between spicy and bland foods (Rolls et al., 2003). Texture, as you have likely found, is an important part of the eating experience.

What if you could get all the nutrition you need by swallowing one small tablet each day? Would you still be motivated to eat so as to enjoy the taste and texture of food, even if you did not need it? Researchers have answered this question by studying *tube feeding,* a technique used with hospitalized patients who cannot chew or swallow on their own. Tube feeding satisfies the body's nutritional needs by delivering nutrients directly to the stomach. When healthy volunteers completed a tube-feeding experiment, they were allowed to snack freely; some received nutrition through a tube while others in the control condition believed they were being tube-fed but actually were not. Interestingly, volunteers reported a similar appetite and consumed just as much food under these two conditions (Stratton et al., 2003). It appears that the pleasure of food is motivation enough to eat, even if we do not actually need the nutrients.

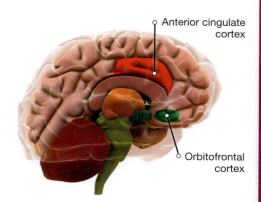

{FIG. 11.4}   **The Pleasure of Taste**   When fat receptors of the tongue are stimulated, the cingulate cortex—a region of the brain involved in emotional processing—is activated. The orbitofrontal cortex is involved in linking food taste and texture with reward.

American astronauts in the 1960s may not have been thrilled about their meals. Even though the tubes contained actual foods the astronauts enjoyed on earth, such as beef with vegetables, they lost most of their appeal when pureed and served in a tube.

PSYCH @

The Dessert Menu

The key to maintaining a healthy weight is to maintain energy balance. That is, over time we are advised against eating more calories than we burn. Although this text is certainly not a diet book, applying some of the research described in this module can help you improve your eating habits.

As one example, some cognitive psychologists have focused on how our thoughts about certain foods can become intrusive (Kavanagh et al., 2005). Hearing the words "potato chips" brings them to mind, but then a full-blown craving can develop as obsessive thoughts about them sink in. The craving seemingly becomes an intrusion upon your thoughts that will not go away unless satisfied. If you feel distracted by food cravings, do not try ignoring them—that may simply make matters worse. Instead, try focusing on something that requires active visual-spatial thought, because imagery can help you deal with your cravings. Imagining the sights and smells of the foods you crave can actually help (Harvey et al., 2005). If you are alone, or do not mind looking a bit silly, you can try something as simple as this exercise: Pretend the tips of your index and middle fingers are two feet, and have them walk across your forehead in small steps while following them with your eyes. Believe it or not, this is very similar to a technique that has been shown to reduce cravings by one-third (McClelland et al., 2006).

· · · · · · · · · · · · · · · · · · · ·

FOOD VARIETY AND EATING   To what extent does food availability affect how much we eat? The question is more difficult to answer than you might think. Imagine sitting down to your favorite meal. Many of us would eat a lot, but then watching each helping disappear would probably serve as a reminder that it is approaching time to stop. But what if someone interfered with your ability to keep track of how much you had eaten? This scenario is not what we would expect in normal situations, but it would allow for an ideal test of how food availability affects how much you will eat.

Psychologists have created such a situation in the laboratory through a technique known as the *bottomless bowl* of soup. Volunteers were asked to eat soup until they had enough. In the experimental condition, a tube continued to fill the soup bowl from the bottom so that it could not be detected by the volunteers. These individuals stopped eating after consuming, on average, over 70% more than those participants who knowingly refilled their bowls. Even more interesting is what happened—or did not happen—in terms of feelings and thoughts: The individuals eating from bottomless bowls did not *feel* any more satiated, nor did they *believe* they had eaten any more than the individuals in the control group. It turns out we are not so good at putting on the brakes when we cannot keep track of how much we have consumed (Wansink et al., 2005).

The results of the bottomless soup bowl study can be explained by **unit bias**, *the tendency to assume that the unit of sale or portioning is an appropriate amount to consume*. In some cases, this assumption works well. A single banana comes individually wrapped and makes for a healthy portion; it is an ideal unit (Geier et al., 2006). In contrast, packaged and preportioned foods often come in far larger than healthy sizes. A bottle of soda today is likely to be 20 ounces, but a few decades ago the same brand of soda came in a 6-ounce bottle. Despite the huge difference in volume, each is seen as constituting one unit of soda. As a consequence, individuals are now likely to consume more than three times as much soda in one sitting as their elders would have.

EATING AND THE SOCIAL CONTEXT   Eating is more than just a physical drive—there are social motives for eating as well. Have you ever gone to a party feeling not a hint of hunger, yet you spent the first hour sampling each of the snacks laid out on the dining room table? The presence of other people certainly seems to increase our motivation to eat, a situation that is probably very familiar to you. In addition, the presence of other people can *decrease* food intake. Whether other people make you want to eat more or less depends on the situation. To distinguish one situation from the other, researchers have narrowed social influences down to three main factors (Herman et al., 2003):

- *Social facilitation: Eating more.* Dinner hosts may encourage guests to take second and even third helpings, and individuals with a reputation for big appetites will be prodded to eat the most. Perhaps the strongest element of social facilitation is just the time spent at the table: The longer a person sits socializing, the more likely he or she is to continue nibbling (Berry et al., 1985).

Compare a modern soft drink serving (top) to the historical serving size (bottom). Despite the massive increase in volume, modern consumers still consider the unit of packaging as a normal-sized serving.

- *Impression management: Eating less.* Sometimes people self-consciously control their behavior so that others will see them in a certain way—a phenomenon known as *impression management.* For example, you probably know that it is polite to chew with your mouth closed. Similarly, the *minimal eating norm* suggests that another aspect of good manners—at least in some social and cultural settings—is to eat small amounts to avoid seeming rude (Herman et al., 2003).
- *Modeling: Eating whatever they eat.* At first exposure to a situation, such as a business dinner, a new employee may notice that no one eats much and everyone takes their time. The newcomer will see the others

as *models*, and so he too will restrain his eating. Later, he may be introduced to his friend's family reunion where everyone is having a second or third helping. In this case, he will be likely to eat more, even if he is already feeling full (Herman et al., 2003).

Clearly, eating is not just a matter of maintaining homeostasis. It is best described as a behavior motivated by biological, social, and individual psychological factors.

Quick Quiz 11.1b
Psychological Aspects of Hunger

KNOW...

1 The minimal eating norm is the observation that people tend to:

A eat as little as possible in just about every social situation imaginable.

B view eating reasonable portions as the polite thing to do.

C encourage one another to eat too much.

D eat as much as possible as to flatter the cook.

UNDERSTAND...

2 Sometimes being around others can:

A lead you to eat more than you normally would.

B lead you to eat less than you normally would.

C both a or b, depending on what others were doing.

D neither a nor b; others do not influence our eating.

APPLY...

3 In Europe, the typical container of fruit and yogurt is roughly 6 ounces. In the United States, the same food item is usually packaged in 8-ounce containers. The unit bias suggests that:

A a French person in the United States would be likely to eat the entire container, even though it contains 25% more than the typical French serving.

B an American visiting Paris would almost certainly miss the extra 2 ounces of yogurt.

C a French person visiting the United States would carefully evaluate the differences in packaging to ensure that he or she does not consume more than usual.

D all people would be unsatisfied with the 6-ounce serving in France.

ANALYZE...

4 How does research using tube feeding show that tastes and textures are an important part of satiation?

A Tube feeding has been shown to increase taste sensations.

B Even though the tube-fed volunteers received all the nutrition they needed, they were still motivated to eat.

C The texture of food delivered via tube can be seen by volunteers, which decreases their appetite.

D Tube-fed volunteers stop eating because their nutrition needs have been met.

Answers can be found on page ANS-4.

Disorders of Eating

Our dietary habits are influenced by biological dispositions, our beliefs and perceptions about eating and our bodies, and sociocultural factors. Unfortunately, these motivational systems do not always lead us to good health.

OBESITY **Obesity** *is a disorder of positive energy balance, in which energy intake exceeds energy expenditure.* Some refer to this phenomenon as an epidemic in the United States, and it has spread across the world as well. In 2008, 49 of the 50 U.S. states had at least a 20% prevalence rate of obesity (Figure 11.5; Centers for Disease Control and Prevention [CDC], 2010). One of the major problems in controlling obesity is the difficulty in ensuring long-term maintenance of weight loss. The weight-loss options we encounter on an almost daily basis are numerous—but some are good, while others are simply gimmicks. The gimmicks often claim to be proven, easy solutions for weight loss. For example, advertisements tell people that they can lose weight without exercising, just by taking a pill. People are also told that diet and exercise are the only way to lose weight. Even when they follow this advice of dieting and exercising, many people find shedding pounds to be an arduous, if impossible, task.

Why can weight management be so difficult? One problem is that both the drive to eat and the incentive value of food increase with deprivation (Raynor & Epstein, 2003). This trend makes patterns of overeating notoriously difficult to change. Several studies have shown that girls and adolescents who self-report dieting are heavier later in life (Field et al., 2003; Stice et al., 2005). The restraint involved in dieting—especially avoiding certain highly reinforcing foods—may actually make the foods even more reinforcing in the long run.

It is normal to be sensitive to the reinforcing, pleasurable aspects of food, but some individuals are clearly more prone to overeating than others. Research suggests that people who are obese have an increased sensitivity to food and food-related cues. For instance, when children who are obese are allowed to smell or eat just a small sample of candy bars, cakes, and savory nuts, they eat more of these items when given the opportunity than do normal-weight children (Jansen et al., 2003). Also, obese people have significantly higher metabolic activity in those regions of the brain that respond to sensations of the mouth, lips, and tongue (Wang et al., 2002). These findings suggest that people with obesity have more intense, rewarding sensory experiences when it comes to food. But note that this statement is a correlation: It does not tell us whether increased sensitivity to food cues causes obesity, or vice versa.

ANOREXIA AND BULIMIA What we eat, or do not eat, has both short- and long-term physical and psychological consequences. In the late 1940s, a group of scientists in Minnesota recruited young men who were conscientious objectors to service in World War II. In lieu of going overseas to fight, the men participated in a study examining the effects of extreme food deprivation on physiology and behavior. The men were placed on a diet and activity regimen that brought them down to 75% of their original weight. As the study progressed, the participants not only lost weight but also experienced reduced pulse, respiration, and blood pressure. The men became depressed and, when finally allowed to eat again, they developed abnormal feeding patterns such as binging (Kalm & Semba, 2005).

These effects of food deprivation mirror what we find in eating disorders such as **anorexia nervosa**, *an eating disorder that involves (1) self-starvation, (2) intense fear of weight gain and a distorted perception of body image, and (3) a denial of the serious consequences of severely low weight.* Other problems associated with anorexia include consecutive loss of menstrual periods (amenorrhea), and for males a loss of sexual motivation. The disorder usually occurs during mid to late adolescence and has been on the rise during the 20th century (see Table 11.1; Hudson et al., 2007).

Bulimia nervosa *is an eating disorder that is characterized by periods of food deprivation, binge-eating, and purging.* Binging involves short but intense episodes of massive calorie consumption marked by a lack of regulation of how many calories the body actually needs. The binging is followed by purging (self-induced vomiting, the most common type), fasting, laxative or diuretic use, or intense exercise. People with anorexia may also purge, but this is

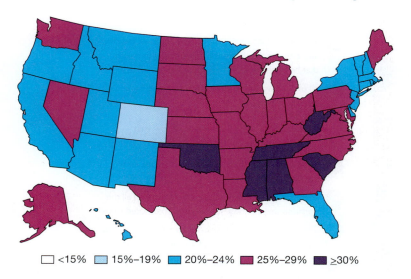

☐ <15%   ☐ 15%–19%   ■ 20%–24%   ■ 25%–29%   ■ ≥30%

{FIG. 11.5} **Obesity Rates in the United States** Data from the CDC indicate that of the 50 U.S. states, only Colorado has an obesity rate less than 20%.

Table 11.1 :: **Statistical Characteristics of Eating Disorders**

	Women and Men combined	
Lifetime prevalence of anorexia	Women: 0.9%	Men: 0.3%
Lifetime prevalence of bulimia	Women: 1.5%	Men: 0.5%
Percentage of people with anorexia who are receiving treatment	34%	
Percentage of people with bulimia who are receiving treatment	43%	
Average duration of anorexia	1.7 years	
Average duration of bulimia	8 years	

Source: Hudson et al., 2007.

less common than in those who have bulimia. Bulimia nervosa is most prevalent in late adolescence and young adulthood (Hudson et al., 2007).

Males, although less prone to these problems than females, also develop eating disorders. Adolescents and young men may starve themselves during periods of high exercise to lose weight and achieve muscle mass (Ricciardelli & McCabe, 2004).

One concern regarding eating disorders is the role that culture plays in their onset. Specifically, people with regular exposure to Western culture are more likely to develop bulimia than members of cultures without such exposure (Keel & Klump, 2003). Although anorexia may be influenced by sociocultural factors, such as the idealized view of a thin figure, this condition does not follow the same sociocultural trend as bulimia.

People with anorexia experience severely distorted views of their body. Although dangerously underweight they continue to both fear and *feel* being fat. Both males and females may become anorexic.

Quick Quiz 11.1c
Disorders of Eating

KNOW...

1. High energy intake and low energy expenditure leads to _____.
   - A anorexia
   - B obesity
   - C bulimia
   - D weight loss

2. What is one difference between anorexia and bulimia?
   - A Anorexia involves periods of self-starvation, whereas bulimia does not.
   - B Bulimia involves purging (such as self-induced vomiting), whereas this is less characteristic in anorexia.
   - C Anorexia occurs in females only, whereas bulimia occurs in both females and males.
   - D Anorexia and bulimia are actually two terms for the same disorder.

UNDERSTAND...

3. Why do psychologists believe that obese people respond differently to food reinforcement than do people of normal weight?
   - A Obese people typically have less exposure to diverse food groups.
   - B Brain imaging studies show less activity in obese individuals' brains in response to food compared to the brains of people of normal weight.
   - C Brain imaging studies show greater activity in obese individuals' brains in response to food compared to the brains people of normal weight.
   - D Obese people do not respond differently to food reinforcement than people of normal weight.

APPLY...

4. Which of the following is the most likely predictor of someone's chances of developing an eating disorder or obesity?
   - A Activity of the parietal somatosensory cortex
   - B Decreased sensitivity to the reward value of food
   - C Exposure to idealized versions of body type and thinness
   - D Fat receptors on the tongue

Answers can be found on page ANS-4.

Module Summary

(((•—[Listen
to the audio file
of this module at
MyPsychLab

Now that you have read this module
you should:

KNOW ...

● **The key terminology of motivation and hunger:**

anorexia nervosa (p. 404)   incentives (p. 398)

bulimia nervosa (p. 404)   motivation (p. 397)

drives (p. 398)   obesity (p. 404)

glucose (p. 398)   satiation (p. 398)

homeostasis (p. 397)   unit bias (p. 402)

UNDERSTAND ...

● **The biological, cognitive, and social processes that
shape eating patterns.** Ghrelin and CCK are released
into the bloodstream from the stomach; ghrelin signals
hunger, whereas CCK signals fullness (satiety). Energy is
delivered through the bloodstream in the form of glucose,
while the hormone insulin helps the cells throughout the
body store this fuel. These substances are monitored by
the hypothalamus, which signals hunger when not enough
glucose is available to the cells. You should also have an
understanding of the effects of psychological cues, such as
the unit bias and the variety of available foods, as well as
social cues, such as the minimal eating norm.

● **The major eating and weight-control problems people
face.** This module discussed issues related to obesity and
the difficulties that individuals face when trying to slim
down. For example, restricting food intake may actually
increase the reward value of food. Other problems include
anorexia and bulimia, both of which involve periods of
self-starvation and a fear of gaining weight. Bulimia also
includes purging, such as through vomiting or the use of
laxatives.

APPLY ...

● **Your knowledge of hunger regulation to better
understand and evaluate your own eating patterns.**
Do you finish an entire package of a food item, as the
minimal eating norm would suggest? Or do you check
to ensure you are getting an appropriate serving size?
Try this activity to find out exactly how you eat. Starting
first thing tomorrow, keep a food diary for the next three
days. In other words, keep a record of everything you eat
over this period, recording when you ate, what you ate,
and what made you feel like eating. It is important to be
honest with yourself and to be reflective: Did you eat
because your stomach rumbled, because you were craving
something, or perhaps because the food was just there?
It is okay to list more than one reason for each entry in
your food diary. At the end of the three-day period, tally
how often each reason for eating appeared in your diary.
Make note of what proportion of the time you ate for
each reason. Ask yourself: Are the results surprising? Do
they make you want to think more about the reasons you
eat? (Note: You can also try to work from memory and
recreate a food diary from the past three or four days, but
the results might not be as accurate).

ANALYZE ...

● **The roles of texture and taste in satiation.** A number
of innovative studies have demonstrated that tastes and
textures do play a role in signaling the end of a meal. For
example, we know that people can receive the necessary
nutrition through tube feeding, yet they still choose to eat
so as to experience the sensations associated with food.

Sexual Motivation

KNOW ...	UNDERSTAND ...	APPLY ...	ANALYZE ...
The key terminology associated with sexual motivation	Similarities and differences in sexual responses in men and women	Information from surveys to understand your own views of sexuality	Different explanations for what determines sexual orientation

Why do humans have sex? Psychologists Cindy Meston and David Buss have asked just this question in their research on human sexual motivation. Specifically, they asked college students why they have sex and tabulated the many different responses offered by both males and females (Meston & Buss, 2007). There are so many possible answers to this very open-ended question—how many do you think they came up with? Certainly more than if we asked the same about why birds, bees, or meerkats have sex. Here are some of the reasons the students came up with:

- "I wanted to get back at my partner for cheating on me."
- "Because of a bet."
- "I wanted to end the relationship."
- "It feels good."

- "I wanted to show my affection toward the other person."
- "I wanted to feel closer to God."

Although we will never know for sure, birds, bees and meerkats likely have sex to reproduce (a reason that was *far* down the list for college students). The motivation to have sex naturally has its complex, underlying physiology. As we will see in this module, however, human sexual motivation is expressed and experienced in diverse ways—at least 237 different ways, according to Meston and Buss's research.

Focus Questions

1 How do psychologists explain the diverse sexual motivations of humans?

2 How do psychologists explain variations in sexual orientation?

One fascinating aspect of the human mind is its ability to hold strong beliefs in the absence of any supporting evidence. No shortage of examples can be found when it comes to beliefs about sexuality. For example, many people once believed that women who are menstruating can spoil a ham by touching it or that masturbation can cause blindness or insanity.

We have come a long way toward a modern and scientific understanding of human sexual motivation and behavior. Current views are still far from completely informed and enlightened, however; cultural norms and values will always play a role in discussions of sexuality. Nevertheless, researchers have made significant progress toward developing a biopsychosocial model of sexuality that recognizes the biological basis of sex as well as the personal and social issues that are an inherent part of the topic.

Each individual differs in his or her **libido**—*the motivation for sexual activity and pleasure.* What accounts for these individual differences in sex drive? This is not an easy question to answer because differences can be explained by a combination of biological and sociocultural factors. It is generally believed that men are more interested in sex than are women. On average, men become sexually aroused more often, fantasize more, masturbate more, and desire more sexual partners than do women (Ellis & Symons, 1990). Even so, the term "on average" leaves out important details—namely, the wide variation in individuals' sexual interests. Some women might desire sex just as much as the most sexually motivated men, while some men show no interest in sex at all. These observations and many others come from extensive research psychologists have conducted using a wide range of methods.

Human Sexual Behavior: Psychological and Biological Influences

Humans have many motives for pursuing and having sex, and one notable observation is that sex frequently occurs *without* an end goal of reproduction. In other words, sex serves many purposes other than what seems to be its primary biological purpose. But sex is not unique in this regard; people eat when they are not hungry and drink when they are not thirsty, without considering the nutritional purpose of their behavior. However, sex for purposes other than reproduction appears to be rare in nonhuman species. Interestingly, masturbation occurs in some primate species, and the bonobo chimpanzee engages in frequent genital contact, touching, and other sexual behaviors without actually copulating (de Waal & Lanting, 1997; Starin, 2004).

By comparison, among humans, expressions of sexual motivation are vast and diverse. Sexual themes are common in television, movies, humor, advertising, and other media, and discussions of sex and sexuality influence social life, the workplace, and politics. Obviously, sex is a very important and relevant topic for psychology, but it is also one of the most challenging to study. Sex generally happens in private, and many people prefer to keep it that way. Nonetheless, psychologists use a variety of methods to understand the complexities of human sexual behavior, including interviews, questionnaires, physiological measures, and even direct observations of behavior. Interviews and questionnaires are the least intrusive techniques and, therefore, are the most commonly used.

PSYCHOLOGICAL MEASURES OF SEXUAL MOTIVATION One of the first scientists to tackle the topic of human sexual behavior was zoology professor Alfred Kinsey. Kinsey began his research on human sexuality by interviewing his students about their sexual histories. Between 1938 and 1952, Kinsey and his colleagues at Indiana University interviewed thousands of people and published their results in a pair of books known informally as the *Kinsey Reports* (1948, 1953). By modern standards, Kinsey's methods were quite flawed and rather controversial. Kinsey tended to make sweeping generalizations about his findings that were based on very limited samples. Despite these practices, Kinsey's work on sexuality continues to influence discussion on sexual behavior and motivation.

The fact that Kinsey dared to apply science to sexuality was offensive to many people at the time. During an era when the phrase "sexual orientation" did not even exist, Kinsey reported that 37% of the males whom he interviewed had at least one homosexual experience resulting in orgasm; this was absolutely shocking at the time. (The corresponding figure for females in his studies was 13%.) Contrary to the conventional thinking of his time, Kinsey believed that heterosexuality and homosexuality fell on a continuous scale (Table 11.2). His studies opened up further opportunities for current researchers to find out what motivates human sexual behavior. Since Kinsey conducted his investigations, however, the methods used for such research have changed—to include more representative samples, for example—and the extensive interviews have been largely replaced with anonymously completed questionnaires that encourage participants to provide more candid responses.

Table 11.2 :: A Continuum of Sexual Orientation

Kinsey and his associates defied the convention of identifying people as either heterosexual or homosexual by measuring sexual interests on a continuous scale.

0	1	2	3	4	5	6
Exclusively heterosexual	Predominantly heterosexual; only incidentally homosexual	Predominantly heterosexual; more than incidentally homosexual	Equally heterosexual and homosexual	Predominantly homosexual; more than incidentally heterosexual	Predominantly homosexual; only incidentally heterosexual	Exclusively homosexual

Source: Reprinted with permission of the Kinsey Institute for Research in Sex, Gender, and Reproduction, Inc.

The questionnaire method of studying human sexual motivation has continued since Kinsey's time. At the beginning of this module, we introduced a study conducted by psychologists Cindy Meston and David Buss, who asked more than 1,500 college students to identify their reasons for having sex. We listed a few reasons provided by the students—some conventional (to express affection) and others perhaps more surprising (to feel closer to God). We return to this study to discuss some general themes that emerged—notably, the four shown in Figure 11.6.

As you can see in Figure 11.6, physical, personal, and social factors underlie sexual motivation. For the respondents in Meston and Buss's study, physical reasons were related to pleasure of the sex itself as well as to orgasm. Many respondents used sex for what might be described as instrumental reasons—sex was a means of accomplishing a goal such as financial or personal gain, or revenge. College students were also motivated by emotional reasons and because of feelings of insecurity. Reproduction ranked very far down the list, which might seem surprising for a study whose results were published under the title "Why Humans Have Sex" (Meston & Buss, 2007). Also note that this study surveyed college students, who represent a relatively small slice of humanity. Other survey-based studies of sexual motivation have found additional factors that motivate sexual behavior, such as expressing value and nurturance toward one's partner, experiencing stress relief, enhancing one's perception of personal power and, of course, having children (Hill & Preston, 1996).

1. For physical reasons.
"The person's physical appearance turned me on."
"I want to achieve an orgasm."

2. To help attain a goal.
"I wanted to get a raise."
"I wanted to hurt an enemy."

3. For emotional reasons.
"I realized I was in love."
"I wanted to intensify my relationship."

4. Because of insecurity.
"I felt obligated to."
"I wanted to be nice."

{FIG. 11.6} **Why Have Sex?** Self-reported reasons for having sex by college undergraduates (Meston & Buss, 2007).

There are also reasons for avoiding sex. Each year thousands of teenagers experience unplanned or unwanted effects of sexual behavior, such as pregnancy, sexually transmitted diseases, or being in a relationship that may be abusive or simply too complex for a younger person to handle. Sexual abstinence clubs have been cropping up across high school and college campuses.

MYTHS IN MIND
Sex After Sixty?

Living in a culture that emphasizes youth can make it difficult to talk about—or even think about—the sexual lives of older people. Sex often seems like something that only younger people care about, starting with the surge of hormones in adolescence and lasting until parenthood. Recent years, however, have brought us a wave of advertisements showing older couples discussing sexual intimacy. Since sexuality is such an important part of life, it is worth asking what happens to sex and sexuality as people age.

In one survey (Lindau et al., 2007), almost three-fourths of the 57- to 64-year-old respondents reported sexual

Research confirms that many senior adults remain sexually active.

contact with a partner in the past year, as did half of the 64- to 75-year-olds and one-fourth of the respondents between ages 75 and 85. Sexuality does not always require a partner: Almost half of the men and one-fourth of the women in the survey reported masturbating within the past year.

Does sexuality decline in the senior years? It seems that for many people, it does. Nevertheless, these data clearly show that many seniors remain sexually active into their 80s. This sexuality is not without problems; approximately 40% of women in the survey cited lack of desire as a problem, and almost the same percentage of men reported erectile problems.

. . . .

The survey and interview methods discussed to this point have provided a rich set of data about human sexuality. Other researchers have approached this topic from a biological standpoint by looking at the physiological and brain basis of sexual motivation (Meston & Frohlich, 2000).

BIOLOGICAL MEASURES OF SEX Several decades of work have revealed that sexual motivation is controlled by a distinct set of biological processes. Starting in the 1950s, researchers William Masters and Virginia Johnson described the human sexual response cycle based on their observations of 27 male and 118 female prostitutes who agreed to masturbate or have intercourse while under observation (Masters & Johnson, 1966). Participants were monitored with heart rate and blood pressure equipment, as well as with more peculiar devices such as the penile plethysmograph or vaginal photoplethysmograph, which are designed to measure blood flow to the genitalia in men and women, respectively. Masters and Johnson's initial study allowed them to develop their methods and work with participants who, according to the researchers, were less likely to be sexually inhibited than nonprostitutes. Masters and Johnson followed up this study with observations of hundreds of men and women to characterize the physiological changes that occur during sex.

Figure 11.7 summarizes Masters and Johnson's (1966) observations of human sexual responding in males and females. The **sexual response cycle** *describes the phases of physiological change during sexual activity, which comprises four primary stages: excitement, plateau, orgasm, and resolution.* Dividing the sexual response cycle into phases allowed the researchers to describe the cascade of physiological changes that occur during sexual behavior. The

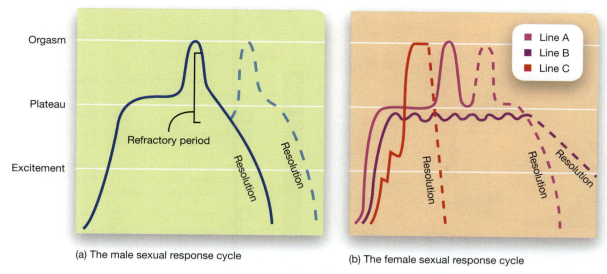

Orgasm
Plateau
Excitement

Refractory period
Resolution
Resolution

(a) The male sexual response cycle

Line A
Line B
Line C

Resolution
Resolution
Resolution

(b) The female sexual response cycle

{FIG. 11.7} **Sexual Response Cycles** (a) Masters and Johnson's studies showed that males typically experience a single orgasm followed by a refractory period—a time during which orgasm cannot be physically achieved again. Then they experience resolution, unless they continue sexual activity. (b) Women typically have a more varied sexual response profile than men. Here are a few examples. Line A indicates a woman who has multiple orgasms, Line B a woman who does not experience orgasm, and Line C a woman who has a single orgasm. **Click on this figure in your eText to see more details.**

cycle applies to both male and female sexual responses, although there are differences between sexes in how these stages are experienced and their duration. The work of Masters and Johnson and those who have followed in their footsteps reveal a complex picture of male and female sexual responses.

One topic of particular interest is how males and females differ in their patterns of orgasm. In one study, 21% to 32% of women reported that they did not experience orgasm during masturbation or sexual intercourse (Dunn et al., 2005), whereas only 2% of men did not experience orgasm. Men usually experience a single orgasm followed by a **refractory period**, *a time period during which erection and orgasm are not physically possible.* In contrast, some women experience multiple orgasms without a refractory period.

What about the subjective experience of orgasm? Do women and men *feel* differently during orgasm? This challenging question was taken up by a group of researchers who asked college students to write detailed descriptions of their orgasm experiences. Researchers removed clues to the sex of each writer by changing terms such as "penis" or "vagina" to "genitals." Then, male and female physicians, psychologists, and medical students judged whether each description came from a male or female. The judges were no better than chance at guessing the gender of the authors, and neither female nor male judges were any better than the other at guessing (Vance & Wagner, 1976). This outcome suggests that, to some degree, males and females have similar subjective experiences during orgasm.

Although sexual activity involves the whole body, researchers have recently focused on brain activity in women who experienced orgasm while being monitored by functional MRIs (Komisaruk et al., 2006). Stimulation of the breasts, nipples, and vaginal areas causes sensory nerves to send signals to the hypothalamus. The hypothalamus, in turn, stimulates the pituitary gland to release a hormone called *oxytocin*, which plays a role in orgasm and post-orgasm physiology. Blood levels of oxytocin surge just after orgasm and may remain elevated for at least five minutes (Carmichael et al., 1994). Oxytocin is released during orgasm in males as well (Murphy et al., 1990). In addition, the dopamine-rich reward centers of the brain become highly active during orgasm (Holstege et al., 2003).

SEXUAL DYSFUNCTIONS In some cases, physiological processes are involved in sex malfunction. In males, this may include *erectile dysfunction (ED)*—the inability to achieve or maintain an erection. Evidence supports the idea that ED is often caused by cardiovascular problems such as hypertension (Jackson et al., 2006). When this is the case, physicians may prescribe medications, such as Viagra, that enhance blood flow to the genitals. For females, physiological problems may lead to lack of arousal or painful intercourse, despite the fact the individual may want to engage in sexual activity. In some of these cases, medical treatments such as estrogen replacement therapy may provide relief.

Medical treatments are not the only option for addressing sexual dysfunctions. In some cases, male or

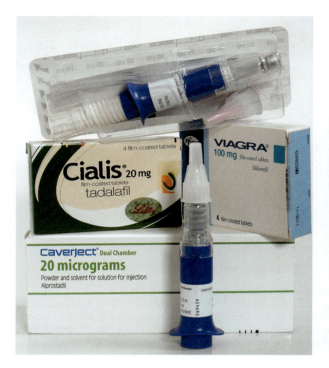

Medications for erectile dysfunction are now commonplace. The majority of users are middle-aged and older males. However, these drugs are also sometimes used by younger males in both heterosexual and homosexual relationships, often without a prescription.

female sexual dysfunction may arise from depression or anxiety. In these circumstances, cognitive and behavioral techniques can often resolve the problems.

SEX AND TECHNOLOGY In the past two decades, electronic media such as the Internet, text messaging, instant messaging, and social networking sites have become common outlets for sexual expression. Electronic media are often used for viewing pornography, having online sexual encounters, and meeting others for sex offline. Adolescents, as well as both single and married adults, may engage in *cybersex*—that is, the use of the Internet and computer equipment for sending sexually explicit images and messages to a partner. An estimated one in three adults today has engaged in cybersex (Daneback et al., 2005).

Unplanned pregnancy and STDs are obviously not an immediate risk of cybersex. However, people tend to communicate with less inhibition via digital media compared to face-to-face encounters. This opens up the possibility for impulsive behavior such as sending sexually explicit pictures and messages ("sexting"). Many teens have suffered some rather harsh consequences for sexting. Some states consider sexting to be a form of underage pornography and those convicted could be required to register as sex offenders.

Quick Quiz 11.2a
Human Sexual Behavior: Psychological and Biological Influences

KNOW …

1 _____ refers to one's motivation for sexual behavior and pleasure.

- **A** Libido
- **B** Excitement
- **C** Orgasm
- **D** Cybersex

2 According to research on sexual motivation in college students, which of the following is not a primary reason students offer for having sex?

- **A** Emotional reasons
- **B** Physical reasons
- **C** Social reasons
- **D** Reproduction

3 In what order do the phases of the sexual response cycle occur?

- **A** Plateau, orgasm, resolution, excitement
- **B** Excitement, plateau, orgasm, and resolution
- **C** Orgasm, resolution, excitement, plateau
- **D** Excitement, orgasm, resolution, plateau

UNDERSTAND …

4 The male sexual response cycle includes a(n) _____ during which erection and orgasm are not physically possible, whereas the female sexual response cycle most often does not.

- **A** plateau
- **B** refractory period
- **C** oxytocin release
- **D** sensitive period

5 If a researcher wanted to study how brain activity changes during sexual activity, which of the following methods would be most suitable?

- **A** behavioral observation
- **B** functional MRI scan
- **C** survey or questionnaire
- **D** interview

Answers can be found on page ANS-4.

Sexual Orientation: Biology and Environment

Sexual orientation *is a consistent preference for sexual relations with members of the opposite sex (heterosexuality), same sex (homosexuality), or either sex (bisexuality).* Current definitions of sexual orientation focus on the psychological aspects of sexuality (e.g., desire, emotion, identification) rather than strictly behavioral criteria (Bailey et al., 2000). For example, a person can have a sexual orientation but never have sexual contact throughout his or her life.

Sexual orientation is not exclusively determined by patterns of sexual behavior. It also includes aspects of identity and emotional connection. Scientists are discovering that sexual orientation is an outcome of complex gene and environmental interactions.

Psychologists have long struggled to find a satisfactory explanation for variations in sexual orientation. Sigmund Freud (1905) advanced the theory that male homosexuality could be traced to the presence of a domineering mother and weak father figure. As recently as 1987, Ellis and Ames argued that homosexuality could be caused by experiencing seduction from an older sibling or playmate. Both theories lack scientific evidence to confirm their validity. An ongoing debate is now considering why a significant number of humans prefer emotional and sexual relationships with members of the same sex. Researchers question whether sexual orientation is based on choices people make or on biologically related factors such as genetics or differences in brain anatomy. Thus modern scientific explanations of homosexuality focus on interactions between biological and sociocultural factors.

SEXUAL ORIENTATION AND THE BRAIN

In the early 1990s, neuroscientist Simon LeVay compared the brains of deceased gay and heterosexual males. In his work, he found that an area of the hypothalamus was, on average, smaller in gay men compared to heterosexual men (Figure 11.8; LeVay, 1991). LeVay's results created a storm of controversy among both scientists and the public. Many people incorrectly interpreted his findings as proof that homosexuality was biologically, and therefore genetically, determined. In fact, the differences in the hypothalamus *could* have been due to environmental factors—LeVay's study was not designed to test either conclusion. As with many other topics you have encountered in this text, disentangling

the "nature versus nurture" issues in relation to sexual orientation is a challenge that many researchers are now addressing. Modern research on the brain has shown how environmental factors, even those occurring in the prenatal environment, contribute to anatomical and functional differences in the brain (Roselli & Stormshak, 2009).

Scientists have been skeptical of LeVay's results, in part because they have proved difficult to replicate (Lasco et al., 2002). The region of the hypothalamus he identified was only smaller *on average* in gay men versus heterosexuals, and the ranges in size were overlapping. In addition, the purportedly homosexual men whom LeVay studied died of complications associated with HIV, which could have accounted for the differences in their brains. Although its results are not considered definitive, LeVay's study stimulated considerable scientific curiosity and debate about links between the brain and sexual orientation. Work on animal subjects (sheep) has shown that 8% to 10% percent of rams show preferences for mounting other rams. The only difference researchers have found between male-preferring and female-preferring rams is a smaller region of the hypothalamus (Roselli et al., 2004).

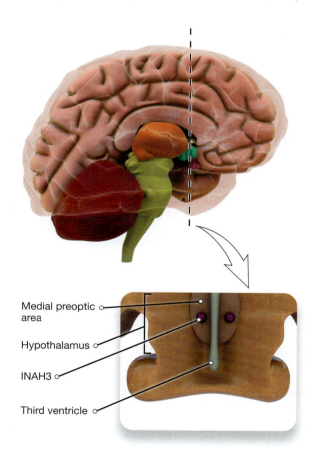

Medial preoptic area

Hypothalamus

INAH3

Third ventricle

{FIG. 11.8} **Sexual Orientation and the Brain** An early study of the brain basis of sexual orientation found that homosexual males had a smaller subregion (INAH3) of the hypothalamus within the medial pre-optic area (LeVay, 1991).

Researchers have also been intrigued by findings suggesting that a band of nerve fibers connecting the left and right brain hemispheres, called the anterior commissure, is larger in homosexual men and women than in heterosexual men (Allen & Gorski, 1992). Like the results of LeVay's work, this finding has proved difficult to replicate. Even if the hypothalamus and the anterior commissure differ between homosexual and heterosexual people, we are left to wonder what those differences really mean in terms of sexual orientation. Perhaps there is no definitive characteristic of brain anatomy that determines sexual preferences; perhaps it is the *patterns* of brain activity that reveal differences.

Imaging studies show that sexual stimuli elicit different patterns of brain activity in homosexual and heterosexual people. In one study, homosexual men and heterosexual women showed greater activation of the medial preoptic area of the hypothalamus while smelling a male derivative of testosterone found in underarm sweat. This brain region, which is involved in sexual behavior in many different species, including humans, did not become activated when heterosexual men smelled male underarm sweat (Savic et al, 2005). Homosexual males and heterosexual females show greater activity in the brain's reward centers when viewing pictures of genitalia of sexually aroused males. The same pattern of brain activity is found in homosexual women and heterosexual men viewing pictures of female genitalia (Ponseti et al., 2006). These findings may not provide the final answer about the brain basis of sexual orientation, but they do indicate that differences in sexual motivation may be based on differences in specific patterns of brain activity.

WORKING THE SCIENTIFIC LITERACY MODEL
Hormones and Sexual Orientation

Hormones are another place to look for clues about the biological basis of sexual orientation. Although popular culture often equates sexuality directly with hormone levels, we should examine what scientists have learned through research on these chemicals.

What do we know about hormones and sexual orientation?

Testosterone *is a hormone that is involved in the development of sex characteristics and the motivation of sexual behavior.* This hormone is found in both males and females, albeit typically at higher levels in males, and is known to influence sexual behavior in several ways. First, surges in testosterone are associated with elevated sexual arousal in both males and females. Second, testosterone has long-term effects on sexual development.

Researchers have long noted that prenatal hormone levels influence sex-specific behavior and sexual preferences in nonhuman species (Morris et al., 2004). During human development—and in particular during the second and fifth months of pregnancy, when the fetal brain is developing rapidly—the amount of testosterone the fetus encounters influences behavior later in life. An excess amount of testosterone results in boys who are more masculine; if the fetus is female, high testosterone exposure is associated with an increased chance of showing male typical behavior, and sometimes homosexual orientation. Low circulating levels of testosterone during prenatal development results in feminization—whether the fetus is genetically female or male. Males exposed to low prenatal testosterone levels are more likely to identify with feminine pursuits and show homosexual preferences (Rahman, 2005).

How can scientists study hormones and sexual orientation?

One detail you may be wondering about is how anyone could even know how much testosterone he or she was exposed to before being born. This level is not something you would expect to find recorded on your medical record, unlike your length and weight. Interestingly, some external features can be measured in adulthood that correlate with prenatal testosterone exposure. One measure compares the relative length of the index finger (second digit—2D) and ring finger (fourth digit—4D) (Manning et al., 1998). Heterosexual females tend to have index and ring fingers of equal length (an equal 2D:4D ratio). Heterosexual males have longer ring fingers than index fingers. On average, homosexual males tend to have feminized (equal) 2D:4D ratios and lesbians have masculine ratios, although this pattern has not been found in all studies (Rahman, 2005).

The point here is not that finger length has some particular relevance to sexual orientation. Rather, these differences in finger length ratios reflect prenatal exposure to testosterone, which in turn influences sexual orientation.

Can we critically evaluate this finding?

The possibility that finger lengths—or something else so easy to measure—could be indicative of something as complex as sexual orientation is exciting to researchers who are interested in understanding what leads people toward different sexual preferences. Sexual orientation is a complex aspect of human (and some nonhuman) behavior. Nonetheless, most researchers of 2D:4D ratios use a categorical approach by identifying participants as either heterosexual or homosexual. However, as described in Table 11.2, psychologists since Alfred Kinsey's studies have viewed sexual orientation as ranging on a continuum, rather than as a point on an absolute either/or scale. Different results might emerge from sexual orientation research if a continuous—rather than categorical—measure of sexual orientation is used (Kraemer et al., 2006). Also, as discussed in Module 2.1, being able to replicate research results is a critical component of the scientific process. Not all research on finger length ratios suggests that heterosexual and homosexual people differ in this measure (Grimbos et al., 2010).

Why is this relevant?

Many common beliefs remain about why people are homosexual, and many of these beliefs are entirely erroneous, if not potentially harmful. An example is the belief that homosexuality is a choice and, therefore, can be changed. In reality, there are no valid scientific data to back this claim. Biologically informed ideas about how homosexuality arises provide a more complete, accurate picture, and give society the necessary perspective for better understanding sexual minorities.

Another interesting finding relating to prenatal testosterone exposure is that gay males tend to have a larger number of older brothers than do heterosexual males. An intriguing hypothesis for why this pattern emerges has to do with an expecting mother's immune system. At birth, some mixing of blood between mother and newborn occurs. If the newborn is male, the mother is thus exposed to proteins that are specific to males, which triggers an immune response by the mother. If the subsequent fetuses are male, the maternal immune system may transport the antibodies of her immune system that she built up from the previous birth across the placenta. The result is an inhibition of testosterone circulation in the developing male. The limited testosterone exposure may result in a feminized brain. The absence of a corresponding birth order effect in lesbians suggests that the immune response by the mother specifically affects male fetuses (Blanchard, 2008).

GENETICS AND SEXUAL ORIENTATION Sexual orientation may be influenced by a combination of genes. Evidence for this comes from twin studies that have identified higher genetic correlations between identical twins compared with fraternal twin pairs. Several twin studies examining the genetic basis of sexual orientation have been conducted. Genetic correlations between .30 and .60 for homosexuality have been reported for both men and women, suggesting that approximately half of the individual differences found in sexual orientation are due to genetic factors (Figure 11.9; Bailey & Pillard, 1995; Bailey et al., 1993; Kirk et al., 2000). This result tends to hold true for gay men across multiple studies. In contrast, the research is inconsistent when it comes to females—studies have also failed to confirm a genetic relationship between genes and homosexuality in women (Bailey et al., 2000; Långström et al., 2010).

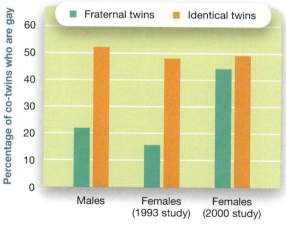

{FIG. 11.9} **Genetics and Sexual Orientation** Twin studies tend to show consistently higher genetic correlations for sexual orientation between male identical twins compared to fraternal twins. This finding indicates that male homosexuality has a genetic basis. Results of studies comparing female identical and fraternal twins are not as consistent.

Thus genes appear to play at least some role in sexual orientation, but particularly for men. However, this statement does not mean that sexual orientation is *determined* by genetics. The brain and endocrine system are remarkably sensitive to the environment, and they interact with a variety of sociocultural factors (Meston & Ahrold, 2010). Nevertheless, current evidence suggests that cultural influences have a meager effect, at best, on sexual orientation. There are more homosexual people in urban areas than in rural regions, probably because homosexual people are more likely to settle in urban areas. Students who attend same-sex schools are more likely to have homosexual experiences than students in mixed-sex schools, but this does not increase the likelihood of a homosexual orientation when students from same-sex schools reach adulthood (Wellings et al., 1994). Moreover, young males of the Sambia tribe in New Guinea are required to engage in sexual acts with adult males, but this practice does not increase the likelihood of homosexual orientation in adulthood (Bailey, 2003). The implications of research findings related to sexual orientation and the cultural and biological basis of homosexuality are many. At the very least, the evidence suggests that sexual orientation is neither purely an environmental outcome nor solely a cultural creation. In all likelihood, complex gene–environment interactions determine sexual orientation.

Quick Quiz 11.2b
Sexual Orientation: Biology and Environment

KNOW…

1 Some research on the brain basis of sexual orientation has found reduced size in regions of the _____ in homosexual men.

   A hippocampus   **C** hypothalamus

   B cerebral cortex   **D** amygdala

APPLY…

2 Biological theories of sexual orientation have suggested that testosterone levels during _____ may influence whether males become homosexual or heterosexual.

   A prenatal development

   B puberty

   C adulthood

   D periods of sexual intercourse

ANALYZE…

3 Brain differences between homosexual and heterosexual adults should be interpreted as:

   A a result of both genetic and environmental factors.

   B due solely to inherited, genetic differences.

   C proof that the brain structure between homosexual men and heterosexual women is identical.

   D due solely to environmental factors.

Answers can be found on page ANS-4.

Module Summary

Now that you have read this module
you should:

KNOW ...

● *The key terminology associated with sexual motivation:*

libido (p. 408)   sexual response cycle (p. 410)
refractory period (p. 411)   testosterone (p. 414)
sexual orientation (p. 412)

UNDERSTAND ...

● *Similarities and differences in sexual responses in men
and women.* The similarities in sexual response cycles
found in men and women can be explained by a common
reproductive physiology in both sexes. However, males
experience a distinct phase called the refractory period,
during which erection or orgasm are not physiologically
possible.

APPLY ...

● *Information from surveys to understand your own
views of sexuality.* People express sexuality for many
different reasons, in different ways, and with varying
frequency. How do you feel about sexuality? You can apply
what we have learned from research to understand if
you take a generally permissive attitude (people have the
right to do what they want) or a more conservative one.
Respond to each of the items below by assigning a score
on a scale from 1 (strongly agree) to 5 (strongly disagree).
Note that it is not necessary to be sexually active to
complete this scale—simply respond to the general
principle of each item.

1. I do not need to be committed to a person to have
   sex with him or her.

2. Casual sex is acceptable.

3. I would like to have sex with many partners.

4. One-night stands are sometimes enjoyable.

5. It is okay to have ongoing sexual relationships with
   more than one person at a time.

6. Sex as a simple exchange of favors is okay if both
   people agree to it.

7. The best sex is with no strings attached.

8. Life would have fewer problems if people could have
   sex more freely.

9. It is possible to enjoy sex with a person and not like
   that person very much.

10. It is okay for sex to be just a good physical release.

Once you have assigned a number to each item, average
your responses to get your overall score. In one study of
slightly more than 200 college students, men averaged a
score of 3.63 and women averaged a score of 4.47 on this
scale (Hendrick et al., 2006). How do you compare? Given
what you have learned about the biological and cultural
factors that influence sexuality, are you surprised by the
gender difference? Which other factors might influence
the norms?

ANALYZE ...

● *Different explanations for what determines sexual
orientation.* Several lines of evidence point to biological
factors contributing to homosexuality. For example,
small differences in brain anatomy are observed between
homosexual and heterosexual males. Exposure to
testosterone in the prenatal environment may contribute
to homosexual orientation as well; homosexuality
has been attributed to low testosterone levels during
prenatal development in males, and exposure to higher
than normal levels of testosterone for homosexual
females. Also, twin studies indicate that homosexuality
has a significant genetic component, particularly in males.
These findings point to biological factors interacting with
environmental ones.

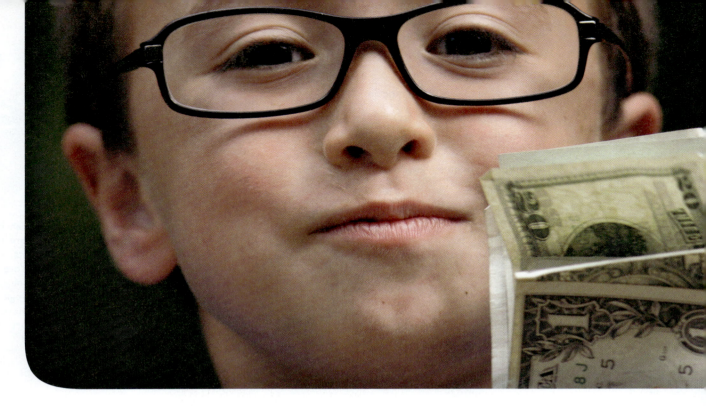

Module 11.3

Social and Achievement Motivation

Learning Objectives	KNOW ...	UNDERSTAND ...	APPLY ...	ANALYZE ...
After reading this module you should:	The key terminology of social and achievement motivation	How people experience a need to belong How thoughts about mortality can motivate people	Theories of motivation to understand your personal motivation to achieve in school or your career	Claims that a sense of belonging is something people *need* versus something they *want*

Most college students have to work, whether they hold a part-time job during the school year, engage in summer work, or even work full-time while taking one or two classes. But how convenient would it be if attending school was a paying job in itself?

Some primary and secondary schools actually have begun to treat school a little more like a job. For example, a group of New York City schools instituted a program that pays students for good grades. Providing monetary incentives for good grades is not anything new; this is something many parents have tried. What is unique about the New York City program is that the parents are not giving out the money. The money, raised privately by a man named Roland Fryer, is distributed to high-performing students who attend relatively poor schools in disadvantaged neighborhoods. Fourth graders can earn as much as $25 for high marks earned on 10 standardized tests. Seventh graders enjoy higher amounts as rewards—as much as $50 per exam. Supporters of the program reason

that the reward system encourages good behavior and helps to reduce poverty—noble causes indeed. These types of systems can be found on a smaller scale in other locations. For example, schools might offer a monetary reward for perfect attendance or for each book read.

Focus Questions

 How critical are incentives in motivating us to achieve?

 Is our intrinsic desire to succeed undermined by incentives?

· · · · · · · · · · · · · · · · · ·

In addition to satisfying basic biological drives, motivation entails meeting our complex social and personal needs. In this module, we explore our motivation for a sense of belongingness and to achieve.

The Need to Belong

Everyone acknowledges that humans require satisfaction of at least a few basic needs for survival, such as adequate food, water, clothing, and shelter. The basic needs that keep the body functioning are fundamental for all species. Other necessities also exist, beginning with the need to have meaningful social relationships and continuing with uniquely human needs for self-esteem and self-actualization (discovering and achieving purpose in life).

Figure 11.10 shows how psychologist Abraham Maslow (1943) conceived of this increasing complexity of motivational needs. At the base of the "hierarchy of needs" are physiological motives that must be satisfied before all others are considered. After these needs are addressed, an individual may turn to higher-level needs such as the need for love and belonging, self-esteem, and achievement. Researchers have explored how and why we are motivated to become affiliated with others, but it was not until recently that psychologists have begun to treat this issue as a "fundamental need to belong"—a need as basic as nourishment and protection (Baumeister & Leary, 1995).

Self-actualization needs: to find self-fulfillment and realize one's potential

Aesthetic needs: symmetry, order, and beauty

Cognitive needs: to know, understand, and explore

Esteem needs: to achieve, be competent, gain approval and recognition

Belongingness and love needs: to be with others, be accepted, and belong

Safety needs: to feel secure and safe, out of danger

Physiological needs: hunger, thirst, fatigue, etc.

{FIG. 11.10} **Maslow's Hierarchy of Needs** According to Abraham Maslow, human needs are organized as a hierarchy, with basic needs at the bottom, and personal fulfillment and other uniquely human characteristics at the top. **Click on this figure in your eText to see more details.**

BELONGING IS A NEED, NOT A WANT

The **need to belong** (sometimes known as *affiliation motivation*) *is the motivation to maintain relationships that involve pleasant feelings such as warmth, affection, appreciation, and mutual concern for each person's well-being.* In addition, an individual must have the sense that these feelings are part of a permanent relationship, such as a friendship, kinship, or shared group membership (Baumeister & Leary, 1995). A strong sense of belonging brings more than warmth and happiness; it appears to be fundamental in the same way that food and shelter are needs—these are all things that humans cannot survive without.

Although we all probably want to have pleasant interactions, it is the second part of the definition—a sense of permanence—that emphasizes the type of needs we have. Specifically, an individual who has many positive social interactions with a series of different individuals does not enjoy the same satisfaction and other benefits as an individual who interacts with only a few people, but regularly and for a long period of time. For example, an executive who flies all over the continent may have fascinating conversations with fellow passengers every week, yet feel extremely lonely. Meanwhile, imagine a couple living on a rural farm who see only a few neighbors during the week and participate in church on weekends. The permanence of their family, community, and church is significant, and they will probably be much more satisfied with their sense of belongingness over the long run.

Psychologists hypothesize that close, permanent relationships are as important as food and water are for normal psychological functioning.

George Clooney's character in *Up in the Air* shunned all permanent relationships, opting instead for brief, passing encounters. He was soon confronted with his own need to belong.

Psychologists have found that social connectedness is a good predictor of overall health, whereas loneliness is a risk factor for illnesses such as heart disease and cancer (Cacioppo et al., 2003). Loneliness elevates a person's risk for having hypertension, a weaker immune system, and high levels of stress hormones. This relationship holds true even when lonely and nonlonely individuals have the same amount of social interaction—it is the sense of belonging that counts (Hawkley et al., 2003). Even very simple indicators such as living alone or an individual's rating of the statement "I feel lonely" predict chances of survival after heart attacks and bypass surgeries (Herlitz et al., 1998; Rozanski et al., 1999). Most people now accept that cigarette smoking has severe direct effects on health, but few recognize that loneliness is equally good at predicting one's life expectancy (House, et al., 1988).

The need to belong is evident from the great lengths to which people go to form and maintain relationships. Generally, friendships and romantic relationships have their foundations in warm feelings and mutual attraction, so we might be tempted to say that people maintain relationships because they are positive experiences. But consider this point: If humans were motivated to form bonds because belonging is pleasant or felt good, what should we expect people to do when a relationship turns unpleasant or even abusive? Statistics suggest that people receiving the abuse are often very reluctant to end their relationships, even if the perceived "good moments" are interspersed with ongoing abuse. Some of this reluctance is explained by well-founded fear of revenge, a sense of financial dependence, or frustration with the services that are available to help (Anderson & Saunders, 2003; Grauwiler, 2008; Kim & Gray, 2008). Why, then, is ending the relationship so difficult to do? This reluctance can be explained in part by the strength of emotional bonds. Breaking an emotional attachment is a difficult

and painful thing to do. In many cases, the breakup involves a period of depression and psychological stress that exceeds the emotional toll of the abuse (Anderson & Saunders, 2003). In short, the need to belong can be so strong that people find it is easier to endure the abuse than to break the bond.

Parenting also illustrates the sacrifices that individuals will make to satisfy their belongingness needs. Children require personal, social, and financial sacrifices, not to mention the physical discomfort associated with pregnancy and labor. Parenthood does not provide the health benefits of other types of relationships, and it can be associated with higher levels of emotional distress and depression and lower levels of marital satisfaction, at least while the children are young (e.g., Evenson & Simon, 2005; Umberson et al., 2010). Despite these inconveniences and the associated emotions, having children is one of the most celebrated aspects of adult life in many cultures—thanks in large part to the need to belong.

The stresses of parenting can actually lead an individual to report lower levels of happiness. However, having children remains one of the most celebrated aspects of adult life.

WORKING THE SCIENTIFIC LITERACY MODEL

Terror Management Theory and the Need to Belong

As far as scientists can tell, humans are unique among life on earth in that we are aware of our own mortality. This realization creates a uniquely human problem that one researcher described very bluntly: If humans are just like any other form of life, then we "may be no more significant or enduring than any individual potato, pineapple, or porcupine" (Pyszczynski et al., 2004, p. 436). This is a provocative way of asking, If we all must die, what makes humans think we are more important than other forms of life? For most people, it is easy to answer this question: Our personal identities, our family and friends, a sense of spiritual or religious purpose, and a sense of nationalism and patriotism distinguish us from pineapples and porcupines. **Terror management theory** *is a psychological perspective asserting that the human fear of mortality motivates behavior, particularly those that preserve self-esteem and sense of belonging.*

What do we know about terror management theory?

Life-threatening experiences certainly are terrifying and emotional. However, we can maintain a sense of calm in our lives because we use *anxiety buffers*—concepts and beliefs that prevent death-related anxiety. These elements include a *worldview*, such as religious and political beliefs, and a sense of self-esteem. Thus the thought of death is a motivation to belong to something more enduring and much larger than oneself. We can rely on spiritual or religious purpose, the future generations of family, or the continuation of our native culture or way of life to bolster our sense of self-worth (Pyszczynski et al., 2004).

How can scientists study terror management?

To measure the motivational power of terror management, researchers induce *mortality salience*—an increased awareness of death—with simple reminders. For example, volunteers may write a paragraph or two about what happens when people die, while a control group writes about something unpleasant that does not make mortality more apparent (salient), such as the discomfort of a root canal or other dental pain. In experiments, simply writing about death is enough to motivate individuals to increasingly defend their own worldview (their spiritual and political beliefs; Weise et al., 2008).

The fact that mortality salience increases defensiveness is one thing, but perhaps even more interesting are the tactics that psychologists have used to reduce the impact of mortality salience. For example, when psychologists followed the mortality salience stimulus by asking participants to think positive thoughts about their parents, the effects of the mortality salience disappeared (Cox et al., 2008). This and other related experimental procedures suggest that belonging to something more permanent—a family, a

community, or a religion—really does help manage death-related anxiety.

Can we critically evaluate this evidence?

When mortality salience research began two decades ago, many critics questioned whether it was really thoughts of death that created these experimental effects, or whether the effects simply represented a reaction to the unpleasantness of the study materials. Terror management theorists quickly responded by pointing out that the same effects do not arise among members of control groups who have been exposed to unpleasant stimuli ranging from dental pain to the anxiety of public speaking. Perhaps just as convincing is the fact that a recent meta-analysis of 277 studies confirmed that responses to mortality salience can be reliably produced in the laboratory (Burke et al., 2010).

Why is this relevant?

These same processes seem to be at work outside of experiments, and can help explain behaviors we see in the news. For example, U.S. voters receiving mortality salient treatments were more likely than others to support President George W. Bush's invasion of Iraq during his 2004 bid for reelection (Cohen et al, 2005), and more willing to accept civilian casualties in the ongoing wars (Pyszczynski et al., 2006). Similarly, Iranian students who experienced mortality salience were more likely to support political violence than Iranian students in a control group. Apparently, mortality salience is a powerful motivator regardless of one's nationality or political persuasion.

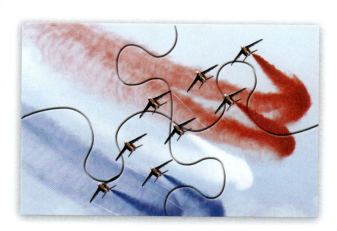

Quick Quiz 11.3a
The Need to Belong

KNOW ...

1 _____ suggests that individuals are motivated to belong to families, religious groups, and nationalities as a means to control their death-related anxiety.

   A Mortality salience

   B Terror management theory

   C Affiliation motivation

   D External motivation

2 Affiliation motivation is:

   A the drive to have as many friends as possible.

   B the desire to be around other people as often as possible.

   C the need to have at least a few permanent meaningful relationships.

   D the desire to be isolated from others.

UNDERSTAND ...

3 What happens when researchers induce mortality salience using essay writing procedures?

   A Participants motivation states are not changed.

   B Participants are increasingly motivated to defend their own worldview.

   C Participants decrease their sense of attachment to their families.

   D Participants are motivated to change their perceptions of death.

ANALYZE ...

4 What point did Maslow intend to communicate when he placed love and belonging in the middle of his hierarchy of needs?

   A Individuals generally must take care of physiological needs first, but must satisfy love and belonging needs before developing healthy self-esteem.

   B Love and belonging are not essential human needs.

   C Individuals generally must first have a healthy self-esteem before they can satisfy love and belonging needs.

   D Love and belonging are more important than physiological needs.

Answers can be found on page ANS-4.

Achievement Motivation

Achievement motivation *is the drive to perform at high levels and to accomplish significant goals.* It often involves the *need to compete* with and outperform other individuals. It can be seen in the *desire to master* a task, with or without other incentives or rewards. Achievement motivation can be observed in a student's approach to school, an entrepreneur's desire to build a business, or an athlete's hopes of winning a gold medal (McClelland, 1985).

Complete the **Survey** *What Motivates You?* at **MyPsychLab**

If you consider your own experiences, you can probably identify situations in which you feel highly motivated and others that fail to get you going. This is a normal part of motivation, and we see wide variation in the amount and type of motivation people experience. For example, **mastery motives** *are motives that reflect a desire to understand or overcome a challenge* (e.g., a genuine desire to *master* a task), whereas **performance motives** *are generally those motives that are geared toward gaining rewards or public recognition.* Another way to contrast motives is to compare approach and avoidance goals. **Approach goals** *are enjoyable and pleasant incentives that we are drawn toward, such as praise or financial reward.* **Avoidance goals** *are unpleasant outcomes such as shame, embarrassment, or emotional pain, which we try to avoid.* If you combine these two perspectives, you will see why some psychologists refer to motivation as a 2×2 framework (see Table 11.3; Elliot & McGregor, 2001).

Have you ever found yourself starting a paper the day before it was due? Or studying for a test into the early morning hours rather than starting your preparation a few days earlier? These types of *procrastination* are highly correlated to the goals in the 2×2 achievement framework. Researchers have found that students are most likely to procrastinate when they are working on avoidance goals. Apparently, it is very difficult to write a term paper if your only motivation is to avoid failing or appearing unintelligent; these motives are very different from actually *wanting* to write a paper. Procrastination is least likely when mastery and approach goals are combined. When students are genuinely interested in learning about a topic and expect to gain something by completing the project, it is much easier for them to get started right away (Howell & Watson, 2007).

As a student, you have probably experienced all of these motivations, finding some subjects so interesting you want to learn more (approach, mastery) and others

This person is clearly procrastinating—there is a good chance that his work is a performance-avoidance goal.

Table 11.3 :: Motivation to Achieve

An individual's motivation to achieve is a combination of two factors: the desire to master something (versus simply performing) and the desire to gain (approach) or avoid something.

	MASTERY: "I WANT TO LEARN THIS …"	PERFORMANCE: "I JUST WANT A GOOD GRADE"
APPROACH	… because it's so interesting.	… so they will know how smart I am.
AVOIDANCE	… because I would hate to feel uninformed.	… so I don't look dumb.

so dull that you would never study them if they were not required for a degree (approach, performance). It might be tempting to assume that you can experience only one form of motivation at a time, but that does not seem to be the case (Elliott & Murayama, 2008). There is no reason why you cannot be motivated to learn and simultaneously experience a motivation to finish your degree.

At the beginning of this module we described a program in New York City that involves paying young students for good test scores. Although the students making the money may not complain, this strategy has been criticized by many people. As you can see from Table 11.3, this program appears to focus far more on performance motives than on mastery motives. From the outset, critics warned that the strategy would not encourage students to enjoy learning, but rather to discover that passing tests is all that is required to receive rewards. They warned that this type of system would not maintain the motivation to pursue and achieve mastery. After all, psychologists have long observed that those who are motivated by intrinsic factors, such as gaining knowledge or experiences for the sake of enjoyment, may actually lose interest in activities if external incentives become available.

BIOPSYCHOSOCIAL PERSPECTIVES

Cultural Differences in Motivation to Achieve

Our discussion of achievement to this point has been neutral when it comes to culture. In reality, what people value in terms of achievement is influenced by culture. For example, whether an individual values the utility of learning a new skill is culturally influenced.

In one investigation, psychologists recruited U.S.-born and East Asian college students who identified themselves as having a low interest in mathematics to participate in a study on achievement motivation. The students read materials about how to use a unique method for computing multiplication problems. Within the instructional materials for the math problems were passages that explained the utility of the technique, including its importance for improving memory and succeeding in graduate school and employment. Half of the participants from each culture participated in this condition, while the second half were assigned to a control group who learned the math technique but did not have the utility of doing so explained to them. All students computed sample problems using the method introduced in the instructional materials and rated whether they found the technique to be useful. The researchers found that in comparison to U.S. students, East Asian students with little interest in math reported greater interest in learning the task, and they tried harder when told it would be useful for future schooling and employment prospects (Shechter et al., 2011). These results do not imply that Westerners do not value skills that will help them succeed. In fact, this same group of researchers found that U.S. students found the math technique to be more valuable if it helped with more immediate demands, such as managing finances and measuring ingredients.

· · · · · · · · · · · · · · · · · · ·

Quick Quiz 11.3b
Achievement Motivation

KNOW …

1 If a student is a pre-med major because he is curious about how the body works and how it recovers from disease, psychologists would say that he has _____ motives. If the student is studying pre-med only because he thinks this major will impress people, then psychologists would say that he has _____ motives.

  A mastery; performance   **C** performance; avoidance
  B performance; mastery   **D** avoidance; mastery

2 People are least likely to procrastinate when they are genuinely interested in the task and believe they can gain something from it. This is known as a(n) _____ goal.

  A mastery-avoidance   **C** performance-avoidance
  B mastery-approach   **D** avoidance-mastery

APPLY …

3 If you are studying math problems because you really want to win an award, psychologists would say you have _____ goals; if you are just hoping that you do not get the lowest score in the class, you are exhibiting _____ goals.

  A avoidance; approach   **C** approach; avoidance
  B approach; mastery   **D** approach; mastery

Answers can be found on page ANS-4.

Module Summary

Now that you have read this module you should:

Listen
to the audio file
of this module at
MyPsychLab

KNOW ...

- **The key terminology of social and achievement motivation:**

achievement motivation (p. 422)
approach goals (p. 422)
avoidance goals (p. 422)
mastery motives (p. 422)

need to belong (p. 419)
performance motives (p. 422)
terror management theory (p. 421)

UNDERSTAND ...

- **How people experience a need to belong.** Psychologists have discovered a number of ways in which people are motivated to enter into personal relationships. People seek out friendships, romantic relationships, and group membership to satisfy this need.

- **How thoughts about mortality can motivate people.** Terror management theory explains that the threat of death can motivate people to become more religious and patriotic, and to bolster their self-esteem. This effect can be seen in a number of studies showing that participants have a more favorable disposition toward their own groups and a more negative attitude toward outsiders.

APPLY ...

- **Theories of motivation to understand your personal motivation to achieve in school or your career.** How would you describe your motivation for school? Are you just trying to earn good grades, or do you find yourself motivated because you are interested in learning? Complete the four brief questionnaires included in **Table 11.4** to see how your motives stack up relative to other students. If you are really motivated to learn, you may want to revisit earlier modules in the text that describe skills and techniques for more effective studying. (Module 6.3 and Module 7.2 may help!)

ANALYZE ...

- **Claims that a sense of belonging is something people need versus something they want.** Although belonging may not be the most basic type of need on the hierarchy of needs—those positions are usually assigned to food, water, and shelter—it is a significant need nonetheless. Research has shown that doing without has some drastic consequences. Not only is loneliness related to depression, but it is also associated with a reduced life span. The fact that belonging is essential to good health and longevity provides strong support for classifying it as a need, not just something people want.

Table 11.4 :: Application Activity

Thinking about your Psychology course, respond to each statement by assigning a score on a scale of 1 ("Not at all true of me") to 7 ("Very true of me"). Then find your average response for each set of three questions. Compare your scores to the averages for each score.

	MASTERY	PERFORMANCE
APPROACH	1. I want to learn as much as possible from this class. 2. It is important for me to understand the content of this course as thoroughly as possible. 3. I desire to completely master the material presented in this class. Average score: 5.52	1. It is important for me to do better than other students. 2. It is important for me to do well compared to others in this class. 3. My goal in this class is to get a better grade than most of the other students. Average score: 4.82
AVOIDANCE	1. I worry that I may not learn all that I possibly could in this class. 2. Sometimes I'm afraid that I may not understand the content of this class as thoroughly as possible. 3. I am often concerned that I may not learn all that there is to learn in this class. Average score: 3.89	1. I just want to avoid doing poorly in this class. 2. My goal in this class is to avoid performing poorly. 3. My fear of performing poorly in this class is often what motivates me. Average score: 4.49

Source: These items and the averages are provided in Elliott & McGregor, 2001.

Emotion

KNOW ...	UNDERSTAND ...	APPLY ...	ANALYZE ...
The key terminology associated with emotion	Different theories of human emotions	Your knowledge of theories of emotion to new examples	Evidence for and against the use of lie detector tests
	Cultural similarities and differences in emotional expressions		

One day, 18-year-old John Sharon and his girlfriend went on a drinking binge and wound up in the Arizona desert. There, John experienced a series of violent seizures. He finally managed to call home for help, but by the time his father arrived, something had changed; John was beginning to think he was God. No, John Sharon was not mentally ill, despite what was presumably a period of delusional thinking. Instead, physicians diagnosed John with temporal lobe epilepsy (TLE).

As neuroscientist V. S. Ramachandran describes it, TLE is a disorder that involves the transmission of sporadic electrical signals through the temporal lobe; this condition often affects the brain's limbic system, which is known to contribute to the experience of emotions. In essence, Ramachandran believes that John's epilepsy occasionally sends a major jolt of energy through the portion of his brain that allows him to experience intense joy. Apparently, the jolt is stronger than a typical brain would ever create, so the only way John can describe his emotional experience

is to say that it is the most beautiful and intense experience imaginable. Just talking about the feelings can actually bring tears to his eyes. Also, rather than perceiving TLE as a disabling condition, John feels sorry for people who cannot share his experiences.

It turns out that John is not alone. Many people have experienced this profound emotional response following TLE seizures and, curiously, they tend to describe them in religious or spiritual terms.

Focus Questions

 What role does the brain play in our emotional experiences?

 How do the labels we give our emotions, such as fear, happiness, and sadness, relate to their corresponding physical sensations?

Like many well-known terms in psychology, emotion is challenging to define scientifically. We will follow common convention in psychology and define **emotion** *as a psychological experience involving three components: (1) subjective thoughts and experiences with (2) accompanying patterns of physical arousal and (3) characteristic behavioral expressions.* For example, anger may involve thoughts and feelings of frustration, aggravation, and possibly ill will. Anger is accompanied by increased heart rate and is expressed with clenched teeth and fists, or tightly pursed lips and a pinched brow. Each of our different emotions is accompanied by characteristic experiences, expressions, and physiological reactions. In this module we explore biological, psychological, and sociocultural influences on our emotional experiences and expressions.

Many of our emotional experiences come from hard-wired responses, and some basic ones such as anger and happiness appear across the human spectrum. See if you can make a prediction: If facial expressions are universal to all humans, which kinds of expressions would you expect to see on the faces of people who have been blind and deaf since birth or very early in life? Would they have the same basic expressions as everyone else, despite the fact that they have never seen a smile or frown,

☑●—⌐ Complete the **Survey** *How Do You Deal with Your Emotions?* at **MyPsychLab**

Children who are born both deaf and blind show the same facial expressions and emotions as people who see and hear. This is one of many pieces of evidence that our emotions have a strong, biological basis.

and never heard laughter or crying? As you can see from the photo, it appears that they do. Because these individuals have not seen or heard these expressions before, it is likely that at least these basic expressions are hard-wired into our genetic makeup, rather than something learned from watching others. ☑

Biology of Emotion

The physiology of emotion involves both the brain and the rest of the body (Rainville et al., 2006). Many of our emotional reactions involve the *autonomic nervous system* (ANS; see Module 3.3), which conveys information between the spinal cord and the blood vessels, glands, and smooth muscles of the body. The ANS maintains processes such as heart rate, respiration, and digestion, which, as you have almost certainly experienced, are also affected by emotional events. Both the ANS and specialized regions of the brain are interconnected in complex ways, giving rise to our *experience* of emotion.

THE AUTONOMIC RESPONSE: FIGHT OR FLIGHT? Let's examine two situations that might provoke fear. First, imagine you are taking a peaceful walk and suddenly encounter a charging, snarling dog. The physiological aspect of this emotional experience would involve a division of the ANS called the *sympathetic nervous system,* which generally increases your energy and alertness to enable you to handle frightening or dangerous situations—that is, it activates the *fight-or-flight response.* This sudden burst of energy involves increased heart rate, respiration, sweat, and alertness. To fuel this response, the sympathetic nervous system draws energy away from bodily functions that can wait until the end of an emergency, such as immune responses and sexual arousal (see Figure 11.11).

Parasympathetic		Sympathetic
Pupils constricted	**Eyes**	Pupils dilated
Salivating	**Mouth**	Dry
No goose bumps	**Skin**	Goose bumps
Dry	**Palms**	Sweaty
Constricted passages	**Lungs**	Dilated passages
Decreased rate	**Heart**	Increased rate
Directed toward internal organs and muscles	**Blood**	Directed to muscles
Decreased activity	**Adrenal glands**	Increased activity
Stimulated	**Digestion**	Inhibited

{FIG. 11.11}   **The Autonomic Nervous System and Emotional Responding**   The ANS is involved in emotional responding. The sympathetic division prepares the body to respond to stress, and the parasympathetic division restores the body to normal conditions.

Autonomic arousal prepares the body to respond to real or perceived threats.

Now imagine a giant auditorium where you are about to give a speech. You may feel anxiety building as audience members trickle in. This situation bears no resemblance to facing down a charging dog, yet your sympathetic nervous system produces many of the same effects. These two scenarios illustrate that similar emotional responses apply to life-threatening situations as well as those that are merely perceived as threatening, such as public speaking.

Once you finish the speech, or when you realize that the dog is tethered to a tree out of reach, you will most likely feel the calming effects regulated by another division of the ANS called the *parasympathetic nervous system*. The parasympathetic nervous system typically uses energy more sparingly, bringing your heart rate and respiration back to resting rates and focusing on non-emergency tasks, such as digestion (Figure 11.11).

The physiological responses we have described thus far mostly apply to what occurs below the neck. This certainly does not diminish their psychological importance—activity in the autonomic nervous system has actually been regarded as sufficient evidence to determine whether someone is being truthful or is lying. In other words, these responses serve as a primary measure used in the polygraph.

PSYCH @ CRIMINAL INVESTIGATIONS

Is the Polygraph a Valid Lie Detector?

The *polygraph*, casually referred to as the "lie detector," measures respiration, blood pressure, and palm sweat—autonomic nervous system responses that should increase when someone lies. Most U.S. courts do not accept polygraph results as valid evidence. Regardless, the system is used in some situations, such as when evaluating statements made by convicted sex offenders, in divorce cases, and occasionally in employee screening and evaluation. Although many support its use, controlled studies of polygraph recordings suggest that they provide evidence of arousal (that is what they are designed to do), but they are not valid indicators of lying (Iacono, 2001; Saxe, 1994).

Some researchers are turning to brain imaging in their search for a more reliable lie detection method (Simpson, 2008). Researchers have reported increased brain activity in regions of the frontal and parietal lobes when subjects are being deceptive, compared to when they tell the truth. In some studies, patterns of brain activity have been used to discriminate false from true statements 78% of the time (Langleben et al., 2005). That level is not perfect, of course, but it suggests this technology is potentially more reliable than the polygraph.

The polygraph measures physiological arousal during a series of questions, some of which are worded specifically to detect whether the subject is lying. But are these devices reliable means of lie detection?

The meaning behind facial expressions changes with subtle modifications. For example, one version of smiling is genuine, while another is reserved for social graces. Can you tell which is which from this photo? Psychologist Paul Ekman (pictured) has discovered many nuances in our facial "microexpressions."

A comparatively inexpensive method of assessing untruthfulness is to examine facial expressions and other non-verbal cues. Paul Ekman and his colleagues found that federal officers and judges, sheriffs, and psychologists are able to detect deception at greater-than-chance levels, and with interest and experience, some individuals seem to be better at spotting lies (Ekman, et al., 1999). In fact, Ekman has shown that people can be trained to detect the very subtle nonverbal "microexpressions" indicative of lying.

· · · · · · · · · · · · · · · · · · ·

THE EMOTIONAL BRAIN: PERCEPTION AND ACTION

Along with responses governed by the ANS, our emotional experiences involve several brain areas, some of which were mentioned in the story that opened this module. For example, the *limbic system* is critical to emotional processing. It includes the hippocampus, hypothalamus, amygdala, and various cortical regions (also described in Module 3.3).

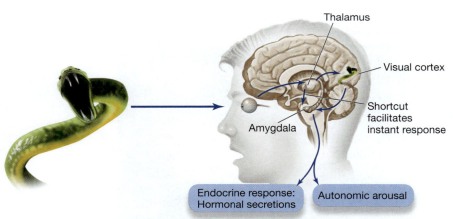

Thalamus

Visual cortex

Shortcut facilitates instant response

Amygdala

Endocrine response: Hormonal secretions

Autonomic arousal

{FIG. 11.12} **Emotion and the Amygdala** The amygdala is a key brain structure in the processing of emotion. Neuroscientist Joseph LeDoux has described this processing as functioning through both "slow" and "fast" pathways. Fast pathways are routed from sensory areas of the brain through the amygdala and directly to the autonomic nervous system for quick action. The slow pathway is routed through the cortex where the situation is processed at a higher level of awareness.

The *amygdala* is of particular interest to scientists who study emotion for two reasons. First, it is involved in assessing and interpreting situations to determine which types of emotions are appropriate. Second, it seems to connect the perception or interpretation of these situations to brain regions that stimulate the physiological responses required for action (Feldman Barrett & Wager, 2006; Sergerie et al., 2008). For example, the amygdala is active when we view any type of threatening stimulus or situation, such as an angry or fearful facial expression. Once a threat is detected, the amygdala stimulates the body into action by sending messages to the sympathetic branch of the ANS, causing increased pulse, respiration, and sweat, as well as by sending messages to motor centers controlling startle or freezing reactions.

Neuroscientists believe that emotional responses such as fear can follow two separate pathways. Sensory information first goes through the thalamus, and then may go directly to the amygdala, which immediately stimulates hormonal and autonomic responses. This route is sometimes called the *fast pathway* because the body is readied for action before the stimulus is even fully perceived and interpreted. Second, the thalamus relays information to the sensory areas of the brain, such as those devoted to vision, which then stimulate the amygdala and physiological responses. This *slow pathway* involves conscious recognition of the stimulus and situation (Figure 11.12). Although it plays a critical role in emotion processing, the amygdala is not the only brain region responsible for our emotions, as patients with amygdala damage continue to have emotional reactions (Anderson & Phelps, 2000).

As you know from John Sharon's story at the beginning of the module, emotions other than fear can arise from electrical activity in the brain. The full range of our emotional experiences involves different areas of the cerebral cortex. Generally speaking, people who are prone to depression and more negative emotion tend to have more activity in the right frontal lobes, whereas people who are prone to happiness and positive emotion tend to have more activity in the left frontal lobe (Urry et al., 2004). Each of our complex, primary emotions, such as fear, anger, happiness, and surprise, seems to involve a component of the limbic system. Even so, it is very difficult to distinguish each emotion just by looking at brain images of a person experiencing that emotion. Brain imaging studies have shown that our emotions involve regions distributed all over the brain (Feldman Barrett & Wager, 2006). Given these details, you probably would not be surprised to find that different forms of epilepsy, other brain diseases, and even brain injuries can lead to changes in emotional processing.

KNOW …

1 The _____ is a set of brain regions involved in emotional processing.

- **A** cortex
- **B** hindbrain
- **C** limbic system
- **D** parietal lobe

2 After narrowly avoiding a car accident, your arousal returns to a baseline state because of activity in the _____.

- **A** sympathetic nervous system
- **B** parasympathetic nervous system
- **C** hypothalamus
- **D** amygdala

ANALYZE …

3 A judge is dismissing evidence based on a lie detector test. What can you conclude about her decision?

- **A** Her decision is wrong because lie detector tests are valid.
- **B** Her decision is correct because lie detector tests are only 99% accurate.
- **C** Her decision is correct because lie detector tests are not sufficiently valid to use as a basis for legal decisions.
- **D** Her decision is wrong because lie detector tests are far more reliable than other techniques for detecting deception, such as brain imaging.

Answers can be found on page ANS-4.

The Psychological Experience of Emotions: Competing Theories

One challenge for psychologists has been to determine the relationship between bodily arousal and the psychological experience of emotion. Imagine you are home alone late at night, and a faint sound comes from the back of the house. Your heart starts to race as you leap from the couch and try to determine whether the noise was just the cat knocking something over, a breeze blowing through an open window, or an intruder breaking into your home. Why did you have this surge of fear and panic? Did the possibility of an intruder cause your heart to race? Or did your racing heart cause you to consider that it could be an intruder? The James-Lange and Cannon-Bard theories of emotion represented early attempts to answer these questions, and both remain relevant to modern-day explanations of our emotions.

THE JAMES-LANGE AND CANNON-BARD THEORIES OF EMOTION According to the **James-Lange theory of emotion**, *our physiological reactions to stimuli (the racing heart) precede and give rise to the emotional experience (the fear)*. Notice that the subjective experience of fear follows the physiological response. The James-Lange theory goes one step further, claiming that your sense of fear is *determined* by how your body responds. This idea may contradict your own common-sense experiences of emotion. It may seem to make more sense that your subjective sense of fear comes first—your heart races *because* you feel frightened. Psychologists Walter Cannon and Philip Bard disagreed with the James-Lange theory on the principle that a physiological reaction cannot give rise to an emotion. Our hearts can race in a variety of situations, even when running up a flight of stairs, so this response alone is not enough to create emotions such as surprise, anger, or fear.

An alternative to the James-Lange theory is the **Cannon-Bard theory of emotion**, *which states that emotions such as fear or happiness occur simultaneously with their physiological components* (Figure 11.13 on p. 430). This may sound like common sense to you. Based on your own emotional experiences, it may seem impossible that a physiological reaction could precede awareness of feeling afraid, happy, surprise, or angry. It might *seem* like common sense that our physiological reactions and awareness of emotional experience occur together. In fact, common sense does not always win out; not all evidence supports the Cannon-Bard theory, either.

The James-Lange theory—that our mental, subjective experiences are influenced by bodily responses that precede them—is consistent with the **facial feedback hypothesis**: *If emotional expressions influence subjective emotional experiences, then the act of forming a facial expression should elicit the specific, corresponding emotion.* In other words, if you are smiling, then you should find things more pleasant. Give this exercise a try (see Figure 11.14 on p. 430): Hold a pencil in your mouth sideways without letting your lips touch it—just your teeth. Research participants who held a pencil in their mouths in this way were essentially smiling whether they meant to or not. As the facial feedback hypothesis predicted, they reported elevated levels of happiness (Strack et al., 1988).

You might argue that the positive emotional experience came from the silliness of holding a pencil in this way. However, psychologists tested a control condition to rule out this hypothesis: Hold the pencil in your mouth using only your lips—do not let your teeth come into contact with the pencil. This is a method of producing a sad face and, sure enough, it leads to decreased mood (Larsen et al, 1992).

Based on these results, it appears that facial feedback affects some of our emotional responses. Not all emotions are affected by facial feedback, however. Take surprise, for

PsychTutor

Click here in your eText for an interactive tutorial on **Basic Emotions**

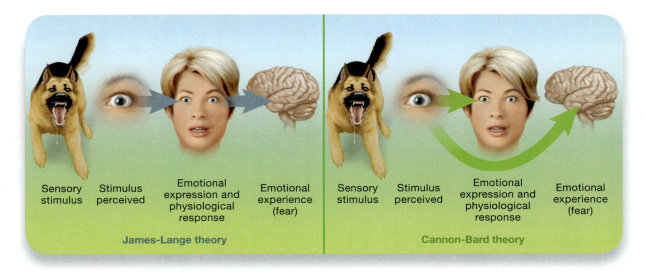

{FIG. 11.13}   **Competing Theories of Emotion**   What is the correct order of events when it comes to emotional experiences? The James-Lange and Cannon-Bard theories differ in their predictions. **Click on this figure in your eText to see more details**.

example. When you are surprised, your eyes widen, your brows rise, and your jaw drops. But surprise is often experienced with very little facial expression, and researchers have shown that the facial feedback hypothesis is not as applicable to surprise as it is to happiness and sadness (Reisenzein & Studtman, 2007). These findings are inconsistent with the James–Lange theory, which predicts that the facial expression would happen *before* the emotion is actually felt. Furthermore, people with spinal cord damage may lack the physiological accompaniments of emotions, but they still report feeling emotions as intensely as they did before their injuries (Cobos et al., 2002).

SCHACHTER'S TWO-FACTOR THEORY   To this point, we have considered only subjective and physiological experiences that accompany emotions. In reality, our emotions also involve thoughts, memories, beliefs, and interpretations of experiences. According

to Stanley Schachter, these cognitive aspects of emotional experiences are critical. Schachter agreed with James and Lange that our physical reactions give rise to our emotional experiences. However, many different emotions can elicit physical arousal, so our interpretation of why we are aroused is what creates the emotional experience. Schachter's **two-factor theory of emotion** *holds that patterns of physical arousal and the cognitive labels we attach to them form the basis of our emotional experiences* (Figure 11.15). Physical arousal is the first factor to come into play (as James and Lange predict), and along with this state comes a cognitive label

(a)   (b)

{FIG. 11.14}   Psychologists have found that inducing a facial expression, such as a frown or a smile, can have mild effects on how people feel. This lends support to the facial feedback hypothesis.

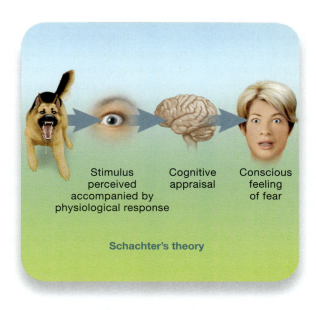

{FIG. 11.15}   **Two-Factor Theory of Emotion**   According to Schachter and Singer, emotions are experiences composed of physiological responses and the cognitive labels we give them.

for the experience, such as "I am afraid." Combining the two factors, the physical and cognitive, gives rise to the emotional experience of fear.

Schachter's theory gives us a more complete account of emotional experience. John Sharon's case from the beginning of the module illustrates this theory in action: John had a bodily experience (intense brain activity caused by the temporal lobe seizure) that resulted in a euphoric, deeply spiritual experience. Looking around the Arizona desert, he saw no clear reason to feel such bliss, so perhaps he concluded that it must be God. This scenario demonstrates that the label we put on emotional experiences frames how we perceive and interpret the experiences.

Quick Quiz 11.4b
The Psychological Experience of Emotions: Competing Theories

UNDERSTAND...

1 Which of the following is a weakness of the James-Lange theory of emotion?

   A Cognitive appraisal is not a component.

   B The theory does not address the subjective feeling of emotion.

   C The theory ignores the role of physiological reactions.

   D Awareness always precedes physiological reactions during emotions.

APPLY ...

2 Joseph's mother tells him to smile more if he wants to feel better. She is applying the _____ theory of emotion.

   A Cannon-Bard   **C** James-Lange

   B two-factor   **D** slow/fast path

3 Steven is paralyzed from the neck down and does not experience the autonomic responses that usually accompany fear. Despite this injury, he continues to experience fear. Which theory of emotion is contradicted by this observation?

   A Cannon-Bard   **C** James-Lange theory

   B Two-factor theory   **D** Physiological theory

Answers can be found on page ANS-4.

The Role of Culture in Emotions

Have you ever traveled to a region where you could not speak the language? If so, you probably found yourself relying on facial expressions and other nonverbal cues to decide whether a local was trustworthy or friendly. Facial expressions probably help a foreign traveler determine who to ask for directions or which vendor to approach or avoid

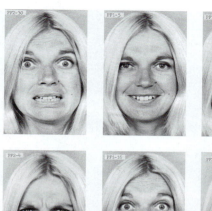
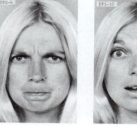
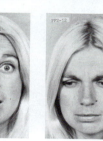

Although this photo spread depicts just one individual, people across many different cultures can accurately identify each emotional expression. Another basic emotion is contempt, which is not as easy to identify from facial expressions.

in a market. Cultural psychologists, and almost any world traveler for that matter, have long known that humans show many similar emotional expressions regardless of their language and background. Researchers have ventured out into some of the most remote regions of the world and confirmed that humans all recognize basic emotions such as fear, anger, happiness, sadness, surprise, and disgust (Ekman et al., 1987; Elfenbein & Ambady, 2003; Izard, 1994).

EMOTIONAL DIALECTS AND DISPLAY RULES
Humans have basic, universal ways of expressing some core emotions. Nevertheless, people raised within a specific culture show characteristics that are specific to their region (Elfenbein & Ambady, 2003). Put simply, cultural groups have unique **emotional dialects**—*which are variations across cultures in how common emotions are expressed.* For example, people from North America and from Gabon (a country in West Africa) both experience contempt. However, North Americans are more likely to lower their brow, and Gabonese people are more likely to raise their upper lip when expressing this emotion.

The situation or context is a major factor in determining when members of different cultures express certain emotions. **Display rules** *refer to the unwritten expectations we have regarding when it is appropriate to show a certain emotion.* Imagine biting into what looks like a delicious chocolate chip cookie that actually turns out to be disgusting. Your expression of disgust would be easily recognized around the world. Now, imagine this event happening in a situation where you are trying to make a good impression—perhaps you are in your instructor's office

Even in the most formal occasions, and even among royalty, it can be impossible to stifle emotions. Web surfers were thrilled to catch England's Prince Harry succumbing to a fit laughter during this formal state ceremony. What could have been so funny?

appealing a grade and she offers you a homemade treat. If it turned out to taste awful, you would likely attempt to inhibit your feeling of disgust. Culture-specific display rules can be found the world over. The British norm of "keeping a stiff upper lip" and the adage "never let them see you sweat" are examples (Elfenbein et al., 2007).

WORKING THE SCIENTIFIC LITERACY MODEL

Cultural Variations in Emotion Interpretation

Even through cultural and language barriers, people recognize a smile or a frown with relative ease. However, interpreting *why* someone is smiling or frowning involves the additional step of interpretation, which can differ among cultures.

What do we know about cultural influences on the interpretation of emotions?

How emotional expressions are interpreted by others can be subtle and complex. In Module 8.1, we discussed how Asian people tend to explain events in terms of how objects are related to one another. For example, a dog might be recognized, first and foremost, as an animal that bonds with humans and is disliked by cats. In contrast, Westerners tend to categorize the world based on a focal object or event—so a dog might first be recognized as a domesticated mammal with canine teeth (Masuda et al., 2008). Do these different ways of thinking translate into differences in how people of various cultures interpret emotions?

How can science explain cultural variations in emotion interpretation?

To answer this question, psychologists asked students from both Western and Asian universities to judge the emotion of the central figure in the scenes depicted in Figure 11.16. Western students tended to focus on the facial expression of the central figure. Thus, if the individual was smiling, they would report he was happy, and they did not interpret his happiness with respect to how the surrounding people appeared to feel. In contrast, Asian students interpreted the central figure's emotion in reference to what people in the background might be feeling (Masuda et al., 2008).

The tendency for Asian students to focus on people in the background was further confirmed in two different ways. First, the participants were later asked whether they recognized the background figures, and Asian students were more accurate than Western students in remembering whether they saw specific individuals in the background.

{FIG. 11.16}   How is the man in the middle of these pictures feeling?

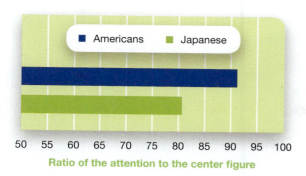

Ratio of the attention to the center figure

{FIG. 11.17} **East–West Differences in Interpreting Emotion** In comparison to Asian people, Westerners spend more time looking at the focal individual in a scene and interpret his or her emotions without reference to surrounding individuals (Masuda et al., 2008).

Also, using a device that tracks the actual eye movements of the participants, the researchers discovered that Asian students spent more time actually looking at the entire picture, rather than just the central character (Figure 11.17; Masuda et al., 2008).

Can we critically evaluate these findings?

Our emotional expressions include many components that we attend to, including context, facial expressions, body posture, and tone of voice. Given these additional elements, it would seem reasonable to ask whether findings from looking at a picture in a laboratory experiment actually apply to more complex situations that include movement and sounds and other events that are missing from the still pictures. In fact, some evidence indicates that similar results would be found when listening to voices. For instance, Japanese people have been observed not only to attend to facial expressions when interpreting emotion, but also to pay particularly close attention to tone of voice (Tanaka et al., 2010).

Why is this relevant?

Display rules emerge within a culture because reading and understanding emotional expressions can be such an important part of socializing. Although cross-cultural research demonstrates that all people share some common core emotions, the existence of emotional dialects and display

rules can complicate the interpretation of emotions in people who may be unfamiliar. Indeed, people's accuracy in interpreting the emotional expressions of people from different cultures can be much lower in comparison to their interpretation of the expressions of members of their own culture (Elfenbein & Ambady, 2002). Thus culturally-based display rules and emotional dialects can also lead to misunderstandings when cultures clash. Awareness of this possibility should be elevated when traveling to an unfamiliar place or when hosting guests from afar.

Quick Quiz 11.4c
The Role of Culture in Emotions

KNOW …

1 A(n) _____ refers to when it is appropriate to show a specific emotion.

   Ⓐ emotional dialect   Ⓒ context rule
   Ⓑ display rule   Ⓓ display dialect

UNDERSTAND …

2 Which of the following is an example of an emotional dialect?

   Ⓐ Experiencing anger
   Ⓑ Avoiding laughter in church
   Ⓒ Raising one's chin in contempt
   Ⓓ Smiling as a sign of happiness

3 Which of the following is an example of a display rule?

   Ⓐ Biting one's lip in embarrassment
   Ⓑ Dropping one's jaw in surprise
   Ⓒ Suppressing anger during a debate
   Ⓓ Expressing happiness to a loved one

Answers can be found on page ANS-4.

Module Summary

Now that you have read this module you should:

((•— Listen
to the audio file
of this module at
MyPsychLab

KNOW ...

● **The key terminology associated with emotion:**

Cannon-Bard theory of emotion (p. 429)

display rules (p. 431)

emotion (p. 426)

emotional dialects (p. 431)

facial feedback hypothesis (p. 429)

James-Lange theory of emotion (p. 429)

two-factor theory of emotion (p. 430)

UNDERSTAND ...

● **Different theories of human emotions.** For decades, scientists have sought a solid theory of human emotion. By now you should be able to explain three primary attempts to explain this phenomenon. The James-Lange theory predicts that physiological responses such as a racing heart will precede the emotional experience, such as fear. In contrast, the Cannon-Bard theory predicts that both physiology and the emotional experiences will occur together. Two-factor theory incorporates a cognitive component of appraisal. First, we have a physiological reaction to a stimulus or situation, next we appraise it by determining which emotion is appropriate, and then comes the conscious experience of the emotion we label as fear, anger, happiness, or whatever it may be.

● **Cultural similarities and differences in emotional expressions.** Whichever theory best applies, emotions such as fear, anger, happiness, sadness, surprise, and disgust appear to be human universals—all people experience them regardless of culture. At the same time, we cannot completely explain human emotions without references to cultural variation in the form of dialects and display rules.

APPLY ...

● **Your knowledge of theories of emotion to new examples.** Give this exercise a try. Spend 10 seconds looking at the Sanskrit figure on the left in **Figure 11.18** while slowly nodding your head. Now, spend about 10 seconds looking at the figure on the right while slowly moving your head from side to side.

{FIG. 11.18} **Application Activity**

Now, imagine that you had to choose one image to display on the wall of your home. Which one would you choose—the one on the left or the one on the right?

What is important about this exercise is not which figure you chose; rather, it is the application of emotion theories to the problem. Consider the facial feedback study, and try to explain how the head movements could potentially influence one's preference for a symbol. This module provided examples of what researchers have found using similar techniques.

ANALYZE ...

● **Evidence for and against the use of lie detector tests.** For decades, the polygraph has been used as a method for lie detection. Scientists have scrutinized the test to evaluate its validity as a reliable detector of truthfulness and deception. The modern consensus is that the polygraph reliably measures physiological arousal, but does not achieve a universally acceptable level of accuracy in detecting lies.

Module 11.1 :: Hunger and Eating

Focus Questions:

1 **What are some ways that our physical and social environments affect eating?** Eating is the product of psychological and social processes. The simple availability of food—especially a variety of foods—can increase hunger. People tend to eat whatever portions are served based on the assumption that one scoop or one package makes a reasonable serving size. Meanwhile, being around other people may cause us to eat either more or less than we normally would, depending on the behavior of others and the context.

2 **What makes us feel hungry or full?** If you assumed that a growling stomach causes hunger, research shows you would be at least partially correct. At the same time, the physiology of hunger also involves glucose, insulin, ghrelin, and CCK—as well as the subregions within the hypothalamus that serve as on/off switches for hunger.

👁—**Watch** *In the Real World Application: Eating Disorders* in the **MyPsychLab video series**

Module 11.2 :: Sexual Motivation

Focus Questions:

1 **How do psychologists explain the diverse sexual motivations of humans?** This question can be answered from several different points of view, including the psychological and biological perspectives. First, people offer many different reasons for having sex—including personal and social motives and, of course, for reproduction. Second, from a biological perspective, researchers have identified the basic physiological processes that occur during arousal and sex.

2 **How do psychologists explain variations in sexual orientation?** No definitive scientific explanation for variations in sexual orientation has been advanced. Twin studies do suggest a genetic contribution, and some intriguing neurological differences between homosexual and heterosexual people have been found. Furthermore, hormone levels, particularly during prenatal development, appear to influence sexual orientation. Psychologists do know that homosexuality *cannot* be explained by having incidental same-sex experiences when young.

👁—**Watch** *The Big Picture: What Drives Us?* in the **MyPsychLab video series**

Module 11.3 :: Social and Achievement Motivation

Focus Questions:

1 **How critical are incentives in motivating us to achieve?** As the research shows, several types of motives for achievement exist, and incentives are just one way to foster motivation. People may also be motivated to avoid negative consequences, or simply because they enjoy the challenge.

2 **Is our intrinsic desire to succeed undermined by incentives?** When comparing these different motivational states, psychologists have found that people who are intrinsically motivated put forth more effort and are less frustrated when they encounter setbacks. Those who are working solely to achieve incentives may not take the correct path to get there. For example, students who are interested only in the outcome of their work might be tempted to cheat to get good grades.

👁—**Watch** *What's in It for Me? Meeting Our Needs* in the **MyPsychLab video series**

Module 11.4 :: Emotion

Focus Questions:

1 **What role does the brain play in our emotional experiences?** The structures and circuitry of the limbic system underlie the brain basis of our emotions. Many of the structures of the limbic system, including the amygdala, are located in the temporal lobes. Under normal circumstances, the limbic system is involved in both expressing emotions, such as feeling afraid, and inhibiting emotions, such as attempting to stifle smiling and laughter. The amygdala is involved in processing emotional reactions and stimulating the autonomic nervous system to react.

2 **How do the labels we give our emotions, such as fear, happiness, and sadness, relate to their corresponding physical sensations?** The primary emotions described in this module include fear, happiness, sadness, anger, disgust, and surprise. Each gives rise to different physical experiences, although we may also have mixed emotions, such as feeling happy and sad at the same time. The relationships between the physical sensations that accompany emotions, our appraisal of the situation, and the labels we use to describe our reactions constitute the basics of emotional experience.

👁—**Watch** *The Basics: Theories of Emotion and Motivation* in the **MyPsychLab video series**

1 Gerald is trying to watch how much he eats and avoid eating junk food. According to your text, what can he do to reduce his craving for cookies when he is craving them?

A Try to ignore the craving

B Imagine visual images that have nothing to do with food.

C Stand on his head

D Stick himself in the arm with a pin

2 In general, what effect does the presence of other people have on the amount of food an individual eats?

A The presence of others makes people eat less.

B The presence of others makes people eat more.

C The presence of others has no effect on the amount people typically eat.

D The presence of others can make people eat more or less than usual, depending on the situation.

3 Alfred Kinsey is famous for being one of the first scientists to study _____.

A human sexuality   C peer pressure

B obesity in children   D facial expressions

4 Researchers have found that homosexual men tend to have a greater number of older brothers than heterosexual men. Which hypothesis has been proposed to account for this finding?

A The mother's immune system is exposed to male-specific proteins during pregnancy, which then limits the amount of testosterone available during later pregnancies.

B Parents tend to deemphasize masculinity in young sons if they already have several sons.

C Being raised with older male brothers influences the developing sexuality of male children.

D Younger brothers eventually inherit a gene that predisposes them to homosexuality.

5 Which of the following factors increases an individual's risk for illness, heart disease, and even cancer?

A Mortality salience

B Loneliness

C Performance motives

D Avoidance goals

6 Louis practices shooting baskets after school because he doesn't want his friends to make fun of him for being bad at basketball. Louis's motivation to practice is most accurately described as driven by a(n) _____ goal.

A shame   C avoidance

B mastery   D approach

7 Many people who have temporal lobe epilepsy describe the seizures as _____.

A painful

B "raw fear"

C out-of-body experiences

D religious experiences

8 Controlled studies of polygraph recordings indicate that they should be most accurately described as detecting _____.

A parasympathetic activity

B lies

C arousal

D negative emotions

9 Gillian drinks a lot of coffee while studying all night. The caffeine in the coffee causes Gillian's heart to start racing and her hands to begin shaking. Suddenly, Gillian begins to feel fear and anxiety for no apparent reason. Gillian's experience is best explained by which theory of emotions?

A Maslow's hierarchy of needs

B James-Lange theory of emotion

C Facial feedback

D Cannon-Bard theory

10 Which of the following statements is true about how humans display emotions?

A While some basic emotions are universally recognized, different cultures have unique ways of displaying some emotions.

B All emotional displays are understood across all cultures.

C There are no emotional displays that are universally understood across all cultures.

D Emotional displays are determined by context, but not by culture.

What do we know about theories of emotion?

Figures 11.13 and **11.14 on page 430** review the three major theories of emotion covered in this chapter. If you are trying to differentiate between them, it may help to remember that they vary in the order of the various responses. According to the James-Lange theory, if you saw an aggressive dog (stimulus), your heart would race (physiological response) and you would feel fear (emotional response). But according to the Cannon-Bard theory, you would see the aggressive dog (stimulus), and then experience a racing heart and a feeling of fear simultaneously (physiological and emotional response). In the cognitive category, Schacter-Singer's two-factor theory holds that the dog (stimulus) would cause your heart to race (physiological response); you would label that response "I am afraid" (cognitive response) and then feel fear (emotional response).

A common thread running through these theories is the agreement on the biological basis for emotional responding. The limbic system is a key player in the body's response to a stimulus, and specialized structures in the brain stimulate the body by sending messages to the autonomic nervous system **(Figure 11.11 on page 426)**

Why is this relevant?

Watch the accompanying video excerpt on the theories of motivation and emotion. You can access the video at MyPsychLab or by clicking the play button in the center of your eText. If your instructor assigns this video as a homework activity, you will find additional content to help you in MyPsychLab. You can also view the video by using your smart phone and the QR code below, or you can go to the YouTube link provided.

After you have read this chapter and watched the video, imagine you are walking alone late at night and hear footsteps behind you. Think about your emotional reaction to this situation. Consider the major theories of emotion: James-Lange theory, Cannon-Bard theory, and Schacter-Singer theory. From the perspective of these major theories of emotion, describe how each would predict the sequence of events that would occur as you experience a reaction to this situation.

How can science help explain emotional responses?

As discussed on **page 429**, research on the facial feedback hypothesis supports the idea that our emotional responses are influenced by the bodily processes that precede them. When we smile, mood can be elevated and when we frown, mood can be dampened. Nevertheless, research also shows that people with certain types of spinal cord damage, who lack a sympathetic nervous system response, can still feel a full range of emotions. Thus, a physiological response does not always precede an emotional experience.

Brain imaging studies suggest that all of the emotions we feel regularly involve components of the limbic system, and that certain areas of the brain are more active depending on the emotion being experienced. Research (described on **page 428**) shows that people with depression have more brain activity in the right frontal lobe, whereas people prone to positive thoughts have more activity in the left frontal lobe.

Emotional experience is also influenced by cultural factors. Scientists have observed some emotions across all cultures, although emotional dialects and display rules alter how and when they are expressed.

Can we critically evaluate claims about emotional responses?

While the facial feedback hypothesis provides some support for the James-Lange theory of emotion, the fact that some emotions can be experienced in the absence of facial expression seems inconsistent with the theory, as is the fact that people who cannot experience physiological responses can still feel emotion. Also, in a development related to the physiology of emotions, investigators have often relied on responses of the autonomic nervous system (measured by a polygraph) as a "lie detector test." When we explored the polygraph in **Psych @ Criminal Investigations on page 427**, we asked whether a polygraph can actually tell if someone is lying. If someone perspires during a polygraph test, does that mean he or she has something to hide? While polygraphs do, indeed, provide evidence of physiological arousal, there is no evidence that they can reliably prove or disprove when someone is lying. By comparison, brain imaging research has led to a higher success rate showing patterns between brain activity and lying, although so far this rate is only approximately 78%.

youtube.com/
scientificliteracy

MyPsychLab

Your turn to Work the Scientific Literacy Model: You can access the video at MyPsychLab or by clicking the play button in the center of your eText. If your instructor assigns this video as a homework activity, you will find additional content to help you at MyPsychLab. You can also view the video by using your smart phone and the QR code, or you can go to the YouTube link provided.

12 :: PERSONALITY

Contemporary Approaches to Personality

KNOW ...	UNDERSTAND ...	APPLY ...	ANALYZE ...
The key terminology associated with contemporary approaches to personality	The behaviorist and social-cognitive views of personality	The Big Five personality traits to understand your own personality	The strengths and weaknesses of trait theories
			The relative roles of personality traits and psychological and physical states in determining behavior

What does your living space say about you? That alphabetized bookshelf and bathroom full of grooming products suggest conscientiousness. The photos of Mount Everest and major European cities reveal an openness to experiencing new and exciting things. The three pet cats and extensive DVD collection? Possibly signs of an introverted homebody.

It might sound like we are just making assumptions here, but it turns out scientific research backs up the notion that personality can be measured by examining the details of our dwellings. Psychologist Sam Gosling and his students have, with permission, closely scrutinized people's offices and bedrooms for clues about their personality (Gosling, 2008; Gosling et al., 2002). Teams of seven or eight observers entered people's bedrooms and offices and rated the personality types of the occupants with a standardized personality test. Not only did the observers reach close consensus on many measures of personality, but their ratings also matched up with how the occupants rated their *own* personality. You may be looking around at your own room now—and one thing that might come to mind is that some belongings have been there a very long time and symbolize the "core" of who you are. Other clues, such as the clothing strewn all

over the floor, may simply reflect that you lead a busy life. Either way, your personal surroundings reveal important information about you. These findings lead to some important questions we will address in this module.

Focus Questions

 What are the basic traits that make up human personality?

 To what extent are our preferences, thoughts, and behaviors determined by situational factors versus more stable personality traits?

· · · · · · · · · · · · · · · · · ·

Personality *is a characteristic pattern of thinking, interacting, and reacting that is unique to each individual, and remains relatively consistent over time and situations.* Psychologists have long searched for a theory of personality that would describe and explain how people develop these patterns of behaviors, but the search has proven to be very challenging. The first two modules in this chapter focus on contemporary, scientific research on personality. In Module 12.3, we will offer some historical perspectives that lack scientific rigor, but provide a sense of how far the field of personality psychology has come.

Some psychologists study personality by using an **idiographic approach**, *meaning that they focus on creating detailed descriptions of individuals and their unique personality characteristics.* An idiographic approach might involve focusing on a rare type of individual. Such an investigation could range from a detailed study of a serial killer to a profile of someone with an exceptionally creative talent. However, the idiographic approach can actually be applied to anyone. What makes the idiographic approach distinct is that is it person centered, and might include how an individual perceives his or her own personality, as well as how others perceive that individual's personality (Carlson, et al., 2010).

In contrast to psychologists who adopt the idiographic approach, other psychologists are interested in describing personality in terms that can apply to any member of the population. After all, if we can understand which characteristics are typical, then we can better understand what makes individuals unique. Which traits do all people seem to have? What proportion of a group is shy or outgoing? These questions reflect a **nomothetic approach**, *which examines personality in large groups of people, with the aim of making generalizations about personality structure.* One advantage of the nomothetic approach is that it allows psychologists to ask questions about the genetic and cultural basis of personality traits, a topic we will explore in the next module.

The difference between the idiographic and nomothetic approaches is sometimes unclear, because they share some similarities (Grice et al., 2006). Even so, psychologists—especially those who want to know general characteristics about personality—find the distinction useful. In this module, we focus on the nomothetic approach to personality, which typically relies on descriptive labels to identify individuals' patterns of behavior—shy versus outgoing, optimistic versus pessimistic, and so on. Thousands of adjectives may be applied to describe personality, but which ones can best be used to describe people?

The Trait Perspective

Several decades ago, some very patient psychologists tallied nearly 18,000 English words that could be used to describe an individual's physical and psychological attributes (Allport & Odbert, 1936). One reason for searching out these thousands of terms was to identify potential **personality traits**, *which are labels applied to specific attributes of personality, such as "shy," "cheerful," "outgoing," and "adventurous."* According to the trait approach, we can understand individuals—and what makes them alike or sets them apart—based on how well each of these traits describes that person. To accomplish this labeling, trait researchers have devised a variety of personality tests. Some tests present a list of trait labels and ask an individual to rate how well the trait describes him or her. Other measures of personality present specific behaviors that represent traits. Items on these kinds of personality tests might, for example, ask you to rate your agreement with statements such as "I like to meet new people" to assess how outgoing you are.

The advantage of measuring traits through personality tests is that individuals can be described as scoring high or low on a specific trait. As a consequence, we can compare and contrast individual personalities: Whereas one student might be considered outgoing and talkative, for example, his roommate might be considered quiet, shy, and reserved. Of course, a potential problem with this approach is that we cannot expect to understand personality if we have to consider the applicability of 18,000 attributes for each individual. A technique called **factor analysis** *reveals statistical similarities among a wide variety of items.* For instance, when applied to personality descriptors, the terms *friendly*, *warm*, and *kind* have very similar meanings. These related traits can be grouped in a cluster, referred to as a *factor*. The factors derived from this analysis comprise broad personality trait labels, such as *extraversion*, that psychologists use when measuring personality.

THE FIVE FACTOR MODEL Using factor analysis, psychologist Raymond Cattell (1946) narrowed the list of key personality traits to 16, thereby simplifying and standardizing the number of dimensions psychologists needed to describe the composition of personality. But even 16 factors might be more than we need to describe personality. McCrae and Costa (1987), creators of the *NEO Personality Inventory*, found that personality could be reduced to five major dimensions called the **Five Factor Model** (or just the Big Five personality factors) *which is a trait-based approach to personality measurement that includes extraversion, emotional stability (also referred to by the opposite quality, neuroticism), conscientiousness, agreeableness, and openness* (see Figure 12.1). The Five Factor Model is probably the most popular of the trait-based approaches, and it has been cited in hundreds of research articles.

PsychTutor

Click here in your eText for an interactive tutorial on **The Big Five**

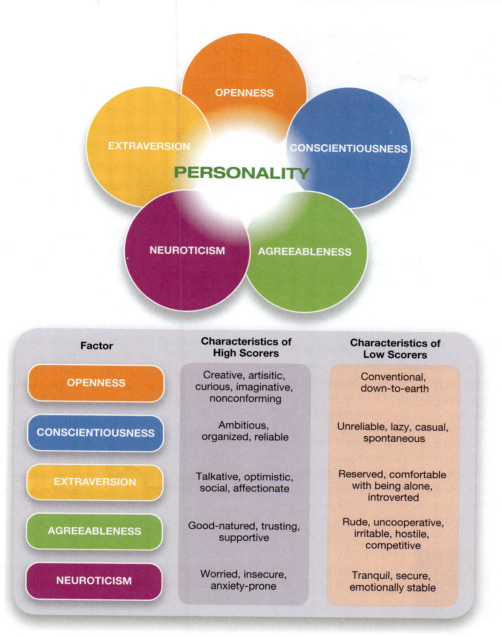

Factor	Characteristics of High Scorers	Characteristics of Low Scorers
OPENNESS	Creative, artisitic, curious, imaginative, nonconforming	Conventional, down-to-earth
CONSCIENTIOUSNESS	Ambitious, organized, reliable	Unreliable, lazy, casual, spontaneous
EXTRAVERSION	Talkative, optimistic, social, affectionate	Reserved, comfortable with being alone, introverted
AGREEABLENESS	Good-natured, trusting, supportive	Rude, uncooperative, irritable, hostile, competitive
NEUROTICISM	Worried, insecure, anxiety-prone	Tranquil, secure, emotionally stable

{FIG. 12.1} **The Big Five Personality Dimensions** A widely used measure of personality is the NEO PI-R. Typically, people rate themselves on multiple questions that measure the traits of openness, conscientiousness, extraversion, agreeableness, and neuroticism. (To help you remember the Big Five, note that the first letters of the traits spell out OCEAN.)

Responses on the Big Five can predict many real-world behaviors. For example, extraverted people tend to report happier moods than do introverts (Lischetzke & Eid, 2006), and extraverted college students are likely to achieve high status in student groups such as fraternities and sororities (Anderson et al., 2001). On the downside, extraverts are more prone to risk taking and substance abuse problems (Martsh & Miller, 1997). Conscientious individuals, however, are likely to have positive health-related behaviors, longevity, and higher levels of achievement (Chamorro-Premuzic & Furnham, 2003; Roberts et al., 2005). Thus the Big Five are not just important for describing individuals, but are also useful for understanding people's behavior, thoughts, and emotions. It is encouraging that what people report about their personalities generally corresponds to their actual behavior. However, a separate but related issue is whether people accurately portray what they are like to other people.

WORKING THE SCIENTIFIC LITERACY MODEL
How Accurate Are Self-Ratings?

Self-reports of personality are relatively accurate predictors of actual behavior—but this correlation does depend on test takers portraying themselves accurately. For this reason, it is important for researchers to ask, Do people tend to present themselves as they really are on such tests, or do they present an idealized version of themselves?

What do we know about personality and self-presentation?

Social networking sites such as Facebook provide ample opportunities for people to publicly express what they are really like, but people could almost as easily project what they *want* to be like. In an effort to put their best foot forward, people may be tempted to mislead others (Toma et al., 2008). A few short hikes a year might translate into an interest in "mountaineering," and a "well-read" individual might simply have a stack of *People* magazines and a few mystery novels on the coffee table. If the person in question happens to be your best friend, you might know the truth, but the dozens or hundreds of casual "friends" on the networking site might be misled. So how can we know whether people are accurate in their self-presentations on such sites?

How can science determine whether people provide accurate characterizations of their personality?

A group of psychologists rated personality traits from the profiles of 236 people who use online social network sites, including Facebook (Back et al., 2010). The participants were young adults who were asked to give honest ratings of themselves on the Big Five dimensions. They took a similar personality test and were asked to "describe yourself as you ideally would like to be." The students allowed the researchers to view their personal online profiles, which the researchers then used to rate the participants' personalities. It turns out that the researchers' personality ratings based on the participants' network profiles matched up with how the participants rated themselves. In contrast, the ratings by the researchers did not match up with what the participants rated as their ideal personalities. Thus the participants expressed who they really were, rather than presenting idealized versions of themselves in their online profiles. In other words, extraverts came across as extraverts, and introverts as introverts, on online social networking sites. This study mirrors a similar one showing that people accurately portray what they are like on their personal websites (Vazire & Gosling, 2004).

Can we critically evaluate this research?

The Facebook study was done exclusively on college students and community volunteers aged 17 to 22 years. Thus there is a limit to how far the results can be generalized to others. Perhaps high school students or older adults use Facebook differently than college-aged students. Also, not everyone would agree to allow a team of psychologists to examine his or her social networking information. Perhaps individuals who are prone to presenting an idealized version of themselves would avoid participating in this kind of study. Of course, Facebook is also just one of many different activities available to us in the ever-growing digital sphere. What researchers find about Facebook may not generalize to all forms of digital communication and entertainment.

Why is this relevant?

Perhaps you can take some comfort in the findings of the Facebook study—though you should not be surprised to find that a friend or two in your network are exceptions. If you participate in a social networking site, you might want to revisit your postings and see whether you think you have portrayed yourself accurately, as the study described would predict, or whether a hint of idealization has crept into your profile. Also, if your life is an open book to the online world, you might keep in mind that many potential employers, even if they are not advised to do so, search the Internet for additional information on job applicants. Is the portrayal of your online self appropriate?

While young adults seem to post accurate self-descriptions on social networking sites, the same may not be true for other types of electronic media.

PSYCH @
The Virtual World

Many popular video games put players in a virtual world where characters are created and controlled by the gamer. In the game *World of Warcraft*, for example, players construct a character who has a profession, a physical appearance, and personality characteristics. This character then navigates through its virtual world interacting with other characters, gains resources, and attempts to defeat monsters. This venue offers a chance for players to create an avatar having attributes they wish they had—an idealized version of the self.

Psychologists gathered up a sample of *World of Warcraft* players and asked them to take two versions of the Big Five personality inventory: a standard version and an idealized version similar to the one described on page 441 (Bessiere et al., 2007). The gamers also answered questions about the personality of their *World of Warcraft* character. It turns out that the characters created in *World of Warcraft* have qualities that were more similar to an idealized version of the self, particularly along the dimensions of extraversion, neuroticism, and conscientiousness. Another interesting finding was that players who reported having low psychological well-being, particularly depression, were especially prone to creating an idealized self. It appears that in contrast to Facebook, the gaming venue is seen as an appropriate outlet for indulging in a little fantasy about the self.

Gamers may use the virtual world to create idealized versions of themselves.

PERSONALITY TRAITS OVER THE LIFE SPAN   One issue that psychologists have long pondered is whether personality traits are fixed or whether they change significantly over the life span. To address that question, we should consider personality from its beginnings. Newborn infants typically are not described with the same range of adjectives that we use for adults; adults may be thought of as talkative, ambitious, greedy, and arrogant, whereas infants probably are not. However, within their first few months of life, infants do show the beginnings of personality characteristics. As described in Module 10.2, *temperament* refers to personality-like attributes that appear to be present at birth, and includes such characteristics as activity level, mood, attention span. and distractibility (Rothbart & Bates, 2006; Thomas & Chess, 1977). Some infants are generally active and happy, whereas others are more tranquil and still others are easily upset. If traits are stable, long-term characteristics, then we would expect to find that temperament is a good predictor of adult personality. To some extent, this is the case: Infant temperament predicts the adult personality traits of neuroticism, extraversion, and conscientiousness (Evans & Rothbart, 2007). The temperament styles found in infancy seem to represent an innate, biological basis upon which personality is built.

Just because there is consistency between temperament and personality does not mean that personality cannot change. Young adults tend to experience fewer negative emotions than do adolescents, reflecting decreases in neuroticism (Donnellan et al., 2007). In addition, emotional stability, conscientiousness, agreeableness, and social dominance (an aspect of extraversion) all increase in early adulthood (Roberts et al, 2006; see Figure 12.2 on p. 444). Later in life, self-ratings of personality traits remain remarkably consistent. In one meta-analysis (an analysis of multiple already published studies), researchers compiled data from 152 studies involving more than 50,000 participants who were tracked for at least one year. Children in this study were found to be less stable in their personality traits, but by middle age people showed relatively little change in their personality traits over time (Roberts & Del Vecchio, 2000).

PERSONALITY TRAITS AND STATES   Trait labels may go a long way toward describing what people are like. However, many psychologists are quick to point out that no matter how useful traits may seem, people's behavior is also determined by situational factors and context. You may know someone whom you would describe as very calm and tranquil, yet when the restaurant waiter brings him the wrong dish he loudly protests. Definitions of personality typically include an element of consistency, but this does

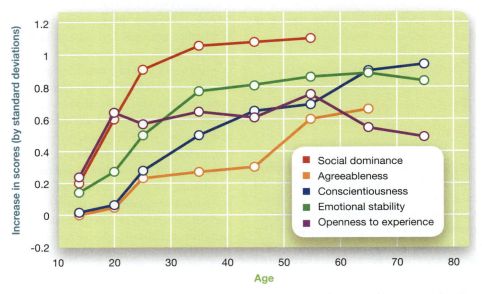

{FIG. 12.2} **Personality Stability and Change over the Life Span** Average scores of emotional stability, conscientiousness, agreeableness, and social dominance (an aspect of extraversion) all increase through adulthood. Openness to experience generally rises through early adulthood and remains steady through the life span (Roberts et al., 2006).

not mean that people are always consistent in the ways they behave. In contrast to a personality trait, a **state** *is a temporary physical or psychological engagement that influences behavior.* Perhaps your normally calm friend lashed out at the waiter because he was hungry to the point of irritability. In this case, the situation motivates his behavior more than his usual calm demeanor—something that is not unusual. Even people who seem so consistent in how they express their neuroticism, agreeableness, or extraversion will not behave in the same way across all situations, and this observation has led to some strong criticisms of trait theories of personality (Mischel, 1968; Mischel & Shoda, 1998).

How states and situational factors influence our behavior is a challenging topic. How many different situations or states do you find yourself in during any particular day? You can be awake or asleep, confident or unsure, you may have money or no money, and you may be in a crisis situation or completely relaxed. The list could go on forever—and as you might have guessed, psychologists have tried to see just how long it goes. In one study, 77 college students were asked to describe as many situations they might encounter at any given time. Their total reached more than 7,000. Perhaps you can now see why many psychologists would rather focus on five personality dimensions. Fortunately, Saucier and colleagues (2007) took these 7,000 situations and reduced them to 4 general aspects of situations that are most likely to influence our behavior:

1. Locations (e.g., being at work, school, or home)
2. Associations (e.g., being with friends, alone, or with family)

3. Activities (e.g., awake, rushed, studying)
4. Subjective states (e.g., mad, sick, drunk, happy)

These situations influence how and when our personality traits are expressed. Identifying these situations is important because they contribute to our psychological states, and they interact with personality traits to determine our behavior.

NORMAL AND ABNORMAL PERSONALITY: THE MMPI-2 As you have read, the Big Five traits present a model of normal personality. In other words, this model can be applied to describe how most individuals behave in a variety of situations. In addition to these "normal" traits, personality psychologists are interested in the range of traits that predispose people to experience psychological problems. Identifying them is the goal of

In some situations—such as boot camp—individual personality traits are hidden as the situation makes increasing demands on how to behave.

tests such as the **Minnesota Multiphasic Personality Inventory (MMPI-2)**, *a multiple-question personality inventory that is used to characterize both normal personality dimensions and profiles that fit various psychological disorders* (something we will cover in greater detail in Chapters 13 and 14). The MMPI-2 provides a multidimensional profile of each individual who completes it. As you can see in Figure 12.3, profiles such as *schizophrenia* and *psychopathic deviancy* are included in the MMPI.

The main purpose of the MMPI is to discriminate between "normal" and "abnormal" characteristics. While tests of the Big Five have been constructed with specific traits in mind, the developers of the MMPI took a very different approach; specifically, they did not construct the items on the MMPI to resemble specific traits in any obvious way. Instead, the researchers identified a set of individuals who had been diagnosed with a variety of psychological disorders and asked them to respond to hundreds of true/false items on a personality inventory. Then they asked people in a sample taken from the general population to do the same. Researchers identified a number of response patterns among individuals with disorders that did not occur in the general sample. These patterns or profiles are now used to identify individuals whose personality is associated with a variety of psychological problems.

The MMPI is widely used for psychological evaluation, where the intent is to treat individuals who may potentially have mental problems. However, it has created some controversy when used for other purposes. In at least two court cases (*Karraker v. Rent-A-Center, Inc.* and *Miller v. City of Springfield*), employers that used the MMPI for promotion or hiring decisions have been found guilty of violating the Americans with Disabilities Act (ADA). The ADA prohibits the use of medical information in making employment decisions. In each of these cases, the plaintiffs accused a company (Rent-A-Center) and a police department (City of Springfield) of refusing to hire them based on the results of the MMPI, which contained medical information. The plaintiff in the *Miller* case scored high on the depression scale and argued that the refusal to hire her was based on this score. In both cases, judges sided with the plaintiffs.

OTHER METHODS FOR MEASURING PERSONALITY In addition to personality inventories, two additional methods for measuring personality include *interviews* and *behavioral assessments*. In a personality interview, a psychologist asks a structured set of questions and analyzes the responses to create an individual personality profile. When using a behavioral assessment, a psychologist will create a personality profile by observing an individual in a specific context or situation. Behavioral assessments are often used for the purposes of employee hiring and job placement, as well as for observing younger children who may not be suited to taking a self-report personality inventory. These methods are valuable in that they involve careful and close observations of an individual, which can allow for a rich and detailed understanding of the individual. However, a drawback to both is that responding directly to an interviewer or knowing that one is being watched can alter an individual's behavior. A fourth method for measuring personality includes projective tests, which we will cover in-depth in Module 12.3.

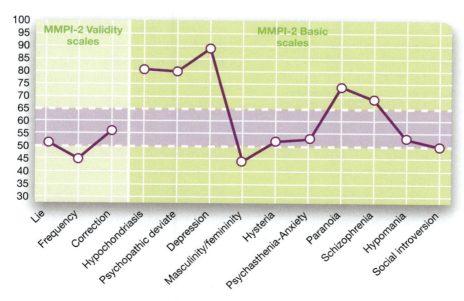

{FIG. 12.3} **A Sample MMPI-2 Profile** The pink shaded area between points 50 and 65 represent the normal range. Scores above or below these points indicate an abnormal personality (relative to the population norm) for a given dimension.

Quick Quiz 12.1a
The Trait Perspective

KNOW...

1. Which of the following statements best describes the difference between the nomothetic and idiographic approaches to personality?

   A. The nomothetic approach focuses on traits found across large groups, whereas the idiographic approach focuses on individuals.

   B. The idiographic approach focuses on traits found across large groups, whereas the nomothetic approach focuses on individuals.

   C. The idiographic approach relies on measures such as the Big Five, whereas the Big Five is of no use to a nomothetic approach.

   D. The idiographic approach allows psychologists to ask questions about the genetic and cultural basis of personality traits.

UNDERSTAND...

2. A major difference between the Big Five and the MMPI is:

   A. the Big Five is ideally suited for measuring abnormal personality traits.

   B. the Big Five is an idiographic approach, whereas the MMPI takes a nomothetic approach to measuring personality.

   C. the MMPI accounts for states and situational factors, whereas the Big Five does not.

   D. the MMPI can be used to measure abnormal personality traits.

APPLY...

3. You are the type of person who tends to go to the same restaurant and order the same thing, sticking to your daily routine. You have even turned down opportunities to travel to new destinations. Which of the Big Five factors would account for this description of your personality?

   A. Agreeableness   C. Openness

   B. Conscientiousness   D. Neuroticism

ANALYZE...

4. Your friend, who is normally introverted, is outraged at the taxi driver who is trying to overcharge you. He is cursing at the driver in a verbal altercation. This event is most likely due to his _____.

   A. temperament   C. idealized self

   B. subjective state   D. Big Five personality traits

5. The theory that our personalities consist of a stable set of traits is very useful to psychologists, but there are some notable problems with trait theories. Which of the following is *not* a problem?

   A. Trait theories typically rely on self-reported behaviors, rather than actual observed behaviors.

   B. Situational factors, in addition to personality traits, also determine our behavior.

   C. Factor analysis is not considered a valid technique in the study of personality.

   D. Historically, psychologists have not agreed on the traits that make up someone's personality.

Answers can be found on page ANS-4.

Behaviorist and Social-Cognitive Perspectives

In addition to pondering the utility of the trait approach, psychologists have been asking other key questions about personality: How do our thoughts and experiences affect personality? Which types of personality characteristics lead to psychological problems and, conversely, which traits are the healthiest? Trait descriptions remain part of some of these perspectives, albeit with some important differences that help broaden our understanding of personality.

In Module 1.2 we introduced behaviorism, an approach to psychology that emphasized the need to focus exclusively on observable relationships between stimuli and responses. Although the study of personality was not a primary interest to behaviorists, some individuals attempted to apply behavioral principles to it. Behavioral psychologists were less concerned with labeling personality traits and shunned the use of self-report inventories to measure personality. Notably, B. F. Skinner believed that personality consists of various response tendencies that occur in different situations. For example, if the situation is a small social gathering, your responses might include dominating the conversation, deferring topics of conversation to the other individuals, asking a lot of questions, or remaining silent. The option you pick is based on your past experiences—that is, whether a given response has been reinforced or punished in this situation. If you have a history of being reinforced for asking questions, you will likely repeat the behavior each time you are in this situation. A behaviorist might note that using the personality dimension of "extraversion" is an unnecessary addition—it is just a label that does not help us understand the simple relationship between stimulus and response. Thus the behaviorist perspective emphasizes the importance of the situation, rather than a relatively stable personality trait, in determining behavior (Figure 12.4).

Many psychologists would agree with Skinner's position that learning contributes to personality. One such individual is Albert Bandura, who advanced a social cognitive theory of personality. The fundamental difference between Bandura's theory and a strict behaviorist approach is that Bandura sees people as actively shaping and determining their environments, rather than the other way around. His social-cognitive learning theory explores the dynamics between people, personality, and their environment (Bandura, 2001). People who rate low on neuroticism, for instance, are likely to view the world in a nonthreatening light. Their initial reaction to an event, such as a person honking a car horn, will not be to assume that someone is threatening them. In contrast, individuals who rate high on neuroticism may find the honking threatening. How individuals respond to this situation may in part determine which type of environment they choose to be in. For example, people who likely feel threatened are apt to *choose* to be in a more comfortable and tranquil environment where there are fewer automobiles. Thus, according to this perspective, people actively choose their environments in part because they react differently to different situations. These observations led Bandura to propose the theory of **reciprocal determinism**—*the idea that behavior, internal (personal) factors, and external factors interact to determine one another, and that our personalities are based on interactions among these three aspects* (see Figure 12.4).

To see how this theory works, consider the small social gathering described earlier. The behaviorist account delineates a simple relationship between asking questions (the behavior) and having a gathering go well (the consequence). The idea of reciprocal determinism incorporates internal and personal factors such as beliefs, expectations, and personal disposition. Someone who is outgoing chooses to be in an environment in which there will be others with whom to interact, and has a history of finding the experience to be rewarding. Socializing with others reinforces not just behaviors, but

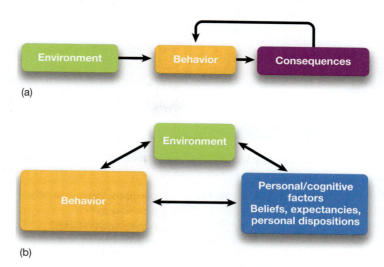

(a)

(b)

{FIG. 12.4} **(a) Behaviorist Account of Personality.** Behaviorists thought that what psychologists call personality was an expression of relationships between behavior, rewards, and punishment. Behaviorists avoided referring to personality traits and dispositions, but rather focused on how past experiences predict future behaviors. For example, whether someone tends to be pessimistic might be based on past experiences of feeling a lost sense of control. **(b) Reciprocal Determinism and the Social-Cognitive Approach.** According to Albert Bandura and colleagues, personality is a product of dynamic interactions between behavior and reinforcement, and, importantly, the beliefs, expectancies, and dispositions of the individual. **Click on this figure in your eText to see more details.**

also the beliefs and expectations that being with others will be enjoyable (see Figure 12.4).

Quick Quiz 12.1b :: Behaviorist and Social-Cognitive Perspectives

1 Which of the following concepts developed by Bandura refers to interactions that occur among behavior, internal, and external factors as an explanation for personality?

- **A** Reciprocal determinism
- **B** Positive psychology
- **C** Intersubjectivity
- **D** Egocentrism

2 Kaitlin describes herself as unmotivated. She has not felt rewarded by her attempts to succeed at school or work and, therefore, has given up trying. How might a psychologist who adopts a strict behaviorist approach account for Kaitlin's behavior?

- **A** Kaitlin believes that she cannot succeed and, therefore, avoids putting herself in situations where she might fail.
- **B** Kaitlin has a history of not being reinforced for trying to succeed and, therefore, has stopped trying.
- **C** Kaitlin focuses too much on negatives and does not have a positive outlook on life.
- **D** Kaitlin has low levels of the trait known as extraversion.

3 Alternative approaches to personality such as the behaviorist and cognitive approaches complement trait theories of personality because:

- **A** behavior and personal experience, which influence personality, are major parts of the alternative approaches.
- **B** trait theories focus on the negatives of personality.
- **C** it is easier to observe behavior than to ask someone to fill out a personality inventory.
- **D** trait theories focus only on the positive aspects of personality.

Answers can be found on page ANS-4.

Module 12.1

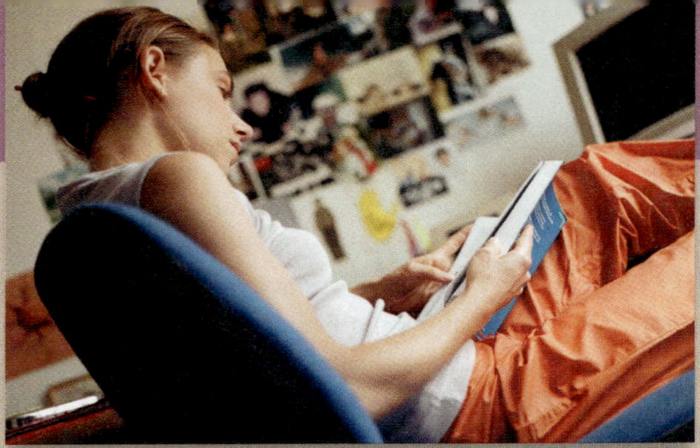

Now that you have read this module
you should:

KNOW ...

- **The key terminology associated with contemporary approaches to personality:**

Five Factor Model (Big Five
  personality factors) (p. 440)

factor analysis (p. 440)

idiographic approach (p. 440)

Minnesota Multiphasic Personality
  Inventory (MMPI-2) (p. 445)

nomothetic approach (p. 440)

personality (p. 439)

personality traits (p. 440)

reciprocal determinism (p. 447)

state (p. 444)

of specific behaviors and habits that correspond to each trait. Before you begin this exercise, review **Figure 12.1** (p. 441), which outlines some of the major characteristics of high and low scores on each of the five factors.

UNDERSTAND ...

- **The behaviorist and social-cognitive views of personality.** A strict behavioral account of personality identifies the stimuli and situational factors that control the various responses that can be elicited. When this perspective is adopted, there is little use of trait terminology, such as neuroticism or conscientiousness, and no reference to cognitive factors such as beliefs or thoughts. The social-cognitive approach to personality also accounts for situational factors and behavior, but adds a cognitive element that interacts with the environment in such a way that situations, behavior, and thoughts are determined in reciprocal fashion.

APPLY ...

- **The Big Five personality traits to understand your own personality.** Psychologists usually describe individuals based on their scores on personality tests involving the Big Five traits, such that someone might rate high, medium, or low on each trait. Use **Table 12.1** to describe your own personality in terms of the Big Five, and cite examples

ANALYZE ...

- **The strengths and weaknesses of trait theories.** Trait theories of personality tend to make reliable predictions about actual behavior. Furthermore, research shows that individuals who complete trait inventories tend to agree on their results with the people who know them well, and with the findings by researchers who observe their rooms or Facebook pages. Thus there is a great deal of agreement about who exhibits which traits. In contrast, behaviorists would argue that traits are really just descriptions of behavior, so they do not explain how such behaviors arise.

- **The relative roles of personality traits and psychological and physical states in determining behavior.** The debate over whether personality traits influence behavior or whether situational factors play a bigger role in behavior has been ongoing in the field of personality psychology. In reality, both sets of factors are important. Personality traits can be remarkably consistent, yet the situations we find ourselves in can lead to unexpected behavior.

Table 12.1 :: Applying the Five Factor Model

For each trait, try to determine if you would score low, medium, or high if you were to complete a test based on the Five Factor Model. Cite specific examples of behaviors and preferences that support your ranking.

FACTOR	LOW, MEDIUM, OR HIGH?	SPECIFIC EXAMPLES
Openness		
Conscientiousness		
Extraversion		
Agreeableness		
Neuroticism		

Module 12.2

Cultural and Biological Approaches to Personality

Learning Objectives

After reading this module you should:

KNOW ...	UNDERSTAND ...	APPLY ...	ANALYZE ...
The key terminology associated with cultural and biological approaches to personality	How evolution has influenced personality	Your knowledge to understand personality differences among cultures and between men and women	Claims that males and females have fundamentally different personalities

Some psychologists have deemed the United States WEIRD in comparison to some other societies (Henrich et al., 2010). Hearing this label applied to the U.S. may come as a surprise. Traveling from one town to the next often yields only slightly different variations of urban landscape, restaurants, suburbs, cars, styles, and people—there certainly seem to be people and places far more exotic. In this case, however, WEIRD is an acronym for "Western, Educated, Industrialized, Rich, and Democratic." Armed with that understanding, you might now be more inclined to agree that the United States is rather WEIRD.

As it turns out, most psychological studies of personality are conducted on WEIRD people. Standardized measures of personality are administered to college undergraduates at Western universities, papers are published, and the data inform psychologists' conceptions of human personality. What does this work show? For one, WEIRD people look favorably upon projecting a positive image of the self, and showing others how good they are. In contrast, East Asian people tend to focus on acknowledging ways that they can improve (Heine & Buchtel, 2009). This cultural difference has been found to persist across multiple studies. But *perhaps* such differences between the WEIRD and the non-WEIRD are due to genetic factors.

Focus Questions

 Does culture influence the types of personality traits we find across human societies?

 How do biological processes such as genes, the nervous system, and evolution account for individual differences in personality?

One goal among personality psychologists is to characterize what human beings are like—to boil the essence of what it is to be human down to a set of core attributes along whose dimensions people vary. Thus, from a psychological perspective, the study of personality is the study of human nature. To fully understand human personality, then, we need to examine more than just college sophomores at U.S. universities; instead, our studies must include people of all ages from many different cultures and geographic regions (Church, 2010; McAdams & Pals, 2006). Also, if all people can be described according to the Big Five dimensions, then we should expect to find a genetic basis for them, as well as an evolutionary explanation for how the traits came about. Furthermore, we ought to find a brain and chemical basis for personality traits. In this module, we expand our discussion of personality to address these questions and issues.

Culture and Personality

What are people from Germany, Sweden, or Japan like? Even if you have never set foot in any of these countries, you may have a general sense of what they are like and your descriptions would likely indicate that you believe each is unique in some way. We tend to have specific adjectives we use to describe people from broad regions of the world and even within more narrow geographic regions. For example, who do you think is more likely to be aggressive or seemingly rude while driving in heavy traffic—a person from Boston, Massachusetts, or someone from Savannah, Georgia? In Module 12.1, we differentiated situations, states, and traits. If you answered that the person from Boston is more likely to behave aggressively in traffic, does this behavior reflect a personality trait difference? Perhaps—but we cannot rule out the possibility that the Bostonian is aggressive because other people around him are also being aggressive (a situation) or because the stress of living in a crowded urban environment with complicated traffic patterns brings out some negative emotions (a state). In reality, many of the stereotypes we may hold about people from other regions or nations may be due to situational and state factors rather than differences in personality. Personality psychologists who study other cultures are typically interested in whether there are true cross-cultural differences in personality traits, rather than differences attributable to the effects of states or situations on behavior. They also study people of various cultures and nations to see which personality traits are shared.

Complete the **Survey** *What Has Shaped Your Personality?* at **MyPsychLab**

CULTURAL VARIATIONS IN THE BIG FIVE   One major challenge to doing cross-cultural work is finding a standardized measure of personality that can be translated and administered in languages other than English. The first module in this chapter introduced the Big Five personality dimensions, which include neuroticism, extraversion, openness, agreeableness, and conscientiousness (refer back to Figure 12.1 on page 441). These factors were discovered by researchers working in WEIRD places—the United States, Canada, and Europe. Researchers realize that just because a factor such as conscientiousness appears in data from the United States, it does not necessarily mean that the same factor would appear everywhere in the world. To find out whether the Big Five traits are truly universal, a large team of psychologists measured the Big Five dimensions in more than 17,000 people speaking 28 different languages and inhabiting 56 countries on 6 continents (they did not visit Antarctica). As it turns out, translations of the Big Five personality were validated across cultures (Schmitt et al., 2007; see also McCrae et al., 2005). This study suggests that when it comes to the basic composition of personality, the WEIRD and the non-WEIRD are quite alike: We are united in having at least five of the same personality characteristics. Remember, however, that the traits of the Big Five also vary by degree—some individuals are more open to experience, conscientious, and neurotic than others.

Another question addressed in this large-scale study was whether trait averages differ among cultures. The researchers found numerous cross-cultural differences in average personality ratings. People from Serbia and Croatia tend to be the most extraverted of the nations sampled, whereas the most introverted people came from Bangladesh and France. People from Chile and Belgium were the most open to experience, while respondents from Japan and Hong Kong rated very low on the openness scale. Looking at a more worldwide distribution,

Psychologists find many commonalities in personality dimensions from people of diverse cultures. However, there may be some culturally unique personality dimensions.

people from East Asia were the least extraverted. People from Africa were the most agreeable and conscientious of all nations (see Figure 12.5; Schmitt et al., 2007). Many of the findings in these large scale cross-cultural studies defy cultural stereotypes (Terracciano et al., 2005). For example, we might be inclined to think that cultures consisting of people who score high on conscientiousness would have the strongest economies, but no such relationship was found. In fact, nations that scored highest on conscientiousness had a relatively poor global economic standing.

CULTURALLY UNIQUE PERSONALITY TRAITS

One issue with research using the Big Five for cross-cultural studies is that it inevitably imposes a structure of personality onto other cultures. The majority of published studies using the Big Five have used U.S. undergraduate students as subjects—a WEIRD population that is probably not representative of the rest of the world (Henrich et al., 2010). Although the five-factor structure has been found in other cultures, we could also be missing something. What if members of other cultures have more than five factors? This condition could certainly be overlooked if all we test for is the Big Five. As it turns out, researchers in China have identified some different factors, including interpersonal relatedness—which is composed of harmony, tradition, and relationships with others—as well as a dependability factor (Cheung et al., 1996). The Big Five inventory is not constructed in a way that would reveal something like interpersonal relatedness. Thus people of other cultures or nations may also have unique personality characteristics that are undetected by the instruments we use (Heine & Buchtel, 2009).

BIOPSYCHOSOCIAL PERSPECTIVES

Cultural Differences in Self-Perception

Following are common terms people use to describe themselves and others. The terms represent ends of a spectrum. As you look at each pair, think about which side is most representative of Americans.

Independent	Conforming
Assertive	Yielding
Competitive	Cooperative
Above average	Normal

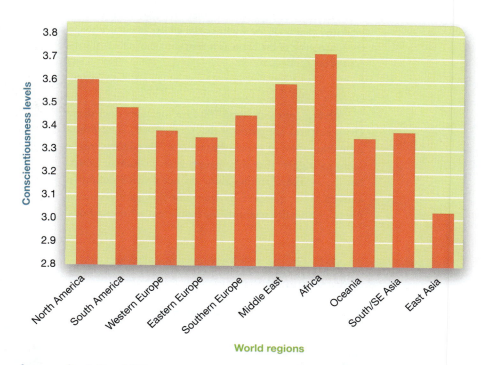

{FIG. 12.5} **Cultural Differences in Levels of Conscientiousness** This graph shows how average self-reported levels of conscientiousness differ among thousands of people studied across numerous cultures and nations (from Schmitt et al., 2007).

Most Americans would probably lean toward the items on the left. But would you find the same result if you had used the same scale to rate members of another nationality or culture, such as Chinese or Latin American? Many cross-cultural psychologists believe that the personal and social values of members of some cultures range along a continuum from *individualism* to *collectivism*. **Individualism** *refers to the view that personal identity, goals, and attributes are of greater value than group identity, goals, and attributes.* In contrast, **collectivism** *is a view that places greater value on defining the self in terms of group membership and goals.* Whether someone lives within a society where individualism or collectivism is emphasized and valued will influence their personality attributes.

Returning to the pairs of words, Americans (and other Westerners) tend to score high on measures of assertiveness, competitiveness, and other attributes that point to a self-focused orientation. The value we tend to place on these attributes can be seen in early development, as parents and others encourage children to discover what makes them unique and special. This approach contrasts with that employed in East Asian societies, which teach children the importance of discovering how they are connected to others, and to value group over personal accomplishment. This is especially the case among people from China (Oyserman et al., 2002).

The distinction between collectivism and individualism has even been identified within the brain. In one study, researchers scanned the brains of people as they made judgments about themselves; the patterns of activity could be used to independently determine whether individuals were from individualistic or collectivistic cultures (Chiao et al., 2009).

However, it is not clear whether these are differences that are inherited genetically, or whether the effects of culture shape the functioning of the brain as it relates to the individualistic–collectivist continuum.

· · · · · · · · · · · · · · · · · · · ·

Overall, research using Big Five measures does show cross-cultural consistency (McCrae, 2001). The common expression of personality traits across cultures might seem to suggest that they have a basis in human DNA, but cross-cultural studies alone do not provide definitive answers to this question. To determine how genes contribute to personality, scientists use a different set of methods.

Quick Quiz 12.2a
Culture and Personality

How Genes Affect Personality

Friends and relatives may have commented on the physical resemblance you share with your parents or siblings. For biological relatives, there is little doubt that physical

resemblances are based on genetics. But what about personality? If you catch yourself behaving in ways similar to a parent or a sibling, do you or others around you conclude that "It must be genetic"? It is tempting to do so, but then similarities among relatives could also be due to sharing so many aspects of the environment. Psychologists conduct twin studies and employ other research techniques to distinguish genetic and environmental sources of individual differences in personality.

TWIN STUDIES Twin studies using the Big Five have found that identical (monozygotic) twins show a stronger correlation for each personality trait than do fraternal (dizygotic) twins. As you can see from Figure 12.6, the genetic correlations for identical twin pairs are approximately .50 for all five factors, significantly higher than the correlations for fraternal twin pairs (who

Gerald Levey and Mark Newman are identical twins who were reared apart. When they eventually met it turns out they had many similarities—for example, both chose the same profession.

Highly detailed and specific similarities between identical twins who were reared apart tend to draw a great deal interest. Nevertheless, identical twins may also be very different. Paula Bernstein and Elyse Schein are identical twins who were separated at birth, and upon uniting at age 35 discovered they were very different from each other.

average approximately .20). Although the environment contributes to variation in personality, research on the genetic basis of personality consistently shows that genes are responsible for many of the differences we see among individuals (Tellegen et al., 1988).

After studying Figure 12.6 and thinking about twins a bit, you might wonder whether the stronger similarities between identical twin pairs are due to something other than genes. Identical twins are often treated in very similar ways, especially during their younger and formative years. Nontwin siblings or fraternal twins reared together share a very similar environment, but perhaps the environments shared by identical twins reared together is even more similar by comparison. If this is true, then the strong correlations seen in Figure 12.6 between identical twin pairs might be environmentally based. It turns out that twin studies conducted on identical twins who were reared apart yield the same basic findings as studies of twins who were reared together—they are more alike than fraternal twins or nontwin siblings (Tellegen et al., 1988). The genetic correlations range from .39 to .58, indicating that despite growing up in different environments the identical twins converged toward having similar personalities.

Although the results of twin studies reveal that heredity plays an important role in personality development, parenting and other environmental influences certainly matter. As discussed in Modules 10.2 and 10.4, the environments that parents provide and their style of parenting certainly do influence the ways their children behave. Another point to consider is that twin studies do not tell us which specific genes may account for individual differences. Newer molecular methods are used to answer this type of question.

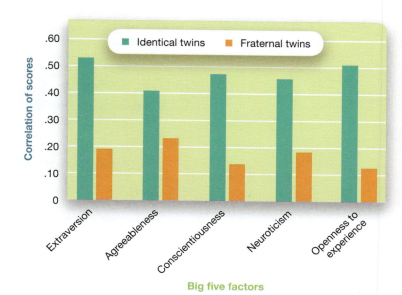

{FIG. 12.6} **Genes and Personality** Identical twin pairs show higher genetic correlations than do fraternal twins for each of the Big Five personality traits. **Click on this figure in your eText to see more details**.

What do we know about specific genes and personality?

To think about how genes relate to personality, it is easiest to start with familiar brain chemicals with known functions. For example, serotonin, among other things, regulates mood and emotion. One of the genes that codes for serotonin activity has been found on human chromosome 17. Specifically, this gene codes for proteins that transport serotonin molecules within the tiny spaces (synapses) between nerve cells. Many of our genes are polymorphic (*poly* = "multiple"; *morph* = "form"), meaning that there are different versions of the same gene that lead to different physical or behavioral characteristics. Two possible variations of the "serotonin transporter gene" have been identified: a short copy and a long copy. People who inherit short copies from one or both parents are predisposed to anxiety, shyness, and negative emotional reactions in interpersonal situations (Battaglia et al., 2005; Lesch et al., 1996).

How do scientists study genes and personality?

One method for studying genes and personality is to compare responses on self-report questionnaires of personality in people who have inherited different copies of the serotonin transporter gene. People who inherit short copies of the gene tend to report greater levels of anxiety and

WORKING THE SCIENTIFIC LITERACY MODEL
From Molecules to Personality

Scientists have identified specific genes underlying blood type, susceptibility to many diseases, and other characteristics. But is it possible to do the same for personality? Sophisticated technologies that allow researchers to sequence specific genes and identify their functions at a molecular level have created inroads into this mystery. While scientists have not identified a specific gene or genes involved in the expression of neuroticism, agreeableness, or any other trait, genes that code for specific brain chemicals that are related to personality have been identified.

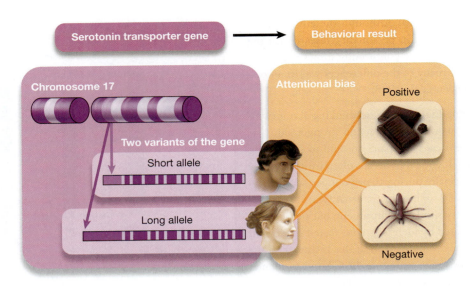

Serotonin transporter gene → Behavioral result

Chromosome 17

Two variants of the gene

Short allele

Long allele

Attentional bias

Positive

Negative

{FIG. 12.7} **Genes, Serotonin, and Personality** People who inherit two copies of the long version of the serotonin transporter gene fixate on positive images and avoid looking at negative images. People who inherit the short version of this gene are not biased toward attending to positive imagery.

neuroticism compared to people who inherit two long copies. However, these differences depend on which of the many different varieties of self-report questionnaires are used (Schinka et al., 2004).

Another way to study how genes and personality are related is to conduct experiments. In one study, participants provided a hair sample so researchers could extract DNA to determine which combination of serotonin transporter genes they had inherited. The participants completed a task that monitored their attentional focus to pictures of positive (e.g., a smiling infant), negative (a black widow spider), or neutral (a kitchen table) stimuli. (To avoid contaminating the experiment, the participants were not informed of the DNA test results.) Previous research has shown that people who have problems with anxiety focus their attention on threatening stimuli more than nonanxious people (Bar-Haim et al., 2007). It turns out that participants who had inherited two short versions of the serotonin transporter gene did not avoid looking at the negative images, whereas those who inherited two long copies looked more at positive images (Figure 12.7; Fox et al., 2009). Not only are short copies of this gene related to self-reported levels of anxiety, but they are also relevant to immediate reactions to stimuli that may be perceived as threatening.

Can we critically evaluate this evidence?

An advantage of molecularly based genetic work over the twin studies described earlier is that this research holds the possibility of revealing cause-and-effect links between genes and personality. To date, however, this linkage still only remains a possibility. At this point the general consensus is that a vast number of genes, each of which has

only a very small effect, account for individual differences in personality (Terracciano et al., 2010). The fact that genes are correlated to personality may lead you to wonder whether your personality is *caused* by the specific genes you inherit for, say, serotonin activity. It is important to remember that genes *interact* with the environment to produce behavior.

Why is this relevant?

Knowledge about how genes and personality are related can help psychologists identify risk factors for developing mental disorders. As we will see in Module 13.3, genetic studies of personality help us better understand the biological basis of psychological disorders such as anxiety and depression. This work raises some interesting possibilities, such as the potential to screen individuals to assess their risk of developing a disorder. In turn, at-risk individuals might be better helped with early detection and treatment. Also, links between DNA and personality may lead some psychologists to speculate and test hypotheses about how our personalities have evolved.

KNOW …

1 _____ refers to the view that personal identity, goals, and attributes are of greater value than group identity, goals, and attributes, whereas _____ places greater value on defining the self in terms of group membership and goals.

Ⓐ Motivation; agreeableness

Ⓑ Individualism; collectivism

Ⓒ Autonomy; dependence

Ⓓ Collectivism; individualism

UNDERSTAND …

2 Even when identical twins are reared apart, they still tend to be very similar in personality. How is this strong evidence that genes contribute to personality?

Ⓐ Identical twins who were reared apart were most likely treated in very similar ways.

Ⓑ The similarities remain, even though there were probably significant differences in how the siblings were raised.

Ⓒ There are fewer similarities when twins are reared together.

Ⓓ Actually, identical twins who are raised apart show very little similarity.

3 Which of the following statements best describes what psychologists now know about the genetic basis of personality?

Ⓐ Hundreds of genes have been identified that are directly linked to specific personality traits.

Ⓑ Technology is not sophisticated enough to link genes and personality characteristics.

Ⓒ Some genes have been identified that are related to certain aspects of personality function.

Ⓓ Genes do not contribute to personality characteristics.

Answers can be found on page ANS-4.

The Role of Evolution in Personality

The presence of universal, genetically based personality dimensions across different cultures suggests that personality evolved to promote survival and reproductive success (Figueredo et al., 2009). Being anxious, bold, curious, open, extraverted, introverted, or conscientious could be adaptive responses to a complex physical and social environment. For example, some evolutionary psychologists suggest that neuroticism is important when it comes to competing for mates. If neuroticism is important to survival in general, and to reproductive success in particular, then it should confer some advantage on individuals expressing this trait. People who are neurotic are more likely to be jealous (Melamed, 1991). In some environments, jealousy is an adaptive response—if one is not vigilant about their mate, the individual may run the risk of infidelity. Thus, although jealousy can be very unattractive and even drive couples apart, it _can_ keep one's partner in a relationship (Buss, 2000). Jealousy is one way that individuals advertise that their mate is unavailable—and can be expressed both to one's partner _and_ to anyone jeopardizing the relationship. Evolutionary psychologists speculate that jealousy is a trait that evolved for guarding mates. It is easy enough to speculate, of course—but it is preferable to put some science behind the study of evolution and personality.

ANIMAL BEHAVIOR: THE EVOLUTIONARY ROOTS OF PERSONALITY One compelling argument for the evolution of personality is the presence of personality traits in numerous nonhuman species. For example, scientists have studied one particular species of bird (_Parus major_) that lives in Europe and Asia. These birds display two different types of behavior when they encounter new environments. One personality type is bold in its exploration of new environments and less responsive to external stimuli. The other type is more timid, less exploratory, and more reactive to external stimulation. These two personality types are known to have a strong genetic basis. Which of the two personality types is adaptive depends on what kind of year the birds are having. If there are limited resources, aggressive birds have greater reproductive success. In years where resources are plentiful, timid birds have greater success, possibly because the aggressive birds succumb to the downsides of being less responsive to external stimulation, such as predators (Dingemanse et al., 2004).

Do nonhuman species have the same types of personality traits as humans? It turns out that several of the Big Five personality traits have been found in a rich diversity of species—such as hedgehogs, ants, rhinos, and primates (Gosling, 2001). Clearly these animals cannot fill out the paper-and-pencil version of a personality inventory such as the Big Five. Instead, individuals who are familiar with the animals rate their behaviors according to the five factors. Typically, observers strongly agree on their ratings of extraversion and neuroticism in the animals studied (Gosling, 2001).

Our closest primate cousins are a good place to look for personality characteristics in nonhumans. In one study, a list of adjectives was taken from the Big Five test and people who were familiar with the

Psychologists are finding that measures of human personality are applicable to diverse species such as hyenas, octopuses, and chimpanzees, among many others.

chimpanzee subjects rated how well the adjectives applied to each chimp on a 1 to 7 scale. Of the Big Five traits, extraversion, conscientiousness, and agreeableness were reliably found in the chimps (Weiss et al., 2007). Some researchers even argue you do not need a backbone to have a personality. Octopuses, for example, show stable individual differences in measures of activity, reactivity, and avoidance (Mather & Anderson, 1993).

EVOLUTION AND INDIVIDUAL DIFFERENCES IN PERSONALITY TRAITS

So how are individual differences in personality relevant to evolution? Personality tends to vary from one individual to the next, and situational factors are important in determining how we behave. These observations are difficult to reconcile with an evolutionary interpretation (Buss, 2009). As you can imagine, being open to new experiences might serve one well in survival and, possibly, in reproductive success. In contrast, avoiding new experiences may be a better strategy in other circumstances.

Evolution involves changes in traits that occur within reproducing populations over many generations; it occurs at the level of populations. Thus individual differences have traditionally been regarded as evolutionary "noise" (Tooby & Cosmides, 1990). Genetically speaking, one individual within an entire breeding population cannot have much of an effect on how a trait evolves—unless this individual alone somehow breeds with most, if not all, receptive members. Therefore, the relationship between personality and

evolution may mean that individual differences are not so random.

For example, when it comes to your surroundings, do you think your current environment is a matter of accident and circumstance? Consider these questions:

- Did you do a random search of colleges and universities to decide where you would go?
- In high school and college, did you randomly point at students to decide who would be your casual acquaintances, lifelong friends, and romantic partners?
- Did you randomly select from a list of clubs or sports to determine which one you would spend hours of your free time on?

If you made completely random choices, you might describe feeling like a fish out of water. We assume you answered "no" to these obvious questions, but this exercise illustrates that we *choose* particular environments and typically there are reasons for making those choices: Our personalities guide decisions about with whom we associate, where we choose to go to school, and whether we spend hours every afternoon engaged in mastering chess, football drills, or dance routines. The extravert and the introvert, the neurotic and the tranquil, and the conscientious and the careless gravitate toward the respective niches they best fill.

This pattern has been confirmed in studies that monitored the language and social interactions of college students in their natural environments. Psychologists using special recording devices that monitor language and social interactions every 12 minutes found that over

Sometimes opposites may attract, but in general, people form social bonds with others who share similar personality traits.

MYTHS IN MIND
Men Are From Mars, Women Are From Venus

Much is often made about apparent differences in how men and women think and behave. This comparison can sometimes get stretched pretty far, such as the implication inherent in the title of the 1992 self-help book *Men Are From Mars, Women Are From Venus* (Gray, 1992). The notion that men and women may as well be from different planets is strongly reinforced by the popular media.

To what extent does science back up this hypothesis when it comes to personality? On the one hand, there is strong evidence that men and women differ on their Big Five personality ratings. Women generally report higher levels of extraversion, conscientiousness, agreeableness, and neuroticism than men. This finding has been noted in comparisons made across dozens of cultures (Schmitt et al., 2008). On the other hand, these gender differences are quite small and may be mostly explained by economic factors—not something you will read about in popular self-help books. Truth can be less interesting than fiction, but in this case is far more valuable to know. It turns out that the countries showing the *largest* gender differences in personality also have greater access to resources such as health care, education, and wealth. Men and women in countries with fewer social and economic resources tend to be more similar in their self-reported personality scores. This phenomenon may occur because prosperity gives members of either gender greater flexibility to diverge and allows individual differences to flourish (Schmitt et al., 2008). A good title will sell a lot of self-help books, but does little to inform the general public about what scientific studies truly reveal about human behavior.

a 4-week period, college students were remarkably consistent in the social environments they chose (Mehl & Pennebaker, 2003). They—and the rest of us—select environments that suit their personality characteristics and actively avoid those that might lead to discomfort. To the extent that fish make choices, few would opt for giving life on land a shot.

The importance of personality to social bonding is not trivial. Friendships, professional relationships, and especially romantic relationships succeed (or fail) because of the compatibility (or incompatibility) of personalities. You have likely heard the phrase "Opposites attract." The few examples you may be thinking of notwithstanding, for the most part we pair up with those who are most like us. Psychologists have found that across various cultures spouses tend by be very similar in personality dimensions (McCrae et al., 2008). In the human and animal kingdom, we call this phenomenon *assortative mating*—choosing sexual partners who are similar to the individual doing the searching.

In summary, the consistent appearance of core personality traits across cultures and species indicates that these traits have been important to survival. At the same time, personality is flexible. Thus evolution appears to also have favored variation in personality that allows us to fill diverse social and environmental niches.

Men and women tend to differ in some personality dimensions. However, these differences are often greatly exaggerated—especially in the pop psychology industry.

APPLY...

1 What is an important piece of evidence supporting an evolutionary basis of personality?

   A Changes in personality can be seen over generations.

   B Personality traits are stable in the sense that they are common among humans and can be found in nonhuman species.

   C Personality traits are not stable and cannot be found in nonhuman species.

   D No valid evidence supports an evolutionary approach to personality.

ANALYZE...

2 When it comes to personality, the phrase "opposites attract" seems to be the exception, rather than the rule. People typically match up pretty closely when it comes to choices of romantic partners. Which evolutionary principle has been used to explain this phenomenon?

   A Natural selection   **C** Adaptation

   B Assortative mating   **D** Survival of the fittest

3 Which of the following statements best summarizes personality differences between men and women?

   A Averages of some traits such as extraversion and neuroticism may differ in some samples, with societal factors strongly contributing to the differences.

   B Males and females inherit separate sets of genes that cause their differences in personality.

   C Research shows that men and women really do not differ in personality.

   D Males are generally agreeable, whereas women are generally conscientious.

Answers can be found on page ANS-4.

The Brain and Personality

Modern scientific methods of investigating the brain and behavior have revealed some interesting connections. We hear media stories about new discoveries revealing how brain structures contribute to specific behaviors or personality traits. What might surprise you is that biological explanations for personality go back as far as recorded history.

EARLY APPROACHES TO THE BIOLOGY OF PERSONALITY Ancient medicine (circa 400 B.C.) was guided by the theory of humorism. According to this theory, the body consisted of four humors—including blood, phlegm, black bile, and yellow bile. Physical illness and disorders of personality were attributed to imbalances among the four humors. For example, too much black bile resulted in melancholy.

Science took a positive step forward when physicians, and those who would eventually become psychologists, decided that the skull and its contents were a better place to look to better understand personality. In the late 1700s, the German doctor Franz Gall developed phrenology—the theory that personality characteristics corresponded to individual differences in brain structure that could be assessed by measuring the shape and contours of the skull surface (see Module 1.2). Phrenology held sway well into the 1800s. Its practitioners were correct in postulating that different psychological functions were localized in specific regions of the brain, but it turns out that the shape of the skull has little, if anything, to do with personality.

As knowledge about the brain has grown, psychologists have been better able to link personality characteristics with specific brain regions. Hans Eysenck, a pioneer in this area, proposed that arousal states of the brain are the basis of extraversion and that the reactivity of the limbic system (the emotional circuits), reticular activating system, and cortex are correlated with extraversion (Eysenck, 1967). People who have decreased reactivity in these brain regions are basically "underaroused." As a consequence, they seek out novel social and emotional stimulation. Introverts, by comparison, have higher reactivity within these brain regions and, therefore, seek less stimulation than do extraverts.

Even the two hemispheres of the brain may "differ" in personality. The left and right hemispheres differ in the processing of positive and negative emotions, for example (Sutton & Davidson, 1997). Activity in the left prefrontal cortex is associated with positive responses, whereas activity in the right prefrontal cortex is associated with responding to threats and unfamiliar stimuli. It turns out that individuals differ in which side of the prefrontal cortex dominates—those with more active left hemispheres tend to experience more positive emotions, whereas people whose right hemispheres dominate tend to be more anxious (Figure 12.8). Although these findings are intriguing, it is important to avoid thinking of individuals as being "right brained" versus "left brained"; doing so oversimplifies how the brain really works.

CONTEMPORARY RESEARCH: IMAGES OF PERSONALITY IN THE BRAIN Modern-day researchers use imaging technology to test for relationships between personality and the brain. A common assumption made by many scientists is that the size of a brain region corresponds to the magnitude of behavior it controls or mediates. So does the size of various areas have any relationship to the degree to which people are extraverted or neurotic? When it comes to personality, this seems to be the case. Neuroscientists have tested whether each of the Big Five personality traits is associated with a different brain region, and whether these regions correspond to the behaviors and motivations associated with these traits. For example, extraverts tend to be more driven to seek out rewards than introverts, and neurotic individuals tend to experience more negative emotions than emotionally stable individuals. The reward and emotion centers of the brain are fairly well mapped.

In one study using magnetic resonance imaging (MRI), researchers took detailed measures of brain volume in more than 100 participants who also rated themselves on the Big Five inventory. The scientists then looked for associations between brain anatomy and the self-rated personality traits of each participant. It turns out that ratings on four of the Big Five traits—neuroticism, extraversion, agreeableness, and conscientiousness—corresponded to the size of predicted brain regions (DeYoung et al., 2010). People who rated themselves as high on conscientiousness had a correspondingly large region called the middle frontal gyrus, which is known to be involved in self-regulation and engaging in planned actions. A region of the brain called the medial orbitofrontal cortex, which is involved in reward processing, was larger in people who scored high on extraversion (see Figure 12.9).

The complexity of personality and of the brain makes it unreasonable to suppose we could ever point at a single region and declare it to be the center of any single personality trait. That said, we have come a long way from the days when personality was described in terms of the four humors of blood, phlegm, and black and yellow bile.

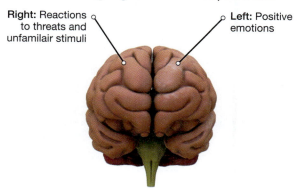

Right: Reactions to threats and unfamilair stimuli

Left: Positive emotions

{FIG. 12.8} **The Relationship Between the Right and Left Brain Hemispheres and Personality** The right and left hemispheres of the cerebral cortex show some general differences related to personality. Activity in the left frontal lobe is associated with positive emotion, whereas activity in the right frontal lobe is associated with responses to threats and unfamiliar stimuli. Individuals may differ in terms of which side predominates in response to emotional events.

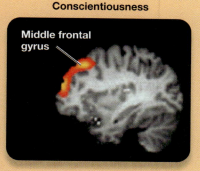

Extraversion

Medial orbitofrontal cortex

Conscientiousness

Middle frontal gyrus

{FIG. 12.9} **Measuring Personality and Brain Anatomy** People's self-ratings of the Big Five traits correspond to their brain volume in specific regions. Here we see two (among several) regions of the brain where size is positively correlated with ratings of extraversion and conscientiousness (DeYoung et al., 2010).

Quick Quiz 12.2d
The Brain and Personality

KNOW…

1 An outdated approach claiming that behavior and personality were based on the sizes of various regions of the skull surface was called:

- **A** magnetic resonance imaging.
- **B** alchemy.
- **C** phrenology.
- **D** humorism.

2 Hans Eysenck proposed that arousal states of the brain are the basis of extraversion, citing the importance of all but which of the following systems?

- **A** Limbic system
- **B** Parasympathetic nervous system
- **C** Reticular activating system
- **D** Cortex

APPLY…

3 Some evidence suggests that the two hemispheres of the brain control differing general features of personality. Imagine someone injured the left lobe of the cerebral cortex, reducing its ability to function. What kinds of change might you expect?

- **A** Fewer negative emotions, because the left hemisphere dominates when expressing negative emotions
- **B** Fewer positive emotions, because the left hemisphere processes positive emotional expressions
- **C** No effect; the right hemisphere is the emotion-dominant hemisphere
- **D** Fewer negative and positive emotions, because the left hemisphere processes all emotional experiences

Answers can be found on page ANS-4.

Module Summary

Now that you have read this module you should:

Listen to the audio file of this module at **MyPsychLab**

KNOW ...

- *The key terminology associated with cultural and biological approaches to personality:*

collectivism (p. 451) individualism (p. 451)

UNDERSTAND ...

- *How evolution has influenced personality.* Evolutionary psychologists speculate that traits such as neuroticism and extraversion evolved because they solved environmental and social problems encountered by our distant ancestors. Although this hypothesis is difficult to test directly, different sources of evidence lend support to it. The widespread occurrence of these personality traits among different species indicates that they are adaptive. Also, modern-day humans use individual differences in personality structure to decide on mating and possibly long-term partner choices.

APPLY ...

- *Your knowledge to understand personality differences among cultures and between men and women.* Assign a value of true or false to each of the following statements (check your answers on page ANS-4):

Generally speaking:

1. Canadians are much more agreeable than Americans.
2. Men and women have vastly different personalities.
3. Americans are pushy.
4. People from England are reserved.
5. Swiss people are conventional and closed off to new experiences.
6. Women are more warm and compassionate than men.
7. Chinese people value group cohesiveness.

ANALYZE ...

- *Claims that males and females have fundamentally different personalities.* Claims of major gender differences in personality are sometimes made to support popular-book sales. In reality, the general consensus in psychological science is that males and females are more alike than different when it comes to personality. Both, of course, share common personality dimensions. Although females may tend to be, on average, more conscientious and extraverted than males, there is little evidence to support claims that men and women are fundamentally different in personality.

Psychodynamic and Humanistic Approaches to Personality

Learning Objectives

After reading this module you should:

KNOW ...	UNDERSTAND ...	APPLY ...	ANALYZE ...
The key terminology related to the psychodynamic and humanistic approaches to personality	How people use defense mechanisms to cope with conflicting thoughts and feelings The developmental stages Freud used to explain the origins of personality	Both psychodynamic and humanistic perspectives to explain personality	Whether projective tests are valid measures of personality The strengths and weaknesses of psychodynamic perspectives

In the spring of 2010, the website wikileaks.org posted a graphic video recording from a U.S. military helicopter. The video involved images in which the helicopter gunned down a group of men on the ground and voice recordings of the crew gaining permission to fire and coordinating the attack. These scenes alone would be disturbing to many individuals, but what drew the most attention—and public criticism—was the tone of the helicopter crew's dialog. The pilot and gunner could be clearly heard joking about the fate of the men on the ground, daring them to run or raise a weapon, and then chuckling as they surveyed dead bodies on the ground.

The sharp contrast of the gruesome images with the light banter of the crew led many to question the psychological makeup of the soldiers involved. How can someone joke about the violent deaths of others, even if they are enemies? One argument suggests that these specific soldiers must be sadistic, somehow enjoying the killing. Others defend the soldiers by saying that they are typical individuals, that killing is psychologically troubling, and that the responses heard on the video are a means

of coping with the stress of combat. Possibly, almost anyone in the same shoes would do the same thing.

Focus Questions

 Is personality fundamentally guided by dark, aggressive impulses or by a desire for more positive experiences?

 Do people really use psychological defenses like humor to protect themselves from emotionally troubling events?

· · · · · · · · · · · · · · · · · ·

Over time, the field of psychology has seen many different approaches to personality, but one theme that unites various perspectives on personality is the search for what makes individuals unique and how these differences arise. In this module, we will explore a perspective on personality that is quite unlike what we learned about in the two preceding modules. While trait perspectives on personality search for the best way to accurately describe individuals, **psychodynamic theories** *focus on how personality arises through complex interactions involving conscious and unconscious processes that occur from early development on through adulthood.* Personality is one of many psychological topics that the psychodynamic approach addresses. Psychodynamic psychologists also address mental health and therapies, a topic we will explore further in Chapter 14.

The Psychodynamic Perspective

The psychodynamic approach to personality began with Sigmund Freud in the late 1800s. Freud was an Austrian physician who attempted to examine patients' personalities, just as medical specialists might examine their patients' physical health. Freud was interested in how personality is structured, how it functions, and how disorders arise. Because he came from a medical perspective, Freud's studies of personality were largely based on individual cases of people who sought his help for psychological difficulties they were experiencing.

The theories introduced by Freud have evolved considerably through time. Some have been abandoned, while remnants of others can be found in modern psychology. The psychodynamic perspective on personality does not consist of a single theory, but rather has evolved into a family of different theories that, despite their differences, are based on a few key observations (see Westen, 1998):

1. *Unconscious thoughts, memories, and emotions operate simultaneously and are major influences on our behavior.* Although we spend most of our time with the feeling that we are in control of our bodies and actions, closer examination suggests that unconscious thoughts and emotions can motivate our behavior. These different unconscious processes occur simultaneously. For example, we think and feel at the same time. Sometimes our thoughts and emotions are in sync, and at other times they may be in conflict.

2. *Personality takes shape in early childhood and children learn to regulate their emotions during this period of development.* Psychodynamic theorists place a great deal of importance on early childhood experiences. Although adults may change their behavior with effort, personality is thought to be formed well before adulthood. An important part of childhood is learning appropriate and acceptable ways of experiencing and expressing thoughts and emotions.

PsychTutor

Click here in your eText for an interactive tutorial on **Freud: Id, Ego, Superego**

Psychodynamic theories of personality emphasize early childhood development, especially in terms of emotion. In particular, the dynamic between parent and child is thought to determine how personality develops.

3. *Mental representations of the self and others shape how the individual acts.* The nature of key social relationships, particularly with the parents, determines personality development. During childhood, individuals learn about relationships from interacting with family or other caregivers, and they learn about themselves from the way they are treated.

Although these observations are not unique to psychodynamic psychology, they represent some of the core beliefs that shaped psychodynamic thinking. Keep them in mind as you read about personality theories, starting with Freud's approach.

THE STRUCTURE OF PERSONALITY   Like many other psychodynamic theorists, Freud hypothesized that the human psyche consists of multiple, sometimes conflicting, processes. He theorized that three hypothetical, interacting parts exist: the *id*, the *ego*, and the *superego* (Figure 12.10). Each part has its own unique principle guiding it, and each contributes unique factors to an individual's personality.

The **id** *represents a collection of basic biological drives, including those directed toward sex and aggression.* Freud believed the id was fueled by an energy called *libido*. Although this term is more commonly used in reference to sexual energy, the libido also controls other biological urges such as hunger. The id motivates people to seek out experiences that bring pleasure, with little regard for the appropriateness or consequences of their realization. As a consequence, the id is said to operate according to

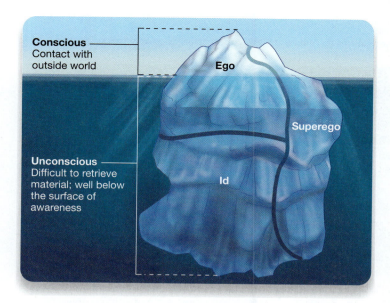

Conscious
Contact with
outside world

Ego

Superego

Unconscious
Difficult to retrieve
material; well below
the surface of
awareness

Id

{FIG. 12.10} **The Freudian Structure of Personality** A popular depiction of how Freud viewed personality features an iceberg, with the unconscious mind residing below the surface and conscious awareness at only the tip of the iceberg. The id is completely submerged, whereas the ego and the superego operate at both unconscious and conscious levels. **Click on this figure in your eText to see more details.**

the *pleasure principle*. The search for instant gratification motivated by the id may not always be appropriate from a social perspective, however—and that is where the ego comes into play.

The **ego** *is the component of personality that keeps the impulses of the id in check*—to delay the gratification sought by the id until it is socially appropriate. The ego represents the ability to understand that an individual cannot eat, engage in sexual activity, or otherwise give in to the id all the time. Therefore, it is said to operate according to the *reality principle*.

The third component of the human psyche, the **superego**, *was thought to develop during our upbringing; it serves as an inner voice we hear when we shame ourselves for acting inappropriately or lavish praise on ourselves for doing something good*. The moral composition of the superego is primarily learned from the authority of one's parents.

Interestingly, Freud emphasized that the influence of the id is present at birth, whereas the superego must develop with experience. This concept would seem to suggest that people are born to be bad—thus some have argued that Freud had a rather grim view of human personality. Once the three components are in place, the id, ego, and superego operate simultaneously, at times in harmony and at others in conflict. In fact, this *intrapsychic conflict* is one of the hallmarks of Freud's theory. Consider the soldiers described at the

beginning of the module: From Freud's perspective, everyone has an id that provides the aggressive drives to act as a soldier, even though the superego might nag that "Killing is wrong," and the ego may simply concentrate on the reality of the current situation. Understanding intrapsychic conflict in this manner can help a psychoanalyst (i.e., someone who approaches therapy from a psychodynamic perspective) understand an individual's personality. What is especially important is uncovering conflicts that are unresolved, which might result in guilt if the superego wins out, or in hostility if the id is victorious.

UNCONSCIOUS PROCESSES AND PSYCHODYNAMICS
How can the id be a driving force if we are not aware of it? Freud's answer was that our behavior is controlled by both unconscious and conscious processes. The *unconscious* mind includes impulses and drives that we are not directly aware of, whereas *conscious* thoughts are those for which you are aware.

Consider an example of how conscious and unconscious processes operate simultaneously. A person who was raised to believe in gender and ethnic equality is aware of his beliefs about women, men, and members of other ethnicities. He is riled when he overhears a degrading sexist or ethnic remark. This person's conscious awareness of his thoughts and emotions suggests that he fully believes in equality. A psychodynamic psychologist might say his attitude toward others is based on a well-developed superego. However, when this same person hears a story about a doctor, he might assume the doctor is male if this was not directly specified in the story. In addition, he may consistently choose to sit away from members of other ethnicities when he rides the subway. These responses would suggest that the individual's conscious belief in equality may not similarly reside in his unconscious mind.

Recent laboratory experiments have revealed rather significant discrepancies between conscious and unconscious attitudes, thoughts, and emotions (Banaji & Heiphetz, 2010). The conflicts that arise because of these discrepancies are dealt with in a variety of ways—in particular, through the use of what have been termed defense mechanisms.

DEFENSE MECHANISMS
Because Freud was a physician interested in mental problems, he focused a

Table 12.2 :: Defense Mechanisms and Examples

According to psychodynamic views of personality, the ego uses defense mechanisms to reduce anxiety caused by urges or impulses originating from the id.

DEFENSE MECHANISM	DEFINITION	FREUDIAN APPLICATION	MODERN EXAMPLE*
Repression/suppression	Actively drowning out thoughts, memories, or wishes.	Feelings of anger toward the same-sexed parent are rejected.	Using fMRI technology, researchers have observed distinct patterns of brain activity when subjects are asked to forget information (Anderson et al., 2004).
Denial	Resistance to perceiving what actually occurs.	Feelings of aggression toward the same-sexed parent are avoided.	People tend to believe they are less vulnerable than the "average person" to misfortunes such as losing a job or getting a debilitating illness (Perloff & Fetzer, 1986).
Isolation	Creating a mental gap between a threatening thought and other feelings or thoughts.	Anxiety associated with toilet training and disapproval from parents is avoided by dismissing parental wishes.	People who are given little time to process evaluations from others are more likely to dismiss negative feedback than people given a lot of time to process their evaluations (Hixon & Swann, 1993).
Reaction formation	Altering an unacceptable impulse into its opposite.	Anxiety that accompanies hostility toward one's same-sexed parent is reduced by expressing affection.	Men who report negative attitudes toward homosexuality show greater physical arousal in response to images of men engaged in homosexual activity than do non-homophobic men (Adams et al., 1996).

*Some of these examples, such as repression, are the source of ongoing debate among psychologists.
Source: Some examples and the theme of this table are based on Baumeister et al., 1998.

great deal of attention on the conflicts and experiences that invoke anxiety. He was particularly interested in the idea that so many conflicts occurred unconsciously. To explain this phenomenon, he and his daughter Anna (also a key figure in early psychodynamic psychology) identified a number of **defense mechanisms**, *which are unconscious strategies the ego uses to reduce or avoid anxiety, guilt, and other unpleasant* feelings (Freud, 1936). Table 12.2 lists a number of these defense mechanisms, some of which appear to have scientific support. For example, the person who avoids sitting next to someone of a different ethnicity while on the subway may try to *rationalize* his actions by convincing himself that his choice was based on seating space rather than ethnicity. In the case of soldiers at war, perhaps they rely on humor not to express hostility, but rather to reduce the psychological impact of their experiences and actions. As a matter of fact, there is strong correlational evidence suggesting that a good sense of humor helps people manage stress (Martin, 2001).

PSYCHOSEXUAL DEVELOPMENT We do not come into the world knowing how to manage daily life, nor do we know right from wrong. To Freud, the infant is a bundle of impulses; it is only through experience that the ego and superego can emerge. Freud explained

that these aspects of personality develop through a series of stages, which occur mostly in the first five years of life (as summarized in Table 12.3). In each stage, pleasurable sensory experiences are focused in different parts of the body, and the id is driven to experience as much as possible.

For example, the oral stage is the phase in which infant attention focuses on sensations of the mouth. Freud believed that all people experience at least some difficulties during their psychosexual development as they transition from one stage to the next. Imagine what it must be like for an infant in the oral stage: For the first year, everything is great—you cry and you get fed. Then one day, weaning suddenly begins and your mother tells you that you have to wait to eat. You have never been told "no" before! This is a normal part of development, and it essentially helps the infant develop an ego and adjust to social realities. For some individuals, this process is more difficult and may result in a **fixation**, *in which an individual becomes preoccupied with obtaining the pleasure associated with a particular stage.* Freud might explain that habits such as biting your fingernails or excessive gum chewing stem from unresolved conflict during the oral stage. He would attribute these habits to very early life experiences that remain in the unconscious mind, labeling it an "oral fixation."

Table 12.3 :: Stages of Psychosexual Development According to Freud

STAGE	PLEASURE FOCUS	FIXATION RESULTS
Oral (0–18 months)	Actions of the mouth—sucking, chewing, swallowing	Excessive pleasure derived from eating, drinking, smoking, and other oral activities
Anal (18–36 months)	Bowel elimination, control	Excessive cleanliness or sloppiness
Phallic (3–6 years)	Genitals	Castration anxiety (males), or penis envy (females)
Latency (6 years until puberty)	Sexual interests in period of dormancy	None
Genital (puberty and after)	Sexual experiences with other people	None

Freud proposed that individuals go through the following sequence of psychosexual stages:

- *Oral stage.* During this stage, pleasure is derived from actions involving the mouth. Breastfeeding is the most obvious pleasurable activity in which infants partake. Fixation at this stage might result from overindulgence or deprivation from breastfeeding when it is needed. According to Freud, adults who are orally fixated may be prone to excesses of eating, drinking, and smoking or, conversely, may try to avoid oral stimulation as much as possible.

- *Anal stage.* Stimulation relating to bowel movements is the source of pleasure during this stage. Toilet training plays a central role in the passage through this stage. Fixation results in being excessively neat and organized (*anal-retentive*) or, on the opposite end of the spectrum, a person who becomes sloppy and messy.

- *Phallic stage.* This stage is a focal point of psychosexual development, as it is when children begin to show interest in their own genitals. Freud believed that children in the phallic stage become sexually attracted to the opposite-sexed parent, leading to one of two events depending on the sex of the child. The male child develops a sense of competition with his father, and then begins to fear that his father will castrate him in the course of competing for the affection of the mother (the *Oedipal complex*). The female fixation manifests itself in what Freud termed *penis envy*, in which girls are believed to fantasize about having a penis.

- *Latent stage.* During this stage, the libido is dormant. Relationships center on building friendships with same-sex peers.

- *Genital stage.* This stage, which is marked by the onset of puberty, continues throughout adulthood. It is during this time that interest in mature, sexual relationships with others begins. Unresolved conflicts at earlier stages of psychosexual development may impede the development of mature sexual relationships at this stage and into adulthood.

According to Freud, during the oral stage of psychosexual development pleasure is derived from actions of the mouth—particularly breastfeeding. Later, during the anal stage, attention turns toward potty training.

Modern psychodynamic psychologists generally do not agree that Freud's stages of psychosexual development are directly applicable to personality development. Clinical psychologists, however, attest to observing patterns that are consistent with Freud's observations of each stage of psychosexual development (Westen, 1998). For example, one study reported that children are more likely to show affection to the same-sexed parent and aggression toward the opposite-sexed parent (Watson & Getz, 1990). This is reminiscent of the Oedipal complex, although you should notice there is no reference to sexual attraction toward the opposite-sexed parent.

EXPLORING THE UNCONSCIOUS WITH PROJECTIVE TESTS

The unconscious mind is an enduring theme among psychodynamic psychologists, but it presents a problem when it comes to tapping into individuals' personality characteristics: How can we become aware of something that is, by definition, unavailable to consciousness? Freud employed techniques such as *dream analysis*; that is, he viewed dreams as direct links to the unconscious mind. According to Freud, because the id does not use language, the conscious mind can make sense of dreams only by interpreting what they symbolize. Freud also noticed clues to the unconscious in the little things people do, a gesture, a slip of the tongue, or even a joke. To Freud, all of these behaviors are clues to what is going on in the unconscious mind.

Since Freud's time, psychodynamic psychologists have attempted to develop more standardized techniques for probing the unconscious. These **projective tests** *are personality tests in which ambiguous images are presented to an individual to elicit responses that reflect unconscious desires or conflicts.* They are called "projective" because the image itself might not represent anything in particular, but rather how an individual describes the stimulus is thought to be a projection of her own thoughts and personality.

One of the most familiar projective tests (see Figure 12.11) is the **Rorschach inkblot test,** *in which subjects are asked to describe what they see on the inkblot, and psychologists attempt to interpret what the subject projects onto the stimulus by using a standardized scoring and interpretation method* (Exner, 1991). Another projective test is the **Thematic Apperception Test** (TAT), *which asks respondents to tell a*

{FIG. 12.11} **The Rorschach Inkblot Test** Some psychologists attempt to measure personality characteristics by analyzing the verbal responses clients use to describe what they see in an inkblot such as this. **Click on this figure in your eText to see more details.**

story about a series of 31 pictures involving ambiguous interpersonal situations (Figure 12.12). For example, a picture might show a man and woman looking at each other with blank expressions. Subjects are asked to tell a story about the picture. Are they a married couple discussing a divorce? Or are they acting students who are preparing for a scene in a play? The type of response the subject makes is thought to be a projection of their personality functioning.

Two particularly important concepts come into play when it comes to evaluating psychological testing: reliability and validity (see Module 2.1). The *reliability*

{FIG. 12.12} **The Thematic Apperception Test** In this projective test, the individual is asked to tell a story about what is happening in the image. The responses to this task are thought by some to reveal something important about personality.

{FIG. 12.13} **Figure Drawing as a Projective Test** Figure drawing is another projective technique used by many psychologists. The content of the drawings is analyzed and interpreted by the therapist. It turns out that these drawings are somewhat related to artistic ability and intelligence, but not personality (Lilienfeld et al., 2000). This is a problem of validity. The figure drawing technique does not appear to measure what it claims to measure: personality. **Click on this figure in your eText to see more details**.

of a test refers to how consistently it yields similar results. In the case of projective tests, we would expect to have reliability between therapists who evaluate the responses—two or more therapists who analyze responses to projective tests should come up with the same or very similar conclusions. The *validity* of a test refers to how well the test measures what it is intended to measure. Projective tests are supposed to measure personality functioning. But what if they actually measure something else, such as creativity, imagination, or someone's mood at the time that person takes the test? For some projective tests, this appears to be the case. For example, the *figure-drawing test* shown in Figure 12.13 does not seem to measure personality—at least not exclusively—but rather some combination of artistic ability and intelligence (see Lilienfeld et al., 2000). Unfortunately, time and again research has indicated serious limitations regarding the reliability and validity of projective tests (Garb et al., 2005; Lilienfeld et al., 2000).

Despite criticisms from some researchers, many clients and therapists claim that they have experienced significant breakthroughs toward understanding personality by using projective tests. A survey in the mid-1990s estimated that 43% of clinical psychologists and psychiatrists made frequent use of projective tests (Watkins et al., 1995). More recently, a survey of school psychologists showed that the TAT and Rorschach were used by 30% and 14% of these professionals, respectively, but their popularity appears to be declining (Hojnoski et al., 2006). Despite this trend, some researchers continue to look for projection in other areas. It may be that an entirely new way of approaching the concept of projection is needed.

There are clearly problems with the reliability and validity of some projective tests, but the basic idea of projection remains compelling to many psychologists in practice. Could there be some way to measure projection with greater accuracy? In fact, it is possible that the way you perceive others is actually a projection of your own personality.

What do we know about the way people perceive others?

People have a seemingly natural inclination to make assumptions about what others are like, even if only very limited information is available. Other people—even those whom we hardly know—might be regarded as friendly, aggressive, selfish, or trustworthy, for example. We have a natural inclination to use terms such as these to organize how we think about other people. Psychologists have recently asked whether our perceptions of others actually say just as much about our own characteristics. In other words, is the way we perceive others shaped by our own personal qualities?

The trait of Machiavellianism provides a great example. People who exhibit this trait are generally willing and able to manipulate and deceive others to get what they want. Interestingly, they are more likely than the general population to see others as being cynical and selfish (Christie & Geis, 1970). Thus psychologists suggest that the degree to which an individual sees people as selfish and cynical is, to an extent, a projection of his own Machiavellianism (Wood et al., 2010).

How can scientists study how projection relates to personality?

Although projection was initially a psychodynamic idea, contemporary researchers have begun to apply it to other approaches, such as the trait approach. In one study, a research team had participants rate their own personality according to the Big Five (see Module 12.1 for the Big Five), narcissism, and symptoms of psychological depression. They found several correlations showing that the way people view themselves is, in fact, related to how they view others. For example, the participants who rated themselves as agreeable (meaning they make an effort to get along with others and avoid conflict) also tended to rate others as conscientious, emotionally stable, and open to new experiences. The researchers identified a general trend in which people who view themselves positively (as agreeable, intelligent, and satisfied with life) are likely to view others the same way (Wood et al., 2010). In other words, how an individual perceives others appears to be a projection of how the individual views herself.

Can we critically evaluate this research?

The results of this study indicate that self-ratings and ratings of others are correlated. However, the correlations themselves are not very large, meaning that psychologists cannot make *precise* predictions about a rater's personality based on that individual's ratings of others, but rather can make only *general* statements. In addition, the projection is in a fairly broad domain—the projection seems to occur only in terms of positive and negative attributes. Once again, this places limitations on how much psychologists can really learn about an individual based on that person's perceptions of others.

Why is this relevant?

Standard projective tests such as the Rorschach inkblot test and the Thematic Apperception Test are fraught with problems and controversy. It would be unheard of for modern medical doctors to diagnose disorders using procedures that are as unreliable and of as questionable validity as these tests. Thus it is important that if psychologists plan to continue using projective tests to measure personality, they should continue to search openly for new, objective methods that might reveal meaningful information about the individuals taking them. Psychology need not necessarily abandon projective tests altogether, as the benefits of adding rigor and scrutiny to them has shown that they can be of value (e.g., Schultheiss & Brunstein, 2001).

Quick Quiz 12.3a
The Psychodynamic Perspective

1 According to Freud, the _____ is the personality component that is responsible for seeking to satisfy basic biological needs.

- **A** id
- **B** ego
- **C** superego
- **D** libido

2 Which of the following is *not* a point of emphasis for psychodynamic theories of personality?

- **A** The role of unconscious motives
- **B** The importance of early social relationships
- **C** Learning how to cope with and regulate emotion
- **D** Using trait descriptions to describe personality

3 According to Freud, which of the following is the order in which the stages of psychosexual development occur?

- **A** Oral, anal, phallic, latency, genital
- **B** Oral, anal, genital, phallic, latency
- **C** Anal, oral, phallic, latency, genital
- **D** Latency, oral, anal, genital, phallic

4 A defense mechanism would be employed:

- **A** by the id to create conflict.
- **B** by the superego to reduce or avoid conflict.
- **C** by the ego to reduce or avoid conflict.
- **D** by the superego to create conflict.

5 Steven lied to about his brother to avoid getting in trouble with his parents, but now he is experiencing extreme guilt. According to Freud, this guilt would arise due to the activity of the _____.

- **A** Oedipal complex
- **B** ego
- **C** superego
- **D** libido

6 Why have some psychologists questioned the reliability of projective tests?

- **A** Judges very often agree on how to interpret an individual test.
- **B** Judges often do not agree on how to interpret an individual test.
- **C** The tests may not measure what they claim to measure.
- **D** These tests often provide disturbing details about a person's unconscious.

Answers can be found on page ANS-4.

Alternatives to the Psychodynamic Approach

Freud attracted many followers, but some of his contemporaries took psychodynamic psychology in different directions. They recognized that sex and aggression are not the only motives relevant to personality development; indeed, other motivational forces, such as the need for belonging and the need for achievement are important aspects of personality. Like Freud, however, these theorists emphasized the existence of multiple, unconscious processes and the importance of development.

One example of these new directions was **analytical psychology**, *a branch of psychology that describes personality as it relates to what are called unconscious archetypes.* These archetypes are mental representations of personality figures, relationships, and experiences. Swiss psychologist Carl Jung (1875–1961) founded analytical psychology after breaking from Freud professionally and personally. In contrast to Freud, Jung emphasized how the unconscious mind also harnesses creativity. Jung believed that in addition to having a personal unconscious, humans also possess a **collective unconscious**—*a collection of memories that can be traced to our ancestral past.* These memories take the form of *archetypes*, which are images and symbols that are thought to have universal meaning among all humans. According to Jung, all people have an archetype for a mother or father, and a notion of a God. One such archetype, called the *Hero*, represents the universal human belief, often expressed as myth and folklore, in a special force or being that wins mighty battles against hated foes. The archetypes that Jung identified were thought to organize human thoughts and behavior, and therefore personality.

Others who followed in Freud's footsteps included Alfred Adler (1870–1937) and Karen Horney (1885–1952), both of whom placed far less emphasis on sexual conflict and personality development than did Freud. Adler viewed the social environment as critical to personality development. He believed that people develop an **inferiority complex**, *an abnormal personality that results from struggling with feelings of inferiority in one's social environment.* Horney (pronounced "HORN-eye"), like Adler, saw social dynamics as critical to personality. Instead of sexual conflicts, Horney viewed interpersonal conflict between children and their parents as important to personality development. Also, she rightfully took exception to the notion that females experience penis envy toward males.

As you can see, psychodynamic theorists have separated themselves in a number of important ways. Contemporary psychodynamic psychologists work mostly in the field of clinical psychology, a remnant of Freud's interest in mental disorders. And, despite some differences,

According to Carl Jung, the "Hero" archetype is a universal notion of the individual who embodies good and strength.

modern psychodynamic psychologists do share many of the core attributes mentioned at the beginning of the module: an emphasis on unconscious thought and emotion, internal conflicts, and the influence of early experiences on adult personality (Westen, 1998).

Freud's theories have been widely criticized as sexist, pseudoscientific, and overly focused on the darks sides of humanity. They are also regarded as untestable, meaning that they do not generate hypotheses that can be confirmed or disconfirmed. For instance, if we were to tell you that, while growing up, you were sexually attracted to your opposite-sexed parent, you could say one of two things: You could either confirm that this was the case, or you could deny it. In the latter case, a Freudian psychoanalyst could simply say you were employing a defense mechanism and *repressing* the memories. Thus this idea cannot be falsified. Moreover, regarding the concept of repression, contemporary research on memory has failed to produce evidence that people are any more likely to forget negative life events than other memories (see McNally, 2005).

Finally, Freud has been criticized for developing an enormous, comprehensive theory about human personality based on his interactions with a relatively small, unrepresentative group of individuals. He provided little beyond anecdotal evidence that his explanations for pathological personality could be applied to normally developing people or to people from different cultural backgrounds.

These are just a few critiques of Freud's theory, but they signal serious problems with his ideas. Thus it is not surprising that other psychologists took psychodynamic theory in different directions. Current psychodynamic psychology is applied mainly to psychotherapy, which recent research shows can be an effective treatment for certain psychological problems (Shedler, 2010). We will encounter psychodynamics again in Module 14.2.

In defense of Freud and psychodynamic psychology, one does not have to look far to find fault in many older theories and ideas in psychology and other sciences. In other words, decades-old scientific theories are often regarded as "pseudoscience" by modern standards. Also, Freud recognized several very important principles that continue to influence the field of psychology today, including the role played by the unconscious and the significance of early experiences in the development of the adult personality.

Quick Quiz 12.3b
Alternative Psychodynamic Approaches

KNOW...

1 The aspect of consciousness proposed by Carl Jung that is a store of archetypes representing symbols and experiences common to all cultures is called the _____.

   A preconscious
   B subconscious
   C analytical conscious
   D collective unconscious

APPLY...

2 Alexandra's older sister is praised for being good at math, but Alexandra struggles with the subject. What would the resulting feelings of being "not good enough" be called?

   A Negative reinforcement
   B Negative archetype
   C Inferiority complex
   D Oedipal complex

ANALYZE...

3 Which of the following is not a critique of Freud's psychodynamic approach to personality?

   A It focuses on situations we cannot control.
   B It does not yield many scientifically testable hypotheses.
   C It was based on a very limited sample of subjects.
   D It has not been found useful or applicable to clinical psychology.

Answers can be found on page ANS-4.

Humanistic Perspectives

Other psychologists keen on understanding human personality focused on what contributes to happiness and fulfillment. Abraham Maslow (1908–1970) believed that all humans seek to fulfill a hierarchy of needs, which begins with satisfying basic motivations for food and physical safety, and progresses toward more psychologically complex experiences such as feeling a sense of security and love for others and by others. When basic needs for love are met, human beings seek to achieve self-esteem. The most advanced stage of personality development is reached with **self-actualization**, *which involves reaching our fullest potential* (Maslow, 1968; see also Module 11.3). During the mid 20th century, Maslow and others created a movement called **humanistic psychology** *that emphasized the unique and positive qualities of human experience and potential*. This perspective was viewed as an alternative to psychodynamic theory as well as to

behaviorism, both of which did not acknowledge an important role for free will in human behavior.

Like Maslow, Carl Rogers (1902–1987) held a more optimistic view of humanity. According to his **person-centered perspective**, *people are basically good, and given the right environment their personality will develop fully and normally*. Humans, he said, have the motivation and potential to expand their horizons, mature, and fulfill each of their capacities. During his career Rogers became increasingly focused on a particular aspect of personality, the **self-concept**—*that is, the collection of feelings and beliefs we have about who we are*. Those persons with a positive self-concept are aware of their qualities, including both their limitations and their abilities. Those individuals with a negative self-concept focus on what they want to be (their "ideal self"), rather than on what they actually are. For example, a person with limited ability to play music may insist on joining a band, but may develop a negative self-concept because he is focusing on an ideal version of himself, rather than on his real self.

In conclusion, humanistic ideas offer an alternative approach to personality that stands in stark contrast to psychodynamic theory. One advantage to Rogers' work is that his theories were tested empirically, which was not the case with Freud's work. Many who prefer the humanistic approach do so not for scientific reasons, however, but because they value the more optimistic view of human nature and the potential for free will that are lacking in the psychodynamic approach.

Quick Quiz 12.3c
Humanistic Perspectives

KNOW...

1 According to Maslow, what is the most advanced stage of personality development?

   A Collective unconscious
   B Self-actualization
   C Hierarchy of needs
   D Action potential

2 In contrast to psychodynamic theory, humanistic theory emphasizes:

   A free will.
   B how personalities are determined by biology.
   C how personality is determined by the environment.
   D how defense mechanisms affect behavior.

APPLY...

3 Justin has struggled to pass his mathematics courses and decides to pursue a degree in creative writing, an area in which he has a long history of succeeding. According to Carl Rogers, in this instance Justin is showing a(n) _____.

   A positive self-concept
   B negative self-concept
   C inferiority complex
   D Oedipal complex

Answers can be found on page ANS-4.

Module Summary

Now that you have read this module you should:

KNOW ...

- **The key terminology related to the psychodynamic and humanistic approaches to personality:**

analytical psychology (p. 469)
collective unconscious (p. 469)
defense mechanisms (p. 464)
ego (p. 463)
fixation (p. 464)
humanistic psychology (p. 470)
id (p. 462)
inferiority complex (p. 469)
person-centered perspective (p. 470)

projective tests (p. 466)
psychodynamic theories (p. 462)
Rorschach inkblot test (p. 466)
self-actualization (p. 470)
self-concept (p. 470)
superego (p. 463)
Thematic Apperception Test (TAT) (p. 466)

UNDERSTAND ...

- **How people use defense mechanisms to cope with conflicting thoughts and feelings.** According to the psychodynamic perspective, defense mechanisms activate whenever our unconscious drives come into conflict with the ego or the superego. These mechanisms may involve repressing urges, displacing them, or even finding subtle, more acceptable ways of expressing them.

- **The developmental stages Freud used to explain the origins of personality.** To explain personality development according to Freud, we begin with the concept of libido—the id's energy source for the drives that originate at different focal points of the body from infancy to adolescence. Each of the stages of psychosocial development—oral, anal, phallic, latent, and genital—is associated with a unique form of conflict as the ego and superego develop. Failure to resolve the corresponding conflict can result in a fixation.

APPLY ...

- **Both psychodynamic and humanistic perspectives to explain personality.** If you are applying the psychodynamic approach to understand someone's personality, you would likely consider the role that unconscious processes play in determining behavior, as well as the conflicts that exist between a person's impulses and his need to regulate them. Review Freud's structure of the mind in **Figure 12.10** (p. 463) and the psychosexual stages of development in **Table 12.3** (p. 465). What might each of the following situations mean from Freud's perspective?

  1. A student cannot concentrate on her homework until every little item on her desk is in its appropriate place.

  2. An individual commits violent acts against others without feeling any remorse.

     In contrast, humanistic psychologists tend to believe that we are not constrained by our impulses and unconscious drives, but rather are free to act and reach our fullest potential. Thus they may rely on something like Maslow's hierarchy of needs to describe how a person is developing. How far has a person developed in each of these scenarios? Check your answers on page ANS-4.

  3. A student cannot concentrate on homework because he is so busy checking his Facebook news feed.

  4. A lawyer gives up a lucrative legal practice to start a nonprofit legal defense organization supporting economically disadvantaged people.

ANALYZE ...

- **Whether projective tests are valid measures of personality.** In this module you learned about projective tests such as the Rorschach inkblot test and the Thematic Apperception Test, which some believe allow psychologists to tap into unconscious processes. Although research does suggest that we process information without being aware of it, projective tests do not appear to be valid ways of accessing what is being processed.

- **The strengths and weaknesses of psychodynamic perspectives.** Psychodynamic theories can provide some compelling explanations for human motivation. For example, it is easy to understand how social and moral conflicts arise when couched in terms of a struggle between the id and the ego. At the same time, this approach does not have a lot of scientific support. It is not possible to objectively identify the structure of an individual's personality from this perspective; instead, psychodynamic theorists must rely on subjective interpretations. Attempts at developing more objective projective tests have been largely unsuccessful.

Module 12.1 :: Contemporary Approaches to Personality

Focus Questions:

1 What are the basic traits that make up human personality?
An English-language dictionary includes thousands of terms that could be used to describe what people are like. With the help of a statistical technique called factor analysis, psychologists have whittled these many possibilities down to arrive at a significantly reduced number of traits, though not all agree on what those traits should be. In recent times, the Big Five (neuroticism, extraversion, openness, agreeableness, and consciousness) has been a widely used model of personality. Measures such as the MMPI will arrive at a different answer as to how many traits to include, because this inventory includes clinical scales that describe abnormal personality functioning. For example, depression, hysteria, and paranoia scales are of great use for a clinician, but are less relevant to the general population.

2 To what extent are our preferences, thoughts, and behaviors determined by situational factors versus more stable personality traits? Well-established and -developed personality tests tend to measure personality effectively. Even so, our behavior cannot be completely explained by a personality inventory such as the Big Five. At any given time, our location, the people with whom we associate with, our activities, our subjective states, and many other factors influence how we behave, which is often in ways that are inconsistent with what a personality test might predict.

👁 **Watch** *The Basics: Personality Theories* in the **MyPsychLab** **video series**

Module 12.2 :: Cultural and Biological Approaches to Personality

Focus Questions:

1 Does culture influence the types of personality traits we find across human societies? As we learned in the beginning of this module, WEIRD (Western, Educated, Industrialized, Rich, Democratic) individuals are representative of people of other cultures insofar as the traits making up the Big Five also characterize differences among people sampled across many different languages and nations. That said, individuals from within different cultures vary in the degree to which they express these traits. Also, psychologists have found that when they do not apply the Big Five structure to other cultures, different, possibly culturally unique traits arise.

2 How do biological processes such as genes, the nervous system, and evolution account for individual differences in personality? Decades of work using twin comparisons show that individual differences in personality are partly accounted for by genetic factors—typically, the concordance rates approximate .50. Molecular studies allow us to look at specific genes that correlate with personality. Genes that code for serotonin activity in the brain are related to traits such as shyness and neuroticism; they predict how individuals will respond to negative events. Psychologists are now finding that the core personality traits in humans can be also found in a diverse array of nonhuman species, suggesting that these traits are remarkably old from a genetic perspective. In addition, the unique and flexible combinations of personality traits within each individual may allow for humans (and many nonhumans) to attract others and fill needs presented by rapidly changing environmental and social situations.

👁 **Watch** *Special Topics: Twins and Personality* in the **MyPsychLab video series**

Module 12.3 :: Psychodynamic and Humanistic Approaches to Personality

Focus Questions:

1 Is personality fundamentally guided by dark, aggressive impulses or by a desire for more positive experiences? The story that opened this module described soldiers laughing during a brutal attack. Does this behavior make the soldiers fundamentally dangerous or sadistic people? According to Freud's approach, everyone has aggressive impulses, represented by the id. If we are not aware of our own impulses, it is simply because our defense mechanisms—such as humor—are working appropriately. From the humanistic perspective, however, people are seen as basically good and strive to reach their potential.

2 Do people really use psychological defenses like humor to protect themselves from emotionally troubling events? Sigmund Freud and Anna Freud both emphasized the role of defense mechanisms in preventing unconscious impulses from evolving into conscious thoughts and actions. This effort may involve rationalizing, denying, or even joking about the intrapsychic conflict that results. In the case of humor, some research suggests that it is an effective way to cope with stress (Martin, 2001).

👁 **Watch** *What's in It for Me? Psychological Resilience* in the **MyPsychLab video series**

👁 **Watch** the complete video series online at **MyPsychLab**

Episode 13: Personality
1. *The Big Picture: What Is Personality?*
2. *The Basics: Personality Theories*
3. *Special Topics: Twins and Personality*
4. *Thinking Like a Psychologist: Testing Personality*
5. *In the Real World Application: Putting Popular Personality Assessments to the Test*
6. *What's in It for Me? Personality Resilience*

1 Some psychologists use a(n) _____ approach to studying personality, which is a person-centered method in which researchers focus on individual people and their unique personalities.

- (A) nomothetic
- (B) factor-analysis
- (C) idiographic
- (D) reciprocal

2 Which of the following statements is true about personality traits over the life span?

- (A) The first signs of personality do not appear until a child is approximately 2 years of age.
- (B) Early temperament is not a useful predictor of adult personality.
- (C) Young adults tend to experience more negative emotions compared to adolescents.
- (D) By middle age, adult personality traits show very little change over time.

3 Unlike the strict behaviorists' view, Bandura's theory of reciprocal determinism:

- (A) emphasizes the importance of learning.
- (B) acknowledges that people shape and determine their environments.
- (C) emphasizes the importance of traits.
- (D) assumes that traits are not stable over time.

4 Kwan comes from an Asian country where the importance of family connections is emphasized, and group success is generally considered more important than individual accomplishment. Kwan's culture appears to emphasize which view?

- (A) Individualism
- (B) Collectivism
- (C) Martyrism
- (D) Conformism

5 What do twin studies indicate about the role of genes in personality?

- (A) Heredity plays an important role in personality.
- (B) Dizygotic twins are more likely than monozygotic twins to share personality traits.
- (C) Personality is almost entirely determined by parenting and other environmental factors.
- (D) Personality appears to be related to two different copies of a serotonin transporter gene.

6 Research into animal personalities suggests that:

- (A) unlike human personality traits, animal personality traits have no genetic basis.
- (B) humans are the only animals who have true emotions.
- (C) the Big Five personality traits can be observed only in primates.
- (D) the Big Five personality traits occur in many different types of animals.

7 Ancient scholars believed in the theory of humorism, which postulated that personality was controlled by the:

- (A) date and time of a person's birth.
- (B) shape and contours of a person's skull.
- (C) balance of four fluid substances within the body.
- (D) balance of the right and left hemispheres of the brain.

8 In old cartoons, characters were sometimes shown with a devil on one shoulder telling them to do something selfish or immoral, such as stealing or lying. On the other shoulder, the animators would draw an angel, which would tell the character not to listen to the devil and to act morally instead. In Freudian terms, the angel represents which part of the character's psyche?

- (A) Ego
- (B) Superego
- (C) Id
- (D) A defense mechanism

9 Daniel's psychiatrist shows him a series of cards with abstract inkblots on them and asks Daniel to describe what he sees. When Daniel asks about the test, his psychologists explains that it is called the _____.

- (A) Rorschach Inkblot Test
- (B) Minnesota Multiphasic Personality Inventory (MMPI)
- (C) Thematic Apperception Test (TAT)
- (D) Figure-Drawing Test

10 As a response to both behaviorism and psychodynamic theory, Abraham Maslow (among others) initiated a movement called _____, which emphasized the unique and positive qualities of human experience and potential.

- (A) phrenology
- (B) humanistic psychology
- (C) analytical psychology
- (D) self-actualization

✓●—[**Study** and **Review** at **MyPsychLab**

Work the Scientific Literacy Model :: Understanding Personality?

What do we know about personality?

Review what it means to approach the study of personality from an idiographic or nomothetic perspective on **page 440**. The nomothetic approach is what allows researchers to arrive at global characterizations of personality, such as the five factor model. (**Review Figure 12.1**). Research using the Big Five indicates that individuals tend to have relatively stable traits from day to day—an observation that, as demonstrated in twin studies, indicates a strong genetic component to personality. But as we mention, personality is also affected by factors like culture, environment, and the situation. **On pages 443–444** we discussed the dynamic relationship between states and traits. This is a complicated but important idea. Remember that traits are stable characteristics, while states are temporary but highly influential determinants of behavior that are influenced by context. States influence how and when personality traits are expressed. For example, you may normally be highly agreeable, but if you start your morning by losing your bus pass, and then wait in a long line at the coffee shop, you may be in a state of anger by the time the barista hands you a cappuccino instead of the iced coffee you ordered.

How can science help explain personality?

Researchers use a variety of tests to understand personality. The five factor model and other trait approaches rely on statistical analyses, such as factor analysis, to determine the structure of personality. However, some question the validity of self-reports: Can people be trusted to evaluate their own characteristics, and do they report their behavior accurately? As we described on **page 442**, research shows that people's self-reporting on trait inventories matches with the reports of people who know them well, and studies on self-presentation on Facebook also suggests that people accurately report their personality characteristics. Projective personality tests like the Rorschach inkblot test are commonly used by psychodynamic psychologists. Research has shown that we do process information without being aware of it; although psychologists have generally struggled to demonstrate that projective tests are reliable or valid. Psychologists argue that our personality dimensions evolved to solve adaptive problems in our physical and social environments. So, for example, each of the Big Five traits is thought to have an adaptive function. Evidence for this argument comes from several sources, namely that of studies showing that numerous non-human species also share some of the basic personality dimensions that people have.

Why is this relevant?

Watch the accompanying video excerpt on testing personality. You can access the video at MyPsychLab or by clicking the play button in the center of your eText. If your instructor assigns this video as a homework activity, you will find additional content to help you in MyPsychLab. You can also view the video by using your smart phone and the QR code below, or you can go to the YouTube link provided.

After you have read this chapter and watched the video, identify and explain the four major approaches to personality assessment, including the advantages and disadvantages of each type.

Can we critically evaluate claims about personality?

Some popular psychology authors have argued that men and women are so different that they might as well be from different planets—but is this supported by research? The answers is no, at least not when it comes to personality characteristics. The **Myths in Mind on page 457** raised the point that although women and men differ on their Big Five personality ratings, the differences are actually quite small and are often based on states or situational factors. Similar claims have been made about culturally-based personalities. The research shows that there is remarkable consistency across cultures on core personality traits; however, it would be wrong to assume that culture has no affect on personality. **Figure 12.5 on page 451** illustrated a notable and interesting variation in the degree to which personality traits are expressed across cultures. Finally, when it comes to projective tests and probing the unconscious mind, it seems as though some projective tests are not measuring personality, but artistic ability, intelligence or something altogether different, so it is wise to be skeptical of their results.

MyPsychLab

Your turn to Work the Scientific Literacy Model: You can access the video at MyPsychLab or by clicking the play button in the center of your eText. If your instructor assigns this video as a homework activity, you will find additional content to help you at MyPsychLab. You can also view the video by using your smart phone and the QR code, or you can go to the YouTube link provided.

youtube.com/
scientificliteracy

13 :: PSYCHOLOGICAL DISORDERS

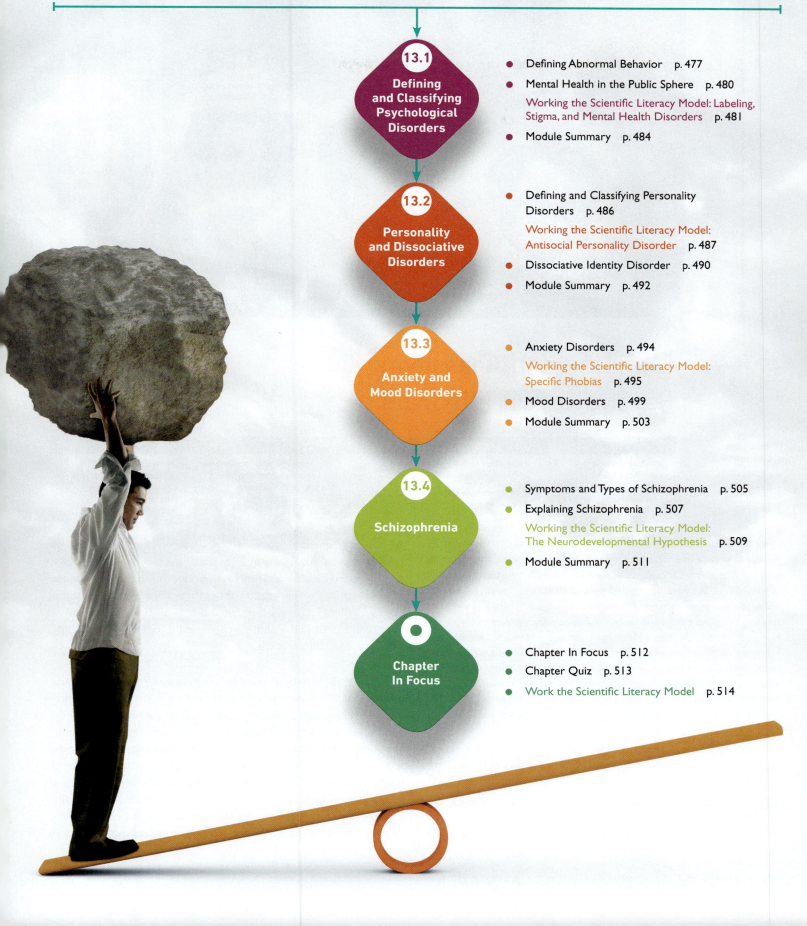

Defining and Classifying Psychological Disorders

Learning Objectives

After reading this module you should:

KNOW ...	UNDERSTAND ...	APPLY ...	ANALYZE ...
The key terminology associated with defining and classifying psychological disorders	How disorders are viewed as either dimensional or categorical The differences between the concepts of psychological disorders and insanity	Your knowledge to understand the symptoms, stereotypes, and stigma surrounding psychological disorders	Whether the benefits of labeling psychological disorders outweigh the disadvantages

Since 2001, the U.S. military has awarded more than 40,000 Purple Heart medals to service members who have been wounded in the line of duty in Iraq and Afghanistan. Thousands of men and women have been wounded in these wars, but have been lucky enough to come back alive. Some of these soldiers must learn to use prosthetic limbs, some have lost vision or hearing, and others will experience chronic pain for the rest of their lives. However, not a single Purple Heart has been awarded to a soldier who has returned with psychological wounds such as post-traumatic stress disorder (PTSD). This condition, involving chronic anxiety, nightmares, depression, suicidal impulses, and rage, is estimated to affect as many as 20% of men and women returning from military service (Ramchand et al., 2010). Should the military recognize psychological wounds as well as physical?

Focus Questions

 Why do people frequently regard physical and psychological conditions as fundamentally different?

 Which guidelines or criteria allow psychologists to diagnose a mental disorder such as PTSD?

· · · · · · · · · · · · · · · · · · ·

We routinely encounter information about psychological disorders such as depression or autism from many sources, including news, talk shows, and advertisements for prescription drugs. The amount of information floating around about these disorders is vast, and it can be challenging to sift through and critically analyze this enormous volume. To understand psychological disorders, we will apply two complementary models.

First is the **medical model**: *using our understanding of medical conditions to think about psychological conditions.* Just as diabetes has a set of symptoms, probable causes, and likely outcomes, so do psychological disorders. There are also preventive measures, interventions, and treatments targeted toward psychological disorders, just as there are for conditions such as diabetes or cancer. Today it might seem natural to talk about psychological problems in these terms, but, in fact, the medical model has not always been the norm. Throughout history and in various cultures, other explanations have been proposed for what we now call psychological

Table 13.1 :: Biological, Psychological, and Sociocultural Factors Influence Both Physical and Mental Disorders

	DIABETES	MAJOR DEPRESSION
Biological	Genetic influences on pancreatic function; excessive refined sugars	Genetic influences on neurotransmitter production and function; sleep disruption; lack of positive emotional arousal
Psychological	Poor food choices; sedentary lifestyle; alcohol abuse	Negative self-concept; pessimism; negative life experiences
Sociocultural	Familial and cultural foods and traditions; limited budget for groceries; lack of physical and nutritional education in the schools; lack of role models	Lack of social support; social withdrawal; lack of psychological services; stigma regarding psychological treatments

disorders. For example, someone who experiences hallucinations would likely be diagnosed with a psychological disorder in the United States. However, in another place or time, that same individual might be viewed as possessed by evil spirits, the victim of a curse, or even a prophet.

The second model we adopt includes the multiple perspectives of the *biopsychosocial model* (Table 13.1), first introduced in Module 1.1. For example, one biological factor contributing to depression involves disrupted activity of neurotransmitters such as serotonin. Psychological factors include persistent negative beliefs about the self (e.g., *nothing I do makes any difference in the world*) and feelings of hopelessness. Social factors such as impoverished neighborhoods and stressful family problems contribute to the development of depression as well. As is the case with many physical disorders such as diabetes, psychological disorders can rarely be traced to a single cause, so the biopsychosocial approach helps us develop a comprehensive understanding of psychological disorders.

This chapter focuses on psychological disorders, which, generally speaking, comprise abnormal behavioral and cognitive functioning. Before we go any further, however, we need to identify what is meant by *abnormal* when it comes to human behavior and experience.

Defining Abnormal Behavior

Abnormal psychology *is the psychological study of mental illness,* but the term "abnormal" needs some clarification. A person who cuts or burns himself until he sustains serious injury is behaving abnormally, as very few people inflict such damage on themselves. Someone who obtains a medical degree before the age of 20 is also unusual, statistically speaking, but she may show no signs of any mental illness. The difference between these two "unusual" individuals is that the person who harms

himself is exhibiting **maladaptive behavior**, *or behavior that hinders a person's ability to function in work, school, relationships, or society.* To distinguish between the abnormal and the unusual, the American Psychiatric Association (2000) provides three main criteria to identify maladaptive behavior:

- The behavior causes distress to self or others.
- The behavior impairs the ability to function in day-to-day activities.
- The behavior increases the risk of injury, death, legal problems or punishment for breaking rules, or other detrimental consequences.

As you can see, abnormal psychology is a broad term, so to define more specific varieties of abnormal behavior, mental health professionals rely on a carefully designed system of diagnosis.

Complete the **Survey** *Are You Normal?* at **MyPsychLab**

PSYCHOLOGY'S PUZZLE: DIAGNOSING PSYCHOLOGICAL DISORDERS To diagnose psychological disorders, psychologists and psychiatrists rely on the ***Diagnostic and Statistical Manual for Mental Disorders* (fourth edition, Text Revision)** (which we will abbreviate as DSM-IV), *the manual that establishes criteria for the diagnosis of mental disorders.* Created and updated by expert panels from the American Psychiatric Association, the DSM-IV offers a set of clear guidelines for determining the presence and severity of some 350 mental disorders. For each disorder in the DSM-IV, the guidelines convey three important pieces of information about an individual's experience: a set of symptoms; the **etiology**, *or the origins or causes of symptoms;* and the *prognosis,* or how these symptoms will persist or change over time, with or without professional treatment.

The DSM-IV uses five divisions to characterize psychological disorders (Table 13.2 on p. 478); each division is referred to as an axis (plural = axes, pronounced "ax-eeze"). The axes are broad categories that

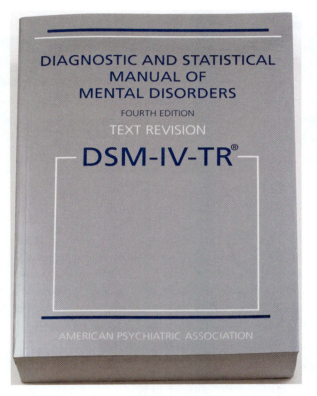

The DSM-IV (1994) and its revised version, the DSM-IV-TR (2000), are used by mental health professionals for diagnosing mental disorders. The first edition was published in 1952; a fifth edition is scheduled to be published in 2013.

post-traumatic stress disorder (PTSD; see Table 13.3) are specific types of anxiety disorders. Given that more than 350 disorders are identified in the DSM-IV, we will examine only the most prominent in this text.

As you can see in Table 13.3, the diagnostic criteria identify a likely cause, the psychological experiences that follow, and a time course for the symptoms. In the case of suspected PTSD, this information helps psychologists decide whether the patient should be diagnosed with the disorder, a different psychological disorder, or none at all.

The DSM-IV addresses problems associated with the physical, mental, and social functioning of an individual. Its widespread use attests to how useful the biopsychosocial model is in understanding mental health. In addition, many insurance companies will not cover treatment for mental health problems without a formal diagnosis.

Despite its advantages, however, the DSM-IV has some limitations. Mental health professionals do not unanimously agree on how to classify many disorders, and disputes often arise over whether some conditions should be included or excluded from the manual. Disorders covered in the DSM-IV are primarily based on observations of clients or patients, rather than on potentially more objective markers of mental disorders such as genes, neurotransmitters, or brain abnormalities—a practice that leaves room for subjectivity and for individuals to potentially fake psychological problems. Thus a growing number of psychologists believe that biological markers, some

are divided into numerous subtypes. For example, Axis I includes mood and anxiety disorders; anxiety disorder is a general category, while phobias (excessive fears) and

Table 13.2 :: The Five Axes of the DSM-IV and Sample Disorders

AXIS I: CLINICAL DISORDERS : OTHER CONDITIONS THAT MAY BE A FOCUS OF CLINICAL ATTENTION
Disorders Usually First diagnosed in Infancy, Childhood, or Adolescence (*excluding Mental Retardation, which is diagnosed on Axis II*)
The first axis includes what most people traditionally think of as psychiatric disorders and behavioral problems. It includes disordered mood or thought, anxiety, as well as substance abuse problems.

AXIS II: PERSONALITY DISORDERS: MENTAL RETARDATION
Personality disorders are described in Module 13.2. These involve persistent patterns of maladaptive behavior that are disturbing and difficult to change. For example, individuals with personality disorders may be unusually self-centered, immune to other's feelings, or in need of excessive attention.

AXIS III: GENERAL MEDICAL CONDITIONS (WITH ICD-9-CM CODES)
For this axis, a physician may provide information about medical conditions that a mental health worker should consider. For example, a person with diabetes may experience symptoms from the physical disorder that could be confused with symptoms of a psychiatric disorder.

AXIS IV: PSYCHOSOCIAL AND ENVIRONMENTAL PROBLEMS
Sometimes individuals experience problems in their immediate environment or social circles. These stressors can create difficulties that, like medical problems, may mimic psychological symptoms. However, complaints arising from psychosocial problems do not necessarily constitute enough evidence for the diagnosis of an Axis I disorder.

AXIS V: GLOBAL ASSESSMENT OF FUNCTIONING (GAF) SCALE
Clinicians use this scale to assess the overall psychological, interpersonal, and work-related functioning on a scale from 100 (very high-level functioning) to 1 (severely impaired functioning).

Table 13.3 :: Diagnostic Criteria for 309.81 Posttraumatic Stress Disorder

A. The person has been exposed to a traumatic event in which both of the following were present:
   1. the person experienced, witnessed, or was confronted with an event or events that involved actual or threatened death or serious injury, or a threat to the physical integrity of self or others
   2. the person's response involved intense fear, helplessness, or horror. Note: In children, this may be expressed instead by disorganized or agitated behavior

B. The traumatic event is persistently reexperienced in one (or more) of the following ways:
   1. recurrent and intrusive distressing recollections of the event, including images, thoughts, or perceptions. Note: In young children, repetitive play may occur in which themes or aspects of the trauma are expressed.
   2. recurrent distressing dreams of the event. Note: In children, there may be frightening dreams without recognizable content.
   3. acting or feeling as if the traumatic event were recurring (includes a sense of reliving the experience, illusions, hallucinations, and dissociative flashback episodes, including those that occur on awakening or when intoxicated). Note: In young children, trauma-specific reenactment may occur.
   4. intense psychological distress at exposure to internal or external cues that symbolize or resemble an aspect of the traumatic event
   5. physiological reactivity on exposure to internal or external cues that symbolize or resemble an aspect of the traumatic event

C. Persistent avoidance of stimuli associated with the trauma and numbering of general responsiveness (not present before the trauma), as indicated by three (or more) of the following:
   1. efforts to avoid thoughts, feelings, or conversations associated with the trauma
   2. efforts to avoid activities, place, or people that arouse recollections of the trauma
   3. inability to recall an important aspect of the trauma
   4. markedly diminished interest or participation in significant activities
   5. feeling of detachment or estrangement from others
   6. restricted range of affect (e.g., unable to have loving feelings)
   7. sense of foreshortened future (e.g., does not expect to have a career, marriage, children, or a normal life span)

D. Persistent symptoms of increased arousal (not present before the trauma), as indicated by two (or more) of the following:
   1. difficulty falling asleep or staying asleep
   2. irritability or outbursts of anger
   3. difficulty concentrating
   4. hypervigilance
   5. exaggerated startle response

E. Duration of the disturbance (symptoms in Criteria B, C, and D) is more than 1 month.

F. The disturbance causes clinically significant distress or impairment in social, occupational, or other important areas of functioning.

Specify if:

   Acute: if duration of symptoms is less than 3 months

   Chronic: if duration of symptoms is 3 months or more

Specify if:

   With Delayed Onset: if onset of symptoms is at least 6 months after the stressor

Source: American Psychiatric Association, 2000.

of which could be detected by brain scans, should be indentified and incorporated into diagnostic criteria (Hyman, 2007).

Because of the thousands of studies that have been published since the 2000 revision of the DSM-IV, we now have a better understanding of many of the disorders in the manual. Therefore, the American Psychiatric Association plans to release a new edition—the DSM-V—in May 2013. This new edition will likely reflect the substantial advances in neuroscience and genetics that have contributed to our knowledge of psychological disorders. In addition, the current DSM-IV treats most symptoms in an either/or fashion: Either you have the symptom or you do not. It is anticipated that the DSM-V will allow

for a broader range of symptoms and severity because, as you will see, symptoms are not always so clear-cut.

CATEGORICAL VERSUS DIMENSIONAL VIEWS OF DISORDERS Another challenge when classifying mental disorders is that the either/or distinction between normal and abnormal does not reflect the complexity of human behavior. Many symptoms of psychological disorders consist of typical thoughts and behaviors, except that they are more severe and longer-lasting than usual, and they may occur in inappropriate contexts or without any clear reasons. These symptoms fit what is called a *dimensional* view of psychological disorders because the normal–abnormal distinction is a matter of degree. For example, someone who has

PsychTutor
Click here in your eText for an interactive tutorial on **Unusual vs. Pathological**

an unusually stressful experience that brings about heightened anxiety may feel fine after several days. In contrast, when stress and anxiety are very severe, lasting for weeks at a time, and begin to change how a person leads his or her life, then the condition may become recognized as a psychological disorder. In this case, it may become a type of anxiety disorder such as PTSD. This is certainly true for many veterans returning from active military duty, and it can also be true for people who survive violent crimes, accidents, and other traumatic events.

In contrast, a *categorical* view of psychological disorders regards different mental conditions as separate types; that is, differences between normal and abnormal functioning are of kind, rather than degree (Esterberg & Compton, 2009). According to this approach, a disorder is not just an extreme version of normal thoughts and behaviors, but rather something altogether different. Down syndrome is an example of a categorical disorder because it involves an unusual genetic condition: An individual either has the extra 21st chromosome linked to Down syndrome or does not. Because Down syndrome is categorical, you would not expect to find someone who has a "partial" form of the disorder. However, that is not the case for dimensional disorders; individuals might show a range of symptoms that are indicative of PTSD, depression, and many other disorders discussed in this chapter.

Quick Quiz 13.1a
Defining Abnormal Behavior

KNOW…

1 The _____ uses an understanding of physical conditions to think about psychological conditions.

   (A) biopsychosocial model   (C) categorical view

   (B) dimensional view   (D) medical model

UNDERSTAND…

2 Viewing a psychological disorder as an extreme case of otherwise normal behavior reflects the _____.

   (A) dimensional view   (C) categorical view

   (B) medical model   (D) biopsychosocial model

3 Which of the following is *not* a psychiatric criterion for mental illness?

   (A) Expression of behavior that causes distress to self or others

   (B) The condition must be categorical

   (C) Impairment of functioning

   (D) Increased risk of lost freedom, pain, or death

Answers can be found on page ANS-4.

Mental Health in the Public Sphere

Psychological disorders represent a significant health concern. Roughly 25% of American adults will experience a disorder within a given year (Kessler et al., 2005). Even if you are one of those fortunate individuals who is unaffected by psychological disorders, you will benefit from being able to read about and understand mental health issues. Two mental health issues that affect the public sphere include the insanity defense and the public perception of individuals who have mental illness.

THE INSANITY DEFENSE Consider the following cases:

In 2006, Andrea Yates was committed to a psychiatric hospital in Texas for murdering her five children. On June 20, 2001, Yates drowned her children in the bathtub, one at a time, and placed them side by side on her bed. Prior to the murders, Yates had suffered from long, treacherous bouts of postpartum depression. In her testimony, she stated that her children were not developing as she had hoped, and her guilt led her to the horrifying acts. She was given a life sentence in 2002, but successfully appealed and was found not guilty by reason of insanity.

Between 1978 and 1991, Jeffrey Dahmer murdered at least 15 men. Before some of them died, Dahmer attempted to turn his victims into zombies by pouring acid into holes he drilled into their skulls. He also engaged in sexual and cannibalistic acts with the corpses. Dahmer went to trial in 1992 and was sentenced to 15 consecutive life terms in prison.

It may come as a surprise that Jeffrey Dahmer was not considered insane. *Insanity* is a legal concept and is not directly related to psychological diagnoses and treatment. In fact, *insanity* depends on legal definitions that vary by state. Nevertheless, the overarching concept is generally the same; the **insanity defense** *is the legal strategy of claiming that a defendant was unable to differentiate between right and wrong when the criminal act was committed.*

The precedent for the insanity defense was set in Great Britain in 1843. A jury agreed that Daniel M'Naghten had assassinated the Prime Minister's secretary, but did not send him to jail because they believed him incapable of knowing what he did was wrong. M'Naghten was committed to a mental institution, and the plea "not guilty by reason of insanity" is now known as the *M'Naghten rule.*

Nearly 150 years after the M'Naghten trial, Jeffrey Dahmer's jury voted 10-2 to find him guilty, rejecting his insanity defense. Although it would seem that only an insane person could commit such atrocities, Dahmer

Andrea Yates was found not guilty by reason of insanity. The jury believed she could not distinguish right from wrong at the time of the murders.

Jeffrey Dahmer, however, was found to be sane. His admission of guilt and remorse suggested he did understand that what he did was wrong.

expressed remorse and guilt for his crimes and admitted to knowing his actions were wrong. He drank heavily to lower his inhibitions and mute his emotions as he murdered his victims. He was legally sane because he knew he was committing a crime. Andrea Yates, in contrast, was ultimately found to be insane. Although we may find her acts unimaginable, the jury agreed that Yates believed she was doing the right thing at the time. The insanity defense is a rare occurrence—it is advanced in fewer than 1% of federal cases—and it has a success rate of only 20% of the time when it is used (Melton et al., 2007).

WORKING THE SCIENTIFIC LITERACY MODEL
Labeling, Stigma, and Mental Disorders

The DSM-IV provides names or *labels* for psychological disorders, and this system helps to facilitate communication among mental health professionals: A label indicates a set of symptoms, probable causes, and potential treatments. However, these diagnostic labels can also have their drawbacks, the worst of which is stigmatization.

What do we know about the stigma of mental disorders?

Stigmas include negative stereotypes about what it means to have a psychological disorder,

and stigmatization may lead to discrimination, unjustified fears, and alienation. Attaching such labels can also lead people to misinterpret normal behavior as symptoms of a disorder. Even mental health professionals can be influenced this practice, as shown by David Rosenhan's classic study from the 1970s. In his investigation, eight normal, healthy individuals volunteered to go to psychiatric hospitals with complaints about auditory hallucinations. All eight were admitted to the hospitals for either schizophrenia or manic depression (bipolar disorder). After their admission, these so-called patients behaved normally, complaining of no psychiatric symptoms whatsoever. Nonetheless, they remained hospitalized for an average of 19 days until being released as "in remission" (Rosenhan, 1973). Apparently, the initial diagnosis led the hospital staff to misinterpret even normal behavior as symptoms of an illness.

How can science explain the personal effects of stigmatization?

Contemporary research is examining the use of diagnostic labels from multiple perspectives. One important question is how the diagnostic label affects the individual's self-perception. To answer this question, a group led by Jill Holm-Denoma recruited 53 volunteers who were seeking treatment for the first time and followed them through the process. Participants rated their positive and negative emotions at five times: before and after an intake session, before and after a feedback session in which they were informed and educated about their diagnosis, and one more time before beginning a treatment session. Referring

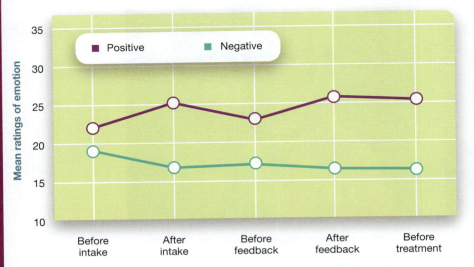

{FIG. 13.1} **Mean Values for Positive and Negative Emotions According to the Visual Analog Scale** Researchers found that individuals did not experience an increase in negative emotions upon learning their psychological diagnosis. In fact, positive emotions increased slightly.

However, we see that stigma and stereotyping can have negative effects, leading to prejudice and the misattribution of behaviors. In an ideal world, we would be able to keep the labels and get rid of the stigma altogether. That may not be entirely possible, but psychologists and community groups are making progress in this regard.

Why is this relevant?

So how do psychologists work against mental illness stigmas? Researchers from a number of academic areas have identified some techniques that work in reducing stigmatization. For example, research shows that personal contact and knowledge of biopsychosocial explanations of mental illness are associated with lower stigma (Boyd et al., 2010). Education seems to matter, too: When individuals are instructed about the first-person experience of mental illness, they show greater acceptance than groups that simply learn the facts about mental illness (Mann & Himelien, 2008). On campus, you might find a chapter of a student organization known as Active Minds, a group that has had success in reducing the stigma associated with mental illness at some campuses (McKinney, 2009). Keep these findings in mind as you read the rest of this chapter; as an informed student you will be less likely to judge others and more likely to seek help yourself, or recommend it to others, if it is ever needed.

to Figure 13.1, you can see how their feelings changed over time. Positive emotions (represented by the purple line) increased significantly after the intake session; even more important, they increased again after the feedback session. There were no significant changes to the negative feelings, as shown by the relatively straight green line (Holm-Denoma et al., 2008). These results provide correlational evidence that learning about one's own diagnosis might increase positive emotional experiences during treatment.

Can we critically evaluate this information?

It is tempting to ask whether the labels applied to psychological disorders are beneficial or harmful, but this question may actually oversimplify the situation. For one, the advantages of this system are clear for professionals: Labels are a necessary means of identifying and describing the problems they encounter. There is also evidence to suggest that labels help individuals understand their own situation, and the labels may hold out hope for successful treatment. Some psychologists who are in favor of labels have argued that Rosenhan's study merely exaggerated the problem: If a patient is complaining of hallucinations, what else is the psychiatrist supposed to do?

BIOPSYCHOSOCIAL PERSPECTIVES

Are Symptoms Universal?

As described at the beginning of the module, PTSD can be a debilitating disorder that includes physical symptoms of tension and anxiety along with cognitive and emotional symptoms, such as recurring thoughts, images, and nightmares. With these tell-tale signs, mental health professionals in the United States have little trouble identifying and diagnosing the condition for those returning home from the wars in Iraq and Afghanistan. But what about those who experience these same wars in their own neighborhoods and villages? Consider these questions:

● Yes or no: Do individuals in other parts of the world—Asia or Africa, for example—experience the physiological symptoms of PTSD?

● Yes or no: Do individuals in other parts of the world experience similar cognitive and emotional symptoms and concerns when it comes to PTSD?

Several teams of researchers have asked these very questions in war-torn villages of Afghanistan, as well as in the aftermath of the 2004 Indian Ocean tsunami that struck Sri Lanka. They found very clear evidence of the physiological symptoms of PTSD, but they were surprised at the difference in the cognitive and emotional symptoms experienced by members of various cultures. People from the United States tended to report difficult internal experiences such as flashbacks, Afghans

Survivors of major disasters are at risk for developing PTSD. Cultural factors influence the nature of the anxiety that people experience in the wake of such disasters.

and Sri Lankans were more likely to experience symptoms that extended beyond the individual—their worries were largely focused on their families and communities. Thus, to truly understand PTSD, we need to examine all aspects of the biopsychosocial model. While the physical stressors may be similar, psychologists who work with individuals from different cultures should pay close attention to culturally relevant terms and experiences when helping people cope with trauma (Fernando, 2008; Miller et al., 2006).

· · · · · · · · · · · · · · · · · ·

Quick Quiz 13.1b :: Mental Health in the Public Sphere

UNDERSTAND...

1 As described in this section, insanity:

A is itself a psychological disorder.

B describes a person with *any* psychological disorder.

C is not recognized by the legal profession or judicial system.

D means that an individual could not distinguish between right and wrong when he or she broke a law.

APPLY...

2 Which of the following statements about PTSD is true?

A People of all cultures experience the exact same concerns after trauma.

B Some cultures are immune to stress reactions.

C Physiological symptoms of PTSD may be common among people of different cultures, but the specific concerns people have can vary.

D PTSD occurs in only cultures that use a medical model.

ANALYZE...

3 Which statement best describes the effects of labeling someone with a mental disorder?

A Labeling always leads to negative perceptions of the individual with the disorder.

B Labeling can have either positive or negative effects, depending on factors such as context and cultural expectations.

C Knowing that someone has a mental disorder always leads to caring and compassionate responses.

D Labeling does not work because the DSM-IV categories are not adequate.

Answers can be found on page ANS-4.

Module Summary

Now that you have read this module you should:

((•)) Listen to the audio file of this module at **MyPsychLab**

KNOW ...

● **The key terminology associated with defining and classifying psychological disorders:**

abnormal psychology (p. 477)

Diagnostic and Statistical Manual for Mental Disorders (DSM-IV) (p. 477)

etiology (p. 477)

insanity defense (p. 480)

maladaptive behavior (p. 477)

medical model (p. 476)

UNDERSTAND ...

● **How disorders are viewed as either dimensional or categorical.** Disorders are defined and identified according to patterns of symptoms. Some symptoms and disorders are categorical because an individual clearly has the symptoms or does not. However, many, if not most, psychological disorders are dimensional in nature—they vary by degree of severity.

● **The differences between the concepts of psychological disorders and insanity.** Many people get their information about psychological disorders from fiction or sensationalized events in the news, so it is important to make distinctions between the psychological concept of a disorder and the legal concept of insanity. Most people with psychological disorders are not considered insane; in fact, only a small minority of people ever could be. Within the legal system, individuals may be declared insane if they were unable to tell right from wrong when they

committed an offense. This designation in no way provides a diagnosis of any specific type of mental disorder.

APPLY ...

● **Your knowledge to understand the symptoms, stereotypes, and stigma surrounding psychological disorders.** Researchers have created some simple measures of stigma. See how you compare to others by completing the scale in **Table 13.4**.

ANALYZE ...

● **Whether the benefits of labeling psychological disorders outweigh the disadvantages.** To evaluate the importance of the DSM-IV's labels, it would be helpful to consider their functions. They organize large amounts of information about symptoms, causes, and outcomes into terminology that mental health professionals can work with. From a practical point of view, this system meets the requirements of the insurance companies that pay for psychological services. One downside to this process is that once the label is applied, people have the tendency to misinterpret behaviors that are perfectly normal.

Table 13.4 :: Attitudes Toward Mental Illness

Complete the following scale to measure your attitude toward mental illness. For each of the items, circle the number that best describes how much you agree or disagree with the statement.

ITEM	COMPLETELY DISAGREE				COMPLETELY AGREE
If I had a mentally ill relative, I wouldn't want anyone to know.	1	2	3	4	5
Most of my friends would see me as being weak if they thought that I had a mental illness.	1	2	3	4	5
I would be very embarrassed if I were diagnosed as having a mental illness.	1	2	3	4	5
Mentally ill people scare me.	1	2	3	4	5
I would cross the street if I saw a mentally ill person coming in order to avoid passing him/her.	1	2	3	4	5
I think that mentally ill people are strange and weird.	1	2	3	4	5
Find your total score by adding up the numbers you circled and dividing by 6.					

Interpretation: This scale measures stigma towards individuals who have a mental illness. Compare your score to a large sample of high school students. Their average on this same scale was 2.13, with higher scores indicating greater levels of stigma. For those with a family member diagnosed with a mental disorder, the mean dropped to 2.05.

Source: Watson et al., 2005.

Personality and Dissociative Disorders

KNOW ...	UNDERSTAND ...	APPLY ...	ANALYZE ...
The key terminology associated with personality and dissociative disorders	The phenomenon of dissociation and how a dissociative disorder might occur	The biopsychosocial model to understand the causes of personality disorders	The status of dissociative identity disorder as a legitimate diagnosis

Since childhood, Aileen Wuornos was a victim of countless incidents of sexual and emotional abuse. She had no stable home or family, and her history of abuse gave her little reason to develop trust in others. Wuornos moved from place to place, never received much education, and gained few skills that could help her lead a normal adult life. Over the years, she was arrested for numerous relatively minor offenses. Wuornos eventually turned to prostitution. Over a one-year period spanning 1989 and 1990, she murdered seven men, some of whom she had lured into her car by posing as a stranded motorist. Wuornos was declared sane and fit to stand trial. She was convicted and sentenced to death in the state of Florida, and eventually gave up on appealing her case.

It may surprise some that a remorseless murderer could be *sane* in any sense of the word. In fact, psychologists who evaluated Wuornos and testified in her defense diagnosed her with antisocial and borderline personality disorders (*Wuornos v. State of Florida,* 1994).

In October 2002, Aileen Wuornos was executed by lethal injection. Her case raises numerous issues and questions about psychological disorders.

Focus Questions

1. What are personality disorders, and how do they differ from normal personality traits?

2. Which aspects of antisocial personality disorder, in *some* cases, lead to violent behavior?

• • • • • • • • • • • • • • • • • •

Chapter 12 described the psychological approaches to personality—the relatively stable patterns of thinking, behaving, and relating to others that make each person unique. In this module, we will begin by examining what happens when individuals experience problems during personality development and the effects it can have on their lives—and on others' lives as well. This discussion will be followed by examination of a very different type of disorder known as *dissociative disorders*. Despite their differences, these two categories of disorders are similar in that they are among the most intriguing and challenging to understand.

Defining and Classifying Personality Disorders

Mental health professionals identify **personality disorders** *as particularly unusual patterns of behavior for one's culture that are maladaptive, distressing to oneself or others, and resistant to change.* Sometimes these disorders are observed in people who tend to be quirky and difficult to get along with, yet do not present a threat to themselves or others. In other individuals, these problematic aspects of personality may have severe manifestations. For example, some people feel no empathy toward others, even those in great distress. Others hold excessive expectations of gaining the attention and admiration of others, and will feel severely rejected if their demands are not met. People may become rapidly attached to another person, only to reject that individual, sometimes violently, at any moment. These are examples of dimensional qualities; in other words, any of these characteristics may apply to *anyone* at some point, so it is important to remember that the actual disorders represent extreme and persistent cases.

As Table 13.5 shows, the DSM-IV identifies clusters of personality disorders involving (1) odd or eccentric behavior; (2) dramatic, emotional, and erratic behavior; and (3) anxious, fearful, and inhibited behavior.

BORDERLINE PERSONALITY At the core of any personality disorder is emotional dysfunction, and one of the clearest examples of this is borderline personality disorder (Blashfield & Intoccia, 2000). **Borderline personality disorder (BPD)** *is characterized by intense extremes between positive and negative emotions, an unstable sense of self, impulsivity, and difficult social relationships.* Each of these characteristics seems to be connected to a tendency to think in all-or-none terms. For example, a person with BPD may fall in love quickly, professing deep commitment and affection, but just as quickly become disgusted by someone's imperfections. Friends, family, colleagues, and even public figures can also be idealized and despised in the same way. Thus the all-or-none thinking associated with BPD prevents an individual from rationally understanding that, no matter how much a person means to the individual, there are bound to be periods of conflict in the relationship.

As a part of their troubled relationships, people with BPD can become paranoid, suspecting that everyone else has similarly unpredictable feelings. Thus their fear of abandonment is typically very intense, and it may drive them to go to extremes to prevent the loss of a relationship. It may also lead to risky sexual behavior as the individual desperately tries to secure relationships. One of the most distinguishing features of BPD is the tendency toward *self-injury,*

Table 13.5 :: Varieties of Personality Disorders

CLUSTER	DESCRIPTION
Odd, eccentric	**Paranoid Personality Disorder** is a pattern of distrust and suspiciousness such that others' motives are interpreted as malevolent.
	Schizoid Personality Disorder is a pattern of detachment from social relationships and a restricted range of emotional expression.
	Schizotypal Personality Disorder is a pattern of acute discomfort in close relationships, cognitive or perceptual distortions, and eccentricities of behavior.
Dramatic, emotional, erratic	**Antisocial Personality Disorder** is a pattern of disregard for, and violation of, the rights of others.
	Borderline Personality Disorder is a pattern of instability in interpersonal relationships, self-image, and affects, and marked impulsivity.
	Histrionic Personality Disorder is a pattern of excessive emotionality and attention seeking.
	Narcissistic Personality Disorder is a pattern of grandiosity, need for admiration, and lack of empathy.
Anxious, fearful, inhibited	**Avoidant Personality Disorder** is a pattern of social inhibition, feelings of inadequacy, and hypersensitivity to negative evaluation.
	Dependent Personality Disorder is a pattern of submissive and clinging behavior related to an excessive need to be taken care of.
	Obsessive-Compulsive Personality Disorder is a pattern of preoccupation with orderliness, perfectionism, and control.

Personality Disorder Not Otherwise Specified is a category provided for two situations: 1) the individual's personality pattern meets the general criteria for a Personality Disorder and traits of several different Personality Disorders are present, but the criteria for any specific Personality Disorder are not met; or 2) the individual's personality pattern meets the general criteria for a Personality Disorder, but the individual is considered to have a personality Disorder that is not included in the classification (e.g., passive-aggressive personality disorder).

Source: American Psychiatric Association, 2000.

According to Greek mythology, Narcissus discovered his image reflecting from the surface of a pool of water. Unable to tear himself away from the beauty of his own face, Narcissus wasted away and died at the water's edge. In modern times, narcissism describes a person who has an inflated sense of self-importance.

which may involve cutting or burning oneself. In some cases, these episodes of self-injury may appear to be suicide attempts and, in fact, they sometimes are true attempts.

NARCISSISTIC PERSONALITY   **Narcissistic personality disorder (NPD)** *is characterized by an inflated sense of self-importance and an intense need for attention and admiration, as well as intense self-doubt and fear of abandonment.* These narcissistic feelings leave little room for empathy. In fact, people with NPD are known to manipulate and arrange their relationships to make sure their own needs are met, no matter the toll it takes on others. Because of these tendencies, you can see evidence of the disorder in all aspects of behavior. For example, evidence of NPD may even be found in your classroom: Students with narcissistic tendencies are more likely to engage in academic dishonesty than others. Moreover, their sense of entitlement and specialness allows them to cheat without feeling any guilt or remorse (Brunell et al., 2011).

HISTRIONIC PERSONALITY   Emotional dysfunction can also be seen in **histrionic personality disorder (HPD)**, *which is characterized by excessive attention seeking and dramatic behavior.* "Histrionic" comes from a Latin word meaning "like an actor or like a theatrical performance"—an apt label for this disorder. People who have HPD are typically very successful at drawing people in with flirtatiousness,

provocative sexuality, and flattery, but they are simply playing the roles they believe are necessary to be the center of attention. Thus people with HPD are characterized by extreme shallowness and emotional immaturity.

WORKING THE SCIENTIFIC LITERACY MODEL
Antisocial Personality Disorder

Antisocial personality disorder (APD) *refers to a condition marked by a habitual pattern of willingly violating others' personal rights, with very little sign of empathy or remorse.* It is a difficult condition to deal with because the actions of people with APD are often distressful and alarming, and they are rarely, if ever, motivated to change.

What do we know about antisocial personality disorder?

People with APD tend to be physically and verbally abusive, destructive, and frequently find themselves in trouble with the law. Men are three times more likely to be diagnosed with APD than women, and symptoms of the disorder typically appear during childhood and adolescence. These symptoms include patterns of harming or torturing people or animals, destroying property, stealing, and being deceitful (Lynam & Gudonis, 2005). Although it is not a DSM-IV diagnosis, the term *psychopath* is a more familiar way of describing this and similar patterns of behavior, and its use often brings to mind the cold-blooded, remorseless murderer. More accurately, the term refers to a person who embodies cognitive and emotional qualities of egocentrism, callousness, and manipulative tendencies (Hare & Neumann, 2008). Psychopathy and antisocial personality disorder refer to a very similar set of abnormal personality traits.

For some people, the antisocial acts they commit are severe. This tendency was clearly evident in the words of Aileen Wuornos when she refused to appeal her death sentence:

> *I killed those men, robbed them as cold as ice. And I'd do it again, too … There's no chance in keeping me alive or anything, because I'd kill again. I have hate crawling through my system. (CNN, 2002)*

Keep in mind that serial killers represent only a very small subset of people with antisocial and psychopathic tendencies. In fact, people who have either antisocial tendencies or full-blown manifestations of APD can be found throughout society. Given their high potential for harming others, scientists have sought to understand what makes them different from normal citizens.

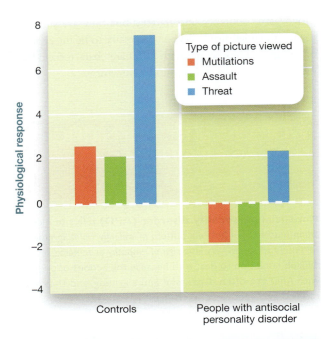

{FIG. 13.2} **Emotional Responses of Individuals with Antisocial Personality Disorder** This graph shows the strength of autonomic response to three types of pictures: mutilations, assault, and threat. Responses are much greater among control subjects (those who do not have APD; the three bars on the left) than among the individuals with antisocial personality disorder (the three bars on the right).

How can science explain antisocial personality disorder?

You may have heard stories of people who have snapped under stress and committed horrific acts—this type of situation is very different from what would be expected from someone with APD. In fact, researchers have discovered that people with antisocial personality disorder are *under*-reactive to stress. For example, a flash of light, a loud sound, or the sudden appearance of an angry face will startle most people. In contrast, people with APD show very weak startle responses—such as blinking—when exposed to unpleasant stimuli. In one study, researchers recorded the eletrical signals of the eyeblink muscles while presenting disturbing images to a group of people with APD and a control group without APD. You can see the results in Figure 13.2, in which the strength of the startle response is indicated by the height of the bars. The group of people with APD (the bars on the right side) have much weaker responses than the group without APD (on the left; Levenston et al., 2000).

A similar pattern was found when psychologists compared people with psychopathy who had been convicted of violent crimes with nonpsychopathic controls in a procedure involving aversive classical conditioning. People with psychopathy and control participants looked at brief presentations of photographs of human faces (the conditioned stimulus) followed by a brief but painful application of pressure to the body (the unconditioned stimulus).

What *should* happen is that participants will acquire a negative emotional reaction (the conditioned response) to the faces. But people with psychopathy did not react this way. They showed very little physiological arousal, their emotional brain centers remained quiet, and overall they did not seem to mind looking at pictures of faces that had been paired with pain (Birbaumer et al., 2005). In contrast, people in the control group did not enjoy this experience. In fact, following several pairings of pictures of faces with pain, the control group showed increased physiological arousal and activity of the emotion centers of the brain, and understandably reported disliking the experience of the experiment.

Can we critically evaluate this information?

We must be careful not to assume that all people with APD are violent criminals. Antisocial qualities can be found in white-collar criminals who cheat and lie for profit. For example, Wall Street power broker Bernard Madoff admitted to stealing billions of dollars from investors who trusted him with their money. Madoff has shown very little remorse for ruining the fortunes of many individuals and institutions—including charities. Some have suggested that, although he committed no violent crime, the level of deceit, maliciousness, and egocentrism he exhibited is psychopathic in nature.

Why is this relevant?

Identifying how physiology and brain function differ in people with APD and psychopathy is certainly helpful for psychologists who are trying to understand the underlying basis for these disturbing behavioral patterns. People with APD tend to be highly resistant to psychological therapies. As a consequence, given the high level of danger they can pose, drug treatments that can alter the physiological processes underlying the disorder may be needed. Also, antisocial patterns are often detectable during childhood and adolescence, which are critical periods of brain development. Perhaps therapies will be more highly beneficial if started at an early age, rather than in adulthood.

THE BIOPSYCHOSOCIAL APPROACH TO PERSONALITY DISORDERS

It is often difficult to identify the causes of personality disorders because they seem to arise from multiple causes over a long period of time. Rather than pinpointing the exact moment a disorder began, psychologists speak in general terms about the types of events that contribute to personality disorders. Adding to the difficulty is the fact that multiple causes are likely at play, and it may be possible for two people to develop the same symptomatic thoughts and behaviors through entirely different routes. The biopsychosocial model provides the most comprehensive view, so we will examine personality disorders from three different perspectives.

Psychological Factors Do people with personality disorders think differently from normal people? Persistent beliefs about the self are a major part of the human personality. A person with a narcissistic personality seeks to avoid negative attention at all costs because it brings unpleasant hostile or depressive reactions. To ward off these feelings, the person continues seeking attention. A similar pattern may be apparent in someone who has a histrionic personality. Attention seeking through engaging in flattery and wearing provocative clothing may help individuals with HPD avoid the negative feelings they associate with being unnoticed. Thus they are likely to resort to these behaviors in the future, even at the expense of developing genuine relationships.

Adults with psychopathy and children with *conduct disorders* (often a precursor to psychopathy) have difficulty learning tasks that require decision making and following of complex rules. Brain imaging studies show that children with conduct disorders perform worse at these tasks and have reduced activity in the frontal lobes compared with healthy controls and even children with attention-deficit/hyperactivity disorder (ADHD) (Finger et al., 2008). Thus it appears that cognitive factors and their underlying brain processes can also help explain personality disorders.

Sociocultural Factors Children begin to develop social skills and emotional attachments at home and in their local neighborhood. Not surprisingly, then, troubled homes and neighborhoods can contribute to the development of psychopathy or antisocial personality disorder (Meier et al., 2008). Because individuals with a history of physical, sexual, and emotional abuse have been treated as objects rather than as sensitive human beings, they may not empathize with others, including animals. Less severe cases of conditions such as BPD may arise from profound *invalidation* during childhood, meaning that a child's caregivers did not respond to his or her emotions as if they were real or important (Crowell et al., 2009). As a result, adults with BPD never master the ability to identify and control emotions, so they tend to react more strongly to everyday life stressors (Glaser et al., 2008).

Biological Factors Not everyone who experiences extreme stress and abuse develops a personality disorder, of course. So why do some adapt successfully while others develop personality disorders? The answer may lie in how the stress interacts with biological predispositions for personality disorders. A number of specific genes seem to contribute to emotional instability through serotonin systems in the brain (Crowell et al., 2009). Research also points to unique activity in the limbic system and frontal lobes—brain regions that are associated with emotional responses and impulse control, respectively (Brendl et al., 2005).

COMORBIDITY AND PERSONALITY DISORDERS

Personality disorders present serious challenges to mental health professionals, who have struggled to reach consensus on how to categorize specific subtypes. One issue is the high levels of comorbidity among personality disorders. **Comorbidity** *is the presence of two disorders simultaneously, or the presence of a second disorder that affects the one being treated.* For example, a person who is being treated for heart disease may also have diabetes, and the presence of both diseases in the same individual can complicate treatment. Similarly, substance abuse is often comorbid with personality disorders (Goldstein et al., 2007; Gudonis et al., 2009). Their intertwining presents a challenge for treatment: Is it the personality disorder or the substance abuse that is at the root of the problem? Comorbidity rates have led some psychologists to suggest that the DSM-IV identifies far too many different types of personality disorders (Clark, 2007). These disagreements aside, APD and BPD are the most reliable to diagnose; that is, two or more mental health professionals are highly likely to agree on whether someone has APD or BPD.

KNOW …

1 Which of the following is *not* a characteristic of personality disorders?

  A Traits that are inflexible and maladaptive

  B Significant functional impairment or subjective distress

  C Marked deviation from cultural expectations

  D Typically diagnosed with medical tests

2 Which of the following individuals demonstrates the definition of comorbidity?

  A A person who has both borderline personality disorder and a substance abuse disorder

  B A person who is histrionic who both seeks excessive attention and is emotionally hyper-reactive

  C A person with borderline personality disorder who is impulsive and tends to be in unstable relationships

  D A person who experiences a personality disorder that turns out to be fatal

UNDERSTAND …

3 _____ refers to a condition marked by a habitual pattern of willingly violating others' personal rights, with very little sign of empathy or remorse.

  A Borderline personality disorder

  B Narcissistic personality disorder

  C Histrionic personality disorder

  D Antisocial personality disorder

4 _____ involves intense extremes between positive and negative emotions, an unstable sense of self, impulsivity, and difficult social relationships.

  A Borderline personality disorder

  B Narcissistic personality disorder

  C Histrionic personality disorder

  D Antisocial personality disorder

APPLY …

5 Which of the following biopsychosocial factors is least likely to be related to personality disorders?

  A Stress reactivity

  B History of abuse

  C Decreased activity of the frontal lobes

  D Enjoyment of pain

Answers can be found on page ANS-4.

Dissociative Identity Disorder

Have you ever been so engaged in driving, reading a book, or playing a game that you were totally unaware of what was going on around you? Have you ever had difficulty determining whether an event really happened, or whether it was something you dreamed? Chances are that at least one of these experiences is familiar to you. Psychologists refer to them as *dissociative experiences* because they are characterized by a sense of separation—a dissociation—between you and your surroundings. Dissociative experiences may arise while you are intensely focused on one activity, or when you drift off while not doing anything in particular, such as daydreaming during a long lecture. People differ in their tendencies to dissociate, but such experiences seem completely normal.

In a few cases, some people have such extreme experiences that they may be diagnosed with a **dissociative disorder**, *a category of mental disorders characterized by a split between conscious awareness from feeling, cognition, memory, and identity* (Kihlstrom, 2005). Dissociative disorders include the following conditions:

- *Dissociative fugue:* A period of profound autobiographical memory loss. People in fugue states may go so far as to develop a new identity in a new location with no recollection of their past.
- *Depersonalization disorder:* A belief that one has changed in some fundamental way, possibly ceasing to be "real."
- *Dissociative amnesia:* A severe loss of memory, usually for a specific stressful event, when no biological cause for amnesia is present.

Probably the most familiar member of this category is **dissociative identity disorder** (**DID**; sometimes referred to as multiple personality disorder), *in which a person claims that his or her identity has split into one or more distinct alter personalities, or alters.* Alters may differ in name, gender, sexual orientation, personality, behavior, memory, perception, and autobiographical sense of self. The dissociation of alter identities can be so strong that one alter may have no memory of events experienced by other alters.

In most cases, dissociative disorders such as DID are thought to be brought on by extreme stress. Some psychologists have hypothesized that, during a traumatic episode (for example, during a sexual assault), an individual may cope by trying to block out the experience and focus on another time and place. Psychologists have speculated that with repeated experiences, this type of dissociation could become an individual's habitual way of coping with the trauma (van der Kolk, 1994). Most cases of DID do include reports of a stressful event or series of events that precipitated the onset of the condition (Putnam, 1989). These events generally include elements of violence and intentional humiliation, such as rape, insertion of objects into the body, or forms of sexual torture.

Although DID appears in melodramatic and comedic films on a regular basis, it is actually a very rare disorder. Only approximately 1% of psychiatric patients have been diagnosed with DID (Rifkin et al., 1998). Therefore, this disorder's prevalence in the general population is a very small fraction of 1%. Because so few people develop DID, and because even the disorder itself seems implausible to some, many psychologists doubt the validity of this diagnosis altogether. Here we will examine the evidence for the disorder as well as the skeptics' arguments against it.

A condition like DID is very difficult to test for. One approach to testing for DID is to check for memory dissociations between alter identities. For example, in one study patients viewed words and pictures and were tested for recall of the stimuli either when they were experiencing the same alter as when they learned, or when they were experiencing a different alter. The results suggested that some types of learning do not transfer between alter identities (Eich et al., 1997). This finding would suggest that the two alters are truly separate identities. Skeptics, however, might point out that similar results can be produced in the general population simply by instructing volunteers (who do not claim to have DID) to imagine themselves in different contexts (Sahakyan & Kelley, 2002). Another approach to examining DID is to record patterns of brain activity. One study using positron emission tomography (PET) actually found differing frontal lobe activity for people with DID while they were experiencing each of their alters (Reinders et al., 2003). (In case you wondered, the researchers obtained consent to participate in the study by *both* alters.) Although the results of both of these studies are thought provoking, they do not provide solid evidence for a biological basis of DID.

Skeptics of DID note that a physical cause or symptom of the disorder has never been identified, which makes it more difficult to test objectively. In addition, it is far easier to fake a disorder that relies so heavily on self-reports than it is to fake diabetes or a heart attack. As a consequence, even if psychologists accept DID as a true disorder, it can be difficult to ascertain who is really experiencing it and who is faking.

Some other observations offer compelling reasons to be skeptical about diagnosing DID. First, in 1970, there were 79 documented cases of DID (then referred to as multiple personality disorder). In 1986, there were around 6,000; by 1998, the number had risen to more than 40,000 (Lilienfeld & Lynn, 2003). Second, 80% of patients diagnosed with DID were unaware of having the disorder before starting therapy (Putnam, 1989). These observations suggest that DID may have its origins in the context of therapy, rather than being a response to trauma.

Why did the rate of DID skyrocket from 79 cases to more than 40,000 cases per year in less than three decades? This increased prevalence could simply be a product of awareness: After professionals learned how to identify the disorder, they could begin to diagnose it more effectively. However, it is also possible that the drastic increase seen from 1970 through the 1980s is due to social and cultural effects, such as the popularization of a film called *Sybil,* which purported to tell the true story of a woman with DID. Diagnoses of DID rose shortly after this film was released.

Why are so many cases of DID accounted for by so few therapists? Perhaps only a small number of psychologists are trained to properly diagnosis DID, but that does not seem likely given the uniform use of the DSM-IV. A more plausible explanation is that a small subset of psychologists find the disorder compelling and are more willing to diagnose it, so they may (perhaps unintentionally) provoke dissociative symptoms in the context of therapy (Frankel, 1993).

Researchers have examined social and therapist effects on DID by observing what happens when the disorder is introduced to other parts of the world. In these cases it appears that DID—whether a disorder or not—has a strong sociocultural component. For example, the disorder was nonexistent in Japan in 1990 (Takahashi, 1990), but Japanese psychologists began diagnosing patients with DID when the disorder was described by North Americans (An et al., 1998). In India, the disorder is recognized, but how the disorder manifests itself is different from in America: Americans with DID switch from alters upon suggestion, whereas people in India who have DID switch alters only upon awakening (North et al., 1993). These observations point to a predominantly sociocultural disorder in which cultural beliefs and therapists determine how the symptoms are manifested (Lilienfeld et al., 1999).

One final problem with DID is that the validity of the disorder largely rests on the public belief that many of the people with it are repressing a traumatic experience. In reality, studies examining more than 10,000 trauma victims found that any forgetting that did occur could be explained by infantile or childhood amnesia (they were simply too young to remember) or just normal forgetting (Pope et al., 2000). The fact is that most trauma victims remember their experiences (Cahill & McGaugh, 1998). Thus many psychologists find it unlikely that traumatic experiences can directly lead to DID.

Quick Quiz 13.2b :: Dissociative Identity Disorder

1 Dissociative identity disorder is best described as:

A a lost grasp on reality.

B a lack of regard for the feelings of others.

C a splitting of identity.

D a problem with memory, attention, and the ability to form coherent thoughts.

2 Fugue is a form of dissociative disorder most commonly associated with:

A a belief that you no longer exist or are real.

B loss of sensation in an appendage with no physical or neurological evidence.

C housing multiple personalities in one body.

D loss of identity and memories of the self.

3 Which of the following is believed to typically bring on dissociative identity disorder?

A A physical injury to the head   **C** Old age

B Extreme stress or trauma   **D** Genetics

4 Skeptics have argued against the validity of DID in a number of different cases. What is their reasoning?

A The disorder appears to be based on cultural expectations.

B Most people who experience trauma do not dissociate.

C The vast majority of cases come from a very small number of therapists.

D Skeptics have cited all of these arguments.

Answers can be found on page ANS-4.

Module Summary

Module 13.2

((•—[**Listen** to the audio file of this module at **MyPsychLab**

Now that you have read this module you should:

- **The key terminology associated with personality and dissociative disorders:**

antisocial personality disorder (APD) (p. 487)

borderline personality disorder (BPD) (p. 486)

comorbidity (p. 489)

dissociative disorder (p. 490)

dissociative identity disorder (DID) (p. 490)

histrionic personality disorder (HPD) (p. 487)

narcissistic personality disorder (NPD) (p. 487)

personality disorders (p. 486)

2. What is at least one psychological factor, consisting of emotions, thoughts, and experiences?

3. What are at least two social or cultural factors, including relationships, cultural expectations, and so on?

Check your answers on page ANS-4.

- **The phenomenon of dissociation and how a dissociative disorder might occur.** Dissociation can be explained in everyday phenomena such as daydreaming. However, a dissociative disorder may occur when perceptions of mind, body, and surroundings are severely and chronically separated, such as in purported cases of dissociative identity disorder.

- **The biopsychosocial model to understand the causes of personality disorders.** Take antisocial personality disorder and psychopathy for example:

1. Can you name one or two biological influences associated with APD and psychopathy?

- **The status of dissociative identity disorder as a legitimate diagnosis.** The lack of a physical basis for the disorder and its unusual rate and patterns of diagnosis rightly bring about skepticism. For example, diagnoses of DID increased dramatically after a film depicted a purported case of DID. Ensure that your evaluation (of any condition, not just DID) is not biased by fictional or sensationalized accounts you have seen or read. However, it is also important to remember that many of the mental disorders for which we have a greater understanding were at one time considered mysterious and controversial.

Anxiety and Mood Disorders

Learning Objectives

After reading this module you should:

KNOW ...	UNDERSTAND ...	APPLY ...	ANALYZE ...
The key terminology related to anxiety and mood disorders	The different types of anxiety disorders How anxiety or mood disorders can be self-perpetuating	Your knowledge of anxiety and mood disorders to be alert to people in need	Whether maladaptive aspects of psychological disorders might arise from perfectly normal, healthy behaviors

Waking up to a headache, fever, or sore throat, unpleasant as it is, is not at all unusual. But what about waking up to obsessive–compulsive disorder (OCD)? When it comes to mental disorders, people typically think of signs that something is "not quite right" about a person's behavior, and what follows may be a *gradual* unfolding of more noticeable personality, behavioral, or emotional problems. Although this is how mental disorders typically develop, sudden onset of OCD—a serious anxiety disorder—has been documented in cases in which young children were exposed to bacterial streptococcal infections. Shortly after exposure to the infection, some children quickly developed symptoms of OCD, including extremely repetitive behaviors and having irrational fears and obsessions (Snider & Swedo, 2004). But why might a relatively common infection result in such rapid behavior and emotional changes in *some* children? The answer seems to be that when the immune system mounts its reaction to the bacterial infection, it also damages cells in the *caudate*, a part of the brain related to impulse control, as well as related structures in the same vicinity. As we will see in this module, one theory about OCD is that compulsive, repetitive behaviors (such as hand washing) are ways of dealing with

the lost sense of impulse control—a loss that occurs when the caudate is damaged (Huyser et al., 2009). If this theory is correct, then, at least in this case, a psychological disorder can be acquired virtually overnight.

Focus Questions

 OCD has a specific set of symptoms, yet is only one type of anxiety disorder. What are some other ways that problems with anxiety can manifest themselves?

 Depression, another very common disorder, also has a biological basis. Which abnormalities are related to depression?

· · · · · · · · · · · · · · · · · · ·

If you have had any personal experiences with psychological disorders—maybe you, a family member, a friend, or a co-worker has experienced one—then there is a good chance you will come across a description of it in this module.

Anxiety Disorders

Anxiety disorders *are a category of disorders involving fear or nervousness that is excessive, irrational, and maladaptive.* They also are among the most frequently diagnosed disorders, affecting more than 40 million Americans aged 18 and older, whereas mood disorders affect nearly 21 million adults (National Institutes of Mental Health [NIMH], 2008). Many people experience both types of disorders either simultaneously or at different times in their lives, so we will examine both in this module.

Everyone experiences feelings of anxiety. Indeed, anxiety is based on a normal physiological and psychological response to stressful events known as the *fight-or-flight response* (Nesse & Ellsworth, 2009). We experience this response as a racing, pounding heartbeat with increased respiration, which allows for quick energy use. Some people also notice a knot in the stomach and sweaty or clammy hands. These physical changes reflect a shift in energy away from non-emergency tasks like digestion and toward fighting or fleeing. This basic fight-or-flight response seems to be common to all mammals, and it is actually a very adaptive response to threats such as predators.

If the processes underlying anxiety are adaptive, then our challenge is to identify symptoms that go beyond typical psychological responses and become maladaptive. As discussed in Module 13.1, the distinction between a typical psychological state and a disorder combines extremes in duration and severity, and a disordered state may be a disproportionate response to real-life events, or it may occur without any precipitating event whatsoever.

VARIETIES OF ANXIETY DISORDERS

I had to cross that bridge twice a day to drop off my daughter at school. One Friday traffic slowed to a crawl and I noticed my heart thumping. Out of nowhere, the idea hit me: I was going to die on that bridge and there was nothing I could do about it… . The more I tried to calm myself, the worse it got. Everything was a blur. I somehow made it the last 50 feet and pulled over. That whole experience couldn't have been more than five minutes but it seemed like forever. Next Monday I felt skittish approaching the bridge. I kept thinking about my heart beating even though I tried paying attention to other things. Next thing I know I'm thinking, "I'm having a heart attack—a real heart attack this time."

For a while, I avoided the bridge by having my wife make the trip, but that didn't solve the problem … I was in a meeting in the library when I thought I felt my heart racing again. Before long, I'd locked myself in the restroom wondering if this would be the time it killed me.

—JMD, a 44-year-old journalist

The primary symptoms of all anxiety disorders include the basic feelings of anxiety, and you can certainly see those in JMD's story. What separates anxiety disorders from other forms of anxiety is a combination of an unjustifiable degree, duration, and source of anxiety. In all anxiety disorders, the experience creates distress for the individual and interferes with normal daily functioning at work, at school, and in personal relationships.

As you can see in the description of JMD's experiences, there does not seem to be any real source for his anxiety, but it certainly causes distress. Anxiety is interfering with his daily functioning, including his family life and his work. Therefore, it does seem like some type

Fight or flight . . . or freeze or faint? In addition to fight-or-flight responses, mammals can also react by freezing—as in the "deer in the headlights" response—or by fainting, as some will do at the sight of blood (Bracha et al., 2004).

of anxiety disorder. To be more specific about symptoms and treatment, psychologists have identified several major types of anxiety disorders.

Generalized Anxiety Disorder **Generalized anxiety disorder (GAD)** *involves frequently elevated levels of anxiety that are not directed at or limited to any particular situation*—the anxiety is *generalized* to just about anything. Additionally, people with GAD often feel irritable and have difficulty sleeping and concentrating, which are not unusual experiences for people with any type of anxiety problem. What makes GAD distinct from other anxiety disorders is that people who have it often struggle to identify the specific reasons for why they are anxious (Turk et al., 2005). Moreover, the anxiety that people with GAD experience does not seem to go away, even if a particular problem or issue is resolved. Rather, the anxiety becomes redirected toward some other concern. The onset of GAD can be attributed to a variety of factors, not all of which are clear, but major life changes commonly precede its onset (Newman & Llera, 2011).

Panic Disorder **Panic disorder** *is an anxiety disorder marked by repeated episodes of sudden, very intense fear.* This condition is distinct from GAD because the anxiety occurs in short segments, but can be much more severe. The key feature of this disorder is *panic attacks*—brief moments of extreme anxiety that include a rush of physical activity paired with frightening thoughts. A panic attack escalates when the fear of death causes increased physical arousal, and the increased physical symptoms feed the frightening thoughts. The escalation rarely goes on for more than 10 minutes, after which the individual will eventually return to a more relaxed state.

People with panic disorder often develop an intense fear that the panic will strike again, which can lead to **agoraphobia**, *an intense fear of having a panic attack or lower-level panic symptoms in public.* As a result of this fear, the individual may begin to avoid public settings so as to avoid the embarrassment and trauma of a panic attack. In its most extreme forms, agoraphobia leads an individual to stay inside his or her home almost permanently.

WORKING THE SCIENTIFIC LITERACY MODEL
Specific Phobias

In contrast to GAD, where an individual's anxiety can be applied to just about any situation, a **phobia** *is a severe, irrational fear of a very specific object or situation.* Some of the most common phobias are listed in Table 13.6. The best-known form of phobia is probably **specific phobias**, *which involve an intense fear of an object, activity, or organism.* These include fears of things such as specific animals, heights, thunder, blood, and injections or other medical procedures. (Social phobias, which are very common, are a different category of phobias that are discussed later.)

What do we know about specific phobias?

Phobias are developed through unpleasant or frightening experiences—for example, a person who is bitten by a dog might develop a phobia of dogs. But negative experiences tell only part of the story—not all dog bite victims develop phobias. The overwhelming majority of the triggers for phobias are objects or situations we may *need* to fear, or at the very least be cautious about. This linkage leads

Table 13.6 :: What Are We So Afraid of?

	CURRENTLY EXPERIENCING THE PHOBIA	HAVE EXPERIENCED THE PHOBIA AT ONE TIME
Animals (snakes, birds, or other animals)	4.7%	50.3%
Natural environment (e.g., heights, storms, water)	5.9%	62.7%
Blood or bodily injury (including injections)	4.0%	42.5%
Situations (e.g., dentists, hospitals, crowded places)	5.2%	55.6%
Other specific objects	1.0%	10.6%

Source: Stinson et al., 2007.

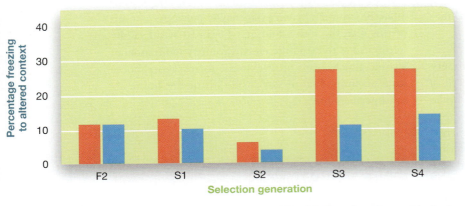

{FIG. 13.3} **Anxiety Levels Are Inherited in an Animal Model** Over the course of just a few generations, mice from the highly fearful genetic strain show increasingly strong fear responses as indicated by the height of the red bars.

psychologists to believe there is a genetic component to a fear of heights, snakes, and other potential dangers from our evolutionary history (Öhman & Mineka, 2001); in other words, we may be *biologically predisposed* to fear some objects (see Module 6.1).

How can science explain specific phobias?

If organisms really are biologically prepared to fear, then scientists should be able to find a genetic basis for for this tendency. One approach to studying how genes influence fear and anxiety comes from selective breeding techniques. To use this approach, one group of researchers tested a strain of mice for fear conditioning and ranked the mice from least to most easily conditioned. Specifically, they used a classical conditioning technique in which the mice heard a tone followed by an electrical shock. Fear was measured by the length of time the mice held still in fear in response to the tone—mice typically show fear by freezing in place (Ponder et al., 2007).

The most fearful mice were then allowed to breed with each other across four generations. The least fearful animals were also paired up and allowed to breed. As Figure 13.3 shows, across these four generations, fear responses became more and more distinct, with the third and fourth generations being very different from each other—the mice bred from the most fearful families became even more easily conditioned than their great grandparents. Thus the researchers showed that the disposition to learn certain types of fears can be genetically influenced.

Can we critically evaluate this information?

What can a study of frightened mice tell us about human fears? Although this research informs us that the genes of mice can be selectively bred to increase susceptibility to acquire fear responses, humans are a very different species. Though valuable, this particular study does not specify how anxiety and fear are coded in the human genome. Therefore, it is reasonable to look for evidence related specifically to humans. Further, this research might lead you to believe that humans have developed biological tendencies to fear dangerous things in general, but that does not seem to be the case. As described in Module 6.1, the objects and events people tend to fear have been a part of human experience for thousands of years—long enough to influence our genetic makeup. This would explain why so many people rapidly develop phobias of snakes or spiders—the threats our ancestors faced—whereas relatively few people develop phobias about other potential dangers, such as guns.

Why is this relevant?

It is important for mental health professionals to understand that phobias have a genetic component. This relationship suggests that not all fears should be treated equally, nor should all individuals with phobias be treated the same way. By isolating genetic tendencies and determining how they affect the nervous system, researchers will be able to develop more specialized forms of treatment for phobias, and potentially for other anxiety disorders as well.

In the novel and miniseries IT, by Stephen King, an evil life form would become a clown to lure children into a trap. This type of imagery can be the basis for which many people come to experience fear of certain objects—even clowns.

Social Phobias **Social anxiety disorder** *is an irrational fear of being observed, evaluated, or embarrassed in public.* A person experiencing a social anxiety disorder can go out in public, but prefers familiar places and routines. Even if he is very competent, an individual with social anxiety disorder will avoid many other situations because the anxiety levels are too high. Consider the day of a college student who has social anxiety:

- This student always shows up to class right as it begins so he does not have to risk awkward conversation with classmates he does not know. Even worse, what if everyone else is having conversations and he has to sit alone without talking to anyone?
- Despite being very hungry, the student will not go into the cafeteria because his roommate is not around. He

cannot face the prospect of sitting with strangers, especially without his roommate. He finds a quiet spot near the library and gets lunch from a vending machine.
- Walking across a quiet part of campus, he sees his professor approaching. Not knowing if the professor would recognize him, he wonders if he should say hello. Thinking about this issue makes him so tense, he pretends to stop and read a text message to avoid eye contact.

As you can see, the day is a series of very unpleasant, tense moments in situations that most people would find completely ordinary. The distress the student feels and the degree to which he shapes his life around his social phobia suggest that he has social anxiety disorder. To make a formal diagnosis of this disorder, a psychologist would need to evaluate the student's full set of symptoms and their duration.

Obsessive–Compulsive Disorder Other anxiety disorders may include fears about the future as well, but their trademark features are intrusive thoughts and behaviors that seem to be stuck in a continuous replay cycle. The disorder you read about in the introduction to this module is known as **obsessive–compulsive disorder (OCD)**: *a disorder characterized by unwanted, inappropriate, and persistent thoughts (obsessions); repetitive stereotyped behaviors (compulsions); or a combination of the two* (see Table 13.7). We introduced this disorder at the outset by describing how it can occur suddenly in children. Nevertheless, OCD typically does not strike until young adulthood. Most of us have had unwanted thoughts such as an annoying song that was stuck in our head, but obsessions are generally inappropriate thoughts that can last for months or even years. A person might imagine himself picking up germs from everything he touches, or blurting out forbidden sexual feelings to a co-worker. Attempts to ignore these thoughts just make them worse, so the individual might seek relief through socially acceptable ways (being friendly with his co-worker) or in secret (sending anonymous messages). Recall

Table 13.7 :: Prevalence of Symptoms in a Survey of 293 Individuals with Obsessive–Compulsive Disorder

PERCENTAGE OF SAMPLE EXPERIENCING OBSESSION	SPECIFIC TYPES OF OBSESSIONS
58%	A fear of being contaminated
56%	Persistent doubting
48%	Need to arrange things in a symmetrical pattern
45%	Aggressive thoughts
PERCENTAGE OF SAMPLE EXPERIENCING COMPULSION	**SPECIFIC TYPES OF OBSESSIONS**
69%	Checking
60%	Cleaning
56%	Repeating actions

Source: Pinto et al., 2006.

from the module opener that the caudate region of the brain seems to be responsible for stifling inappropriate impulses. The compulsive behaviors that people with OCD engage in are thought to be a way of asserting control over their anxiety and impulses.

Compulsive behaviors often arise from specific obsessions. Someone who is obsessively worried about starting a fire might develop compulsive checking behaviors. For example, before she can leave her house, she might check that all lamps and appliances are unplugged. She may make the rounds two more times, ensuring that the electrical cords are secured by fasteners at least two feet from the outlet. Finally, she might turn off the light to leave but, to avoid the possibility that the light switch is halfway between on and off, she might count out a series of one to seven in which she turns the light off repeatedly, followed by one last downward swipe to ensure the switch is fully off. Only then can she feel secure in leaving the house.

How would you classify JMD's case from the beginning of this section? He does not seem to exhibit symptoms of GAD because his fears are short term and limited in scope, rather than general and long-lasting. Between panic disorder and phobias, panic disorder seems to be the best fit for his condition. Even though he associates the anxiety with a bridge, his fear apparently can happen anywhere—even in the library—so we can rule out a specific phobia. JMD's symptoms match the description of panic disorder because they involve short-lived episodes of unjustifiable but very intense panic. In the end, this is a diagnosis that only a professionally trained clinical psychologist or psychiatrist would be able to make.

THE VICIOUS CYCLE OF ANXIETY DISORDERS One of the most difficult aspects of anxiety disorders is that they tend to be self-perpetuating (Figure 13.4). In a sense, having an anxiety disorder today sets you up to have an anxiety disorder next week as well (Hofmann, 2007). For example, in JMD's description of his first panic attack, he described a lull in traffic that gave him a moment to think about bodily sensations. The thoughts about a heart attack kept his physiological arousal at a very high level, which in turn seemed to confirm his fears and kept his thoughts racing. It was not a fear of the bridge or the traffic that set his anxiety off, but rather his fear of having a heart attack. That is why the panic attacks can occur in multiple situations.

This vicious cycle appears in other anxiety disorders as well. For example, think about a young girl who tries to pet a neighbor's cat, but the cat scratches her. The incident did not leave a lasting physical scar, but years later the girl still feels nervous around cats. She is reluctant to even enter a house if the owners have a cat, but if she does, she remains nervous until the cat is taken away to another room or let outside. How might this behavior contribute to a vicious cycle? The sight of a cat triggers an anxiety response. When the cat is removed from the situation, or when the girl avoids the situation altogether, the anxiety fades. This process of reducing the fear, in turn, can actually reinforce the phobia.

Quick Quiz 13.3a
Anxiety Disorders

KNOW...

1. Which of the following is not classified as an anxiety disorder?
   - **A** Panic attack
   - **B** GAD
   - **C** Depression
   - **D** Social phobia

2. The difference between obsessions and compulsions is that:
   - **A** obsessions are repetitive behaviors, whereas compulsions are fears about specific events.
   - **B** obsessions are repetitive, unwanted thoughts, whereas compulsions are repetitive behaviors.
   - **C** obsessions are temporary, whereas compulsions are practically permanent.
   - **D** obsessions and compulsions are the same thing.

UNDERSTAND...

3. Allison has an intense fear of flying, so much so that she cannot even bear to close her eyes and imagine that she is on a plane. From this brief description, Allison may be experiencing:
   - **A** a specific phobia.
   - **B** a social phobia.
   - **C** a generalized phobia.
   - **D** normal levels of anxiety.

{FIG. 13.4} **The Vicious Cycle of Panic Attacks Click on this figure in your eText to see more details.**

Notice increased heart rate

Fear of heart problem

4 Which condition is marked by a strong feeling of tension and worry, no matter what the situation may be?

A A specific phobia

B A panic attack

C Generalized anxiety disorder

D Normal feelings of anxiety

5 The idea that anxiety disorders can be self-perpetuating means that:

A anxiety in one situation always causes anxiety in another situation, regardless of what is happening in those situations.

B the emotions associated with anxiety lead to physiological responses, which in turn lead to more anxious emotions, creating a vicious cycle.

C you choose when and what to be anxious about.

D anxiety is always limited to one situation or place.

6 If anxiety leads to the onset of so many different disorders, how can it be a beneficial, adaptive process?

A It cannot be an adaptive process.

B The physiological response underlying anxiety prepares us to fight or flee.

C Anxiety is a good way to gain sympathy.

D The anxiety response evolved to help attract mates.

Answers can be found on page ANS-4.

Mood Disorders

There was a two-week period when I was on top of the world. I thought I could do anything. I took on extra tasks at work that I had no idea how to do and had no time to do them. I went around boasting about how well my work was going, bought a car I couldn't afford or didn't even want. I was so energized that I couldn't fall asleep. I wound up taking four or five people out for drinks and buying rounds for everyone, sometimes having 18 to 20 drinks a day before passing out for an hour or two and then waking up to start all over again. But I didn't think it was slowing me down. The only ill effect it seemed to have was that I was getting really annoyed with everyone—everyone was slowing me down. It was like having road rage but it occurred in my house, at my work, at the store. Nobody could move fast enough. And I started to get so annoyed that I decided I just needed to sleep. So I took a few sleeping pills, but that didn't do it. The next night I took about twice as many and I finally succeeded in getting myself admitted to the hospital—the psychiatric unit to be exact.

Then everything crashed. I just started crying nonstop for about three days; they put me on medication and said it would take about two weeks to work. In that time, I lost

Many people have experienced problems with a mood disorder. Those with depression may experience extended periods of sadness and hopelessness that have no apparent cause.

about 5 or 10 pounds from my total lack of appetite. Even when they decided I was okay to go home, I wasn't really ready to function. I laid in bed; I refused to answer the phone or respond to emails from friends. I guess I hit bottom when I was halfway up the stairs in my house. I was so confused: I couldn't figure out if I really wanted to go all the way up, or if I just wanted to go back down. I was so confused by that simple decision that I just sat down and cried on the middle steps.

—NS, 35-year-old research scientist

Statistics show that NS is not alone with his experiences, which are symptoms of a condition known as bipolar disorder: Mood disorders such as bipolar disorder and depression are particularly common, affecting roughly 9.5% of adults in the U.S.—nearly 21 million people (Kessler et al., 2005). Due to a combination of biological, cognitive, and sociocultural differences, rates of depression are twice as high among women as among men, and three times as high among people living in poverty (Hyde et al., 2008). There is also a genetic susceptibility to mood disorders. In this section we discuss the two major types of mood disorders—major depression and bipolar disorder.

MAJOR DEPRESSION AND BIPOLAR DISORDER Feelings of sadness and depression are normal aspects of human experience. By comparison, clinical depression can be very severe and may occur even when there are no events or circumstances we normally associate with depressed mood. **Major depression** *is a disorder marked by prolonged periods of sadness, feelings of worthlessness and hopelessness, social withdrawal, and cognitive and physical sluggishness.* With this definition, it should be clear that depression involves more than just feeling sad for a long period of time—cognition becomes depressed as well. Thus affected

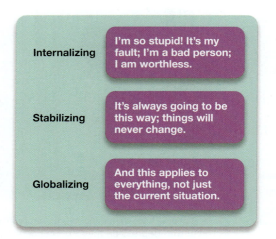

Internalizing — I'm so stupid! It's my fault; I'm a bad person; I am worthless.

Stabilizing — It's always going to be this way; things will never change.

Globalizing — And this applies to everything, not just the current situation.

{FIG. 13.5} **Three Elements of the Depressive Explanatory Style** The three elements of the depressive explanatory style are internalizing, stabilizing, and globalizing.

individuals have difficulty concentrating and making decisions while memories shift toward unpleasant and unhappy events. Physiologically, affected individuals may be lethargic and sleepy, yet experience insomnia. They may experience a change in appetite and the onset of digestive problems such as constipation. People who are feeling sad do not necessarily experience all of these cognitive and biological symptoms, so major depression is clearly a distinct psychological disorder.

Bipolar disorder (formerly referred to as manic depression) *is characterized by extreme highs and lows in mood, motivation, and energy.* It shares many symptoms with major depression—some distinguish the two by referring to major depression as *unipolar*—but it occurs only a third as often as depression (NIMH, 2008).

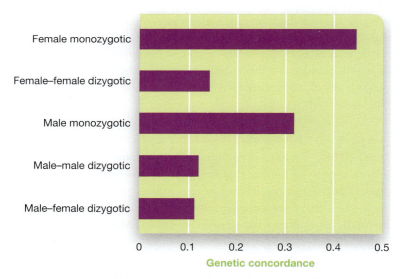

{FIG. 13.6} **Genetic Relatedness and Major Depression** Identical (monozygotic) twins have a greater chance of both developing major depression compared to fraternal (dizygotic) twins. Notice that the genetic correlation is highest for female monozygotic twins.

Bipolar disorder involves depression at one end and *mania* (an extremely energized, positive mood) at the other end. Mania may take several forms: Some individuals talk so fast that their thoughts cannot keep up; others run up credit card bills of thousands of dollars with the idea that somehow they can afford it. People experiencing mania may be sexually charged or ready to start a fight. Because these moods are so energetic, the individual often does not feel distress about the mania until it has passed, at which time they may feel a great deal of remorse and embarrassment.

Bipolar disorder encompasses both ends of an emotional continuum, and individuals with bipolar disorder can move from one end to the other at different rates. Some people with bipolar disorder experience only a few manic episodes in their lives, whereas others go through mania several times each year. Still others, known as "rapid cyclers," experience very abrupt mood swings, sometimes within hours.

COGNITIVE AND NEUROLOGICAL ASPECTS OF DEPRESSION Depression affects cognition as well as emotion. People with depression can become confused and have difficulty concentrating and making decisions. In addition, a characteristic *depressive explanatory style* emerges, in which a depressed individual explains life with three qualities: internal, stable, and global (Sweeney et al.,1986). Imagine an individual with depression does something as minor as losing his keys, and refer to Figure 13.5 to see the depressive explanatory style at work.

There is a substantial amount of research on the biological aspects of depression. For example, twin studies suggest an underlying genetic risk for developing major depression (Figure 13.6). In addition, brain imaging research has identified two primary regions of interest related to depression: (1) the *limbic system*, which is active in emotional responses and processing, and (2) the dorsal (back) of the frontal cortex, which generally plays a role in controlling thoughts and concentrating. As is the case with panic disorder, a vicious cycle appears to occur with depression. The overactive limbic system responds strongly to emotions and sends signals that lead to a decrease in frontal lobe activity (see Figure 13.7), and the decrease in frontal lobe functioning reduces the ability to concentrate and control what one thinks about (Gotlib & Hamilton, 2008).

Various neurotransmitters of the brain—especially serotonin, dopamine, and norepinephrine—appear to

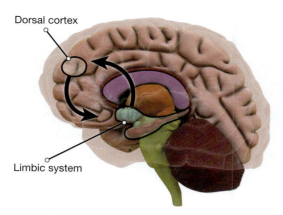

Dorsal cortex

Limbic system

Level of daily stress

Vulnerability to negative events

Disrupted social ties

Neighborhood characteristics → Depression

{FIG. 13.8} **Can Your Neighborhood Cause Depression?** Several environmental factors are associated both with troubled neighborhoods and depression.

{FIG. 13.7} **Depression and the Brain** Brain imaging research has shown higher than normal levels of activity in the limbic system of people with depression while responding to negative emotional information. This response slows activity in the dorsal cortex, making it more difficult for the individual to control thoughts—especially thoughts that might break the vicious cycle.

increase the risk of depression. In Module 14.3, we will discuss drug therapies that are used to alter the levels and activity of these neurotransmitters. These brain regions and their neurotransmitters actually tie in to other physiological systems. The negative emotions of depression co-occur with stress reactions throughout the body, thereby involving the endocrine system in the disorder. In addition, prolonged bouts of depression can compromise functioning of the immune system. As a result, individuals with depression are at higher risk for viral illnesses and heart disease, and have higher mortality rates, even when accounting for health behaviors and suicide (Penninx et al., 1999; Roblaes et al., 2005). The process can flow the other way as well. For example, cancer patients receiving drugs that affect these systems often wind up experiencing the symptoms of depression (Irwin & Miller, 2007).

SOCIOCULTURAL INFLUENCES ON MOOD DISORDERS
Biological and cognitive factors of depression interact with environmental influences. In particular, socioeconomic and environmental factors leave some individuals more vulnerable to mood disorders. As Figure 13.8 shows, just living in a specific neighborhood can be a risk factor for three main reasons (Cutrona et al., 2006). First, poor neighborhoods are associated with higher daily stress levels due to substandard housing and facilities, increased crime rates, and lack of desirable businesses (e.g., high numbers of adult bookstores and bars, combined with low numbers of revenue-generating family establishments). Second, people living in these neighborhoods are more vulnerable to stressors such as unemployment

because they often lack connections, mentors, and job opportunities that professionals have access to in high-end neighborhoods. Third, disrupted social ties are more prevalent in poor neighborhoods. Low rates of home ownership combined with difficulty making rent can lead to high turnover; people may not know their neighbors very well and, therefore, take less interest in one another's well-being.

Perhaps while reading this section you thought of a friend or acquaintance who grew up in a stressful environment yet shows no symptoms of depression or other mental illness. Researchers looking at the genetic basis of depression may have an answer as to why some people react to such circumstances by developing depression while others avoid the condition. People who inherit "short" copies of a gene responsible for serotonin (5-HTT) activity are predisposed to depressive episodes in response to stress, whereas those who inherit "long" copies are less prone to depression ("short" and "long" refer to the structure of the different versions of the genes). Individuals who inherit short copies of the 5-HTT gene are also more prone to suicide attempts (Caspi et al., 2003; see also Module 3.1). Keep in mind that we are talking about risk factors here—not inevitable consequences of the genes inherited.

SUICIDE It is difficult to imagine a worse outcome from a mood disorder than suicide. For many people, it is equally difficult to imagine how anyone could reach such a low point. Nonetheless, suicide remains a serious public health concern. Recent statistics rank suicide as the 11th most frequent cause of death in the United States (Centers for Disease Control and Prevention [CDC], 2010).

There is significant variation in who is most likely to die by suicide. Suicide is four times more likely among males than among females, and two to three times more likely among Native Americans and European Americans than among individuals of other ethnicities. In addition, many people believe that

Table 13.8 :: Warning Signs of Suicide

Learn how to recognize the danger signals. Be concerned if someone you know:

- Talks about committing suicide
- Has trouble eating or sleeping
- Exhibits drastic changes in behavior
- Withdraws from friends or social activities
- Loses interest in school, work, or hobbies
- Prepares for death by writing a will and making final arrangements
- Gives away prized possessions
- Has attempted suicide before
- Takes unnecessary risks
- Has recently experienced serious losses
- Seems preoccupied with death and dying
- Loses interest in his or her personal appearance
- Increases alcohol or drug use

Source: American Psychological Association, 2011.

adolescents are particularly vulnerable to suicide, but the highest suicide rates are actually observed among the elderly population: The suicide rate for people 65 and older is nearly 60% higher than the rate for teens. That certainly does not diminish the seriousness of adolescent suicide—given that teens have a much lower mortality rate in general, suicide ranks as the third leading cause of death in this group (CDC, 2010). Fortunately, research, treatment, and public awareness have significantly reduced the suicide rate among youth since the 1980s (Gould et al., 2003).

Suicide often comes as a surprise to the family and friends of the victim, although in some cases clear warning signs are evident (Table 13.8). Among people in their teens and early 20s, the most significant risk factors are mood disorders, recent and extremely stressful life events, a family history of mood disorders (with or without suicide), easy access to a lethal means of suicide (most significantly, firearms), and the presence of these factors in conjunction with substance abuse (Gould et al., 2003; Moscicki, 2001). For younger individuals, being the victim of bullying and ostracism is a risk factor, but it is a greater concern when youth are both the victims and the perpetrators of bullying (Klomek et al, 2007). Family and friends have reported that in the weeks before a suicide, individuals have behaved in ways that are now recognized as warning signs. For example, an individual may verbally express despair and hopelessness (*I just want to give up; Nothing matters anymore; They'll be sorry when I'm gone*), give away personal possessions, suddenly withdraw from work or school, have crying spells, or obtain a means of committing the act.

PSYCH @
The Suicide Helpline

Thousands of people contact suicide telephone helplines every day. Is there even a "best practice" when it comes to helping an individual who is suicidal? The first telephone suicide helplines were religious based and emphasized empathy and active listening. Although this is certainly a helpful approach, it may not meet the needs of every caller. Suicide prevention specialists are also equipped with more active strategies for dealing with distressed callers. For example, the Los Angeles Suicide Prevention Center has served as a model for many call centers in the United States. There, the crisis specialists take a problem-solving approach, including evaluation, referral, treatment, and follow-up.

It turns out that good crisis telephone responders effectively use both styles, depending on the circumstances. First-time callers tend to benefit more from an active listener, who will be nonjudgmental, compassionate, and reflective. Repeat callers also need compassion, but tend to benefit more if the listener engages in problem-solving strategies (Mishara et al., 2007; Mishara & Daigle, 1997).

Some helpful resources can be found at http://www.suicidepreventionlifeline.org/ and the National Suicide Prevention Lifeline 1-800-273-TALK (8255).

· · · · · · · · · · · · · · · · · ·

Quick Quiz 13.3b :: Mood Disorders

1 _____ is characterized by periods of intense depression as well as periods with elevated mood and energy levels.

 A Major depression

 B Unipolar depression

 C Bipolar disorder

 D Generalized anxiety disorder

2 Depression is associated with lower activity in the frontal lobe, which may result in:

A lack of appetite.

B difficulty concentrating and thinking.

C periods of elevated mood and energy.

D constipation.

3 First-time callers to suicide prevention lines benefit most from:

 A empathy and active listening.

 B firm, demanding instructions.

 C extensive problem-solving interventions.

 D direct referral to the hospital.

Answers can be found on page ANS-4.

Module Summary

Module 13.3

((•●—[**Listen** to the audio file of this module at **MyPsychLab**

Now that you have read this module you should:

KNOW …

- **The key terminology related to anxiety and mood disorders:**

agoraphobia (p. 495)
anxiety disorders (p. 494)
bipolar disorder (p. 500)
generalized anxiety disorder (GAD) (p. 495)
major depression (p. 499)

obsessive-compulsive disorder (OCD) (p. 497)
panic disorder (p. 495)
phobia (p. 495)
social anxiety disorder (p. 497)
specific phobias (p. 495)

UNDERSTAND …

- **The different types of anxiety disorders.** Although anxiety disorders share many similarities in symptoms, they differ in terms of what brings about the symptoms and the intensity of the symptoms. The cues that trigger anxiety range widely: In generalized anxiety disorder, just about anything may cause anxiety; in specific phobias, an individual fears only certain objects. Likewise, the intensity can range from near-constant worrying to the brief periods of highly intense anxiety in phobias and panic disorder.

- **How anxiety or mood disorders can be self-perpetuating.** Both depression and anxiety are characterized by a vicious cycle: With anxiety, anxious or fearful thoughts can lead to physiological arousal; physiological arousal can lead to escape and avoidance to get rid of the immediate fear, which in turn reinforces the anxious thoughts. In depression, a similar pattern can occur with depressed thoughts, self-blame, and social withdrawal.

APPLY …

- **Your knowledge of anxiety and mood disorders to be alert to people in need.** To do so, write down at least five warning signs for suicide, and identify the number of the suicide helpline. Check your answers on page ANS-4.

ANALYZE …

- **Whether maladaptive aspects of psychological disorders might arise from perfectly normal, healthy behaviors.** To analyze this issue, we need to examine the specific symptoms that occur in someone who has a phobia and is showing an adaptive response (fear, anxiety) but to an inappropriate stimulus or situation. It is perfectly reasonable and healthy to be cautious about heights, for example, in the sense that falls can be dangerous, even life-threatening. This reaction is maladaptive only when the fear response is so intense or out of context that it interferes with daily life. Imagine a house painter who cannot climb a ladder or scaffold; unless he overcomes his fear (or finds very short houses to work on), he will have to make major adjustments to accommodate his fear.

Schizophrenia

Learning Objectives

After reading this module you should:

KNOW ...	UNDERSTAND ...	APPLY ...	ANALYZE ...
The key terminology associated with schizophrenia	How different neurotransmitters affect individuals with schizophrenia The genetic and environmental contributions to schizophrenia	Your knowledge to identify different forms of schizophrenia	Claims that schizophrenia is related to genius or violent behavior

After reading about numerous mental disorders you would not be faulted for thinking the brain is a fragile structure. It certainly can be. However, consider a brain that comprehends unfathomably complex mathematics and creatively disentangles and models natural patterns. Yet, this same brain often struggles to distinguish reality from fiction and spins itself into an entirely confused and random state. Such is the brain of John Nash, a mathematician and Nobel laureate in economics. To academics, Nash has long been known first for his intellectual ideas. To the general public, he is best recognized as a genius who has schizophrenia. Both are true. By his middle and late twenties Nash was an established giant in the fields of mathematics and economics (he completed his doctorate at 22 years of age). Around this time he also started showing tell-tale symptoms of schizophrenia, including paranoia and delusional thinking. Among his many unusual experiences, Nash

heard voices that were not there and believed there were government conspiracies against him. Despite his mental illness (and, contrary to popular belief, not because of it), Nash is one of the greatest scholars of our time.

Focus Questions

 Why and how do people develop such a devastating disorder like schizophrenia?

 What scientific evidence suggests that schizophrenia is associated with brain abnormalities?

· · · · · · · · · · · · · · · · · · ·

Approximately 7.6 out of 1,000 adults (not quite 1% of the population) will experience schizophrenia at some point in their lives (Saha et al., 2005). Schizophrenia is among the most debilitating of psychological conditions, and it has affected people for at least as long as written history. Writings from early history describe people who seem to have lost touch with reality, who hear voices from within, and who produce bizarre speech and behaviors. It is these symptoms of schizophrenia that may give rise to false beliefs that individuals are possessed by demons or spirits. As we will see, a scientific understanding of the disorder can help correct such false beliefs.

Symptoms and Types of Schizophrenia

Schizophrenia *refers to a collection of disorders characterized by chronic and significant breaks from reality, a lack of integration of thoughts and emotions, and serious problems with attention and memory.* One obvious sign of breaking from reality is the experience of **hallucinations**, *which are false perceptions of reality such as hearing internal voices.* Patients may also experience **delusions**, *which are false beliefs about reality.* For example, a person with schizophrenia may have a *delusion of grandeur*, believing that he is Jesus, the Pope, or the President. Consider the following personal account of a man named Kurt Snyder, who wrote a book about his experiences with schizophrenia during college:

> *I thought about fractals and infinity for many years. I always told myself I was on the verge of discovery, but I simply had to think a little bit harder about it. I just wasn't thinking hard enough. The reality is that the problems I was trying to solve were far beyond my mental abilities, but I didn't recognize this fact. Even though I had no evidence to substantiate my self-image, I knew in my heart that I was just like Einstein, and that someday I would get a flash of inspiration. I didn't recognize the truth—that I am not a genius. I kept most of my mathematical ideas to myself and spoke to very few people about them. I was paranoid that someone else would solve the riddle first if I provided the right clues. (Snyder, 2006, p. 209)*

Kurt's experiences, and those of many other individuals diagnosed with schizophrenia, attest to the mind-altering experiences that characterize this disorder.

Schizophrenia occurs throughout the world, and affects an estimated 0.4% to 0.7% of its population

(Bhugra, 2005). Men are more likely to have the disorder (7:5 ratio) and tend to develop it earlier in life than women (Aleman et al., 2003). The onset of schizophrenia, in the form of an acute psychotic episode, typically occurs during late adolescence or young adulthood (DeLisi, 1992). More subtle signs, as discussed later in this module, can also appear very early—even as a toddler.

In addition to disorganized thinking, numerous other symptoms accompany schizophrenia. For some individuals, the symptoms cluster into different patterns, leading mental health professionals to identify subtypes of the disorder:

Kurt Snyder began experiencing schizophrenia in college. *Me, Myself, and Them* is his personal account of living with schizophrenia.

- **Paranoid schizophrenia**: *Symptoms include delusional beliefs that one is being followed, watched, or persecuted, and may also include delusions of grandeur.*
- **Disorganized schizophrenia**: *Symptoms include thoughts, speech, behavior, and emotion that are poorly integrated and incoherent. People with disorganized schizophrenia may also show inappropriate, unpredictable mannerisms.*
- **Catatonic schizophrenia**: *Symptoms include episodes in which a person remains mute and immobile—sometimes in bizarre positions—for extended periods. Individuals may also exhibit repetitive, purposeless movements.*
- **Undifferentiated schizophrenia**: *This category includes individuals who show a combination of symptoms from more than one type of schizophrenia.*
- **Residual schizophrenia**: *This category reflects individuals who show some symptoms of schizophrenia but are either in transition to a full-blown episode or in remission.*

Some mental health professionals prefer to classify symptoms into positive and negative categories, rather than use the subtypes identified in the preceding list (Harvey & Walker, 1987). **Positive symptoms** *refer to behaviors that should not occur, such as confused and paranoid thinking, and inappropriate emotional reactions.*

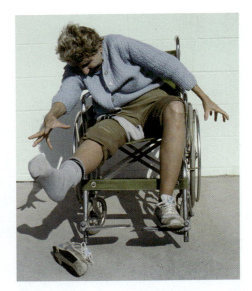

People who experience catatonic schizophrenia will remain immobile, even if in a bizarre position, for extended periods of time.

Positive symptoms involve the presence of maladaptive behavior. In contrast, **negative symptoms** *involve the absence of adaptive behavior.* Absent or flat emotional reactions and lack of speech and motivation are examples of negative symptoms.

Individuals with schizophrenia experience several problems with cognitive functioning. These range from basic startle responses, such as eye blinking (Perry et al., 2002), to the skills involved in standardized achievement tests—test scores tend to drop during adolescence as the disorder begins its course (Fuller et al., 2002). Many complex cognitive abilities involve the prefrontal cortex, a brain region showing significant neurological decline in individuals with schizophrenia (Wright et al., 2000). One such ability is working memory, the memory system that allows us to keep track of a train of thought, organize the sequence of a conversation, and handle multiple memory tasks for a short period of time. Therefore, working memory deficits may partially explain the disorganized thoughts and speech characteristic of schizophrenia (Park et al., 1999).

Social interaction is difficult for many people with schizophrenia. They typically have difficulty reasoning about social situations and show relatively poor social adjustment (Done et al., 1994). In addition, their emotional expressions and ability to react to the emotions of others may be impaired (Penn & Combs, 2000). For example, people with schizophrenia may maintain a neutral mask-like expression on their faces, and show little response to smiles or other expressions from people around them.

MYTHS IN MIND
Schizophrenia Is Not a Sign of Violence or Genius

Schizophrenia is a widely recognized term, but it may also be the most misunderstood label in psychology. Many people use schizophrenia to mean "split personality," but are actually referring to dissociative identity disorder (see Module 13.2). Other myths are more difficult to dispel, such as the belief that "madness" goes along with genius, or that schizophrenia makes a person dangerous. These myths persist because of high-profile cases such as those involving Ted Kaczynski and John Nash. Kaczynski, a bright mathematician, became famous as the "Unabomber" after sending mail bombs to prominent researchers at various universities. Nash, who was introduced at the beginning of this module, is another math genius, but has lived a peaceful, productive life as a researcher at Princeton University; the film *A Beautiful Mind* is based on the story of his life.

Few individuals with schizophrenia commit offenses even approaching the degree of violence brought about by Kaczynski. Moreover, when violence does occur, substance abuse and other factors tend to play a role (Douglas et al., 2009; Fazel et al., 2009). What may be most surprising is that people with mental illness are actually more likely to be *victims* of crime—up to 11 times more likely than non-mentally ill people (Teplin et al., 2005). Perhaps people with schizophrenia should be concerned about the rest of the population.

Ted Kaczynski's case is unusual because his illness led him to send bombs to researchers through the mail. Most people with schizophrenia do not present a threat to others.

John Nash is a math genius and the subject of *A Beautiful Mind*. Stories like Nash's lead some to incorrectly associate genius with certain types of mental illness, including schizophrenia.

Also, despite the two well-publicized cases of Ted Kaczynski and John Nash, people with schizophrenia typically score slightly below average on IQ tests (Woodberry et al., 2008).

· · · · · · · · · · · · · · · · · ·

Quick Quiz 13.4a
Symptoms and Types of Schizophrenia

KNOW...

1 A person with schizophrenia who experiences delusions that she is royalty is experiencing a(n) _____ symptom.

  A positive   **C** catatonic

  B negative   **D** undifferentiated

2 A patient who is nonresponsive and remains still in odd postures may be diagnosed with which subtype of schizophrenia?

  A Disorganized   **C** Catatonic

  B Undifferentiated   **D** Residual

APPLY...

3 An individual showing poor integration of thinking and emotion visits a psychiatrist claiming that all of her neighbors are watching her. Into which category of schizophrenia might the psychiatrist classify the individual?

  A Residual   **C** Disorganized

  B Undifferentiated   **D** Paranoid

ANALYZE...

4 Which of the following statements best summarizes the relationship between schizophrenia and violence?

  A Generally, people with schizophrenia are no more likely to become violent than non-mentally ill people, and if violence occurs, other factors, such as substance abuse, are likely to contribute to its cause.

  B People with schizophrenia are twice as likely to be violent as non-mentally ill people.

  C People with schizophrenia are far more peaceful than non-mentally ill people.

  D People with schizophrenia cannot differentiate right from wrong, and therefore are prone to violence.

5 There have been several famous cases of people with superior intellectual abilities as well as schizophrenia. Does this mean that schizophrenia is the cause or the result of genius?

  A No; in fact, the average IQ of people with schizophrenia may be slightly lower than average.

  B Yes; in fact, the average IQ of people with schizophrenia is approximately 15% higher than average.

  C Yes, because people who are that smart are likely to develop schizophrenia simply because they know too much.

  D No, because schizophrenia is associated with very low IQs.

Answers can be found on page ANS-4.

Explaining Schizophrenia

So far we have described schizophrenia based on its psychological and physical characteristics. Researchers are also very curious about the underlying sources of these characteristics and have employed a wide range of techniques to discover what causes schizophrenia. Although a single definitive answer has not yet emerged, it seems clear that a complete answer will draw from the entire biopsychosocial model.

GENETICS Studies using twin, adoption, and family history methods have shown that as genetic relatedness increases, the chance that a relative of a person with schizophrenia will also develop the disorder increases (see Figure 13.9). For example, if one identical twin has schizophrenia, the other twin has a 25% to 50% chance of developing it. This rate is significantly higher than the 10% to 17% rate found in dizygotic (fraternal) twin pairs (Gottesman, 1991).

For decades, behavioral genetic studies have shown that genes contribute to schizophrenia, but they cannot identify the specific genes that contribute to the disorder. However, with the benefit of recent technological advances and the data from the Human Genome Project, researchers are beginning to make progress at the molecular level. For example, scientists have discovered a distinct pattern of genetic irregularities that is found in 15% of individuals with schizophrenia, compared

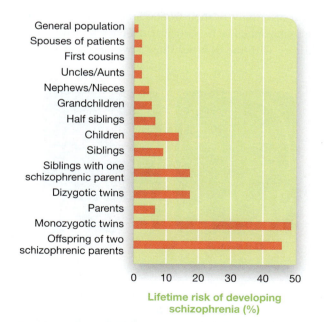

{FIG. 13.9} **Genetic Influences for Schizophrenia** The more genetic similarity an individual has to a person with schizophrenia, the more likely that he or she will also develop the disorder.

with only 5% of healthy controls (Walsh et al., 2008). On the one hand, this relationship suggests a possible genetic contribution to schizophrenia. On the other hand, the genetic abnormality was not found in 85% of the individuals. Thus, like most psychological disorders, schizophrenia cannot be diagnosed by testing for a single gene. Another way to examine the biological factors involved in schizophrenia is to examine brain anatomy and chemistry.

SCHIZOPHRENIA AND THE NERVOUS SYSTEM One very noticeable neurological characteristic of people with schizophrenia is apparent in the size of the brain ventricles, the fluid-filled spaces occurring within the core of the brain. People with schizophrenia have ventricular spaces that are 20% to 30% larger than the corresponding spaces in people without schizophrenia (see Figure 13.10) (Gottesman & Gould, 2003). The larger ventricular spaces correspond to a loss of brain matter. In fact, the volume of the entire brain is reduced by approximately 2% in those individuals with schizophrenia—a small but significant difference. In particular, the reduced volume can be found in structures such as the amygdala and hippocampus (Wright et al., 2000). It is important to remember that the anatomical changes associated with schizophrenia may not *cause* the disorder; rather, they might just tend to occur in people who have it.

The brains of people with schizophrenia are not just different in size; they also function differently. Individuals with schizophrenia have been shown to have a lower level of activity in their frontal lobes than those without schizophrenia. In particular, people who have a long history with the disorder show lower levels of activity

Psychologists have long noted that individuals who are being treated with antipsychotic drugs that block dopamine tend to be heavy smokers. One possible reason is that both the rewarding experiences and the impaired concentration associated with dopamine are reduced by the medication. Heavy nicotine use stimulates the reward and cognitive centers of the brain, thereby helping compensate for the dampening effects the medication has on dopamine (Winterer, 2010).

in their frontal lobes either when they are at a resting state or when their frontal lobes are activated by a cognitive task (Hill et al., 2004). As you just read, these individuals tend to have smaller amygdala and hippocampal regions. These differences also correspond to reduced activity of these structures during cognitive tasks (Hempel et al., 2003).

Imbalances in chemicals coursing through the brain seem to lead to the disordered thinking and emotions associated with schizophrenia. Specifically, individuals with schizophrenia have overactive receptors for the neurotransmitter dopamine (Heinz & Schlagenhauf, 2010). The excess dopamine may be involved in producing the positive symptoms of schizophrenia, such as hallucinations and delusions, but not the negative symptoms such as flattened emotion and lack of speech (Andreasen et al., 1995).

Another neurotransmitter, called *glutamate*, appears to be *underactive* in brain regions, including the hippocampus and the frontal cortex, of individuals with schizophrenia. Coincidently, glutamate receptor activity is also inhibited by the drug PCP (angel dust), which in high doses can cause symptoms that mirror those of schizophrenia.

In summary, scientists have found several neurological differences associated with schizophrenia. The science behind all of these factors is very important, but researchers are still far from having a clear picture about the biological basis of this disorder. To further our understanding of the disorder we need to examine how these biological variables interact with environmental influences to put people at greater risk for developing schizophrenia.

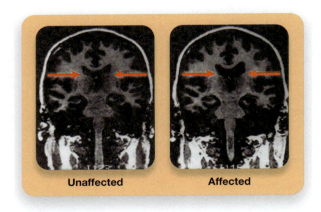

Unaffected **Affected**

{FIG. 13.10} **Brain Volume in One Monozygotic Twin with Schizophrenia and Another Without Schizophrenia** The brains of two genetically identical individuals, one affected with schizophrenia and the other unaffected, are shown here. The arrows point to the spaces created by the ventricles of the brain. Note the significant loss of brain matter in the affected individual.

ENVIRONMENTAL AND CULTURAL INFLUENCES ON SCHIZOPHRENIA

Research on the neuroscience of schizophrenia has made inroads toward discovering its causes. But remember a few observations: First, many people who *do not* have mutant versions of the genes involved in schizophrenia may still develop the disorder and, second, an identical twin has roughly a 50% chance of developing schizophrenia if her twin has it. Finally, although approximately 1% of the world population may have the disorder, as much as 10% of the population is at a *genetic risk* for developing schizophrenia (Meehl, 1990). These observations indicate that schizophrenia is not strictly a genetic disorder, and they suggest that we should consider some environmental factors that influence early brain development.

Environmental and Prenatal Factors When we think about environmental influences, we have to stretch back as far as possible—even before birth. For example, people with schizophrenia are statistically more likely to have been born during winter months (Tochigi et al., 2004). One plausible explanation for this link is that the brain develops a great deal during the second trimester, which would coincide with the onset of flu season for wintertime births. Furthermore, extreme stress such as loss of a spouse and even exposure to war during pregnancy may increase the chances that the infant will subsequently develop schizophrenia. From examples like these, psychologists speculate that perhaps maternal exposure to the influenza virus and fetal exposure to stress hormones may put a person at risk for schizophrenia (Brown & Derkits, 2010; King et al., 2010).

Even well after prenatal development, certain events can increase one's risk of developing schizophrenia. For example, a very small proportion of people who use marijuana develop psychotic symptoms, possibly because the drug interacts with the genes involved in schizophrenia (Caspi et al., 2005). Head injuries occurring prior to age 10 also put people who are genetically vulnerable to schizophrenia at greater risk for developing the disorder (AbdelMalik et al., 2003). "Psychosocial stress" is a broad term covering numerous challenges posed by the environment. Examples of psychosocial stressors include poverty, unemployment, discrimination, divorce, and death of a loved one. Being raised in an urban environment, where psychosocial stressors are more abundant, puts individuals at greater risk for developing schizophrenia (van Os et al., 2004).

Cultural Factors In Module 13.1, we introduced the topic of cultural perceptions of mental illness. Differing cultural perspectives are evident when it comes to schizophrenia. For example, ethnicity influences the types of experiences that individuals report having. Anglo-Americans tend to focus on the mental experiences of the disorder, such as disorganized thinking and emotions. In contrast, Mexican Americans focus more on how schizophrenia affects the body, such as by producing tension or tiredness. They conceive of the disorder as any other form of illness, whereas Americans tend to view mental disorders as separate from other types of illness (Weisman et al., 2000).

You have probably heard the term "running amok" to describe violent and out-of-control behavior. This term is actually Indonesian in origin. Psychiatrist Emil Kraepelin concluded that amok is more similar to what we call psychosis, albeit with some notable differences. For example, auditory hallucinations—a very common symptom of schizophrenia as Westerners know it—seem to be virtually absent in Indonesians. Kraepelin attributed this difference to the low use of speech in this culture (Jilek, 1995).

Beliefs about mental illness are linked to varying cultural views of the world (McGruder, 2004). Many people throughout the world, such as the Swahili of Tanzania, believe that what we call schizophrenia is really a sign that spirits have invaded the body. In some cultures, the self is perceived as not wholly separate from an individual, but rather "permeable" to other entities or beings. Spirits, which are thought to overpower humans, can therefore invade the body.

WORKING THE SCIENTIFIC LITERACY MODEL
The Neurodevelopmental Hypothesis

Schizophrenia is obviously a complex disorder, and no one explanation has been able to account for all the variations in symptoms, severity, and duration of this disorder. Perhaps a combination of factors is to blame.

What do we know about the neurodevelopmental hypothesis?

As with most disorders, schizophrenia is best explained by interactions of various biopsychosocial factors. Because these factors begin to influence behavior even before birth, researchers have invested great efforts into studying the **neurodevelopmental hypothesis** (of schizophrenia)—*the hypothesis that irregular biological and environmental factors interact during infant and child development to produce schizophrenic symptoms* (Walker et al., 2010). It is important to distinguish this approach from other possibilities, such as a *neurodegenerative hypothesis* proposing that the brain deteriorates to produce schizophrenia. As its name implies, the neurodevelopment hypothesis says that the brain grows into a schizophrenic state rather than degenerating into one.

How can science test the neuro-developmental hypothesis?

The neurodevelopmental hypothesis draws from research on genetics and prenatal factors. However, the developmental emphasis of the hypothesis gains strength from behavioral evidence collected during childhood and adolescence. There are even a few early warning signs. For example, when psychologists viewed home movies of infants and children who subsequently developed schizophrenia, they noted that these children showed some unusual motor patterns, primarily on the left side of the body, such as jerky, repeated, and unnecessary arm movements (Walker et al., 1994). Siblings who did not have schizophrenia did not show these same motor patterns.

In adolescence, psychologists can detect the schizophrenia *prodrome,* a collection of characteristics that resemble mild forms of schizophrenia symptoms. For example, a teenager might become increasingly socially withdrawn and have some difficulty with depression and anxiety. But the most telling—and most perplexing—problems include experiences that resemble hallucinations and delusions, with the exception that the affected individual does not fully believe them. For example, a teen might say, "I seem to keep hearing my mother calling my name before I fall asleep, even when I know she isn't home. It is strange ..." (Walker et al., 2010, p. 206).

Can we critically evaluate this information?

Unusual body movements certainly do not mean a child will develop schizophrenia in early adulthood. Nevertheless, it is at least one irregular developmental pattern that might reflect neurological abnormalities. Its emergence would be consistent with that predicted by the neurodevelopmental approach, which relies heavily on the idea that vulnerability to schizophrenia is present at birth (Walker et al., 2010). Similarly, at some point in adolescence, while most individuals will report at least one of these collections of symptoms, those who report all of them are at a greatly increased risk for schizophrenia.

Why is this relevant?

What might be some advantages to understanding the early development of schizophrenia? By identifying developmental patterns and catching them early, it may be possible to alter the progression of the disorder, thereby preventing schizophrenia from developing, or at least controlling its severity. In recent years, a number of attempts to prevent schizophrenia from developing in high-risk populations have been made, but have not proved effective (McGlashan et al., 2006; McGorry et al., 2002). To accomplish this goal, researchers will have to rely on all levels of explanation: genetics, the function and structure of the brain, neurotransmitters, prenatal influences, and psychosocial factors.

Quick Quiz 13.4b
Explaining Schizophrenia

KNOW ...

1 The neurodevelopmental hypothesis states that:

A biological factors are solely responsible for schizophrenia.

B social factors are solely responsible for schizophrenia.

C irregular biological and environmental factors interact during early development and are responsible for schizophrenia.

D prenatal exposure to the influenza virus definitely causes schizophrenia.

UNDERSTAND ...

2 Which of the following statements is most accurate concerning the biochemical basis of schizophrenia?

A The neurotransmitter dopamine is overly active.

B Dopamine is underactive.

C Serotonin levels are too low.

D There is too much glutamate activity.

3 Evidence for the neurodevelopmental hypothesis includes the fact that young children who eventually develop schizophrenia:

A report hallucinations as early as four years of age.

B show unusual motor patterns such as jerky, repeated movements.

C lapse into periods of catatonia.

D had the flu during preschool.

Answers can be found on page ANS-4.

Module Summary

Now that you have read this module
you should:

Listen to
the audio file of
this module at
MyPsychLab

KNOW ...

● **The key terminology associated with schizophrenia:**

catatonic schizophrenia (p. 505)
delusions (p. 505)
disorganized schizophrenia
    (p. 505)
hallucinations (p. 505)
negative symptoms (p. 506)
neurodevelopmental hypothesis
    (of schizophrenia) (p. 509)

paranoid schizophrenia (p. 505)
positive symptoms (p. 505)
residual schizophrenia (p. 505)
schizophrenia (p. 505)
undifferentiated schizophrenia
    (p. 505)

UNDERSTAND ...

● **How different neurotransmitters affect individuals
with schizophrenia.** Part of how we can explain
schizophrenia is by identifying the neurotransmitters that
are affected by the disorder. Abnormal dopamine and
glutamate levels are found in schizophrenia; review the
effects of these neurotransmitters on page 508.

● **The genetic and environmental contributions to
schizophrenia.** The neurodevelopmental hypothesis
claims that at least some neurological abnormalities
are present at birth, although it does not state to what
degree these abnormalities are genetic or environmental.
Nevertheless, some research suggests that prenatal
exposure to the flu or to significant amounts of stress
hormones are all risk factors for this type of mental illness.
Genetics seem to play a role, as twin studies show that if
one identical twin has schizophrenia, the other has a 50%

chance of developing the disorder—a substantial increase
over the 1% occurrence rate in the general population.

APPLY ...

● **Your knowledge to identify different forms of
schizophrenia.** Try the activity in **Table 13.9**: Identify
which symptoms in the left column most closely match
the form of schizophrenia (if any) in the right column.

Check your answers on page ANS-4.

ANALYZE ...

● **Claims that schizophrenia is related to genius or
violent behavior.** As you have read, some high-profile
cases highlight people with schizophrenia who are
intellectually brilliant. In reality, however, research tells us
that the average intelligence of people with schizophrenia
is not much different from those of the general population;
in fact, it is a little bit lower than the norm. Similarly, the
belief that schizophrenia leads to violence derives from a
small group of high-profile examples. In truth, there does
not seem to be increased risk of violence associated with
schizophrenia alone.

Table 13.9 :: Application Activity for Module 13.4

1. Rosalita was helped to a chair and she has sat there, virtually motionless,
   for about 2 hours.
2. Eyanna refuses to go to the dentist. "Last time I went," she said, "they put a
   transmitter in my teeth so that the agents can control my thoughts."
3. Jeff has begun experiencing extreme dissociations. He even began acting
   differently and referring to himself as "Steve."
4. Jinhai's language is very difficult to understand. He seems to be talking perfectly well but many of the words he is using are made up and other words
   are totally out of place.

A. This is not schizophrenia.
B. Paranoid schizophrenia
C. Catatonic schizophrenia
D. Disorganized schizophrenia
E. Residual schizophrenia

Module 13.1 :: Defining and Classifying Psychological Disorders

Focus Questions:

1 Why do people frequently regard physical and psychological conditions as fundamentally different? There is more than one explanation for this tendency, and the first is relatively clear: Humans have a long history of separating mind and body. Mental illnesses are regarded a product of the mind, and a widespread belief holds that we should have much more control over our minds than over our bones, skin, and internal organs. This position is also reinforced by the institutional separation of doctors and psychologists. The two parties meet in some contexts, such as in psychiatry, but otherwise have little to do with each other.

2 Which guidelines or criteria allow psychologists to diagnose a mental disorder such as PTSD? Psychologists rely on behaviors, input from the affected individual and, sometimes, input from family members. The DSM-IV guides their decisions by providing lists of symptoms, the time course of mental illnesses, and other factors that help them distinguish normal from abnormal functioning.

◉—[**Watch** *The Big Picture: What Is Abnormal, Anyway?* **MyPsychLab video series**

Module 13.2 :: Personality and Dissociative Disorders

Focus Questions:

1 What are personality disorders, and how do they differ from normal personality traits? Personality disorders consist of patterns of thinking and behavior that are maladaptive, cause distress to self and others, and are particularly resistant to change. As seen in Table 13.5 (page 486), different categories and types of personality disorders have been identified. These disorders differ from normal personality traits in that they are characterized by unusual behavioral patterns, improper emotional and impulsive outbursts, and socially inappropriate behavior.

2 Which aspects of antisocial personality disorder, in *some* cases, lead to violent behavior? A lack of regard for how one's behavior affects people appears to be the culprit. People with this disorder often have a habitual pattern of violating others' personal rights. Often, very little empathy or remorse accompanies or follows such acts. Although people who have antisocial personality disorder are at higher risk for demonstrating these patterns of behavior, not all people diagnosed with the disorder are violent.

◉—[**Watch** *Special Topics: DSM-IV* **MyPsychLab video series**

Module 13.3 :: Anxiety and Mood Disorders

Focus Questions:

1 What are some other ways that problems with anxiety can manifest themselves? Numerous types of anxiety disorders, with somewhat similar symptoms and a wide range of possible causes, have been identified. They include generalized anxiety disorder, which consists of long-term anxiety without a specific, identifiable source, and phobias, which are short-term bouts of anxiety that arise when a particular feared object or situation is present. Like phobias, panic disorder is a very intense form of anxiety that may sometimes lead to agoraphobia; in fact, many people experience both anxiety disorders.

2 Which abnormalities are related to depression? Depression and anxiety are closely related disorders, and are often diagnosed together in the same individual. Behavioral symptoms of depression include changes in mood, sleep, and appetite. Cognitively, people with depression tend to adopt a negative explanatory style that includes beliefs that problems are internally based and cannot be controlled by the individual.

◉—[**Watch** *The Basics, Part 1: Living with Disorder* **MyPsychLab video series**

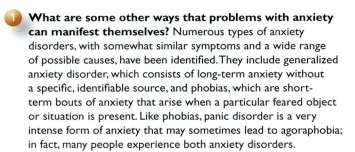

Module 13.4 :: Schizophrenia

Focus Questions:

1 Why and how do people develop such a devastating disorder like schizophrenia? As you read in this module there are multiple contributing factors to schizophrenia. It is not possible to take a single case, such as John Nash's, and identify one particular event or gene that caused the disorder. As the neurodevelopmental hypothesis predicts, numerous gene, brain, and environmental interactions occurring from very early in life interact to bring about schizophrenia.

2 What scientific evidence suggests that schizophrenia is associated with brain abnormalities? The science behind schizophrenia gives us firm grounds for explaining the disorder, and avoiding the potentially disastrous consequences of misunderstanding the source of its symptoms. Several abnormalities of brain structure and function have been linked to schizophrenia, which help explain the symptoms and aid in the development of treatments.

◉—[**Watch** *Thinking Like a Psychologist: Assessing the Effectiveness of Treaments* **MyPsychLab video series**

1 Psychologists and psychiatrists use the criteria laid out in the most recent edition of the _____ to diagnose psychological disorders.

A Dimensional and Categorical Atlas of Mental Health

B International Diagnostic Guidelines

C Guide to Psychopathology and Abnormal Behavior

D Diagnostic and Statistical Manual for Mental Disorders

2 Your textbook mentions that which of the following methods can be successful in reducing the stigma of mental illness?

A Educating the public about the biopsychosocial explanations of mental illness

B Limiting contact with individuals suffering from the most debilitating mental illnesses

C Encouraging the use of diagnostic labels

D Limiting the general public's access to information about specific mental illnesses

3 Aaliyah's few friends complain that she is often melodramatic and emotionally immature. Aaliyah loves attention (especially from men) and is constantly flirting, often inappropriately. If Aaliyah was diagnosed with a psychological disorder, which of the following would be the most likely candidate?

A Narcissistic personality disorder

B Borderline personality disorder

C Histrionic personality disorder

D Antisocial personality disorder

4 Which of the following disorders do many psychologists believe is *not* a valid diagnosis?

A Dissociative identity disorder

B Schizophrenia

C Histrionic personality disorder

D Post-traumatic stress disorder

5 In addition to suffering from panic attacks, people with panic disorder often develop an intense fear of:

A having a panic attack when they are alone.

B public places.

C germs.

D leaving the stove on.

6 Huynh washes his hands 100 or more times each day. The constant washing causes the skin on his hands to dry and crack, yet he continues to engage in this behavior. Huynh's behavior is an example of _____.

A an obsession

B agoraphobia

C a compulsion

D a negative symptom

7 All other things equal, a person living in a _____ neighborhood, who also inherited the _____ copy of the 5-HTT gene, would have the greatest risk of developing depression.

A middle-class; long

B poor; short

C middle-class; short

D poor; long

8 _____ are false beliefs about reality, whereas _____ are false perceptions of reality such as hearing internal voices.

A Positive symptoms; negative symptoms

B Negative symptoms; positive symptoms

C Hallucinations; delusions

D Delusions; hallucinations

9 Suppose a friend described schizophrenia as having a "split personality." How would you respond?

A "This is a common misconception caused by people confusing schizophrenia with dissociative identity disorder."

B "Only disorganized schizophrenia is characterized by a splitting of personalities."

C "That point is controversial; psychologists cannot agree on whether schizophrenia involves a splitting of personality."

D "That is an accurate description of schizophrenia."

10 Which of the following statements is true about the average brain of individuals with schizophrenia when they are compared to the brains of individuals who do not have the disorder?

A There are no known anatomical differences.

B The overall size of the brain is actually larger than normal in people with schizophrenia.

C Dopamine activity is lower than normal in people with schizophrenia.

D The fluid-filled spaces at the core of the brain are larger in people with schizophrenia.

What do we know about schizophrenia?

Recall that psychologists evaluate mental disorders such as schizophrenia using two complementary models. The medical model assumes that, like diseases of the body, psychological disorders have a standard set of symptoms, probable causes, and likely outcomes. On **page 505**, you can review the several subtypes of schizophrenia, such as paranoid, catatonic, or disorganized schizophrenia, each of which has its own set of symptoms. **Table 13.1 on page 477** offers a snapshot of another approach that psychologists use to develop a comprehensive view of each disorder—the biopsychosocial model. It is likely that genetics, environment, and the brain all play key roles in the development of the disorder.

When diagnosing most mental disorders, psychiatrists and psychologists rely on the DSM-IV, which offers a set of guidelines for identifying the symptoms and severity of mental illnesses. For example, two symptoms experienced by individuals with schizophrenia are hallucinations and delusions. These terms are sometimes used interchangeably, but they mean different things. Recall that hallucinations are false perceptions of reality (hearing voices), whereas delusions are false or erroneous beliefs about reality (believing that one is God).

Why is this relevant?

Watch the accompanying video excerpt on psychological disorders. You can access the video at MyPsychLab or by clicking the play button in the center of your eText. If your instructor assigns this video as a homework activity, you will find additional content to help you in MyPsychLab. You can also view the video by using your smart phone and the QR code below, or you can go to the YouTube link provided.

After you have read this chapter and watched the video, consider the following question: Why do most researchers consider schizophrenia a brain disorder? Which evidence suggests that schizophrenia could begin in the womb?

How can science help explain schizophrenia?

On **page 506**, we mentioned that the disorganized thought processes characteristic of schizophrenia may be explained by brain research that suggests a decline in the functioning of the prefrontal cortex in people with this disease. Twin studies suggest a strong genetic influence in the emergence of schizophrenia, although specific genes cannot entirely explain why some people do or do not develop the disease. Biological research, as shown in **Figure 13.10**, demonstrates that people with schizophrenia have larger ventricle spaces, which correspond to a loss of brain matter. Research has also revealed that imbalances of chemicals in the brain may account in part for some symptoms of the disorder. Important research on environmental and prenatal factors has also helped further our understanding of the disease. For instance, researchers have found that babies born in the winter months are statistically more likely to develop schizophrenia, suggesting a possible link between the effects of influenza season and fetal brain development. When it comes to environmental factors, those who are genetically at risk for the disorder and who suffer head injuries before age 10 years have an increased chance of developing the disease, as do those individuals who are raised in an environment characterized by psychosocial stress.

Can we critically evaluate claims about schizophrenia?

The complexity of schizophrenia seems to call for an approach that uses multiple perspectives. On **page 509**, we explored the neurodevelopmental hypothesis, which proposes that a combination of genetic and environmental factors work together during infant and child development to make people more susceptible to the disease. For instance, psychologists can identify symptoms in adolescence that predict schizophrenia. Detecting early precursors to the disorder might allow people to alter the progression of schizophrenia.

While schizophrenia is a familiar disorder to most people, it is often misunderstood. **Myths in Mind on page 506** dispels the notion that, despite famous cases such as those of John Nash and Ted Kaczynski, people with schizophrenia are likely to be either geniuses or violent offenders. To the contrary, people with schizophrenia tend to score below average on standardized intelligence tests and are less likely to be perpetrators of crime (and more likely to be victims of it).

MyPsychLab   **Your turn to Work the Scientific Literacy Model:**   You can access the video at MyPsychLab or by clicking the play button in the center of your eText. If your instructor assigns this video as a homework activity, you will find additional content to help you at MyPsychLab. You can also view the video by using your smart phone and the QR code, or you can go to the YouTube link provided.

youtube.com/ scientificliteracy

14 :: THERAPIES

Treating Psychological Disorders

Learning Objectives	KNOW ...	UNDERSTAND ...	APPLY ...	ANALYZE ...
After reading this module you should:	The key terminology associated with mental health treatment	The major barriers to seeking help for psychological disorders The importance of empirically supported treatments	Your knowledge to understand your own attitudes toward help-seeking	Whether self-help options, such as popular books, are a useful therapy option

What do you think of when you imagine a person providing psychological therapy? By now, you should have a fairly accurate idea of what this practice entails, although the general public typically understands the process of therapy based on the entertainment industry's portrayals of it, rather than through the work of actual mental health workers and their professional organizations. Celebrity therapists are seen and heard providing advice to people at a moment's notice and with no context or time spent truly evaluating each individual's problems. Dr. Laura (Schlessinger), who has a master's degree and license in marriage and family counseling (although her doctorate is in physiology), often uses her show as a political platform as much as a venue for offering advice. Dr. Phil (McGraw), who also received clinical training, typically works the entertainment (and even weight loss) circuit. Dr. Drew (Pinsky) has hosted call-in shows and is the doctor in residence in the show *Celebrity Rehab*. In addition to public portrayals of doing drug rehabilitation, Dr. Drew uses his medical degree to work with actual patients, off camera. It is no wonder that the general public is confused about what, exactly, psychological therapy is and who can conduct it.

Focus Questions

 How helpful is the advice given by popular media and self-help gurus?

 Who typically conducts psychological therapy and which credentials are needed to do so?

· · · · · · · · · · · · · · · · · ·

In Chapter 13 we described some of the psychological disorders that affect millions of lives. Nearly everyone has friends, family, neighbors, or co-workers who could benefit from psychological treatment. In this module, we address much of the background on **psychotherapy**—*the processes for resolving personal, emotional, behavioral, and social problems so as to improve well-being.* We will address who uses psychotherapy, who provides it, and how it is evaluated.

Large-scale surveys indicate that a growing number of Americans are seeking help for psychological problems. Researchers estimate that approximately 13% of adults in the U.S. population received some form of mental health treatment between 2004 and 2008, including more than 57% who could be diagnosed with a psychological disorder (National Institute of Mental Health [NIMH], 2011). This group included people who are being treated for serious psychiatric conditions, as well as people seeking help for common issues such as stress, marital and relationship problems, loneliness, dissatisfaction at work, problems with impulsiveness, or persistent anxiety.

Not all groups of people are equally likely to seek treatment. In general, women participate in psychotherapy more often than men, and people aged 35 through 55 seek treatment more often than younger adults and the elderly (Addis & Mahalik, 2003; Olfson & Marcus, 2010). Researchers within the United States have found that Caucasians are more likely to seek psychotherapy than are African American and Hispanic individuals (see Figure 14.1; Olfson & Marcus, 2010; Olfson et al., 2002). Finally, people raised and living in the United States and Canada are generally more likely to seek therapy than people from most other regions, as demonstrated in research on college students from countries as diverse as Israel, Hungary, Japan, and Korea (Cohen et al., 1998; Masuda et al., 2005; Yoo & Skovholt, 2001).

Barriers to Psychological Treatment

Thousands of individuals could benefit from psychological treatment but delay getting help for many years, or simply go without any treatment at all (Wang et al., 2005). A nationwide survey shows that more than one-third of all U.S. adults with a diagnosable disorder do not receive treatment (NIMH, 2011). Why have so many gone without help? Researchers have begun to focus on *barriers* to treatment—financial, cognitive, cultural, and other factors that prevent individuals from receiving therapy.

EXPENSE AND AVAILABILITY Two of the main barriers to mental health treatment are time and expense (Colonna-Pydyn et al., 2007; Craske et al., 2005). Psychotherapy can be expensive, often costing more than $100 per hour, making it difficult or impossible to afford for people without health insurance. Because therapy may require weekly sessions spanning several months, even middle-class families would have to sacrifice to cover the typical cost of therapy. In addition, there is a widespread perception that the drugs used to treat psychological disorders are expensive, and there is some

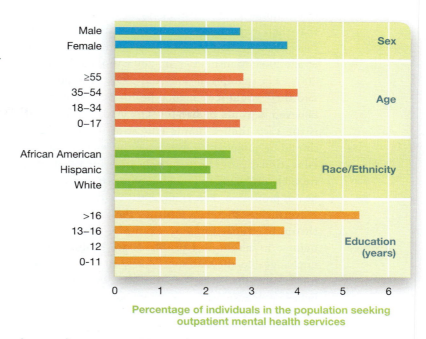

{FIG. 14.1} **Who Seeks Treatment?** Whether someone seeks outpatient psychological therapy services depends on numerous factors, including ethnicity, sex, education level, and age.

truth to that assumption. For example, brand-name drugs used to treat schizophrenia may cost as much as $400 per month. Therapy is also associated with numerous indirect costs, such as time away from work, transportation, and possibly even child care. As a result, many individuals from lower-income families do without treatment until a major incident or problem occurs. This explains why members of some socioeconomic groups are more likely than others to initiate treatment at a hospital emergency room rather than scheduling an appointment with a psychologist or other provider (Snowdon, 1999).

To help overcome these barriers, some community organizations provide offices in lower-income areas where private psychotherapists are scarce and needed. Community mental health centers often provide therapy on a sliding scale, which means the cost of a one-hour session may range from $5 to $150, depending on the patient's income and insurance status. As for the perception that drugs are expensive, many treatments can also be made affordable through use of generic products. Although brand-name antidepressants such as Prozac and Zoloft may cost more than $1.50 per dose, they must compete with the generic versions that are sold as fluoxetine and sertraline, respectively, for as little as $0.20 per dose.

MINIMALIZATION, MISUNDERSTANDING, OR MISTRUST It is quite common for people who avoid treatment to *minimize* their condition, meaning that they tend to view their symptoms as less severe than others might believe. Also, people may not be aware that their experiences, although distressful, can be successfully treated by therapy or medication (Craske et al., 2005; Mansfield et al., 2005; Vanheusdan et al., 2008). For example, in one study, 99% of respondents said they would seek mental health treatment if they believed it would be helpful (Fox et al., 2001). If this is the case, then a simple educational intervention should be sufficient to overcome the barriers. In fact, educational programs can help individuals identify treatable problems and build confidence in the mental health profession (Fox et al., 2001; Sharp et al., 2006). Nevertheless, there are limits to the gains achievable through education: For example, when people believe psychological problems are biological and unchangeable, they are more likely to stigmatize and judge individuals who seek treatment than when they believe psychosocial factors contribute to the disorder (Walker & Read, 2002).

STIGMA ABOUT MENTAL HEALTH   Even among individuals who believe they need treatment, many resist seeking help because of the *stigma*—a collection of negative stereotypes, discussed in Module 13.1—associated with psychological disorders (Corrigan, 2004; Vogel et al., 2009). Imagine a business executive taking time off to have a heart murmur treated—people would likely be very supportive of her. Now consider someone who leaves work early once a week for therapy sessions to treat an anxiety disorder. Would she be as likely to reveal the purpose of her absence? And would her co-workers be as forthcoming with support? Maybe not. Mental health stigmas affect not only adults' decisions about caring for their own problems, but also their decisions on behalf of their children. Indeed, many adults also refuse treatment for their children (Hinshaw, 2005; Vogel et al., 2007).

Sadly, some of the fear of stigma may be justified even though the stigma is not: Stigma against people with mental disorders can result in job and housing discrimination, as well as avoidance by family, peers, and co-workers. However, being a member of a social group that actively supports psychological treatment can reduce, and in the best circumstances eliminate, many of the fears about stigmatization (Vogel et al., 2007).

GENDER ROLES   In the United States and elsewhere, men often go without treatment due to a conflict between stereotypes of psychological treatments and *gender roles*. Masculine gender roles emphasize emotional strength—which is in conflict with acknowledging and talking through emotions and interpersonal problems. These gender roles also emphasize independence, so even if a problem is acknowledged, males would be more likely to believe they should just "get over it" (Berger et al., 2005; Mahalik et al., 2003). Getting men to seek help has presented such a long-standing challenge that the NIMH has staged public awareness campaigns of this issue. The "Real Men, Real Depression" marketing campaign targets men of various ages and ethnicities, and the initial evidence indicates that this and similar campaigns succeed in getting people in need to find help (Bell et al., 2010; Rochlen et al, 2006).

INVOLUNTARY AND COURT-ORDERED TREATMENT   Although many individuals voluntarily seek mental health care, a substantial number have been required to contact mental health services by the courts, social services agencies, or employers. In the United States, more than 40 states have laws that allow court-ordered outpatient treatments for people with severe disorders (Applebaum, 2005), and similar laws exist in Canada, Australia, and many other countries where psychiatric and psychological services are widely available. The majority of these cases stem from erratic or disturbing behavior resulting in legal trouble. Other reasons for involuntary treatment include driving while intoxicated and domestic violence.

Although these conditions are all cause for concern, there does appear to be bias in how these mandatory referrals are made. A survey of records indicated that individuals who are lower in socioeconomic status and from African American or Latino backgrounds are significantly more likely to receive court-ordered treatment (Takeuchi & Cheung, 1998). Multiple reasons appear to explain this bias. One major reason is the financial barrier: Individuals with higher incomes have more resources, often including health insurance, than those with lower incomes, so they can afford to obtain treatment on their own. In contrast, people from lower-income groups may have less access to information about services and may not be able to afford them. Therefore, when people face large barriers, a court order is sometimes the only way to work around it.

Obviously, forcing someone into treatment brings up serious ethical and legal questions. Individuals who receive these orders often feel coerced. Nonetheless, the evidence shows that a significant number of people benefit from mandated treatment, as indicated by their adherence to treatment and reduced encounters with law enforcement (Hough & O'Brien, 2005; Pollack et al., 2005; Swartz & Swanson, 2004).

Given that many individuals do not have access to therapies due to financial barriers, in many communities the juvenile and adult corrections systems are the only means of guaranteeing treatment. As a result, the public may begin to believe that (1) mental health is not a significant problem, but crime is; and (2) people with mental illness are prone to crime and violence. Neither assumption is correct.

Quick Quiz 14.1a
Barriers to Psychological Treatment

KNOW...

1. The processes for resolving personal, emotional, behavioral, and social problems so as to improve well-being are known as _____ .

   Ⓐ psychotherapy
   Ⓑ barriers to help-seeking
   Ⓒ minimalizing
   Ⓓ compensation

UNDERSTAND...

2. Which type of barrier is in evidence when people believe their problems are not important enough for a therapist?

   Ⓐ Financial
   Ⓑ Minimalizing
   Ⓒ Mistrust
   Ⓓ Delay

APPLY...

3. Based on the statistics presented in this module, which of the following individuals would be most likely to seek out help from a mental health professional?

   Ⓐ An Asian male in his 60s
   Ⓑ A Hispanic female in her 40s
   Ⓒ A Caucasian male in his early 30s
   Ⓓ A Caucasian female in her late 20s

4. Knowing someone with a psychological disorder is likely to _____ your stereotypes about the disorder.

   Ⓐ exaggerate
   Ⓑ have no effect on
   Ⓒ reduce
   Ⓓ diminish both your understanding and

Answers can be found on page ANS-4.

Mental Health Providers and Settings

A wide variety of treatment settings are available for people in need of mental health care. The type of treatment people receive depends on several factors, including their age, the type and severity of the disorder, and the existence of any legal issues and concerns that coincide with the need for treatment. Mental health services include inpatient care, outpatient office visits, and the use of prescription drugs (see Figure 14.2 and also Module 14.3). Care may be received from many different types of mental health professionals with varying backgrounds. ⚕

MENTAL HEALTH PROVIDERS In popular culture, the terms *psychologist* and *psychiatrist* are often (and erroneously) used as if they meant the same thing. In fact, some major distinctions separate the two and, even among psychologists, there are a variety of providers.

Perhaps the best-known providers are **clinical psychologists**, *mental health professionals with doctoral degrees who diagnose and treat mental health problems ranging from the everyday to the chronic and severe.* **Counseling psychologists** *are mental health professionals who typically work with people needing help with common problems such as stress, coping, and mild forms of anxiety and depression, rather than severe mental disorders.* Psychologists who practice from either perspective typically earn a doctoral degree, including a PhD, PsyD, or EdD, although some states will certify counselors who hold a master's degree. Practitioners of clinical and counseling psychology work in many capacities and settings. They may provide individual or group therapy in an office or institution such as a hospital, or they may conduct psychological testing and research. Other people with different levels of training and background also conduct therapy; for example, *clinical social workers* and *psychiatric nurses* conduct therapy to help people cope with psychological problems.

☑ ● Complete the **Survey** *How Do You Take Care of Your Mental Health?* at **MyPsychLab**

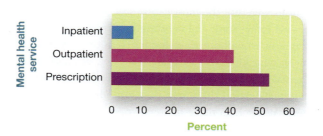

{FIG. 14.2} **Types of Treatment People Use** Prescription drugs are the most prevalent mental health option followed by outpatient visits with a therapist, and then inpatient care (numbers are for adults aged 18 and older in the United States who sought mental health treatment). **Click on this figure in your eText to see more details.**

Today, some people with severe mental disorders reside in an institution or hospital that specializes in mental health care. These settings are dramatically different than they were just a few decades ago, when they were called "insane asylums" and other unfortunate names.

Psychiatrists *are physicians who specialize in mental health, and who diagnose and treat mental disorders primarily through prescribing medications that influence brain chemistry.* (Currently, except in Louisiana and New Mexico, licensed clinical psychologists cannot prescribe medications in the United States.) Like clinical psychologists, psychiatrists work in a variety of settings, but they are most frequently found in hospitals and other institutional settings, treating people with relatively severe psychological disorders.

INPATIENT TREATMENT AND DEINSTITUTIONALIZATION

Throughout much of human history, people experiencing severe disorders—now known by names such as psychosis, schizophrenia, or Alzheimer's disease—were often separated from society. They may have been physically removed from the city or, in the 1800s and 1900s, locked in an asylum. These actions hardly qualify as treatments because there was no hope that the individuals would get better. Instead, the twin goals were to protect the public and to provide basic care for individuals whose families could not do so (Wright, 1997).

Sadly, history tells us that many of the mental institutions were not the most caring places; in fact, they appeared rather stark and depressing. Patients were mostly warehoused without receiving much in the way of treatment, education, or recreation. This lack of physical and mental stimulation seems to have sealed the fate of the patients, putting them in a position where they would never recover. To make matters worse, some institutions relied on restraints such as chains and straightjackets, and the employee profile fit the modern idea of a jailhouse guard rather than a nurse or therapist.

By the 1950s, a grass-roots campaign had formed in response to the obvious shortfalls of this treatment. Known as **deinstitutionalization**, *this movement pushed for returning people from mental institutions to their communities and families and enabling them to receive treatment on an outpatient basis.* The results were largely successful, and the movement convinced several sectors of society—namely government, the public, and social scientists—that asylums were causing more problems than they solved.

Deinstitutionalization has not done away with the need for inpatient care, but modern science has provided many ways to improve the experience from warehousing to actual treatment. In the decades since this movement began, many of the people admitted to psychiatric hospitals have entered the facilities only for *evaluation* and *stabilization.* In as little as three or four days, a patient admitted after a suicide attempt may be fully evaluated, begin medication and therapy, receive education about emergency resources such as suicide hotlines, and then be released to the care of his or her family. Thus inpatient treatment is now geared more toward protecting the individual patient from harm, and providing as quick a return to society as possible.

Of course, some people still require serious, long-term care. Rather than spend their lives in an asylum, many of these individuals live in *residential treatment centers,* which tend to resemble a dormitory or motel more than an asylum. Low-level **residential treatment centers** *provide psychotherapy and life skills training so that the residents can become integrated into society to the greatest extent possible.* Medium- to high-level centers place increasing restrictions on individuals, so they may have the appearance of a hospital equipped like a medium-security prison. These facilities are intended for individuals with a more dangerous history—perhaps people who have committed physical or sexual assault.

OUTPATIENT TREATMENT AND PREVENTION

Outpatient therapy and inpatient housing simultaneously grew in popularity through the early

20th century. Their emergence paved the way for deinstitutionalization, which was essentially a call to move the mentally ill to the community where they could receive outpatient treatment. After deinstitutionalization began, however, homelessness and substance abuse became a major problem for the severely mentally ill. People with less intense problems sometimes found themselves facing financial barriers and stigma when they sought help.

To meet these needs, some psychologists began spending time away from individual, one-on-one therapy to see what they could do for the community at large—thus arose a field now known as **community psychology**, *an area of psychology that focuses on identifying how individuals' mental health is influenced by the neighborhood, economics, social groups, and other community-based variables.* By operating at this level, community psychologists can emphasize prevention and screening. They may initiate public awareness campaigns, develop group therapies and other resources, advocate for jobs and education, and offer free or low-cost group counseling in neighborhoods where private mental health services are not available. For example, to prevent depression, community psychologists may conduct research into the environmental and neighborhood factors that contribute to stress, anxiety, and depression, and then work with community groups to resolve these problems. In addition, they may develop programs to counter negative cognitive patterns and bolster positive thinking in schools and in afterschool programs.

PSYCH @

The University Mental Health Counseling Center

University campuses are typically regarded as lively, energetic environments. We would not attribute 100% of this image to the faculty; rather, it is the students who create this dynamic climate. However, the stresses of university life can bring about temporary struggles with mental well-being. Traditional-age college students experience the stresses of managing a heavy workload, beginning a career path, developing an adult identity, and finding a way to pay for college, while nontraditional students often have to juggle work and family obligations along with school (Mowbray et al., 2006). Also, some students face lifelong struggles with mental illness. Approximately 15% of college students exhibit symptoms of depression. In fact, the number of students diagnosed with depression has increased more than 50% for the past two decades, along with the number reporting anxiety and other psychological problems (American College Health Association, 2007).

University counseling centers typically employ a resident psychologist or psychiatrist, along with a staff of counselors trained to help with psychological problems. The size of this staff, of course, depends on the size of the university and the availability of funding. Although most universities offer counseling for their students, recent surveys indicate that counseling centers are so busy they have resorted to waiting lists for students seeking help. Some have been asked to treat disorders much more severe than most counseling centers are designed to accommodate (Gallagher, 2007; Voelker, 2003). Despite the existence of these waiting lists, surveys indicate that only 20% of students would go to the counseling center on their own; instead, students are far more likely to seek help from friends (75%) or family (63%) (Jed Foundation, 2009).

· · · · · · · · · · · · · · · · · · ·

Quick Quiz 14.1b
Mental Health Providers and Settings

KNOW ...

1. Which type of provider is permitted to prescribe medications in all 50 states?
   - **A** Psychiatrist
   - **B** Clinical psychologist
   - **C** Clinical social worker
   - **D** Medical psychologist

2. _____ study how individuals' mental health is influenced by the neighborhood, economics, social groups, and other community-based variables.
   - **A** Residential treatment centers
   - **B** Community psychologists
   - **C** Psychiatrists
   - **D** Social workers

3. The social movement against keeping the mentally ill in asylums is known as _____ .
   - **A** empirically validated treatments
   - **B** social work
   - **C** deinstitutionalization
   - **D** community psychology

Answers can be found on page ANS-4.

Evaluating Treatments

The U.S. Food and Drug Administration (FDA) requires that manufacturers demonstrate the safety and usefulness of many over-the-counter drugs and *all* drugs that require prescriptions. To provide this evidence, drug makers must pay to have experiments conducted by their staff or researchers at major universities and medical centers. These randomized, blind, controlled studies are done to determine whether a drug has its intended effects and which side effects it produces. It may be somewhat surprising to learn that there is comparatively little oversight over something as important as psychological therapy. How important is it to know whether a certain psychological intervention will produce results, cause damage, or be a waste of money? This question is one that that psychologists have spent decades tackling. In the mid-1990s, the American Psychological Association set up task forces to evaluate different therapy practices; as of 2005, these task forces had made their findings and recommendations available online (APA, 2009). To answer the question as to whether therapy works, psychologists need to conduct sound, controlled research.

EMPIRICALLY SUPPORTED TREATMENTS

Empirically supported treatments (also called evidence-based therapies) *are treatments that have been tested and evaluated using sound research designs* (Chambless & Ollendick, 2001; De Los Reyes & Kazdin, 2008). The most rigorous way of testing whether a certain therapy works is through an experiment. Recall from Module 2.2 that an experiment would involve randomly assigning volunteers to a treatment group (e.g., a type of therapy) and to a control group. Ideally, experiments are also double-blind, which in this case means that neither the patient nor the individual evaluating the patient is aware of which treatment the patient is receiving. Although this design represents the ideal steps in the laboratory and is easy to implement in a drug study, it can be very challenging to employ these methods when studying psychological therapies. A therapist, of course, knows which type of treatment she administers. Also, every patient and every therapist are unique. Part of the effectiveness of therapy comes from the *therapeutic alliance*—the relationship that emerges in therapy. Therefore, even though a therapist may implement the same steps and procedures in a therapy, each session is likely to be different. Due to these and other factors, few studies meet rigorous criteria required for empirical support (DeRubeis & Crits-Cristoph, 1998).

This approach to testing the effectiveness of different therapies is modeled after the drug testing procedures that are carried out in laboratories. Some psychologists believe that evaluating psychotherapy in the same way we test drugs ignores some of the nuances and complexity that exist in the process of therapy (Westen & Bradley, 2005). Perhaps it comes as some surprise that professional psychologists scrutinize their practices at such a high level, especially given the common perception of psychologists and the process of therapy as portrayed by celebrity therapists with television and radio shows.

WORKING THE SCIENTIFIC LITERACY MODEL
Can Self-Help Treatments Be Effective?

Many people opt to address their psychological problems by using a wide variety of resources that do not involve visiting an actual therapist. When disorders are severe, it is clearly very important to seek professional help. But for milder psychological distress, is self-help a viable option?

What do we know about self-help treatments?

At the beginning of this module, we discussed how celebrity therapists affect public perceptions of the process of mental health treatment. The fact that these media-savvy individuals receive so much attention suggests that perhaps some people find it helpful to listen to their advice. In addition, plenty of other self-help resources can be found elsewhere, such as on the Internet and the self-help section at the local bookstore (Strecher, 2007). It is not currently possible to determine whether people enjoy personal mental health benefits from viewing and listening to popular programs featuring celebrity therapists. In contrast, **bibliotherapy**, *the use of self-help books and other reading materials as a form of therapy,* has been experimentally tested.

How can science help us learn more about self-help treatments?

One study seeking to answer this question involved assessing the effectiveness of bibliotherapy over a three-month period in 170 elderly primary care patients who were experiencing depression. The patients were evenly divided into two groups: one that read a self-help book on depression, and another that received the standard care received by all patients. After three months, the group who read the self-help book in addition to the standard care showed no signs of reduced depression compared to the control group (Joling et al., 2010).

Nevertheless, this particular question cannot be definitively answered with a single study. There are far too many factors to consider, such as the type and severity of psychological problem, the choice of self-help book, and a multitude of dispositional factors of each individual who tries bibliotherapy.

An ideal place to search for answers in this situation is to consult a meta-analysis, which combines numerous studies testing a similar hypothesis. One such analysis combined six separate studies that had tested whether the book *Feeling Good* reduced depressive symptoms. The researchers found that over four weeks, those who read the book had reduced depression compared to those who did not (see Figure 14.3; Anderson et al., 2005). Thus there may be reason to believe that, at least among people who are not experiencing major depression, bibliotherapy can be helpful. Even so, psychologists caution that the effects of bibliotherapy tend to be very minor (Morgan & Jorm, 2008).

Can we critically evaluate this evidence?

It may strike you as impersonal to turn to a computer, television, or book for assistance with mental health problems. In reality, the impersonal nature of these treatments may be the primary advantage when it comes to getting information about mental health. For example, people use electronic resources because they provide a relatively anonymous venue for gaining information (Rainie & Packel, 2001).

Another issue is that it is always important to consider the source. Self-help gurus may be focused more on the business and entertainment side of things rather than on producing long-term positive benefits to those in need. In addition, some of these individuals do not have professional degrees in psychology or other mental health fields. As a consequence, we should not expect all self-help materials to have the same success rates; it is even possible that some could do more harm than good. Before judging a specific self-help treatment as effective or not, we should determine whether it is supported by sound scientific research.

Why is this relevant?

Major advantages of using self-help options include that they are typically low in cost, are convenient and provide anonymity for those who want it. Self-help options are easy to find. In fact, many people consult online resources to get help for depression, anxiety, substance abuse problems, and sexual health (Fox, 2005). If you do turn to self-help resources for your psychological problems, remember to choose wisely and stay committed to the program. Research has shown that not all treatments are

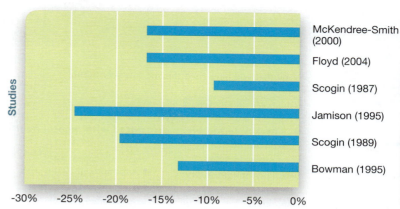

{FIG. 14.3} **Results of Six Studies Evaluating the Self-Help Book *Feeling Good*** Research on the book *Feeling Good* shows successful results in reducing symptoms of depression. Comparisons across six studies (identified by author name and publication date) indicate statistically significant improvement in each case (Anderson et al., 2005).

successful, and that compliance and follow-through with some forms of self-help are probably quite a bit lower than in face-to-face therapy sessions (O'Kearney et al., 2006). Thus the ideal course of treatment is probably to speak with a professional at least once—especially if symptoms are severe—to find out whether self-help is appropriate for your situation.

Quick Quiz 14.1c :: Evaluating Treatments

1 _____ is the relationship that emerges in therapy and is an important aspect of effectiveness.

  A Client insight   **C** Therapeutic alliance

  B Bibliotherapy   **D** Friendship

2 What does it mean to say that a therapy has "empirical support"?

  A Insurance companies prefer it.

  B Therapists prefer to use it.

  C Research studies confirm that it is effective compared to no treatment and possibly compared to other alternatives.

  D Research studies demonstrate that it can do a better job than drugs.

3 Which of the following conclusions best summarizes the effectiveness of bibliotherapy?

  A It has no benefit whatsoever.

  B It is more effective than other forms of therapy.

  C It works, but is addictive.

  D Overall, evidence suggests it may be helpful for mild problems, but results are not always consistent.

Answers can be found on page ANS-4.

Module Summary

Module 14.1

Listen to the audio file of this module at **MyPsychLab**

Now that you have read this module you should:

KNOW ...

● *The key terminology associated with mental health treatment:*

bibliotherapy (p. 522)
clinical psychologist (p. 519)
community psychology (p. 521)
counseling psychologist (p. 519)
deinstitutionalization (p. 520)
empirically supported treatments (p. 522)
psychiatrist (p. 520)
psychotherapy (p. 516)
residential treatment center (p. 520)

UNDERSTAND ...

● *The major barriers to seeking help for psychological disorders.* These barriers include expense, availability, ethnicity, gender, and attitudes toward therapy. For example, males are more likely to view help-seeking as a sign of weakness and, in the United States, African American and Latino individuals are less likely to receive treatment than European Americans.

● *The importance of empirically supported treatments.* Psychotherapies need to be tested for their effectiveness using appropriate and rigorous experimental designs. Empirically supported treatments demonstrate that the technique being evaluated works better than doing nothing at all, and that it works better than existing treatments that are suspected to be less effective.

APPLY ...

● *Your knowledge to understand your own attitudes toward help-seeking.* Complete the scale in **Table 14.1** to see how you compare to others. College student averages are 1.6 for males and 1.9 for females.

ANALYZE ...

● *Whether self-help options, such as popular books, are a useful therapy option.* Self-help books alone are not likely to be life-changing or stand-alone treatments for serious problems with depression, anxiety, and substance abuse, for example. Even so, research on bibliotherapy indicates that in some cases, when used in conjunction with other methods, reading self-help books can bring about modest improvements.

Table 14.1 :: The Attitudes Toward Seeking Professional Psychological Help Scale

Read each item carefully and circle the response in the column that indicates the degree to which you agree or disagree with the item. Next, average the circled numbers to arrive at your total score.

ITEM	AGREE	PARTLY AGREE	PARTLY DISAGREE	DISAGREE
If I believed I was having a mental breakdown, my first inclination would be to get professional attention.	3	2	1	0
The idea of talking about problems with a psychologist strikes me as a poor way to get rid of emotional conflicts.	0	1	2	3
If I were experiencing a serious emotional crisis at this point in my life, I would be confident that I could find relief in psychotherapy.	3	2	1	0
There is something admirable in the attitude of a person who is willing to cope with his or her conflicts and fears without resorting to professional help.	0	1	2	3
I would want to get psychological help if I were worried or upset for a long period of time.	3	2	1	0
I might want to have psychological counseling in the future.	3	2	1	0
A person with an emotional problem is not likely to solve it alone; he or she is likely to solve it with professional help.	3	2	1	0
Considering the time and expense involved in psychotherapy, it would have doubtful value for a person like me.	0	1	2	3
A person should work out his or her own problems; getting psychological counseling would be a last resort.	0	1	2	3
Personal and emotional troubles, like many things, tend to work out by themselves.	0	1	2	3

Source: Fischer & Farina (1995).

Module 14.2

Psychological Therapies

Learning Objectives

After reading this module you should:

KNOW ...	UNDERSTAND ...	APPLY ...	ANALYZE ...
The key terminology related to psychological therapies	The general approaches to conducting major types of psychotherapy	Your knowledge to identify major therapeutic techniques	The pros and cons of the major types of psychotherapy

Medical doctors are generally required to follow the Hippocratic Oath—an agreement that states they will cause no harm to their patients. One way of honoring this oath is to use the safest and most effective treatments. We do not generally associate the Hippocratic Oath with psychologists, but they also follow the basic tenet. Like physicians, psychologists must be aware of the possibility that a specific type of treatment might worsen a condition and, therefore, should be avoided.

For example, *Scared Straight* was a program developed in the 1970s that involved exposing at-risk youth to prisons and prisoners. The interventions were based on the premise that shocking or scaring the youths with the harsh realities of prison life would deter criminal activity. These scare tactics involved blunt descriptions of prison violence, along with verbal aggression directed at adolescents attending the sessions. The program may have succeeded in scaring and shocking adolescents, but the youths who attended these sessions did not necessarily go down a straight path. Many were later convicted of crimes and incarcerated. According to some analyses, participation in the program is actually associated with an increased chance that adolescents would commit crimes (Petrosino et al., 2003).

Scared Straight and other methods for helping people can, in fact, do more harm than good (Lilienfeld, 2007). Although a rare case, this example reminds us that therapy can be done in many different ways, and we should be cautious in determining which ones are best.

Focus Questions

1 Which options for therapy are available?

2 Are all well-established options equally effective at treating problems?

· · · · · · · · · · · · · · · · · ·

In Module 14.1, we introduced *psychotherapy* as the processes for resolving personal, emotional, behavioral, and social problems so as to improve well-being. Psychotherapy is a broad term, as mental health providers practicing psychotherapy can choose from many different approaches when conducting therapy. In this module, we will study several of these approaches. You will find that the methods are diverse, but what unifies them under the category of psychotherapy—rather than biological or medical therapy—is the fact that they all address problems through communication between client and therapist.

Most forms of psychotherapy work best with a specific type of problem or psychological disorder. Physicians once prescribed antibiotics for all sorts of problems, using trial and error. It eventually became clear that antibiotics had no effect on viruses like the flu or the common cold, but work very well for bacterial infections such as strep throat. Similarly, we will find that therapists can match their techniques with specific types of problems to produce the best results.

Insight Therapies

Psychologists have long believed that self-knowledge and understanding can lead to positive changes in behavior. This is certainly the case for **insight therapies**, *which is a general term referring to psychotherapy that involves dialogue between client and therapist for the purposes of gaining awareness and understanding of psychological problems and conflicts.* We begin our look at insight therapies with **psychodynamic therapies**, *forms of insight therapy that emphasize the need to discover and resolve unconscious conflicts.*

PSYCHOANALYSIS: EXPLORING THE UNCONSCIOUS **Psychoanalysis** *is an insight therapy developed by Sigmund Freud that became the precursor to modern psychodynamic therapies.* If you read Module 12.3, then you are familiar with some of the core concepts of Freud's approach, such as *unconscious motivation.* Freud hypothesized that certain fundamental urges, such as sexuality, appetites, and aggression, are constantly influencing how we think and behave, even when we are not aware of them. He proposed that many unconscious motivations are so unacceptable that people develop ways of keeping them out of conscious awareness. Moreover, because people are already repressing sexual and aggressive impulses, any unpleasant and distasteful experiences can be suppressed as well, such as frightening, intimidating, or humiliating moments (Freud, 1896/1954). Needless to say, Freud believed that each individual's unconscious mind could be an ominous place.

As an insight therapy, the primary goal of psychoanalysis is to help the client understand past experiences, relationships, and personal conflicts, and then apply that understanding to improve mental and emotional functioning. Freud and his followers based their practice on some core ideas summarized in Table 14.2.

These core ideas may sound straightforward, except for one crucial point: Accessing the unconscious mind is tricky business. The patient cannot tell you much about it because, by definition, *unconscious* means that the patient is not aware of it. Freud and his associates came up with several methods and concepts they believed would help them access the unconscious realm so as to cure unhealthy minds. For example, the therapeutic method of **free association** *instructs the patient to reveal any thoughts that arise, no matter how odd or meaningless they may seem.* The purpose of this exercise is to allow the patient a chance to avoid self-censorship and perhaps reveal something important. This has likely happened to you in conversation—when you suddenly find yourself talking about a totally different topic than the one that started it, yet you have no idea how you changed subjects. Free association allows the same sort of phenomenon to occur, but with just the patient speaking. On the surface, the transitions from topic to topic may not seem important, but if the therapist *analyzes* the content and the connections of free association, it is thought that important ideas will be revealed.

> … [D]reams are not a somatic (bodily), but a mental, phenomenon. (Freud, 1920, p. 90)

If Freud is correct, dreams can be a useful source of information about unconscious conflicts. However, the unconscious mind cannot simply describe past conflicts because it lacks a language to do so. Instead, Freud proposed, emotions take on symbolic qualities, which is why dreams so often feature bizarre imagery and very loose storylines. To make sense of this jumble, a trained psychoanalyst might conduct **dream analysis**, *a method of understanding unconscious thought by interpreting the manifest content (what happens in the dream) to get a sense of the latent content (the unconscious elements that motivated the dream).*

Table 14.2 :: Core Ideas Forming the Basis of Psychoanalysis

Adults' psychological conflicts have their origins in early experiences.
These conflicts affect the thoughts and emotions of the individual, and their source often remains outside of conscious awareness.
The unconscious conflicts and their effects are called *neuroses* (anxieties).
By accessing the unconscious mind, the analyst and patient can gain a better understanding of the early conflicts that lead to neuroses.
Once the conflicts are brought to the surface, the analyst and the patient can work through them together.

We can illustrate what Freud hoped to discover with one particular dream analysis he wrote about: A patient dreamed he was riding his bicycle down a street when suddenly a dachshund ran him down and bit his ankle as he attempted to pedal away. Meanwhile, two elderly ladies sat by and laughed at the incident. This is the manifest content, but what might the dream *mean*—what is the latent content? Freud pointed out that in his waking life the patient had repeatedly seen a woman walking a dog and, although he was very attracted to her, he felt great anxiety about approaching her. The man had consciously devised a plan to use the dog as an excuse to strike up a conversation with the woman. Unfortunately, the anxiety caused by fear of rejection manifested itself in an unpleasant dream about being attacked by a dog, accompanied by the humiliation of being laughed at (Freud, 1920, pp. 165–166).

The process of discovering unconscious conflict through psychoanalysis can create considerable discomfort. If you have managed to keep painful memories unconscious, why would you want to bring them back up again? According to Freud, psychoanalysis patients engage in what he called **resistance**—*a tendency to avoid directly answering crucial questions posed by the therapist*. Patients may get angry at the analyst, or even become cynical about the whole process. Others may edit their own thoughts before speaking, or may try to joke around to change the subject. This leads to an interesting dynamic between patient and psychoanalyst called **transference**—*a psychoanalytic process that involves patients directing the emotional experiences that they are reliving toward the therapist*. If the unconscious conflict angers the patient, she may direct it toward the analyst. If the patient is addressing a hidden sexual conflict, then his transference may involve sexual feelings for the analyst. The analyst uses transference to move the therapy forward by pointing out parallels between the client's behavior directed toward the analyst and that directed toward significant others.

Transference is a significant milestone in the process of psychotherapy. Once it is reached, therapist and patient can begin to process specific problems and discuss ways of coping with them. The therapist and patient *work through* the issues that have arisen from the long sessions of free association, dream analysis, resistance, and transference.

MODERN PSYCHODYNAMIC THERAPIES Today, Freudian-based psychoanalysis is practiced by a relatively small number of therapists. Nevertheless, Freud's ideas have remained influential and several newer therapies have evolved from traditional psychoanalysis. One example is **object relations therapy**, *a variation of psychodynamic therapy that focuses on how early childhood experiences and emotional attachments influence later psychological functioning*. In contrast to psychoanalysis, object relations therapy does not center on repressed sexual and aggressive conflicts. Instead, the focus is on *objects,* which may be real or imagined people in a child's life, as well as the child's understanding of herself. The early relations between the child and these objects results in the development of a mental model for the child; as a consequence, she will form and maintain relationships as an adult based on her representations of childhood relationships. The object relations therapist's job is to help the client understand the underlying patterns in relationships, which often involve issues of trust, fear of abandonment, or dependence on others. Once therapy produces insight, then the client and the therapist can work through any problems they may have identified.

Both object relations therapy and psychoanalysis share the goal of helping individuals gain insight into how and why their current functioning was affected by early events. In addition to these approaches, other variations on the process of therapy have been developed.

HUMANISTIC THERAPY One particularly significant alternative to psychoanalysis comes from humanistic psychology. In the 1950s, humanistic psychologists broke from psychoanalytic approaches, creating a new discipline based on at least five fundamental differences (listed in Table 14.3 on p. 528). Perhaps the biggest difference is the shifted focus from long-lasting, unconscious conflicts to the individual's strengths and potential for growth. This shift was thought to empower individuals with the ability to overcome their problems. Also, rather than interpreting the hidden meanings of dreams and free associations, the humanistic therapist's role is to listen and understand.

American psychologist Carl Rogers (1902–1987) developed a version of humanistic therapy called **person/client-centered therapy**, *which focuses on individuals' abilities to solve their own problems and reach their full potential with the encouragement of the therapist*. As a humanist, Rogers believed that all individuals could develop and reach their full potential. However, people experience psychological problems when others impose *conditions of worth,* meaning that they appear to judge or lose affection for a person who does not live up to expectations.

Table 14.3 :: Contrasting Psychoanalytic and Humanistic Views of Major Psychological Issues and Debates

ISSUE	PSYCHOANALYSIS	HUMANISTIC THERAPY
Conscious versus unconscious	Focuses on unconscious drives	Focuses on conscious experience
Determinism versus free will	Behavior is determined by repressed sexual and aggressive instincts	Behavior is chosen freely
Weaknesses versus strengths	Everyone has neuroses	Everyone has strengths
Responsibility for change	The analyst interprets and explains to the patient what is wrong	The therapist asks the client what is wrong and attempts to help clarify issues
Mechanism of change	Insight into unconscious conflicts allows problems to be worked through	Unconditional positive regard allows a person to develop and heal

Such an individual might be a father who is never satisfied with his child's report card or a wife who gets angry at her spouse over failing to keep his promises. If loved ones give the impression that they no longer respect the person or that they love the person less because of the individual's actions, then they have imposed conditions of worth.

Conditions of worth can produce long-term consequences to psychological health because the individual is then likely to change his behavior in an attempt to regain affection. If this happens frequently, then the individual is no longer living his own life, but rather merely living out the expectations of others. That, to Carl Rogers, is a key aspect of any psychological dysfunction.

The critical aspect of client–centered therapy lies within the dialogue that unfolds between therapist and client. The therapist must show *unconditional positive regard* through genuine, empathetic, and nonjudgmental attention. If the therapist can remove all conditions of worth, clients may begin to express themselves without fear and begin to develop inner strength. Finally, with self-confidence and strength, clients can accept disagreement with others and focus on living their lives to the fullest.

EVALUATING INSIGHT THERAPIES As discussed in Module 14.1, therapies should be used only if there is empirical support that they actually work. Psychodynamic therapies meet some of the rigorous criteria for empirically supported therapies, though surprisingly few studies in this area have been conducted with proper research design and control conditions. Ultimately, the effectiveness of insight therapies depends on the condition being treated. Studies that have used the most rigorous research designs have shown that

psychodynamic therapy has not been effective in treating severe depression or schizophrenia, but it has shown promise for treating panic disorder, dependence on opiate drugs (e.g., heroin), and borderline personality disorder (Gibbons et al., 2008). Psychodynamic therapy may help with major depression if combined with drug treatment—an approach we will describe in greater detail in Module 14.3.

At the beginning of this module we noted that some therapies have been developed to treat specific disorders. An example is *interpersonal therapy,* a style of psychodynamic therapy that was developed by psychologists Henry Stack Sullivan and Gerald Klerman to treat depression (Weissman, 2006). Sullivan and Klerman believed that emotional reactions and depression are rooted in interpersonal relationships. For example, the root of depression may stem from having poorly developed friendships or conflict with a spouse or other loved one. Thus interpersonal therapy focuses on social relationships. This perspective stands in contrast to traditional psychoanalytic approaches that center on conflicts within the individual. Although developed to treat depression, interpersonal therapy has also been successfully applied to clients seeking help with diverse conditions such as anxiety, bulimia nervosa, and borderline personality disorder.

Insight therapies can help people gain understanding and awareness of the nature of their psychological problems. As we will soon read, many people with conditions ranging from mild to severe succeed in handling problems without digging toward the root causes. Also, insight therapy may be unsuitable for individuals who are not prone to self-reflection, including children, people with severe disorders such as schizophrenia, and even those who simply are less inclined to be self-reflective.

KNOW …

1. _____ refers to a phenomenon of psychoanalysis in which the client begins directing emotional responses toward the therapist.

   A Resistance
   B Befriending
   C Objectifying
   D Transference

2. In psychoanalysis, resistance occurs when:

   A a patient develops sexual attraction for the analyst.

   B a patient begins to divert the analysis by joking, becoming cynical, or perhaps just refusing to answer questions.

   C a therapist begins to have the same feelings as the patient.

   D the therapist refuses to continue a therapy session.

UNDERSTAND …

3. In psychoanalysis, treatment for psychological problems seems to come from:

   A the patient working through a problem once it has been uncovered through dream analysis or free association.

   B the patient receiving unconditional positive regard.

   C the therapist understanding and explaining the manifest content of a dream.

   D the therapist diagnosing the psychological disorder and providing appropriate drug therapy.

APPLY …

4. A kindergarten teacher (unintentionally) places conditions of worth on her students. What does this mean?

   A She always lets her students know how much she values them.

   B She regularly tries to draw compliments out of her students.

   C She acts as if a student no longer matters to her or the school if he misbehaves.

   D She provides monetary rewards for good behavior.

ANALYZE …

5. What has research concluded in regard to the effectiveness of insight therapies?

   A Insight therapies are always very effective.

   B Insight therapies are never effective.

   C Insight therapies do not help people gain awareness of the nature of their psychological problems, so they tend to not be effective.

   D The effectiveness of insight therapies depends on the conditions that are being treated.

Answers can be found on page ANS-4.

Behavioral, Cognitive, and Group Therapies

Behavioral therapies *address problem behaviors and thoughts, and the environmental factors that trigger them, as directly as possible.* At the heart of behavioral therapies is the belief that patterns of behavior are the result of conditioning and learning, including maladaptive behaviors that lead people to require therapy. Thus these behaviors can also be reduced or modified by applying the principles of learning that account for how they were originally acquired.

EXPOSURE AND SYSTEMATIC DESENSITIZATION

We can examine how behavioral therapy works by considering one of the most common types of social anxiety, public speaking. Most individuals experience at least some anxiety about public speaking, but in some people this anxiety increases to the point that just thinking about making a speech can induce intense worry and arousal, and even panic attacks. External cues, such as the professor who assigns a speech, fellow students, the ticking clock, and the dreaded podium at the front of the class, may all elicit anxiety in such cases. In addition, internal stimuli such a racing heart, sweaty palms, and shakiness can make anxiety spin out of control—perhaps to the point of triggering a full-blown panic attack.

We can use classical conditioning, described in Module 6.1, to help us understand how anxiety is acquired as well as how it can be reduced. The anxiety-provoking internal and external stimuli become *conditioned stimuli* (see Figure 14.4 on p. 530). The more intense these stimuli, the more likely it is that a panic attack will occur. Using behavioral therapy, the psychologist might help the individual focus on the conditioned stimuli that precede the panic attacks, and work to control responses to them prior to an upcoming public speaking engagement. Often, a client in treatment with a behavioral therapist undergoes **exposure treatments**—*a process in which exposure to the feared situation is completed gradually and under controlled conditions.* Examples include mental imagery, actual pictures or models of the feared stimulus, and confronting the actual feared situation. When conducted appropriately, exposure therapy mimics the process of extinction in classical conditioning, in which the feared event (the CS) is no longer paired with the aversive event (the US). Such extinction treatments can result in a loss of the troublesome fear response (Norrholm et al., 2008).

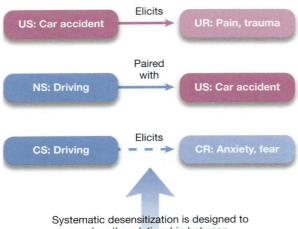

Systematic desensitization is designed to weaken the relationship between conditioned stimuli that elicit maladaptive responses such as extensive fear or anxiety.

{FIG. 14.4} **Classical Conditioning and Systematic Desensitization** Classical conditioning can contribute to fears that we acquire, such as driving after having a car accident. Systematic desensitization is designed to reduce or eliminate these conditioned responses.

Exposure treatments can create stress for the client, even if the therapist begins with a very low-level cue. For this reason, therapists using exposure therapy will typically incorporate relaxation techniques into their treatment. **Systematic desensitization** *is a technique in which gradual exposure to a feared stimulus or situation is blended with relaxation training* (Wolpe, 1990). The gradual exposure allows for an individual to practice relaxing under conditions that elicit mild anxiety, and then slowly progress to greater levels of anxiety-provoking stimuli. If the individual can eventually relax during moderately high levels of exposure to the feared stimulus or situation, then the anxiety response can be extinguished. Behavioral therapists and their clients follow three main steps in conducting systematic desensitization, which are outlined in Table 14.4.

In some cases, the client may elect to undergo a process called *flooding*. In this procedure, the client goes straight to the most challenging part of the hierarchy, exposing himself to the scenario that causes the most anxiety and panic. Thus he may elect to give a long speech in front of 100 strangers. The idea here is that, rather than avoiding the anxiety-provoking situation, the client dives right in and (one hopes) discovers that there are no truly negative consequences to giving a well-prepared speech.

Fear and anxiety responses can be acquired through observing others (Olsson & Phelps, 2007). Fortunately, these responses can also be reversed by observation. Thus another technique used in exposure therapy is observational learning or "modeling" (Bandura, 1977). With this method, the client observes another person engage with the feared object or situation. For example, an ophidiophobe (a person with a phobia of snakes) might observe another person as he handles a snake. In some cases, such as with a fear of heights or flying, virtual reality technology has been used to provide exposure treatments.

Table 14.4 :: Applying Steps of Systematic Desensitization to Fear of Public Speaking

1. *Build an anxiety hierarchy.* This involves the therapist assisting the client in creating a list of stimuli that arouse fear responses, starting with the stimulus or situation that evokes the least amount of anxiety and ending with the stimulus that elicits the most anxiety.

   Think about and visualize:
   1. Doing library research for a presentation
   2. Preparing slides and note cards
   3. Practicing the presentation alone
   4. Practicing the presentation with a small group of friends
   5. Leaving for campus on the day of the presentation
   6. Class starting
   7. Being called up to give the presentation
   8. Setting up and looking out at the audience
   9. Beginning to speak
   10. Delivering the presentation

2. *Relaxation training.* During this phase. the client learns to respond to relaxation suggestions from the therapist as they work through the hierarchy. This is typically done using mental imagery while the client is visiting the therapist's office.

3. *Work through the hierarchy.* Steps 1 and 2 are combined here as the therapist works through the hierarchy with the client while engaging in relaxation techniques.

WORKING THE SCIENTIFIC LITERACY MODEL

Virtual Reality Therapies

Exposure and systematic desensitization techniques have long been a part of behavioral treatments for fear and anxiety. Nevertheless, some difficulties may arise with these conditions. First, people with fear and anxiety about a specific object or situation usually avoid any contact with it—so even taking the first step toward a therapist's office can be challenging. This issue explains why most people who may have post-traumatic stress disorder (PTSD) never seek treatment (Kessler, 2000). Also, although it is sometimes used in office settings, mental imagery is typically the method employed with these therapeutic techniques, but it may not transfer well to the actual anxiety-provoking situation. Technological advances are helping address these problems.

What do we know about virtual reality exposure?

Recently, some behavioral therapists have started incorporating virtual reality into their treatment options. **Virtual reality exposure (VRE)** is a treatment that uses graphical displays to create an experience in which the client seems to be immersed in an actual environment. The reality it creates helps address two problems associated with traditional systematic desensitization methods described previously. First, people who use mental imagery alone can easily become avoidant and fail to comply with the therapist's suggestions. Second, and most importantly, VRE exposure can provide a real-time approximation of the feared situation. Over the past decade, this technology has becoming increasingly common in helping soldiers returning from the wars in Iraq and Afghanistan—many of whom have developed PTSD.

How can scientists study virtual reality exposure?

Psychologists at Emory University in Atlanta have been using a simulator called Virtual Iraq, which was developed to deliver two possible scenarios—being in a Middle Eastern city or driving a Humvee through a desert road in simulated war conditions (Figure 14.5). The weather, time of day, background noise, civilians, aerial craft, and ground vehicles can be programmed by the therapist to change as desired during the exposure

sessions. There is also the option to provide simulated gunfire and bomb explosions. Smell cues are available using an air compressor that pumps in odors of burning rubber, garbage, diesel fuel, and gunpowder (Cukor et al., 2009). Using this technology, psychologists have conducted multiple VRE sessions with combat veterans.

In one set of trials, 20 active-duty soldiers who were diagnosed with PTSD following combat activity underwent VRE therapy. Their PTSD symptoms were measured before and after therapists guided them through VRE treatment in the Virtual Iraq simulator. At the conclusion of their therapy, the soldiers' PTSD symptoms declined by 50%, with 16 of the soldiers no longer meeting the criteria for the disorder (Rizzo et al., 2010). The results included fewer disturbing thoughts about stressful events that occurred during military service; fewer disturbing dreams; reduced physical reactions such as heart pounding, sweating, and trouble breathing; and less avoidance of activities that trigger memories of military service. VRE using the Virtual Iraq simulator appeared to work.

Can we critically evaluate this evidence?

From an experimental standpoint, this study should have used a placebo (control) group that received no treatment, or a comparison group that received some other

{FIG. 14.5} **Virtual Reality Exposure** Combat veterans diagnosed with PTSD have participated in virtual reality therapies involving simulated exposure to traumatic events. Therapists work with clients to help them process and cope with their fears.

treatment method, such as insight therapy. Without a control group, we are left to wonder how other variables might have influenced the improvement in PTSD symptoms, such as the mere passage of time or the simple fact that people were expressing interest and concern for the veterans.

Why is this relevant?

Treating PTSD with highly specialized systems such as the one just described for veterans is *far* from the only application of VRE. Psychologists are now applying this technology to a broad range of situations, including common fears such as flying in an airplane and heights. A major advantage is that VRE also allows clients and therapists to have close control over the systematic exposure to the feared situation, and it allows the therapist to tailor the situation to the client's needs (Hodges et al., 2001).

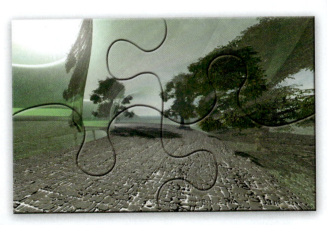

The drug Antabuse is used in aversive conditioning for alcohol consumption. When it is taken and the person subsequently consumes alcohol, Antabuse causes nausea and vomiting. If successful, Antabuse treatment leads to a conditioned aversion to alcohol.

(Garbutt, 2009). As you can imagine, the client would need to have a fairly strong motivation to quit, and must be willing to take the drug knowing that it would make her ill. If she cheats and skips the drug one day, then the treatment will not have much chance of working. Thus, even though aversive conditioning can help people quit, it still requires willpower to complete the treatments.

AVERSIVE CONDITIONING Behavioral therapies can also be used to remove unwanted behaviors. Most people have at least one behavior they would like to reduce or eliminate, whether it be a nervous reaction such as fingernail biting, or a serious health concern such as smoking. Behavioral principles tell us that these habits are maintained because they bring rewards. As long as they are enjoyable or reduce stress, these habits will be difficult to break. For the more engrained habits and addictions, people may require therapy to help them reduce problem behaviors.

Aversive conditioning *is a behavioral technique that involves replacing a positive response to a stimulus with a negative response, typically by using punishment.* One aversive conditioning treatment involves using the drug Antabuse (disulfiram) to reduce problem alcohol consumption. Antabuse causes nausea and vomiting when combined with alcohol, so the drug classically conditions an aversion to alcohol. Antabuse works for some individuals, but there are several reasons why it is not entirely effective

COGNITIVE-BEHAVIORAL THERAPIES Behavioral therapies are very effective ways of changing or eliminating maladaptive behaviors, but they do not *directly* address problematic thoughts. Two psychodynamic-trained psychologists, Albert Ellis (1962) and Aaron Beck (1963), found that individuals with depression have the tendency to interpret and think about their lives in a negative light. As Ellis, Beck, and other psychotherapy researchers learned more about the thought patterns of people with depression, it became apparent that therapies should be directed at reducing and changing negative cognition into more realistic and rational thought patterns. Over time, they formalized procedures for carrying out this new approach known as cognitive-behavioral therapy.

Cognitive-behavioral therapy *is a form of therapy that consists of procedures such as exposure, cognitive restructuring, and stress inoculation training* (NIMH, 2009). Exposure—the behavioral technique described earlier in this module—is an important component to the process. This is particularly true in situations where specific events or contexts create problems, such as the death of a loved one or surviving a traumatic experience. Exposure allows the client and the therapist to understand the feelings associated with the event, whereas avoidance leaves the stressor in place, perhaps allowing the problem to worsen.

Next, *cognitive restructuring* occurs as the client's beliefs and interpretations about events are shifted or restructured so that they can be viewed from a more rational, and less emotional, perspective. For example, someone who develops depression after losing her job might come to believe the layoff was deserved. She can work with the therapist to clarify whether this is a rational explanation for the situation. As a result of these discussions, the therapist and client may put a restructuring plan in place. When thoughts of unnecessary self-blame occur, the client should stop and say to herself, "It was actually poor management; I could not have stopped it." Alternatively, if she is partially responsible, she must learn to think about how she can make amends, prevent future mistakes, and not beat herself up over past failures. In either case, the restructuring involves moving from thoughts like *I am a bad person; I deserve this; nobody can help me*, to a more productive and rational set of thoughts.

Finally, people who experience stress and anxiety may benefit from relaxation techniques, as they allow the client to regain emotional control and perspective on the negative experiences. This phase of treatment, sometimes called *stress inoculation training*, helps the client put traumatic memories into perspective in a way that promotes the individual's well-being.

One thing you may not have noticed about cognitive-behavioral therapy: These techniques all require the client—not just the therapist—to do serious work. The therapist can help by teaching a client ways to identify problematic thoughts and some techniques for restructuring the problem. Ultimately, however, the client must manage all the work once he leaves the psychologist's office. Thus cognitive-behavioral therapy may actually involve homework, reading, and studying.

GROUP AND FAMILY THERAPIES Therapy can take on many different dynamics. In some situations, clients may benefit greatly by participating in *group therapy* sessions. One advantage with this approach is that group therapy tends to be less costly than individual sessions. Also, groups may be organized in many different ways to suit different purposes. Members may share a particular problem, such as interpersonal conflicts, substance use, or adjustment problems. Therapists may organize groups of a particular age cohort, such

as adolescents or middle-aged adults. Therapists are typically trained to implement group techniques adapted from the major types of therapy discussed earlier in this module, such as cognitive-behavioral therapy.

Groups are typically formed among individuals who are strangers to one another at the outset. At other times, individuals may best be helped by undergoing therapy with family members.

Psychologists who conduct *family therapy* help people cope with numerous types of problems. They may need to focus specifically on dynamics involving each individual family member. Alternatively, people may seek family therapy because they need help dealing with one particular individual, such as an abusive parent or a troubled adolescent. Clearly, family therapy is very different from individual psychotherapy. The problems that an individual brings into psychotherapy sessions are typically not isolated in a social sense. Problems with anger, depression, or anxiety often stem from a broader social context—in particular, that of the family. Family therapists take a **systems approach**, *an orientation toward family therapy that involves identifying and understanding what each individual family member contributes to the entire family dynamic.*

As an example, think of a family whose members include a son being treated for schizophrenia. The son may have spent many months in individual psychotherapy sessions. How family members react to him when he experiences acute episodes of schizophrenia alters his behavior, for better or for worse. Also, how he is treated after he has received treatment and the schizophrenia is in remission can have a significant impact on his well-being. Remission rates among people with schizophrenia who are given emotional support at home are quite high (Hooley, 2007). In this situation, then, the family therapist's job is to help the entire family make adjustments to the disorder, whether the symptoms are present or are in remission.

EVALUATING COGNITIVE, BEHAVIORAL, AND GROUP THERAPIES Behavioral therapies have been shown to be particularly effective at treating symptoms associated with anxiety disorders, such as obsessive–compulsive disorder and specific phobias (Chambless & Ollendick, 2001). They have also proved useful for increasing or decreasing targeted problematic behaviors.

Cognitive-behavioral therapy has been particularly effective in treating depression, which is not too surprising given that this method of therapy was specifically developed to treat this type of mental disorder

PsychTutor
Click here in your eText for an interactive tutorial on **Evaluation of Therapies**

(Hollon et al., 2002). In addition, cognitive-behavioral therapies have been successful in treating such conditions as anxiety, obesity, and eating disorders. It seems that at present cognitive and behavioral therapies are quite versatile in their applications and amenable to treating a wide variety of disorders. A specific strength is that this type of therapy focuses on definable and concrete relationships between events and the emotions and reactions experienced by clients. This connection gives psychologists and therapists a solid basis from which to work in the therapeutic process. Given this perspective, it may turn out that cognitive and behavioral therapies are generally effective tools that can be used to treat most psychological problems. The time course of cognitive therapy is also typically much shorter than psychoanalysis, which is helpful to people who have limited insurance coverage for mental health issues.

Nevertheless, cognitive and behavioral therapies alone may not alter the numerous problem behaviors associated with a major disorder. For example, behavioral therapy may be used to help individuals with schizophrenia cope with auditory hallucinations, but it does not eliminate them (Thomas et al., 2010).

CLIENT AND THERAPIST FACTORS Generally speaking, psychotherapy works. What may be equally, if not more, important than the specific style of therapy used, however, are those factors that are inherent to therapists and clients themselves. For example, the bond that exists between therapist and client is an important part of successful therapy. The trust, disclosure, and collaboration between therapist and client seem to be critical in achieving positive outcomes in therapy. Why is this? Do people get better because a positive bond forms between therapist and client? Or does the bond form because symptoms are reduced during the therapy sessions? Although a good client–therapist relationship may initiate solid progress in therapy, bonds between clients and therapists often form *after* psychological symptoms have been reduced (Tang & DeRubeis, 1999).

Also, when the client and the therapist agree on goals and a personal bond forms in the treatment process, the outcome is more likely to be positive (Orlinsky et al., 2004). Not surprisingly, outcomes of therapy tend to be better when therapists show warmth and concern. Clients who are well adjusted and are willing to recognize and work on their problems are more likely to benefit from therapy (Prochaska & Norcross, 2002).

Quick Quiz 14.2b
Behavioral, Cognitive, and Group Therapies

KNOW...

1 _____ involves a process in which the client faces feared situations gradually and under controlled conditions.

- **A** Client-centered therapy
- **C** Insight therapy
- **B** Family therapy
- **D** Exposure therapy

2 _____ consists of key procedures including exposure, cognitive restructuring, and stress inoculation training.

- **A** Cognitive-behavioral therapy
- **B** Family therapy
- **C** Virtual reality exposure therapy
- **D** Exposure therapy

UNDERSTAND...

3 Aversive conditioning works to reduce or eliminate unwanted behaviors by:

- **A** replacing a negative response to a stimulus with a positive response, typically by using reinforcement.
- **B** replacing a positive response to a stimulus with a negative response, typically by using reinforcement.
- **C** replacing a positive response to a stimulus with a negative response, typically by using punishment.
- **D** replacing a negative response to a stimulus with a positive response, typically by using punishment.

APPLY...

4 Neil is facing difficulties with anger and depression, and his parents are having trouble managing his behaviors and responding appropriately. To address all of these concerns, the most beneficial treatment in this situation would be _____.

- **A** cognitive-behavioral therapy
- **B** family therapy
- **C** virtual reality exposure therapy
- **D** exposure therapy

ANALYZE...

5 A major strength of cognitive-behavioral therapy is that:

- **A** it has been particularly effective in treating depression, anxiety, and eating disorders.
- **B** it prevents resistance from occurring.
- **C** it is not affected by the quality of the client–therapist relationship.
- **D** it develops transference between client and therapist.

6 Cognitive-behavioral therapies seem to be effective because they:

- **A** help individuals restructure their maladaptive thoughts and beliefs.
- **B** teach individuals to brood over problems effectively.
- **C** systematically desensitize phobias.
- **D** None of the above.

Answers can be found on page ANS-5.

Module Summary

Now that you have read this module you should:

KNOW ...

- **The key terminology related to psychological therapies:**

aversive conditioning (p. 532)
behavioral therapy (p. 529)
cognitive-behavioral therapy (p. 532)
dream analysis (p. 526)
exposure treatments (p. 529)
free association (p. 526)
insight therapy (p. 526)
object relations therapy (p. 527)
person/client-centered therapy (p. 527)

psychoanalysis (p. 526)
psychodynamic therapy (p. 526)
resistance (p. 527)
systematic desensitization (p. 530)
systems approach (p. 533)
transference (p. 527)
virtual reality exposure (VRE) (p. 531)

UNDERSTAND ...

- **The general approaches to conducting major types of psychotherapy.** Each therapy seems to be different. Psychoanalysis, for example, works by uncovering hidden conflicts, whereas humanistic therapy is said to work by removing conditions of worth that can hinder a person's growth. Behavioral and cognitive therapies focus on how the physical and social environments affect behaviors and thought patterns, and seek to alter one or both to make positive changes. Therapies also take place with groups and families.

APPLY ...

- **Your knowledge to identify major therapeutic techniques.** Imagine you are helping someone with a phobia find a therapist for treatment, and you speak with three professionals about the approach they would take. Match their response with the corresponding school of thought. Note: Not all the schools of therapy will be used. Check your answers on page ANS-5.

1. I would ask the individual to describe his train of thought when he encounters the feared object. Then I would ask him to explain why it is irrational to think that way, and we would try to replace his irrational thoughts with more reasonable, less anxiety-provoking beliefs.

2. I would ask the patient to think about his earliest childhood experiences with the object, and then to speak freely about those memories at length. We would try to discover the significance of that object in his early development.

3. We would take an active approach. One important step is to teach the client how to be calm and relaxed while gradually introducing the feared stimulus.

   A. Humanistic therapy

   B. Cognitive-behavioral therapy

   C. Psychodynamic therapy

   D. Family therapy

   E. Behavioral therapy

ANALYZE ...

- **The pros and cons of the major types of psychotherapy.** See **Table 14.5** below.

Table 14.5 :: Pros and Cons of the Major Types of Therapy

	PROS	CONS
Insight therapies	• Can provide deep understanding of the self	• Long term and often very expensive • Can have limited application to people with serious disorders
Behavioral and cognitive therapies	• Typically time- and cost-efficient • Addresses immediate thoughts and behavioral problems • Addresses both mild and severe problems	• Does not necessarily offer deeper understanding of psychological problems
Group/family therapies	• Allows individuals to empathize and relate to others with similar problems • Gives family members insight into how each individual contributes to both positive and negative aspects of family life	• Does not fully address individual issues (although group and family therapies are often used in combination with individualized therapy)

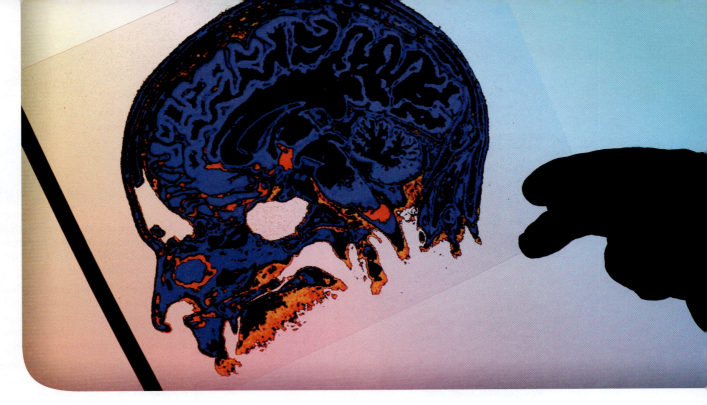

Biomedical Therapies

KNOW ...	UNDERSTAND ...	APPLY ...	ANALYZE ...
The key terminology associated with biological treatments	How the drugs described in this module affect brain functioning How various medical therapies that do not involve drugs work	Your knowledge of drug therapies to different psychological conditions	Whether St. John's wort, a popular herbal remedy for depression, works

The term "psychosurgery" is likely to make people cringe. It probably brings to mind thoughts of old, barbaric methods of permanently "numbing" the minds of mistreated psychiatric patients. For the first time in decades, however, a new surgical technique for treating obsessive–compulsive disorder has been approved. Patients who do not improve with extensive psychotherapy and drugs may elect to undergo *cingulotomy*, a surgery that involves destroying four small, raisin-sized sets of nerve cells deep inside the brain.

Gerry Radano is one patient who has undergone this treatment (Carey, 2009; Radano, 2007). Radano became a recluse in her losing battle with obsessive–compulsive disorder. Like many people with this condition, her fear of contamination was so great that she no longer ventured outdoors. After losing her job, isolating herself from family and friends, and being labeled as "incurable," Radano elected to undergo brain surgery. Her condition improved greatly.

A few hundred individuals have undergone the same procedure, though not all have benefited from it. Such brain surgery may seem extreme but, based on current assessments, it appears to carry no more physical risks than do standard drug treatments. In this module, we explore several biological treatment options for psychological disorders, some of them quite surprising.

Focus Questions

1. Are there medical techniques available that do not involve destroying specific sets of brain cells?

2. Are drugs and other technological procedures "miracle cures" for psychological problems?

• • • • • • • • • • • • • • • • • •

Many of the mental health problems we have covered in this text are caused in part by malfunctioning processes of the nervous system. Thus it is fitting that many treatments would target brain chemistry and the activity of nerve cells in an attempt to correct the problems. **Psychopharmacotherapy** *refers to the process of treating psychological* *disorders with drugs.* Drugs are by far the most frequently used biomedical option, but they are often employed in conjunction with psychotherapy. Surgery or electrically stimulating the brain are options, although they are typically used only in situations where no other available treatments have succeeded. In this module, we explore and evaluate each of these biomedical treatment options, and examine how they may be used in conjunction with psychotherapies.

Drug Treatments

Psychotropic drugs *are medications designed to alter psychological functioning.* The original drug treatments for psychological problems were initiated in institutional and clinical settings, primarily targeting very severe cases. Since then, drug treatments have become mainstream practice for people experiencing even relatively mild psychological problems and symptoms. This expansion has made certain psychotropic drugs, such as those used to treat depression, among the most prescribed forms of medicine in the United States (Olfson & Marcus, 2009).

Psychotropic drugs have been developed to take many different courses of action. First, all psychotropic drugs are designed to cross the **blood–brain barrier**, *a network of tightly packed cells that only allow specific types of substances to move from the bloodstream to the brain* (see Figure 14.6). This barrier is a very important adaptation we have for protecting delicate brain cells against harmful infections and other substances. Psychotropic drugs are designed to cross this barrier, and then affect one or more specific neurotransmitters. Because drugs are designed with various end results in mind, including changing mood, thinking, and behavior, we will examine these drugs by grouping them according to the specific problems they treat.

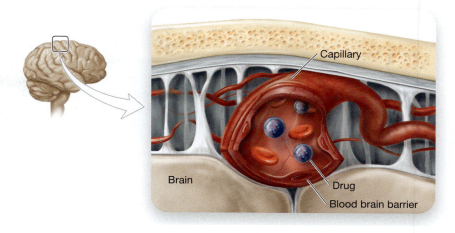

{FIG. 14.6} **How Psychotropic Drugs Reach the Brain** To reach the brain and have their designed effect, psychotropic drugs must cross the blood–brain barrier, a network of densely packed cells that restrict the flow of substances between the capillaries and brain cells.

ANTIDEPRESSANTS AND MOOD STABILIZERS

As the name suggests, **antidepressant drugs** (or antidepressants) *are medications prescribed to elevate mood and reduce other symptoms of depression.* In general, antidepressant drugs target areas of the brain that, when functioning normally, are rich in monoamine neurotransmitters—serotonin, norepinephrine, and dopamine. With multiple neurotransmitters involved, antidepressants come in several varieties, each with its own way of altering brain chemistry (Figure 14.7).

Monoamine oxidase inhibitors (MAOIs) *are a type of antidepressant that deactivates monoamine oxidase, an enzyme that breaks down serotonin, dopamine, and norepinephrine at the synaptic clefts of nerve cells* (see Figure 14.7). When the MAO enzyme is inhibited, fewer dopamine, serotonin and norepinephrine neurotransmitters are metabolized, which in turn leaves more of them available at

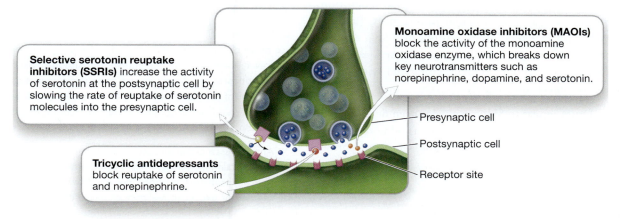

Selective serotonin reuptake inhibitors (SSRIs) increase the activity of serotonin at the postsynaptic cell by slowing the rate of reuptake of serotonin molecules into the presynaptic cell.

Monoamine oxidase inhibitors (MAOIs) block the activity of the monoamine oxidase enzyme, which breaks down key neurotransmitters such as norepinephrine, dopamine, and serotonin.

Tricyclic antidepressants block reuptake of serotonin and norepinephrine.

Presynaptic cell

Postsynaptic cell

Receptor site

{FIG. 14.7} **Antidepressant Effects at the Synapse** The major antidepressant drugs have different ways of increasing the transmission of neurotransmitters such as serotonin, dopamine, and norepinephrine at the synapses.

the synapses. MAOIs are used less frequently than other antidepressants, in part because they can have dangerous interactions with fermented foods (e.g., aged cheeses, smoked meats, alcoholic beverages) and other medications. If you look at the label of just about any over-the-counter medication, you will probably find listed warnings against using MAOIs when taking the nonprescription drug.

Tricyclic antidepressants *were among the earliest types of antidepressants on the market and appear to work by blocking the reuptake of serotonin and norepinephrine* (Figure 14.7, p. 537). Much like MAOIs, this class of antidepressants affects transmission of serotonin and norepinephrine. Unfortunately, as with MAOIs, many side effects are associated with tricyclic antidepressants. Thus newer drugs that have similar results but fewer side effects have been developed.

Selective serotonin reuptake inhibitors (SSRIs) *are a class of antidepressant drugs that block the reuptake of the neurotransmitter serotonin.* You might be familiar with Prozac (fluoxetine), an SSRI that appeared on the market in 1987 and since has been among the most commonly used. Other SSRIs include Zoloft (sertraline) and Paxil (paroxetine). SSRI side effects, which include loss of sexual interest and function, are less numerous and less severe than the adverse reactions associated with other antidepressants on the market.

Keep in mind that blocking neurotransmitter reuptake is a *hypothesis* about how these drugs work, not a fact. Nevertheless, SSRIs may do more than just block the reuptake of serotonin. Recent research has connected reduced hippocampal volume to depression. Interestingly, SSRIs have been shown to lead to *neurogenesis*—the growth of brand-new neurons—in precisely this part of the brain. Researchers have hypothesized that once the drugs accomplish this renewal—a process that may take weeks—cognition and emotion resume normal functioning (Jacobs, 2004). This regeneration of neurons may help explain why the effects of antidepressants can take a relatively long time to become evident, compared with drugs that take effect immediately.

Drugs similar to SSRIs have also been developed to inhibit the reuptake of both serotonin and norepinephrine. They are called selective serotonin-norepinephrine reuptake inhibitors (SNRIs).

Mood stabilizers *are drugs used to prevent or reduce the manic side of bipolar disorder.* **Lithium** *was one of the first mood stabilizers to be prescribed regularly in psychiatry.* From the 1950s to the 1980s, it was the standard drug treatment for depression and bipolar disorder. Lithium, a salt compound, can be quite effective, but it can also be toxic to the kidneys and endocrine system. Today, doctors generally prefer to prescribe other drugs because they seem to be more effective and safer than lithium (Thase & Denko, 2008). For example, people with bipolar disorder now take anticonvulsant medications such as *valproate* (marketed under the brand name Depakote), or anti-psychotic medications, which we will cover later. Although all of these medicines are effective in preventing manic episodes, they are also associated with significant side effects, including weight gain or restlessness, which leads to many individuals failing to take their medications as prescribed.

MYTHS IN MIND

Antidepressant Drugs Are Happiness Pills

A common belief is that antidepressants are happiness in pill form—that their chemical magic not only causes depression to disappear, but also brings on optimism and a rush of positive emotion. In reality, antidepressant drugs can alleviate depression (when they work), but they do not make people happier than they were before becoming depressed.

The "happiness pill" misconception about antidepressants has led some individuals to believe that taking a high dose of antidepressants will induce a euphoric high, much like cocaine or heroin. This is also a myth. Although some people have attempted to abuse antidepressants by taking high doses (even crushing and snorting them for quicker delivery to the brain), there is no evidence that an intense rush of happiness results. Remember that SSRIs typically take a couple of weeks to work. Taking a high dose, or snorting crushed-up pills, neither magnifies their effect nor reduces the two-week waiting period before effects become evident.

SSRIs and other major antidepressants also do not induce other characteristic effects of addictive drugs, including withdrawal, tolerance, and compulsive use. Although discontinuing antidepressant drugs can have some unpleasant effects, they are not of the same magnitude or variety of withdrawal effects expected from drugs such as heroin, nicotine, or alcohol (Shelton, 2006).

Antidepressants support the neurochemistry that allows for normal brain functioning, which includes the possibility of experiencing happiness. In short, individuals without depression should not expect to feel greater happiness if they take the drugs.

. . . .

ANTIANXIETY DRUGS Sometimes referred to as tranquilizers, **antianxiety drugs** *are prescribed to alleviate nervousness and tension, and to prevent and reduce panic attacks.* Widely prescribed examples include Xanax (alprazolam), Valium (diazepam), and Ativan (lorazepam). These drugs affect the activity of gamma-aminobutyric acid (GABA), an inhibitory neurotransmitter that reduces neural activity, see Module 3.2). They appear to temporarily alter the structure of GABA receptors, allowing more GABA molecules to inhibit neural activity. The effects of antianxiety drugs such as Xanax are relatively short-lived. They take effect within minutes of ingestion and may last for only a few hours. Given that these drugs facilitate inhibition of the nervous system, it is not surprising that their side effects include drowsiness and impaired attention, especially when they are taken at high doses. These drugs also have the potential to induce abuse and withdrawal symptoms.

ANTIPSYCHOTIC DRUGS **Antipsychotic drugs** *are used to treat disorders such as schizophrenia, and are sometimes prescribed to people with severe mood disorders.* Several classes of antipsychotic drugs are distinguished.

As discussed in Module 13.4, symptoms of schizophrenia are related to increased activity of dopamine, possibly because of the presence of an overabundance of receptors for dopamine in key brain regions. The first generation of antipsychotic medications (e.g., Thorazine, Halodol) was designed to block dopamine receptors. These drugs are not without side effects, however: Dopamine is also associated with movement, so blocking its transmission can result in a syndrome called **tardive dyskinesia**, *a neurological condition marked by involuntary movements and facial tics.*

The newer generation of medications is referred to as *atypical antipsychotics* or second-generation antipsychotics. The various atypical antipsychotics on the market vary in their exact effects, but generally speaking they primarily seem to reduce dopamine and serotonin activity. Atypical antipsychotics work for almost half of the individuals who take them, reducing the severity of symptoms but not necessarily eliminating them altogether (Leucht et al., 2009). Unfortunately, studies show that their effects weaken over time, such that symptoms can return.

Second-generation antipsychotics have the advantage of carrying a low risk for tardive dyskinesia as compared to first-generation drugs such as Thorazine. Nevertheless, they are not without risk. For example, the atypical antipsychotic drug Zyprexa was hailed as a major breakthrough for individuals with schizophrenia, but this drug causes drastic weight gain and has been linked to the onset of diabetes. Clozapine, the first atypical antipsychotic drug, is also known to compromise the body's white blood cells.

People often make the assumption that biomedical therapies are limited to prescription drugs or procedures that only a physician can provide. In reality, people often self-prescribe and administer treatments for depression consisting of over-the-counter remedies. As with any other treatment, we should examine the evidence to determine the effectiveness of these options. In this case, we will examine St. John's wort.

What do we know about St. John's wort?

St. John's wort (*Hypericum perforatum*) is an herbal remedy available in drugstores that has a long history of use as a treatment for various conditions. It is very popular in European countries, and is commonly purchased in the United States. Despite its widespread use as a mood enhancer, there is mixed evidence supporting the effectiveness of St. John's wort. Carefully controlled, long-term studies are required to definitively settle the question about whether it works as an antidepressant.

How can scientists study St. John's wort?

Several groups of researchers have been testing whether St. John's wort can alleviate depression. One group, whose members worked at multiple research centers, provided a 6-week treatment plan for 332 mild to moderately depressed individuals. They were randomly assigned into two groups receiving different doses of St. John's wort, or a third group which received a placebo. The study, which was performed under double-blind conditions, revealed that a 6-week regimen of St. John's wort significantly reduces depressive symptoms compared to individuals taking a placebo (Kasper et al., 2006).

One important question about St. John's wort is whether it is more effective than prescription antidepressant drugs. To address this issue, an 8-week randomized, placebo-controlled study similar to the one just described was conducted on

340 people with major depression, but with one group receiving an SSRI. In this study, the SSRI was only moderately effective compared with the placebo, which is not an uncommon finding even in carefully controlled studies. St. John's wort was no more effective than the placebo (Hypericum Depression Trial Study Group, 2002).

Can we critically evaluate this evidence?

St. John's wort, just like prescription antidepressant drugs, produces mixed results. For some people, it seems to be effective; for others, it does little or nothing. However, due to conflicting results, we should consider one of the most important confounds: Because herbal supplements are not regulated by government agencies, the quality may vary a great deal among brands. If that is true, it could explain why studies of St. John's wort have produced conflicting results (Klaus et al., 2008). Another issue to consider is that depression varies by degree. It appears that St. John's wort has a greater chance of working for people with mild to moderate depression, rather than major depression, as shown by a review of 37 double-blind, randomized trials (Linde et al., 2005).

Why is this relevant?

Knowledge about these experiments can help individuals with depression make informed choices about how to elevate their mood. However, individuals considering the herbal remedy still need to consult with their doctors. The FDA warns that St. John's wort can produce unfavorable reactions with medications used to treat heart disease, seizures, and some cancers. Also, drug treatments, whether herbal or prescription, may not be the only therapeutic option—especially for people experiencing relatively mild or moderate levels of depression.

BIOPSYCHOSOCIAL PERSPECTIVES

Ethnicity, Drugs, and Psychological Treatment

Consider whether you agree or disagree with the following statements:

- Having psychological problems or a mental illness is a sign of weakness.
- Problems with mental illness should be kept private and within the family.
- People who have a mental illness are not defined by their condition (in other words, although their illness is a part of an individual, it does not determine his identity and worth).
- Seeking mental health treatment and taking prescription drugs for mental health issues is acceptable.

Each of these statements addresses contemporary concerns people have about being treated for mental illness. Any individual could agree or disagree with them, but research indicates that, as a group, people from different ethnic backgrounds tend to have similar perspectives on what it means to have a mental illness and how treatment should proceed. In general, Caucasian people tend to believe that mental health issues are not a sign of weakness, although (as reviewed in Module 14.1) males are less likely to feel this way. Caucasians also tend to feel less concerned about the stigma of having mental health problems compared to Latinos or African Americans, and seeking treatment and taking drugs for mental health issues is generally acceptable among the members of this group.

African Americans tend to regard severe problems with mental health as family business, and are less likely to seek either psychotherapy or drug treatment, even when they are available. People of Latino descent are also less likely to seek psychological and drug treatments, and show concern about stigmas associated with having mental illness (Carpenter-Song et al., 2010; Olfson & Marcus, 2009). Latinos have adopted a cultural label of *ataque de nervios* (attack of the nerves) to refer to mental illness; this term does not carry the potential social damage that can be caused by being labeled as having depression or schizophrenia.

Cross-ethnic comparisons show differing views on mental illness, drug treatments, and psychological therapies. In addition, people of different racial and ethnic backgrounds may *respond* differently to drug treatments. The frequency with which certain genes that are associated with the receptor activity and the metabolism of neurotransmitters associated with depression (serotonin, dopamine, norepinephrine) differ among ethnic groups (Dong et al., 2009). Even very small genetic variations may help explain individual differences in the ways that people respond to psychiatric drugs. Clearly, the biopsychosocial view of therapies paints a broad and complex picture of drug and psychological treatments.

EVALUATING DRUG THERAPIES It can be tempting to conclude that because drugs are designed to target the root physical causes of psychological disorders, they should be more effective than psychotherapy. This general conclusion is not warranted, although in some cases drugs do offer quicker and more effective results than do psychotherapies. Research generally shows that drugs are more effective when combined with other types of therapy. For example, psychotherapy alone may not be sufficient for treating severe disorders such as schizophrenia. Therapists have found that people with schizophrenia tend to have difficulty imagining themselves in past and future situations—abilities that would otherwise enable them to engage in self-reflection and understanding (D'Argembeau et al., 2008). Drugs may help reduce these symptoms and facilitate the process of talking therapy.

Antidepressants have become increasingly accepted among the general public in part due to the pervasive marketing campaigns from drug companies (see Figure 14.8). However, taking antidepressant medication in no way ensures that the symptoms of depression will subside. Approximately 50% to 60% of people who take antidepressants improve within a few months—but 30% of people improve to similar levels by taking a placebo (Hollon et al., 2002). Similar to the outcomes found in drug studies, 50% to 60% of people benefit from psychotherapy in treating depression. Thus we cannot conclude that drugs either are more effective or should replace traditional psychotherapy. Combining the two types of treatment is often the best course of action for people who are struggling with depression. Notably, the combination of psychodynamic therapies and antidepressants is more effective in treating major depression than medication alone (Burnand et al., 2002; de Jonghe et al., 2001). Even though many individuals may experience great benefits from taking psychotropic medications, they typically remain cautious about using them.

Although modern antidepressants have been around for more than 20 years, and antipsychotic medications have been available for more than 50 years, many people remain skeptical about the safety of psychotropic drugs (Dijkstra et al., 2008). Attitudes have been changing, however, as increasing numbers of people have come to believe that biology is a

{FIG. 14.8} **Direct-to-Consumer Advertising of Antidepressants** Antidepressant medication prescriptions written in the United States nearly doubled between 1996 and 2005 (from 5.8% to 10.1% of the populations sampled). A ban on direct-to-consumer advertising for drugs was lifted in 1997, which may account for a substantial part of this increase.

primary cause of disorders such as major depression (Blumner & Marcus, 2009). Even so, consumer caution is certainly warranted. The antipsychotic drug Zyprexa, for example, has some severe side effects that were withheld from the public based on examination of internal documents from Eli Lilly, the company that patented and sells the drug. The high-stakes financial interests of drug companies are often in conflict with the best interests of the people who need the drugs. These conflicting needs lead to the type of problem encountered with Zyprexa, and can also lead to exaggerated claims about the effectiveness of some medications. This set of problems will be difficult to overcome because the work of the researchers who evaluate the drugs is often funded by the manufacturers of the drugs themselves.

Researchers are finding some beneficial alternatives to drugs, especially for individuals who do not have severe forms of depression. Numerous studies have shown that exercise is more effective than placebo at relieving depressive symptoms, and it is almost as effective as standard SSRI medications (Brené et al., 2007). If this is true, there are at least two reasons to believe exercise might be preferred to medication. First, the obvious health benefits of exercise (e.g., cardiovascular fitness, muscle tone) provide for a higher quality of life in general. Second, the change in lifestyle that comes with a regular exercise program actually prevents relapse of depressive symptoms better than medication (Babyak et al., 2000).

So what is it about exercise that alleviates depressive symptoms? Several mechanisms are probably at work. In the short term, running is associated with the release of endorphins, which reduce pain sensation and increase mood. The effects of endorphins are relatively short term; they generally dissipate the same day as the exercise. Over time, active individuals typically increase their energy levels and participate in enjoyable activities, both of which can act against the social withdrawal and negative cognitive style associated with depression. Finally, neuroscience research indicates that exercise actually increases activity in the brain's reward circuitry and facilitates neurogenesis in the hippocampus, a function that is also attributed to SSRI medications (Brené et al., 2007).

PsychTutor

Click here in your eText for an interactive tutorial on **Medications and Their Limitations**

Quick Quiz 14.3a
Drug Treatments

KNOW …

1 Tardive dyskinesia is:

  A a side effect of antipsychotics that involves motion control problems.

  B an antidepressant that breaks down enzymes in the synapse.

  C the growth of new neurons in the adult brain.

  D a side effect of antidepressant drugs.

UNDERSTAND …

2 _____ affect the nervous system by blocking reuptake of serotonin in neurons.

  A MAOIs

  B Antianxiety medications

  C Mood stabilizers

  D SSRIs

3 Monoamine oxidase inhibitor drugs work by:

  A boosting the ability of an enzyme to break down serotonin and norepinephrine molecules.

  B inhibiting the ability of an enzyme to break down serotonin and norepinephrine molecules.

  C selectively blocking the reuptake of serotonin.

  D creating new dopamine molecules.

ANALYZE …

4 Generally speaking, which of the following is the most accurate statement about psychotropic drugs?

  A They are superior to talking therapy.

  B Their effects are rarely evident until weeks after taking them.

  C They are more effective if combined with some form of talking therapy.

  D Lifestyle changes are not necessary for alleviating problems with depression.

5 Imagine that a friend asks you what you have heard about St. John's wort because he is considering using it to alleviate his depression. Which of the following is probably the safest conclusion you can draw?

  A Many people have reported improvements with St. John's wort, but the effects are typically mild and improvements may depend on the quality of the brand.

  B St. John's wort is superior to prescription antidepressant medications.

  C Your friend may as well take a placebo: St. John's wort has never proved effective at reducing symptoms of depression.

  D St. John's wort is superior to cognitive-behavioral therapies.

Answers can be found on page ANS-5.

Technological and Surgical Methods

Drugs are the most widely used method of biomedical therapy offered to people seeking help for psychological problems. Nevertheless, other options are available, most of which are used for more severe symptoms and disorders. Today, these procedures are generally safe and carefully tested and scrutinized, though that has not always been the case.

You have likely heard of the *frontal lobotomy*. The story behind this procedure is chilling. Many neurologists of the 1800s and 1900s experimented with surgically removing regions of the cortex in the hope of "curing" psychological problems. Portuguese surgeon Antonio Moniz came to believe that the prefrontal cortex was the source of many psychological problems, and he reasoned that destroying this region would cure the problems. Moniz used either chemicals or a wire loop to destroy the frontal lobe. The procedure

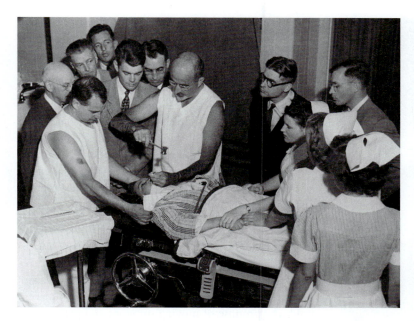

Walter Freeman performing a frontal lobotomy surgery.

was imported to the United States by Walter Freeman, a surgeon who modified Moniz's technique in a way he considered simpler but equally effective. Freeman used an ice pick to pierce the orbit of the eye, lodge it within the brain, and move it around until the frontal lobes were detached from the rest of the brain (Valenstein, 1973). This manipulation was done without anesthesia and on an outpatient basis. Freeman believed the procedure to be miraculously successful (despite the high percentage of patients who died from internal bleeding and other complications). Freeman and the few others who were willing to perform lobotomies used the procedure on some 4,000 people despite resistance from the medical community and public.

By the 1970s, the prefrontal lobotomy was all but eliminated in the United States. Although the frontal lobotomy has given an unfortunate reputation to just about *any* medical procedure intended to improve psychological functioning, there are several available techniques that are safe and often quite effective.

FOCAL LESIONS   At the opening of this module, we discussed how some people elect to undergo experimental surgical procedures to treat psychiatric problems. These techniques typically involve creating small *lesions* in specific brain regions. A lesion is a damaged area of tissue, such as a cluster of nerve cells. Brain lesions are never used on human subjects for basic research purposes. However, in some cases, when all other treatments have not worked to satisfaction, a surgeon may create small brain lesions in patients. Some people with depression, obsessive–compulsive disorder, and other anxiety disorders have

undergone lesion surgery directed at a cluster of cells located in the anterior cingulate cortex, which is overactive in people with these disorders (Cosgrove & Rauch, 2003; Fitzgerald et al., 2005; Steele et al., 2008). This procedure, mentioned in the opening of this module, is called an *anterior cingulotomy* and has no more risks or side effects than do many of the drugs used to treat these disorders. Also, the use of brain imaging technology allows surgeons to carry out the procedure with great precision.

ELECTROCONVULSIVE THERAPY

Electroconvulsive therapy (ECT) *is a psychiatric treatment in which an electrical current is passed through the brain to induce a temporary seizure.* This procedure was introduced in the 1930s and has been viewed negatively for much of its history, in part because in its early days it was generally unsafe. Over the years, however, procedures for delivering ECT have improved dramatically. For example, patients are now given sedatives and muscle relaxers to reduce the discomfort they may experience during the therapy and to prevent injury related to the convulsions. Thus ECT has gone from being viewed as a torturous "shock treatment" to a relatively normal and safe procedure, although it is still reserved for the most severe cases of disorders such as depression and schizophrenia. The side effects are relatively mild, typically consisting of some amnesia, but only for events occurring around the time of the treatment.

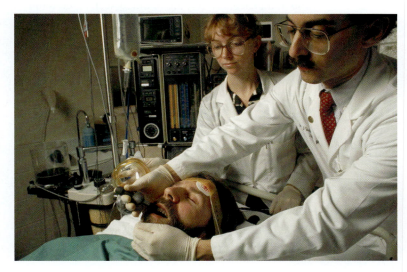

People with depression or bipolar disorder may elect to undergo electroconvulsive therapy if other treatments have not been successful.

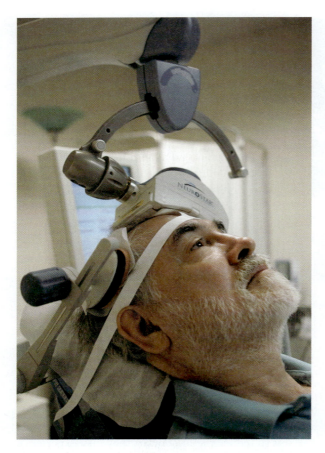

Delivering brief pulses of a strong magnetic field to the cerebral cortex has been shown to help alleviate symptoms of severe depression, and possibly other disorders.

Why does ECT work? Which changes in the nervous system does ECT stimulate? Scientists are not sure why inducing what is basically a controlled seizure can have positive outcomes for many individuals. It is possible that the procedure invigorates the expression of genes that code for important chemicals relating to mood, such as serotonin.

TRANSCRANIAL MAGNETIC STIMULATION

Transcranial magnetic stimulation (TMS) *is a therapeutic technique in which a focal area of the brain is exposed to a powerful but safe magnetic field.* TMS does not involve anesthesia or induce a seizure. Clinical researchers have discovered that stimulating parts of the frontal lobes of the cortex reduces depressive symptoms (Chistyakov et al., 2005). The FDA has approved the use of this technique for treating major depression in people who have not improved using drugs or ECT. This technique holds considerable promise, and it may turn out to be of value in reducing symptoms of other mental disorders, such as schizophrenia (Slotema et al., 2010; Zaman et al., 2008).

DEEP BRAIN STIMULATION

Deep brain stimulation (DBS) *is a technique that involves electrically stimulating highly specific regions of the brain.* Thin electrode-tipped wires are routed to the region of the brain needing stimulation. A small battery connected to the wires is then inserted just beneath the skin surface. Unlike many of the drugs reviewed previously, DBS produces instantaneous results, though there are some troublesome side effects to consider. In particular, some patients have experienced internal bleeding and infection. Also, even though the wires and electrodes are placed with the utmost precision, it is possible that behavioral side effects can occur, such as depression, aggression, penile erection, and laughter (Kringelbach et al., 2007).

Scientists are not sure exactly how DBS works. It has primarily been applied to people who have movement disorders such as Parkinson's disease. More recently, it has been used to help treat depression and obsessive–compulsive disorder. Deep brain stimulation holds the promise of moving surgeons and patients beyond the need to perform any type of lesion surgery, such as the cingulotomy (Kringelbach & Aziz, 2009).

EVALUATING TECHNOLOGICAL AND SURGICAL METHODS   Technological and surgical methods are typically reserved for severe cases involving people who are diagnosed with a full-blown disorder such as depression, schizophrenia, or obsessive–compulsive disorder. Some of these methods continue to be controversial because procedures such as the frontal lobotomy and ECT are the first examples to come to mind. Lobotomies are a thing of the past, however, and ECT is now a safe procedure. Surgeries that involve destroying brain tissue are still used in extreme cases, but less invasive methods such as DBS and TMS are also becoming more widely available. Many members of the public believe that ECT causes lasting cognitive impairments, but the evidence for this contention is contradicted by the majority of research on people who have been treated with it (Rose et al., 2003).

Combining the treatments covered in this chapter is common, such as seeing a therapist and taking prescribed antidepressants, or combining drugs with ECT. Why do people need more than one form of treatment? In some cases, there is an urgent need to take action—for example, if the individual is suicidal. Also, for more serious cases a single treatment may provide very little benefit. For example, the drug lithium has such a long history of use because it works so well, with relapse rates hovering around 20% (Keller & Baker, 1991). In contrast, half of people who undergo ECT end up relapsing back into depression, although combining antidepressants can help improve long-term outcomes of ECT (Sackeim et al., 2009).

Quick Quiz 14.3b :: Technological and Surgical Methods

UNDERSTAND ...

1 If a doctor wanted to activate a very *specific* brain region in the hope of alleviating symptoms of a mental disorder, she would most likely use which of the following procedures?

- **A** Focal lesion
- **B** Cingulotomy
- **C** Electroconvulsive therapy
- **D** Deep brain stimulation

2 Which of the following techniques results in intentionally killing nerve cells?

- **A** Deep brain stimulation
- **B** Electroconvulsive therapy
- **C** Focal lesion
- **D** Transcranial magnetic stimulation

ANALYZE ...

3 A new age guru openly criticizes medical procedures for treating psychological problems, citing the frontal lobotomy as his only evidence. Which statement best contradicts his critique?

- **A** The frontal lobotomy is no longer used and has been replaced with scientifically supported treatments.
- **B** Frontal lobotomies are now relatively safe to perform.
- **C** Frontal lobotomies actually work very well for schizophrenia, but not for bipolar disorder.
- **D** The argument is irrelevant, as medical procedures are being phased out in favor of new age treatments.

Answers can be found on page ANS-5.

Module Summary

Module 14.3

((•— **Listen** to the audio file of this module at **MyPsychLab**

Now that you have read this module you should:

KNOW ...

- **The key terminology associated with biological treatments:**

antianxiety drugs (p. 539)
antidepressant drugs (p. 537)
antipsychotic drugs (p. 539)
blood–brain barrier (p. 537)
deep brain stimulation (DBS) (p. 544)
electroconvulsive therapy (ECT) (p. 543)
lithium (p. 538)
monoamine oxidase inhibitors (MAOIs) (p. 537)

mood stabilizers (p. 538)
psychopharmacotherapy (p. 536)
psychotropic drugs (p. 537)
selective serotonin reuptake inhibitors (SSRIs) (p. 538)
tardive dyskinesia (p. 539)
transcranial magnetic stimulation (TMS) (p. 544)
tricyclic antidepressants (p. 538)

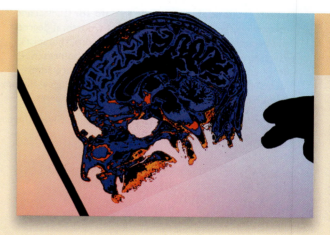

UNDERSTAND ...

- **How the drugs described in this module affect brain functioning.** Antidepressant drugs typically target monoamine neurotransmitter activity, with differing mechanisms of action (review **Figure 14.7**). Many of the antipsychotic drugs on the market reduce dopamine activity in the brain. Antianxiety drugs tend to target GABA receptors and increase activity of this inhibitory neurotransmitter.

- **How various medical therapies that do not involve drugs work.** Other procedures available for treating mental illness include electroconvulsive therapy, transcranial magnetic stimulation, deep brain stimulation, and focal lesions. In some cases, particularly ECT, researchers are still unsure about which aspect of the treatment produces the therapeutic results. Stimulation techniques increase the brain activity in targeted areas, whereas lesions prevent brain activity. By targeting the areas responsible for specific behaviors, thoughts, or emotions, treatments can have dramatic effects on behavior.

APPLY ...

- **Your knowledge of drug therapies to different psychological conditions.** Match the drugs listed in the left column with the condition they are typically prescribed to treat on the right. Check your answers on page ANS-5.

DRUG	CONDITION
1. Lithium	a. Anxiety
2. An SSRI	b. Depression
3. Xanax	c. Schizophrenia
4. Clozapine	d. Bipolar disorder

ANALYZE ...

- **Whether St. John's wort, a popular herbal remedy for depression, works.** Research into the effects of St. John's wort has produced mixed results. The herb may work for people with mild to moderate levels of depression, but in the case of severe depression, it seems less successful. Most psychologists would encourage people to seek professional treatment for depression rather than to self-medicate. The pharmaceutical treatments have been researched more thoroughly and are produced and packaged under more highly controlled regulations.

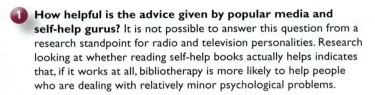

Module 14.1 :: Treating Psychological Disorders

Focus Questions:

1 **How helpful is the advice given by popular media and self-help gurus?** It is not possible to answer this question from a research standpoint for radio and television personalities. Research looking at whether reading self-help books actually helps indicates that, if it works at all, bibliotherapy is more likely to help people who are dealing with relatively minor psychological problems.

2 **Who typically conducts psychological therapy, and which credentials are needed to do so?** Clinical and counseling psychologists earn advanced, doctoral degrees and become licensed to become professional therapists. Psychiatrists earn medical degrees, are able to prescribe drugs, and typically work with people with more severe mental illnesses. Others who conduct psychological therapy include clinical social workers and psychiatric nurses.

👁—[**Watch** In the Real World Application: Self-Help Therapy in the **MyPsychLab video series**

Module 14.2 :: Psychological Therapies

Focus Questions:

1 **Which options for therapy are available?** The types of therapies include insight approaches, such as psychoanalysis and humanistic therapies; behavioral and cognitive-behavioral therapy; and group and family therapy. These are all general categories of therapy—within each, you would likely find different specific approaches. For example, object relations therapy is an offshoot of psychoanalysis, and the systems approach is a specific approach to family therapy.

2 **Are all well-established options equally effective at treating problems?** Different problems typically call for different types of therapies. For example, addiction treatment typically involves individualized sessions, often using cognitive-behavioral approaches, as well as group therapy sessions. Cognitive-behavioral therapies have also proved extremely useful in treating problems relating to mood and anxiety. Behavioral therapies have proved successful in treating certain types of anxiety issues—including phobias of specific objects or situations. Also, one specific subtype of behavioral therapy—aversive conditioning—may prove useful when the client is trying to reduce cravings for something such as alcohol.

👁—[**Watch** What's in It for Me? Finding a Therapist If You Need One in the **MyPsychLab video series**

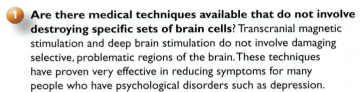

Module 14.3 :: Biomedical Therapies

Focus Questions:

1 **Are there medical techniques available that do not involve destroying specific sets of brain cells?** Transcranial magnetic stimulation and deep brain stimulation do not involve damaging selective, problematic regions of the brain. These techniques have proven very effective in reducing symptoms for many people who have psychological disorders such as depression.

2 **Are drugs and other technological procedures "miracle cures" for psychological problems?** While drug treatments have been very effective for many people with mental disorders, they are much less beneficial if they are not combined with psychological therapy. The same caveat applies to technological procedures such as brain stimulation and surgery. To date, no one can lay claim that any drug or procedure offers a "miracle cure".

👁—[**Watch** Thinking Like a Psychologist: Assessing the Effective Treatments in the **MyPsychLab video series**

👁—[**Watch** the complete video series online at **MyPsychLab**

Episode 17: Psychological Disorders and Therapies
1. The Big Picture: What Is Abnormal, Anyway?
2. The Basics, Part 1: Living with Disorder
3. The Basics, Part 2: Therapies in Action
4. Special Topics: DSM-IV
5. Thinking Like a Psychologist: Assessing the Effectiveness of Treatments
6. In the Real World Application: Self-Therapy
7. What's in It for Me? Finding a Therapist If You Need One

1   Which of the following is believed to be the key reason why men in the United States often go without psychological treatment?

A   Psychotherapy is less effective for men than it is for women.

B   Psychological problems tend to be less severe for men than for women.

C   Men often believe that seeking treatment conflicts with masculinity.

D   Psychological problems are more likely to resolve on their own for men than for women.

2   Rita is a mental health professional who has a Master's degree. She generally works with people who are having difficulty dealing with mild depression or anxiety, or are generally having trouble with stress or coping; she does not work with individuals who have more severe mental disorders such as schizophrenia or major depression. Rita is most likely a _____.

A   counseling psychologist

B   psychiatrist

C   clinical psychologist

D   forensic psychologist

3   The rigorous testing of specific psychotherapies is difficult, in part because:

A   clients do not want to receive experimental treatments.

B   most people prefer self-help treatments.

C   therapists cannot be blind to the type of therapy they are administering.

D   few therapists are willing to participate in such studies.

4   Carl Rogers developed a type of therapy called _____, which focuses on individuals' abilities to solve their own problems and reach their full potential with the encouragement of the therapist.

A   object relations therapy

B   psychoanalysis

C   insight therapy

D   person/client-centered therapy

5   To treat his fear of spiders, Nate's therapist has him lie still for 30 minutes while several tarantulas crawl on him. This extreme therapy is an example of _____.

A   aversive conditioning

B   flooding

C   systematic desensitization

D   virtual reality exposure

6   Family therapists take a _____ approach, an orientation toward family therapy that involves identifying and understanding what each individual family member contributes to the entire family dynamic.

A   client-centered

B   psychoanalytic

C   systems

D   systematic desensitization

7   In general, antidepressant drugs are believed to work by:

A   decreasing monoamine activity in the brain.

B   increasing monoamine activity in the brain.

C   increasing GABA activity in the brain.

D   decreasing GABA activity in the brain.

8   Research into the effectiveness of antidepressants indicates that the most effective treatment for many people is:

A   taking antidepressant drugs alone.

B   psychotherapy without any pharmaceutical therapy.

C   taking antidepressants combined with antipsychotic drugs.

D   combining antidepressant drugs with psychotherapy.

9   In the middle of the 20th century, Walter Freeman and others infamously treated thousands of patients with a procedure known as _____.

A   shock therapy

B   the frontal lobotomy

C   deep brain stimulation

D   anterior cingulotomy

10   Which of the following statements is true about electroconvulsive therapy (ECT)?

A   ECT can be an effective treatment for severe cases of depression.

B   ECT is no longer considered a valid or ethical form of treatment.

C   ECT is still performed in the same way it was delivered in the 1930s and 1940s.

D   ECT triggers a controlled stroke.

✓●—[**Study** and **Review** at **MyPsychLab**

What do we know about treating psychological disorders?

Although we categorize disorders and define them separately, the reality is that clinicians often treat psychological disorders with a mixture of therapeutic techniques. **Table 14.5** summarizes the major types of psychotherapies, and you can review the major psychotropic drugs and psychosurgeries on **pages 536–544**. If you are having trouble remembering the specifics of these therapies, you can think about them in terms of their treatment goals. For instance, while psychoanalysis and humanistic therapy are both insight therapies, the goal of psychoanalysis is to develop insight into the problem by revealing unconscious conflicts, whereas the humanistic approach attempts to gain a richer understanding of those factors that bring about personal growth and self-actualization by focusing on conscious and subjective experience. The cognitive-behavioral model aims to change the thoughts and feelings that lead to unwanted behaviors, and the goal of the behavioral approach is to change an unwanted behavior through principles of classical conditioning and observational learning. Finally, biomedical therapies aim to alleviate symptoms and, potentially, treat the neurological basis of the client's problems.

Why is this relevant?

Watch the accompanying video excerpt on psychological therapies. You can access the video at MyPsychLab or by clicking the play button in the center of your eText. If your instructor assigns this video as a homework activity, you will find additional content to help you in MyPsychLab. You can also view the video by using your smart phone and the QR code below, or you can go to the YouTube link provided.

After you have read this chapter and watched the video, compare and contrast the following forms of psychotherapy: cognitive, humanistic, and behavioral. Identify the focus of each approach as well as areas of agreement and difference.

How can science help explain psychological therapies?

First, it is important to note that many therapies stem from basic scientific research. For example, systematic desensitization comes directly out of basic research on classical conditioning. Similarly, drug treatments are derived from an understanding of neurotransmitter functioning in the brain. Scientific research shows that empirically based therapies—that is, those treatments that are tested for effectiveness using appropriate scientific research design—have high success rates. The most rigorous approach to studying treatment methods would be double-blind experiments; ideally, such investigations would involve control groups and follow patients over a long period of time. These methods are certainly used with the biologically based treatments, but great difficulties arise when researchers think about implementing these methods with psychotherapy. In particular, the therapist cannot be blinded to the type of treatment being provided. In addition, the effectiveness of psychotherapy may arise from the therapeutic alliance—the unique relationship between therapist and patient that would be quite challenging to manipulate.

Can we critically evaluate claims about psychological therapies and treatments?

Psychotherapy is clearly a powerful tool in the treatment of psychological disorders. But what if someone cannot or will not see a mental health care professional? Encouraging research on self-help treatments suggests that these methods can be helpful if the treatment itself is valid, and combining the self-help treatment with at least one face-to-face therapy session would likely achieve a better rate of success.

The **Myths in Mind** feature on **page 538** discussed the misconception that antidepressants can alleviate depression and deliver a dose of euphoria in the form of a magic pill. While studies support the use of antidepressants across a range of psychological problems, they are by no means the first and only treatment for such patients. Herbal supplements such as St. John's wort might be effective for treating depression, but when considering studies of these products, we have to keep in mind confounding variables such as the strength of the supplement (most of these products are unregulated in the United States) and the degree of depression in the individual. Controlled and long-term studies of St. John's wort indicate that the supplement is no more effective than a placebo at treating people who are diagnosed with depression.

MyPsychLab

Your turn to Work the Scientific Literacy Model: You can access the video at MyPsychLab or by clicking the play button in the center of your eText. If your instructor assigns this video as a homework activity, you will find additional content to help you at MyPsychLab. You can also view the video by using your smart phone and the QR code, or you can go to the YouTube link provided.

youtube.com/scientificliteracy

15 :: SOCIAL PSYCHOLOGY

Module 15.1

Social Influences on Behavior and Attitudes

Learning Objectives

After reading this module you should:

KNOW ...	UNDERSTAND ...	APPLY ...	ANALYZE ...
The key terminology associated with social influence	Why individuals conform to others' behaviors and thoughts How individuals and groups can influence attitudes and behaviors	Your knowledge of cognitive dissonance to see how well your beliefs match your behaviors	Whether guards who participate in abuse are inherently bad people, or if their behavior is the product of social influences

In early 2004, military policeman Joe Darby turned over a set of photographs to the Army's criminal investigation unit. As he described it:

> To be honest, at first I thought they were pretty funny ... To me, that pyramid of naked Iraqis, when you first see it, is hilarious ... But some of the other pictures didn't sit right with me. The ones of prisoners being beaten, or the one with a naked Iraqi sitting on his knees in front of another naked Iraqi, some of the more sexually-explicit-type stuff to humiliate the prisoners ... After about three days, I made a decision to turn the pictures in. (Hylton, 2006)

This action led to an investigation and eventually the conviction of the guards for violating laws and Army regulations regarding the abuse of prisoners at the Abu Ghraib prison in Iraq.

Handing over the pictures was not an easy thing for Darby to do. He understood that turning over the photos would put him at serious risk for retaliation. There was also concern for his family. What if someone tried to harm Darby's wife for a decision he made on his own without her knowledge? How would he live with that? Finally, there was the matter of his career. Would he be able to continue in the military? Or would people view him as a traitor—someone who could not be trusted?

Eventually, the Army conducted a security assessment and determined that the threat to Darby's family in his hometown was too great. Darby, his wife, and children were placed in protective custody. Today, they remain in an undisclosed location and they constantly have an armed military escort whenever they go out—even for something as simple as a trip to the grocery.

The violations at Abu Ghraib are certainly not the only cases of prisoner abuse to have occurred. Unfortunately incidents like this happen frequently in the criminal justice system and military prisons and it is often very difficult for people to come forward and report the abuse for fear of retaliation. Victims and social psychologists alike wonder why these abuses happen, what we might do to prevent them, and how we might help make it easier to report these incidents.

Focus Questions

1 Were the guards at the Abu Ghraib prison callous and brutal people, or did the situation lead them to behave that way?

2 Would a decent and honest person refuse to harm others, even if he or she were instructed to do so by an authority figure?

Social psychology *is a broad field of study that includes how individuals perceive and think about other people, as well as how the presence of other people can influence individuals' behaviors.* Most of us feel as if we are in charge of our own behavior—that we are free to determine what we do and do not do, and that we act for good reasons, not just to go along with the crowd. But the research in this field challenges these ideas at many levels; social psychology provides strong evidence that some behavior depends more on *where we are* than on *who we are*.

Norms, Roles, and Conformity

No matter which culture is involved, humans are remarkably sensitive to whether behavior is socially acceptable or unacceptable. When you walk down the street, is it appropriate to make eye contact with strangers? In some situations, doing so would make you vulnerable to hostility or could insult passers-by. When you step into an elevator, do you stand with your back to the door and announce the floors to fellow passengers? You might get some odd looks

if you did. Here, we investigate how our behavior is influenced by what is deemed acceptable and expected.

NORMS AND ROLES   **Social norms** *are the (usually unwritten) guidelines for how to behave in social contexts.* Norms include everything from the little nuances of public behavior and the manners we use in polite company, to the topics that are suitable for conversation and the types of clothing deemed appropriate. Some norms exist at the societal level, whereas other norms operate at the level of smaller groups. For example, most colleges have a few norms that are specific to that campus, such as how to dress for class, how to address the faculty, and how to behave in the classroom.

Social roles *are specific sets of behaviors that are associated with a position within a group.* The key word here is "specific": While norms are general rules that apply to members of a group, roles are guidelines that apply to specific positions within the group. Because roles are so specific, we often have labels for them—such as professor, student, coach, parent, and prison guard.

Volunteers were randomly assigned to play guards or prisoners in the Stanford Prison Study in 1971. Each group took their roles so seriously that the researchers called off the experiment before it was even halfway completed.

One of the most famous psychological studies depicts the power that roles have over our behavior. The Stanford Prison Study, as it has come to be known, revealed how normal people can take on virtually any type of role (Haney et al., 1973; Haney & Zimbardo, 1998). The participants for the study were pre-screened to establish that they were psychologically healthy, and then were randomly assigned to play the role of either prisoner or prison guard. Because of the pre-screening, the two groups were virtually identical in terms of personality, mental health, and intelligence.

The role playing began as soon as the prisoners were "arrested" and brought to the basement of the Stanford University psychology building, where they were incarcerated in a made-up prison. The students assigned to be guards were issued uniforms and given the task of overseeing the prisoners, and they soon began to take their jobs very seriously. Prison guards established rules and issued orders. Some of prisoners complied; others resisted. As guards enforced the rules, some became abusive, and their methods of control escalated until some were requiring prisoners to do push-ups, clean toilets by hand, or spend hours without clothes in solitary confinement.

Remember, this was *role playing*, not a real prison with real criminals and guards. In fact, these men all fit the same general profile in terms of personality, mental health, and intelligence. Despite their inherent similarities to the prisoners, the guards either became brutal and callous or simply stood by while others carried out the abuse. At the same time, many prisoners acquiesced and passively accepted the brutal treatment. It is not as though they shrugged it off as a game; many exhibited stress-related symptoms including screaming, crying, and some even became ill. The researchers called off the experiment after six days, even though it had originally been planned to last two weeks. As you can probably imagine, this experiment brought to light a need for psychologists to closely scrutinize the ethical implications of their research. The Stanford Prison Study, conducted in 1971, would not be deemed ethical by today's research standards, and neither it nor anything like it would ever be repeated. However, instead of burying any record of it, psychologists continue to use the results to address important social psychological questions.

What led to this type of behavior? Remember, the guards and prisoners alike were bright, well-adjusted people. They volunteered for the study to make a little money or because they thought it would be an adventure. The only thing separating them from each other and from their real lives was the role that was assigned to them at random. Therefore, the differences must have been due to what they believed were the proper behaviors for their assigned roles.

You can likely see the connection between the Stanford experiment and the prisoner abuse scandal at Abu Ghraib. American soldiers were put in a prison and told to guard the prisoners. Without the appropriate supervision and instructions, even mild-mannered, good-natured people can do cruel and terrible things to others. It is not just about *who* they are that matters; it is *where* they are and *what role* they play.

MIMICRY AND CONFORMITY   Other people can be a great source of information about how to behave. **Mimicry** *occurs when one person copies another's behavior.* It can be a very useful skill at times, such as in a foreign country where you do not know the language and no one is around to help you translate. How will you get by? Many international travelers make it a long way on mimicry. If you want to ride public transportation, just watch what the other passengers are doing. Do they buy tickets before boarding, or do they pay a driver once they board? Following another's lead is often the best way to go, even if you are just walking into a new restaurant in your neighborhood.

There is another form of mimicry that many people find even more interesting; it is most often called nonconscious mimicry but also goes by the more colorful term—the *chameleon effect*. The chameleon effect occurs when individuals mimic another's behavior without meaning to or realizing that they are doing it (Chartrand & Bargh, 1999). Furthermore, the imitated behavior usually does not have any obvious use; it is as if it "just happens." For example, you might find that if someone else is whispering, you probably will whisper as well, even if it is to ask, "Why are we whispering?" In fact, researchers have documented even more subtle forms of mimicry, such as walking slower in the presence of the elderly, or scratching one's head after someone else does the same (Dijksterhuis & Bargh, 2001).

It turns out that some situations produce more mimicry than others. Specifically, we are more likely to mimic others when we need to make a good impression, want to be liked, or want to be part of a group (Lakin & Chartrand, 2003). Interestingly, this tactic actually seems to work. The person who is being imitated usually does wind up with a favorable view of the imitator (Chartrand & Bargh, 1999). Some observers have even dubbed mimicry the "social glue" that binds groups together (Lakin et al., 2003).

The study of mimicry focuses on how we are influenced by a single individual, but being part of a group can affect our behaviors as well. Simply being among other people can influence us even if we are not aware of it. **Conformity** *refers to a change in behavior to fit in with a group.* Unlike the chameleon effect, conformity can be—and often is—a conscious decision.

Table 15.1 :: Personal and Situational Factors Contribute to Conformity

PEOPLE TEND TO BE LESS LIKELY TO CONFORM WHEN …	PEOPLE TEND TO BE MORE LIKELY TO CONFORM WHEN …
Only one other person is in the vicinity	There is a larger group in the vicinity
There are only male group members	There is a high proportion of female group members
There are only strangers in the room	There are friends, family, or acquaintances in the vicinity
There are extremely clear and simple tasks	The task is unclear or ambiguous
There is one other nonconformist in the room	Others conform first
Responses are made anonymously	Responses are made publicly

One of the first scientific studies of conformity was performed in the 1950s by Solomon Asch. Imagine you show up to participate in a study of perception and you are asked to take a seat among five other people. What you do not know is that the group of five are *confederates* (individuals working for the experimenter) that have already been told what to say. For the perception task, the group is shown the three lines in Figure 15.1, and each individual is asked which line is the same length as the standard line. Despite the obvious, correct choice (line B), the other people in the room all give the same incorrect answer. When it is your turn, do you go against the group? Or do you conform? In Asch's research, approximately 75% of these perfectly capable participants conformed to the group and gave the wrong answer at least once during the testing, and approximately 25% conformed regularly (Asch, 1951, 1955, 1956).

Why would individuals give what they knew was the wrong answer? Some of the reasons are obvious. After the experiments, many of the conforming participants said that they might have misunderstood the test, or thought that there was a "trick" or an optical illusion involved. Others simply wanted to avoid making a scene or being the odd one out. Thus we may conclude that conformity sometimes occurs because people think they are missing something, while other times it arises because individuals want to avoid social discomfort. In fact, there are numerous factors that influence whether someone conforms or goes against the grain (see Table 15.1).

Quick Quiz 15.1a
Norms, Roles, and Conformity

KNOW…

1. Social roles differ from norms in that:
   - Ⓐ they are expectations for a specific individual in a situation.
   - Ⓑ they are expectations for how nearly everyone should behave in a situation.
   - Ⓒ they cannot be enforced.
   - Ⓓ they are created by the individuals instead of being taught by society.

UNDERSTAND…

2. The chameleon effect occurs when:
   - Ⓐ individuals withdraw from social interactions.
   - Ⓑ individuals try to use subtle means of persuasion.
   - Ⓒ individuals turn their backs on a group member.
   - Ⓓ individuals unintentionally mimic another's behavior.

ANALYZE…

3. How did the Stanford Prison Study researchers come to the conclusion that roles, and not individual personalities, were the main influence on the volunteers' behavior?
   - Ⓐ The volunteer "prison guards" were specifically instructed to respond brutally.
   - Ⓑ The "prisoners" were actually actors hired by the researchers.
   - Ⓒ The prisoners and prison guards were psychologically similar prior to the start of the experience.
   - Ⓓ The researchers actually believed that personality is more important than social roles.

Answers can be found on page ANS-5.

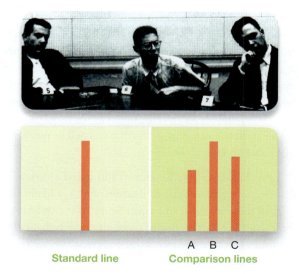

{FIG. 15.1} **Perceptual Judgment Task in Asch's Conformity Studies** Which of the comparison lines is the same length as the standard line? The correct answer is line B, and most people find that to be obvious. However, in Asch's experiments, many people conformed with the confederates and gave the wrong answer. **Click on this figure in your eText to see more details.**

Standard line   Comparison lines

A B C

Group Influence and Authority

Whether you know it or not, there is a really good chance that your performance at work or play is to some extent determined by the others in your group. Social psychologists have studied a number of ways this influence can work. For example, groups can improve your performance, or they may lead you to slack off. Some groups unite their members—even if their ideas are foolhardy—while other situations are divisive. Similar patterns of social influence have been seen among corporations, in presidential cabinet meetings, and, believe it or not, among all sort of species in the animal kingdom—even the lowly cockroach! Because groups are an important part of education, work, and play, it is important to understand the social influences on individual performance.

SOCIAL LOAFING AND SOCIAL FACILITATION

You probably have at least one college professor who sees a lot of value in group projects. Group assignments can be more sophisticated and cover a wider range of topics because more minds are engaged in the task. However, every class charged with completing a group project involves at least one student who feels she has done the entire project herself and at least one student who spent group meeting time sending text messages while his colleagues struggled to solve problems. Sound familiar? In addition to the individual stars and stragglers, most professors have seen a group of B students put together an outstanding A+ project while another group of B students barely manages to get a C on their project.

Do groups facilitate an individual's work? Or do they make an individual's work poorer? Oddly enough, the answer to both questions is "yes." But not to worry—that just means psychologists need to describe both effects, and then explain which personal and situational factors lead to one or the other.

Social loafing *occurs when an individual working as part of a group or team reduces his or her effort.* The individual may or may not be aware that he is loafing, but the behavior affects the group process nonetheless. Two of the most remarkable findings about social loafing are that it can appear in all sorts of tasks, including physical activities (swimming, rope-pulling), cognitive activities (problem solving, perceptual tests), and creativity (song-writing) and that it seems to occur equally across all types of groups, regardless of age, gender, and nationality (Karau & Williams, 2001; Latane et al., 2006).

Given the universal nature of social loafing, researchers have been able to identify a number of situational

influences with the potential to turn just about anyone into a loafer:

- *My effort will not help my performance.* Loafing may occur if an individual believes she is not capable of doing well.
- *My performance will not make a difference to the group's performance.* Loafing tends to occur when an individual believes he could do well but the group as a whole would do poorly, or perhaps that the group would do fine without him.
- *The group may get rewarded but it won't matter to me.* The group might get paid, but each individual's share is perceived as too small. Or perhaps conflict between group members can lead to loafing. Either way, the loafing members just want to get the group effort over with.
- *No one else is trying very hard.* Social loafing can be contagious. If one group member loafs, others may loaf as well (Karau & Williams, 2001).

If you think about the reverse of these situational influences, you should be able to predict what prevents social loafing: If an individual believes her contribution will help the group succeed and get rewarded, and if she values the rewards, then she is likely to put forth her best effort (Goren et al., 2003).

Not all groups have problems with social loafing; in fact, in some groups the reverse happens. **Social facilitation** *occurs when an individual's performance is better in the presence of others than when alone.* For example, a runner who completes a mile in a little more than 5 minutes by himself might finally break the 5-minute mark when running with his track teammates. Although that relationship is easy enough to understand, there is one interesting finding that challenges researchers: The presence of others does not always help performance. In fact, in some cases it can hurt the outcome. As a general rule, however, it seems that when individuals have mastered a task, the audience can help, whereas for novices, having an audience can hurt performance (Bell & Yee, 1989; MacCracken & Stadulis, 1985).

Psychologists have developed and tested a variety of theories to explain social facilitation, and it is likely that each of these explanations contributes to the overall effect (Uziel, 2007). The first of these processes is that being in groups can lead individuals to experience heightened arousal. This effect prepares individuals to do well on tasks for which they are confident in their own abilities.

In contrast, if individuals are uncertain about their skill, the arousal can turn into nervousness and actually impair performance (Zajonc, 1965). Interestingly, this effect is seen in animals as simple as the cockroach. Zajonc and colleagues (1969) had cockroaches run a maze or go down a runway for reinforcement. They found social facilitation for the runway task (the easy task), in that the cockroaches completed the runway faster when other cockroaches were around. In contrast, the cockroaches did worse in the maze when other roaches were present, which is the usual finding with complex tasks in front of an audience. Roaches aside, among humans impaired performance in the presence of others may be due to heightened self-awareness. This proposed relationship reflects the finding that social facilitation effects are increased when people are told they are being evaluated. For easy tasks, evaluation provides an incentive to do well, but for complex tasks, it can create anxiety and disrupt performance (Cottrell, 1972).

GROUPTHINK   Despite the old proverb, two heads are not always better than one, and six can be downright harmful. Probably the best example of this case is the phenomenon of **groupthink**, *a decision-making problem in which group members avoid arguments and strive for agreement.* At first, this might sound like a good thing. Conflicts can be unpleasant for some people and they can certainly get in the way of group decision making. But groupthink does not always promote good decision making. This is because when everyone avoids argument, three main problems occur. First, the group often becomes overconfident and gains a sense of excitement about its progress. Second, group members may minimize or ignore potential problems and risks. Third, they may apply social pressure to members who are not fully in support of the idea in an effort to get them to conform (Ahlfinger & Esser, 2001; Janis, 1972).

Some groups are more susceptible to groupthink than others, as Table 15.2 shows. Laboratory research revealed that when groupthink occurs, there is almost always a strong or "directive" leader—specifically, an individual who suppresses dissenters and encourages the group to consider fewer alternative ideas (Ahlfinger & Esser, 2001). Experimental research has confirmed that the more the group members have in common—especially in terms of

shared sociopolitical perspectives—the more likely they are to fall into the patterns of groupthink (e.g., Schulz-Hardt et al., 2000).

Despite the similarities among the groups that have succumbed to groupthink, plenty of cases can be cited where groups with strong leaders and a shared background *did not* fall into groupthink patterns. Also, one should realize that groupthink does not always lead to bad decisions (Kerr & Tindale, 2004). In some cases of groupthink, the group might have stumbled on the best solution early in the decision process, so any alternatives that were introduced really would not be needed.

OBEDIENCE TO AUTHORITY   One of the most direct forms of social influence is authority, and social psychologists are particularly interested in what leads an individual to **obedience**—*complying with instructions or orders from an individual who is in a position of authority.* Authority comes from a combination of social roles and social context. Individuals are likely to obey parents, teachers, bosses, and law enforcement officials because we generally agree that those titles indicate authority. However, authority can be situational. For example, if you walk into an examination room for a physical and the physician asks you to undress, you most likely will comply. Your reaction is likely to be much different if your physician asks this of you upon running into you at the supermarket.

Social psychologists have asked just how much influence an authority figure can have over an individual's behavior. It is one thing for an employee to complete a report for her supervisor. It is quite another thing for her to engage in behaviors that conflict with her values—perhaps inflicting pain on another—just because her boss requested it. To explore just how far people will go to obey authority figures, psychologist Stanley Milgram conducted in 1961 what is now known as a classic study on obedience. Read about the procedures first:

- A recruit shows up at the psychologist's lab. Another man is already there, and the two men draw slips of paper to find out who is the teacher and

Table 15.2 :: Risk Factors for Groupthink

- The group is highly cohesive; group members come from similar backgrounds and approach the problems from the same general perspective.
- There is a strong leader in the group, someone who can control the conversation and can keep the focus on his or her idea, whether it is the appointed leader or a very strong personality.
- The group ignores outside experts and dismisses expert opinions that do not agree with the group. They seek information only that will support their ideas.

Source: McCauley, 1987.

who will be the learner. In this case, the recruit is assigned to be the teacher. He is not informed that the other man is an actor who works for the experimenter (a confederate).

- The teacher is told to read a series of word pairs to the learner, who is in a separate room. When given one word, the learner is asked to repeat its pair. The learner is hooked up to an electrical shock apparatus. If the learner cannot remember the words, the teacher is to administer an electric shock. Unbeknownst to the teacher, the learner will only be acting as if he received the shocks.
- Each time the learner gets the answer wrong, the teacher is to increase the voltage on the electric shocks. Each switch appears to increase the voltage all the way up to a maximum of 450 volts.
- At the first shock, the learner protests. With each increase in voltage, the learner's response becomes stronger and stronger—he cries out, screams in pain, says his heart is bothering him, demands to leave the study, and eventually falls silent.
- If along the way the teacher becomes concerned about harming the learner, the psychologist-experimenter simply says either, "Please continue" or, "The experiment requires that you continue."

Now it is time to make a couple of predictions. First, what proportion of the volunteers do you think would follow directions and increase the voltage to the maximum 450-volt shock? In other words, if 100 people went through the study, how many do you think would give the full shock to the learner? Second, what type of person do you think would give the highest voltage shock?

Before the original experiments, a group of experts—psychiatrists and psychologists—estimated that only a small percentage of the population would obey the psychologist's instructions to continue with the experiment and administer the shocks. Further, they believed that anyone who did fully comply would have psychological problems; they would most likely be sadistic or antisocial people.

Now comes the big surprise: Almost everyone in Milgram's study—more than 75% of the participants—continued administering the shocks past the points where the participant screamed and begged to leave the study. Sixty-five percent continued to increase the shocks until they reached 450 volts—the highest amount possible.

Were these evil, sadistic individuals? Footage of this experiment shows the participants in great distress; they became very tense, and many of them tried to help the learner even as they continued to give the shocks. So why would they obey the authority?

You should notice that this study included a number of strong social cues. The experimenter was a scientist wearing a lab coat in his own lab; a figure of authority. Also, if the authority believed it was acceptable to continue, many of the participants felt that they could continue even though they did not want to. Milgram tested different variations of this experiment by having the experimenter wear street clothes instead of a lab coat or by having a second authority figure express concern for the leaner. Whenever the figure of authority was weakened, obedience was greatly reduced (Milgram, 1963, 1974; Miller, 1986). Social norms were also at work in the Milgram studies. When there were one or more confederates acting as a co-teacher, the participants tended to conform. When the co-teacher complied with the authority's request, 92.5% of the participants gave the highest possible shock; when two co-teachers refused to comply, only 10% gave the highest possible shock.

As with the Stanford Prison Study, for ethical reasons psychologists today would not conduct experiments such as the one described here. Also, much

The "shock generator" that the teacher operated to punish the learner.

The "learner" gets set up to participate in the experiment. He is being hooked up to the device that the teacher believes will deliver a shock.

The experimenter explains to the "teacher" what the experimental procedure entails and how to use the shock generator.

Although most subjects were highly obedient, some, such as this person, refused to continue complying with the experimenter's orders.

like the Stanford Prison Study, the results of Stanley Milgram's work continue to be discussed because they teach lessons about human behavior that should never be forgotten. Milgram designed these studies in an attempt to understand atrocities committed during the World War II. What might cause a normal, well-adjusted family man to become a torturer or murderer in a concentration camp? Although Milgram's laboratory experiment does not match the magnitude of those real-world events, one can draw parallels between them. Both situations have clear authority figures built into the social context, complete with uniforms (lab coat versus military) and official locations (university laboratory versus military camp). Social influences worked throughout both cases: In Milgram's studies, the scientist knew what to do; in World War II Germany, propaganda described Jews, intellectual dissidents, and homosexuals as the source of all the suffering in depression-era Germany. Finally, both situations involved social norms' influence, whether they were in the form of teachers or an entire army.

Quick Quiz 15.1b
Group Influence and Authority

KNOW...

1 _____ is complying with instructions from an individual who has authority.

   A Obedience

   B Groupthink

   C Conformity

   D Mimicry

UNDERSTAND...

2 Which of the following does not explain why social loafing may occur?

   A The individual believes that even if the group succeeds, there will be very little reward in it for each individual group member.

   B The individual believes that the group will fail no matter what his or her contribution is.

   C The individual believes that he or she has little to contribute to a group.

   D The other group members refuse to work with the individual.

3 Groupthink is *least* likely to occur when:

   A group members have very different sociopolitical values.

   B group members become excited about their progress.

   C a leader emerges who suppresses dissent.

   D the group refuses to consider alternatives.

APPLY...

4 While working on a group project in class, Dustin tries extra hard and volunteers to take on more work than the rest of the group. Based on this, fellow group members decide to slack off a little. Dustin is demonstrating _____, while his group is demonstrating _____.

   A social loafing; social facilitation

   B social facilitation; obedience

   C social facilitation; social loafing

   D obedience; social loafing

Answers can be found on page ANS-5.

Attitudes and Actions

Phrases such as "everyone is entitled to his or her own opinion" reflect the generally accepted belief that people form their own attitudes. Most of us like to think that we develop our own opinions and are largely free from bias. In reality, it is likely that we have a *bias blind spot*; in other words, we tend to be blind to social influences on our beliefs (Pronin et al., 2002). In some circumstances, however, just the opposite also occurs.

Social psychologists have developed some interesting research that shows how important groups are in forming our beliefs and opinions. Think about the roles of political labels on attitudes. Do you consider yourself liberal or conservative? Have you joined a political movement because you identify with all the beliefs of the group? Or could it be that membership in a political party shapes one's beliefs?

CONFORMING TO GROUP ATTITUDES   To answer these questions, researchers have tested attitude changes on fictional political issues, such as a proposed law to pay very generous unemployment benefits. When told the law was backed by Democrats, political conservatives denounced the proposal as too expensive, while the liberals supported it. When the experimenters presented the same proposal to participants as a Republican initiative, the conservatives were more approving, but liberals said that it did not pay enough. Thus researchers were able to demonstrate that individuals were responding not to the actual proposal (to pay an $800 monthly benefit) but rather to the political party that proposed it (Cohen, 2003).

These trends are also at work in nonfictional politics, of course, provided two conditions are met. First, the issue at hand needs to be highly identified with the group. It is not likely that the opinions of either liberals or conservatives would be affected if they were told a proposal was supported by their university's badminton club; welfare programs and badminton have little, if any, connection to each other in most people's minds. However, there are clear differences in how the two political parties treat social programs. Second, there must be some ambiguity in the issue. If the proposal is very clear—such as a complete ban on abortion or capital punishment—then the party label will have little influence. In fact, those issues are what lead many individuals to their party choice. By comparison, issues such as the exact amount of welfare payments are beyond what most voters concern themselves with, so they turn to the party for guidance.

GROUP POLARIZATION Sometimes groups affect attitudes through direct means, such as informing their members what the official party line is on issues such as abortion and stem-cell research. At other times, dynamic effects of group membership intensify members' attitudes, thereby increasing the differences between groups. **Group polarization** *occurs when members of a group discuss characteristic attitudes of their group and, as a result, their views become stronger.* When this happens in two competing groups, their opinions become polarized, meaning that the two groups become further apart in their opinions (see Figure 15.2).

To see how this effect works, imagine students from the Young Republicans and College Democrats met to discuss a campus issue, such as the role of ethnicity in college admissions. If you were to administer an attitude scale before the discussion, you would likely find that the two groups differ somewhat. If you administered the scale again after the discussion, you might find that the two groups had moved even further apart, with each group become more extreme in its position. Although the effect of group polarization seems to fade away after a discussion, the effect is very predictable and has been found in a number of experiments (Isenberg, 1986; Liu & Latané, 1998).

Why do groups become polarized? Several forces appear to be at work within a group, beginning with the simple fact that in group discussions, individuals hear the group's position articulated over and over again (Brauer et al., 1995). In the process, individuals are likely to hear more and more of the arguments for their position, but will probably encounter no support and certainly arguments against the other position. In a few cases, polarization may occur because the individuals want to identify closely with their group, almost as if it were a competition to be the most "group-like" individual in the discussion (Krizan & Baron, 2007).

COGNITIVE DISSONANCE Our actions, beliefs, and attitudes are not independent entities. Rather, they are dynamically related. Sometimes a state of tension can exist between two thoughts or beliefs. For example someone who spends years pursuing admission into law school, only to be rejected, will experience tension between his goals and the reality of the situation. He may, in turn minimize the importance of becoming a lawyer— thereby reducing the tension—by claiming "there are too many of them anyway." This is an example of **cognitive dissonance**, *which occurs when an individual has two thoughts (cognitions) that are inconsistent with each other (dissonance) and, as a result, experiences motivation to reduce the discrepancy.* As in the example above, cognitive dissonance brings about tension. Although this tension will be greater for some people than others, and greater in some situations than others, the key point is that it provides motivation for an individual to reduce the cognitive dissonance either by changing a behavior or changing an attitude. The psychological study of cognitive dissonance can be traced back to a fascinating, true story described by Leon Festinger and colleagues (1956).

Marian Keech, a stay-at-home mother in Chicago, experienced a number of premonitions she described as secret messages from the planet Clarion. The beings from Clarion were trying to warn her of impending doom; apparently there was to be a huge flood on December 21, 1954, that would wipe out life on Earth. Convinced of the validity of this prophecy,

Before a medical marijuana debate:

After debate:

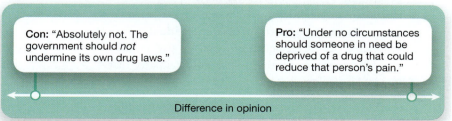

{FIG. 15.2} **Group Polarization** Imagine a formal debate on a topic such as the legalization of marijuana for medical purposes. Over the course of a debate, members of the two sides tend to become more distinct or polarized in their opinions—a process known as *group polarization*.

Mrs. Keech and her followers gave away their possessions, quit their jobs, and made other preparations for the coming event. If they listened to the Clarions, they would be contacted at midnight on the eve of the disaster, then whisked away in a spaceship and saved from the peril that lay ahead.

On the night of December 20, the group members gathered to wait for contact from an alien. As the clock reached 5 minutes after midnight, the group members agreed that the clock was probably about 10 minutes fast. The true time, they claimed, was 5 until midnight. Another 5 minutes passed without contact. An hour passed, and another, and another.

Finally, at 4:45 A.M., there had been no contact from Clarion, no spaceship, and no signs of rain or flooding. Faced with that kind of evidence, you might expect that Mrs. Keech and her followers would return to their normal lives, perhaps a bit embarrassed. To the contrary, Mrs. Keech had another revelation. God had been so moved by their efforts that He decided to spare them and called off the flood. What seemed to be irrefutable evidence against the group's belief was the very information they believed proved they were right.

When their prediction failed, there was tension between the knowledge that they had invested so much in the prophecy and yet the prophecy was not correct. Mrs. Keech and many of her followers reduced the cognitive dissonance through *justification of effort*, telling themselves that their efforts were justified because those efforts prevented the flood. This story might remind you of a more recent event, in which Harold Camping, a self-styled prophet, predicted a world-ending, 5-month-long rapture to commence on May 21, 2011. Faced with contrary evidence as that day came to a close, Camping deemed it an "invisible judgment day" and revised his prediction to a single, all-out doomsday scheduled for October 21, 2011. (Note: This text went to press before this date, so if you are reading these words, it appears Mr. Camping was wrong again.)

Consider another example to see how cognitive dissonance might work: A boy in a convenience store wants a pack of gum but has no money to purchase it. He notices the clerk is busy with other customers, so he decides to slip the gum into his pocket. Two thoughts occur nearly simultaneously: *I am stealing the gum* and *stealing is wrong*. These two thoughts are at odds with each other, and the dissonance creates tension. What can the boy do? One way to reduce the dissonance is to change the behavior and return the gum. Then, the boy would think *Stealing is wrong*, and *That is why I put the gum back*. The dissonance—and the tension it causes—is gone. But what

Attitudes
Concern for the elderly
Social justice

Actions
Volunteering at a nursing home
Donating to famine relief

{FIG. 15.3} **The Circle of Attitudes and Actions** We all know that attitudes can affect our behaviors, but did you know that your behavior can change your attitude?

often happens is that the attitude changes. In this case, the boy might change his thoughts about stealing by thinking *It is only a few cents so it won't affect this big company* or *Other kids in my neighborhood steal candy from here all the time*. This transformation explains why cognitive dissonance is so important to the study of attitudes. The boy's attitude toward stealing loses some of its negativity ("It is not *that* bad") and the behavior stays the same (Gosling at al., 2006; McKimmie et al., 2009). Thus it is not always the attitude that affects the behavior; sometimes the behavior can affect the attitude (see Figure 15.3).

There are a number of ways that cognitive dissonance reduction can affect attitudes. In the shoplifting example, the boy resorted to *trivializing* by telling himself that the action was not significant enough to cause concern. In other cases, an individual may completely change his or her attitude to avoid tension. In addition, we have all probably engaged in *denial of responsibility* at one point or another. This effect occurs when an individual maintains the same attitude about the action, but changes his belief about his own role in the action, saying *I had no choice* or *I was forced to do it* (Gosling et al., 2006).

WORKING THE SCIENTIFIC LITERACY MODEL
Two-Step Persuasion Techniques

The study of social influence clearly shows that our behaviors are flexible and can change to fit the social environment. It follows that these processes can in turn be used as tools for persuasion.

What do we know about persuasion?

The simplest way to demonstrate persuasion through social influence is through an old salesperson's trick called the **foot-in-the-door technique**, *which involves making a*

"Would you you sign a petition for this cause?" "Sure!"

"Could you also give an hour of your time to volunteer for the cause?"

"Would you be willing to volunteer four days each week to help our cause?"

"Well, how about just spending an hour with us this Saturday afternoon?"

{FIG. 15.4} **Two-Step Persuasion Techniques to Encourage Community Service** The foot-in-the-door technique (top) starts with a small request and then moves on to a larger request. The door-in-the-face technique (bottom) does the reverse. It begins with a highly demanding request and then appears to settle for a much smaller one.

simple request followed by a more substantial request. To the traveling salesmen of a few decades ago, literally getting one's foot in the door meant that a homeowner could not shut you out. In social psychology, it may involve any request for something simple—which is the metaphorical foot in the door—followed by a more substantial request (Burger, 1999; Cialdini, 2000).

To see this technique in action, refer to Figure 15.4. If we asked individuals to commit to an hour at a fundraising booth, we might be frustrated with the results. But if we ask someone for a very small commitment—perhaps just signing a petition—it likely will be easier to convince that person to come back for a full hour later.

Taking an opposite approach to persuasion, the **door-in-the-face technique** *begins with a large request that is likely to be turned down, followed by a smaller request that is likely to be accepted.* Rather than asking someone to volunteer an hour of her time, ask her for a huge commitment—perhaps volunteering four days every week. The individual is likely to

say no, but when given the chance to sign up for a more reasonable amount of time, she may feel relieved and jump at the chance.

How can science explain persuasion?

These techniques belong to a family of methods that involve a two-step sequence of requests. They may sound very simple, but they clearly work when applied correctly. Researchers have examined dozens of studies on these techniques and found that they are highly effective and reliable (Beaman, 1983; Dillard et al., 1984; Pascual & Guéguen, 2005). But the question remains: Why do they work?

Psychologist Robert Cialdini argues that these techniques work best when the individual is operating mindlessly—that is, without thinking carefully (Cialdini & Goldstein, 2004). Several reasons explain why this might be the case. One possibility is that the first step in the request depletes individuals' desire or ability to intentionally control their behavior so that they find it harder to resist requests. Imagine that your self-control is a form of energy. In the first step of the process, you have to expend some of that energy in saying "no" (for the door-in-the-face technique) or by some activity if you answer "yes" (for the foot-in-the-door technique). If the second request follows quickly, you have not had time to refuel your self-control; thus you are more likely to comply with the second request.

To test this hypothesis with the foot-in-the-door technique, researchers randomly assigned volunteers to two groups: One group completed a questionnaire about dietary habits while the other did not. The research team measured the depletion of self-control by having the volunteers complete a second task in which they had to come up with arguments for something they did not believe in (a tuition increase). The members of the group that had completed the initial questionnaire apparently had depleted their self-regulatory energy—they produced significantly fewer arguments than the control group. Sure enough, they were also more likely to comply with an additional request to keep a food diary for two weeks (Fennis, et al., 2009).

Can we critically evaluate this evidence?

The research shows that two-step compliance techniques really work, but what are their limitations? It is doubtful that you could use these techniques to persuade individuals to behave in a way they normally would not. For example, no amount of foot-in-the-door manipulations would convince an innocent person to rob a bank. Furthermore, these techniques probably have limited effects when other paths of influence are in place. In other words, a boss might be able to lure a new employee to work overtime, but the employee may not be able to get a paid vacation from the boss.

Why is this relevant?

These two-step techniques can be applied to a number of situations. Cialdini and his colleagues showed that the foot-in-the-door technique could be used to recruit volunteers to work with juvenile delinquents (Cialdini et al., 1975), while other researchers were able to bolster support for a canned food drive (Burger & Caldwell, 2003) and a center for disabled children (Davis & Knowles, 1999) by making sequential requests.

CENTRAL AND PERIPHERAL ROUTES TO COMPLIANCE
The foot-in-the-door and door-in-the-face techniques may sound like little more than trickery, even if they are both scientifically validated techniques. Whatever happened to persuading people by explaining the facts? Researchers have asked that very question and, in the process, they have discovered that there are two paths to persuasion (Cacioppo et al., 1986; Petty et al., 1997). As Figure 15.5 shows, you can take the **central route (to persuasion)** *in which individuals take time, evaluate evidence, and use valid logic and arguments.* We like to think that most of our attitudes and beliefs are arrived at through the central route. In reality, though, we arrive at many of our beliefs through the persuasion techniques described above. These make up the **peripheral route (to persuasion)**, *in which quick judgments are made based on limited evidence, and emotions and vague impressions are used more than logic.*

How do you know which path to take? Generally, when people believe a topic is very important and when they have time to make decisions, the central route is more persuasive. Because this route involves more

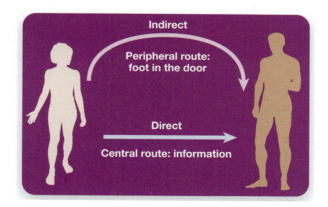

{FIG. 15.5} **Central and Peripheral Routes to Persuasion** There are two ways to persuade people. The central route provides information, while the peripheral route uses social psychological techniques such as the foot-in-the-door method to influence attitudes and behavior. **Click on this figure in your eText to see more details.**

reasoning, it appeals to those with high intelligence and those who like to think about and solve problems. When topics that are less important to an individual and decisions are likely to be made quickly, the peripheral route may be more persuasive.

Those who work in marketing, advertising, political campaigning, and public relations are constantly developing and implementing persuasion strategies. A first step is to identify the degree to which the message should be central or peripheral. In many cases, individuals who have little evidence to support their claim can encourage others to use peripheral processing by increasing emotional appeals and urging quick judgments. Anyone with a television is sure to have encountered the "act now" technique, which encourages individuals to act quickly without further deliberation. Although it does not affect everyone it reaches, this method is effective in swaying those who are close to purchasing a product to follow through. Similarly, messages that play on fear can overpower messages that are based solely on rational evidence, provided that the warnings seem like real threats (Nabi, 2002).

Quick Quiz 15.1c :: Attitudes and Actions

KNOW…

1 We tend to think of our beliefs as being our own, and as being immune to group influences. This phenomenon is known as _____.

- **A** groupthink
- **B** the bias blind spot
- **C** social facilitation
- **D** self determinism

2 _____ occurs when an individual has two thoughts that are inconsistent with each other, creating a motivation to reduce the discrepancy.

- **A** Groupthink
- **B** Social facilitation
- **C** Cognitive dissonance
- **D** Obedience

UNDERSTAND…

3 What makes the central route to persuasion distinct from the peripheral route?

- **A** The central route relies on information and evaluation of options, whereas the peripheral route is based on intuition and quick decisions.
- **B** The central route is based on reinforcement, whereas the peripheral route is based on punishment.
- **C** The peripheral route takes longer than the peripheral route.
- **D** The central route is based on intuition and quick decisions, whereas the peripheral route relies on information and evaluation of options.

4 Sequential persuasion techniques like the foot-in-the-door technique may work because they:

- **A** rely on authority figures.
- **B** wear down one's sense of self-control or self-regulation.
- **C** rely on deception.
- **D** offer no alternatives.

APPLY…

5 Greg asked you to sign a petition for his student fundraising group. After he gets your signature, he asks you for a small donation. Which technique does Greg seem to be using?

- **A** Foot-in-the-door
- **B** Central route
- **C** Door-in-the-face
- **D** None of the above

Answers can be found on page ANS-5.

Module Summary

Now that you have read this module
you should:

((•━┤ **Listen** to
the audio file of
this module at
MyPsychLab

KNOW ...

● *The key terminology associated with social influence:*

central route (to persuasion)
  (p. 561)
cognitive dissonance (p. 558)
conformity (p. 552)
door-in-the-face technique (p. 560)
foot-in-the-door technique (p. 559)
group polarization (p. 558)
groupthink (p. 555)
mimicry (p. 552)

obedience (p. 555)
peripheral route (to persuasion)
  (p. 561)
social facilitation (p. 554)
social loafing (p. 554)
social norms (p. 551)
social psychology (p. 551)
social roles (p. 551)

UNDERSTAND ...

● *Why individuals conform to others' behaviors and thoughts.* At its most basic level, conforming begins with mimicry, in which people simply imitate others' behaviors. Mimicry seems to help form social bonds and encourages prosocial behavior. Conformity usually describes the way an individual's more complex beliefs and behaviors evolve to become like the group's. This change often happens unconsciously; in fact, we are said to have a bias blind spot that prevents us from seeing how our beliefs are shaped by group membership.

● *How individuals and groups can influence attitudes and behaviors.* In addition to conformity, attitudes and behaviors can be changed through persuasion techniques. The two-step procedures of the foot-in-the-door and door-in-the-face techniques are applied by an individual who is intending to persuade or convince another person. In addition, unintentional phenomena exist. For example, in groupthink, the excitement of a group's progress leads individuals to think alike and to be overconfident in their group's decisions.

APPLY ...

● *Your knowledge of cognitive dissonance to see how well your beliefs match your behaviors.* Complete the questionnaire in **Table 15.3** to begin this process.

ANALYZE ...

● *Whether guards who participate in abuse are inherently bad people, or if their behavior is the product of social influences.* The evidence from social psychological research clearly shows that individuals can change their behaviors drastically to fit a role, to comply with what the rest of the group is doing, and to follow instructions from authority figures. When all of these social influences are in play, it would not be at all unusual for a person to behave much differently—even more cruelly— than the individual ever believed he or she could.

Table 15.3 :: Attitudes Scale
Rate the following items on a scale from 1 (strongly disagree) to 5 (strongly agree).

A1. World hunger is a serious problem that needs attention.	1 2 3 4 5
A2. Our country needs to address the growing number of homeless.	1 2 3 4 5
A3. The right to vote is one of the most valuable rights of American citizens.	1 2 3 4 5
A4. Our government should pay more attention to how its citizens want their taxes to be spent.	1 2 3 4 5
Total points for A1 to A4:	

Next rate whether you perform the following behavior on a *regular* basis using a scale of 1 (never) to 5 (on a regular and frequent basis).

B1. Do you personally do anything to lessen world hunger (e.g., donate food or money, volunteer time, write your representative)?	1 2 3 4 5
B2. Do you personally do anything to help the homeless?	1 2 3 4 5
B3. Did you vote in the most recent elections for which you were eligible to do so, including city and county elections?	1 2 3 4 5
B4. Do you personally convey your feelings to the government (e.g., write your representatives or participate in protests)?	1 2 3 4 5
Total points for B1 to B4:	

Now subtract your B score from your A score. Approximately 99% of people have a positive score, which indicates that their behavior does not exactly match their ideals. If you are like most people, your behaviors come up short and you likely feel cognitive dissonance; the larger the number, the more dissonance you should feel. Thus you should feel compelled to explain why the numbers are so different—maybe you have some very good reasons. These explanations should help you reduce the cognitive dissonance.

Source: Adapted from Carkenord & Bullington, 1993.

Social Cognition

Learning Objectives

After reading this module you should:

KNOW ...	UNDERSTAND ...	APPLY ...	ANALYZE ...
The key terminology associated with social cognition	How we form first impressions and how these impressions influence us	Your understanding of the different ways we explain our own behavior versus the behavior of others	The common belief that stereotypes can only be derogatory

One February night in 1999, four New York City plainclothes police officers were patrolling a Bronx neighborhood in search of a rape suspect when they saw a lone man walking down the street. The officers thought he was behaving suspiciously, so they decided to question him. Upon orders from the police to stop, the man ducked into the vestibule of an apartment building, reaching for the door with one hand and putting the other into his pocket. Officers feared he was reaching for a gun. One officer opened fire on the man, and the other three followed, firing a total of 41 shots, 19 of which hit the man and killed him on the spot.

Tragically, the victim of the shooting was a peaceful and unarmed 24-year-old man named Amadou Diallo. By all accounts, Diallo was a friendly, industrious, and law-abiding man from Guinea, West Africa, who had come to New York in hopes of attaining a college education. How could such a horrible fate happen to an innocent man?

Much of New York was in an uproar over the shooting, and the turmoil was only heightened after the four police officers were found not guilty of any criminal wrongdoing in court. Half of all New Yorkers disagreed with the verdict, and that figure reached almost 80% among Africans and African Americans (Connelly, 2000). People of all backgrounds attributed the shooting to hostile prejudice. Fellow police officers defended their colleagues, even if they did not witness the scene, blaming the stressful environment in which they work. Obviously, this was a tragic event for the Diallo family and friends. Events like these raise some important questions.

Focus Questions

 Which processes make it possible for people to form such quick impressions—right or wrong—of others?

 The officers denied that race played a role in the killing of Amadou Diallo, but is it possible that Diallo's race could have affected the officers' reactions *without* their knowledge?

This module focuses on a combination of the social and cognitive perspectives called *social-cognitive psychology.* This field includes the *cognitions* (perceptions, thoughts, and beliefs) an individual may have about *social contexts* (other people, groups, or situations). The many different social contexts we encounter makes for an enormous diversity of experiences, so it makes for an exciting area to study.

To understand social-cognitive research, it is important to begin with the theory that there are two varieties of thought. **Intuitive thought** is *quick, effortless, automatic thinking* (in fact, it requires great effort when you try to control it). Intuitions tend to be based on associations; an individual encounters a person or situation and some things just "pop" into mind. **Deliberative thought** is *a more careful, effortful and rational process.* In other words, it is slower, requires some effort, and usually takes place one step at a time (Chaiken & Trope, 1999; Kahneman, 2003; Todorov et al., 2005).

Intuitive thinking precedes deliberation. Consider a situation in which a person is trying to control his temper at work because he feels he is the only person doing his job. What happens when this man discovers a co-worker got promoted before him? His intuitive thought—that automatic impulse—might be that he is justified in yelling at the boss and insulting the co-worker. His intuitive thought may very well be correct that he should be angry, but then deliberative thought begins. This type of thought reminds him that what he says and does will eventually mean keeping or losing his job. If he goes overboard, he might just get fired.

The distinction between intuitive and deliberate thought has had quite an impact on social-cognitive research: Imagine if instead of a man angry about his role in the workplace, we are talking about police officers on patrol. Which automatic, intuitive thoughts might they have when they encounter a man on a dark street? Will they have time for deliberative thought before they act? As we will see in this module, intuitive and deliberative thought processes can be applied to topics ranging from one's first impression of a person to stereotypes about entire groups of individuals.

Person Perception

Person perception *refers to the processes by which individuals form judgments and categorize other people* (Kenny, 2004). It begins immediately in our social encounters, and is guided by our past experiences with others. The power of first impressions can be explained by the automatic side of social cognition. Upon first encountering someone, we have very little information on which to evaluate him or her. As a consequence, we rely on **schemas**—*clusters of knowledge and expectations about individuals and groups* (schemas were also covered in Module 7.3). The person's gender, race, and style of dress all activate schemas, and these schemas bring certain traits to mind automatically.

THIN SLICES OF BEHAVIOR Two remarkable aspects of first impressions are how fast they are formed and how accurate they can be. Imagine this scenario: You walk into a classroom for a review session for the final exam. After 30 seconds, you realize that you are

Based on these photos, which instructor would you anticipate is interesting or boring? Easy or challenging? Thin-slices research tells us that it takes less than 30 seconds of video to decide—and to be reasonably accurate.

early, and the previous class has not yet been dismissed. Nonetheless, in the 30 seconds that elapsed you have already had time to size up the professor; she has made her first impression on you. As she leaves the classroom, a student assistant announces that he will be distributing course evaluation forms. As the forms are passed down the aisle, you take one. Of course, you will not fill it out—that would be dishonest. But what if you did?

This very quick way of assessing individuals has been researched through a technique called **thin slices**—*basing judgments of others on very limited information*. In studies of this process a researcher might present very short video clips or even a still photo of an individual—these are the "thin slices" of behavior that participants use to make judgments of personal qualities. These judgments can be compared to the judgments made by others who have much more information—either because they saw more of the video or, in our example, because they attended the course for an entire semester.

Using the thin-slices method, researchers found that participants who watched 30 seconds of a college lecture (without sound) gave instructor ratings that were remarkably similar to the end-of-semester ratings of that same class (Ambady & Rosenthal, 1993; Tom et al., 2010). Additional research has shown even higher levels of agreement when rating high school teachers and using even thinner slices—even as short as 6 seconds!

Thin-slices research tells us that we are very quick to size people up, even if the only information comes

According to research on thin slices, our perceptions of others are formed immediately and with only physical appearance as a source of information. It turns out that our initial perceptions can be quite accurate. We have a strong tendency to judge personality characteristics based on physical appearances.

from snippets of overheard conversations (Holleran et al., 2009; Mehl et al., 2006). You may find it surprising that we make judgments of trustworthiness, competence, likeability, and aggressiveness in as little as half a second of exposure to a photograph (Willis & Todorov, 2006). Further exposure to a face does not change ratings much, although it does have the tendency to increase the judges' confidence in their ratings. In other words, the impression is more or less the same, but the judges feel they have more reason to believe it.

Taken together, thin-slice research demonstrates just how quickly impressions are formed. The process of person perception upon first encountering someone often yields accurate information about what he or she is like—but, of course, first impressions are not always the most reliable. Furthermore, relying too much on information from first impressions can affect how relationships develop.

SELF-FULFILLING PROPHECIES AND OTHER EFFECTS OF FIRST IMPRESSIONS First impressions certainly produce quick and long-lasting effects on how we perceive others, but their biggest impact comes from how they shape our social behaviors. Researchers have linked some very simple cues, such as facial appearance, to everything from how a jury treats a defendant to how people will vote. For example, one study asked participants to act as jurors and evaluate evidence against a defendant. These participants were less likely to find a defendant guilty when shown a photograph of a person who simply appeared more trustworthy (Porter et al., 2010). Participants in another study made judgments about the competence of congressional candidates just by looking at their faces, and those judgments predicted a surprisingly high 70% of the election outcomes (Todorov et al., 2005).

An individual's impression of others can also lead to a **self-fulfilling prophecy**, *which occurs when a first impression affects the observer's behavior and, as a result, the first impression comes true*. In fact, this phenomenon has been under scientific investigation for a long time in the context of teacher–student interactions. When teachers have high expectations of a student, they behave differently toward that student: Teachers will tend to spend less time addressing behavior (especially for boys), present more challenging work, and give more reinforcement and constructive criticism than they will for a student whom they perceive to have less promise (Jussim, 1986). This finding holds true whether the teachers form their own expectations about a student or researchers give teachers randomly assigned high or low achievement test scores for the students (Brophy & Good, 1970; Rosenthal & Jacobson, 1968). The self-fulfilling prophecy is complete when students with low expectations placed on them receive lower grades from their teachers and lower scores on standardized tests because of this differential treatment.

Fortunately, the fact that self-fulfilling prophecies sometimes come true does not mean we are destined to fulfill them. In reviewing the research, psychologists have identified several variables that can reduce the effects of self-fulfilling prophecies, including grade level (older student are less susceptible) and familiarity (being in a familiar setting also reduces the effects). In addition, some evidence suggests that, in the classroom setting, teachers' perceptions are often correlated with performance because they are accurate perceptions, not because of the self-fulfilling prophecy. Moreover, when researchers have observed the self-fulfilling prophecy, it tends to have a small to moderate effect (Jussim & Harber, 2005).

ATTRIBUTIONS   In some sense, all people are armchair psychologists, describing and explaining behavior in an intuitive and unscientific way. It turns out that people value the *reason* for someone's behavior more than the behavior itself. For example, if someone steps on your toe by accident, you would probably be more likely to forgive him than if he did it on purpose.

Attributions are the explanations we make about the causes of behavior. Much in the same way that first impressions tend to be automatic judgments about personal qualities, attributions tend to start out as automatic, intuitive explanations. Think about what might happen in a close call while driving: As you drive alone, a car suddenly swerves in front of you, requiring you to slam on the brakes and turn the wheel sharply. Quick—what is the first thing that comes to mind about the other driver? That is how quickly most attributions are initially formed.

To shed light on how attributions work, psychologists distinguish two main types. First, with an **internal attribution** (also known as a dispositional attribution), *the observer explains the actor's behavior as due to some intrinsic quality of the actor:* He is lazy, she wants attention, and so on (see Figure 15.6). Second, with an **external attribution** (also known as a situational attribution), *the observer explains the actor's behavior as the result of the social context* (Heider, 1958).

Truthfully, most behaviors are a complex blend of disposition *and* situation; nonetheless, we have clear biases in the type of attribution we use when we explain why others behave as they do. Specifically, we often commit the **fundamental attribution error**—*a tendency to make internal attributions for others' behaviors while ignoring external influences* (Ross, 1977).

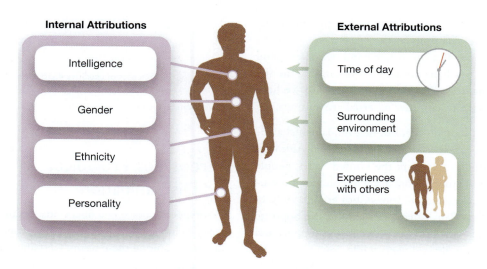

{FIG. 15.6}   **Internal and External Attributions**   Internal attributions are based on qualities or actions of the individual, whereas external attributions focus on the context in which the individual is situated. **Click on this figure in your eText to see more details.**

Think about that driver swerving in traffic. Which kind of personal qualities would correspond to bad driving? He must be selfish, hostile, or severely lacking in intelligence. These are all internal, dispositional qualities and they *might* be true, but they might not. But did you even consider external causes—perhaps a blown-out tire? Most often we will not, unless we actually take the time to make a more thoughtful attribution.

When explaining our own behavior, our attributions are much more generous. For example, if we swerve into the adjacent lane while driving, we are likely to blame an object in the road or someone else recklessly trying to merge onto the highway. These kinds of external attributions prevent us from putting the blame on ourselves, a phenomenon known as the **self-serving bias**: *We will use internal attributions for ourselves when we do something well, but external attributions when we fail or commit errors.* If we successfully avoid an accident, we are likely to credit it to our alertness and driving skill—both internal, dispositional attributions that led to a successful outcome.

There is a distinct asymmetry to these biases. People tend to explain others' behavior in terms of internal attributions, but explain their own behavior based on which type—internal or external—makes them feel good about themselves. Individuals with severe forms of depression and anxiety appear much less susceptible to the self-serving bias—by perhaps as much as 50% (Mezulis et al., 2004). Thus the self-serving bias might actually reduce our chances for psychological distress. Of course, other factors probably contribute to these biases as well. For example, it could be a simple matter of time: On the one hand, we watch others' actions as they occur, so we make quick judgments. On the other hand, we may spend time planning our behavior and understanding the situational events that led up to our actions, so we have much more time to consider external attributions.

Finally, we should point out that fundamental attribution error is largely a cultural phenomenon. Although it is easy to find examples in the United States, people from East Asia are much more likely to consider the situation when making attributions (Choi et al., 1999). In fact, people from Japan may even exhibit the opposite trend: They may attribute successes to the support and assistance from family and peers while downplaying the role of personality, intelligence, or talent (Akimoto & Sanbonmatsu, 1999).

PsychTutor
Click here in your eText for an interactive tutorial on **Attribution Theory**

Quick Quiz 15.2a
Person Perception

KNOW…

1 _____ is very quick, effortless, and automatic, whereas _____ is a more careful and effortful process.

A Deliberative thought; intuitive thought

B Intuitive thought; deliberative thought

C Internal attribution; external attribution

D External attribution; internal attribution

2 Which of the following best defines person perception?

A A broad field of study that includes how individuals perceive and think about other people, as well as how the presence of other people can influence individuals' behaviors

B The processes by which individuals form judgments and categorize other people

C An attribution where the observer explains the actor's behavior as the result of the social context

D Clusters of knowledge and expectations about individuals and groups

UNDERSTAND…

3 Which of the following statements about thin slices is most accurate?

A Thin slices lead to inaccurate impressions of others.

B In many instances, lasting and often accurate impressions of others form in just a few moments.

C Thin-slice impressions are 100% accurate.

D Thin slices work only when rating the attractiveness of others.

APPLY…

4 Donald, once poor, inherited $5 million and decided to donate $1,000 to a local charity. Donald believes he took this step because he is a kind and generous man. Donald might be demonstrating _____.

A the fundamental attribution error

B hindsight bias

C self-serving bias

D concepts of cognitive dissonance

Answers can be found on page ANS-5.

Stereotypes, Prejudice, and Discrimination

Stereotypes, prejudice, and discrimination are hot topics in social psychology. At first glance, many people fail to make distinctions among these terms. Certainly they all go together, but they represent different concepts. A **stereotype** *is a set of beliefs about a group of people*; as a combination of ideas and opinions, stereotypes may be viewed as a type of schema. With stereotypes in place, individuals are likely to experience **prejudice**, *an attitude based on stereotypes that includes emotions and value judgments as well*. Finally, **discrimination** *is a behavior based on prejudice.*

There are some parallels between stereotypes and attributions. For example, you can probably identify a rival high school or college sports team. The other team would be considered the **outgroup**—*a collection of people who are perceived as different*. The outgroup does not have to be disliked or in competition with your own group; just the perception of difference is enough to make the distinction between groups. Your own classmates, who make up your *ingroup*, are perceived as having more positive qualities. Thus there is a similarity between the self-serving bias and what we call the **ingroup bias**, *which occurs when we attribute positive qualities to the social group we belong to*.

Given the pervasive nature of prejudice and the profound consequences it can have, it is important to have a thorough understanding of ways to identify and measure prejudice and its social and cognitive origins.

MYTHS IN MIND
All Stereotypes Are Based on Negative Characteristics

The first examples that come to mind when stereotyping a group are usually based on negative characteristics. However, a hidden danger of stereotypes is found in benevolent or "well-intentioned" stereotyping, and it has been studied a great deal with regard to sexism. For example, researchers have distinguished between *hostile sexism*, or stereotypes that have negative views of one or both sexes, and *benevolent sexism*, which includes positive views of one or both sexes (Glick & Fiske, 1996, 2001). To examine this concept in the social context, consider the somewhat dated saying that women are "the fairer sex." A person using this phrase may mean it as a compliment, implying that women are virtuous and empathetic. As a number of psychologists have pointed out, even well-intended stereotypes can place restrictions on an individual's behavior. By considering them to be "virtuous," women may be held to different sexual standards than men, and, as a result, may be seen as dependent on men for money or protection. Further, women may be hindered in careers that call for assertive and sometimes aggressive behaviors (such as running a major corporation or working in front-line law enforcement) because the "fairer sex" stereotype is pervasive in the organization (Glick & Fiske, 1996, 2001). Thus negative effects of stereotyping can occur even when the intentions of an individual may have been complimentary.

• • • • • • • • • • • • • • • • • •

SOCIAL TRENDS IN STEREOTYPES AND PREJUDICE Everyone is familiar with the legacy of racial prejudice in the United States. Arguments over the legitimacy of slavery are 150 years in the past and it has been decades since public schools were integrated, yet racial prejudice remains a major concern among all demographic groups in this country (Jones, 2008). The emphasis on race has also increased our awareness of other forms of stereotyping. For example, psychologists have researched stereotypes and prejudice related to weight and body size, sexual orientation, and religious affiliation.

Racial, ethnic, and other outgroup stereotypes are pervasive and, unfortunately, seem to thrive in times of hardship. **Scapegoating** *occurs when people use stereotypes to misplace and exaggerate blame on others*. For example, during economic slumps, an outgroup is often targeted for taking jobs from the ingroup or for draining resources from the local economy. In general, people tend to overvalue the qualities of their ingroup and undervalue the qualities of other groups (Cialdini & Richardson, 1980).

Caucasian people in the United States are increasingly concerned about whether they appear prejudiced (Plant et al., 2010) and are more likely than ever to say that racism is a problem (Jones, 2008). Today young African Americans and Latinos are more likely to obtain diplomas and higher education degrees than even a generation ago. They are also expected to live longer than the preceding generations and are more likely to achieve middle-class socioeconomic status, such as a comfortable income and home ownership. Despite the positive message that these trends send, racial and ethnic differences persist in the United States. For example, Africans and African Americans experience more physical and aggressive treatment from police (Smith, 2004).

Even among those who publicly denounce prejudice and discrimination, there are some who may be trying to disguise their true feelings and still others who are unaware of their own subtle prejudices. For example, researchers have found subtle but very reliable differences in facial expressions and brain activity when participants (both Black and White) looked at Black versus White faces, even among those who express little or no prejudice (Cunningham et al., 2004; Eberhardt, 2005; Vanman et al., 2004). Consistent with research on thin slices, Black participants could also identify which White actors in a silent videotape were more prejudiced than others—after only 20 seconds of viewing (Richeson & Shelton, 2005)!

Records of police encounters over the past 30 years confirm what many minorities in the United States have

PsychTutor
Click here in your eText for an interactive tutorial on **Prejudice vs. Discrimination**

long claimed: Police use more aggressive techniques on minority suspects than White suspects (Inn, Wheeler, & Sparling, 1977; Smith, 2004; Weitzer & Tuch, 2004). In fact, Black suspects have historically been five times more likely to die in police confrontations than White suspects (Department of Justice, 2001).

The lesson should be a powerful one: Even if one abhors prejudice, he or she may implicitly hold the stereotypes that lead to prejudice and discrimination. As research with police shooting shows, it is important to acknowledge implicit stereotypes and automatic judgments, because otherwise the results may be tragic.

WORKING THE SCIENTIFIC LITERACY MODEL
Explicit Versus Implicit Measures of Prejudice

Research has left us with a contradiction: Public opinion says that prejudice is unpopular, yet social scientists and psychologists have produced data demonstrating it occurs quite frequently. How could this be?

What do we know about measuring prejudice?

One explanation is that members of the public have simply learned to conceal their prejudice to be polite or politically correct. Another intriguing possibility is that some people are deceiving themselves; perhaps they harbor prejudice but do not realize it. Is that even possible? To address this question, psychologists have distinguished between measures of explicit and implicit prejudice. **Explicit prejudice** *occurs when individuals confess to or openly demonstrate their stereotypes.* **Implicit prejudice** *includes forms of stereotyping and prejudice that are kept silent, either intentionally or because individuals are unaware of their own prejudices* (Greenwald & Banaji, 1995; Nosek, 2007). The methods of measuring implicit prejudice are trickier, yet psychologists can infer that it exists based on the research cited earlier.

How can science study implicit prejudice?

One means of measuring implicit prejudice is the *Implicit Associations Test* (IAT; Greenwald et al., 1998). The IAT measures how fast people can respond to images or words flashed on a computer screen. To complete the test, a person uses two fingers and two computer buttons. As Figure 15.7 shows, one button represents two ideas—that is where the associations come into play. In round 1, if the computer presents a Caucasian face, the subject should press the button on the right. If the subject sees a positive word, such as "peace," he should press the same button. In other words, Caucasian features and pleasant words are paired on one button. The other button pairs Black individuals with negative words. With these associations, it takes an average of 800 milliseconds (four-fifths of a second) to press the correct button.

Round 2 rearranges the associations. If the participant sees a White person, he is still supposed to press the right button, but this time he also uses that button for negative words, such as "pain" or "war." If the computer presents a Black person or a positive word, such as "peace," the subject is to press the left button. In this situation, subjects took 1,015 milliseconds to press the correct button, or more than one-fifth of a second longer than in round 1.

Why does it take longer to respond when there is a Black/positive button than when there is a Black/negative button? The researchers reasoned that our racial schemas associate more negativity with Blacks than with Whites. Thus, even if those associations are *implicit*—in other words, the individual is not aware of those associations—they still affect the participants' responses.

Can we critically evaluate this evidence?

Although the data gathered with this instrument show *reliable* results, some psychologists have questioned the test's validity: Is the IAT really a measure of prejudice? Its developers point to the repeated findings that show consistent trends indicating favoritism toward the ingroup and bias against the outgroup. Some interpret these findings differently, however. The stereotypes about race are familiar to virtually all members of a culture, so perhaps the IAT is actually measuring what an individual knows about stereotypes rather than what he or she believes is true. Simply knowing about a stereotype does not mean an individual believes it, uses it to judge people (prejudice), or uses the stereotype to discriminate.

Why is this relevant?

The development of the IAT has fostered a great deal of research and has been applied to at least a dozen forms of stereotyping, including stereotypes of social

(a)

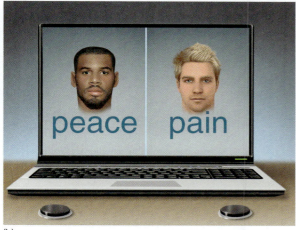

(b)

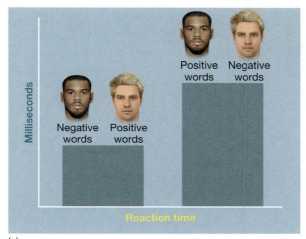

(c)

{FIG. 15.7} **The IAT Procedure** To complete one condition in the IAT (a), participants must use one button to identify Black faces and negative words and another button to identify White faces and positive words. In other condition (b), the positive and negative words are switched to be paired with the other race (Black/positive and White/negative). Average response times are faster when Black is paired with negative words and White is paired with positive words (c). Is this a sign of hidden prejudice?

classes (Rudman et al., 2002), sexual orientation (Banse et al., 2001), and even fraternity and sorority members (Wells & Corts, 2008). The results of all these tests illustrate that implicit prejudice seems to be more prevalent than what people are willing to express in explicit tests (Nosek et al., 2002). The IAT is also being applied to clinical settings. For example, one research group developed an IAT that measures attitudes about alcohol use. This instrument can successfully predict how much alcohol someone is likely to consume, even when explicit measures fail to do so (Ostafinet et al., 2008).

PSYCH @

The Law Enforcement Academy

Imagine that instead of linking positive or negative terms with Black faces in the IAT, you were asked to make a decision to shoot or not to shoot a potential criminal. A number of researchers have used video-game-like tasks to put participants in these situations. In these video simulations, a figure will suddenly appear, perhaps wielding a weapon or perhaps just holding a cell phone. It turns out that the split second of indecision in the IAT corresponds to more mistaken shootings of the innocent Black people than innocent Whites (Correll et al., 2007; Correll et al., 2006).

Certainly a video game pales in comparison to the adrenaline-fueled confrontation that occurred in the case of Amadou Diallo described at the beginning of this module. It is easy to imagine the stress of a real confrontation, combined with the complexity of a real-world situation, leads to an even higher chance of a mistaken shooting occurring (Saus et al., 2006). To combat any implicit influence of race on an officer's decision to shoot, most law enforcement agencies require extended training of their employees. For example, Denver police cadets must complete

The split-second differences in the IAT may be related to officers' increased use of deadly force with Black suspects, including cases where the suspect is unarmed. Here, a police officer undergoes virtual reality training designed to reduce shooting errors.

72 hours of training related to shoot/do not shoot decisions. This and other programs use a combination of walk-through sets, where cardboard figures suddenly appear, and other situations with actors, some of whom are armed with foam pellet guns. Most important, the data show that extensive training works for police officers; even student volunteers in the lab can be trained to reduce shooting errors through such means (Correl et al., 2007; Plant & Peruche, 2005).

· · · · · · · · · · · · · · · · · · ·

Quick Quiz 15.2b
Stereotypes, Prejudice, and Discrimination

1 The concept of self-serving bias is similar to _____, in which we attribute positive qualities to the social group we belong to.

- **A** ingroup bias
- **B** outgroup bias
- **C** discrimination
- **D** implicit bias

2 _____ prejudice refers to situations in which a person stereotypes a group of people based on hidden, unacknowledged feelings.

- **A** Explicit
- **B** Discriminative
- **C** Associative
- **D** Implicit

3 Unconscious forms of prejudice are thought to be measured with the implicit associations test. This test is based on:

- **A** the types of words people typically make up when they see a person of a specific race.
- **B** how long it takes people to respond to positive or negative words along with Black or White faces.
- **C** changes in heart rate that accompany photos of people from different racial backgrounds.
- **D** increased activity in the emotional centers of the brain that are associated with specific races.

4 Which of the following statements about stereotypes and prejudice is false?

- **A** Stereotypes can be expressed outwardly and very explicitly.
- **B** All stereotypes are of negative characteristics.
- **C** Stereotypes are often experienced implicitly.
- **D** Prejudice has become increasingly unpopular in the United States.

Answers can be found on page ANS-5.

Module Summary

Now that you have read this module you should:

Listen to the audio file of this module at **MyPsychLab**

KNOW ...

- **The key terminology associated with social cognition:**

deliberative thought (p. 565)
discrimination (p. 569)
explicit prejudice (p. 570)
external (situational) attribution (p. 567)
fundamental attribution error (p. 567)
implicit prejudice (p. 570)
ingroup bias (p. 569)
internal (dispositional) attribution (p. 567)

intuitive thought (p. 565)
outgroup (p. 569)
person perception (p. 565)
prejudice (p. 569)
scapegoating (p. 569)
schemas (p. 565)
self-fulfilling prophecy (p. 566)
self-serving bias (p. 568)
stereotype (p. 568)
thin slices (p. 566)

UNDERSTAND ...

- **How we form first impressions and how these impressions influence us.** We quickly form impressions, even with only thin slices of behavior are available to us. These impressions can be surprisingly accurate, but in some cases they may lead to self-fulfilling prophecies.

APPLY ...

- **Your understanding of the different ways we explain our own behavior versus the behavior of others.** One way to do so is to consider your own behavior and personality as compared to that of a friend or a classmate. Try the exercise in **Table 15.4** and compare your results with someone from your class.

ANALYZE ...

- **The common belief that stereotypes can only be derogatory.** Stereotypes can also be kind—even an attempt to compliment can be based on an assumption about group membership. However, referring to women as the "fairer sex" or assuming that someone is intelligent or athletic can be insulting and produce other negative effects.

Table 15.4 :: Description of Self and Others

First, consider your own personality and behaviors. For each of these 10 rows, put an X by the one personality trait that best describes your behavior *or* put the X beside "Depends on the situation."

Next, think about a classmate. For each row, put an O by the one personality trait that best describes your classmate *or* put the O beside "Depends on the situation."

1.	Serious	Joyful	Depends on the situation
2.	High-energy	Low-key	Depends on the situation
3.	Plans for the future	Lives for the present	Depends on the situation
4.	Reserved	Emotionally expressive	Depends on the situation
5.	Dignified and formal	Casual and relaxed	Depends on the situation
6.	Skeptical of others	Trusting	Depends on the situation
7.	Cautious	Bold and daring	Depends on the situation
8.	Conscientious and orderly	Carefree and spontaneous	Depends on the situation
9.	Argumentative	Agreeable	Depends on the situation
10.	Realistic	Idealistic	Depends on the situation
	Add up the Xs in these two columns here: _____		Add up the Xs in this column _____
	Add up the Os in these two columns here: _____		Add up the Os in this column _____

Finally, compare the number of Xs and Os on the left side of the table. Did you have more Os than Xs? According to research, most people from the United States will have more Os on the left side because they tend to attribute others' behavior to personality traits. The same individuals should have more Xs than Os on the right side of the table due to a tendency to see one's own behavior as situational. Compare your scores with others in your class—especially with those of classmates from cultures other than your own.

Source: Adapted from Nisbett et al., 1973.

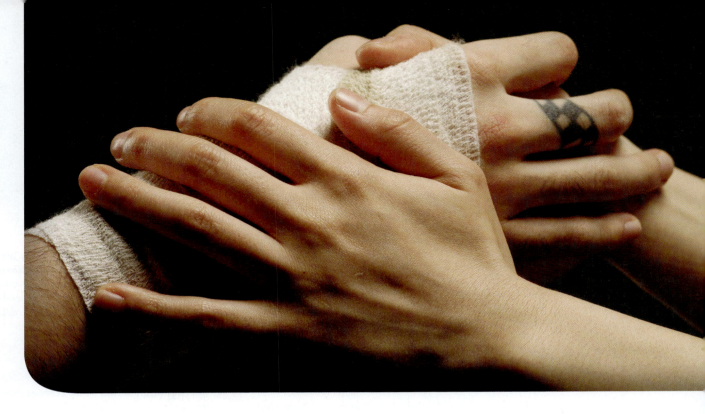

**Module
15.3**

Helping and Harming Others

**Learning
Objectives**

After reading
this module
you should:

KNOW ...	UNDERSTAND ...	APPLY ...	ANALYZE ...
The key terminology in the study of helping and aggression	Cognitive and evolutionary theories of helping Biopsychosocial influences on aggression	Your knowledge to assess your own levels of altruism	The role of biological factors and testosterone in aggressive behavior

People are remarkably sensitive to watching others experience pain. However, if you had never actually felt pain before, do you think you could possibly be sensitive to pain in *others*? It seems plausible that, without having personal experience of being jabbed with a needle or stubbing a toe, it would be impossible to recognize pain in others.

A way of finding an answer to this question would be to ask the very rare group of individuals who have a condition called congenital insensitivity to pain (CIP)—a problem brought about by a gene mutation that renders useless the specialized types of nerve cells that transmit pain messages to the brain. These individuals experience no pain whatsoever. A broken bone or a deep cut would elicit no crying, agony, or even flinching. Remarkably, people with CIP actually *can* share in pain that they could not possibly feel. As long as they can see and hear emotional cues that someone is in pain, they have the same kind of "sympathy pain" that everyone else does (Danziger et al., 2009). One fascinating implication of this finding is that human beings are hard-wired to respond to others in a caring way. People with CIP exhibit this behavior in the complete absence of any personal experience.

Focus Questions

 In addition to responding to pain, in which other ways does the human motive to care and feel for others apply?

 How do psychologists account for people's failure to express compassion for someone in pain or need?

· · · · · · · · · · · · · · · · · ·

Group membership is a fundamental need of human life (Baumeister & Leary, 1995). It is difficult to imagine a day without being part of a family, a class, a work team, a neighborhood, or a community. But for any of these groups to function effectively, the members have to figure out how to get along. *Prosocial behaviors* are those behaviors that promote social functioning, group cohesion, or the well-being of the individuals within the group. Sometimes these behaviors are easy and enjoyable, at other times they are responses to emergencies, and sometimes serious challenges must be overcome to demonstrate prosocial behaviors. In contrast, *antisocial behaviors* may serve one individual or a small group at the expense of the greater community. In this module, we examine the personal and group qualities that make coexistence peaceful or tumultuous, as well as the extent to which people will go to help or hurt one another.

Empathy, Altruism, and Helping

The words *humanity* and *humanitarian* describe feelings and actions of compassion, and the existence of these terms highlights that many people see our compassionate sides as a uniquely human quality. People are highly motivated to look out for each other. **Empathy** *is the emotional concern one individual has for another's well-being.* It includes feelings of compassion or distress for the condition of others (Batson et al., 2007). One psychological characteristic making empathy possible is perspective-taking—attempting to understand another's situation by imagining what it would be like to be that person. In experiments where volunteers are asked to imagine the thoughts and feelings of another, they report strong feelings of concern and even show emotional physiological responses (Batson et al., 2007; Davis, 2004).

A second factor just as important as perspective-taking is the value we place on other people's welfare. As shown in Figure 15.8, this value may lead directly to empathy or may contribute to perspective-taking. Although most adults place at least some value on every person's life, we would definitely experience less empathy for a convicted murderer than for a friend (Batson et al., 2007).

Empathy is evident from various physiological processes (Decety, 2010). Humans have a specialized type of nerve cell that could possibly serve as a basis for empathy. These cells, called *mirror neurons*, respond to the actions and expressions of others and are correlated with the ability to understand another's intentions and emotions (Kaplan & Iacoboni, 2006). Similarly, the neurons involved in pain perception are active when

Starting from a very young age, human children recognize when others are in need of help and respond accordingly.

an individual sees another in pain, or even when he or she just imagines the pain (Minio-Paluello et al., 2006). Other psychologists have measured increased emotional responses, such as a faster pulse rate and the slight changes in skin moisture that give us clammy hands, when volunteers observe emotional reactions in others (Levenson & Reuf, 1997). In fact, when the more empathetic volunteers watched someone experiencing distress, their physiological responses tended to match those of the person experiencing the distress, a phenomenon the researchers referred to as *shared physiology*.

SOCIAL-COGNITIVE APPROACHES TO HELPING

The capacity for empathy would seem to be a prerequisite for helping others; the more empathy an individual reports, the more likely the person is to help. This is true even if helping requires very little effort (Davis et al., 1999). At the individual level, the willingness to help may depend on the situation—some situations seem more urgent than others—and it can depend on the individual—some individuals regularly feel more empathy than others.

In addition to empathy, group membership can have a strong effect on helping. Referring back to the model of empathy in Figure 15.8, we see two variables that lead to empathy—valuing the other's welfare and adopting the other's perspective. It seems likely that both would

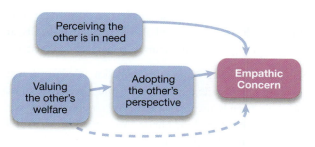

{FIG. 15.8} **Factors Contributing to Empathy** According to Batson and colleagues (2007), empathy stems from our capacity to perceive that another person is in need and to value that individual's welfare. Empathy can be expressed with or without the ability to actually adopt the perspective of another person.

relate to group membership as well. Do you think you would be more likely to value and understand people in your own groups than strangers? As you may surmise, research shows that our empathy extends more toward those in our own groups (Hewstone et al., 2002). Even so, this finding does not mean that we always refuse to help people outside of our groups. When strangers or members of other groups are in need, people are more likely to help when they can find similarities or likeable qualities. Also, individuals who feel they have a strong, secure bond with family and friends seem to be more likely to help others regardless of their group membership (Mikulincer & Shaver, 2005; Sturmer et al., 2005).

Much of our helping behavior can be explained by **social-exchange theory**, *which states that an individual will consider the costs and benefits of helping another before he or she acts.* This approach treats helping much like a financial arrangement between individuals and society. The currency in these arrangements is not necessarily monetary, however—benefits may include positive feelings and social approval for one's deeds. Also, the cost and benefit ratios of these arrangements can be highly variable. Simple acts of charity, such as dropping coins in the Salvation Army collection pot or leaving out a few canned goods for a food drive, bring the benefit of feeling good about oneself at very little cost. By comparison, a decision to donate a kidney to a loved one involves weighing considerable physical and emotional costs and risks against the great benefits of increasing someone's longevity and easing that person's suffering.

☑● Complete
the **Survey** *Could
You Be a Hero?* at
MyPsychLab

Wesley Autrey leapt in front of a New York subway to save Cameron Hollopeter, who had fallen on the tracks after having a seizure. Autrey literally covered Hollopeter and held him still between the tracks as the train cars rolled just inches above his body. His heroism received coverage from the network television news and the major newspapers, and he was even invited to appear on television shows such as *Late Show with David Letterman*. Autrey's act was an amazing example of altruism, as he could not have possibly considered any benefit to himself at the moment of his brave act.

Helping behavior can also take the form of **altruism**—*helping others in need without receiving or expecting reward for doing so.* Highly visible examples can be seen in a heroic deed, like that of Wesley Autrey, who jumped in front of a subway train to save a complete stranger. Altruism is not always that dramatic; even an anonymous donation of a few dollars could be considered altruistic. From a social-cognitive perspective, we can explain altruism using the **social responsibility norm**: *Society teaches us that the value of helping goes beyond the benefits an individual might receive, and that individuals who cannot help themselves require special help.* With this norm in place, people feel compelled to help children, the elderly, and those with medical crises. Such acts do, indeed, give us the sense that humans are special in their ability to give with such selfless motivation. Psychologists working within the evolutionary perspective, however, suggest that it is impossible for someone to act based on truly selfless motives. ☑

EVOLUTIONARY APPROACHES TO ALTRUISM

Survival and reproduction are keys to evolutionary success, so behaviors that put individuals at risk must ultimately serve these purposes. After all, if an organism sacrifices itself for another, it will not be able to pass on the genes that influence altruistic behavior.

The concept of *costly signaling* explains acts of altruism as signals to others that the helper would be a valuable mate (McAndrew, 2002). Helping others can be risky, but it can also be a way to assert status and make a statement that the person doing the helping is trustworthy. Of course, this kind of altruism is a gamble; it may have big payoffs, but it is potentially very *costly*. Balancing payoff and risk for behaving altruistically presents a puzzle: Why would anyone help others if all it did was jeopardize evolutionary success? The answer lies in the concept of **kin selection**, *which predicts that altruistic behavior is most likely to occur when it gives a genetic benefit to the individual* (Hamilton, 1964). For example, if a mother sacrifices herself for her child, her altruism raises the chances that her genes will survive—not in her, of course, but in her offspring. It follows that her offspring will also behave altruistically, at least to the extent that altruistic behavior is inherited.

One challenge to the process of kin selection is that helping behavior extends well beyond genetic relatives. We help friends, neighbors, and even complete strangers. You have likely heard the phrase, "You scratch my back, I'll scratch yours." **Reciprocal altruism** *refers to helping behavior extended to nongenetic relatives, with the possibility that the favor may be later returned* (Trivers, 1971). The phenomenon of reciprocal altruism may sound like something uniquely human, but it also occurs in nonhuman species.

Reciprocal altruism can be found among vampire bats. When adult bats return to the cave after gathering blood from their hosts, locating their hungry offspring can be challenging. Bats will feed unrelated offspring if they cannot find their own brood—an example of reciprocal altruism.

FAILING TO HELP: THE BYSTANDER EFFECT In 1964, word spread through the news that a woman named Kitty Genovese had died in New York City after a brutal attack, despite the 40 witnesses who could have intervened or called for help. Although some have disputed the number of witnesses (Manning et al., 2007), what is clear is that Genovese died tragically and nobody intervened. The thought of unresponsive witnesses stimulated a new line of research into the **bystander effect**, *which occurs when an individual in a group does not provide help, either because the person believes someone else will help or because the other people in the group are not helping either.*

We now know that, unfortunately, there are times when individuals see someone in need and yet they do not help, even when helping would be safe and easy to do. Dozens of studies have explored this effect by simulating emergencies. For example, in one study, an individual volunteer was ushered into a small room while one to three other "volunteers" (who were actually research confederates) were said to be waiting in similar rooms to have a conversation over intercoms. As they waited, one confederate reported being prone to seizures and subsequently asked for help as a seizure apparently began. Researchers found that, the more confederates there were, the longer it took the true participant to react to his calls for help (Latane & Darley, 1968).

There are at least three possible explanations for the bystander effect. A crowd can freeze bystanders due in part to a sort of stage fright—*What happens if I try to intervene and wind up embarrassing myself* (Karakashian et al., 2006)? Individuals may look around and see other bystanders not

reacting and ask, *What if the others know something I do not?* Maybe there is not any trouble after all (Prentice & Miller, 1996). A final possibility is that they experience **diffusion of responsibility** (see Figure 15.9): *this occurs when people feel less responsible for an individual in need when in the presence of a group.* It is as if a person asks himself, "If no one else is helping, then why should I care?" (Darley & Latane, 1968). Each of these possibilities helps explain why otherwise empathic people do not help people who may be in need.

What breaks the spell and allows bystanders to intervene? It turns out that individuals with specific training, such as CPR, are more likely to help, probably because they feel better equipped (Huston et al., 1981). Similarly, being among friends and family may reverse the bystander effect, presumably because the members of the group share greater concern for each other than for strangers (Levine & Crowther, 2008).

Because of the bystander effect, if you were to ask researchers Darley and Latane (1968), "If I'm in serious trouble, am I better off with one person around or with seven people around?", their answer would be a very confident "one." Therefore, it is important to know that if you do find yourself in need with a crowd around, you can reduce the risk of the bystander effect by acting against the anonymity and diffusion of responsibility. First, ask for help from a specific person. Make eye contact as you ask for help so the person cannot deny

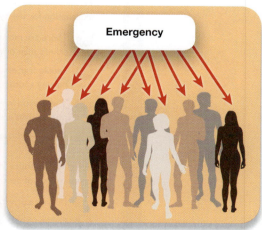

{FIG. 15.9} **Diffusion of Responsibility** If one person witnesses an emergency, it is as if 100% of the responsibility for helping falls on that person. If 10 people witness an emergency, that responsibility is diffused, so it is as if each person feels only 10% of the responsibility—which may not be enough to motivate a person to act. **Click on this figure in your eText to see more details.**

responsibility. Next, be specific when you ask for help. Say "call 911" so the person can spring into action without thinking (Schroeder et al., 1995).

One point that bears repeating is the norm of social responsibility: In most societies, the expectation is that when a person is able, he or she will provide help. Although *helping* is the norm, not everyone will go out of their way to help others. Others, unfortunately, will behave in ways that harm other individuals—the topic that we turn to in the next section.

Quick Quiz 15.3a
Empathy, Altruism, and Helping

1 Behavior that places the helper at significant risk or certain harm for the benefit of another is referred to as _____.

 A altruism

 B empathy

 C costly signaling

D social responsibility norm

2 Society teaches that the value of helping goes beyond the benefits an individual might receive, and that individuals who cannot help themselves require special help. Based on _____, people feel compelled to help individuals who cannot help themselves such as the elderly and people with medical crises.

 A altruism

 B empathy

 C costly signaling

D the social responsibility norm

3 Which of the following is the most plausible explanation for the bystander effect?

A There are more people who are unwilling to help others than originally thought.

B People fear embarrassment that could come from helping another.

C The person in need is likely to be unrelated, and nonrelatives are not worth helping.

D All of the above are likely.

4 Which of the following is an example of the phenomenon of costly signaling in action?

A Making a private donation to a hospital

B Failing to help because others are around

C Showing off one's wealth

D Chasing down a thief who has stolen a stranger's purse

Answers can be found on page ANS-5.

Aggression

At its most basic level, **aggression** *is any behavior intended to hurt or harm an individual* (Anderson & Bushman, 2002). Aggression toward others comes in a variety of forms. People can be either physically or verbally aggressive. Aggression can occur in socially sanctioned contexts, such as sporting events, or in contexts that violate the rights of others, as in assault. Aggression can involve provoking others, or it can be reactive, as when responding to insults or threats. Like altruism, aggression is influenced by both the person and the situation. Because research shows some interesting and important links between biological factors and aggression, we will start our exploration of this behavior there.

WORKING THE SCIENTIFIC LITERACY MODEL
Biological Influences on Aggression

People have long speculated that aggressive tendencies can be inherited, even before scientists uncovered modern concepts of genes and evolution. Many also believe that hormones are the reason why young males are the most aggressive demographic group. But how much credit should we give to biological explanations of aggression?

What do we know about the biology of aggression?

Families seem to differ in their aggressive tendencies, and at an individual level some people react with especially high levels of defensiveness and aggression when threatened. The heritability of aggressive behaviors among humans is estimated to be approximately .50 (Rhee & Waldman, 2002). Scientists have identified specific brain regions, chemicals, and genes that interact with environmental triggers to aggressive responses. A key to understanding the biological basis of aggression is to identify how the environment triggers these biological factors.

How can science explain the biology of aggression?

Aggressive behavior is related to functioning of the amygdala, which is part of the brain's limbic system. Men who are prone to violence show abnormal activity in the limbic regions of the brain (Pardini & Phillips, 2010). Furthermore, amygdala responding appears to be related to testosterone levels. The amygdala has receptors for testosterone, and testosterone levels affect the activation of the amygdala in response to threatening situations (Derntl et al., 2009).

Correlational research has found that more aggressive males tend to have unusually high testosterone levels, and are also prone to crime, drug use, and impulsiveness (Dabbs et al., 2001). Numerous potential candidate genes are thought to play a role in this relationship (Craig & Halton, 2009). One gene is known to code for the receptors that androgens bind to. This gene varies in length between individuals, with some people inheriting "short" versions and others inheriting "long" versions of it. (The length of the gene is due to the number of repeat molecular sequences that comprise the DNA molecule; long versions have more repeats.)

Researchers suspected that this gene might be implicated in human aggressive tendencies—notably male aggression. In one study, investigators examined the androgen receptor gene of 645 men, 374 of whom had been convicted of murder or rape, and compared it to the androgen receptor gene of the 271 controls, who had no violent history. The criminal males were statistically more likely to have inherited the short version of the androgen receptor gene. Additionally, the men who were especially violent offenders (e.g., who committed rape and then murder) had the shortest copies of this gene (Rajender et al., 2008).

Can we critically evaluate this evidence?

Testosterone has gained the reputation as the hormone driving male aggression. In reality, testosterone is also found in women, in whom it serves most of the same functions as in men. Furthermore, large-scale literature reviews suggest only a very mild overall relationship exists between testosterone and aggression. Testosterone levels appear to be related to problematic behaviors in only certain subsamples of people, such as younger adolescent boys and people with emotional problems (Book et al., 2001; Craig & Halton, 2009). In addition, aggression is just one of many behaviors associated with testosterone; this hormone is also involved in psychological processes that have nothing to do with aggression. For example, testosterone and its receptors are abundant in many regions of the brain involved in thinking and memory, so the hormone plays a role in those functions.

Although research indicates that people who are aggressive have unusual activity in the areas of the brain associated with emotion, it is important not to simplify the issue. Research certainly does show that amygdala responding is related to aggression, and that abnormal conditions of this brain

structure can result in emotional and behavioral problems. This line of thinking can be taken too far, however. Just four decades ago, clinical researchers at a juvenile mental hospital in Australia surgically removed the amygdalae from youths who were prone to aggression-related problems. It was not until 2007 when this type of surgery was formally banned (White & Williams, 2009).

Why is this relevant?

The costs of violent aggression are high. An estimated 2.2 million people require medical treatment for violence-related incidents each year in the United States, at an estimated cost of $37 billion in health care and lost work productivity (Corso et al., 2007). The additional costs of incarceration and legal proceedings make the investigation of aggression and its causes a critical area of study. Testosterone is certainly related to aggression, but its level can fluctuate under many other circumstances, including just about any competition where opponents vie for dominance. In fact, in one peculiar study, researchers found that testosterone levels of John McCain supporter temporarily dropped after it was announced that Barack Obama had won the 2008 presidential election (Stanton et al., 2009).

PERSONALITY AND AGGRESSION People vary in their tolerance and even preference for violence. Some individuals enjoy the unmitigated violence of ultimate fighting or the over-the-top theatrics of professional wrestling, while at the other end of the spectrum are individuals who cannot bring themselves to honk their car horn when it is clearly justified.

Dozens of studies have examined how different personality traits are related to aggression, and their results reveal two distinct patterns. First, some individuals seem to be naturally prone to aggression in just about any situation, whether they are provoked or not. Psychologists refer to this tendency as *trait aggression,* because the hostility seems to be as much as a trait for these individuals as shyness or politeness is for others. Other people can still be aggressive, but only when they feel threatened or provoked. These *reactive-aggressive* individuals tend to be more competitive, self-centered, impulsive, and quick to anger than the rest of the population (Bettencourt et al., 2006).

THE SITUATIONAL CAUSES OF AGGRESSION

Even for those individuals who are low in trait aggression, situational factors have a great deal of effect on their aggressive behaviors. It is probably not surprising that the biggest cause is interpersonal provocation such as insults or physical attack (Berkowitz, 2003). For children, aggressive behavior may be a response to bullying. For adults, it may be a response to grown-up forms of bullying in the workplace, or any other form of perceived maltreatment from one's supervisors or peers (Baron, 1999; LeBlanc & Barling, 2004).

The **frustration-aggression hypothesis** *describes another major contributor to aggression, which occurs when an individual is prevented from achieving a goal—especially if the goal should be within reach—and experiences frustration as a result.* Prolonged frustration or meaningless frustration is especially likely to trigger aggressive responses. Even when there is a perfectly reasonable explanation for the frustration, aggression is still likely to occur (Dill &

Anderson, 1995). One of the most familiar forms of frustration-related aggression is road rage. When drivers are stuck in traffic and when they feel threatened by careless, slow, or aggressive drivers, they are more likely to become aggressive themselves (Dukes et al., 2001; Galovski et al., 2006).

BIOPSYCHOSOCIAL PERSPECTIVES
Cultures of Honor

The following scenario is modified from Nisbett and Cohen (1996):

> *Shortly after arriving at the party, Jill pulled her husband Steve aside, obviously bothered by something. Jill told Steve that Larry had already made two passes at her that evening. Steve kept an eye on Larry and within five minutes Larry tried to kiss Jill.*

How would you complete this story? Would Steve privately confront Larry and point out that his behavior is inappropriate? Or would Steve react violently toward him?

Psychologists have found that how people finish this story depends on at least two things: (1) whether they have been wronged prior to reading it, and (2) their geographic region of upbringing in the United States. Here is how researchers from the University of Michigan identified these two factors: Students from the northern and southern United States were recruited to participate in a study. Whenever a volunteer would arrive for the study, an actor who was actually a part of the study bumped into the student and mumbled an obscenity at him. Shortly afterward, the student read a passage similar to the one presented above. The provocation of the bump from a stranger led Southern males to complete the story with more violent themes compared to Northern males. In addition, the researchers collected saliva samples and analyzed testosterone levels following the incident; Southerners had higher testosterone levels than did Northerners.

Why the difference between studies of two different geographical regions? Scholars discuss the idea of *cultures of honor*—social groups that expect individuals to protect themselves and their property by whatever means necessary (Cohen et al., 1996; Nisbett & Cohen, 1996). This perspective stands in contrast to the *culture of law,* which relies on a judicial system, penal codes, and law enforcement officers. In cultures of honor, individuals, especially males, are expected to react strongly to even mild insults or conflicts, to ensure they do not lose social status or seem like pushovers in front of their community (see Figure 15.10).

The frustration-aggression hypothesis states that aggression arises from frustration—the inability to reach a goal when it should be relatively easy to do. This is especially clear in road rage caused by traffic jams and slow drivers.

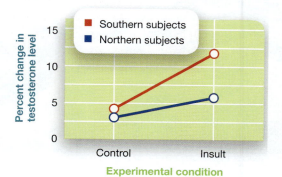

{FIG. 15.10} **Men from a Culture of Honor React More Strongly to Perceived Insults** Compared to Northerners, the testosterone levels of Southern research participants increased greatly after they were bumped before an experiment.

Such cultures are usually found among people living far away from urban centers, where governmental law enforcement is weakest. In the United States, western and rural southeastern regions of the country seem to give precedence to honor over law. In the Southeast, for example, the rate for murders based on honor and interpersonal conflict (i.e., not murders associated with other felonies, such as armed robbery) far exceeds the rates for the rest of the country. Moreover, communities in the South are far more accepting of men who have committed murder in the name of protecting their family, property, or reputation (Nisbett & Cohen, 1996). Similarly, higher rates of aggressive behavior and its acceptance have been found a variety of settings ranging from rural and nomadic societies to urban gangs. The one thing all cultures of honor have in common is a reluctance to rely on legal systems.

· · · · · · · · · · · · · · · · · · ·

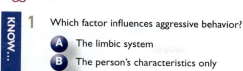

Quick Quiz 15.3b
Aggression

KNOW...

1 Which factor influences aggressive behavior?

- **A** The limbic system
- **B** The person's characteristics only
- **C** The situation only
- **D** All of the above factors influence aggressive behavior

UNDERSTAND...

2 Aggressive behavior has its brain basis in the _____.

- **A** adrenal glands
- **B** brain stem
- **C** mirror neurons
- **D** limbic system

APPLY...

3 If you were raised in a culture of honor, you are most likely to:

- **A** avoid aggressive acts at all costs.
- **B** rely solely on the legal system to provide justice.
- **C** insult or attack others without provocation.
- **D** be accepting of situations in which someone took revenge on another person.

4 Which scenario is best explained by the frustration-aggression hypothesis?

- **A** You are stuck in heavy traffic and you start to threaten other motorists.
- **B** You threaten another person who is behaving inappropriately toward a family member.
- **C** You have excessively high levels of testosterone so you seek out aggressive situations.
- **D** All of these situations can be explained using the frustration-aggression hypothesis.

ANALYZE...

5 Which conclusion has been drawn concerning the research on testosterone and aggression?

- **A** There is only a very mild relationship between testosterone and aggression.
- **B** Testosterone is a very strong predictor of aggressive behavior.
- **C** Testosterone is related to problematic behaviors in only subsamples of people.
- **D** Both a and c are correct options.

Answers can be found on page ANS-5.

Module Summary

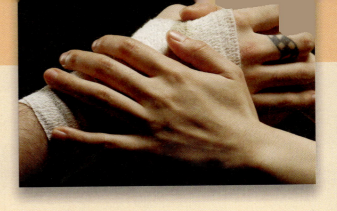

Module 15.3

Now that you have read this module you should:

Listen to the audio file of this module at **MyPsychLab**

KNOW ...

- **The key terminology in the study of helping and aggression:**

aggression (p. 578)
altruism (p. 576)
bystander effect (p. 577)
diffusion of responsibility (p. 577)
empathy (p. 575)

frustration-aggression hypothesis (p. 580)
kin selection (p. 576)
reciprocal altruism (p. 576)
social-exchange theory (p. 576)
social responsibility norm (p. 576)

UNDERSTAND ...

- **Cognitive and evolutionary theories of helping.** According to social-exchange theory, people weigh the financial and personal costs of helping and altruism. Evolutionary accounts explain altruism as a result of kin selection, in which helping relatives ultimately benefits reproductive fitness. Reciprocal altruism occurs in cases where helping is directed toward nonrelatives, with the expectation that favors will eventually be returned.

- **Biopsychosocial influences on aggression.** Recall the example from Nisbett and Cohen (1996), who found that young adults with ties to rural areas of the southeastern United States tend to be more aggressive than Northerners. These psychologists explain this difference in terms of a culture of honor.

APPLY ...

- **Your knowledge to assess your own levels of altruism.** Complete a brief version of the Self-Report Altruism Scale in **Table 15.5**. Average scores from a sample of 50 college students was 27. How do you match up?

ANALYZE ...

- **The role of biological factors and testosterone in aggressive behavior.** The limbic system (e.g., amygdala) and testosterone levels are correlated with aggression. Testosterone levels peak in competitive situations and during aggressive encounters. Genetic links between testosterone levels and violence have also been identified. However, not all violent people have high testosterone levels, and testosterone has more functions than just playing a role in aggression. Receptors for testosterone are also found in the brain regions responsible for thinking and memory.

Table 15.5 :: Excerpt from the Self-Report Altruism Scale

Rate each item in the far left column on a scale ranging from 0 (Never) to 4 (Very Often). Then add up the points to calculate your total score.

	NEVER	ONCE	MORE THAN ONCE	OFTEN	VERY OFTEN
1. I have given directions to a stranger.	0	1	2	3	4
2. I have given money to a charity.	0	1	2	3	4
3. I have given money to a stranger who needed it (or asked me for it).	0	1	2	3	4
4. I have donated goods or clothes to a charity.	0	1	2	3	4
5. I have done volunteer work for a charity.	0	1	2	3	4
6. I have donated blood.	0	1	2	3	4
7. I have helped carry a stranger's belongings (books, parcels, etc.).	0	1	2	3	4
8. I have delayed an elevator and held the door open for a stranger.	0	1	2	3	4
9. I have allowed someone to go ahead of me in a lineup (at photocopy machine, in the supermarket).	0	1	2	3	4
10. I have let a neighbor whom I didn't know too well borrow an item of some value to me (e.g., a dish, tools, etc.)	0	1	2	3	4
11. I have helped a classmate who I did not know that well with a homework assignment when my knowledge was greater than his or hers.	0	1	2	3	4
12. I have helped an acquaintance to move households.	0	1	2	3	4

Source: Rushton, Chrisjohn, & Fekken, 1981.

Module 15.1 :: Social Influences on Behavior and Attitudes

Focus Questions:

1 Were the guards at Abu Ghraib callous and brutal people, or did the situation lead them to behave that way? In order to answer this, we would need to have extensive knowledge of the individuals' previous behavior. However, psychological research suggests that very typical individuals can change their behavior drastically depending on the situation. This behavior may include abuse committed by prison guards, as in the case of the Stanford Prison Study.

2 Would a decent and honest person refuse to harm others, even if he or she were instructed to do so by an authority figure? Milgram's research on obedience to authority makes it clear that psychologically normal individuals can be persuaded to perform unsettling acts simply because an authority figure suggests it.

👁—**Watch** *The Basics: Under the Influence of Others* in the **MyPsychLab video series**

Module 15.2 :: Social Cognition

Focus Questions:

1 Which processes make it possible for people to form such quick impressions—right or wrong—of others? Person perception is a constant part of social life. Social cognition—that is, thinking and reasoning about the behavior of others—involves intuitive and deliberate thought. Research indicates that intuitive thoughts can be initiated with thin slices of behavior; it only takes a moment to form an impression.

2 The officers in the module-opening vignette denied that race played a role in the killing of Amadou Diallo, but is it possible that Diallo's race could have affected the officers' reactions *without* their knowledge? The results of the Implicit Association Test (IAT) suggest that people can hold stereotypes at a subconscious level, so it is possible that these implicit associations might contribute to snap decisions without a person's knowledge.

👁—**Watch** *The Big Picture: The Social World* in the **MyPsychLab video series**

Module 15.3 :: Helping and Harming Others

Focus Questions:

1 In addition to responding to pain, in which other ways does the human motive to care and feel for others apply? Humans are remarkably sensitive to others in need. Empathy occurs in a wide variety of contexts and is directed toward both kin and complete strangers. Humans, and some nonhuman species, have specialized physiological responses underlying helping and empathy.

2 How do psychologists account for people's failure to express compassion for someone in pain or need? Even people who are compassionate and generally concerned about the welfare of others can fail to show it. This possibility has been demonstrated in studies of the bystander effect, in which the mere presence of others reduces the chance that an individual will intervene to help someone. Failure to help is not necessarily a character flaw—the apathy of bystanders can result from normal responses such as "stage fright," fear of embarrassment, or second-guessing.

👁—**Watch** *Thinking Like a Psychologist: Changing Attitudes and Behaviors* in the **MyPsychLab video series**

👁—**Watch** the complete video series online at **MyPsychLab**

Episode 16: Social Psychology

1. *The Big Picture: The Social World*
2. *The Basics: Under the Influence of Others*
3. *Special Topics: Mental Shortcuts in a Social Context*
4. *Thinking Like a Psychologist: Changing Attitudes and Behaviors*
5. *In the Real World Application: Are Stereotypes and Prejudice Inevitable?*
6. *What's in It for Me? Attraction*
7. *What's in It for Me? Persuasion*

✓● Study and Review at MyPsychLab

1 In Solomon Asch's famous experiment in which participants were asked to visually judge the length of lines, why did many participants give the incorrect answer at least part of the time?

A The lines were too close in length to accurately judge their relative lengths.

B The participants conformed their answers to those offered by others in the room.

C The participants were hoping to stand out as unique.

D The participants were intentionally trying to sabotage the study.

2 When making a difficult decision, group members sometimes strive for agreement so as to avoid arguments, a phenomenon known as _____.

A social loafing

B obedience

C social facilitation

D groupthink

3 Approximately what percentage of participants delivered the maximum possible shock in Milligram's obedience study?

A 0%

B 6%

C 15%

D 65%

4 Kyle is an independent filmmaker who has always believed that big Hollywood movies are garbage. Recently, however, he agreed to work on a big-budget Hollywood movie because the pay was very good. Now he tells his friends, "Not all Hollywood movies are that bad." Kyle's change in attitude is likely the result of _____.

A cognitive dissonance

B conformity

C groupthink

D group polarization

5 The fundamental attribution error is the tendency to attribute the actions of others to _____, while ignoring the role of _____.

A ingroup factors; outgroup factors

B outgroup factors; ingroup factors

C their disposition; the situation

D the situation; their disposition

6 Conceptually, _____ is the opposite of the fundamental attribution error.

A cognitive dissonance

B the self-fulfilling prophecy

C outgroup bias

D self-serving bias

7 Which of the following is a criticism of the Implicit Associations Test (IAT)?

A The IAT may measure only familiarity with a stereotype, not actual prejudice.

B The IAT actually measures explicit prejudice, not implicit prejudice.

C The IAT is not reliable when subjects are retested.

D Subjects can change their responses to make themselves appear less prejudiced.

8 Some researchers believe that humans' capacity for empathy is based on the nerve cells called _____.

A sympathy neurons

B mirror neurons

C empathy cells

D altruism neurons

9 The concept of _____ explains why parents would risk their own lives to rescue one of their children.

A self-serving bias

B a culture of honor

C reciprocal altruism

D kin selection

10 In a(n) _____, individuals are expected to protect themselves and their property by whatever means necessary.

A androcracy

B culture of honor

C judicial system

D social exchange

Work the Scientific Literacy Model :: Understanding Social Cognition

What do we know about social cognition?

Review **Figure 15.6** on **page 567** for a recap of internal and external attributions, and take a moment to think about how you attribute behavior in your daily life. Consider the fundamental attribution bias by thinking about this scenario: Imagine you are at the movies and another person in the theater snaps at you and your friends for talking too loudly. You might assume that she is simply unpleasant and uptight (internal attribution) rather than assuming that she was having a bad day (external attribution). In contrast, an example of the self-serving bias would be snapping at your roommate for talking on the phone too loudly, but rationalizing your behavior because you were feeling cranky after a long shift at work—not to mention your roommate was being rude first.

You may be surprised to learn that the terms "stereotype," "prejudice," and "discrimination" are not interchangeable. Remember that a stereotype is a generalized set of beliefs about a group of people (a type of schema), prejudice is a prejudgment of members of a group based solely on their membership in that group (an attitude), and discrimination is actual positive or negative behavior that is based on that prejudice (actions).

Why is this relevant?

Watch the accompanying video excerpt on stereotypes and prejudice. You can access the video at MyPsychLab or by clicking the play button in the center of your eText. If your instructor assigns this video as a homework activity, you will find additional content to help you in MyPsychLab. You can also view the video by using your smart phone and the QR code below, or you can go to the YouTube link provided.

After you have read this chapter and watched the video, discuss the factors that contribute to prejudice and discrimination and identify some techniques for reducing the development of prejudice and discrimination.

How can science help explain stereotypes and prejudice?

Recent research has shown that people are increasingly concerned about appearing prejudiced, yet there is still evidence of pervasive stereotypes. For instance, examination of police records reveals that Black suspects are over 5 times more likely to die in a police encounter than White suspects. Psychologists interpret this type of evidence to suggest that many of us unknowingly or implicitly harbor prejudice. The discussion on **page 569** supports this claim with a study in which researchers found subtle but remarkable differences in facial expressions and brain activity when subjects looked at Black and White faces, even when the participants claimed that they were not prejudiced. Similarly, on **page 570** we described the Implicit Associations Test, which researchers say can reveal implicit prejudice through a series of responses to images or words flashed on a computer screen (see **Figure 15.7**). For example, a person who believes he is free from prejudice might exhibit an implicit (unconscious) association between positive words and images of White faces, and negative words with images of Black faces.

Can we critically evaluate claims about stereotypes, prejudice, and discrimination?

Even "positive" stereotypes can be harmful. In the **Myths in Mind** feature on **page 569**, you were asked to think about how seemingly harmless stereotyping, such as labeling women as nurturers, can affect the group being stereotyped. If all women are nurturing and gentle, then certainly women would be out of place in a field like finance or politics, where leaders often have to make unpopular and assertive decisions. This kind of categorization can have other negative effects as well, such as the exclusion of women from executive or other high-level positions.

Are stereotypes just too powerful to fight? Keep in mind that training can undermine stereotypes. The **Psych @** feature on **page 571** described the success that law enforcement retraining has had in changing shoot/do not shoot procedures, and the encouraging data that suggest this kind of training can work even with people who are not making life-and-death decisions. Also, keep in mind that the research on implicit prejudice, while interesting, raises some questions about validity and whether the IAT is testing prejudice or simply the knowledge of pervasive stereotypes.

youtube.com/
scientificliteracy

MyPsychLab

Your turn to Work the Scientific Literacy Model: You can access the video at MyPsychLab or by clicking the play button in the center of your eText. If your instructor assigns this video as a homework activity, you will find additional content to help you at MyPsychLab. You can also view the video by using your smart phone and the QR code, or you can go to the YouTube link provided.

16 :: HEALTH, STRESS, AND COPING

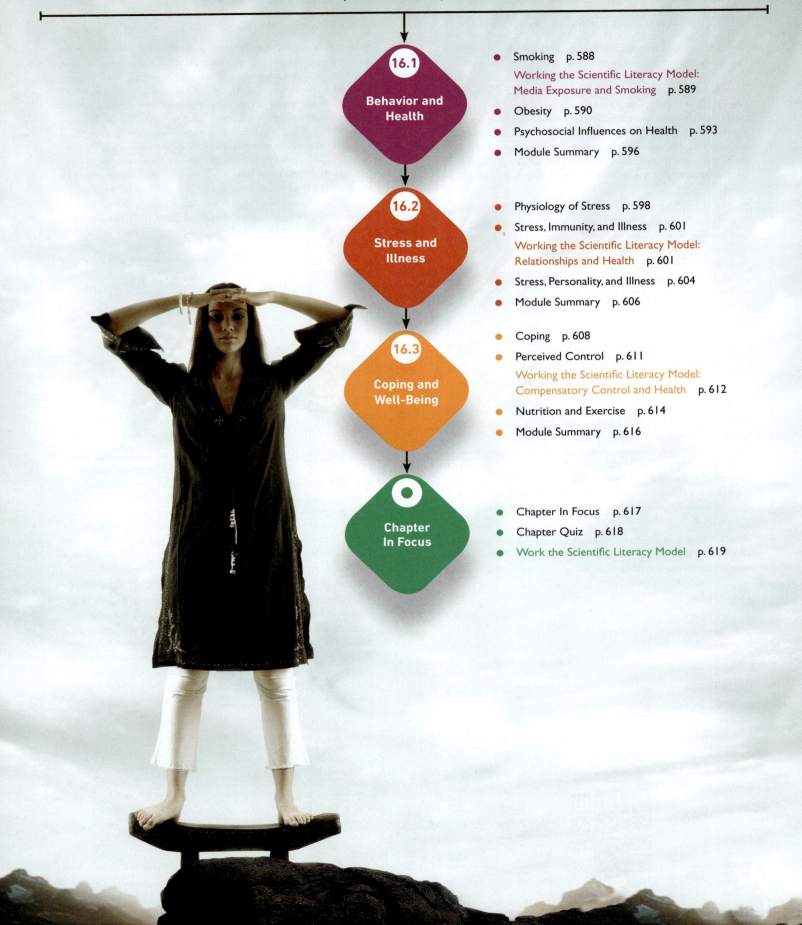

Behavior and Health

Module 16.1

Learning Objectives

After reading this module you should:

KNOW ...	UNDERSTAND ...	APPLY ...	ANALYZE ...
The key terminology related to health psychology	How genetic and environmental factors influence obesity	Your knowledge to exert more control over your own health	Whether associations with people who smoke affect smoking in adolescents

Should a person's body weight be a basis for how much tax the person pays? Some politicians, hospital administrators, and other members of society advocate a "fat tax"—taxing individuals for their excess weight, or for the nonessential food items that contribute to being overweight. Sugary soft drinks contribute hundreds of calories to our daily diet without providing any nutrition, and do little to leave a person feeling full and satisfied. So, like cigarettes, should additional taxes be attached to these products for the same reasons that cigarettes are so heavily taxed? Some health care providers are pursuing such a plan. In 2009, for example, state employees in Alabama who were obese discovered that they had to lose weight by year's end or face increased monthly health insurance costs. On one hand, this may sound like blatant discrimination and focusing on just one of many economic burdens associated with obesity. On the other hand, there is a parallel precedent for fat tax plans—namely, the massive taxes on cigarettes that serve to discourage smoking and help cover the costs of treating smoking-related illnesses.

Focus Questions

1. Which factors contribute to weight problems, and how much control over them can people expect to have?

2. To what extent is physical health based on psychological processes such as choice and decision?

• • • • • • • • • • • • • • • • • •

To what degree do you believe your behavior affects your health? Each day we make choices that shape our physical and mental health. We decide what to eat and what to avoid eating, whether to exercise or be inactive. Some people choose to light up a cigarette whenever the chance arises, or they create as many opportunities as possible to satisfy their intense cravings. The choices people make about their career paths similarly influence their health. Workplace stress levels for

Table 16.1 :: Estimated Annual Deaths in the United States Due to Behavior-Related Risk Factors

This table presents the estimated number of deaths annually in the United States due to specific behavior-related risk factors such as diet, exercise, and tobacco and alcohol use. To put this in context, there are between 2.4 million and 2.5 million deaths in the United States each year (CDC, 2009a). The 248,000 male deaths related to tobacco use represent approximately 10% of all deaths in the United States each year.

RISK FACTOR	MALE	FEMALE	TOTAL
Tobacco use	248,000	219,000	467,000
High blood pressure	164,000	231,000	395,000
Overweight and obesity	114,000	102,000	216,000
High blood sugar	102,000	89,000	190,000
High LDL cholesterol	60,000	53,000	113,000
Alcohol use	45,000	20,000	64,000

Source: Adapted from Danaei et al., 2009.

air traffic controllers are quite different from those experienced by librarians. The numerous and complex connections between behavior and health certainly have created an important niche for *health psychologists*, who study both positive and negative impacts that humans' behavior and decisions have on their health, survival, and well-being.

The need for health psychologists has increased considerably over the 20th century, as most premature deaths today are attributable to lifestyle factors (see Table 16.1). A century ago, people in the United States were likely to die from influenza, pneumonia, tuberculosis, measles, and other contagious diseases. Advances in medicine have served to keep these conditions under much better control. Instead, people are now much more likely to die from tobacco use, alcohol use, obesity, and inactivity. In fact, more than half of all deaths in the United States in 2006 were caused by heart disease, cancer, stroke, and diabetes—all of which are linked to behavior (Centers for Disease Control and Prevention [CDC], 2009a).

Smoking

Smoking cigarettes causes life-shortening health problems including lung, mouth, and throat cancer; heart disease; and pulmonary diseases such as emphysema. The life expectancy of the average smoker is between 7 and 14 years shorter than that of a nonsmoker (CDC, 2002; Streppel et al., 2007). The costs in lives and money attributable to smoking are massive, as shown in Table 16.2. Despite the starkly ominous figures, an estimated 20.6% (6 million) of U.S. adults smoke cigarettes (CDC, 2009b).

The tobacco industry attempts to make everyone think of cigarettes as a familiar part of life; it spends more than $36 million each day on cigarette advertisements (Federal Trade Commission, 2007).

Table 16.2 :: Health Costs of Tobacco Use

- Tobacco use causes an estimated 5 million deaths worldwide each year.
- Cigarette smoking is the leading preventable cause of death in the United States.
- One in five U.S. deaths is due to cigarette smoking.
- Cigarette smoking is costly: More than $193 billion is lost each year to this habit ($97 billion in lost work productivity and $96 billion in health care expenses).

Source: CDC, 2009b.

WORKING THE SCIENTIFIC LITERACY MODEL
Media Exposure and Smoking

If smoking is so dangerous, why do people do it? This is a perplexing question not only for psychologists, but also for many smokers. One reason may be the exposure young people have to other people who smoke: parents, friends, and even characters on television and in the movies.

What do we know about media influences on smoking?

Many different factors influence whether someone becomes a smoker, including family and local culture, personality character-istics, and socioeconomic status. Thus people may smoke because this behavior is associated with certain traits or societal roles, such as attractiveness, rebelliousness, and individualism. Each day approximately 2,000 adolescents in the United States try their first cigarette, and many will go on to become full-time smokers (Heatherton & Sargent, 2009). An important question that health psychologists grapple with concerns the societal factors that lead young people to smoke. Many such factors come into play. Instead of reviewing all of them here, we will focus on a single influence: exposure to smoking in movies and entertainment. Actors in many popular television shows and movies smoke. Although smoking in films has declined over the past couple of decades, there are still numerous widely popular movies in which characters smoke (Sargent & Heatherton, 2009).

How can science help us analyze the effects of smoking in the movies?

To what extent does smoking in movies contribute to adolescent smoking? This question has been ad-dressed using a variety of methods. In one study, re-searchers conducted a random-digit-dialing survey of 6,522 U.S. adolescents from all major geographic regions and socioeconomic groups. The adoles-cents reported their age and indicated whether they smoked, and were asked to identify whether they had seen specific popular movies that featured smoking. The more exposure the adolescents had to movies

that featured smoking, the more likely they were to have tried smoking (see Figure 16.1). This relationship persisted even after the researchers controlled for important vari-ables such as socioeconomic status, personality, and paren-tal and peer influences on smoking (Heatherton & Sargent, 2009). Although this study showed a clear correlation link-ing smoking in movies and adolescent smoking, it did not explain *why* this correlation exists.

It appears that how people identify with smokers may influence their decision to smoke. An experimental study showed that adolescents who had positive responses to a protagonist who smoked were much more likely to associate smoking with their own identities. This cor-relation was observed in both adolescents who already smoked and even those who did not smoke (Dal Cin et al., 2007).

Can we critically evaluate this evidence?

It is very difficult to establish that watching movie stars smoke cigarettes *causes* adolescents to smoke, even though the correlations might suggest that it does. When researchers tracked the amount of smoking featured in popular movies from 1990 to 2007, they found that as the incidence of smoking in movies rose, smoking among adolescents increased after a short period of time. Likewise, when smoking in movies decreased, a decline in adolescent smoking followed (Sargent & Heatherton, 2009). However, the problem with these correlations is that multiple explanations could be put forth for why they exist. Although the researchers would like to demonstrate

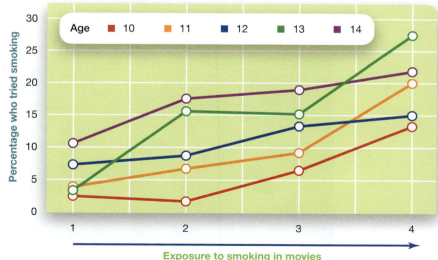

{FIG. 16.1} **Smoking and the Movies** The more 10- to 14-year-olds view smoking in movies, the more likely they are to smoke (Heatherton & Sargent, 2009).

that smoking in movies influences audience members, perhaps the truth is the other way around: People who are already willing to smoke might be more attracted to movies that feature smoking.

Why is this relevant?

Smoking by young people raises serious concerns about the health and well-being of those individuals who start smoking at such an early age. In addition, cigarette-related illness imposes a major societal burden in terms of lost work productivity and rising health care costs. As the research shows, cigarette smoking in movies is just one of many influences on smoking behavior. Of course, it may be one influence that could be easier to control than, say, peer pressure. With scientific research in hand, advocacy groups such as Smoke Free Movies and the National Association of Attorneys General have a sound basis for arguing against smoking in movies—especially those that adolescents are likely to watch.

There is some good news related to smoking rates. The prevalence of smoking in the United States declined steadily over the 1990s and early 2000s (CDC, 2010d). State and local laws are reducing the risks posed by secondhand smoke exposure by banning smoking in many public places—especially restaurants and public buildings. As mentioned at the beginning of the module, steep taxes applied to unhealthy products such as tobacco also act as a deterrent against their use. Not only does such a policy tend to reduce the number of smokers, but it also raises funds for health care and anti-smoking campaigns.

Quick Quiz 16.1a
Smoking

KNOW...

1 What does a health psychologist study?

A The positive impacts that our behavior has on our health

B The negative impacts that our behavior has on our heath

C The chance that we will survive based on our decisions

D Both the positive and the negative impacts that our behavior and decisions have on our health and survival

2 In modern times, the leading causes of death in industrialized nations such as the United States are _____.

A viral infections

B bacterial infections

C lifestyle factors

D each of these are equal contributors

ANALYZE...

3 Which of the following statements is the best evidence that viewing smoking in movies plays a causal (rather than correlational) role in influencing people's perception of smoking and willingness to try smoking?

A Long-term trends show that increased or decreased incidence of smoking by adolescents follows increases or decreases in rates of smoking in movies.

B The more adolescents smoke, the more smoking occurs in movies.

C Advertisements for smoking occur more frequently, along with smoking by film actors.

D Adolescent smoking occurs at roughly the same rate regardless of how smoking is depicted in films.

Answers can be found on page ANS-5.

Obesity

You have likely heard the term "freshman 15"—the supposed number of pounds incoming college students can expect to gain during their first year of school. This term has stuck because weight gain during the first year of college (at least in the United States) has seemingly become so common, if not expected. It is unclear exactly how the term originated, and research has shown that the 15-pound estimate is actually inflated. In reality, those male and female students who gain weight during their early college career put on an average of 6 pounds (Gropper et al., 2009).

What accounts for this phenomenon? Several factors that are probably all too familiar to many readers: increased food intake, decreased physical activity, and, for many students, increased levels of alcohol consumption. The lifestyle changes that students face during college affect physical health. In addition, college in general, and the first year in particular, present new challenges that bring on a great deal of both positive and negative stress. The freshman 15 (or 6) and other health-related issues are based on lifestyle decisions we make. Six pounds is not a lot of weight—but habits formed during any period of time, freshman year or otherwise, can be difficult to break.

According to the National Institutes of Health (NIH, 2009), roughly two-thirds of U.S. adults are overweight or obese. Moreover, from 1960 to 2004, obesity rates increased from 13.3% to 32.1% for adults between 20 and 74 years of age. Obesity is a significant problem in the United States as well as other regions of the world—particularly urban areas—in which the culture of fast food and processed, prepackaged meals has spread. The World Health Organization (WHO, 2009) estimates that 1 billion people across the world are overweight and 300 million are obese.

Excess weight is not just a cosmetic problem. Obesity is associated with numerous detrimental health consequences, such as cardiovascular disease, diabetes, osteoarthritis (degeneration of bone and cartilage material), and some forms of cancer.

So what weight is considered healthy and what is considered problematic? The **body mass index (BMI)** *is a statistic commonly used for estimating a healthy body weight that factors in an individual's height*. In everyday usage, the BMI is used to screen people for weight categories that indicate whether they are considered normal weight, underweight, overweight, or obese. Many proposals for a fat tax use the BMI as the basic calculation of appropriate weight.

What causes obesity? As discussed in Module 11.1, weight is gained because of a *positive energy balance*, meaning that too many calories come in and not enough are expended. Obviously overeating can lead to obesity. But why might a 6-foot-tall male weigh 170 pounds while enjoying massive amounts of food and a relatively inactive lifestyle, while another person of similar height and lifestyle weighs in at 200 pounds? Several factors explain this phenomenon, including genetic, neurological, and environmental variables.

GENETICS AND BODY WEIGHT   Twin, family, and adoption studies all suggest that genes account for between 50% and 90% of the variation in body weight

(Maes et al., 1997). Genetic factors influence body type, metabolism, and other physiological processes that contribute to body weight and size.

Some researchers have suggested that genes contribute to the development of a **set point**, *a hypothesized mechanism that serves to maintain body weight around a physiologically programmed level*. The set point is not an exact number of pounds, but rather a relatively small range encompassing 10% to 20% of one's weight. Your initial set point is controlled by genetic mechanisms, but your actual weight can be modified by environmental factors—namely, what and how much you eat. According to set point theory, if an individual gains 10% of his body weight (e.g., increasing from 150 to 165 pounds) his set point would make a corresponding shift upward—the body acts as though its normal weight is now the larger 165 pounds. Metabolism slows correspondingly, such that this person now requires additional energy expenditure to take the weight off. This process explains why people who gain extra weight may shed a few pounds with relative ease, but find it overwhelmingly difficult to continue losing or even maintaining their weight once they reach an initial goal.

Set point theory has a long tradition in the field of nutrition, but its validity is challenged by research suggesting that weight gain and difficulty with weight loss are unrelated to a physiological set point. Rather, individual differences in physical activity may be a stronger determinant of who succeeds at losing weight and keeping it off. Specifically, people who gain weight expend less energy in their normal day-to-day activities (Weinsier et al., 2002). Thus the difficulty with losing the weight may be related to lower activity levels, rather than any elevation of a set point.

SOCIAL FACTORS   In addition to genetic factors, similarities in body weight among family members are naturally influenced by what and how much they are eating. What children eat is largely based on what their parents provide and allow them to eat, and eating patterns developed in childhood are generally carried into adulthood.

Sociocultural influences on eating certainly extend beyond the family. Food advertisements trigger eating—after watching a commercial for buttery microwave popcorn, you have probably found yourself rummaging around in the kitchen in search of that last bag you hope is still there. If your popcorn supply is depleted, you are still far more likely to snack after watching commercials about food (Harris et al., 2009). Researchers have found that children who see food commercials while watching a 30-minute cartoon program consume 45% more snack food than do children who view nonfood commercials. The researchers estimated that this difference could lead to an additional 10 pounds of extra weight gained each year (Harris et al., 2009). Also, increased incidences of overweight and obesity are disproportionately found among children who grow up in poverty, where low-cost, high-fat diets are commonplace (Miech et al., 2006).

The cost of health care rises with body mass index. Questions over who is responsible for paying these costs have generated heated debate. Should a person who is overweight or obese be obligated to pay more tax toward health care to offset the higher cost of his or her care? Many people would certainly answer this question with a resounding "yes." Of course, health care costs may also rise because individuals develop diseases that have little to do with their lifestyle. Research on employment statistics indicates that workers who are overweight or obese are paid less than thin colleagues with similar qualifications—a finding that has led economists to suggest that the disparity in wage earnings is about equal to the size of the difference in medical costs incurred by thin versus overweight and obese people (Bhattacharya & Bundorf, 2005).

THE SEDENTARY LIFESTYLE Modern conveniences have reduced the amount of physical activity required of most people. Many jobs involve very little physical activity, and home entertainment has evolved into activities that typically require nothing more than sitting and, often, snacking. Such pleasurable activities can easily replace exercise.

Many children and adolescents are indoctrinated into this lifestyle from their early years. In turn, childhood obesity rates have risen drastically, accompanied by the

The number of hours children spend playing video games is directly related to increased body weight. Would a tax on video game purchases help curb this problem?

availability of an even greater variety of sedentary activities, such as video games. Researchers have found that the amount of time that children spend playing video games is positively correlated with levels of obesity (Stettler et al., 2004). Some individuals remain optimistic that this trend may be reversed, pointing out the availability of video games that involve physical activity, although these options claim only a small portion of the overall market.

The popularity of video games, and their potential to encourage a sedentary lifestyle, has not gone unnoticed by lawmakers. Over the past few years, some politicians have proposed bills that would add a fat tax onto the purchases of video games and equipment (ABC News, 2008). While modern conveniences and increased preferences for entertainment that demands very little physical activity certainly are not helping the obesity epidemic, such tax increases are unlikely to make substantial inroads on weight loss if people do not increase their activity levels.

BIOPSYCHOSOCIAL PERSPECTIVES
Obesity

Genetics, social influences, and lifestyle factors all play roles in obesity. But what about broader influences, such as socioeconomic status and ethnicity? To address this question, start by classifying the following statements about obesity as either true or false:

1. In the United States, obesity rates are unrelated to ethnicity.

2. In the United States, obesity in children is linked to socioeconomic factors.

3. Obesity is related to socioeconomic factors in U.S. adults.

4. Obesity can have a negative, long-term impact on the brain.

Nutritious, nonprocessed foods tend to be more expensive, which might have led you to predict that obesity would be more prevalent in people in lower socioeconomic brackets (e.g., low income or poverty). Also, diet seems to be influenced by sociocultural factors, including the types of foods people grow up eating. What do the data say about these issues?

The following answers are based on obesity trend statistics reported by the CDC (2010b, 2010c):

1. *False.* Black and Hispanic adults have, on average, a greater prevalence of obesity in the United States (Figure 16.2).

2. *True.* As household income increases, obesity decreases in both boys and girls in the United States. However, since at least 1988 childhood obesity has increased across populations at all income levels. (Note: These

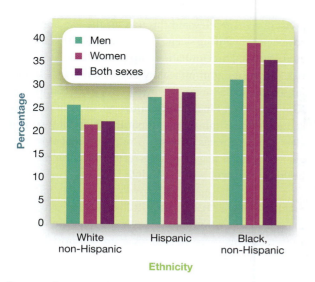

{FIG. 16.2} **Obesity Rates in Adults by Ethnicity and Gender in the United States, 2006–2008**

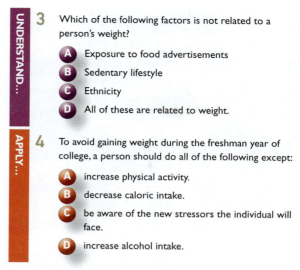

Answers can be found on page ANS-5.

relationships represent overall trends; they are not consistent across all ethnic groups.)

3. *False.* Recent CDC statistics show that most obese adults are not members of low-income groups, and that obesity among people of all socioeconomic categories is on the rise. There are even some patterns based on gender. Men at high income levels are more likely to be obese than men at lower levels. Conversely, among women, obesity increases at lower income levels.

4. *True.* Obesity can have a negative, long-term impact on the brain. Researchers have found that people who are obese have, on average, 8% less brain tissue than people who are lean. The average brain of an individual with obesity in his 70s looks approximately 16 years older than a lean person of the same age (Raji et al., 2010.)

· · · · · · · · · · · · · · · · · · · ·

Quick Quiz 16.1b
Obesity

KNOW...

1. _____ is a hypothesized mechanism that serves to maintain body weight around a physiologically programmed level.

  A BMI   **C** Obesity

  B Set point   **D** A sedentary lifestyle

2. In the United States, researchers have found that obesity rates are related to ethnicity in what way?

  A Obesity rates are not related to ethnicity.

  B Caucasian adults have a greater prevalence of obesity.

  C Hispanic adults have a greater prevalence of obesity.

  D Asian adults have a greater prevalence of obesity.

UNDERSTAND...

3. Which of the following factors is not related to a person's weight?

  A Exposure to food advertisements

  B Sedentary lifestyle

  C Ethnicity

  D All of these are related to weight.

APPLY...

4. To avoid gaining weight during the freshman year of college, a person should do all of the following except:

  A increase physical activity.

  B decrease caloric intake.

  C be aware of the new stressors the individual will face.

  D increase alcohol intake.

Psychosocial Influences on Health

The environments where we work, live, and play and the people with whom we interact influence both our physical and mental health. College dormitories are a prime example, especially in the fall of each academic year. Frequently, dormitory space is overbooked, leaving some students without an established living space, and forcing people to live in cramped conditions. Single rooms may be converted into doubles, and "suites" may appear where there were none. Perhaps not surprisingly, these conditions lend themselves to the increased spread of influenza and other viruses amid a fairly stressed group of individuals. In addition, these conditions affect the way that individuals interact with one another.

Years ago psychologists compared students who lived in well-designed dormitory arrangements versus those living in improvised and poorly designed conditions. The crowded, poorly designed accommodations caused students to lose their sense of control over whom they could interact with or avoid. The researchers found that students living in the stressful environment were less socially interactive with strangers, had difficulty with working in small groups, and gave up more easily in a competitive game (Baum & Valins, 1977). The students living in the less than ideal conditions seemed to feel helpless, which in turn affected how they interacted with others. For most students, better accommodations await them at home, and larger spaces open up at the end of the semester. However, for many living with very low incomes, the stresses of poor housing may be permanent.

People who are of low socioeconomic status are at increased risk for poor health. Numerous factors, including limited access to health care, stress, poor nutrition, and discrimination, collectively place children growing up in these communities at greater risk for developing health problems.

POVERTY AND DISCRIMINATION

Health and wealth increase together, and it appears that socioeconomic factors have numerous positive and negative effects. People who live in affluent communities not only enjoy better access to health care, but also have a greater sense of control over their environments and have the resources needed to maintain a lifestyle of their choosing. Individuals who lack this sense of control live in circumstances that can compromise their health. People who experience poverty, discrimination, and other social stressors have higher incidences of depression, anxiety, and other mental health problems (Tracy et al., 2008).

Furthermore, health problems are magnified by stress. Heart disease is prevalent in socioeconomically disadvantaged populations, and children who experience adverse socioeconomic circumstances (e.g., less than 12 years of education or living in a low-income household) are at greater risk for developing heart disease in adulthood (Fiscella et al., 2009; Galobardes et al., 2006). This relationship likely reflects the compound effects of stress, as well as the poorer diet that is often found among individuals residing in communities of low socioeconomic status.

Discrimination is another stressor that can compromise both physical and mental health. This kind of stressor is particularly problematic because it is often uncontrollable and unpredictable. Being a target of prejudice and discrimination is linked to increased blood pressure, heart rate, and secretions of stress hormones, which when experienced over long periods of time compromise physical health. For example, when people perceive that they are the targets of racism, their blood pressure remains elevated throughout the day, and it recovers poorly during sleep (Brondolo et al., 2008; Steffen et al., 2003). Discrimination also puts people at greater risk for engaging in unhealthy behaviors such as smoking and substance abuse (Bennett et al., 2005; Landrine & Klonoff, 1996). Finally, discrimination, or even the perception of discrimination, can put the body on sustained alert against threats. The stress response that this state elicits can have negative, long-term effects on physical health, as you will read in Module 16.2.

FAMILY AND SOCIAL ENVIRONMENT

Our close, interpersonal relationships have a major impact on health. In fact, chronic social isolation is as great a mortality risk as smoking, obesity, and high blood pressure (House et al., 1988). Marriage is typically the primary social relationship that people establish and has been shown to have long-term health benefits. Married people tend to live longer and have better mental and physical health than do nonmarried adults. Married couples enjoy the benefits of social support, combined resources, and they tend to have better health habits (Kiecolt-Glaser & Newton, 2001).

This is good news for married couples, but are both members of a heterosexual marriage benefiting equally from their union? It turns out that men enjoy greater health benefits from marriage. Unmarried women have a 50% higher mortality rate than do married women, whereas unmarried men have a 250% higher mortality rate (Ross et al., 1990). Several possible reasons for this disparity in the health benefits gained from marriage have been suggested. One likely contributor is the greater role that women take in recognizing and supporting healthy behaviors in others.

Of course, marriage can also be a considerable source of stress. Marital problems are among the most stressful experiences that people can have. Married couples who are experiencing ongoing problems with their relationship tend to experience more depression and greater incidences of physical illness than happily married couples (Kiecolt-Glaser & Newton, 2001). Marital problems and divorce also affect the emotional and physical health of children, particularly if they are younger during problematic periods of a marriage or during the parents' actual divorce. Adolescents of divorced parents are at a slightly higher risk of engaging in delinquent behaviors (Amato, 2001). While divorce can negatively affect the health of children, parents who continue engaging in high-quality parenting during marital discord protect children from many of the negative effects on health attributable to divorce (Hetherington et al., 1998).

SOCIAL CONTAGION You have almost surely found yourself eating food simply because others around you were doing so, even if you were not actually hungry. The simple presence of other people is a puzzling social influence on our behavior—easy to observe, but challenging to explain. Social scientists have discovered an even more puzzling pattern of behaviors spreading among individuals. Body weight seems to spread socially, and not just the pound or so gained from packing in extra food at a birthday party just because others around you were also eating. Body weight changes can spread widely among individuals within social groups. Fluctuations can go in either direction—weight may increase or decrease. The same even appears to happen with smoking—either starting or quitting. It may be that many of our health and lifestyle choices are influenced by what others around us are doing.

These phenomena are examples of **social contagion**, *the often subtle, unintentional spreading of a behavior as a result of social interactions.* Social contagion of body weight, smoking, and other health related behaviors has been documented in the Framingham Heart Study. The National Heart Institute began this ongoing study in 1948 to track 15,000 residents of Framingham, Massachusetts. Participants made regular visits to their doctors, who recorded important health statistics such as heart rate, body weight, and other standard physical measures. Scientists working with the Framingham data noticed that over time, clusters of people from this study group became increasingly similar in certain characteristics—such as body weight increases or

Social contagion in the dorms. Your college roommate may influence your GPA more than you know—for better or for worse. At Dartmouth College, students are randomly assigned to their dorm rooms rather than matched on various characteristics, as is customary at many schools. This practice makes Dartmouth's roommate pairs a diverse mixture. Professor Bruce Sacerdote (2001) found that GPA levels are influenced by one's roommate. Students with high GPAs elevate the GPAs of their lower-scoring roommates, and vice versa.

decreases, starting or quitting smoking, and even levels of happiness (Christakis & Fowler, 2007, 2008; Fowler & Christakis, 2008). It turns out that the groups who showed similar patterns in their health statistics were also friends with one another. It was as though the behaviors spread in the same way a virus would. Although genetic factors certainly do influence our health, this work seems to show just how powerful social factors can be.

Quick Quiz 16.1c :: Psychosocial Influences on Health

KNOW …

1 Which psychological term refers to the often subtle, unintentional spreading of a behavior as a result of social interactions?

A Health psychology   **C** Discrimination

B Social contagion   **D** Observational learning

2 Based on the research discussed in this module, which of the following is the lowest risk factor for health problems?

A Being an unmarried adult

B Experiencing discrimination

C Having an identical twin who is overweight

D Being a married adult

UNDERSTAND …

3 Which of the following statements about how discrimination influences health is most accurate?

A Discrimination is unrelated to poor health.

B People who experience discrimination are likely to compensate for it by making positive health-related choices.

C An immediate increase in heart rate is the biggest problem associated with experiencing discrimination.

D Experiencing discrimination stimulates the stress response, which can bring about long-term health problems.

Answers can be found on page ANS-5.

Module Summary

Now that you have read this module you should:

KNOW ...

- **The key terminology related to health psychology:**

body mass index (BMI) (p. 591) social contagion (p. 595)

set point (p. 591)

UNDERSTAND ...

- **How genetic and environmental factors influence obesity.** Twin and adoption studies indicate that inheritance plays a strong role as a risk factor for obesity (or, for that matter, as a predictor of healthy body weight). Furthermore, environmental influences on weight gain are abundant. Cultural, family, and socioeconomic factors influence activity levels and diet, even in very subtle ways, such as through social contagion.

APPLY ...

- **Your knowledge to exert more control over your own health.** To what extent do you believe you can do this? Complete the scale in **Table 16.3** and follow the instructions to calculate your total scores.

EVALUATE ...

- **Whether associations with people who smoke affect smoking in adolescents.** Correlational trends certainly show that smoking in popular movies is positively related to smoking among adolescents (e.g., increased exposure is related to increased incidence of smoking). Controlled laboratory studies suggest a cause-and-effect relationship exists between identification with story protagonists who smoke and smoking behavior by young viewers.

Table 16.3 :: The Health Locus of Control Scale

Each of the following items is a belief statement about your health with which you may agree or disagree. Beside each statement is a scale that ranges from strongly disagree (1) to strongly agree (6). For each item, we would like you to circle the number that represents the extent to which you agree or disagree with that statement. Please make sure that you answer *every item* and that you circle *only one* number per item. This is a measure of your personal beliefs; obviously, there are no right or wrong answers.

ITEM	STRONGLY DISAGREE					STRONGLY AGREE
1. If I get sick, it is my own behavior that determines how soon I get well again.	1	2	3	4	5	6
2. No matter what I do, if I am going to get sick, I will get sick.	1	2	3	4	5	6
3. I am in control of my health.	1	2	3	4	5	6
4. Most things that affect my health happen to me by accident.	1	2	3	4	5	6
5. When I get sick, I am to blame.	1	2	3	4	5	6
6. Luck plays a big part in determining how soon I will recover from an illness.	1	2	3	4	5	6
7. The main thing that affects my health is what I myself do.	1	2	3	4	5	6
8. My good health is largely a matter of good fortune.	1	2	3	4	5	6
9. If I take care of myself, I can avoid illness.	1	2	3	4	5	6
10. No matter what I do, I'm likely to get sick.	1	2	3	4	5	6
11. If I take the right actions, I can stay healthy.	1	2	3	4	5	6
12. If it's meant to be, I will stay healthy.	1	2	3	4	5	6

First, add up the total of your circled responses for the odd-numbered items only: _____

Now add up the total of your circled responses for the even-numbered items only: _____

Here is how you should interpret your scores: The first scale based on odd-numbered items measures the degree to which you believe you have control over your own health. The average of this scale in the original study was 24.1, with higher values indicating a greater sense of control over one's health. The second scale based on even-numbered items measures the degree to which you believe chance is involved in your health. Again, higher scores indicate a greater sense that luck is involved, and the average in the original study was 15.1.

Source: Adapted from Wallston et al., 1978.

Stress and Illness

Learning Objectives

After reading this module you should:

KNOW ...	UNDERSTAND ...	APPLY ...	ANALYZE ...
The key terminology associated with stress and illness	The physiological reactions that occur under stress How the immune system is connected to stress responses	A measure of stressful events to your own experiences	The claim that ulcers are caused by stress

The frustration and embarrassment of choking under pressure is undeniable. Whether the stakes are a championship title or admission to an elite university, a sudden, inexplicable shift to subpar performance can be devastating. According to psychologist Sian Beilock, the culprit in such a case may be the negative effects that stress has on working memory—the short-term capacity to hold and manipulate information. Calculating a 15% tip for a bill of $43.84 at a restaurant, or while the pizza delivery person waits, requires working memory processes. The pressure of your date or the pizza delivery person looking on impatiently may result in your appearing either foolishly generous or just plain cheap.

Beilock has conducted experiments on how stress affects the cognitive resources needed for problem solving. For example, in one study, research volunteers were asked to solve math problems. Some were told that if they solved the problems correctly, they would earn money for themselves as well as for a partner they were paired with; if they did not perform well, both the volunteer and the partner would lose money. Beilock and her colleagues have found that this type of pressure draws resources away from the working memory processes needed for success (Beilock, 2008, 2010). Stressful thoughts readily occupy working memory space and cause the unfortunate experience of choking under pressure. Stress, both good and bad, is a part of everyday life for most people.

Focus Questions

1. How does stress affect the brain and body?

2. How do individuals differ in how they handle stress?

• • • • • • • • • • • • • • • • • •

On any given day, we are likely to experience frustration, conflict, pressure, and change. All of these experiences, and others as well, involve stress. **Stress** *is a psychological and physiological reaction that occurs when perceived demands exceed existing resources to meet those demands.*

Stress refers to both events (stressors) and experiences in response to these events (the stress response). Stressors can take a wide variety of forms, such as acute events (giving a speech, experiencing an assault, getting in a car accident) and chronic events (illness, marital problems, ongoing job-related challenges).

We can probably all agree that events such as car accidents and relationship troubles are stressful. However, psychologists have discovered that two individuals can react very differently even if they have experienced the same stressful event. To explain why and how people differ, psychologists Richard Lazarus and Susan Folkman developed a cognitive appraisal theory of stress (Lazarus & Folkman, 1984). Here, the term *appraisal* refers to the cognitive act of assessing and evaluating the potential threat and demands of an event, and these appraisals occur in two steps. First, the individual perceives a potential threat and begins the *primary appraisal* by asking herself, "Is this a threat?" If the answer is no, then she will not experience any stress; but if the answer is yes, she will experience a physiological stress reaction (perhaps a racing heart beat and sweaty palms) as well as an emotional reaction (perhaps anxiety and fear). As these events unfold, the *secondary appraisal* begins—she must determine how to cope with the threat. During the secondary appraisal, she may determine that she knows how to cope with the stressor or that the stressor goes beyond her ability to cope.

Complete the **Survey** *Will This Survey Stress You Out?* at **MyPsychLab**

Imagine that a teenager experiences his first traffic accident. During his primary appraisal of the event, he will probably assess the situation as stressful even though it was a minor collision; his stomach may feel like it is in a knot and he may begin to worry about the consequences. As the stress sets in, his secondary appraisal may help him cope if he remembers that he has insurance to cover the damage, he considers that nobody was injured, and remembers how his parents have always been supportive and understanding. With these thoughts, he can develop ways of coping with the stress, therefore keeping it at manageable levels.

Life changes are a major source of stress, whether they bring about positive or negative emotions. Also, whether something is stressful varies by degree. Psychologists have actually ranked stressful events according to their magnitude, as can be seen in the Social Readjustment Rating Scale (SRRS) in Table 16.4 (Holmes & Rahe, 1968). The highest-stress events include death of a spouse and divorce, while holidays and traffic tickets occupy the lower end of the spectrum. According to the psychologists who developed this scale, as the points in the left column of Table 16.4 accumulate, a person's risk for becoming ill increases. For example, 300 or more points put people at significant risk for developing heart problems, ulcers, and infections. As we will see, our stress responses are closely linked to numerous physiological systems, such as cardiovascular and immune system functioning.

Life-stress experiences for adults will not necessarily generalize across all age groups. Recognizing this fact, some psychologists have focused specifically on what is stressful to college students. The right-hand column of Table 16.4 ranks stressful events reported by college students.

Some level of stress can actually be helpful—without it, motivation to perform can decline. Conversely, as Sian Beilock and many other psychologists have shown, too much stress taxes cognitive resources, resulting in poorer

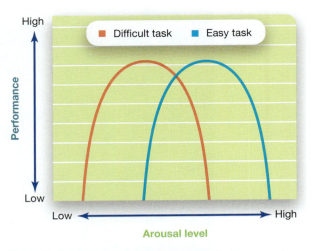

{FIG. 16.3} **Arousal and Performance** Performance is related to at least two critical factors—the difficulty of the task and the level of arousal/stress while they are being performed. For easy tasks, moderately high arousal helps; for difficult tasks, lower levels of arousal are optimal.

performance. Task complexity is an important factor to consider when it comes to describing the relationship between stress and performance. Generally speaking, higher levels of arousal facilitate solving relatively simple problems, while complex tasks are better performed under lower levels of arousal (see Figure 16.3).

To reiterate the definition of this term, stress occurs when perceived demands exceed the resources we believe we have to cope with the demands. In either case, our bodies have evolved important physiological and neural mechanisms to regulate our responses to stress.

Physiology of Stress

Stress is *felt* as much as it is experienced. You can literally feel yourself react to acute stressors, such as giving an oral presentation in class, as well as chronic stressors, such as the cumulative effect of a challenging school year. Walter Cannon, an early researcher into the phenomenon of stress, noted that the physical responses to stressors were somewhat general, despite the fact that stress can come from a variety of sources that may be biological, cognitive, or social in nature. Cannon described this general reaction as a *fight-or-flight response,* a set of physiological changes that occur in response to psychological or physical threats.

Hans Selye (1956) looked beyond the immediate fight-or-flight response and saw the unfolding of a larger pattern of responding to stress. He named this pattern the **general adaptation syndrome (GAS):** *a theory of stress responses involving stages of alarm, resistance, and exhaustion.* As GAS illustrates, a stressful event, such as a mild shock if you are a rat, or a pop quiz if you are a college student, first elicits an *alarm* reaction. Alarm consists of your

Table 16.4 :: Life Stress Inventories for the General Adult Population and for College Students

RATING	ITEM	RATING	ITEM
	ORIGINAL SOCIAL READJUSTEMENT RATING SCALE (HOLMES & RAHE, 1967)		A LIFE STRESS INVENTORY GENERATED BY COLLEGE STUDENTS (RENNER & MACKIN, 1998)
100	Death of a spouse	100	Being raped
73	Divorce	100	Finding out that you are HIV-positive
65	Marital separation	98	Being accused of rape
63	Jail term	97	Death of a close friend
63	Death of a close family member	96	Death of a close family member
53	Personal injury or illness	94	Contracting a sexually transmitted disease (other than AIDS)
50	Marriage	91	Concerns about being pregnant
47	Fired at work	90	Finals week
45	Marital reconciliation	90	Concerns about your partner being pregnant
45	Retirement	89	Oversleeping for an exam
44	Change in health of family member	89	Flunking a class
40	Pregnancy	85	Having a boyfriend or girlfriend cheat on you
39	Sex difficulties	85	Ending a steady dating relationship
39	Gain of new family member	85	Serious illness in a close friend or family member
39	Business readjustment	84	Financial difficulties
38	Change in financial state	83	Writing a major term paper
37	Death of close friend	83	Being caught cheating on a test
36	Change to different line of work	82	Drunk driving
35	Change in number of arguments with spouse	82	Sense of overload in school or work
31	Mortgage exceeding $10,000	80	Two exams in one day
30	Foreclosure of mortgage or loan	77	Cheating on your boyfriend or girlfriend
29	Change in responsibilities at work	76	Getting married
29	Son or daughter leaving home	75	Negative consequences of drinking or drug use
29	Trouble with in-laws	73	Depression or crisis in your best friend
28	Outstanding personal achievement	73	Difficulties with parents
26	Wife begins or stops work	72	Talking in front of a class
26	Begin or end school	69	Lack of sleep
25	Change in living conditions	69	Change in housing situation (hassles, moves)
24	Revision of personal habits	69	Competing or performing in public
23	Trouble with boss	68	Getting in a physical fight
20	Change in work hours or conditions	66	Difficulties with a roommate
20	Change in residence	65	Job changes (applying, new job, work hassles)
20	Change in schools	65	Declaring a major or concerns about future plans
19	Change in recreation	62	A class you hate
19	Change in church activities	61	Drinking or use of drugs
18	Change in social activities	60	Confrontations with professors
17	Mortgage or loan less than $10,000	58	Starting a new semester
16	Change in sleeping habits	57	Going on a first date
15	Change in number of family get-togethers	55	Registration
15	Change in eating habits	55	Maintaining a steady dating relationship
13	Vacation	54	Commuting to campus or work, or both
12	Christmas	53	Peer pressures
11	Minor violations of the law	53	Being away from home for the first time
	Total	52	Getting sick
		52	Concerns about your appearance
		51	Getting straight A's
		48	A difficult class that you love
		47	Making new friends, getting along with friends
		47	Fraternity or sorority rush
		40	Falling asleep in class
		20	Attending an athletic event (e.g., football games)
			Total

recognition of the threat and the physiological reactions that accompany it. As the stressful event continues, the second part of this adaptive response, known as *resistance*, is characterized by coping with the event (freezing for the rat, and for you gathering your thoughts and mentally preparing for the quiz). The third and final stage is *exhaustion*—the experience depletes your physical resources and your physiological stress response declines.

Since the work of Cannon and Selye, psychologists have further uncovered the highly complex physiological interactions that occur during and after stress. In their search, two key pathways have been identified: the autonomic pathway and the HPA axis, which we discuss next.

THE STRESS PATHWAYS You can likely attest to the fact that stress involves your whole body. During stressful times the heart races, palms get sweaty, and the stomach feels like it is tied in a knot. These sensations are the result of activity in the *autonomic pathway,* which originates in the brain and extends to the body where you *feel* stress the most. Recall from Module 3.3 that the nervous system consists of the central nervous system (brain and spinal cord) and the peripheral nervous system, which includes the autonomic nervous system. In response to stress, the hypothalamus stimulates the sympathetic nervous system, which then causes the adrenal glands (found in a region called the adrenal medulla) to release epinephrine and norepinephrine, which then trigger bodily changes associated with the fight-or-flight response (see Figure 16.4).

Another physiological system involved in the stress response is the **hypothalamic–pituitary–adrenal (HPA) axis**, *a neural and endocrine circuit that provides communication between the nervous system (the hypothalamus) and the endocrine system (pituitary and adrenal glands).* Think of the HPA axis as a series of steps leading to the body's stress response. When you perceive that you are in a stressful situation, the hypothalamus releases a substance called corticotrophin-releasing factor, which stimulates the pituitary gland to release adrenocorticotrophic hormone. This hormone in turn stimulates the release of **cortisol**, *a hormone secreted by the adrenal cortex that prepares the body to respond to stressful circumstances.* For example, cortisol may stimulate increased access to energy stores or lead to decreased inflammation. In summary, both the sympathetic nervous system (through the release of epinephrine and norepinephrine) and the HPA axis (through the release of cortisol) function to prepare us to respond to stress.

With rare medical exceptions, humans mount both autonomic and HPA axis responses to stress. These responses are highly adaptive and promote survival under stress. However, as we will see later, chronic stress responses, which can occur under circumstances such as having legal or financial problems, impact long-term health (Chrousos & Gold, 1992). Also, individuals differ in how their autonomic nervous system responds to stress. These individual differences may be traceable to our early experiences with stressful events. Human and animal studies reveal that childhood stress, such as deprivation of maternal care, has lasting effects on the stress response system (Chrousos, 2009). Researchers have discovered that chemicals called glucocorticoids (cortisol is a type of glucocorticoid), which are a part of the HPA axis, are also modified by social stress during early development. To identify this relationship, researchers conducted autopsies on people who had experienced extensive childhood abuse and eventually committed suicide. Compared with the autopsies of controls, the brains of the deceased individuals who had been abused had significantly fewer receptors for glucocorticoids (McGowan et al., 2009). Fewer receptors for these chemicals have also been found in well-controlled rat studies involving maternal deprivation. As we can see, stress can have very negative effects on brain functioning and development.

{FIG. 16.4} **Stress Pathways of the Body** The stress pathways of the body include the autonomic nervous system and the HPA axis. Both systems converge on the adrenal glands. The autonomic response involves stimulation of the adrenal medulla by the sympathetic nervous system, resulting in the release of epinephrine and norepinephrine—chemicals that stimulate the fight-or-flight response. Activity of the HPA axis results in stimulation of the adrenal cortex, which releases cortisol into the bloodstream. **Click on this figure in your eText to see more details.**

OXYTOCIN: TO TEND AND BEFRIEND

Not all stress responses are about fighting or fleeing; in fact, some have just the opposite focus. Stress sometimes leads people to seek close contact and social support, a phenomenon known as the *tend and befriend* response (Tamres et al., 2002; Taylor, 2002). This reaction may be promoted by the release of **oxytocin**, *a stress-sensitive hormone that is typically associated with maternal bonding and social relationships*. Oxytocin influences social bonding in both males and females, but women seem to rely more on this particular physiological adaptation to cope with stress (Taylor, 2006). This unique stress response for females is thought to have evolutionary significance. For females of many species, the responsibility to avoid harm and protect offspring under stressful circumstances has likely survival advantages over fighting or running away.

Quick Quiz 16.2a
Physiology of Stress

KNOW…

1 Which of the following is not a component of Selye's general adaptation syndrome?

  A Resistance   **C** Flight

  B Alarm   **D** Exhaustion

2 Which of the following is a major player in the chemical response comprising the autonomic fight-or-flight stress response system?

  A Cortisol   **C** Dopamine

  B Epinephrine   **D** Oxytocin

UNDERSTAND…

3 A major difference between the tend and befriend stress response and the responses mediated by the autonomic pathway and the HPA axis is that:

  A the tend and befriend response involves cortisol activity.

  B men are more likely to express the tend and befriend response.

  C the tend and befriend response facilitates care for offspring and others in a social group.

  D the tend and befriend response is a negative stress reaction, whereas the autonomic pathway and HPA axis responses are positive reactions.

4 High _____ levels and low _____ levels are associated with elevated stress.

  A cortisol; oxytocin   **C** epinephrine; cortisol

  B epinephrine; oxytocin   **D** cortisol; vasopressin

APPLY…

5 According to the Social Readjustment Rating Scale (SRRS), which of the following is most likely to cause you the most stress?

  A A jail term

  B The death of a family member

  C A pregnancy

  D A divorce

Answers can be found on page ANS-5.

Stress, Immunity, and Illness

Stress and physical health are closely related. The immune system, which is responsible for protecting the body against infectious disease, has numerous connections with the nervous system, including the stress response systems just discussed (Maier & Watkins, 1998). **Psychoneuroimmunology** *is the study of the relationship between immune system and nervous system functioning.* You have likely had the unfortunate experience of getting sick in the midst of a period of high stress. In fact, one study suggests that final exams may be bad for you. In this investigation, medical students provided blood samples during the term and again during the final exam period. Analysis of these blood samples showed reduced immune responses during the high-stress period at the end of the term (Kiecolt-Glaser, 1984). This is not an isolated phenomenon; dozens of experimental and correlational studies have shown, for example, that stress predicts whether people will succumb to the cold virus (Cohen et al., 1998). Another issue that health psychologists have explored is the relationship between intimate relationships and physical health.

WORKING THE SCIENTIFIC LITERACY MODEL
Relationships and Health

Social relationships can be a major source of both positive and negative stress, and they can provide a great deal of support during our most stressful times. Given the links between stress and health, it seems reasonable to ask: How do our personal relationships relate to health?

What do we know about relationships and health?

Weddings, holidays, and family and class reunions can bring great joy and closeness, yet can be very stressful. Friendships and romantic relationships can also bring about considerable negative stress when there is conflict or disagreement, or when individuals feel misunderstood or disregarded. Periods of social distress can distract someone from work, school, and other daily activities. In addition, this type of stress can even affect how the body responds to illness or injury.

Two hormones, *oxytocin* and *vasopressin*, are involved in social behavior and bonding. We previously discussed the

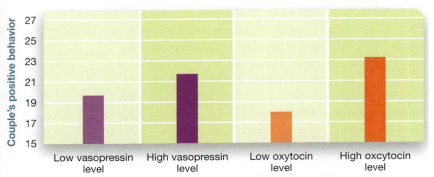

Couple's positive behavior

| 27 | 25 | 23 | 21 | 19 | 17 | 15 |

Low vasopressin level | High vasopressin level | Low oxytocin level | High oxcytocin level

{FIG. 16.5} **Relationship Quality Is Related to Physiological Responses** Higher oxytocin and vasopressin levels are associated with positive social interactions between married couples.

role of oxytocin in moderating stress responses, primarily in females. People with high vasopressin levels also tend to report better relationship quality with their spouses (Walum et al., 2008). Interestingly, both of these hormones also interact with the immune system, specifically to reduce inflammation.

How can science explain connections between relationships and health?

These observations suggest the possibility that oxytocin and vasopressin might be related to better physical health in the context of close social relationships. A common, if not surprising method for measuring immunity and health is to see how quickly people recover from a minor wound. In one study, the effect of marital stress on wound healing was tested in a group of 37 married couples (Gouin et al., 2010). Each couple was asked to sit together with no other couples or researchers present and complete a series of marital interaction tasks, including a discussion of the history of their marriage and a task in which both spouses were instructed to discuss something they wished to change about themselves. These interactions were videotaped and the researchers also took blood samples to measure oxytocin and vasopressin levels. Each participant also consented to receiving a suction blister on the forearm, which is a very minor wound created with a medical vacuum pump.

During the marital interaction tasks, those who engaged their partner with positive responses including acceptance, support, and self-disclosure had higher levels of oxytocin and vasopressin. Those who responded with hostility, withdrawal, and distress had lower levels (Figure 16.5). In addition, the suction blister wounds healed more quickly over an 8-day period in individuals with high oxytocin and vasopressin levels. (Suction wounds heal to 100% within 12 days.)

The health-promoting effects of oxytocin are also evident from placebo-controlled studies. In another experiment, married couples were given either an intranasal solution of oxytocin or a placebo. The couples then engaged in discussion about conflict within their marriage. Those who received a boost of oxytocin showed more positive, constructive behavior during their discussion compared to couples in the placebo group. The researchers also measured cortisol levels from saliva samples obtained from each individual. Those in the oxytocin group had lower levels of this stress hormone compared to couples in the placebo group (Ditzen et al., 2009).

Can we critically evaluate this evidence?

It might be tempting to conclude that a boost of oxytocin or vasopressin could be the key to marital happiness, stress reduction, and physical health. Although the studies you just read about are related to these important qualities, it is important to avoid oversimplifying what their results mean. Claims that homeopathic oxytocin remedies can make anyone happier and better at love, marriage, sex, and even "mind reading" should be looked at with skepticism. Advertisements for such products are not hard to find. However, scientists are still in the relatively early stages of learning just how oxytocin and vasopressin affect social behavior in humans, and how they are related to immune system function (Gouin et al., 2010; Macdonald & Macdonald, 2010).

Why is this relevant?

Although these studies were conducted with married couples, the physiological and physical healing benefits of close, positive social relationships extend to romantic relationships, friendships, and family. Procedures for healing physical injury currently focus on repair to damaged areas and preventing infection from setting in. In addition to these critical steps, it appears that managing psychological stress is also important for facilitating recovery from wounds (Gouin & Kiecolt-Glaser, 2011).

CORONARY HEART DISEASE High stress levels appear to put people at greater risk for developing **coronary heart disease**—*a condition in which plaques form in the blood vessels that supply the heart with blood and oxygen, resulting in restricted blood flow.* For example, one study followed 12,000 healthy males for a nine-year period and found that men who experienced ongoing stress with their families or at work were 30% more likely to die from coronary heart disease than were men who were not chronically stressed (Matthews & Gump, 2002). Coronary heart disease begins when injury and infection damage the arteries of the heart. This damage triggers the *inflammatory response* by the immune system—white blood cells travel to affected areas in an attempt to repair the damaged tissue. These cells gather cholesterol and form dangerous plaques, which can rupture, break off, and block blood flow. So how does stress fit into this picture? Stress causes an increased release of those molecules that cause the inflammation that leads to heart complications (Segerstrom & Miller, 2004).

Stress influences heart functioning in other, indirect ways as well. For example, stress influences the decisions we make at the grocery store and in trips to the kitchen—decisions that can impact health. Seeking out food in response to stress puts people at increased risk for developing health problems, particularly if the stress is frequent and the food is of poor quality. However, as we learned earlier, males and females differ in how they handle stress. In one study, psychologists offered male research participants snacking options of healthy foods (peanuts and grapes) or unhealthy options (M&Ms and potato chips) while they were given an unsolvable anagram puzzle (stressful) or a solvable anagram (nonstressful). Perhaps counter to what you might predict, men in the *no-stress* condition ate more junk food than did the men who were stressed by the unsolvable anagram (Zellner et al., 2007). This finding contrasts with the tendencies of female participants—in a similar experiment, women ate more junk food when stressed (Zellner et al., 2006).

An unsolvable anagram is an acute stressor that is easy to leave behind. By comparison, job, family, and other potential sources of stress are much more challenging to manage. So how do real-life chronic stressors affect eating? It turns out that chronic stress leads to greater consumption of calorie-rich, less-healthy foods. This finding probably fits with your own experiences. Unfortunately, the stress response in the nervous system underlies our decisions to opt for doughnuts rather than apple slices. Why do we turn to tasty, calorie-rich foods when stressed? The answer may seem obvious—it's called "comfort food" for a reason. However, stress actually alters the physiological pathways that lead us to food. Evolution has equipped us with a tendency to increase food intake under times of stress. Recall that when the HPA axis is stimulated under stressful circumstances it releases glucocorticoids such as cortisol. Researchers now think that this stress response leads us to regard calorie-rich food as more rewarding than when we are not stressed (Adam & Epel, 2007).

MYTHS IN MIND
Stress and Ulcers

People typically associate ulcers—open sores in the lining of the esophagus, stomach, and small intestine—with people working in high-stress jobs, such as police officers or air traffic controllers. The belief that stress causes people to develop ulcers is widespread. In actuality, most ulcers are caused by a bacterium, *Helicobacter pylori*, which can cause inflammation of the lining of various regions of the digestive tract. This bacterium is surprisingly common, and approximately 10% to 15% of people who are exposed to it will develop an ulcer resulting from inflammation. Thus stress does not *cause* ulcers, although it can worsen their symptoms. Also, smoking, alcohol, pain relievers, and a poor diet—anything that can irritate the digestive system—increases problems associated with ulcers.

Contrary to popular belief, chronic stress, like that experienced by air traffic controllers, will not cause a stomach ulcer.

• • • • • • • • • • • • • • • • • •

AIDS Acquired-immune deficiency syndrome (AIDS) is a disease caused by infection with the human immunodeficiency virus (HIV). This disease saps the immune system's ability to fight off infections, to such an extent that even conditions that are relatively harmless to most of the population can be devastating to an individual with AIDS. Patients in industrialized countries with more medical options have a better prognosis than those living in impoverished areas. Retroviral therapies have greatly increased the longevity, health, and overall quality of life of patients. However, people who are HIV positive need regular vaccination treatments. Unfortunately, stress impedes the body's ability to respond to vaccinations. In turn, studies have shown that those who experience serious emotional distress are less responsive to HIV treatments. Stress-induced elevation of norepinephrine can also worsen the condition of the various illnesses associated with AIDS. Patients who have elevated activity of the autonomic nervous system are slower to respond to antiretroviral therapies, which increases their risks of developing certain types of cancer such as B-cell lymphoma (Cole et al., 1998).

CANCER   Researchers are finding numerous links between psychosocial factors and cancer progression (Antoni & Lutgendorf, 2007). Several factors, such as the type of cancer and an individual's age, account for why some people rapidly succumb to cancer while others are able to win the battle. In addition, stress levels affect the progression of cancer. Why is this? It appears that norepinephrine supports cancer cell growth, and that cortisol magnifies this effect. Hormones from the autonomic nervous system stimulate cells that reside in tumors, which ultimately results in growth and proliferation of these masses (Antoni et al., 2006). Thus, when someone experiences stress, the autonomic nervous system and HPA axis naturally respond, but their reactions compromise how well the individual can fight the disease.

For many people, stress levels can be changed and the course of a disease such as cancer can be slowed. For example, individuals who have undergone assertiveness training and learn anger management techniques show reduced autonomic activity and hormonal activity associated with the HPA axis (Antoni et al., 2007). Also, those who are optimistic cope by using humor and have a positive outlook on the disease (and thus less stress) show physiological benefits such as greater immune response (Lutgendorf et al., 2007).

Psychologists are finding that the stress–illness relationship is a very complex one, involving numerous physiological systems. Also, the effects of mental stress on physical functioning are diverse. Recall that stress can come in a variety of forms—at the very least, we can divide it into acute and chronic variations. It appears that stress also has dual influences on immunity. Acute stressors tend to activate the immune system, whereas chronic exposure to stress generally causes suppression of the immune system (Segerstrom & Miller, 2004).

Stress, Personality, and Illness

How people handle and cope with stress often depends on their personality. This relationship is evident very early in life, even during infancy. Children who are easily distressed tend to be more prone to illness during adulthood. Even cognitive activity in our early years is related to adult health. For example, children who are able to better focus their attention on tasks tend to be healthier in adulthood (Kubzansky et al., 2009). Furthermore, infants who are securely attached to their mothers show reduced activity in their sympathetic nervous systems when their mothers are absent (Frigerio et al., 2009). As personality takes shape in adulthood, we can further see how different personalities deal with stress and how stress relates to health.

First consider your own responses to a common stressful event. Imagine you have a one-hour break between classes, during which you need to get lunch and also visit one of your professors across campus. When you arrive at your professor's office, you see a line of other students awaiting their turn, and the current occupant is blathering on and on about something completely unrelated to schoolwork. How would you tend to react in this situation? Would you become agitated, angry, resentful, and fidgety? Or would you be more inclined to strike up a conversation with others in line to help pass the time? Your answer will likely depend on various factors—but each of us tends to have a common style of responding to stressful events.

The **Type A personality** *describes people who tend to be impatient and worry about time, and are easily angered, competitive and highly motivated.* In contrast, the **Type B personality** *describes people who are more laid back and characterized by a patient, easygoing, and relaxed disposition* (Friedman & Rosenman, 1974). The concept of Type A and B did not originate in psychology. Rather, cardiologists suspected that people who were prone to stress had poorer physical health. They identified these individuals as Type A, and their studies revealed that people who fall in the Type A category are far more likely to have heart attacks than are Type B people. This initial finding has been replicated many times, though the correlation between levels of Type A characteristics and coronary heart disease is only moderate. This less than strong relationship likely reflects the fact that other factors, not just how a person copes with stress, may further elevate the risk of coronary heart disease. People who have a Type A personality also engage in behaviors that compromise physical health, such as drinking large quantities of alcohol, smoking, and sleeping less than people with a Type B personality. Thus numerous correlated factors may explain the relationship between Type A personality and risk of coronary heart disease.

The distinction between Type A and B personalities has not satisfied all behavioral scientists and physicians. Being quick to anger is a characteristic of Type A individuals, but so is being hyper-motivated to succeed at work. Perhaps there is something more specific about personality that increases one's risk for developing heart disease. More recent research has shown that people who are prone to hostility and anger are at greater risk for developing coronary heart disease (Razzini et al., 2008). Other personality characteristics linked to coronary heart disease include anxiety and depression.

Outlook on life seems to influence physical health as well. People who are optimistic tend to have a positive outlook on life and have a constructive way of explaining the causes of everyday events. Pessimists have a more negative perception of life and tend to see the glass as half-empty. Optimism is correlated with better physical health than pessimism. For example, optimists had a lower incidence of coronary heart disease in a large cohort of men studied in the Veterans Affairs Normative Aging Study (Kubzansky et al., 2001). Pessimism can even compromise health when it comes to viral responses. Women who tend toward pessimism and test positive for the HPV virus (a papilloma virus known to cause cervical cancer) have lower counts of white blood cells that fight disease than do optimistic women with the HPV virus. If stressed, pessimistic women run a greater risk of developing cervical cancer (Antoni et al., 2006).

Much of the research on personality and health is correlational in nature—the two variables are related but what accounts for their relationship is not always possible to determine. The fact that early childhood experiences predict later health outcomes suggests that personality style determines health during adulthood.

Quick Quiz 16.2c
Stress, Personality, and Illness

KNOW...

1 People with _____ personality type are patient and easygoing, and have relaxed disposition, whereas _____ personality individuals tend to be impatient and are easily angered, competitive, and highly motivated.

- **A** Type A; Type B
- **B** stressed; relaxed
- **C** Type B; Type A
- **D** relaxed; stressed

2 The health risk most likely to be associated with Type A personality is _____.

- **A** AIDS
- **B** cancer
- **C** coronary heart disease
- **D** the cold virus

ANALYZE...

3 Which of the following observations is a fair critique of the Type A and Type B categorization of personality types?

- **A** They were not developed by psychologists.
- **B** They apply only to hospital patients.
- **C** They reflect the fact that people tend to lie on personality tests.
- **D** Their connection to health outcomes may be more reflective of lifestyle factors such as sleep and alcohol consumption than of personality style.

Answers can be found on page ANS-5.

Module 16.2

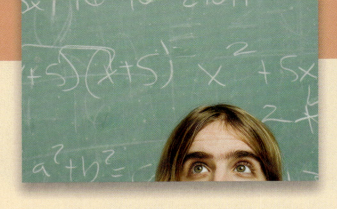

Now that you have read this module you should.

KNOW …

- **The key terminology associated with stress and illness:**

coronary heart disease (p. 603)

cortisol (p. 600)

general adaptation syndrome (GAS) (p. 598)

hypothalamic–pituitary–adrenal (HPA) axis (p. 600)

oxytocin (p. 601)

psychoneuroimmunology (p. 601)

stress (p. 597)

Type A personality (p. 605)

Type B personality (p. 605)

UNDERSTAND …

- **The physiological reactions that occur under stress.** When a person encounters a stressor, the hypothalamus stimulates the sympathetic nervous system to act, triggering the release of epinephrine and norepinephrine from the adrenal medulla. This reaction is often referred to as the fight-or-flight response. Another part of the stress response system is the HPA axis, in which the hypothalamus stimulates the pituitary gland to release hormones that in turn stimulate the adrenal cortex to release cortisol, which prepares the body to deal with stressful situations.

- **How the immune system is connected to stress responses.** Cortisol suppresses the immune system, leaving people more vulnerable to illness and slowing recovery time from illness and injury.

APPLY …

- **A measure of stressful events to your own experiences.** You can compare your own life stress experiences with those of a large sample of college students. To complete this activity, look at the right-hand column of **Table 16.4** on page 599. Using the values next to each stressful event listed, add up the numbers that apply to your experiences and compute your total stress score. Renner and Mackin (1998) gathered data on a sample of 257 undergraduate college students using the same instrument (range: 17–45 years; mean: 19.75 years). They reported an average stress score of 1,247 (standard deviation: 441), with scores ranging from 182 to 2,571. How did you compare with their sample?

ANALYZE …

- **The claim that ulcers are caused by stress.** Ulcers are damaged areas of the digestive tract often caused by infection with the bacterium *Helicobacter pylori*. Stress and other factors, such as diet and alcohol consumption, can worsen the condition of ulcers, but stress alone does not cause them.

Module

16.3

Coping and Well-Being

Learning Objectives

After reading this module you should:

KNOW ...	UNDERSTAND ...	APPLY ...	ANALYZE ...
The key terminology associated with coping and well-being	How control over the environment influences coping and outlook Positive and negative styles of coping	Your knowledge to better understand your own tendencies when dealing with stressful situations	Whether activities such as relaxation techniques, meditation, and biofeedback actually help people cope with stress and problems

What is the best way to cope with a personal disaster, such as losing your job? Writing about how the event makes you feel may not seem like a priority, but according to psychologist James Pennebaker, it may be one of the best strategies for coping and regaining the emotional resources needed to move on. Pennebaker, a leading researcher on the psychological benefits of writing, decided to intervene when a local computing and electronics firm laid off 60 professional workers. All he asked the workers to do was to write. But their instructions on *how* to write were different: Half the volunteers were randomly assigned to write about their "deepest thoughts and feelings surrounding the job loss, and how their lives, both personal and professional, had been affected" (Spera et al., 1994, p. 725). In contrast, the control group members were told to write about their plans for the day and how they planned to find another job, which is much less personal and emotional. After a month of weekly 20-minute writing sessions, the group members who were writing about their emotions were getting hired much more frequently than the control group members. This was a double-blind, randomized study, so the differences between the groups can be traced to the writing. Similar methods have been used in Pennebaker's studies of first-year college students, people

grieving the loss of a loved one, and other groups experiencing stressful transitions. The result was the same each time—group members who wrote meaningful narratives of their emotions and thoughts came out ahead, not just in terms of mental health, but physically and in terms of their performance at work or school.

Focus Questions

1. What are the different ways people cope with stress?
2. Which factors make coping especially challenging?

· · · · · · · · · · · · · · · · · ·

In this module, we will present some widely used solutions for coping with stress and behavioral methods that may potentially help in improving health. We will also discuss some topics that might be less familiar, but may prove useful in how you cope with stress and negative events. Finally, we will discuss how stress and successful coping are closely related to our sense of control.

Coping

Equally important in understanding how stress works is understanding how to cope with it. **Coping** *refers to the processes used to manage demands, stress, and conflict.* Some of us approach a problem or stressor, such as large monetary debt or a setback at work, by taking a *problem-solving* approach. In other words, we cope by defining the problem and working toward a solution. However, not all stressors are brought about by problems that have identifiable solutions. For example, *emotional coping* is probably better suited to dealing with an issue such as the loss of a loved one. Neither of these styles of coping is superior to the other—the two are often combined and their suitability depends on the nature of the problem (Folkman & Lazarus, 1980).

Not all coping techniques actually help; some may simply replace one problem with another. For example, some people turn to alcohol or drugs to temporarily avoid feelings of stress, and some turn to food. Ice cream, chocolate, and salty snacks are popular—but probably unhealthy—methods of coping. In this section, we will examine the major ways of coping by focusing first on the positive approaches, and then on some of the negative ways that people cope.

POSITIVE COPING STRATEGIES   Psychology may have a reputation for focusing on the negative, including how damaging stress can be. In reality, psychologists also study what makes people thrive, even in the face of extreme stress. This area of study, which has recently become known as **positive psychology**, *uses scientific methods to study human strengths and potential.* Research in this area has identified numerous adaptive and constructive ways in which people cope with problems; these strategies produce meaningful solutions to stressful problems or, at the very least, healthy ways of living with them.

Optimism *is the tendency to have a favorable, constructive view on situations and to expect positive outcomes.* The effectiveness of optimism for coping with stress is particularly evident in studies of freshmen adjusting to their first semester of college. Students who were optimistic by nature experienced relatively low levels of stress and depression and were also proactive in seeking out peers for support and companionship. Overall, their adjustment to college was better than the adjustment of those students who were pessimistic in nature (Brissette et al., 2002). People who are optimistic in the face of adversity are better able to approach problems from various angles and come up with constructive solutions. Some evidence also indicates that they are more physiologically equipped to deal with stress than are pessimists. Optimists are better protected against coronary heart disease than pessimists (Kubzansky et al., 2001), and optimism is associated with quicker recovery following surgery (Hochhausen et al., 2007).

Coping is also influenced by **resilience**, *the ability to effectively recover from illness or adversity.* Individuals differ in their ability to bounce back from events such as disaster, disease, or major loss. Resilient people tend to have one or more factors stacked in their favor. Financial and social resources, opportunities for rest and relaxation, and other positive life circumstances contribute to resiliency. Even so, amazing stories of resiliency can be found among individuals living with unimaginable stress. Thus personality and emotional characteristics are also important contributors to resiliency in the face of adversity. One amazing example is that of Victor Frankl, an early- and mid-20th-century Austrian psychiatrist. Frankl was already an influential physician and therapist when he, his wife, and family were forced into concentration camps during World War II. Frankl found himself in the role of helping people adjust to life in the concentration camp. He encouraged others to tap into whatever psychological resources they had left to cope with very bleak circumstances. Frankl not only helped others find resiliency, but also became more aware of his own resiliency as he had to find meaning in his own circumstances. Eventually Frankl's wife and parents were deported to different concentration camps, where they were murdered. Despite his own enormous losses, Frankl continued helping others to cope and find solace under the worst of circumstances (Frankl, 1959).

Psychologists have long focused on the negative outcomes of stress, but stories such as Frankl's demonstrate that stress and trauma can also lead people to recognize and use positive qualities. In fact, psychologists describe the phenomenon of **post-traumatic growth**, *the capacity to grow and experience long-term positive effects in response to negative events* (Tedeschi & Calhoun, 2004). It happens in response to events such as automobile accidents, sexual and physical assault, combat, and severe and chronic illnesses. Individuals who experience post-traumatic growth often report feeling a greater sense of vulnerability, yet over time develop an increased inner strength. They also report finding greater meaning and depth in their relationships, a greater sense of appreciation for what they have, and an increased sense of spirituality (Tedeschi & Calhoun, 2004).

Post-traumatic growth is not an alternative reaction to post-traumatic stress. Rather, the two conditions occur together. Clinicians recognize that the growth occurs during the process of coping, not because of the event itself. Often a clinical psychologist trained in working with trauma victims helps facilitate the growth process and assists the individual in finding the interpersonal and social resources needed for healing.

MEDITATION, RELAXATION, AND BIOFEEDBACK

As you have been reading this chapter, your circulatory system has been pumping blood and maintaining blood pressure, your lungs have been breathing in air, and your digestive system may have been working on a recent meal, all without the tiniest bit of conscious effort. Certainly you can hold your breath for a moment using conscious effort, but can you hold your heartbeat? Change your blood pressure? If you are like most of us, you cannot control all of these autonomic functions, but that does not mean that it is impossible.

Biofeedback *is a therapeutic technique involving the use of physiological recording instruments to provide feedback that increases awareness of bodily responses.* The psychologists who developed this technique believed that by seeing or hearing a machine's representation of bodily processes, people could gain awareness of stress responses and bring them under voluntary control. For example, a patient with chronic stress could use feedback on his blood pressure, heart rate, and tension of his facial muscles to monitor and, possibly, control his stress responses. As you can imagine, this ability would have very useful applications to clinical psychology. However, after some very promising findings, the excitement over biofeedback was reeled in a bit, in part because it was found that simple relaxation techniques were just as useful.

Many people report significant benefits by using *relaxation* and *meditation* techniques to cope with stress and life's difficult periods. Relaxation and meditation techniques are designed to calm emotional responses as well as physiological reactions to stress. People frequently regard meditation as either a religious or new-age ritual—something that takes years of practice from which only "experts" can benefit. This is hardly an accurate summary of meditation. Meditation comes in two general varieties: (1) *mindfulness*, which involves attending to all thoughts, sensations, and feelings without attempting to judge or control them, and (2) *concentrative*, in which the individual focuses on a specific thought or sensation, such as an image or a repeated sound (Cahn & Polich, 2006). Meditation is most successful when performed in a quiet environment, when the person assumes a relaxed position (but not sufficient to support napping), and when he or she remains passive except for mindfulness activity or focusing attention. Meta-analysis

Biofeedback involves the use of physiological monitoring, which allows the patient to see and sometimes hear the output of his or her physiological reactions.

of literature indicates that meditation is very effective in reducing blood pressure, which reduces the potential for long-term problems with hypertension and cardiovascular disease (Rainforth et al., 2007).

Brain imaging work may take us a step closer to actually visualizing the connections between mind and body. A complex form of meditation called *integrated mind–body training* was developed from traditional Chinese medicine; it involves bodily interaction with thinking and emotion. This probably sounds mystical and beyond scientific scrutiny. In fact, Chinese scientists conducted brain scans on students who practiced integrated mind-body training. Over the course of the training, the students' brains did seem to develop an increased ability to control bodily physiology. A region of the midfrontal cortex called the *anterior cingulate* was particularly

Meditation is practiced in many cultures, typically to serve the function of promoting health and stress reduction.

relevant; this area is involved in various aspects of processing reward and emotion. In this study, activity within the anterior cingulate was associated with the participants' increased control over parasympathetic nervous system responses. The increased parasympathetic activity accounted for the heightened sense of relaxation experienced while meditating. This result was not found in students who engaged in a simpler relaxation technique that did not involve integrating mind–body interactions (Tang et al., 2009). Thus scientific studies of meditation appear to confirm its health benefits, and are also bringing us closer to understanding precisely how the nervous system is linked with other bodily processes (Cahn & Polich, 2006).

PSYCH @

Church

Many people use religion as their primary coping mechanism during stressful situations, both large and small. They may use any combination of religious practices, depending on the specific nature of the faith: prayer, meditation, religious counseling, and social support from family and congregations. All of these efforts can provide strength and comfort during difficult times, but they may also be associated with greater overall happiness. Many psychologists have become increasingly curious about the possible health benefits associated with religion and spirituality. Numerous studies have found that people who are very religious and are actively engaged with religious practices do, in fact, live a bit longer than do people who are less religious or nonreligious (McCullough et al., 2000).

A hasty interpretation of these results might lead one to conclude that religion causes people to live longer—that the experiences of prayer and church going lead to the greater longevity. However, the studies in this area actually produce correlational, not experimental, data—psychologists cannot randomly assign people to be religious or not. Consequently, we must consider alternative explanations. For example, lifestyle factors are also at play. Younger and older people of Muslim, Jewish, or Christian faith are more likely to engage in healthy behaviors, including wearing seatbelts, visiting the dentist, and avoiding consumption of alcohol and cigarette smoking (reviewed in McCullough & Willoughby, 2009). Religions also tend to have negative views of criminal activity, drug abuse, and risky sexual activity. Thus the increased longevity is probably related to the greater self-control and self-regulation that are characteristic of many religious belief systems.

Generally, people who are religious show greater well-being and lower levels of depression (Smith et al., 2003). The determination of whether religion protects people from depression depends on the point of view taken, however. People who cope with problems using positive aspects of religion (e.g., viewing stressors with kindness or collaborating with others in solving problems) are less prone to depression than religious people who adopt negative appraisals of their problems and concerns, such as viewing problems as a result of God's punishment (Ano & Vasconcelles, 2005; McCullough & Willoughby, 2009).

· · · · · · · · · · · · · · · · · · · ·

NEGATIVITY AND PESSIMISM Adversity elicits a wide range of emotions and reactions. **Negative affectivity** *refers to the tendency to respond to problems with a pattern of anxiety, hostility, anger, guilt or nervousness.* We occasionally might hear of someone who deals with a difficult breakup by socially withdrawing from others, becoming angry and resentful, and oftentimes growing hostile enough to threaten and harass the other person with phone calls, repeated texting, or spreading of rumors. Although the anger and upset feelings are perfectly normal reactions, clearly these hostile behaviors are a negative way of coping. However, for some individuals, this manner of dealing with adversity is consistent, and occurs across a broad number of situations, even ones that are trivial by comparison to a breakup.

Based on this description of an individual with negative affectivity, you might expect that he or she is not too popular. Actually, negative affectivity has severe physical consequences, not just social ramifications. Negative affectivity has been linked to frequent physical complaints (headaches, pain, stomachaches;

Is the glass half-full or half-empty? Long-term studies have shown that people who have a pessimistic view tend to have increased medical problems and reduced longevity compared to optimists.

Watson & Pennebaker, 1989). Even worse, people with a negative coping style are at greater risk for illness, ulcers, asthma and coronary heart disease (Friedman & Booth-Kewley, 1987).

Related to negative affectivity is what psychologists refer to as **pessimistic explanatory style**, *which is the tendency to interpret and explain negative events as internally based and as a constant, stable quality* (Burns & Seligman, 1989). The pessimism even bubbles to the surface when events occur beyond one's personal control, such as a natural disaster or war. It is certainly evident in common events as well—for example, a laid-off employee who struggles to find a job may attribute the problem to his perceived inability to network properly or because he is just doomed to failure. In addition, similar to those with negative affectivity, individuals with a pessimistic explanatory style are at risk for health problems such as reduced immunity (Kamen-Siegel et al., 1991). Notably, pessimism appears to have long-term consequences on health. Researchers at the Mayo Clinic administered personality tests assessing optimism and pessimism to patients who came into the clinic for general medical issues during the 1960s. Thirty years later, the data on optimism and pessimism were compared to patient survival, and the researchers found a 19% increase in mortality risk in people who were consistently pessimistic (Maruta et al., 2000). Perhaps a good attitude does more than help individuals cope emotionally with illness; perhaps it actually helps them overcome it.

Quick Quiz 16.3a
Coping

KNOW...

1 _____ is the tendency to respond to problems with a pattern of anxiety, hostility, anger, guilt, or nervousness.

- **A** A coping style
- **B** Negative affectivity
- **C** Pessimism
- **D** An aggression complex

2 What does it mean to say someone is resilient?

- **A** The person has the ability to effectively recover from illness or adversity.
- **B** The person tends to be calm when challenged or stressed.
- **C** The person shows the tendency to have a favorable, constructive view on situations and to expect positive outcomes.
- **D** The person uses only positive processes to manage demands, stress, and conflict.

UNDERSTAND...

3 _____ is a positive coping strategy, while _____ is a negative style of coping.

- **A** Meditation; resilience
- **B** Pessimistic explanatory style; negative affectivity
- **C** Meditation; alcohol
- **D** Post-traumatic growth; resilience

APPLY...

4 Your partner suddenly broke up with you and did not offer an explanation. If you attribute the breakup to your not being a very outgoing person, you are demonstrating _____.

- **A** negative affectivity
- **B** a pessimistic explanatory style
- **C** resilience
- **D** a coping style

5 Under which circumstance would a problem-solving coping strategy best apply?

- **A** To reduce the pain of a breakup
- **B** To cope with a death in the family
- **C** To adjust to living in a new city
- **D** To deal with losing one's driver's license

ANALYZE...

6 What is the most accurate conclusion regarding the effects of meditation on stress and well-being?

- **A** Mediation is the absolute best way to combat stress and protect your body from disease.
- **B** Advanced training in mediation will decrease stress in a manner similar to simple relaxation techniques.
- **C** Mediation helps the practitioner control his or her physiological responses, thereby decreasing stress and preventing health problems such as cardiovascular disease.
- **D** Mediation is not a commonly used way of managing stress.

Answers can be found on page ANS-5.

Perceived Control

As Dr. Pennebaker's story from the beginning of this module illustrates, the most stressful of circumstances are the ones that people have little or no control over. For example, children who reside in abusive homes have no control over their circumstances, nor do the victims of natural disasters. Each situation can result in people acquiring a sense that their behavior has little effect on external events.

Laboratory experiments have demonstrated the negative impact that a lack of control has on health and behavior. A classic example comes from work on avoidance learning in dogs conducted in the 1960s by Martin

Seligman and his colleagues (Seligman & Maier, 1967; see Figure 16.6). In this study, dogs were exposed to an avoidance learning procedure in which they were placed in a chamber with an electric grid on the floor of one side, where the shock was delivered, and a panel that the dogs could jump over to reach a "safe" zone where there was no shock. Some dogs learned that if a tone preceded the shock, they could quickly jump to the safe zone, avoiding the shock altogether. Another group of dogs was first conditioned to the tone paired with an inescapable shock. These dogs were then placed in the avoidance chamber, but did not attempt to avoid the shock when the warning tone was sounded. Rather, they would lie down, whine, and appear resigned to receive the shock. This finding was described as **learned helplessness—** *an acquired suppression of avoidance or escape behavior in response to unpleasant, uncontrollable circumstances.*

Learned helplessness has been offered as an explanation for how people with depression tend to view the world. People with depression are prone to hold beliefs that their actions have no influence on external events, and that their environment and circumstances dictate outcomes. To some extent these beliefs may be true, but when generalized to just about any situation, they can negatively affect mental and physical well-being. The parallels to Seligman's work are rather clear. In some circumstances, humans and some nonhuman species will simply endure pain rather than initiate ways to avoid or escape it.

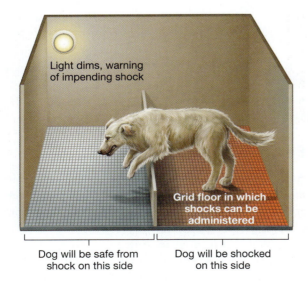

Light dims, warning of impending shock

Grid floor in which shocks can be administered

Dog will be safe from shock on this side

Dog will be shocked on this side

{FIG. 16.6} **The Learned Helplessness Procedure** In Seligman and Maier's study, dogs that could avoid a painful shock would quickly learn to do so. Conversely, dogs that initially learned they could not avoid a shock remained passive when the opportunity to do so was given. The acquired failure to avoid or escape unpleasant circumstances that are perceived as uncontrollable is referred to as learned helplessness. **Click on this figure in your eText to see more details.**

WORKING THE SCIENTIFIC LITERACY MODEL
Compensatory Control and Health

The idea of a random world and a lack of personal control can be discomforting. For example, hurricanes and tornados are often referred to as "acts of God," rather than the result of an unfortunate confluence of meteorological events and human-populated areas. But does having a sense of control lead to better health?

What do we know about how people cope with seemingly random events?

Some people feel as if they are the victims of random events, while others believe themselves to be the beneficiaries of the whims of life. However, the idea that randomness dictates worldly events can create anxiety in people. Even if a person believes randomness is the rule, he or she can become highly motivated to find meaning in the world and, through this search, a sense that the course of events is determined by the will of individuals or God (Kay et al., 2009), In this way, many people cope with stressful life events through **compensatory control**—*psychological strategies people use to preserve a sense of nonrandom order when personal control is compromised* (Kay et al., 2009). For example, people who are skeptical of any divine purpose in the world may change their view in the wake of personal or societal tragedy. These observations are primarily correlational, but researchers have conducted experiments to determine causal relationships between sense of control and beliefs about randomness versus orderliness.

How can science explain compensatory control?

To study compensatory control, researchers have developed a laboratory task that manipulates people's sense of personal control over a situation (Whitson & Galinsky, 2008). In one study, participants completed a concept identification task in which two symbols were presented on a computer screen, and the participant had to guess which symbol correctly represented the concept that the computer had chosen (e.g., the color of the symbol, its shape). The computer provided feedback on whether the participants chose the correct or incorrect symbol after each trial. Half of the participants received accurate feedback, while the other half received completely random feedback—sometimes their correct answers were recorded as incorrect, and vice versa. Participants receiving random feedback reported feeling a lower sense of control on a self-report measure.

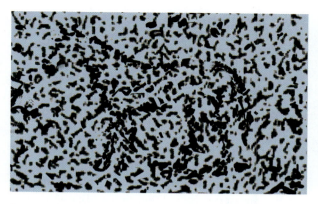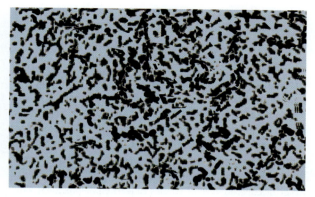

{FIG. 16.7} **Seeing Images Where There Are None** Do you see a figure in the image on the left? You may see a figure resembling a horse. What about on the right? There is no discernible image intended for this image. Psychologists have found that individuals who feel as though they lack control are more likely to detect patterns in the image at right than are people who feel a greater sense of control (Whitson & Galinsky, 2008).

Following the concept identification task, the participants then viewed multiple pictures, such as those shown in Figure 16.7. If you look closely, you will see that one of the pictures has a horse-like figure in it, whereas the other image has no discernible pattern. Participants in both conditions reported seeing faintly drawn figures, such as the horse. However, participants who had a diminished sense of control induced by the random feedback they received on the computer task were more likely to report seeing patterns within completely random images (Whitson & Galinsky, 2008).

It appears that when people feel their sense of control is undermined, they compensate by heightening their search for structure in the world, to the point of calling upon their imagination. This is evident in other domains as well, not just detecting patterns in random, snowy images. People also gain a greater need for structure and become increasingly willing to believe in superstitious rituals and to endorse conspiracy theories when their sense of control is diminished (Figure 16.8; Kay et al., 2009; Whitson & Galinksy, 2008).

Can we critically evaluate this evidence?

A major advantage of the study described here is that the researchers were able to experimentally induce a perceived lack of control in the participants who received random feedback on their performance on the computerized task. The observation that these participants then perceived images within randomness and showed a heightened belief in superstition and conspiracies may help to explain how people respond to lost control outside of the laboratory. Of course, one limitation is that a real-world lack of control, such as that which occurs in the face of natural disaster or loss of a job, has far greater consequences. Thus, as with any laboratory experiment, there is a limit to the degree to which the results generalize.

Also, earlier we commented that belief in a divine force such as God can buffer people from the discomfort produced by the notion that, for the most part, outcomes and events are largely random. It is important to add that this is not a statement on the existence of God, but rather a description of how perception of events can influence what people believe.

Why is this relevant?

Having a sense of control greatly affects how we think about and interpret the world. In addition, it affects our health. Individuals who believe they can predict and influence present and future events tend to have improved physical and mental well-being compared to people who believe the opposite. For

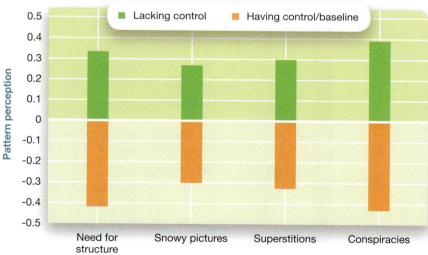

{FIG. 16.8} **Exercising Compensatory Control** When people feel as though they lack control over the world, their need for structure, perception, and beliefs in superstition and conspiracies increases. The orange bars show that participants who perceive that they are in control of events were unlikely to see images in snowy pictures and did not hold superstitious beliefs or endorse conspiracy theories. As the green bars indicate, when the same people perceive that they have lost a sense of control during the experimental procedure, the pattern is completely reversed. The participants report a greater need for structure, perceive images in random arrays, become more superstitious, and endorse conspiracy theories (Kay et al., 2009).

example, patients who are scheduled to undergo medical procedures, such as a colonoscopy, have reduced anxiety for the procedure if they are given clear, informative tutorials about the procedure before it occurs (Luck et al., 1999).

People may also compensate for their lack of control by performing *superstitious rituals*, which can provide a sense of at least partial control over outcomes. This can be seen in everyday examples, such as among athletes who follow the same steps when preparing for a game, as well as in extreme, maladaptive forms, such as in obsessive–compulsive disorder (covered in Module 13.3). Doing nothing is one response, as Seligman and Maier discovered in their studies of learned helplessness. With lost control, people are also more likely to develop beliefs that the world is not random and is controlled and orderly. This perception manifests itself as beliefs about an intervening God as well as greater likelihood of defending social and political institutions that can offer control (Kay et al., 2009).

Quick Quiz 16.3b
Perceived Control

Nutrition and Exercise

"You are what you eat" is a well-worn phrase that was probably around long before scientists confirmed that it was true. However, we now know that what we eat influences brain physiology and functioning. This being the case, psychologists have begun to investigate how diet affects intellectual ability and performance at work and school.

NUTRITION AND COGNITIVE FUNCTION Long-term consumption of fattening and sugary foods can have a negative impact on cognitive functioning. But what about the short-term effects? You have probably heard of the importance of a good breakfast more times than you care to recall. However, breakfast is the most often skipped meal, especially among children and adolescents (Rampersaud et al., 2005). Many people report not having time to eat (or not making time) and a lack of appetite for breakfast foods.

Skipping breakfast may not be a healthy choice for people heading off to school or work. The brain utilizes large amounts of glucose and other nutrients for energy and in the synthesis of neurotransmitters. Overall, research indicates that eating breakfast has a positive effect on cognitive performance (Widenhorn-Müller et al., 2008). But does this mean eating *anything*? Would you be better off eating a huge bowl of sugary cereal than eating nothing on the morning of a major exam? Currently, it is not clear how diet affects cognition and memory on a short-term basis for humans, but studies with rats show that those eating eat a high-fat, non-nutritious diet perform poorly on memory tasks in comparison to rats fed a more nutritious diet (Murray et al., 2009).

The relationship between diet and cognitive functioning has led some researchers on a quest to isolate specific compounds that are best suited to improving cognition. Certain chemicals found in various plants, called flavanols, appear to improve cognitive functioning. The majority of work on these compounds has used animal models or has taken place in a Petri dish. It does appear that these chemicals can protect nerve cells and reduce cell death (Reznichenko et al., 2005). Other dietary supplements, such as the omega-3 fatty acids found in fish, can improve brain functioning when combined with exercise (van Praag et al., 2007; Wu et al., 2008).

NUTRITION AND LONGEVITY Time and again we hear how avoiding foods that are high in saturated fats, sugar, and other non-nutritional ingredients is one way of staying healthy and living longer. Surprisingly, some research suggests that it is *not eating* that improves health and longevity. A large body of evidence indicates that caloric restriction increases longevity and can even slow the onset of age-related conditions such as Alzheimer's disease (Levenson & Rich, 2007). A calorie-restricted diet may involve eating approximately 60% of the normal amount of calories, while continuing to take in the needed nutrients. An obvious drawback to calorie restriction is that cutting back on that much food can be very unpleasant. This has led researchers to search for dietary supplements that could be taken to simulate caloric restriction.

EXERCISE Exercise has considerable physical and psychological benefits, as people ranging from weekend warriors to long-term exercisers can attest. Barring injury, we typically do not hear a committed exerciser express regret about her active lifestyle. So which specific aspects of exercise account for all of its benefits? Obviously, exercise benefits the cardiovascular, muscular, and other physiological systems. How does the nervous system factor in? Activities such as tennis train the nervous system to coordinate movements, but the benefits to the nervous system go well beyond becoming nimble and quick.

Exercise has short-term benefits on mental functioning. For example, researchers in Germany asked college student participants either to do all-out sprints, to jog, or to do nothing. The students who sprinted were able to learn 20% more items on a vocabulary list than the students who jogged or were inactive (Winter et al., 2007). Why did this occur? Perhaps the sprinters were more motivated than the others. This explanation sounds plausible, but the researchers randomly assigned healthy participants to the three groups—so there should not be anything inherent to the sprinter group that would lead them to learn more words. It appears that the type of exercise they engaged in led to increased cognitive performance. Which physiological processes might account for the cognitive edge the sprinters gained from their intense physical activity? The researchers discovered that the students who engaged in intense exercising had increased levels of dopamine, epinephrine, and **brain-derived neurotrophic factor (BDNF)**—*a protein in the nervous system that promotes survival, growth, and formation of new synapses.* Cardiovascular exercise also provides

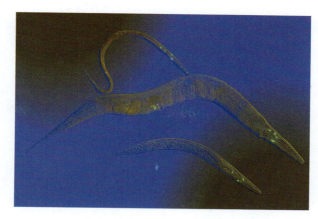

It may strike you as odd that research findings on the benefits of caloric restriction are largely based on roundworms (*Caenorhabditis elegans*). However, the results have been replicated with mice and nonhuman primates, and now studies on humans suggest that eating less—a lot less—can increase longevity.

immediate benefits in cognitive processing speed, again as measured in college-aged students (Hillman et al., 2003). But these immediate benefits of exercise are not limited to younger people. When sedentary adults between 60 and 85 years of age take up weekly exercise, they show improved brain functioning and cognitive performance (Hillman et al., 2008; Kramer et al., 1999).

One important issue to address is whether these short-term effects translate into lifelong cognitive benefits from exercise. Results from long-term studies indicate that a lifestyle that includes regular exercise helps preserve cognitive function and the brain systems that support it (van Praag, 2009). Researchers have found that older people who are at genetic risk for developing Alzheimer's disease and who show cognitive impairments can slow the rate of memory decline by exercising (Lautenschlager et al., 2008). It appears that levels of brain chemicals such as BDNF are boosted by exercise, which helps explain the changes in the brain that account for the cognitive benefits. Furthermore, exercise supports the development of new nerve cells in the hippocampus, a critical area for memory and cognitive activity (van Praag, 2008).

Quick Quiz 16.3c :: Nutrition and Exercise

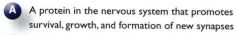

1 What is brain-derived neurotrophic factor (BDNF)?

A A protein in the nervous system that promotes survival, growth, and formation of new synapses

B A calorie-restricted diet that may involve eating approximately 60% of the normal amount of calories, while continuing to take in the needed nutrients.

C A neurotransmitter that reduces stress and increases overall well-being

D A hormone that is released in those individuals with a healthy diet

2 You are about to take a big test. In an effort to reduce your stress and increase your well-being, which of the following actions would be the least beneficial?

A Going for a run

B Increasing your amount of hard study time

C Eating a good breakfast

D Getting a good night's sleep

Answers can be found on page ANS-5.

Module Summary

Listen to the audio file of this module at **MyPsychLab**

Now that you have read this module you should:

KNOW ...

- **The key terminology associated with coping and well-being:**

biofeedback (p. 609)
brain-derived neurotrophic factor (BDNF) (p. 615)
compensatory control (p. 612)
coping (p. 608)
learned helplessness (p. 612)
negative affectivity (p. 610)

optimism (p. 608)
pessimistic explanatory style (p. 611)
positive psychology (p. 608)
post-traumatic growth (p. 608)
resilience (p. 608)

UNDERSTAND ...

- **How control over the environment influences coping and outlook.** Psychologists have discovered that people (and dogs) become more willing to allow unpleasant events to occur if they learn (or believe) that their behavior brings no change. Having at least some degree of control helps people with coping and outlook. When control is threatened, people use compensatory responses, such as detecting order within random images.
- **Positive and negative styles of coping.** Whether someone copes using a positive or negative style is related to personality (e.g., optimism versus pessimism). Positive coping includes the concept of resilience—the ability to recover from adversity, and even benefit from the experience, as is the case with post-traumatic growth.

Coping via negative affectivity and pessimism can have both psychological and physiological disadvantages.

APPLY ...

- **Your knowledge to better understand your own tendencies when dealing with stressful situations.** Are you an optimist or a pessimist? Complete the scale in **Table 16.5** to find out. An average score is about 21, with higher scores indicating greater optimism. Now that you know how your personality compares to others, you may want to reread the section of this module on optimism and pessimism to better understand the implications for your health.

ANALYZE ...

- **Whether activities such as relaxation techniques, meditation, and biofeedback actually help people cope with stress and problems.** Meditation and other relaxation methods have been found to be quite effective in reducing stress. While some training and practice may be necessary, these techniques are by no means inaccessible to those who are motivated to pursue them.

Table 16.5 :: The Life-Orientation Test

	STRONGLY DISAGREE		NEUTRAL		STRONGLY AGREE
1. In uncertain times, I usually expect the best.	0	1	2	3	4
2. If something can go wrong for me, it will.	4	3	2	1	0
3. I always look on the bright side of things.	0	1	2	3	4
4. I'm always optimistic about my future.	0	1	2	3	4
5. I hardly ever expect things to go my way.	4	3	2	1	0
6. Things never work out the way I want them to.	4	3	2	1	0
7. I'm a believer in the idea that "every cloud has a silver lining."	0	1	2	3	4
8. I rarely count on good things happening to me.	4	3	2	1	0
	Now add up the total of the numbers you circled: _____				

Source: Scheier & Carver, 1985.

Module 16.1 :: Behavior and Health

Focus Questions:

1 **Which factors contribute to weight problems, and how much control over them can people expect to have?** Weight problems are linked to genetics, lifestyle, sociocultural, and socioeconomic factors. Obviously people cannot change their genetic makeup, but what children eat at an early age influences their dietary preferences during adulthood. Therefore, youths who are at risk for overweight or obesity will obtain long-term benefits from good nutrition. However, nutrition is also related to socioeconomic factors, which, for people of any age, are not easy to change.

2 **To what extent is physical health based on psychological processes such as choice and decision?** Lifestyle can have an enormous impact on health. Our views on this matter are vastly different from 100 years ago, when many lives were lost to infectious diseases, such as the flu, that now seem to be relatively harmless to those with access to standard medical resources. Table 16.1 on page 588 puts this relationship into context, so take a moment to review it. As you can see, the leading causes of death in the United States are related to dietary factors, alcohol use, and smoking—all factors that humans should be able to control by making well-informed decisions.

👁 **Watch** *The Big Picture: Health Psychology* in the **MyPsychLab video series**

Module 16.2 :: Stress and Illness

Focus Questions:

1 **How does stress affect the brain and body?** Cognitive processes such as working memory are affected by stress, as Sian Beilock's work reviewed at the beginning of this module demonstrated. The command centers for the stress response systems involve the hypothalamus, autonomic nervous system, and endocrine systems (pituitary and adrenal glands). The critical responses are adaptive for coping with the numerous stressful situations we encounter. However, chronic stress and an overworked stress response system can lead to unfavorable health outcomes, such as coronary heart disease and increased disease susceptibility.

2 **How do individuals differ in how they handle stress?** Several sources of variation have been identified. Males and females both have the same stress response systems described above. However, seeking out social companionship and support—a practice known as the tend and befriend

response—is more common in women. Also, people with different personality styles deal with stress differently.

👁 **Watch** *The Basics: Stress and Your Health* in the **MyPsychLab video series**

Module 16.3 :: Coping and Well-Being

Focus Questions:

1 **What are the different ways people cope with stress?** Numerous coping responses are possible. Activities such as relaxation, meditation, exercise, and participation in spiritual activity and prayer are all useful coping strategies. Individual differences in how people cope with stress can also be traced to personality style—such as whether someone tends to adopt an optimistic or pessimistic outlook.

2 **Which factors make coping especially challenging?** Obviously, the severity of a problem is a major influence. As we learned in this module, people who are pessimistic have greater difficulty coping with stress and problems. Also, situations in which we lack control, or perceive a lack of control, present added challenges for coping.

👁 **Watch** *In the Real World Application: Reducing Stress, Improving Health* in the **MyPsychLab video series**

👁 **Watch** the complete video series online at **MyPsychLab**

Episode 15: Stress and Health

1. *The Big Picture: Health Psychology*
2. *The Basics: Stress and Your Health*
3. *Special Topics: Health Disparities*
4. *Thinking Like a Psychologist: Personality and Health*
5. *In the Real World Application: Reducing Stress, Improving Health*
6. *What's in It for Me? The Challenge of Quitting Bad Habits*

✓● Study and Review at MyPsychLab

1 The prevalence of smoking in the United States _____ over the 1990s and early 2000s.

- **A** increased steadily
- **B** decreased steadily
- **C** stayed relatively constant
- **D** increased for men and decreased for women

2 What effect does watching food commercials have on the eating habits of viewers?

- **A** Food commercials generally have little to no effect on eating habits.
- **B** People are more likely to eat the specific product being advertised in the commercial, but not other unrelated foods.
- **C** Snacking in general is more likely after viewers watch a food commercial.
- **D** The eating habits of adults are influenced more by food commercials than are the eating habits of children.

3 High rates of heart disease in socioeconomically disadvantaged communities are likely due to a combination of poor diet and which other factor?

- **A** Stress
- **B** Drug use
- **C** Lead exposure
- **D** Education

4 Sheleigh and Henry are two married adults. Statistically speaking, how is their marriage most likely to affect their health?

- **A** Both likely experience health benefits from being married, but Henry probably benefits more than Sheleigh.
- **B** Both likely experience health benefits from being married, but Sheleigh probably benefits more than Henry.
- **C** Henry and Sheleigh are likely to experience equal health benefits from being married.
- **D** Both Henry and Sheleigh are likely to have worse health outcomes because they are married.

5 The HPA axis involves which three structures?

- **A** Hippocampus, pituitary gland, adrenal glands
- **B** Hypothalamus, pineal gland, adenoids
- **C** Hippocampus, pineal gland, adrenal glands
- **D** Hypothalamus, pituitary gland, adrenal glands

6 The health benefits of close social relationships, such as marriage, appear to be due in part to a hormone called _____.

- **A** HPA
- **B** cortisol
- **C** oxytocin
- **D** *Helicobacter pylori*

7 Which aspect of Type A personality is most closely correlated with increased risk for heart disease?

- **A** Competitiveness
- **B** Anger and hostility
- **C** Patience
- **D** Worrying about time

8 Biofeedback is a therapeutic technique involving:

- **A** focusing on a specific thought or sensation, such as an image or a repeated sound.
- **B** attending to all thoughts, sensations, and feelings without attempting to judge or control them.
- **C** the use of physiological recording instruments to provide feedback that increases awareness of bodily responses.
- **D** bodily interaction with thinking and emotion.

9 Gretta is in an abusive relationship with her boyfriend. Although leaving her boyfriend is an obvious way to end the abuse, Gretta has been in this situation for so long that she no longer feels she has any control over it. Gretta's situation illustrates the concept of _____.

- **A** compensatory control
- **B** learned helplessness
- **C** resilience
- **D** post-traumatic growth

10 Research suggests that a diet consisting of approximately 60% fewer calories than normal, plus nutritional supplements, has what effect?

- **A** It increases longevity.
- **B** It shortens a person's life span by one-third.
- **C** It severely increases the effects of stress on the body.
- **D** It leads to moderate to severe cognitive impairment.

Work the Scientific Literacy Model :: Stress and Health

What do we know about the nature of stress?

Review **Figure 16.4** on **page 600**, which outlined the pathways of stress in the body. All stress starts with an event, so it is important to know the difference between a stressor and stress. Recall that a stressor is an *event* that causes us to experience stress. This event can be either negative, such as getting stuck in traffic, or positive, such as becoming a parent. It is not even necessary for the event to actually occur—just the thought of an upcoming presentation can exert pressure on some students. Our *reaction* to the event is called stress, and it can take physical, emotional, mental, and behavioral forms. **Table 16.4** on **page 599** lists several possible stressors; you may want to try coming up with examples of your own, along with possible stress reactions. One example of a stressor would be taking your psychology final exam. A possible stress reaction: increased heart rate at the thought of the exam, and worrying about the exam the night before. Keep in mind that the same stressor can affect people differently.

On **page 598**, we covered Lazarus and Folkman's cognitive appraisal theory of stress. This theory predicts that we evaluate a stressor in terms of its stakes or importance, and then consider our resources for coping *before* we have a stress reaction.

Why is this relevant?

Watch the accompanying video excerpt on reducing stress. You can access the video at MyPsychLab or by clicking the play button in the center of your eText. If your instructor assigns this video as a homework activity, you will find additional content to help you in MyPsychLab. You can also view the video by using your smart phone and the QR code below, or you can go to the YouTube link provided.

After you have read this chapter and watched the video, imagine a friend has just lost a job which helped him cover tuition costs. Apply Lazarus and Folkman's cognitive theory of stress and describe his potential reactions to this job loss. In your answer, be sure to describe the following: Stressful Event; Primary Appraisal; Secondary Appraisal; Stress Response.

How can science help explain stress and health?

The effects of stress on the immune system have been the focus of some interesting recent research. On **page 600**, we explained how the autonomic nervous system's response to stress can differ depending on the individual. Human and animal studies suggest that chronic stress, like parental deprivation during childhood and trauma, can have negative effects on brain development. Other research has linked chronic stress to coronary heart disease and the progression of various cancers. Even if you are dealing with stressors that seem more mundane, you may have a reduced immune response; this finding came out of a study in which medical students were shown to exhibit reduced immune responses during the stressful period of final exams. Personality also seems to play a role in the stress response, with research on people with Type A and Type B personalities suggesting that highly motivated, competitive, and quick-to-anger people (Type A) are more likely to have heart attacks than laid-back, easygoing Type B people.

Can we critically evaluate claims about stress and health?

Do not assume that all stress is bad. Stress can actually be a good source of motivation. In fact, under some circumstances, such as when you are trying to complete a task of easy to moderate difficulty, stress can enhance performance. The presence of an audience might enhance your performance of a dance routine that you know very well; that same audience could have a negative effect when you are trying to perform a routine you only just learned, however.

Stress may make a difference when it comes to the scores the dance judges award to you, but can it really give you a heart attack? While it is true that Type A people tend to have more heart attacks, people who fall into that category are also more likely to engage in other risky behaviors, such as excessive alcohol consumption and smoking—both of which are also risk factors for heart disease. Similarly, in the **Myths in Mind** feature on **page 603**, we debunked the idea that chronic stress causes ulcers. Ulcers are caused by infection with a type of bacteria, but high levels of stress can certainly worsen their symptoms.

An important consideration when assessing much of the research relating stress to physical and mental health in humans is the fact that it is correlational. However, experiments using animals often do confirm the existence of cause-and-effect relationships between stress and health.

youtube.com/ scientificliteracy

MyPsychLab

Your turn to Work the Scientific Literacy Model: You can access the video at MyPsychLab or by clicking the play button in the center of your eText. If your instructor assigns this video as a homework activity, you will find additional content to help you at MyPsychLab. You can also view the video by using your smart phone and the QR code, or you can go to the YouTube link provided.

17 :: INDUSTRIAL AND ORGANIZATIONAL PSYCHOLOGY

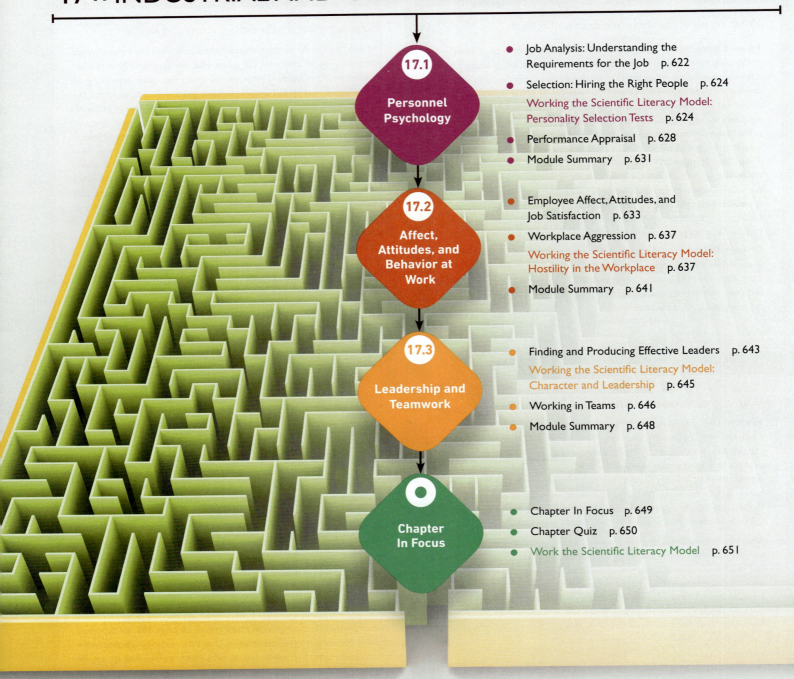

 Module 17.1

Personnel Psychology: Hiring and Maintaining an Effective Workforce

Learning Objectives

After reading this module you should:

KNOW ...	UNDERSTAND ...	APPLY ...	ANALYZE ...
The key terminology of personnel psychology	Interviews, testing, and assessment center methods of personnel selection Methods used in employee performance appraisals	Your knowledge of personnel psychology to identify likely KSAOs for a given job	The relative value of structured versus unstructured interview selection techniques

The Apprentice began airing on network television in 2004, claiming to be the ultimate job interview. This game show pits a number of high-energy, high-ambition contestants against one another in a series of miniature business scenarios across each episode in the season. The winner gets to become an apprentice to real estate mogul Donald Trump. That is quite a way to win a job.

Why did this show become so popular? Perhaps it is because anyone who has been interviewed or tested for a job can relate to the tension it produces. There is the desire to say and do the right things, to impress the employer, and to win the job without selling yourself out. The popularity of *The Apprentice* has led networks around the world to create their own versions of the show with powerful business figures from all corners of the globe. Other job-interview shows have appeared on television, each trying to create bigger and more tension-producing

scenarios: *Hell's Kitchen* is an attempt to find the best young chef, whereas *America's Next Top Model* tries to find a rising star in modeling. These shows stage contests and activities that are much too far-fetched to be part of the typical company's hiring procedures, and we should all be thankful for that. But even after all the effort and expense goes into producing one of these shows, there is little to guarantee that the best candidate has won the job.

Focus Questions

 1 Which techniques ensure that employers hire the most suitable workers?

2 How can employers determine whether workers are doing their jobs well?

The typical American grows up in a household with one or two siblings. Young parents are often amazed and overwhelmed by the way two small children can wreak so much havoc in their lives. While many turn to self-help books for advice, another option might be to hire an efficiency expert to come to the home. Even better, you could become an efficiency expert and run the home with the scientific precision of an assembly line. In fact, this describes the home life of Frank and Lillian Gilbreth, pioneers in the field now known as *industrial and organizational (I/O) psychology*.

Frank was a high school graduate who had worked his way up from bricklayer to construction contractor; Lillian had a master's degree in literature (Purdue University Library, 2009). Although neither had formal scientific training, they learned about applying scientific methods to the workplace from a psychologist and began to systematically study their construction company's laborers. They eventually developed a new bricklaying technique that led to reduced physical strain and injuries, increased the speed of work, and produced a more satisfied and productive work team. Soon, the Gilbreths began studying the methods of all kinds of workers. Frank left construction for business consulting; Lillian earned a doctorate in psychology and joined the faculty of Purdue University.

Despite their busy careers, Lillian and Frank had 12 children together, so it should be no surprise that, as efficiency experts, the Gilbreths literally brought their work home with them. You might say that their household became a company: The parents were the chief executives who made the plans for the family, the older children were the middle managers who oversaw different chores, and the younger children provided hourly labor by doing the actual chores. This story may sound familiar to you: Their son Frank Jr. wrote the autobiographical novel, *Cheaper by the Dozen*, which was released as a film in 1950. Fifty years later, another film came out with the same title and the same large family, but without the efficiency experts involved.

As you can appreciate from previous chapters of this text, the span of psychological science ranges from a laboratory-based discipline to a highly applied, practical one. We will use this chapter to apply psychology to the setting in which most adults spend the majority of their waking hours: the workplace. As defined in Module 1.3, I/O psychology is the scientific study of behavior and thought in work settings. According to the Society of Industrial-Organizational Psychology (SIOP), the field serves three main goals: (1) to help employers deal with employees fairly; (2) to help make jobs more interesting and satisfying; and (3) to help workers be more productive.

The first hints of I/O psychology emerged in the late 1800s from a desire to develop management practices that would have the same degree of precision as engineering. In fact, much of the first scientific research on employee behavior was published in the major academic journal for mechanical engineers (van de Water, 1997). The merging of engineering and psychology into *industrial psychology* made sense at the time because the U.S. economy was based on manufacturing—mining raw materials and turning them into useful products. Industrial psychologists did the same thing with human labor—finding the raw strength and talent and turning it into a productive workforce. This work was largely focused on helping management hire people with potential and making sure they were adequately trained; managing and motivating employees; and evaluating performance. From this moment came a new type of profession: *personnel psychology*. Although the term "personnel psychology" is used less frequently today, this field has become one of the major components of I/O psychology. Psychologists working in this area focus on hiring people with potential, ensuring they are adequately trained, managing and motivating employees, and evaluating performance.

A number of societal forces helped I/O psychology gain a foothold. During the two World Wars, the military and its supporting industries gave I/O psychology a big boost by hiring hundreds of psychologists to work on personnel selection, training, and other related tasks (Katzell & Austin, 1992; van de Water, 1997). Later, in the 1960s, psychologists found more opportunities as the American economic structure began to shift from manufacturing to service industries (Katzell & Austin, 1992). More jobs moved into offices; a growing number of work teams began brainstorming and communicating together to solve problems rather than spreading out to individual stations along an assembly line. In addition, successful employees became very mobile, able to move from job to job based on the strength of their accomplishments. Thus psychology in the workplace began to include more *organizational psychology*, focusing on the culture and organizational qualities of work.

Job Analysis: Understanding the Requirements for the Job

Psychologists contribute to several aspects of hiring and evaluating employees. As you will read, this effort goes far beyond placing an ad in the paper and conducting interviews. For starters, psychologists take a scientific approach; I/O psychologists are systematic, provide operational definitions, collect data, and use many other basic principles adopted by laboratory psychologists. In addition, psychologists may work in all areas of the process, from creating a job description, to finding the right people to fill those positions, to training them, and finally to evaluating the quality of the work and the effectiveness of the personnel procedures.

One of the most important aspects of this process is the **job analysis**, *the process of writing a detailed description of a position in terms of the required knowledge, abilities, skills, and other characteristics required to succeed, as well as evaluating the value of the position for the over-all organization* (Bobko et al., 2008). As part of the job analysis, psychologists identify the **KSAOs**—*the knowledge, skills, abilities, and other traits required for a specific job.* Psychologists turn to a variety of sources for this task, such as *incumbents*

{FIG. 17.1}   **The O*NET Concept Chart**   O*NET provides information about types of jobs and the requirements for workers that may fill them.

(people who already hold the job), their supervisors, and *subject-matter experts (*people who have technical expertise related to the job). Interviewing multiple incumbents, supervisors, and subject-matter experts provides diverse perspectives on a job.

Job analysis might seem simple at first because it is relatively easy to find a collection of tasks and assign them to an individual. This might be the case for jobs that follow a set routine and include a fixed number of tasks—such as a custodial employee who vacuums and removes trash on a daily basis. However, the more complex and varied the task, the more difficult it is to pin down a job description (Dierdorff & Morgeson, 2008). Jobs also tend to change based on technology, the economy, and popular trends, so job analyses should be updated regularly, especially in high-tech positions (Bobko et al., 2008). Finally, incumbents often engage in a process called **job crafting**, *which means taking on or creating additional roles and tasks for a position over time.* Because these extra duties stem from the individual's unique KSAOs, they may distract newcomers from what the essential tasks of the job really are (Wrzesniewski & Dutton, 2001).

There are thousands of different occupations, and no individual psychologist could analyze them all. Fortunately, a substantial number of these jobs have already been thoroughly studied and the corresponding job analyses published on the Internet as part of a U.S. federal government project. This project is available to anyone in the general public—you just need to search for the *Occupational Information Network* or *O*NET* (Crouter et al., 2006; Occupational Information Network, 2009;

http://online.onetcenter.org/). O*NET is a collection of databases that describe jobs from six domains (see Figure 17.1). If you are interested in becoming a clinical psychologist, just go to O*NET, type in this job title, and start searching. There you will find the six categories of descriptors that will help you learn more about the job; if you are an employer, you will find which type of person you may want to hire.

Quick Quiz 17.1a
Job Analysis: Understanding the Requirements for the Job

KNOW…

1 Sometimes an employee expands her job to include new tasks and responsibilities over time. This departure from the original job description is known as:

A job crafting.
C employee drifting.
B workplace expansion.
D job analysis.

2 If you are interested in finding out what is required for any given job, you should refer to _____ for important and accurate information.

A job net
C O*NET
B job crafting
D the occupational index

APPLY…

3 During job analysis, psychologists will identify the essential KSAOs. Which one of the following qualities is *not* a KSAO?

A Knowledge
C Abilities
B Skills
D Organizations

Answers can be found on page ANS-5.

Table 17.1 :: KSAOs for a Job Analysis of Social Work

Knowledge	Psychology, sociology, therapy and counseling, basic law
Skills	Listening, social perceptiveness, critical thinking, service orientation, judgment
Abilities	Oral communication, written communication, problem sensitivity (ability to anticipate problems)
Other traits	Concern for others, ability to control stress, persistence, integrity, dependability

Selection: Hiring the Right People

When the job analysis is complete, employers should have a list of KSAOs in hand and can turn their attention to hiring the best possible workers. The ideal worker would be someone whose KSAOs match those required for the job (see Table 17.1 for an example). Perhaps if you had Donald Trump's resources, you could stage a series of high-stakes competitions to examine how people would act in various challenging situations. Not surprisingly, though, the best methods in the real world only faintly resemble what you might see in entertainment (even if it is "reality" TV).

INTERVIEWING Certainly the most familiar and most widely used employee selection method is the job interview. In the basic interviewing technique known as an **unstructured interview**, *an employer discusses a variety of job- and personality-related topics with a candidate with relatively few prepared questions to guide the conversation.* From this dialog, the employer can draw reasonably accurate conclusions about the applicant's personality (Blackman, 2002). However, the unstructured nature allows the interview to get off track, which raises several problems. For example, different candidates will experience different interviews, making comparisons less reliable.

Structured interviews remove some of the uncertainty by incorporating three main components (see Table 17.2). First, **structured interviews** *present the same set of questions to each job candidate with planned (rather than unstructured) follow-up questions.* Second, these questions are drawn directly from the job analysis to ensure that each is relevant to the position. Finally, the interviewer is trained to follow the same procedures in each interview, and uses a standardized form to ensure each interview session is consistent as possible (Campion et al., 1997).

Many structured interviews also include *situational interview* questions—questions about how the candidate would respond to a situation that is relevant to the job (Latham et al., 1980). These questions can actually be drawn from real situations that incumbents have faced in the past. When developing these questions, psychologists might ask low-quality and high-quality employees how they have responded to that situation in the past. By comparing a candidate's response to the incumbents' responses, psychologists can get a sense of how well a candidate will perform on the job (see Table 17.2).

WORKING THE SCIENTIFIC LITERACY MODEL
Personality Selection Tests

Anyone who has interviewed for a job experiences concern over whether he or she is qualified or the "right" person for the position. Of course, employers are looking for just the right person, too, and many are turning to personality tests to help them in their search.

What do we know about personality selection measures?

One of the most significant aspects of job analysis is the identification of a list of KSAOs that can help employers make decisions about

Table 17.2 :: Sample Situational Interview Question

The following is an item from a situational interview for the position of sales associate at a jewelry store. The question would be presented and the candidate's response would be scored according to the scale below. The higher scores on the scale correspond to more desirable responses.

A customer comes into the store to pick up a watch he had left for repair. The repair was supposed to have been completed a week ago, but the watch is not back yet from the repair shop. The customer becomes very angry. How would you handle this situation?
1   Tell the customer the watch isn't back yet and ask him or her to check with you again later.
3   Apologize, tell the customer that you will check into the problem, and call him or her back later.
5   Put the customer at ease and call the repair shop while the customer waits.

Source: Weekley & Gier, 1987.

which type of person would be the best fit for a job. Therefore, one of the primary aspects of personnel selection is determining whether a person has the right knowledge, abilities, and other personality traits. One of the most popular means of assessing an individual's qualifications for a job is with a test, including testing of personality traits and cognition.

Before a personality test can be used by employers to select employees, I/O psychologists must first determine which personality traits are associated with success or failure in a specific position. This area of research is called **validation studies** *in which researchers administer tests to a large sample of incumbents and evaluate their performance to find correlations between job performance and personality traits or cognitive abilities* (Sackett & Lievens, 2008; Van Iddekinge & Ployhart, 2008).

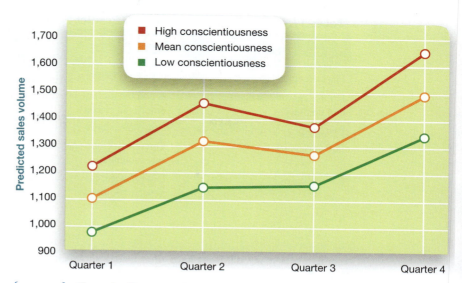

{FIG. 17.2} **Conscientiousness Can Predict Job Performance** The red line shows that high conscientiousness is associated with better job performance than low conscientiousness scores (the green line) among pharmaceutical sales representatives. Performance was measured by the number of prescriptions written for a specific medication by physicians in his or her territory. Data were collected for each quarter during the first year the drug was available (Thoresen et al., 2004).

How can scientists study personality-based selection tests?

Tests of personality traits draw heavily from social-cognitive and trait theories (described in Module 12.1). In fact, many of the self-report tests used in personality research are also used for personnel selection. Meta-analyses (which which combine the results of many earlier studies) as far back as 1991 have supported their use for this purpose (Barrick & Mount, 2005; Salgado, 1997; Tett et al., 1991). One of the more popular personality models is the Big Five (also known as the Five Factor Model; see Table 17.3), and the most popular self-report measure of the Big Five personality traits has been the NEO-PI.

For example, Figure 17.2 shows how conscientiousness predicts success among sales representatives for pharmaceutical companies (Thoresen et al., 2004). In each quarter of the year shown in the figure, those sales representatives who rate high in conscientiousness outperformed their peers with low levels of conscientiousness. Meanwhile, traits of agreeableness and openness did not predict success. Therefore, if we were consulting for a major drug company, we could recommend hiring applicants who score high in conscientiousness.

Can we critically evaluate this evidence?

To critique this research, we can begin with one of the most important concepts in psychological research: Correlational studies do not tell us about cause and effect. It is valuable to know that conscientious people are better at some jobs, but is their success really due to their personality? This research is also limited in that it assumes personality is a relatively stable trait, but perhaps it is possible to create work environments that encourage specific trait-like behaviors. In other words, the right training program or incentives might help a person who is usually low in conscientious to be more conscientious while at work.

Why is this relevant?

Personality inventories measuring the Big Five can be

Table 17.3 :: The Big Five Personality Traits as Measured by the NEO-PI

Neuroticism (versus emotional stability)	Experiencing negative affect (anger, hostility, nervousness) and being emotionally unsettled
Extraversion	Being sociable, affectionate, fun-loving
Openness	Showing imagination, seeking novelty and variety
Agreeableness	Being trusting, having the tendency to get along with others and to avoid conflict
Conscientiousness	Paying attention to procedures and details, following rules, being neat, organized, and timely

Table 17.4 :: How the Big Five Can Predict Performance in a Wide Variety of Jobs

TYPE OF WORK	TRAITS ASSOCIATED WITH HIGH PERFORMANCE	CITATION
Pharmaceutical sales	Conscientiousness	Thoresen et al. (2004)
Fitness center managers and employees	A combination of extraversion and emotional stability	Judge & Erez (2007)
Factory production line workers	Emotional stability	Buttigieg (2006)
Entrepreneurs	Openness, Emotional Stability, and agreeableness	Zhao & Seibert (2006)
Camp counselors	Extraversion, agreeableness, conscientiousness	Loveland et al. (2005)

useful across many different lines of work, as shown in Table 17.4.

Not only can personality tests be used to select specific individuals, but they can also be used to rule out individuals whose profiles suggest that they would be low-performers or disruptive employees across many different types of jobs (Salgado, 2002). For example, researchers studied a division of law enforcement using the California Personality Inventory and found distinguishing personality profiles among officers who were disciplined for inappropriate conduct (Sarchione et al., 1998). Another study investigated university employees and found that those who scored low on conscientiousness but high on extraversion were more likely to exhibit excessive absenteeism (Judge et al., 1997). I/O psychologists can apply similar methods to almost any imaginable career.

One issue you may have considered is that personality is not the *only* determining factor when selecting employees. Employers are also likely to want to know more about the various cognitive skills that applicants may bring.

COGNITION-BASED SELECTION TESTS   As an alternative or supplement to personality tests, some psychologists utilize cognitive selection tests, which are based on topics described in Module 9.1. For example, *situational judgment tests* put applicants in hypothetical situations, much like reality-show contestants find themselves in job-related scenarios (see Table 17.5). These tests, which are correlated with cognitive ability, predict job performance better than

self-report personality tests (McDaniel et al., 2001). In fact, combining situation judgments with direct cognitive tests produces even better results (Clevenger et al., 2001). In meta-analyses across dozens of studies in a variety of fields, tests of cognitive ability have usually been shown to do a better job at predicting performance compared to personality tests (Salgado et al., 2003; Schmidt & Hunter, 1998; see Table 17.6).

Just like personality tests, cognitive tests must go through validation studies that serve to identify who should be selected and who should be turned away. Cognitive tests are far more difficult to fake than personality tests, but a new set of problems can arise from their use. Such instruments may be based on culturally specific skills or knowledge, and they may also induce *stereotype threat*, a phenomenon in which a person unintentionally conforms to a stereotype (Kirnan et al., 2009). For example, a well-qualified woman who applies for an engineering position may become aware of a stereotype implying that men are better at engineering and mathematics. If she then becomes anxious or preoccupied by this stereotype, she may perform below her normal level. More importantly, she may perform below the level of a male who has the same basic ability but does not face stereotype threat. Thus, due to stereotype threat, two individuals with different gender, ethnic, or cultural backgrounds may score very differently on the same test, despite having equal performance measures on the job. This possibility presents an ethical problem in that cognitive tests may discriminate based on ethnicity, gender, or culture rather than on candidates' actual potential.

THE ASSESSMENT CENTER   Personnel selection can be approached from a number of directions, as you can see, and it would seem that the best methods would involve a combination of techniques. **Assessment centers** *capitalize on multiple approaches to personnel selection by combining personality, cognitive, and sometimes*

Table 17.5 :: A Sample Situational Judgment Test Item

A man on a very urgent mission during a battle finds he must cross a stream about 40 feet wide. A blizzard has been blowing and the stream has frozen over. However, because of the snow, he does not know how thick the ice is. He sees two planks about 10 feet long near the point where he wishes to cross. He also knows where there is a bridge about 2 miles downstream. Under the circumstances he should:

A. Walk to the bridge and cross it.

B. Run rapidly across on the ice.

C. Break a hole in the ice near the edge of the stream to see how deep the stream is.

D. Cross with the aid of the planks, pushing one ahead of the other and walking on them.

E. Creep slowly across the ice.

Source: Northrop, 1989, p. 190.

physical ability tests. Although this term suggests a physical location—perhaps an office complex where people come for day-long appointments—an assessment center actually refers to the process, not the location where it takes place.

Some of the unique aspects of assessment centers are the reliance on multiple raters, and the use of raters who have special training in assessment as well as the job that is being filled. This increases the validity of the process considerably (Hough & Oswald, 2000). Like the reality shows mentioned in the module-opening vignette, assessment centers regularly put candidates through **job simulations**—*role-playing activities that are very similar to situations encountered in the actual job.* A related activity is the *in-basket technique,* in which prospective employees sort through a set of incoming tasks and respond to them as if they were actual tasks.

Perhaps the similarity of the judgments and games are what give assessment centers slightly higher validity than either situational judgment tests or cognitive instruments (Hermelin et al., 2007; Krause et al., 2006). Nevertheless, assessment centers are not without drawbacks. Given the number of tests and the complexity of the simulations involved, assessment centers can be time-consuming (they can last multiple days) and expensive (as much as $1,000 per day for a single candidate) to operate.

In summary, there will never be a perfect means of predicting which candidate will be the best possible person for the job. There are more techniques than we have described here, and even more are bound to be used in the future. Despite the inevitable change, several trends seem to be relatively fixed. Personnel selection tools will continue to match individuals with positions based on KSAOs, and the methods used to do so will be tested for validity. It is also likely that these methods will involve some combination of interviewing; tests of personality, cognitive ability, or physical ability; and some form of situational decision making.

Table 17.6 :: Cognition Predicts Training Success and Performance

Workers in a variety of careers completed tests of mental abilities and, for many careers, these scores correlated with performance during and after training.

TYPE OF WORK	CORRELATION WITH TRAINING	CORRELATION WITH PERFORMANCE
Apprentice	—	.26
Chemist	—	.28
Driver	.22	.26
Electrician	.28	.35
Information clerk	.31	.46
Engineer	.23	.28
Manager	.25	—
Mechanics	—	.21
Police	.12	.13
Sales	.34	—
Skilled worker	.28	.17
Typing	.23	.31

Source: Salgado et al., 2003.

Your campus career center may offer a number of valid and reliable tests of career interests and abilities.

PSYCH @

The Career Center

Most universities, colleges, and communities have career centers. These busy hubs of activity link employers to workers, with a focus on the job-hunter. They provide lists of internships and jobs, host career fairs for soon-to-be graduates, and aid students in crafting appealing résumés and personal statements to help them secure a spot in the workforce.

Career center personnel, even if they are not psychologists, often administer personality tests, interest inventories, and sometimes even skill or ability tests. These results are then matched with jobs that are likely to be available in the future, such as nurse or software engineer.

So what might a career center test look like? In a sense, it is the mirror image of a job analysis form on O*NET: Rather than identifying the KSAOs needed to perform a specific job, it asks which KSAOs you can provide—not to mention what your interests might be. Your KSAOs can then be matched against a list of job analyses to find the best match.

You can learn more about the most popular career interest tests at their websites, or visit your campus career center, as many offer these tests for free:

- Strong Interest Inventory: https://www.cpp.com/products/strong/index.aspx

- Jackson Vocational Interest Survey: http://www.jvis.com/

- The U.S. government's O*NET website offers consumer information on vocational testing: http://www.onetcenter.org/guides.html

· · · · · · · · · · · · · · · · · ·

Quick Quiz 17.1b
Selection: Hiring the Right People

KNOW…

1 An assessment center is:

A an office or meeting room that is used for structured interviews.

B a process of screening potential employees using a variety of tests and simulations.

C a method of evaluating how well a current employee is performing.

D a personality test.

UNDERSTAND…

2 A consultant measures 100 employees working in different branches at a government agency to determine whether their personality traits can be used to predict job performance. The consultant is most likely:

A running simulations for assessment centers.

B conducting a validation study.

C job crafting.

D doing structured interviews with each employee to get a sense of his or her personality type.

3 What is one of the unique aspects of assessment centers?

A Reliance on multiple assessment methods

B The size of the building

C Their physical location

D The reliance on a single type of assessment test

ANALYZE…

4 One advantage of structured interviews is that they:

A present the same questions to each candidate to ensure each interview is consistent.

B allow the conversation to drift from topic to topic depending on what is interesting.

C provide valid assessments of cognitive ability.

D remove any possibility of cultural bias and stereotype threat.

Answers can be found on page ANS-5.

Performance Appraisal

Personnel selection may come first, but **performance appraisal**—*the evaluation of current employees*—is every bit as important (Kline & Sulsky, 2009). Evaluation ensures that employees are doing their jobs correctly; if not, then they may need additional training or incentives to bring their performance up to the desired level. When employees do their work well, they need to be recognized with awards, bonuses, or raises and, in some cases, they may be given more challenging tasks or additional responsibilities to keep them engaged. Unfortunately, when employees do not respond to feedback, evaluations can also result in termination. In short, without proper evaluation techniques, productivity suffers. Thus, even though employees often dread the scrutiny of an evaluation, the benefits to the company are typically well worth it.

WHAT NEEDS TO BE EVALUATED? A good deal of employee evaluation is based on a supervisor's overall rating of an employee. An overall rating is often sufficient for evaluating work performance (Viswesvaran et al., 2005) however, employers often want to evaluate some more specific aspects of work performance (Rotundo & Sackett, 2002):

- *Task performance* describes how well an employee performs the assigned duties for his or her position in the organization.
- *Organizational citizenship behavior* (OCB) is the degree to which an employee contributes beyond what is expected (e.g., exceptional teamwork, leadership).
- *Counterproductive behavior* includes actions that interfere with one's own (and sometimes others') productivity, such as absenteeism, lateness, dishonesty, and inappropriate interpersonal behaviors.

Although overall ratings are often sufficient, collecting information from each of these three areas promotes balanced assessments that look at all the contributions an employee makes as well as anything that reduces productivity.

WHO CONDUCTS THE EVALUATION? The traditional approach to employee evaluation is for the immediate supervisor to review the employee's work over a period of time and provide one-on-one feedback. This makes sense because the supervisor knows which tasks have been assigned and how they were performed. However, the supervisor has only one perspective, which may be described as a *top-down* perspective. A clever employee may be substandard in many aspects of the job, yet have the ability to present a positive image to the boss. Therefore it is essential to include other points of view in the evaluation process.

Multisource assessment or **360-degree feedback** *provides evaluation information from many different perspectives within and beyond an organization.* The 360-degree analogy reminds us that the employee receives feedback from all angles (see Figure 17.3). In addition to the traditional supervisory evaluation, multisource assessments include

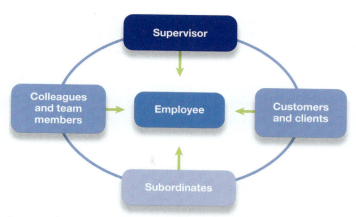

{FIG. 17.3} **Employee Evaluation** The 360-degree feedback method provides evaluation information from all directions.

information from an employee's co-workers, anyone whom he may supervise, and perhaps customers or clientele that he might serve. In many cases, the employee will even rate himself.

In theory, 360-degree feedback is a great method of employee evaluation because it covers all aspects of the job: The supervisor can look over workload and productivity, the peers and supervised employees can report on teamwork and leadership, and customers can report on professionalism and service. Indeed, research on 360-degree feedback generally has shown positive results with the approach (Conway et al., 2001; Facteau et al., 1998). However, problems can arise in this process. For example, power structures in an organization might appear to be threatened. Specifically, some managers do not seem to take subordinate feedback seriously. Also, managers appear to remember feedback from other management more so than feedback from subordinates, and some managers react cynically to subordinate feedback, especially if they believe that the procedure may be unfair (McCarthy & Garavan, 2007; Smither et al., 2005).

PREVENTING BIAS IN EVALUATION If proper controls are lacking, a number of biases and errors have the potential to make the evaluation process more difficult. One such error is the **halo effect**, *in which a rater thinks highly about one aspect of an employee's job or personality and this leads him or her to provide similar ratings for other aspects of the employee's work.* Another error, called the **contrast effect**, *occurs when a rater evaluates one employee who is very strong in a number of dimensions such that, by comparison, the next employee is likely to appear weak, even if he is an average worker by other measures.* Think about these effects in the context of a sales office. One worker may be particularly good at making contacts with new clients, but only has moderate success actually completing the sale. We could see evidence of the halo effect if her manager rated her highly for both making contacts *and* completing sales. Now consider a moderately successful sales representative who is evaluated after the star performer. Despite his consistency, the contrast effect between him and the star salesperson may leave him with a lower rating than he deserves—unless an appropriate rating system is in place.

This module has merely scratched the surface of performance appraisals, but there are some clear messages to take home. First, appraisals are absolutely essential to successful businesses because they promote positive behaviors and create opportunities to correct negative behaviors. Because assessments occur infrequently, however, managers must rely on their memories to evaluate employees, which leaves a large opening for errors. Thus systematic methods should be used along with multiple points of view. With these in place, assessment should be a valuable tool for any employer.

Quick Quiz 17.1c
Performance Appraisal

KNOW...

1 If a psychologist completes a performance appraisal for a superstar employee, then the next employee may seem weak in comparison. This can lead to _____.

  A the contrast effect   C the downsizing effect

  B the halo effect   D stereotype threat

UNDERSTAND...

2 If a psychologist conducts a performance appraisal using feedback from supervisors, subordinates, peers, and clients, he is most likely using the _____ approach.

  A telescoping   C 360 degree feedback

  B compass   D task performance

3 A new start-up company has several employees who need to be evaluated. Which of the following would a personnel psychologist need to assess?

  A Organizational citizenship behavior

  B Counterproductive behavior

  C Task performance

  D All of these

Answers can be found on page ANS-5.

Module Summary

Module 17.1

((• — Listen to
the audio file of
this module at
MyPsychLab

Now that you have read this module
you should:

KNOW ...

- **The key terminology of personnel psychology:**

360-degree feedback (p. 629)
assessment center (p. 626)
contrast effect (p. 629)
halo effect (p. 629)
job analysis (p. 623)
job crafting (p. 623)

job simulations (p. 627)
performance appraisal (p. 628)
structured interview (p. 624)
unstructured interview (p. 624)
validation studies (p. 625)

UNDERSTAND ...

- **Interviews, testing, and assessment center methods of personnel selection.** The two major types of interviews are structured and unstructured. Job candidates also may be tested to assess their personality type and cognitive ability. These results are used to determine whether a candidate is suited to a particular company and, if so, for which specific job she is most suited. Assessment centers often combine both personality and cognitive testing with simulations of actual work situations.

- **Methods used in employee performance appraisals.** 360-degree feedback (also known as multisource assessments) provide the most detailed information on employee performance. They typically involve evaluating task performance, organizational citizenship behavior, and counterproductive behavior.

APPLY ...

- **Your knowledge of personnel psychology to identify likely KSAOs for a given job.** To do so, complete **Table 17.7** below and then check your answers by going to www.onetonline.org and searching for the job title.

ANALYZE ...

- **The relative value of structured versus unstructured interview selection techniques.** In an unstructured interview, an employer discusses a variety of job- and personality-related topics with a candidate, and asks a few prepared questions to guide the conversation. However, comparisons among employees can be difficult to make with this method, and potential sources of bias can creep into the interview. Structured interviews present the same set of questions drawn directly from the job analysis to ensure their relevance to the position. They provide for consistency across candidates and focus on job-related information rather than shared interests. Requiring interviewers to follow a specific set of questions reduces opportunities for bias.

Table 17.7 :: Identifying KSAOs

Pick an occupation. What do you think the KSAOs for this job might be? Try to come up with at least five qualities in each category and write them here or on a separate piece of paper. When you finish, compare your results with the O*NET description—just go to www.onetonline.org and type the occupation into the search bar.

Knowledge	
Skills	
Abilities	
Other traits	

Affect, Attitudes, and Behavior at Work

Learning Objectives

After reading this module you should:

KNOW ...	UNDERSTAND ...	APPLY ...	ANALYZE ...
The key terminology of employee affect and attitudes	Job satisfaction, burnout, and the attitudes and affect that go along with them The risk factors for, and varieties of, workplace aggression	Your knowledge of satisfaction and burnout to ensure you maintain high motivation for college courses and your career	Various methods for preventing burnout and encouraging job satisfaction

Did you know that almost half of new teachers leave the profession within five years (Lambert, 2006)? This means more than half of all teachers spent about the same amount or more time in college than they did in their teaching careers! For Craig, a former teacher, the job seemed perfect because he liked reading and history, he interacted well with teens at the high school level, and he believed he could make positive changes in boys' lives on the wrestling and track teams. He knew that the pay would not be great, but he was so excited that he finished his education degree in four years and charged headlong into his first teaching job.

Craig does not know how it happened, but one day three years later, he looked around at the piles of papers and began to wonder if he should stay up all night grading or call in sick the next day. He would have finished the paperwork during his planning period earlier that day, except that he had to deal with overprotective parents who had no idea—and refused to believe—how poorly their son behaved at school. The apathy of many of his students began to sink in: If they could not bother to try harder on the assignments, then perhaps Craig should not put so much effort into planning classes and giving feedback on rough drafts. He began

to feel emotionally and physically exhausted after each day's work, and felt resentment toward the principal who always sided with the parents and the superintendent. Faced with so many obstacles, he felt as if nothing he could do would matter in the long run. After his fourth year, Craig left teaching for good and took a job in sales.

This is an all-too-familiar scenario for educational professionals. What is interesting about this case is how motivated Craig was at the beginning of his career—he worked very hard for a modest salary, and even volunteered to do more than the typical teacher. But then frustration set in, and along with it came a range of negative physiological, psychological, and social effects.

Focus Questions

 Which factors might lead someone to be highly engaged and satisfied with his or her work?

 What can cause a highly motivated individual to become burned out?

Productivity and success at work are largely due to the behavior of the members who make up the workforce. This aspect of the workplace environment goes beyond the simple question of whether workers are doing their job or not. Indeed, the attitudes and emotional energy that people bring to work ultimately affect their overall productivity and job satisfaction. In this module, we will explore how emotions and behaviors in workplace can affect a company and its workers.

Employee Affect, Attitudes, and Job Satisfaction

I/O psychologists have become increasingly interested in researching *affect*—individuals' emotional responses—regarding their jobs and work in general (Thoresen et al., 2003). The work in this vein includes research on both **positive affect (PA)**, *the tendency to experience positive emotions such as happiness, satisfaction, and enthusiasm,* and **negative affect (NA)**, *the tendency to experience negative emotions, including frustration, anger, and distress.* Even if you have held only one job, chances are you have experienced both varieties of affect. However, some individuals tend to experience more of one type than another, a quality known as *trait affectivity.*

There are at least two important reasons for I/O psychologists' interest in affect, the first of which may be called the *happier is smarter hypothesis*: Employees who have PA traits seem to make better decisions and may also be more creative (Côté, 1999). In addition, a variety

of research shows that PA is associated with teamwork, organizational citizenship, improved negotiating techniques, and general performance (Brief & Weiss, 2002). (Incidentally, the *happier is smarter hypothesis* has been found among college students as well—so remember to think positive about your psychology course.)

I/O psychologists also study affect because when positive or negative affect becomes so consistent that it is as reliable as personality traits, this attitude can influence job satisfaction or dissatisfaction (Connolly & Visweswaran, 2000; Watson & Slack, 1993). Along these lines, PA employees are less likely to quit and, in general, show more organizational commitment (Côté, 1999).

BIOPSYCHOSOCIAL PERSPECTIVES

Affect as a Cultural Trait

You can likely identify positive and negative affect among your individual classmates and friends. As traits, these affective states can occur in spite of events that challenge them, so that a NA individual may feel glum, despite having achieved recent successes. These affective traits are actually quite similar to the Big Five dimensions (see Table 17.4 on page 626); negative affect is related to neuroticism while positive affect is related to extraversion (Judge et al., 2002; Watson & Clark, 1992). Biological psychologists have found that PA individuals experience more activity in the brain's reward circuitry, whereas NA individuals experience more activity in the circuits involved in fear and alert responses (Watson et al., 1999). Adoption and behavioral genetic studies even show a significant heritable component to trait affect (Tellegen et al., 1988).

Psychologist Edward Chang has also examined emotion traits across cultures. What do you think he has found? First consider whether the following statements are true or false:

1. Pessimism is more common among East Asians than among European Americans.

2. Asian Americans are more likely to ruminate (dwell on negative thoughts and experiences) than European Americans.

3. Pessimistic thinking is always a negative quality.

Across a wide variety of studies, Chang and his colleagues have found reliable cultural differences in some affective traits.

1. *True.* Pessimism does seem to be related to culture. East Asian cultures tend to score higher on measures of pessimism than European Americans (Chang et al., 2003).

2. *True.* Asian Americans are more likely to ruminate than their European American counterparts (Chang et al., 2010).

3. *False.* Pessimistic thinking can actually have benefits and lead to better performance on tasks than optimism (Norem & Chang, 2002).

Psychologists have found that employees who show positive affect perform better at work than employees with negative affect.

PsychTutor

Click here in
your eText for an
interactive tutorial
on **Factors in Job
Satisfaction**

JOB SATISFACTION VERSUS BURNOUT   The balance between positive and negative emotions reflects how satisfied people are with their jobs. Positive or negative thoughts about work are expressed as *job attitudes*, a combination of affect and thoughts an employee holds about his or her job (Brief & Weiss, 2002). **Job satisfaction** *refers to the degree to which an employee is content with his or her work*, and is most likely to be achieved by people with positive job attitudes (see Figure 17.4). For many people, starting a new job can produce a sense of intense satisfaction, also known a *honeymoon period* (Boswell et al., 2009). Job satisfaction typically rises and falls throughout a career, however. The lower periods may include the experience of **burnout**, *a combination of persistent emotional and physical exhaustion, cynical attitudes about the job, and a sense that one's work has little meaning* (Table 17.8; Maslach, 2003).

Professions such as teaching, law, and medicine require a conscious commitment and years of education, just as skilled labor and crafts (electricians, plumbers, artisans) require training, practice, and often an apprenticeship. It should not come as a surprise, then, that many people who make this type of commitment enter the workforce with a sense of satisfaction and engagement. But what keeps some people feeling satisfied? And what about those who experience job satisfaction despite taking a job they thought they would eventually dread?

The common-sense notion that enjoyable jobs, co-workers, and supervisors all contribute to job satisfaction does seem to be correct (Mossholder et al., 2005), but job satisfaction goes beyond these factors. For example, a teacher may be highly satisfied with the effect he could have on students, but only marginally satisfied with his income. Satisfaction also depends on the situation you find yourself in—you may be perfectly suited to design computer software but just because you have a job in this field does not guarantee satisfaction.

Satisfaction also reflects whether the job is what the employee expected (Wanous et al., 1992). Moreover, achieving job satisfaction and avoiding burnout depend on how employees are treated, promoted, and challenged. Research shows that it is actually good to challenge workers, particularly those high in cognitive ability, as long as the organization supports their extra efforts (Wallace

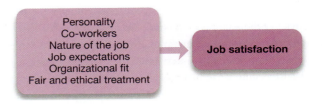

{FIG. 17.4}   **Sources of Job Satisfaction**   Job satisfaction stems from multiple factors, including personal qualities and the work environment.

et al., 2009). In fact, among teachers, more complex teaching strategies are equated with lower levels of burnout, even though they require more effort (Ben-Ari et al., 2003).

Individual differences in affective qualities lead to burnout for some people and job satisfaction for others, regardless of the job. For example, people who are extraverted and emotionally stable (the opposite of neuroticism) tend to be more satisfied with their job (Judge et al., 2002). Also, whether someone is satisfied or experiences burnout depends on his self-appraisals—his beliefs about ability, worth, and level of control (Judge & Bono, 2001). Thus job satisfaction is related to the following factors:

- *Self esteem*, which includes beliefs about one's value and worth as a human being.
- *Self-efficacy*, which involves beliefs about one's ability to accomplish certain goals or complete specific tasks.
- *Locus of control*, which is a set of beliefs about one's ability to control one's work environment and success.

As you can see, a certain degree of job satisfaction seems to be based on an individual's disposition, and this tends to make job satisfaction relatively stable as long as an individual holds a job (Dormann & Zapf, 2001).

The likelihood of experiencing job satisfaction versus burnout is also related to the interaction between the individual and his or her environment (Best et al., 2005; Maslach, 2003). When our skills, energy level, and aspirations match our job, then we are likely to be engaged. A mismatch—such as a teacher who is highly engaged and enthusiastic but works with students who are unmotivated and at a school with low administrative support—can be enough to lead an individual to change jobs (Staw et al., 1986).

Table 17.8 :: Job Satisfaction Versus Burnout

JOB SATISFACTION		BURNOUT
Energy	*←Physical and emotional experience→*	Exhaustion
Optimism	*←Attitudes about job→*	Cynicism
Accomplishment	*←Beliefs about self→*	Lack of accomplishment

Some people may become dissatisfied with a job simply because there is a lack of opportunity to express positive affectivity, or because they are not suited for the job in the first place. Our language is filled with phrases that illustrate this mismatch: *Another day, another dollar*; *it's a living*; *TGIF* (thank God it's Friday). All of these phrases bring to mind a person who works out of necessity but does not find much fulfillment in the workplace. In contrast to these kinds of employed-but-uninspired workers, other people experience factors that actively drive satisfaction down; instead of boredom, they feel distress, dread, and perhaps even anger about their work.

Burnout is the overarching term describing feelings of low job satisfaction. It is characterized by three qualities: physical and emotional exhaustion; a cynical, pessimistic attitude about the organization; and a feeling that nothing of significance has been accomplished. The work environment can accelerate burnout through the nature of the tasks, insufficient resources, and unpleasant social situations (Spector, 2002). And if one employee gets burned out, beware: Burnout has even been shown to be contagious (Westman & Vinokur, 1998).

Exhaustion comes from the nature of the work: Dull, repetitive work can create stress by challenging a worker to maintain her attention despite severe boredom (Maslach, 2003). Similarly, piling on too much work can be stressful, even if the work would be interesting at a slower pace. *Cynicism* derives from a negative or ineffective interpersonal environment; it can be agonizing to walk into the office each morning if you are aware that you will have to face a boss who is out of touch and work on projects that seem to be pointless. Finally, *feelings of ineffectiveness* may arise from any situation in which the employee cannot access the necessary information or resources for the job. This can be a very stressful situation because the employee must constantly invent new ways to do her job or simply accept that she will not be able to perform up to her standards (Breaugh & Colihan, 1994; Hodge et al., 1994). Considerable stress may also be attributable to a lack of information and direction required to know which tasks need to be done, how work will be evaluated, or what purpose the work serves.

Could the factors just described apply to our teacher's story from the beginning of the module? Certainly Craig felt the work piling up, and he believed that he lacked the resources to do his job well. Interpersonally, he felt the administrators did not support his work, and neither the students nor their parents offered much encouragement.

ABSENTEEISM AND TURNOVER   As dissatisfaction and burnout increase, a number of undesirable behaviors may begin to surface. One of the first to appear is **absenteeism**—*regularly missing work for either legitimate or questionable reasons*. According to major surveys, 1.5% to 2.5% of the U.S. workforce is absent on any given workday (Commerce Clearing House, 2006). Although absence due to a major illness or crisis is completely excusable, burnout can lead people to lower their standards for what constitutes an emergency. In other words, a happy worker may miss one day with the flu whereas a burned-out worker might take three days off (Schaufeli et al, 2009; Ybema et al, 2010).

Many consider absenteeism to be the first step driving the problem of **turnover**, *the rate at which existing employees leave the organization* (Griffeth et al., 2000). Turnover is more than just a nuisance for managers who must hire and train new workers; it is also a major expense for organizations. The real cost of turnover includes searching for and hiring a new employee, training that employee, and the loss of productivity until the new worker becomes proficient.

Of course, having disgruntled workers on the job may not be any better than having them skip work. Dissatisfied employees are likely to engage in *counterproductive behaviors* that may reduce productivity for the rest of the organization (Berry et al., 2007). If the stress is social in nature, the disgruntled workers may engage in social forms of disruption aimed at other people. Examples include loud and incessant complaining, starting rumors, and even harassment. In other situations, workers who feel they have been treated unfairly may attempt to reward themselves through theft, or perhaps they may attack the company through vandalism.

REDUCING THE EFFECTS OF BURNOUT   Given the major problems that burnout presents to both employers and employees, researchers have examined

Burnout is characterized by physical and emotion exhaustion, cynicism, and a sense that the work has little importance.

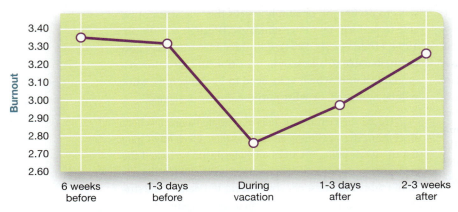

{FIG. 17.5} **Vacation Temporarily Relieves Burnout** Burnout is measured here on a self-report scale ranging from 1 to 7, with 7 indicating the most burnout. As shown by the decline in the center of the graph, a week or more of vacation can greatly reduce burnout. However, burnout returns to nearly the same level in a matter of 3 weeks.

(Richardson & Rothstein, 2008). In addition, employers can offer raises in hopes of making the job more rewarding, although problems with the workload and social environment will not go away just because the paycheck is a little larger. As the phrase TGIF suggests, time away from work is beneficial, and even a single day off can help (Frankenhaeuser et al., 1989; Lounsbury & Hoopes, 1986). The effects of an extended break are even greater (as long as the worker enjoys the vacation) but, as shown in Figure 17.5, the relief from burnout does not last much longer than the holiday itself (Fritz & Sonnentang, 2006; Kühnel & Sonnentang, 2011). After all, the employee who returns from vacation has to walk right back into the situation that led to burnout.

various ways to prevent or reduce burnout and its ill effects. Some key advice is that burnout interventions should occur at the organizational level, because qualities of the job, social environment, and availability of resources have the largest impact on burnout.

For example, physical exercise and cognitive-behavioral stress management skills may help employees manage their reactions to stress more effectively

The real solution to employee dissatisfaction seems to be proactive—addressing the source of the problem before it gets out of control. A significant but limited amount of dissatisfaction seems to be related to personality, so a company can start by hiring people whose KSAOs fit the job and the organization—a selection process described in Module 17.1. Once workers are hired, effective training is essential and mentoring can help make the transitions go smoothly (Payne & Huffman, 2005).

Quick Quiz 17.2a :: Employee Affect, Attitudes, and Job Satisfaction

KNOW...

1 _____ is the rate at which existing employees leave the organization.

A Burnout **C** Turnover

B Negative affect **D** Job satisfaction

2 Absenteeism refers to:

A when an employee regularly misses work for illegitimate reasons.

B when an employee regularly misses work for any reason.

C the rate at which employees leave the company.

D the policy of allowing workers to accumulate sick leave and vacation time.

UNDERSTAND...

3 An employee who is enthusiastic about his job, even when times are tough, is expressing _____.

A positive affect **C** high self-efficacy

B negative affect **D** openness to experience

4 Which outcome would an employer not expect to find with employees who express negative affect?

A Diminished creativity **C** Ineffective teamwork

B Poorer decision making **D** High job satisfaction

APPLY...

5 You are a very capable employee who feels very positive about your work skills. However, layoffs are a constant threat and you play no part in deciding who stays and who goes at your company. Your job satisfaction may suffer because:

A you have low self-efficacy.

B you probably have low self-esteem about your job.

C you lack a sense of control over your work.

D the managers are verbally abusive.

ANALYZE...

6 How do exercise and stress-management skills work to reduce or prevent burnout?

A They provide a distraction from work.

B They make the job more rewarding.

C They help the employee reduce reactions to stress.

D Actually, they do very little to reduce or prevent burnout.

Answers can be found on page ANS-5.

Workplace Aggression

On occasion, a frightening work-related story will dominate the news for a few days—a recently dismissed employee returns to his former workplace seeking violent revenge. The extreme nature of these nationally reported incidents tends to overshadow the vast majority of cases that present a real threat to workers and their businesses. In its more common forms, workplace aggression may involve verbal hostility, obstructionism (making someone's job more difficult), and overt aggression, such as assaults or vandalism (Baron et al., 1999). The victims of workplace aggression are likely to have lower satisfaction and may even quit their jobs, so psychologists have been trying to understand the causes of this undesirable behavior and its long-term effects on individuals and the organizations they work for (Lapierre et al., 2005).

WORKING THE SCIENTIFIC LITERACY MODEL
Hostility in the Workplace

Common sense suggests that, to be productive and satisfied workers, people need to feel safe around their co-workers. However, not all workplaces meet this description. What leads some workers to create a hostile work environment?

What do we know about hostility in the workplace?

In a recent survey, more than 5% of businesses overall (and more than 50% of large establishments with 1,000-plus employees) reported an episode of violence in the previous year (Bureau of Labor Statistics, 2006; see Figure 17.6). However, only 10% to 15% of these cases involved acts by current or recent employees; instead, the majority involved seemingly random criminal acts committed at certain organizations and against members of certain occupations (prison staff, caretakers for the mentally ill, and even teachers) and, in some cases, by clientele (LeBlanc & Barling, 2004).

An obvious response to this problem is to look for screening instruments that might be able to predict who is likely to become aggressive, and particularly those people who might become violent. Achieving this goal can be challenging, however. After all, potential employees probably do not intend to express aggressiveness when they begin their jobs and, even if they did, they would probably not disclose their planned aggression in an interview.

How can scientists study hostility in the workplace?

A number of factors slightly increase a person's risk for being aggressive at work, such as fitting a highly competitive, achievement-oriented personality profile and having a history of aggressive behavior (LeBlanc & Barling, 2004). Research also suggests that males are more prone to aggression than females (Rutter & Hine, 2005). One particularly telling trait for aggression is alcohol abuse. Interestingly, alcohol use by itself does not predict aggression, though the combination of heavy alcohol use and perceived injustice or maltreatment is a very ominous pairing (Greenburg & Barling, 1999; Jockin et al., 2001). Some research has shown that organizational variables are better predictors of workplace aggression than personal traits. One such study looked at both personal and situational variables and found that when organizational policies treated employees unfairly, or when supervisors were strict and abusive, the risk for aggression increased significantly (Inness et al., 2005).

Recently psychologists have turned to a new method of detecting aggressive tendencies: the conditional reasoning test. This method presents current or prospective employees with a series of word problems similar to the standardized reading comprehension tests you have probably completed in school (see Table 17.9 on p. 638; James et al., 2005; James & LeBreton, 2010). The word problems do not explicitly talk about aggression, yet this measure seems to be able to accurately identify potentially aggressive individuals. It appears to work because for each item in the test, one response choice seems reasonable only to the degree that an individual is willing to be aggressive. Can you detect which items in Figure 17.7 (p. 638) are associated with aggressive tendencies? It may not be as easy as you think.

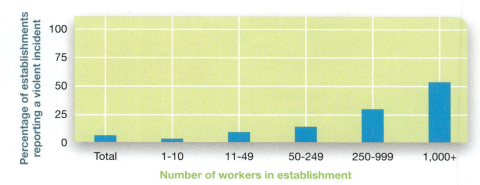

{FIG. 17.6} **Prevalence of Workplace Violence** Percentage of establishments that have experienced an incident of workplace violence in the 12 months prior to the survey, by size of establishment.

Table 17.9 :: Sample Conditional Reasoning Problems

ILLUSTRATIVE CONDITIONAL REASONING PROBLEMS

1. American cars have gotten better in the past 15 years. American carmakers started to build better cars when they began to lose business to the Japanese. Many American buyers thought that foreign cars were better made.

   Which of the following is the most logical conclusion based on the above?

   a. America was the world's largest producer of airplanes 15 years ago.

   b. Swedish carmakers lost business in America 15 years ago.

   c. The Japanese knew more than Americans about building good cars 15 years ago.

   d. American carmakers built cars to wear out 15 years ago so they could make a lot of money selling parts.

2. The old saying, "an eye for an eye," means that if someone hurts you, then you should hurt that person back. If you are hit, then you should hit back. If someone burns your house, then you should burn that person's house.

   Which of the following is the biggest problem with the "eye for an eye" plan?

   a. It tells people to "turn the other cheek."

   b. It offers no way to settle a conflict in a friendly manner.

   c. It can be used only at certain times of the year.

   d. People have to wait until they are attacked before they can strike.

Source: James et al., 2005.

Can we critically evaluate this evidence?

Although psychologists can identify risk factors, it is not clear exactly what actions managers should take when presented with this information. For example, being male is a risk factor—does that mean that companies should hire only females? To complicate matters, some risk factors for aggression—competitiveness and achievement motivation, for example—are also desirable qualities for certain positions.

Why is this relevant?

Despite these challenges, psychologists hope that a thorough understanding of workplace aggression will lead to methods of decreasing violence. In terms of selection, a predictive tool such as the conditional reasoning method may be able to distinguish between non-violent workers and those who present a threat. Once these individuals are on the job, psychologists may eventually be able to monitor the work environment to identify situations that might interact with personalities to produce hostile situations. Thus preventive measures could be put in place before any overt acts of aggression occur.

Traits leading to aggressive actions
- Interpersonal conflict
- Anger
- Males
- Negative affectivity
- Job dissatisfaction
- Perceived injustice
- Alcohol abuse

Interpersonal violence

Possible targets of aggressive actions

Organizational violence

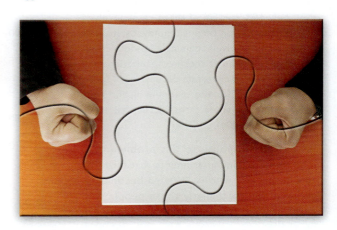

{FIG. 17.7} **Qualities Leading to Workplace Violence** Each of these qualities is associated with increased risk of committing aggressive acts in the workplace. Traits with arrows are significantly more likely to contribute to one target than the other.

SEXUAL HARASSMENT *Sexual harassment* is a well-known term in industrialized societies, so it might surprise you to learn that the term did not come into use until the 1970s. Despite its familiarity, the concept of sexual harassment can be difficult to define because sexuality is such a multi-faceted aspect of human behavior. The best way to distinguish harassment from other behavior is to emphasize the fact that harassment is *unwelcomed* sexual attention. In the United States, this understanding is clearly stated in the official legal definition of **sexual harassment** developed by the Equal Employment Opportunity Commission (EEOC, 2011): *"unwelcome sexual advances, requests for sexual favors, and other verbal or physical harassment of a sexual nature."* Such harassment may come in various forms, such as *quid pro quo harassment* in which a supervisor promises raises or other benefits in return for sexual favors. A *hostile work environment* is a situation in which a worker feels threatened or demeaned by sexual advances, insults, or other comments of a sexual nature.

Over the past decade, the EEOC—the government agency that oversees formal charges of sexual harassment in the United States—has received 12,000 to 15,000 complaints each year, with the vast majority (85% to 90%) being filed by women (EEOC, 2011). However, the number of complaints by males has been slowly increasing. Despite the large numbers, these incidents include only the legal complaints; many more cases likely go unreported because individuals are embarrassed or afraid to file complaints, they believe their case is not severe enough, or they do not have confidence in the formal procedures.

Aside from the sex differences in harassment, few demographic characteristics can be used to identify those individuals who are most likely to harass their fellow workers. Harassment seems to be equally likely to occur in all types of jobs and organizations, but is slightly more likely to occur when the harasser has higher educational levels and status in the organization (Pina et al., 2009). Personality researchers have found that the Big Five personality traits, which are so important to other I/O issues, have little or no relationship to sexual harassment. However, a few more specific traits are related to harassment, such as honesty-humility, which is negatively correlated with harassment (Lee et al., 2004), whereas authoritarianism is positively associated with harassment (Begany & Milburn, 2002).

Because of the gender differences and power issues inherent in the problem of sexual harassment, many psychologists have turned to the sociocultural perspective to explain why it occurs. Many social stereotypes depict men as the predominant breadwinners in the family and as leaders of organizations. For some men, the power ascribed to them by these stereotypes crosses over from home life and organizational roles into the realm of their sexual interests.

Other psychologists adopt a biological perspective, explaining that males and females have evolved differing motives for sex: Men seek quantity and diversity in sexual partners, whereas women look for partners with resources. If this is true, then it might explain both the tendency for males to be the perpetrators of sexual harassment and the frequent power imbalances between males and females that exist in organizations (i.e., predominantly male supervisors) (Pina et al., 2009).

Both the sociocultural and biological views help explain why some men sexually harass, but they are not as successful in explaining why most men do not. Further, they do little to account for the cases in which women are the instigators.

Perhaps the most important aspect of sexual harassment is understanding exactly why it is such a serious problem. First and foremost is the obvious disrespect for an individual that harassment and other forms of aggression exhibit. Research also shows decreases in job satisfaction and commitment to the organization, as well as increases in physical and emotional illness, following sexual harassment (Willness et al., 2007).

MYTHS IN MIND
The Many Misunderstandings About Sexual Harassment

Psychologists investigating sexual aggression, including sexual harassment, have documented a number of pervasive myths. These myths are not just incorrect, but are actually dangerous. People who accept these myths are more likely to commit sexual harassment and other forms of sexual aggression. For the rest of the population, endorsing the myths makes it less likely that victims will receive the support they need. Here are some of the most widely-held myths about sexual harassment:

Myth: Modern work settings include more women and more protections, so harassment has not been a significant problem in recent years.

Reality: Sexual harassment is still a significant problem. Nearly half of all women report harassment at some point, and the EEOC receives as many as 15,000 complaints each year.

Myth: Sexual harassment must be sexual in nature.

Reality: Sexual harassment includes discrimination based on a person's sex, even if no sexual contact is suggested.

Myth: Sexual harassment requires the instigator to have bad intentions.

Reality: Sexual harassment is determined by its consequences, not the aggressor's intentions. If sexual advances are unwelcome but persist anyway, then they constitute harassment. This is true even if the instigator does not consciously mean any harm.

Myth: A person has to physically touch another person for the act to be considered harassment.

Reality: Sexual harassment is any unwanted sexual advance, including phone calls, emails, and notes.

Myth: Women secretly enjoy the sexual attention. Playing hard to get is just part of the game.

Reality: Sexual harassment by definition is unwelcomed and unwanted. Harassment is very different from consensual flirting and dating.

Myth: An individual could avoid being sexually harassed if he or she really wanted.

Reality: Some people suffer harassment quietly for fear of retaliation. The instigator may be physically intimidating or have control over raises and promotions at work.

· · · · · · · · · · · · · · · · · · ·

Quick Quiz 17.2b
Workplace Aggression

KNOW…

1 Recent statistics indicate that more than _____ of businesses overall reported an episode of violence in the previous year.

A 2% **C** 10 %

B 5% **D** 20%

UNDERSTAND…

2 Which is likely to be the best predictor of aggression in the workplace?

A Presence of competitive employees

B Presence of males in the workplace

C Policies in the workplace that treat employees unfairly

D Presence of females in the workplace

3 Which of the following is an accurate statement concerning sexual harassment?

A An individual could avoid being sexually harassed if he or she really wanted.

B Modern work settings include more women and more protections, so harassment has become much less of a problem in recent years.

C Sexual harassment is determined by its consequences, not by the aggressor's intentions.

D A person has to physically touch another person for the act to be considered harassment.

Answers can be found on page ANS-5.

Module Summary

Now that you have read this module you should:

KNOW ...

- **The key terminology of employee affect and attitudes:**

absenteeism (p. 635)
burnout (p. 634)
job satisfaction (p. 634)
negative affect (NA) (p. 633)

positive affect (PA) (p. 633)
sexual harassment (p. 639)
turnover (p. 635)

((•—[**Listen** to
the audio file of
this module at
MyPsychLab

UNDERSTAND ...

- **Job satisfaction, burnout, and the attitudes and affect that go along with them.** Job satisfaction seems to come from a combination of energy, optimism, and a sense of accomplishment, whereas burnout seems to derive from the opposite effects—exhaustion, cynicism, and feeling a lack of accomplishment. To maintain job satisfaction, it helps to have a challenging job with support from management. People with positive affectivity (PA) also tend to feel more satisfied.

- **The risk factors for, and varieties of, workplace aggression.** Aggression can take the form of physical acts, but also includes verbal aggression and some types of obstructionism. Many risk factors may potentially contribute to workplace aggression, such as having a competitive, achievement oriented personality or a history of aggression. In addition, substance abuse (e.g., alcohol), an abusive supervisor, and a sense that the individual has been treated unfairly increase the risk of workplace aggression.

APPLY ...

- **Your knowledge of satisfaction and burnout to ensure you maintain high motivation for college courses and your career.** Psychologists have applied the concept of burnout to college students, who are prone to experiencing exhaustion, cynicism, and decreased efficacy, just as employees are. Complete the college student version of the Maslach Burnout Inventory in **Table 17.10** (Schaufeli et al., 2002) to see how you compare to others. In one study of 191 University of Georgia students, average scores for the three facets of burnout were 17.95 for exhaustion, 11.1 for cynicism, and 26.0 for personal effectiveness (Pisarek, 2009). If you score higher than that, you are at risk for being burned out!

ANALYZE ...

- **Various methods for preventing burnout and encouraging job satisfaction.** The best techniques are probably preventive measures: Hiring people with the right skills and personality for the job reduces the chance for burnout while increasing chances for satisfaction. Stress management skills and time off from work are both helpful for existing employees. Although pay raises may seem like a good idea for boosting job satisfaction, they probably do little to address the actual causes of burnout.

Table 17.10 :: The Student Burnout Inventory

To complete the Student Burnout Inventory, circle the number that best describes you on the following scale. Simply add up the circled numbers in each section to find your scores.

	NEVER		SOMETIMES				ALWAYS
I feel emotionally drained by my studies.	0	1	2	3	4	5	6
I feel used up at the end of a day at university.	0	1	2	3	4	5	6
I feel tired when I get up in the morning and I have to face another day at the university.	0	1	2	3	4	5	6
Studying or attending a class is really a strain for me.	0	1	2	3	4	5	6
I feel burned out from my studies.	0	1	2	3	4	5	6
Total Exhaustion Score =							
I have become less interested in my studies since my enrollment at the university.	0	1	2	3	4	5	6
I have become less enthusiastic about my studies.	0	1	2	3	4	5	6
I have become more cynical about the potential usefulness of my studies.	0	1	2	3	4	5	6
I doubt the significance of my studies.	0	1	2	3	4	5	6
Total Cynicism Score =							
I can effectively solve the problems that arise in my studies.	6	5	4	3	2	1	0
I believe that I make an effective contribution to the classes that I attend.	6	5	4	3	2	1	0
In my opinion, I am a good student.	6	5	4	3	2	1	0
I feel stimulated when I achieve my study goals.	6	5	4	3	2	1	0
I have learned many interesting things during the course of my studies.	6	5	4	3	2	1	0
During class I feel confident that I am effective in getting things done.	6	5	4	3	2	1	0
Total Professional Efficacy Score =							

Source: Schaufeli et al., 2002.

Leadership and Teamwork

Learning Objectives

After reading this module you should:

KNOW ...	UNDERSTAND ...	APPLY ...	ANALYZE ...
The key terminology associated with leadership and teamwork	Which skills and personal qualities predict good leadership Why certain input and process qualities lead to more effective teams	Your knowledge to identify types of leaders with whom you work or study	Whether leaders should focus more on inspiring good work or should stick to rewarding it

Every group of people has leaders: families, schools, nonprofit organizations, corporations—you name it. Some have formal roles, such as parents, principals, and managers; in other situations, leaders emerge through day-to-day activities, inspiring people to work or play harder. But even leaders have leaders, and at least one popular news magazine has attempted to sort out who are the best—the leaders among leaders—in the United States. Leafing through one year's issue (*U.S. News,* 2008), we came across a particularly impressive leader, and one whom we have had the privilege to watch in person: Patricia Head Summitt, who coaches the women's basketball team at the University of Tennessee.

"I don't handle losing very well … I get physically ill," says Summitt, and she adds that the experience of losing is actually a chance to learn about how to improve your own performance. Fortunately for her, Coach Summitt does not lose very often; in fact, she is the winningest basketball coach of male or female teams in the National Collegiate Athletic Association (NCAA). In more than 30 years of coaching at UT, she has won 1,000 games, losing less than 10% of the time. Her teams have made it to the NCAA women's playoffs every year since the inception of the

women's championship tournament in 1982. Summitt's teams have won 14 conference championships and a record 8 national titles.

Given that she is one of the most dominant coaches in college sports history, you might expect that Summitt thinks only of basketball. In reality, she perceives herself as a leader among women in other respects. "I can teach young women that there are no barriers… . you go for it. Whatever you want in life, you go for it," she explains. "Basketball is a great place to learn that." This leadership also accounts for the stellar graduation rate among her players—every single one has completed her coursework and made it to graduation. With such a track record, it is no wonder that Summitt is often invited to speak to community and business leaders.

Focus Questions

 What are the qualities that make a person stand out as a leader?

 Which factors lead teams to work together effectively?

It is difficult to imagine a work environment that does not benefit from high-quality leadership. Consider some of the benefits good leadership provides to an organization:

- A common set of objectives and goals
- A means of identifying, recognizing, and rewarding quality work
- Ethics, and acceptable practices for working toward those goals
- Guidelines for acceptable behavior at work, including how to treat colleagues and clients

Even a self-employed professional who works alone benefits from a clear understanding of these four areas. So if leadership is key, how can companies acquire good leadership? Do they simply need to find someone with all the right qualities? Or could anyone be a leader with the right training?

Finding and Producing Effective Leaders

Leadership emergence *is the degree to which individuals are viewed as leaders by others* (Judge et al., 2002). Leaders generally share a set of personal qualities that distinguish them from the rest of the workforce. When the opportunity arises, the individual who possesses these characteristics will naturally *emerge* from the group and the situation as a leader. In terms of personality, this means that researchers should be able to administer personality tests to members of a number of organizations and pick out the leaders simply by looking at the patterns in the test results (Foti & Hauenstein, 2007). In reality, identifying leaders is not so clear-cut, although relatively stable personality and cognitive traits do significantly predict who becomes a leader. From the Big Five personality dimensions (Table 17.3 on p. 625; also discussed in Module 12.1), high emotional stability, extraversion, openness, and conscientious are associated with leader emergence (Judge et al., 2002).

In addition to predicting leader emergence, it is important to predict which leaders will be most effective. The Big Five model has a fairly good track record of predicting who will be an effective leader, along with *self-monitoring*—the tendency to reflect on and regulate one's own behavior in response to social cues (Day & Schleicher, 2006). Individuals who score high on self-monitoring measures are likely to think about what makes an effective leader, and then monitor their own behavior to ensure they are exhibiting those traits. In doing so, a shy individual who knows that extraverts do well as leaders may try to develop habits to overcome his appearance of shyness. In contrast, a low self-monitoring individual is

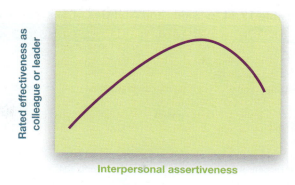

{FIG. 17.8} **Assertiveness Predicts Leadership Effectiveness** The most effective leaders are neither the least assertive nor the most assertive—they have just the "right touch," as indicated by the peak in the middle of the graph (Ames, 2008).

unlikely to notice that his introverted personality is preventing his emergence or effectiveness as a leader.

Despite the success of leaders such as Coach Pat Summitt, a commonly held stereotype says that men make better leaders than women. In fact, surveys suggest that in the United States, employees prefer to work for male bosses and women still face more difficulties in attaining leadership positions (Eagly, 2007). However, this stereotype does not stand up to investigation. On average, women show more desirable leadership styles and traits than men (Eagly, 2007), and both men and women attain the same levels of effectiveness (Eagly et al., 1995). Perhaps the survey results indicate that people expect leaders to be assertive—a characteristic that tends to be associated with masculinity.

Assertiveness *is the degree to which an individual will work to achieve or protect one's interests.* Television and films are filled with stereotypes of bosses ranging from meek pushovers to power-wielding bullies, and neither make for very good management in fiction or in real life. As Figure 17.8 shows, leaders with the "right touch" can be assertive when it is called for, but not all the time (Ames, 2008).

To pull together the various traits and capabilities that produce effective leadership, researchers Hogan and Warrenfeltz (2003) developed the comprehensive model of leadership skills that is summarized in Table 17.11 on page 644. As you read through the list of these skills, think about how they may apply to the people you know in leadership positions. Do these qualities capture what good leaders do? And are poor leaders lacking in one or more of these areas? Research confirms that this is the case, at least to a certain extent. Meta-analyses have found strong correlations between these four domains and performance (Ones et al., 1993; Vinchur et al., 1998).

Table 17.11 :: Skills and Abilities of Successful Leaders

DOMAIN	WHAT IT REPRESENTS	SAMPLE CAPABILITIES
Intrapersonal	High standards of performance for oneself	Is able to control emotions Is willing to take a stand Has career ambition and perseverance Shows integrity, ethics Shows self-confidence
Interpersonal	Social skills and role-playing ability	Has talent for building relationships Is sensitive to office politics Exhibits listening and negotiating skills Shows good communication
Business	Abilities and technical knowledge needed to plan and coordinate efforts	Has intelligence and technical skill Shows experience and understanding how the organization functions Has decision-making ability Sets priorities and goals
Leadership	Influence and team-building skills	Supports and motivates workers Sets standards for others' behaviors Develops and communicates a vision for the organization Motivates others

Source: Adapted from Hogan & Warrenfeltz, 2003.

PsychTutor

Click here in your eText for an interactive tutorial on **Leadership**

LEADERSHIP STYLES   There are many ways to lead successfully, and psychologists have identified several different styles of leader (Bass, 1997). Typically, the most desirable style is **transformational leadership**, *which is a combination of charisma, intellectualization, and a focus on individuals within an organization.* Charisma blends together charm, attractiveness, and communication ability, which collectively produce an extremely influential personality. *Charismatic leaders* energize the organization by making a job seem to be extremely important and meaningful, thereby inspiring others through positive emotions (Shamir et al., 1993).

Transformational leadership also involves *intellectual stimulation,* which encourages deliberate thought regarding work tasks and the job in general. Through intellectualization, the worker does not mindlessly perform tasks, but asks what the function of the task might be, and considers alternative and creative approaches to the task.

The transformational style is linked to a number of positive outcomes. For example, intellectualization and individual focus helps workers understand their tasks and roles more fully, which in turn leads to a greater sense of psychological well-being (Nielsen et al., 2008). In this environment, workers feel a heightened sense of commitment to their jobs and to others in the workplace. Ultimately, the transformational style leads to better productivity, thanks to the collective effects of motivated, thoughtful employees (Bass et al., 2003; Jung &

Sosik, 2002). As such, it is often considered to be a preferred type of management.

Whereas transformational leadership involves inspiration and vision, transactional leadership treats social exchanges like business transactions. Specifically, **transactional leadership** *encourages employee or team member behaviors through rewards and punishments.* An active approach to transactional leadership would involve a leader closely watching workers, rewarding those who follow instructions and meet expectations. Alternatively, transactional leaders can be passive, practicing *management by exception.* With this approach, leaders let workers go about their tasks and intervene only when an exception—some sort of problem—arises. Compared to transformation, transactions are much less inspiring; nevertheless, this style can be effective in certain situations, particularly those that require close attention to detail.

The final approach to leadership may not count as leadership at all. Translated from French, *laissez-faire* is roughly equivalent to the English phrase "leave it alone." Thus **laissez–faire leadership** *describes the style of someone who has been appointed to a position of leadership, but who does not engage in many (if any) leadership processes*—he or she simply leaves the workers alone.

In the end, both the transformational and transactional styles of leadership can be effective, and a great many managers use both. The important results to remember are the correlations with each leadership style: Transformational leadership has the strongest association with satisfied, motivated employees or team members, whereas a laissez-faire style does not (Lowe et al., 1996).

Employees look to leaders to learn how to be productive and which tasks to take on. But leaders are also role models for what is acceptable and what is unacceptable. Since that is the case, should we look for leaders with character?

What do we know about character and leadership?

In the early 2000s, a number of highly publicized scandals erupted surrounding corporate executives, including events at major corporations such as Enron and Tyco. A few years later, the financial crisis in the United States began with the failure of many of the country's largest financial institutions. To many people, it appeared that we were experiencing a crisis in leadership (Riggio et al., 2010). This problem was not due to the inability to lead—in fact, many of the affected companies had very strong leaders—but rather to the moral and ethical qualities of the choices those leaders made. The response of many psychologists was to search for the *virtues* that we expect from our leaders. Another approach was to investigate *character* in leadership, with definitions of character centered on those individual qualities that guide a leader to make moral and ethical decisions (Thompson & Riggio, 2010).

How can scientists study character and leadership?

One approach to studying character in leadership is to consider the traits or virtues that separate a truly ethical leader from a person who simply leads. Ronald Riggio and his colleagues identified four primary virtues from philosophical and psychological works on leadership: prudence, fortitude, temperance, and justice. *Prudence* is a very practical type of wisdom that involves the ability to "make the appropriate decision that minimizes harm and maximizes good" (Riggio et al., 2010, p. 237). *Fortitude* is the courage to make difficult—even prudent—decisions. Virtuous leaders also display *temperance* in that they can exercise control over

their emotional reactions and make reasonable decisions. Finally, the virtue of *justice* means that a leader should be able to follow rules, but also make decisions based on principles of fairness. The researchers administered a questionnaire to thousands of employees who rated various types of leaders on these virtues, and statistical analyses confirmed that these traits correspond with ethical leadership. Perhaps more importantly, these virtues correlate positively with desirable outcomes, such as a sense of empowerment among employees, and identification with the organization as a whole.

Can we critically evaluate this evidence?

We should be cautious in accepting the virtues of prudence, fortitude, temperance, and justice as the only ones that comprise character in leadership. The research techniques employed suggest that they are important, but other qualities may also play a role in ethical leadership. For example, some researchers have included personal integrity and forgiveness as important qualities (Grahek et al., 2010). In addition, researchers have asked about the nature and nurture of character. To what extent can these qualities be taught?

Why is this relevant?

One obvious application of this information is that leadership virtues can be applied to the study of leadership emergence, and it follows that psychological measures such as the Leadership Virtues Questionnaire might be used for screening potential leaders. Imagine you are in charge of hiring new managers for your organization: Would you like to know who possesses high levels of these four traits? Another application would be in the training of managers. Most definitions of character in leadership emphasize the idea that character comes from experience; therefore it might be possible to train individuals who are strong in other aspects of leadership to also practice these virtues.

Quick Quiz 17.3a
Finding and Producing Effective Leaders

KNOW...

1 Assertiveness is best characterized by:

A how strict a person is.

B the degree to which a person protects his or her interests.

C how closely a leader monitors others.

D adherence to written policies.

UNDERSTAND...

2 Leaders with character exhibit which of the following traits?

A Frugality   **C** Politeness

B Fortitude   **D** Good looks

3 Which of the following best describes the laissez-faire approach to leadership?

A A team leader anticipates errors that people might potentially make and works to avoid them.

B A team leader controls worker behavior through rewards and punishments.

C A team leader strives to make rewards for good work equitable across all team members.

D A team leader spends little time offering direction or feedback on performance.

APPLY...

4 Lauren, your boss, encourages you to work hard by paying you extra when you succeed. What is her style of leadership?

A Transactional   **C** Instinctive

B Transformational   **D** Laissez-faire

ANALYZE...

5 Transactional leadership styles are most effective when:

A the leader is assertive.

B the leader manages by exception.

C the task requires close attention to detail.

D the employees are already highly motivated.

Answers can be found on page ANS-5.

Working in Teams

Modern organizations almost always make use of teams—groups of individuals with shared goals and responsibilities. Most likely you are currently a member of several teams—perhaps a sports team, a group project for class, a drama or dance company, or, naturally, a team of co-workers. The past two decades have seen the rapid growth of **virtual teams**, *production or project teams that are physically separated but operate largely (or completely) by electronic communications*. New software tools facilitate collaboration and conferences over the

The intelligence, conflict resolution skills, and communication abilities of these workers will contribute to the success of their work team.

Internet, so companies are able to save the time and expense of traveling while gaining greater access to experts around the world.

To understand how teams function, psychologists often divide teamwork into three parts: *input*, *process*, and *output*. These areas seem to apply to all teams, so what distinguishes a sports team from a software development project team is simply the specific types of inputs, processes, and outputs.

INPUTS   Team inputs include qualities such as the nature of the organization, management, the type of work the team is assigned, and the individuals who make up the team—basically, anything that is present before the process gets under way. For example, when members know that the team will be provided with motivation and rewards as a group, the outputs are usually more successful, and it is the responsibility of the organization's management to determine how rewards are allocated (Pritchard, 1995). Naturally, teams need members who have strong skills related to the assigned tasks, but did you know that teamwork itself is a skill? Research shows that intelligence, conflict resolution ability, and communication skills are all correlated with successful teams (Stevens & Campion, 1999). Not surprisingly, extraversion, agreeableness, and conscientiousness have also been associated with positive team outcomes (Barrick et al., 1998; Morgeson et al., Reider, & Campion, 2005).

PROCESS: WHAT THE TEAM DOES   Team processes are essential to successful group performance (LePine et al., 2008). Obviously, communication will play an important role anytime multiple people are involved. Equally important, but perhaps less obvious, is the issue of *coordination*, meaning that individuals' tasks fit together in a timely and orderly fashion. Certainly Coach Summitt's basketball players need to be in the right place at the right time, or there will be errant passes, missed shots, and poor defense. The same concepts apply to work teams. Imagine a poorly coordinated assembly line where one group takes longer to complete its task than the next group down the line. Such a breakdown in coordination will leave one group idle and unproductive throughout portions of the shift.

Other social processes that can impede team effectiveness involve concepts you read about in Module 15.1. *Social loafing* is particularly detrimental to group success: It occurs when some group members produce less effort on a team than they do alone. When social loafing occurs, the team does not realize the full benefit from its working members (Latané et al., 1979).

From a more cognitive perspective, group decision making can also be either an asset or a liability. In cases of *groupthink*, individuals within the team develop very strong convictions about an idea. As groupthink builds, all members begin to agree, and proposed actions tend to become riskier and maybe even too far-fetched to be feasible. Because the group seems to be approaching a unanimous decision, individuals become more and more certain about the correctness of their decision, and they maintain this belief until it is finalized. In some cases, this kind of agreement is helpful, but there are consequences when groupthink runs out of control: The decision can be wrong. One of the best-known examples led to the explosion of the space shuttle Challenger (Morehead et al., 1991). In this case, a small group of engineers had warned other workers about fuel tank seals freezing in cold weather. However, the team in charge of the launch convinced themselves that launching was a good idea, despite the risks linked to the seals. The Challenger launched, only to explode before it had been airborne for 2 minutes. Had team members employed correct team decision making, perhaps the disaster could have been avoided. Such an effort might have involved appointing a specific team member to question individual decisions, looking for outsiders to weigh in on the debate, or even breaking into smaller groups for discussions so that the social pressure would not be so great (Priem et al., 1995).

OUTPUT Perhaps the main reason to develop work teams is to increase efficiency. Certainly production teams are more efficient, as are well-coordinated project teams.

When the goal is to innovate, teams—especially teams with diverse members—tend to outperform individuals (Axtell et al., 2006). Conversely, individuals are not subject to groupthink, so in many cases well-qualified people can make better decisions alone than with a group (Gigone & Hastie, 1997).

Outputs comprise more than just the products and services that result from teams; they also include benefits to the individual and the organization as a whole. Individuals may find increased job satisfaction thanks to positive experiences interacting with colleagues, a feeling of shared purpose, and the sense that they have achieved something bigger than they could have done by themselves (Cordery, 1996; West et al., 1998).

Quick Quiz 17.3b
Working in Teams

KNOW...

1. The design and layout of a work facility, along with the way in which bosses and employees are organized, is considered a(n) _____.

   A input   **C** process

   B output   **D** leadership style

UNDERSTAND...

2. _____ has occurred if an employee reduces the amount of work he completes because three fellow team members are assigned to collectively carry out a single task.

   A Social loafing

   B Charisma

   C Self-monitoring

   D Transactional leadership

3. The risk of groupthink can be reduced by all of the following except:

   A appointing an individual to question decisions.

   B breaking into smaller groups to reduce social pressure.

   C asking for input from outsiders.

   D encouraging group members to be very polite.

Answers can be found on page ANS-5.

Module Summary

Module 17.3

Now that you have read this module you should:

Listen to the audio file of this module at **MyPsychLab**

KNOW ...

- **The key terminology associated with leadership and teamwork:**

assertiveness (p. 643)
laissez-faire leadership (p. 644)
leadership emergence (p. 643)
transactional leadership (p. 644)

transformational leadership (p. 644)
virtual teams (p. 646)

UNDERSTAND ...

- **Which skills and personal qualities predict good leadership.** From a personality perspective, leaders tend to be emotionally stable, extraverted, open, and conscientious. Good leaders are able to monitor their own behavior. Transformational leaders—those who are charismatic and intellectual, and who focus on the individuals within an organization—are usually preferable.

- **Why certain input and process qualities lead to more effective teams.** Teams are usually most successful when the members share motivation and rewards. When individual members are intelligent, good communicators, and good problem solvers, the team will perform well.

APPLY ...

- **Your knowledge to identify types of leaders with whom you work or study.** Complete **Table 17.12** (or create your own table on a separate piece of paper) for at least three leaders. Start by writing the definitions and qualities of each type of leader in the left column. Then, in the Instructor column, identify specific behaviors that demonstrate which type of leader your psychology instructor is. If you are employed, do the same for your supervisor. Finally, pick one additional leader, perhaps from your campus administration or from a campus group you belong to and do the same.

ANALYZE ...

- **Whether leaders should focus more on inspiring good work or should stick to rewarding it.** Research shows that leadership styles have their place. Transformational leadership—the more inspirational form—is probably better at fostering creativity, whereas transactional leadership may be better in situations that call for attention to detail.

Table 17.12 :: Leadership Styles Activity

DEFINE:	PSYCHOLOGY INSTRUCTOR	SUPERVISOR	OTHER: _____
Transactional leader			
Transformational leader			
Laissez-faire leader			

Module 17.1 :: Personnel Psychology: Hiring and Maintaining an Effective Workforce

Focus Questions:

1 Which techniques ensure that employers hire the most suitable workers? Television shows such as *The Apprentice* take the unstructured interview and simulation approaches to interviewing to unusual extremes. In the real world, structured interviews, personality tests, and cognitive tests are the norm. In some cases, the very in-depth method of the assessment center may even be used. Regardless of the method applied, I/O psychologists want to see evidence that this method is effective. Sound selection methods have gone through multiple validation studies to prove their effectiveness.

2 How can employers determine whether workers are doing their jobs well? A number of methods for evaluating an employee's performance have been developed. Perhaps the most thorough is the 360-degree feedback method. This approach gathers information on a worker's performance from all angles: supervisors, peers, subordinates, and even individuals outside the organization, such as clients or customers. In addition, employers should be concerned about measuring multiple aspects of a worker's performance, including task performance, organizational citizenship, and counterproductive behaviors.

Module 17.2 :: Affect, Attitudes, and Behavior at Work

Focus Questions:

1 Which factors might lead someone to be highly engaged and satisfied with his or her work? People tend to be most satisfied with their work when they feel competent, in control, and challenged, regardless of the line of work. Satisfaction is most likely when an individual's expectations for a job are met by his or her actual experiences. However, not all people can be expected to feel the same; people high in positive affect are more likely to be satisfied than others.

2 What can cause a highly motivated individual to become burned out? Burnout includes a sense of emotional and physical exhaustion, cynicism, and a sense that the work has little meaning. Burnout can arise from multiple sources, including meaningless tasks, insufficient resources, and unpleasant interactions with co-workers and management.

Module 17.3 :: Leadership, Teamwork, and the Organization

Focus Questions:

1 What are the qualities that make a person stand out as a leader? For Coach Summitt (described at the beginning of the module), it is her charisma and her ability to inspire and motivate that are especially notable. These are properties of a transformational leader, along with the personality traits of extraversion, openness, and conscientiousness. Other situations may call for different types of leadership, but clearly this style works for the competitive world of college sports. Interestingly, many people hold a stereotype that men make better leaders, although research shows that women are every bit as effective.

2 Which factors lead teams to work together effectively? Psychologists focus on inputs, processes, and outputs to determine what makes a team work effectively. Inputs associated with success include clear rewards for the group, skilled team members, and group members whose personality traits (e.g., extraversion and agreeableness) help them interact with others. Processes work best when they are well coordinated, such that individual tasks fit together in a timely and orderly fashion. These factors all contribute to the most desirable outputs: successfully completed projects and satisfied team members.

✓●─ **Study** and
Review at
MyPsychLab

1 Which of the following is *not* one of the main goals of I/O psychology as defined by the Society of Industrial-Organizational Psychology (SIOP)?

A To help employers deal with employees fairly

B To help workers be more productive.

C To help make jobs more interesting and satisfying

D To help employers avoid lawsuits

2 As the United States evolved from a manufacturing economy to one based more on office work, I/O psychologists began to focus more on _____.

A hiring

B training

C the culture and organizational qualities of work

D managing employees

3 Which of the following statements is true regarding the use of personality-based selection tests for hiring?

A Some personality traits can be useful predictors of performance at various jobs.

B Personality traits can be useful predictors of which candidates will do poorly at a job, but do not predict which candidates are likely to succeed.

C Conscientiousness is the only personality trait that correlates with performance across a wide range of jobs.

D Personality-based selection tests are not a useful tool for predicting job performance.

4 An employee who always goes above and beyond what his or her employer asks is demonstrating good _____.

A task performance

B organizational citizenship behavior

C situational judgment

D counterproductive behavior

5 Joaquin's supervisor is always impressed at his ability to come up with creative solutions to problems at work. Because of this talent, the supervisor has a very good opinion of Joaquin as an overall employee, despite the fact that he is frequently late to work and sometimes has poor productivity. The supervisor's overall good opinion of Joaquin is likely the result of _____.

A the contrast effect

B the halo effect

C the 360-degree bias

D the mixed-performance bias

6 "Locus of control" refers to:

A whether an individual feels more in control at home or at work.

B a set of beliefs about the person's ability to control his or her work environment and success.

C a person's beliefs about his or her value and worth as a human being.

D the skills that a person can use to affect his or her work environment.

7 The "Conditional Reasoning Test" could theoretically be used by employers to detect _____ in employees.

A mental illness

B success potential

C aggressive tendencies

D high intelligence levels

8 Which of the following statements is true regarding male versus female leadership?

A On average, women show more desirable leadership styles and traits than men.

B On average, men show more desirable leadership styles and traits than women.

C In the United States, employees prefer to work for female bosses.

D Men are more effective leaders than women.

9 In general, the _____ style of leadership is considered the most desirable.

A transactional

B laissez-faire

C passive

D transformational

10 Which of the following would be an example of a virtual team?

A A group of workers around the globe who coordinate their efforts through teleconferencing and email

B A computer simulation of how employees might interact

C A group of employees who have similar jobs, but who do not actually interact with one another

D A group of employees in which one member does the majority of the work that is claimed by the team

Work the Scientific Literacy Model :: Understanding Employee Affect, Attitudes, and Behavior

What do we know about employee affect, attitudes, and behavior?

For most people, work occupies a significant portion their daily time and energy. Whether an individual enjoys his or her job depends on an interaction between personality characteristics and the job itself. Recall the discussion of positive affect and negative affect on **page 633**. Positive affect (PA) is the tendency to experience emotions such as optimism and enthusiasm, whereas negative affect (NA) is the tendency to experience emotions such as frustration and anger. If you tend to exhibit NA traits, then you will likely feel glum and unsatisfied even after a recent success, such as getting a B+ on an exam. Job satisfaction is directly related to negative or positive affect. **Figure 17.4** on **page 634** highlights several sources of job satisfaction, and its negative counterpart—job burnout—is profiled in **Table 17.8** on **page 643**. Affect can even influence behavior at work, as employees are more likely to engage in counterproductive behavior, such as aggression and absenteeism, if they are unhappy with their job.

How can science help explain the importance of employee affect and attitudes?

Research shows that people with PA traits tend to outdo their NA co-workers when it comes to creativity, teamwork, and decision making. In fact, interesting research has revealed that people with negative and positive affect tendencies are simply wired differently. Reward centers in the brain are more active in PA individuals, whereas the brains of NA individuals have increased activity in fear and alert response circuitry. Studies show that feeling satisfied in your job is related to internal factors such as self-esteem, the belief in your ability to accomplish tasks (self-efficacy), and your belief about whether you control your own work environment and successes (locus of control). At the opposite end of the spectrum is burnout—a sense of mental and physical exhaustion, a cynical attitude, and the belief that one's work has little meaning. In addition, researchers have investigated the idea that intellectually challenging people with high cognitive ability contributes to a sense of job satisfaction. Even highly skilled people may burn out on their jobs, however. You can see the results of a study on burnout in **Figure 17.5** on **page 636**, which suggested that vacation time can alleviate the negative feelings associated with burnout, at least temporarily.

Why is this relevant?

Watch the accompanying video excerpt on motivation. You can access the video at MyPsychLab or by clicking the play button in the center of your eText. If your instructor assigns this video as a homework activity, you will find additional content to help you in MyPsychLab. You can also view the video by using your smart phone and the QR code below, or you can go to the YouTube link provided.

Once you have read this chapter and watched the video, consider the following. Several aspects of the work environment have been found to increase job involvement, work motivation, and job satisfaction. Identify and describe these conditions. How is money related to work motivation?

Can we critically evaluate claims about affect, attitudes, and behavior at work?

Should employees limit their hiring to people with sunny dispositions or positive affective traits? Keep in mind that some emotional traits are culturally influenced. The **Biopsychosocial Perspectives** feature on **page 633** notes that negative traits such as pessimism seem to be related to culture, and that some measure of pessimistic thinking can actually lead to better performance on certain tasks than optimistic thinking. Burnout can happen to both positive and negative thinkers, and it can negatively influence individual performance, organizational morale, and even aggressive behavior.

Can employers buy their workers' loyalty? Does a big paycheck equal job satisfaction? While a raise might temporarily motivate a dissatisfied employee, it has the same effect as a vacation on a burned-out worker—a temporary one. The real solution seems to be taking a proactive approach. Organizations need to hire the right people for positions within the company, use training and mentoring to motivate them, and offer strategies and programs (such as gym memberships and other health benefits) to help their workers manage stress.

youtube.com/
scientificliteracy

MyPsychLab

Your turn to Work the Scientific Literacy Model: You can access the video at MyPsychLab or by clicking the play button in the center of your eText. If your instructor assigns this video as a homework activity, you will find additional content to help you at MyPsychLab. You can also view the video by using your smart phone and the QR code, or you can go to the YouTube link provided.

Answer Key

CHAPTER 1

Quick Quiz 1.1a :: p. 5
1. B   2. C   3. D   4. C

Quick Quiz 1.1b :: p. 11
1. A   2. B   3. A

Apply Activity 1.1 :: p. 12
1. The appeals to your wallet and to your environmental conscience sound great, but it might be too good to be true!
2. The manufacturer is trying to make money. That does not make the company evil, but it might lead its marketing staff to exaggerate the benefits offered by its products.
3. We do not have any evidence that the product works, just the manufacturer's claim. Until you find the evidence, you must tolerate ambiguity—you cannot say if it is effective or not.

Quick Quiz 1.2a :: p. 19
1. D   2. B   3. A   4. B

Quick Quiz 1.2b :: p. 25
1. A   2. D   3. A   4. C

Apply Activity 1.2 :: p. 26
1. C   2. A   3. B   4. E   5. D

Quick Quiz 1.3 :: p. 31
1. B   2. D   3. B   4. A   5. A

Apply Activity 1.3 :: p. 32
1. C   2. D   3. B   4. E   5. A

Chapter Quiz :: p. 34
1. A   2. A   3. A   4. C   5. D   6. C
7. A   8. C   9. B   10. D   11. B   12. B
13. A   14. C   15. D

CHAPTER 2

Quick Quiz 2.1a :: p. 45
1. A   2. B   3. C   4. A

Quick Quiz 2.1b :: p. 46
1. B   2. C   3. A

Apply Activity 2.1 :: p. 47
1. The problem with the instrumentation is one of reliability. One key measure of reliability in research is the degree to which a measurement provides consistent, stable responses. In this case, the recording device does not meet this criterion.
2. The problem with Dr. Nielson's happiness measure probably concerns its validity. The different observers were always in agreement on how they recorded the children's behavior, so their measure is reliable. However, given what the second group of researchers found, it is possible that Dr. Nielson's group is actually measuring how energetic children are, rather than how happy they are. (As you may have thought, this could also go the other way around: The researcher who was recording whether children were energetic may have been unknowingly measuring whether they were happy.)

Quick Quiz 2.2a :: p. 50
1. B   2. C   3. D

Quick Quiz 2.2b :: p. 52
1. B (this is a strong negative correlation. The strength of the relationship is strongest because it is closer to -1.0 than either +.54 or +.10. Correlation coefficients cannot go above 1.0)
2. A   3. C

Quick Quiz 2.2c :: p. 54
1. C   2. B   3. A   4. A

Apply Activity 2.2 :: p. 55
1. independent; dependent
2. positive; negative

Quick Quiz 2.3a :: p. 60
1. B   2. C   3. B

Quick Quiz 2.3.b :: p. 61
1. D   2. B

Apply Activity 2.3 :: p. 62
1. It is not really informed consent if the volunteers are exposed to risks before signing the consent form. The "informed" part of informed consent means that individuals are fully informed about risks they may experience as a result of participating in the study.
2. This research design is unethical because it requires volunteers to answer all of the questions in a survey. Participants generally have the right to quit at any time, or to decline to answer any specific questions they choose. This issue is particularly important with sensitive topics such as sexuality.

Quick Quiz 2.4a :: p. 67
1. B   2. D   3. A   4. C

Quick Quiz 2.4b :: p. 68
1. C   2. A

Apply Activity 2.4 :: p. 69
1. Negatively skewed   2. 90–94
3. 9 (4 between 80–84 and 5 between 85–89).

Chapter Quiz :: p. 71
1. A   2. B   3. D   4. D   5. B   6. D
7. C   8. A   9. C   10. B

CHAPTER 3

Quick Quiz 3.1a :: p. 78
1. B   2. C   3. A   4. A

Quick Quiz 3.1b :: p. 82
1. C   2. B   3. A   4. D

Apply Activity 3.1 :: p. 83
1. Evolutionary psychologists predict that males will be more jealous about sexual infidelity because they are more interested in the reproductive qualities in a mate. This statement does not mean that women will not experience jealousy; rather, it indicates that men will have a stronger response on average.
2. This graph does show that men have stronger responses to infidelity, so these results support the hypothesis.

Quick Quiz 3.2a :: p. 88
1. C   2. B   3. B   4. C

Quick Quiz 3.2b :: p. 93
1. B   2. B   3. D   4. A

Apply Activity 3.2 :: p. 94
1. The monoamines are a group of neurotransmitter including serotonin, dopamine, and norepinephrine.
2. If monoamine oxidase breaks down the monoamine neurotransmitters, then an inhibitor would prevent it from breaking down the neurotransmitters. The result would be more monoamine neurotransmitters in the synapse.
3. Yes, an MAOI might produce effects resembling those of an SSRI, at least to the extent that both drugs have similar end results. Both types of drugs increase the amount of a neurotransmitter in the synapse, but do so in different ways.

Quick Quiz 3.3a :: p. 97
1. D   2. A   3. C

Quick Quiz 3.3b :: p. 105
1. C   2. B   3. A   4. D   5. A

Quick Quiz 3.3c :: p. 108
1. B   2. C   3. A   4. A

CHAPTER 4

Apply Activity 4.1 :: p. 123
A: Correct Rejection. There is no monster in the closet, and the child is confident that she has not heard anything. B: Miss. There really are monsters in the closet, but the child has not heard them. C: Hit. There really is a monster in the closet. D: False Alarm. There is no monster in the closet, but the child insists that she heard something.

Apply Activity 4.2 :: p. 136
The pictorial depth cues include:
1. a linear perspective (the tracks converging as they reach the horizon)
2. a texture gradient (the rocks, grass and other nearby objects can be seen in greater detail than objects farther away)
3. height in plane (the features that are in the top half of the picture are perceived as far away relative to objects in the bottom region of the photo); and
4. relative size. Railroad ties are known to be the same size, but the ones that are closer appear larger than those that are far off.

CHAPTER 5

Apply Activity 5.2 :: p. 179
1. False 2. True 3. True 4. False 5. False
6. True 7. True

CHAPTER 6

Apply Activity 6.1 :: p. 208
1. CS = theme song, US = kiss, UR = excitement, CR = excitement
2. CS = instrument used by the eye doctor, US = puff of air, UR = blinking, CR = blinking
3. CS = advertisement, US = delicious meal, UR = pleasure from the meal, CR = cravings

Apply Activity 6.2 :: p. 220
1. Negative punishment explains Steven's change in behavior. This process is considered punishment because Steven's behavior of cheating stopped; it is considered negative punishment because the consequence was to remove something he found reinforcing (being at school).
2. Positive reinforcement explains Ericka's pursuit of math. The personal and social rewards are stimuli that added (positively related) to her doing math, which increased her interest in and pursuit of this subject.
3. We are negatively reinforced for closing the car doors, turning off lights, and fastening the seat belt. Each of these behaviors removes the unpleasant buzzing or dinging sound. In turn, the behaviors increase because they allow us to either avoid or escape the annoying sounds.
4. Hernan is using positive punishment. The nail and cuticle biting decrease because he introduces an unpleasant stimulus, the terrible-tasting lotion.

Apply Activity 6.3 :: p. 231
1. Even though his time is limited, John can still incorporate a distributed practice approach to his studying. If he has only 12 hours to study within a 48-hour period, he should distribute his efforts into, perhaps, four 3-hour periods. (There will even be time to sleep!)
2. Janet should try changing the order of the processes. Perhaps her professor's insistence on covering this topic in the same order did not work for her. Thus altering the order of how each of the four processes of observational learning apply would likely help her better understand them.
3. Darius needs to try to determine the purpose of learning the material. It is not busy work. He should focus on understanding how the schedules of reinforcement apply to real-world situations.

CHAPTER 7

Apply Activity 7.1 :: p. 248
1. If Dr. Richard blocks long-term potentiation, then the rat is unlikely to form any long-term memories. At best, they will be weak memories, and the rat will only partially remember the maze.
2. A damaged hippocampus can lead to anterograde amnesia. However, if the damage happens after the rat has committed the maze path to memory, then memory for this specific information should be unaffected by the procedure.

Quick Quiz 7.2.a :: p. 253
1. B   2. A   3. B   4. B   5. A
Quick Quiz 7.2.b :: p. 255
1. A   2. C   3. D
Quick Quiz 7.2.c :: p. 257
1. B   2. B   3. A

Quick Quiz 7.3a :: p. 263
1. D   2. A   3. C

Quick Quiz 7.3.b :: p. 266
1. B   2. A   3. A   4. D   5. B

Apply Activity 7.3 :: p. 267
Of the 225 exonerations, 77% of the cases included erroneous eyewitness testimony—more than any other contributing factor. Given this high correlation, we believe research on eyewitness testimony should continue to find ways of reducing errors. The results of this research should be applied to investigative techniques used by law enforcement officers.

Chapter Quiz :: p. 269
1. C   2. D   3. A   4. C   5. C   6. B
7. B   8. D   9. C   10. D

CHAPTER 8
Quick Quiz 8.1a :: p. 277
1. B   2. B   3. D   4. A
Quick Quiz 8.1b :: p. 279
1. C   2. B

Apply Activity 8.1 :: p. 280
1. For most people, a trout would be a better example for a fish. Hammerheads and eels have unique shapes, but trout are very "fish-like"—they are better prototypes for this category.
2. For many Americans, prototypical sports might include baseball, football, and basketball. For much of the rest of the world, the prototypical sport is probably soccer. Sports that are not considered prototypical by many would include golf, badminton, and even curling.
3. When people respond to this category, they usually settle on prototypical items that are difficult or impossible to re-place—for example, photo albums and other memorabilia, prized possessions, and heirlooms.

Quick Quiz 8.2a :: p. 285
1. B   2. C   3. B   4. A
Quick Quiz 8.2b :: p. 290
1. D   2. B   3. C   4. D   5. C   6. A

Quick Quiz 8.3a :: p. 295
1. D   2. C   3. B   4. A
Quick Quiz 8.3b :: p. 302
1. B   2. A   3. D   4. C   5. A

Apply Activity 8.3 :: p. 303
1. This is a morpheme. We can tell in at least two ways. First, it contains multiple phonemes. Second, it can be added to words in a meaningful way such as in "dislike" and "disprove."
2. On one hand, you might consider /s/ a phoneme because it represents a single sound. On the other hand, you might consider it a morpheme because it can be added to words in a meaningful way (to make a noun plural). Thus, in this case /s/ can be either a phoneme or a morpheme.
3. This is a phoneme. It represents the sound of c in cat. However, /k/ is not a morpheme because it does not have any intrinsic meaning.

Chapter Quiz :: p. 305
1. C   2. D   3. A   4. A   5. C   6. B
7. A   8. D   9. D   10. B

CHAPTER 9
Quick Quiz 9.1a :: p. 311
1. B   2. B   3. C   4. D   5. A   6. C
Quick Quiz 9.1b :: p. 317
1. B   2. C   3. A   4. D   5. D

Apply Activity 9.1 :: p. 318
Student A = typical; Student B = typical; Student C = low; Student D = high

Quick Quiz 9.2a :: p. 323
1. A   2. B   3. C
Quick Quiz 9.2b :: p. 326
1. C   2. B   3. A   4. C
Quick Quiz 9.2c :: p. 327
1. B   2. D

Apply Activity 9.2 :: p. 328
Katrina obviously scores high in analytical intelligence—this is apparent in her academic success. She is also likely to score very high in creativity, as she has made significant discoveries and contributions to the field of chemistry. Unfortunately, she does not seem to do as well with practical intelligence. Katrina is probably about average because she may get by at work, but appears to be quite dependent on others at home.

Quick Quiz 9.3a :: p. 332
1. B   2. A   3. D
Quick Quiz 9.3b :: p. 334
1. A   2. D   3. D
Quick Quiz 9.3c :: p. 338
1. D   2. B   3. B
Quick Quiz 9.3d :: p. 340
1. B   2. C   3. D

Chapter Quiz :: p. 343
1. B   2. C   3. B   4. A   5. D   6. D
7. A   8. D   9. A   10. C

CHAPTER 10
Quick Quiz 10.1a :: p. 348
1. C   2. C   3. D   4. A
Quick Quiz 10.1b :: p. 355
1. A   2. B   3. D   4. C

Apply Activity 10.1 :: p. 356
1. Longitudinal   2. Cross-sectional

Quick Quiz 10.2a :: p. 359
1. A   2. C
Quick Quiz 10.2b :: p. 365
1. C   2. A   3. C   4. B   5. C
Quick Quiz 10.2c :: p. 370
1. B   2. D   3. A   4. A

Apply Activity 10.2 :: p. 371
1. Bridgette is in the sensorimotor stage; the major cognitive milestone in this stage is object permanence.
2. Jared is in the concrete operational stage because he needs to have direct physical contact/interaction with the objects to solve the problems.
3. Michael is likely in the preoperational phase; he lacks a concept of conservation.
4. The students would need to have reached the formal operational stage, which is characterized by the type of hypothetical and abstract thought required to answer this question.

Quick Quiz 10.3a :: p. 373
1. B   2. A
Quick Quiz 10.3b :: p. 377
1. C   2. B   3. D
Quick Quiz 10.3c :: p. 381
1. D   2. A   3. C   4. D

Apply Activity 10.3 :: p. 382
1. Jeff displays conventional reasoning in his decision. Although you would likely regard what he did as wrong (as might Jeff), his reasoning for engaging in the behavior is based on whether the act breaks a law.
2. Margaret displays postconventional moral reasoning because she is not personally affected, but is looking out for the well-being of innocent strangers.
3. Julie is likely struggling with identity diffusion.
4. Breanna appears to have reached identity achievement.

Quick Quiz 10.4a :: p. 385
1. C   2. B
Quick Quiz 10.4b :: p. 387
1. D   2. B   3. C
Quick Quiz 10.4c :: p. 391
1. B   2. A   3. A

Apply Activity 10.4 :: p. 392
1. Authoritarian parenting   2. Indulgent permissive   3. Authoritative

CHAPTER 11

CHAPTER 12

Apply Activity 12.2 :: p. 460

1. Canadians are much more agreeable than Americans. (False. They rate about the same on this trait.)
2. Men and women have vastly different personalities. (False. Although there are some differences, they are generally very small.)
3. Americans are pushy. (False. Americans are no more so than members of cultures who do not have this stereotype.)
4. People from England are reserved. (False. See "Americans are pushy.")

5. Swiss people are conventional and closed off to new experiences. (False. Interestingly, Swiss people actually tend to hold this belief about themselves, but data suggest they are no more or less closed off to new experiences than members of countries who do not hold this stereotype.)
6. Women are more warm and compassionate than men. (True. This is generally the case, although the difference between genders is probably small.)
7. Chinese people value group cohesiveness. (True. As you read in this module people in China tend to embrace collectivism.)

As you can see from this activity, there are some very general personality differences that occur between members of large groups. However, the consensus is that our stereotypes of people from entire countries tend to be inaccurate or at best exaggerated (Terracciano et al., 2005).

Apply Activity 12.3 :: p. 471

1. Freud would comment on the student's desire for cleanliness and organization as a fixation at the anal stage of development (Table 12.3).
2. Someone who does not feel remorse probably did not develop much of a superego, if any; thus the individual is unable to control the id or feel guilt when it takes over.
3. A student who checks his Facebook status may just be avoiding work he is not interested in. If the behavior gets to be too much, then he may be struggling to fulfill social needs.
4. An individual who is willing to sacrifice her own luxuries and put her talents to use for others would be self-actualizing.

CHAPTER 13

Apply Activity 13.2 :: p. 492

1. People with psychopathy show reduced startle reflex and reduced activity in the frontal lobes.
2. Individuals with psychopathy have difficulty learning and following rules.
3. People who develop psychopathy or APD are more likely to grow up in distressed homes or neighborhoods where prosocial rules are not easily learned. A history of childhood sexual, physical, or emotional abuse at the hands of adults is also associated with APD and psychopathy.

Apply Activity 13.3 :: p. 503

If someone you know is considering suicide, he or she can call 1-800-273-TALK (8255). Five key signs of suicidal thinking are (1) talking about suicide; (2) withdrawing from friends or social activities; (3) losing interest in school, work, or hobbies; (4) preparing for death by writing a will, making final arrangements, or giving away prized possessions; and (5) losing interest in personal appearance. See Table 13.8 for additional signs.

Apply Activity 13.4 :: p. 511

1. C: The statuesque behavior is catatonia.
2. B: The overly suspicious delusions are signs of paranoia.
3. A: This sounds like a "split personality," which is not a form of schizophrenia (see the discussion of dissociative identity disorder in Module 13.2).
4. D: The scrambled language and thoughts represent disorganized schizophrenia.

CHAPTER 14

Quick Quiz 14.2b :: p. 534
1. D   2. A   3. C   4. B   5. A   6. A

Apply Activity 14.2 :: p. 535
1. B: cognitive-behavioral therapy, because it is aimed at addressing irrational thought patterns and cognitive restructuring.
2. C: psychodynamic therapy, because the emphasis is on gaining insight into early childhood experiences.
3. E: behavioral therapy, because the focus is on modifying observable behavior patterns.

Quick Quiz 14.3a :: p. 542
1. A   2. D   3. B   4. C   5. A

Quick Quiz 14.3b :: p. 545
1. D   2. C   3. A

Apply Activity 14.3 :: p. 545
1. D   2. B   3. A   4. C

Chapter Quiz :: p. 547
1. C   2. A   3. C   4. D   5. B   6. C
7. B   8. D   9. B   10. A

CHAPTER 15

Quick Quiz 15.1a :: p. 533
1. A   2. D   3. C

Quick Quiz 15.1b :: p. 557
1. A   2. D   3. A   4. C

Quick Quiz 15.1c :: p. 562
1. B   2. C   3. A   4. B   5. A

Quick Quiz 15.2a :: p. 568
1. B   2. B   3. B   4. C

Quick Quiz 15.2b :: p. 572
1. A   2. D   3. B   4. B

Quick Quiz 15.3a :: p. 578
1. A   2. D   3. B   4. D

Quick Quiz 15.3b :: p. 581
1. D   2. D   3. D   4. A   5. D

Chapter Quiz :: p. 584
1. B   2. D   3. D   4. A   5. C   6. D
7. A   8. B   9. D   10. B

CHAPTER 16

Quick Quiz 16.1a :: p. 590
1. D   2. C   3. A

Quick Quiz 16.1b :: p. 593
1. B   2. C   3. D   4. D

Quick Quiz 16.1c :: p. 595
1. B   2. D   3. D

Quick Quiz 16.2a :: p. 601
1. C   2. B   3. C   4. C   5. D

Quick Quiz 16.2b :: p. 604
1. C   2. A   3. B   4. B

Quick Quiz 16.2c :: p. 605
1. C   2. C   3. D

Quick Quiz 16.3a :: p. 611
1. B   2. A   3. C   4. B   5. D   6. C

Quick Quiz 16.3b :: p. 614
1. B   2. A   3. C

Quick Quiz 16.3c :: p. 615
1. A   2. D

Chapter Quiz :: p. 618
1. B   2. C   3. A   4. A   5. D   6. C
7. B   8. C   9. B   10. A

CHAPTER 17

Quick Quiz 17.1a :: p. 623
1. A   2. C   3. D

Quick Quiz 17.1b :: p. 628
1. B   2. B   3. A   4. A

Quick Quiz 17.1c :: p. 630
1. A   2. C   3. D

Quick Quiz 17.2a :: p. 636
1. C   2. B   3. A   4. D   5. C   6. C

Quick Quiz 17.2b :: p. 640
1. B   2. C   3. C

Quick Quiz 17.3a :: p. 646
1. B   2. B   3. D   4. A   5. C

Quick Quiz 17.3b :: p. 647
1. A   2. A   3. D

Chapter Quiz :: p. 650
1. D   2. C   3. A   4. B   5. B   6. B
7. C   8. A   9. D   10. A

Glossary

360-degree feedback :: A technique that provides evaluation information for an employee from various perspectives within and beyond an organization; also known as multisource assessment. 629

abnormal psychology :: The psychological study of mental illness. 477

absenteeism :: Regularly missing work, whether for legitimate or questionable reasons. 635

absolute threshold :: The minimum amount of energy or quantity of a stimulus required for it to be reliably detected at least 50% of the time it is presented. 116

acetylcholine :: A neurotransmitter found at junctions between skeletal muscles and nerves, as well as in the brain, where it is involved in the processes of arousal and attention. 89

achievement motivation :: The drive to perform at high levels and to accomplish significant goals. 422

achievement tests :: Tests that measure knowledge and thinking skills that an individual has acquired. 309

acquisition :: The initial phase of learning in which a response is established. 198

acronym :: A pronounceable word that can be broken up so that each letter represents the first letter in a phrase or set of items. 256

action potential :: A wave of electrical activity that originates at the base of the axon and rapidly travels down its length; the firing of a nerve cell. 87

activation–synthesis hypothesis (of dreaming) :: Prediction that dreams arise from brain activity originating from bursts of excitatory messages arising from the brain stem. 164

adrenal glands :: A pair of endocrine glands located adjacent to the kidneys that release stress hormones, such as cortisol and epinephrine. 92

aggression :: Any behavior that is intended to hurt or harm an individual. 578

agonists :: Drugs that enhance or mimic the effects of neurotransmission. 91

agoraphobia :: An intense fear of having a panic attack or lower-level panic symptoms in public. 495

algorithms :: Problem-solving strategies that are based on a series of rules. 282

all-or-none principle :: The observation that individual nerve cells fire at the same strength every time an action potential occurs. 87

altruism :: Behavior that places the helper at significant risk or certain harm for the benefit of another. 576

Alzheimer's disease :: A degenerative and terminal condition resulting in severe damage of the entire brain. 384

amnesia :: A profound loss of at least one form of memory. 246

amygdala :: A structure in the forebrain that facilitates memory formation for emotional events, mediates fear responses, and appears to play a role in recognizing and interpreting emotional stimuli, including facial expressions. 99

analytical psychology :: A branch of psychology that describes personality as the result of unconscious archetypes. 469

anchoring effect :: An effect that occurs when an individual attempts to solve a problem involving numbers and uses pervious knowledge to keep (i.e., anchor) the response within a limited range. 286

anecdotal evidence :: An individual's story or testimony about an observation or event that is used to make a claim as evidence. 45

anorexia nervosa :: An eating disorder that involves (1) self-starvation, (2) intense fear of weight gain and a distorted perception of body image, and (3) a denial of the serious consequences of severely low weight. 404

antagonists :: Drugs that inhibit neurotransmission by blocking the receptors for or synthesis of the neurotransmitter. 91

anterograde amnesia :: The inability to form new memories for events occurring after a brain injury. 246

anthropometrics :: A historical term referring to the method of measuring physical and mental variations in humans. 314

antianxiety drugs :: Drugs prescribed to alleviate nervousness and tension, and to prevent and reduce panic attacks. 539

antidepressant drugs :: Drugs prescribed to elevate mood and reduce other symptoms of depression. 537

antipsychotic drugs :: Drugs used treat disorders such as schizophrenia, and sometimes patients with severe mood disorders. 539

antisocial personality disorder (APD) :: A personality disorder marked by a habitual pattern of willingly violating others' personal rights, with little sign of empathy or remorse. 487

anxiety disorders :: A category of mental disorders involving fear or nervousness that is excessive, irrational, and maladaptive. 494

aphasias :: Language disorders caused by damage to the brain structures that support the use and understanding of language. 296

appeal to authority :: A claim that is based on belief in an expert's testimony, even when no supporting data or scientific evidence is present. 45

appeal to common sense :: A claim that appears to be sound, but lacks supporting scientific evidence. 45

applied psychology :: A branch of psychology that uses psychological knowledge to address problems and issues across various settings and professions, including law, education, clinical psychology, and business organization and management. 28

approach goals :: Enjoyable and pleasant incentives that we are drawn toward, such as praise or financial reward. 422

aptitude tests :: Tests designed to measure an individual's potential to perform well in a specific range of tasks. 309

assertiveness :: The degree to which an individual will work to achieve or protect one's interests. 643

assessment centers :: A method of personnel selection that capitalizes on multiple approaches to selection by combining personality, cognitive, and sometimes physical ability tests. 626

attachment :: An enduring emotional bond formed between individuals. 365

authoritarian parenting :: A parenting style in which parents exercise excessive control over children and are less likely to express warmth toward them. 389

authoritative parenting :: A parenting style characterized by the expression of warmth and responsiveness to the needs of children, but exercising control over certain actions and decisions made by children. 388

autonomic nervous system :: The portion of the peripheral nervous system that is responsible for controlling involuntary activity of the organs and glands. 96

availability heuristic :: A strategy for estimating the frequency of an event based on how easily examples of it come to mind. 286

aversive conditioning :: A behavioral therapy technique that involves replacing a positive response to a stimulus with a negative response, typically by using punishment. 532

avoidance goals :: Unpleasant outcomes that we try to avoid, such as shame, embarrassment, or emotional pain. 422

avoidance learning :: A specific type of negative reinforcement that removes the possibility of an aversive stimulus occurring. 213

axon :: The projection of a neuron that transports information from the neuron to neighboring neurons in the form of an electrochemical reaction. 85

basal ganglia :: A set of forebrain structures involved in facilitating planned movements, skill learning, and are also integrated with the brain's reward system. 99

behavioral genetics :: The study of how genes and environment influence behavior. 76

behavioral genomics :: The study of how specific genes, in their interactions with the environment, influence behavior. 77, 331

behavioral therapy :: A form of therapy that addresses problem behaviors and thoughts, and the environmental factors that trigger them, as directly as possible. 529

behaviorism :: The dominant approach to psychology in the United States starting in the first half of the 20th century, which had a singular focus on studying only observable behavior, with little to no reference to mental events or instincts as possible causes of behavior. 21

belief perseverance :: A cognitive bias that occurs when an individual believes he or she has the solution to the problem or the correct answer for a question, and accepts only evidence that will confirm those beliefs. 287

bibliotherapy :: The use of self-help books and other reading materials as a form of therapy. 522

binocular depth cues :: Distance cues that are based on the differing perspectives of both eyes. 132

biofeedback :: A therapeutic technique involving the use of physiological recording instruments to provide feedback that increases ones awareness of bodily responses. 609

biopsychosocial model :: An approach to explaining behavior as a product of biological, psychological, and sociocultural factors. 5

bipolar disorder :: A type of mood disorder characterized by extreme highs and lows in mood, motivation, and energy; sometimes referred to as manic depression. 500

blood–brain barrier :: A network of tightly packed cells that allow only specific types of substances to travel from the bloodstream to the brain 537

body mass index (BMI) :: A statistic commonly used for estimating a healthy body weight that factors in an individual's height. 591

borderline personality disorder (BPD) :: A psychological disorder involving intense extremes between positive and negative emotions, an unstable sense of self, impulsivity, and difficult social relationships. 486

bottom-up processing :: A perceptual process in which a whole stimulus or concept is constructed from bits of raw sensory information. 120

brain-derived neurotrophic factor (BDNF) :: A protein in the nervous system that promotes survival, growth, and formation of new synapses. 615

brain stem :: A portion of the hindbrain on top of the spinal cord that comprises the medulla, pons, reticular formation, and cerebellum. 98

Broca's area :: A frontal lobe structure that controls humans' ability to articulate the speech sounds that make up words. 296

bulimia nervosa :: An eating disorder characterized by periods of food deprivation, binge-eating, and purging. 404

burnout :: A combination of persistent emotional and physical exhaustion, cynical attitudes about the job, and a sense that one's work has little meaning. 634

bystander effect :: The situation in which, as an individual looks around at other bystanders and notices that no one else is helping, the bystander freezes. 577

Cannon-Bard theory of emotion :: The theory that emotions such as fear or happiness occur simultaneously with their physiological components. 429

case study :: An in-depth report about the details of a specific case. 49

catatonic schizophrenia :: A subtype of schizophrenia including episodes in which a person remains mute and immobile—sometimes in bizarre positions—for extended periods. 505

categories :: Groups of interrelated concepts. 273

cell body :: The part of a neuron that contains the nucleus and the genetic information of the cell; also known as the *soma*. 85

central executive :: The control center of working memory; it coordinates attention and the exchange of information among the three storage components. 240

central nervous system :: The division of the nervous system consisting of the brain and the spinal cord. 96

central route (to persuasion) :: A path to persuasion in which individuals take time, evaluate evidence, and use valid logic and arguments to arrive at attitudes or beliefs. 561

central tendency :: A measure of the central point of a distribution of numbers. 64

cerebellum :: A portion of the hindbrain involved in the coordination, timing, and learning of movements as well as maintaining balance. 98

cerebral cortex :: The convoluted, wrinkled outer layer of the brain that is involved in multiple higher functions, such as thought, language, and personality. 100

chromosomes :: Structures in the cellular nucleus that are lined with all of the genes an individual inherits. 75

chunking :: The process of organizing smaller units of information into larger, more meaningful units. 241

circadian rhythms :: Internally driven daily cycles of approximately 24 hours that affect physiological and behavioral processes. 159

classical categorization :: A theory that claims objects or events are categorized according to a certain set of rules or based on a specific set of features. 273

classical conditioning :: Learning that occurs when a neutral stimulus begins to elicit a response that was originally caused by another stimulus. 196

clinical psychologist :: A mental health professional with a doctoral degree who diagnoses and treats mental health problems ranging from the everyday to the chronic and severe. 519

clinical psychology :: The field of psychology concerned with diagnosing and treating mental and behavioral disorders. 17

cochlea :: A fluid-filled membrane in the ear that is coiled in a snail-like shape and contains the structures that convert sound into neural impulses. 140

cognitive-behavioral therapy :: A form of therapy that consists of procedures such as exposure, cognitive restructuring, and stress inoculation training. 532

cognitive development :: The changing abilities and processes of memory, thought, and reasoning that occur throughout the life span. 360

cognitive dissonance :: The situation in which an individual has two thoughts (cognitions) that are inconsistent with each other (dissonance) and, as a result, experiences motivation to reduce the discrepancy. 558

cohort effects :: Consequences of being born in a particular year or narrow range of years. 347

collective unconscious :: A collection of memories that can be traced to our ancestral past. 469

collectivism :: The tendency to place greater value on defining the self in terms of group membership and goals. 451

coma :: A state marked by complete loss of consciousness and suppressed brain stem reflexes. 178

community psychology :: An area of psychology that focuses on identifying how individuals' mental health is influenced by the neighborhood, economics, social groups, and other community-based variables. 521

comorbidity :: The presence of two disorders simultaneously, or the presence of a second disorder that affects the one being treated. 489

compensatory control :: The psychological strategies people use to preserve a sense of nonrandom order when personal control is compromised. 612

concept :: The mental representation of an object, event, or idea. 273

concrete operational stage :: The third stage of cognitive development, spanning ages 7 to 11 years, when children develop skills in using and manipulating numbers as well as logical thinking. 362

conditioned emotional response :: A set of emotional and physiological responses that develop to a specific type of object or situation. 200

conditioned response (CR) :: A learned response that occurs to the conditioned stimulus. 197

conditioned stimulus (CS) :: A once neutral stimulus that elicits a conditioned response because it has a history of being paired with an unconditioned stimulus. 197

conditioned taste aversion :: The acquired dislike of or disgust for a food or drink because that food or drink was paired with illness. 202

conduction hearing loss :: Hearing loss resulting from damage to any of the physical structures that conduct sound waves to the cochlea. 142

cones :: Photoreceptors in the eye that are sensitive to the different wavelengths of light that we perceive as color. 127

confirmation bias :: A cognitive bias that occurs when an individual searches for only evidence that will confirm his or her beliefs instead of evidence that might disconfirm them. 287

conformity :: The situation in which an individual's behavior changes to fit with the behavior of a group. 552

confounding variables :: Factors outside of the researcher's control that might affect the results of a study. 53

consciousness :: Our subjective thoughts, perceptions, experiences of the world, and self-awareness. 158

conservation :: Knowledge that the quantity or amount of an object is not related to the physical arrangement and appearance of that object. 361

consolidation :: The process of converting short-term memories into long-term memories in the brain. 245

constructive memory :: A process by which we first recall a generalized schema and then add in specific details. 261

continuous reinforcement :: A schedule in which every response made results in reinforcement. 216

contrast effect :: A type of error in the evaluation process in which a rater evaluates one employee who is very strong in a number of dimensions such that, by comparison, the next employee is likely to appear weaker, even though he or she may be an average worker by other measures. 629

control group :: A group in an experiment that does not receive the treatment and, therefore, serves as a comparison to an experimental group. 53

control processes :: Elements of memory systems that shift information from one memory store to another. 237

convenience sample :: A sample consisting of those individuals who are the most readily available. 40

conventional morality :: A type of moral thinking that regards social conventions and rules as guides for appropriate moral behavior, and emphasizes taking directives from parents, teachers, and the law. 376

convergence :: A depth cue that occurs when the eye muscles contract so that both eyes focus on a single object. 132

coping :: Processes used to manage demands, stress, and conflict. 608

core knowledge hypothesis :: A view on development that proposes infants have inborn abilities for understanding some key aspects of their environment. 363

cornea :: A clear layer that covers the front portion of the eye and contributes to our ability to focus our vision on an object. 126

coronary heart disease :: A condition in which plaques form in the blood vessels that supply the heart with blood and oxygen, resulting in restricted blood flow. 603

corpus callosum :: The area of the brain connecting the two cerebral hemispheres. 100

correlational research :: A technique for measuring the degree of association between two or more variables. 50

cortisol :: A hormone secreted by the adrenal cortex that prepares the body to respond to stressful circumstances. 600

counseling psychologist :: A mental health professional who typically works with people needing help with common problems such as stress, coping, and mild forms of anxiety and depression, rather than severe mental disorders. 519

critical thinking :: Exercising curiosity and skepticism when evaluating the claims of others, and with our own assumptions and beliefs. 8

cross-foster :: The act of raising an animal as member of a family that is not of the same species. 300

cross-sectional design :: A research design used to measure and compare samples of people from different age groups at one point in time. 347

crystallized intelligence (Gc) :: A form of intelligence that relies on extensive experience and knowledge and, therefore, tends to be relatively stable and robust. 321

dark adaptation :: A process by which the rods and cones in the eye become increasingly sensitive to light under low levels of illumination. 127

debriefing :: An ethical procedure in which researchers explain the true nature of a study, and especially the nature of and reason for any deception after it has been completed. 58

deception :: Misleading or only partially informing participants in a research study about the true topic or hypothesis under investigation. 58

declarative memory :: Memories we are consciously aware of and can that be verbalized, including facts about the world and one's own personal experiences. 243

deep brain stimulation (DBS) :: A technique that involves electrically stimulating highly specific regions of the brain. 544

defense mechanisms :: Unconscious strategies that the ego uses to reduce or avoid anxiety, guilt, and other unpleasant feelings. 464

deinstitutionalization :: A grass-roots movement that pushed for returning people from mental institutions to their communities and families and enabling individuals to receive treatment on an outpatient basis. 520

déjà vu :: A distinct feeling of having seen or experienced a situation that is impossible or unlikely to have previously occurred. 176

deliberative thought :: An intentional and effortful form of thinking. 565

delusions :: False beliefs about reality. 505

demand characteristics :: Inadvertent cues given off by the experimenter or the experimental context that provide information about how participants are expected to behave in a research study. 41

dementia :: A set of symptoms including mild to severe disruption of mental functioning, memory loss, disorientation, poor judgment, and decision making. 384

dendrites :: The small branches radiating from the cell body of a neuron that receive messages from other cells and transmit the message toward the cell body. 85

denial of responsibility :: The situation in which an individual maintains the same attitude about an action, but changes his belief about his own role in the action. 559

dependence :: A need to take a drug to ward off unpleasant physical withdrawal symptoms; often referred to as addiction. 188

dependent variable :: The observation or measurement that is recorded during the experiment and subsequently compared across all groups in a research study. 53

descriptive statistics :: A set of techniques used to organize, summarize, and interpret data. 64

determinism :: The belief that all events are governed by lawful, cause-and-effect relationships. 14

developmental psychology :: The study of change and stability of human physical, cognitive, social, and behavioral characteristics across the life span. 346

***Diagnostic and Statistical Manual for Mental Disorders* (DSM-IV)** :: The manual that establishes criteria for the diagnosis of mental disorders. 477

difference threshold :: The smallest detectable difference between stimuli. 116

diffusion of responsibility :: The situation in which individual bystanders do not feel the full effect of empathy because so many others are around. 577

discrimination (in learning) :: A process in which an organism learns to respond to one original stimulus but not to new stimuli that may be similar to the original stimulus. 199

discrimination :: Any behavior based on prejudice. 569

discriminative stimulus :: A cue or event indicating that a response, if made, will be reinforced. 214

dishabituation :: An increase in responsiveness following a change in a stimulus or event. 363

disorganized schizophrenia :: A subtype of schizophrenia involving poorly integrated thoughts, speech, behavior, and emotion. 505

display rules :: The unwritten expectations people have regarding when it is appropriate to show a certain emotion. 431

dissociation theory :: An explanation of hypnosis as a unique state in which consciousness is divided into an observer and a hidden observer. 173

dissociative disorder :: A category of mental disorders characterized by a split between conscious awareness from feeling, cognition, memory, and identity. 490

dissociative identity disorder (DID) :: A condition in which people claim that their identity has split into one or more distinct alter personalities, or alters; sometimes referred to as multiple personality disorder. 490

divided attention :: Attending to several stimuli or tasks at once. 121

dizygotic twins :: Twins who were conceived by two different eggs and two different sperm, but still shared the same womb; also known as *fraternal twins.* 76

DNA (deoxyribonucleic acid) :: Molecules formed in a double-helix shape that contain four amino acids: adenine, cytosine, guanine, and thymine. 75

door-in-the-face technique :: A technique that begins with a large request that is likely to be turned down, followed by a smaller request that is likely to be accepted. 560

dopamine :: A monoamine neurotransmitter involved in movement, mood, and processing of rewarding experiences. 89

double-blind study :: An experimental procedure in which neither the participant nor the experimenter knows the exact treatment received by any individual. 43

dream analysis :: A method of understanding unconscious thought by interpreting the manifest content (what happens in the dream) to get a sense of the latent content (the unconscious elements that motivated the dream). 526

drive :: A physiological trigger that tells us we may be deprived of something and causes us to seek out what is needed, such as food. 398

DRM (Deese-Roediger-McDermott) procedure :: A research technique in which participants study a list of highly related words called semantic associates. 263

dual coding :: The phenomenon that occurs when information is stored in more than one form—such as a verbal description and a visual image, or a description and a sound. 256

ecological validity :: The degree to which the results of a laboratory study can be applied to or repeated in the natural environment. 40

ecstasy (MDMA) :: An illegal club/rave drug known to heighten sensory experiences, intensify social bonding, and have hallucinogenic effects. 182

ego :: A component of personality that mediates the id through the reality principle. 463

egocentric :: Perceiving and interpreting the world in terms of the self. 367

elaborative rehearsal :: Prolonging exposure to information by thinking about its meaning. 250

electroconvulsive therapy (ECT) :: A psychiatric treatment in which an electrical current is passed through the brain to induce a temporary seizure. 543

electroencephalogram (EEG) :: A measure of brain activity that uses electrodes attached to the scalp to measure patterns of brain activity. 106

embryonic stage :: The second stage of prenatal development, spanning weeks two through eight of gestation. During this time, the embryo begins developing major physical structures such as the heart and nervous system, as well as the beginnings of the arms, legs, hands, and feet. 349

emotion :: A psychological experience involving three components: (1) subjective thoughts and experiences, (2) accompanying patterns of physical arousal, and (3) characteristic behavioral expressions. 426

emotional dialects :: Variations across cultures in how core emotions are expressed. 431

emotional well-being :: The subjective experience of both positive and negative emotions, which are typically measured by life satisfaction, happiness, and the balance between negative and positive emotional experiences. 390

empathy :: The emotional concern that one individual has for another's well-being. 575

empirically supported treatments :: Also called evidence based therapies; treatments that have been tested and evaluated using sound research designs. 522

empiricism :: A philosophical tenet that knowledge comes through experience. 14

encoding :: The process of storing information in a long-term memory system. 237

encoding specificity principle :: The concept that retrieval is most effective when it occurs in the same context as encoding. 252

endorphin :: A chemical produced by the pituitary gland and the hypothalamus that functions to reduce pain and induce feelings of pleasure. 92

entity theory :: The belief that intelligence is a fixed characteristic and relatively difficult (or impossible) to change. 339

episodic buffer :: A storage component of working memory that combines the images and sounds from the other two components (the phonological loop and visuospatial sketchpad) into coherent, story-like episodes. 240

episodic memory :: A type of declarative memory for personal experiences that seems to be organized around episodes and is recalled from a first-person perspective. 243

escape learning :: A process in which an organization learns that a response removes an unpleasant or undesirable stimulus that is already present. 213

etiology :: The origins or causes of symptoms. 477

evolution :: The change in the frequency of genes occurring in an interbreeding population over generations. 78

evolutionary psychology :: A psychological approach that interprets and explains modern human behavior in terms of forces acting upon our distant ancestors. 21

experimental group :: The group in an experiment that is exposed to the independent variable. 53

explicit prejudice :: The situation in which an individual confesses to or openly demonstrates his or her stereotypes. 570

exposure treatments :: A behavioral therapy process in which exposure to a feared situation is completed gradually and under controlled conditions. 529

external attribution :: The situation in which the observer explains the actor's behavior as a result of the social context. 567

extinction (in classical conditioning) :: The loss or weakening of a conditioned response when a conditioned stimulus and an unconditioned stimulus no longer occur together. 198

extinction (in operant conditioning) :: The weakening of an operant response when reinforcement is no longer available. 214

facial feedback hypothesis :: A prediction that if emotional expressions influence subjective emotional experiences, then the act of forming a facial expression should elicit the specific corresponding emotion. 429

factor analysis :: A statistical technique used by psychologists to reveal statistical similarities underlying a wide variety of items. 320, 440

false memory :: Remembering events that did not occur, or incorrectly recalling details of an event. 263

fast mapping :: The ability to map words onto concepts or objects after only a single exposure. 300

fetal alcohol syndrome :: A condition resulting in abnormalities in mental functioning, growth, and facial development in the offspring of women who use alcohol during pregnancy. 353

fetal stage :: The third stage of prenatal development, spanning week eight of gestation through birth. During this time, the skeletal, organ, and nervous systems become more developed and specialized. 349

first letter technique :: A mnemonic technique that uses the first letters of a set of items to spell out words that form a sentence. 256

Five Factor Model (Big Five personality factors) :: A trait-based approach to personality measurement that includes extraversion, emotional stability (also referred to by the opposite quality, neuroticism), conscientiousness, agreeableness, and openness. 440

fixation :: A preoccupation with obtaining pleasure during psychosexual development, resulting in failure to progress as expected. 464

fixed-interval schedule :: A schedule that reinforces the first response occurring after a set amount of time passes. 216

fixed-ratio schedule :: A schedule in which reinforcement is delivered after a specific number of responses have been completed. 216

flashbulb memory :: An extremely vivid and detailed memory about an event and the conditions surrounding how one learned about the event. 254

fluid intelligence (Gf) :: A type of intelligence that is used to adapt to new situations and solve new problems without relying on previous knowledge. 321

Flynn effect :: The finding of steady population-level increases in intelligence test scores over time. 326

foot-in-the-door technique :: A persuasion technique that involves a request for something simple, followed by a more substantial request. 559

forebrain :: The most visibly obvious region of the whole brain; it consists of multiple interconnected structures that are critical to such complex processes as emotion, memory, thinking, and reasoning. 99

forensic psychology :: The branch of psychology that encompasses work in the criminal justice system, including interactions with the legal system and its professionals. 28

formal operational stage :: The fourth stage of cognitive development, beginning at approximately 11 years of age and continuing into adulthood, that involves advanced cognitive processes such as abstract reasoning and hypothetical thinking. 362

fovea :: The central region of the retina, which contains the highest concentration of cones. The fovea ensures that objects we center our vision upon are the clearest and most colorful relative to objects in the periphery. 127

free association :: A therapeutic method that instructs the patient to reveal any thoughts that arise, no matter how odd or meaningless they may seem. 526

frequency :: The number of observations that fall within a certain category or range of scores. 64

frequency theory :: A theory of hearing stating that the perception of pitch is related to the frequency at which the basilar membrane vibrates. 141

frontal lobe :: Region of the cortex that is involved in higher cognitive functions, such as planning, regulating impulses and emotion, language production, and voluntary movement. 101

frustration-aggression hypothesis :: A prediction that aggression will occur when an individual is prevented from achieving a goal and experiences frustration as a result. 580

functional fixedness :: A problem-solving obstacle that occurs when an individual identifies a potential operator, but can think of only its most obvious function. 284

functionalism :: The study of the purpose and function of behavior and conscious experience. 21

fundamental attribution error :: The tendency to make internal attributions for others while ignoring external attributions. 567

gamma-amino butyric acid (GABA) :: A primary inhibitory neurotransmitter of the nervous system, which prevents neurons from generating action potentials. 89

gate-control theory (of pain) :: A theory that explains our experience of pain as an interaction between nerves that transmit pain messages and those that inhibit these messages. 147

gene :: The basic unit of heredity that is responsible for guiding the process of creating the proteins that make up the body's physical structures, and regulating development and physiological processes throughout the life span. 75

gene knockout (KO) :: A method of removing a specific gene thought to be involved in a trait (such as intelligence) and testing the effects of removing the gene by comparing behavior of animals without the gene with those that have it. 331

general adaptation syndrome (GAS) :: An early theory of stress responses involving stages of alarm, resistance, and exhaustion. 598

general intelligence (g) :: The concept that intelligence is a basic cognitive trait comprising the ability to learn, reason, and solve problems regardless of their nature. 320

generalizability :: The degree to which one set of results can be applied to other situations, individuals, or events. 40

generalization :: A process in which a response that originally occurs to a specific stimulus also occurs to different, though similar stimuli. 199

generalized anxiety disorder (GAD) :: A type of anxiety disorder involving frequently elevated levels of anxiety that are not directed at or limited to any particular situation. 495

genotype :: The genetic makeup of an organism. 75

germinal stage :: The first stage of prenatal development, spanning from conception to two weeks' gestation. 349

gestalt psychology :: An approach emphasizing that psychologists need to focus on the whole of perception and experience, rather than its parts. 23

glial cells :: Specialized cells of the nervous system that are involved in manufacturing myelin, mounting immune responses in the brain, removing wastes, and synchronizing activity of the billions of neurons that constitute the nervous system. 86

glucose :: A sugar that serves as a primary energy source of the brain and the rest of the body. 398

glutamate :: An excitatory neurotransmitter in the nervous system that plays a critical role in the processes of learning and memory. 89

graded membership :: The observation that some concepts appear to make better category members than other concepts. 273

group polarization :: The situation in which members of a group discuss characteristic attitudes and the individuals experience an increase in those attitudes as a result. 558

groupthink :: A decision-making problem in which group members avoid argument and strive for agreement. 555

gustatory system :: System involved in the sensation and perception of taste. 150

habituation :: A decrease in responding with repeated exposure to an event. 363

hallucinations :: False perceptions of reality, such as hearing internal voices. 505

hallucinogenic drugs :: A category of drugs that bring about visual, auditory, and sometimes tactile distortions, and alter how people perceive their own thinking. 183

halo effect :: A type of error in the appraisal process in which a rater thinks highly of an aspect of an employee's job or personality, which in turn leads him or her to unintentionally overrate other aspects of the employee's performance. 629

haptics :: The active, exploratory aspect of touch sensation and perception. 146

Hawthorne effect :: Situations in which behavior changes as a result of being observed. 40

health psychology :: The study of how individual, biological, and environmental factors affect physical health. 29

heritability :: A statistic, expressed as a number between zero and one, that represents the degree to which genetic differences between individuals contribute to individual differences in a behavior or trait found in a population. 76

heuristics :: Problem-solving strategies that stem from previous experiences and provide an educated guess as to what is the most likely solution. 282

hippocampus :: A structure in the brain located below the amygdala in the limbic system; it is responsible for learning and memory. 100

histrionic personality disorder (HPD) :: A category of personality disorder characterized by excessive attention seeking and dramatic behavior. 487

homeostasis :: The body's physiological processes that allow it to maintain consistent internal states in response to the outer environment. 397

hormones :: Chemicals produced by the endocrine system that regulate bodily functions and behavior. 91

humanistic psychology :: A perspective of psychology that focuses on the unique aspects of each individual human, their freedom to act, their rationale thought, and the belief that humans are fundamentally different from other animals. 22, 470

hypnosis :: A procedure of inducing a heightened state of suggestibility. 173

hypothalamic–pituitary–adrenal (HPA) axis :: A neural and endocrine circuit that involves communication between the nervous system (the hypothalamus) and the endocrine system (pituitary and adrenal glands). 600

hypothalamus :: A brain structure that regulates basic biological needs and motivational systems. 92

hypothesis :: A testable prediction about processes that can be observed and measured. 3

hypothesis test :: A statistical test for the difference between the means of the two groups relative to the variability one would expect due to chance in the means. 68

id :: A component of personality underlying basic biological drives, including those related to sex and aggression. 462

identity :: A person's self-image and perception of his or her unique and individual characteristics. 377

identity statuses :: The processes and outcomes of identity development that include elements of both crisis and personal commitment. 378

idiographic approach (to personality) :: An approach to the study of personality that uses detailed descriptions of individuals and their unique personality characteristics. 440

ill-defined problem :: A problem with either an ambiguous initial state or an ambiguous goal state. 282

imagination inflation :: The increased confidence in a false memory following repeated imagination of the event. 264

imitation :: Recreation of a motor behavior or expression, often to accomplish a specific goal. 227

implicit prejudice :: Forms of stereotyping and prejudice that are kept silent either intentionally or because the individual is unaware of their own prejudice. 570

inattentional blindness :: A failure to notice clearly visible events or objects because attention is directed elsewhere. 122

incentives (goals) :: The stimuli we seek to reduce the drives such as those related to social approval and companionship, food, water, and other needs. 398

incremental theory :: The belief that intelligence can be shaped by experiences, practice, and effort. 339

independent variable :: The variable in an experiment that the experimenter manipulates to distinguish between groups participating in the study. 53

indifferent-uninvolved parenting :: A parenting style in which the parents show neither warmth toward nor control over their children. 389

individualism :: The view that personal identity, goals, and attributes are of greater value than group identity, goals, and attributes. 451

indulgent-permissive parenting :: A parenting style in which the parents show warmth toward their children, but do not attempt to control their children, even in positive and helpful ways. 389

industrial/organizational (I/O) psychology :: A branch of applied psychology in which psychologists work for businesses and other organizations to improve employee productivity and the organizational structure of the company or business. 30

inferiority complex :: A feeling that one is inferior to others, often resulting in struggles that influence personality development. 469

informed consent :: A research procedure in which a potential volunteer must be informed (know the purpose, tasks, and risks involved in the study) and give consent (agree to participate based on the information provided) without pressure. 58

ingroup bias :: Attribution of positive qualities to the social groups we belong to (i.e., our ingroup). 569

insanity defense :: A legal strategy of claiming that a defendant was unable to differentiate between right and wrong when the criminal act was committed. 480

insight therapies :: A general term referring to psychotherapy that involves dialogues between client and therapist for the purposes of gaining awareness and understanding of psychological problems and conflicts. 526

insomnia :: A condition marked by a severe lack of sleep. 167

institutional review board (IRB) :: A committee of researchers and officials at an institution charged with the protection of human research participants. 57

intelligence :: The ability to think, understand, reason, and cognitively adapt to and overcome obstacles. 309

intelligence quotient (IQ) :: A measurement in which the mental age of an individual is divided by the person's chronological age and then multiplied by 100. 312

internal attribution :: The observer's explanation of the actor's behavior as some intrinsic quality of the individual. 567

intuitive thought :: Quick, effortless, automatic thinking. 565

iris :: The round muscle that adjusts the size of the pupil and gives the eyes their characteristic color. 126

James-Lange theory of emotion :: The theory that our physiological reactions to stimuli (e.g., a racing heart) precede and give rise to an emotional experience (e.g., fear). 429

jet lag :: The discomfort a person feels when internal sleep cycles are not synchronized with light and dark changes in the environment, such as when an individual travels across several time zones. 163

job analysis :: The process of writing a detailed description of a position in terms of its required knowledge, skills, abilities, and other traits, as well as evaluating the value of the position for the overall organization. 623

job crafting :: The processes of taking on or creating additional roles and tasks for a position over time. 623

job satisfaction :: The degree to which an employee is content with his or her work. 634

job simulations :: Role-playing activities that are very similar to situations encountered on the actual job. 627

kinesthesis :: Our sense of bodily motion and position. 146

kin selection :: The explanation that altruistic behavior is most likely to occur when it confers a genetic benefit to the individual. 576

KSAOs :: The knowledge, skills, abilities, and other traits required for a specific job. 623

laissez-faire leadership :: A leadership style describing someone who has been appointed to a position of leadership, but who does not engage in many (if any) leadership processes. 644

language :: A form of communication that involves the use of spoken, written, or gestural symbols that are combined in a rule-based form. 293

latent content :: In psychoanalytic terms, the underlying meaning of a dream, which is believed by some to be behind the images and symbols in dreams. 164

latent learning :: Learning that is not immediately expressed in terms of a response until the organism is reinforced for doing so. 222

leadership emergence :: The degree to which individuals are viewed as leaders by others. 643

learned helplessness :: An acquired suppression of avoidance or escape behavior in response to unpleasant, uncontrollable circumstances. 612

learning :: A process by which behavior or knowledge changes as a result of experience. 195

learning styles :: The hypothesis that individuals are fundamentally different in how they best acquire information. 324

lens :: The structure that focuses light onto the back of the eye. 126

lesioning :: A technique that inflicts controlled damage to brain tissue so as to study its function. 107

libido :: The motivation for sexual activity and pleasure. 408

limbic system :: A region in the forebrain including several networked structures involved in emotion and memory. 99

linguistic relativity (Whorfian hypothesis) :: The theory that the language we encounter and use determines how we understand the world; also known as the Whorfian hypothesis. 278

lithium :: One of the first mood stabilizers to be prescribed regularly in psychiatry. It is typically prescribed for people with bipolar disorder. 538

longitudinal design :: A research design that follows the development of the same set of individuals through time. 347

long-term memory (LTM) :: A memory store that holds information for extended periods of time, if not permanently. 238

long-term potentiation (LTP) :: An enduring increase in connectivity and transmission of neural signals between nerve cells that fire together. 244

maintenance rehearsal :: Prolonging exposure to information by repeating it. 250

major depression :: A disorder marked by prolonged and unjustified periods of sadness, feelings of hopelessness and worthlessness, social withdrawal, and cognitive and physical sluggishness. 499

maladaptive behavior :: Behavior that hinders a person's ability to function in work, school, relationships, or society. 477

manifest content :: In psychoanalytic terms, the imagery and storylines that make up a dream. 164

marijuana :: A drug derived from the *Cannabis* plant that produces a combination of hallucinogenic, stimulant, and relaxing (narcotic) effects. 184

mastery motives :: Motives that reflect a desire to understand or overcome a challenge (e. g., a genuine desire to master a task). 422

materialism :: The belief that humans, and other living beings, are composed exclusively of physical matter. 14

mean :: The arithmetic average of a set of numbers. 64

median :: A measure of central tendency based on the 50th percentile—the point on the horizontal axis at which 50% of all observations are lower, and 50% of all observations are higher. 64

medical model (of psychological disorders) :: Using one's understanding of medical conditions to think about psychological conditions. 476

meditation :: Any procedure that involves a shift in consciousness to a state in which an individual is highly focused, aware, and in control of mental processes. 175

menarche :: The onset of menstruation. 373

mental age :: The average or typical test score for a specific chronological age. 312

mental set :: A cognitive obstacle that occurs when an individual attempts to apply a routine solution to what is actually a new type of problem. 283

method of loci :: A mnemonic method that connects words to be remembered to locations along a familiar path. 256

midbrain :: A region of the brain residing just above the hindbrain that primarily functions as a relay station between sensory and motor areas. 98

mimicry :: Copying another person's behavior. 552

minimally conscious state (MCS) :: A disordered state of consciousness marked by the ability to make small intentional movements and respond to very basic instructions. 178

Minnesota Multiphasic Personality Inventory (MMPI-2) :: Multiple-question personality inventory used to measure both normal and abnormal personality functioning across several profiles. 445

misinformation effect :: An effect that occurs when information occurring after an event becomes part of the memory for that event. 263

mnemonics :: Techniques that are intended to improve memory for specific information. 256

mode :: A measure of central tendency represented by the category with the highest frequency (the category with the most observations). 65

monoamine oxide inhibitors (MAOIs) :: A type of antidepressant that deactivates monoamine oxidase, an enzyme that breaks down serotonin, dopamine, and norepinephrine at the synaptic clefts of nerve cells. 537

monocular cues :: Depth cues that we can perceive with only one eye. 132

monozygotic twins :: Genetically identical twins conceived from the same egg. 76

mood stabilizers :: Drugs that are used to prevent or reduce the manic side of bipolar disorder. 538

morpheme :: The smallest meaningful units of language. 293

motivation :: Physiological and psychological processes underlying the initiation of behaviors that direct organisms toward specific goals. 397

multiple intelligences :: A model claiming there are eight different forms of intelligence, each independent from the others. 324

myelin :: A fatty sheath that insulates axons from one another, resulting in increased speed and efficiency of neural communication. 86

narcissistic personality disorder (NPD) :: A condition marked by a tendency to have an inflated sense of self-importance and an intense need for attention and admiration, as well as intense self-doubt and fear of abandonment. 487

narcolepsy :: A disorder in which a person experiences extreme daytime sleepiness and even sleep attacks. 169

naturalistic observation :: An unobtrusive observation and recording of behavior as it occurs in the subject's natural environment. 49

natural selection :: A primary mechanism for evolutionary change; the process by which favorable traits become increasingly common in a population of interbreeding individuals, while traits that are unfavorable become less common. 78

nature and nurture relationships :: The inquiry into how heredity (nature) and environment (nurture) influence behavior and mental processes. 19

need to belong :: The motivation to maintain relationships that involve pleasant feelings such as warmth, affection, appreciation, and mutual concern for each person's well-being; sometimes called affiliation motivation. 419

negative affect (NA) :: The tendency to experience negative emotions including frustration, anger, and distress. 633

negative affectivity :: The tendency to respond to problems with a pattern of anxiety, hostility, anger, guilt, or nervousness. 610

negatively skewed distribution :: A type of distribution in which the curve has an extended tail to the left of the cluster. 64

negative punishment :: A decrease in a behavior because it removes or diminishes a particular stimulus. 214

negative reinforcement :: I The strengthening of a behavior because it removes or diminishes a stimulus. 213

negative symptoms (of schizophrenia) :: Symptoms of schizophrenia involving the absence of adaptive behavior. 506

neurodevelopmental hypothesis :: A hypothesis that states irregular biological and environmental factors interact during child development to produce symptoms of schizophrenia. 509

neuron :: One of the major types of cells found in the nervous system, which is responsible for sending and receiving messages throughout the body. 85

neuroplasticity :: The capacity for the brain to change over the course of the life span as the result of individual experiences. 104

neurotransmitters :: Chemicals that function as messengers within the body, thereby allowing neurons to communicate with one another. 86

nightmares :: Particularly vivid and disturbing dreams that occur during REM sleep. 167

night terrors :: Intense bouts of panic and arousal that awaken an individual from sleep, typically in a heightened emotional state. 167

nociception :: Activity of nerve pathways that respond to uncomfortable stimulation. 147

nomothetic approach (to personality) :: An approach to the study of personality that examines personality in large groups of people, with the aim of making generalizations about personality structure. 440

nondeclarative memory :: A form of memory including actions or behaviors that you can remember and perform without awareness. 243

norepinephrine :: A neurotransmitter involved in regulating stress responses, including increasing arousal, attention, and heart rate. 89

normal distribution :: Sometimes called the bell curve; a symmetrical distribution with values clustered around a central, mean value. 64

norms :: Statistics that allow individuals to be evaluated relative to a typical or standard score. 310

obedience :: Complying with instructions or orders from an individual who is in a position of authority. 555

obesity :: A disorder of positive energy balance, in which energy intake exceeds energy expenditure. 404

objective measurements :: The measure of an entity or behavior that, within an allowed margin of error, is consistent across instruments and observers. 38

object permanence :: The ability to understand that objects exist even when they cannot be seen or touched. 360

object relations therapy :: A variation of psychodynamic therapy that focuses on how early childhood experiences and emotional attachments influence later psychological functioning. 527

observational learning :: I A type of learning in which changes in behavior and knowledge result from watching others. 225

obsessive–compulsive disorder (OCD) :: A type of anxiety disorder characterized by unwanted, inappropriate, and persistent thoughts (obsessions); repetitive, stereotyped behaviors (compulsions); or a combination of the two. 497

occipital lobes :: The areas of the cerebral cortex where visual information is processed. 101

olfactory epithelium :: A thin layer of cells that are lined by sensory receptors called cilia (involved in perception of smell). 151

olfactory system :: The sense of smell; the detection of airborne particles with specialized receptors located in the nose. 151

operant conditioning :: A type of learning in which behavior is determined by consequences. 209

operational definitions :: Statements that describe the procedures (or operations) and/or specific measures that are used to record observations in a research study. 39

opiates :: Drugs such as heroin and morphine that reduce pain and induce extremely intense feelings of euphoria; also called narcotics. 184

opponent-process theory (of color vision) :: The theory that we perceive color in terms of opposite ends of the spectrum—red to green, yellow to blue, and white to black. 135

optic nerve :: A collection of neurons that gather sensory information, exit at the back of the eye, and connect with the brain. 127

optimism :: The tendency to have a favorable, constructive view on situations and to expect positive outcomes. 608

outgroup :: Social groups to which we do not belong. 569

oxytocin :: A stress-sensitive hormone associated with maternal bonding and social relationships. 600

panic disorder :: An anxiety disorder marked by repeated episodes of sudden, very intense fear. 495

paranoid schizophrenia :: A subtype of schizophrenia involving delusional beliefs that one is being followed, watched, or persecuted, and may also include delusions of grandeur. 505

parasympathetic nervous system :: A division of the autonomic nervous system that is responsible for maintaining homeostasis (balance) by returning the body to a baseline, nonemergency state. 96

parietal lobes :: A region of the cortex located behind the frontal lobes that is responsible for the sense of touch and bodily awareness. 101

partial (intermittent) reinforcement :: A schedule in which only a certain number of responses are rewarded, or a certain amount of time must pass before reinforcement is available. 216

partial reinforcement effect :: The observation that organisms conditioned under partial reinforcement resist extinction longer than those conditioned under continuous reinforcement. 217

peer review :: A process in which papers submitted for publication in scholarly journals are read and critiqued by experts in the specific field of study. 44

percentile rank :: The percentage of scores below a certain point. 310

perception :: Attending to, organizing, and interpreting stimuli that we sense. 115

perceptual constancy :: The ability to perceive objects as having constant shape, size, and color despite changes in perspective. 129

performance appraisal :: The evaluation of current employees. 628

performance motives :: Motives that are geared toward gaining rewards or public recognition. 422

peripheral nervous system (PNS) :: A major division of the nervous system that transmits signals between the brain and the rest of the body; it is divided into two subcomponents, the somatic system and the autonomic system. 96

peripheral route (to persuasion) :: A path to persuasion in which quick judgments are made based on limited evidence and use emotions and vague impressions more than logic. 561

persistent vegetative state (PVS) :: A state of minimal to no consciousness, in which the patient's eyes may be open, and the individual develops sleep–wake cycles without clear signs of consciousness. 178

personality :: A characteristic pattern of thinking, interacting, and reacting that is unique to each individual, and that remains consistent over time and situations. 439

personality disorder :: A category of mental disorders that include particularly unusual patterns of behavior for one's culture that are maladaptive, distressing to oneself or others, and resistant to change. 486

personality traits :: Labels applied to specific attributes of personality such as "shy," "cheerful," "outgoing," and "adventurous." 440

person-centered perspective :: Humanistic perspective emphasizing that people are basically good and that, given the right environment, they will develop fully and normally. 470

person/client-centered therapy :: A humanistic therapy method that focuses on individuals' ability to solve their own problems and reach their full potential with the encouragement of the therapist. 527

person perception :: The processes by which individuals form judgments and categorize other people. 565

pessimistic explanatory style :: The tendency to interpret and explain negative events as internally based and as a constant, stable quality. 611

phenotype :: The observable characteristics of an organism, including physical structures and behaviors. 75

phobia :: A type of anxiety marked by severe, irrational fear of a particular object or situation. 495

phoneme :: The most basic unit of a speech sound. 293

phonological loop :: A storage component of working memory that relies on rehearsal and stores information as sounds (i.e., as an auditory code). 240

pitch :: The perceptual experience of sound wave frequencies. 138

pituitary gland :: The master gland of the endocrine system that produces hormones and sends commands about hormone production to the other glands of the endocrine system. 92

placebo effect :: A measurable and experienced improvement in health or behavior that cannot be attributable to a medication. 42

place theory of hearing :: A theory stating that how we perceive pitch is based on the location (place) along the basilar membrane that sound stimulates. 141

polysomnography :: A set of objective measurements used to examine physiological variables during sleep. 160

population :: In a research context, the group that researchers want to generalize about. 40

positive affect (PA) :: The tendency to experience positive emotions such as happiness, satisfaction, and enthusiasm. 633

positively skewed distribution :: A type of distribution in which the long tail is on the right of the cluster. 64

positive psychology :: The use of scientific methods to study human strengths and potential. 608

positive punishment :: A process in which a behavior decreases because it adds to or increases a particular stimulus. 213

positive reinforcement :: The strengthening of behavior after potential reinforcers such as praise, money, or nourishment follow that behavior. 213

positive sleep state misperception :: A condition in which an individual substantially overestimates the amount of sleep the person is getting. 169

positive symptoms (of schizophrenia) :: Symptoms of schizophrenia characterized by behaviors that should not occur, such as confused and paranoid thinking, and inappropriate emotional reactions. 505

postconventional morality :: A type of moral reasoning that considers rules and laws as relative while right and wrong are determined by more abstract principles of justice and rights. 376

post-traumatic growth :: The capacity to grow and experience long-term positive effects in response to negative events. 608

pragmatics :: The study of nonlinguistic elements of language use. 295

preconventional morality :: A very basic, egocentric form of moral reasoning characterized by self-interest in seeking reward or avoiding punishment. 376

prejudice :: An attitude that relies on the beliefs found in stereotypes, including emotions and value judgments. 569

preoperational stage :: The second stage of cognitive development, spanning ages two through seven years, that is characterized by understanding of symbols, pretend play, and mastery of the concept of conservation. 361

preparedness :: The biological predisposition to rapidly learn a response to a particular class of stimuli. 202

preserve and protect hypothesis :: The hypothesis that sleep's function is to preserve energy levels during periods of low activity and avoid potentially harmful situations. 162

preterm infants :: Infants born at 36 weeks' gestation or earlier. 352

primary auditory cortex :: A major perceptual center of the brain involved in perceiving what we hear. 141

primary reinforcers :: Stimuli that satisfy basic motivational needs. 212

priming :: The activation of individual concepts in long-term memory. 275

proactive interference :: A type of interference that occurs when the first information learned (e.g., in a list of words) occupies memory, leaving fewer resources left to remember the newer information. 239

problem solving :: Accomplishing a goal when the solution or the path to the solution is not clear. 282

problem-solving theory (of dreaming) :: The theory that thoughts and concerns are continuous from waking to sleeping, and that dreams may function to facilitate finding solutions to problems encountered while awake. 165

procedural memories :: A form of nondeclarative memory that involves patterns of muscle movements (motor memory). 243

projective tests :: Personality tests in which ambiguous images are presented to an individual to elicit responses that reflect unconscious desires or conflicts. 466

prototype :: A mental representation of an average category member. 274

pseudoscience :: Ideas that are presented as science but actually do not utilize basic principles of scientific thinking or procedure. 4

psychiatrist :: A physician who specializes in mental health, and who diagnoses and treats mental disorders primarily through prescribing medications that influence brain chemistry. 520

psychiatry :: A branch of medicine concerned with the treatment of mental and behavioral disorders. 28

psychoactive drugs :: Drugs that affect thinking, behavior, perception, and emotion. 181

psychoanalysis :: An approach developed by Sigmund Freud and his associates that attempts to explain how behavior and personality are influenced by unconscious processes. 18, 526

psychodynamic theory (of personality) :: Early theory of personality that focused on how personality arises through complex interactions involving motivational conscious and unconscious processes that occur from early development on through adulthood. 462

psychodynamic therapies :: Forms of insight therapy that emphasize the need to discover and resolve unconscious conflicts. 526

psychology :: The scientific study of behavior, thought, and experience. 3

psychometrics :: The measurement of psychological traits and abilities—including personality, attitudes, and intelligence. 309

psychoneuroimmunology :: The study of the relationship between immune system and nervous system functioning. 601

psychopharmacotherapy :: The process of treating psychological problems with drugs. 536

psychophysics :: The study of how physical energy such as light and sound and their intensity relate to psychological experience. 16, 116

psychotherapy :: Processes for resolving personal, emotional, behavioral, and social problems so as to improve well-being. 516

psychotropic drugs :: Medications designed to alter psychological functioning. 537

puberty :: The physical transition from childhood to adolescence, culminating in reproductive maturity. 373

punisher :: A reinforcing stimulus whose delivery is contingent upon a response, with the result being a decrease in behavior. 211

punishment :: A process that decreases the future probability of a response. 211

pupil :: The part of the eye that regulates the amount of light allowed to enter by changing its size; it dilates to allow more light to enter and constricts to allow less light in. 126

quasi-experimental research :: A research technique in which the two or more groups that are compared are selected based on predetermined characteristics, not random assignment. 53

random assignment :: A technique for dividing samples into two or more groups. 53

random sample :: A method of obtaining participants for research in which every individual in a population has an equal chance of being included. 40

Raven's Progressive Matrices :: An intelligence test emphasizing problems that are intended not to be bound to a particular language or culture. 313

reciprocal altruism :: Helping behavior that is extended to nongenetic relatives, with the possibility that the favor may be later returned. 576

reciprocal determinism :: A social-cognitive perspective on personality that focuses on how behavior, internal (personal) factors, and external factors interact to determine one another, and that posits our personalities are based on interactions among these three aspects. 447

recovered memory :: A memory of a traumatic event that is suddenly recovered after the memory of that event has been unconsciously for a long period of time. 265

recovered memory controversy :: A heated debate among psychologists about the validity of recovered memories. 265

reflex :: An involuntary muscle reaction to a specific type of stimulation. 354

refractory period (of a neuron) :: A brief period of time (approximately 2 milliseconds) during which a neuron cannot fire following an action potential. 87

refractory period (of the sexual response cycle) :: Time period during which erection and orgasm are not physically possible. 411

rehearsal :: Repeating information until you do not need to remember it anymore. 240

reinforcement :: A process in which an event or reward that follows a response increases the likelihood of that response occurring again. 210

reinforcer :: A stimulus that is contingent upon a response, and increases the probability of that response occurring again. 210

reliability :: A characteristic of a measure that provides consistent and stable answers across multiple observations and points in time. 39

REM sleep :: A stage of sleep characterized by quickening brain waves, deep relaxation, inhibited body movement, and rapid eye movements (REM). 161

replication :: A process of repeating a study and finding a similar outcome each time. 44

representativeness heuristic :: A strategy of making judgments of likelihood based on how well an example represents a specific category. 285

residential treatment centers :: Facilities that provide psychotherapy and life skills training so that the residents can become integrated into society as best as possible. 520

residual schizophrenia :: A subtype of schizophrenia in which the patient shows some symptoms of schizophrenia but either is in transition to a full-blown episode or is in remission. 505

resilience :: The ability to effectively recover from illness or adversity. 608

resistance :: A tendency of psychoanalysis patients to avoid directly answering crucial questions posed by the therapist. 527

resting potential :: The stable, inactive state of a neuron that is not transmitting or receiving messages. 86

restless legs syndrome :: A persistent feeling of discomfort in the legs, accompanied by the urge to continuously shift the legs into different positions. 168

restore and repair hypothesis (of sleep) :: The hypothesis that sleep's function is to restore energy levels and repair any damage the body incurred during wakefulness. 161

retina :: The inner surface of the eye consisting of specialized receptors that absorb light and send signals about properties of light to the brain. 126

retinal disparity :: The difference in relative position of an object as seen by both eyes, which provides information to the brain about depth; also called binocular disparity. 132

retrieval :: Bringing information from long-term memory back into short-term memory. 237

retroactive interference :: Interference that occurs when the most recently learned information overshadows some other information that has not made it into long-term memory. 239

retrograde amnesia :: A condition in which memory for the past is lost. 246

reuptake :: A process whereby neurotransmitter molecules that have been released into the synapse are reabsorbed into the axon terminals of the presynaptic neuron. 88

rods :: Photoreceptors that occupy peripheral regions of the retina, and are highly sensitive under low light levels. 127

Rorschach inkblot test :: A projective test in which subjects are asked to describe what they see in an inkblot, and psychologists attempt to interpret what the subject projects onto the stimulus by using a standardized scoring and interpretation method. 466

sample :: A select group of population members. 40

satiation :: A point in a meal when a person is no longer motivated to eat. 398

savants :: Individuals with low mental capacity in most domains but extraordinary abilities in other specific areas such as music, mathematics, or art. 323

scaffolding :: An approach to teaching in which the teacher matches guidance to the learner or student's needs. 364

scapegoating :: The tendency to misplace and exaggerate blame based on stereotypes. 569

schedules of reinforcement :: Rules that determine when reinforcement is available. 216

schema :: A cluster of knowledge that constitutes one's knowledge about events, objects, and ideas. 260, 565

schizophrenia :: A collection of mental disorders characterized by chronic and significant breaks from reality, a lack of integration of thoughts and emotions, and serious problems with attention and memory. 505

school psychology :: A branch of psychology that involves work with students with special needs, such as emotional, social, or academic problems. 29

scientific literacy :: The ability to understand, analyze, and apply scientific information. 6

scientific method :: A way of learning about the world through collecting observations, proposing explanations for the observations, developing theories to explain them, and using the theories to make predictions about future events. 3

sclera :: The white, outer surface of the eye. 126

secondary reinforcers :: Reinforcing stimuli that acquire their value through learning. 212

sedative drug :: A drug that depresses the activity of the central nervous system; also called "downers." 185

selective attention :: The style of attention that involves focusing on one particular event or task while ignoring other stimuli. 121

selective serotonin reuptake inhibitors (SSRIs) :: A class of antidepressant drugs that block the reuptake of the neurotransmitter serotonin. 538

self-actualization :: Reaching one's fullest potential by meeting needs ranging from basic (satisfying hunger) to complex (engaging in loving relationships). 470

self-awareness :: The ability to recognize one's individuality. 366

self-concept :: A collection of feelings and beliefs a person has about who he or she is. 470

self-fulfilling prophecy :: The situation in which a first impression affects the observer's behavior, and as a result, the first impression comes true. 566

self-reporting :: A research method in which responses are provided directly by the people who are being studied, typically through face-to-face interviews, phone surveys, paper-and-pencil tests, and web-based questionnaires. 38

self-serving bias :: Using internal attributions to take credit for success, while using external attributions to avoid responsibility for failures or mistakes. 568

semantic memory :: A type of declarative memory that includes facts about the world. 244

semantic network :: An interconnected set of nodes (concepts) and the links that join them to form a category. 274

semantics :: The study of how people come to understand meaning from words. 294

sensation :: The process of detecting external events by sense organs and turning those events into neural signals. 115

sensitive period :: A window of time in which exposure to a specific type of environmental stimulation is needed for normal development of a specific ability. 348

sensorimotor stage :: The first stage of cognitive development, spanning birth to age two years, when infants' thinking and understanding about the world is based on sensory experiences and physical actions they perform on objects. 360

sensorineural hearing loss :: Hearing loss that results from damage to the cochlear hair cells (sensory) and the neurons comprising the auditory nerve (neural). 142

sensory adaptation :: The reduction of activity in sensory receptors with repeated exposure to a stimulus. 115

sensory memory :: A memory store that accurately holds perceptual information for a very brief amount of time. 237

serial position effect :: The tendency to recall the first few items form a list and the last few items, but only an item or two from the middle of the list. 238

serotonin :: A monoamine neurotransmitter involved in regulating sleep, appetite, and mood. 89

set point :: A hypothesized mechanism that serves to maintain body weight around a physiologically programmed level. 591

sexual harassment :: Unwelcome sexual advances and other conduct of a sexual nature that implicitly or explicitly affects an individual's employment. 639

sexual orientation :: Consistent preference for sexual relations with members of the opposite sex (heterosexuality), same sex (homosexuality), or either sex (bisexuality). 412

sexual response cycle :: The phases of physiological change during sexual activity, which consists of four primary stages: excitement, plateau, orgasm, and resolution. 410

shaping :: A procedure in which a specific operant response is created by reinforcing successive approximations of that response. 215

short-term memory (STM) :: A memory store with limited capacity and duration (less than a minute). 238

signal detection theory :: A theory stating that whether a stimulus is perceived depends on both sensory experience and judgments made by the subject. 117

single-blind study :: An experimental procedure in which the participants do not know the true purpose of the study, or else they do not know which type of treatment they are receiving (for example, a placebo or a drug). 43

sleep apnea :: A disorder characterized by the temporary inability to breathe during sleep. 168

sleep deprivation :: A state in which a person cannot or does not sleep. 162

sleep displacement :: A situation in which an individual is prevented from sleeping at the normal time but allowed to sleep at an unusual time; thus sleep is *displaced* from its optimal time. 163

sleep state misperception (SSM) :: A condition in which a person substantially underestimates the amount of sleep she gets. 169

social anxiety disorder :: An irrational fear of being observed, evaluated, or embarrassed in public. 497

social-cognitive theory :: The concept that hypnosis arises from beliefs and expectations about the effects of hypnosis. 174

social contagion :: The often subtle, unintentional spreading of a behavior as a result of social interactions. 595

social desirability (socially desirable responding) :: An occurrence in which participants in a research study respond in ways that increase the chances that they will be viewed favorably. 41

social-exchange theory :: An approach that treats helping much like a financial arrangement between individuals and society; before an individual acts, she will consider the costs and benefits of helping. 576

social facilitation :: The situation in which an individual's performance is better in the presence of others than when alone. 554

social loafing :: The situation in which an individual working as part of a group or team reduces his or her effort. 554

social norms :: Unwritten guidelines for how to behave in social contexts. 551

social psychology :: A broad discipline that examines individual behavior in social contexts, including the people, locations, and social expectations that have the potential to change our behavior. 551

social responsibility norm :: The idea that the value of helping goes beyond the benefits an individual might receive, and that individuals who cannot help themselves require special help. 576

social roles :: Specific sets of behaviors that are assigned to an individual within a given social context. 551

somatic nervous system :: A component of the peripheral nervous system that includes the nerves that receive sensory input from the body and that control skeletal muscles; it is responsible for voluntary and reflexive movement. 96

somnambulism :: A disorder that involves wandering and other activities while asleep; also known as sleepwalking. 168

sound localization :: The process of identifying where sound comes from. 140

specific phobias :: Disorders involving an intense fear of an object, activity, or organism. 495

spermarche :: The first ejaculation of sperm, typically occurring during early adolescent development. 373

spontaneous recovery :: The reoccurrence of a previously extinguished conditioned response, typically after some time has passed since extinction. 198

standard deviation :: A measure of variability around the mean. 66

standardized test :: Any test that includes a set of questions or problems that are administered and scored in a uniform (in other words, standardized) way across large numbers of individuals. 310

Stanford-Binet test :: A test intended to measure innate (genetic) intelligence. 312

state :: A temporary physical or psychological engagement that influences behavior. 444

statistical significance :: A situation in which means of groups under comparison are farther apart than one would expect them to be by random chance alone. 68

stereotype :: A set of beliefs about a group of people. 568

stereotype threat :: The situation in which people become aware of stereotypes about their social group, resulting in fear of being reduced to that stereotype. 340

stimulants :: A category of drugs that speed up the nervous system, and typically enhance wakefulness and alertness. 182

storage :: The time and manner in which information is retained between encoding and retrieval. 250

stores :: Elements of memory systems that retain information in memory without using it for any specific purpose. 237

stress :: Psychological and physiological reactions that occur when perceived demands exceed existing resources to meet those demands. 597

structuralism :: An attempt to analyze conscious experience by breaking it down into basic elements, and to understand how these elements work together. 20

structured interview :: An interview procedure in which an employer presents the same set of questions to each job candidate with planned (rather than unstructured) follow-up questions. 624

substance P :: A neurotransmitter involved in pain perception. 90

superego :: A component of personality that directs moral behavior and decisions; it is thought to develop during a child's upbringing, and serves as an inner voice we hear when we shame ourselves for acting inappropriately or lavish praise on ourselves for doing something good. 463

sympathetic nervous system :: A division of the autonomic nervous system that is responsible for the fight-or-flight response of an increased heart rate, dilated pupils, and decreased salivary flow—responses that prepare the body for action. 96

synapse :: A microscopically small space that separates individual nerve cells. 86

synaptic cleft :: A minute space between the terminal button and the dendrite where neurotransmitters cross between presynpatic and postsynaptic cells. 87

synaptic pruning :: A process in which weak and unused nerve cell connections are lost. 359

syntax :: The rules for combining words and morphemes into meaningful phrases and sentences. 294

systematic desensitization :: A technique in which gradual exposure to a feared stimulus or situation is blended with relaxation training. 530

systems approach :: An orientation toward family therapy that involves identifying and understanding what each individual family member contributes to the entire family dynamic. 533

tardive dyskinesia :: A neurological condition marked by involuntary movements and facial tics. 539

temperament :: A general emotional reactivity typically found in infants that serves as a basis for the development of the adult personality. 367

temporal lobes :: A region of the cerebral cortex that is responsible for the processing of sound, including language and music. The temporal lobes are also involved in recognizing faces and objects. 101

teratogen :: A substance, such as a drug, that is capable of producing physical defects in a fetus. 353

terror management theory :: Psychological perspective asserting that the human fear of mortality motivates behavior, particularly those behaviors that preserve self-esteem and sense of belonging. 421

testing effect :: The finding that completing practice tests can improve exam performance, even without additional studying. 257

testosterone :: A hormone that is involved in the development of sex characteristics and the motivation of sexual behavior. 414

thalamus :: A brain structure involved in relaying sensory information. What we see and hear is routed through the thalamus and then proceeds to more specialized regions of the brain for further processing. 100

Thematic Apperception Test :: A projective test that asks respondents to tell a story about a series of 31 pictures involving ambiguous interpersonal situations. 466

theory :: An explanation for a broad range of observations that also generates new hypotheses and integrates numerous findings into a coherent whole. 4

theory of mind :: The ability to recognize the thoughts, beliefs, and expectations of others. 367

thin slices :: A research technique in which a researcher presents a very short video tape or still photo of an individual, which participants then use to make judgments of personal qualities. 566

tolerance :: A process in which repeated drug use results in a need for a higher dose to get the intended effect. 188

top-down processing :: Form of perceptual processing in which prior knowledge and expectations guide what is perceived. 120

transactional leadership :: A leadership style that encourages employee or team member behaviors through rewards and punishments. 644

transcranial magnetic stimulation (TMS) :: A procedure in which researchers send an electromagnetic pulse to a targeted region of the brain, which can either stimulate or temporarily disable it. 107, 544

transduction :: The process in which physical or chemical stimulation is converted into a nerve impulse that is relayed to the brain. 115

transference :: A psychoanalytic process in which patients direct the emotional experiences that they are reliving toward the therapist. 527

transformational leadership :: A leadership style that combines charisma, intellectualization, and a focus on individuals within an organization. 644

trichromatic theory (Young-Helmholtz theory) :: A theory that maintains color vision is determined by three different cone types that are sensitive to short, medium, and long wavelengths of light. 134

tricyclic antidepressants :: One of the earliest types of antidepressants on the market, which were prescribed to block the reuptake of serotonin and norepinephrine. 538

turnover :: The rate at which existing employees leave an organization. 635

two-factor theory of emotion :: A prediction that patterns of physical arousal and the cognitive labels we attach to them form the basis of our emotional experiences. 434

Type A personality :: A term describing people who tend to be impatient and worry about time, and who are easily angered, competitive, and highly motivated. 605

Type B personality :: A term describing people who are more laid back and characterized by a patient, easygoing, and relaxed disposition. 605

unconditioned response (UR) :: A reflexive, unlearned reaction to an unconditioned stimulus. 196

unconditioned stimulus (US) :: A stimulus that elicits a reflexive response without learning. 196

undifferentiated schizophrenia :: A category of schizophrenia that includes individuals who show a combination of symptoms from other types of schizophrenia. 505

unit bias :: The tendency to assume that the unit of sale or portioning is an appropriate amount to consume. 402

unstructured interview :: An interviewing procedure in which an employer discuss a variety of job and personality-related topics with a candidate, with relatively few prepared questions to guide the conversation. 624

validation studies :: Studies in which researchers administer tests to a large sample of incumbents along with an evaluation of their performance to find correlations between job performance and personality traits or cognitive abilities. 625

validity :: The degree to which an instrument or procedure actually measures what it claims to measure. 39

variability :: The degree to which scores are dispersed in a distribution. 66

variable :: The object, concept, or event being measured. 38

variable-interval schedule :: A schedule of reinforcement in which the first response is reinforced following a variable amount of time. 216

variable-ratio schedule :: A schedule of reinforcement in which the number of responses required to receive reinforcement varies according to an average. 216

virtual reality exposure (VRE) :: A therapeutic technique that uses real-time computer graphical displays that create a sense that the client is immersed in an actual environment. 531

virtual teams :: Production or project teams that are physically separated but operate largely (or completely) by electronic communication. 646

visuospatial sketchpad :: A component of working memory that maintains visual images and spatial layouts in a visuospatial code. 240

Wechsler Adult Intelligence Scale (WAIS) :: The most commonly used intelligence tested used on adolescents and adults. 312

well-defined problem :: A problem that has both a clear initial state and a clear goal state. 282

Wernicke's area :: The area of the brain most closely associated with finding the meaning of words. 296

Whorfian hypothesis :: See *linguistic relativity*. 278

working memory :: A model of short-term remembering that includes a combination of memory components that can temporarily store small amounts of information for a short period of time. It is composed of the phonological loop, the visuospatial sketchpad, and the episodic buffer. 240

zeitgeist :: A general set of beliefs of a particular culture at a specific time in history. 14

zone of proximal development :: A concept proposed by Lev Vygotsky explaining that development is ideal when children attempt skills and activities that are just beyond what they can do alone, but they have adults who are attentive to their progress and can provide guidance. 364

zygote :: A cell formed by the fusion of a sperm and an ovum (egg cell). 349

References

ABC News. (2008). Retrieved October 3, 2009, from http://www.abc.net.au/news/stories/2008/01/26/2147188.htm

AbdelMalik, P., Husted, J., Chow, E. W., & Bassett, A. S. (2003). Childhood head injury and expression of schizophrenia and multiply affected families. *Archives of General Psychiatry, 60,* 231–236.

Abematsu, M., Smith I., & Nakashima, K. (2006). Mechanisms of neural stem cell fate determination: Extracellular cues and intracellular programs. *Current Stem Cell Research and Therapy, 1*(2), 267–277.

Abraham, W. (2006). Memory maintenance: The changing nature of neural mechanisms. *Current Directions in Psychological Science, 15,* 5–8.

Abramowitz, E., Barak, Y., Ben-Avi, I., & Knobler, H. (2008). Hypnotherapy in the treatment of chronic combat-related PTSD patients suffering from insomnia: A randomized, zolpidem-controlled clinical trial. *International Journal of Clinical and Experimental Hypnosis, 56*(3), 270–280.

Ackerman, P. L., Beier, M. E., & Boyle, M. O. (2005). Working memory and intelligence: The same or different constructs? *Psychological Bulletin, 131,* 30–60.

Ackerman, P. L., Kanfer, R., & Calderwood, C. (2010). Use it or lose it? Wii brain exercise practice and reading for domain knowledge. *Psychology of Aging, 25,* 753–766.

Adair, G. (1984). The Hawthorne effect: A reconsideration of the methodological artifact. *Journal of Applied Psychology, 69,* 334–345.

Adam, T. C., & Epel, E. S. (2007). Stress, eating, and the reward system. *Physiology and Behavior, 91*(4), 449–458.

Adams, H. E., Wright, L. W., & Lohr, B. A. (1996). Is homophobia associated with homosexual arousal? *Journal of Abnormal Psychology, 105,* 440–445.

Addis, D. R., Wong, A. T., & Schacter, D. L. (2008). Age-related changes in the episodic simulation of future events. *Psychological Science, 19,* 33–41.

Addis, M. E., & Mahalik, J. R. (2003). Men, masculinity, and the contexts of help seeking. *American Psychologist, 58,* 5–14.

Aggarwal, R., & Saeed, S. R. (2005). The genetics of hearing loss. *Hospital Medicine, 66,* 32–36.

Ahlfinger, N. R., & Esser, J. K. (2001). Testing the groupthink model: Effects of promotional leadership and conformity predisposition. *Social Behavior and Personality, 29,* 31–41.

Ainsworth, M. D. S. (1978). The development of infant–mother attachment. In B. M. Caldwell & H. N. Ricciuti (Eds.), *Review of child development research* (Vol. 3, pp. 1–94). Chicago: University of Chicago Press.

Akimoto, S. A., & Sanbonmatsu, D. M. (1999). Differences in self-effacing behavior between European and Japanese Americans: Effect on competence evaluations. *Journal of Cross-Cultural Psychology, 30*(2), 159–177.

Akmajian, A., Demers, R. A., Farmer, A. K., & Harnish, R. M. (2001). *Linguistics: An introduction to language and communication.* Cambridge, MA: MIT Press.

Aleman, A., Kahn, R. S., & Selten, J. P. (2003). Sex differences in the risk of schizophrenia. *Archives of General Psychiatry, 60,* 565–571.

Alger, S. E., Lau, H., & Fishbein, W. (2010). Delayed onset of a daytime nap facilitates retention of declarative memory. *PLoS One, 5*(8), 1–9.

Alladin, A., & Alibhai, A. (2007). Cognitive hypnotherapy for depression: An empirical investigation. *International Journal of Clinical and Experimental Hypnosis, 55*(2), 147–166.

Allen, J. S., Bruss, J., Brown, C. K., & Damasio, H. (2005). Normal neuroanatomical variation due to age: The major lobes and a parcellation of the temporal region. *Neurobiology of Aging, 26*(9), 1245–1260.

Allen, L. S., & Gorski, R. A. (1992). Sexual orientation and the size of the anterior commissure in the human brain. *Proceedings of the National Academy of Sciences, 89,* 7199–7202.

Allport, G., & Odbert, H. W. (1936). Trait names: A psycholexical study. *Psychological Monographs, 47,* 211.

Amato, P. R. (2001). Children of divorce in the 1990s: An update of the Amato and Keith (1991) meta-analysis. *Journal of Family Psychology, 15,* 355–370.

Ambady, N., & Rosenthal, R. (1993). Half a minute: Predicting teacher evaluations from thin slices of nonverbal behavior and physical attractiveness. *Journal of Personality and Social Psychology, 64,* 431–441.

American Academy of Sleep Medicine. (2005). *ICSD-2: International classification of sleep disorders* (2nd ed.): *Diagnostic and coding manual.*

American College Health Association. (2007). The American College Health Association National College Health Assessment (ACHA–NCHA) spring 2006 reference group data report (abridged). *Journal of American College Health, 53,* 195–206.

American Psychiatric Association. (2000). *Diagnostic and statistical manual of mental disorders* (4th ed., text revision). Washington, DC: Author.

American Psychological Association. (2004, September). Getting a good night's sleep with the help of psychology. Retrieved June 10, 2011, from http://www.apa.org/research/action/sleep.aspx

American Psychological Association (APA). (2009). Task force on evidence-based practice. Retrieved from http://www.apa.org/practice/ebp.html

American Psychological Association. (2011). Retrieved from http://www.apa.org/topics/suicide/signs.aspx

Ames, D. (2008). In search of the right touch: Interpersonal assertiveness in organizational life. *Current Directions in Psychological Science, 17*(6), 381–385.

An, K., Kobayashi, S., Tanaka, K., Kaneda, H., Sugibayashi, M., & Okazaki, J. (1998). Dissociative identity disorder and childhood trauma in Japan. *Psychiatry and Clinical Neurosciences, 52,* 111–114.

Ancoli-Israel, S., & Roth, T. (1999). Characteristics of insomnia in the United States: Results of the 1991 National Sleep Foundation Survey. I. *Sleep, 22,* S347–S353.

Anderson, A. K., & Phelps, E. A. (2000). Expression without recognition: Contributions of the human amygdala to emotional expression. *Psychological Science, 11,* 106–111.

Anderson, C., John, O., Keltner, D., & Kring, A. (2001). Who attains social status? Effects of personality and physical attractiveness in social groups. *Journal of Personality and Social Psychology, 81*(1), 116–132.

Anderson, C. A., Berkowitz, L., Donnerstein, E., Huesmann, L. R., Johnson, J. D., Linz, D., Malamuth, N. M., & Wartella, E. (2003). The influence of media violence on youth. *Psychological Science in the Public Interest, 4,* 81–110.

Anderson, C. A., & Bushman, B. J. (2002). Human aggression. *Annual Review of Psychology, 53,* 27–51.

Anderson, C. A., Shibuya, A., Ihori, N., Swing, E. L., Bushman, B. J., Sakamoto, A., Rothstein, H. R., & Saleem, M. (2010). Violent video game effects on aggression, empathy, and prosocial behavior in Eastern and Western countries: A meta-analytic review. *Psychological Bulletin, 136*(2), 151–173.

Anderson, D., & Saunders, D. (2003). Leaving an abusive partner: An empirical review of predictors, the process of leaving, and psychological well-being. *Trauma, Violence, & Abuse, 4*(2), 163–191.

Anderson, L., Lewis, G., Araya, R., Elgie, R., Harrison, G., Proudfoot, J., Schmidt, U., Sharp, D., Weightman, A., & Williams, C. (2005). Self-help books for depression: How can practitioners and patients make the right choice? *British Journal of General Practice, 55,* 387–392.

Anderson, M. C., Ochsner, K. N., Kuhl, B., et al. (2004). Neural systems underlying the suppression of unwanted memories. *Science, 303,* 232–235.

Andreasen, N. C., Arndt, S., Alliger, R., Miller, D., & Flaum, M. (1995). Symptoms of schizophrenia: Methods, meaning, and mechanisms. *Archives of General Psychiatry, 52,* 341–351.

Ano, G. G., & Vasconcelles, E. B. (2005). Religious coping and psychological adjustment to stress:

A meta-analysis. *Journal of Clinical Psychology, 61,* 461–480.

Antoni, M., & Lutgendorf, S. (2007). Psychosocial factors and disease progression in cancer. *Current Directions in Psychological Science, 16,* 42–46.

Antoni, M., Lutgendorf, S., Cole, S., Dhabhar, F., Sephton, S., McDonald, P., Stefanek, M., & Sood, A. (2006). The influence of biobehavioral factors on tumor biology, pathways and mechanisms. *Nature Reviews Cancer, 6,* 240–248.

Antoni, M., Schneiderman, N., & Penedo, F. (2007). Behavioral interventions and psychoneuroimmunology. In R. Ader, R. Glaser, N. Cohen, & M. Irwin (Eds.), *Psychoneuroimmunology* (4th ed., pp. 615–703). New York: Academic Press.

Appelbaum, P. (2005). Assessing Kendra's Law: Five years of outpatient commitment in New York. *Psychiatric Services, 56,* 791–792.

Archer, J. (2004). Sex differences in aggression in real-world settings: A meta-analytic review. *Review of General Psychology, 8*(4), 291–322.

Archer, J., Graham-Kevan, N., &Davies, M. (2005). Testosterone and aggression: A reanalysis of Book, Starzyk, and Quinsey's (2001) study. *Aggression and Violent Behavior, 10*(2), 241–261.

Arendt, J. (2009). Managing jet lag: Some of the problems and possible new solutions. *Sleep Medicine Reviews, 13,* 249–256.

Arija, V., Esparó, G., Fernández-Ballart, J., Murphy, M., Biarnés, E., & Canals, J. (2006). Nutritional status and performance in test of verbal and non-verbal intelligence in 6 year old children. *Intelligence, 34*(2), 141–149.

Arnett, J. J. (2004). *Emerging adulthood: The winding road from the late teens through the twenties.* New York: Oxford University Press.

Arnett, J.J. (2010). Oh, grow up! Generational grumbling and the new life stage of emerging adulthood: Commentary on Trzesniewski & Donnellan (2010). *Perspectives on Psychological Science, 5,* 89–92.

Asch, S. E. (1951). Effects of group pressure upon the modification and distortion of judgments. In H. Guetzkow (Ed.), *Groups, leadership and men: Research in human relations* (pp. 177–190). Oxford, UK: Carnegie Press.

Asch, S. E. (1955). Opinions and social pressure. *Scientific American, 193*(5), 31–35.

Asch, S. E. (1956). Studies of independence and conformity: A minority of one against a unanimous majority. *Psychological Monographs, 70*(9, No. 416).

Aslin, R. N. (2007). What's in a look? *Developmental Science, 10,* 48–53.

Atkinson, R. C., & Shiffrin, R. M. (1968). Human memory: A proposed system and its control processes. In K. W. Spence & J. T. Spence (Eds.), *The psychology of learning and motivation: Advances in research and theory* (Vol. 2, pp. 89–195). New York: Academic Press.

Avena, N. M., Rada, P., & Hoebel, B. G. (2008). Evidence for sugar addiction: Behavioral and neurochemical effects of intermittent, excessive sugar intake. *Neuroscience and Biobehavioral Reviews, 32,* 20–39.

Avidan, G., & Behrmann, M. (2008). Implicit familiarity processing in congenital prosopagnosia. *Journal of Neuropsychology, 2*(1), 141–164.

Awh, E., Barton, B., & Vogel, E. K. (2007). Visual working memory represents a fixed number of items, regardless of complexity. *Psychological Science, 18,* 622–628.

Axtell, C., Holman, D., & Wall, T. (2006). Promoting innovation: A change study. *Journal of Occupational and Organizational Psychology, 79*(3), 509–516.

Babyak, M., Blumenthal, J. A., Herman, S., Khatri P., Doraiswamy M., Moore K., Craighead W. E., Baldewicz T. T., & Krishnan K. R. (2000). Exercise treatment for major depression: Maintenance of therapeutic benefit at 10 months. *Psychosomatic Medicine, 62,* 633–638.

Back, M. D., Stopfer, J. M., Vazire, S., Gaddis, S., Schmukle, S. C., Egloff, B., & Gosling, S. (2010). Facebook profiles reflect actual personality, not self-idealization. *Psychological Science, 21,* 372–374.

Baddeley, A. (2001). Is working memory still working? *American Psychologist, 56,* 851–864.

Baddeley, A. D., Thomson, N., Buchanan, M. (1975). Word length and the structure of short-term memory. *Journal of Verbal Learning & Verbal Behavior, 14*(6), 575–589.

Badman, M. K., & Flier, J. S. (2005). The gut and energy balance: Visceral allies in the obesity wars. *Science, 307,* 1909–1914.

Bahrick, H. (1984). Semantic memory content in permastore: Fifty years of memory for Spanish learned in school. *Journal of Experimental Psychology: General, 113,* 1–29.

Bahrick, L. E., & Watson, J. S. (1985). Detection of intermodal proprioceptive–visual contingency as a potential basis of self-perception in infancy. *Developmental Psychology, 21,* 963–973.

Bailenson, J. N., Shum, M. S., Atran, S., Medin, D. L., & Coley, J. D. (2002). A bird's eye view: Biological categorization and reasoning within and across cultures. *Cognition, 84*(1), 1–53.

Bailey, J. M. (2003). *The man who would be queen.* Washington, DC: Joseph Henry Press.

Bailey, J. M., Dunne, M. P., & Martin, N. G. (2000). Genetic and environmental influences on sexual orientation and its correlates in an Australian twin sample. *Journal of Personality and Social Psychology, 78,* 524–536.

Bailey, J. M., & Pillard, R. C. (1995). Genetics of human sexual orientation. Annual Review of Sex Research, 6, 126–150.

Bailey, J. M., Pillard, R. C., Neale, M. C., & Agyei, Y. (1993). Heritable factors influence sexual orientation in women. *Archives of General Psychiatry, 50,* 217–223.

Balch, W., Myers, D., & Papotto, C. (1999). Dimensions of mood in mood-dependent memory. *Journal of Experimental Psychology: Learning, Memory, and Cognition, 25,* 70–83.

Banaji, M. R., & Heiphetz, L. (2010). Attitudes. In S. T. Fiske, D. T. Gilbert, & G. Lindzey (Eds.), *Handbook of social psychology* (pp. 348–388). New York: John Wiley & Sons.

Bandura, A. (1977). *Social learning theory.* Englewood Cliffs, NJ: Prentice Hall.

Bandura, A. (2001). Social cognitive theory: An agentic perspective. *Annual Review of Psychology, 52,* 1–26.

Bandura, A., Ross, D., & Ross, S. A. (1961). Transmission of aggression through imitation of aggressive models. *Journal of Abnormal and Social Psychology, 63,* 575–582.

Bandura, A., Ross, D., & Ross, S. A. (1963). Imitation of film-mediated aggressive models. *Journal of Abnormal and Social Psychology, 66,* 3–11.

Banse, R., Seise, J., & Zerbes, N. (2001). Implicit attitudes toward homosexuality: Reliability, validity, and controllability of the IAT. *Zeitschrift fur Experimentelle Psychologie, 48,* 145–160.

Barbanoj, M. J., Riba, J., Clos, S., Giménez S., Grasa E., & Romero S. (2008). Daytime Ayahuasca administration modulates REM and slow-wave sleep in healthy volunteers. *Psychopharmacology (Berl.), 196,* 315–326.

Barbet, I., & Fagot, J. (2007). Control of the corridor illusion in baboons (*Papio papio*) by gradient and linear-perspective depth cues. *Perception, 36,* 391–402.

Bard, K. A., Todd, B., Bernier, C., Love, J., & Leavens, D. A. (2006). Self-awareness in human and chimpanzee infants: What is measured and what is meant by the mirror-and-mark test? *Infancy, 9,* 185–213.

Bar-Haim, Y., Lamy, D., Pergamin, L., Bakermans-Kranenburg, M. J., & van Ijzendoorn, M. H. (2007). Threat-related attentional bias in anxious and nonanxious individuals: a metaanalytic study. *Psychological Bulletin, 133,* 1–24.

Barnes, C., & Wagner, D. (2009). Changing to Daylight Saving Time cuts into sleep and increases workplace injuries. *Journal of Applied Psychology, 94*(5), 1305–1317.

Barnes, G. M., Welte, J. W., Hoffman, J. H., & Tidwell, M-C. (2010). Comparisons of gambling and alcohol use among college students and noncollege young people in the United States. *Journal of American College Health, 58,* 443–452.

Baron, R. A. (1999). Social and personal determinants of workplace aggression: Evidence for the impact of perceived injustice and the Type A behavior pattern. *Aggressive Behavior, 25,* 281–296.

Baron, R. A., Neuman, J. H., & Geddes, D. (1999). Social and personal determinants of workplace aggression: Evidence for the impact of perceived injustice and the Type A behavior pattern. *Aggressive Behavior, 25,* 281–296.

Barr, R., Zack, E., Garcia, A., & Muentener, P. (2008). Infants' attention and responsiveness to television increases with repetition and parental interaction. *Infancy, 13,* 30–56.

Barrick, M. R., & Mount, M. K. (2005). Yes, personality matters: Moving on to more important matters. *Human Performance, 18,* 359–372.

Barrick, M. R., Stewart, G. L., Neubert, M. J., & Mount, M. K. (1998). Relating member ability and personality to work-team processes and team effectiveness. *Journal of Applied Psychology, 83*(3), 377–391.

Bartlett, F. C. (1932). *Remembering: A study in experimental and social psychology.* Cambridge, UK: Cambridge University Press.

Bass, B. (1997). Does the transactional–transformational leadership paradigm transcend organizational and national boundaries? *American Psychologist, 52*(2), 130–139.

Bass, B. M., Avolio, B. J., Jung, D. I., & Berson, Y. (2003). Predicting unit performance by assessing transformational and transactional leadership. *Journal of Applied Psychology, 88,* 207–218.

Batson, C., Eklund, J., Chermok, V. L., Hoyt, J. L., & Ortiz, B. G. (2007). An additional antecedent of empathic concern: Valuing the welfare of the person in need. *Journal of Personality and Social Psychology, 93*(1), 65–74.

Battaglia, M., Ogliari, A., Zanoni, A., Citterio, A., Pozzoli, U., Giorda, R., Maffei, C., & Marino, C. (2005). Influence of the serotonin transporter promoter gene and shyness on children's cerebral responses to facial expressions. *Archives of General Psychiatry, 62,* 85–94.

Baum, A., & Valins, S. (1977). *Architecture of social behavior: Psychological studies of social density.* Hillsdale, NJ: Erlbaum.

Baumeister, R. F., Dale, K., & Sommer, K. L. (1998). Freudian defense mechanisms and empirical findings in modern social psychology: Reaction formation, projection, displacement, undoing, isolation, sublimation and denial. *Journal of Personality, 66,* 1081–1124.

Baumeister, R. F., & Leary, M. R. (1995). The need to belong: Desire for interpersonal attachments as a fundamental human motivation. *Psychological Bulletin, 117,* 497–529.

Baumrind, D. (1971). Current patterns of parental authority. *Developmental Psychology Monographs, 4*(1, Pt 2).

Baumrind, D. (1991). Parenting styles and adolescent development. In J. Brooks-Gunn, R. Lerner, & A. C. Petersen (Eds.), *The encyclopedia on adolescence* (pp. 746–758). New York: Garland.

Bauserman, R., & Davis, C. (1996). Perceptions of early sexual experiences and adult sexual adjustment. *Journal of Psychology and Human Sexuality, 8,* 37–59.

Baym, C., Corbett, B., Wright, S., & Bunge, S. (2008). Neural correlates of tic severity and cognitive control in children with Tourette syndrome. *Brain: A Journal of Neurology, 131*(1), 165–179.

Beaman, A. (1983). Fifteen years of foot-in-the-door research: A meta-analysis. *Personality and Social Psychology Bulletin, 9*(2), 181–196.

Beauchamp, G. K., & Mennella, J. A. (2009). Early flavor learning and its impact on later feeding behavior. *Journal of Pediatric Gastroenterology and Nutrition, 48,* S25–S30.

Beck, A. T. (1963). Thinking and depression: I. Idiosyncratic content and cognitive distortions. *Archives of General Psychiatry, 9,* 324–333.

Beck, D. M., & Kastner, S. (2009). Top-down and bottom-up mechanisms in biasing competition in the human brain. *Vision Research, 49,* 1154–1165.

Begany, J. J. &, Milburn, M. A. (2002). Psychological predictors of sexual harassment: Authoritarianism, hostile sexism, and rape myths. *Psychology of Men & Masculinity, 3,* 119–126.

Begley, S. (2007, August 15). The puzzle of hidden ability. *Newsweek.* Retrieved from http://www.newsweek.com/2007/08/15/the-puzzle-of-hidden-ability.html

Beilock, S. L. (2008). Math performance in stressful situations. *Current Directions in Psychological Science, 17,* 339–343.

Beilock, S. L. (2010). *Choke: What the secrets of the brain reveal about getting it right when you have to.* New York: Free Press.

Beilock, S., Rydell, R., & McConnell, A. (2007). Stereotype threat and working memory: Mechanisms, alleviation, and spillover. *Journal of Experimental Psychology: General, 136*(2), 256–276.

Bekinschtein, T. A., Cardozo, J., & Manes, F. F. (2008). Strategies of Buenos Aires waiters to enhance memory capacity in a real-life setting. *Behavioral Neurology, 20,* 65–70.

Bekinschtein, T. A., Shalom, D. E., Forcato, C., Herrera, M., Coleman, M. R., Manes, F. F., & Sigman, M. (2009). Classical conditioning in the vegetative and minimally conscious state. *Nature Neuroscience, 12*(10), 1343–1349.

Bell, P. A., & Yee, L. A. (1989). Skill level and audience effects on performance of a karate drill. *Journal of Social Psychology, 129*(2), 191–200.

Bell, R. A., Paterniti, D. A., Azari, R., Duberstein, P. R., & Epstein, R. M. (2010). Encouraging patients with depressive symptoms to seek care: A mixed methods approach to message development. *Patient Education and Counseling, 78*(2), 198–205.

Belsky, J. (2007). Childhood experiences and reproductive strategies. In R. I. M. Dunbar & L. Barrett (Eds.), *Oxford handbook of evolutionary psychology* (pp. 237–253). New York: Oxford University Press.

Belsky, J., & Rovine, M. (1990). Patterns of marital change across the transition to parenthood. *Journal of Marriage and the Family, 52,* 109–123.

Ben-Ari, R., Krole, R., & Har-Even, D. (2003). Differential effects of simple frontal versus complex teaching strategy on teachers' stress, burnout, and satisfaction. *International Journal of Stress Management, 10*(2), 173–195.

Bennett, G. G., Wolin, K. Y., Robinson, E. L., Fowler, S., & Edwards, C. L. (2005). Racial/ethnic harassment and tobacco use among African American young adults. *American Journal of Public Health, 95,* 238–240.

Benton, D. (2001). Micro-nutrient supplementation and the intelligence of children. *Neuroscience & Biobehavioral Reviews, 25*(4), 297–309.

Berger, J. M., Levant, R., McMillan, K. K., Kelleher, W., & Sellers, A. (2005). Impact of gender role conflict, traditional masculinity ideology, alexithymia, and age on men's attitudes towards psychological help seeking. *Psychology of Men & Masculinity, 6,* 73–78.

Berger, R., & Phillips, N. (1995). Energy conservation and sleep. *Behavioural Brain Research, 69*(1), 65–73.

Berkowitz, L. (2003). Affect, aggression and antisocial behavior. In R. J. Davidson, K. Scherer, & H. H. Goldsmith (Eds.), *Handbook of affective sciences* (pp. 804–823). New York/Oxford, UK: Oxford University Press.

Berlin, B. (1974). *Principles of Tzeltal plant classification.* New York: Academic Press.

Berry, C., Ones, D., & Sackett, P. (2007). Interpersonal deviance, organizational deviance, and their common correlates: A review and meta-analysis. *Journal of Applied Psychology, 92*(2), 410–424.

Berry, S. L., Beatty, W. W., & Klesges, R. C. (1985). Sensory and social influences on ice-cream consumption by males and females in a laboratory setting. *Appetite, 6,* 41–45.

Bertram, L., Lill, C. M., & Tanzi, R. E. (2010). The genetics of Alzheimer's disease: Back to the future. *Neuron, 68,* 270–281.

Bessiere, K., Seay, A. F., & Kiesler, S. (2007). The ideal self: Identity exploration in World of Warcraft. *Cyberpsychology and Behavior, 10,* 530–535.

Best, D. (2009). Secondhand and prenatal tobacco smoke exposure. *Pediatrics, 123,* e1017–e1044.

Best, R., Stapleton, L., & Downey, R. (2005). Core self-evaluations and job burnout: The test of alternative models. *Journal of Occupational Health Psychology, 10,* 441–451.

Bestmann, S. (2008). The physiological basis of transcranial magnetic stimulation. *Trends in Cognitive Sciences, 12*(3), 81–83.

Bettencourt, B. A., Talley, A., Benjamin, A. J., & Valentine, J. (2006). Personality and aggressive behavior under provoking and neutral conditions: A meta-analytic review. *Psychological Bulletin, 132,* 751–777.

Bhatara, A., Tirovolas, A., Duan, L. M., Levy, B., & Levitin, D. J. (2011). Perception of emotional expression in musical performance. *Journal of Experimental Psychology: Human Perception and Performance, 37,* 921–934.

Bhattacharya, J., & Bundorf, M. K. (2005). *The incidence of healthcare costs of obesity.* Working Paper #11303. National Bureau of Economic Research.

Bhugra, D. (2005). The global prevalence of schizophrenia. *Plos Medicine, 2,* 372–373.

Bialystok, E., Craik, F. I. M., Green, D. W., & Gollan, T. H. (2009). Bilingual minds. *Psychological Science in the Public Interest, 10,* 89–129.

Birbaumer, N., Veit, R., Lotze, M., Erb, M., Hermann, C., Grodd, W., Flor, H. (2005). Deficient fear conditioning in psychopathy: A functional magnetic resonance imaging study. *Archives of General Psychiatry, 62*(7), 799–805.

Bishop, S. (2002). What do we really know about Mindfulness-Based Stress Reduction? *Psychosomatic Medicine, 64*(1), 71–83.

Blackman, M. (2002). Personality judgment and the utility of the unstructured employment interview. *Basic and Applied Social Psychology, 24,* 241–250.

Blackwell, L., Trzesniewski, K., & Dweck, C. (2007). Implicit theories of intelligence predict achievement across an adolescent transition: A longitudinal study and an intervention. *Child Development, 78*(1), 246–263.

Blake, R., Palmeri, T. J., Marois, R., & Kim, C-Y. (2005). On the perceptual reality of synesthetic color. In L. C. Robertson & N. Sagiv (Eds.), *Synesthesia* (pp. 47–73). Oxford, UK: Oxford University Press.

Blanchard, R. (2008). Review and theory of handedness, birth order, and homosexuality in men. *Laterality, 13*, 51–70.

Blandin, Y., & Proteau, L. (2000). On the cognitive basis of observational learning: Development of mechanisms for the detection and correction of errors. *Quarterly Journal of Experimental Psychology: Human Experimental Psychology, 53*, 846–867.

Blashfield, R. K., & Intoccia, V. (2000). Growth of the literature on the topic of personality disorders. *American Journal of Psychiatry, 157*, 3.

Bliss, T., & Lømo, T. (1973). Long-lasting potentiation of synaptic transmission in the dentate area of the anaesthetized rabbit following stimulation of the perforant path. *Journal of Physiology, 232*, 331–356.

Bloom, P. (2010). *How pleasure works.* New York: Norton.

Blumner, K., & Marcus, S. (2009). Changing perceptions of depression: Ten-year trends from the General Social Survey. *Psychiatric Services, 60*, 306–312.

Bobko, P., Roth, P., & Buster, M. (2008). A systematic approach for assessing the currency ("up-to-dateness") of job-analytic information. *Public Personnel Management, 37*, 261–277.

Boesch, C. (1991). Teaching among wild chimpanzees. *Animal Behaviour, 41*, 530–532.

Bogaert, A. F. (2008). Menarche and father absence in a national probability sample. *Journal of Biosocial Sciences, 40*, 623–636.

Bogle, K. E., & Smith, B. H. (2009). Illicit methylphenidate use: A review of prevalence, availability, pharmacology, and consequences. *Current Drug Abuse Reviews, 2*, 157–176.

Book, A. S., Starzyk, K. B., & Quinsey, V. L. (2001). The relationship between testosterone and aggression: A meta-analysis. *Aggression and Violent Behavior, 6*(6), 579–599.

Boomsma, D. I., Van Beijsterveldt, C. E. M., & Hudziak, J. J. (2005). Genetic and environmental influences on anxious/depression during childhood: A study from the Netherlands Twin Register. *Genes, Brain, and Behavior, 4*, 466–481.

Boring, E. G. (1923). Intelligence as the tests test it. *New Republic, 35*, 35–37.

Boswell, W., Shipp, A., Payne, S., & Culbertson, S. (2009). Changes in newcomer job satisfaction over time: Examining the pattern of honeymoons and hangovers. *Journal of Applied Psychology, 94*(4), 844–858.

Bouton, M. E. (1994). Context, ambiguity, and classical conditioning. *Current Directions in Psychological Science, 3*, 49–53.

Bowlby, J. (1951). Maternal care and mental health. *World Health Organization Monograph*, Serial No. 2.

Boyd, J. E., Katz, E. P., Link, B. G., & Phelan, J. C. (2010). The relationship of multiple aspects of stigma and personal contact with someone hospitalized for mental illness, in a nationally representative sample. *Social Psychiatry and Psychiatric Epidemiology, 45*(11), 1063–1070.

Bracha, H., Ralston, T., Matsukawa, J., Williams, A., & Bracha, A. (2004, October). Does "fight or flight" need updating? *Psychosomatics: Journal of Consultation Liaison Psychiatry, 45*(5), 448–449.

Bransford, J. D., & Johnson, M. K. (1973). Considerations of some problems of comprehension. In W. Chase (Ed.), *Visual information processing* (pp. 383–438). Oxford, UK Academic.

Brauer, M., Judd, C. M., & Gliner, M. D. (1995). The effects of repeated expressions on attitude polarization during group discussions. *Journal of Personality and Social Psychology, 68*(6), 1014–1029.

Breaugh, J. A., & Colihan, J. P. (1994). Measuring facets of job ambiguity: Construct validity evidence. *Journal of Applied Psychology, 79*, 191–202.

Breiter, H. C., Aharon, I., Kahneman, D., Dale, A., & Shizgal, P. (2001). Functional imaging of neural responses to expectancy and experience of monetary gains and losses. *Neuron, 30*(2), 619–639.

Brendel, G. R., Stern, E., & Silbersweig, D. (2005). Defining the neuro-circuitry of borderline personality disorder: Functional neuroimaging approaches. *Development and Psychopathology, 17*, 1197–1206.

Brené, S., Bjørnebekk, A., Aberg, E., Mathé, A. A., Olson, L., & Werme, M. (2007). Running is rewarding and antidepressive. *Physiology and Behavior, 92*, 136–140.

Bridgeman, B., McCamley-Jenkins, L., & Ervin, N. (2000). Predictions of freshman grade-point average from the revised and recentered SAT I: Reasoning test (College Board Report No. 2000-1). New York: College Entrance Examination Board.

Brief, A., & Weiss, H. (2002). Organizational behavior: Affect in the workplace. *Annual Review of Psychology, 53*(1), 279–307.

Brion, M. J., Victora, C., Matijasevich, A., Horta, B., Anselmi, L., Steer, C., Menezes, A. M., Lawlor, D. A., Davey Smith, G. (2010). Maternal smoking and child psychological problems: Disentangling causal and noncausal effects. *Pediatrics, 126*, e57–e65.

Brissette, I., Scheier, M. F., & Carver, C. S. (2002). The role of optimism and social network development, coping, and psychological adjustment during a life transition. *Journal of Personality and Social Psychology, 82*, 102–111.

Brondolo, E., Libby, D. J., Denton, E., Thompson, S., Beatty, D. L., Schwartz, J. (2008). Racism and ambulatory blood pressure in a community sample. *Psychosomatic Medicine, 70*, 49–56.

Brophy, J. E., & Good, T. L. (1970). Teachers' communication of differential expectations for children's classroom performance. *Journal of Educational Psychology, 61*, 365–374.

Brown, A. (2002). Consolidation theory and retrograde amnesia in humans. *Psychonomic Bulletin & Review, 9*, 403–425.

Brown, A. S. (2003). A review of the déjà vu experience. *Psychological Bulletin, 129*, 394–413.

Brown, A. S., & Derkits, E. J. (2010). Prenatal infection and schizophrenia: A review of epidemiologic and translational studies. *American Journal of Psychiatry, 167*, 261–280.

Brown, B. B., & Klute, C. (2006). Friendships, cliques, and crowds. In G. R. Adams & M. D. Berzonsky (Eds.), *Blackwell handbook of adolescence* (pp. 330–348). Malden, MA: Blackwell.

Brown, J. (1958). Some tests of the decay theory of immediate memory. *Quarterly Journal of Experimental Psychology, 10*, 12–21.

Brown, R., & Kulik, J. (1977). Flashbulb memories. *Cognition, 5*, 73–99.

Brown, W. M., Lee Cronk, L., Grochow, K., Jacobson, A., Liu, C. K., Popović, Z., & Trivers, R. (2005). Dance reveals symmetry especially in young men. *Nature, 438*, 1148–1150.

Brunell, A. B., Staats, S., Barden, J., & Hupp, J. M. (2011). Narcissism and academic dishonesty: The exhibitionism dimension and the lack of guilt. *Personality and Individual Differences, 50*(3), 323–328.

Buck, L. B. (1996). Information coding in the vertebrate olfactory system. *Annual Review of Neuroscience, 19*, 517–544.

Buck, L. B., & Axel, R. (1991). A novel multigene family may encode odorant receptors: A molecular basis for odor recognition. *Cell, 65*, 175–187.

Buckingham, H. (2006). A pre-history of the problem of Broca's aphasia. *Aphasiology, 20*, 792–810.

Bugelski, B. R., & Alampay, D. A. (1961). The role of frequency in developing perceptual sets. *Canadian Journal of Psychology, 15*, 205–211.

Bugg, J. M., Zook, N. A., DeLosh, E. L., Davalos, D. B., & Davis, H. P. (2006). Age differences in fluid intelligence: Contributions of general slowing and frontal decline. *Brain and Cognition, 62*(1), 9–16.

Bureau of Labor Statistics. (2006, October 27). Retrieved September 14, 2009, from http://www.bls.gov/iif/ oshwc/osnr0026.pdf

Burger, J. M. (1999). The foot-in-the-door compliance procedure: A multiple-process analysis and review. *Personality and Social Psychology Review, 3*(4), 303–325.

Burger, J. M., & Caldwell, D. F. (2003). The effects of monetary incentives and labeling on the foot-in-the-door effect: Evidence for a self-perception process. *Basic and Applied Social Psychology, 25*(3), 235–241.

Burke, B. L., Martens, A., & Faucher, E. H. (2010). Two decades of terror management theory: A meta-analysis of mortality salience research. *Personality and Social Psychology Review, 14*(2), 155–195.

Burnand, Y., Andreoli, A., Kolatte, E., Venturini A, & Rosset, N. (2002). Psychodynamic psychotherapy and clomipramine in the treatment of major depression. *Psychiatric Services, 53*, 585–80.

Burns, M., & Seligman, M. (1989). Explanatory style across the life span: Evidence for stability over 52 years. *Journal of Personality and Social Psychology, 56*(3), 471–477.

Burton, L. A., Henninger, D., & Hafetz, J. (2005). Gender differences in relations of mental rotation, verbal fluency, and SAT scores to finger length ratios as hormonal indexes. *Developmental Neuropsychology, 28*, 493–505.

Bushman, B. J., & Anderson, C. A. (2007). Measuring the strength of the effect of violent media on aggression. *American Psychologist, 62*, 253–254.

Buss, A. H., & Perry, M. (1992). The Aggression Questionnaire. *Journal of Personality and Social Psychology, 63*(3), 452–459.

Buss, D. M. (1989). Sex differences in human mating preferences: Evolutionary hypotheses tested in 37 different cultures. *Behavioral and Brain Sciences, 12,* 1–49.

Buss, D. M. (2000). *The dangerous passion: Why jealousy is as necessary as love and sex.* New York: Free Press.

Buss, D. M. (2009). How can evolutionary psychology successfully explain personality and individual differences? *Perspectives on Psychological Science, 4,* 359–366.

Buss, D. M., Shackelford, T. K., Kirkpatrick, L. A., & Larsen, R. J. (2001). A half century of mate preferences: The cultural evolution of values. *Journal of Marriage and the Family, 63,* 491–503.

Buston, P. M., & Emlen, S. T. (2003). Cognitive processes underlying human mate choice: The relationship between self-perception and mate preference in Western society. *Proceedings of the National Academy of Sciences, 100,* 8805–8810.

Butler, A., Kang, S., & Roediger, H. (2009). Congruity effects between materials and processing tasks in the survival processing paradigm. *Journal of Experimental Psychology: Learning, Memory, and Cognition, 35*(6), 1477–1486.

Buttigieg, S. (2006). Relationship of a biodata instrument and a Big 5 personality measure with the job performance of entry-level production workers. *Applied H.R.M. Research, 11*(1), 65–68.

Caci, H., Deschaux, O., Adan, A., & Natale, V. (2009). Comparing three morningness scales: Age and gender effects, structure and cut-off criteria. *Sleep Medicine, 10,* 240–245.

Cacioppo, J. T., Hawkley, L. C., & Bernston, G. G. (2003). The anatomy of loneliness. *Current Directions in Psychological Science, 12,* 71–74.

Cacioppo, J. T., Petty, R. E., Kao, C., & Rodriguez, R. (1986). Central and peripheral routes to persuasion: An individual difference perspective. *Journal of Personality and Social Psychology, 51*(5), 1032–1043.

Cahill, L., & McGaugh, J. L. (1998). Mechanisms of emotional arousal and lasting declarative memory. *Trends in Neuroscience, 21,* 294–299.

Cahn, B. R., & Polich, J. (2006). Meditation states and traits: EEG, ERP and neuroimaging studies. *Psychological Bulletin, 132,* 180–211.

Cairns, R., & Cairns, B. (1994). *Lifelines and risks: Pathways of youth in our time.* New York: Cambridge University Press.

Calkins, L. (2010). Detained and drugged: A brief overview of the use of pharmaceuticals for the interrogation of suspects, prisoners, patients, and POWs in the US. Bioethics, 24, 27–34.

Campion, M., Palmer, D., & Campion, J. (1997). A review of structure in the selection interview. *Personnel Psychology, 50*(3), 655–702.

Cannon, W. B., & Washburn, A. L. (1921). An explanation of hunger. *American Journal of Physiology, 29,* 441–454.

Cao, X., Cui, Z., Feng, R., Tang, Y., Qin, Z., & Mei, B. (2007). Maintenance of superior learning and memory function in NR2B transgenic mice during ageing. *European Journal of Neuroscience, 25*(6), 1815–1822.

Capafons, A., Mendoza, M., Espejo, B., Green, J., Lopes-Pires, C., Selma, M., et al. (2008). Attitudes and beliefs about hypnosis: A multicultural study. *Contemporary Hypnosis, 25*(3), 141–155.

Carey, B. (2009, November 26). Surgery for mental ills offers both hope and risk. *The New York Times.* Retrieved from http://www.nytimes.com

Carkenord, D. M., & Bullington, J. (1993). Bringing cognitive dissonance to the classroom. *Teaching of Psychology, 20*(1), 41–43.

Carlson, E. N., Furr, R. M., & Vazire, S. (2010). Do we know the first impressions we make? Evidence for idiographic meta-accuracy and calibration of first impressions. *Social Psychological and Personality Science, 1,* 94–98.

Carlson, M. L., Breen, J. T., Gifford, R. H., Driscoll, C. L., Neff, B. A., Beatty, C. W., Peterson, A. M., & Olund, A. P. (2010). Cochlear implantation in the octogenarian and nonagenarian. *Otology and Neurotology, 31,* 1343–1349.

Carmichael, M. S., Warburton, V. L., Dixen, & Davidson, J. M. (1994). Relationships among cardiovascular, muscular, and oxytocin responses during human sexual activity. *Archives of Sexual Behavior, 23,* 59–79.

Carmody, T. P., Duncan, C., Simon, J. A., Solkowitz, S., Huggins, J., Lee, S., & Delucchi, K. (2008). Hypnosis for smoking cessation: A randomized trial. *Nicotine & Tobacco Research, 10*(5), 811–818.

Carnagey, N. L., Anderson, C. A., & Bushman, B. J. (2007). The effect of video game violence on physiological desensitization to real-life violence. *Journal of Experimental Social Psychology, 43,* 489–496.

Carpenter-Song, E., Chu, E., Drake, R. E., Ritsema, M., & Alverson, H. (2010). Ethno-cultural variations in the experience and meaning of mental illness and treatment: Implications for access and utilization. *Transcultural Psychiatry, 47,* 224–251.

Carstensen, L. L., Isaacowitz, D., & Charles, S. T. (1999). Taking time seriously: A theory of socioemotional selectivity. *American Psychologist, 54,* 165–181.

Carston, R. (2002). *Thoughts and utterances: The pragmatics of explicit conversation.* New York: Blackwell.

Carter, A. C., Brandon, K., & Goldman, M. S. (2010). The college and noncollege experience: A review of the factors that influence drinking behavior in young adulthood. *Journal of Studies on Alcohol and Drugs, 71*(5), 742–750.

Cartwright, R., Agargun, M., Kirkby, J., & Friedman, J. K. (2006). Relation of dreams to waking concerns. *Psychiatry Research, 141,* 261–270.

Caruso, E. M., Waytz, A., & Epley, N. (2010). The intentional mind and the hot hand: Perceiving intentions makes streaks seem likely to continue. *Cognition, 116*(1), 149–153.

Caspari, I. (2005). Wernicke's aphasia. In L. LaPointe (Ed.), *Aphasia and related neurogenic language disorders* (3rd ed., pp. 142–154). New York: Thieme.

Caspi, A., Hariri, A. R., Holmes, A., Uher, R., & Moffitt, T. E. (2010). Genetic sensitivity to the environment: The case of the serotonin transporter gene and its implications for studying complex diseases and traits. *American Journal of Psychiatry, 167,* 509–527.

Caspi, A., Moffitt, T. E., Cannon, M., Taylor, A., Craig, I. W., Harrington, H., McClay, J., Mill, J., Martin, J. Braithwaite, A. & Poulton, R. (2005). Moderation of the effect of adolescent-onset cannabis use on adult psychosis by a functional polymorphism in the catechol-*O*-methyltransferase gene: Longitudinal evidence of a gene X environment interaction. *Biological Psychiatry, 57,* 1117–1127.

Caspi, A., Sugden, K., Moffitt, T. E., Taylor, A., Craig, I. W., Harrington, H., et al. (2003). Influence of life stress on depression: Moderation by a polymorphism in the 5-HTT gene. *Science, 301,* 386–389.

Cattell, R. B. (1946). *The description and measurement of personality.* New York: Harcourt, Brace & World.

Cattell, R. B. (1971). *Abilities: Their structure, growth, and action.* New York: Houghton Mifflin.

Cavallera, G., & Giudici, S. (2008). Morningness and eveningness personality: A survey in literature from 1995 up till 2006. *Personality and Individual Differences, 44*(1), 3–21.

Cave, E., & Holm, S. (2003). Milgram and *Tuskegee:* Paradigm research projects in bioethics. *Health Care Analysis, 11,* 27–40.

Ceci, S., & Williams, W. (1997). Schooling, intelligence, and income. *American Psychologist, 52*(10), 1051–1058.

Ceci, S., Williams, W., &. Barnett, S. (2009). Women's underrepresentation in science: Sociocultural and biological considerations. *Psychological Bulletin, 135*(2), 218–261.

Centers for Disease Control and Prevention (CDC). (2002). Annual smoking-attributable mortality, years of potential life lost, and productivity losses—United States, 1995–1999. *Morbidity and Mortality Weekly Report, 51*(14), 300–303

Centers for Disease Control and Prevention (CDC). (2009). Tobacco use and pregnancy. Retrieved August 1, 2010, from http://www.cdc.gov/reproductivehealth/tobaccousepregnancy/index.htm

Centers for Disease Control and Prevention (CDC). (2009a, April 17). *National Vital Statistics Reports, 57*(14).

Centers for Disease Control and Prevention (CDC). (2009b). Retrieved June 20, 2011, from http://www.cdc.gov/tobacco/data_statistics/fact_sheets/fast_facts/index.htm

Centers for Disease Control and Prevention (CDC). (2010). Injury prevention and control: Violence prevention. Retrieved from http://www.cdc.gov/ViolencePrevention/suicide/consequences.html

Centers for Disease Control and Prevention (CDC). (2010). NCHS vital statistics system for numbers and deaths. Retrieved June 15, 2011, from http://www.cdc.gov/NCHS/data/nvsr/nvsr58/nvsr58_19.pdf

Centers for Disease Control and Prevention (CDC). (2010). Obesity data and statistics. Retrieved April 2, 2010, from http://www.cdc.gov/obesity/data/trends.html

Centers for Disease Control and Prevention (CDC). (2010). Youth risk behavior surveillance—United States, 2009. *Morbidity and Mortality Weekly Report, 59*(No. SS-5). Retrieved from http://www.cdc.gov/mmwr/pdf/ss/ss5905.pdf

Centers for Disease Control and Prevention (CDC). (2010a, April 5). Compared with whites, Blacks had 51% higher and Hispanics had 21% higher obesity rates. Retrieved from http://www.cdc.gov/Features/dsObesityAdults/

Centers for Disease Control and Prevention (CDC). (2010b). Obesity and socioeconomic status in adults: United States, 2005–2008. *NCHS Data Brief, 50*. Retrieved January 13, 2011, from http://www.cdc.gov/nchs/data/databriefs/db50.htm

Centers for Disease Control and Prevention (CDC). (2010bc). Obesity and socioeconomic status in children and adolescents: United States, 2005–2008. *NCHS Data Brief, 51*. Retrieved January 13, 2011, from http://www.cdc.gov/nchs/data/databriefs/db51.htm

Centers for Disease Control and Prevention (CDC). (2010d, September 10). Vital signs: Current cigarette smoking among adults aged ≥18 years—United States, 2009. Retrieved July 9, 2011, from http://www.cdc.gov/mmwr/preview/mmwrhtml/mm5935a3.htm

Cepeda, N. N., Pashler, H., Vul, E., et al. (2006). Distributed practice in verbal recall tasks: A review and quantitative synthesis. *Psychological Bulletin, 132,* 354–380.

Chaiken, S., & Trope, Y. (1999). *Dual-process theories in social psychology.* New York: Guilford Press.

Chambless, D., & Ollendick, T. (2001). Empirically supported psychological interventions: Controversies and evidence. *Annual Review of Psychology, 52,* 685–716.

Chamorro-Premuzic, T., & Furnham, A. (2003). Personality traits and academic exam performance. *European Journal of Personality, 17,* 237–250.

Chan, B. L., et al. (2007). Mirror therapy and phantom limb pain. *New England Journal of Medicine, 357,* 2206–2207.

Chang, E. C., Sanna, L. J., & Yang, K. (2003). Optimism, pessimism, affectivity, and psychological adjustment in US and Korea: A test of a mediation model. Personality and Individual Differences, 34(7), 1195–1208.

Chang, E. C., Tsai, W., & Sanna, L. J. (2010). Examining the relations between rumination and adjustment: Do ethnic differences exist between Asian and European Americans? Asian American Journal of Psychology, 1(1), 46–56.

Chappel, J. N., Veach, T. L., & Krug, R. S. (1985). The Substance Abuse Attitude Survey: An instrument for measuring attitudes. *Journal of Studies on Alcohol, 46*(1), 48–52.

Charles, S. T., & Carstensen, L. L. (2009). Social and emotional aging. *Annual Review of Psychology, 61,* 383–409.

Charles, S. T., Mather, M., & Carstensen, L. L. (2003). Focusing on the positive: Age differences in memory for positive, negative, and neutral stimuli. *Journal of Experimental Psychology, 85,* 163–178.

Charron, S., & Koechlin, E. (2010). Divided representation of concurrent goals in the human frontal lobes. *Science, 328,* 360–363.

Chartrand, T. L., & Bargh, J. A. (1999). The chameleon effect: The perception–behavior link and social interaction. *Journal of Personality and Social Psychology, 76,* 893–910.

Chaudhari, N., Landin, A. M., & Roper, S. D. (2000). A metabotropic glutamate receptor variant functions as a taste receptor. *Nature Neuroscience, 3,* 113–119.

Chen, I., Vorona, R., Chiu, R., & Ware, J. (2008). A survey of subjective sleepiness and consequences in attending physicians. *Behavioral Sleep Medicine, 6*(1), 1–15.

Chentsova-Dutton, Y. E., & Tsai, J. L. (2007). Cultural factors influence the expression of psychopathology. In S. O. Lilienfeld, W. T. O'Donohue, S. O. Lilienfeld, & W. T. O'Donohue (Eds.), *The great ideas of clinical science: 17 principles that every mental health professional should understand* (pp. 375–396). New York: Routledge/Taylor & Francis Group.

Cheung, B. Y., Chudek, M., & Heine, S. J. (2011). Evidence for a sensitive period for acculturation: Younger immigrants report acculturating at a faster rate. *Psychological Science, 22,* 147–152.

Cheung, F. M., Leung, K., Fan, R. M., Song W, Zhang J-X, Zhang J-P. (1996). Development of the Chinese Personality Assessment Inventory. *Journal of Cross-Cultural Psychology, 27,* 181–199.

Chiao, J. Y., Harada, T., Komeda, H., Li, Z., Mano, Y., Saito, D., Parrish, T. B., Sadato, N., & Iidaka, T. (2009). Neural basis of individualistic and collectivistic views of self. *Human Brain Mapping, 30,* 2813–2820.

Chiesa, A., & Serretti, A. (2010). Mindfulness based cognitive therapy for psychiatric disorders: A systematic review and meta-analysis [Electronic publication ahead of print]. *Psychiatry Research.*

Chistyakov, A. V., Kaplan, B., Rubicheck, O., Kreinin, I., Koren, D., Feinsod, M., & Klein, E. (2005). Antidepressant effects of different schedules of repetitive transcranial magnetic stimulation vs. clomipramine in patients with major depressions: Relationship to changes in cortical excitability. *International Journal of Neuropsychopharmacology, 8,* 223–233.

Choi, I., Nisbett, R. E., & Norenzayan, A. (1999). Causal attribution across cultures: Variation and universality. *Psychological Bulletin, 125*(1), 47–63.

Choi, Y., Shamosh, N. A., Cho, S., DeYoung, C. G., Lee, M., Lee, J., & Lee, K. (2008). Multiple bases of human intelligence revealed by cortical thickness and neural activation. *Journal of Neuroscience, 28*(41), 10323–10329.

Christakis, D. A. (2009). The effects of media usage: What do we know and what should we learn? *Acta Paediatrica, 98,* 8–16.

Christakis, N. A., & Fowler, J. H. (2007). The spread of obesity in a large social network over 32 years. *New England Journal of Medicine, 357,* 370–379.

Christakis, N. A., & Fowler, J. H. (2008). The collective dynamics of smoking in a large social network. *New England Journal of Medicine, 358,* 2249–2258.

Christensen, C., Silberberg, A., Hursh, S., Huntsberry, M., & Riley, A. (2008). Essential value of cocaine and food in rats: Tests of the exponential model of demand. *Psychopharmacology, 198,* 221–229.

Christie, R., & Geis, F. L. (1970). *Studies in Machiavellianism.* New York: Academic Press.

Chrousos, G. P. (2009). Stress and disorders of the stress system. *Nature Reviews Endocrinology, 5,* 374–381.

Chrousos, G. P., & Gold, P. (1992). The concepts of stress and stress system disorders: Overview of physical and behavioral homeostasis. *Journal of the American Medical Association, 267,* 1244–1252.

Church, A. T. (2010). Current perspectives in the study of personality across cultures. *Perspectives on Psychological Science, 5,* 441–449.

Church, R., & Goldin-Meadow, S. (1986). The mismatch between gesture and speech as an index of transitional knowledge. *Cognition, 23*(1), 43–71.

Cialdini, R. B. (2000). *Persuasion: Influence and practice* (4th ed.). New York: Allyn & Bacon.

Cialdini, R. B., & Goldstein, N. J. (2004). Social influence: Compliance and conformity. *Annual Review of Psychology, 55,* 591–621.

Cialdini, R. B., & Richardson, K. D. (1980). Two indirect tactics of image management: Basking and blasting. *Journal of Personality and Social Psychology, 39,* 406–415.

Cialdini, R. B., Vincent, J. E., Lewis, S. K., Catalan, J., Wheeler, D., & Darby, B. (1975). Reciprocal concessions procedure for inducing compliance: The door-in-the-face technique. *Journal of Personality and Social Psychology, 31*(2), 206–215.

Cillessen, A. H. N., & Rose, A. J. (2005). Understanding popularity in the peer system. *Current Directions in Psychological Science, 14,* 102–105.

Clancy, S. A. (2005). *Abducted: How people come to believe they were kidnapped by aliens.* Cambridge, MA: Harvard University Press.

Clark, L. A. (2007). Assessment and diagnosis of personality disorder: Perennial issues and an emerging reconceptualization. *Annual Review of Psychology, 58,* 227–257.

Cleary, A. (2008). Recognition memory, familiarity, and déjà vu experiences. *Current Directions in Psychological Science, 17*(5), 353–357.

Cleary, A. M., Ryals, A. J., & Nomi, J. S. (2009). Can déjà vu result from similarity to a prior experience? Support for the similarity hypothesis of déjà vu. *Psychonomic Bulletin and Review, 16,* 1082–1088.

Clevenger, J., Pereira, G., Wiechmann, D., Schmitt, N., & Harvey, V. (2001). Incremental validity of situational judgment tests. *Journal of Applied Psychology, 86*(3), 410–417.

CNN. (2002). Retrieved December 21, 2010, from http://archives.cnn.com/2002/LAW/10/09/wuornos.execution/index.html

CNN. (2008, January 23). Loaded gun slips through airport security. Retrieved November 11, 2010 from http://www.cnn.com/2008/US/01/23/airport.gun/index.html

Coane, J. H., & Balota, D. A. (2009). Priming the holiday spirit: Persistent activation due to extraexperimental experiences. *Psychonomic Bulletin & Review, 16*(6), 1124–1128.

Cobos, P., Sánchez, M., García, C., Nieves, V. M., & Vila, J. (2002). Revisiting the James versus Cannon debate on emotion: Startle and autonomic modulation in patients with spinal cord injuries. *Biological Psychology, 61,* 251–269.

Cohen, B., Guttmann, D., & Lazar, A. (1998). The willingness to seek help: A cross-national comparison. *Cross-Cultural Research: The Journal of Comparative Social Science, 32,* 342–357.

Cohen, D., Nisbett, R. E., Bowdle, B. F., & Schwarz, N. (1996). Insult, aggression, and the Southern culture of honor: An "experimental ethnography." *Interpersonal Relations and Group Processes, 70,* 945–960.

Cohen, F., Ogilvie, D. M., Solomon, S., Greenberg, J., & Pyszczynski, T. (2005). American roulette: The effect of reminders of death on support for George W. Bush in the 2004 presidential election. *Analyses of Social Issues and Public Policy (ASAP), 5,* 177–187.

Cohen, G. L. (2003). Party over policy: The dominating impact of group influence on political beliefs. *Journal of Personality and Social Psychology, 85*(5), 808–822.

Cohen, N. J., Eichenbaum, H., Deacedo, B. S., & Corkin, S. (1985). Different memory systems underlying acquisition of procedural and declarative knowledge. In D. S. Olton, E. Gamzu, & S. Corkin (Eds.), *Memory dysfunctions: An integration of animal and human research from preclinical and clinical perspectives* (pp. 54–71). New York: New York Academy of Sciences.

Cohen, S., Frank, E., Doyle, B. J., Skoner, D. P., Rabin, B. S. & Gwaltney, J. M. (1998). Types of stressors that increase susceptibility to the common cold. *Health Psychology, 17,* 214–223.

Cole, S., Korin, Y., Fahey, J., & Zack, J. (1998). Norepinephrine accelerates HIV replication via protein kinase A–dependent effects on cytokine production. *Journal of Immunology, 161,* 610–616.

Collins, A. M., & Loftus, E. F. (1975). A spreading-activation theory of semantic processing. *Psychological Review, 82,* 407–428.

Collins, A. M., & Quillian, M. R. (1969). Retrieval time from semantic memory. *Journal of Verbal Learning and Verbal Behavior, 8,* 240–248.

Colom, R., Juan-Espinosa, M., Abad, F., & García, L. (2000). Negligible sex differences in general intelligence. *Intelligence, 28*(1), 57–68.

Colonna-Pydyn, C., Gjesfjeld, C., & Greeno, C. (2007). The factor structure of the Barriers to Treatment Participation Scale (BTPS): Implications for future barriers scale development. *Administration and Policy in Mental Health and Mental Health Services Research, 34,* 563–569.

Comings, D. E., & Blum, K. (2000). Reward deficiency syndrome: Genetic aspects of behavioral disorders. *Progress in Brain Research, 126,* 325–341.

Commerce Clearing House. (2006). Retrieved October 3, 2009, from http://www.cch.com/

Conde-Agudelo, A., Belizan, J. M., & Diaz-Rossello, J. (2011). Kangaroo mother care to reduce morbidity and mortality in low birthweight infants. *Cochrane Database of Systematic Reviews, 3.* doi: 10.1002/14651858.CD002771.pub2

Conn, P. J., Battaglia, G., Marino, M. J., & Nicoletti, F. (2005). Metabotropic glutamate receptors in the basal ganglia motor circuit. *Nature Reviews Neuroscience, 6*(10), 787–798.

Connolly, J. J., & Viswesvaran, C. (2000). The role of affectivity in job satisfaction: A meta-analysis. *Personality and Individual Differences, 29,* 265–281.

Connelly, M. (2000, February 29). Poll Finds That Half in State Disagree With Diallo Verdict. New York Times. Retrieved from http://www.nytimes.com/2000/02/29/nyregion/poll-finds-that-half-in-state-disagree-with-diallo-verdict.html.

Conway, A., Kane, M., & Engle, R. (2003). Working memory capacity and its relation to general intelligence. *Trends in Cognitive Sciences, 7*(12), 547–552.

Conway, J. M., Lombardo, K., & Sanders, K. C. (2001). A meta-analysis of incremental validity and nomological networks for subordinate and peer rating. *Human Performance, 14*(4), 267–303.

Cook, E. W., Hodes, R. L., & Lang, P. J. (1986). Preparedness and phobia: Effects of stimulus content on human visceral conditioning. *Journal of Abnormal Psychology, 95,* 195–207.

Corballis, M. C. (1993). *The lopsided ape.* Oxford, UK: Oxford University Press.

Cordery, J. L. (1996). Autonomous work groups and quality circles. In M. A. West (Ed.), Handbook of work group psychology (pp. 225–246). Chichester, U.K.: John Wiley.

Correll, J., Park, B., Judd, C. M., & Wittenbrink, B. (2007). The influence of stereotypes on decisions to shoot. *European Journal of Social Psychology, 37*(6), 1102–1117.

Correll, J., Urland, G. R., & Ito, T. A. (2006). Event-related potentials and the decision to shoot: The role of threat perception and cognitive control. *Journal of Experimental Social Psychology, 42*(1), 120–128.

Corrigan, P. (2004). How stigma interferes with mental health care. *American Psychologist, 59,* 614–625.

Corso, P. S., Mercy, J. A., Simon, T. R., et al. (2007). Medical costs and productivity losses due to interpersonal and self-directed violence in the United States. *American Journal of Preventative Medicine, 32,* 474–482.

Cosgrove, G. R., & Rauch, S. L. (2003). Stereotactic cingulotomy. *Neurosurgery Clinics of North America, 13,* 225–235.

Côté, S. (1999). Affect and performance in organizational settings. *Current Directions in Psychological Science, 8*(2), 65–68.

Cotman, C. W., & Berchtold, N. C. (2002). Exercise: A behavioral intervention to enhance brain health and plasticity. *Trends in Neuroscience, 25,* 295–301.

Cottrell, N. B. (1972). Social facilitation. In C. G. McClintock (Ed.), *Experimental social psychology* (pp. 185–236). New York: Holt.

Cowan, N., Lichty, W., & Grove, T. R. (1990). Properties of memory for unattended spoken syllables. *Journal of Experimental Psychology: Learning, Memory, and Cognition, 16*(2), 258–269.

Cox, C., Arndt, J., Pyszczynski, T., Greenberg, J., Abdollahi, A., & Solomon, S. (2008). Terror manage-

ment and adults' attachment to their parents: The safe haven remains. *Journal of Personality and Social Psychology, 94*(4), 696–717.

Coyle, T. (2006). Test–retest changes on scholastic aptitude tests are not related to *g. Intelligence, 34*(1), 15–27.

Coyle, T., & Pillow, D. (2008). SAT and ACT predict college GPA after removing *g. Intelligence, 36*(6), 719–729.

Cragan, J. D., Friedman, J. M., Holmes, L. B., Uhl, K., Green, N. S., & Riley, L. (2006). Ensuring the safe and effective use of medications during pregnancy: Planning and prevention through preconception care. *Maternal and Child Health Journal, 10,* S129–S135.

Craig, I., & Plomin, R. (2006). Quantitative trait loci for IQ and other complex traits: Single-nucleotide polymorphism genotyping using pooled DNA and microarrays. *Genes, Brain and Behavior, 5*(suppl 1), 32–37.

Craig, I. W., & Halton, K. E. (2009). Genetics of human aggressive behavior. *Human Genetics, 126,* 101–113.

Craik, F., & Lockhart, R. (1972). Levels of processing: A framework for memory research. *Journal of Verbal Learning & Verbal Behavior, 11,* 671–684.

Craik, F., & Tulving, E. (1975). Depth of processing and the retention of words in episodic memory. *Journal of Experimental Psychology: General, 104,* 268–294.

Craik, F., & Watkins, M. (1973). The role of rehearsal in short-term memory. *Journal of Verbal Learning & Verbal Behavior, 12,* 599–607.

Cramer, R., Lipinski, R., Meteer, J., & Houska, J. (2008). Sex differences in subjective distress to unfaithfulness: Testing competing evolutionary and violation of infidelity expectations hypotheses. *Journal of Social Psychology, 148*(4), 389–405.

Craske, M., Edlund, M., Sullivan, G., Sherbourne, C., Stein, M., & Bystritsky, A. (2005). Perceived unmet need for mental health treatment and barriers to care among patients with panic disorder. *Psychiatric Services, 56,* 988–994.

Crawford, M., Chaffin, R., & Fitton, L. (1995). Cognition in social context. *Learning and Individual Differences, 7*(4), 341–362.

Crawley, A. M., Anderson, D. R., Wilder, A., Williams M., & Santomero A. (1999). Effects of repeated exposures to a single episode of the television program *Blue's Clues* on the viewing behaviors and comprehension of preschool children. *Journal of Educational Psychology, 91,* 630–638.

Critchley, H., Daly, E., Phillips, M., Brammer, M., Bullmore, E., Williams, S., Van Amelsvoort, T., Robertson, D., David, A., & Murphy, D. (2000). Explicit and implicit neural mechanisms for processing of social information from facial expressions: A functional magnetic resonance imaging study. *Human Brain Mapping, 9,* 93–105.

Crouter, A., Lanza, S., Pirretti, A., Goodman, W., & Neebe, E. (2006). The O★Net jobs classification system: A primer for family researchers. *Family Relations, 55*(4), 461–472.

Crowell, S. E., Beauchaine, T. P., & Linehan, M. M. (2009). A biosocial developmental model of borderline personality: Elaborating and extending Linehan's theory. *Psychological Bulletin, 125,* 495–510.

Csibra, G., Davis, G., Spratling, M. W., & Johnson, M. H. (2000). Gamma oscillations and object processing in the infant brain. *Science, 290,* 1582–1585.

Cukor, J., Spitalnick, J., Difede, J., Rizzo, A., & Rothbaum, B. O. (2009). Emerging treatments for PTSD. *Clinical Psychology Review, 29,* 715–726.

Cummings, D. (2006). Ghrelin and the short- and long-term regulation of appetite and body weight. *Physiology & Behavior, 89*(1), 71–84.

Cunningham, W. A., Johnson, M. K., Raye, C. L., Gatenby, J. C., Gore, J. C., & Banaji, M. R. (2004). Separable neural components in the processing of Black and White faces. *Psychological Science, 15,* 806–813.

Cutrona, C., Wallace, G., & Wesner, K. (2006). Neighborhood characteristics and depression: An examination of stress processes. *Current Directions in Psychological Science, 15*(4), 188–192.

D'Argembeau, A., Raffard, S., & Van der Linden, M. (2008). Remembering the past and imaging the future in schizophrenia. *Journal of Abnormal Psychology, 117,* 247–251.

Dabbs, J. M., Riad, J. K., & Chance, S. E. (2001). Testosterone and ruthless homicide. *Personality and Individual Differences, 31,* 599–603.

Dal Cin, S., Gibson, B., Zanna, M. P., Shumate, R., & Fong, G. T. (2007). Smoking in movies, implicit associations of smoking with the self, and intentions to smoke. *Psychological Science, 18,* 559–563.

Daley, T. C., Whaley, S. E., Sigman, M. D., Espinosa, M. P., & Neumann C. (2003). IQ on the rise: The Flynn effect in rural Kenyan children. *Psychological Science, 14*(3), 215–219.

Damisch, L., Stoberock, B., & Mussweiler, T. (2010). Keep your fingers crossed! How superstition improves performance. *Psychological Science, 21,* 1014–1020.

Danaei, G., Ding, E. L., Mozaffarian, D., Taylor B, & Rehm J. 2009 The preventable causes of death in the United States: Comparative risk assessment of dietary, lifestyle, and metabolic risk factors. *PLoS Med, 6*(4), e1000058. doi: 10.1371/journal. pmed.1000058

Daneback, K., Cooper, A., & Månsson, S. (2005). An Internet study of cybersex participants. *Archives of Sexual Behavior, 34,* 321–328.

Dani, C., Poggi, C., Romagnoli, C., & Bertini, G. (2009). Survival and major disability rate in infant born at 22–25 weeks of gestation. Journal of Perinatal Medicine, 37, 599–608.

Danziger, N., Faillenot, I., & Peyron, R. (2009). Can we share a pain we never felt? Neural correlations of empathy in patients with congenial insensitivity to pain. *Neuron, 61,* 203–212.

Darley, J. M., & Latane, B. (1968). Bystander intervention in emergencies: Diffusion of responsibility. *Journal of Personality and Social Psychology, 8,* 377–383.

Dar-Nimrod, I., & Heine, S. J. (2006). Exposure to scientific theories affects women's math performance. *Science, 314*(5798), 435.

Dar-Nimrod, I., Rawn, C. D., Lehman, D. R., & Schwartz, B. (2009). The maximization paradox: The costs of seeking alternatives. *Personality and Individual Differences, 46*(5–6), 631–635.

Darwin, C. (1872). *The expression of emotion in man and animals.* London: John Murray.

Daselaar, S. M., Dennis, N. A., & Cabeza, R. (2007). Ageing: Age-related changes in episodic and working memory. In S. A. R. B. Rombouts, F. Barkhof, & P. Scheltens (Eds.), *Clinical applications of functional brain MRI* (pp. 115–148). New York: Oxford University Press.

Dastoor, S. F., Misch, C. E., & Wang, H. L. (2007). Botulinum toxin (Botox) to enhance facial macroesthetics: A literature review. *Journal of Oral Implantology, 33*(3), 164–171.

Davis, B., & Knowles, E. S. (1999). A disrupt-then-reframe technique of social influence. *Journal of Personality and Social Psychology, 76*(2), 192–199.

Davis, C. L., Tomporowski, P. D., McDowell, J. E., Austin, B. P., Miller, P. H., Yanasak, N. E., et al. (2011). Exercise improves executive function and achievement and alters brain activation in overweight children: A randomized, controlled trial. *Health Psychology, 30,* 91–98.

Davis, D., & Loftus, E. (2009). The scientific status of "repressed" and "recovered" memories of sexual abuse. In K. S. Douglas, J. L. Skeem, & S.O. Lilienfeld (Eds.), *Psychological science in the courtroom: Consensus and controversy* (pp. 55–79). New York: Guilford Press.

Davis, M. H. (2004). Empathy: Negotiating the border between self and other. In L. Z. Tiedens & C. W. Leach (Eds.), *The social life of emotions* (pp. 19–42). New York: Cambridge University Press.

Davis, M. H., Mitchell, K. V., Hall, J. A., Lothert, J., Snapp, T., & Meyer, M. (1999). Empathy, expectations, and situational preferences: Personality influences on the decision to participate in volunteer helping behaviors. *Journal of Personality, 67*(3), 469–503.

Dawson, M., Soulières, I., Gernsbacher, M., & Mottron, L. (2007). The level and nature of autistic intelligence. *Psychological Science, 18*(8), 657–662.

Day, D., & Schleicher, D. (2006). Self-monitoring at work: A motive-based perspective. *Journal of Personality, 74*(3), 685–713.

de Araujo, I. E., & Rolls, E. T. (2004). Representation in the human brain of food texture and oral fat. *Journal of Neuroscience, 24,* 3086–3093.

De Bruin, E., Beersma, D., & Daan, S. (2002). Sustained mental workload does not affect subsequent sleep intensity. *Journal of Sleep Research, 11*(2), 113–121.

de Jonghe, F., Kool, S., van Aalst, G., Dekker J, & Peen J. (2001). Combining psychotherapy and antidepressants in the treatment of depression. *Journal of Affective Disorders, 64,* 217–229.

De Los Reyes, A., & Kazdin, A. (2008). When the evidence says, "yes, no, and maybe so": Attending to and interpreting inconsistent findings among evidence-based interventions. *Current Directions in Psychological Science, 17,* 47–51.

De Valk, H., & Liefbroer, A. C. (2007). Timing preferences for women's family-life transitions: Intergenerational transmission among migrants and Dutch. *Journal of Marriage and Family, 69,* 190–206.

de Waal, F. B. M., & Lanting, F. (1997) *Bonobo: The forgotten ape.* Berkeley and Los Angeles, CA: University of California Press.

Deary, I. R, Irwing, P., Der, G., & Bates, T. C. (2007). Brother–sister differences in the g factor in intelligence: Analysis of full, opposite-sex siblings from the NLSY1979. *Intelligence, 35*(5), 451–456.

Deary, I. J., Johnson, W., & Houlihan, L. M. (2009). Genetic foundations of human intelligence. *Human Genetics, 126,* 215–232.

Deary, I. J., Penke, L., & Johnson, W. (2010). The neuroscience of human intelligence differences. *Nature Reviews Neuroscience, 11,* 201–211.

DeCasper, A. J., & Spence, M. J. (1986). Prenatal maternal speech influences newborns' perception of speech sounds. *Infant Behavior and Development, 9,* 133–150.

Decety, J. (2010). To what extent is the experience of empathy mediated by shared neural circuits? *Emotion Review, 2*(3), 204–207.

Deese, J. (1959). On the prediction of occurrence of particular verbal intrusions in immediate recall. *Journal of Experimental Psychology, 58*(1), 17–22.

Delgado, J. M. R., & Anand, B. K. (1952). Increase of food intake induced by electrical stimulation of the lateral hypothalamus. *American Journal of Physiology, 172,* 162–168.

DeLisi, L. E. (1992). The significance of age of onset for schizophrenia. *Schizophrenia Bulletin, 18,* 209–215.

DeLoache, J. S. (1995). Early understanding and use of symbols: The model model. *Current Directions in Psychological Science, 4,* 109–113.

DeLoache, J. S., Uttal, D. H., & Rosengren, K. S. (2004). Scale errors offer evidence for a perception–action dissociation early in life. *Science, 304,* 1027–1029.

Department of Justice. (2001). *Policing and homicide, 1976–98: Justifiable homicide by police, police officers murdered by felons* (NCJ180987). Washington, DC: Bureau of Justice Statistics.

Derntl, B., Windischberger, C., Robinson, S., Kryspin-Exner, I., Gur, R. C., Moser, E., & Habel, U. (2009). Amygdala activity to fear and anger in healthy young males is associated with testosterone. *Psychoneuroendocrinology, 34*(5), 687–693.

DeRubeis, R., & Crits-Christoph, P. (1998). Empirically supported individual and group psychological treatments for adult mental disorders. *Journal of Consulting and Clinical Psychology, 66,* 37–52.

DeYoung, C. G., Hirsh, J. B., Shane, M. S., Papademetris, X., Rajeevan, N., & Gray, J. R. (2010). Testing predictions from personality neuroscience: Brain structure and the Big Five. *Psychological Science, 21,* 820–828.

Díaz-Morales, J. F. (2007). Morning and evening-types: Exploring their personality styles. *Personality and Individual Differences, 43*(4), 769–778.

Dick, D. M. (2007). Identification of genes influencing a spectrum of externalizing psychopathology. *Current Directions in Psychological Science, 16,* 331–335.

Dick, F., Bates, E., Wulfeck, B., Utman, J. A., Dronkers, N., & Gernsbacher, M. A. (2001). Language deficits, localization, and grammar: Evidence for a distributive model of language breakdown in aphasic patients and neurologically intact individuals. *Psychological Review, 108,* 759–788.

Dierdorff, E., & Morgeson, F. (2007). Consensus in work role requirements: The influence of discrete occupational context on role expectations. *Journal of Applied Psychology, 92*(5), 1228–1241.

Dijksterhuis, A., & Bargh, J. A. (2001). The perception–behavior expressway: Automatic effects of social perception on social behavior. In M. P. Zanna (Ed.), *Advances in experimental social psychology* (pp. 1–40). San Diego, CA: Academic Press.

Dijkstra, A., Jaspers, M., & van Zwieten, M. (2008). Psychiatric and psychological factors in patient decision making concerning antidepressant use. *Journal of Consulting and Clinical Psychology, 76,* 149–157.

Dill, J., & Anderson, C. A. (1995). Effects of justified and unjustified frustration on aggression. *Aggressive Behavior, 21,* 359–369.

Dillard, J. P., Hunter, J. E., & Burgoon, M. (1984). Sequential-request persuasive strategies: Meta-analysis of foot-in-the-door and door-in-the-face. *Human Communication Research, 10*(4), 461–488.

Dingemanse, N. J., Both, C., Drent, P. J., & Tinbergen, J. M. (2004). Fitness consequences in a fluctuating environment. *Proceedings of the Royal Society of London, Series B, 271,* 847–852.

Ditzen, B., Schaer, M., Gabriel, B., Bodenmann, G., Ehlert, U., & Heinrichs, M. (2009). Intranasal oxytocin increases positive communication and reduces cortisol levels during couple conflict. *Biological Psychiatry, 65,* 728–731.

Domjan, M., Cusato, B., & Krause, M. A. (2004). Learning with arbitrary versus ecological conditioned stimuli: Evidence from sexual conditioning. *Psychonomic Bulletin and Review, 11,* 232–246.

Done, D. J., Crow, T. J., Johnstone, E. C., & Sacker, A. (1994). Childhood antecedents of schizophrenia and affective illness: Social adjustment at ages 7 and 11. *British Medical Journal, 309,* 699–703.

Dong, C., Wong, M-L., & Lucinio, J. (2009). Sequence variations of ABCB1, SLC6A2, SLC6A3, SLC6A4, CREB1, CRHR1, and NTRK2: Association with major depression and antidepressant response in Mexican-Americans. *Molecular Psychiatry, 14,* 1105–1118.

Donnellan, M. B., Conger, R. D., & Burzette, R. G. (2007). Personality development from late adolescence to young adulthood: Differential stability, normative maturity, and evidence for the maturity-stability hypothesis. *Journal of Personality 75*(2), 237–264.

Dormann, C., & Zapf, D. (2001). Job satisfaction: A meta-analysis of stabilities. *Journal of Organizational Behavior, 22,* 483–504.

Douglas, K. S., Guy, L. S., & Hart, S. D. (2009). Psychosis as a risk factor for violence to others: A meta-analysis. *Psychological Bulletin, 135,* 679–706.

Dozois, D., Bieling, P., Patelis-Siotis, I., Hoar, L., Chudzik, S., McCabe, K., et al. (2009). Changes in self-schema structure in cognitive therapy for major depressive disorder: A randomized clinical trial. *Journal of Consulting and Clinical Psychology, 77*(6), 1078–1088.

Duan, J., Sanders, A. R., & Gejman, P. V. (2010). Genome-wide approaches to schizophrenia. *Brain Research Bulletin, 83,* 92–102.

Dukes, R. L., Clayton, S. L., Jenkins, L. T., Miller, T. L., & Rodgers, S. E. (2001). Effects of aggressive driving and driver characteristics on road rage. *Social Science Journal, 38,* 323–331.

Dunn, K. M., Cherkas, L. F., & Spector, T. D. (2005). Genetic influences on variation in female orgasmic function: a twin study. *Biology Letters, 1,* 260–263.

Durante, K. M., Li, N. P., & Haselton, M. G. (2008). Changes in women's choice of dress across the ovulatory cycle: Naturalistic and laboratory task-based evidence. *Personality and Social Psychology Bulletin, 34,* 1451–1460.

Durgin, F. H., Baird, J. A., Greenburg, M., Russell, R., Shaughnessy, K., & Waymouth, S. (2009). Who is being deceived? The experimental demands of wearing a backpack. *Psychonomic Bulletin and Review, 16,* 964–969.

Dweck, C. (2002). Beliefs that make smart people dumb. In R. J. Sternberg (Ed.), *Why smart people can be so stupid* (pp. 24–41). New Haven, CT: Yale University Press.

Dweck, C., Chiu, C-y., & Hong, Y-y. (1995). Implicit theories and their role in judgments and reactions: A wolrd from two perspectives. Psychological Inquiry, 6, 267–285.

Dykiert, D., Gale, C., & Deary, I. (2009). Are apparent sex differences in mean IQ scores created in part by sample restriction and increased male variance? *Intelligence, 37*(1), 42–47.

Eagly, A. (2007). Female leadership advantage and disadvantage: Resolving the contradictions. *Psychology of Women Quarterly, 31*(1), 1–12.

Eagly, A., Karau, S., & Makhijani, M. (1995). Gender and the effectiveness of leaders: A meta-analysis. *Psychological Bulletin, 117*(1), 125–145.

Eaton, D. K., Kann, L., Kinchen, S. A., et al. (2010). Youth risk behavior surveillance—United States, 2009. *Morbidity and Mortality Surveillance Summary, 59*(SS-5), 1–148.

Eberhardt, J. L. (2005). Imaging race. *American Psychologist, 60,* 181–190.

Edwards, J. G., Gibson, H. E., Jensen, T., Nugent, F., Walther, C., Blickenstaff, J., & Kauer, J. A. (2010). A novel non-CB1/TRPV1 endocannabinoid-mediated mechanism depresses excitatory synapses on hippocampal CA1 interneurons [Electronic publication ahead of print]. *Hippocampus.*

Eich, E., Macaulay, D., Lowenstein, R. J., & Dihle, P. H. (1997). Memory, amnesia, and dissociative identity disorder. *Psychological Science, 8,* 417–422

Ekman, P., Friesen, W., O'Sullivan, M., Chan, A., Diacoyanni-Tarlatzis, I., Heider, K., et al. (1987, October). Universals and cultural differences in the judgments of facial expressions of emotion. *Journal of Personality and Social Psychology, 53*(4), 712–717.

Ekman, P., O'Sullivan, M., & Frank, M. G. (1999). A few can catch a liar. *Psychological Science, 10,* 263–266.

Elfenbein, H. A., & Ambady, N. (2002). On the universality and cultural specificity of emotion recognition: A meta-analysis. *Psychological Bulletin, 128,* 203–235.

Elfenbein, H. A., & Ambady, N. (2003). Universals and cultural differences in recognizing emotions. *Current Directions in Psychological Science, 12,* 159–164.

Elfenbein, H. A., Beaupré, M., Lévesque, M., & Hess, U. (2007). Toward a dialect theory: Cultural differences in the expression and recognition of posed facial expressions. *Emotion, 7,* 131–146.

Elkins, S. R., & Moore, T. M. (2011). A time-series study of the treatment of panic disorder. *Clinical Case Studies, 10*(1), 3–22.

Elliot, A. J., & McGregor, H. A. (2001). A 2 × 2 achievement goal framework. *Journal of Personality and Social Psychology, 80,* 501–519.

Elliot, A. J., & Murayama, K. (2008). On the measurement of achievement goals: Critique, illustration, application. *Journal of Educational Psychology, 100,* 613–628.

Ellis, A. (1962). *Reason and emotion in psychotherapy.* New York: Lyle Stuart.

Ellis, B. J., & Garber, J. (2000). Psychosocial antecedents of variation in girls' pubertal timing: Maternal depression, stepfather presence, and marital and family stress. *Child Development, 71,* 485–501.

Ellis, B. J., & Symons, D. (1990). Sex differences in sexual fantasy: An evolutionary psychological approach. *Journal of Sex Research, 27,* 527–555.

Ellis, L., & Ames, M. (1987). Neurohormonal functioning and sexual orientation: A theory of homosexuality—heterosexuality. *Psychological Bulletin, 101,* 233–258.

Epley, N., & Gilovich, T. (2001). Putting adjustment back into the anchoring and adjustment heuristic: Differential processing of self-generated and experimenter-provided anchors. *Psychological Science, 12,* 391–396.

Epley, N., & Gilovich, T. (2006). The anchoring-and-adjustment heuristic: Why the adjustments are insufficient. *Psychological Science, 17,* 311–318.

Equal Employment Opportunity Commission (EEOC) (2011). Sexual harassment. Retrieved July 14, 2011, from http://www.eeoc.gov/eeoc/statistics/enforcement/sexual_harassment.cfm

Equal Employment Opportunity Commission (EEOC) (2011). Sexual harassment. Retrieved July 14, 2011, from http://www.eeoc.gov/laws/types/sexual_harassment.cfm

Erickson, K. I., Voss, M. W., Prakash, R. S., Basak, C., Szabo, A., Chaddock, L., et al. (2011). Exercise training increases size of hippocampus and improves memory. *Proceedings of the National Academy of Sciences, 108,* 3017–3022.

Ericsson, K. A., & Polson, P. G. (1988). Memory for restaurant orders. In M. Chi, R. Glaser, & M. Farr (Eds.), *The nature of expertise* (pp. 23–70). Hillsdale, NJ: Erlbaum.

Erikson, E. (1963). *Childhood and society.* New York: Norton.

Eriksson, P. S., Perfilieva, E., Bjork-Eriksson, T., Alborn, A. M., Nordborg, C., Peterson, D. A., & Gage, F. H. (1998). Neurogenesis in the adult human hippocampus. *Nature Medicine, 4*(11), 1313–1317.

Esterberg, M. L., & Compton, M. T. (2009). The psychosis continuum and categorical versus dimensional diagnostic approaches. *Current Psychiatry Reports, 11,* 179– 184.

Evans, D., & Rothbart, M. K. (2007). Developing a model for adult temperament. *Journal of Research in Personality, 41,* 868–888.

Evans, G., & Schamberg, M. (2009). Childhood poverty, chronic stress, and adult working memory. *Proceedings of the National Academy of Sciences, 106,* 6545–6549.

Evenson, R., & Simon, R. (2005). Clarifying the relationship between parenthood and depression. *Journal of Health and Social Behavior, 46,* 341–358.

Exner, J. E. (1991). *The Rorschach: A comprehensive system. Vol. 2: Interpretation (2nd ed.).* New York: Wiley.

Eysenck, H. J. (1967). *The biological basis of personality.* Springfield, IL: Charles C. Thomas.

Facteau, C. L., Facteau, J. D., Schole, L. C., Russell, J. E.A., & Poteet, M. L. (1998). Reactions of leaders to 360 degree feedback from subordinates and peers. *Leadership Quarterly, 9*(4), 427–448.

Fancher, R. (2009). Scientific cousins: The relationship between Charles Darwin and Francis Galton. *American Psychologist, 64,* 84–92.

Fantz, R. L. (1961). The origin of form perception. *Scientific American, 47,* 627–638.

Fazel, S., Långström, N., Hjern, A., Grann, M., & Lichtenstein, P. (2009). Schizophrenia, substance abuse, and violent crime. *Journal of the American Medical Association, 301,* 2016–2023.

Federal Trade Commission. (2007). *Cigarette report for 2004 and 2005.* Washington, DC: Author.

Feldman Barrett, L., & Wager, T. D. (2006). The structure of emotion: Evidence from neuroimaging studies. *Current Directions in Psychological Science, 15,* 79–83.

Feldman, J. (2003). The simplicity principle in human concept learning. *Current Directions in Psychological Science, 12,* 227–232.

Fennis, B. M., Janssen, L., & Vohs, K. D. (2009). Acts of benevolence: A limited- resource account of compliance with charitable requests. *Journal of Consumer Research, 35*(6), 906–924.

Fernandes, M. A., & Moscovitch, M. (2000). Divided attention and memory: Evidence of substantial interference effects at retrieval and encoding. *Journal of Experimental Psychology: General, 129,* 155–176.

Fernando, G. A. (2008). Assessing mental health and psychosocial status in communities exposed to traumatic events: Sri Lanka as an example. *American Journal of Orthopsychiatry, 78*(2), 229–239.

Ferster, C. B., & Skinner, B. F. (1957). *Schedules of reinforcement.* Englewood Cliffs, NJ: Prentice Hall.

Festinger, L., Reicken, H., & Schachter, S. (1956). *When prophecy fails: A social and psychological study of a modern group that predicted the destruction of the world.* Harper-Torchbooks.

Field, A. E., Austin, S. B., Taylor, C. B., Malspeis, S., Rosner, B, Rockett, H. R., Gillman. W., &

Colditz, G. A. (2003). Relation between dieting and weight change among preadolescents and adolescents. *Pediatrics, 112,* 900–906.

Field, T., Diego, M. A., Hernandez-Reif, M., Deeds, O., & Figuereido, B. (2006). Moderate versus light pressure massage therapy leads to greater weight gain in preterm infants. *Infant Behavior and Development, 29,* 574–578.

Figueredo, A. J., Gladden, P. R., Vásquez, G., Wolf, P. S. A., Jones, D.N, et al. (2009). Evolutionary theories of personality. In P.J. Corr & G. Matthews (Eds.), *Cambridge handbook of personality psychology: Part IV. Biological perspectives* (pp. 265–274). Cambridge, UK: Cambridge University.

Finger, E. C., Marsh, A. A., Mitchell, D. G., Reid, M. E., Sims, C., Budhani, S., Kosson, D. S., Chen, G., Towbin, K., Leibenluft, E., Pine, D. S., & Blair, J. R. (2008). Abnormal ventromedial prefrontal cortex function in children with psychopathic traits during reversal learning. *Archives of General Psychiatry, 65*(5), 586–594.

Fiscella, K., Tancredi, D., & Franks, P. (2009). Adding socioeconomic status to Framingham scoring to reduce disparities in coronary risk assessment. *American Heart Journal, 157*(6), 988–994.

Fischer, E. H., & Farina, A. (1995). Attitudes toward seeking professional psychological help: A shortened form and considerations for research. *Journal of College Student Development, 36,* 368-373.

Fischer, P., Kastenmuller, A., & Greitemeyer, T. (2010). Media violence and the self: The impact of personalized gaming characters in aggressive video games on aggressive behavior. *Journal of Experimental Social Psychology, 46,* 192–195.

Fitzgerald, K. D., Welsh, R. C., Gehring, W. J., Abelson, J. L., Himle, J. A., Liberzon, I., & Taylor, S. F. (2005). Error-related hyperactivity of the anterior cingulate cortex in obsessive–compulsive disorder. *Biological Psychiatry, 57,* 287–294.

Fivush, R., & Nelson, K. (2004). Culture and language in the emergence of autobiographical memory. *Psychological Science, 15*(9), 573–577.

Flynn, J. R. (1984). The mean IQ of Americans: Massive gains 1932 to 1978. *Psychological Bulletin, 95,* 29–51.

Flynn, J. R. (1987). Massive IQ gains in 14 nations: What IQ tests really measure. *Psychological Bulletin, 101,* 171–191.

Flynn, J. R. (2007). American IQ gains from 1932 to 2002: The WISC subtests and educational progress. *International Journal of Testing, 7,* 209–224.

Folkman, S., & Lazarus, R. S. (1980). An analysis of coping in a middle-aged community sample. *Journal of Health and Social Behavior, 21,* 219–239.

Fontanilla, D., Johannessen, M., Hajipour, A. R., Cozzi, N.V., Meyer, B. J., & Ruoho, A. E. (2009). The hallucinogen N, N-dimethyltryptamine (DMT) is an endogenous sigma-1 receptor regulator. *Science, 323*(5916), 934–937.

Foroud, T., Edenberg, H. J., & Crabbe, J. C. (2010). Genetic research: Who is at risk for alcoholism? *Alcohol Research & Health, 33*(1–2), 64–75.

Foti, R., & Hauenstein, N. (2007). Pattern and variable approaches in leadership emergence and

effectiveness. *Journal of Applied Psychology, 92*(2), 347–355.

Fournier, A. K., Ehrhart, I. J., Glindemann, K. E., & Geller, E. (2004). Intervening to decrease alcohol abuse at university parties: Differential reinforcement of intoxication level. *Behavior Modification, 28*(2), 167–181.

Fouts, R. S. (1997). *Next of kin: What chimpanzees tell us about who we are.* New York: Avon Books.

Fowler, J. H., & Christakis, N. A. (2008). Dynamic spread of happiness in a large social network: Longitudinal analysis over 20 years in the Framingham Heart Study. *British Medical Journal, 337,* a2338.

Fox, E., Ridgewell, A., & Ashwin, C. (2009). Looking on the bright side: Biased attention and the human serotonin transporter gene. *Proceedings of the Royal Society, B., 276,* 1747–1751.

Fox, J., Blank, M., Rovnyak, V., & Barnett, R. (2001). Barriers to help seeking for mental disorders in a rural impoverished population. *Community Mental Health Journal, 37,* 421–436.

Fox, S. (2005). Health information online. Pew Internet and American Life Project. Retrieved from http://www.pewinternet.org

Fraley, R. C., Brumbaugh, C. C., & Marks, M. J. (2005). The evolution and function of adult attachment: A comparative and phylogenetic analysis. *Journal of Personality and Social Psychology, 89,* 731–746.

Frankel, F. H. (1993). Adult reconstruction of childhood events in the multiple personality literature. *American Journal of Psychiatry. 150,* 954–958.

Frankl, V. (1959). Man's search for meaning. New York: Washington Square Press.

Frankenhaeuser, M., Lundberg, U., Fredrikson, M., Melin, B., Tuomisto, M., Myrstern, A., Hedman, M., Bergman-Losman, B., & Willin, L. (1989). Stress on and off the job as related to sex and occupational status in white-collar workers. *Journal of Organizational Behavior, 10,* 321–346.

Franks, N., & Richardson, T. (2006). Teaching in tandem-running ants. *Nature, 439,* 153.

Freire, A., Lee, K., & Symons, L. (2000). The face-inversion effect as a deficit in the encoding of configural information: Direct evidence. *Perception, 29,* 159–170.

Freud, A. (1936). *The ego and the mechanisms of defense.* London: Hogarth Press & Institute of Psycho-Analysis.

Freud, S. (1896/1954). *The origins of psychoanalysis: Letters to Wilhelm Fliess.* London: Imago.

Freud, S. (1905/2000). *Three essays on the theory of sexuality.* New York: Basic Books Classics.

Freud, S. (1920). *A general introduction to psychoanalysis.* New York: Liveright Publishing.

Friedman, H. S., & Booth-Kewley, S. (1987). The "disease-prone personality": A meta-analytic view of the construct. *American Psychologist, 42*(6), 539–555.

Friedman, M., & Rosenman, R. H. (1974). *Type A behavior and your heart.* New York: Knopf.

Frigerio, A., Ceppi, E., Rusconi, M., Giorda, R., Raggi, M. E., & Fearon, P. (2009). The role played by the interaction between genetic factors and attachment in the stress response in infancy. *Journal of Child Psychology and Psychiatry, 50,* 1513–1522.

Fritz, C., & Sonnentag, S. (2006). Recovery, well-being, and performance-related outcomes: The role of workload and vacation experiences. *Journal of Applied Psychology, 91,* 936–945.

Fuller, R., Nopoulos, P., Arndt, S., O'Leary, D., Ho, B. C., & Andreasen, N. C. (2002). Longitudinal assessment of premorbid cognitive functioning in patients with schizophrenia through examination of standardized scholastic test performance. *American Journal of Psychiatry, 159,* 1183–1189.

Furnham, A., & Chamorro-Premuzic, T. (2004). Estimating one's own personality and intelligence scores. *British Journal of Psychology, 95*(2), 149–160.

Gais, S., Molle, M., Helms, K., & Born, J. (2002). Learning-dependent increases in sleep spindle density. *Journal of Neuroscience, 22,* 6830–6834.

Galanter, E. (1962). Contemporary psychophysics. In R. Brown, E. Galanter, E. H. Hess, & G. Mandler (Eds.), *New directions in psychology* (p. 231). New York: Holt, Rinehart, & Winston.

Gallagher, R. P. (2007). *National Survey of Counseling Center Directors (2007).* Washington, DC: International Association of Counseling Services. Retrieved from http://www.iacsinc.org/

Gallo, D., Roberts, M., & Seamon, J. (1997). Remembering words not presented in lists: Can we avoid creating false memories? *Psychonomic Bulletin & Review, 4,* 271–276.

Gallup Poll. (2009, February 11). On Darwin's birthday, only 4 in 10 believe in evolution. Data retrieved from http://www.gallup.com/poll/114544/darwin-birthday-believe-evolution.aspx

Galobardes, B., Smith, G. D., & Lynch, J. W. (2006). Systematic review of the influence of childhood socioeconomic circumstances on risk for cardiovascular disease in adulthood. *Annals of Epidemiology, 16*(2), 91–104..

Galovski, T. E., Malta, L. S., & Blanchard, E. B. (2006). Theories of aggressive driving. In T. E. Galovski, L. S. Malta, & E. B. Blanchard (Eds.), *Road rage: Assessment and treatment of the angry, aggressive driver* (pp. 27–44). Washington, DC: American Psychological Association.

Gangestad, S. W., Thornhill, R., & Yeo, R. A. (1994). Facial attractiveness, developmental stability, and fluctuating asymmetry. *Ethology and Sociobiology, 15,* 73–85.

Garb, H. N., Wood, J. M., Lilienfeld, S. O., & Nezworski, M. T. (2005). Roots of the Rorschach controversy. *Clinical Psychology Review, 25,* 97–118.

Garbutt, J. (2009). The state of pharmacotherapy for the treatment of alcohol dependence. *Journal of Substance Abuse Treatment, 36,* S15–S23.

Garcia, J., Ervin, F. R., & Koelling, R. A. (1966). Learning with prolonged delay of reinforcement. *Psychonomic Science, 5,* 121–122.

Gardner, H. (1983). *Frames of mind: The theory of multiple intelligences.* New York: Basic Books.

Gardner, H. (1999). *Intelligence reframed: Multiple intelligences for the 21st century.* New York: Basic Books.

Gardner, R. A., Gardner, B. T., & VanCantfort, T. E. (1989). *Teaching sign language to chimpanzees.* Albany, NY: State University of New York Press.

Garling, T., Kirchler, E., Lewis, A., & van Raaij, F. (2009). Psychology, financial decision making, and financial crises. *Psychological Science in the Public Interest, 10*(1), 1–47.

Garry, M., & Polaschek, D. (2000). Imagination and memory. *Current Directions in Psychological Science, 9,* 6–10.

Garry, M., Manning, C., Loftus, E., & Sherman, S. (1996). Imagination inflation: Imagining a childhood event inflates confidence that it occurred. *Psychonomic Bulletin & Review, 3*(2), 208–214.

Gaser, C., & Schlaug, G. (2003). Brain structures differ between musicians and non-musicians. *Journal of Neuroscience, 23,* 9240–9245.

Gazzaniga, M. S. (1967). The split-brain in man. *Scientific American, 217,* 24–29.

Gazzaniga, M. S. (2000). Cerebral specialization and interhemispheric communication. *Brain, 123,* 1293–1326.

Geake, J. G., & Hansen, P. C. (2010). Functional neural correlates of fluid and crystallized intelligence. *Neuroimage, 49,* 3489–3497.

Geier, A., Rozin, P., & Doros, G. (2006). Unit bias: A new heuristic that helps explain the effect of portion size on food intake. *Psychological Science, 17*(6), 521–525.

Gershoff, E. T. (2002). Parental corporal punishment and associated child behaviors and experiences: A meta-analytic and theoretical review. *Psychological Bulletin, 128,* 539–579.

Gershoff, E. T., & Bitensky, S. H. (2007). The case against corporal punishment of children: Converging evidence from social science research and international human rights law and implications for U.S. public policy. *Psychology, Public Policy, and the Law, 13,* 231–272.

Giacino, J., Ashwal, S., Childs, N., Cranford, R., Jennett, B., Katz, D., et al. (2002). The minimally conscious state: Definition and diagnostic criteria. *Neurology, 58*(3), 349–353.

Gibbons, M., Crits-Christoph, P., & Hearon, B. (2008). The empirical status of psychodynamic therapies. *Annual Review of Clinical Psychology, 4,* 93–108.

Giedd, J. N. (2008). The teen brain: Insights from neuroimaging. *Journal of Adolescent Health, 42,* 335–343.

Gigone, D., & Hastie, R. (1997). Proper analysis of the accuracy of group judgments. *Psychological Bulletin, 121*(1), 149–167.

Gilligan, C. (1982). *In a different voice: Psychological theory and women's development.* Cambridge, MA: Harvard University Press.

Gilovich, T., & Griffin, D. (2002). Introduction: Heuristics and biases: Then and now. In T. Gilovich, D. Griffin, & D. Kahneman (Eds.), *Heuristics and biases: The psychology of intuitive judgment* (pp. 1–18). New York: Cambridge University Press.

Gilovich, T., Vallone, R., & Tversky, A. (1985). The hot hand in basketball: On the misperception of random sequences. *Cognitive Psychology, 17,* 295–314.

Giorgio, A., Watkins, K. E., Chadwick, M., James, S., Winmill, L., Douaud, G., De Stefano N., Matthews P. M., Smith S. M., Johansen-Berg H., James A. C., et al. (2010). Longitudinal changes in grey and white matter during adolescence. *Neuroimage, 49,* 94–103.

Glaser, J. P., Os, J. V., Mengelers, R., & Myin-Germeys, I. (2008). A momentary assessment study of the reputed emotional phenotype associated with borderline personality disorder. *Psychological Medicine, 30,* 1–9.

Glenberg, A., Smith, S., & Green, C. (1977). Type I rehearsal: Maintenance and more. *Journal of Verbal Learning & Verbal Behavior, 16,* 339–352.

Glenn, N. D. (1990). Quantitative research on marital quality in the 1980s: A critical review. *Journal of Marriage and the Family, 52,* 818–831.

Glick, P., & Fiske, S. T. (1996). The Ambivalent Sexism Inventory: Differentiating hostile and benevolent sexism. *Journal of Personality and Social Psychology, 70,* 491–512.

Glick, P., & Fiske, S. T. (2001). An ambivalent alliance: Hostile and benevolent sexism as complementary justifications for gender inequality. *American Psychologist, 56,* 109–118.

Glindemann, K. E., Ehrhart, I. J., Drake, E. A., & Geller, E. S., (2007). Reducing excessive alcohol consumption at university fraternity parties: A cost-effective incentive/reward intervention. *Addictive Behaviors, 32*(1), 39–48.

Glindemann, K. E., Wiegand, D. M., & Geller, E. S. (2007). Celebratory drinking and intoxication: A contextual influence on alcohol consumption. *Environment and Behavior, 39*(3), 352–366.

Godden, D., & Baddeley, A. (1975). Context-dependent memory in two natural environments: On land and underwater. *British Journal of Psychology, 66,* 325–331.

Gogtay, N., Giedd, J. N., Lusk, L., Hayashi, K. M., Greenstein, D., Vaituzis, C., et al. (2004). Dynamic mapping of human cortical development during childhood through early adulthood. *Proceedings of the National Academy of Sciences, 101,* 8174–8179.

Goh, J. O., Chee, M. W., Tan, J. C., Venkatraman, V., Hebrank, A., Leshikar, E. D., et al. (2007). Age and culture modulate object processing and object-scene binding in the ventral visual area. *Cognitive, Affective, & Behavioral Neuroscience, 7,* 44–52.

Goldin, P. R., & Gross, J. J. (2010). Effects of mindfulness-based stress reduction (MBSR) on emotion regulation in social anxiety disorder. *Emotion, 10,* 83–91.

Goldman-Rakic, P. S. (1996). The prefrontal landscape: Implications of functional architecture for understanding human mentation and the central executive. *Philosophical Transactions of the Royal Society of London (B Biological Sciences), 351*(1346), 1445–1453.

Goldstein, R. B., Compton, W. M., Pulay, A. J., Ruan, W. J., Pickering, R. P., Stinson, F. S., & Brant, B. F. (2007). Antisocial behavioral syndromes and DSM-IV drug use disorders in the United States: Results from the National Epidemiologic Survey on Alcohol Related Conditions. *Drug and Alcohol Dependence, 90,* 145–158.

Goodall, J. (1999) *Reason for hope: A spiritual journey.* New York: Warner Books.

Gopnik, A. (2010). *The philosophical baby.* New York: Farrar, Straus, & Giroux

Goren, H., Kurzban, R., & Rapoport, A. (2003). Social loafing vs. social enhancement: Public goods provisioning in real-time with irrevocable commitments. *Organizational Behavior and Human Decision Processes, 90,* 277–290.

Gosling, P., Denizeau, M., & Oberlé, D. (2006). Denial of responsibility: A new mode of dissonance reduction. *Journal of Personality and Social Psychology, 90,* 722–733.

Gosling, S. D. (2001). From mice to men: What can we learn about personality from animal research? *Psychological Bulletin, 127,* 45–86.

Gosling, S. D. (2008). *Snoop: What your stuff says about you.* New York: Basic Books.

Gosling, S. D., Ko, S. J., Mannarelli, T., & Morris, M. E. (2002). A room with a cue: Personality judgments based on offices and bedrooms. *Personality Processes and Individual Differences, 82,* 379–398.

Gotlib, I., & Hamilton, J. (2008). Neuroimaging and depression: Current status and unresolved issues. *Current Directions in Psychological Science, 17,* 159–163.

Gottesman, I. (1991). *Schizophrenia genesis.* New York: W. H. Freeman.

Gottesman, I., & Gould, T. D. (2003). The endophenotype concept in psychiatry: Etymology and strategic intentions. *American Journal of Psychiatry, 160,* 636–645.

Gottfredson, L. (1997). Why *g* matters : Complexity of everyday life. *Intelligence, 24,* 79–132.

Gottman, J. M., & Levenson, R. W., (1992). Marital processes predictive of later dissolution: Behavior, physiology and health. *Journal of Personality and Social Psychology, 63,* 221–233.

Gottman, J., & Levenson, R. W. (2002). A two-factor model for predicting when a couple will divorce: Exploratory analyses using 14-year longitudinal data. *Family Process, 41*(1), 83–96.

Gouin, J. P., & Kiecolt-Glaser, J. K. (2011). The impact of psychological stress on wound healing: Methods and mechanisms. *Immunology and Allergy Clinics of North America, 31,* 81–93.

Gouin, J-P., Carter, C. S., Pournajafi-Nazarloo, H., Glaser, R., Malarkey, W. B., Loving, T. J., Stowell, J., & Kiecolt-Glaser, J. K. (2010). Marital behavior, oxytocin, vasopressin, and wound healing. *Psychoneuroendocrinology, 35,* 1082–1090.

Gould, M. S., Greenberg, T., Velting, D. M., & Shaffer, D. (2003). Youth suicide risk and preventive interventions: A review of the past 10 years. *Journal of the American Academy of Child and Adolescent Psychiatry, 42,* 386–405.

Gould, S. J. (1981). *The mismeasure of man.* New York: W. W. Norton

Gould, S. J., & Lewontin, R. C. (1979). The spandrels of San Marco and the panglossian paradigm: A critique of the adaptationist approach. *Proceedings of the Royal Society of London, 205,* 581–598.

Gouzoulis-Mayfrank, E., & Daumann, J. (2006). The confounding problem of polydrug use in recreational ecstasy/MDMA users: A brief overview. *Journal of Psychopharmacology, 20,* 188–193.

Graham, K., & Wells, S. (2004). Aggression among young adults in the social context of the bar. *Addiction Research and Theory, 9,* 193–219.

Grahek, M. S., Thompson, A., & Toliver, A. (2010). The character to lead: A closer look at character in leadership. *Consulting Psychology Journal: Practice and Research, 62*(4), 270–290.

Granpeesheh, D., Tarbox, J., & Dixon, D. R. (2009). Applied behavior analytic interventions for children with autism: A description and review of treatment research. *Annals of Clinical Psychiatry, 21,* 162–173.

Grant, J. A., & Rainville, P. (2009). Pain sensitivity and analgesic effects of mindful states in Zen meditators: A cross-sectional study. *Psychosomatic Medicine, 71,* 106–114.

Grauwiler, P. (2008). Voices of women: Perspectives on decision-making and the management of partner violence. *Children and Youth Services Review, 30*(3), 311–322.

Gray, J. (1992). *Men are from Mars, women are from Venus.* New York: Harper-Collins.

Gray, P., Kahlenberg, S., Barrett, E., Lipson, S., & Ellison, P. (2002). Marriage and fatherhood are associated with lower testosterone in males. *Evolution and Human Behavior, 23*(3), 193–201.

Gray, R., Petrou, S., Hockley, C., & Gardner, F. (2007). Self-reported health status and health-related quality of life of teenagers who were born before 29 weeks' gestational age. *Pediatrics, 120,* e86–e93.

Greenberg, L., & Barling, J. (1999). Predicting employee aggression against coworkers, subordinates and supervisors. *Journal of Organizational Behavior, 20,* 897–913.

Greenwald, A. G., & Banaji, M. R. (1995). Implicit social cognition: Attitudes, self- esteem, and stereotypes. *Psychological Review, 102*(1), 4–27.

Greenwald, A. G., McGhee, D. E., & Schwartz, J. L. K. (1998). Measuring individual differences in implicit cognition: The implicit association test. *Journal of Personality and Social Psychology, 74,* 1464–1480.

Greven, C. U., Harlaar, N., Kovas, Y., Chamorro-Premuzic, T., & Plomin, R. (2009). More than just IQ: School achievement is predicted by self-perceived abilities—but for genetic rather than environmental reasons. *Psychological Science, 20,* 753–762.

Grice, J. W., Jackson, B. J., & McDaniel, B. L. (2006). Bridging the idiographic–nomothetic divide: A follow-up study. *Journal of Personality, 74,* 1191–1218.

Grice, P. (1975). Logic and conversation. In P. Cole & J. Morgan (Eds.), *Syntax and semantics* (p. 3). New York: Academic Press.

Griffeth, R., Hom, P., & Gaertner, S. (2000). A meta-analysis of antecedents and correlates of employee turnover: Update, moderator tests, and research implications for the next millennium. *Journal of Management, 26*(3), 463–488.

Griffiths, R. R., Richards, W. A., Johnson, M. W., McCann, U. D., & Jesse, R. (2008). Mystical-type experiences occasioned by psilocybin mediate the attribution of personal meaning and spiritual significance 14 months later. *Journal of Psychopharmacology, 22,* 621–632.

Grigorenko, E. L., Geissler, P. W., Prince, R., Okatcha, F., Nokes, C., & Kenny, D. A. (2001). The organization of Luo conceptions of intelligence: A study of implicit theories in a Kenyan village. *International Journal of Behavior Development, 25,* 367–378.

Grimbos, T., Dawood, K., Burriss, R. P., Zucker, K. J., & Puts, D. A. (2010). Sexual orientation and the second to fourth finger length ratio: A meta-analysis in men and women. *Behavioral Neuroscience, 124,* 278–287.

Gropper, S. S., Simmons, K. P., Gaines, A., Drawdy, K., Saunders, D., Ulrich, P., & Connell, L. J. (2009). The freshman 15: A closer look. *Journal of American College Health, 58,* 223–231.

Grossman, I., Na, J., Varnum, M. E., Park, D. C., Kitayama, S., & Nisbett, R. E. (2010). Reasoning about social conflicts improves into old age. *Proceedings of the National Academy of Sciences, 107,* 7246–7250.

Gudonis, L. C., Derefinko, K., & Giancola, P. R. (2009). The treatment of substance misuse in psychopathic individuals: Why heterogeneity matters. *Substance Use & Misuse, 44*(9–10), 1415–1433.

Guedj, E., Aubert, S., McGonigal, A., Mundler, O., & Bartolomei, F. (2010). Déjà-vu in temporal lobe epilepsy: Metabolic pattern of cortical involvement in patients with normal brain MRI. *Neuropsychologia, 48*(7), 2174–2181.

Gutchess, A. H., Hedden, T., Ketay, S., Aron, A., & Gabrieli, J. D. (2010). Neural differences in the processing of semantic relationships across cultures. *Social Cognitive and Affective Neuroscience, 5,* 254–263.

Haber, J., & Jacob, T. (2007). Alcoholism risk moderation by a socio-religious dimension. *Journal of Studies on Alcohol and Drugs, 68*(6), 912–922.

Hackenberg, T. D. (2009). Token reinforcement: A review and analysis. *Journal of the Experimental Analysis of Behavior, 91,* 257–286.

Haidt, J. (2001). The emotional dog and its rational tail: A social intuitionist approach to moral judgment. *Psychological Review, 108,* 814–834.

Hakuta, K., Bialystok, E., & Wiley, E. (2003). Critical evidence: A test of the critical-period hypothesis for second-language acquisition. *Psychological Science, 14,* 31–38.

Hall, E., Esty, E., & Fisch, S. (1990). Television and children's problem-solving behavior: A synopsis of an evaluation of the effects of Square One TV. *Journal of Mathematical Behavior, 9*(2), 161–174.

Halpern, D. F. (1996). *Thought and knowledge: An introduction to critical thinking.* Mahwah, NJ: Lawrence Erlbaum.

Halpern, D., & LaMay, M. (2000). The smarter sex: A critical review of sex differences in intelligence. *Educational Psychology Review, 12*(2), 229–246.

Halpern-Felsher, B. L., Cornell, J. L., Kropp, R. Y., & Tschann, J. M. (2005). Oral versus vaginal sex among adolescents: Perceptions, attitudes, and behavior. *Pediatrics, 4,* 845–851.

Hamilton, W. D. (1964). The genetical evolution of social behavior. I. *Journal of Theoretical Biology, 7,* 1–16.

Hane, A. A., Feldstein, S., & Dernetz, V. H. (2003). The relation between coordinated interpersonal timing and maternal sensitivity in four-month-old infants. *Journal of Psycholinguistic Research, 32,* 525–539.

Haney, C., & Zimbardo, P. (1998). The past and future of U.S. prison policy: Twenty-five years after the Stanford Prison Experiment. *American Psychologist, 53,* 709–727.

Haney, C., Banks, C., & Zimbardo, P. (1973). Interpersonal dynamics in a simulated prison. *International Journal of Criminology & Penology, 1,* 69–97.

Hare, R. D., & Neumann, C. S. (2008). Psychopathy as a clinical and empirical construct. *Annual Review of Clinical Psychology, 4,* 217–246.

Harley, T. A. (2001). *The psychology of language: From data to theory.* New York: Psychology Press.

Harlow, H. F. (1958). The nature of love. *American Psychologist, 13,* 673–685.

Harlow, H. F., Dodsworth, R. O., & Harlow, M. K. (1965). Total social isolation in monkeys. *Proceedings of the National Academy of Sciences, 54,* 90–97.

Harris, J. L., Bargh, J. A., & Brownell, K. D. (2009). Priming effects of television food advertising on eating behavior. *Health Psychology, 28*(4), 404–413.

Harter, S., & Monsour, A. (1992). Developmental analysis of conflict caused by opposing attributes in the adolescent self-portrait. *Developmental Psychology, 28,* 251–260.

Harvey, A., Tang, N., & Browning, L. (2005). Cognitive approaches to insomnia. *Clinical Psychology Review, 25*(5), 593–611.

Harvey, K., Kemps, E., & Tiggemann, M. (2005). The nature of imagery processes underlying food cravings. *British Journal of Health Psychology, 10*(1), 49–56.

Harvey, P., & Walker, E. (Eds.). (1987). *Positive and negative symptoms of psychosis: Description, research, and future directions.* Hillsdale, NJ: Lawrence Erlbaum Associates.

Haselton, M. G., Mortezaie, M., Pillsworth, E. G., Bleske-Rechek, A., & Frederick, D. A. (2007). Ovulatory shifts in human female ornamentation: Near ovulation, women dress to impress. *Hormones and Behavior, 51,* 40–45.

Hatsopoulos, N. G., & Donoghue, J. P. (2009). The science of neural interface systems. *Annual Review of Neuroscience, 32,* 249–266.

Hawkley, L. C., Burleson, M. H., & Berntson, G. G. (2003). Loneliness in everyday life: Cardiovascular activity, psychosocial context, and health behaviors. *Journal of Personality and Social Psychology, 85,* 105–120.

Hayes, K. J., & Hayes, C. (1951). The intellectual development of a home-raised chimpanzee. *Proceedings of the American Philosophical Society, 95,* 105–109.

Heatherton, T. F., & Sargent, J. D. (2009). Does watching smoking in movies promote teenage smoking? *Current Directions in Psychological Science, 18,* 63–67.

Hebb, D. O. (1947). The effects of early experience on problem solving at maturity. *American Psychologist, 2,* 306–307.

Heider, F. (1958). *The psychology of interpersonal relations.* New York: Wiley.

Heine, S. J., & Buchtel, E. E. (2009). Personality: The universal and the culturally specific. *Annual Review of Psychology, 60,* 369–394.

Heinz, A., & Schlagenhauf, F. (2010). Dopaminergic dysfunction in schizophrenia: Salience attribution revisited. *Schizophrenia Bulletin, 36,* 472–485.

Hempel, A., Hempel, E., Schönknecht, P., Stippich, C., & Schröder, J. (2003). Impairment in basal limbic function in schizophrenia during affect cognition. *Psychiatry Research, 122,* 115–124.

Hendrick, C., Hendrick, S. S., & Reich, D. A. (2006). The brief sexual attitudes scale. *Journal of Sex Research, 43,* 76–86.

Henrich, J., Heine, S. J., & Norenzayan, A. (2010) The weirdest people in the world? *Behavioral and Brain Sciences, 33,* 61–135.

Herlitz, J., Wiklund, I., Caidahl, K., Hartford, M., Haglid, M., & Karlsson, B. W. (1998). The feeling of loneliness prior to coronary artery bypass grafting might be a predictor of short- and long-term postoperative mortality. *European Journal of Vascular and Endovascular Surgery, 16,* 120–125.

Herman, C. P., Roth, D. A., & Polivy, J. (2003). Effects of the presence of others on food intake: A normative interpretation. *Psychological Bulletin, 129,* 873–886.

Herman, L. M., Kuczai, S., & Holder, M. D. (1993). Responses to anomalous gestural sequences by a language-trained dolphin: Evidence for processing of semantic relations and syntactic information. *Journal of Experimental Psychology: General, 122,* 184–194.

Hernandez, A. E., & Li, P. (2007). Age of acquisition: Its neural and computational mechanisms. *Psychological Bulletin, 133,* 638–650.

Hernandez-Reif, M., Diego, M., & Field, T. (2007). Preterm infants show reduced stress behaviors and activity after 5 days of massage therapy. *Infant Behavior and Development, 30,* 557–561.

Herrnstein, R., & Murray, C. (1994). *The bell curve: Intelligence and class structure in American life.* New York: Free Press.

Hetherington, E. M., Bridges, M., & Insabella, G. M. (1998). What matters? What does not? Five perspectives on the association between marital transitions and children's adjustment. *American Psychologist, 53,* 167–184.

Hewstone, M., Rubin, M., & Willis, H. (2002). Intergroup bias. *Annual Review of Psychology, 53,* 575–604.

Heyes, C. M., & Galef, B. G. Jr. (Eds.). (1996). *Social learning in animals: The roots of culture.* San Diego: Academic Press.

Hilgard, E. (1994). Neodissociation theory. In S. J. Lynn & J. W. Rhue (Eds.), Dissociation: Clinical and theoretical perspectives (pp. 32–51). New York: Guilford Press.

Hill, C. A., & Preston, L. K. (1996). Individual differences in the experience of sexual motivation: Theory and measurement of dispositional sexual motives. *Journal of Sex Research, 33,* 27–45.

Hill, K. E., Mann, L., Laws, K. R., Stippich, C., & Schröder, J. (2004). Hypofrontality in schizophrenia: A meta-analysis of functional imaging studies. *Acta Psychiatrica Scandinavica, 110,* 243–256.

Hillman, C. H., Erickson, K. I., & Kramer, A. F. (2008). Be smart, exercise your heart: Exercise effects on brain and cognition. *Nature Review Neuroscience, 9,* 58–65.

Hillman, C. H., Snook, E. M., & Jerome, G. J. (2003). Acute cardiovascular exercise and executive control function. *International Journal of Psychophysiology, 48*(3), 307–314.

Hingson, R. W., Zha, W., & Weitzman, E. R. (2009, July). Magnitude of and trends in alcohol-related mortality and morbidity among U.S. college students ages 18–24, 1998–2005. *Journal of Studies on Alcohol and Drugs, 16*(suppl), 12–20.

Hinshaw, S. (2005). The stigmatization of mental illness in children and parents: Developmental issues, family concerns, and research needs. *Journal of Child Psychology and Psychiatry, 46*(7), 714–734.

Hirst, W., Phelps, E., Buckner, R., Budson, A., Cuc, A., Gabrieli, J., et al. (2009). Long-term memory for the terrorist attack of September 11: Flashbulb memories, event memories, and the factors that influence their retention. *Journal of Experimental Psychology: General, 138*(2), 161–176.

Hixon, J. G., & Swann, W. B. (1993). When does introspection bear fruit? Self-reflection, self-insight, and interpersonal choices. *Journal of Personality and Social Psychology, 64,* 35–43.

Hobson, J., Pace-Schott, E., & Stickgold, R. (2000). Dreaming and the brain: Toward a cognitive neuroscience of conscious states. *Behavioral and Brain Sciences, 23*(6), 793–842.

Hochhausen, N., Altmaier, E. M., McQuellon, R., Davies, S. M., Papadopolous, E., Carter, S., Henslee-Downey, J, et al. (2007). Social support, optimism, and self-efficacy predict physical and emotional well-being after bone marrow transplantation. *Journal of Psychosocial Oncology, 25*(1), 87–101.

Hodges, L. F., Anderson, P., Burdea, G. C., Hoffman, H. G., & Rothbaum, B. O. (2001). VR as a tool in the treatment of psychological and physical disorders. *IEEE Computer Graphics and Applications, 21*(6), 25–33.

Hofer, M. A. (2006). Psychobiological roots of early attachment. *Current Directions in Psychological Science, 15,* 84–88.

Hofmann, S. (2007). Cognitive factors that maintain social anxiety disorder: A comprehensive model and its treatment implications. *Cognitive Behaviour Therapy, 36,* 193–209.

Hogan, R., & Warrenfeltz, R. (2003). Educating the modern manager. *Academy of Management Learning & Education, 2*(1), 74–84.

Hojnoski, R. L., Morrison, R., Brown, M., & Matthews, W. J. (2006). Projective test use among school psychologists: A survey and critique. *Journal of Psychoeducational Assessment, 24*(2), 145–159.

Holleran, S. E., Mehl, M. R., & Levitt, S. (2009). Eavesdropping on social life: The accuracy of stranger ratings of daily behavior from thin slices of natural conversations. Journal of Research in Personality, 43, 660–672.

Hollon, S., Thase, M., & Markowitz, J. (2002). Treatment and prevention of depression. *Psychological Science in the Public Interest, 3,* 39–77.

Holm-Denoma, J. M., Gordon, K. H., Donohue, K. F., Waesche, M. C., Castro, Y., Brown, J. S., Jakobsons, L. J., Merrill, J. K., Buckner, J. D., & Joiner, T. E. (2008). Patients' affective reactions to receiving diagnostic feedback. *Journal of Social and Clinical Psychology, 27*(6), 555–575.

Holmes, T. H., & Rahe, R. H. (1967). The Social Readjustment Rating Scale. *Journal of Psychosomatic Research, 11,* 213–218.

Holstege, G., Georgiadis, J. R., Paans, A. M. J., Meiners, L. C., van der Graaf, F. H. C. E., &, Reinders, A. A. T. (2003). Brain activation during human male ejaculation. *Journal of Neuroscience, 23,* 9185–9193.

Holyoak, K. J., & Morrison R. G. (2005). Thinking and reasoning: A reader's guide. In K. J. Holyoak & R. G. Morrison (Eds.), *The Cambridge handbook of thinking and reasoning* (pp. 1–9). New York: Cambridge University Press.

Hooley, J. (2007). Expressed emotion and relapse of psychopathology. *Annual Review of Clinical Psychology, 3,* 329–352.

Hooven, C. K., Chabris, C. F., Ellison, P. T., & Kosslyn, S. M. (2004). The relationship of male testosterone to components of mental rotation. *Neuropsychologia, 42,* 782–790.

Hoover, A. E., Démonet, J. F., & Steeves, J. K. (2010). Superior voice recognition in a patient with acquired prosopagnosia and object agnosia. *Neuropsychologia, 48,* 3725–3732.

Hopkins, B., & Westra, T. (1989). Maternal expectations of their infants' development: Some cultural differences. *Developmental Medicine and Child Neurology, 31,* 384–390.

Horn, J. L., & Cattell, R. B. (1967). Age differences in fluid and crystallized intelligence. *Acta Psychologica, 26,* 107–129.

Horn, L. R., & Ward, G. (2004). *The handbook of pragmatics.* Malden, MA: Blackwell.

Horne, J., & Minard, A. (1985). Sleep and sleepiness following a behaviourally "active" day. *Ergonomics, 28*(3), 567–575.

Horner, V., & Whiten, A. (2005). Causal knowledge and imitation/emulation switching in chimpanzees (*Pan troglodytes*) and children (*Homo sapiens*). *Animal Cognition, 8,* 164–181.

Hough, L., & Oswald, F. (2000). Personnel selection: Looking toward the future—remembering the past. *Annual Review of Psychology, 51,* 631–664.

Hough, W., & O'Brien, K. (2005). The effect of community treatment orders on offending rates. *Psychiatry, Psychology and Law, 12,* 411–423., 39–77.

House, J. S., Landis, K. R., & Umberson, D. (1988). Social relationships and health. *Science, 241,* 540–545.

Howe, M. L. (2003). Memories from the cradle. *Current Directions in Psychological Science, 12*(2), 62–65.

Howell, A. J., & Watson, D. C. (2007). Procrastination: Associations with achievement goal orientation and learning strategies. *Personality and Individual Differences, 43*(1), 167–178.

Hrobjartsson, A., & Gotzsche, P. (2010). Placebo interventions for all clinical conditions. *Cochrane Database of Systematic Reviews, 1,* CD003974.

Hubel, D. H., & Wiesel, T. N. (1962). Receptive fields, binocular interaction and functional architecture in the cat's visual cortex. *Journal of Physiology, 160,* 106–154.

Hudson, J., Hiripi, E., Pope, H., & Kessler, R. (2007). The prevalence and correlates of eating disorders in the National Comorbidity Survey replication. *Biological Psychiatry, 61*(3), 348–358.

Huffman, M. A. (1996). Acquisition of innovative cultural behaviors in nonhuman primates: A case study of stone handling, a socially transmitted behavior in Japanese macaques. In C. M. Heyes & B. Galef (Eds.), *Social learning in animals: The roots of culture* (pp. 267–289). San Diego: Academic Press.

Hunt, E., & Carlson, J. (2007). Considerations relating to the study of group differences in intelligence. *Perspectives on Psychological Science, 2*(2), 194–213.

Huston, T. L., Ruggiero, M., Conner, R., & Geis, G. (1981). Bystander intervention into crime: A study based on naturally-occurring episodes. *Social Psychology Quarterly, 44,* 14–23.

Huyser, C., Veltman, D. J., de Haan, E., & Boer, F. (2009). Paediatric obsessive- compulsive disorder, a neurodevelopmental disorder? Evidence from neuroimaging. *Neuroscience and Biobehavioral Reviews, 33,* 818–830.

Hyde, J. (2005). The gender similarities hypothesis. *American Psychologist, 60*(6), 581–592.

Hyde, J., Mezulis, A., & Abramson, L. (2008). The ABCs of depression: Integrating affective, biological, and cognitive models to explain the emergence of the gender difference in depression. *Psychological Review, 115,* 291–313.

Hylton, W. S. (2006, September). Prisoner of conscience. Retrieved from http://www.gq.com/news-politics/newsmakers/200608/joe-darby-abu-ghraib

Hyman, S. E. (2007). Can neuroscience be integrated into the DSM-V? *Nature Reviews Neuroscience, 8,* 725–732.

Hypericum Depression Trial Study Group. (2002). Effect of *Hypericum perforatum* (St. John's wort) in major depressive disorder: A randomized controlled trial. *Journal of the American Medical Association, 287,* 1807–1814.

Iacono, W. G. (2001). Forensic "lie detection": Procedures without scientific basis. *Journal of Forensic Psychology Practice, 1,* 75–85.

Ingersoll, R., & Smith, T. (2003). The wrong solution to the teacher shortage. *Educational Leadership, 60,* 30–33.

Inn, A., Wheeler, A. C., & Sparling, C. L. (1977). The effects of suspect race and situation hazard on police officer shooting behavior. *Journal of Applied Social Psychology, 7,* 27–37.

Inness, M., Barling, J., & Turner, N. (2005). Understanding supervisor-targeted aggression: A within-person, between-jobs design. *Journal of Applied Psychology, 90,* 731–739.

Innocence Project. (2010, November). Retrieved from http://www.innocenceproject.org/Content/Eyewitness_Identification_Reform.php

Irwin, M., & Miller, A. (2007). Depressive disorders and immunity: 20 years of progress and discovery. *Brain, Behavior, and Immunity, 21,* 374–383.

Isenberg, D. J. (1986). Group polarization: A critical review and meta-analysis. *Journal of Personality and Social Psychology, 50*(6), 1141–1151.

Iudicello, J. E., Woods, S. P., Vigil, O., Scott J. C., Cherner M., Heaton R. K., Atkinson J. H., Grant I.; HIV Neurobehavioral Research Center (HNRC) Group. (2010). Longer term improvement in neurocognitive functioning and affective distress among methamphetamine users who achieve stable abstinence. *Journal of Clinical and Experimental Neuropsychology, 32,* 704–718.

Iyengar, S. S., Wells, R. E., & Schwartz, B. (2006). Doing better but feeling worse: Looking for the "best" job undermines satisfaction. *Psychological Science, 17*(2), 143–150.

Izard, C. E. (1994). Innate and universal facial expressions: Evidence from developmental and cross-cultural research. *Psychological Bulletin, 115,* 288–299.

Izard, V., Sann, C., Spelke, E. S., & Streri, A. (2009). Newborn infants perceive abstract numbers. *Proceedings of the National Academy of Sciences, 106,* 10382–10385.

Jackson, G., Rosen, R. C., Kloner, R. A., & Kostis, J. B. (2006). The second Princeton consensus on sexual dysfunction and cardiac risk: New guidelines for sexual medicine. *Journal of Sexual Medicine, 3,* 28–36.

Jacobs, B. (2004). Depression: The brain finally gets into the act. *Current Directions in Psychological Science, 13,* 103–106.

Jaffé, R., & Moritz, R. F. (2010). Mating flights select for symmetry in honeybee drones (*Apis mellifera*). *Naturwissenschaften, 97,* 337–343.

Jaffee, S., & Hyde, J. S. (2000). Gender differences in moral orientation: A meta-analysis. *Psychological Bulletin, 126,* 703–726.

James, L. R., & LeBreton, J. M. (2010). Assessing aggression using conditional reasoning. Current Directions in Psychological Science, 19(1), 30–35.

James, L. R., McIntyre, M. D., Glisson, C. A., Green, P. D., Patton, T. W., LeBreton, J. M., Frost, B. C., Russell, S. M., Sablynski, C. J., Mitchell, T. R., & Williams, L. J. (2005). A conditional reasoning measure for aggression. *Organizational Research Methods, 8*(1), 69–99.

Janis, I. L. (1972). *Victims of groupthink: A psychological study of foreign policy decisions and fiascoes.* Boston: Houghton Mifflin.

Jansen, A., Theunissen, N., Slechten, K., Nederkoorn, C., Boon, B., Mulkens, S., (2003). Overweight children overeat after exposure to food cues. *Eating Behaviors, 4,* 197–209.

Jed Foundation. (2009). Retrieved from http://www.jedfoundation.org/

Jensen, A. R. (2002). Galton's legacy to research on intelligence. *Journal of Biosocial Science, 34,* 145–172.

Jilek, W. G. (1995). Emil Kraepelin and comparative sociocultural psychiatry. *European Archives of Psychiatry and Clinical Neuroscience, 245,* 231–238.

Jockin, V., Arvey, R. D., & McGue, M. (2001). Perceived victimization moderates self- reports of workplace aggression and conflict. *Journal of Applied Psychology, 86,* 1262–1269.

Johns, M. W. (1991). A new method for measuring daytime sleepiness: The Epworth sleepiness scale. *Sleep, 14*(6), 540–545.

Johns, M., Schmader, T., & Martens, A. (2005). Knowing is half the battle: Teaching stereotype threat as a means of improving women's math performance. *Psychological Science, 16,* 175–179.

Johnson, K. E., & Mervis, C. B. (1997). Effects of varying levels of expertise on the basic level of categorization. *Journal of Experimental Psychology: General, 126,* 248–277.

Johnson, W., Bouchard, T. J., Krueger, R. F., McGue, M., & Gottesman, I. I. (2004). Just one *g*: Consistent results from three test batteries. *Intelligence, 32,* 95–107.

Johnson, W., te Nijenhuis, J., & Bouchard, T. (2008). Still just 1 *g*: Consistent results from five test batteries. *Intelligence, 36,* 81–95.

Joling, K. J., van Hout, H. P., Van't Veer-Tazelaar, P. J., van der Horst, H. E., Cuijpers, P., van de Ven, P. M., & van Marwijk, H. W. (2010). How effective is bibliotherapy for very old adults with subthreshold depression? Randomized controlled trial [Electronic publication ahead of print]. *American Journal of Geriatric Psychiatry.*

Jones, H. P., Karuri, S., Cronin, C. M., Ohlsson, A., Peliowski, A., Synnes, A., & Lee, S. K. (2005) Actuarial survival of a large Canadian cohort of pre-term infants. *BMC Pediatrics, 5*(40), 1–13.

Jones, J. (2008, August 4). Majority of Americans say racism against Blacks is widespread. Retrieved from http://www.gallup.com/poll/109258/majority-americans-say-racism-against-blacks-widespread.aspx

Jones, K. L., & Smith, D. W. (1973). Recognition of the fetal alcohol syndrome in early infancy. *Lancet, 2,* 999–1001.

Jonides, J., Lacey, S., & Nee, D. (2005). Processes of working memory in mind and brain. *Current Directions in Psychological Science, 14,* 2–5.

Judge, T. A., & Bono, J. E. (2001). Relationship of core self-evaluations traits—self esteem, generalized self efficacy, locus of control, and emotional stability—with job satisfaction and job performance: A meta-analysis. *Journal of Applied Psychology, 86,* 80–92.

Judge, T. A., Bono, J. E., Ilies, R., & Gerhardt, M. W. (2002). Personality and leadership: A qualitative and quantitative review. *Journal of Applied Psychology, 87*(4), 765–780.

Judge, T. A., Heller, D., & Mount, M. K. (2002). Five-factor model of personality and job satisfaction: A meta-analysis. *Journal of Applied Psychology, 87,* 530–541.

Judge, T., & Erez, A. (2007). Interaction and intersection: The constellation of emotional stability and extraversion in predicting performance. *Personnel Psychology, 60,* 573–556.

Judge, T., Martocchio, J., & Thoresen, C. (1997). Five-factor model of personality and employee absence. *Journal of Applied Psychology, 82,* 745–755.

Julius, D., & Basbaum, A. I. (2001). Molecular mechanisms of nociception. *Nature, 413,* 203–210.

Jung, D. I., & Sosik, J. J. (2002). Transformational leadership in groups: The role of empowerment, cohesiveness, and collective effectiveness. *Small Group Research, 33,* 313–336.

Jussim, L. (1986). Self-fulfilling prophecies: A theoretical and integrative review. *Psychological Review, 93,* 429–445.

Jussim, L., & Harber, K. D. (2005). Teacher expectations and self-fulfilling prophecies: Knowns and unknowns, resolved and unresolved controversies. *Personality and Social Psychology Review, 9*(2), 131–155.

Kagan, J., Snidman, N., & Arcus, D. (1998). Childhood derivatives of high and low reactivity in infancy. *Child Development, 69,* 1483–1493.

Kahneman, D. (2003). A perspective on judgment and choice: Mapping bounded rationality. *American Psychologist, 58,* 697–720.

Kahneman, D., & Miller, D. T. (1986). Norm theory: Comparing reality to its alternatives. *Psychological Review, 93,* 136–153.

Kalm, L. M., & Semba, R. D. (2005). They starved so that others be better fed: Remembering Ancel Keys and the Minnesota experiment. *Journal of Nutrition, 135,* 1347–1352.

Kamen-Siegel, L., Rodin, J., Seligiman, M. E., & Dwyer, J. (1991). Explanatory style and cell-mediated immunity in elderly men and women. *Health Psychology, 10*(4), 229–235.

Kaminski, J., Call, J., & Fischer, J. (2004). Word learning in a domestic dog: Evidence for "fast mapping." *Science, 304*(5677), 1682–1683.

Kaplan, J. T., & Iacoboni, M. (2006). Getting a grip on other minds: Mirror neurons, intention understanding, and cognitive empathy. *Social Neuroscience, 1*(3–4), 175–183.

Karakashian, L. M., Walter, M. I., & Christopher, A. N. (2006). Fear of negative evaluation affects helping behavior: The bystander effect revisited. *North American Journal of Psychology, 8,* 13–32.

Karau, S. J., & Williams, K. D. (2001). Understanding individual motivation in groups: The collective effort model. In M. E. Turner (Ed.), *Groups at work: Theory and research* (pp. 113–141). Mahwah, NJ: Lawrence Erlbaum Associates.

Kasper, S., Anghelescu, I. G., Szegedi, A., Dienel, A., & Kieser, M. (2006). Superior efficacy of St. John's wort extract WS 5570 compared to placebo in patients with major depression: A randomized, double-blind, placebo-controlled, multi-center trial [ISRCTN77277298]. *BMC Medicine, 4,* 14.

Katzell, R. A., & Austin, J. T. (1992). From then to now: The development of industrial-organizational psychology in the United States. *Journal of Applied Psychology, 77*(6), 803–835.

Kaufman, A. S. (2001). WAIS-III IQs, Horn's theory, and generational changes from young adulthood to old age. *Intelligence, 29*(1), 131–167.

Kavanagh, D. J., Andrade, J., & May, J. (2005) Imaginary relish and exquisite torture: The elaborated intrusion theory of desire. *Psychological Review, 112*(2), 446–467.

Kawai, M. (1965). Newly acquired pre-cultural behavior of a natural troop of Japanese monkeys on Koshima Island. *Primates, 6,* 1–30.

Kay, A. C., Whitson, J. A., Gaucher, D., & Galinsky, A. D. (2009). Compensatory control: Achieving order through the mind, our institutions, and the heavens. *Current Directions in Psychological Science, 18,* 264–268.

Kazdin, A. E., & Benjet, C. (2003). Spanking children: Evidence and issues. *Current Directions in Psychological Science, 12,* 99–103.

Keel, P. K., & Klump, K. L. (2003). Are eating disorders culture-bound syndromes? Implications for conceptualizing their etiology. *Psychological Bulletin, 129*(5), 747–769.

Keller, M. B., & Baker, L. A. (1991) Bipolar disorder: Epidemiology, course, diagnosis, and treatment. *Bulletin of the Menninger Clinic, 55,* 172–181.

Kelly, Y., Sacker, A., Schoon, I., & Nazroo, J. (2006). Ethnic differences in achievement of developmental milestones by 9 months of age: The Millennium Cohort Study. *Developmental Medicine and Child Neurology, 48,* 825–830.

Kenny, D. A. (2004). PERSON: A general model of interpersonal perception. *Personality and Social Psychology Review, 8,* 265–280.

Kerr, N. L., & Tindale, R. S. (2004). Group performance and decision making. *Annual Review of Psychology, 55,* 623–655.

Kessler, R. C. (2000). Posttraumatic stress disorder: The burden to the individual and to society. *Journal of Clinical Psychiatry, 61*(suppl 5), 4–12.

Kessler, R. C., Chiu, W. T., Demler, O., & Walters, E. E. (2005). Prevalence, severity, and comorbidity of twelve-month DSM-IV disorders in the National Comorbidity Survey Replication (NCS-R). *Archives of General Psychiatry, 62,* 617–627.

Kiecolt-Glaser, J. (1984). Psychosocial modifiers of immunocompetence in medical students. *Psychosomatic Medicine, 46*(1), 7–14.

Kiecolt-Glaser, J. K., & Newton, T. L. (2001). Marriage and health: His and hers. *Psychological Bulletin, 127,* 472–503.

Kihlstrom, J. F. (1997). Hypnosis, memory and amnesia. Philosophical Transactions of the Royal Society of London B: Biological *Sciences, 352,* 1727–1732.

Kihlstrom, J. F. (2005). Dissociative disorders. *Annual Review of Clinical Psychology, 1,* 227–253.

Kim, J., & Gray, K. A. (2008). Leave or stay? Battered women's decision after intimate partner violence. *Journal of Interpersonal Violence, 23,* 1465–1482.

King, S., St. Hilaire, A., & Heidkamp, D. (2010). Prenatal factors in schizophrenia. *Current Directions in Psychological Science, 19,* 209–213.

Kirk, K. M., Bailey, J. M., Dunne, M. P., & Martin, N. G. (2000). Measurement models for sexual orientation in a community twin sample. *Behavioral Genetics, 30,* 345–356.

Kirnan, J., Alfieri, J., Bragger, J., & Harris, R. (2009). An investigation of stereotype threat in employment tests. *Journal of Applied Social Psychology, 39*(2), 359–388.

Kirsch, I., & Lynn, S. (1998). Dissociation theories of hypnosis. *Psychological Bulletin, 123*(1), 100–115.

Klaczynski, P. A. (1993). Reasoning schema effects on adolescent rule acquisition and transfer. *Journal of Educational Psychology, 85,* 679–692.

Klaus, L., Berner, M. M., & Levente, K. (2008). St. John's wort for major depression. In *Cochrane Database of Systematic Reviews: Reviews 2008, 4.* Chichester, UK: John Wiley & Sons.

Kleider, H., Pezdek, K., Goldinger, S., & Kirk, A. (2008). Schema-driven source misattribution errors: Remembering the expected from a witnessed event. *Applied Cognitive Psychology, 22*(1), 1–20.

Kleim, J. A., Jones, T. A., & Shallert, T. (2003). Motor enrichment and the induction of plasticity before or after brain injury. *Neurochemical Research, 28,* 1757–1769.

Kleinman, R. E., Hall, H., Green, H., Korzec-Ramirez, D., Patton, K., Pagano, M. E. (2002). Diet, breakfast, and academic performance in children. *Annals of Nutrition and Metabolism, 46*(suppl 1), 24–30.

Kline, T., & Sulsky, L. (2009). Measurement and assessment issues in performance appraisal. *Canadian Psychology/Psychologie canadienne, 50*(3), 161–171.

Klomek, A., Marrocco, F., Kleinman, M., Schonfeld, I., & Gould, M. (2007). Bullying, depression, and suicidality in adolescents. *Journal of the American Academy of Child & Adolescent Psychiatry, 46,* 40–49.

Kluger, B. M., & Triggs, W. J. (2007). Use of transcranial magnetic stimulation to influence behavior. *Current Neurology and Neuroscience Reports, 7*(6), 491–497.

Koelsch, S. (2010). Towards a neural basis of music-evoked emotions. *Trends in Cognitive Science, 14,* 131–137.

Kohlberg, I. (1984). *The psychology of moral development: Essays on moral development* (Vol. II). San Francisco: Harper & Row.

Köksal, F., Domjan, M., Kurt, A., Sertel, Ö, Örüng, S., Bowers, R., & Kumru, G. (2004). An animal model of fetishism. *Behaviour Research and Therapy, 42,* 1421–1434.

Komisaruk, B. R., Beyer-Flores, C., & Whipple, B. (2006). *The science of orgasm.* Baltimore, MD: Johns Hopkins University Press.

Kornell, N. (2009). Optimising learning using flashcards: Spacing is more effective than cramming. *Applied Cognitive Psychology, 23,* 1297–1317.

Kornell, N., & Bjork, R. A. (2007). The promise and perils of self-regulated study. *Psychonomic Bulletin & Review, 14*(2), 219–224.

Kostic, B., & Cleary, A. M. (2009). Song recognition without identification: When people cannot "name that tune" but can recognize it as familiar. *Journal of Experimental Psychology: General, 138,* 146–159.

Kotchoubey, B., Kaiser, J., Bostanov, V., Lutzenberger, W., & Birbaumer, N. (2009). Recognition of affective prosody in brain-damaged patients and healthy controls: A neurophysiological study using EEG and whole-head MEG. *Cognitive, Affective, & Behavioral Neuroscience, 9,* 153–167.

Kouprina, N., Pavlicek, A., Mochida, G. H., Solomon, G., Gersch, W., Yoon, Y. H., et al. (2002). Accelerated evolution of the ASPM gene controlling brain size begins prior to human brain expansion. *PloS Biology, 2,* 0653–0663.

Kraemer, B., Noll, T., Delsignore, A., Milos, G., Schnyder, U., & Hepp, U. (2006). Finger length ratio (2D:4D) and dimensions of sexual orientation. *Neuropsychobiology, 53,* 210–214.

Krahé, B., & Bieneck, S. (In press). The effect of music-induced mood on aggressive affect, cognition, and behavior. *Journal of Applied Social Psychology.*

Kramer, A. F., Hahn, S., Cohen, N. J., Banich, M. T., McAuley, E., Harrison, C. R., Chason, J., Vakil, E., Bardell, L., Boileau, R. A., & Colcombe, A. (1999). Ageing, fitness and neurocognitive function. *Nature, 400,* 418–419.

Krause, D., Kersting, M., Heggestad, E., & Thornton, G. (2006). Incremental validity of assessment center ratings over cognitive ability tests: A study at the executive management level. *International Journal of Selection and Assessment, 14,* 360–371.

Kraut, R., Kiesler, S., Boneva, B., Cummings, J., Helgeson, V., & Crawford, A. (2002). Internet paradox revisited. *Journal of Social Issues, 58,* 49–74.

Kraut, R., Patterson, M., Lundmark, V., Kiesler, S., Mukopadhyay, T., & Scherlis, W. (1998). Internet paradox: A social technology that reduces social involvement and psychological well-being? *American Psychologist, 53,* 1017–1031.

Krendl, A. C., Richeson, J. A., Kelley, W. M., & Heatherton, T. F. (2008). The negative consequences of threat: A functional magnetic resonance imaging investigation of the neural mechanisms underlying women's underperformance in math. *Psychological Science, 19,* 168–175.

Kringelbach, M. L., & Aziz, T. Z. (2009). Deep brain stimulation: Avoiding errors of psychosurgery. *Journal of the American Medical Association, 301,* 1705–1707.

Kringelbach, M. L., Jenkinson, N., Owen, S. L. F., & Aziz, T. Z. (2007). Translational principles of deep brain stimulation. *Nature Reviews Neuroscience, 8,* 623–635.

Kristensen, P., & Bjerkedal, T. (2007). Explaining the relation between birth order and intelligence. *Science, 316,* 1717–1718.

Krizan, Z., & Baron, R. S. (2007). Group polarization and choice-dilemmas: How important is self-categorization? *European Journal of Social Psychology, 37*(1), 191–201.

Kruger, J., Wirtz, D., & Miller, D. (2005). Counterfactual thinking and the first instinct fallacy. *Journal of Personality and Social Psychology, 88*(5), 725–735.

Krystal, A. (2009). A compendium of placebo-controlled trials of the risks/benefits of pharmacological treatments for insomnia: The empirical basis for U.S. clinical practice. *Sleep Medicine Reviews, 13*(4), 265–274.

Kubzansky, L. D., Martin, L. T., & Buka, S. L. (2009). Early manifestations of personality and adult health: A life course perspective. *Health Psychology, 28,* 364–372.

Kubzansky, L. D., Sparrow, D., Vokonas, P., & Kawachi, I. (2001). Is the glass half empty or half full? A prospective study of optimism and coronary heart disease in the normative aging study. *Psychosomatic Medicine, 63,* 910–916.

Kühnel, J., & Sonnentag, S. (2011). How long do you benefit from vacation? A closer look at the fade-out of vacation effects. *Journal of Organizational Behavior, 32*(1), 125–143.

Kyllonen, P. C. (1996). Is working memory capacity Spearman's g? In I. Dennis & P. Tapsfield (Eds.), *Human abilities: Their nature and measurement* (pp. 49–75). New Jersey: Erlbaum.

Lakin, J. L., & Chartrand, T. L. (2003). Using nonconscious behavioral mimicry to create affiliation and rapport. *Psychological Science, 14,* 334–339.

Lakin, J. L., Jefferis, V. E., Cheng, C. M., & Chartrand, T. L. (2003). The chameleon effect as social glue: Evidence for the evolutionary significance of nonconscious mimicry. *Journal of Nonverbal Behavior, 27,* 145–162.

Lakoff, G., & Johnson, M. (1999). *Philosophy in the flesh: The embodied mind and its challenge to Western thought.* New York: Basic Books.

Lalumiere, M. L., & Quinsey, C. L. (1998). Pavlovian conditioning of sexual interest in human males. *Archives of Sexual Behavior, 27*(3), 241–252.

Lam, L. T., & Peng, Z. (2010). Effect of pathological use of the Internet on adolescent mental health: A prospective study. *Archives of Pediatric and Adolescent Medicine, 164,* 901–906.

Lambert, L. (2006, May 9). Half of teachers quit in 5 years. *The Washington Post.* Retrieved from http://www.washingtonpost.com/wp-dyn/content/article/2006/05/08/AR2006050801344.html

Laming, D. (2010). Serial position curves in free recall. *Psychological Review, 117*(1), 93–133.

Landrigan, C. P., Rothschild, J. M., Cronin, J. W., Kaushal, R., Burdick, E., Katz, J. T., Lilly, C. M., Stone, P. H., Lockley, S. W., Bates, D. W. & Czeisler, C. A. (2004). Effect of reducing interns' work hours on serious medical errors in intensive care units. *New England Journal of Medicine, 351*(18), 1838–1848.

Landrine, H., & Klonoff, E. A. (1996). The Schedule of Racist Events: A measure of racial discrimination and a study of its negative physical and mental health consequences. *Journal of Black Psychology, 22*(2), 144–168.

Laney, C., Heuer, F., & Reisberg, D. (2003). Thematically-induced arousal in naturally-occurring emotional memories. *Applied Cognitive Psychology, 17,* 995–1004.

Lang, A., Craske, M., Brown, M., & Ghaneian, A. (2001). Fear-related state dependent memory. *Cognition & Emotion, 15,* 695–703.

Lang, E. V., Benotsch, E. G., Fick, L. J., Lutgendorf, S., Berbaum, M. L., Berbaum, K. S., Logan, H., & Spiegel, D. (2000). Adjunctive nonpharmacological analgesia for invasive medical procedures: A randomised trial. *Lancet, 355,* 1486–1490.

Langhans, W. (1996a). Metabolic and glucostatic control of feeding. *Proceedings of the Nutritional Society, 55,* 497–515.

Langhans, W. (1996b). Role of the liver in the metabolic control of eating: What we know—and what we do not know. *Neuroscience and Biobehavioral Review, 20,* 145–153.

Langleben, D. D., Loughead, J. W., Bilker, W. B., Ruparel, K., Childress, A. R., Busch, S. I., & Gur, R. C. (2005). Telling truth from lie in individual subjects with fast event–related fMRI. *Human Brain Mapping, 26,* 262–272.

Långström, N., Rahman, Q., Carlström, E., & Lichtenstein, P. (2010). Genetic and environmental effects on same-sex sexual behavior: A population study of twins in Sweden. *Archives of Sexual Behavior, 39,* 75–80.

Lapierre, L. M., Spector, P. E., & Leck, J. D. (2005). Sexual versus nonsexual workplace aggression and victims' overall job satisfaction: A meta-analysis. *Journal of Occupational Health Psychology, 10*(2), 155–169.

Larsen, R., Kasimatis, M., & Frey, K. (1992). Facilitating the furrowed brow: An unobtrusive test of the facial feedback hypothesis applied to unpleasant affect. *Cognition & Emotion, 6*(5), 321–338.

Lasco, M. S., Jordan, T. J., Edgar, M. A., Petito, C. K., Byne, W., et al. (2002). A lack of dimorphism of sex or sexual orientation in the human anterior commissure. *Brain Research, 936*, 95–98.

Latane, B., & Darley, J. M. (1968). Group inhibition of bystander intervention in emergencies. *Journal of Personality and Social Psychology, 10*(3), 215–221.

Latané, B., Williams, K., & Harkins, S. (1979). Many hands make light the work: The causes and consequences of social loafing. *Journal of Personality and Social Psychology, 37*(6), 822–832.

Latane, B., Williams, K., & Harkins, S. (2006). Many hands make the light work: The causes and consequences of social loafing. In J. M. Levine & R. L. Moreland (Eds.), *Small groups* (pp. 297–308). New York: Psychology Press.

Latham, G. P., Saari, L. M., Pursell, E. D., & Campion, M. A. (1980). The situational interview. *Journal of Applied Psychology, 65*(4), 422–427.

Laumann, E., Gagnon, J. H., Michael, R. T., & Michaels, S. (1994). *The social organization of sexuality: Sexual practices in the United States.* Chicago: University of Chicago Press.

Lautenschlager, N. T., Cox, K. L., Flicker, L., Foster, J., van Bockxmeer, F. M., Xiao, J., Greenop, K., & Almeida, O. P. (2008). Effect of physical activity on cognitive function in older adults at risk for Alzheimer disease: A randomized trial. *Journal of the American Medical Association, 300*, 1027–1037.

Lavie, P. (2001). Sleep–wake as a biological rhythm. *Annual Review of Psychology, 5*, 277–303.

Lawlor, D., Clark, H., Ronalds, G., & Leon, D. (2006). Season of birth and childhood intelligence: Findings from the Aberdeen Children of the 1950s cohort study. *British Journal of Educational Psychology, 76*(3), 481–499.

LeBlanc, M. M., & Barling, J. (2004). Workplace aggression. *Current Directions in Psychological Science, 13*, 9–12.

Lederman, S. J., & Klatzky, R. L. (2004). Haptic identification of common objects: Effects of constraining the manual exploration process. *Perception and Psychophysics, 66*, 618–628.

LeDoux, J. (1994). Emotion, memory and the brain. *Scientific American, 270*, 50–57.

Lee, J. C. (2010). Memory reconsolidation mediates the updating of hippocampal memory content. *Frontiers in Behavioral Neuroscience, 4*, 1–10.

Lee, K, Gizzarone, M., & Ashton, M. (2004). Personality and the likelihood to sexually harass. *Sex Roles, 49*, 59–69.

Leighton, J. P., & Sternberg, R. J. (2003). Reasoning and problem solving. In A. F. Healy & R. W. Proctor (Eds.), *Handbook of psychology: Experimental psychology* (Vol. 4, pp. 623–648). Hoboken, NJ: John Wiley & Sons.

LePine, J. A., Piccolo, R. F., Jackson, C. L., Mathieu, J. E., & Saul, J. R. (2008). A meta-analysis of teamwork processes: Tests of a multidimensional model and relationships with team effectiveness criteria. *Personnel Psychology, 61*(2), 273–307.

Lesch, K-P., Bengel, D., Heils, A., et al. (1996). Association of anxiety-related traits with a polymorphism in the serotonin transporter gene regulatory region. *Science, 273*, 1527–1531.

Leucht, S., Arbter, D., Engel, R., Dienel, A., & Kieser, M. (2009). How effective are second-generation antipsychotic drugs? A meta-analysis of placebo-controlled trials. *Molecular Psychiatry, 14*(4), 429–447.

LeVay, S. (1991). A difference in hypothalamic structure between heterosexual and homosexual men. *Science, 253*, 1034–1037.

Levenson, C. W., & Rich, N. J. (2007). Eat less, live longer? New insights into the role of caloric restriction in the brain. *Nutrition Review, 65*, 412–415.

Levenson, R. W., & Ruef, A. M. (1997). Physiological aspects of emotional knowledge and rapport. In W. J. Ickes (Ed.), *Empathic accuracy* (pp. 44–72). New York: Guilford Press.

Levenston, G. K., Patrick, C. J., Bradley, M. M., & Lang, P. J. (2000). The psychopath as observer: Emotion and attention in picture processing. *Journal of Abnormal Psychology, 109*(3), 373–385.

Levin, R. (1994). Sleep and dreaming characteristics of frequent nightmare subjects in a university population. *Dreaming, 4*, 127–137

Levin, R., & Nielsen, T. A. (2007). Disturbed dreaming, posttraumatic stress disorder, and affect distress: A review and neurocognitive model. *Psychological Bulletin, 133*, 482–528.

Levine, M., & Crowther, S. (2008). The responsive bystander: How social group membership and group size can encourage as well as inhibit bystander intervention. *Journal of Personality and Social Psychology, 95*(6), 1429–1439.

Levitin, D. J. (2008). *The world in six songs: How the musical brain created human nature.* New York: Dutton.

Lewin, C., Wolgers, G., & Herlitz, A. (2001). Sex differences favoring women in verbal but not in visuospatial episodic memory. *Neuropsychology, 15*(2), 165–173.

Lewis, R. L., & Gutmann, L. (2004). Snake venoms and the neuromuscular junction. *Seminars in Neurology, 24*, 175–179.

Li, C. (2010). Primacy effect or recency effect? A long-term memory test of Super Bowl commercials. *Journal of Consumer Behaviour, 9*(1), 32–44.

Libertus, M. E., & Brannon, E. M. (2009). Behavioral and neural basis for number sense in infancy. *Current Directions in Psychological Science, 18*, 346–351.

Liégeois, F., Badeweg, T., Connelly, A., Gadian, D. G., Mishkin, M., & Vargha-Khadem, F. (2003). Language fMRI abnormalities associated with FOXP2 gene mutation. *Nature Neuroscience, 6*, 1230–1237.

Lilienfeld, S. (2007). Psychological treatments that cause harm. *Perspectives on Psychological Science, 2*, 53–70.

Lilienfeld, S. O., & Arkowitz, H. (2009, February). Lunacy and the full moon. *Scientific American, 20*, 64–65.

Lilienfeld, S. O., & Lynn, S. J. (2003). Dissociative identity disorder: Multiple personality, multiple controversies. In S. O. Lilienfeld, J. M. Lohr, & S. J. Lynn (Eds.), *Science and pseudoscience in clinical psychology* (pp. 109–142). New York: Guilford Press.

Lilienfeld, S. O., Lynn, S. J., Kirsch, I., Chaves, J. F., Sarbin, T. R., Ganaway, G. K., & Powell, R. A. (1999). Dissociative identity disorder and the sociocognitive model: Recalling the lessons of the past. *Psychological Bulletin, 125*, 507–523.

Lilienfeld, S. O., Wood, J. M., & Garb, H. N. (2000). The scientific status of projective techniques. *Psychological Science in the Public Interest, 1*, 27–66.

Lillard, A. (1998). Ethnopsychologies: Cultural variations in theories of mind. *Psychological Bulletin, 123*, 3–32.

Lim, W., Plucker, J., & Im, K. (2002). We are more alike than we think we are: Implicit theories of intelligence with a Korean sample. *Intelligence, 30*(2), 185–208.

Lin, C., Davidson, T., & Ancoli-Israel, S. (2008). Gender differences in obstructive sleep apnea and treatment implications. *Sleep Medicine Reviews, 12*(6), 481–496.

Lindau, S. T., Schumm, L. P., Laumann, E. O., Levinson, W., O'Muircheartaigh, C. A., & Waite, L. J. (2007). A study of sexuality and health among older adults in the United States. *New England Journal of Medicine, 357*(8), 762–774.

Linde, K., Berner, M., Egger, M., & Mulrow, C. (2005). St. John's wort for depression: Meta-analysis of randomised controlled trials. *British Journal of Psychiatry, 186*, 99–107.

Linebarger, D., & Walker, D. (2005). Infants' and toddlers' television viewing and language outcomes. *American Behavioral Scientist, 48*(5), 624–645.

Lischetze, T., & Eid, M. (2006). Why extraverts are happier than introverts: The role of mood regulation. *Journal of Personality, 74*, 1127–1161.

Liu, J. H., & Latané, B. (1998). Extremitization of attitudes: Does thought- and discussion-induced polarization cumulate? *Basic and Applied Social Psychology, 20*(2), 103–110.

LoBue, V., Rakison, D. H., & DeLoache, J. S. (2010). Threat perception across the life span: Evidence for multiple converging pathways. *Current Directions in Psychological Science, 19*, 375–379.

Loftus, E. (1975). Leading questions and the eyewitness report. *Cognitive Psychology, 7*, 560–572.

Loftus, E. F., & Davis, D. (2006). Recovered memories. *Annual Review of Clinical Psychology, 2*, 469–498.

Logothetis, N. K. (2007). The ins and outs of fMRI signals. *Nature Neuroscience, 10*(10), 1230–2.

Lounsbury, J. W., & Hoopes, L. L. (1986). A vacation from work: Changes in work and nonwork outcomes. *Journal of Applied Psychology, 71*, 392–401.

Loveland, J., Gibson, L., Lounsbury, J., & Huffstetler, B. (2005). Broad and narrow personality traits in relation to the job performance of camp counselors. *Child & Youth Care Forum, 34*, 241–255.

Lowe, K. B., Kroeck, K. G., & Sivasubramaniam, N. (1996). Effectiveness correlates of transformational and transactional leadership: A meta-analytic review. *Leadership Quarterly, 7*, 385–391.

Lowenstein, L. F. (2002). Fetishes and their associated behavior. *Sexuality and Disability, 20,* 135–147.

Luck, A., Pearson, S., Maddern, G., & Hewett, P. (1999). Effects of video information on precolonoscopy anxiety and knowledge: A randomised trial. *Lancet, 354,* 2032–2035.

Luders, E., Narr, K., Bilder, R., Szeszko, P., Gurbani, M., Hamilton, L., Toga, A. W., & Gaser, C. (2008). Mapping the relationship between cortical convolution and intelligence: Effects of gender. *Cerebral Cortex, 18*(9), 2019–2026.

Luo, L., & Craik, F. I. (2008). Aging and memory: A cognitive approach. *Canadian Journal of Psychiatry, 53,* 346–353.

Lutgendorf, S. K., Costanzo, E., & Siegel, S. (2007). Psychosocial influences in oncology: An expanded model of biobehavioral mechanisms. In R. Ader, R. Glaser, N. Cohen, & M. Irwin (Eds.), *Psychoneuroimmunology* (4th ed., pp. 869–895). New York: Academic Press.

Lynam, D. R., & Gudonis, L. (2005). The development of psychopathology. *Annual Review of Clinical Psychology, 1,* 381–407.

Lynn, R. (2006). *Race differences in intelligence: An evolutionary analysis.* Augusta, GA: Washington Summit Publishers.

Lynn, R. (2009). What has caused the Flynn effect? Secular increases in the Development Quotients of infants. *Intelligence, 37*(1), 16–24.

Lynn, S. J., & Kirsch, I. (1996). False memories, hypnosis, and fantasy-proneness. *Psychological Inquiry, 7,* 151–155.

Lynn, S., Nash, M., Rhue, J., Frauman, D., & Sweeney, C. (1984). Nonvolition, expectancies, and hypnotic rapport. *Journal of Abnormal Psychology, 93,* 295–303.

Lyznicki, J. M., Doege, T. C., Davis, R. M., & Williams, M. A. (1998). Sleepiness, driving, and motor vehicle crashes. *Journal of the American Medical Association 279,* 1908–1913.

Maccoby, E. E., & Martin, J. A. (1983). Socialization in the context of the family: Parent–child interaction. In P. H. Mussen & E. M. Hetherington, *Handbook of child psychology: Vol. 4. Socialization, personality, and social development* (4th ed., pp. 1–101). New York: Wiley.

MacCracken, M. J., & Stadulis, R. E. (1985). Social facilitation of young children's dynamic balance performance. *Journal of Sport Psychology, 7,* 150–165.

Macdonald, K., & Macdonald, T. M. (2010). The peptide that binds: A systematic review of oxytocin and its prosocial effects in humans. *Harvard Review of Psychiatry, 18,* 1–21.

MacSweeney, M., Capek, C. M., Campbell, R., & Woll, B. (2008). The signing brain: The neurobiology of sign language. *Trends in Cognitive Science, 12,* 432–440.

Maes, H. H., Neale, M. C., & Eaves, L. J. (1997). Genetic and environmental factors in relative body weight and human adiposity. *Behavioral Genetics, 27,* 325–351.

Maess, B., Koelsch, S., Gunter, T. C., & Friederici, A. D. (2001). Musical syntax is processed in Broca's area: An MEG study. *Nature Neuroscience, 4,* 540–545.

Magaletta, P. R., Mulvey, T. A., & Grus, C. L. (2010). What can I do with a degree in psychology? Retrieved from http://www.apa.org/workforce/presentations/2010-psychology-degree.pdf

Maguire, E. A., Gadian, D. G., Johnsrude, I. S., Good, C. D., Ashburner, J., Frackowiak, R. S., & Frith, C. D. (2000). Navigation-related structural changes in the hippocampus of taxi drivers. *Proceedings of the National Academy of Sciences, 97,* 4398–4403.

Mahalik, J., Good, G., & Englar-Carlson, M. (2003). Masculinity scripts, presenting concerns, and help seeking: Implications for practice and training. *Professional Psychology: Research and Practice, 34,* 123–131.

Maier, N. F. (1930). Reasoning in humans. I. On direction. *Journal of Comparative Psychology, 10*(2), 115–143.

Maier, N. F. (1931). Reasoning in humans. II. The solution of a problem and its appearance in consciousness. *Journal of Comparative Psychology, 12*(2), 181–194.

Maier, S. F., & Watkins, L. R. (1998). Cytokines for psychologists: Implications of bidirectional immune-to-brain communication for understanding behavior, mood, and cognition. *Psychological Review, 105,* 83–107.

Mampe, B., Friederici, A. D., Christophe, A., & Wermke, K. (2009). Newborns' cry melody is shaped by their native language. *Current Biology, 19,* 1994–1997.

Mangels, J. A., Butterfield, B., Lamb, J., Good, C., & Dweck, C. S. (2006). Why do beliefs about intelligence influence learning success? A social cognitive neuroscience model. *Social Cognitive and Affective Neuroscience, 1,* 75–86.

Mann, C. E., & Himelein, M. J. (2008). Putting the person back into psychopathology: An intervention to reduce mental illness stigma in the classroom. *Social Psychiatry and Psychiatric Epidemiology, 43*(7), 545–551.

Mannes, S. M., & Kinstch, W. (1987). Knowledge organization and text organization. *Cognition and Instruction, 4,* 91–115.

Manning, J. T., Scutt, D., Wilson, J., & Lewis-Jones, D. I. (1998). The ratio of the 2nd to 4th digit length: A predictor of sperm numbers and levels of testosterone, LH and oestrogen. *Human Reproduction, 13,* 3000–3004.

Manning, R., Levine, M., & Collins, A. (2007). The Kitty Genovese murder and the social psychology of helping: The parable of the 38 witnesses. *American Psychologist, 62*(6), 555–562.

Mansfield, A. K., Addis, M. E., & Courtenay, W. (2005). Measurement of men's help seeking: Development and evaluation of the barriers to help seeking scale. *Psychology of Men & Masculinity, 6,* 95–108.

Marcia, J. E. (1980). Identity in adolescence. In J. Adelson (Ed.), *Handbook of adolescent psychology* (pp. 159–187). New York: Wiley.

Marino, L. (2002). Convergence of complex cognitive abilities in cetaceans and primates. *Brain, Behavior, and Evolution, 59,* 21–32.

Marsh, R., Gerber, A. J., & Peterson, B. S. (2009). Neuroimaging studies of normal brain development and their relevance for understanding childhood neuropsychiatric disorders. *Journal of the American Academy of Child and Adolescent Psychiatry, 47,* 1233–1251.

Martin, L. (1986). "Eskimo words for snow": A case study in the genesis and decay of an anthropological example. *American Anthropologist, 88,* 418–423.

Martin, R. A. (2001). Humor, laughter and physical health: Methodological issues and research findings. *Psychological Bulletin, 127,* 504–519.

Martin, R. A. (2002). Is laughter the best medicine? Humor, laughter and physical health. *Current Directions in Psychological Science, 11,* 216–220.

Martin, R. A. (2007). *The psychology of humor: An integrative approach.* Burlington, MA: Elsevier Academic Press.

Martsh, C. T., & Miller, W. R. (1997). Extraversion predicts heavy drinking in college students. *Personality and Individual Differences, 23,* 153–155.

Maruff, P., Falleti, M. G., Collie, A., Darby, D., & McStephen, M. (2005). Fatigue-related impairment in the speed, accuracy and variability of psychomotor performance: Comparison with blood alcohol levels. *Journal of Sleep Research, 14,* 21–27.

Maruta, T., Colligan, R. C., Malinchoc, M., & Offord, K. P. (2000). Optimists vs pessimists: Survival rate among medical patients over a 30-year period. *Mayo Clinic Proceedings, 75,* 140–143.

Maslach, C. (2003). Job burnout: New directions in research and intervention. *Current Directions in Psychological Science, 12,* 189–192.

Maslach, C., Jackson, S. E., & Leiter, M. P. (1996). *Maslach burnout inventory* (3rd ed.). Palo Alto, CA: Consulting Psychologists Press.

Maslow, A. (1943). A theory of human motivation. *Psychological Review, 50,* 370–396.

Maslow, A. (1968). *Toward a psychology of being* (2nd ed.). New York: Van Nostrand.

Masters, W., & Johnson, V. (1966). *Human sexual response.* Oxford, UK: Little, Brown.

Masters, W. H., & Johnson, V. E. (1966). Human Sexual Response. Boston: Little, Brown.

Masuda, A., Suzumura, K., Beauchamp, K. L., Howells, G. N., & Clay, C. (2005). United States and Japanese college students' attitudes towards seeking professional psychological help. *International Journal of Psychology, 40,* 303–313.

Masuda, T., Ellsworth, P. C., Mesquita, B., Leu, J., Tanida, S., & van de Veerdonk, E. (2008). Placing the face in context: Cultural differences in the perception of facial emotion. *Journal of Personality and Social Psychology, 94,* 365–381.

Mather, J. A., & Anderson, R. C. (1993). Personalities of octopuses (*Octopus rubescens*). *Journal of Comparative Psychology, 107*(3), 336–340.

Matsumoto, D., Yoo, S., Fontaine, J., Anguas-Wong, A., Arriola, M., Ataca, B., et al. (2008). Mapping expressive differences around the world: The relationship between emotional display rules and individualism versus collectivism. *Journal of Cross-Cultural Psychology, 39*(1), 55–74.

Matthews, K., & Gump, B. B. (2002). Chronic work stress and marital dissolution increase risk of post-trial mortality in men from the Multiple Risk

Factor Intervention Trial. *Archives of Internal Medicine, 162,* 309–315.

Maxfield, M., Pyszczynski, T., Kluck, B., Cox, C., Greenberg, J., Solomon, S., et al. (2007). Age-related differences in responses to thoughts of one's own death: Mortality salience and judgments of moral transgressions. *Psychology and Aging, 22*(2), 341–353.

Mazzoni, G., & Memon, A. (2003). Imagination can create false autobiographical memories. *Psychological Science, 14,* 186–188.

McAdams, D. P., & Pals, J. L. (2006). A new Big Five: Fundamental principles for an integrative science of personality. *American Psychologist, 61,* 204–217.

McAndrew, F. T. (2002). New evolutionary perspectives on altruism: Multilevel- selection and costly-signaling theories. *Current Directions in Psychological Science, 11*(2), 79–82.

McAnulty, G., Duffy, F. H., Butler, S., Bernstein, J. H., Zurakowski, D., & Als, H. (2010). Effects of newborn individualized developmental care and assessment program (NIDCAP) at age 8 years: Preliminary data. *Clinical Pediatrics (Philadelphia), 49,* 258–270.

McAnulty, G., Duffy, F. H., Butler, S., Parad, R., Ringer, S., Zurakowski, D., & Als, H. (2009). Individualized developmental care for a large sample of very preterm infants: Health, neurobehaviour and neurophysiology. *Acta Paediatrica, 98,* 1920–1926.

McCarthy, A., & Garavan, T. (2007). Understanding acceptance of multisource feedback for management development. *Personnel Review, 36,* 903–917.

McCauley, C. (1987). The nature of social influence in groupthink: Compliance and internatalization. *Journal of Personality and Social Psychology, 57,* 250–260.

McClelland, A., Kemps, E., & Tiggemann, M. (2006). Reduction of vividness and associated craving in personalized food imagery. *Journal of Clinical Psychology, 62*(3), 355–365.

McClelland, D. C. (1985). How motives, skills, and values determine what people do. *American Psychologist, 40,* 812–825.

McCormick, L. M., Keel, P. K., Brumm, M. C., Bowers, W., Swayze, V., Andersen, A., & Andreasen, N. (2008). Implications of starvation-induced change in right dorsal anterior cingulate volume in anorexia nervosa. *International Journal of Eating Disorders, 41*(7), 602–610.

McCracken, L. M., Gauntlett-Gilbert, J., & Vowles, K. E. (2007). The role of mindfulness in a contextual cognitive–behavioral analysis of chronic pain-related suffering and disability. *Pain, 131,* 63–69.

McCrae, R. R. (2001). Trait psychology and culture. *Journal of Personality, 69,* 819–846.

McCrae, R. R., Martin, T. A., Hrebickova, M., Urbanek, T., Boomsma, D. I., Willemsen, G., & Costa, P. T., Jr. (2008). Personality trait similarity between spouses in four cultures. *Journal of Personality, 76,* 1137–1164.

McCrae, R. R., & Costa, P. (1987). Validation of the Five-Factor Model of personality across instruments and observers. *Journal of Personality and Social Psychology, 52*(1), 81–90.

McCrae, R. R., Terracciano, A., et al. (2005). Personality profiles of cultures: Aggregate personality traits. *Journal of Personality and Social Psychology, 89,* 407–425.

McCullough, M. E., Hoyt, W. T., Larson, D. B., Koenig, H. G., & Thoresen, C. E. (2000). Religious involvement and mortality: A meta-analytic review. *Health Psychology, 19,* 211–222.

McCullough, M. E., & Willoughby, B. L. (2009). Religion, self-regulation, and self-control: Associations, explanations, and implications. *Psychological Bulletin, 135,* 69–93.

McDaid, C., Duree, K. H., Griffin, S. C., Weatherly, H. L. A., Stradling, J. R., Davies, J. O, Sculpher, M. J., & Westwood, M. E. (2009). A systematic review of continuous positive airway pressure for obstructive sleep apnoea–hypopnoea syndrome. *Sleep Science Reviews, 13,* 427–436.

McDaniel, M., Morgeson, F., Finnegan, E., Campion, M., & Braverman, E. (2001). Use of situational judgment tests to predict job performance: A clarification of the literature. *Journal of Applied Psychology, 86*(4), 730–740.

McGlashan, T. H., Zipursky, R. B., Perkins, D., Addington J., Miller T., Woods S. W. (2006). Randomized double-blind clinical trial of olanzapine versus placebo in patients prodromally symptomatic for psychosis. *American Journal of Psychiatry, 163,* 790–799.

McGorry, P. D., Yung, A. R., Phillips, L. J., Yuen, H. P., Francey, S., Cosgrave, E. M. (2002). Randomized controlled trial of interventions designed to reduce the risk of progression to first-episode psychosis in a clinical sample with subthreshold symptoms. *Archives of General Psychiatry, 59,* 921–928.

McGowan, P. O., Sasaki, A., D'Alessio, A. C., Dymov, S., Labonte, B., Szyf, M., Turecki, G., & Meaney, M. J. (2009). Epigenetic regulation of the glucocorticoid receptor in human brain associates with childhood abuse. *Nature Neuroscience, 12*(3), 342–348.

McGruder, J. (2004). Disease models of mental illness and aftercare patient education: Critical observations from meta-analyses, cross-cultural practice and anthropological study. *British Journal of Occupational Therapy, 67,* 310–318.

McKimmie, B. M., Terry, D. J., & Hogg, M. A. (2009). Dissonance reduction in the context of group membership: The role of metaconsistency. *Group Dynamics: Theory, Research, and Practice, 13*(2), 103–119.

McKinney, K. G. (2009). Initial evaluation of Active Minds: A student organization dedicated to reducing the stigma of mental illness. *Journal of College Student Psychotherapy, 23*(4), 281–301.

McNally, R. (2005). Debunking myths about trauma and memory. *Canadian Journal of Psychiatry/La Revue canadienne de psychiatrie, 50*(13), 817–822.

McNally, R. J., Lasko, N. B., Clancy, S. A., Macklin, M. L., Pitman, R. K., & Orr, S. P. (2004). Psychophysiological responding during script-driven imagery in people reporting abduction by space aliens. *Psychological Science, 15,* 493–497.

Meehl, P. (1990). Toward an integrated theory of schizotaxia, schizotypy, and schizophrenia. *Journal of Personality Disorders, 4,* 1–99.

Mehl, M. R., Gosling, S. D., & Pennebaker, J. W. (2006). Personality in its natural habitat: Manifestations and implicit folk theories of personality in daily life. *Journal of Personality and Social Psychology, 90*(5), 862–877.

Mehl, M. R., & Pennebaker, J. W. (2003). The sounds of social life: A psychometric analysis of students' daily social environments and natural conversations. *Journal of Personality and Social Psychology, 84,* 857–870.

Mehler, J., & Bever, T. G. (1967). Cognitive capacity of very young children. *Science, 158,* 141–142.

Meier, M. H., Slutske, W. S., Arndt, S., & Cadoret, R. J. (2008). Impulsive and callous traits are more strongly associated with delinquent behavior in higher risk neighborhoods among boys and girls. *Journal of Abnormal Psychology, 117,* 377–385.

Melamed, T. (1991). Individual differences in romantic jealousy: The moderating effect of relationship characteristics. *European Journal of Social Psychology, 21,* 455–461.

Melton, G. B., Petrila, J., Poythress, N. G., & Slobogin, C. (2007). Psychological evaluations for the courts: A handbook for mental health professionals and lawyers (3rd ed.). New York: Guilford Press.

Meltzoff, A. N., & Moore, M. K. (1977). Imitation of facial and manual gestures by human neonates. *Science, 198,* 75–78.

Melzack, R., & Wall, P. D. (1965). Pain mechanisms: A new theory. *Science, 150,* 971–979.

Melzack, R., & Wall, P. D. (1982). *The challenge of pain.* New York: Basic Books.

Messer, D. (2000). State of the art: Language acquisition. *The Psychologist, 13,* 138–143.

Meston, C. M., & Ahrold, T. (2010). Ethnic, gender, and acculturation influences on sexual behaviors. *Archives of Sexual Behavior, 39,* 179–189.

Meston, C. M., & Buss, D. M. (2007). Why humans have sex. *Archives of Sexual Behavior, 36,* 477–507.

Meston, C. M., & Frohlich, P. F. (2000). The neurobiology of sexual function. *Archives of General Psychiatry, 57,* 1012–1030.

Meston, C. M., Levin, R. J., Sipski, M. L., Hull, E. M., & Heiman, J. R. (2004). Women's orgasm. *Annual Review of Sex Research, 15,* 173–257.

Mezulis, A. H., Abramson, A. Y., Hyde, J. S., & Hankin, B. L. (2004). Is there a universal positivity bias in attributions? A meta-analytic review of individual, developmental, and cultural differences in the self-serving attributional bias. *Psychological Bulletin, 130,* 711–747.

Miech, R. A., Kumanyika, S. K., Stettler, N., Link, B. G., Phelan, J. C., & Chang, V. W. (2006). Trends in the association of poverty with overweight among US adolescents, 1971–2004. *Journal of the American Medical Association, 295*(20), 2385–2393.

Mikulincer, M., & Shaver, P. R. (2005). Attachment security, compassion, and altruism. *Current Directions in Psychological Science, 14,* 34–38.

Milgram, S. (1963). Behavioral study of obedience. *Journal of Abnormal and Social Psychology, 67,* 371–378.

Milgram, S. (1974). *Obedience to authority: An experimental view.* US: Harpercollins.

Miller, A. G. (1986). *The obedience experiments: A case study of controversy in social science.* New York: Praeger.

Miller, G. (1956). The magical number seven, plus or minus two: Some limits on our capacity for processing information. *Psychological Review, 63*(2), 81–97.

Miller, I. J., Jr., & Reedy, F. E. (1990). Variations in human taste bud density and intensity perception. *Physiology and Behavior, 47,* 1213–1219.

Miller, J. M., & Krosnick, J. A. (1996). News media impact on the ingredients of presidential evaluations: A program of research on the priming hypothesis. In D. Mutz & P. Sniderman (Eds.). *Political persuasion and attitude change* (pp. 79–99). Ann Arbor, MI: University of Michigan Press.

Miller, K. E., Omidian, P., Quraishy, A., Quraishy, N., Nasiry, M., Nasiry, S., Karyar, N. M., & Yaqubi, A. (2006). The Afghan Symptom Checklist: A culturally grounded approach to mental health assessment in a conflict zone. *American Journal of Orthopsychiatry, 76*(4), 423–433.

Miller, L. J., Myers, A., Prinzi, L., & Mittenberg, W. (2009). Changes in intellectual functioning associated with normal aging. *Archives of Clinical Neuropsychology, 24,* 681–688.

Milling, L. (2009). Response expectancies: A psychological mechanism of suggested and placebo analgesia. *Contemporary Hypnosis, 26*(2), 93–110.

Minio-Paluello, I., Avenanti, A., & Aglioti, S. (2006). Left hemisphere dominance in reading the sensory qualities of others' pain? *Social Neuroscience, 1,* 320–333.

Mischel, W. (1968). *Personality and assessment.* New York: Wiley.

Mischel, W., & Shoda, Y. (1998). Reconciling processing dynamics and personality dispositions. *Annual Review of Psychology, 49,* 229–258.

Mishara, B. L., Chagnon, F., Daigle, M., Balan, B., Raymond, S., Marcoux, I., Bardon, C., Campbell, J. K., & Berman, A. (2007). Which helper behaviors and intervention styles are related to better short-term outcomes in telephone crisis intervention? Results from a silent monitoring study of calls to the U.S. 1-800-SUICIDE Network. *Suicide and Life Threatening Behavior, 37,* 308–321.

Mishara, B. L., & Daigle, M. S. (1997). Effects of different telephone intervention styles with suicidal callers at two suicide prevention centers: An empirical investigation. *American Journal of Community Psychology, 5,* 861–885.

Mizushige, T., Inoue, K., & Fushiki, T. (2007). Why is fat so tasty? Chemical reception of fatty acid on the tongue. *Journal of Nutritional Science and Vitaminology, 53*(1), 1–4.

Molina, J., & Mendoza, M. (2006). Change of attitudes towards hypnosis after a training course. *Australian Journal of Clinical & Experimental Hypnosis, 34*(2), 146–161.

Montgomery, G. H., DuHamel, K. N., & Redd, W. H. (2000). A metaanalysis of hypnotically induced analgesia: How effective is hypnosis? *International Journal of Clinical and Experimental Hypnosis, 48*(2), 138–153.

Montgomery, I., Trinder, J., Fraser, G., & Paxton, S. (1987). Aerobic fitness and exercise: Effect on the sleep of younger and older adults. *Australian Journal of Psychology, 39*(3), 259–271.

Morehead, G., Ference, R., & Neck, C. P. (1991). Group decision fiascoes continue: Space Shuttle Challenger and a revised groupthink framework. *Human Relations, 44,* 539–550.

Morgan, A. J., & Jorm, A. F. (2008). Self-help interventions for depressive disorders and depressive symptoms: A systematic review. *Annals of General Psychiatry, 7,* 13.

Morgan, H. L., Turner, D.C., Corlett, P.R. et al. (2010). Exploring the impact of ketamine on the experience of illusory body ownership. *Biological Psychiatry, 69,* 35–41.

Morgeson, F. P., Reider, M. H., & Campion, M. A. (2005). Selecting individuals in team settings: The importance of social skills, personality characteristics, and teamwork knowledge. *Personnel Psychology, 58*(3), 583–611.

Morin, C., Bootzin, R., Buysse, D., Edinger, J., Espie, C., & Lichstein, K. (2006). Psychological and behavioral treatment of insomnia: Update of the recent evidence (1998–2004). *Sleep: Journal of Sleep and Sleep Disorders Research, 29*(11), 1398–1414.

Morleo, M., Woolfall, K., Dedman, D., Mukherjee, R., Bellis, M. A., & Cook, P. A. (2011). Underreporting of foetal alcohol spectrum disorders: An analysis of hospital episode statistics [Electronic publication ahead of print]. *BMC Pediatrics, 11.*

Morris, J., Jordan, C., & Breedlove, S. (2004, October). Sexual differentiation of the vertebrate nervous system. *Nature Neuroscience, 7*(10), 1034–1039.

Moscicki, E. K. (2001). Epidemiology of completed and attempted suicide: Toward a framework for prevention. *Clinical Neuroscience Research, 1,* 310–323.

Mossholder, K., Settoon, R., & Henagan, S. (2005). A relational perspective on turnover: Examining structural, attitudinal, and behavioral predictors. *Academy of Management Journal, 48*(4), 607–618.

Mowbray, C., Megivern, D., Mandiberg, J., Strauss, S., Stein, C., Collins, K., et al. (2006). Campus mental health services: Recommendations for change. *American Journal of Orthopsychiatry, 76,* 226–237.

Murphy, C., Cain, W. S., & Bartoshuk, L. M. (1977). Mutual action of taste and olfaction. *Sensory Processes, 1,* 204–211.

Murphy, M. R., Checkley, S. A., Seckl, J. R., & Lightman, S. L. (1990). Naloxone inhibits oxytocin release at orgasm in man. *Journal of Clinical Endocrinology and Metabolism, 71*(4), 1056–1058.

Murray, A. J., Knight, N. S., Cochlin, L. E., McAleese, S., Deacon, R. M., Rawlins, J. N., & Clarke, K. (2009). Deterioration of physical performance and cognitive function in rats with short-term high-fat feeding [Electronic publication ahead of print]. *FASEB Journal: Journal of the Federation of American Societies for Experimental Biology.*

Murtagh, D. R., & Greenwood, K. M. (1995). Identifying effective psychological treatments for insomnia: A meta-analysis. *Journal of Consulting and Clinical Psychology, 63,* 79–89.

Nabi, R. L. (2002). Anger, fear, uncertainty, and attitudes: A test of the cognitive-functional model. *Communication Monographs, 69*(3), 204–216.

Nairne, J. S. (1996). Short-term/working memory. In E. Bjork, R. A. Bjork, E. Bjork, & R. A. Bjork (Eds.), *Memory* (pp. 101–126). San Diego, CA: Academic Press.

Naj, A. C., Jun, G., Beecham, G.W., Wang, L-S., Vardarajan, B.N., Buros, J., et al. (2011). Common variants of MS4A4/MS4A6E, CD2AP, CD33 and EPHA 1 are associated with late-onset Alzheimer's disease. *Nature Genetics, 43,* 436–441.

Nakajima, A., & Tang, Y-P. (2005). Genetic approaches to the molecular/neuronal mechanisms underlying learning and memory in the mouse. *Journal of Pharmacological Sciences, 99,* 1–5.

Nakamura, M., Kanbayashi, T., Sugiura, T., & Inoue, Y. (2011). Relationship between clinical characteristics of narcolepsy and CSF orexin-A levels. *Journal of Sleep Research, 20*(1, Pt1), 45–49.

Nash, R., Wade, K., & Lindsay, D. (2009). Digitally manipulating memory: Effects of doctored videos and imagination in distorting beliefs and memories. *Memory & Cognition, 37*(4), 414–424.

National Association for College Admission Counseling (NACAC). (2008). Report of the Commission on the Use of Standardized Tests in Undergraduate Admission. Retrieved from http://www.nacacnet.org/PublicationsResources/Research/Documents/TestingComission_FinalReport.pdf

National Institute of Drug Abuse. (2010). NIDA InfoFacts: Salvia. Retrieved November 24, 2010, from http://www.drugabuse.gov/Infofacts/salvia.html

National Institutes of Health. (2009, July). *Taste disorders.* NIH Publication No. 09-3231A. Retrieved June 8, 2011, from http://www.nidcd.nih.gov/health/smelltaste/taste.html

National Institutes of Health (NIH). (2009). Statistics related to overweight and obesity. Retrieved February 15, 2010, from http://win.niddk.nih.gov/statistics/#preval

National Institutes of Mental Health (NIMH). (2008). Retrieved from http://www.nimh.nih.gov/health/publications/the-numbers-count-mental-disorders-in-america/index.shtml

National Institute of Mental Health (NIMH). (2009). Retrieved from http://www.nimh.nih.gov/health/publications/post-traumatic-stress-disorder-ptsd/psychotherapy.shtml

National Institute of Mental Health (NIMH). (2011). Retrieved from http://www.nimh.nih.gov/statistics/3USE_MT_ADULT.shtml

National Science Foundation. (2010). National science indicators. Retrieved from http://www.nsf.gov/statistics/seind10/c7/c7s2.htm

Neisser, U. (2000). Snapshots or benchmarks? In U. Neisser & I. Hyman (Eds.), *Memory observed: Remembering in natural contexts* (2nd ed., pp. 68–74). New York: Worth Publishing.

Neisser, U. (Ed.). (1998). *The rising curve.* Washington, DC: American Psychological Association.

Neisser, U., Boodoo, G., Bouchard, T. J., Boykin, A. W., Brody, N., Ceci, S. J., Halpern, D. F., Loehlin, J. C., Perloff, R., Sternberg, R. J., & Urbina, S. (1996). Intelligence: Knowns and unknowns. *American Psychologist, 51,* 77–101.

Neisser, U., & Harsch, N. (1992). Phantom flashbulbs: False recollections of hearing the news about Challenger. In E. Winograd & U. Neisser (Eds.), *Affect and accuracy in recall: Studies in flashbulb memories* (pp. 9–31). Cambridge, UK: Cambridge University Press.

Nelson, C. A., Zeanah, C. H., Fox, N. A., Marshall, P. J., Smyke, A. T., & Guthrie, D. (2007). Cognitive recovery in socially deprived young children: The Bucharest early intervention project. *Science, 318,* 1937–1940.

Nesse, R., & Ellsworth, P. (2009). Evolution, emotions, and emotional disorders. *American Psychologist, 64,* 129–139.

Newcombe, N. S., Drummey, A., Fox, N. A., et al. (2000). Remembering early childhood: How much, how, and why (or why not). *Current Directions in Psychological Science, 9*(2), 55–58.

Newman, M. G., & Llera, S. J. (2011). A novel theory of experiential avoidance in generalized anxiety disorder: A review and synthesis of research supporting a contrast avoidance model of worry. *Clinical Psychology Review, 31,* 371–382.

Nguyen, H., & Ryan, A. (2008). Does stereotype threat affect test performance of minorities and women? A meta-analysis of experimental evidence. *Journal of Applied Psychology, 93*(6), 1314–1334.

Nicholas, J. G., & Geers, A. E. (2007). Will they catch up? The role of age at cochlear implantation in the spoken language development of children with severe to profound hearing loss. *Journal of Speech, Language, and Hearing Research, 50,* 1048–1062.

Nielsen Research Reports. (2010). Retrieved April 10, 2011, from http://blog.nielsen.com/nielsen-wire/consumer/u-s-homes-add-even-more-tv-sets-in-2010/

Nielsen, K., Randall, R., Yarker, J., & Brenner, S. (2008). The effects of transformational leadership on followers' perceived work characteristics and psychological well-being: A longitudinal study. *Work & Stress, 22*(1), 16–32.

Nielsen, M., & Tomaselli, K. (2010). Overimitation in Kalahari Bushman children and the origins of human cultural cognition. *Psychological Science, 21,* 729–736.

Nielson, K., Yee, D., & Erickson, K. (2005). Memory enhancement by a semantically unrelated emotional arousal source induced after learning. *Neurobiology of Learning and Memory, 84,* 49–56.

Niparko, J. K., Tobey, E. A., Thal, D. J., Eisenberg, L. S., Wang, N. Y., Quittner, A. L., Fink, N. E. (2010). Spoken language development in children following cochlear implantation. *Journal of the American Medical Association, 303,* 1498–1506.

Nisbett, R. (2009). *Intelligence and how to get it: Why schools and cultures count.* New York: W. W. Norton.

Nisbett, R. E., Caputo, C., Legant, P., & Marecek, J. (1973). Behavior as seen by the actor and as seen by the observer. *Journal of Personality and Social Psychology, 27*(2), 154–164.

Nisbett, R. E., & Cohen, D. (1996). *Culture of honor: The psychology of violence in the South.* Boulder, CO: Westview Press.

Nisbett, R. E., & Masuda, T. (2003). Culture and point of view. *Proceedings of the National Academy of Sciences, 100,* 11163–11170.

Norem, J. K., & Chang, E. C. (2002). The positive psychology of negative thinking. *Journal of Clinical Psychology, 58*(9), 993–1001.

Norrholm, S. D., Vervliet, B., Jovanovic, T., Boshoven, W., Myers, K. M., Davis, M., Rothbaum, B., & Duncan, E. (2008). Timing of extinction relative to acquisition: A parametric analysis of fear extinction in humans. *Behavioral Neuroscience, 122,* 1016–1030.

North, C. S., Ryall, J. E. M., Ricci, D. A., & Wetzel, R. D. (1993). *Multiple personalities, multiple disorders.* New York: Oxford University Press.

Northrop, L. C. (1989). *The psychometric history of selected ability constructs.* Washington, DC: U.S. Office of Personnel Management.

Norton, A., Zipse, L., Marchina, S., & Schlaug, G. (2009). Melodic intonation therapy: Shared insights on how it is done and why it might help. *Annals of the New York Academy of Sciences, 1169,* 431–436.

Nosek, B. A. (2007). Implicit–explicit relations. *Current Directions in Psychological Science, 16,* 65–69.

Nosek, B. A., Banjai, M., & Greenwald, A. G. (2002). Harvesting implicit group attitudes and beliefs from a demonstration web site. *Group Dynamics: Theory, Research, and Practice, 6,* 101–115.

Nyi, P. P., Lai, E. P., Lee, D. Y., Biglete, S. A., Torrecer, G. I., & Anderson, I. B. (2010). Influence of age on *Salvia divinorum* use: Results of an Internet survey. *Journal of Psychoactive Drugs, 42,* 385–392.

O'Connor, A. R., & Moulin, C. J. (2006). Normal patterns of déjà experience in a healthy, blind male: Challenging optical pathway delay theory. *Brain and Cognition, 62,* 246–249.

O'Connor, A., & Moulin, C. (2008). The persistence of erroneous familiarity in an epileptic male: Challenging perceptual theories of déjà vu activation. *Brain and Cognition, 68*(2), 144–147.

O'Connor, A. R., & Moulin, C. J. (2010). Recognition without identification, erroneous familiarity, and déjà vu. *Current Psychiatry Reports, 12,* 165–173.

O'Connor, D. B., Archer, J., & Wu, F. C. W. (2004). Effects of testosterone on mood, aggression and sexual behavior in young men: A double-blind, placebo-controlled, cross-over study. Journal of Clinical Endocrinology and Metabolism, 89, 2837–2845.

O'Kearney, R., Gibson, M., Christensen, H., & Griffiths, K. M. (2006). Effects of a cognitive-behavioural Internet program on depression, vulnerability to depression and stigma in adolescent males: A school-based controlled trial. *Cognitive Behavior Therapy, 35,* 43–54.

O'Leary, C. M., Nassar, N., Kurinczuk, J. J., de Klerk, N., Geelhoed, E., Elliot, E. J., & Bower, C. (2010). Prenatal alcohol exposure and risk of birth defects. *Pediatrics, 126,* e843–e850.

Occupational Information Network. (2009). Retrieved September 1, 2009, from http://online.onetcenter.org/

Öhman, A., & Mineka, S. (2001). Fears, phobias, and preparedness: Toward an evolved module of fear and fear learning. *Psychological Review, 108,* 483–522.

Olds, J., & Milner, P. (1954). Positive reinforcement produced by electrical stimulation of the septal area and other regions of the rat brain. *Journal of Comparative and Physiological Psychology, 47,* 419–428.

Olfson, M., & Marcus, S. C. (2009). National patterns in antidepressant medication treatment. *Archives of General Psychiatry, 66,* 848–856.

Olfson, M, & Marcus, S. C. (2010). National trends in outpatient psychotherapy. *American Journal of Psychiatry, 167,* 1456–1463.

Olfson, M., Marcus, S. C., Druss, B., & Pincus, H. A. (2002). National trends in the use of outpatient therapy. *American Journal of Psychiatry, 159,* 1914–1920.

Olivo, E., Dodson-Lavelle, B., Wren, A., Fang, Y., & Oz, M. (2009). Feasibility and effectiveness of a brief meditation-based stress management intervention for patients diagnosed with or at risk for coronary heart disease: A pilot study. *Psychology, Health & Medicine, 14*(5), 513–523.

Olson, K. R., Lambert, A. J., & Zacks, J. M. (2004). Graded structure and the speed of category verification: On the moderating effects of anticipatory control for social vs. non-social categories. *Journal of Experimental Social Psychology, 40*(2), 239–246.

Olsson, A., & Phelps, E. (2007). Social learning of fear. *Nature Neuroscience, 10,* 1095–1102.

Ones, D., Viswesvaran, C., & Schmidt, F. (1993). Comprehensive meta-analysis of integrity test validities: Findings and implications for personnel selection and theories of job performance. *Journal of Applied Psychology, 78*(4), 679–703.

Ophir, E., Nass, C., & Wagner, A. D. (2009). Cognitive control in media multitaskers. *Proceedings of the National Academy of Sciences, 106,* 15583–15587.

Orlinsky, D. E., Rønnestad, M. H., & Willutzki, U. (2004). Fifty years of psychotherapy process outcome research: Continuity and change. In M. J. Lambert (Ed.), *Bergin and Garfield's handbook of psychotherapy and behavior change* (5th ed., pp. 307–389). New York: Wiley.

Orne, M. T. (1962). On the social psychology of the psychological experiment: With particular reference to demand characteristics and their implications. *American Psychologist, 17,* 776–783.

Ostafin, B. D., Marlatt, G., & Greenwald, A. G. (2008). Drinking without thinking: An implicit measure of alcohol motivation predicts failure to control alcohol use. *Behaviour Research and Therapy, 46*(11), 1210–1219.

Owen, A. M., & Coleman, M. R. (2008). Functional neuroimaging of the vegetative state. *Nature Reviews Neuroscience, 9,* 235–243.

Owen, A. M., Coleman, M. R., Boly, M., et al. (2006). Detecting awareness in the vegetative state. *Science, 313,* 1402.

Oxford English dictionary. (2011). Retrieved June 16, 2011, from http://dictionary.oed.com/entrance.dtl

Oyserman, D., Coon, H. M., & Kemmelmeier, M. (2002). Rethinking individualism and collectivism: Evaluation of theoretical assumptions and meta-analyses. *Psychological Bulletin, 128,* 3–72.

Packard, V. (1957). *The hidden persuaders.* New York: Washington Square Press.

Padden, C. A., & Humphries, T. L. (2005). *Inside Deaf culture.* Cambridge, MA: Harvard University Press.

Paivio, A. (1991). Dual coding theory: Retrospect and current status. *Canadian Journal of Psychology, 45,* 255–287.

Paller, K. (2004). Electrical signals of memory and of the awareness of remembering. *Current Directions in Psychological Science, 13,* 49–55.

Pallesen, S., Hilde, I., Havik, O., & Nielsen, G. (2001). Clinical assessment and treatment of insomnia. *Professional Psychology: Research and Practice, 32*(2), 115–124.

Pardini, D. A., & Phillips, M. (2010). Neural responses to emotional and neutral facial expressions in chronically violent men. *Journal of Psychiatry and Neuroscience, 35,* 390–398.

Park, D. C., & Huang, C-M. (2010). Culture wires the brain: A cognitive neuroscience perspective. *Perspectives on Psychological Science, 5,* 391–400.

Park, S., Püschel, J., Sauter, B. H., Rentsch, M., & Hell, D. (1999). Spatial working memory deficits and clinical symptoms of schizophrenia: A 4-month follow-up study. *Biological Psychiatry, 46,* 392–400.

Park, T. J., Lu, Y., Jüttner, R., Smith, E. S., Hu, J., Band, A., et al. (2008). Selective inflammatory pain insensitivity in the African naked mole-rat (*Heterocephalus glaber*). *PLoS Biology, 6,* e13.

Parsons, H. M. (1974). What happened at Hawthorne?: New evidence suggests the Hawthorne effect resulted from reinforcement contingencies. *Science, 183,* 922–932.

Pascual, A., & Guéguen, N. (2005). Foot-in-the-door and door-in-the-face: A comparative meta-analytic study. *Psychological Reports, 96*(1), 122–128.

Pasher, H., McDaniel, M., Rohrer, D., & Bjork, R. (2008). Learning styles: Concepts and evidence. *Psychological Science in the Public Interest, 9,* 105–119.

Patterson, D., & Jensen, M. (2003). Hypnosis and clinical pain. *Psychological Bulletin, 129*(4), 495–521.

Paul, D. B., & Blumenthal, A. L. (1989). On the trail of little Albert. *Psychological Record, 39,* 547–553.

Paulesu, E., Frith, C., & Frackowiak, R. (1993). The neural correlates of the verbal component of working memory. *Nature, 362,* 342–345.

Payne, J. D., & Kensinger, E. A. (2010). Sleep's role in the consolidation of emotional episodic memories. *Current Directions in Psychological Science, 19,* 290–295.

Payne, S. C., & Huffman, A. H. (2005). A longitudinal examination of the influence of mentoring on organizational commitment and turnover. *Academy of Management Journal, 48*(1), 158–168.

Peeters, M., & Giuliano, F. (2007). Central neurophysiology and dopaminergic control of ejaculation. *Neuroscience and Biobehavioral Reviews, 32,* 438–453.

Penn, D. L., & Combs, D. (2000). Modification of affect perception deficits in schizophrenia. *Schizophrenia Research, 46,* 217–229.

Penninx, B., Geerlings, S., Deeg, D., van Eijk, J., van Tilburg, W., & Beekman, A. (1999). Minor and major depression and the risk of death in older persons. *Archives of General Psychiatry, 56,* 889–895.

Perlman, D., Salomons, T., Davidson, R., & Lutz, A. (2010). Differential effects on pain intensity and unpleasantness of two meditation practices. *Emotion, 10*(1), 65–71.

Perloff, L. S., & Fetzer, B. K. (1986). Self-other judgments and perceived vulnerability to victimization. *Journal of Personality and Social Psychology, 50,* 502–510.

Perry, W., Feifel, D., Minassian, A., Bhattacharjie, B. S., & Braff, D. L. (2002). Information processing deficits in acutely psychotic schizophrenia patients medicated and unmedicated at the time of admission. *American Journal of Psychiatry, 159,* 1375–1381.

Peterson, L., & Peterson, M. (1959). Short-term retention of individual verbal items. *Journal of Experimental Psychology, 58,* 193–198.

Petrosino, A., Turpin-Petrosino, C., & Buehler, J. (2003). "Scared Straight" and other juvenile awareness programs for preventing juvenile delinquency. *Annals of the American Academy of Political and Social Science, 589,* 41–62.

Petty, R. E., Wegener, D. T., & Fabrigar, L. R. (1997). Attitudes and attitude change. *Annual Review of Psychology, 48,* 609–647.

Pezaris, E., & Casey, M. (1991). Girls who use "masculine" problem-solving strategies on a spatial task: Proposed genetic and environmental factors. *Brain and Cognition, 17*(1), 1–22.

Phelps, E. A. (2004). Human emotion and memory: Interactions of the amygdala and hippocampal complex. *Current Opinion in Neurobiology, 14,* 198–202.

Piaget, J., & Inhelder, B. (1956). *The child's conception of space.* Boston: Routledge & Kegan Paul.

Pina, A., Gannon, T., & Saunders, B. (2009). An overview of the literature on sexual harassment: Perpetrator, theory, and treatment issues. *Aggression and Violent Behavior, 14*(2), 126–138.

Pinker, S. (1994). *The language instinct.* New York: William Morrow.

Pinker, S. (1999). *Words and rules: The ingredients of language.* New York: Basic Books.

Pinto, A., Mancebo, M., Eisen, J., Pagano, M., & Rasmussen, S. (2006). The Brown longitudinal obsessive compulsive study: Clinical features and symptoms of the sample at intake. *Journal of Clinical Psychiatry, 67,* 703–711.

Pisarik, C. T. (2009). Motivational orientation and burnout among undergraduate college students. *College Student Journal, 43*(4, Pt B), 1238–1252.

Pittas, A. G., Hariharan, R., Stark, P. C., Hajduk, C. L., Greenberg, A. S., & Roberts, S. B. (2005). Interstitial glucose level is a significant predictor of energy intake in free-living women with healthy body weight. *Journal of Nutrition, 135,* 1070–1074.

Plant, E., Devine, P. G., & Peruche, M. B. (2010). Routes to positive interracial interactions: Approaching egalitarianism or avoiding prejudice. *Personality and Social Psychology Bulletin, 36*(9), 1135–1147.

Plant, E. A., & Peruche, B. (2005). The consequences of race for police officers' responses to criminal suspects. *Psychological Science, 16,* 180–183.

Plomin, R., Corley, R., DeFries, J. C., & Fulker, D. W. (1997). Nature, nurture, and cognitive development from 1 to 16 years: A parent–offspring adoption study. *Psychological Science, 8,* 442–447.

Plomin, R., & Crabbe, J. (2000). DNA. *Psychological Bulletin, 126*(6), 806–828.

Plomin, R., & Spinath, F. M. (2004). Intelligence: Genetics, genes, and genomics. *Journal of Personality and Social Psychology, 86*(1), 112–129.

Poe, G. R., Walsh, C. M., & Bjorness, T. E. (2010). Cognitive neuroscience of sleep. *Progress in Brain Research, 185,* 1–19.

Pollack, D., McFarland, B., Mahler, J., & Kovas, A. (2005). Outcomes of patients in a low-intensity, short-duration involuntary outpatient commitment program. *Psychiatric Services, 56,* 863–866.

Ponder, C. A., Kliethermes, C. L., Drew, M. R., Muller, J. J., Das, K. K., Risbrough, V. B., Crabbe, J. C., Gilliam, T. C., & Palmer, A. A. (2007). Selection for contextual fear conditioning affects anxiety-like behaviors and gene expression. *Genes, Brain & Behavior, 6*(8), 736–749.

Ponseti, J., Bosinski, H. A., Wolff, S., Peller, M., Jansen, O., Mehdorn, H. M., Büchel, C., & Siebner, H. R. (2006). A functional endophenotype for sexual orientation in humans. *NeuroImage, 33,* 825–833.

Pope, H. G., Jr., Oliva, P. S., & Hudson, J. I. (2000). Repressed memories: B. Scientific status. In D. L. Faigman, D. H. Kay, M. J. Saks, & J. Sanders (Eds.), *Modern scientific evidence: The law and science of expert testimony* (pp. 154–195). St. Paul, MN: West.

Porter, R. H., & Winberg, J. (1999). Unique salience of maternal breast odors for newborn infants. *Neuroscience and Biobehavioral Reviews, 23,* 439–449.

Prentice, D. A., & Miller, D. T. (1996). Pluralistic ignorance and the perpetuation of social norms by unwitting actors. In M. P. Zanna (Ed.), *Advances in experimental social psychology* (Vol. 29, pp. 161–209). San Diego, CA: Academic Press.

Priem, R. L., Harrison, D. A., & Muir, N. (1995). Structured conflict and consensus outcomes in group decision making. *Journal of Management, 21*(4), 691–710.

Pritchard, R. (Ed.). (1995). *Productivity measurement and improvement: Organizational: case studies.* Westport, CT: Praeger/Greenwood.

Prochaska, J. O., & Norcross, J. C. (2002). Stage of change. In J. C. Norcross (Ed.), *Psychotherapy relationships that work* (pp 303–313). New York: Oxford.

Pronin, E., Lin, D. Y., & Ross, L. (2002). The bias blind spot: Perceptions of bias in self versus others. *Personality and Social Psychology Bulletin, 28*(3), 369–381.

Pronin, E., Wegner, D. M., McCarthy, K., & Rodriguez, S. (2006). Everyday magical powers: the role of apparent mental causation in the overestimation of personal influence. *Journal of Personality and Social Psychology, 91*, 218–231.

Propper, R. E., Stickgold, R., Keeley, R., & Christman, S. D. (2007). Is television traumatic? Dreams, stress and media exposure in the aftermath of September 11, 2001. *Psychological Science, 18*, 334–340.

Purdue University Library. (2009). The Frank and Lillian Gilbreth website. Retrieved September 2, 2009, from http://www.lib.purdue.edu/spcol/manuscripts/gilbreth.html

Putnam, F. W. (1989). *Diagnosis and treatment of multiple personality disorder.* New York: Guilford Press.

Pyszczynski, T., Abdollahi, A., Solomon, S., Greenberg, J., Cohen, F., & Weise, D. (2006). Mortality salience, martyrdom, and military might: The Great Satan versus the Axis of Evil. *Personality and Social Psychology Bulletin, 32*(4), 525–537.

Pyszczynski, T., Greenberg, J., Solomon, S., Arndt, J., & Schimel, J. (2004). Why do people need self-esteem? A theoretical and empirical review. *Psychological Bulletin, 130*(3), 435–468.

Qiu, Y. H., Wu, X. Y., Xu, H., & Sackett, D. (2009). Neuroimaging study of placebo analgesia in humans. *Neuroscience Bulletin, 25*, 277–282.

Rabbitt, P., Ibrahim, S., Lunn, M., Scott, M., Thacker, N., Hutchinson, C., & Jackson, A. (2008). Age-associated losses of brain volume predict longitudinal cognitive declines over 8 to 20 years. *Neuropsychology, 22*(1), 3–9.

Raber, J. (2008). AR, apo E, and cognitive function. *Hormones and Behavior, 53*, 706–715.

Rachman, S. (1966). Sexual fetishism: An experimental analogue. *Psychological Record, 16*, 293–296.

Rada, P., Avena, N. M., & Hoebel, B. G. (2005). Daily bingeing on sugar repeatedly releases dopamine in the accumbens shell. *Neuroscience, 134*(7), 737–744.

Radano, G. M. (2007). *Contaminated: My journey out of obsessive compulsive disorder.* Lorraine: Bar-Le-Duc Books.

Rahman, Q. (2005). The neurodevelopment of human sexual orientation. *Neuroscience and Biobehavioral Reviews, 29*, 1057–1066.

Rainforth, M. V., Schneider, R. H., Nidich, S. I., Gaylord-King, C., Salerno, J. W., & Anderson, J. W. (2007). Stress reduction programs in patients with elevated blood pressure: A systematic review and meta-analysis. *Current Hypertension Reports, 9*, 520–528.

Rainie, L., & Packel, D. (2001). More online, doing more: The Pew Internet & American Life Project. Retrieved from http://www.pewinternet.org

Rainville, P., Bechara, A., Naqvi, N., & Damasio, A. R. (2006). Basic emotions are associated with distinct patterns of cardiorespiratory activity. *International Journal of Psychophysiology, 61*, 5–18.

Rajender, S., Pandu, G., Sharma, J. D., Gandhi, K. P. C., Singh, L., Thangaraj, K., et al. (2008). Reduced CAG repeats length in androgen receptor gene is associated with violent criminal behavior. *International Journal of Legal Medicine, 122*, 367–372.

Raji, C. A., Ho, A. J., Parikshak, N. N., Becker, J. T., Lopez, O. L., Kuller, L. H., Hua, X., Leow, A. D., Toga, A. W., & Thompson, P. M. (2010). Brain structure and obesity. *Human Brain Mapping, 31*, 353–364.

Ramachandran, V. S., & Altschuler, E. L. (2009). The use of visual feedback, in particular mirror visual feedback, in restoring brain function. *Brain, 132*, 1693–1710.

Ramachandran, V. S., & Gregory, R. L. (1991). Perceptual filling in of artificially induced scotomas in human vision. *Nature, 350*, 699–702.

Ramchand, R., Schell, T. L., Karney, B. R., Osilla, K. C., Burns, R. M., & Caldarone, L. B. (2010). Disparate prevalence estimates of PTSD among service members who served in Iraq and Afghanistan: Possible explanations. *Journal of Trauma and Stress, 23*, 59–68.

Rampersaud, G. C., Pereira, M. A., Girard, B. L., Adams, J., & Metzl, J. (2005). Breakfast habits, nutritional status, body weight, and academic performance in children and adolescents. *Journal of the American Diet Association, 105*(5), 743–760.

Ranganathan, M., & D'Souza, D. C. (2006). The acute effects of cannabinoids on memory in humans: A review. *Psychopharmacology, 188*, 425–444.

Rasch, B., & Born, J. (2008). Reactivation and consolidation of memory during sleep. *Current Directions in Psychological Science, 17*(3), 188–192.

Rasmussen, E. B., & Newland, M. C. (2008). Asymmetry of reinforcement and punishment in human choice. *Journal of the Experimental Analysis of Behavior, 89*, 157–167.

Rauscher, F. H., & Shaw, G. L. (1998). Key components of the "Mozart effect." *Perceptual and Motor Skills, 86*, 835–841.

Rauscher, F. H., Shaw, G. L., & Ky, K. N. (1995). Listening to Mozart enhances spatial–temporal reasoning: Towards a neurophysiological basis. *Neuroscience Letters, 185*, 44–47.

Raynor, H. A., & Epstein, L. (2003). The relative-reinforcing value of food under differing levels of food deprivation and restriction. *Appetite, 40*, 15–24.

Razzini, C., Bianchi, F., Leo, R., Fortuna, E., Siracusano, A., & Romeo, F. (2008). Correlations between personality factors and coronary artery disease: From type A behaviour pattern to type D personality. *Journal of Cardiovascular Medicine, 9*(8), 761–768.

Rechtschaffen, A. (1998). Current perspectives on the function of sleep. *Perspectives in Biological Medicine, 41*, 359–390.

Reinders, A. T. S., Nijenhuis, E. R. S., Paans, A. M. J., Korf, J., Willemsen, A. T. M., & den Boer, J. A. (2003). One brain, two selves. *NeuroImage, 20*, 2119–2125.

Reisenzein, R., & Studtmann, M. (2007). On the expression and experience of surprise: No evidence for facial feedback, but evidence for a reverse self-inference effect. *Emotion, 7*, 612–627.

Remafedi, G., Resnick, M., Blum, R., & Harris, L. (1992). Demography of sexual orientation in adolescents. Pediatrics, 89, 714–721.

Rendell, L., & Whitehead, H. (2001). Culture in whales and dolphins. *Behavioral and Brain Sciences, 24*, 309–382.

Renner, M., & Mackin, R. (1998). A life stress instrument for classroom use. *Teaching of Psychology, 25*(1), 46–48.

Rescorla, R. A., & Wagner, A. R. (1972). A theory of Pavlovian conditioning: Variations in the effectiveness of reinforcement and nonreinforcement. In A. H. Black & W. F. Prokasy (Eds.), *Classical conditioning II: Current research and theory* (pp. 64–99). New York: Appleton-Century-Crofts.

Reyna, V. F., & Farley, F. (2006). Risk and rationality in adolescent decision making: Implications for theory, practice, and public policy. *Psychological Science in the Public Interest, 7*, 1–44.

Reznichenko. L., Amit, T., Youdim, M. B., & Mandel, S. (2005). Green tea polyphenol (−)-epigallo-catechin-3-gallate induces neurorescue of long-term serum-deprived PC12 cells and promotes neurite outgrowth. *Journal of Neurochemistry, 93*, 1157–1167.

Rhee, S., & Waldman, I. D. (2002). Genetic and environmental influences on antisocial behavior: A meta-analysis of twin and adoption studies. *Psychological Bulletin, 128*(3), 490–529.

Rhodes, G. (2006). The evolutionary psychology of facial beauty. *Annual Review of Psychology, 57*, 199–226.

Rhodes, G., Louw, K., & Evangelista, E. (2009). Perceptual adaptation to facial symmetries. *Psychonomic Bulletin and Review, 16*, 503–508.

Ricciardelli, L. A., & McCabe, M. P. (2004). A biopsychosocial model of disordered eating and the pursuit of muscularity in adolescent boys. *Psychological Bulletin, 130*, 179–205.

Rich, A. N., Kunar, M. A., Van Wert, M. J., Hidalgo-Sotelo, B., Horowitz, T. S., & Wolfe, J. M. (2008). Why do we miss rare targets? Exploring the boundaries of the low prevalence effect. *Journal of Vision, 8*, 1–17.

Richardson, K., & Rothstein, H. (2008). Effects of occupational stress management intervention programs: A meta-analysis. *Journal of Occupational Health Psychology, 13*(1), 69–93.

Richert, R. A., Robb, M. B., Fender, J. G., & Wartella, E. (2010). Word learning from baby videos. Archives of Pediatrics & Adolescent Medicine, 164, 432–437.

Richeson, J. A., & Shelton, J. N. (2005). Thin slices of racial bias. *Journal of Nonverbal Behavior, 29*, 75–86.

Rideout, V. J., & Hamel, E. (2006). *The media family: Electronic media in the lives of infants, toddlers, preschoolers and their parents.* Menlo Park, CA: Kaiser Family Foundation.

Rieger, G., & Savin-Williams, R. C. (2011 February 25). Gender nonconformity, sexual orientation, and psychological well-being [Electronic publication ahead of print]. *Archives of Sexual Behavior.*

Rifkin, A., Ghisalbert, D., Dimatou, S., Jin, C., & Sethi, M. (1998). Dissociative identity disorder in psychiatric inpatients. *American Journal of Psychiatry, 155,* 844–845.

Riggio, R. E., Zhu, W., Reina, C., & Maroosis, J. A. (2010). Virtue-based measurement of ethical leadership: The Leadership Virtues Questionnaire. *Consulting Psychology Journal: Practice and Research, 62*(4), 235–250.

Risen, J. L., & Gilovich, T. (2008). Why people are reluctant to tempt fate. *Journal of Personality and Social Psychology, 95,* 293–307.

Ritterband, L., Thorndike, F., Gonder-Frederick, L., Magee, J., Bailey, E., Saylor, D., et al. (2009). Efficacy of an Internet-based behavioral intervention for adults with insomnia. *Archives of General Psychiatry, 66*(7), 692–698.

Rivera, S. M., Wakeley, A., & Langer, J. (1999). The drawbridge phenomenon: Representational reasoning or perceptual preference. *Developmental Psychology, 35,* 427–435.

Rizzo, A. S., Difede, J., Rothbaum, B. O., Reger, G., Spitalnick, J., Cukor, J., & McLay, R. (2010). Development and early evaluation of the Virtual Iraq/Afghanistan exposure therapy system for combat-related PTSD. *Annals of the New York Academic of Sciences, 1208,* 114–125.

Robb, M. B., Richert, R. A., & Wartella, E. A. (2009). Just a talking book? Word learning from watching baby videos. *British Journal of Developmental Psychology, 27,* 27–45.

Roberson, D. M. J., & Davidoff, J. (2000). The "categorical perception" of colors and facial expressions: The effect of verbal interference. *Memory & Cognition, 28,* 977–986.

Roberson, D. M. J., Davies, I. R. L., & Davidoff, J. (2000). Color categories are not universal: Replications and new evidence in favor of linguistic relativity. *Journal of Experimental Psychology: General, 129,* 369–398.

Roberts, B.W., & DelVecchio, W. F. (2000). The rank-order consistency of personality from childhood to old age: A quantitative review of longitudinal studies. *Psychological Bulletin, 126,* 3–25.

Roberts, B. W., Walton, K., & Bogg, T. (2005). Conscientiousness and health across the life course. *Review of General Psychology, 9*(2), 156–168.

Roberts, B., Walton, K., & Viechtbauer, W. (2006). Patterns of mean-level change in personality traits across the life course: A meta-analysis of longitudinal studies. *Psychological Bulletin, 132*(1), 1–25.

Roberts, R., Roberts, C., & Duong, H. (2009). Sleepless in adolescence: Prospective data on sleep deprivation, health and functioning. *Journal of Adolescence, 32*(5), 1045– 1057.

Robertson, S. I. (2001). *Problem solving.* New York: Psychology Press.

Robinson, L., Platt, B., & Riedel, G. (2011, February 16). Involvement in the cholinergic system in conditioning and perceptual memory [Electronic publication ahead of print]. *Behavioral and Brain Research.*

Roblaes, T., Glaser, R., & Kiecolt-Glaser, J. (2005). Out of balance: A new look at chronic stress, depression, and immunity. *Current Directions in Psychological Science, 14,* 111–115.

Rochlen, A., McKelley, R., & Pituch, K. (2006). A preliminary examination of the "Real Men. Real Depression" campaign. *Psychology of Men & Masculinity, 7*(1), 1–13.

Roediger, H., Agarwal, P. K., Kang, S. K., & Marsh, E. J. (2010). Benefits of testing memory: Best practices and boundary conditions. In G. M. Davies, D. B. Wright (Eds.), *Current issues in applied memory research* (pp. 13–49). New York: Psychology Press.

Roediger, H., & McDermott, K. (1995). Creating false memories: Remembering words not presented in lists. *Journal of Experimental Psychology: Learning, Memory, and Cognition, 21,* 803–814.

Rogers, J. M. (2009). Tobacco and pregnancy. *Reproductive Toxicology, 28,* 152–160.

Rogers, J., Kochunov, P., Zilles, K., et al. (2010). On the genetic architecture of cortical folding and brain volume in primates. *Neuroimage, 53,* 1103–1108.

Rogoff, B., Mistry, J., Goncu, A., & Mosier, C. (1993). Guided participation in cultural activity by toddles and caregivers. *Monographs for the Society of Research in Child Development, 58* (serial no. 236).

Rollins, B. C. (1989). Marital quality at midlife. In S. Hunter & M. Sundel (Eds.), *Midlife myths* (pp. 184–194). Newbury Park, CA: Sage.

Rolls, E. T. (2010). Neural representation of fat texture in the mouth. In J-P Montmayeur & J. le Coutre (Eds.), *Fat detection: Taste, texture, and post ingestive effects* (pp. 197–223). Boca Raton, FL: CRC Press.

Rolls, E. T., Verhagen, J. V., & Kadohisa, M. (2003). Representations of the texture of food in the primate orbitofrontal cortex neurons responding to viscosity, grittiness, and capsaicin. *Journal of Neurophysiology, 90,* 3711–3724.

Rosch, E. H. (1973). Natural categories. *Cognitive Psychology, 4,* 328–350.

Rosch, E., & Mervis, C. B. (1975). Family resemblances: Studies in the internal structure of categories. *Cognitive Psychology, 7,* 573–605.

Rosch, E., Mervis, C. B., Gray, W., Johnson, D., & Boyes-Braem, P. (1976). Basic objects in natural categories. *Cognitive Psychology, 8,* 382–439.

Rose, A. J., Swenson, L. P., & Waller, E. M. (2004). Overt and relational aggression and perceived popularity: Developmental differences in concurrent and prospective relations. *Developmental Psychology, 40,* 378–387.

Rose, D., Wykes, T., Leese, M., Bindman, J., & Fleischmann, P. (2003). Patients' perspectives on electroconvulsive therapy: Systematic review. *British Medical Journal, 326,* 1363–1368.

Rose, N., Myerson, J., Roediger, H., & Hale, S. (2010). Similarities and differences between working memory and long-term memory: Evidence from the levels-of-processing span task. *Journal of Experimental Psychology: Learning, Memory, and Cognition, 36*(2), 471–483.

Roselli, C. E., Larkin, K., Schrunk, J. M., & Stormshak, F. (2004). Sexual partner preference, hypothalamic morphology and aromatase in rams. *Physiology and Behavior, 83,* 233–245.

Roselli, C. E., & Stormshak, F. (2009). Prenatal programming of sexual partner preference: The ram model. *Journal of Neuroendocrinology, 21,* 359–364.

Rosenhan, D. L. (1973). On being sane in insane places. *Science, 179*(4070), 250–258.

Rosenthal, R., & Fode, K. L. (1963). The effect of experimenter bias on the performance of the albino rat. *Behavioral Science, 8,* 183–189.

Rosenthal, R., & Jacobson, L. (1966). Teachers' expectancies: Determinates of pupils' IQ gains. *Psychological Reports, 19,* 115–118.

Rosenthal, R., & Jacobson, L. (1968). *Pygmalion in the classroom: Teacher expectation and pupils' intellectual development.* New York: Holt, Rinehart & Winston.

Ross, C. E., Mirowsky, J., & Goldsteen, K. (1990). The impact of the family on health: The decade in review. *Journal of Marriage and the Family, 52,* 1059–1078.

Ross, L. (1977). The intuitive psychologist and his shortcomings: Distortions in the attribution process. In L. Berkowitz (Ed.), *Advances in experimental social psychology* (Vol. 10). New York: Academic Press.

Ross, M., & Wang, Q. (2010). Why we remember and what we remember: Culture and autobiographical memory. *Perspectives on Psychological Science, 5*(4), 401–409.

Rothbart, M. K., & Bates, J. E. (2006). Temperament. In W. Damon, R. Lerner, & N. Eisenberg (Eds.), *Handbook of child psychology: Vol. 3. Social, emotional, and personality development* (6th ed., pp. 99–166). New York: Wiley.

Rotundo, M., & Sackett, P. R. (2002). The relative importance of task, citizenship, and counterproductive performance to global ratings of job performance: A policy-capturing approach. *Journal of Applied Psychology, 87*(1), 66–80.

Rouder, J. N., & Ratcliff, R. (2004). Comparing categorization models. *Journal of Experimental Psychology: General, 133,* 63–82.

Rouder, J. N., & Ratcliff, R. (2006). Comparing exemplar- and rule-based theories of categorization. *Current Directions in Psychological Science, 15,* 9–13.

Rozanski, A., Blumenthal, J. A., & Kaplan, J. (1999). Impact of psychological factors on the pathogenesis of cardiovascular disease and implications for therapy. *Circulation, 99,* 2192–2217.

Rozin, P. (1987). Psychobiological perspectives on food preferences and avoidances. In M. Harris & E. B. Ross (Eds.), *Food and evolution* (pp. 181–205). Philadelphia: Temple University Press.

Rubin, D., & Wenzel, A. (1996). One hundred years of forgetting: A quantitative description of retention. *Psychological Review, 103,* 734–760.

Rudman, L. A., Feinburg, J., & Fairchild, K. (2002). Minority members' implicit attitudes: Automatic ingroup bias as a function of group status. *Social Cognition, 20,* 294–320.

Rumelhart, D. E., & McClelland, J. L. (1986). *Parallel distributed processing* (Vol. 1). Cambridge, MA: MIT Press.

Rushton, J., Chrisjohn, R. D., & Fekken, G. (1981). The altruistic personality and the Self-Report Altruism Scale. *Personality and Individual Differences, 2*(4), 293-302.

Rutter, A., & Hine, D. W. (2005). Sex differences in workplace aggression: An investigation of moderation and mediation effects. *Aggressive Behavior, 31*(3), 254–270.

Rydell, R., McConnell, A., & Beilock, S. (2009). Multiple social identities and stereotype threat: Imbalance, accessibility, and working memory. *Journal of Personality and Social Psychology, 96*(5), 949–966.

Sacerdote, B. (2001). Peer effects with random assignment: Results for Dartmouth roommates. *Quarterly Journal of Economics, 116*, 681–704.

Sack, K. (1998). Georgia's governor seeks musical start for babies. *The New York Times,* January 15, 1998, p. A12.

Sack, R. L., Brandes, R. W., Kendall, A. R., & Lewy, A. J. (2000). Entrainment of free-running circadian rhythms by melatonin in blind people. *New England Journal of Medicine, 343,* 1070–1077.

Sackeim, H. A., Dillingham, E. M., Prudic, J., Cooper, T., McCall, W. V., Rosenquiest, P. Isenberg, K., Garcia, K., Mulsant, B. H., & Haskett, R. F. (2009). Effect of concomitant pharmacotherapy on electroconvulsive therapy outcomes: Short-term efficacy and adverse effects. *Archives of General Psychiatry, 66,* 720–737.

Sackett, P., & Lievens, F. (2008). Personnel selection. *Annual Review of Psychology, 59,* 419–450.

Sagberg, F. (1999). Road accidents caused by drivers falling asleep. *Accident Analysis & Prevention, 31,* 639–649.

Saha, S., Chant, D., Welham, J., & McGrath, J. (2005). A systematic review of the prevalence of schizophrenia. *PLoS Med, 2*(5), e141. doi: 10.1371/journal.pmed.0020141

Sahakyan, L., & Kelley, C. M. (2002). A contextual change account of the directed forgetting effect. *Journal of Experimental Psychology: Learning, Memory, & Cognition, 28,* 1064–1072.

Saigal, S., & Doyle, L. W. (2008). An overview of mortality and sequelae of preterm birth from infancy to adulthood. *Lancet, 371*(9608), 261–269.

Salgado, J. F. (1997). The five-factor model of personality and job performance in the European community. *Journal of Applied Psychology, 82,* 30–43.

Salgado, J. F. (2002). The Big Five personality dimensions and counterproductive behaviors. *International Journal of Selection and Assessment, 10*(1–2), 117–125.

Salgado, J., Anderson, N., Moscoso, S., Bertua, C., de Fruyt, F., & Rolland, J. (2003). A meta-analytic study of general mental ability validity for different occupations in the European Community. *Journal of Applied Psychology, 88*(6), 1068–1081.

Salo, R., Ursu, S., Buonocore, M. H., Leamon, M. H., & Carter, C. (2010). Impaired prefrontal cortical functioning disrupted adaptive cognitive control in methamphetamine abusers: An fMRI study. *Biological Psychiatry, 65,* 706–709.

Salvatore, J. E., I-Chun Kuo, S., Steele, R. D., Simpson, J. A., & Collins, W. A. (2011). Recovering from conflict in romantic relationships: A developmental perspective. *Psychological Science, 22,* 376–383.

Sarchione, C., Cuttler, M., Muchinsky, P., & Nelson-Gray, R. (1998). Prediction of dysfunctional job behaviors among law enforcement officers. *Journal of Applied Psychology, 83*(6), 904–912.

Sargent, J. D., & Heatherton, T. F. (2009). Comparison of trends for adolescent smoking in movies: 1990–2007. *Journal of the American Medical Association, 301,* 2211–2213.

Saucier, G., Bel-Bahar, T., & Fernandez C. (2007). What modifies the expression of personality tendencies? Defining basic domains of situation variables. *Journal of Personality, 75*(3), 479–504.

Saus, E., Johnsen, B., Eid, J., Riisem, P., Andersen, R., & Thayer, J. (2006). The effect of brief situational awareness training in a police shooting simulator: An experimental study. *Military Psychology, 18,* s3–s21.

Savage-Rumbaugh, S., & Lewin, R. (1994). *Kanzi: The ape at the brink of the human mind.* New York: Wiley.

Savic, I., Berglund, H., Lindström, P., & Gustafsson, J. (2005, May). Brain response to putative pheromones in homosexual men. *PNAS: Proceedings of the National Academy of Sciences of the United States of America, 102*(20), 7356–7361.

Savin-Williams, R. C., & Cohen, K. M. (2004). Homoerotic development during childhood and adolescence. *Child Adolescent Psychiatric Clinics of North America, 13,* 529–549.

Saxe, L. (1994). Detection of deception: Polygraph and integrity tests. *Current Directions in Psychological Science, 3,* 69–73.

Schaufeli, W. B., Bakker, A. B., & Van Rhenen, W. (2009). How changes in job demands and resources predict burnout, work engagement and sickness absenteeism. *Journal of Organizational Behavior, 30*(7), 893–917.

Schaufeli, W. B., Martínez, I. M., Marques Pinto, A., Salanova, M., & Bakker, A. B. (2002). Burnout and engagement in university students: A cross-national study. *Journal of Cross-Cultural Psychology, 33*(5), 464–481.

Scheier, M. F., & Carver, C. S. (1985). Optimism, coping, and health: Assessment and implications of generalized outcome expectancies. *Health Psychology, 4*(3), 219–247.

Schenck, C. H., Lee, S. A., Bornemann, M. A., & Mahowald, M. W. (2009). Potentially lethal behaviors associated with rapid eye movement sleep behavior disorder: Review of the literature and forensic implications. *Journal of Forensic Science, 54,* 1475–1484.

Schenck, C. H., & Mahowald, M. (2002). REM sleep behavior disorder: Clinical, developmental, and neuroscience perspectives 16 years after its formal identification. *Sleep, 25,* 120–138.

Schenck, C. H., Milner, D. M., Hurwitz, T. D., et al. (1989). A polysomnographic and clinical report on sleep-related injury in 100 adult patients. *American Journal of Psychiatry, 146,* 1166–1173.

Schierenbeck, T., Riemann, D., Berger, M., & Hornyak, M. (2008). Effect of illicit recreational drugs upon sleep: Cocaine, ecstasy and marijuana. *Sleep Medicine Reviews, 12*(5), 381–389.

Schinka, J. A., Busch, R. M., & Robichaux-Keene, N. (2004). A meta-analysis of the association between the serotonin transporter gene polymorphism (5HTTLPR) and trait anxiety. *Molecular Psychiatry, 9,* 197–202.

Schlaug, G., Jancke, L., Huang, Y., & Steinmetz, H. (1995). In vivo evidence of structural brain asymmetry in musicians. *Science, 267,* 699–701.

Schlaug, G., Marchina, S., & Norton, A. (2009). Evidence for plasticity in white matter tracts of chronic aphasic patients undergoing intense intonation-based speech therapy. *Annals of the New York Academy of Sciences, 1169,* 385–394.

Schlaug, G., Renga, V., & Nair, D. (2008). Transcranial direct current stimulation in stroke recovery. *Archives of Neurology, 65,* 1571–1576.

Schmader, T., Johns, M., & Forbes, C. (2008). An integrated process model of stereotype threat effects on performance. *Psychological Review, 115*(2), 336–356.

Schmidt, F. L., & Hunter, J. E. (1998). The validity and utility of selection methods in personnel psychology: Practical and theoretical implications of 85 years of research findings. *Psychological Bulletin, 124,* 262–274.

Schmidt, G. L., DeBuse, C. J., & Seger, C. A. (2007). Right hemisphere metaphor processing? Characterizing the lateralization of semantic processes. *Brain and Language, 100,* 127–41.

Schmidt, R., & Bjork, R. (1992). New conceptualizations of practice: Common principles in three paradigms suggest new concepts for training. *Psychological Science, 3*(4), 207–217.

Schmitt, D. P., Allik, J., McCrae, R. R., Benet-Martinez, V., et al. (2007). The geographic distribution of Big Five personality traits: Patterns and profiles of human self-descriptions across 56 nations. *Journal of Cross-Cultural Psychology, 38,* 173–212.

Schmitt, D. P., Realo, A., Voracek, M., & Allik, J. (2008). Why can't a man be more like a woman? Sex differences in Big Five personality traits across 55 cultures. *Journal of Personality and Social Psychology, 94,* 168–182.

Schmolk, H., Buffalo, E. A., & Squire, L. R. (2000). Memory distortions develop over time: Recollections of the O. J. Simpson trial verdict after 15 and 32 months. *Psychological Science, 11,* 39–45.

Schoenberger, N. E., Kirsch, I., Gearan, P., Montgomery G., Pastyrnak S., et al. (1997). Hypnotic enhancement of a cognitive behavioral treatment for public speaking anxiety. *Behavior Therapy, 28,* 127–140.

Schottenbauer, M. A., Momenan, R., Kerick, M., & Hommer, D. W. (2007). Relationships among aging, IQ, and intracranial volume in alcoholics and control subjects. *Neuropsychology, 21,* 337–345.

Schredl, M. (2001). Night terrors in children: Prevalence and influencing factors. *Sleep and Hypnosis, 3*(2), 68–72.

Schredl, M. (2003). Effects of state and trait factors on nightmare frequency. *European Archives of Psychiatry and Clinical Neuroscience, 253*(5), 241–247.

Schroeder, D. A., Penner, L. A., Dovidio, J. F., & Piliavin, J. A. (1995). *The psychology of helping and altruism: Problems and puzzles.* New York: McGraw-Hill.

Schroers, M., Prigot, J., & Fagen, J. (2007). The effect of a salient odor context on memory retrieval in young infants. *Infant Behavior and Development, 30,* 685–689.

Schultheiss, O. C., & Brunstein, J. C. (2001). Assessing implicit motives with a research version of the TAT: Picture profiles, gender differences, and relations to other personality measures. *Journal of Personality Assessment, 77,* 71–86.

Schulz-Hardt, S., Frey, D., Luthgens, C., & Moscovici, S. (2000). Biased information search in group decision making. *Journal of Personality and Social Psychology, 78,* 655–669.

Schummers, J., & Browning, M. D. (2001). Evidence for a role for GABA(A) and NMDA receptors in ethanol inhibition of long-term potentiation. *Brain Research, 94,* 9–14.

Schwartz, B., Ward, A., Monterosso, J., Lyubomirsky, S., White, K., & Lehman, D. R. (2002). Maximizing versus satisficing: Happiness is a matter of choice. *Journal of Personality and Social Psychology, 83*(5), 1178–1197.

Scoboria, A., Mazzoni, G., Kirsch, I., & Jimenez, S. (2006). The effects of prevalence and script information on plausibility belief and memory of autobiographical events. *Applied Cognitive Psychology, 20*(8), 1049–1064.

Seale, J. P., Shellenberger, S., Rodriguez, C., Seale, J. D., & Alvarado, M. (2002). Alcohol use and cultural change in and indigenous population: A case study from Venezuela. *Alcohol and Alcoholism, 37,* 603–608.

Segerstrom, S. C., & Miller, G. E. (2004). Psychological stress and the immune system: A meta-analytic study of 30 years of inquiry. *Psychological Bulletin, 130,* 601–630.

Seidenberg, M. S., & Pettito, L. A. (1979). Signing behavior in apes: A critical review. *Cognition, 7,* 177–215.

Seligman, M. E. P. (1971). Phobias and preparedness. *Behavior Therapy, 2,* 307–320.

Seligman, M., & Maier, S. (1967). Failure to escape traumatic shock. *Journal of Experimental Psychology, 74,* 1–9.

Selye, H. (1956). *The stress of life.* New York: McGraw-Hill.

Senghas, A. (2003). Intergenerational influence and ontogenetic development in the emergence of spatial grammar in Nicaraguan Sign Language. *Cognitive Development, 18,* 511–531.

Senghas, A., Kita, S., & Ozyurek, A. (2004). Children creating core properties of language: Evidence from an emerging sign language in Nicaragua. *Science, 305*(5691), 1779–1782.

Shad, M. U., Bidesi, A. S., Chen, L-A., Thomas, B. P., Ernst, M., & Rao, U. (2011). Neurobiology of decision-making in adolescents. *Behavioural Brain Research, 217,* 67–76.

Shamir, B., House, R. J., & Arthur, M. B. (1993). The motivational aspects of charismatic leadership: A self-concept theory. *Organization Science, 4,* 1–17.

Sharot, T., Martorella, E. A., Delgado, M. R., & Phelps, E. (2007). How personal experience modulates the neural circuitry of memories of September 11. *Proceedings of the National Academy of Sciences of the United States of America, 104,* 389–394.

Sharp, W., Hargrove, D., Johnson, L., & Deal, W. (2006). Mental health education: An evaluation of a classroom based strategy to modify help seeking for mental health problems. *Journal of College Student Development, 47*(4), 419–438.

Shechter, O. G., Durik, A. M., Miyamoto, Y., & Harackiewicz, J. M. (2011). The role of utility value in achievement behavior: The importance of culture. *Personality and Social Psychology Bulletin, 37,* 303–317.

Shedler, J. (2010). The efficacy of psychodynamic therapy. *American Psychologist, 65,* 98–109.

Shelton, R. C. (2006). The nature of discontinuation syndrome associated with antidepressant drugs. *Journal of Clinical Psychiatry, 67,* 3–7.

Shepperd, J. A., & Koch E. J. (2005). Pitfalls in teaching judgment heuristics. *Teaching of Psychology, 32,* 43–46.

Sherman, J. W., Kruschke, J. K., Sherman, S. J., Percy, E. J., Petrocelli, J. V., & Conrey, F. R. (2009). Attentional processes in stereotype formation: A common model for category accentuation and illusory correlation. *Journal of Personality and Social Psychology, 96,* 305–323.

Siegel, J. (1995). Phylogeny and the function of REM sleep. *Behavioural Brain Research, 69,* 29–34.

Siegel, J. (2005). Clues to the functions of mammalian sleep. *Nature, 437*(7063), 1264–1271.

Siegel, S. (1984). Pavlovian conditioning and heroin overdose: Reports by overdose victims. *Bulletin of the Psychonomic Society, 22,* 428–430.

Siegel, S., Hinson, R. E., Krank, M. D., & McCully, J. (1982). Heroin "overdose" death: Contribution of drug-associated environmental cues. *Science, 216,* 436–437.

Siegler, R. S. (1992). The other Alfred Binet. *Developmental Psychology, 28*(2), 179–190.

Silva, A. J., Paylor, R., Wehner, J. M., & Tonegawa, S. (1992). Impaired spatial learning in alpha-calcium-calmodulin kinase II mutant mice. *Science, 257,* 206–211.

Silva, M., Groeger, J., & Bradshaw, M. (2006). Attention–memory interactions in scene perception. *Spatial Vision, 19,* 9–19.

Silverman, I., Choi, J., & Peters, M. (2007). The hunter-gatherer theory of sex differences in spatial abilities: Data from 40 countries. *Archives of Sexual Behavior, 36,* 261–268.

Silverman, I., & Eals, M. (1992). Sex differences in spatial abilities: Evolutionary theory and data. In J. H. Barkow & L. Cosmides (Eds.), *The adapted mind: Evolutionary psychology and the generation of cultures* (pp. 533–549). New York: Oxford University Press.

Simons, D. J., & Chabris, C. F. (1999). Gorillas in our midst: Sustained inattentional blindness for dynamic events. *Perception, 28,* 1059–1074.

Simpson, J. R. (2008). Functional MRI lie detection: Too good to be true? *Journal of the Academy of Psychology and the Law, 236,* 91–98.

Singer, M. A., & Goldin-Meadow, S. (2005). Children learn when their teacher's gestures and speech differ. *Psychological Science, 16,* 85–89.

Sinha, R. (2009). Modeling stress and drug craving in the laboratory: Implications for addiction treatment development. *Addiction Biology, 14*(1), 84–98.

Skinner, B. F. (1948). Superstition in the pigeon. *Journal of Experimental Psychology, 38,* 168–172.

Skinner, B. F. (1985). Cognitive science and behaviorism. *British Journal of Psychology, 76,* 291–301.

Skipper, J. I., Goldin-Meadow, S., & Nusbaum, H. C. (2007). Speech-associated gestures, Broca's area, and the human mirror system. *Brain and Language, 101,* 260–277.

Slotema, C. W., Blom, J. D., Hoek, H. W., & Sommer, I. E. (2010). Should we expand the toolbox of psychiatric treatment methods to include repetitive transcranial magnetic stimulation (rTMS)? A meta-analysis of the efficacy of rTMS in psychiatric disorders. *Journal of Clinical Psychiatry, 71,* 873–884.

Smith, B. W. (2004). Structural and organizational predictors of homicide by police. *Policing: An International Journal of Police Strategies and Management, 27,* 539–557.

Smith, E. S., Blass, G. R., Lewin, G. R., & Park, T. J. (2010). Absence of histamine-induced itch in the African naked mole-rat and "rescue" by substance P. *Molecular Pain, 6,* 29.

Smith, J., & Tolson, J. (2008). Recognition, diagnosis, and treatment of restless legs syndrome. *Journal of the American Academy of Nurse Practitioners, 20*(8), 396–401.

Smith, T. B., McCullough, M. E., & Poll, J. (2003). Religiousness and depression: Evidence for a main effect and the moderating influence of stressful life events. *Psychological Bulletin, 129,* 614–636.

Smith, T. W., & Spiro, A. III. (2002). Personality, health, and aging: Prolegomenon for the next generation. *Journal of Research in Personality, 36,* 363–394.

Smither, J. W., London, M., & Reilly, R. R. (2005). Does Performance Improve Following Multisource Feedback? A Theoretical Model, Meta-Analysis, And Review Of Empirical Findings. *Personnel Psychology, 58*(1), 33–66.

Snider, L. A., & Swedo, S. E. (2004). PANDAS: Current status and directions for research. *Molecular Psychiatry, 9,* 900–907.

Snowdon, L. R. (1999). African American service use for mental health problems. *Journal of Community Psychology, 27,* 303–313.

Snyder, K. (2006). Kurt Snyder's personal experience with schizophrenia. *Schizophrenia Bulletin, 32,* 209–211.

Souchay, C., Moulin, C., Clarys, D., Taconnat, L., & Isingrini, M. (2007). Diminished episodic memory awareness in older adults: Evidence from feeling-of-knowing and recollection. *Consciousness and Cognition: An International Journal, 16*(4), 769–784.

Sourander, A., Klomek, A. B., Ikonen, M., Lindroos, J., Luntamo, T., Koskelainen, M., Ristkari, T., & Helenius, H. (2010). Psychosocial risk factors associated with bullying and cyberbullying among adolescents: A population-based study. *Archives of General Psychiatry, 67,* 720–728.

Sousa-Poza, A., & Sousa-Poza, A. A. (2000). Well-being at work: A cross-national analysis of the levels and determinants of job satisfaction. *Journal of Socio-Economics, 29,* 517–538.

Spanos, N., Cobb, P., & Gorassini, D. (1985). Failing to resist hypnotic test suggestions: A strategy for self-presenting as deeply hypnotized. *Psychiatry: Journal for the Study of Interpersonal Processes, 48*(3), 282–292.

Spearman, C. (1923). *The nature of intelligence and the principles of cognition.* London: Macmillan.

Spector, P. (2002). Employee control and occupational stress. *Current Directions in Psychological Science, 11,* 133–136.

Spelke, E. (2005). Sex differences in intrinsic aptitude for mathematics and science? A critical review. *American Psychologist, 60*(9), 950–958.

Spelke, E. S., & Kinzler, K. D. (2007). Core knowledge. *Developmental Science, 10,* 89–96.

Spera, S. P., Buhrfeind, E. D., & Pennebaker, J. W. (1994). Expressive writing and coping with job loss. *Academy of Management Journal, 37,* 722–733.

Sperling, G. (1960). The information available in brief visual presentations. *Psychological Monographs, 74*(11, Whole No. 498), 1–29.

Sperry, R. W. (1982). Some effects of disconnecting the cerebral hemispheres. *Science, 217,* 1223–1226, 1250.

Squire, L. R. (1986). Mechanisms of memory. *Science, 232*(4758), 1612–1619.

Squire, L. R. (1989). On the course of forgetting in very long-term memory. *Journal of Experimental Psychology: Learning, Memory, and Cognition, 15*(2), 241–245.

Squire, L. R., Wixted, J. T., & Clark, R. E. (2007). Recognition memory and the medial temporal lobe: A new perspective. *Nature Reviews Neuroscience, 8*(11), 872–83.

Staffen, W., Kronbichler, M., Aichhorn, M., Mair, A., & Ladurner, G. (2006). Selective brain activity in response to one's own name in the persistent vegetative state. *Journal of Neurology, Neurosurgery, and Psychiatry, 77,* 1383–1384.

Stahl, C., Unkelbach, C., & Corneille, O. (2009). On the respective contributions of awareness of unconditioned stimulus valence and unconditioned stimulus identity in attitude formation through evaluative conditioning. *Journal of Personality and Social Psychology, 97,* 404–420.

Stanford, E. P., Happersett, C. J., Morton, D., Molgaard, C., & Peddecord, K. M. (1991). Early retirement and functional impairment from a multi-ethnic perspective. *Research and Aging, 13,* 5–38.

Stanhope, N., Cohen, G., & Conway, M. (1993). Very long-term retention of a novel. *Applied Cognitive Psychology, 7,* 239–256.

Stanton, S. J., Beehner, J. C., Saini, E. K., Kuhn, C. M., & Labar, K. S. (2009). Dominance, politics, and physiology: Voters' testosterone changes on the night of the 2008 United States presidential election. *PLoS One, 21,* e7543.

Starin, E. D. (2004). Masturbation observations in Temminck's red colobus. *Folia Primatologica, 75,* 114–117.

Stark, C. E., Okado, Y., & Loftus, E. F. (2010). Imaging the reconstruction of true and false memories using sensory reactivation and the misinformation paradigms. *Learning and Memory, 17,* 485–488.

Staw, B. M., Bell, N. E., & Clausen, J. A. (1986). The dispositional approach to job attitudes: A lifetime longitudinal test. *Administrative Science Quarterly, 31,* 56–77.

Steele, C. (1997). A threat in the air: How stereotypes shape intellectual identity and performance. *American Psychologist, 52*(6), 613–629.

Steele, J. D., Christmas, D., Eliamel, M. S., & Matthews, K. (2008). Anterior cingulotomy for major depression: Clinical outcome and relationship to lesion characteristics. *Biological Psychiatry, 63,* 670–677.

Steele, K. M., Ball, T. N., & Runk, R. (1997). Listening to Mozart does not enhance backwards digit span performance. *Perceptual and Motor Skills, 84,* 1179–1184.

Steele, K. M., Bass, K. E., & Crook, M. D. (1999). The mystery of the Mozart effect: Failure to replicate. *Psychological Science, 10,* 366–369.

Steffen, P. R., McNeilly, M., Anderson, N., & Sherwood, A. (2003). Effects of perceived racism and anger inhibition on ambulatory blood pressure in African Americans. *Psychosomatic Medicine, 65,* 746–750.

Steinberg, L. (1987). The impact of puberty on family relations: Effects of pubertal status and pubertal timing. *Developmental Psychology, 23,* 451–460.

Steinberg, L. (2007). Risk taking in adolescence: New perspectives from brain and behavioral science. *Current Directions in Psychological Science, 16,* 55–59.

Steinberg, L. (2008). A social neuroscience perspective on adolescent risk-taking. *Developmental Review, 28,* 78–106.

Sternberg, R. J., Castejón, J. L., Prieto, M. D., Hautamäki, J., & Grigorenko, E. L. (2001). Confirmatory factor analysis of the Sternberg Triarchic Abilities Test in three international samples: An empirical test of the triarchic theory of intelligence. *European Journal of Psychological Assessment, 17*(1), 1–16.

Stettler, N., Signer, T. M., & Suter, P. M. (2004). Electronic games and environmental factors associated with childhood obesity in Switzerland. *Obesity Research, 12,* 896–903.

Stevens, M. J., & Campion, M. A. (1999). Staffing work teams: Development and validation of a selection test for teamwork settings. *Journal of Management, 20,* 503–530.

Stevenson, R. J., Oaten, M. J., Caste, T. I., Repacholi, B. M., & Wagland, P. (2010). Children's response to adult disgust elicitors: Development and acquisition. *Developmental Psychology, 46,* 165–177.

Stice, E., Presnell, K., Shaw, H., & Rohde, P. (2005). Psychological and behavioral risk factors for obesity onset in adolescent girls: A prospective study. *Journal of Consulting and Clinical Psychology, 73,* 195–202.

Stickgold, R., & Walker, M. P. (2007). Sleep-dependent memory consolidation and reconsolidation. *Sleep Medicine, 8,* 331–343.

Stine-Morrow, E. A. L. (2007). The Dumbledore hypothesis of cognitive aging. *Current Directions in Psychological Science, 16,* 295–299.

Stinson, F. S., Dawson, D. A., Chou, P. S., et al. (2007). The epidemiology of DSM-IV specific phobia in the USA: Results from the National Epidemiologic Survey on Alcohol and Related Conditions. *Psychological Medicine, 37,* 1047–1059.

Stokoe, W. C., Casterline, D. C., & Croneberg, C. G. (1976). *A dictionary of American Sign Language on linguistic principles* (2nd ed.). Linstok Press: Silver Spring, MD.

Stout, J. G., Dasgupta, N., Hunsinger, M., & McManus, M. (2011). STEMing the tide: Using in-group experts to inoculate women's self-concept and professional goals in science, technology, engineering, and mathematics (STEM). *Journal of Personality and Social Psychology, 100,* 255–270.

Strack, F., Martin, L. L., & Stepper, S. (1988). Inhibiting and facilitating conditions of the human smile: A nonobtrusive test of the facial feedback hypothesis. *Journal of Personality and Social Psychology, 54,* 768–777.

Strahan, E. J., Spencer, S. J., & Zanna, M. P. (2002). Subliminal priming and persuasion: Striking while the iron is hot. *Journal of Experimental Social Psychology, 38,* 556–568.

Strassman, R. (2001). *DMT: Spirit molecule.* Rochester, VT: Park Street Press.

Stratton, R. J., Stubbs, R. J., & Elia, M. (2003). Short-term continuous enteral tube feeding schedules did not suppress appetite and food intake in healthy men in a placebo-controlled trial. *Journal of Nutrition, 133,* 2570–2576.

Strecher, V. (2007). Internet methods for delivering behavioral and health-related interventions (e-health). *Annual Review of Clinical Psychology, 3,* 53–76.

Streissguth, A. P., & Connor, P. D. (2001). Fetal alcohol syndrome and other effects of prenatal alcohol: Developmental cognitive neuroscience implications. In C. A. Nelson & M. Luciana (Eds.), *Handbook of developmental cognitive neuroscience* (pp. 505–518). Cambridge, MA: MIT Press.

Streppel, M. T., Boshuizen, H. C., Ocke, M. C., Kok, F. J., & Kromhout, D. (2007). Mortality and life expectancy in relation to long-term cigarette, cigar, and pipe smoking: The Zutphen study. *Tobacco Control, 16,* 107–113.

Stuart, E. W., Shimp, T. A., & Engle, R. W. (1987). Classical conditioning of consumer attitudes: Four experiments in an advertising context. *Journal of Consumer Research, 14*(3), 334–349.

Sturmer, S., Snyder, M., & Omoto, A. M. (2005). Prosocial emotions and helping: The moderating role of group membership. *Journal of Personality and Social Psychology, 88,* 532–546.

Substance Abuse and Mental Health Services Administration (SAMHSA). (2010). *Results from the 2009 National Survey on Drug Use and Health: National Findings* (Office of Applied Studies, NSDUH Series H-38A, HHS Publication No. SMA 10-4586 Findings). Rockville, MD: SAMHSA.

Sulloway, F. (2007). Birth order and intelligence. *Science, 316,* 1711–1712.

Sumnall, H. R., Measham, F., Brandt, S. D., & Cole, J. C. (2010). *Salvia divinorum* use and phenomenology: Results from an online survey [Electronic publication ahead of print]. *Journal of Psychopharmacology.*

Sundet, J. (2004). The end of the Flynn effect: A study of secular trends in mean intelligence scores of Norwegian conscripts during half a century. *Intelligence, 32,* 349.

Suomi, S. J., & Harlow, H. (1972). Social rehabilitation of isolate-reared monkeys. *Developmental Psychology, 6,* 487–496.

Super, D. E., Savickas, M. L., & Super, C. M. (1996). The life-span, life-space approach to careers. In D. Brown, L. Brooks, & Associates (Eds.), *Career choice and development: Applying contemporary theories to practice* (3rd ed., pp. 121–178). San Francisco: Jossey-Bass.

Sutton, S. K., & Davidson, R. J. (1997). Prefrontal brain asymmetry: A biological substrate of the behavioral approach and inhibition systems. *Psychological Science, 8,* 204–210.

Swami, V., Furnham, A., Maakip, I., Ahmad, M., Nawi, N., Voo, P., et al. (2008). Beliefs about the meaning and measurement of intelligence: A cross-cultural comparison of American, British and Malaysian undergraduates. *Applied Cognitive Psychology, 22*(2), 235–246.

Swartz, M., & Swanson, J. (2004). Involuntary outpatient commitment, community treatment orders, and assisted outpatient treatment: What's in the data? *Canadian Journal of Psychiatry / La Revue canadienne de psychiatrie, 49,* 585–591.

Sweeney, P. D., Anderson, K., & Bailey, S. (1986). Attributional style in depression: A meta-analytic review. *Journal of Personality and Social Psychology, 50,* 974–991.

Swithers, S. E., Baker, C. R., & Davidson, T. L. (2009). General and persistent effects of high-intensity sweeteners on body weight gain and caloric compensation in rats. *Behavioral Neuroscience, 123,* 772–780.

Swithers, S. E., & Davidson, T. L. (2005). Obesity: Outwitting the wisdom of the body? *Current Neurology and Neuroscience Reports, 5,* 159–162.

Symons, C. S., & Johnson, B. T. (1997). The self-reference effect in memory: A meta-analysis. *Psychological Bulletin, 121,* 371–394.

Takahashi, Y. (1990). Is multiple personality really rare in Japan? *Dissociation, 3,* 57–59.

Takeuchi, D., & Cheung, M. (1998). Coercive and voluntary referrals: How ethnic minority adults get into mental health treatment. *Ethnicity & Health, 3,* 149–158.

Talarico, J., & Rubin, D. (2003). Confidence, not consistency, characterizes flashbulb memories. *Psychological Science, 14,* 455–461.

Talmi, D., Grady, C., Goshen-Gottstein, Y., & Moscovitch, M. (2005). Neuroimaging the serial position curve: A test of single-store versus dual-store models. *Psychological Science, 16,* 716–723.

Tamres, L., Janicki, D., & Helgeson, V. S. (2002). Sex differences in coping behavior: A meta-analytic review. *Personality and Social Psychology Review, 6,* 2–30.

Tanaka, A., Koizumi, A., Imai, H., Hiramatsu, S., Hiramoto, E., & de Gelder, B. (2010). I feel your voice: Cultural differences in the perception of emotion. *Psychological Science, 21,* 1259–1262.

Tang, T. Z., & DeRubeis, R. J. (1999). Sudden gains and critical sessions in cognitive-behavioral therapy for depression. *Journal of Consulting and Clinical Psychology, 67,* 894–904.

Tang, Y., Shimizu, E., Dube, G., Rampon, C., Kerchner, G., Zhuo, M., et al. (1999). Genetic enhancement of learning and memory in mice. *Nature, 401*(6748), 63–69.

Tang, Y.-Y., Ma, Y., Fan, Y., Feng, H., Wang, J., Feng, S., Lu, Q., Hu, B., Lin, Y., Li, J., Zhang, Y., Wang, Y., Zhou, L., & Fan, M. (2009). Central and autonomic nervous system interaction is altered by short-term meditation. *Proceedings of the National Academy of Sciences, 105,* 8865–8870.

Tashiro, A., Makino, H., & Gage, F. H. (2007). Experience-specific functional modification of the dendate gyrus through adult neurogenesis: A critical period during an immature stage. *Journal of Neuroscience, 27,* 3252–3259.

Taylor, A. J., & Hort, J. (2004). Measuring proximal stimuli involved in flavour perception. In A. J. Taylor & D. R. Roberts (Eds.), *Flavor perception* (pp. 1–38). Oxford, UK: Blackwell.

Taylor, C. A., Lee, S. J., Guterman, N. B., & Rice, J. C. (2010). Use of spanking for 3-year-old children and associated intimate partner aggression or violence. *Pediatrics, 126,* 415–24.

Taylor, S. E. (2002). *The tending instinct: How nurturing is essential to who we are and how we live.* New York: Holt.

Taylor, S. E. (2006). Tend and befriend: Biobehavioral bases of affiliation under stress. *Current Directions in Psychological Science, 15,* 273–277.

Teasdale, T. W. & Owen, D. R. (2005). A long-term rise and recent decline in intelligence test performance: The Flynn effect in reverse. *Personality and Individual Differences, 39*(4), 837–843.

Tedeschi, R. G., & Calhoun, L. G. (2004). Post-traumatic growth: Conceptual foundations and empirical evidence. *Psychological Inquiry, 15,* 1–18.

Tellegen, A., Lykken, D. T., Bouchard, T. J., Wilcox, K. J., Segal, N. L., & Rich, S. (1998). Personality similarity in twins reared apart and together. *Journal of Personality and Social Psychology, 54,* 1031–1039.

Teplin, L. A., McClelland, G. M., Abram, K. M., & Weiner, D. A. (2005). Crime victimization in adults with severe mental illness: Comparison with the National Crime Victimization Survey. *Archives of General Psychiatry, 62,* 911–921.

Terao, Y., & Ugawa, Y. (2002). Basic mechanisms of TMS. *Journal of Clinical Neurophysiology, 19*(4), 322–343.

Terracciano, A., Abdel-Khalek, A. M., Adám, N., et al. (2005). National character does not reflect mean personality trait levels in 49 cultures. *Science, 310,* 96–100.

Terracciano, A., Sanna, S, Uda, M., et al. (2010). Genome-wide association scan for five major dimensions of personality. *Molecular Psychiatry, 15,* 647–656.

Tett, R. P., Jackson, D. N., & Rothstein, M. (1991). Personality measures as predictors of job performance: A meta-analytic review. *Personnel Psychology, 44,* 703–742.

Thacher, P. (2008). University students and "the all-nighter": Correlates and patterns of students' engagement in a single night of total sleep deprivation. *Behavioral Sleep Medicine, 6*(1), 16–31.

Thase, M. E., & Denko, T. (2008). Pharmacotherapy of mood disorders. *Annual Review of Clinical Psychology, 4,* 53–91.

Thomas, A., & Chess, S. (1977). *Temperament and development.* New York: Brunder/Mazel.

Thomas, N., Rossell, S., Farhall, J., Shawyer, F., & Castle, D. (2010). Cognitive behavioural therapy for auditory hallucinations: Effectiveness and predictors of outcome in a specialist clinic [Electronic publication ahead of print]. *Behavioural and Cognitive Psychotherapy.*

Thomas, S. B., & Quinn, S. C. (1991). The Tuskegee syphilis study, 1932 to 1972: Implications for HIV education and AIDS risk education programs in the black community. *American Journal of Public Health, 81,* 1498–1505.

Thompson, A., & Riggio, R. E. (2010). Introduction to special issue on defining and measuring character in leadership. *Consulting Psychology Journal: Practice and Research, 62*(4), 211–215.

Thoresen, C., Bradley, J., Bliese, P., & Thoresen, J. (2004). The Big Five personality traits and individual job performance growth trajectories in maintenance and transitional job stages. *Journal of Applied Psychology, 89,* 835–853.

Thoresen, C., Kaplan, S., Barsky, A., Warren, C., & de Chermont, K. (2003). The affective underpinnings of job perceptions and attitudes: A meta-analytic review and integration. *Psychological Bulletin, 129,* 914–945.

Thornton, A., & Raihani, N. J. (2010). Identifying teaching in wild animals. *Learning & Behavior, 38*(3), 297–309.

Tobias, M. C., O'Neill, J., Hudkins, M., Bartzokis, G., Dean, A. C., & London, E. D. (2010). White-matter abnormalities in brain during early abstinence from methamphetamine abuse. *Psychopharmacology, 209,* 13–24.

Tochigi, M., Okazaki, Y., Kato, N., & Sasaki, T. (2004). What causes seasonality of birth in schizophrenia? *Neuroscience Research, 48,* 1–11.

Todorov, A., Mandisodza, A. N., Goren, A., & Hall, C. (2005). Inferences of competence from faces predict election outcomes. *Science, 308,* 1623–1626.

Tolman, E. C., & Honzik, C. H. (1930). Degrees of hunger, reward and non-reward, and maze learning in rats. *University of California Publications in Psychology, 4*241–4256.

Tom, G., Pettersen, P., Lau, T., et al. (1991). The role of overt head movement in the formation of affect. *Basic and Applied Social Psychology, 12,* 281–289.

Tom, G., Tong, S., & Hesse, C. (2010). Thick slice and thin slice teaching evaluations. *Social Psychology of Education, 13*(1), 129–136.

Toma, C. L., Hancock, J. T., & Ellison, N. B. (2008). Separating fact from fiction: An examination of deceptive self-deception in online dating profiles. *Personality and Social Psychology Bulletin, 34,* 1023–1036.

Tomblin, J. B., O'Brien, M., Shriberg, L. D., Williams, C., Murray, J., Patil, S., Bjork, J., Anderson, S., & Ballard, K. (2009). Language features in a mother and daughter of a chromosome 7;13 translocation involving FOXP2. *Journal of Speech, Language, and Hearing Research, 52,* 1157–1174.

Tooby, J., & Cosmides, L. 1990. On the universality of human nature and the uniqueness of the individual: The role of genetics and adaptation. *Journal of Personality, Special Issue: Biological Foundations of Personality—Evolution, Behavioural Genetics, and Psychophysiology, 58,* 17–67.

Tracy, M., Zimmerman, F. J., Galea, S., et al. (2008). What explains the relation between family poverty and childhood depressive symptoms? *Journal of Psychiatric Research, 42*(14), 1163–1175.

Trajanovic, N., Radivojevic, V., Kaushansky, Y., & Shapiro, C. (2007). Positive sleep state misperception: A new concept of sleep misperception. *Sleep Medicine, 8*(2), 111–118.

Tranel, D., & Damasio, A. (1985). Knowledge without awareness: An autonomic index of facial recognition by prosopagnosics. *Science, 228,* 1453–1454.

Trinder, J. (1988). Subjective insomnia without objective findings: A pseudo-diagnostic classification? *Psychological Bulletin, 103,* 87–94.

Trivers, R. L. (1971). The evolution of reciprocal altruism. *Quarterly Review of Biology, 46,* 35–57.

Tulving, E. (1972). *Episodic and semantic memory.* Oxford, UK: Academic Press.

Tulving, E., & Markowitsch, H. J. (1998). Episodic and declarative memory: Role of the hippocampus. *Hippocampus, 8,* 198–203.

Turk, C., Heimberg, R., Luterek, J., Mennin, D., & Fresco, D. (2005). Emotion dysregulation in generalized anxiety disorder: A comparison with social anxiety disorder. *Cognitive Therapy and Research, 29*(1), 89–106.

Turkheimer, E., Haley, A., Waldron, M., D'Onofrio, B., & Gottesman, I. I. (2003). Socioeconomic status modifies heritability of IQ in young children. *Psychological Science, 14,* 623–628.

Tversky, A., & Kahneman, D. (1973). Availability: A heuristic for judging frequency and probability. *Cognitive Psychology, 5,* 207–232.

Tversky, A., & Kahneman, D. (1982). The framing of decisions and the psychology of choice. *Science, 211*(4481), 453–458.

U.S. Department of Health and Human Services. (2001). *Youth violence: A report of the Surgeon General.* Rockville, MD: U.S. Public Health Service, Office of the Surgeon General. Retrieved June 2, 2010, from http://www.surgeongeneral.gov/library/youthviolence/report.html

U.S. News. (2008, March 9). America's best leaders. Retrieved October 1, 2009, from http://www.usnews.com/features/news/special-reports/best-leaders.html

Ullman, M. T., Corkin, S., Coppola, M., Hickok, G., Growdon, J. H., Koroshetz, W. J., & Pinker, S. (1997). A neural dissociation within language: Evidence that the mental dictionary is part of the declarative memory, and that grammatical rules are processed by the procedural system. *Journal of Cognitive Neuroscience, 9,* 266–276.

Umberson, D., Pudrovska, T., & Reczek, C. (2010). Parenthood, childlessness, and well-being: A life course perspective. *Journal of Marriage and Family, 72*(3), 612–629.

Unsworth, N., & Engle, R. W. (2005). Working memory capacity and fluid abilities: Examining the correlation between Operation Span and Raven. *Intelligence, 33,* 67–81.

Urry, H. L., Nitschke, J. B., Dolski, I., Jackson, D. C., Dalton, K. M., Mueller, C. J., et al. (2004). Making a life worth living: Neural correlates of well-being. *Psychological Science, 15,* 367–372.

Uziel, L. (2007). Individual differences in the social facilitation effect: A review and meta-analysis. *Journal of Research in Personality, 41*(3), 579–601.

Valenstein, E. S. (1973). *Brain control: A critical examination of brain stimulation and psychosurgery.* London: Wiley-Interscience.

Valkenburg, P. M., & Peter, J. (2009). Social consequences of the Internet for adolescents: A decade of research. *Current Directions in Psychological Science, 18,* 1–5.

van Beek, Y., Genta, M. L., Costabile, A., & Sansavini, A. (2006). Maternal expectations about infant development and pre-term and full-term infants: A cross-national comparison. *Infant Behavior and Development, 15,* 41–58.

van de Water, T. (1997). Psychology's entrepreneurs and the marketing of industrial psychology. *Journal of Applied Psychology, 82*(4), 486–499.

Van den Bussche, E., Van den Noortgate, W., & Reynvoet, B. (2009). Mechanisms of masked priming: A meta-analysis. *Psychological Bulletin, 135,* 452–477.

van der Kolk, B. A. (1994). The body keeps score: Memory and the evolving psychobiology of posttraumatic stress. *Harvard Review of Psychiatry, 1,* 253–265.

Van Iddekinge, C., & Ployhart, R. (2008). Developments in the criterion-related validation of selection procedures: A critical review and recommendations for practice. *Personnel Psychology, 61,* 871–925.

van IJzendoorn, M., & Juffer, F. (2005). Adoption is a successful natural intervention enhancing adopted children's IQ and school performance. *Current Directions in Psychological Science, 14*(6), 326–330.

van Os, J., Pedersen, C. B., & Mortensen, P. B. (2004). Confirmation of synergy between urbanicity and familial liability in the causation of psychosis. *American Journal of Psychiatry, 161,* 2312–2314.

van Praag, H. (2008). Neurogenesis and exercise: Past and future directions. *Neuromolecular Medicine, 10,* 128–140.

van Praag, H. (2009). Exercise and the brain: Something to chew on. *Trends in Neuroscience, 32,* 283–290.

van Praag, H., Lucero, M. J., Yeo, G. W., Stecker, K., Heivand, N., Zhao, C., Yip, E., Afanador, M., Schroeter, H., Hammerstone, J., & Gage, F. H. (2007). Plant-derived flavanol (−)epicatechin enhances angiogenesis and retention of spatial memory in mice. *Journal of Neuroscience, 27,* 5869–5878.

van Straten, A., & Cuijpers, P. (2009). Self-help therapy for insomnia: A meta-analysis. *Sleep Medicine Reviews, 13*(1), 61–71.

Vance, E. B., & Wagner, N. N. (1976). Written descriptions of orgasm: A study of sex differences. *Archives of Sexual Behavior, 5,* 87–98.

Vanheusden, K., Mulder, C., van der Ende, J., van Lenthe, F., Mackenbach, J., & Verhulst, F. (2008). Young adults face major barriers to seeking help from mental health services. *Patient Education and Counseling, 73*(1), 97–104.

Vanman, E. J., Saltz, J. L., Nathan, L. R., & Warren, J. A. (2004). Racial discrimination by low-prejudiced Whites: Facial movements as implicit measures of attitudes related to behavior. *Psychological Science, 15,* 711–714.

Vargha-Khadem, F., Gadian, D. G., Copp, A., & Mishkin, M. (2005). FOXP2 and the neuroanatomy of speech and language. *Nature Reviews Neuroscience, 6,* 131–138.

Vaughn, L. K., Denning, G., Stuhr, K. L., et al. (2010). Endocannabinoid signaling: Has it got rhythm? *British Journal of Pharmacology, 160,* 530–543.

Vazire, S., & Gosling, S. D. (2004). E-perceptions: Personality impressions based on personal websites. *Journal of Personality and Social Psychology, 87,* 123–132.

Verwey, M., & Amir, S. (2009). Food-entrainable circadian oscillators in the brain. *European Journal of Neuroscience, 30*(9), 1650–1657.

Villar, J., Merialdi, M., Gülmezoqlu, A. M., Abalos, E., Carroli, G., Kulier, R., & de Onis, M. (2003). Characteristics of randomized controlled trials included in systematic reviews of nutritional interventions reporting maternal morbidity, mortality, preterm delivery, intrauterine growth restriction and small for gestational age and birth weight outcomes. *Journal of Nutrition, 133,* 1632–1639.

Vinchur, A., Schippmann, J., Switzer, F., & Roth, P. (1998). A meta-analytic review of predictors of job performance for salespeople. *Journal of Applied Psychology, 83*(4), 586–597.

Viswesvaran, C., Schmidt, F. L., & Ones, D. S. (2005). Is there a general factor in ratings of job performance? A meta-analytic framework for disentangling substantive and error influences. *Journal of Applied Psychology, 90*(1), 108–131.

Voelker, R. (2003). Mounting student depression taxing campus mental health services. *Journal of the American Medical Association, 289,* 2055–2056.

Vogel, D. L., Wade, N. G., & Ascheman, P. (2009). Measuring perceptions of stigmatization by others for seeking psychological help: Reliability and validity of a new stigma scale with college students. *Journal of Counseling Psychology, 56,* 301–308.

Vogel, D. L., Wade, N. G., Wester, S. R., Larson, L., & Hackler, A. H. (2007). Seeking help from a mental health professional: The influence of one's social network. *Journal of Clinical Psychology, 63,* 233–245.

Vogel, E., Woodman, G., & Luck, S. (2001). Storage of features, conjunctions, and objects in visual working memory. *Journal of Experimental Psychology: Human Perception and Performance, 27,* 92–114.

Volkow, N. D. (2010). Congressional Caucus on Prescription Drug Abuse. Retrieved November 24, 2010, from http://nida.nih.gov/Testimony/9-22-10Testimony.html

Von Békésy, G. (1957). Sensations on the skin similar to directional hearing, beats and harmonics of the ear. *Journal of the Acoustical Society of America, 29*(4), 489–501.

vonFrisch, K. (1967). *The dance language and orientation of bees.* Cambridge, MA: Harvard University Press.

Vygotsky, L. (1978). *Mind in society: The development of higher psychological processes.* (M. Cole, V. John-Steiner, S. Scribner, & E. Soubermen, Eds.). Cambridge MA: Harvard University Press.

Wade, K., Garry, M., Read, J., & Lindsay, S. (2002). A picture is worth a thousand lies: Using false photographs to create false childhood memories. *Psychonomic Bulletin & Review, 9,* 597–603.

Wagner, G. A., & Morris, E. K. (1987). "Superstitious" behavior in children. *Psychological Record, 37,* 471–488.

Waite, L. J., & Gallagher, M. (2000). *The case for marriage: Why married people are happier, healthier and better off financially.* New York: Doubleday.

Wakefield, A. J., Murch, S. H., Anthony, A., Linnell, J., Casson, D. M., Malik, M., et al. (1998). Retracted: Ileal-lymphoid-nodular hyperplasia, non-specific colitis, and pervasive developmental disorder in children. *Lancet, 351,* 637–641.

Walker, E. G., Savole, T., & Davis, D. (1994). Neuromotor precursors of schizophrenia. *Schizophrenia Bulletin, 20,* 441–451.

Walker, E. G., Shapiro, D., Esterberg, M., & Trotman, H. (2010). Neurodevelopment and schizophrenia: Broadening the focus. *Current Directions in Psychological Science, 19,* 204–208.

Walker, I., & Read, J. (2002). The differential effectiveness of psychosocial and biogenetic causal explanations in reducing negative attitudes toward "mental illness." *Psychiatry: Interpersonal and Biological Processes, 65*(4), 313–325.

Walker, R. (2009, October 18). The song decoders. *New York Times.* Retrieved from http://www.nytimes.com/2009/10/18/magazine/18Pandora-t.html

Wallace, J., Edwards, B., Arnold, T., Frazier, M., & Finch, D. (2009). Work stressors, role-based performance, and the moderating influence of organizational support. *Journal of Applied Psychology, 94,* 254–262.

Wallston, K. A., Wallston, B. S., & DeVellis, R. (1978). Development of the Multidimensional Health Locus of Control (MHLC) scales. *Health Education Monographs, 6,* 160–170.

Walsh, T., McClellan, J. M., McCarthy, S. E., Addington, A. M., Pierce, S. B., et al. (2008). Rare structural variants disrupt multiple genes in neurodevelopmental pathways in schizophrenia. *Science, 320,* 539–543.

Walum, H., Westberg, L., Henningsson, S., et al. (2008). Genetic variation in vasopressin receptor 1a gene (AVPR1A) associated with pair-bonding behavior in humans. *Proceedings of the National Academy of Sciences, 105,* 14153–14156.

Wang, G. J., Volkow, N. D., Felder, C., Fowler, J. S., Levy, A. V., Pappas, N. R., Wong, C. T., Zhu, W., & Netusil, N. (2002). Enhanced resting activity of the oral somatosensory cortex in obese subjects. *Neuroreport, 13,* 1151–1155.

Wang, P. S., Berglund, P., Olfson, M., Pincus, H. A., Wells, K. B., & Kessler, R. C. (2005). Failure and delay in initial treatment contact after first onset of mental disorders in the National Comorbidity Survey Replication. *Archives of General Psychiatry, 62,* 603–613.

Wang, X., Lu, T., Snider, R. K., & Liang, L. (2005). Sustained firing in auditory cortex evoked by preferred stimuli. *Nature, 435,* 341–346.

Wanous, J., Poland, T., Premack, S., & Davis, K. (1992). The effects of met expectations on newcomer attitudes and behaviors: A review and meta-analysis. *Journal of Applied Psychology, 77*(3), 288–297.

Wansink, B., Painter, J. E., & North, J. (2005). Bottomless bowls: Why visual cues of portion size may influence intake. *Obesity Research, 13,* 93–100.

Ware, M. A., Wang, T., Shapiro, S. et al. (2010). Smoked cannabis for chronic neuropathic pain: A randomized controlled trial. *Canadian Medical Association Journal, 182,* E694–E701.

Wark, D. (2006). Alert hypnosis: A review and case report. *American Journal of Clinical Hypnosis, 48*(4), 291–300.

Warren, M. P., & Brooks-Gunn, J. (1989). Mood and behavior during adolescence: Evidence for hormonal factors. *Journal of Clinical Endocrinology and Metabolism, 69,* 77–83.

Watkins, C. E., Campbell, V. L., Neiberding, R., & Hall-mark, R. (1995). Contemporary practice of psychological assessment by clinical psychologists. *Professional Psychology: Research and Practice, 26,* 54–60.

Watson, A. C., Miller, F. E., & Lyons, J. S. (2005). Adolescent Attitudes Toward Serious Mental Illness. *Journal of Nervous and Mental Disease, 193,* 769–772.

Watson, D., & Clark, L. (1992). On traits and temperament: General and specific factors of emotional experience and their relation to the five-factor model. *Journal of Personality, 60*(2), 441–476.

Watson, D., & Pennebaker, J. W. (1989). Health complaints, stress and distress: Exploring the central role of negative affectivity. *Psychological Review, 96,* 234–264.

Watson, D., & Slack, A. K. (1993). General factors of affective temperament and their relation to job satisfaction over time. *Organizational Behavior and Human Decision Processes, 54,* 181–202.

Watson, D., Wiese, D., Vaidya, J., & Tellegen, A. (1999). The two general activation systems of affect: Structural findings, evolutionary considerations, and psychobiological evidence. *Journal of Personality and Social Psychology, 76,* 820–838.

Watson, J. B. (1930). *Behaviorism.* Chicago: University of Chicago Press.

Watson, J. B., & Rayner, R. R. (1920). Conditioned emotional reactions. *Journal of Experimental Psychology, 3,* 1–14.

Watson, M. W., & Getz, K. (1990). The relationship between Oedipal behaviors and children's family role concepts. *Merrill-Palmer Quarterly, 36,* 487–505.

Weekley, J. A., & Gier, J. A. (1987). Reliability and validity of the situational interview for a sales position. *Journal of Applied Psychology, 72*(3), 484–487.

Weeks, D. L., & Anderson, L. P. (2000). The interaction of observational learning with overt practice: Effects on motor skill learning. *Acta Psychologica, 104,* 259–271.

Weinsier, R. L., Hunter, G. R., Desmond, R. A., Byrne, N. M., Zuckerman, P. A., & Darnell, B. (2002). Free-living activity expenditure in women successful and unsuccessful at maintaining a normal body weight. *American Journal of Clinical Nutrition, 75,* 499–504.

Weise, D., Pyszczynski, T., Cox, C., Arndt, J., Greenberg, J., Solomon, S., et al. (2008, May). Interpersonal politics: The role of terror management and attachment processes in shaping political preferences. *Psychological Science, 19,* 448–455.

Weisman, A. G., Lopez, S. R., Ventura, J., Nuechterlein, K. H., Goldstein, M. J., & Hwang, S. (2000). A comparison of psychiatric symptoms between Anglo-Americans and Mexican-Americans with schizophrenia. *Schizophrenia Bulletin, 26,* 817–824.

Weiss, A., King, J. E., & Hopkins, W. D. (2007). A cross-setting study of chimpanzee (*Pan troglodytes*) personality structure and development: Zoological parks and Yerkes National Primate Research Center. *American Journal of Primatology, 69*(11), 1264.

Weiss, E., Kemmler, G., Deisenhammer, E., Fleischhacker, W., & Delazer, M. (2003). Sex differences in cognitive functions. *Personality and Individual Differences, 35*(4), 863–875.

Weissman, M. M. (2006). A brief history of interpersonal psychotherapy. *Psychiatric Annals, 36*(8), 553–557.

Weitzer, R., & Tuch, S. A. (2004). Race and perceptions of police misconduct. *Social Problems, 51,* 305–325.

Wellings, K., Field, J., Johnson, A. M., & Wadsworth, J. (1994). *Sexual behaviour in Britain: The national survey of sexual attitudes and lifestyles.* Penguin: Harmondsworth.

Wells, B., & Corts, D. P. (2008). Attitudes towards fraternities and sororities: Evidence of implicit, in-group favoritism. *College Student Journal.*

Wells, G. L., & Quinlaven, D. S. (2009). Suggestive eyewitness identification procedures and the Supreme Court's reliability test in light of eyewitness science: 30 years later. *Law and Human Behavior, 33,* 1–24.

Wells, G. L., & Petty, R. E. (1980). The effects of overt head movements on persuasion: Compatibility and incompatibility of responses. *Basic and Applied Social Psychology, 1*(3), 219–230.

Wenk, G. (2010). *Your brain on food: how chemicals control your thoughts and feelings.* Oxford, UK: Oxford University Press.

West, M. A., Borrill, C. S., & Unsworth, K. L. (1998). Team effectiveness in organizations. In C. L. Cooper & I. T. Robertson (Eds.) International Review of Industrial and Organizational Psychology, 13, 1–48.

Westen, D. (1998). The scientific legacy of Sigmund Freud: Toward a psychodynamically informed psychological science. *Psychological Bulletin, 124,* 333–371.

Westen, D., Blagov, P. S., & Harenski, K. (2006). Neural bases for motivated reasoning: An fMRI study of emotional constraints on partisan political judgment in the 2004 U.S. presidential election. *Journal of Cognitive Neuroscience, 18,* 1974–1958.

Westen, D., & Bradley, R. (2005). Empirically supported complexity: Rethinking evidence-based practice in psychotherapy. *Current Directions in Psychological Science, 14,* 266–271.

Westman, M., & Eden, D. (1997). Effects of a respite from work on burnout: Vacation relief and fade-out. *Journal of Applied Psychology, 82,* 516–527.

Westman, M., & Vinokur, A. (1998). Unraveling the relationship of distress levels within couples: Common stressors, empathic reactions, or crossover via social interaction? *Human Relations, 51*(2), 137–156.

White, A. M. (2003). What happened? Alcohol, memory blackouts, and the brain. *Alcohol Research & Health, 27,* 186–196.

White, R., & Williams, S. (2009). Amygdaloid neurosurgery for aggressive behaviour, Sydney, 1967–1977: Chronological narrative. *Australas Psychiatry, 17,* 405–209.

Whitson, J. A., & Galinsky, A. D. (2008). Lacking control increases illusory pattern perception. *Science, 322,* 115–117.

Whorf, B. L. (1973). *Language, thought, and reality: Selected writings of Benjamin Whorf,* edited by J. B. Carroll. Oxford, UK: Technology Press of MIT.

Wichman, A. L., Rodgers, J. L., & Maccallum, R. C. (2007). Birth order has no effect on intelligence: A reply and extension of previous findings. *Personality and Social Psychology Bulletin, 33,* 1195–1200.

Widenhorn-Müller, K., Hille, K., Klenk, J., & Weiland, U. (2008). Influence of having breakfast on cognitive performance and mood in 13- to 20-year-old high school students: Results of a crossover trial. *Pediatrics, 122,* 279–284.

Wijdicks, E. F. (2006). Minimally conscious state vs. persistent vegetative state: The case of Terry (Wallis) vs. the case of Terri (Schiavo). *Mayo Clinic Proceedings, 81,* 1155–1158.

Willingham, D. T. (2004). Reframing the mind: How Howard Gardner became a hero among educators by simply by redefining talents as "intelligences." *Education Next, 4*(3), 19–24.

Willis, J., & Todorov, A. (2006). First impressions: Making up your mind after a 100-ms exposure to a face. *Psychological Science, 17,* 592–598.

Willness, C. R., Steel, P., & Lee, K. (2007). A meta-analysis of the antecedents and consequences of workplace sexual harassment. *Personnel Psychology, 60*(1), 127–162.

Wimmer, H., & Perner, J. (1983). Beliefs about beliefs: Representation and constrained function of wrong beliefs in young children's understanding of deceptions. *Cognition, 13,* 103–128.

Winter, B., Breitenstein, C., Mooren, F. C., Voelker, K., Fobker, M., Lechtermann, A., Krueger, K.,

Fromme, A., Korsukewitz, C., Floel, A., & Knecht, S. (2007). High impact running improves learning. *Neurobiology of Learning and Memory, 87,* 597–609.

Winterer, G. (2010). Why do patients with schizophrenia smoke? *Current Opinion in Psychiatry, 23,* 112–119.

Witelson, S. F., Beresh, H., & Kigar, D. L. (2006). Intelligence and brain size in 100 postmortem brains: Sex, lateralization and age factors. *Brain: A Journal of Neurology, 129*(Pt 2), 386–398.

Witelson, S. F., Kigar, D. L., & Harvey, T. (1999). The exceptional brain of Albert Einstein. *Lancet, 353,* 2149–2153.

Wobber, V., Hare, B., Maboto, J., Lipson, S., Wrangham, R., & Ellison, P. T. (2010). Differential changes in steroid hormones before competition in bonobos and chimpanzees. *Proceedings of the National Academy of Sciences of the United States of America, 107*(28), 12457–12462.

Wolfe, J. M., Horowitz, T. S., Van Wert, M. J., Kenner, N. M., Place, S. S., & Kibbi, N. (2007). Low target prevalence is a stubborn source of errors in visual search tasks. *Journal of Experimental Psychology: General, 136*(4), 623–638.

Wolpe, J. (1990). *The practice of behavior therapy.* Elmsford, NY: Pergamon Press.

Wood, D., Harms, P., & Vazire, S. (2010). Perceiver effects as projective tests: What your perceptions of others say about you. *Journal of Personality and Social Psychology, 99*(1), 174–190.

Wood, J. M., Bootzin, R. R., Rosenhan, D., Nolen-Hoeksema, S., & Jourden, F. (1992). Effects of the 1989 San Francisco earthquake on frequency and content of nightmares. *Journal of Abnormal Psychology, 101,* 219–224.

Woodberry, K. A., Giuliano, A. J., & Seidman, L. J. (2008). Premorbid IQ in schizophrenia. *American Journal of Psychiatry, 165,* 579–587.

World Health Organization (WHO). (2009). Retrieved November 23, 2009, from http://www.who.int/dietphysicalactivity/publications/facts/obesity/en/

Wright, D. (1997). Getting out of the asylum: Understanding the confinement of the insane in the nineteenth century. *Social History of Medicine, 10,* 137–155.

Wright, I. C., Rabe-Hesketh, S., Woodruff, P. W., David, A. S., Murray, R. M., & Bullmore, E. T. (2000). Meta-analysis of regional brain volumes in schizophrenia. *American Journal of Psychiatry, 157,* 16–25.

Wrzesniewski, A., & Dutton, J. E. (2001). Crafting a job: Revisioning employees as active crafters of their work. *Academy of Management Review, 26,* 179–201.

Wu, A., Ying, Z., & Gomez-Pinilla, F. (2008). Docosahexaenoic acid dietary supplementation enhances the effects of exercise on synaptic plasticity and cognition. *Neuroscience, 155,* 751–759.

Wu, L., Niu, Y., & Yang, J. (2005). Tectal neurons signal impending collision of looming objects in the pigeon. *European Journal of Neuroscience, 22*(9), 2325–2331.

Wuornos v. State of Florida, 19 Fla. Law W. S 455 (September 22, 1994).

Yamamoto, B. K., Moszczynska, A., & Gudelsky, G. A. (2010). Amphetamine toxicities: Classical and emerging mechanisms. *Annals of the New York Academy of Science, 1187,* 101–121.

Yamazaki, T., & Tanaka, S. (2009). Computational models of timing mechanisms in the cerebellar granular layer. *Cerebellum, 8,* 423–432.

Ybema, J. F., Smulders, P. W., & Bongers, P. M. (2010). Antecedents and consequences of employee absenteeism: A longitudinal perspective on the role of job satisfaction and burnout. *European Journal of Work and Organizational Psychology, 19*(1), 102–124.

Yoo, S. K., & Skovholt, T. M. (2001). Cross-cultural examination of depression expression and help-seeking behavior: A comparative study of American and Korean college students. *Journal of College Counseling, 4,* 10–19.

You, J., Fung, H. H. L., & Isaacowitz, D. M. (2009). Age differences in dispositional optimism. *European Journal of Aging, 6,* 247–252.

Zajonc, R. B. (1965). Social facilitation. *Science, 149,* 269–274.

Zajonc, R. B., Heingartner, A., & Herman, E. M. (1969). Social enhancement and impairment of performance in the cockroach. *Journal of Personality and Social Psychology, 13*(2), 83–92.

Zaman, R., Thind, D., & Kocmur, M. (2008). Transcranial magnetic stimulation in schizophrenia. *Neuroendocrinological Letters, 1,* 147–160.

Zeidan, F., Gordon, N., Merchant, J., & Goolkasian, P. (2010). The effects of brief mindfulness meditation training on experimentally induced pain. *Journal of Pain, 11*(3), 199–209.

Zelazo, N. A., Zelazo, P. R., Cohen, K. M., & Zelazo, P. D. (1993). Specificity of practice effects on elementary neuromotor patterns. *Developmental Psychology, 29,* 686–691.

Zellner, D. A., Loaiza, S., Gonzalez, Z., Pita, J., Morales, J., Pecora, D., & Wolf, A. (2006). Food selection changes under stress. *Physiology and Behavior, 87*(4), 789–793.

Zellner, D. A., Saito, S., & Gonzalez, J. (2007). The effect of stress on men's food selection. *Appetite, 49*(3), 696–699.

Zernicke, K. A., Cantrell, H., Finn, P. R., & Lucas, J. (2010). The association between earlier age of first drink, disinhibited personality, and externalizing psychopathology in young adults. *Addictive Behaviors, 35*(5), 414–418.

Zhao, H., & Seibert, S. (2006). The Big Five personality dimensions and entrepreneurial status: A meta-analytical review. *Journal of Applied Psychology, 91,* 259–271.

Zhong, C., & DeVoe, S. E. (2010). You are how you eat: Fast food and impatience. *Psychological Science, 21*(5), 619–622.

Zimmerman, F. J., & Christakis, D. A. (2005). Children's television viewing and cognitive outcomes a longitudinal analysis of national data. *Archives of Pediatrics and Adolescent Medicine, 159,* 619–625.

Credits

Photo Credits

CHAPTER 1

Page 1: Colin Anderson/Photographer's Choice /Getty Images; **2** FotosearchRF/Glow Images; **3** *l* AF archive/Alamy; **3** *r* Flirt/SuperStock; **3** *c* sextoacto /Shutterstock; **4** Dennis MacDonald/Alamy; **5** *l* Ellie Rothnie/Alamy; **5** *r* Taras Livyy/iStockphoto; **8** TayaCho/iStockphoto; **9** Zacarias Pereira da Mata /Shutterstock; **10** Shiva/Shutterstock; **13** Roberto A Sanchez/iStockphoto; **14** Ljupco Smokovski /Shutterstock; **15** *cr* AP Photo; **15** *cl* Bettmann /CORBIS; **15** *tr* Editorial Image, LLC/Alamy; **15** *tl* Library of Congress; **15** *c* pio3/Shutterstock; **15** *br* Science and Society/SuperStock; **15** *bl* The APA logo is a trademark of the American Psychological Association. Reproduced with permission. No further reproduction or distribution is permitted without written permission from the American Psychological Association.; **16** Pictorial Press Ltd /Alamy; **17** *b* Classic Image/Alamy; **17** *tl* JONG KIAM SOON/Shutterstock; **17** *tr* konstantynov /Shutterstock; **18** Mary Evans/SIGMUND FREUD COPYRIGHTS/Alamy; **19** Science and Society /SuperStock; **20** *l* akg-images/Newscom; **20** *r* Mary Evans Picture Library/Alamy; **21** Time Life Pictures /Mansell/Time Life Pictures/Getty Imag es; **22** *b* Michael Rougier/Time & Life Pictures/Getty Images; **22** *t* Nina Leen/Time Life Pictures/Getty Images; **27** Colin Anderson/Glow Images; **29** Spencer Grant /Alamy

CHAPTER 2

Page 36: Tim Flach/Stone+/Getty Images; **37** PhotosIndia.com/Glow Images; **38** *l* age fotostock /SuperStock; **38** *r* Ewa Walicka/Shutterstock; **41** Engineering and drafting school, ca. 1925. Western Electric Company photograph album. Baker Library Historical Collections. Harvard Business School. (olvwork278414); **43** *t* kkgas/iStockphoto; **43** *b* stuartbur/iStockphoto; **48** Blend Images/Alamy; **49** CREATISTA/Shutterstock; **52** *l* gary yim /Shutterstock; **52** *r* Fancy/Glow Images; **56** National Archives; **59** MONA LISA PRODUCTION /SCIENCE PHOTO LIBRARY; **63** Imagesource /Glow Images

CHAPTER 3

Page 73: Colin Anderson/Photographer's Choice /Getty Images; **73** Janis Litavnieks/iStockphoto; **73** Lisa Thornberg/iStockphoto; **74** Colin Anderson /Glow Images; **74** Roberto A Sanchez/iStockphoto; **76** *t* Creatas Images/Getty Images/Thinkstock; **76** *b* Martin Harvey/Alamy; **77** Comstock Images/Getty Images/Thinkstock; **79** *c* Brazil Photos.com/Alamy; **79** *r* MartiniDry/Shutterstock; **79** *l* Shawn Hempel /Shutterstock; **80** University of Western Australia; **81** *b* Bob Daemmrich/PhotoEdit, Inc.; **81** *t* Roberto A

Sanchez/iStockphoto; **84** Rod Williams/naturepl. com; **86** Sebastian Kaulitzki/Alamy; **90** Neil Bromhall/naturepl.com; **91** Thinkstock/Getty Images; **92** Martin Nemec/Shutterstock; **95** Colin Anderson/ Glow Images; **100** Dorling Kindersley/Getty Images; **105** Tony Hutchings/Photographer's Choice/Getty Images; **106** akg-images/Newscom; **107** DORIS TSAO/MCT/Landov

CHAPTER 4

Page 113: Colin Anderson/Glow Images; **114** Tim Pannell/Glow Images; **116** Flashon Studio /Shutterstock; **117** Jostein Hauge/Shutterstock; **118** DG Photography/Alamy; **120** *b* Patti McConville /Alamy; **120** *t* Tonnywu76/Dreamstime; **122** *br* Chris Chabris; **122** *l* Purestock/Alamy; **122** *tr* Photo by Matt Milless; **122** *tr* Simons, D. J., & Chabris, C. F. (1999). "Gorillas in our midst: Sustained inattentional blindness for dynamic events. Perception," 28, 1059-1074. Figure provided by Daniel Simons.; **124** Eliza Snow/iStockphoto; **130** *c* Brian Prawl /Shutterstock; **130** *r* Forget Patrick/Sagaphoto. com/Alamy; **131** *b* Caspar Benson/Glow Images; **131** *t* Michael Nichols/National Geographic/Getty Images; **132** *t* Museo Civico Ala Ponzone, Cremona, Italy/The Bridgeman Art Library International; **132** *b* PA Photos/Landov; **133** *r* David Davis/Shutterstock; **133** photofriday/Shutterstock; **134** The Art Gallery Collection/Alamy; **136** *b* Thinkstock/Getty Images; **137** IGphotography/iStockphoto; **143** Robert Clark/National Geographic Stock; **145** tuja66 /iStockphoto; **149** Radius/Glow Images

CHAPTER 5

Page 157: Mike Harrington/Stone/Getty Images; **158** Sylvia Serrado/Glow Images; **160** HANK MORGAN/SCIENCE PHOTO LIBRARY; **162** Yuri Arcurs/Shutterstock; **166** Blend Images /Alamy; **167** Steve Prezant/Glow Images; **168** Custom Medical Stock Photo/Alamy; **172** Adam Haglund/Glow Images; **173** AP PHOTO /Bookstaver; **174** *t* Paula Connelly/iStockphoto; **174** *b* susaro/iStockphoto; **176** Colin Anderson /Brand X Pictures/Getty Images; **178** *l* AP Photo /Schindler Family Photo; **178** *r* Reuters/Landov; **180** Benne Ochs/Glow Images; **181** Advertising Archive/Courtesy Everett Collection; **182** Multnomah County Sheriff/Splash/Newscom; **184** *b* AP Photo /Don Ryan; **184** *t* Ted Kinsman/Photo Researchers, Inc.; **186** The National Institute on Drug Abuse; **189** Trinette Reed/Glow Images

CHAPTER 6

Page 194: Colin Anderson/Glow Images; **195** Christina Kennedy/Alamy; **200** Archives of the History of American Psychology, The Center for the History of Psychology/The University of Akron; **201** *r* Courtesy of Dr. Herta Flor; **201** *bl* Mark Kostich

/iStockphoto; **201** *tl* Özgür Donmaz/iStockphoto; **201** *cl* Silvia Boratti/iStockphoto; **204** *tl* Image courtesy of The Advertising Archives; **205** *l* Shaun Lowe/iStockphoto; **205** *r* Lee O'Dell/Shutterstock; **206** Michael Domijan, University of Texas at Austin; **209** PhotoAlto/Alamy; **212** *bl* Iurii Konoval /Shutterstock; **212** *tl* Lana Sundman/Alamy; **212** *br* Morgan Lane Photography/Shutterstock; **212** *tr* Richard Goldberg/Shutterstock; **214** Mike Clarke /iStockphoto; **215** Bork/Shutterstock; **218** ktd011 /iStockphoto; **221** Courtesy of Victoria Horner and the Chimpanzee Sanctuary and Wildlife Conservation Trust, Ngamba Island, Uganda.; **221** *inset* Courtesy of Victoria Horner and the Chimpanzee Sanctuary and Wildlife Conservation Trust, Ngamba Island, Uganda.; **224** *b* TommL/iStockphoto; **224** *t* wavebreakmedia ltd/Shutterstock; **226** Cathy Keifer/Shutterstock; **227** *t* Danita Delimont Creative /Alamy; **227** *bl* Miles Barton/Naturepl.com; **227** *br* Yuri Arcurs/Shutterstock; **228** From A. Bandura & R. Walters/Photo Courtesy of Albert Bandura; **228** From A. Bandura & R. Walters/Photo Courtesy of Albert Bandura; **228** From A. Bandura & R. Walters /Photo Courtesy of Albert Bandura; **228** From A. Bandura & R. Walters/Photo Courtesy of Albert Bandura; **228** From A. Bandura & R. Walters/Photo Courtesy of Albert Bandura; **228** From A. Bandura & R. Walters/Photo Courtesy of Albert Bandura; **228** From A. Bandura & R. Walters/Photo Courtesy of Albert Bandura; **228** From A. Bandura & R. Walters /Photo Courtesy of Albert Bandura; **229** *b* Dwayne Newton/PhotoEdit, Inc.; **229** *t* Jacom Stephens /iStockphoto

CHAPTER 7

Page 235: Blend Images/Alamy; **236** Radius Images /Alamy; **238** Gilbert Lundt; Jean-Yves Ruszniewski /TempSport/Corbis; **239** Clayton Hansen /iStockphoto; **243** Monkey Business Images /Shutterstock; **246** Kamira/Shutterstock; **249** Andrea Zanchi/iStockphoto; **252** theerapics/iStockphoto; **254** Beth Dixson/Alamy; **256** Lori Howard /Shutterstock; **257** Andersen Ross/Gettyimages; **259** Matteo Malavasi/iStockphoto; **261** Glow Images; **263** *l* Courtesy of Elizabeth Loftus; **263** *r* Courtesy of Elizabeth Loftus; **265** *r* Courtesy of Wade, K., Garry, M., Read, J., & Lindsay, S.; **265** *l* Courtesy of Wade, K., Garry, M., Read, J., & Lindsay, S.

CHAPTER 8

Page 271: Colin Anderson/Glow Images; **272** WoodyStock/Alamy; **274** *c* Al Mueller/Shutterstock; **274** *l* chatursunil/Shutterstock; **274** *r* Leo /Shutterstock; **276** Anthia Cumming/iStockphoto; **277** *r* Nicole S. Berry, Janxin Leu; **277** *l* Nisbett & Masuda (2003, PNAS); **277** *c* Nisbett & Masuda (2003, PNAS); **278** Park et al. "Culture Wires the Brain: A Cognitive Neuroscience Perspective."

Text Credits

Endpapers "The National Science Education Standards define scientific literacy as the ability to . . ." (bullet list of 4 aspects of scientific literary as discussed in paragraph 3, p. 22) From *National Science Education Standards*, National Academy of Sciences, 1996. http://www.nap.edu/openbook.php?record_id=496. Reprinted by permission of National Academies Press.

CHAPTER 1

Figure 1.8 "A Phrenology Map" From p. 106 in *Psychology: From Inquiry to Understanding,* 2nd ed. by Scott O. Lilienfeld, Steven J. Lynn, Laura L. Namy, & Nancy J. Woolf. Copyright © 2011. Printed and electronically reproduced by permission of Pearson Education, Inc., Upper Saddle River, New Jersey.

Figure 1.10 "Where Professional Psychologists Work" 2007 Doctorate Employment Survey, American Psychological Association.

Figure 1.11 "Work Settings for People Earning Master's and Bachelor's Degrees in Psychology" Magaletta, P.R., Mulvey, T. A. & Grus, C. L. (2010). What Can I Do with a Degree in Psychology? Retrieved http://www.apa.org/workforce/presentations/2010-psychology-degree.pdf.

CHAPTER 3

Figure 3.1 "Human Chromosomes" Figure 3.21, p. 113 in *Psychology: From Inquiry to Understanding,* 2nd ed. by Scott O. Lilienfeld, Steven J. Lynn, Laura L. Namy, & Nancy J. Woolf. Copyright © 2011. Printed and electronically reproduced by permission of Pearson Education, Inc., Upper Saddle River, New Jersey.

Figure 3.2 "DNA Molecules" Figure 3.22, p. 114 in *Psychology: From Inquiry to Understanding,* 2nd ed. by Scott O. Lilienfeld, Steven J. Lynn, Laura L. Namy, & Nancy J. Woolf. Copyright © 2011. Printed and electronically reproduced by permission of Pearson Education, Inc., Upper Saddle River, New Jersey.

Figure 3.2 "Major Events at the Synapse" Slightly adapted from figure 3.2, p. 86 in *Psychology: From Inquiry to Understanding,* 2nd ed. by Scott O. Lilienfeld, Steven J. Lynn, Laura L. Namy, & Nancy J. Woolf. Copyright © 2011. Printed and electronically reproduced by permission of Pearson Education, Inc., Upper Saddle River, New Jersey.

Figure 3.2 "Mental Rotation Tasks" From p. 344 in *Psychology: From Inquiry to Understanding,* 2nd ed. by Scott O. Lilienfeld, Steven J. Lynn, Laura L. Namy, & Nancy J. Woolf. Copyright © 2011. Printed and electronically reproduced by permission of Pearson Education, Inc., Upper Saddle River, New Jersey.

Figure 3.3 "Gene and Environment Interactions" Adapted from Caspi, A., et al. (2003). Influence of life stress on depression: Moderation by a polymorphism in the 5-HTT gene. Science, 301, 386-389. Copyright © 2003 by American Association for the Advancement of Science. Reprinted by Rightslink on behalf of the publisher.

Figure 3.7 "Men and Women React Differently to Infidelity" Adapted from Cramer, R., Lipinski, R., Meteer, J., & Houska, J. (2008). Sex differences in subjective distress to unfaithfulness: Testing competing evolutionary and violation of infidelity expectations hypotheses. *The Journal of Social Psychology,* 148(4), 389-405. Copyright © 2008. Reprinted by permission of Taylor & Francis Group, http://www.informaworld.com.

Figure 3.8 "A Neuron and its Key Components" (with "node" label removed) Slightly adapted from figure 3.1, p. 85 in *Psychology: From Inquiry to Understanding,* 2nd ed. by Scott O. Lilienfeld, Steven J. Lynn, Laura L. Namy, & Nancy J. Woolf. Copyright © 2011. Printed and electronically reproduced by permission of Pearson Education, Inc., Upper Saddle River, New Jersey.

Figure 3.9 "Sensory and Motor Neurons" Slightly adapted from figure 3.16, p. 101 in *Psychology: From Inquiry to Understanding,* 2nd ed. by Scott O. Lilienfeld, Steven J. Lynn, Laura L. Namy, & Nancy J. Woolf. Copyright © 2011. Printed and electronically reproduced by permission of Pearson Education, Inc., Upper Saddle River, New Jersey.

Figure 3.10 Slightly adapted "The Inner and Outer Regions of Nerve Cells Differ in Electrical Charge" Slightly adapted from figure 3.3, p. 88 in *Psychology: From Inquiry to Understanding,* 2nd ed. by Scott O. Lilienfeld, Steven J. Lynn, Laura L. Namy, & Nancy J. Woolf. Copyright © 2011. Printed and electronically reproduced by permission of Pearson Education, Inc., Upper Saddle River, New Jersey.

Figure 3.11 "The Time Course and Phases of a Nerve Cell Going from Resting to Action Potential" Adapted from Sternberg, 2004.

Figure 3.12 "The Lock and Key Analogy for how Neurotransmitters and Receptors Match" Figure 3.11, p. 89 in *Psychology: From Inquiry to Understanding,* 2nd ed. by Scott O. Lilienfeld, Steven J. Lynn, Laura L. Namy, & Nancy J. Woolf. Copyright © 2011. Printed and electronically reproduced by permission of Pearson Education, Inc., Upper Saddle River, New Jersey.

Figure 3.15 Slight adaptation of "The Endocrine System" Slightly adapted from figure 3.18, p. 103 in *Psychology: From Inquiry to Understanding,* 2nd ed. by Scott O. Lilienfeld, Steven J. Lynn, Laura L. Namy, & Nancy J. Woolf. Copyright © 2011. Printed and electronically reproduced by permission of Pearson Education, Inc., Upper Saddle River, New Jersey.

Figure 3.16 "The Organization of the Nervous System" Figure 2.1, p. 38 from *Psychology: An Exploration,* 1st ed. by Saundra Ciccarelli & J. Noland White. Copyright © 2010. Reprinted and electronically reproduced by permission of Pearson Education, Inc., Upper Saddle River, New Jersey.

Figure 3.17 "The Autonomic Nervous System" Figure 3.17, p. 102 in *Psychology: From Inquiry to Understanding,* 2nd ed. by Scott O. Lilienfeld, Steven J. Lynn, Laura L. Namy, & Nancy J. Woolf. Copyright © 2011. Printed and electronically reproduced by permission of Pearson Education, Inc., Upper Saddle River, New Jersey.

Figure 3.18 Slight adaptation of "The Hindbrain and Midbrain" Slightly adapted from figure 3.15, p. 100 in *Psychology: From Inquiry to Understanding,* 2nd ed. by Scott O. Lilienfeld, Steven J. Lynn, Laura L. Namy, & Nancy J. Woolf. Copyright © 2011. Printed and electronically reproduced by permission of Pearson Education, Inc., Upper Saddle River, New Jersey.

Figure 3.19 "The Basal Ganglia" Figure 3.7 from *Psychology: From Inquiry to Understanding,* 1st ed. by Scott O. Lilienfeld, Steven J. Lynn, Laura L. Namy, and Nancy J. Woolf. Copyright © 2009. Printed and electronically reproduced by permission of Pearson Education, Inc., Upper Saddle River, New Jersey.

Figure 3.20 "The Limbic System" (dropped the label "cingulate cortex") Slightly adapted from figure 3.14, p. 99 in *Psychology: From Inquiry to Understanding,* 2nd ed. by Scott O. Lilienfeld, Steven J. Lynn, Laura L. Namy, & Nancy J. Woolf. Copyright © 2011. Printed and electronically reproduced by permission of Pearson Education, Inc., Upper Saddle River, New Jersey.

Figure 3.21 Slight adaptation of "Gray and White Matter of the Brain" Adaptation of Morieb, 2001 as reprinted in *Psychology: From Inquiry to Understanding,* 1st ed. by Scott O. Lilienfeld, Steven J. Lynn, Laura L. Namy, and Nancy J. Woolf. Copyright © 2009. Printed and electronically reproduced by permission of Pearson Education, Inc., Upper Saddle River, New Jersey.

Figure 3.22 "The Corpus Callosum" Slightly adapted from figure 3.10, p. 95 in *Psychology: From Inquiry to Understanding,* 2nd ed. by Scott O. Lilienfeld, Steven J. Lynn, Laura L. Namy, & Nancy J. Woolf. Copyright © 2011. Printed and electronically reproduced by permission of Pearson Education, Inc., Upper Saddle River, New Jersey.

Figure 3.23 Slight adaptation of "The Four Lobes of the Cerebral Cortex" Slightly adapted from figure 3.11, p. 95 in *Psychology: From Inquiry to Understanding,* 2nd ed. by Scott O. Lilienfeld, Steven J. Lynn, Laura L. Namy, & Nancy J. Woolf. Copyright © 2011. Printed and electronically reproduced by permission of Pearson Education, Inc., Upper Saddle River, New Jersey.

Figure 3.24 "The Body as Mapped on the Motor Cortex and Somatosensory Cortex" (slightly adapted) Figure 12.9, p. 438 from *Human Anatomy and Physiology,* 7th ed. by Elaine N. Marieb & Katja Hoehn. Copyright © 2007. Printed and electronically reproduced by permission of Pearson Education, Inc., Upper Saddle River, New Jersey.

Figure 3.25 "Brain Specialization" (slightly adapted) Slightly adapted from figure 3.13, p. 96 in *Psychology: From Inquiry to Understanding,* 2nd ed. by Scott O. Lilienfeld, Steven J. Lynn, Laura L. Namy, & Nancy J. Woolf. Copyright © 2011. Printed and electronically reproduced by permission of Pearson Education, Inc., Upper Saddle River, New Jersey.

Figure 3.26 "A Split-Brain Experiment" Slightly adapted from figure 3.20, p. 111 in *Psychology: From Inquiry to Understanding,* 2nd ed. by Scott O. Lilienfeld, Steven J. Lynn, Laura L. Namy, & Nancy J. Woolf. Copyright © 2011. Printed and electronically reproduced by permission of Pearson Education, Inc., Upper Saddle River, New Jersey.

Figure 3.27 "Musical Intonation Therapy" Adapted from Helm-Estabrooks, N., Nicholas M., & Morgan, A. (1989). *Melodic Intonation Therapy Program.* Austin, TX: PRO-ED.

Figure 3.28 "Measuring Brain Activity" Figure 3.19, p. 107 in *Psychology: From Inquiry to Understanding,* 2nd ed. by Scott O. Lilienfeld, Steven J. Lynn, Laura L. Namy, & Nancy J. Woolf. Copyright © 2011. Printed and electronically reproduced by permission of Pearson Education, Inc., Upper Saddle River, New Jersey.

CHAPTER 4

Figure 4.5 "The Kanizsa Square" From "Object Processing in the Infant Brain" by C. S. Hermann & A. D. Friederici (April 13, 2001), *Science*, 292 (5515), 165. Copyright © 2001 by AAAS. Reprinted by permission of AAAS.

Figure 4.8 "Expectations Influence Perception" Figure, "Expectations Influence Perception" from "The Role of Frequency in Developing Perceptual Sets" by D. A. Alampay & B. R. Bugelski (1961) *Canadian Journal of Psychology*, 15, 205-211. Copyright © 1961 by Canadian Psychological Association. Permission granted for use of material.

Figure 4.9 "Light Waves in the Electromagnetic Spectrum" Figure 3.1, p. 79 from *Psychology: An Exploration*, 1st ed. by Saundra Ciccarelli and J. Noland White. Copyright © 2010. Reprinted and electronically reproduced by permission of Pearson Education, Inc., Upper Saddle River, NJ.

Figure 4.11 "The Human Eye and Its Structures" Adapted from Dorling Kindersley.

Figure 4.13 "Arrangement of Photoreceptors in the Retina" Figure 3.4(a), p. 81 from *Psychology: An Exploration*, 1st ed. by Saundra Ciccarelli and J. Noland White. Copyright © 2010. Reprinted and electronically reproduced by permission of Pearson Education, Inc., Upper Saddle River, NJ.

Figure 4.15 "Nearsightedness and Farsightedness" (your adaptation of image as adapted from St. Luke's Cataract & Laser Institute) Adapted from figure 4.16, p. 138 in *Psychology: From Inquiry to Understanding*, 2nd ed. by Scott O. Lilienfeld, Steven J. Lynn, Laura L. Namy, and Nancy J. Woolf. Copyright © 2011. Printed and electronically reproduced by permission of Pearson Education, Inc., Upper Saddle River, New Jersey.

Figure 4.16 "Pathways of the Visual System in the Brain" "Crossing of the Optic Nerve" (Fig. 3.4, p. 96) from *Psychology*, 3rd edition by Saundra Ciccarelli & J. Noland White. Copyright © 2012. Printed and electronically reproduced by permission of Pearson Education, Inc., Upper Saddle River, New Jersey.

Figure 4.17 "Measuring the Activity of Feature Detection Cells" Figure 4.18, p. 139 in *Psychology: From Inquiry to Understanding*, 2nd ed. by Scott O. Lilienfeld, Steven J. Lynn, Laura L. Namy, and Nancy J. Woolf. Copyright © 2011. Printed and electronically reproduced by permission of Pearson Education, Inc., Upper Saddle River, New Jersey.

Figure 4.18a "Perceptual Constancies" Figure 4.7, p. 128 in *Psychology: From Inquiry to Understanding*, 2nd ed. by Scott O. Lilienfeld, Steven J. Lynn, Laura L. Namy, and Nancy J. Woolf. Copyright © 2011. Printed and electronically reproduced by permission of Pearson Education, Inc., Upper Saddle River, New Jersey.

Figure 4.19 "Find the T among this Scattered array of offset Ls" From "Why Do We Miss Targets? Exploring the Boundaries of The Low Prevalence Effect" by A. N. Rich et al. (2008) *Journal of Vision*, 8, 1-17. Copyright © 2008. Reprinted by permission of Association for Research in Vision and Opthamology.

Figure 4.22b Illustration of "Motion Parallax" From *Sensation and Perception*, 6th ed. by Coren. Copyright © 1989. Reprinted by permission of John Wiley & Sons, Inc.

Figure 4.26 "The Negative Afterimage: Experiencing Opponent-Process Therapy" Figure 4.24, p. 143 in *Psychology: From Inquiry to Understanding*, 2nd ed. by Scott O. Lilienfeld, Steven J. Lynn, Laura L. Namy, and Nancy J. Woolf. Copyright © 2011. Printed and electronically reproduced by permission of Pearson Education, Inc., Upper Saddle River, New Jersey.

Figure 4.27 "Characteristics of Sound: Frequency and Amplitude" Figure 4.27, p. 148 in *Psychology: From Inquiry to Understanding*, 2nd ed. by Scott O. Lilienfeld, Steven J. Lynn, Laura L. Namy, and Nancy J. Woolf. Copyright © 2011. Printed and electronically reproduced by permission of Pearson Education, Inc., Upper Saddle River, New Jersey.

Figure 4.28 "A Comparison of Hearing Across Different Species" Based on Fay (1988) and Warfield (1973).

Figure 4.30 "How we localize sound" Figure 4.31, p. 151 in *Psychology: From Inquiry to Understanding*, 2nd ed. by Scott O. Lilienfeld, Steven J. Lynn, Laura L. Namy, and Nancy J. Woolf. Copyright © 2011. Printed and electronically reproduced by permission of Pearson Education, Inc., Upper Saddle River, New Jersey.

Figure 4.32 "A Cochlear Implant" "Cochlear Implant" (Fig. 3.9, p. 104) from *Psychology*, 3rd edition by Saundra Ciccarelli & J. Noland White. Copyright © 2012. Printed and electronically reproduced by permission of Pearson Education, Inc., Upper Saddle River, New Jersey.

Figure 4.34 "The Sense of Kinesthesis" Figure 8.5, p. 229 from *Biological Psychology*, 10th ed. by Kalat. Copyright © 2009 by Wadsworth, a part of Cengage Learning, Inc. Reprinted by permission. http://www.cengage.com/permissions.

Figure 4.35 "Cross-Section of Skin and Free Nerve Endings that Respond to Pain" Figure 3.12, p. 109 from *Psychology*, 3rd edition by Saundra Ciccarelli & J. Noland White. Copyright © 2012. Printed and electronically reproduced by permission of Pearson Education, Inc., Upper Saddle River, NJ.

Figure 4.36 "A Mirror Box Used in Therapy for People Who Have Lost Limbs" (your rendering of photo from study by Ramachandran & Rogers-Ramachandran, 1996). Adapted from p. 157 in *Psychology: From Inquiry to Understanding*, 2nd ed. by Scott O. Lilienfeld, Steven J. Lynn, Laura L. Namy, and Nancy J. Woolf. Copyright © 2011. Printed and electronically reproduced by permission of Pearson Education, Inc., Upper Saddle River, New Jersey. Pearson adaptation derived from Ramachandran and Rogers-Ramachandran (1996). Synaesthesia in phantom limbs induced with mirrors. Proceedings of the Royal Society of London, 263, 377-386.

Figure 4.37 "Mirror box therapy compared to mental visualization and a control condition" Figure 1 from "Mirror Therapy and Phantom Limb Pain" by B. L. Chan et al. (2007) *New England Journal of Medicine*, 357, 2206-2207. Copyright © 2007. Reprinted by permission of Massachusetts Medical Society.

Figure 4.38 "Papillae and Taste Buds" Figure 4.32, p. 152 in *Psychology: From Inquiry to Understanding*, 2nd ed. by Scott O. Lilienfeld, Steven J. Lynn, Laura L. Namy, and Nancy J. Woolf. Copyright © 2011. Printed and electronically reproduced by permission of Pearson Education, Inc., Upper Saddle River, New Jersey.

Figure 4.39 "Density of Taste Buds in a Supertaster and a Normal Taster" (image of tongue only, not photos) Adapted from p. 153 in *Psychology: From Inquiry to Understanding*, 2nd ed. by Scott O. Lilienfeld, Steven J. Lynn, Laura L. Namy, and Nancy J. Woolf. Copyright © 2011. Printed and electronically reproduced by permission of Pearson Education, Inc., Upper Saddle River, New Jersey.

Table 4.4 Chapter 4 "Common Sounds" NIDCD.

CHAPTER 5

Figure 5.2 "How Sleep Requirements Change with Age" From Roffwarg, H. P., Defazio, J. N., and Dement, W. C., (1966), "Ontogenetic Development of the Human Sleep-Dream Cycle" in *Science*, April 29, 1966, 152 (3722): 604-619. Copyright © 1966 by AAAS. Reprinted by permission of AAAS.

Figure 5.4 "Order and Duration of Sleep Stages Through a Typical Night" Adapted from *Some Must Watch While Some Must Sleep* by W. D. Dement. W. C. Freeman & Company, 1974.

Figure 5.5 "The Costly Effects of Sleep Deprivation" From "Effect of Reducing Interns' Work Hours on Serious Medical Errors in Intensive Care Units" by C. P. Landrigan et al. (2004) *New England Journal of Medicine*, 351 (18), 1838-1848. Copyright © 2004. Reprinted by permission of Massachusetts Medical Society.

Figure 5.6 "How to Prepare for an Eastward Flight Crossing Six Time Zones" From Revell, V. L. & Eastman, C. I. (2005) How to trick Mother Nature into letting you fly around or stay up all night. *Journal of Biological Rhythms*, 20 (4). Copyright © 2005 by Sage Publications. Reprinted by permission of Sage Publications.

Figure 5.8 "The Influence of the 9/11 Terrorist Attacks on Dream Content" From Propper, R. E., Stickgold, R., Keeley, R., & Christman, S. D. (2007) Is television traumatic? Dreams, stress and media exposure in the aftermath of September 11, 2001. *Psychological Science*, 18, 334-340. American Psychological Association.

Figure 5.9 "Sleep Apnea" From figure 5.3, p. 173 in *Psychology: From Inquiry to Understanding*, 2nd ed. by Scott Lilienfeld, Steven J. Lynn, Laura L. Namy, & Nancy J. Woolf. Copyright © 2011. Reprinted by permission of Pearson Education, Inc., Upper Saddle River, NJ.

Figure 5.10 "Meditation Reduces Negative Emotion" Figure 2 from Goldin, P. R. & Gross, J. J. (2010) Effects of mindfulness-based stress reduction (MBSR) on emotion regulation in social anxiety disorder. Emotion, 10 (1), 83-91. American Psychological Association.

Figure 5.12 "Frequency of Drug Use among High School Seniors" The Monitoring the Future Study, University of Michigan.

Figure 5.14 "Celebrating with Alcohol" From Glindemann, K. E., Wiegand, D. M., & Geller, E. (2007). Celebratory drinking and intoxication: A contextual influence on alcohol consumption. Environment and Behavior, 39 (3), 352-366. Copyright © 2007 by Sage Publications, Inc. Reprinted by permission of Sage Publications.

Table 5.1 "The American Psychiatric Association's Criteria for Primary Insomnia" Adapted from

Diagnostic and Statistical Manual of Mental Disorders, 4th ed., American Psychiatric Association, 2000.

Table 5.2 "Non-Pharmacological Techniques for Improving Sleep" Based on recommendations from the American Psychological Association, 2004.

Table 5.3 "Epworth Sleepiness Scale" Copyright © 1990-1997 by M W Johns. Use of the ESS by governmental agencies, as well as by organisations and individuals in a commercial or for-profit context, requires entry into a license agreement and the payment of applicable license fees. Refer to www.epworthsleepinessscale.com for further details.

Table 5.5 "What are Your Feelings about Drug Abuse?" Table 3, p. 50 from "The Substance Abuse Attitude Survey: An Instrument for Measuring Attitudes" by J. N. Chappel, T. L. Veach, and R. S. Krug. (1985). Journal of Studies on Alcohol, 46 (1), 58-52. Copyright © 1985. Reprinted with permission from Research Documentation, Inc., publisher of the Journal of Studies on Alcohol, now the Journal of Studies on Alcohol and Drugs (www.jsad.com).

CHAPTER 6

Figure 6.10 "Diet Soda Consumption is Associated with Increased, not Decreased Prevalence of Obesity" 6: Consumptive data for soft drinks comes from USDA Economic Research Service. Obesity prevalence data comes from National Center for Health Statistics. (Figure from Swithers et al., 2009.)

Figure 6.13 "An Operant Chamber" From p. 213 in *Psychology: From Inquiry to Understanding*, 2nd ed. by Scott Lilienfeld, Steven J. Lynn, Laura L. Namy, & Nancy J. Woolf. Copyright © 2011. Reprinted by permission of Pearson Education, Inc., Upper Saddle River, NJ.

Figure 6.15 "Schedules of Reinforcement" From figures 6.8 & 6.9 in *Psychology: From Inquiry to Understanding*, 2nd ed. by Scott Lilienfeld, Steven J. Lynn, Laura L. Namy, & Nancy J. Woolf. Copyright © 2011. Reprinted by permission of Pearson Education, Inc., Upper Saddle River, NJ.

Figure 6.17a "Learning without Reinforcement" Figure 4.9, p. 141 from *Psychology: An Exploration*, 1st ed. by Saundra Ciccarelli & J. Noland White. Copyright © 2010. Adapted by permission of Pearson Education, Inc., Upper Saddle River, NJ.

Figure 6.17b "Learning without Reinforcement" Adapted from "Degrees of Hunger, Reward and Non-Reward and Maze Learning in Rats" by E. C. Tolman & C. H. Honzik, (1930), University of California Publications in Psychology, 4241-4256.

CHAPTER 7

Figure 7.1 "The Atkinson-Shiffrin Model" From "Human Memory: A Proposed System and Its Control Processes" by R. C. Atkinson & R. M. Shiffrin in *The Psychology of Learning and Motivation: Advances in Research and Theory*, Vol 2 (pp. 89-195) ed. by K. W. Spence & J. T. Spence. Copyright © 1968 by Elsevier. Reprinted by permission of Elsevier.

Figure 7.13 "Context-Dependent Learning" From p. 262 in *Psychology: From Inquiry to Understanding*, 2nd ed. by Scott Lilienfeld, Steven J. Lynn, Laura L. Namy, & Nancy J. Woolf. Copyright © 2011. Reprinted by permission of Pearson Education, Inc., Upper Saddle River, NJ.

Figure 7.15 "Ebbinghaus's Forgetting Curve" Ebbinghaus, 1885.

Figure 7.16 "Bahrick's Long-Term Forgetting Curve" From Bahrick, H. P. (1984). Semantic memory content in permastore: Fifty years of memory for Spanish learned in school. *Journal of Experimental Psychology: General*, 113 (1), 1-29. American Psychological Association.

Figure 7.18 "Schemas Affect how We Encode and Remember" Kleider, H., Pezdek, K., Goldinger, S., & Kirk, A. (2008). Schema-driven source misattribution errors: Remembering the expected from a witnessed event. Applied Cognitive Psychology, 22(1) 1-20. Copyright © 2008 by John Wiley & Sons. Reprinted by permission of John Wiley & Sons.

Figure 7.19 "A Sample Word List and its Critical Lure for the DRM Procedure" From Roediger, H., & McDermott, K. (1995). Creating false memories: Remembering words not presented in lists. *Journal of Experimental Psychology: Learning, Memory, and Cognition*, 21, 803-814. American Psychological Association.

Figure 7.20 "The Role of Eyewitness Errors in Wrongful Conviction" Reprinted by permission of The Innocence Project (http://www.innocenceproject.org).

CHAPTER 8

Figure 8.3 "A Semantic Network Diagram for the Category 'Animal'" Based on Collins & Quillian (1969).

Figure 8.5 "Priming affects the Speed of Responses on a Lexical Decision Task" Figure 1, p. 1126 from "Priming the Holiday Spirit: Persistent Activation due to Extraexperimental Experiences" by J. H. Coane & D. A. Balota (2009) *Psychonomic Bulletin & Review*, 16 (6), 1124-1128. Copyright © 2009 by Springer. Reprinted by permission of Springer.

Figure 8.6 "Your Culture and Point of View" (image of cow, chicken, grass) adapted from "Culture and Point of View" by R. E. Nisbett & T. Masuda (2003) *Proceedings of the National Academy of Sciences*, 100 (19), 11163-11170. Copyright © 2003. Reprinted by permission of National Academy of Sciences.

Figure 8.9 "The Nine Dot Problem" Maier, N. F. (1930). Reasoning in humans. I. On direction. *Journal of Comparative Psychology*, 10(2), 115-143. American Psychological Association.

Figure 8.15 "Ratings of Perceived Contradictions in Political Statements" (your figure 2) Figure 2 from "Neural Bases of Motivated Reasoning: An fMRI Study of Emotional Constraints on Partisan Political Judgment in the 2004 U.S. Presidential Election" by D. Westen, P. S. Blagov, & K. Harenski (2006), *Journal of Cognitive Neuroscience*, 18 (11), 1947-1058. Copyright © 2006 by the Massachusetts Institute of Technology. Reprinted by permission of MIT Press Journals.

Figure 8.16 "Satisfaction of Maximers and Satisficers" Dar-Nimrod, I., Rawn, C. D., Lehman, D. R., & Schwartz, B. (2009). The Maximization Paradox: The costs of seeking alternatives. *Personality and Individual Differences*, 46(5-6), 631-635. Copyright © 2009 by Elsevier. Reprinted by permission of Elsevier.

Figure 8.17 "Syntax Allows Us to Understand Language by the Organization of the Words" adaptation) Adapted from *The Language Instinct* by S. Pinker, HarperCollins, 1994.

Figure 8.19 "Inheritance Pattern for the Mutated FOXP2 Gene in the KE Family" Adapted from Vargha-Khadem et al. (2005) and Watkins et al. (2002).

Table 8.3 "Contradictory and Exculpatory Statements for Democratic and Republican Presidential Candidates" Table 1 from "Neural Bases of Motivated Reasoning: An fMRI Study of Emotional Constraints on Partisan Political Judgment in the 2004 U.S. Presidential Election" by D. Westen, P. S. Blagov, & K. Harenski (2006), *Journal of Cognitive Neuroscience*, 18 (11), 1947-1058. Copyright © 2006 by the Massachusetts Institute of Technology. Reprinted by permission of MIT Press Journals.

CHAPTER 9

Figure 9.4 "Sample Problem from Raven's Progressive Matrices" NCS Pearson, 1998.

Figure 9.7 "General Intelligence is Related to Various Outcomes" Adapted from Hernstein & Murray, 1994; Gottfredson, 1997.

Figure 9.9 "Measuring Fluid Intelligence" from "Specific Impairments of Planning" From "Specific Impairments of Planning" by T. Shallice (1982), Philosophical Transcripts of the Royal Society of London B 298, 199-209. Copyright © 1982 by The Royal Society. Reprinted by permission of The Royal Society.

Figure 9.11 "The Triarchic Theory of Intelligence" Figure 9.3, p. 323 in *Psychology: From Inquiry to Understanding*, 2nd ed. by Scott O. Lilienfeld, Steven J. Lynn, Laura L. Namy, and Nancy J. Woolf. Copyright © 2011. Printed and electronically reproduced by permission of Pearson Education, Inc., Upper Saddle River, New Jersey.

Figure 9.12 "Differing Perspectives on Intelligence" (figure 1) from "Reframing the Mind: How Howard Gardner Became a Hero among Educators by Simply Redefining Talents as "'Intelligences'" From "Reframing the Mind: How Howard Gardner Became a Hero among Educators by Simply Redefining Talents as "'Intelligences'" by D. T. Willingham (2004), *Education Next: A Journal of Opinion and Research*, by Hoover Institution on War, Revolution, and Peace, 4 (3), 19-24. Copyright © 2004 in the format Textbookj via Copyright Clearance Center. Reprinted by permission of the publisher.

Figure 9.13 "The Flynn Effect" from "Searching for Justice: The Discovery of IQ Gains over Time" Flynn, J. R. (1999). Searching for justice: The discovery of IQ gains over time. *American Psychologist*, 54, 5-20.

Figure 9.14 "Intelligence and Genetic Relatedness" adapted from "Intelligence: Genetics, Genes, and Genomics" Adapted from "Intelligence: Genetics, Genes, and Genomics" by R. Plomin & F. M. Spinath. (2004) *Journal of Personality & Social Psychology*, 86 (1), 112-129.

Figure 9.16 "Birth Order and Intelligence" adapted from "Explaining the Relation between Birth Order and Intelligence" Adapted from "Explaining the Relation between Birth Order and Intelligence" by P. Kristensen and T. Bjerkedal (2007) *Science*, Vol. 316, No. 5832: 1717-1718. Copyright © 2007 by AAAS. Reprinted by permission of AAAS.

Figure 9.19 "Personal Beliefs Influence Grades" from "Implicit Theories of Intelligence Predict Achievement Across an Adult Transition: A Longitudinal Study and an Intervention" "Implicit Theories of Intelligence Predict Achievement Across an Adult Transition: A Longitudinal Study and an Intervention" by L. S. Blackwell, K. H. Trzesniewski, & C. S. Dweck (2007) *Child Development*, 78 (1), 246-263. Copyright © 2007 by John Wiley and Sons. Reprinted by permission of John Wiley and Sons.

CHAPTER 10

Figure10.2 Slight adaptation of "The Process of Implantation during Pregnancy" Slightly adapted from figure 10.1, p. 365 in *Psychology: From Inquiry to Understanding,* 2nd ed. by Scott O. Lilienfeld, Steven J. Lynn, Laura L. Namy, & Nancy J. Woolf. Copyright © 2011. Printed and electronically reproduced by permission of Pearson Education, Inc., Upper Saddle River, New Jersey.

Figure 10.3 "Fetal Brain Development" Redrawn and adapted from The Dana Foundation. http://www.dana.org/news/brainhealth/detail.aspx?id=10050.

Figure 10.6 "Testing Conservation" Slightly adapted from figure 10.8, p. 374 in *Psychology: From Inquiry to Understanding,* 2nd ed. by Scott O. Lilienfeld, Steven J. Lynn, Laura L. Namy, & Nancy J. Woolf. Copyright © 2011. Printed and electronically reproduced by permission of Pearson Education, Inc., Upper Saddle River, New Jersey.

Figure 10.8 "Testing Infants' Understanding of Quantity" Figure 1 from "Newborn Infants Perceive Abstract Numbers" by V. Izard, C. Spann, E. S. Spelke, & A. Streri (2009), *Proceedings of the National Academy of Sciences*, 106, 10382-10385. Copyright © 2009. Reprinted by permission of PNAS.

Figure 10.9 "The Strange Situation" Slightly adapted from figure 10.17, p. 386 in *Psychology: From Inquiry to Understanding,* 2nd ed. by Scott O. Lilienfeld, Steven J. Lynn, Laura L. Namy, & Nancy J. Woolf. Copyright © 2011. Printed and electronically reproduced by permission of Pearson Education, Inc., Upper Saddle River, New Jersey.

Figure 10.10 "Piaget's Test for Egocentric Perspective in Children" Slightly adapted from figure 10.7, p. 374 in *Psychology: From Inquiry to Understanding,* 2nd ed. by Scott O. Lilienfeld, Steven J. Lynn, Laura L. Namy, & Nancy J. Woolf. Copyright © 2011. Printed and electronically reproduced by permission of Pearson Education, Inc., Upper Saddle River, New Jersey.

Figure 10.11 "Physical Changes that Accompany Puberty in Male and Female Adolescents" Slightly adapted from figure 10.4, p. 369 in *Psychology: From Inquiry to Understanding,* 2nd ed. by Scott O. Lilienfeld, Steven J. Lynn, Laura L. Namy, & Nancy J. Woolf. Copyright © 2011. Printed and electronically reproduced by permission of Pearson Education, Inc., Upper Saddle River, New Jersey.

Figure 10.12 "Extended Brain Development" Adaptation of figure 4.25, p. 102 in *Biological Psychology*, 10th ed. by Kalat (2009, Wadsworth) after *The Prefrontal Cortex*, by J. M. Fuster (1989, Raven Press).

Figure 10.13 "What Drives Teenagers to Take Risks?" Adapted from Figure 2, p. 630 in "Peer Influence on Risk-Taking, Risk Preference, and Risky Decision-Making in Adolescence and Adulthood: An Experimental Study" by M. Gardner & L. Steinberg (2005). *Developmental Psychology,* 41 (4), 652-635.

Figure 10.14 "Alzheimer's Disease Risk" From "Lifetime Risk of Dementia and Alzheimer's Disease: The Impact of Mortality on Risk Estimates in the Framingham Study" by S. Seshadri et al. (1997) Neurology, 49 (6), 1498-1504. Copyright © 1997 by Wolters Kluwer Health. Reprinted by permission of Wolters Kluwer Health.

Figure 10.15a "How Alzheimer's Affects the Brain" http://www.nia.nih.gov/Alzheimers/Publications/Unraveling/Part2/changing.htm

Figure 10.17 "Divorce Trends in the U.S. since 1950" United States Census Bureau.

Figure10.19 "Emotion, Memory & Aging" "At the Intersection of Emotion and Cognition: Aging and the Positivity Effect" by L. L. Carstensen & J.A. Mikels, (2005) Current Directions in *Psychological Science*, 14 (3). Copyright © 2005 by Sage Publications. Reprinted by permission of SAGE Publications.

Chapter 10 "The Student Burnout Inventory" from "Burnout and Engagement in University Students: A Cross-National Study" From "Burnout and Engagement in University Students: A Cross-National Study" by W. B. Schaufeli, I. M. Martinez, A. Marques Pinto, M. Salanava, & A. B. Bakker (2002) *Journal of Cross-Cultural Psychology*, 33(5), 464-481. Copyright © 2002 by Sage Publications. Reprinted by permission of SAGE Publications.

CHAPTER 11

Figure 11.3 Chapter 1 "The Hypothalamus and Hunger" Figure 10.3, p. 379 from *Psychology: Themes & Variations*, Briefer Edition (with Concept Charts) 8th ed. by Weiten. Copyright © 2011 by Wadsworth, a part of Cengage Learning, Inc. Reproduced by permission. www.cengage.com/permissions.

Figure 11.5 "Obesity Rates in the U.S." http://www.cdc.gov/obesity/data/trends.html#State

Figure 11.6 "Why Have Sex?" Based on Meston, C. M. & Buss, D. M. (2007). Why Humans Have Sex. *Archives of Sexual Behavior*, 36, 477-507.

Figure 11.9 "Genetics and Sexual Orientation" Bailey & Pillard (1995), Bailey et al. (1993), Bailey et al. (2000).

Figure 11.13 "Competing Theories of Emotion" Adapted from Dr. Silvia Helena Cardosa, http://www.cerebromente.org.br/m05/mente/tub6.gif.

Figure 11.15 "How is the person in the middle of these pictures feeling?" Masuda, T., Ellsworth, P. C., Mesquita, B., Leu, J., Tanida, S., & van de Veerdonk, E. (2008). "Placing the face in context: Cultural differences in the perception of facial emotion." *Journal of Personality and Social Psychology*, 94, 365-381.

Figure 11.16 "East-West Differences in Interpreting Emotion" Masuda, T., Ellsworth, P. C., Mesquita, B., Leu, J., Tanida, S., & van de Veerdonk, E. (2008). "Placing the face in context: Cultural differences in the perception of facial emotion." *Journal of Personality and Social Psychology*, 94, 365-381.

Table 11.2 "A Continuum of Sexual Orientation" From *Sexual Behavior in the Human Male*, Kinsey Institute for Research in Sex, Gender & Reproduction. Copyright 1948 by William B. Saunders. Reprinted by permission of The Kinsey Institute for Research in Sex, Gender and Reproduction.

Table 11.4 "Application Activity" Elliot, A. J. & McGregor, H. A. (2001). A 2 x 2 achievement goal framework. *Journal of Personality and Social Psychology*, 80, 501-519.

Table 11.11 "Statistical Characteristics of Eating Disorders" From "The Prevalence and Correlates of Eating Disorders in the National Comorbidity Survey Replication" by J. Hudson, et al. (2007), Journal of Social and Clinical Psychology, 27 (6), 555-575. Copyright © by Elsevier. Reprinted by permission of Elsevier.

CHAPTER 12

Figure 12.1 "The Big Five Personality Dimensions" After McCrae & Costa, 1987.

Figure 12.2 "Personality Stability and Change over the Lifespan" From Roberts, B., Walton, K., & Viechtbauer, W. (2006). Patterns of mean-level change in personality traits across the life-course: A meta-analysis of longitudinal studies. *Psychological Bulletin*, 132(1), 1-25.

Figure 12.3 "A Sample MMPI-2 Profile" The registered trademark symbol ("R" in a circle) must follow the MMPI in line 1 and Inventory in line 1). Adapted from the MMPI-2 (Minnesota Multiphasic Personality Inventory-2) *Manual for Administration, Scoring, and Interpretation*, Revised Edition. Copyright © 2001 by the Regents of the University of Minnesota. All rights reserved. Used by permission of the University of Minnesota Press. "MMPI" and "Minnesota Multiphasic Personality Inventory" are registered trademarks owned by the Regents of the University of Minnesota.

Figure 12.4(b) "Reciprocal Determinism and the Social-Cognitive Approach" Figure 11.2, p. 394 from *Psychology: An Exploration*, 1st ed. by Saundra Ciccarelli and J. Noland White. Copyright © 2010. Reprinted and electronically reproduced by permission of Pearson Education, Inc., Upper Saddle River, NJ.

Figure 12.5 "Cultural Differences in Levels of Conscientiousness" From "The Geographic Distribution of Big Five Personality Traits: Patterns and Profiles of Human Self-Description Across 56 Nations" by D.P. Schmitt, J. Allik, R. R. McCrae, and V. Benet-Martinez (2007) *Journal of Cross-Cultural Psychology*, 38(2), 173-212. Copyright © 2007 by Sage Publications. Reprinted by permission of SAGE Publications.

Figure 12.6 "Genes and Personality" From *Genes and Environment in Personality Development* by J. C. Loehlin. Copyright © 1992. Reprinted by permission of Sage Publications, Inc.

Figure 12.7 ""Genes, Serontonin, and Personality" From "Looking on the Bright Side: Biased Attention and the Human Serotonin Transporter Gene" by E. Fox, A. Ridgewell, & C. Ashwin (2009) *Proceedings of the Royal Society*, B., 276, 1747-1751. Copyright © 2009. Reprinted by permission of The Royal Society and the author.

Figure 12.10 "The Freudian Structure of Personality" Figure 14.1, p. 546 in *Psychology: From Inquiry to Understanding,* 2nd ed. by Scott O. Lilienfeld, Steven J. Lynn, Laura L. Namy, and Nancy J. Woolf. Copyright © 2011. Printed and electronically reproduced by permission of Pearson Education, Inc., Upper Saddle River, New Jersey.

Table 12.2 "Defense Mechanisms and Examples" "Freudian Defense Mechanisms and Empirical Findings in Modern Social Psychology: Reaction Formation, Projection, Displacement, Undoing,

Isolation, Sublimation and Denial" by R.F. Baumeister, K. Dale, and K. L. Sommer, (1998), *Journal of Personality,* (1998) 66, 1081-1124. Copyright © 1998 by John Wiley and Sons. Reprinted by permission of John Wiley and Sons.

CHAPTER 13

Figure 13.1 "Mean Values for Positive and Negative Emotions According to the Visual Analog Scale" from "Patients' Affective Reactions to Receiving Diagnostic Feedback" Figure 1, p. 564 from "Patients Affective Reactions to Receiving Diagnostic Feedback" by J. M. Holm-Denoma, et al. (2008) *Journal of Social and Clinical Psychology,* 27 (6), 555-575. Copyright © 2008 by Guilford Publications. Reprinted by permission of Guilford Publications.

Figure 13.2 "Emotional Responses of Individuals with Anti-Social Personality Disorder" from "The psychopath as observer: Emotion and attention in picture processing" Adapted from Levenston, G. K., Patrick, C. J., Bradley, M. M., & Lang, P. J. (2000). The psychopath as observer: Emotion and attention in picture processing. *Journal of Abnormal Psychology,* 109 (3), 373-385.

Figure 13.2 "Warning Signs of Suicide" American Psychological Association (2011). http://www.apa.org/topics/suicide/signs.aspx

Figure 13.3 "Anxiety Levels are Inherited in an Animal Model" from "Selection for Contextual Fear Conditioning Affects Anxiety-Like Behaviors and Gene Expression" From "Selection for Contextual Fear Conditioning Affects Anxiety-Like Behaviors and Gene Expression" by C. A. Ponder, C. L. Kliethermes, M. R. Drew, J. Muller, K. Das, V. B. Risbrough, J. C. Crabbe, T. C. Gilliam, & A. A. Palmer (2007) *Genes, Brain & Behavior,* 6(8), 736-749. Copyright © 2007 by John Wiley and Sons. Reprinted by permission of John Wiley and Sons.

Figure 13.5 "Genetic Relatedness and Major Depression" from "A Swedish National Twin Study of Major Lifetime Depression" Adapted from Table 1 in Kenneth S. Kendler, Margaret Gatz, Charles O. Gardner, and Nancy L. Pedersen, "A Swedish National Twin Study of Lifetime Major Depression," *American Journal of Psychiatry,* January 2006; 163: 109-114. Copyright © 2010. Reprinted by permission of American Psychiatric Publishing, Inc.

Figure 13.7 "Depression and the Brain" in "Neuroimaging and Depression: Current Status and Unresolved Issues" From "Neuroimaging and Depression: Current Status and Unresolved Issues" by I. Gotlib & J. Hamilton (2008) *Current Directions in Psychological Science,* 17, 159-163. Copyright © 2008 by Sage Publications. Reprinted by permission of SAGE Publications.

Figure 13.8 "Can Your Neighborhood Cause Depression?" from "Neighborhood Characteristics and Depression: An Examination of Stress Processes" From "Neighborhood Characteristics and Depression: An Examination of Stress Processes" by C. Cutrona, G. Wallace, & K. Wesner (2006) *Current Directions in Psychological Science,* 15 (4), 188-192. Copyright © 2006 by Sage Publications. Reprinted by permission of Sage Publications.

Table 13.2 "The Five Axes of the DSM-IV and Sample Disorders" Reprinted with permission from the *Diagnostic and Statistical Manual of Mental Disorders,*

Fourth Edition, Text Revision (Copyright © 2000). American Psychiatric Association.

Table 13.3 "Diagnostic Criteria for Post-Traumatic Stress Disorder" Reprinted with permission from *The Diagnostic and Statistical Manual of Mental Disorders,* Fourth Edition, Text Revision, (Copyright © 2000). American Psychiatric Association.

Table 13.4 "Attitudes toward Mental Illness" from "Measuring Stigma toward Mental Illness: Development and Application of the Mental Illness Stigma Scale" From "Measuring Stigma toward Mental Illness: Development and Application of the Mental Illness Stigma Scale" by E. N. Day, K. Edgren & A. Eshleman (2007) *Journal of Applied Social Psychology,* 37, 2191-2219. Copyright © 2007 by John Wiley and Sons. Reprinted by permission of John Wiley and Sons.

Table 13.5 "Varieties of Personality Disorders" Reprinted with permission from *The Diagnostic and Statistical Manual of Mental Disorders,* Fourth Edition, Text Revision (Copyright © 2000). American Psychiatric Association.

Table 13.6 "What are We So Afraid Of?" from "The Epidemiology of DSM-IV Specific Phobia in the USA: Results from the National Epidemiologic Survey on Alcohol and Related Conditions" Adaptation of Table 3 from "The Epidemiology of DSM-IV Specific Phobia in the USA: Results from the National Epidemiologic Survey on Alcohol and Related Conditions" by F. S. Stinson, et al. (2007) *Psychological Medicine,* 37, 1047-1059. Copyright © 2007 by Cambridge University Press. Reprinted with the permission of Cambridge University Press.

Table 13.7 "Prevalence of Symptoms in a Survey of 293 Individuals with OCD" from "The Brown Longitudinal Obsessive Compulsive Study: Clinical Features and Symptoms of the Sample at Intake" Derived from "The Brown Longitudinal Obsessive Compulsive Study: Clinical Features and Symptoms of the Sample at Intake" by A. Pinto, et al. (2006) *Journal of Clinical Psychiatry,* 67, 703-711. Published by Physicians Postgraduate Press, Inc.

CHAPTER 14

Figure 14.1 "Who Seeks Treatment?" from "National Trends in Outpatient Psychotherapy" Adapted from Table 1 in Mark Olfson and Steven C. Marcus, "National Trends in Outpatient Psychotherapy," *American Journal of Psychiatry,* December 2010; 167: 1456-1463. Copyright © 2010. Reprinted by permission of American Psychiatric Publishing, Inc.

Figure 14.2 "Types of Treatment People Use" http://www.nimh.nih.gov/statistics/3USE_MT_ADULT.shtml.

Figure 14.3 "Results of Six Studies of the Self-Help Book *Feeling Good*" Based on Anderson et al. (2005).

Table 14.1 "Seeking Professional Help" From "Attitudes toward Seeking Professional Psychological Help: A Shortened Form and Considerations for Research" by E. H. Fischer & A. Farina (1995) Journal of College Student Development, 36, 368-373. Copyright © 1995 by American College Personnel Association. Reprinted by permission.

CHAPTER 15

Figure 15.8 Chapter 15 "Factors Contributing to Empathy" from "An Additional Antecedent of

Empathic Concern: Valuing the Welfare of the Person in Need" Figure 1, p. 73 from Batson, C., Eklund, J., Chermok, V. L., Hoyt, J. L., & Ortiz, B. G. (2007). "An Additional Antecedent of Empathic Concern: Valuing the Welfare of the Person in Need." *Journal of Personality and Social Psychology,* 93(1), 65-74.

Figure 15.10 "Men from a Culture of Honor React More Strongly to Perceived Insults" from "Insult, Aggression, and the Southern Culture of Honor: An 'Experimental Ethnography'" Figure 2, p. 952 from "Insult, Aggression, and the Southern Culture of Honor: An 'Experimental Ethnography'" by D. Cohen, R. E. Nisbett, B. F. Bowdle & N. Schwarz (1996) *Journal of Personality and Social Psychology,* 70 (5), 945-960.

Table 15.2 "Some of the risk factors for groupthink" from "The nature of social influence in groupthink: Compliance and Internalization" From McCauley, C. (1987). The nature of social influence in groupthink: Compliance and internalization. *Journal of Personality and Social Psychology,* 57, 250-260.

Table 15.3 "Attitudes Scale" adapted from "Bringing Cognitive Dissonance to the Classroom" Adapted from "Bringing Cognitive Dissonance to the Classroom" by D. M. Carkenord & J. Bullington (1993) *Teaching of Psychology,* 20(1), 41-43. Copyright © 1993 by Taylor & Francis Group. Reprinted by permission of Taylor & Francis Group, http://www.informaworld.com.

Table 15.4 "Description of Self and Others" from "Behavior as Seen by the Actor and as Seen by the Observer" Adapted from Nisbett, R. E., Caputo, C., Leganta, P., & Marecek, J. (1973). Behavior as seen by an actor and as seen by the observer. *Journal of Personality and Social Psychology,* 27(2), 154-164.

Table 15.5 "The Self-Report Altruism Scale" (slightly adapted) From "The Altruistic Personality and the Self-Report Altruism Scale" by J. Rushton, R. D. Chrisjohn, & G. Fekken. (1981) *Personality and Individual Differences,* 2 (4), 293-302. Copyright © 1981 by Elsevier. Reprinted by permission of Elsevier.

CHAPTER 16

Figure 16.1 "Smoking and the Movies" from "Does watching smoking in movies promote teenage smoking?" From "Does Watching Smoking in Movies Promote Teenage Smoking?" by T. F. Heatherton & J. D. Sargent (2009) *Current Directions in Psychological Science,* 18, 63-67. Copyright © 2009 by Sage Publications, Inc. Reprinted by permission of SAGE Publications.

Figure 16.2 "Obesity Rates in Adults by Ethnicity and Gender in the United States (2006-2008)" CDC (2010, April 5). Compared with Whites, Blacks had 51% higher and Hispanics had 21% higher obesity rates. Retrieved from http://www.cdc.gov/Features/dsObesityAdults.

Figure 16.3 "Arousal and Performance" (graph depicting difficult task/easy task) From p. 39 in *Psychology,* 3rd ed. by Saundra Ciccarelli and J. Noland White. Copyright © 2012. Printed and electronically reproduced by permission of Pearson Education, Inc., Upper Saddle River, New Jersey.

Figure 16.5 "How Social Interactions Can Affect Health" from "Marital Behavior, Oxytocin, Vasopressin, and Wound Healing" Figure 3 from "Marital Behavior, Oxytocin, Vasopressin, and

Wound Healing" by J. P. Gouin, C. S. Carter, H. Pournajafi-Nazarloo, R. Glaser, W. B. Malarkey, T. J. Loving, J. Stowell, & J. K. Kiecolt-Glaser (2010) *Psychoneuroendocrinology*, 35 (7), 1082-1090. Copyright © 2010. Reprinted by permission of Elsevier.

Figure 16.6 "Inescapable Stressors Lead to Learned Helplessness" (figure of dog in cube) From p. 606 in *Psychology: From Inquiry to Understanding*, 2nd ed. by Scott O. Lilienfeld, Steven J. Lynn, Laura L. Namy, and Nancy J. Woolf. Copyright © 2011. Printed and electronically reproduced by permission of Pearson Education, Inc., Upper Saddle River, New Jersey.

Figure 16.7 "Seeing Images Where There are None" from "Lacking Control Increases Illusory Pattern Perception" From "Lacking Control Increases Illusory Pattern Perception" by J. A. Whitson & A. D. Galinsky (2008) *Science*, 322, 115-117. Copyright © 2008. Reprinted with permission from AAAS.

Figure 16.8 "Exercising Compensatory Control" from "Compensatory Control: Achieving Order Through the Mind, Our Institutions, and the Heavens" Figure 1 from "Compensatory Control: Achieving Order Through the Mind, Our Institutions, and the Heavens" by A. C. Kay, J. A. Whitson, D. Gaucher, & A. D. Galinsky (2009) *Current Directions in Psychological Science*, 18(5), 264-268. Copyright © 2009 by Sage Publications. Reprinted by permission of SAGE Publications.

Table 16.1 "Estimated Annual Deaths in the United States Due to Behavior-Related Risk Factors" from "The Preventable Causes of Death in the United States: Comparative Risk Assessment of Dietary, Lifestyle, and Metabolic Risk Factors" Derived from data noted in Danaei G, Ding EL, Mozaffarian D, Taylor B, Rehm J, et al. (2009), "The Preventable Causes of Death in the United States: Comparative Risk Assessment of Dietary, Lifestyle, and Metabolic Risk Factors." PLoS Med 6(4): e1000058. doi:10.1371/journal.pmed.1000058.

Table 16.2 "Health Costs of Tobacco Use" http://www.cdc.gov/tobacco/data_statistics/fact_sheets/fast_facts/index.htm. Retrieved June 20, 2011.

Table 16.3 "The Health Locus of Control Scale" adapted from "Development of the Multidimensional Health Locus of Control (MHLC) Scales" Adapted from "Development of the Multidimensional Health Locus of Control (MHLC) Scales" by K. A. Wallston, B. S. Wallston, & R. DeVellis (1978), *Health Education & Behavior*, 6(1), 160-170. Copyright © 1978 by Sage Publications. Reprinted by permission of SAGE Publications.

Table 16.4 "Life-Stress Inventories for the General Adult Population and for College Students" from "A Life-Stress Instrument for Classroom Use" From "A Life-Stress Instrument for Classroom Use" by M. Renner & R. Mackin (1998) *Teaching of Psychology*, 25 (1), 46-48. Copyright © 1998. Reprinted by permission of Taylor & Francis Group. http://www.informaworld.com.

Table 16.4 "Life-Stress Inventories for the General Adult Population and for College Students" from "The Social Readjustment Rating Scale" From "The Social Readjustment Rating Scale" by T. H. Holmes & R. H. Rahe (1967), *Journal of Psychosomatic Research*, 11, 213-218. Copyright © 1967. Reprinted by permission of Elsevier.

Table 16.5 "The Life-Orientation Test" from "Optimism, Coping and Health: Assessment and Implications of Generalized Outcome Expectancies" Scheier, M. F., & Carver, C.S. (1985). Optimism, coping and health: Assessment and implications of generalized outcome expectancies. *Health Psychology*, 4(3), 219-247. American Psychological Association.

CHAPTER 17

Figure 17.1 "The O★NET Concept Chart" O★NET products including O★NET OnLine and O★NET Career Exploration Tools were developed by the U. S. Department of Labor. http://www.onetcenter.org/content/html.

Figure 17.2 "Conscientiousness Can Predict Job Performance" from "The Big Five Personality Traits and Individual Job Performance Growth Trajectories in Maintenance and Transitional Job Stages" From "The Big Five Personality Traits and Individual Job Performance Growth Trajectories in Maintenance and Transitional Job Stages" by C. Thoresen, J. Bradley, P. Bliese, & J. Thoresen (2004) *Journal of Applied Psychology*, 89, 835-853. American Psychological Association.

Figure 17.5 "Vacation Temporarily Relieves Burnout" from "Effects of a Respite from Work on Burnout: Vacation Relief and Fade-Out" From "Effects of a Respite from Work on Burnout: Vacation Relief and Fade-Out" by M. Westman & D. Eden (1997) *Journal of Applied Psychology*, 82, 516-527. American Psychological Association.

Figure 17.6 "Prevalence of Workplace Violence" from "Workplace Violence in 2005" From "Workplace Violence in 2005," *The Editor's Desk*, October 30, 2006. Bureau of Labor Statistics, US Department of Labor. http://www.bls.gov/opub/ted/2006/oct/wk5/art01.htm.

Figure 17.7 "Qualities Leading to Workplace Violence" from "Predicting Workplace Aggression: A Meta-Analysis" Adapted from "Predicting Workplace Aggression: A Meta-Analysis" by M. Hershcovis, N. Turner, J. Barling, K. A. Arnold, K. E. Dupre, M. Sinness & N. Sivanathan (2007) *Journal of Applied Psychology*, 92 (1), 228-238. American Psychological Association.

Figure 17.8 "Assertiveness Predicts Leadership Effectiveness" from "In Search of the Right Touch: Interpersonal Assertiveness in Organizational Life" From "In Search of the Right Touch: Interpersonal Assertiveness in Organizational Life" by D. Ames (2008) *Current Directions in Psychological Science*, 17(6), 381-385. Copyright © 2008 by Sage Publications. Reprinted by permission of SAGE Publications.

Table 17.2 "Sample Situational Interview Question" from "Reliability and Validity of the Situational Interview for a Sales Position" From "Reliability and Validity of the Situational Interview for a Sales Position" by J. A. Weekley & J. A. Gier (1987) *Journal of Applied Psychology*, 72 (3), 484-487. American Psychological Association.

Table 17.5 "A Sample Situational Judgment Test Item" From *The Psychometric History of Selected Ability Constructs* by L. C. Northrop (1998). U. S. Department of Personnel Management, Washington, DC.

Table 17.6 "Cognition Predicts Training Success and Performance" from "A Meta-Analytic Study of General Mental Ability Validity for Different Occupations in the European Community" From "A Meta-Analytic Study of General Mental Ability Validity for Different Occupations in the European Community" by J. Salgado, N. Anderson, S. Moscoso, C. Bertua, F. de Fruyt, & J. Rolland (2003) *Journal of Applied Psychology*, 88 (6), 1068-1081. American Psychological Association.

Table 17.9 "Sample Conditional Reasoning Problems" from "A Conditional Reasoning Measure for Aggression" From "A Conditional Reasoning Measure for Aggression" by L. R. James et al. (2005) *Organizational Research Methods*, 8(1), 69-99. Copyright © 2005 by Sage Publications. Reprinted by permission of SAGE Publications. Table 17.10.

Table 17.11 "Skills and Abilities of Successful Leaders" (adapted) from "Educating the Modern Manager" From "Educating the Modern Manager" by R. Hogan & R. Warrenfeltz (2003), Academy of Management Learning & Education, 2 (1), 74-84. Copyright © 2003. Reprinted by permission of Academy of Management.

Name Index

Note: Boldface page numbers indicate figures, photos, and tables.

Subject Index

Note: Boldface page numbers indicate figures, photos, and tables.

preparedness, 201

prescription drug abuse, 185–186

preserve and protect hypothesis, 162

preterm infants, 352–353

prevention, 521

primary auditory cortex, 141–142

primary reinforcers, 212

primary sex traits, 373

priming, 275–276

The Principles of Psychology (James), 21

proactive interference, 238

problem-solving, 282–285

problem-solving theory of dreaming, 165–166

procedural memories, 243, 386

procrastination, 422–423

professions, 27–31

projection, 467–468

projective tests, 466–468

prosocial behaviors, 574–575

prosopagnosia, 131

prototypes, 273–274

proximity/similarity principle, 120

Prozac, 538

pseudoscience, 4

Psi Chi, **15**

psilocybin, 180, **181**, 183

psychiatric nurses, 519

psychiatrists, 520

psychiatry, 28

psychoanalysis. *See also* psychodynamic psychology
    on dreaming, 164
    Freud and, 18, 526–527

psychodynamic psychology, 462–470, 526–527.
    See also psychoanalysis

psychological disorders
    anxiety disorders, 493–499
    attitudes toward, **484**
    categorical *vs.* dimensional views, 479–480
    dissociative identity disorder, 490–492
    DSM-IV and, 477–479
    insanity defense, 480–481
    maladaptive behavior, 477
    medical *vs.* biopsychosocial model, 476–477
    mood disorders, 499–502
    personality disorders, 486–490
    PTSD, 476, **479**, 483, 531–532
    schizophrenia, 504–510
    stigma of, 481–482

psychology
    contemporary beginnings, 20–24
    defined, 3
    philosophical and scientific origins, 14–19
    professions, 27–31
    specializations, 26

psychometrics, 309

psychoneuroimmunology, 601

psychopathy, 201–202, 487–488

psychopharmacotherapy, 536–537

psychophysics, 16, 116

psychosexual development, 464–466

psychosocial development, 368–370

psychosomatic medicine, 17

psychosurgery, 536

psychotherapy
    barriers to, 517–519
    behavioral therapies, 529–532
    biomedical therapies, 536–542
    cognitive-behavioral therapies, 532–534
    comparisons, **535**
    group and family therapies, 533–534
    insight therapies, 526–529
    providers and settings, 519–521
    statistics, 517
    technological and surgical methods, 542–544
    treatment evaluation, 521–523
    virtual reality therapy (VRE), 531–532

psychotropic drugs, 537

psycoactive drugs, 181

PTSD. *See* post-traumatic stress disorder

puberty, 373

punishers, 211

punishment, 210–211, 213–214, 218–219

pupil (eye), 126

Purdy, Jesse, 27

Q

quasi-experimental research, 53

questionnaires, 50, **54**

R

race/racism, 337, 569–572, 594. *See also* ethnicity

Radano, Gerry, 536

Ramachandran, V. S., 425

random assignment, 53

random samples, 40

rationalization, 464

Raven, John, 313

Raven's Progressive Matrices, 313–314

reaction formation, **464**

reactive aggression, 580

reality principle, 463

reciprocal altruism, 576–577

reciprocal determinism, 447

reconsolidation, 245

recovered memories, 265

reflexes, 354–355

refractory period, 87, 411

rehearsal (memory), 240, 250–252

reinforcement, 210–216

reinforcers, 210–211

relaxation, 609

reliability, 39, 47, 310, 466–467

religion, 610

REM behavior disorder, 158, 168

REM sleep, 161, 164

replication, 44–45

representativeness heuristic, 285

repression, **464**, 469

research
    bias, 40–43
    correlational, 50–52
    descriptive, 49–50
    ethics, 56–61
    evidence, 45–46
    experimental, 52–54
    generalizability, 40
    objective measurements, 38–40
    replication, 44–45
    sharing results, 43–44

researcher bias, 40, 42

research psychologists, 28

residential treatment centers, 520

residual schizophrenia, 505

resilience, 608

resistance, 527

resting potentials, 86–87

restless legs syndrome, 168

restore and repair hypothesis, 161–162

retina, 126

retinal disparity, 132

retrieval (memory), 237, 250–253

retroactive interference, 238

retrograde amnesia, 246–247

reuptake, 88

Riggio, Ronald, 645

Rodriguez, Alex, **428**

rods (eye), 126–127

Rogers, Carl, **15**, 22–23, 470, 527–528

roles, 551–552

romantic relationships, 380–381, 602

rooting reflex, 355

Rorschach inkblot test, 466

Rosenhan, David, 481

Rutherford, Beth, 265

S

salvia, 183–184

same-sex relationships, 380–381

samples, 40

satiation, 398

satisficers, 289–290

saturation (color), 125

savants, 323–324

scaffolding, 364

scapegoating, 569–570

Scared Straight, 525

scatterplots, 50, **51**

schedules of reinforcement, 216–217

Schein, Elyse, **452**

schemas, 260–262, 565

Schiavo, Terri, 177–178

schizophrenia, 504–510, 544

Schlessinger, Laura, 516

Scholastic Assessment Test (SAT), 308–310

school psychology, 29

subliminal messages, 118

substance abuse, 188. *See also* drugs

substance P, 90

suicide, 501–502

Sullivan, Henry Stack, 528

Summitt, Patricia Head, 642

superego, 463

superstition, 217–218, 614

supertasters, 150–151

suprachiasmatic nucleus (SCN), 159

surveys, 50, **54**

Sybil, 491

symmetry, 80

sympathetic nervous system, 96, 426–427

synapses, 86

synaptic cleft, 87

synaptic pruning, 359

synaptogenesis, 359

syntax, 294

systematic desensitization, 530

systems approach, 533–534

systems consolidation, 245

T

Talmi, Deborah, 238

tardive dyskinesia, 539

taste, sense of, 150–152, 401–402

teaching, 227

teamwork, 646–647

temperament, 367–368, 443

temporal lobe epilepsy (TLE), 425

temporal lobes, 101

tend and befriend response, 600–601

teratogens, 353

terror management theory, 420–421

testing effect, 257

testosterone, 92–93, 414–415, 579, 580

test-retest reliability, 310

thalamus, 100

Thematic Apperception Test (TAT), 466–467

theories, 4–5, 12

theory of mind, 367

thin slices method, 566

Thorazine, 539

Thorndike, Edward, **15**, 210–211

thought processes, 565

360-degree feedback, 629

Thurstone, L. L., 323, **325**

Titchener, Edward, 20–21

TMS (transcranial magnetic stimulation), 107

tolerance (to drugs), 188

Tolman, Edward, 222–223

top-down processing, 120–121

touch, sense of, 146–149

trait affectivity, 633

trait aggression, 580

transactional leadership, 644–645

transcranial magnetic stimulation (TMS), 107, 544

transduction, 115

transference, 527

transformational leadership, 644–645

traumatic brain injury, 206–207

treatment evaluation, 521–523

trichromatic theory, 134–135

tricyclic antidepressants, 538

Triplett, Norman, 24

tube feeding, 401

turnover (employment), 635

Tuskegee syphilis study, 56

twins, 76–77, 83, 330–331, 452–453, 507

Twitmyer, Edwin, 21

two-factor theory of emotion, 430–431

Type A personality, 605

Type B personality, 605

U

ulcers, 603

unconditional positive regard, 528

unconditioned response (UR), 196–197

unconditioned stimulus (US), 196–197

unconscious processes, 463, 466–468, 526

undifferentiated schizophrenia, 505

unit bias, 402

university mental health counseling centers, 521

unstructured interviews, 624

V

vaccinations, 353–354

validation studies, 625

validity, 39–40, 47, 466–467

Valium, 539

variability, 66, **68**

variable-interval schedule of reinforcement, 216–217

variable-ratio schedule of reinforcement, 216

variables, 38, 48–49, 53

vasopressin, 601–602

ventral stream, 129

video games, 229–230

violence, 228–230, 637–638

virtual reality therapy (VRE), 531–532

virtual reality training, 571–572

virtual teams, 646

vision disorders, 128

visual system

  artists and, 133–134

  color perception, 134–135

  depth perception, 132–133

  eye, 125–129

  facial recognition, 131–132

  object recognition, 129–131

visuospatial sketchpad, 240, 242

volley principle, 141

Vygotsky, Lev, 364

W

Wade, Kimberly, 259

Washburn, Margaret, **15**

Watson, John B., **15**, 21–22, 200, 222

wavelength (light), 125

Wechsler Adult Intelligence Scale (WAIS), 312–313

Wechsler, David, 312

well-defined problems, 282

Wernicke, Karl, 17

Wernicke's aphasia, 103, 296–297

Wernicke's area, 17, 103, 296–297

Wertheimer, Max, **15**

Whiten, Andrew, 221

Whorfian hypothesis, 278

Wiltshire, Stephen, **324**

wish fulfillment, 164

Witelson, Sandra, 315

Witmer, Lightner, **15**

word-length effect, 241–242

working memory model, 240–242, 251–252, 597

workplace aggression, 637–638

World of Warcraft, 443

Wundt, Wilhelm, **15**, 20–21, 23

Wuornos, Aileen, 485, 487

X

Xanax, 539

Y

Yates, Andrea, 480–481

Young-Helmholtz theory, 134–135

Young, Thomas, 134

Young, Vince, 311

Z

zeitgeist, 14

Zoloft, 538

zone of proximal development, 364

zygotes, 349

Zyprexa, 541